Everyday Jewish Life
in Imperial Russia

MW00581442

FEB 05 2014

PUBLICATION OF THIS BOOK
IS SUPPORTED BY THE

Valya and Robert Shapiro Endowment

FEB 05 2014

PUBLICATION OF THIS BOOK
IS SUPPORTED BY A GRANT FROM

Jewish Federation of Greater Hartford

The Tauber Institute Series
for the Study of European Jewry

Jehuda Reinharz, *General Editor*
Sylvia Fuks Fried, *Associate Editor*
Eugene R. Sheppard, *Associate Editor*

The Tauber Institute Series is dedicated to publishing compelling and innovative approaches to the study of modern European Jewish history, thought, culture, and society. The series features scholarly works related to the Enlightenment, modern Judaism and the struggle for emancipation, the rise of nationalism and the spread of antisemitism, the Holocaust and its aftermath, as well as the contemporary Jewish experience. The series is published under the auspices of the Tauber Institute for the Study of European Jewry—established by a gift to Brandeis University from Dr. Laszlo N. Tauber—and is supported, in part, by the Tauber Foundation and the Valya and Robert Shapiro Endowment.

For the complete list of books that are available in this series, please see www.upne.com

ChaeRan Y. Freeze and Jay M. Harris, editors
Everyday Jewish Life in Imperial Russia: Select Documents, 1772–1914

David N. Myers and Alexander Kaye, editors
The Faith of Fallen Jews: Yosef Hayim Yerushalmi and the Writing of Jewish History

Federica K. Clementi
Holocaust Mothers and Daughters: Family, History, and Trauma

*Ulrich Sieg
Germany's Prophet: Paul de Lagarde and the Origins of Modern Antisemitism

David G. Roskies and Naomi Diamant
Holocaust Literature: A History and Guide

*Mordechai Altshuler
Religion and Jewish Identity in the Soviet Union, 1941–1964

Robert Liberles
Jews Welcome Coffee: Tradition and Innovation in Early Modern Germany

*A Sarnat Library Book

Sharon Faye Koren
Forsaken: The Menstruant in Medieval Jewish Mysticism

Nils Roemer
German City, Jewish Memory: The Story of Worms

David Assaf
Untold Tales of the Hasidim: Crisis and Discontent in the History of Hasidism

Jehuda Reinharz and Yaacov Shavit
Glorious, Accursed Europe: An Essay on Jewish Ambivalence

Eugene M. Avrutin, Valerii Dymshits, Alexander Ivanov, Alexander Lvov, Harriet Murav, and Alla Sokolova, editors
Photographing the Jewish Nation: Pictures from S. An-sky's Ethnographic Expeditions

Michael Dorland
Cadaverland: Inventing a Pathology of Catastrophe for Holocaust Survival

Walter Laqueur
Best of Times, Worst of Times: Memoirs of a Political Education

*Rose-Carol Washton Long, Matthew Baigell, and Milly Heyd, editors
Jewish Dimensions in Modern Visual Culture: Antisemitism, Assimilation, Affirmation

Berel Lang
Philosophical Witnessing: The Holocaust as Presence

David N. Myers
Between Jew and Arab: The Lost Voice of Simon Rawidowicz

Sara Bender
The Jews of Białystok during World War II and the Holocaust

Nili Scharf Gold
Yehuda Amichai: The Making of Israel's National Poet

Hans Jonas
Memoirs

Everyday Jewish Life in Imperial Russia

SELECT DOCUMENTS
[1772-1914]

Edited by
ChaeRan Y. Freeze
and Jay M. Harris

BRANDEIS UNIVERSITY PRESS
WALTHAM, MASSACHUSETTS

BRANDEIS UNIVERSITY PRESS
An imprint of University Press of New England
www.upne.com
© 2013 Brandeis University
All rights reserved
Manufactured in the United States of America
Designed by Eric M. Brooks
Typeset in Miller and Torino by Passumpsic Publishing

For permission to reproduce any of the material
in this book, contact Permissions, University Press
of New England, One Court Street, Suite 250,
Lebanon NH 03766; or visit www.upne.com

The publisher and editors gratefully acknowledge
permission to reprint the following:
Cover illustration: *Jewish Woman Selling Oranges*
by Aleksander Gierymski, 1881. Property of the
Silesian Museum in Katowice.

Acknowledgments continue at the back of the book.

Library of Congress Cataloging-in-Publication Data
available upon request

5 4 3 2 1

For my parents,
Min Chul & Suk Za Yoo;
my brother, Jun;
and my beloved daughter,
Natalia Hanna

For Ilan & Ariel,
Rebecca, & David
through whom I am
blessed with "all"

Contents

Preface

On the eve of 1885, Zinaida Poliakova—daughter of a wealthy banker and railway mogul, Lazar Solomonovich Poliakov—confided to her diary: "Tomorrow is New Year's Day. Will it bring me something good? I won't complain but do wish myself a better year."[1] In some respects, 1885 proved to be a year like any other for her: the relentless tedium of her mother's complaints, family bickering, fancy balls in Moscow (where Poliakova "danced until 3:30 [in the morning]"),[2] the thrill of attending theatrical performances, magnificent operas, endless social calls, and trips abroad for spa treatments. Social routine and the monotony of domestic life—so disparaged by modernists[3]—had deprived this young, female diarist of a real life. "Six months have gone by since I last wrote in my journal," Poliakova remarked at the close of another year, "but during this entire time, not the slightest change has taken place in our way of life."[4]

The flow of daily life dominates this diary, but news about extraordinary economic and political events sometimes intrudes: "Today the *Moscow News* and the *St. Petersburg News* reported the official announcement of the Malkiel bankruptcy. I feel very sorry for them since it is hard for anybody to fall from wealth to poverty, but especially for them."[5] Although Russia underwent rapid industrialization in the mid-1880s, not all Russians had recouped their losses from the European-wide recession of the mid-1870s. Indeed, few sensed that Russia was on the verge of an economic boom. "There are fewer people on the street than usual," reads another entry, dated 21 March 1885. "Papa explains that things are not well."[6] World politics also found their way into Poliakova's diary. A month later, she expressed relief that the wealthy journalist, Madam Ol'ga Alekseevna Novikova,[7] had received assurances from Prime Minister William Gladstone that England and Russia would not go to war over a border dispute in Afghanistan.

The "everyday" (*Alltagsleben*) in Poliakova's diaries reflected one kind of Jewish experience in Imperial Russia. Prosaic details—from the latest Parisian fashions to Anton Rubinshtein's concerts, from reading habits to conflicts with domestic servants—overlapped with her attempts to understand her experiences and fashion her own elite identity. For Poliakova and other Jews living in tsarist Russia, the everyday meant interaction with an emerging modernity: the quotidian confronted them with a new world and drove them to seek creative, strategic ways to negotiate their place in it. In other words, Russian Jewry became "modern" not only by confrontation with "crisis" but through ordinary life, as will be seen throughout this volume. This individual interaction generated differing conceptions of the world and created a new set of distinctive *mentalités*, attitudes, and values.

For a variety of reasons, a wide range of primary sources that draw directly on the ordinary lives of Jews in the Russian Empire have long remained inaccessible.[8] To be sure, there are some valuable collections of primary documents on East European Jewry, such as Lucy Dawidowicz's *The Golden Tradition: Jewish Life and Thought in Eastern Europe*. Her compendium focuses on the autobiographies, memoirs, and essays of prominent figures "whose genius was so adapted to the receptivities of the moment . . . that they became fermenters, initiators of movements, setters of precedent."[9] In brief, her volume seeks to understand the great "isms" through the writings of the dominant players. A section on

"East European Jewry" also appears in Paul Mendes-Flohr and Jehuda Reinharz's *The Jew in the Modern World*, which includes documents (statutes, programs, essays, and poetry) on religious, cultural, and political movements in tsarist Russia and on the role of ideology in the modernization of Jewish society.[10] In addition, several recently translated memoirs provide personal perspectives on the social and political changes that reshaped the lives of Jews in Eastern Europe.[11]

This volume represents the first comprehensive effort to integrate both archival and classical Jewish sources in order to bridge the conventional divide between the discourse of intellectual elites and the social ideals and experiences that guided the behavior of ordinary people. The archival documents come from ten central and provincial repositories in the former Soviet Union (Russia, Ukraine, and Lithuania). Moreover, we have included a selection from an unprecedented profusion of first-person documents, written by ordinary men and women or recorded and transmitted through literate intermediaries (lawyers, journalists, ethnographers, and the like). These materials come from personal archives, petitions to state institutions, court depositions, private materials intercepted and deposited in secret police archives, and a multitude of public declarations that appeared in the contemporary press.

Reading the Sources Critically

Archival documents are not oracles: they must be used with caution and skepticism. Although the files include first-person depositions (especially when drawn from provincial archives), documents in central repositories often appear in the form of "extracts" (detailed summaries, with detailed paraphrases and quotations of original testimony). Still, however accurate and detailed the extract, it nonetheless mediates the original, whether through excisions or summaries, and thus necessarily

obfuscates the structure and style of the original. That problem is exacerbated by the fact that the Russian documents are frequently translations from Yiddish, the primary language of many petitioners and witnesses. In some instances, Jews simply flooded the Russian bureaucracy with Yiddish petitions, not bothering with a translation. As one bureaucrat complained: "Nobody here reads the language!" If they desired to have their petitions considered, they should "submit them in Russian—and on stamped [official] paper!"[12] Even when "learned Jews" (*uchenye evrei*), state rabbis, or other Russian-speaking representatives acted as translators, the text inevitably transforms the original language and distorts the perspective of the original. One translator for the Ministry of Education explained the limitations of his work this way: "I have attempted as far as possible to maintain the special style of this present letter; however, a few expressions cannot be conveyed at all in Russian."[13] Jewish discourse inevitably shaped the official narrative. At the same time, as Natalie Z. Davis has noted, although some would assume "that the minute a learned agent of the state puts his hand on another's words, they are so remade and reshuffled that their original form is effaced," this was not always the case.[14] Written versions had to evoke the personal tone of oral testimonies in order to be credible and to elicit sympathy.

The documents reproduced here can be divided into two main types: (1) those that echo individual voices—personal petitions, complaints, court testimonies, and the like; and (2) those that describe the activities of individuals or groups (for example, police reports on Jewish revolutionaries) and events (such as a Jewish riot to protest the opening of a secular school). It is important to offer both types of documents—both to hear authentic Jewish voices and to help reconstruct contemporary perceptions (whether Jewish or otherwise).

These documents were also chosen because of their "typicality" or "articulateness." On the one hand, they are typical — that is, representative of a particular category of documents or a collection. On the other hand, priority was given to documents that, although substantively representative, are particularly articulate in revealing the common concerns, as well as internal tensions and differences, in Jewish society. For example, the archives preserve many dozens of applications to institutionalize mentally ill relatives in the Jewish hospital in Vil'na. The typical cases stressed the threat that these individuals posed to their family or themselves because of violent behavior; the patients' voices, however, were generally absent save on the examination form. Even then, their statements were mediated by the doctors who recorded their answers. One case that diverged from this pattern was a petition of Ida Suits of St. Petersburg, who contested her diagnosis in a remarkably articulate personal petition that questioned the competence of the doctors and her sister's motives. Such a statement, while extraordinary, provides an alternative perspective on the human drama, missing in most of the other such cases.

Important as new archival sources are, it is essential to include the classical sources, too — above all, the little-used responsa literature and the legal decisions of prominent rabbinic authorities in the Russian Empire. Jewish law extends into all areas of life: the sexual, hygienic, culinary, sartorial, and, of course, family and business matters. Traditional Jews often turned to their local rabbis for instructions regarding such matters; the latter would in turn refer the truly challenging questions to the "giants of the generation" who wrote detailed explanations about the requirements of the law. Although these responses (which were often published) became part of the literature of the elites, they also reflected many aspects of the everyday.

This volume focuses on responsa that explore social and religious issues (such as the impact of environmental hazards on the mikvah and on drinking water) to illuminate how observant Jews and rabbinic authorities coped with contemporary realities.[15] From child abandonment and domestic brutality to acts of extraordinary kindness and decency, Jewish life comes alive in the many questions directed at rabbinic authorities. To be sure, the genre of responsa poses numerous challenges, not least of which are the modes of rabbinic argumentation. Moreover, since these were not intended as historical documents, rabbis often omitted names and other identifying details. Nevertheless, the responsa provide a rich counterpart to the particulars of archival cases. This volume draws upon several of the most important responsa collections by prominent rabbis of unquestioned authority in the Russian empire such as R. Naftali Zvi Yehudah Berlin (1816–1893) of Volozhin, R. Isaac Elhanan Spektor (1817–1896) of Kovno, and R. Hayim Ozer Grodzinski (1863–1940) of Vil'na.

To complement the archival and responsa core, the volume includes a generous amount of unofficial, nonrabbinical texts — private documents, musings that reflect on the lives of individual Jews. These sources include diaries and letters that represented individual experiences and perceptions. Readers will also find new translations of printed materials, including memoirs and autobiographies that looked backward in time, as well as works that had an immediate impact — such as popular religious and secular advice manuals on child rearing, sexuality, religious rituals, and food.

As a rule, the collection includes the main body of the text. Each archival document also includes information about the author, addressee, style (that is, petition, denunciation, complaint, appeal, and so forth), date, and signatories. The end of an archival document is followed by a summary of the final resolution of the case (if available). The responsa literature also includes details about authorship, approximate time period, and other identifying characteristics.

How should one approach these documents? It is of course possible to read them to gain information about the Russian-Jewish past, normally steeped in a heady mixture of nostalgia and politics. But one should not naively take these sources as equivalent to photographs of how things really were. Each is, after all, the product of one or more individuals: it represents how those actors perceived, understood, constructed, and represented their experience, whether real or imagined. Texts are inevitably interventions in the flux of ordinary life, reflecting the strategies, languages, and ideals of people who are seeking to make a point, win a case, or otherwise manage reality.

Decoding the Everyday

The wide range of documents offered here thus provides a new perspective on the everyday life of Jews in Imperial Russia, from the late eighteenth century to the early twentieth century. The everyday has long attracted interest in the fields of critical theory,[16] history,[17] and cultural studies,[18] but only recently has this been the case in Jewish history.[19] For historians, attention to the everyday has signaled a shift from the grand narratives of political history to the quotidian social experience of ordinary people.[20] At the same time, scholarship has also moved beyond the sociological mode of the 1970s and 1980s. Current work is less focused on class than on culture and less insistent on collective mobilization than on individual negotiation of the stubborn realities of the everyday—as reflected in political choices, religious behavior, making love, and making a living.

The shift from the general to the particular, however, raises important methodological questions. First, the focus on the individual, the local, and the singular inevitably raises the issue of typicality. The privileged lifestyle of Zinaida Poliakova, for instance, was hardly typical of the average Jew living in Moscow,

much less in the Pale of Settlement. Indeed, each of the documents here and the situation it describes are particular and individual—from R. Yosef Zekhariah Stern's responsum regarding a doctor's alleged rape of a married woman (document 83) to the separation case of the Grinshteins in Odessa (document 121). Can such personal, individual narratives provide knowledge of the past without seeming purely anecdotal?

Although typicality remains an issue, it is important to recognize that the particular cannot be considered apart from the general. As Henri Lefebvre argues in *Critique of Everyday Life*, even the most mundane act (such as a woman buying sugar) represents "an infinitely complex social event," one that reflects the intricate interconnection between everyday practices and the macro (culture, economics, and society).[21] Singular events thus help us to decode the terms of the grand narrative and to resist the temptation of collapsing individuals into a single unified story, by exposing the contradictions, discrepancies, and diversity of individual experiences. Petitions by skilled Jewish artisans and their families to halt their expulsion from St. Petersburg and other cities outside the Pale of Settlement (documents 146 and 147), for instance, offer a real-world counterpoint to arid summaries of the imperial policy of "selective integration," which allowed "useful" categories of Jews (such as the wealthiest first-guild merchants retired soldiers, university students, and skilled artisans) to reside beyond the Pale of Settlement. These personal appeals reveal not only the difficulties of implementing policy at the grass-roots level but how partial ("selective") Jewish emancipation of the individual could divide families through differing rights of residency.[22]

Focusing on the micro also allows historians to see the faces in the crowd. The nameless *meshugener* (insane person) or village idiot who roamed the town streets—a common trope in Jewish literature—was actually a real person, with his or her own name, family, and story. Documents from everyday life help to humanize narratives and see the complexities behind the stereotypes. For instance, when Enta Pushner submitted a request in 1895 to institutionalize her mother in the Vil'na Jewish Hospital, she provided a graphic description of the street urchins who tormented her mentally ill mother, the sixty-year-old Dvoira Zlotoiabko (document 69). Enta protested the family's decision to lock her mother in a cold cellar out of fear that her indecent, violent, and dangerous behavior (especially her impulse to wield knives) might harm her two small children.[23] Such cases illuminate the unenviable life of the mentally ill — a neglected segment of Jewish society — that prompted debates in the medical profession about nervous disorders among Jews and the need to prevent consanguineous marriages.[24] These documents personalize faceless statistics and humanize the subjects of professional and public discourse.

A second issue is the tendency to decontextualize the quotidian: even if the everyday is now in the foreground, it is important to provide the background context of everyday life — the values, ideals, and myths that permeated Jewish society. That also means providing a full picture — not only of the lives of ordinary people but also those who held status, influence, and power — the *grosse Leute*.[25] In the Russian case, this meant the religious and spiritual leaders who, in the opinion of their supporters, embodied the loftiest ideals (whether of traditional society or the Jewish intelligentsia) even as their growing number of detractors often saw them as impediments to progress. How individuals appropriated and transformed societal ideals to meet everyday needs can be enormously illuminating. For instance, Yehoshua Heschel Levine's 1856 biography of the Gaon of Vil'na — the *misnagdic* model of learning and piety — shows the tensions surrounding Torah study in the mid-nineteenth century (document 4). Levine, one

of a small group of scholars seeking to justify their inclusion of secular studies, depicted the Gaon as an enlightened scholar who sanctioned secular learning, albeit as subordinate to the Torah. Levine thus sought to navigate between "the extreme non-religious Haskalah on the one hand, [and] uncompromising orthodoxy that entirely rejected any dealings with the secular science on the other."[26] While works like Levine's do not necessarily describe "real" behaviors, they do reveal what some believed to be the norms to be emulated, contested, or reformed. At the same time, elites and ordinary people — for all their differences — also had much in common, as members of the same culture and community.

A third issue concerns a tendency to overlook or discount what Lefebvre calls "liminal moments" that transcend and reconfigure the quotidian: the everyday does not preclude the extraordinary. Indeed, "instances of intense experience" (such as love, desire, disgust, and alienation) can critique the everyday and enable actors to imagine possibilities of a different future. Such "moments" do not sunder but "transform (partially or momentarily)."[27] The extraordinary and the sensational likewise constitute individual experience. Litigants and petitioners invoke norms as points of reference and speak in the idiom of their culture, thereby revealing the intricate details of their world. Indeed, the most divisive, sensitive, and unresolved issues can be highly instructive for revealing tensions, anxieties, and pressures.[28] The extraordinary can "catapult the individual into a different existential frame";[29] religious conversion, for example, forces the neophyte to learn a new set of everyday practices and to adopt behavioral norms that conflict with deeply ingrained habits.[30]

A fourth issue pertains to the complex social meaning of the everyday. Above all, the everyday must not be seen just as a passive pattern of routinized conformity but also as potential sites of resistance and transformation. In the words of Michel de Certeau, "the practice of daily life" involves strategies to hinder, evade, and deflect "an imposed purpose."[31] Personal responses to reality do not necessarily entail opposition but may also involve an active and creative process. For example, reading is not an act of docile consumption but one laden with activity: readers "inhabit and explore texts according to their own whims," generating opportunities to engage in creative interaction by daydreaming, ascribing new meaning to old texts, and so forth.[32] To be sure, such opportunities could be circumscribed, especially where a regime exercised tight censorship; yet even there readers could decode the Aesopian language and try to surmise what the author really intended to say.[33] This volume, in particular, seeks to recognize the agency of historical actors, including those at the bottom of the social ladder, and to show how their words and deeds transformed the everyday, both inside and outside the limits of law and convention.

Finally, the concept of montage—the juxtaposition of disparate elements—provides a useful way to understand the "simultaneity of difference."[34] In the summer of 1885, as Zinaida Poliakova was busy deciding whether to travel to Samara for special kumiss treatments or to the spas in Francisbad,[35] farmers in nineteen Jewish agricultural colonies in the Ekaterinoslav district were experiencing a terrible drought and desperately petitioning the state for food and fodder (document 142). Living in different locales in the vast Russian Empire, with unequal access to legal rights, wealth, and technologies, Jews like Poliakova and the Jewish farmers had very different *mentalités* and concerns. The primary objects of this book, then, are to find real Russian Jews within the undifferentiated abstraction called Russian Jewry and explore how authors decoded their varying experiences in Imperial Russia.

The volume is organized thematically, with a chronological framework to each chapter.

It consists of 182 documents divided into six parts: (1) religious life; (2) family; (3) health and sexuality; (4) education and culture; (5) work and leisure; and (6) Jews, neighbors, and the Russian state. We recognize that most documents are relevant to more than one part. For example, Ben Zion Dinur's memoir about his yeshiva experiences (document 109) could appear in the part on religious life, the one on education and culture, or even the one on family. The placement of a document in a particular part reflects its main theme as well as our own editorial need to create a sense of balance and cohesion. The general introduction is intended to provide a broad historical framework for understanding the documents that follow; thus, the introductions to the parts introduce only the main topics that are covered there. To aid the reader in matching documents to topics, we have included a detailed index. The bibliography also lists some basic secondary works; a comprehensive guide to the scholarly literature on Russian Jewry is available online.[36]

Abbreviations of Archives

DAKO	Derzhavnyi arkhiv Kyïvskoi oblasti
DAOO	Derzhavnyi arkhiv Odesskoï oblasti
DAZhO	Derzhavnyi arkhiv Zhytomyrskoï oblasti
DAmK	Derzhavnyi arkhiv mista Kyïeva
TsIAM	Tsentral'nyi istoricheskii arkhiv Moskvy
TsDIAK-Ukraïny	Tsentral'nyi derzhavnyi istorichnyi arkhiv Ukraïny, Kyïev
TsGIA-St. Petersburg	Tsentral'nyi gosudarstennyi istoricheskii arkhiv, St. Petersburg
RGIA	Rossiiskii gosudarstvennyi istoricheskii arkhiv, St. Petersburg
LVIA	Lietuvos Valstybes Istorijos Archyvas, Vilnius

Obsolete Russian Units of Measurement

Arshin	71.12 centimeters
Funt	409.5 grams
Verst	1.07 kilometers (approximately)
Pud	16.38 kilograms
Sazhen	2.1336 meters
Vedro	13.12 liters
Silver ruble	
	Legal monetary unit in imperial Russia. The paper ruble, which also circulated, was valued at approximately 1.60 to the silver ruble in 1890.

A Note on Translations and Names

The Hebrew-language materials were translated by Jay Harris and Saadya Sternberg, the Yiddish by Yuri Vedenyapen, and the Russian by ChaeRan Y. Freeze. We have followed the Library of Congress system of transliteration with the omission of diacritical marks. All Jewish names in Russian archives have been transliterated according to this system. Many archival texts spelled Jewish names differently (reflecting Hebrew, Yiddish, and Russian versions of names and nicknames) and inconsistently (reflecting typographical errors and misspellings). Only one spelling has been selected for consistency. Names of important Jewish figures generally follow the spellings in Gershon David Hundert, *The YIVO Encyclopedia of Jews in Eastern Europe* (New Haven: Yale University Press, 2008) except in instances of commonly used names. Square brackets in notes indicate editors' annotations.

NOTES

1. Zinaida Poliakova, "Dnevniki," in *Sem'ia Poliakovykh*, ed. Larisa Vasil'eva (Moscow: Atlantida, 1995), 150. Lazar Solomonovich Poliakov (b. 1842), an honorary citizen, was a prominent railroad magnate and head of an illustrious banking family in Russia.

2. Ibid., 153.

3. Rita Felski, "Introduction," *New Literary History* 33, no. 4 (2002): 611–12, and *Doing Time: Feminist Theory and Postmodern Culture* (New York: New York University Press, 2000), 77–98.

4. Poliakova, "Dnevniki," 159.

5. Ibid., 148. E. S. Mir and Mina Abramovna Malkiel were occasional guests at the Poliakov home.

6. Ibid., 152.

7. On Novikova, see Joseph Baylen, "Madame Olga Novikov: Propagandist," *American Slavic and East European Review* 10, no. 4 (1951): 255–71.

8. Some obstacles have included linguistic barriers, the complexities of rabbinic literature (which require a thorough knowledge of Jewish law to sort out), and the restrictions on Jewish archival materials until the collapse of the Soviet Union.

9. Lucy Dawidowicz, ed., *The Golden Tradition. Jewish Life and Thought in Eastern Europe* (Syracuse, NY: Syracuse University Press, 1996), 6.

10. Paul Mendes-Flohr and Jehuda Reinharz, *The Jew in the Modern World: A Documentary History*, 3rd ed. (Oxford: Oxford University Press, 2010). Walter Ackerman's *Out of Our People's Past* (New York: United Synagogue of America, 1977) also includes a relevant selection of documents in a section titled "Russia: The Winter of Despair."

11. For example, see Pauline Wengeroff, *Rememberings: The World of a Russian-Jewish Woman in the Nineteenth Century*, trans. Henny Wenkart, ed. Bernard D. Cooperman (Potomac: University Press of Maryland, 2000), and *Memoirs of a Grandmother: Scenes from the Cultural History of the Jews of Russia in the Nineteenth Century*, trans. Shulamit S. Magnus with an introduction, notes, and commentary. (Stanford: Stanford University Press, 2010); Puah Rakowski, *My Life as a Radical Jewish Woman: Memoirs of a Zionist Feminist in Poland*, ed. Paula Hyman (Bloomington: Indiana University Press, 2001); Yehezkel Kotik, *Journey to a Nineteenth-Century Shtetl: The Memoirs of Yekhezkel Kotik*, ed. David Assaf (Detroit: Wayne State University Press, 2002).

12. John D. Klier, "Polish Shtetls under Russian Rule, 1772–1914," *Polin* 17 (2004): 102 (quoting TsDIAK-Ukraïny f. 442, op. 49, d. 271, g. 1870, ll. 1–2).

13. RGIA, f. 733, op. 189, d. 321, l. 15.

14. Natalie Zemon Davis, *Fiction in the Archives: Pardon Tales and Their Tellers in Sixteenth-Century France* (Stanford: Stanford University Press, 1987), 20–22.

15. Environmental hazards were neither new nor unique to Jews of Imperial Russia. Yet, as the documents below show, modern manufacturing and Jewish religious law made the challenge of dealing with them greater for modern Jews than for either early modern Jews or modern non-Jewish subjects of the Russian Empire.

16. See Henri Lefebvre, *Critique of Everyday Life: Volume I* [1947], trans. John Moore (London: Verso, 1991), and *Everyday Life in the Modern World*, trans. Sacha Rabinovitch (New Brunswick, NJ: Transaction, 1984); Michel de Certeau, *The Practice of Everyday Life*, trans. Steven Rendall (Berkeley: University of California Press, 1984).

17. See Alf Lüdke, *The History of Everyday Life: Reconstructing Historical Experiences and Ways of Life* (Princeton: Princeton University Press, 1995); Richard van Dülmen, *Kultur und Alltag in der Frühen Nejzeit*. 3 vols. (Munich: C. H. Beck, 1990–94); Martin Dinges, "'Historische Anthropologie,' und 'Gesellschaftsgeschichte,'" Von dem Lebensstilkonzept zu einer 'Alltagskulturgeschichte' der frühen Neuzeit?" *Zeitschrift für Forschung* 24 (1997): 197–214.

18. For example, see the special issue titled "Everyday Life" in *New Literary History* (33, no. 4 [2002]).

19. On material culture and the everyday, see Jenna Weissman Joselit, *The Wonders of America: Reinventing Jewish Culture, 1880–1950* (New York: Hill and Wang, 1994). On the *Alltagsgeschichte* of German Jewry, see Marion Kaplan, *Jewish Daily Life in Germany, 1618–1945* (Oxford: Oxford University Press, 2005).

20. Ben Highmore, *Everyday Life and Cultural Theory* (London: Routledge, 2002), 27.

21. Lefebvre, *Critique of Everyday Life*, 1: 57. See also Highmore, *Everyday Life and Cultural Theory*, 25.

22. Archival cases show, for example, that children of artisans who enjoyed the right to reside outside the Pale of Settlement could be expelled on reaching their majority if they lacked "an independent handicraft or trade" (document 145). The bureaucratic obstacles to obtaining registration papers often led to geographic separation. See document 54.

23. LVIA, f. 383, op. 5, d. 341, ll. 2–9 ob.

24. ChaeRan Y. Freeze, *Jewish Marriage and Divorce in Imperial Russia* (Hanover, NH: University Press of New England for Brandeis University Press, 2002), 26–30.

25. Alf Lüdtke, *The History of Everyday Life*, 20.

26. Immanuel Etkes, *The Gaon of Vilna: The Man and His Image* (Berkeley: University of California Press, 2002), 43.

27. Quoted in Michael Sheringham, *Everyday Life: Theories and Practices from Surrealism to the Present* (Oxford: Oxford University Press, 2006), 157.

28. Maurice Blanchot, "Everyday Speech," *Yale French Studies* 73 (1987): 12.

29. Rita Felski, "Introduction," *New Literary History* 33, no. 4 (2002): 617.

30. ChaeRan Y. Freeze, "The Mariinsko-Sergievskii Shelter for Converted Jewish Children in St. Petersburg," in *Jews in the East European Borderlands: Essays in Honor of John D. Klier*, ed. Eugene Avrutin and Harriet Murav (Boston: Academic Studies, 2012), 27–49.

31. De Certeau, *The Practice of Everyday Life*, 40.

32. Sheringham, *Everyday Life*, 226.

33. Indeed censorship could inspire more imagination, especially among educated readers seeking to decode the Aesopian language used to evade censors.

34. Highmore, *Everyday Life and Cultural Theory*, 94.

35. Poliakova, "Dnevniki," 157.

36. ChaeRan Y. Freeze, "Russia," in *Oxford Bibliographies in Jewish Studies*, ed. David Biale (New York: Oxford University Press, 2012); http://www.oxfordbibliographies.com.

Acknowledgments

It is our pleasure to acknowledge the many institutions and people to whom we owe a debt of gratitude for the completion of this project. This book was published with the generous Collaborative Research Grant provided by the National Endowment for the Humanities. This grant made it possible to hire researchers and assistants in the archives and libraries of the former Soviet Union, as well as translators in Israel and the United States. We would especially like to thank our research partners: Leonid Vaintraub (Moscow), Sarunas Liekis (Vilnius), and Agnessa Muktan (St. Petersburg). We are also grateful to the dedicated translators of Hebrew and Yiddish: Saadya Sternberg and Yuri Vedenyapen respectively. Grants from the Tauber Institute for the Study of European Jewry and the Near Eastern and Judaic Studies Department at Brandeis University helped us to obtain critical documents to fill in the gaps at the end and to defray the cost of indexing. A remarkably generous subsidy from the Jewish Federation of Greater Hartford helped to underwrite the production costs.

We are also sincerely grateful to the production team at the University Press of New England; to our editor Phyllis D. Deutsch for her sage advice, patience, and constructive suggestions; and to Jeanne Ferris for her remarkable, meticulous copyediting of a book that quoted three languages. We are deeply indebted to Sylvia Fuks Fried, executive director of the Tauber Institute for the Study of European Jewry, for her numerous readings of the book and unwavering support. Sincere gratitude also goes to Jehuda Reinharz, the general editor of the Tauber Institute Series, for his belief in this massive project.

I (ChaeRan Freeze) want to thank my colleagues: Paula Hyman of blessed memory, Lois Dubin, Shaul Stampfer, Immanuel Etkes, Eugene Sheppard, Jonathan Decter, and Ilana Szobel; Tauber staff members Miriam Hoffman for administrative support, Eva Gurevich for meticulous reading of page proofs, and Golan Moskowitz for spending hours typing edits, tracking down footnotes, and assisting with the bibliography; my graduate students Patrick Brown, Yana Drozdovski, April French, and Ira Sammuth Krakhman; Yeshaya Metal of YIVO; Rena Olshansky and Bernard Olshansky of blessed memory; and my uncle Shin Woong Kim and Grandmother Wi Jun Lee of blessed memory. Olga Litvak's steadfast friendship, intellectual companionship, and careful reading of the introduction will always be remembered with gratitude. Special thanks to my dear friend Rabbi Ben Zion Gold who read Ita Kalish's memoirs with me every week to ensure that the translations were correct. I especially appreciated the opportunity to work with my co-author, Jay Harris, whose knowledge of traditional Jewish sources and history made this project immensely richer. Despite his heavy workload, he always came through and was a source of great strength and encouragement. My deepest debt of gratitude goes to my family: my husband, Gregory Freeze, for his profound love, kindness, and patience with my infinite questions about Russian translations; my darling Sebastian and Natalia for their joyful distractions and reminders to stop working; Katie and Christopher for their kind letters of encouragement; and last but not least my devoted parents, Min Chul and Suk Za Yoo, and brother, Theodore Jun, for my childhood adventures in Ethiopia, a remarkable education, and belief in my choice of Jewish history as my life-time love. My gratitude also goes to my sister-in-law Juyeon for her love and friendship.

I (Jay Harris) wish to also acknowledge Immanuel Etkes, Michael Silber, and Shaul Stampfer for their interest in this project and the many discussions (many years ago) about it. Olga Litvak's generous help represents a kindness difficult to repay. My colleagues Shaye Cohen, Rachel Greenblatt, Bernard Septimus, and Ruth Wisse each contributed in different ways to helping bring this project to fruition. My wife, Cheryl, and my kids (to whom this book is dedicated) were an ever-present source of encouragement. Most of all, I want to acknowledge the greatest collaborator anyone could hope for: ChaeRan Freeze. She cheerfully pushed this project forward—taking on more than she bargained for—even as my administrative tasks increasingly pulled me away from it. I hope she can forgive me for all the delays. While a work such as this is never really finished—it could easily be one hundred times longer—it is a pleasure *le-va-rekh 'al ha-mugmar* with her.

Everyday Jewish Life
in Imperial Russia

[Introduction]
The Imperial Context

A traveler to Russia rarely encountered Jews prior to the westward expansion of the Russian Empire in the last quarter of the eighteenth century. The conflict over the so-called Judaizing heresy in the late fifteenth century (a controversial episode, mainly involving religious heterodoxy rather than attraction to Judaism) made Russian leaders wary of encouraging settlement in their lands.[1] Even Peter the Great (r. 1689–1725), who aspired to transform Russia into a modern European power, welcomed only a few exceptional Jewish converts to his realm. Despite the formal bans issued by his successors, Jewish merchants often found their way to trade fairs in the Ukraine (1728) and Smolensk province (1731) and eventually settled on private estates, evading official expulsion with the cooperation of the local gentry. Recommendations by the powerful Senate to permit the temporary sojourn of Jews in "Little Russia" (Ukraine) and Riga for economic purposes did not impress Empress Elizabeth, who famously declared: "I desire no mercenary profit from the enemies of Christ."[2] For most Russians, the figure of the Jew was merely an abstract idea; Russian Orthodoxy remained "uncontaminated by Poland's anti-Jewish stereotypes."[3] The partitions of Poland (1772–95), which brought not only new lands but other peoples into the Russian Empire, changed all this, as will be shown below.

Like other minorities, Russian Jews were subject to the ambivalent, evolving aspirations of a modernizing state. In the prereform era (1800–1855), the Russian Empire sought to integrate Jews into the state with the goal of ensuring stability in the new borderlands. As the documents here demonstrate, Jews—even the most traditional—were ineluctably drawn into the vortex of imperial law and administration. They registered their vital information (births, deaths, marriages, and divorces) for the state, paid taxes, and served in the military; increasingly, from midcentury on they utilized the reformed state courts, attended public schools and universities, and read Russian newspapers and literature; and, in growing numbers, they embraced the promise of selective integration, which allowed Jews in "useful" social categories to leave the Pale of Settlement. Although driven by a bureaucratic impulse to simplify and standardize, St. Petersburg nevertheless sought to maintain the boundary between the center and periphery—for fear that the interior might be overrun with an "excessive presence of Jews."[4] But once the government breached the dam in the mid-nineteenth century, it could hardly contain the floodwaters: the Great Reforms (1860s–70s) unleashed expectations of fundamental change among Jews, as among other segments of the population, and paved the way for a public debate about the so-called Jewish Question. For some, however, selective emancipation—which liberated categories of individuals "from the jurisdiction of the Jewish community" at the expense of the collective—was unacceptable.[5] Like other minorities in postreform Russia (1870–1904), Jewish activists increasingly demanded full civic rights and cultural autonomy, aspirations that the regime was less and less disposed to satisfy, but that became central to Jewish life and politics in late Imperial Russia.

Enlightened Absolutism and Its Russian-Jewish Subjects (1762–1800)

After a palace coup brought Catherine the Great (r. 1762–96) to the throne, she embraced both the ideals of the *philosophes* and the prerogatives of absolute despotism. Her main goal was to transform Russia into what Marc Raeff has called a "well-ordered *Polizeistaat*"—a state that would ensure good governance and the well-being of its subjects.[6] Based on the deliberations of the Legislative Committee, which provided valuable instructions and input, the Catherinean regime embarked on its ambitious plan of state building, economic development, and social and cultural change.[7]

Even prior to the territorial annexation of Poland in 1772, which brought sizable numbers of Jews into the empire for the first time, Catherine had already begun to consider the question of Jewish immigration and status. Once the issue of Jewish settlement arose in the Senate, the empress wrote—in her usual third person—of a dilemma rooted in the diverging interests of an enlightened ruler (favorably disposed toward the immigration of any group) and anxiety about the complications that this might entail:

> Every matter in the Senate was carried [out] according to a schedule, with the exception of matters of extreme urgency, and as luck would have it, at this session a project to permit Jews into Russia was first on the agenda. Catherine was in a difficult position if she should give her approval to such a proposal, even though it was universally recognized as beneficial. . . . Catherine simply answered the procurator-general, when he approached her for her decision: "I desire that this matter be postponed to another time." Thus, it is often not enough to be enlightened, to have the best of intentions and the means of carrying them out, however often [people] might express bold decisions about wise conduct.[8]

While she could prevaricate before 1772, the first Polish partition (followed by the second in 1793 and the third in 1795) made it imperative that Catherine define the status of Jews in the empire. The partitions gave Russia lands from the right bank of the Dnieper River (Podolia, Volhynia, and Kiev provinces) to eastern Belorussia, and from Polish Livonia (Vitebsk and Mogilev provinces) to Lithuania. In the process, Russia acquired the largest Jewish populations in Europe, numbering almost a million.[9]

In the spirit of autocratic goodwill, Catherine promised to guarantee the Jews "all the freedoms which they now enjoy with regard to their religion and their property . . . for the humanity of Her Imperial Highness makes it impossible for her to exclude only them from her general benevolence for all."[10] The extension of religious tolerance was an act of pragmatic *raison d'état*: Catherine's empire embraced an astonishing array of faiths—not only Russian Orthodoxy, but also Catholicism, Protestantism, Islam, Buddhism, Karaism, Judaism, and others. Determined to expand the demographic base (for economic, taxation, and conscription reasons), an enlightened ruler like Catherine had no intention of resorting to mass expulsions or forced conversions. To facilitate absorption and minimize conflict, her regime recognized the structure and status of each confession in order to ensure order and stability in non-Russian areas and the borderlands.

In the Jewish case, however, the state found that its imperial method—to co-opt existing elites and institutions and make them into instruments of control—did not work well. In contrast to groups like Baltic German Protestants and Polish Catholics, Jews did not have an ecclesiastical hierarchy or administration that could serve as a surrogate for the Russian bureaucracy. On the contrary, the Jewish administrative structure in Poland-Lithuania (made up of the intracommunal Council of the Four Lands, regional councils, and local

BALTIC SEA

St. Petersburg

LIVONIA

PSKOV

Moscow

Volga

COURLAND

Riga

Liutsin

Rezhitsa

Sebezh

Nevel'

Dvinsk

Moscva

W. Dvina

VITEBSK

Tel'shi

Shavli

Novo-
Aleksandrovsk

Ponevezh

Drissa

Polotsk

Gorodok

Velizh

SMOLENSK

Oka

KOVNO

Rossieny

Disna

Vil'komir

Sventsiany

Lepel'

Senno

Vitebsk

KALUGA

Kovno

Vil'na

VILNA

Vileika

Orsha

Gor'kii

Mstislavl'

Troki

Oshmiany

Borisov

Mogilev

Chausy

Klimovichi

OREL

Lida

Igumen

MOGILEV

Staryi Bykhov

Cherikov

Grodno

Minsk

Novogrudok

Bobruisk

Sokolka

Volkovysk

Slutsk

Rogachev

Belostok

Slonim

Don

Be'lsk

Pruzhany

MINSK

Rechitsa

Gomel'

KURSK

Kobrin

Pripyat

Mozyr'

Warsaw

Brest

Pinsk

CHERNIGOV

Desna

Donets

KINGDOM
OF
POLAND

R U S S I A N

Ovruch

VOLHYNIA

Chernigov

POLTAVA

KHAR'KOV

Kovel

Vladimir-Volynskii

Novograd-
Volynskii

Radomysl'

Kiev

Lutsk

Rovno

Zhitomir

Vistula

Dubno

Ostrog

KIEV

Kanev

DON

Kremenets

Zaslavl'

Berdichev

Vasil'kov

Poltava

GALICIA

Starokonstantinov

Skvira

Tarashcha

Cherkassy

Dniester

PODOLIA

Litin

Lipovets

Chigirin

Dnieper

Proskurov

Letichev

Vinnitsa

Zvenigorodka

Aleksandriia

EKATERINOSLAV

Prut

Kamenets-
Podol'skii

Novaia
Ushitsa

Gaisin

Uman'

Elisavetgrad

Ekaterinoslav

A U S T R I A N

Bratslav

E M P I R E

Khotin

Mogilev-Podol'skii

Iampol'

Ol'gopol'

S. Bug

Soroki

Balta

KHERSON

TAURIDA

E M P I R E

Bel'tsy

Anan'ev

Orgeev

Siret

Kishinev

Tiraspol'

Bendery

Odessa

Kherson

BESSARABIA

Akkerman

Danube

Izmail

R O M A N I A

B L A C K   S E A

OTTOMAN EMPIRE

Legend:
□ Pale of Settlement
▭ Kingdom of Poland
Reserved for Jewish
settlement

0   50   100   150 miles
0   50   100   150 km

kahals [community councils]) had already begun to decline in the late seventeenth century; by the time of the partitions of 1772–95, only the *kahal* remained intact, and even it was weak and ineffective.[11] The state, poorly represented on the periphery, made this diminished *kahal* its key administrative link to the Jews. The governor of Mogilev, M. V. Kakhovskii, expressed shock on meeting such an "alien" people and offered this description of the *kahal*: "In every town (*mestechko*), both seigniorial and state, the Jews have their own elders who are elected among their own; they elect those who are sufficiently learned in the Talmud and all those who are fully capable. . . . The *kahal* collects taxes for its poor, and for expenditures [on litigation] in case the entire *kahal* or one of its members is summoned to court in a criminal case, to avoid legal punishment through the contribution of money."[12] Although formally abolished in 1844, the *kahal* continued to function informally, especially in such matters as tax collection, social discipline, and (until 1873) military conscription.

As in Poland, the *beit din* (rabbinical court) continued to operate alongside the *kahal*, albeit with more limited jurisdiction. In theory, rabbinical courts were only to resolve cases concerning "Jewish religious laws, rites, and liturgy"; all other civil and criminal matters belonged to the purview of the state magistrates and municipal councils.[13] In practice, however, the *beit din* exercised much broader powers in the Jewish community, going beyond the boundaries of family and religious law. One hostile observer (a Jewish convert to Christianity) complained: "This court examines all Jewish cases, and in spite of the fact that it is not invested with any state authority, it judges Jews in a dictatorial manner—definitively, without an appeals [court], and so severely that there is probably nothing like it."[14] But while St. Petersburg became increasingly critical of the *beit din* and questioned its

usefulness, local authorities defended it. As late as 1854, the governors of Kherson, Ekaterinoslav, and Bessarabia described the Jewish courts favorably and argued that they "freed the state from having to deal with petty suits."[15] Not until the judicial reform of 1864, which established a westernized legal system with a jury of peers, did the *beit din* encounter a serious challenge to its authority and jurisdiction.

Apart from establishing administrative links, the Russian government had to define the estate (*soslovie*) status of Jews and to fit them into the larger estate system that prescribed the juridical status, with attendant privileges and obligations, of each social estate.[16] Eager to increase Russia's urban population (minuscule by European standards—just 5 percent of the population), Catherine required Jews to enroll in the urban estates either as merchants (*kuptsy*) or petty townspeople (*meshchane*) on equal terms with their Christian counterparts.[17] Since Jews were concentrated in commerce and the crafts, these categories seemed appropriate. Those possessing more than 500 rubles in capital could join the merchant guilds and enjoy exclusion from the onerous poll tax registry—the great chasm separating the privileged from the rest of the population. Those lacking such wealth fell into the poll-tax category of petty townspeople and engaged in petty trade, crafts, and service work (often supplemented by selling produce from garden plots and orchards, and animal husbandry).[18] Townspeople were subject not only to the poll tax, but also to corporal punishment, conscription, and restrictions on geographic mobility. But the empire conferred freedom of movement on none (save the nobility), a restriction hotly contested by Jewish merchants seeking to conduct business in the Russian interior.[19]

Emboldened by their right to register as merchants, as well as by the Senate decree of 1777 permitting merchants to "move from one city to another," a trickle of Jews moved to Moscow and Smolensk.[20] Their success provoked the ire of native merchants and triggered demands to exclude Jews from the Russian interior. Most famously, a petition by Moscow merchants complained that Jews routinely sold foreign goods at lower prices by smuggling them across the border and avoiding the customs toll. The merchants accused Jews of manipulating coinage: "Any gold or silver coin, especially Dutch gold coins passing through their hands, never returns intact, but is always cut or debased." The petition also accused Nota Khaimovich Notkin, a wealthy contractor for Count Semen Zorich of Shklov and Count Grigorii Potemkin, of being the worst offender: Notkin allegedly enriched himself "through various subterfuges and forgeries," extracting "goods worth 500,000 rubles from local merchants." The merchants claimed that Notkin had fled abroad with all his capital, having "subjected many merchant households to pitiful ruination; some merchants died of grief, leaving behind poor wives and children without support." The governor of Moscow confirmed that several people filed proceedings against Notkin but denied that their claims added up to the staggering sums cited in the merchants' petition (document 125). Nevertheless, official policy became more restrictive. In revising the terms for Jewish residency on 21 December 1791, Catherine declared: "We find that the Jews do not have any right to register in the merchant estate in the towns and ports of the Russian interior, and only by Our ukase are they permitted to have the rights of citizenship and petty townspeople status in Belorussia."[21] She limited the provinces open to Jewish settlement to Minsk, Iz'iaslav, Kiev, Chernigov, and Novgorodsk-Seversk and opened two new areas to the south, Ekaterinoslav and the Tauride district—measures that some historians see as the beginning of the Pale of Settlement.[22] Others have attributed Catherine's decision to anxiety provoked by the French Revolution, which made her suspicious of the nascent intelligentsia and "French contagion."[23]

Registration in the urban estates did not mean an egalitarian distribution of the tax burden. On the contrary, Jewish townspeople were singled out for higher levies, as in the statute of 23 June 1794, which required Jews to pay a tax "double that assessed from townspeople and merchants of the various Christian confessions."[24] To add insult to injury, the Karaite sect, which sought actively to define itself as separate from the Jews, received a special exemption. Jews were not alone: Peter the Great imposed double taxation on the Old Believers,[25] with half going to the state coffers and the other half "to the Synod as a fine for the schism."[26] Indeed, groups like the Old Believers (not Russian Orthodox) and Jews (not Karaites) were called on to render extra payments at the state's whim. As if to pay lip service to enlightened ideals, however, the law added that Jews "who do not wish to remain, to such are granted the liberty to leave our Empire, on the basis of the Charter of the Towns, upon payment of a three-year double tax."[27] In contrast to their fellow townspeople, Jews at least were exempt from military service, but they had to pay a tax of 500 rubles for the privilege.

Although the majority of Jews resided in small market towns, some made their home in villages, engaging in dairy farming, milling, innkeeping, and distilling alcohol. According to one estimate, the share of the population made up of rural Jews increased from 19 percent to 36 percent as one traveled east from the heartland of Poland.[28] The coercive urbanization of these rural inhabitants on paper generated a host of legal complications, leading to periodic expulsions and relocations.[29] State decrees also sought to prevent Jews from distilling or selling alcohol, which officials saw as a key cause of rural impoverishment.[30]

The first half of the nineteenth century marked the transition from enlightened absolutism to preparations for the Great Reforms. Alexander I (r. 1801–25), who came to power after the assassination of his much-maligned father (Paul I, r. 1796–1801), was very much the heir of his enlightened grandmother, Catherine II. His primary objective was to realize her original plan, to move from state building to legal codification. And although the distractions of war prevented him from achieving most of these objectives, he did lay the institutional foundations of modern Imperial Russia—a meritocratic bureaucracy and education (especially university) system, the annexation of still more territories, and the integration of minorities into the empire. Alexander died intestate in 1825. After some confusion about who was his legal successor (leading to the famous "Decembrist" uprising), his brother Nicholas I (r. 1825–55) came to the throne in an age of "restoration" (encapsulated in the slogan "Orthodoxy, Autocracy, Nationality," discussed below). Traditional historiography portrayed the Nikolaevan reign as the "apogee of autocracy"—marked by the reassertion of royal prerogatives, privileges for Orthodoxy, and the strengthening of serfdom.[31] Modern scholarship has drastically revised that view and characterized this era as one of prereforms.[32] Although the state did more planning than implementing, it assembled data and deliberated options that would significantly facilitate and expedite far-reaching measures during the Great Reforms of the late 1850s and 1860s.

The prereform state devoted considerable attention to its Jewish minority—which was hardly monolithic, divided as it was into religious subcultures: Hasidism and *misnagdism* (and to a much lesser extent *musar*, which emerged later). The Hasidim, concentrated in the southwest and a few northwest provinces (parts of modern Ukraine, Poland,

and Belarus), traced their origins to a spiritual movement permeated with mysticism, magic, and heightened messianic expectation in eighteenth-century Poland. As the printing revolution moved eastward in the seventeenth century, it made the esoteric works of kabbalah, previously the purview of elites, accessible to a broader circle of learned Jews.[33] So popular were the works of kabbalah that, already in the sixteenth century, leaders like R. Moshe Isserles (1520–72) complained that men who could barely get through a portion of the Bible with Rashi's commentary were "jumping to study kabbalah."[34] As a result of this new mystical orientation, many Jews came to believe that the commandments could no longer be performed with perfunctory routine; each act had to be fulfilled with proper intention (*kavanah*), for the fate of human history depended on it. Mystics proliferated across Poland, living ascetic lives free of "frivolity"; they focused instead on "constant mourning over the exile and the continuous flight from sin."[35] Some formed separate prayer groups, praying according to the Lurianic rite;[36] others became miracle workers (*baalei shem*) who healed the sick, wrote amulets for all occasions, and exorcised demons. Many were revered leaders of their communities, not the itinerant charlatans portrayed in traditional scholarship.[37]

One of the most charismatic and talented was R. Israel Baal Shem (called the Besht, meaning "master of the good name"), who became prominent in hasidic lore and historiography as the founder of Hasidism. Recent studies have shown that, contrary to the images of the Besht as a humble mystic who disguised his holy identity or as a populist rebel who stood up against the religious establishment, the Baal Shem was a prominent communal leader who enjoyed the advantages of his position. Archival records show that the Besht, who moved in 1740 to the prominent town of Międzybóż (in modern Ukraine), was held in such high esteem that his community provided him with housing and tax exemptions extended only to the scholarly elite.[38] Tales about his extraordinary gifts also emphasize his charisma, profound knowledge of esoteric magic and kabbalah, powers of healing and prophecy, and heavenly ascents. The Besht introduced several innovations heralding a new spirit in a religious climate saturated with pessimism and gloom. As Moshe Rosman has shown, Hasidism made the "mystical ethos" part of everyday religion and emphasized communal interaction over isolation.[39] Whereas previous kabbalists emphasized Torah study and continual concentration on God (an endless battle against corporeal distractions that served as the primary path to *devekut*, or "cleaving the soul to the divine"), the Besht advocated ecstatic prayer and the sanctification of the mundane. By discovering the "divine potential inherent within the [everyday]," even in the realm of evil, the Besht emphasized the concept of transforming evil into good—achieved through "uplifting wayward thoughts" and "worship through corporeality."[40] This mode of prayer also shifted the emphasis from self-abnegation to joy in worship and the sanctification of mundane activities. And although the Besht restricted his teachings to a small circle of learned disciples, his model of leadership—a *baal shem* who sought "to relieve individual suffering"[41] and a mystic who cared deeply about the public's welfare—paved the way for Hasidism to become a mass movement.

By the late eighteenth century, the Hasidim had developed a doctrine of the *tsaddik*, transforming charismatic leaders from isolated mystics into intermediaries between the divine and ordinary people.[42] In the words of Moshe Idel, "the *tsaddikim* did not conceive of ecstasy as their ultimate goal; rather, they had an additional spiritual aim: the drawing down of the divine effluence for the benefit of the community."[43] Equally important, the masses could no longer be passive beneficiaries but, because they could not achieve *devekut* on their own, must adhere to a hasidic

leader.[44] This intimate relationship between the *tsaddik* and his flock led to the creation of powerful courts in towns across Poland, Ukraine, Belorussia, and Galicia. From the ostentatious courts of the Twersky dynasty in Kiev province (document 1) to the austere court of Simhah Bunem of Przysucha (document 3), each court had its own special character. In part, this continuity was rooted in the hereditary principle of succession (although that was not universally observed), which sustained traditions from generation to generation.[45] Pinhas Minkovsky, who served as the cantor in R. Duvid Twersky's court in Tal'noe, recalled their distinct way of life:

> On a wide expanse in the center of the city of Tal'noe [. . .] there extended a large court, surrounded on all sides by a fence, akin to a small town in and of itself, that, amazingly, contained large and beautiful buildings, like small palaces: a palace for the rebbetzin; a palace for their only son, R. Motele. [. . .] Each one of these buildings was beautifully and tastefully appointed, with the finest appurtenances, expensive furnishings, with servants (male and female), while one building stood entirely vacant. This was the guesthouse of the court, where guest *tsaddikim* and in-laws and relatives would be housed. [. . .] And, it goes without saying, the residence of the *tsaddik* himself outranked them all in beauty and splendor (document 1).

The Twersky court attracted not only disciples but also the attention of the Russian state. Denunciations by Jewish progressives about the exorbitant tribute collected from the local population and their so-called fanaticism sparked several investigations. The secret police reports reveal not only a widespread reverence for the Twersky rebbes (among gentiles as well as Jews), but also a surprising reluctance among local officials to interfere in their activities, despite directives from St. Petersburg (document 2).

Hasidic court life was rich and colorful. Pilgrimages to the rebbe, special Sabbaths and festival meals, especially the rebbe's *tish* and sermon, singing and dancing, storytelling, and other customs were all integral to hasidic daily life. Followers also sought private meetings (*yekhides*) with their rebbe to unburden their heavy souls and receive his blessings. Yekhezkel Kotik, a memoirist and aspiring Jewish intellectual who sharply criticized hasidic men for abandoning their families and livelihoods to visit their rebbes, could not conceal his fondness for their "riotous festivities" and joyful worship.[46] In a less sentimental portrayal of the court of her grandfather, R. Simhah Bunem, in Otwock, Ita Kalish described the family tensions and heartaches behind the bustling scene. Her special attention to the female members of the household, especially the savvy fashion mavens who subverted the rebbe's stringent rules about female modesty, provides a perspective on the gendered dynamics of hasidic life (document 3).

Hasidic courts relied not only on theological persuasion but also on pragmatic, sociopolitical strategies to recruit followers and maintain influence over far-flung communities. As recent studies have shown, the Hasidim first established a social presence by creating separate institutions such as prayer houses and ritual slaughter establishments, thereby undermining the local hierarchy and siphoning off proceeds from the tax on kosher meat (*korobochnyi sbor*). This was all accomplished with the sanction of the Russian state.[47] Next the Hasidim gained a foothold in the existing communal institutions—from the ritual slaughter house to local synagogues—by introducing their own customs and rituals.[48] The success of the Hasidim depended partly on the patronage of the mercantile elites with whom they forged marriage alliances. R. Israel of Kozienice promised that "even merchants, whose work is not always for the sake of God, by cleaving to the *tsaddikim* are . . . raised to God."[49]

As the Hasidim began making inroads into Belorussia, the *misnagdim*[50] actively opposed them, starting in 1772 in Shklov and spreading to other northern towns in tsarist Russia. Abandoning conventional strategies of derision and mockery, the *misnagdim* now resorted to harsher measures: bans, persecution, the burning of hasidic books, the dissemination of anti-hasidic pamphlets, and denunciations of the Hasidim to the Russian government. Their aim was nothing less than the total elimination of the Hasidim from Jewish life. Their view that the Hasidim were heretics who "must be brought low" (in the words of one anti-hasidic text) stemmed from both theological and social concerns.[51] One key criticism was the hasidic elevation of prayer over Torah studies as the central value of spiritual life. In contrast to rabbinic prayer, which was "essentially petitionary in nature," hasidic prayer sought to annihilate "the individual ego" and unite with the divine.[52] In the eyes of the *misnagdim*, this transformation of prayer had several pernicious consequences: prayer consumed countless hours (at the expense of Torah studies) and encouraged the Hasidim to have boundless faith in the ability of ordinary human beings to achieve *devekut* with God through mystical prayer. The *misnagdic* rabbis were more pessimistic. R. Phinehas of Polotsk, for example, taught that spiritual life in exile meant a "great distance [between man and God], the inadequacies of human cognition, and the [inaccessible depth of the object of prayer, i.e., God]."[53] The Gaon of Vil'na himself urged that worshipers unable to achieve *kavanah* (proper intention) in prayer must at the very least "recite each word distinctly and keep in mind the meaning of the words."[54] The *misnagdim* also protested that the Hasidim not only changed the liturgy to the Lurianic rite but also engaged in gesticulations and physical motions of ecstasy during prayer (even somersaults)—behavior that the *misnagdim* found bizarre and irreverent. In general, the hasidic penchant for merrymaking and gratification in earthly pleasure was diametrically opposed to the ascetic values of the *misnagdim*.[55] The dispute had its material dimension: the separate hasidic prayer houses and *shehitah* (ritual slaughter) cut into budgetary revenues, especially from the fees on synagogue pews and the kosher meat tax. The latter funded communal expenses, such as rabbinical salaries and educational and charitable institutions.[56] Suspicions about the hasidic use of honed knives for slaughter led some communities (for example, in Shklov) to ban the consumption of their meat: "What their *shohetim* kill may not be eaten; it is carrion, the dishes they use are polluted and forbidden."[57]

In 1798 denunciations to state authorities led to the arrest of two hasidic leaders (R. Shneur Zalman of Liady and R. Asher Perlov of Stolin) and caused a deep bitterness that lingered even after the cessation of overt hostilities (following the death of the Gaon of Vil'na in 1797 and the official recognition of hasidic prayer houses by the state in 1804). Although divisions narrowed in the nineteenth century, underlying tensions occasionally flared up in towns like Dvinsk over issues such as kashrut and veneration of the *tsaddik* or the local rebbe. The memoirs of Sarah Menkin Foner (1854–1935) describe this tense truce: "The adults kept the hatred hidden, but between the children there was always feuding and quarreling." Even if the violence of earlier times had passed, the simmering tensions gave rise to childish barbs, quarrels, and family discord.[58]

By the early nineteenth century, what had begun as an anti-hasidic movement had turned into a cultural movement in its own right. At the core of *misnagdic* life was the reinvigoration of Torah studies and the cultivation of *yirah* (fear of God). No one symbolized these values more than Eliyahu ben Shelomoh Zalman (1720–97), better known as the Gaon of Vil'na, credited by many with galvanizing opposition to Hasidism.[59] Yehoshua Heschel Levine, who wrote the first biography of the Gaon in *Sefer aliyot Eliyahu* (The Ascents of Eliyahu) in 1856, portrayed him as a Jewish scholar (*talmid hakham*) par excellence who became an iconic symbol of learning and piety (document 4). This hagiography drew on testimonies of the Gaon's disciples and family members and exalted his extraordinary memory, intellectual acumen, and asceticism. As some scholars argue, the myths that arose after the Gaon's death reflected the needs of their authors more than the historical figure. Levine, for example, recast the Gaon as a Jewish intellectual who sanctioned secular knowledge, albeit in subordination to the Torah, "a strategy that project[ed] the confrontation between Haskalah and orthodoxy back . . . more than fifty years earlier."[60] In any case, the Gaon's image served to define the lofty ideals of *misnagdism*, even if his actual lifestyle and views (especially on family life) were hardly conventional for his time.[61]

The determination to elevate Torah study also dominated the writing of R. Hayyim of Volozhin (1749–1821). His monumental *Nefesh ha-hayyim* (Breath of life, 1824) drew heavily on *Keter Torah* (Crown of Torah, 1788) by R. Phinehas of Polotsk and provided not only a critique of Hasidism but also a clear statement of the *misnagdic* ethos. Alarmed that Hasidism had gained a foothold among scholarly elites, R. Hayyim of Volozhin employed popular kabbalistic notions to endow Torah studies with special mystical meaning. Whereas the worlds could exist without prayer (for "prayer is the life of the hour"), he argued that they would perish without the Torah, which is "eternal life." According to him, the study of Torah not only facilitated the personal experience of cleaving to God but could also have a profound influence on upper worlds.[62] To promote full-time Torah study, in 1803 R. Hayyim established the yeshiva in Volozhin, transforming an institution that had been dependent on the local rabbi and his contract into a free-standing institution with its own administrative and financial structures. Other yeshivot followed in Mir, Telz [Tel'shi],[63] Slobodka, Ponevezh, and elsewhere, becoming hotbeds of Jewish intellectual activity, not always entirely within the acceptable bounds of the curriculum.[64]

Full-time study was not a prerequisite for partaking in the lofty ideals of *misnagdism*. Learned householders, who had to work to earn a living, reserved time to study or participated in local associations. Troubled by the distractions that prevented members from fulfilling their obligations, in 1859 the Grodno Association adopted the following ordinance: "Whereas in [recent] years our Association has shown signs of succumbing to the burden of earning a livelihood so that we are unable to assemble for the study of Talmud regularly, we have all decided to allot to each member of our Holy Society the task of completing for himself several pages of the Talmud so that the entire Talmud may be completed by the feast of Simhat Torah."[65] The less learned gravitated to the study of *aggadah* (anthologized in a popular early modern collection called *Ein Yaakov*) or the Psalms. In the town of Belostok, the Psalm Reading Association agreed to chant together following a leader, especially since "we the undersigned are not learned."[66] Women could also earn a spiritual reward, either by serving as primary breadwinners (thereby freeing their husbands to study) or by supporting Torah scholars and the yeshivot (monetarily or in kind).

The tendency to focus exclusively on Torah study and neglect the cultivation of ethics or morality in the sphere of human relations troubled R. Israel Lipkin of Salant (better known as R. Salanter, 1810–83), the founder of the *musar* movement. According to one account, R. Salanter recalled an encounter on Yom Kippur with a man who "was so filled with the fear of God" that he failed to answer a question posed by the rabbi: "After I passed him, I thought to myself, 'Is it my fault that you are a God-fearing man and filled with

trembling at the Day of Judgment? What has that to do with me? Are you not required to answer my questions pleasantly and patiently, because such is the way of goodness and kindness?'"[67] To address what he perceived as a gap between all-consuming piety and neglect of basic human decency, R. Salanter emphasized the importance of ethical education. The goal was to curb the "appetite" (*ta'avah*) that led individuals to succumb to "the *yetzer* (evil inclination) and its tricks." Although he held that the love of God should inspire good behavior, he acknowledged that the only force that could successfully tame the appetite was "fear of God" (*yirah*) or of divine punishment.[68] His psychological approach to ethical education provided the foundation for the three schools of *musar* that developed in the late nineteenth century, under his disciples Yitshak Blazer (1837–1907), Simhah Zisl Ziv Broda (1824–98), and Naftali Amsterdam (1832–1906).[69]

The state was hardly knowledgeable about this diverse religious landscape—which, in fact, did not fully crystallize until the mid-nineteenth century. However, it did begin to assemble basic information about the general contours of its Jewish subjects. Under Paul I, the Senate collected reports from marshals of the nobility in the western provinces, the main focus being the countryside. Rural Jews—leaseholders, tavern owners, and innkeepers—came to embody the "Jew" in official discourse, even though these groups were hardly representative. The marshals of Minsk province cited frequent crop failures as a cause of peasant poverty but placed most of the blame on Jews who sold "liquor to the peasants on credit" (with surety consisting of property needed to earn a livelihood), with the result that this practice left them "in squalor" and incapable of "engaging in agriculture."[70] The marshals of Podolia concurred and even suggested reducing the Jews to serfs as a solution—a self-serving recommendation that state officials rejected.[71] Despite occasional expulsions from the countryside and other measures, a plethora of court documents from Vil'na reveals that the state struggled in vain to suppress Jewish distillation and distribution of liquor: cases of Jewish illegal distillation in basements and sheds jammed court dockets throughout the nineteenth century (documents 135–136).

The government of Alexander I also considered several proposals to deal with the Jewish population. From his father's reign, Alexander inherited a comprehensive survey by I. G. Frizel (the governor of Lithuania) and a report by Senator Gavriil Derzhavin (who, after a personal tour of Belorussia in 1799, echoed the economic claims of the marshals).[72] Derzhavin also relied on advice from notable Jewish advisors, including Dr. Il'ia Frank, who invoked Moses Mendelssohn as the inspiration for religious, educational, and communal reform. In Frank's view, the Talmud was to blame for the isolation of Jews from all other nations; hence, to transform the Jews, the state should establish schools to teach Jews in Russian, German, and Hebrew: "By just such means did Mendelssohn enlighten himself, and afterward he had recourse to such means in order to enlighten his German fellow believers, and the most fortunate success crowned his endeavors."[73] As for the autonomous structure of Jewish society, Derzhavin argued that the kahal (a "state within a state") oppressed the poor through the threat of exclusion and therefore must be abolished (as had already been done in the Prussian and Habsburg states). Citing tsarist policy toward Muslims ("We have established a mufti for Islam; so why not a head for the Jewish faith?"), Derzhavin proposed to create a Jewish analogue to the Spiritual Muslim Assembly that Catherine II had established in 1788.[74]

In 1802 Alexander I appointed trusted confidants to a special Committee for the Organization of Jewish Life (known as the Jewish Committee), with the charge to "recommend measures to correct the existing state of the Jews."[75] Wild rumors circulated that these five officials[76] wielded unlimited power to "deal with [the Jews] at their discretion" and provoked so much anxiety in Jewish communities that Viktor Kochubei agreed to meet with deputies from each kahal. The deputies from Kiev and Minsk vigorously protested harsh measures toward rural Jews (expulsions and restrictions on alcohol leases) and warned that these would have catastrophic consequences.[77] Their remonstrations fell on deaf ears, however. Declaring that "nowhere are there designed for them [the Jews] measures more moderate or more indulgent," the Jewish Committee submitted a proposal that the emperor subsequently promulgated as the Statute of 1804 (Polozhenie dlia evreev).[78] The statute reflected both the ambitions of a state eager to integrate its subjects into a unified legal and administrative structure and the peculiarities of a multiconfessional empire that tolerated and even encouraged differences. In this case, Petersburg drew on policies already enacted for its Muslim subjects in Kazan and Orenburg, while leaving more room for Jewish autonomy.[79]

Although traditional scholarship has tended to dismiss the statute and other measures under Alexander as ineffectual, they did signal a step toward administrative integration along with a recognition of confessional difference. On one level, the state began to define Jewish legal status (creating, in James Scott's felicitous phrase, "legible identities").[80] The statute required Jews to register in one of four categories (farmers, manufacturers and artisans, merchants, or townspeople) and threatened to punish violators as "vagrants" liable to the full "severity of the law." Although enforcement was initially weak, over time the number of "vagrancy cases" (those arrested for failure to register) steadily increased in the court records.[81] In addition, the statute required that Jews adopt a hereditary surname (article 32) and to use such in official documents, so as to "better manage their civil status, protect their property, and resolve civil disputes among them."[82] The requirement was hardly original; in 1787 Joseph II had required Jews in the Habsburg realm to adopt surnames.[83] In choosing surnames, Russian Jews gravitated toward place names (such as Korostyshev), occupations (Shneiderman, meaning tailor), or physical traits (Kleiner, meaning small).[84] The state's insistence on the proper spelling of personal names and surnames aimed to combat the tendency of Jews to use nicknames and double names to trick the evil eye.[85] In striving to record (and therefore govern) Jews, the statute allowed some communal autonomy by permitting the triennial election of the communal rabbi and *kahal* elders (article 50).

The bulk of the statute focused on educational and economic reforms, echoing the call for enlightenment, civic amelioration, and productivization in Joseph II's Edict of Tolerance. Like the Hapsburg law, the statute allowed Jews to enroll in schools and universities on an equal footing with other students, but, given the dearth of primary and secondary schools in Russia, in fact Jews could not take advantage of this invitation.[86] The law allowed Jews to retain their distinctive beliefs, but it required them to discard their garb and don German or Polish dress on enrolling at the gymnasium level (to ensure "unanimity and decorum"). Jews who rejected the option of a state education could send their children to special Jewish schools, funded by their own communities — but only if these schools included the study of Russian, Polish, or German[87] (the goal being to facilitate business transactions and other public interaction). Henceforth only public documents (account books, contracts, bills of sale, and so forth) in one of those official languages were valid in legal proceedings.[88] Nevertheless, as the Vil'na court records show, Jews routinely presented translations of Yiddish documents instead of original Russian ones.[89] The language requirement also applied to elected officials and representatives of the Jewish community, a policy previously applied to Muslim mullahs in 1788 and 1789.[90]

The physiocratic view of the Jewish economy as unproductive, even harmful, also figured prominently in the statute. Earlier recommendations to restrict Jewish commercial activities resurfaced in several articles, including article 34: "No Jew, starting on 1 January 1807 . . . may hold any kind of lease (*arenda*) on a tavern, drinking house, or inn in any hamlet or village, either in his own or another's name, nor sell alcoholic drinks or live in them under any pretenses whatsoever, even in transit."[91] The looming war with Napoleon prompted Alexander I to soften these stipulations and to permit Jews to continue their current activities almost until the end of his reign. At the same time, the state offered positive incentives, such as exemption from double taxation, for Jews who became "useful" farmers, factory workers, and artisans. Attempts to resettle Jews in agricultural settlements, especially in the southern regions of the empire, continued under subsequent rulers and created new Jewish communities that were very different from the older establishments (documents 141–144).

In June 1812 Napoleon's Grande Armée invaded Russia, confident of a quick, decisive victory. Six years earlier, the Austrian ambassador to Paris, Prince Klemens von Metternich, had raised doubts about the loyalty of Russia's subjects in the western provinces: "There is no doubt that he [Napoleon] will not fail to present himself as a liberator to the Christian people of Poland and as a messiah to its immense Jewish population."[92] In the event, such predictions proved erroneous: the Jews remained loyal to the tsar. "On the first day of Rosh Hashanah, before *musaf*, I realized that if France will win the war, riches will increase among the Jews and they will prosper," wrote R. Shneur Zalman of Liady to his disciples. However, he warned of a heavy price: "But they will become estranged from God, blessed be He. But if Alexander, the tsar of Russia, will win the war, the Jews will become impoverished but their hearts will be joined with God, blessed be He."[93] R. Shneur Zalman cited Napoleon's newly created Grand Duchy of Warsaw to demonstrate the impact of the Napoleonic Civil Code on the traditional Jewish way of life. The code demanded not only a transformation in Jewish dress, language, and customs, but also military conscription (with no exemptions save for one rabbi and cantor in each community). Faced with the difficulties of conscription among unwilling Jews, however, the government substituted a sizable fee in lieu of service.[94] Moreover, the Napoleonic wars ravaged many Lithuanian and Belorussian market towns where Jews resided. The Polish historian Julian Niemcewicz visited Pinsk in 1819 and, even years after the war, found a desolate, moribund city:

> The [political] integration of the Dnieper and Black Sea basins did not greatly revive economic activity. . . . Their sole cargo is salt, sold at the price of one ducat (*czerwony zloty*) per barrel. The entire trade is in the hands of a Jew by the name of Rabinowicz. The ships, for the most part, return empty. Some carry a little liquor and when they reach Niz, that is, the region of Mozyr, they load tar and coal. Pinsk is thus one big salt warehouse for the entire area of Lithuania, but I have seen there neither warehouse nor commercial traffic.[95]

As the dust of war settled, Alexander I turned his attention to newly acquired territories, including Bessarabia and the Kingdom of Poland (created at the Congress of Vienna out of the former Duchy of Warsaw and other French protectorates). Although Alexander resisted Polish demands to extend the borders of the kingdom to include the former Grand Duchy of Lithuania, he did acquiesce to the Poles' aspirations for self-government and a progressive constitution that promised "no distinction in the enjoyment of civil and political rights,"[96] although these promises were not always honored. St. Petersburg also introduced measures to transform Jews into model subjects worthy of these privileges. This meant dismantling the infrastructure of Jewish autonomy: the abolition of the *kahal* in 1822 (to be replaced with Congregation Boards) and a ban on Jewish associations, including the powerful burial societies.[97] The Russian state also expected Jews to study the Polish language in the new school system and sought to wean them from trade in favor of agriculture.[98] Although a large proportion of the Jews in the kingdom were hasidic, small circles of financiers, physicians, and intellectuals emerged in Warsaw and advocated greater integration into Polish society and culture.[99] These Polish lands later turned into hotbeds of discontent and nationalism, erupting in rebellion against tsarist rule in 1830–31 and 1863. Alexander I, increasingly conservative in his waning years, regarded the developments in Poland with concern and declined to undertake any radical experiments within the empire itself. He died childless, leaving the Jewish Question to his successors to resolve.

Ascending to the throne in 1825, Nicholas I crushed the Decembrist uprising and proclaimed a conservative agenda of incremental change: "Not by impudent dreams, which are always destructive, but changes in the fatherland are being achieved from above and gradually, shortcomings overcome, and abuses corrected."[100] At least publicly, the Nikolaevan regime represented a deliberate antithesis of enlightenment, revolution, and indeed the West more generally. The minister of education, the classicist Sergei Semenovich Uvarov, formulated the basic principles of the regime as "Orthodoxy, Autocracy, Nationality." While the first two elements were easy to decode, the term "nationality" (*narodnost'*) referred vaguely to a unique social order, interpreted by many as a euphemism for serfdom. However, it could also be read to mean

"Russian" — at the expense of the empire's national minorities.[101]

Despite the counter-enlightenment and archconservative rhetoric, the Nikolaevan regime was not so much counter-reform as pre-reform — a government that collected data, analyzed problems, trained officials, and laid the foundations for the Great Reforms of the late 1850s and 1860s. To be sure, Nicholas was exceedingly cautious: in his view, the vast problems confronting Russia — from serfdom to discontent among national minorities — had to be approached with the utmost care and secrecy, lest the administration raise wild hopes and only aggravate the problem of popular unrest. Given his distrust of educated society and even his own bureaucracy, Nicholas relied heavily on close advisors, secret committees, and information collected by the Third Section, a kind of political police that sought to maintain vigilant surveillance over state and society.[102] Nicholas also created additional sections in His Majesty's Own Chancery to address difficult questions, bypassing the regular bureaucracy altogether.[103] The most significant change involved the state peasantry, the target of far-reaching reform by Count Pavel Dmitrievich Kiselev (the same Kiselev who later chaired the Jewish Committee). The overarching aim was to promote social development in the broadest terms, including the creation of village schools and public health facilities, the promotion of newer and more efficient agricultural methods, a more equitable system of taxation and conscription, and even limited self-government.[104]

That "modernizing" impulse also informed government attempts to address the Jewish Question. As with other national and religious minorities (including Lutherans and Catholics), the Nikolaevan regime sought to impose clear administrative uniformity and to integrate non-Russian, non-Orthodox groups into the imperial system. The goal was not to assimilate, but to integrate them — to create unique administrative structures that allowed the regime to exercise some control over these alien elements in the imperial system.[105] In the case of Jews, who had evaded decades of attempts at administrative control, Nicholas perceived a particularly harmful element much in need of control: "They are absolute leeches, fastening themselves everywhere and completely exhausting these unfortunate provinces."[106] As his first measures reveal, Nicholas sought to discipline the Jews with a firm military hand. Thus the conscription edict of 1827 marked the first attempt to transform the Jews into proper subjects. Harrowing images of the Nicholaevan conscription, especially the drafting of minors and the twenty-five-year term of service (for all conscripts, not just Jews), remain etched in the Jewish imagination. For the first time, Jewish males from the poll-tax population between the ages of twelve and twenty-five became liable to conscription; only the privileged (such as registered artisans and guild merchants) enjoyed exemptions. The unsavory task of filling the quota fell to the *kahal*, which selected the most "undesirable" (or expendable) youths for conscription. As communal authorities of Grodno reported in 1827, they had drafted "idlers who paid no taxes and others not tolerated by the community," while the elders in Minsk selected vagrants, servants, and those with no occupation "but playing cards."[107]

The main burden of military service, however, fell on orphaned and impoverished children.[108] Minors, who were too young for the regular army regiments, joined the cantonist battalions first created under Peter the Great. Yehudah Leib Katsenelson (Buki ben Yagli) recalled the feeling of pity when he saw these "soldier-children, Hebrew children, dainty and pretty children, and all of them with their sidelocks shorn."[109] Complaints about illegal recruitment from devastated parents and relatives denouncing corrupt leaders and other unscrupulous Jews soon flooded the offices of the provincial governors (documents 154–155). They reflected not only painful rifts in the community, divided by class and privilege, but also bitter disputes within poor families. In 1834, for example, Gershko Shor registered his second wife's son from a previous marriage in the family poll tax registry but not his own sixteen-year-old from a previous marriage. To all appearances, he had given her son sanctuary from conscription—the government exempted "only sons" from the draft. As Shor's second wife told the governor of Kiev, her husband agreed "to pay the [poll] tax for my son until he came of age, and as a woman I placed my hopes on this, being naive [about] this kind of deception." In fact her husband had registered four other male "souls" in the family census (presumably in exchange for bribes), thereby depriving her son of his only-son status. Having lost key documents in a fire, Shor's wife had no basis for a legal suit and could only implore the emperor to intercede personally: "Your Highness, as a defenseless widow and a complete orphan, I beseech you to protect my son from illegal recruitment in place of another family."[110] Those who lacked power and influence sometimes resorted to desperate measures of evasion, ending up in court on charges of self-mutilation, forgery of documents, and fraud (documents 158–159).

In contrast to Jews in the Kingdom of Poland, who saw military service as the prelude to civic emancipation, Jews in the Pale held no such illusions.[111] Quite apart from the lengthy term and harsh conditions, the army's practice of coercive conversion aroused horror and trepidation. Although in principle soldiers had the right to practice their religion in the military, Jewish cantonists were subject to intense missionary pressure that emanated from the emperor himself. Orthodoxy—one of the three central pillars of Nikolaevan ideology—served to promote uniformity and discipline in the army. In 1843, for instance, Nicholas sent this confidential instruction to his minister of war: "Embark on the conversion to Christianity of those who are in the

schools of the military [settlements], cantonists of the Jewish faith through reliable priests, adding if necessary to the special instructions that have been required by Count [N.] Protasov [chief procurator of the Holy Synod]. But [do so] in order that this matter is given special attention and pursued with all possible caution, gentleness, and without the slightest coercion."[112] One year later, Nicholas expressed deep disappointment that only 34 cantonists out of 3,007 in the Karabinernyi Regiment had converted: "Report again to His Excellency [head of the Karabinernyi Regiment] that His Imperial Majesty is not pleased with the poor success in converting the lower-ranking cantonists of the Jewish confession to the Russian faith."[113] In another instance, in 1847, the tsar complained that, "too few are converting to the Russian Orthodox faith."[114]

Military commanders had several explanations for the lethargic pace of conversion. No doubt some military officers, whether from sloth or caution, were reluctant to force young recruits to convert. Military authorities preferred to blame the local priests, castigated for paying "little attention to this subject"; insofar as the clergy were subordinate to the ecclesiastical authorities, such assertions conveniently shifted the blame from the army to the Church. At least some clergy, however, were zealous about conversion. For example, Bishop Iakov of Saratov proposed to create a Hebrew text of the Bible to prove the clergy's arguments more effectively, require parents to correspond to their sons in Russian, and transfer cantonists who had been subjected to meddling by local Jews to other places in the empire.[115] And some military commanders frankly declared that conversion was by no means a simple matter, even when cantonists were young and presumably still had "an open mind." In fact, the commanders observed, "the youth are deeply immersed in their Judaism."[116] Petitions by parents on behalf of their cantonist sons also revealed the deeply held conviction among the Jews that they had the right to practice their own faith (document 157).[117]

When some commanders, despite the injunction to avoid coercion, did conduct wholesale conversions to satisfy Nicholas's expectations, they met with resistance and evasion. The archival records show that some soldiers who had been forcefully converted obstinately refused to observe the rites of Russian Orthodoxy[118] or even returned to Judaism at the first opportunity (document 20).[119] Under state law, however, such reversion was apostasy, and it was punishable as a criminal offense until the Manifesto on Freedom of Conscience in April 1905, after which hundreds converted back to Judaism.[120]

Despite the notorious Nikolaevan penchant for bureaucratic obfuscation,[121] the bureaucratic narratives are permeated with contradictions that expose the gap between imperial wish and local reality. Whereas the state imagined the military as the ideal site to transform the cantonist into a loyal subject of a patriarchal society, the effort contravened the principle of "unquestioned paternal obedience" by requiring Jewish cantonists "to abjure the faith of their fathers" and embrace Russian Orthodoxy. And ultimately coercive conversion also proved counterproductive: it sought to erase confessional and social boundaries and to transform Jews into Russians, but it had the opposite effect—it actually heightened Jewish self-awareness.[122] Even when the military did appear to achieve its goal of transforming Jewish conscripts into "Russians" (so that they would be indistinguishable from their neighbors after being released from the army), the converts retained bonds with their Jewish relatives. That is apparent in cases of former cantonists who married Russian Orthodox women, yet maintained ties to their Jewish kin. In 1879, for instance, a domestic servant named Shendlia (no surname) arrived in Starokonstantinov (in Volhynia province) to leave her six-year-old daughter with her

older brother—a Jewish cantonist who had converted to Russian Orthodoxy. Desperate, the mother beseeched him to take her daughter while she went to Odessa to work as a cook; her employers refused to hire her if she brought along the child. Her brother, now residing in Kiev, took in the child.[123]

The 1827 law on Jewish conscription was but a prelude to a systematic policy of integration under Nicholas I, the goal being to impose order and state control over Jewish daily life. Imperial integration meant, above all, giving a clear definition to the juridical status of Jews. As part of a general campaign to compile and consolidate the myriad laws of the empire, the emperor directed the Jewish Committee to examine the statutes concerning the Jews, a task already begun toward the end of Alexander I's rule. In 1830 the Second Department, under the de facto leadership of Mikhail Speranskii, published the *Complete Collection of the Laws of the Russian Empire*, and three years later it produced the *Digest of Laws* (effective from 1835). For the first time since the Law Code of 1649, the empire now had both an authoritative collection of all laws and a handbook that systematized existing law into a thematic digest. The *Digest* was a direct blow against bureaucratic arbitrariness in favor of the rule of law, and it also fostered a new level of legal consciousness.[124] In 1835 the state promulgated the Statute on the Jews, which dealt specifically with the Jews and their status.[125] The *Digest* and this statute now provided a clear legal basis for petitions and litigation; to bolster their case, Jews could now invoke specific laws—sometimes even citing laws intended for other groups. It was no longer necessary to appeal only to the emperor's pity or identity as dispenser of extralegal moral justice. One boundary that the statute clearly demarcated was the Pale of Settlement (*cherta osedlosti*), the fifteen western provinces in which Jews (with some exceptions) were to reside until 1917.[126] Although the Kingdom of Poland was not included in the Pale, the government banned Polish Jews from entering the Russian interior but did allow movement between the Pale and the kingdom. In reality, despite state efforts to restrict Jewish mobility, some Jews simply ignored boundaries and caused the regime to conduct an endless battle to apprehend and expel illegal residents from the Russian interior.[127] Others pursued a legal strategy, petitioning the authorities for permission to move on grounds of usefulness to the state, family reunification, and so forth (document 127).

The state also attempted to restructure the institutions governing Jewish communal life. Although critical of the Jews' various religious holidays and customs (as the main obstacle to Jews becoming productive subjects), the government nonetheless employed a religious framework to implement reform. The Jewish Committee informed the emperor: "The religion of the Jews is the principal, and possibly the sole, force shaping the social and family position of this people."[128] So pervasive was Judaism in every aspect of Jewish life that, the committee noted, Western European governments deemed it the most effective "instrument by which to transform the Jewish people."[129] Given this premise, some countries had established religious consistories in the capitals and provinces as an administrative tool for governing the Jewish population.[130] According to Kiselev, the committee's chairman, this approach not only succeeded in consolidating authority into one central institution (thereby facilitating state oversight) but also helped to eliminate "previous biases that alienated the Jews from the rest of civil society."[131] The fundamental question was how to obtain similar results in Russia.

Following the example of the Kingdom of Poland, in 1844 the committee abolished the *kahal*, striking a blow at the traditional basis for Jewish autonomy. Although the *kahal* continued to perform some of its former duties (in particular, tax collection and conscription), it no longer enjoyed the status and power of an official body. In 1845 the committee proposed to establish a "special central institution, which would have a moral influence on the Jews," and which could "give force to the decrees promulgated by the government to transform this people."[132] This rationale underlay the formation of a consistory-like administrative system (based on the French model), headed by the Rabbinic Commission and augmented by a provincial rabbinate operating under the Ministry of Interior. The commission was to deal with matters of marriage and divorce, education, and synagogues; the provincial rabbinate was to oversee general matters such as record keeping, as well as the initial disposition of marriage and divorce cases.[133] In principle, the ancient régime in Russia — until its demise with the Bolshevik seizure of power in 1917 — gave each confession responsibility for marriage and divorce. Here Imperial Russia differed sharply from most European countries, which gradually placed marriage under state control. Indeed, it is easy to understand why the tsarist regime was loath to assume control and impose a standard marital code on a multinational, multiconfessional empire, given the mind-boggling complexity of such matters as well as their provocative political implications. Although some officials advocated secularizing marriage and divorce, and although the state did include some related matters in criminal law (for example, bigamy), the government generally left marital questions for the religious authorities to sort out and resolve.

In recording vital statistics, the state was distinctly more interventionist. As early as 1835, the government declared that only the official state rabbi (*kazennyi ravvin*) and his assistant had the right to perform and record Jewish marriages, divorces, circumcisions, and burials. In 1853 the state added the fateful clause that "marriages and divorce not performed by the state rabbi and his assistant will be considered illegitimate."[134] The assignment of record keeping was hardly accidental; it co-incided with a systematic attempt by the Russian state to standardize registration and ensure full compliance.[135] Thus it distributed to the clergy of each confession printed, bound metrical books (*metricheskie knigi*), with individual entry numbers. This format made it virtually impossible to falsify entries by excising or adding pages *post factum*. Although the documentation was irksome and costly, Jews soon realized the importance of timely and accurate registration in the metrical books. All this became painfully apparent to the widow Lipa Froima Gol'dberg when she later sought to demonstrate her marriage to Leib Gol'dberg. As so often happened in these cases, a spiritual rabbi (*dukhovnyi ravvin*)—who did not enjoy official status but held spiritual authority in the community—had officiated at the wedding but neglected to register the marriage with the state rabbi. As a result, the wedding was never recorded in the metrical books and therefore had no legal validity. This oversight cost Lipa Gol'dberg dearly. After her husband's death, she applied to receive his military pension; when she could not produce the metrical record of marriage, however, the state summarily rejected her petition on the simple grounds that she had no proof of their marriage.[136]

The civil registration of religious marriages inevitably invited resistance, manipulation, and abuse: some evaded registration at all costs, while others took advantage of spelling mistakes to evade the draft.[137] Still others shirked the obligation to support former wives by declaring their marriages null and void (because they were not recorded in the metrical books). Jewish law deemed such marriages valid, however, and thus the unfortunate wives in such cases could not remarry without a formal *get* (bill of divorcement), turning them into *agunot*—anchored for life.[138] Such challenges forced Jewish women to turn to the state, the same agent that created such tension and disorder in the family.

The tensions between imperial ambitions and Jewish realities led to a critical shift in the 1840s and 1850s: from a strategy of collective to individual integration through education.[139] The shift shaped the policy of official enlightenment among the Jews and dovetailed with the Haskalah (enlightenment and romantic) movement that sought to disseminate secular knowledge and modern sensibilities among the Jews. A small coterie of *maskilim* in the Russian Empire—whose knowledge of Hebrew and German facilitated their engagement with Haskalah literature published in Prussia, Galicia, and Poland—began to develop their own ideologies and programs to address their specific circumstances in the empire.[140]

The autobiographies of the *maskilim*—many of whom came from scholarly backgrounds—portrayed their first encounter with the Haskalah as a journey from "blighted stupidity" to rational thought. "I was weary and exhausted from studying the Talmud, its disputations and various absurdities," wrote Moshe Leib Lilienblum (1843–1910). "When I heard of something new that was rational, I was drawn to it, just like an escaped prisoner coming upon a field of flowers" (document 104). But the *maskilim* did not have to look far for sources of rationalist philosophy: they had only to reexamine the neglected philosophical texts of the medieval and renaissance Jewish canon, which were as important to the East European Haskalah as works from the West.[141] Books thus served as the conduit for self-discovery and also represented a critical facet of a *maskil*'s identity.[142] Enraptured by Hebrew grammar books that elucidated the system of logic in language, Avraham Ber Gottlober (1811–99) waxed eloquent: "As I opened the book *Talmud leshon ivri* [Ben-Zeev's grammar], I seemed as if dreaming whilst awake. Like first fruits before summer I drank in his words which were sweet as honey in my mouth, and I put it not down until completing the entire first section."[143] Unlike their earlier counterparts in Western Europe, the first generation of *maskilim* in the Russian Empire remained strict in their religious observance and conservative in their social mores; they recognized the exhilarating possibilities of the new intellectual vistas yet did not feel compelled to sacrifice Judaism in the process. After reading Mendelssohn's commentary on the book of Ecclesiastes, Mordechai Aaron Guenzburg (1795–1846) upheld the freedom of reason but also recognized the limitations of action:

> The book of Ecclesiastes, which first inspired the spirit of enquiry within me, taught me that it is not considered a sin if a man inquires wisely about the matters that arise in his spirit from time to time. This does not mean that he may ever issue practical edicts based solely on his opinion, God forbid; he must hold to faith and never let go, he must live by its word. . . . [Instead] his inquiries will be his pleasing hobby, by which he shall sharpen his mind and strengthen his sentiments; one's thought is free like a wild creature, but one's actions are tightly bound to the sanctuary of the Torah.[144]

Still, Guenzburg and other *maskilim* began to use fiction to liberate their irrepressible fantasies and anxieties.[145] Here, in the safe domain of early Hebrew and (later) Yiddish literature, the *maskilim* explored their sexual angst, religious doubts, political frustration, anger, and fear. As Guenzburg's own autobiography illustrates, the description of his disastrous wedding night was not simply a critique of early marriage; rather, the text—replete with misogynistic portrayals of women—wrestled with deeper anxieties about Jewish masculinity (or lack thereof), female desire, sexuality, and political powerlessness (document 78).[146]

Eager to transform Jewish society, the *maskilim* leaped at the opportunity to participate and even lead in the Nikolaevan reforms, which confirmed their own desire to reform traditional Jewish education, to modernize Jewish family practices, and to update Jewish dress without undermining the foundations of Judaism as they understood it. With great anticipation, Samuel Fuenn (Fin) of Vil'na wrote in 1840: "Now our master, the emperor, has taken it upon himself to be the tiller of our soil, to uproot from it all rank and bitter weeds, to cleanse the hearts of the Jewish people of all evil schemes and to sprinkle blessed dew upon thirsting, yearning soil."[147] This trust in the state, Olga Litvak observes, was "neither entirely instrumental nor politically misplaced."[148] After all, the *maskilim* were the beneficiaries of imperial power, which compensated for their relative weakness, especially in their protracted and bitter struggle against Hasidism—which they cast as the main impediment to their ambitious visions for educational reform.[149]

On the eve of the state school reforms, Jewish education in Russia still resembled what had developed in early modern Poland. This gendered system limited formal instruction to males and also served to create hierarchy and status in society.[150] Although most boys had an opportunity to study in a *heder*, only the elites actually acquired proficient knowledge of Hebrew and rabbinic literature. In contrast, the children of ordinary Jews learned just enough about the mechanics of reading Hebrew to participate in religious life; hence most Jewish men lacked the literacy skills to comprehend any Hebrew texts beyond the rudimentary prayer book.[151] Nor were all the long hours in the *heder* (from morning until evening) devoted to learning; most students also had to perform chores for the *melamed*'s wife or supervise other children. The revolutionary Lazar Gol'denberg fondly recalled his favorite days in the *heder*, when the rebbe left to say kaddish in the synagogue, leaving the children in the kitchen to pluck chickens with his wife. To their delight, she read popular Yiddish stories such as *Bove korelevich* (Bove the prince) aloud to them: "The more rapturous the other places in the books, the more rapidly the children's fingers worked, picking up a cloud of *pukh* [fluff] in the kitchen until after an hour or an hour and a half of work, the rebbe's wife and all the children were absolutely covered with feathers and we resembled a hen with chicks" (document 28). Few Jewish intellectuals, however, shared Gol'denberg's nostalgia for their childhood education. In the discourse of the Haskalah, the *heder* institutionalized the backwardness of Jewish life. "From the abyss of nothingness there now arises in my memory a low and narrow house full of smoke and poisonous vapors, with a large stove near the opening of the house voiding heat to the surroundings," reminisced Yehudah Leib Katzenelson. "On the stove and on the bed by its side, the family of the *melamed* swarms and rolls about—a choir of half naked children shoving and quarreling—a long and thin woman with a man's face and eyes that drip fury."[152] Critics identified a plethora of shortcomings in the *heder*: unsanitary conditions (deprivation of "air, light or activity"), long hours, incompetent *melamdim* inclined to inflict corporal punishment on the young, and an archaic and useless curriculum.[153] State inspection reports offered similar criticisms, especially from mid-century on. In 1870, for example, an inspector in Vil'na claimed that the *heder* caused real harm to the children's health and added that "the Russian language is so alien to the *heder* that I could hardly understand not only the boys but also the *melamdim*" (document 105). The study of European languages, integral to the Romantic vision of cultural renewal, was more widespread among Jewish women than men, in turn affecting (as will be seen) their path toward modernity.

Most boys completed their schooling in their early teens, leaving the schools and houses of study for jobs and apprenticeships. But children who demonstrated aptitude in their studies would often continue past the age of bar mitzvah. Private tutors and study in the

beit midrash (study house) offered the usual venues for advanced study. Talented Talmud students who devoted themselves to a regime of study earned the right to study alone in the *beit midrash*—or, as Shmarya Levin phrased it, the chance to "sleep" there: "[They] slept in the synagogue and study house. . . . They slept mostly on sacks stuffed with hay and straw. Blankets were unknown. . . . In the winter they used to lie down around the two big stoves at the entrance to the synagogue. In the mornings, they had to get up very early—before the first services began. And it was unbecoming to stop studying before midnight."[154] In many of the yeshivot, students depended on the generosity of householders to provide meals known in Yiddish as the *esn teg* ("eating days"). In addition to the privilege of sleeping in the houses of worship, students benefited from the efforts of communal leaders who sought to shield them from the draft.[155] The goal of these yeshivot was to produce Talmud scholars, not community rabbis. However, challenging economic conditions often led students into the rabbinate, especially at the end of the nineteenth century—frequently to the chagrin of their parents and teachers.[156] A vivid picture of life at the Telz yeshiva—from the application process to everyday routines in the study halls and dormitories—is provided in Ben Zion Dinur's memoirs: "The very study in the Telz yeshiva was a powerful experience: a large hall, broad and wide, row after row of benches in four columns along the hall and *shtenders* [lecterns] in front of each seat on the bench. Not a single place was vacant" (document 109).

Because religious law did not mandate the instruction of females, Jewish girls remained outside the formal educational system. Although some towns did establish a special *heder* for girls in a room adjacent to the boys' *heder*, in most instances female education was private (with tutors), informal, and practical, with an emphasis on both reading and writing.[157] Significantly, women stayed outside the rabbi's disciplinary gaze (and hence were free from the close monitoring that characterized male reading) and could study any language they desired (again, "unsupervised").[158] Families hired tutors to teach their girls how to read and write in Yiddish, skills that served them well in the business and leisure world.[159] Avraham Paperna (1840–1919) recalled how Hindele, the daughter of one of his family's boarders, read and copied a *brivensteller* (manual for letter writing) a hundred times over when she had nothing else to read.[160] In the privacy of their homes, female Yiddish readers devoured both religious literature (such as the popular *Tsene u-rene*) and such other genres as legends and fairy tales (for example, *Centura Ventura* and *Maaseh Bove*). The transition to modern belles-lettres was a natural step.[161] In prosperous families, even among the Hasidim, women learned foreign languages and literature. Nokhem Meyer Shaykevitch (1849–1905), who wrote under the name Shomer, recalled with admiration: "My mother Hadassah was the most renowned of the women of Niesvizh for her knowledge of arithmetic and four languages: Yiddish, Russian, German, and Polish."[162] A few girls from elite families even mastered Hebrew. And the *maskilim* took advantage of women's marginality by opening the first modern schools for girls, including one in Vil'na. This initiative stemmed less from a desire to educate women than from the recognition that the modern curriculum elicited less hostility from traditionalists because it was for girls, who were exempt from the obligation of Torah study.[163]

The campaign to reform Jewish education gained momentum in the 1840s when the state decided to create a system of government-sponsored Jewish schools. In 1828 Yitshak Ber Levinson (1788–1860) had received a grant from the state that enhanced the reputation of his *Te'udah be-Yisrael* (Testimony of Israel), which advocated general education among the Jews.[164] Leveraging the power of the state, the *maskilim* also succeeded in establishing modern schools in Odessa, Kishinev, Vil'na, Minsk, Mitau, Kherson, and Riga.[165] Max Lilienthal (1815–82), the headmaster of the new school in Riga, soon attracted the attention of Minister of Education Sergei Uvarov as someone capable of implementing Jewish educational reform. Lilienthal, a German-educated rabbi, embodied Uvarov's ideal of an enlightened Jew but was a complete stranger to coreligionists in Russia. Lilienthal described the "swarming beehive of Jews" in Vil'na like an anthropologist making his first encounter with an alien community: "A committee led me to the vestry, where I found some hundred men assembled, all dressed in the *zhubetses*[166] and their fur caps. I felt so lonesome in the midst of these strange faces—the only *daytshl* in the crowd of Polish Jews."[167] Not only this "crowd of Polish Jews" but the Jewish intellectuals who had initially welcomed him enthusiastically found Lilienthal supercilious and ignorant in both religious and worldly matters.[168] In Mordechai Aaron Guenzburg's words: "This is not the man whom we need: he knows less Torah than young students and even his philosophical knowledge is not great."[169]

The educational reforms met with fierce opposition not simply because of Lilienthal but also for two more fundamental reasons. First, despite his assurances that the Jews would "receive all the rights of citizenship" without qualification, the state in fact did not promise to improve their legal status.[170] Moreover, Lilienthal could not entirely alleviate genuine fears about the specter of conversion that seemed likely to ensue from the new knowledge and culture. Lilienthal's interlocutor, the *shtot maggid* (town preacher), pointed to the disastrous consequences in Germany following the reforms of the great Mendelssohn: "But the whole mass of people will not know how to discern between the ashes and the jewel, dear doctor. . . . [Our religion] will be surrendered in the course of time, and will you be the instrument for such a calamitous and sinful destruction?"[171] Despite these inauspicious beginnings, the government-sponsored schools spread rapidly through the Pale, offering courses in the Jewish religion (*zakon bozhii*), language instruction (Hebrew, Russian, and German), mathematics, geography, history, and calligraphy.[172] Private schools and trade schools also opened in due course, promising to teach practical skills by gender — such as needlework for girls and woodworking for boys (document 110). In the northwest provinces, Jewish reformers fought to preserve these separate Jewish state schools in order to facilitate gradual acculturation with the preservation of Jewish religious classes. Starting in the 1860s, Russian officials in Vil'na increasingly sought to abolish these institutions, arguing that they fostered "a spirit of separatism" and impeded the process of Russification that they believed was the most effective means to instill loyalty to the empire.[173]

In 1847 the government established state rabbinical seminaries in Vil'na and Zhitomir (centers of Jewish publishing houses) to train state rabbis and teachers for Jewish schools. The seven-year program was impressive, at least on paper. During the first three years, students took secular courses equivalent to the curriculum of a Russian lower school (studying, for example, Russian, arithmetic, and geography) and Jewish subjects such as the Pentateuch with the commentaries of Rashi, the early prophets, the book of Proverbs, and so forth. The next four years were devoted to more advanced gymnasium subjects (including history, physics, and foreign languages) and basic halakhic texts. At the end of these seven years, students could enroll in the one-year pedagogical course for teachers or the three-year program for rabbinical training (document 118).[174] Initially, the standard of religious education was low, partly because the faculty members lacked proper training (many were autodidacts) and

partly because of the poor preparation and quality of the students; by the 1860s, however, all the autodidacts had been replaced by teachers with formal education. The fact that the headmaster and teachers were Christian fueled suspicions among Jews of a government scheme to convert students. Avraam Uri Kovner claimed that his parents enrolled his older brother only out of a "desire to be rid of an extra mouth to feed," since the seminary offered a first-class dormitory and assistance to poor students. Kovner recalled that his parents gave their son a cold reception when he came home on holidays: "My parents, considering him lost for the Jewish religion, were indeed ashamed of him. They tolerated him like an unavoidable evil: they never greeted him, caressed him, especially mother, despite the fact that he was an extremely talented and hard-working student, quiet and modest, and most important — he did not cost them anything" (document 117).

Notwithstanding communal opposition, the state rabbinical seminaries produced a new generation of formally educated — diplomaed — Jewish intellectuals, who came to "constitute the literary, intellectual, and political elite of Russian Jewry."[175] Paperna recalled first learning about the Vil'na state rabbinical school through Iakov Gurliand's *Kavod ha-bayit* (which "the witty Kopylniks called *beit-ha-kavod* or lavatory"). To his amazement, Paperna learned that this school of ill repute was staffed by "the best teachers of Jewish literature such as the Katsenelenbogens, father and son [Tvsi Hirsch and Hayim Leib], M[ordechai] Plungianskii, Idel Shereshevskii, and the poets A[vraham] Lebenson, and S. Zalkind, under the general leadership and supervision of the learned Jew . . . the famous writer, Samuel Iosif Fin [Fuenn]." Gurliand's list of first graduates also impressed the young Paperna: they had gone on to serve as state rabbis (for example, Zelik Minor, in Moscow, and Aaron Pumpinaksii, in Riga), writers (such as Lev Levanda), and other influential public figures.[176] The most talented students, such as Kovner's brother, used their education as a springboard to higher education. Savelii Grigor'evich Kovner (1838–96) went on to earn a university degree and became famous for his three-volume *History of Ancient Medicine* (1878–88). As petitions from university graduates reveal, those who received state stipends at the seminary had to repay the debt by serving as state rabbis or schoolteachers. But having left the Pale for better prospects, they had neither the desire to enlighten their coreligionists nor to resume their former way of life (document 119).

The state's ambition of merging (*sliianie*) Jews with the general population also extended to the private sphere of the family and dress customs. These reforms resonated with *maskilim*, who had their own axe to grind with traditional practices. For the first time, the Statute on the Jews raised the legal minimum age of marriage to sixteen for females and eighteen for males.[177] Although child marriages (involving boys under sixteen or girls under thirteen) were rare, they did occur among a special subgroup—the scholarly elite class from which the *maskilim* emerged. There was one important exception: the "panic marriages" (*nisuei behalah*) of young children that, starting in 1827, were triggered by rumors that the state planned to raise the minimum age of marriage.[178] Bitter about their lost youth and unhappy marriages, the *maskilim* waged an unrelenting war against adolescent marriages.[179] For example, the influential autobiography by Mordechai Aaron Guenzburg castigated early marriages for forcing "nature to flower prematurely," which in his case meant sexual dysfunction (document 78). Lilienblum described himself as a child of fourteen who still delighted in climbing on beams of the synagogue when his father engaged him to the daughter of a wealthy family in Miroslav [Miraslav in Yiddish] (document 104). Ironically, the Orthodox establishment also came to favor later marriage.

According to R. Naftali Zvi Yehudah Berlin (1816–93), the head of the Volozhin yeshiva, early marriages were harmful for both sexes: "Girls who begin giving birth when they are young become weak and sickly. And the same is true of males who use their sexual organs for procreation in the days of their youth; their health also fails."[180] Notably, Berlin was not yet sixteen years old when his own first child was born. Although the state could not prevent all underage marriages, it now had the means—metrical books—to detect, punish, and therefore discourage the practice.

Russian officials also sought to modernize Jewish dress and thus efface ethnic and religious differences in public spaces. Under Alexander I, the state required gymnasium and university students to wear German dress to create "unanimity and decorum." Initially, the Nikolaevan state imposed a dress code only on those traveling outside the Pale. The Statute on the Jews said: "During their travel outside the Pale (with the exception of those in statute 8 [people who transported goods over land and water]), Jews are required to wear clothing used in the places of their temporary residences without any distinction from other inhabitants, along with those of the same civil status."[181] After further deliberation, the Jewish Committee concluded that the so-called Jewish dress had nothing to do with religion but represented a style adopted from early modern Poles. Although the latter had discarded these relics ("during political revolution"), the Jews "preserved [this dress] to distinguish themselves from the ruling group." This distinctive dress, the committee continued, "created a sharp boundary between the indigenous residents and the Jews," impeding closer relations with the Christian population.[182] To eliminate this ethnic clothing, the state proposed to make gradual changes and to begin with a special tax that differed according to region: in Odessa, first-guild merchants who donned Jewish dress would pay 40 rubles a year, second-guild merchants 20 rubles, third-guild merchants 4 rubles, and townspeople and artisans 75 kopecks. In contrast, the Jews of Podolia (whom the state considered more fanatical) faced astronomical taxes: first-guild merchants would pay 250 rubles, second-guild merchants 150 rubles, and so forth. The only exemptions were for those under ten and over sixty years of age.

By 1851 the language of the bans had become harsher and more absolute, perhaps as a reminder that by the following year all Jews would have to change their dress: "All distinctions between Jewish dress and that of indigenous residents must be eliminated."[183] The state strictly forbade the wearing of *peyes* (sidelocks) but permitted Jews to put on *tallis*, *tefillin*, and yarmulkes in the synagogue and prayer houses so as not to infringe on religious practice in private space.[184] Women who shaved their heads before getting married faced a fine of five silver rubles.[185] This ruling aroused much consternation in Zhitomir, where Jews complained that the police used excessive force to enforce the law, traumatizing women who wanted to obey the law but felt obliged to be modest (document 75).[186] The state expected stiff resistance to the new dress code, but officials in Kiev claimed that some Jews welcomed the opportunity to shed their traditional costumes.[187] According to Paperna, Jews in Kopyl were perplexed that the state should suddenly take an interest "in their physiognomy and the style of their clothing." Their fervent prayers yielded no results and failed to stop a wrathful police officer from detaining the most respected residents, while the police "unceremoniously cut off [the] bottom half of the homespun coats to the thigh, cleanly shaved off beards, and mercilessly cut off *peyes* at the very roots."[188]

The conflict over clothing was not merely an issue between Jews and the state: it also erupted between Jewish men seeking to police the boundaries of modesty (*tsniut*) and Jewish women eager to follow the latest fashion. This internecine conflict was acrimonious,

even violent, especially in upper-class hasidic society. Ita Kalish recalled how her conservative grandfather, Simhah Bunem, hired a tailor to make modest clothes for the women in his household. The first wife of Kalish's Uncle Yisroel Yitshkok maneuvered to circumvent the restrictions of her father-in-law:

This first wife was the beautiful daughter of a Lodz magnate, a woman of good taste and keen sense of humor, which frequently helped her dodge the severe injunctions of her father-in-law. They were mainly concerned with her manner of dress. The garments she received from the Vurke court she wore only in the circle of her husband's family and Hasidim. In her father's house in Lodz, she would exchange the veil for a modern bonnet and the housecoat for a beautiful, modern dress. Soon R. Simhah Bunem learned of the strategies of his daughter-in-law, and placed her under the supervision of his intimate, Leybush Turker (document 3).

However, Turker colluded with her to ensure that she was dressed appropriately when he came to check on her dress. Another aunt scandalized the Warka family with her "lemon-yellow satin dress, embroidered with blue velvet flowers, with a long train," more suitable for an actress than a member of the rebbe's family (document 3). Government reports also reveal that followers of the Tsaddik Duvid Twersky had no qualms about attacking hasidic women who wore crinolines on the street. According to one report in 1862, "one girl barely escaped with her life from the fury of the mob. She managed with difficulty to get home under the escort of the police attendants and a soldier" (document 77). Thus the attempt to exhibit modern sensibilities through dress—almost twenty years after the imposition of the dress code—still provoked wrath in her community.

By the end of the Nikolaevan era, two key notions—utility and reclassification (*razbor*)

—emerged to shape policy toward the Jews. The discrepancy between the inscribed identities of Jews as townspeople and their actual occupations and residence struck Kiselev, chairman of the Jewish Committee, as a serious problem. He therefore proposed to emulate the Prussian model and divide Jews into two categories: useful and nonuseful. The first group included "all guild merchants, licensed artisans, farmers, and true townspeople with a permanent urban residence."[189] All remaining Jews fell into the second category. Within four years, non-useful Jews were to join one of the four useful categories or face strict penalties, including conscription.[190] Not only non-useful Jews but also state officials such as Count Mikhail Semenovich Vorontsov (governor general of the province of Novaia Rossiia) found the plan opprobrious and impractical. Fresh from a vacation in England, Vorontsov sent this note to the minister of interior: "Thinking objectively, one has to be shocked that these numerous traders are considered non-useful and consequently harmful, when they undoubtedly help both the agricultural industry and commerce through their petty but much maligned trade in the Polish provinces, where no native petty merchant class has ever existed, or exists now."[191] Due to the realities on the ground and mounting pressures of the disastrous Crimean War (1853–56), the state abandoned this grand scheme to classify the Jews.

The Era of Great Reforms (1855–81)

The debacle of the Crimean War forced many Russians, even archconservatives, to recognize that the empire was in urgent need of fundamental reforms. If its post-Napoleonic "great power" status had precluded reforms (for fear of replicating the revolution-prone model of Western Europe), its humiliating defeat in 1856 demonstrated the urgent need for a fundamental transformation. In the words of a moderate Slavophile, Iurii Sa-

marin, "we were vanquished not by the foreign armies of the Western alliances, but by our own internal weaknesses."[192] The new emperor, Alexander II, has been heralded as the Tsar-Liberator (above all, for the emancipation of the serfs in 1861), but in fact he was a cautious conservative, driven only by military defeat to admit the need for reform, and always highly protective of autocratic authority. Not Alexander but the *gosudarstvenniki* (liberal bureaucrats) were the real engineers of reform: trained under the Nikolaevan regime, the *gosudarstvenniki* quickly occupied high positions in the new regime.[193] The reformers also mobilized public support and, with a new era of glasnost, enabled not only traditional social groups such as the nobility and peasantry but also other segments of society — the professions, women, even minorities — to voice their grievances and aspirations. The Great Reforms — including the emancipation of the serfs (1861), the establishment of local self-government (*zemstvo*) and western-style courts (1864), the creation of new urban government (1870), and the adoption of universal military training (1874) — aimed to "liberate the vital forces of self-development and progress."[194] The leitmotif of reform was the unserfment (*raskreposhchenie*) of all society, not just seigneurial peasants. Given the manifest failure of the centralized bureaucracy (so painfully evident in the Crimean War), it was imperative to allow society to assume a greater role in economic development, the construction of an infrastructure, and even in local self-governance. In social terms, the reforms were "all-estate" rather than "non-estate": reformers sought to mobilize but not immediately merge the different social estates. This kind of social gradualism, they hoped, would promote modernization without unleashing excessive, dangerous rates of social change.

The Great Reforms, directly and indirectly, had a profound impact on Jewish society, creating unprecedented opportunities for social and geographic mobility and professional advancement. At the same time, the reforms unleashed dangerous expectations and ambitions for more radical change, thereby planting the seeds of revolution, national aspirations, and violence.[195]

As the new regime began to consider its policy toward Jews, it revived the earlier idea of utility and classification in devising its new policy of "selective integration."[196] Above all, it led to a partial dismantling of the Pale: for the first time, the state allowed "useful" categories of Jews—first-guild merchants, university graduates, and skilled artisans—to resettle outside the Pale. The driving force behind this policy was a twofold dynamic: the state's goal of merging Jews with the general population and the Jews' aspirations for greater legal rights (above all, the right to settle in the Russian interior, especially in Moscow and St. Petersburg). These aspirations informed a petition from first-guild Jewish merchants, who stressed not only their economic usefulness but also the obstacles to their true integration: "But in the western provinces, there is not the sort of group with which such a rapprochement of the Jews could occur." Slyly, the petitioners argued that only through contact with native Russians (not Poles, Lithuanians, Ukrainians, or Belorussians) could Jews ever hope to become true Russians and "acquire the most outstanding of their laudable qualities."[197]

Although only a small proportion of Jews left the Pale[198] and resettled in central Russia, mainly in Moscow and St. Petersburg, this new Jewish public culture (*obshchestvennost'*) embraced the lifestyle and values of its Russian counterpart. A small but influential group of so-called new Jews consisted of wealthy merchants, honorary citizens, and even nobles. The financial elite—comprised of such families as the Ginsburgs, Poliakovs, and Zaks—established banking houses, financed the construction of the railroads, and extended significant loans to the state and nobility.[199] As mentioned in the preface, the di-

aries of Zinaida Poliakova, daughter of the railway mogul and banker Lazar Poliakov, provide a rare window into the family's assimilation into Russian aristocratic culture and society (document 114). She emulated elite Russian women of her day: she spoke several foreign languages, dressed in the latest European styles, socialized at noble balls and soirées, attended concerts and theatrical performances, read novels, wrote letters, and displayed proper social etiquette and grace. Although scornful of university-educated Jews who spoke abominable Russian and writers who harped on the problem of Jewish-Christian relations, Poliakova never denied her Jewish identity. Still, she longed for a Judaism that was more accommodating to her family's Russian way of life, especially regarding kashrut, which her mother forced her to observe strictly. To separate themselves from the mass population of uncultured Jews in the Pale and even in the capitals, the Poliakovs admitted only the *crème de la crème* to their social circle. The family's deliberate distancing of itself from other Jews and such decisions as the donation of money to Russian universities (despite their strict quotas for Jewish students) provoked controversy and anger in the Jewish community.[200] This new plutocracy predictably became the target of vilification by the Jewish intelligentsia, which denounced them for "wallowing in decadence, gluttony, and in one case, near incest."[201]

Another distinct category in the Russian interior consisted of university students, who left the Pale to train for white-collar employment (to be sure, outside the civil service, which remained closed to Jews). As university enrollments exploded in the postreform era, the student subculture created a new space that knew "neither Jews nor Hellenes" (document 120) and which allowed social interactions across ethnic and religious boundaries.[202] "The relationship between students was simple, more like circles," recalled Vladimir Garkavy about his university days in Moscow (document 120). The zemstvo reforms created new opportunities and rising demand for doctors, dentists, veterinarians, engineers, and journalists. Jewish professionals moved to towns in the Russian interior, where they found few coreligionists, let alone a Jewish community. That is apparent in the marital separation case of a veterinarian in Vladimir province (document 38). By the 1880s, however, the quotas—although not unique to Jews—were signaling a significant retreat from selective integration and the onset of a new, less generous policy to deal with the Jewish Question.[203]

There were also Jews in the capital who had neither wealth nor education: the merchants and artisans who earned a precarious livelihood and who had to demonstrate membership in a particular occupation or estate.[204] That was by no means easy or automatic. For instance, after receiving a report from the police that Iosel' Azgud (a former sausage maker and then a taxidermist) was not pursuing his trade but was instead working as a butcher, the craftsmen's guild of St. Petersburg excluded him from its membership. Facing expulsion, Azgud explained that the butcher shop belonged to his father-in-law whom he visited regularly; more important, Azgud's illness with typhoid for several months had forced him to lay off his apprentices. Azgud blamed the police of the fourth precinct for reaching a false conclusion without investigating his circumstances (document 146).[205] Families of artisans and merchants were also vulnerable to expulsion: if children who reached their majority, widows, and widowers failed to demonstrate that they had an independent livelihood, handicraft, or trade, they would lose their residency rights (document 145). Similarly, after 1874 soldiers could no longer rely on prior military service to ensure residency outside the Pale. Nikolaevan soldiers and their families had enjoyed this privilege since 1867, but fears of "an excessive Jewish presence in the interior

provinces" led the state to revoke this right.[206] Confronted with residency issues, some Jews in St. Petersburg and Moscow converted to Christianity, while others simply resorted to living illegally in the city.[207]

Although hailed by some Jewish intellectuals as a sign of social progress, selective integration actually posed a grave threat to their ethos and vision for Russian Jewry. A new generation of Jews came to associate modernity not with cultural renovation but with emancipation from the jurisdiction of the Jewish community, from moral responsibility, even from Judaism itself.[208] But not even the most prescient Jewish intellectual could have foreseen the extent to which the Great Reforms would gradually serve to release individual Jews, even the most traditional, from the discipline of the community.

One major transformation concerned Jewish adjudication—a direct result of the judicial reforms of 1864, which established efficient western-style courts with jury trials. To be sure, Jews had turned to gentile courts earlier; after 1864, however, plaintiffs in civil and criminal cases and from all social classes turned to state courts, which had become far more accessible in terms of rights and costs than in the past. Conflicts with neighbors, whether Jewish or gentile, could now be resolved expeditiously.[209] As the Rabbinic Commission observed, Jews "were more likely to turn to these institutions with their civil suits, rather than the rabbinic courts, because the decision of the latter lacks any executive power" to ensure enforcement.[210] The courts thus not only inspired a spirit of litigiousness—even among domestic servants (document 139)—but also undermined the authority of rabbinical courts. The use of professional lawyers also became more common, even in the provinces. According to a report by the Jewish Committee in Volhynia (1881), Jewish lawyers had appeared in "every town and village," promising to help Jews "draft petitions and other legal instruments."[211]

Another consequence of the Great Reforms was an explosion of information and public discourse through the liberalization of censorship. The Jewish press in Hebrew, Yiddish, and Russian,[212] not only disseminated local and international news, serialized literature, and published ideological essays, but also created a vibrant print culture and venue for the dissemination and exchange of ideas.[213] Reading newspapers became a part of daily life among educated Jews. Typical is Jocheved Bat Rachel Tarshish's recollection of her mother's leisure hours: "During her free hours, she liked to read Yiddish novels and the Russian-language monthly *Voskhod*. She was a regular subscriber and also held on to back issues for many years until the Ukrainian marauders scattered their pages across the town."[214] Likewise, Sarah Azariahu recalled how she "thirstily fell upon the 'thick-bellied' Russian monthlies such as *Russkaia mysl'*, *Russkie bogatstvo*, the Jewish monthly *Voskhod*" and other publications.[215]

Readers not only consumed newspapers and journals, but also devoured a vast array of Jewish and Russian literature. And even interludes of strict censorship failed to repress the writers' creativity or the readers' interest.[216] Although Hebrew literature dates back to the prereform era, it coexisted with the beginnings of modern Yiddish literature: a "highbrow" Yiddish literature and the first modern Yiddish newspaper, *Kol mevaser* (A heralding voice, 1862–71). The reading public consisted primarily of elites: the *maskilim* and the emerging Jewish *haute bourgeoisie* "who were anxious to read about their world and their people"—a corrective to claims by writers and later scholars that their works were "strictly for the masses." A "lowbrow" book industry appeared alongside this older tradition in the early 1880s and catered directly to readers seeking pure entertainment in, for example, the popular romance novels of Shomer.[217] Whatever Jews chose to read,

the literature "open[ed] their eyes to a world beyond the shtetl limits."[218]

The Great Reforms also made some concessions to minority aspirations for greater autonomy, and that too helped to draw Jews into the ethnic politics of the northwest. It bears emphasizing that the Jews in the diverse Russian Empire lived amid other national minorities who were likewise eager to demand their rights and defend their interests. Everyday interactions with neighbors usually revolved around mundane matters, such as haggling over prices at the marketplace or negotiating the terms of short-term promissory notes (document 130). However, there were also moments—such as the Polish Uprising of 1863—when Jews found themselves caught between two competing camps: in that case, between the Poles and Lithuanians on one side, and Russian officialdom on the other. As Lev Levanda's fictional protagonist warns in the novel *A Turbulent Time*, Jews could not stand aside as neutral bystanders: "But you should know that a time is approaching—a turbulent time. . . . A time is approaching when they will lean on us with a knife against our throats, demanding a categorical answer to the questions: 'Who are you? What are you? For whom are you? With whom do you stand?'"[219] These historical moments of reckoning exposed the vulnerability of a multinational empire and left Jews to question how they were to fit in. Some Jews rallied to the Polish banner, sympathetic to the national aspirations of Polish patriots with whom they shared a language, culture, and history. As the documents reveal, however, that was not true of other Jews, who were forced to provide lodging, provisions, and money to the rebels—actions that made them liable to prosecution once the Russians had crushed the rebellion (documents 162–164). Subsequently the state embarked on a process of radical Russification, as it sought to create loyal Russian subjects and to prevent the development of a "distinct and autonomous Jewish nationality in Russia."[220]

From Counter-Reform to Modernization

In the 1870s the state retreated from the Great Reforms (the last significant reform—universal military training—was in 1874) and laid plans to revise substantially the terms of the reforms. Far more programmatic changes came after the assassination of Alexander II on 1 March 1881: his son Alexander III (r. 1881–94) was a strong devotee of state authority and highly critical of the Great Reforms. By the 1880s the spirit of the Great Reforms (which had sought to empower society to help advance growth and development) had given way to the reassertion of *étatisme* and state authority, to an unabashed emphasis on the need for bureaucratic power and even arbitrariness (*proizvol*).[221] Under the aegis of Alexander III and his son Nicholas II (r. 1894–1917) the state reimposed strict censorship, marginalized the role of society (even the privileged elites), and envisioned bureaucracy and autocracy as the twin dynamos of development and economic growth that could enable Russia to reclaim its status as a great power.

Long mischaracterized as an age of reaction, in fact this new era of dynamic autocracy sought not to restore but to build anew—in the first instance, its instruments of governance. Apart from reasserting the prerogatives of autocracy, the regime began to expand exponentially its administration and police, as well as their power over civil society. After first restoring tight censorship and suppressing the revolutionary movement that had slain Alexander II, the regime of Alexander III began to construct a new system of control at the central and local level. The most famous measures included those designed to reduce judicial independence in the 1880s, the appointment of a new network of the land captains (*zemskii nachal'nik*) in 1889 (to govern at the local level), and new restrictions on rural self-government in 1890 and city government in 1892.

A second main focus was economic growth—the precondition for a strong military and the reassertion of Russia's status as a leading power. Although growth under Alexander II had been substantial, it paled in comparison with the accelerated industrialization that began in the mid-1880s: nearly one-third of all industrial growth between 1860 and 1914 came in the brief period 1885–99, during which Russia enjoyed the highest growth rates of any European power in the nineteenth century. Growth peaked under the stewardship of Minister of Finance Count Sergei Iul'evich Witte, whose policy of protective tariffs, foreign investment and loans, high levels of grain exports, and monetary stability (culminating in the adoption of the gold standard of 1897) helped to ensure a steady influx of capital and rapid economic growth. The state itself, in contrast to the earlier period, now became the primary agent of industrial growth, largely displacing the private sector and even assuming key control over such sectors as communications and transportation.

But that growth came at great cost and risk. This peril was most evident in the agrarian sector: monetary deflation, high taxes, and falling grain prices all combined to impose enormous economic stress on agricultural producers, whether they be great landowners or peasants with tiny plots. The famine of 1891, which affected large swaths of the empire and left an enormous number of victims, seemed to symbolize the crisis, especially its devastating impact on the peasantry. Although the impoverishment of the peasant was a far more complex problem whose form and intensity were highly variable, it became a given in public discourse, serving to mobilize the privileged and the poor and encourage them to blame the state alone for their problems. Nor was the industrial sector immune: the recession that commenced in 1899, triggered largely by the business cycle that affected European investors, soon turned large numbers of migrant workers into a mass of unemployed discontents. Thus state policy yielded significant change and growth, but those very dynamics also brought risk and destabilization to the old order.

The Jewish Question

One dramatic dimension of accelerated state building during the era of counter-reforms was the reversal in state policy toward the Jews. Although sheer bureaucratic inertia kept alive some planning for further concessions (for example, efforts of the Kakhanov Commission), the state now abandoned its goal of selective integration in favor of strict controls on the Jews' social and geographic mobility. Based on the recommendations of provincial commissions, in 1882 Alexander III promulgated the Temporary Regulations (also known as the May Laws), which remained in force until the Revolution of 1917. Eager to blame peasant discontent on "Jewish impudence and exploitation of the native Christian population,"[222] the regulations prohibited new Jewish settlements outside cities and towns, the registration of property and mortgages under Jewish names, the leasing and management of properties by Jews, and work by Jews on Sundays and Christian holidays. Although some local authorities used the law to expel Jews from the countryside, others complained about their inability to enforce these measures, which most Jews viewed as only "temporary and would be changed tomorrow, if not today."[223] In 1887, the regime also imposed a strict *numerus clausus* in Russian schools and universities and sought to limit the number of Jews serving in local government and the professions.[224] However, the Ministry of Enlightenment did not consistently enforce the quotas at the postsecondary

level. It even allowed some Jews to "bypass the quota system," which led to an increase in their numbers at the universities in Kiev, Warsaw, and Dorpat by 1896.[225]

After Alexander III replaced the liberal General Governor Mikhail Dolgorukov with Grand Duke Sergei Aleksandrovich, the tsar's brother, in 1891, the Jews of Moscow immediately discerned a sharp change in the attitudes of the new regime. Earlier, the privileged Jews of Moscow felt secure in their position, as Roza Vinaver observed: "For us children, it was persuasive that no one would touch us [even after the assassination of Tsar Alexander II] as long as Prince Dologoruk[ov] went to have dinner with the Poliakovs."[226] Not so under the grand duke, who in 1891 ordered the expulsion of some 20,000 Jews from Moscow, including some artisans who had resided in the city for over twenty years. Nikolaevan soldiers, who had previously enjoyed the right to reside in the capital after retiring from military service, learned that they were no longer to remain in the city. In 1899 the government ruled that Jews were not to comprise more than 33 percent of first-guild merchants in Moscow and added still other bureaucratic obstacles to impede their residence in the city.[227]

The surge of antisemitism was evident not only in state policy but in society as well, where the Jewish Question now became a prominent topic of public discourse. Members of the Russian intelligentsia—from the most liberal to the archconservative—generally held the view that the Jews represented a hostile force to Russia. In works thinly disguised as secular philosophy or scholarly expositions, writers such as the Slavophile Ivan Aksakov castigated Jewish separatism and inability to merge with the surrounding population.[228] Themes of Jews' exploitation of Russians and diabolical schemes to take over Russia also found expression in the press. Relying on the apostate Iakov Brafman's infamous work, *Book of Kahal* (1869), the newspaper *Kievlianin* claimed that the Jews had completely taken over Odessa, much to the detriment of the Christian population:

> In their hands is a large part of the trade. . . . [T]hey have priority in all other fields of endeavor. . . . [S]oon all the land of Bessarabia and Kherson provinces will pass under their control; everywhere there is ruin [as a result] of the Jews — doctors, grain-brokers, those who serve in virtually every office, on the railroad and in other institutions. Rich Jews use their wealth and influence to secure advantageous occupations, positions, jobs, and work for their little brothers, to the detriment of Russians, be they government officials, landowners, doctors, tradesmen, craftsmen, or common laborers.[229]

Two years later, the newspaper — which ironically recommended the abolition of the Pale of Settlement so that Ukraine would not be overrun by Jews — published "The Jewish Cemetery in Prague" in four installments; this was the first time a prototype of *The Protocols of the Elders of Zion* appeared in Russia.[230]

But by far the most ominous and terrifying development was the explosion of pogroms in the early 1880s. Although antisemitism was hardly new to the western provinces of the Russian Empire, the shift from everyday "systemic" violence "through which conflict and competition [were] regularly pursued in society" to mass "catastrophic" violence that was seemingly unprecedented was dramatic.[231] The phenomenon was complex, with multiple causes (antisemitic public discourse, state policy restrictions on Jews, and traditional religious prejudice), but certainly one of the most important factors was economic: the combination of rapid industrialization and agrarian crisis put enormous stress on the lower classes, especially peasants and migrant workers. Placed under such stress, the lower classes were disposed to blame those most closely associated with industry, commerce, and finance: the Jews. The result was grow-ing hostility that exploded into a wave of riots directed primarily at Jewish property. The police discerned this shift in popular attitudes, reporting that a dispute with a Jew over a hat or rotten plums in the marketplace could now erupt into mass violence against Jews (document 130).[232]

The pogroms of 1881 were precipitated by the assassination of Alexander II (which rumor attributed to Jewish revolutionaries), but they gained momentum over the next three years by drawing on peasants' economic distress and tendency to blame Jews for their hardships. Traveling by train from Elizavetgrad, where the first wave of pogroms erupted, to other Ukrainian towns, unemployed itinerant workers also vented their rage and frustration by pillaging and destroying Jewish property.[233] A police report from the Ukrainian town of Balta warned that an influx of some five thousand migrant workers threatened to ignite anti-Jewish violence "based on the most insignificant reason." The report noted that the dissenting Old Believers "are far more inclined than Ukrainians to carry out anti-Jewish disorders" (document 169). Significantly, the Dubossary ritual murder case that preceded the Kishinev pogroms of 1903 greatly agitated the Old Believers, whose antagonism toward Jews was religious but also economic, as the two groups competed for the same resources (document 169).

In contrast to the southern provinces, most northwest towns in Belorussia and Lithuania had a much lower level of violence against Jews, but they were not entirely free of pogroms. When tempers flared, incidents ensued but were "brief and involved a small number of people," making it easier for local police to restore order.[234] The rural character of Belorussian provinces, which experienced far less industrialization and urbanization than other parts of the empire, resulted in less acrimonious relations between Jews and peasants. Indeed, modern Belorussian literary culture portrayed Jews as a "familiar and beneficial presence" rather than as threatening or pernicious.[235]

The violence in the south, especially starting with the Kishinev pogroms in 1903, became increasingly savage: no longer content with looting and destroying property, the *pogromshchiki* committed physical assault, rape, mutilation, and cold-blooded murder (document 167–170). The local police in the south, overwhelmed by the violence, described the mass hysteria among the Jews. "They greatly exaggerate the danger and attach significance to every trivial threat by the peasants and every foolish rumor," complained a police chief after his office had been inundated with telegrams, denunciations, and petitions (document 169). The tendency to dismiss such fears as "exaggerated" led to police inaction that only emboldened the *pogromshchiki* to believe that they could act with impunity. To the alarm of state authorities, Jews began to take matters into their own hands, especially after the Kishinev pogroms. "Masses of Jews are appealing to me with requests for permission to bear firearms," warned the chief of the gendarme administration in Rostov-na-Donu in 1903 (document 170). He also reported an increase in Jewish purchases of revolvers and the formation of "armed detachments for the sole purpose of defending themselves in the event of a pogrom" (ibid.). Fearful of greater disorder, the police disbanded some self-defense groups (for example, in Odessa), but that only intensified anger and suspicion among the Jews. Whatever the sentiments of the police and local authorities, they were simply unprepared to deal with these mass outbreaks, let alone to render justice in the already overwhelmed courts.[236] All this coincided with the general surge in peasant disorders (*besporiadki*), most directed against noble landowners, and the general breakdown of state control that would culminate in the Revolution of 1905–7.

Ironically, the Jews in the Pale—the target of these pogroms—were themselves victims of industrialization, as the new industrial and commercial sectors began to have an impact on their traditional spheres of activity. Their exposure increased as an ever-growing number of Jews migrated from small towns and rural areas to the cities, with the largest concentrations in Warsaw, Odessa, Lodz, Vil'na, and Kishinev.[237] According to the 1897 census, 48.7 percent of Jews resided within the prescribed urban centers, where they dominated crafts like tailoring, weaving, shoemaking, carpentry, and the production of food and beverages.[238] The overconcentration of Jews in the production of consumer goods was due largely to their exclusion from higher-paying mechanized factories because of their need to rest on the Sabbath and lack of technical skills, the recruitment by workers of fellow Christians from their home villages, and fears of the Jewish workers' revolutionary potential.[239] To the dismay of Jewish artisans, their shop-made shoes, clothing, and other products could not compete in quality and price with manufactured goods in the new industrial age. To some degree, the concentration of Jews in consumer goods increased competition and ethnic tension in a market with stagnant domestic demand. Given their limited purchasing power, consumers restricted expenditures to the bare necessities. The result was a surfeit of Jewish artisans; as one contemporary observed, "there were enough Jewish tailors to supply clothing for half the urban population of the Russian Empire."[240]

The excess supply amid weak demand increased the vulnerability of master artisans to the caprice of the marketplace and drove them, in turn, to exploit their journeymen and apprentices ever more ruthlessly. Long hours (sixteen to eighteen hours a day in the northwest cities), meager wages, and seasonal employment left many workers in dire poverty. Since the labor legislation of 1897—which limited labor to eleven and a half hours a day—did not apply to private artisan shops, working hours and conditions were not regulated. Even in regulated factories, long hours nonetheless prevailed as declining profit margins generated growing pressures. In 1901, for instance, protests broke out spontaneously at the Gal'pern matchbox factory in Pinsk after the foreman ordered the female workers to pack thinner matches in bigger boxes. "Those changes significantly reduced our wages," complained twenty-year-old Sora Breitbord, who was paid per unit of packed boxes. "For example, before I received up to thirty-five kopecks, but now no more than twenty kopecks" (document 149). Such conditions carried significant negative implications for the Jewish underclass and the traditional family order. With only meager incomes, neither young men and women nor their parents could afford a wedding, much less support a family with children, which led to a significant rise in the age of marriage. By the late nineteenth century, married men found it impossible to support their families on a single income and increasingly had to rely on what their wives and children earned in the nonmechanized shops and factories such as one in which Breitbord worked. The cramped housing conditions, exacerbated by rapid urban growth, drove families to share "the semi-darkness of cellars" or "similar hovels that had wet walls and floors."[241]

Emigration and Revolution

Disillusioned by the failure of the Great Reforms that led to economic despair, the rise of violent antisemitism, official discrimination, and the state's inability to manage social disorders, Jews sought different solutions to their plight.

One option was emigration: some 2.3 million Jews left the Russian Empire between 1875 and 1914 for far-flung destinations including the United States, Canada, Argentina, South Africa, Western Europe, Australia, and Palestine.[242] Official emigration from the Russian Empire, however, was not a simple

process. To obtain passports and exit certificates, one had to produce a metrical record of birth — an impossible task for parents who had failed to register their children for fear of the draft or through mere negligence (document 179). The state also required a statement of personal integrity from the local police, certifying that no suits or complaints had been filed against the individual or family members. Some prospective emigrants discovered that they could not leave the country unless they paid 300 rubles for the failure of a male family member to appear for military service (document 181). To assist prospective emigrants, the Jewish Colonization Association (JCA) had created over five hundred offices in St. Petersburg and the Pale of Settlement by 1913. "Every day, from eight o'clock in the morning until noon, I would sink up to my neck in the troubles of the Jewish people," recalled Zalman Rubashov (later Shazar) about his work in the central JCA office in St. Petersburg. "I would read, search, reply, catalogue and send my answers to the secretaries for their signature. . . . [about] Jews who want to emigrate and don't know where to turn; migrants who are deceived by ruthless agents and find no protection . . . an abandoned woman whose husband left her and traveled across the sea, forgetting her and her children and leaving them to suffer unheard."[243]

By the early twentieth century, the Zionist Organization had also established two bureaus to recruit immigrants to Palestine — one located in Odessa and the other in Jaffa (in Palestine). Unlike the JCA, which opened its door to the most impoverished Jews, the Zionists were far more selective, shunning "the miserable poor who are not worthy of bringing blessing to the country and who dishonor us." Rather, as Menahem Sheinkin (who headed the office in Jaffa) put it, they needed muscular Jews, "a larger number of healthy, solid elements who can afford to establish themselves, make a living, and generate life."[244]

In contrast to the mass of emigrants, some

Jews decided to stake their future in Russia and determined to remake the empire according to their diverse political visions. As early as the 1860s a few Jews, educated in state schools and universities, embraced the new *Weltanschauung* of Russian radical youth. Repudiating the principles and romanticism of their fathers, the sons expressed unbounded faith in science, materialism, and utilitarianism. "In these days negation is the most useful thing of all — so we deny," declares Bazarov, the nihilist protagonist of Ivan Turgenev's *Fathers and Sons* (1862). Among the first Jewish students to join radical circles were Veniamin Osipovich Portugalov (1835–96) and Lev Moiseevich Zelenskii, medical students (like Bazarov) who hailed from wealthy Jewish merchant families in Poltava and joined the Bekman circle,[245] demanding student rights and self-government. Portugalov was especially vocal in his support of Jewish equality but soon found himself under arrest.[246] Although embracing different ideas, the early radicals of the 1860s shared a hatred of authority.[247]

This generation of radicals differed from their forebears not only in their determination to act (not just theorize) but also in their inclusion of the "women's question." It was partly a matter of female education; as Nikolai Pirogov (1810–81) argued, the "archaic and inane treatment of women's education must change and women must take a role in society more nearly corresponding to their human worth and mental capabilities."[248] But for women, education was not the only concern: issues of parental despotism, unhappy marriages, and unfulfilled lives dominated their discussions. Like their male counterparts, women were drawn to Nikolai Chernyshevskii's novel *What Is to Be Done?* (1863), which espoused a doctrine of personal emancipation and sexual freedom and stressed individual effort, above all through "books, tutoring by friends, and circles."[249] The Hebrew writer Moshe Kamionsky expressed alarm at

how easily young women were seduced by this book, especially a decade later, when radicals organized a coherent political movement:

> And the nihilists knew how to catch in their nets girls and women too, young Jewish ones; many of our nation's daughters [. . .] have been swept up in this movement. In it, they have found an answer to the *women's question*, which was then being raised, as the movement's members championed equality of rights for women and had decided that men had no right to govern them. . . . It thus came as no surprise that the Hebrew maidens, who faced in their own homes enormous resistance to their newfound tendencies, would run away from home and strike out on their own, dedicating themselves to being midwives or schoolteachers among the populace.[250]

He bemoaned a decline in their morals as "young Hebrew women slept in student dormitories of the new movement, Jews or Christians together indiscriminately."

In the early 1870s Jewish revolutionaries joined the populist (*narodnik*) movement, comprising a "staggering 20 percent" of the Chaikovskii circle, the best organized group of revolutionaries.[251] Eager to repay their debt to the people for their privileged lives, students left for the countryside to "merge" with the peasantry and enlighten them about their revolutionary potential. "I decided to become [Russian] Orthodox," wrote Osip Aptekman before going to the people. "I was baptized and felt myself literally renewed. . . . So I had drawn near the peasants, among whom I was to live."[252] Chaim Zhitlovsky did not change his faith but recalled the initial revulsion when he discovered the "Jewish role" in oppressing the peasantry, the very people whom the populists so idealized:

> Samuil Solomonovich Poliakov builds railways in Russia. These railways, according to Nekrasov's famous poem that reflects the

socioeconomic fact, are built on the skeleton of the Russian peasantry. My uncle, Mikhail, brews spirits in his distillery for the Russian people. . . . My niece, Liza, sells the spirits to the peasant. The whole shtetl lives from the *Russian* peasant. My father [in Vitebsk] employs him to cut down Russian woods, which he buys from the greatest exploiter of the Russian muzhik — the Russian noble. . . . Wherever my eyes rested, I saw only *one* thing . . . the harmful effect of Jewish tradesmen on the Russian peasantry.[253]

Although the populists were primarily Russians from privileged backgrounds, Jewish radicals like Mark Natanson, Samuil Kliachko, Solomon Chudnovskii, and Pavel Axelrod rose to leadership positions in the populist movement.

But by the late 1870s, frustrated by their inability to rouse the peasantry and signs of a breakdown in the commune (the bedrock of populist socialism), populists turned to political terrorism — first through the movement called Land and Freedom (Zemlia i Volia) and then through the one called the People's Will (Narodnaia Volia). According to Lev Iakovlevich Shternberg, a key theoretician of the *narodovoltsy*, as long as autocracy prevented free political expression, terrorism was not only legitimate but critical for achieving the goals of the revolution "with the fewest possible victims and in the shortest possible time."[254] On 1 March 1881 Narodnaia Volia, after six failed attempts, finally achieved its most ambitious act of terror — the assassination of Alexander II.

Among the conspirators arrested for the assassination was a young Jewish woman named Gesia Gel'fman, a graduate of the midwifery course at St. Vladimir University in Kiev, who had been arrested earlier in another political case in 1877 (document 171). Her friend Ol'ga Liubatovich recalled meeting Gel'fman for the first time in 1875 at the end of an arduous journey from Odessa to Moscow and Tula: "I lay down on this stranger's bed and dropped off to sleep. Eventually, I was awakened by a kiss. Through my sleepy eyes, I saw the head of a young woman — curly-haired, friendly, beaming with incredible kindness." When Gel'fman admitted to renting the apartment in which the bombs used in the assassination had been stored, her fate was sealed. "She languished under the threat of execution for five months," Liubatovich recalled. In the end, Gel'fman could not survive the trauma when the authorities took away her child to a foundling home, "where they abandoned her without taking a receipt or having her tagged." Liubatovich added bitterly, "this despite the fact that many people (myself included) had offered to raise the child."[255] At the Second Congress of the Union for Equal Rights, some Jews blamed the populists for instigating the pogroms as a way to awaken the peasantry, to which Moisei Aronovich Krol, a devoted populist, retorted: "If we are to start digging into the history of the parties and going through their dirty linen, we could come up with details more shocking."[256]

By the time of the Revolution of 1905–7, several revolutionary parties were competing for dominance. Various neopopulist groups merged to create the Party of Socialist Revolutionaries (PSR). Although primarily focused on the peasantry, the PSR also conducted agitation among the working class that had grown rapidly and exhibited a high degree of radicalism from the mid-1890s onward. The PSR, unlike its rivals, not only rejected the industrialist vision of Marxism (while espousing socialist ideals) but also embraced terrorism as an integral part of its strategy for overthrowing autocracy. Grigorii Gershuni, the founder of the terrorist unit (the "Combat Organization"), declared: "Robbed of every chance of responding to these crimes [of tsarism], we, the conscious minority, hold it to be not only our right but our holy duty, despite all the horror with which we regard this weapon, to answer violence with violence; to avenge the spilling of the blood of the people with the blood of the oppressors."[257] Although the ultimate goal of terrorism was to "awaken the sleepiest philistines"[258] to political consciousness, it was also about vengeance — responding in kind to the state's violence and oppression.

The desire for vengeance inspired Mariia (Mania) Shkol'nik to join the Combat Organization of the PSR. She attributed the decision to assassinate the general governor of Kiev to his alleged role in oppressing Jews and the people: "The executive committee . . . then ordered Shpaizman and me to organize the assassination of the governor general of Kiev, [Nikolai] Kleigels, who had brutally repressed every manifestation of discontent among peasants, workers, and students, who had organized Jewish pogroms, and who had become univerally hated" (document 174). Shkol'nik worked closely with Evno Azef (1869–1918), the son of a poor Jewish tailor who became a leader in the Combat Organization and simultaneously colluded with the secret police. Like Shkol'nik, Klara Klebanova from Chernigov also joined the terrorist "Maximalist" wing, headed by the charismatic Mikhail Sokolov, better known as "the Bear" (*medved'*).[259] Indeed, Jewish women made up some 30 percent of the female Socialist Revolutionaries (SRs) terrorists and played a significant role in the group's acts of violence.[260] Klebanova's admiration of Sokolov's audacious acts of terror (which included bank robberies, as well as attacks on factory owners and landowners) was not shared by everyone in the party, however. Indeed, the PSR leader Victor Chernov castigated Maximalist proclamations as "pogrom-like" and dangerous for party discipline.[261] Although personally opposed to the Maximalist program, Chernov noted that other senior PSR members were more tolerant toward the younger generation's penchant for violence. Klebanova's sister, Dora Lazurkina, was also repulsed by PSR

terrorism and joined the Russian Socialist Democratic Labor Party (RSDLP), a Marxist party and an attractive alternative for Jewish radicals who embraced its focus on the workers, rejection of a special Russian path, internationalist spirit, and lack of nationalistic overtones.[262]

The RSDLP shared the PSR's fundamental socialist ideals but scoffed at its belief in a peasant revolution, which Lenin dismissed as "idiocy," and also rejected its methods of terror.[263] Instead, the RSDLP embraced Marxism, with its vision of a proletarian revolution, and therefore focused on the working class. But the party split in 1903 at its Second Congress over the question of how to bring this revolution about. The dispute derived from an earlier belief among party members that the country, given its political backwardness, must traverse a two-stage revolution: first a bourgeois revolution (a political revolution, establishing a bourgeois democracy and enabling the growth of capitalism) and then a socialist revolution (a social revolution, establishing proletarian rule and erecting a socialist order). One faction of the party (the majority, but mislabeled the Mensheviks [minority]) argued that, because the rest of society by 1900–1903 had risen in opposition to the regime, the party should focus on raising the workers' consciousness — that is, laying the foundation for the second, proletarian revolution. The Mensheviks believed in creating the largest possible party, one that consisted of sympathizers and supporters, not just full-time party activists. The minority, shrewdly adopting the name Bolsheviks (majority), actually feared this "all-class, all-nation" movement precisely because it was not under the party's control and seemed certain to sell out prematurely for an incomplete political revolution. To perform this extraordinary, ahistorical role (whereby the proletariat made the bourgeois revolution), it was essential that the workers be led by full-time professional revolutionaries, who alone should be admitted to party membership. Eventually a third alternative appeared—adumbrated by Leon Trotsky in 1904; this vision of permanent revolution jettisoned the two-stage thesis and favored instead a simultaneous political and social revolution.

Although many Jews were active in the PSR and RSDLP, others became active in the Bund. The roots of the Bund lay in northwestern cities such as Vil'na and Minsk in the 1880s, when the Jewish intelligentsia began to organize workers in their own backyards—a practical strategy adopted from their Polish socialist counterparts. Initially the goal had been to create small study circles (*kruzhki*) to train an elite worker intelligentsia through propaganda. This was seen as the spread of many ideas to a few people—as opposed to its converse, agitation, or the spread of a few ideas to many people. Propaganda meant creating educational programs for the workers, who would study Russian, literature, natural history, political economy, Marxism, and even arithmetic.[264] Timofei Kopelzon recalled the impact of reading tracts like *What Do People Live By*, written by a member of the Polish socialist movement, Shimen Dikshtein: "The booklet became a kind of Torah among us, and we used to read it and debate it in all the workers' circles."[265] Not only workers benefited from the circles; in them, the intelligentsia also learned about the aspirations and needs of the workers. John (Joseph) Mill, a member of the early Vil'na Group, recalled:

I led several workers' circles of about eight to ten persons each. Only one was uniform, being made up exclusively of seamstresses; the rest brought together male and female workers of various trades. This made it easier to find out what was happening in individual shops and factories and provided opportunities to discuss the workers' conditions in order to discover ways and means to improve them. Theoretical propaganda and education, in this manner, went hand in hand with preparations for practical worker politics.[266]

Although the intelligentsia admired the zeal to learn among workers in the circles, some suspected that the socialist message was secondary to the desire for education and, as Pesach Liebman Hersch (known by his pseudonym, P. Libman) remarked later, "in every Jewish worker is concealed an *ekstern* [auditor]"—not a revolutionary proletarian.[267]

In response, Arkadii Kremer (1865–1935) and Samuel Gozhanskii (1867–1943) proposed a new program in the early 1890s: a shift in emphasis from propaganda to agitation—that is, from creating a worker intelligentsia to mobilizing a mass working-class movement. This strategy also meant conducting agitation in Yiddish rather than Russian, a challenging task for the highly Russified intelligentsia. One activist described Kremer's own painful attempt at Yiddish: "He tried to speak Yiddish 'as the people speak it,' but he thought that meant to scatter swear words and curses throughout his speech."[268] The change in strategy elicited anger and disbelief, especially among female workers who took solace from these groups that provided education, culture, and respite from their miserable living conditions. It also met with opposition among veteran Russian revolutionaries such as Vera Zasulich, who complained about the "cultural barriers" that emerged with the shift to Yiddish and mass agitation: "Their level of development is terribly low, although, in the main, they are capable, but they are not acquainted with Russian, or any other literature. All they have is what they learned in gymnasia. They often acquire a whole world-outlook from a few books, but it is so narrow, so stereotyped. I find them boring."[269] The shift to agitation accompanied a new focus on strikes, which tapped into the deep grievances of the workers. Here the Bundists found fertile soil, especially among the lowest-paid workers in the matchbox and cigarette factories.[270] The girls at the Gal'pern matchbox factory mentioned above, for instance, needed little incitement to strike after their boss increased the size of the matchboxes and decreased the size of the matches, making it far more difficult to earn a few kopecks for each box. Whether they were influenced by the mimeographed fliers and street meetings organized by the Bund, or acted spontaneously on their own (as many claimed), the young female workers did indeed go on strike (document 149). According to one study, between 1895 and 1904 the Pale witnessed at least 2,267 Jewish strikes, with more than one strike per day from 1900 on.[271]

In the beginning, the Bund also resorted to legal methods to justify the strike movement: it uncovered various violations of the law by factory owners (such as long working hours) as the basis for protest. Workers employed legal methods such as announcing strikes two weeks in advance. According to a bristle worker: "Usually we struck at the beginning of a *zman* (period of employment); we sought legal methods in order to appear to be in the right with the police."[272]

To the Bund's dismay, Sergei Zubatov (1864–1917), director of the Security (*Okhrana*) Bureau in Moscow, appropriated the idea of a legal working-class movement by creating police unions to compete with the Bund. He persuaded some members of the Bund including Mania Vil'bushevich to form the Jewish Independent Worker's Party (ENRP), which embraced legalism and engaged in cultural and educational activities rather than in subversive politics. In exchange for their cooperation, Zubatov promised that the government would support the workers' demands for better working conditions and help to resolve conflicts between workers and their employers. For instance, when gendarmes in Minsk learned about an impending metal craftsmen's strike for a twelve-hour workday, the gendarme colonel proposed a joint meeting with the strikers and employers.[273] "A group of people who share my views (with Mariia

[Mania] Vil'bushevich at their head) conducted agitation for days on end until they were hoarse, and began to prove the whole usefulness of the intervention by Colonel Vasil'ev in the strike," reported Zubatov to his superiors. He claimed that the gendarmes had achieved a "reconciliation" whereby the workers learned about "the entire incorrectness of the unauthorized work stoppage" and shop owners were told to have a legal working day. Zubatov boasted that these tactics not only angered the revolutionaries (who saw them as "a political slap on the face") but also resonated with the workers: "At the same time, the apartments of those representing peaceful tactics [such as Vil'bushevich] began to be inundated by workers, who came to talk things over and to learn about the new methods of action" (document 173). In reality, the police unions swerved out of control, succeeding in mobilizing workers but not in directing them to state ends. Enthusiasm among the workers for legalism gave way to disillusionment and fury. For example, the ENRP distributed leaflets to Jewish shop clerks of both genders in Minsk that described the failure of the government to enforce the limits on maximum working hours: "The government has rejected the request to close all shops at 9 p.m. In addition, police officers collected a signed statement from many shop clerks swearing that they agreed to sit in their shops until 11 p.m. [. . .] We must call a strike because we see clearly that no one wants to help us; therefore we must help ourselves—through force and unity, through our own struggle" (document 173). By 1903 the state had abandoned the strategy of coopting the workers for its own purposes and even sent its progenitor, Zubatov, into exile.

Movements like the Bund provided a common forum in which single men and women could meet. Drawn together by a shared ideology and social activism, the men and women often developed intense loyalties and romantic bonds. For instance, when Daniel Charney (1888–1959) traveled to Minsk to bail his older brother out of prison and witnessed the comradely intimacy at a banquet held on the latter's behalf, he was utterly amazed: his brother warmly embraced both male and female comrades as though they were lifelong friends.[274] Although the sexual revolution and family question were central to the radical movements, the Bund insisted on a strict code of morality (in the name of revolutionary discipline) that mirrored traditional Jewish norms. Although the Bund endorsed the equality of the sexes in principle and even allowed women to participate as leaders, couriers, smugglers, and street agitators, rank-and-file members took traditional gender roles in daily activities as given and therefore relegated women to subsidiary roles in the nursery and kitchen.[275] Like many revolutionaries, the Bundists deferred the woman's question for resolution after the larger socialist revolution.

Formally created in 1897, the Bund had been active in both the Russian and Jewish labor movements and exercised a strong influence on the RSDLP — for example, disseminating the Kremer pamphlet *On Agitation* (1894) and providing prominent leaders for the Russian Marxist movement. In 1903, however, that collaboration suddenly came to an end. The internationalist wing of the Bund opposed having a separate organization outside the RSDLP, arguing that national divisions would distract the Jewish working class from "learning to believe and to feel that all proletarians without national or religious distinction are brothers."[276] However, others pointed out that, in the words of John Mill, "the Jewish worker suffers in Russia not merely as a worker but as a Jew."[277] This faction was also troubled by the "assimilationist tendencies" of the Jewish proletariat and its members' ignorance of Jewish culture.[278] The Bund, in this faction's view, should therefore provide a secular Jewish identity, one that is not bound to religion, yet not alien to Jewish national culture. Mark Liber declared at the Fourth Congress of the Bund: "Our task is to prepare the Jewish proletariat for national autonomy, to develop its national self-consciousness. To a considerable extent, we have until now been cosmopolitans. We must become nationalists. There is no need to be afraid of this word. *National* is not *nationalistic*. . . . [National agitation] can only raise political consciousness without in any way hindering class consciousness; likewise, it can in no way lead to isolation or exclusiveness."[279] Not only the Bund but other national groups (such as the Georgians) demanded autonomy within the RSDLP, including programmatic clauses on the right to use one's native language for education, governance, and public expression.

Zionism, the Bund's main rival, did not attract a mass following before the First World War but had its roots in the Hebrew and national renaissance of the 1880s. Disillusioned with emancipation, its proponents saw national rebirth as the solution to their abject position in Russia. Following Peretz Smolenskin's return to Vienna after visiting Russia in 1881, he decried a servile Jewish *mentalité* that resulted from the Jews' low status: "We have no sense of national honor; our standards are those of a second-class people. We find ourselves rejoicing when we are granted a favor and exulting when we are tolerated and befriended." Smolenskin argued that now was the time to confront inner weakness and to "turn from the path of disaster we once chose, for we can still be saved."[280] Appalled by the shocking reports of pillaging in the south, Lilienblum (see document 104) similarly acknowledged that when he "became convinced that it was not a lack of high culture that was the cause of our tragedy — for aliens we are and aliens we shall remain. . . . When my eyes were opened by the new ideal, my spirit rose to a new task."[281] That new task was articulated powerfully by Leon Pinsker (a Russified physician in Odessa) in his influential *Autoemancipation* (1882). The Jews needed a land of their own, a *"home*, if not a *country* of our own."[282] Although insisting that the Holy Land was not the inevitable place, Pinsker could not restrain the romantic longing for Eretz Israel among other Jewish nationalists. "I am for Zion," proclaimed Lilienblum, employing the language of the divine:

> To be sure, it is a great and complicated task, but is a nation born all at once? We must work for the development of our land, and we have no right to shirk this divine task . . . Our God, Who has sustained us and has not left us to the mercy of the lions among whom we dwelt these thousands of years, will give us strength for our efforts to find rest. [. . .] This is the land in which our fathers have found rest since time immemorial — and as they lived so will we live.[283]

To prepare for a return to the Holy Land, Lilienblum and Pinsker began to establish local Hovevei Zion (Lovers of Zion) societies, which had the task of promoting emigration and the creation of Jewish settlements in Palestine. Dire circumstances compelled even traditional rabbis like Samuel Mogilever (1824–98) to press for cooperation with secular coreligionists: "A great fire, a fearful conflagration, is raging in our midst, and we are all threatened. [. . .] If brethren put out their hands to us in aid, doing all in their power to deliver us from our dire straits, are there such among us as would dare spurn them? If all factions will really understand this thought, this covenant of brothers will surely stand."[284]

In 1884 representatives of secular and traditional circles held the first organizational meeting in Katowice (German Poland); they were thus able to avoid detection by tsarist police. A struggle for the identity of the movement erupted almost immediately. To placate the Orthodox minority, representatives elected Mogilever (who insisted on a key leadership role) as honorary president of the organization and Pinsker as chairman, the person with the real decision-making author-

ity. After all, argued the more secular members, the rabbis were "impractical men who know nothing about organizing a popular movement [and] are familiar only with the dicta of the *Shulhan Arukh*."[285] But to succeed, they would have to cooperate with rabbis who remained committed to the cause and demanded fealty to tradition as a prerequisite for their continued involvement. Eventually, a tense *modus vivendi* emerged: the Hovevei Zion settlements in Palestine would maintain traditional observance as the official and public policy. Tensions came to a head in the Jewish year 5648 (1887–1888), which, according to the traditional calculation, was a sabbatical year; all agricultural activity had to cease. The settlers assumed that the rabbis would find a way to permit work because they could ill afford to refrain from all their labor. Although some rabbis prepared to find the necessary *heter* (permission), others adamantly refused; indeed, the controversy made it impossible to ignore the deep fault lines in the movement. The exchange of letters between Pinsker and Naftali Berlin documents one aspect of this larger controversy and reveals the repercussions of the controversy on the Russian home front (document 175).

In order to establish an organizational foothold in Russia, Hibbat Tsiyyon (the official name adopted in 1887) had to constitute itself in 1890 as the "Society for the Support of Jewish Farmers and Artisans in Syria and Palestine" and register as a charity — an image and role that its members were eager to shed. Menahem Ussishkin of Moscow (1863–1941) complained in a letter to Lilienblum that the organization merely engaged in charity and created dependence among its settlers in Eretz Israel: "I still maintain what I said to you at Druskieniki and have written to you two or three times: so long as the matter of the resettlement of Eretz Israel is merely one of *charity*, so long as the business of the leaders of Hibbat Tsiyyon is to grant *assistance* to the indigent in the settlements . . . ages will pass and the settlers will [still be saying] . . . give, give — in appeals, letters, telegrams; the leaders of Hibbat Tsiyyon will go on [as they have hitherto] until they have doled out the last penny."[286] Despite their extreme poverty and heavy reliance on foreign support (especially that of Baron Edmond de Rothschild), these early migrants succeeded in creating the first fifteen Hibbat Tsiyyon agricultural settlements (*moshavot*) in Eretz Israel. They were more resilient than the community of Gedera that was created by the Biluim — a group of university students from Kharkov who emigrated between 1882 and 1884.[287]

Members of the First Aliyah laid the foundations for a secular Jewish revival in Eretz Israel, especially the resurrection of Hebrew as the vernacular of everyday life.[288] "The kindergarten shall restore to our people its native tongue," wrote the Hebrew teacher Yitzhak Epstein. "In ten years, an adult will not learn a foreign language properly, though he devote much time and effort to it, but in three years an infant will learn a language so that it becomes for him — if he does not abandon it completely — a native tongue." Eliezer Ben Yehuda (1858–1922), who forced his wife speak to their child exclusively in Hebrew, warned that "as long as women do not speak Hebrew, there is no hope for a revival of spoken Hebrew."[289] Although Hebrew instruction for women had begun in Russia and Poland in the 1880s, there was still great opposition to this dramatic reversal. Puah Rakovsky remembered: "Jewish parents, even the Zionist among them, disparaged Hebrew instructions for girls. The religious [were] opposed to the very idea of it, while the progressives, so-called, and the non-religious were mostly assimilationist."[290] Despite taunts that they were just "a bunch of farmers' wives reading novels," the women of the First Aliyah paved the way for women to work as nursery school and elementary school teachers and to instill Hebrew in the next generation.[291]

The emphasis on reviving a national He-brew culture, which could serve as a substitute for traditional Talmudic culture, lay at the center of the vision of cultural or spiritual Zionism promulgated by Ahad Ha'am (Asher Ginzburg, 1856–1927).[292] In his influential article "This Is Not the Way," he chided Hibbat Tsiyyon for its single-minded preoccupation with the material concerns of its settlements in Eretz Israel at the expense of revitalizing "cultural and national sentiments." His trip to visit Palestine in 1891 only confirmed his conviction about the poverty of Hibbat Tsiyyon's purely practical enterprises:

> I cannot convey the smallest part of what I felt and passed through in the few days since arriving here — where every step, every stone, is a piece of blood-soaked history, where one sees nothing but historical sites on every side, and what sites! Mount Zion, the Temple Mount, the Mount of Olives. . . . And it is only when you are here that you sense how laughable and odd is the modern Palestinian *materialism* [of Hibbat Tsiyyon] with its [implied] belief that the Jews can ever give up Jerusalem![293]

The task at hand was not to resettle Jewish refugees on the land but to "prepare the hearts" of those who could usher in a Hebrew renaissance — the goal of his semi-secret Bnei Moshe society in Odessa. Once transplanted in Eretz Israel, this national culture would "create a new spiritual bond between the scattered sections of the people and by virtue of its spiritual influence will move them to a new national life."[294]

This yearning for a Hebrew renaissance had already developed among the *maskilim* as the state retreated from its institutional support of the Haskalah in the 1870s and 1880s. Writers such as Sholem Y. Abramovitsh became increasingly wary of the emancipation of the individual, which had come at the expense of the collective. At the heart of Abramovitsh's stories was the fear that modern, emancipated Jews would lose sight of their kin, culture, and religion in their pursuit of personal freedom. Indeed, his novel, *Fathers and Sons*, portrays Alexander II as a crook who deceived aspiring *maskilim* into trading public power for private freedom. For Abramovitsh, the seeds of regenerating Jewish life lay in the unreformed Jews in the eternal Pale of Settlement, a sort of Russian-Jewish Eden.[295] Writers such as Yitskhok Leybush Peretz, Ben Ami, and Mordekhai Ze'ev Feierberg employed native motifs such as the *akedah* to explore this topic and create a new messianic topography of the *shtetl*, a space of Russian Jewry's death and national rebirth. Following Lilienblum and Smolenskin, Zionist writers also struggled to reclaim Jewish masculinity. The new Nietzschean ideal of empowerment and self-discipline was elaborated in the works of Yosef H. Brenner, and Grigorii Arieli-Orlov, whose fictional Jewish soldiers shed their impotence and second-class status on their way to Palestine.[296]

Although traditional members of Hibbat Tsiyyon accepted the necessity of cooperation with their secular coreligionists, they could not ignore the criticism that Zionist nationalism aimed to "eradicate the foundations of religion." The Lubavitcher rebbe made this clear: "And their entire desire and intention is to remove the burden of the Torah and the commandments and to uphold their nationalism. This is to be their Judaism."[297] The difficulty of collaborating with secular Zionists, already manifest in the 1880s, led in 1902 to the creation of Mizrahi (the religious wing of Zionism) by R. Yitzhak Yaakov Reines (1839–1915). As Reines explained to his Orthodox critics, the goal of political Zionism was "to improve the condition of the nation and to uplift its honor," not to hasten redemption: "For the redemption in itself is above any and every natural phenomenon or human endeavor, and belongs entirely to the lofty realm of miracles and wonders."[298] Whether this was merely rhetoric or sincere belief, Reines hoped that at the very least a strong Mizrahi

movement could ultimately bring secular Zionists back into the religious fold.[299]

Other Orthodox leaders rejected such ideas and proposed a conservative platform that offered succor to a weak and frightened regime and that therefore might enable them to regain influence. Invoking the scripts of deference, loyalty, and utility, they promised to wean Jewish youth from the pernicious revolutionary movements in exchange for greater authority over their communities.[300] This new rhetoric of religious and political conservatism emerged in the early 1880s. It figured prominently, for example, in an 1882 letter from a group of Orthodox Jewish émigrés in London to Konstantin P. Pobedonotsev, the close advisor of Alexander III and the most prominent public spokesman for the autocracy. The letter urged the state, in its own political self-interest, to support the Orthodox, not the "*maskilim*" (here, meaning secular Jews)—who, it warned, sought only to erode the foundations of faith and tradition. The consequences were dangerous to both state and society: "The lack of faith among the Jews not only encourages nihilism, but spreads atheism, [which leads to] a corruption of morals among the general population."[301] By 1912 the non-Zionist Orthodox had created their own organization, Agudat Yisrael, with its central concept of *da'at Torah* or rabbinic leadership in all areas of Jewish life. Agudat Yisrael consolidated its position after World War I, especially with its new connections to the German rabbinate.[302]

From Revolution to War (1905–14)

At the beginning of the twentieth century, the regime had few allies, having alienated even the moderate and privileged—from noble landowners to white-collar professionals, from factory workers to peasants, from Baltic peoples to national minorities in the Caucasus. All its opponents began to organize and mobilize; even conservative nobles and urban elites convened a series of illegal meetings to press their demands. Faced with rising opposition from within (the "all-nation liberation movement"), the inept regime stumbled into the disastrous Russo-Japanese War (1904–5), which was expected to enhance its prestige but, thanks to catastrophic defeats, had just the opposite effect. Defeated abroad and challenged from within, the regime appeared increasingly vulnerable and, by the fall of 1904, felt compelled to retreat and make concessions during the so-called spring of Petr Dmitrievich Sviatopolk-Mirskii (1857–1914), the third minister of interior in two years.

In early 1905 discontent turned into revolution. The precipitant was the infamous Bloody Sunday (9 January 1905), the outcome of a large demonstration, led by the priest Grigorii Gapon, and a march on the Winter Palace to petition for an improvement in the demonstrators' legal rights and material well-being. When the tsar's troops panicked and fired on them, killing scores of unarmed people, the repression ignited demonstrations around the empire and seemed to confirm the radicals' claim that autocracy was responsible for Russia's woes. Between January and October 1905, every segment of society mobilized—city and village, center and periphery, privileged and nonprivileged—and by October the entire empire had been shut down by a general strike. The breakdown of political authority seemed complete.[303]

In response, after months of prevaricating and offering minor concessions, the emperor capitulated: on 17 October he signed the October Manifesto, promising a constitutional monarchy with representational government, religious freedom, civil liberties, and the right to organize political parties. But rather than calming the popular classes, the manifesto only unleashed greater demands from minorities (for autonomy), peasants (for land), and workers (for higher wages and better working conditions). The revolution, however, mobilized not only the left but also the

right: conservative, monarchist forces began to create their own parties, and the propertied classes formed their own organizations to defend their own interests.[304] The upheaval also unleashed ethnic violence; the weakened autocracy was no longer able to maintain law and order in the center, still less in the borderlands.

With the end of the Russo-Japanese War and with the rise in interclass and interethnic divisions, the state gradually mobilized the forces of repression to restore order and suppress the individual elements in the all-nation liberation movement. Amid the turmoil and signs that revolution was about to erupt once again, the Jewish response was predictably varied. Some Jews, wearied by the chaos, "rejected all projects of utopian reconstruction" and abandoned the political stage to focus on "bettering this world" through the creation of a vibrant public sphere that would foster modern Jewish institutions, politics, and culture.[305] Although the state still interfered in the private voluntary associations (legalized on 4 March 1906 by the Temporary Regulations on Societies and Unions), Jewish cultural activists took advantage of the new freedoms to organize libraries, drama circles, literary clubs, historical societies, and fire brigades. Such organizations, characteristic of the period, offered "an alternative to the synagogue and to the more established forms of Jewish associations, even as the world of the traditional learned elite comprise[d] its own special subculture."[306] For instance, those unable to use Russian lending libraries because of the fees (twenty-five to fifty kopecks per month, with a deposit of one to three rubles) or the absence of Yiddish books now crowded into the modern Jewish libraries. "The word 'library' was like a magical incantation," wrote the memoirist Falik Zolf, "a siren that enticed people there, and no force in the world could keep them back."[307] The library of the Jewish Section of the Russian Society for the Protection of Women described the most popular books among its wards in St. Petersburg in 1905: "Fiction serves as the favorite and most accessible reading material for the readers. They read 1,406 fiction books and 263 books in all other areas. A few readers always take some popular science book along with a work of fiction; however, such readers comprise an insignificant number. Turgenev, Tolstoy, Pushkin, and Dostoyevsky are usually popular."[308]

Many Jews, of course, continued to be prominent in the revolutionary parties (the Bund, PSR, and RSDLP), while others—especially professionals, such as doctors and lawyers—gravitated toward the new liberal party of Constitutional Democrats (called Kadets, after the Russian abbreviation). Still others supported new organizations in defense of Jewish rights and interest, most notably the Union for the Attainment of Full Rights for the Jewish People in Russia (*Soiuz dlia dostizheniia polnopraviia evreiskago naroda v Rossii* [hereafter SP]). This organization, created in 1905, was the first successful effort to bring together representatives of a wide spectrum of political groups—including liberals, socialists, nationalists, and autonomists. Their goal was to lobby not only for Jewish civic rights but also for "the right of the Jewish people for national cultural self-determination."[309] In other words, they rejected the terms of emancipation that had been offered to their coreligionists in Germany—assimilation in exchange for civic equality.[310] Jewish liberals like Maxim Vinaver and the laywer, Genrikh Sliozberg, who initially dominated the SPR, sought to mobilize wary Jewish leaders to participate in the new parliamentary system, which produced two Dumas (in 1906 and 1907). In a resolution at the Third Congress, the SP acknowledged that "the Jewish population participates in the electoral campaign without the conviction that it will be able to send a corresponding number of freely chosen representatives to the State Duma and [operates]

under the onerous awareness that the Duma itself will not correspond to the demands of a true, popularly chosen parliament." Nonetheless, Jewish leaders recognized that the "participation of all other national groups, as well as reactionary parties, in the electoral campaign obliges Jews to stand up for their civil and national rights, to be concerned that they not be left defenseless in a future assembly of popular representatives."[311] To the bitter disappointment of elected Jewish members, who had worked tirelessly for Jewish rights, both Dumas were dissolved, opening the door to the coup d'état of 3 June 1907, an illegal change in the franchise to increase the representation of the propertied classes and to reduce that of the disprivileged—workers, peasants, and minorities.

For the next seven years so-called constitutional autocracy—an oxymoron—labored to rebuild its power and to keep oppositionist forces divided and weak. Under Prime Minister Petr Arkad'evich Stolypin (1862–11), the government sought to construct a working relationship with the Third Duma (1907–12), which, because of the new franchise, had a conservative majority. Although this coalition initially worked (producing, most famously, the Stolypin agrarian reform, which undermined the commune to empower the "rich and the sober"), it began to disintegrate even before Stolypin's assassination in a Kiev theater in September 1911. The government, faced by rising opposition (even in the Duma), continued its efforts to undo the concessions granted during the revolution of 1905–7. Particularly important, and dangerous, was the attempt to instrumentalize the minority question—to retract concessions to minorities (such as the Finns) and, so the regime hoped, mobilize Russian nationalist spirit in support of autocracy.

Nowhere were the anti-minority tactics more apparent than in the case of Jews. Although Stolypin had initially broached the subject of concessions (to reconcile this important group—if only to allay criticism from foreign bankers, who provided much-needed loans), Nicholas II was adamantly opposed and, indeed, inclined to blame the whole revolution of 1905–7 on the Jews. As the domestic situation deteriorated, the regime openly played the antisemitic card in the infamous Beilis ritual murder case in Kiev (1911–13). With authorization from the minister of justice in St. Petersburg, local prosecutors charged Mendel Beilis with the murder of a thirteen-year-old boy, Andrei Iushchinskii, "out of religious fanaticism for ritual purposes." This became Russia's Dreyfus affair, a cause célèbre that provoked international outrage and criticism at home, even a formal inquiry by the regime's own hand-picked Duma. By the time the Fourth Duma (1914–17) convened, the Duma had become a hotbed of opposition, openly critical of the regime, investigating official malfeasance, and disseminating rumors about the imperial family and its unseemly friend and close advisor—Grigorii Rasputin. The political imbroglio in St. Petersburg had its popular counterpart: a spike in workers' strikes; growing peasant intransigence; and rising demands for independence, not mere autonomy, among national minorities. These sentiments would only intensify with Russia's entry into World War I.

On 19 July 1914, the Jewish writer Rahel Khin wrote in her diary at 7:00 a.m.: "Again, I did not sleep through the night. At 5:00 a.m., I settled down to write to the children. When I think about them—I go crazy from rage and torment. Yesterday evening, Stas arrived and leaves this morning at 8:00. They say that Moscow will be jampacked like a military camp (but on Friday when we were there, it was empty). War has not been declared yet but we wait hour by hour. God! Is it possible that the children won't come? God, perform a miracle!" At 10:00 a.m., Khin wrote one dreaded line: "Germany declared war on us."[312] The outbreak of World War I shattered the world as the Jews had known it more than any other

event. Apart from the catastrophic defeats on the military front, the war demonstrated that the ancien régime had utterly failed to win the allegiance of, much less assimilate, national minorities.[313] Indeed, the war and the regime itself only exacerbated ethnic tensions. In particular, the army's division of the population into supposedly reliable and unreliable subjects seemed to legitimize the public's antisemitism and encourage the anti-Jewish violence that took many forms—including pogroms, forced expulsion, hostage taking, and mass deportation of Jews (along with other suspect groups, such as Poles, Armenians, and Latvians). The German High Command played its own role, disseminating propaganda on the enemy front to heighten suspicion of Yiddish-speaking Jews.[314] Ironically, the war dismantled the infamous Pale of Settlement, unleashing a flood of refugees (many Jewish) into the Russian interior. In short order, more than half a million Jews found themselves uprooted and displaced, forced to share physical space with Russians and placing an enormous burden on both central and local authorities.[315] For many Russians, indeed, the mass migration—whether through deportation or flight—brought the first mass encounter between them and Jews.[316]

Conclusion

As this introduction and the documents below suggest, the world of Russian Jews was anything but traditional and unchanging. Because of both internal and external dynamics, the Jewish people experienced profound change in the 142 years that elapsed between the first Polish partition and the outbreak of World War I. Both the Jews and their environment changed, partly in response to each other, and the net result was a very different Jewish world than the one that the Russian Empire had acquired in the last quarter of the eighteenth century.

One important facet in the Jews' everyday

life was the transformation in their status and rights: the imperial state both raised expectations and disappointed them because the autocracy was incapable of managing the social change that it had unleashed on the Jews. The revisionist Zionist Vladimir Jabotinsky recalled how the lawyer Sliozberg once described the impact of the smallest clause in state laws on Jewish everyday life:

"I envy you—for you the Jewish Question is a dream about the future. But for me a clause in this or that statute concerning the liquor trade is also a big part of the Jewish Question." Sliozberg probably had no idea that that night, after the meeting, we, his opponents, the young people of our camp, had a long conversation among ourselves about this statement. Prosaic, as if issued from a chancellery, and pronounced without passion, it struck us like a thunderbolt. It reminded us of the terrible tragedy of everyday existence, of the fact that in three lines of an official text there was sometimes contained a nearly fatal verdict for hundreds of thousands of people. It reminded us of the enormous idealistic value of realism.[317]

Although this legal history has long been mapped (with detailed exegesis of state law), far less attention has been given to the Jews' response. As this volume demonstrates, decrees from St. Petersburg always elicited some kind of reaction, rarely abject acceptance—whether it be calculated compliance, evasion, or resistance. As a result, local authorities became intimately familiar with their Jews as they sought to enforce these laws (or turn a blind eye), deal with the Jews' daily problems with neighbors, and even appreciate the role that some Jews played in their provinces. This was most apparent during World War I, when governors questioned the wisdom of expelling all Jews from their jurisdictions. For instance, the governor of Kurliand, who had just received the order to expel all Jews "with-

out exception," asked whether Jewish doctors and nurses should be included. He must have also informed the head of the Dvinsk military district about the role of Jews in the local economy and war effort, for the latter sent a request to his superiors: "Since all the trade in the province, devastated by war, lies in the hands of the Jews, who are the suppliers of military sections, military institutions, and medical establishments, I ask for permission to leave them; in addition, I would ask for a general permission to leave those Jews who would be considered absolutely loyal."[318]

Another major facet of Jewish daily life in nineteenth-century Russia was the confrontation with modernity. Modern improvements in communication (a more efficient postal system and telegraph), transportation (the railroad), and other technology rapidly changed expectations and relationships. For example, in the case of Burshtein versus Betgilel in the Kiev Orphans' Court (document 53), Samuil Betgilel accused his mother-in-law of failing to send him a telegram about his wife's death and of sending a letter by post instead, which delayed his arrival by train from St. Petersburg to Kiev, giving her time to gain guardianship over his minor daughter.

The processes of economic modernization such as rapid industrialization and urbanization also brought significant changes to Jewish life. In environmental terms, the growth of factories without proper oversight raised new health hazards, as shown in R. Yitzhak Elhanan Spektor's responsum about a foul-smelling natural spring near a turpentine factory that women used as a mikvah (document 80) and Yiddish advice books that warned Jews not to drink harmful water "that contains factory waste" (document 66). For a small minority including Lazar Poliakov's family, the demands of industrialization with its significant banking and financial needs promised greater wealth and opportunity. However, for the majority of the Jews in the Pale of Settlement, the rise of mechanized factories and new technologies meant the demise of their traditional occupations, leading to dire impoverishment. If the documents reveal anything, it is the intimate details of a wretched poverty that prompted desperate Jews to resort to extreme measures such as the abandonment of children, crime, conversion, and emigration.[319]

Modernity also nurtured new reading habits, introducing Jews to the latest news, philosophies, ideologies, and sensibilities that often challenged traditional mores and values. As the documents show, even the strictest hasidic court of R. Simhah Bunem of Otwock was not immune to these trends (document 3): the *shammes* presented the rebbe's daughter, Ita Kalish, with Moses Mendelssohn's translation and commentary on the Bible (the *Biur*). Ben Zion Dinur also relates a scene in his memoirs when he, his cousin, and brother arrived at the Telz yeshiva without having submitted an application in advance. To their surprise, the rabbis pointed out: "'But notices were printed in [the Hebrew newspapers] *Ha-melits* and *Ha-tsefirah*.' And R. Eliezer asks his cousin, "Your father does not read newspapers either?" (document 109).

As a result of these cultural changes, a new class of educated and acculturated Jewish families emerged in large towns and the capitals, adopting the Russian or Polish language, dress, food ways, reading habits, and social manners. But in contrast to their coreligionists in Germany or France, Russian Jews kept their Jewish identity firmly rooted in the Russian confessional definition, a status that only conversion could transform legally. For instance, Zinaida Poliakova, who hobnobbed with the Russian nobility, expressed astonishment at the free merging of religious identities in Western Europe: "It is surprising that a mixed marriage between Leona Gol'dshmit and Viscount Deforfie can be held in Paris. She is Jewish but the groom is a Catholic and serves as a secretary at the French embassy in Berlin."[320] Even Jewish converts had difficulties casting off their status as converted Jews (*kreshchenyi evrei*)—a designation that state officials insisted on attaching to their names in government documents and letters. Perhaps it is not surprising, then, that it was in Russia, where Jews were not permitted to forget their collective identity, that a vibrant Jewish national culture and politics developed—not only in the form of Zionism but other expressions as well, such as diaspora nationalism and Bundism.

In many ways, everyday Jewish life was not unlike that of the surrounding cultures. Jews shared universal experiences with their neighbors: the birth of children, the pleasure of friendship, the pain at the loss of a loved one. However, as "stepchildren of the tsar,"[321] Jews were also saddled with legal disabilities that marred their quality of life and impeded their aspirations for greater civic rights. In this respect the story of the Jews of Imperial Russia was an unfinished one, characterized by unfulfilled ambitions and frustrated desires. "But my heart tells me that in time the Russians will love us. We shall *force* them to love us. With what? With love itself," declares Lev Levanda's fictional character Sarin, as he pines for an affective merger with the Russian nation (*narodnost'*) in the novel *Turbulent Times*. But that idealism was shattered during the last quarter of the nineteenth century. Following the violence of the pogroms of 1881, Levanda wrote in despair and disillusionment: "What can one do if those with whom one so wants to merge shun the merger . . . with crowbars and clubs in their hands?"[322] His desire for an affective merger with the Russian nation had failed, ending in violence and bloodshed. As the regime headed toward the abyss and the very foundations of the old order crumbled, the Jews waited anxiously for the red dawn that promised land, peace, and bread, as well as equality among citizens and friendship among nations.

NOTES

1. On the Judaizer heresy, see Natalia A. Kazakova and Iakov S. Lur'e, *Antifeodal'nye ereticheskie dvizheniia na Rusi XIV-nachala XVI veka* (Moscow: Izd-vo Akademii Nauk SSSR, 1955); Iakov S. Lur'e, "Unresolved Issues in the History of Ideological Movements of the Late 15th Century," in *Medieval Russian Culture*, ed. H. Birnbaum and M. S. Flier (Berkeley: University of California Press, 1984), 150–71; John Klier, "Judaizing without Jews? Moscow-Novgorod, 1470–1504," in *Culture and Identity in Muscovy, 1359–1584*, ed. Ann Kleimola and Gail Lenhoff (Moscow: IZZ-Garant, 1997): 336–49.

2. *Polnoe sobranie zakonov rossiiskoi imperii. Sobranie pervoe* (hereafter *PSZ* 1), 45 volumes (St. Petersburg, 1830–1843), 11: 8,840 (16 December 1743).

3. John Klier, *Russia Gathers Her Jews: The Origins of the "Jewish Question" in Russia, 1772–1825* (DeKalb: Northern Illinois University Press, 1986), 28–9.

4. Benjamin Nathans, *Beyond the Pale: The Jewish Encounter with Late Imperial Russia* (Berkeley: University of California Press, 2002), 63–64; see also 181–83. This was most evident in the refusal to extend the right of residency to retired Jewish soldiers in the military reforms of 1874—a right they enjoyed as Nikolaevan soldiers, who served in the army under the reign of Nicholas I.

5. Olga Litvak, *Conscription and the Search for Modern Russian Jewry* (Bloomington: Indiana University Press, 2006), 7.

6. Marc Raeff, *The Well-Ordered Police State: Social and Institutional Change through Law in the Germanies and Russia, 1600–1800* (New Haven: Yale University Press, 1983).

7. For examples of these "instructions" sent from different social groups, see Gregory L. Freeze, *From Supplication to Revolution: A Documentary Social History of Imperial Russia* (Oxford: Oxford University Press, 1988), 11–99.

8. Quoted in Klier, *Russia Gathers Her Jews*, 35–36; Klier added the word [people].

9. Edward C. Thaden, *Russia's Western Borderlands, 1710–1870* (Princeton: Princeton University Press, 1984).

10. Quoted in Andreas Kappeler, *The Russian Empire* (London: Pearson Education, 2001), 58.

11. The Council of the Four Lands was effectively abolished in 1764, and attempts to resurrect a regional representative body failed. Threats to the *kahal*'s authority came not only from the Polish magnates who interfered increasingly in Jewish internal affairs but also from ordinary Jews who bypassed the *kahal* to litigate in gentile courts—a pattern that later intensified in the Russian Empire. The rise of Hasidism and its challenge to local authority also weakened the *kahal*.

12. Quoted in Gavriil R. Derzhavin, *Sochineniia*, ed. Iakov Grot (St. Petersburg: Tipografiia imperatorskoi akademii nauk, 1878), 7: 335.

13. Quoted in Iulii Gessen, "Bet-din," in *Evreiskaia entsiklopediia*, ed. Lev Katsenelson and Baron David Gintsburg, reprint (St. Petersburg: Izdatel'skii tsentr "TERRA," 1991), 4:411; see also RGIA, f. 821, op. 8, d. 17.

14. A. A. Alekseev, *Ocherki domashnei i obshchestvennoi zhizni evreev, ikh verovanie, bogosluzhenie, prazdniki, obriady, Talmud i kagal* (St. Petersburg: Izdanie knigoprodavtsa I. L. Tuzova 1896), 214.

15. Quoted in Gessen, "Bet-din," 4:412.

16. Gregory L. Freeze, "The *Soslovie* (Estate) Paradigm and Russian Social History," *American Historical Review* 91, no. 1 (1986): 11–36.

17. Klier, *Russia Gathers Her Jews*, 67. The decree of 1780 required Jews to register in an urban center, and a decree of 1781 allowed Jews who enrolled in the merchant estate to pay the same amount of taxes as their Christian counterparts.

18. Freeze, *From Supplication to Revolution*, 52–53.

19. Richard Pipes, "Catherine II and the Jews," *Soviet Jewish Affairs* 5 (1975): 14.

20. *PSZ* 1, 21: 15577, 25 July 1777.

21. *PSZ* 1, 23: 17006, 23 December 1791.

22. Classical historians such as Simon Dubnow took this position. See Dubnow, *History of the Jews in Russia and Poland from the Earliest Times until the Present Day* (Philadelphia: Jewish Publication Society of America, 1916), 314–20.

23. Pipes, "Catherine II and the Jews," 17. Pipes suggests that Jewish merchants, known for their

smuggling activities, may have been seen as a threat to state efforts to interdict seditious literature.

24. *PSZ* 1, 23:17224, 23 June 1794.

25. The Old Believers emerged out of the Great Schism in the Russian Orthodox Church in 1654–66, when Patriarch Nikon introduced reforms to make Russian Orthodox practices conform to those of the Greek Orthodox Church. The Old Believers opposed these reforms and embraced traditional rites and customs. See Robert O. Crummey, *The Old Believers and the World of the Antichrist: The Vyg Community and the Russian State, 1694–1855* (Madison: University of Wisconsin Press, 1970); Georg Bernhard Michels, *At War with the Church: Religious Dissent in Seventeenth-Century Russia* (Stanford: Stanford University Press, 1999).

26. A. Ia. "Podushnaia podat' v Rossii," in *Entsiklopedicheskii slavar' Brokgauza i Efrona* (St. Petersburg, 1890–1907), http://www.vehi.net/brokgauz/index.html.

27. *PSZ* 1, 23:17224, 23 June 1794.

28. Bernard D. Weinryb, *The Jews of Poland: A Social and Economic History of the Jewish Community in Poland from 1100 to 1800* (Philadelphia: Jewish Publication Society of America, 1973), 117.

29. Klier, *Russia Gathers Her Jews*, 67.

30. Ibid., 81–115.

31. A. E. Presniakov, *Apogei samoderzhaviia* (The Hague: Mouton, 1925).

32. See Bruce Lincoln, *Nicholas I: Emperor and Autocrat of All the Russias* (DeKalb: Northern Illinois University Press, 1989), and the literature cited in his book.

33. Gershon Hundert, "Jewish Popular Spirituality in the Eighteenth Century," *Polin* 15 (2002): 93–94.

34. Quoted in Byron L. Sherwin, *Sparks Amidst the Ashes: The Spiritual Legacy of Polish Jewry* (Oxford: Oxford University Press, 1997), 31.

35. Hundert, "Jewish Popular Spirituality in the Eighteenth Century," 94.

36. The prayerbook that followed the Lurianic rite was first published in Poland in 1781. It included rites attributed to the kabbalist Isaac Luria, such as "special devotional texts (kavanot) before major prayers and benedictions, some Sephardic order

and content, and greater attention to the recitation of Temple rituals" (Stefan C. Reif, "Liturgy," in *The YIVO Encyclopedia of Jews in Eastern Europe*, ed. Gershon D. Hundert (New Haven: Yale University Press, 2008), 1: 1076.

37. Immanuel Etkes, *The Besht: Magician, Mystic, and Leader* (Waltham, MA: Brandeis University Press, 2005), 7–8. To be sure, there were complaints about false *baalei shem* in the mid-eighteenth century; however, recent studies have demonstrated that the Besht was not considered to be one of them.

38. Moshe Rosman, *Founder of Hasidism* (Berkeley: University of California Press, 1996), 17–26.

39. Ibid., 1.

40. Etkes, *The Besht*, 254.

41. Ibid., 256.

42. See also Ada Rapoport-Albert, "God and the Zaddik as Two Focal Points of Hasidic Worship," in *Essential Papers on Hasidism*, ed. Gershon Hundert (New York: New York University Press, 1991), 299–329; Samuel Dresner, *The Zaddik: The Doctrine of the Zaddik According to the Writings of Rabbi Yaakov Yosef of Polnoy* (New York: Schocken, 1960), 75–147.

43. Moshe Idel, *Hasidism between Ecstasy and Magic* (Albany: State University of New York Press, 1995), 1.

44. Immanuel Etkes, "The Zaddik," in *Hasidism Reappraised*, ed. Rapoport-Albert (London: The Littman Library of Jewish Civilization, 1996), 159–67.

45. Ada Rapoport-Albert, "Hasidism after 1772," in *Hasidism Reappraised*, ed. Rapoport-Albert, 103. See also Immanuel Etkes, *Ba'al ha-Tanya: Rabi Shne'ur Zalman mi-Ladi ve-reshitah shel Hasidut Habad* (Jerusalem: Zalman Shazar Center, 2011).

46. Yekhezkel Kotik, trans. Margaret Birstein, Sharon Makover-Assaf, and Dena Ordan, *Journey to a Nineteenth-Century Shtetl*, ed. David Assaf (Detroit: Wayne State University Press, 2002), 284.

47. Adam Teller, "Hasidism and the Challenge of Geography: The Polish Background to the Spread of the Hasidic Movement," *AJS Review* 30, no. 1 (2006): 1–29; Glenn Dynner, *Men of Silk: The Hasidic Conquest of Polish Society* (Oxford: Oxford University Press, 2008), 55–88.

48. Avraham Ber Gottlober, *Zikhronot u-masa'ot* (Jerusalem: Bialik Institute, 1976), 1: 59.

49. Quoted in Dynner, *Men of Silk*, 115.

50. The Hebrew word for the opponents was *mitnagdim*; the Yiddish word *misnagdim* will be used henceforth.

51. Quoted in Immanuel Etkes, The *Gaon of Vil'na: The Man and His Image*, trans. Jeffrey M. Green (Berkeley: University of California Press, 2002), 80.

52. Allan Nadler, *The Faith of the Mithnagdim: Rabbinic Responses to Hasidic Rapture* (Baltimore: John Hopkins University Press, 1997), 54.

53. Quoted in ibid., 76.

54. Quoted in ibid., 67.

55. Ibid., 78–102.

56. Iulii Gessen, "Korobochnyi sbor," in *Evreiskaia entsiklopediia*, ed. Katsenelson and Gintsburg, 9: 758–71. The tax varied by town in the early nineteenth century: for a pound of beef, residents paid 2 kopecks in Chernigov and in Nezhin, but 1.5 kopecks in Konotop—amounts that added up when paid into a common coffer.

57. Quoted in Mordecai L. Wilensky, "Hasidic-Mitnaggedic Polemics in the Jewish Communities: The Hostile Phase," in *Essential Papers on Hasidism: Origins to Present*, ed. Gershon Hundert (New York: New York University Press, 1991), 254.

58. Sarah Menkin Foner, *A Woman's Voice: Sarah Foner, Hebrew Author of the Haskalah*, trans. Morris Rosenthal (Wilbraham, MA: Daily International, 2001), 15–16.

59. Etkes, *The Gaon of Vil'na*, 36.

60. Ibid.

61. Shaul Stampfer, *Families, Rabbis, and Education: Traditional Jewish Society in Nineteenth-Century Eastern Europe* (Oxford: Littman Library of Jewish Civilization, 2010), 324–41.

62. Cited in Etkes, *The Gaon of Vilna*, 178.

63. The name "Telz yeshiva" will be used throughout instead of "Tel'shi yeshiva," as this was how it was known.

64. Shaul Stampfer, *Ha-yeshivah ha-Lita'it be-hithavutah ba-me'ah ha-tesha-'esreh* (Jerusalem: Zalman Shazar Center 1995); Immanuel Etkes and Shlomo Tikochinski, eds., *Yeshivot Lita: pirke zikhronot* (Jerusalem: Zalman Shazar Center, 2004).

65. Quoted in Isaac Levitats, *The Jewish Community in Russia, 1772–1844* (New York: Columbia University Press, 1943), 191–92.

66. Quoted in ibid., 194.

67. Quoted in Immanuel Etkes, "Rabbi Israel Salanter and His Psychology of Mussar," in *Jewish Spirituality*, 2nd ed., ed. Arthur Green (New York: Crossroad, 1987), 2: 219.

68. Quoted in ibid., 211–15.

69. Dov Katz, *The Musar Movement: Its History, Leading Personalities, and Doctrines*. Trans. Leonard Oschsy, 5 vols. (Tel Aviv: Orly Press, 1975); David E. Fishman, "The Musar Movement in Interwar Poland," in *The Jews of Poland between Two World Wars*, ed. Ysrael Gutman et al. (Hanover, NH: University Press of New England, 1989), 247–71.

70. Sergei Bershadskii, "Polozhenie o evreiakh 1804 goda," *Voskhod* 15 (January 1895): 92–93. See also Klier, *Russia Gathers Her Jews*, 87.

71. Klier, *Russia Gathers Her Jews*, 88.

72. For a description of Frizel's survey, see ibid., 88–95.

73. Quoted in ibid., 99.

74. Derzhavin, *Sochineniia*, 7: 290.

75. Quoted in Klier, *Russia Gathers Her Jews*, 120.

76. The emperor's "young friends" included Minister of the Interior Viktor Kochubei, Adam Czartoryski, Valerian Zubov, and Severyn Potocki. Other close advisors included Gavriil Derzhavin (later replaced by Petr Lopukhin); Mikhail Speranski, then Kochubei's assistant, also played a role in the deliberations.

77. TsDIAK-Ukraïny, f. 633, op. 1, d. 433, ll. 8–12; d. 1690, ll. 20 ob.–21; Klier, *Rossiia sobiraet svoikh evreev: proiskhozhdenie evreiskogo voprosa v Rossii: 1772–1825* (Moscow: Mosty Kul'tury, 2000), 213–16.

78. Quoted in Klier, *Russia Gathers Her Jews*, 130.

79. For a comparative perspective on Russian policies toward the Muslim population, see Heinz-Dietrich Löwe, "Poles, Jews, and Tatars: Religion, Ethnicity, and Social Structure in Tsarist National-

ity Policies," *Jewish Social Studies* 6, no. 3 (2000): 52–96.

80. On the idea of legibility, see James Scott, *Seeing Like a State: How Certain Schemes to Improve the Human Condition Have Failed* (New Haven: Yale University Press, 1998). This idea was adapted for the Russian-Jewish case by Eugene Avrutin, *Jews and the Imperial State: Identification Politics in Tsarist Russia* (Ithaca: Cornell University Press, 2010).

81. *PSZ* 1, 28: 21547, 9 December 1804. For an example of vagrancy and fake passport cases in the Vil'na courts, see LVIA, f. 448, op. 1, d. 1678.

82. *PSZ* 1, 28: 21547, 9 December 1804. On Jewish surnames, see Avrutin, "The Politics of Jewish Legibility: Documentation Practices and Reform During the Reign of Nicholas I," *Jewish Social Studies* 11, no. 2 (2005): 136–169. See also Alexander Beider, *A Dictionary of Jewish Surnames from the Russian Empire* (Teaneck, NJ: Avotaynu, 1993).

83. Alexander Beider, "Names and Naming," in *The YIVO Encyclopedia of Jews in Eastern Europe*, ed. Hundert, 1: 1250.

84. Ibid, 1: 1251. Jews of the Kiev and Grodno region adopted names ending in -skii (such as Belotsekovskii, Fastovskii, Umanskii), while those in Mogilev, Volhynia, and Podolia chose the Yiddish suffix -er (for example, Klebaner and Moshnyager). Those in western Lithuania elected to forgo suffixes altogether, using names such as Kekst, Upin, and Kibort.

85. For examples of problems with spelling of names, see GAKO, f. 1, op. 1, d. 700, g. 1899; f. 1, op. 139, d. 146; f. 1, op. 147. d. 289; f. 1, op. 128, d. 219; f. 1, op. 138, d. 580. See also Avrutin, *Jews and the Imperial State*, 150–53.

86. On education under Alexander I, see James Flynn, *The University Reforms of Tsar Alexander I, 1802–1835* (Washington: Catholic University of America Press, 1988).

87. *PSZ (1)*, 28: 21547, 9 December 1804.

88. Ibid. Tatars were also required to use Russian in business and official business (see Löwe, "Poles, Jews, and Tatars," 57–58).

89. For example, see LVIA, f. 448, op. 2, d. 349753; f. 448, op. 2, d. 34752.

90. Alan W. Fisher, "Enlightened Despotism and Islam under Catherine II," *Slavic Review* 22, no. 4 (1968), 549.

91. *PSZ (1)*, 28:21547, 9 December 1804. .

92. Quoted in Salo Baron, *The Russian Jew under Tsars and Soviets*, 2nd ed. (New York: Macmillan, 1976), 22.

93. Quoted in "Menahem Mendel of Rymanow, "A Hasid Prays for Napoleon," in Lucy Dawidowicz, ed., *The Golden Tradition: Jewish Life and Thought in Eastern Europe* (Northvale, NJ: J. Aronson, 1989), 95.

94. John Stanley, "The Politics of the Jewish Question in the Duchy of Warsaw, 1807–1812," *Jewish Social Studies* 44, no. 1 (1982), 47–62.

95. Quoted in Mordechai Nadav, *The Jews of Pinsk 1506–1880* (Stanford: Stanford University Press, 2008), 336. Nadav found no record of a merchant named Rabinowicz, only of a Saul Levin. Niemcewicz may have confused two common surnames or perhaps meant "the son of the rabbi" (the meaning of Rabinowicz).

96. Frank Thackeray, *Antecedents of Revolution: Alexander I and the Polish Kingdom* (New York: Columbia University Press, 1980), 16.

97. François Guesnet, *Polnische Juden im 19 Jahrhundert* (Köln: Böhlau, 1998); Klier, *Russia Gathers Her Jews*, 179–80.

98. Klier, *Russia Gathers Her Jews*, 178–79.

99. Guesnet, *Polnische Juden im 19 Jahrhundert*.

100. Quoted in Kornilov, *Kurs istorii Rossii XIX veka*, (Moscow: Izdatel'stvo M. and S. Sabashnikovykh, 1918), 2: 18.

101. Lincoln, *Nicholas I*, 242–52.

102. Ibid., 89.

103. Ibid., 100–103.

104. N. M. Druzhinin, *Gosudarstvennye krest'iane i reforma P. D. Kiseleva*, 2 vols. (Moscow: Izd-vo Akademii nauk SSSR, 1946–58).

105. For example, see Robert Crews, *For Prophet and Tsar: Islam and Empire in Russia and Central Asia* (Cambridge: Harvard University Press, 2006).

106. Quoted in Lincoln, *Nicholas I: Emperor and Autocrat of All the Russias* (Bloomington: Indiana University Press, 1978), 247.

107. Quoted in Levitats, *The Jewish Community in Russia*, 63.

108. Michael Stanislawski, *Tsar Nicholas and the Jews, 1825–55* (Philadelphia: Jewish Publication Society of America, 1983), 13–34; Yohanan Petrovsky-Shtern, *Jews in the Russian Army, 1827–1917: Drafted into Modernity* (Cambridge: Cambridge University Press, 2008), 24–60.

109. Yehudah Leib Katsenelson, *Mah she-ra'u 'einai ve-sham'u oznai*, Jerusalem: Mosad Bialik, 1947), 14.

110. TsDIAK-Ukraïny, f. 442, op. 157, d. 994, l. 12. Since the file ends without a resolution, her appeal evidently failed.

111. On military reforms in the Kingdom of Poland, see Petrovsky-Shtern, *Jews in the Russian Army*, 24–29.

112. RGIA, f. 797, op. 13, d. 39104a, l. 288.

113. RGIA, f. 797, op. 13. d. 31904a, l. 126–26 ob.

114. RGIA, f. 796, op. 128, d. 1380, g. 1847, l. 2.

115. RGIA f. 797, op. 13, d. 31904a, l. 228–233 ob.

116. RGIA, f. 797, op. 13, d. 31904a, ll. 161, 164–67 ob. See also Petrovsky-Shtern, *Jews in the Russian Army*, 93–104.

117. Petrovsky-Shtern estimates that 20,000 to 25,000 Jewish soldiers underwent coerced conversions under Nicholas I (*Evrei v russkoi armii, 1827–1914* [Moscow: Novoe literaturnoe obozrenie, 2003], 168).

118. For examples, see RGIA, f. 796, op. 133, d. 624, g. 1852, ll. 1–4; op. 139, d. 2960, g. 1858, ll. 2–4, 7–9 ob.

119. See Petrovsky-Shtern, *Jews in the Russian Army*, 120–24.

120. On the manifesto of 17 April 1905 and the return to Judaism, see Eugene Avrutin, "Returning to Judaism after the 1905 Law on Religious Freedom in Tsarist Russia," *Slavic Review* 65, no. 1 (2006): 90–110.

121. P. A. Valuev, "Duma russkogo vo vtoroi polovine 1855 goda," *Russkaia starina* 70, no. 9 (1893): 503–14.

122. Litvak, *Conscription and the Search for Modern Russian Jewry*, 20.

123. The case, however, took an unhappy turn: the ailing brother left the child to the care of his Russian wife, Maria Volkova, who insisted that the child be completely assimilated into Russian life. When the child's grandmother came to visit, she was horrified by what she found and wrote to the Starokonstantinov district court: "[The child] always looks dirty and Volkova beats her because she wants her to speak only in Russian. What a strange demand of a six-year-old [girl], who does not know how to speak Yiddish, let alone Russian." When asked by the court investigator if she knew who her parents were, the little girl echoed the words that she heard repeatedly in her household: "I do not know who my parents are, but they say that they are *zhidy* [yids]" (DAZhO, f. 160, op. 1, d. 421, l. 1–1 ob).

124. Lincoln, *Nicholas I*, 103; Raeff, *Michael Speransky, Statesman of Imperial Russia, 1772–1839* (The Hague: M. Nijhoff, 1957) Richard Wortman, *The Development of a Russian Legal Consciousness* (Chicago: University of Chicago Press, 1976).

125. For a summary of the 1835 statute, see Stanislawski, *Tsar Nicholas I and the Jews*, 35–43.

126. First-guild merchants could travel and reside in the Russian interior for up to six months (longer than the one-month restriction of previous laws); Jews could also travel outside the Pale for "the acquisition of inheritance, the securing of rights at judicial venues, and study at academic institutions" (Stanislawski, *Tsar Nicholas I and the Jews*, 37).

127. Avrutin, *Jews and the Imperial State*, 98–115.

128. RGIA, f. 1269, op. 1, d. 14, l. 13.

129. RGIA, f. 1269 op. 1, d. 15, l. 36; f. 821, op. 8, d. 283, l. 28. For a comparative perspective on the integration of Muslims into the empire utilizing their religious institutions, see Crews, *For Prophet and Tsar*.

130. The same policy applied to other religious groups, such as Lutherans. See Paul Werth, *At the Margins of Orthodoxy: Mission, Governance, and Confessional Politics in Russia's Volga-Kama Region* (Ithaca: Cornell University Press, 2002); Gregory L. Freeze, "Evangelische Kirche," *Handbuch der Baltischen Geschichte*, vol. 2 (forthcoming).

131. RGIA, f. 821, op. 8, d. 283, l. 28.

132. RGIA, f. 1269, op. 1, d. 15, l. 31.

133. On these new institutions, see ChaeRan Y. Freeze, *Jewish Marriage and Divorce in Imperial Russia* (Hanover, NH: University Press of New England for Brandeis University Press, 2002), 73–130.

134. Lev Levanda, *Polnyi khronologicheskii sbornik zakonov i polozhenii kasaiushchikhsiia evreev* (St. Petersburg: Tipografiia K. V. Trubnikova, 1874), 303.

135. Ibid., 97, 106–18; Avrutin, *Jews and the Imperial State*, 53–85.

136. DAKO, f. 158, op. 150, d. 536, l. 1–1 ob. For examples of Jews who exploited the absence of a record to abandon a spouse without a Jewish divorce or paying support, see C. Freeze, *Jewish Marriage and Divorce in Imperial Russia*, 124–28.

137. Avrutin, *Jews and the Imperial State*, 62–64, 82–85.

138. On the manipulation of "illegal marriages," see C. Freeze, *Jewish Marriage and Divorce in Imperial Russia*, 124–28.

139. Litvak, *Conscription and the Search for Modern Russian Jewry*, 38–41.

140. On the Haskalah in Galicia, which was especially influential on Russian Jewish *maskilim*, see Jay M. Harris, *Nachman Krochmal: Guiding the Perplexed of the Modern Age* (New York: New York University Press 1991); Jeremy Dauber, *Antonio's Devils: Writers of the Jewish Enlightenment and the Birth of Modern Hebrew and Yiddish Literature* (Stanford: Stanford University Press, 2004), 209–310.

141. Immanuel Etkes, "Li-she'elat mevasre ha-Haskalah be-mizrah Eropah," in *Ha-dat veha-hayim*, ed. Immanuel Etkes (Jerusalem: Zalman Shazar Center, 1993), 41–44.

142. Iris Parush, *Reading Jewish Women: Marginality and Modernization in Nineteenth-Century East European Jewish Society* (Waltham, MA: Brandeis University Press, 2004), 106.

143. Quoted in ibid., 118. Parush discusses the reading biographies of the *maskilim* in great depth (97–132).

144. Quoted in ibid., 106.

145. For example, see Litvak, *Conscription and the Search for Modern Russian Jewry*.

146. See Olga Litvak, *Haskalah: The Romantic Movement in Judaism* (New Brunswick, NJ: Rutgers University Press, 2012).

147. Quoted in Litvak, *Conscription and the Search for Modern Russian Jewry*, 23.

148. Ibid., 10.

149. The struggle of the Jewish intelligentsia against Hasidism in the arena of education continued into the reign of Alexander II. As Daniel Neufeld, the editor in chief of the Polish-language periodical *Jutrzenka*, wrote in a stinging remark in 1862: "The interest of these [hasidic] authorities is in banning learning and the study of local languages, even Hebrew, for they sense that if these sectarians look at any book whatsoever, it will open their eyes and they will become as God, distinguishing between good and evil, as a result of which they will cease to pay tribute to these authorities" (quoted in Marcin Wodzinski, *Haskalah and Hasidism in the Kingdom of Poland: A History of Conflict*, trans. Sarah Cozens and Agnieszka Mirowska [Oxford: Littman Library of Jewish Civilization, 2005], 183).

150. Stampfer, *Families, Rabbis, and Education*, 147.

151. Shaul Stampfer, "What Did Knowing Hebrew Mean in Eastern Europe?" in *Hebrew in Ashkenaz*, ed. Lewis Gilbert (Oxford: Oxford University Press, 1993), 129–40.; Parush, *Reading Jewish Women*, 23–34.

152. Quoted in Parush, *Reading Jewish Women*, 63.

153. Steven J. Zipperstein, "Transforming the Heder: Maskilic Politics in Imperial Russia," in *Jewish History: Essays in Honour of Chimen Abramsky*, ed. Ada Rapoport-Albert and Steven J. Zipperstein (London: Halban, 1988), 87–109.

154. Shmarya Levin, *Childhood in Exile*, trans. Maurice Samuel (New York: Harcourt, Brace, 1929), 258–60.

155. Stampfer, *Families, Rabbis, and Education*, 159.

156. Ibid.

157. Shaul Stampfer, "Gender Differentiation and Education of Jewish Women in Nineteenth-Century Eastern Europe," *Polin* 7 (1992): 63–87; Eliyana Adler, *In Her Hands: The Education of Jewish Girls in Tsarist Russia* (Detroit: Wayne State University Press, 2011).

158. Parush, *Reading Jewish Women*, 6.

159. Stampfer, "Gender Differentiation and Education of Jewish Women in Nineteenth-Century Eastern Europe," 64–65.

160. Avraham Paperna, "Iz Nikolaevskoi epokhi," in *Evrei v Rossi XIX*, ed. Viktor Kelner (Moscow: Novoe literaturnoe obozrenie, 2000), 145.

161. Parush, *Reading Jewish Women*, 134.

162. Quoted in Parush, *Reading Jewish Women*, 42.

163. Simeon Kreis, "Batei sefer yehudiyim be-safah ha-Rusit be-Rusiyah ha-Tsarit," PhD diss., Hebrew University of Jerusalem, 1994, 23–24.

164. Stanislawski, *Tsar Nicholas I and the Jews*, 49–59.

165. Kreis, "Batei sefer yehudiyim be-safah ha-Rusit be-Rusiyah ha-Tsarit," 20–26.

166. *Zhupitses*, winter coats that broadened out from the waist downward.

167. Max Lilienthal, "My Educational Mission in Russia," in *The Golden Tradition*, ed. Dawidowicz, 149.

168. Stanislawski, *Tsar Nicholas I and the Jews*, 93–95.

169. Quoted in Stanislawski, *Tsar Nicholas I and the Jews*, 94.

170. Quoted in ibid., 71.

171. Quoted in Lilienthal, "My Educational Mission in Russia," 152.

172. Stanislawski, *Tsar Nicholas I and the Jews*, 101.

173. Mikhail Dolbilov, "Russifying Bureaucracy and the Politics of Jewish Education in the Russian Empire's Northwest Region (1860–1870s)," *Acta Slavica Iaponica* 24 (2007): 135.

174. DAZhO, f. 396, op. 1, d. 1, g, 1844, l. 1.

175. Stanislawski, *Tsar Nicholas I and the Jews*, 107. See also Verena Dohrn, "Das Rabbinerseminar in Wilna, 1847–1873: Zur Geschichte der ersten staatlichen höheren Schule für Juden im Russischen Reich," *Jahrbücher für Geschichte Osteuropas* 45, no. 3 (1997): 379–400.

176. Paperna, "Iz Nikolaevskoi epokhi," 148–50.

177. Levanda, *Polnyi khronologichsekii sbornik zakonov*, 193–200.

178. Israel Halpern, "Nisuei bahalah be-mizrah eiropah," *Zion* 27 (1962): 36–58.

179. David Biale, "Eros and Enlightenment: Love against Marriage in the East European Jewish Enlightenment," *Polin* 1 (1986): 49–67.

180. Quoted in Ibid., David Biale, "Eros and Enlightenment: Love Against Marriage in the East European Jewish Enlightenment, *Polin* 1 (1986): 59–67.

181. *PSZ* 2, 10:8054, 13 April 1935. See also Iulii Gessen, "Odezhda," in *Evreiskaia entsiklopediia*, ed. Katsenelson and Gintsburg, 12: 46; Avrutin, *Jews and the Imperial State*, 39.

182. Quoted in Gessen, "Odezhda," 12:47. See also Avrutin, *Jews and the Imperial State*, 41.

183. Quoted in Gessen, "Odezhda," 12:48.

184. Avrutin, *Jews and the Imperial State*, 44–45.

185. Gessen, "Odezhda," 12:48–49; Avrutin, *Jews and the Imperial State*, 42–50.

186. Avrutin, *Jews and the Imperial State*, 43–44.

187. Ibid., 42. Avrutin cites some remarkable reports from GARF, f. 109, eksp. 1, op, 20, d. 136, ll. 5b, 25b, 27b.

188. Paperna, "Iz Nikolaevskoi epokhi," 54. Even in 1867–68 Jews were fined for wearing *peyes* and Jewish clothing in Lida (see LVIA, f. 381, op. 17, d. 433a.

189. Stanislawski, *Tsar Nicholas I and the Jews*, 156.

190. Ibid.; Dubnow, *History of the Jews in Russia and Poland from the Earliest Times until the Present Day*, 1:142–43.

191. Quoted in O. M. Lerner, *Evrei v novorossiskom krae* (Odessa: Tipografiia G. M. Levinsona, 1901), 48–49.

192. Quoted in Gregory L. Freeze, *Russia, A History* 2nd ed. (Oxford: Oxford University Press, 2002) 172.

193. Ibid., 210.

194. Ibid., 178.

195. Ibid., 171.

196. Nathans, *Beyond the Pale*, 45–79.

197. Quoted in ibid., 52.

198. In 1858, there were only 11,980 Jews in European Russia; by 1898, the number had risen to 128,343, out of over five million Jews in the empire (ibid., 83).

199. Ibid., 128–29.

200. ChaeRan Y. Freeze, "Crafting an Elite Russian-Jewish Identity: The Diaries of Zinaida Poliakova," unpublished paper.

201. Nathans, *Beyond the Pale*, 130.

202. Ibid., 201–34

203. Ibid., 243.

204. Ibid., 182.

205. GARF, f. 102, op. 76a, d. 785, l. 6–6 ob.

206. Nathans, *Beyond the Pale*, 63.

207. For instance, see TsGIAM-Moscow, f. 203, op. 362, ll. 6, 33, 34, 45, 45.

208. Litvak, *Conscription and the Search for Modern Russian Jewry*.

209. Eugene Avrutin, "Jewish Neighborly Relations and Imperial Russian Legal Culture," *Journal of Modern Jewish Studies* 9, no. 1 (2010): 1–16.

210. RGIA, f. 821, op. 1, d. 281, ll. 87–89 ob.

211. RGIA, f. 821, op. 9, d. 137, l. 50.

212. Early periodicals and newspapers included the weekly Hebrew-language *Ha-karmel*, edited by Samuel Fuenn from 1860 to 1880; *Ha-melits*, founded by Aleksander Zederbaum in 1860, which became a daily in 1886; the Russian-language *Rass-vet*, founded by Osip Rabinovich in 1860, which was replaced by *Sion* a year later and by *Den* in 1869; and the Yiddish-language *Kol mevaser* (1862–71).

213. Alexander Orbach, *New Voices of Russian Jewry: A Study of the Russian-Jewish Press of Odessa in the Era of the Great Reforms* (Leiden: E. J. Brill, 1980); Sarah A. Stein, *Making Jews Modern: The Yiddish and Ladino Press in the Russian and Ottoman Empires* (Bloomington: Indiana University Press, 2004); Oren Soffer, *En le-falpel!: 'iton "Ha-tsefirah" veha-modernizatsyah shel ha-siah ha-hevrati ha-politi* (Jerusalem: Mosad Bialik, 2007).

214. Quoted in Parush, *Reading Jewish Women*, 178.

215. Sarah Azariahu, *Pirkei hayim* (Tel Aviv, 1948), 9.

216. Dmitrii Elyashevich, *Pravitel'stvennaia politika i evreiskaia pechat' v Rossii, 1797–1917: ocherki tsenzury* (St. Petersburg: Mosty-Kul'tury, 1999).

217. Alyssa Quint, "'Yiddish Literature for the Masses'? A Reconsideration of Who Read What in Jewish Eastern Europe," *AJS Review* 29, no. 1 (2005): 63, 64, 69.

218. Ibid., 85.

219. Lev Levanda, "Goriachee vremia," *Evreiskaia biblioteka* 1 (1871): 53. See ChaeRan Y. Freeze, "The Politics of Love in Lev Levanda's *Turbulent Times*," in *Gender and Jewish History: Essays in Honor of Paula Hyman*, ed. Marion Kaplan and Deborah Dash Moore (Bloomington: Indiana University Press, 2010), 187–202.

220. Mikhail Dolbilov, *Russkii krai, chuzhaia vera: etnokofessional'naia politika imperii v Litve i Belorussi pri Aleksandre II* (Moscow: Novoe literaturnoe obozrenie, 2010).

221. P. A. Zaionchkovskii, *Rossiiskoe samoderzhavie v kontse XIX v.* (Moscow: Izd-vo "Mysl'," 1970).

222. GARF, f. 102, op. 76a, d. 54, l. 1.

223. Ibid., l. 330b.

224. The law allowed Jewish students to comprise only 10 percent of secondary schools within the Pale of Settlement, 5 percent in the Russian interior, and 3 percent in Moscow and St. Petersburg. Nathans, *Beyond the Pale*, 266–67.

225. Ibid., 271.

226. Roza Grigorievna Vinaver, "Vospominaniia," (unpublished memoir, 1944), 9.

227. Onisim Gol'dovskii, "Evrei v Moskve (po neopublikovannym domunetam)," in *Moskva evreiskaia*, ed. Konstantin Burmistrov (Moscow: Dom evreiskoi knigi, 2003), 394–410; Lev Aizenberg, "Velikii Kniaz' Sergei Aleksandrovich, Vitte, i evrei—Moskovskie kuptsy (iz istorii izgnaniia evreev iz Moskvy)," in *Evrei v Moskve: Sbornik materialov*, ed. Iurii Snopov and Artur Klempert (Moscow: Mosty kul'tury, 2003), 352.

228. John Klier, *Imperial Russia's Jewish Question, 1855–1881* (Cambridge: Cambridge University Press, 1995), 364–416.

229. Quoted in ibid., 197.

230. Ibid., 198. *The Protocols of the Elders of Zion* was a work that described a spurious Jewish conspiracy to take over the world. See Norman Cohn, *Warrant for Genocide: The Myth of the Jewish World Conspiracy and the Protocols of the Elders of Zion* (Chico, CA: Scholars, 1981); Stephen E. Bronner, *A Rumor about the Jews: Reflections on Antisemitism and the Protocols of the Learned Elders of Zion* (New York: St. Martin's, 2000); Michael Hagemeister, "The *Protocols of the Elders of Zion*: Between History and Fiction," *New German Critique* 103, no. 35 (2008): 83–95.

231. David Nirenberg, *Communities of Violence: Persecution of Minorities in the Middle Ages* (Princeton: Princeton University Press, 1996), 122–24.

232. On a violent riot that began when a peasant woman refused to pay a Jewish woman after tasting some apples, see Darius Staliūnas, "Anti-Jewish Disturbances in the North-Western Provinces in the early 1880s," *East European Jewish Affairs* 34, no. 2 (2004): 126.

233. Irwin Michael Aronson, "The Anti-Jewish Pogroms in Russia in 1881," in *Pogroms: Anti-Jewish Violence in Modern Russian History*, ed. John Klier and Shlomo Lambroza (Cambridge: Cambridge University Press, 1992), 44–61.

234. Staliūnas, "Anti-Jewish Disturbances in the North-Western Provinces in the Early 1880s"; Claire Le Foll, "The Missing Pogroms of Belorussia, 1881–82: Conditions and Motives of an Absence of Violence," in *Anti-Jewish Violence: Rethinking the Pogrom in East European History*, ed. Jonathan Dekel-Chen, David Gaunt, Natan M. Meir, and Israel Bartal (Bloomington: Indiana University Press, 2011), 159–71; Vladas Sirutavičius and Darius Staliūnas, "Was Lithuania a Pogrom-Free Zone? (1881–1940)," in *Anti-Jewish Violence*, 144–58.

235. Le Foll, "The Missing Pogroms of Belorussia," 168.

236. Irwin Michael Aronson, *Troubled Waters: The Origins of the 1881 Anti-Jewish Pogroms in Russia* (Pittsburgh: University of Pittsburgh Press, 1990), 145–60.

237. Mark Kupovetsky, "Demografiia evreiskogo naseleniia rossiiskoi imperii, 1772–1917," in Itskhak Oren, Mikhael Zand, Shmuel Ettinger, eds. *Kratkaia evreiskaia entsiklopediia*, 11 vols. (Jerusalem: Keter, 1976–1992), 7: 382–90.

238. Arcadius Kahan, *Essays in Jewish Social and Economic History*, ed. Roger Weiss (Chicago: University of Chicago Press, 1986), 28.

239. Ezra Mendelsohn, *Class Struggle in the Pale: The Formative Years of the Jewish Worker's Movement in Tsarist Russia* (Cambridge: Cambridge University Press, 1970), 6, 20–22.

240. Genrikh Sliozberg, *Pravovoe i ekonomicheskoe polozhenie evreev v Rossii* (St. Petersburg, 1907), 17.

241. Mendelsohn, *Class Struggle in the Pale*, 13.

242. Approximately 551,503 migrants went to America in 1875–98 and 1,705, 984 to the countries listed in the text in 1899–1914. See Gur Alroey, *Bread to Eat and Clothes to Wear: Letters from Jewish Migrants in the Early Twentieth Century* (Detroit: Wayne State University Press, 2011), 211–12.

243. Quoted in ibid., 16.

244. Quoted in ibid., 20.

245. Iakov Nikolaevich Bekman and Mitrofan Danilovich Muravsky founded the Bekman circle, which boasted eight members by 1856. This secret student society sought to "arouse a general revolution in Russia beginning with the emancipation of the peasants." Erich E. Haberer, *Jews and Revolution in Nineteenth-Century Russia* (Cambridge: Cambridge University Press, 1995), 19–20.

246. Ibid., 19–21.

247. Richard Stites, *The Women's Liberation Movement in Russia: Feminism, Nihilism, and Bolshevism, 1860–1930* (Princeton: Princeton University Press, 1978).

248. Quoted in ibid., 30.

249. Ibid., 93.

250. Quoted in Parush, *Reading Jewish Women*, 179.

251. Haberer, *Jews and Revolution in Nineteenth-Century Russia*, 94.

252. Quoted in Franco Venturi, *Roots of Revolution* (New York: Universal Library, 1960), 503.

253. Quoted in Jonathan Frankel, *Prophecy and Politics: Socialism, Nationalism, and the Russian Jews, 1862–1917* (Cambridge: Cambridge University Press, 1981), 263.

254. Quoted in Manfred Hildermeier, *The Russian Socialist Revolutionary Party before the First World War* (New York: St. Martin's, 2000), 52.

255. "Olga Liubatovich," in Barbara A. Engel and Clifford N. Rosenthal, eds., *Five Sisters: Women against the Tsar: The Memoirs of Five Young Anarchist Women of the 1870s* (New York and London: Routledge, 1975), 184–87.

256. Quoted in Frankel, *Prophecy and Politics*, 136.

257. Quoted in Hildermeier, *The Russian Socialist Revolutionary Party before the First World War*, 54.

258. Quoted in ibid.

259. Paul H. Avrich and Klara Klebanova, "The Last Maximalist: An Interview with Klara Klebanova," *Russian Review* 32, no. 4 (1973): 413–20.

260. Amy Knight, "Female Terrorists in the Russian Socialist Revolutionary Party," *Russian Review* 38, no. 2 (1979): 145.

261. Quoted in Hildermeier, *The Russian Socialist Revolutionary Party before the First World War*, 119.

262. Leonard Shapiro, "The Role of the Jews in the Russian Revolutionary Movement," *Slavonic and Eastern European Review* 40 (1961): 148–67.

263. Hildermeier, *The Russian Socialist Revolutionary Party before the First World War*, 87.

264. Frankel, *Prophecy and Politics*, 180.

265. Quoted in ibid., 194.

266. Quoted in Henry J. Tobias, *The Jewish Bund in Russia from Its Origins to 1905* (Stanford: Stanford University Press, 1972), 26.

267. Quoted in Frankel, *Prophecy and Politics*, 180.

268. Quoted in Frankel, *Prophecy and Politics*, 201.

269. Quoted in Frankel, *Prophecy and Politics*, 205.

270. Mendelsohn, *Class Struggle in the Pale*, 83.

271. Ibid.

272. Mendelsohn, *Class Struggle in the Pale*, 94.

273. Jeremiah Shneiderman, *Sergei Zubatov and Revolutionary Marxism: The Struggle for the Working Class in Russia* (Cornell: Cornell University Press, 1976).

274. Daniel Charney, *Vilne: memuarn* (Buenos Aires, 1951), 67.

275. Harriet Davis-Kram, "Sisters of the Bund," *Contemporary Jewry* 5, no. 2 (1980): 27–43.

276. Quoted in Frankel, *Prophecy and Politics*, 224.

277. Quoted in ibid., 190.

278. "Di diskusye," *Undzer tsayt* 3 (December 1927): 88; Frankel, *Prophecy and Politics*, 180.

279. Quoted in Frankel, *Prophecy and Politics*, 221.

280. Quoted in Arthur Hertzberg, *The Zionist Idea* (New York: Atheneum, 1982), 192.

281. Quoted in ibid., 169–70. Lilienblum was already disillusioned about the prospects of emancipation after the pogrom in Odessa in 1870.

282. Quoted in ibid., 193.

283. Quoted in ibid., 172.

284. Quoted in ibid., 402.

285. Ehud Luz, *Parallels Meet: Religion and Nationalism in the Early Zionist Movement (1882–1904)*, trans. Lenn J. Schramm (Philadelphia: The Jewish Publication Society, 1988), 64.

286. Quoted in David Vital, *The Origins of Zionism* (Oxford: Clarendon Press, 1975), 185.

287. Yosef Salmon, "Ideology and Reality in the Bilu 'Aliyah,'" *Harvard Ukrainian Studies* 2, no. 4 (1978): 430–66; Chaim Chissin, *A Palestine Diary: Memoirs of a Bilu Pioneer, 1882–1887* (New York: Herzl Press, 1976).

288. See: Arieh Bruce Saposnik, *Becoming Hebrew: the Creation of a Jewish National Culture in Ottoman Palestine* (New York: Oxford University Press, 2008); Natan Efrati, *Mi-leshon yehidim li-leshon umah: ha-dibur ha-'ivri be-Erets Yisrael ba-shanim 642–682 (1881–1922)* (Jerusalem: Akademyah la-lashon ha-'Ivrit, 2004).

289. Margalit Shilo, "The Transformation of the Role of Women in the First Aliyah, 1882–1903," *Jewish Social Studies* 2 (Winter 1996): 69, 72.

290. Quoted in Parush, *Reading Jewish Women*, 219.

291. Shilo, "The Transformation of the Role of Women in the First Aliyah," 70; see also 71–73.

292. Steven Zipperstein, *Elusive Prophet: Ahad Ha'am and the Origins of Zionism* (Berkeley: University of California Press, 1993).

293. Quoted in Vital, *The Origins of Zionism*, 194; brackets added by Vital.

294. Quoted in Zipperstein, *Elusive Prophet*.

295. Litvak, *Conscription and the Search for Modern Russian Jewry*, 102–39.

296. Ibid, 140–70.

297. Quoted in Shimoni, *The Zionist Ideology* (Hanover: University Press of New England, 1995), 137.

298. Quoted in ibid., 143.

299. Ibid., 142.

300. C. Freeze, *Jewish Marriage and Divorce in Imperial Russia*, 241–79.

301. Quoted in Yaakov Lifschitz, *Zikhron Yaakov* (Kowno-Sloboda: N. Lifshits, 1924) 2: 77.

302. Gershon Bacon, *The Politics of Tradition: Agudat Yisrael in Poland, 1916–39* (Jersualem: Hebrew University Magnes, 1996).

303. On the Revolution of 1905–7, see Stefani Hoffman and Ezra Mendelsohn, eds., *The Revolution of 1905 and Russia's Jews* (Philadelphia: University of Pennsylvania Press, 2008).

304. See, for example, the declarations of the noble landowners in G. Freeze, *From Supplication to Revolution*, 200–206.

305. Jeffrey Veidlinger, *Jewish Public Culture in the Late Russian Empire* (Bloomington: Indiana University Press, 2009), 1; See also, Gennady Estraikh, "Yiddish in Imperial Russia's Civil Society," in *Jews in the Eastern European Borderlands: Essays in Honor of John D. Klier*, ed. Eugene M. Avrutin and Harriet Murav (Brighton, MA: Academic Studies Press, 2012), 50–66.

306. Litvak, *Conscription and the Search for Modern Russian Jewry*, 141–42.

307. Quoted in Veidlinger, *Jewish Public Culture in the Late Russian Empire*, 34.

308. RGIA, f. 1335, op. 1, d. 3, l. 18.

309. "K sez"du zhurnalistov," *Pravo* (1905): 1226. On the SP, see Christoph Gassenschmidt, *Jewish Liberal Politics in Tsarist Russia, 1900–1914* (New York: New York University Press, 1995).

310. Gassenschmidt, *Jewish Liberal Politics in Tsarist Russia*, xiii.

311. "Rezoliutsii III delegatskogo s"ezda Soiuza ravnopraviia evreev," *Pravo* 8 (February 26 1906): 708–10.

312. Rahel M. Khin, "Iz dnevnikov 1913–1917," *Minuvshee istoricheskii al'manakh* 21 (1997): 540.

313. Eric Lohr, "The Russian Army and the Jews: Mass Deportations, Hostages, and Violence during World War I," *Russian Review* 60, no. 3 (2001): 404–19.

314. George Katkov, *Russia 1917: The February Revolution* (New York: Harper and Row Publishers, 1967), 56.

315. Lohr, "The Russian Army and the Jews," 409–14; see also Michael Cherniavsky, *Prologue to Revolution, Notes of A. N. Iakhontov on the Secret Meetings of Council of Ministers, 1915* (Englewood Cliffs, Prentice-Hall, 1967), 71, 194–95,

316. William Fuller, *The Foe Within: Fantasies of Treason and the End of Imperial Russia* (Ithaca: Cornell University Press, 2006), 179.

317. Quoted in Iakov I. Aizenshtat, "Ze'ev Zhabotinskii — iurist," in *Evrei v kul'ture russkogo zarubezh'ia: sbornik statei, publikatsii, memuarov i esse 1919–1939*, ed. Mikhail Parkhomovskii (Jerusalem: M. Parkhomovskii 1992), 1: 420.

318. RGVIA, f. 1932, op. 2, d. 159, ll. 24–27.

319. For example, see ChaeRan Y. Freeze, "Lilith's Midwives: Jewish Newborn Child Murder in Nineteenth-Century Vil'na," *Jewish Social Studies* 16, no. 2 (Winter 2010): 1–27.

320. Poliakova, "Dnevniki," 177.

321. Litvak, *Conscription and the Search for Modern Russian Jewry*, 13.

322. Quoted in Frankel, *Prophecy and Politics*, 87.

[I]

Religious Life

After the first partition of Poland in 1772, which for the first time brought a large number of Jews into the Russian Empire, Catherine II promised her subjects "all the freedoms which they now enjoy with regard to their religion."[1] Over the next century and a half, Russia gave rise to a rich variety of Judaism unmatched in contemporary Europe. Religion permeated every fiber of Jewish daily life, a sacred rhythm overshadowing the mundane: the three daily services,[2] the washing of hands before meals, benedictions for food, Sabbath rituals, and the celebration of Jewish holidays. Most Jews remained strictly observant; even the most acculturated maintained dietary laws (kashrut) and celebrated traditional holidays, albeit perhaps in restricted form.[3] The precipitous decline in religious piety that accompanied modernization in Western Europe was far less pronounced in the Russian Empire—not only among Jews, but among gentiles as well. In large measure that is because Russia was a multiconfessional empire, which used the existing institutions of each religion to maintain order.

That "confessionality" applied to Jews as well. Family and communal pressure played a critical role in keeping Jews in the fold, although some converted to Christianity (out of religious conviction or utilitarian motives—such as marriage, professional mobility, and desire to escape the Pale or prison). Significantly, however, the state sought to buttress that family role; it not only delegated matters of religion and family to the purview of Jewish law, but it left intact traditional institutions such as the *kahal* (officially abolished in 1844), rabbinical courts, and a multitude of associations (*havurot*), including the influential burial society (*hevra kadisha*). Although the state slowly began to abolish or marginalize such bodies, it was impossible for Jews, even the most acculturated, to extricate themselves fully from Judaism. Life-cycle events such as circumcision, marriage, divorce, and burial inevitably remanded individuals to the jurisdiction of Jewish law and authorities.

This part examines the rich diversity of religious experiences in the Russian Empire: the different subcultures of the Hasidim (with a focus on the Twersky dynasty) and their opponents, the *misnagdim*; spiritual piety and public worship; contemporary dilemmas and Jewish law; religious conversion to Christianity; and the relationship between Judaism and the Russian state.

NOTES

1. Quoted in Andreas Kappeler, *The Russian Empire*, 58. (Full citation given in introduction.)

2. The three daily services, which provide a time of reference in many memoirs, are in the morning (*Shacharit*), afternoon (*Minchah*), and evening (*Maariv*).

3. On the practices of acculturated families in St. Petersburg, see Benjamin Nathans, *Beyond the Pale: The Jewish Encounter with Late Imperial Russia* (Berkeley: University of California Press, 2002).

147. Especially telling, Nathans shows, was the invitation of Roza Vinaver (the wife of the lawyer and politician Maksim Vinaver) to A. G. Gorn'feld, the editor of *Russkoe bogatstvo*, for Passover: "Most Esteemed Arkadii Georgievich, I hasten to remind you that, as a loyal and pious Jew, you are called upon to fulfill your duty, which we will make as pleasant as possible. It is all happening on the 21th of March at 9 p.m., and incidentally I suggest that on that day you eat only lightly (I am sure that this 'lightly' will have to be examined under a microscope). Your devoted Roza Vinaver." See also document 29.

The Diversity of Religious Experience

[1]

The Cantor of Duvid Twersky's Hasidic Court in Tal'noe: The Memoirs of Pinhas Minkovsky

Pinhas Minkovsky, "Mi-sefer hayay," *Reshumot* 1 (1919): 97–122; 4 (1926): 123–44.

I

While I do not know what will be—to what extent the memoirs of the Shatz[1] Minkovsky will stand the test of time—I can well recall what was: the entire town of Belaia Tserkov' knew the wunderkind who stole hearts with the sweetness of his voice and the beauty of his song, Pini Motel Gadis.[2] The town's elders, denizens of the houses of learning, who were in the habit of reckoning and tracking transmigrating souls, and seeking the "source" and "root," "nourishment" and "influence" in the souls of all the living, were not at all surprised by the extensive blessing they found in this young man. First of all, he was a direct descendant on his father's side of R. Yom Tov Lipmann, the Tosafot Yom Tov.[3] On his mother's side was "refined dough" filled with rabbis, *tsaddikim*, Hasidim. Thus, how surprising is it that all his teachers sang his praises? As for his beautiful voice—the "source" and the "root" of that was well known: his grandfather, R. Gadi, was the head of the Shu"Bim[4] of Zhitomir [. . .] and was famous for his Musafs for the High Holy Days and for the sweetness of his chant as one of the most excellent prayer leaders of his generation. And his father, Motel Gadis, was the *hazzan* in the great prayer house in Belaia Tserkov,' one of the sharpest prayer leaders in the Jewish world. Although he was not highly skilled in "the wisdom of the notes"[5] as it is known now among us, he was punctilious regarding every note and point in the liturgy, and would sweat and sweat some more until he was satisfied that he could unlock the musical idea that Yeruham ha-Katan, Nisi Belzer, Haskele Zhitomir, and Moshe Radomlisher[6] had concealed within those notes and points. In any event, he not only knew how to accompany another singer in melodies composed by others, he could also compose his own improvised accompaniment, called "Tishkon."[7] [. . .]

When Pini's first teachers realized his talents as a student of Torah they began to prophesy that he would be a rabbi and leader in Israel. And the prophecy might have come true were it not for "Zamriel," the angel of melody, who negated the words of these prophets. For when Pini was eight years old they prevailed upon him to sing on Passover; as he came to the *bimah* as the representative of the community and sang "Yah 'Eli ve-goali,"[8] all the listeners, especially the women, were astonished and began offering a different prophecy — that the boy would grow up to be one of the great chanters [. . .] maybe even as great as Nisi Blumenthal of Odessa.[9]

In those days every *shtetl* in our district benefited from a range of guests who came one after the other, or two or three all at once: collectors who came to collect the "tax" from their communities' "subscribers"; itinerant preachers hated by the Hasidim and beloved by their Lithuanian opponents; "regulars" of the Rebbe of Chabad; pursers who would empty the monies from the R. Meir *Baal ha-Nes* collection boxes;[10] emissaries of different *tsaddikim* who come to collect money to sustain their "courts"; and on and on. Each of these visitors would inject some life into these forsaken *shtetlakh*, and with their arrival they would arouse the residents to come up awkwardly with something to respond to them.

But the more honored guests, whose arrival truly revived the dead [. . .], were the *tsaddikim* themselves, the sons of R. Mordechai of Chernobyl, known as the Maggid of Chernobyl,[11] who divided the territory among them, and ruled to a high standard; their followers built "altars" to them with what was left of their money and energy. When one of them came to town he brought great joy to his Hasidim, and anger to his opponents. His admirers sensed an "extra soul" within them not only on the Sabbath in shul, or during the [Sabbath] meal *ofn tish*,[12] and telling wonder stories on Saturday night, but every evening during the week, as the *tsaddik* would visit the wealthy leaders among his followers. Each day that he stayed in town was [for his followers] like an extended holiday of [embracing] Hasidism, and a unique [spiritual] arousal; this was the object of scorn and sarcasm on the part of the *misnagdim*, and also provided much material for the young *maskilim* to fill

up the pages of *Ha-Melits*.[13] [. . .] In short, everyone — Hasidim, *misnagdim*, and *maskilim* — were filled with work and vitality.

Guests beneath them in stature but greater in number were the famous *hazzanim* who would travel from city to city and from community to community, with wonder stories about the charms of their voices and the beauty of their melodies preceding them. Among them were Haskele Zhitomir, Moshe Radomlisher, and others, and especially Yeruham ha-Katan and Nisi Belzer, who were then the pillars of Jewish song; in all of Russia there was not a single synagogue that had not heard their melodies, at least on the High Holidays. These giants also became a kind of "holy men" and represented a unique form of Hasidism, for every *hazzan* was close with a particular *tsaddik*, and the latter's admirers extolled the virtues only of their *tsaddik*'s *hazzan*, and not any other. This refers only to the heads of the hasidic communities and their intimates; the rest of the community did not distinguish this way, and when a famous *hazzan* came to town they felt then the way we in the modern community feel when the dancer Isadora Duncan, the actress Sarah Bernhardt, or other such luminaries come to town.

It is self-evident that the primary mavens regarding these guest *hazzanim* and their entourages were the local *hazzanim*, and you will understand that when such honored guests came to our *shtetl*, Belaia Tserkov,' my father's house was filled with tumult, and melody and song. And I confess today: I, the kid Pini Motel Gadis, forgot all about my hunger and thirst, my rebbe's *heder* and my Torah learning, and I swallowed, like a first fruit, every new tune, every new melody, that the guest *hazzan* and his choir would sing in our home, even before the great and honored day came, namely the Sabbath, which was set aside from the time of creation for song and prayer. And I remember well the furious face of my rebbe, and his voice suffused with wrath and admonition: "Aha, a *hazzan* and his entourage come to town, and R. Pinhas does not know where in the world he is." But who cared about this block of wood, who had ears but could not hear, when my soul soared into the upper heavens [. . .] before the great wonders my ears absorbed from the mouths and throats of the giants before me.

But my withdrawal from daily life due to these *hazzanim* was like nothing compared to my withdrawal before the third class of guests, the modern choral *hazzanim* with their choirs, dressed and groomed like priests, [. . .] who began to spread among the communities of Israel, to travel to the towns and share their new songs previously unheard by the *haredim* because of the ban and [also unheard] by the masses as well. If the old *hazzanim*, masters of singing with feeling, stole the hearts of the people with the beauty of their melody, the sharpness of their trills, and the tearful pouring out of their souls, the moderns, masters of orderly singing, seduced their hearers (and, even more, their viewers) with their external beauty and priestly dress.

While the new melodies of the *Songs of Zion* of Sulzer[14] did not touch the souls of the audience, who viewed them as "chattering of priests," all the same they were excited by the orderliness, the unity and rich harmonies of sound and coloration, and even more by the chiseled responses. Who could previously have imagined that after the leader exclaimed "Barkhu et adonai ha-mevorakh" that a mass of voices would not respond "Barukh adonai ha-mevorakh . . . ,"[15] and that, instead, only a choir would solemnly bow its head and respond in a well-orchestrated manner, "Barukh . . ." with the congregation remaining silent? [. . .] In sum, the congregation was not so much excited by the beauty of the song of the choral *hazzanim*, but by the splendor of their orderliness.

In this period, in Jewish literature and in the world of enlightened thought generally, there prevailed a spirit of negation and uprooting with respect to the older ways, and it

was a way to establish one's enlightened bona fides to belittle a commandment openly, or at least some Jewish custom. This spirit was the foundation of the new music of the modern *hazzanim* who adopted a new and foreign title: "cantor." Who were the first cantors? They were the *meshorerim*[16] of the *hazzanim* who sang with feeling. The best of them was the *hazzan* Spitzberg, who accompanied the nobleman of traditional song, Yeruham ha-Katan;[17] he was sent from Berdichev to [study with Salomon Sulzer in Vienna], in order to become adept at the new singing by the very R. Moshe Yitzhak Horowitz who built the first modern temple in the heart of the Volhynian hasidic world.

Spitzberg and his generation of modern cantors were all trained from youth in the traditional music of the synagogue, and they felt its depths and the "soul-pouring" dimensions of the music no less than did the traditional audience. [. . .] But the motto of the time was "anything but Jewish." Thus, perforce they were alienated from their inner yearning for traditional melody that was filled with Jewish flavor and Eastern, Semitic juices. So, all those who turned overnight into enlightened ones wanted to show the signs of their enlightenment publicly by embracing orderly, Western music, which never touched their souls in the slightest. Thus, both the cantors and the audience betrayed themselves, their taste, and their education. [. . .] But when the Haskalah of the 1860s came to a crisis,[18] the mask came off this disguise and also revealed the lie in the world of music: the Jewish flavor, which was necessarily hidden in a remote corner of the soul, newly awoke and removed the bonds of German imitation from the music of our sanctuary. But that [period of] imitation left great destruction in its wake. For during this time the original choral cantors, who drew in their [knowledge of Jewish] music from the source, died or became too old, and those who came after them took in their knowledge only secondhand. Thus, the former had the skills but not the desire, while the latter had the desire but not the skills.

The first modern temple that aroused horror among virtually all the Jews of Russia was the one in Berdichev.[19] To be sure, it was preceded by one in Odessa. But who took account of Odessa, this new city with its influx of refugees from Brody, who came from the West to a place where they were unrecognized and could do whatever they wanted? Besides, everyone knew that "the fires of hell burn for seven miles around Odessa."[20] Thus, [the temple in] Odessa did not pain the hearts of the *haredim* all that much, for they always looked on Odessan Judaism as something alien and beyond the pale. But Berdichev—the heart of Volhynian and Ukrainian Hasidism, with *maggidut* of *tsaddikim* who were the grandchildren of the Besht, the Twerskys, and the Friedmans,[21] the home of R. Levi Yitzhak,[22] author of the *Kedushas Levi*—and there a choral temple would be founded [. . .]? This brought the pious of the entire region, including Belaia Tserkov', to outright despair. [. . .]

In this turbulent period, a choral cantor with his choir appeared for the first time in our *shtetl*, and caused quite a stir. He stayed at the Cantor's Inn, which was already well known throughout the world of *hazzanim*, as the proprietor, R. Hayyim Zuckernik, was the most ardent music lover in the town. Not only did he refuse to profit even one penny from the *hazzanim* who were his guests, but [he] did much besides to benefit them: he went to great lengths to get the leaders of the community institutions to invite them to [lead] the Sabbath services, arranged concerts for them in his hall, and provided for them from his own pocket. But when the first choral cantor came to town "his plans came to nothing,"[23] for he knew in advance that no synagogue or study hall would open its doors to these creatures who would profane the sacred. [T]hus he had no choice but to turn to the wealthy who had already left their piety behind in the hopes that one of them would consent to turn his home for one Sabbath into a temporary temple, and invite the first choral cantor to lead the service for a group of young men who had become heretics, or were suspected of it. And thus it was. His suggestion found favor in the eyes of the impious Herz Horowitz, and especially in the eyes of his wife, who was jealous of her friends from Berdichev, and a passion flared within her to taste at least one "choral" Sabbath in her home and to invite all her friends who had uncovered their hair and yearned to be rescued from the boredom of the *shtetl*, who dearly wished to be seen in public in all their splendor, just like the women of the temple in Berdichev.

A big fight broke out in my father's house regarding the grave question: to attend or not? To be sure, no one would dare suspect my father of coming actually to pray with the sinners. [. . .] But to even hear and spend the hours of Sabbath prayers in such a house, would that not be the height of frivolity? But could one imagine missing the opportunity to hear the new music—causing clamor throughout the world—of the musical genius Salomon Sulzer? I too was torn; after all the discussion and the scorn that I heard from the mouths of the pious about the music of the priests [. . .] who have no place in the world to come, who sin and bring others to sin, and yet here they are in your town, in your street, practically in your house, and you will not go to see and hear them? The temptation was too great for me to resist, and Satan incited me to go, see, and hear, for this was not an everyday occurrence. [. . .] And the whole town was stirring; in every study hall and *kloyz* they argued and debated, screaming about the abomination and pouring scorn on the "jewel" Herz Horowitz who turned his home into a place of rebellion. My father quietly conferred with his loved ones about what to do, as he too could not overcome his passion to hear the new music from the world-famous liturgy of Sulzer. To his delight they advised him not to ask the rabbi—who would surely not permit it—but just to go and hear. After the fact, what is done is done, and they would not remove him from his position for this sin.

In this turbulent state we arrived at the appointed hour, and Horowitz's house was lit up with bright lights, and was filled from end to end. We slipped in as if embarrassed, and stood in a corner and watched. The door opened and from the other room entered the cantor and his choir—dressed in black, with mitres and white collar ties, all groomed, holding books of musical notation in their hands—and they encircled the pulpit, each standing surely in his place. All the assembled were deeply impressed by this appearance—the cleanliness, the orderliness—and especially was I; my soul was practically set aloft by this show. None of the congregation came for actual prayers; they were all standing as if nailed to the floor, or swaying in awe. The street outside was packed with men, women, and children, who were crowding around and silencing everyone, so that they too might hear the choral music. Sulzer's chords sounded so beautiful and intoxicated me. [. . .] I was ashamed of my impoverished taste that allowed me to draw joy from the humble melodies I heard in my father's house. My father too stood like a marble statue, his expertise and understanding departing him in the songs of the cantor; he was excited, but did not know why. [In the cantor's prayers] there was no anguish, no *nusach*,[24] no trills, and no sharpness—it was all new and foreign to him. And yet he was touched by a kind of beauty whose quality he did not understand, to the point of feeling totally inferior, not just regarding himself, but also the other great *hazzanim* from whose waters he drank, who were heretofore giants of music to him. When the music stopped, he remained perplexed and deep in contemplation, shaking his shoulders, his brow frowning, and his eyes moving to and fro, as if to say, "Behold there is music in the world and I did not know."

I envied the "altos" and "sopranos" [of the choir] who could read music, who excelled at harmonizing in the new fashion. I introduced myself to them, and invited them to my father's house, and they presented me to the cantor. Upon testing my voice, he suggested that my father entrust me to him. But my father, for all of his sense of inferiority vis-à-vis the cantor, and for all of his desire to educate me to be a great musician, strongly rebuked me, "You want to be an ignoramus like them? Torah study comes before singing!"

In those days three types of people were granted special privileges, rooted in "ah, that's different!" For example, if a Jew were riding in his carriage on the Sabbath, he should be ready to receive scorn and disdain. But if the traveler were a doctor, all would be fine with him, because "a doctor is different." Or if a Jewish man was walking in the streets on the Sabbath in the company of some young, buttoned-up officer, with two Christian women leaning on his arm, accompanied by a big dog barking as Jews were enjoying their desserts, all those at the table would turn their eyes to the window, astonished and irate at the man who would dare disturb the Sabbath rest in such a coarse way. But, when they saw that the man was the state rabbi, they would immediately calm down, wave their finger, and say, "ah, a *kazennyi*[25] is different!"

The third type to receive such "privileges" was the new choral cantor. The old prayer leaders were expected to conform to all minutiae relating to prayers [. . .] and once [community leaders] had had enough of him, or his voiced failed, or they just wanted someone else in his stead, they would arm themselves with all imaginable religious weapons to get rid of him,[26] for it is no small matter to come before the pulpit and lead the nation of Israel in prayer! But the choral cantor was liberated from all that, and the "table" was as if "unset" for him. [. . .][27] It came to the point that in one city filled with all kinds of traditional Hasidim, a cantor moved into a neighborhood surrounded by a mix of

Hasidim—Volhynians, Ukrainians, Bukovinians—and when the old ladies would leave for Sabbath morning prayers with their grandchildren [. . .] they were astonished to see a bare-headed Jew [violating the Sabbath by] stoking the coals in the furnace. They yelled and cursed at him, but the man did not desist, and responded, "Animals, why are you shouting? Do you not know that I am a choral cantor?" Immediately they were mollified, saying, "a choral cantor is different."

Given the prevalence of such attitudes toward cantors among the pious, it is no surprise at all that my father absolutely rejected the cantor's suggestion that he entrust me to him.

IV

Here I should provide a brief description of the Tal'noe "court" and its influence among the Hasidim.

On a wide expanse in the center of the city of Tal'noe [. . .] there extended a large court, surrounded on all sides by a fence, akin to a small town in and of itself, that, amazingly, contained large and beautiful buildings, like small palaces. A palace for the rebbetzin; a palace for their only son, R. Motele; one for the son-in-law, R. Meir'l (son of one of the wealthy of Berdichev); one for the keeper of the court, R. Yankele Hana-Hayils; and other distinctive structures for the grandchildren and great-grandchildren of the Besht, who lived here all their lives and were supported by the community and the *tsaddik*. Each one of these buildings was beautifully and tastefully appointed, with the finest appurtenances, expensive furnishings, with servants (male and female), while one building stood entirely vacant. This was the guesthouse of the court, where guest *tsaddikim* and in-laws and relatives would be housed. [. . .] And, it goes without saying, the residence of the *tsaddik* himself outranked them all in beauty and splendor.

The rebbe's *kloyz*, which held up to 2,000 people, was built within the court, aside from the large hall and corridor extending from the southern wall of the *kloyz*, with an open doorway for the *tsaddik* to pray with his community in solitude.[28] A large and long wooden building stood in the center of the court, and this was the dining hall, used by the *tsaddik* and those close to him on Sabbaths and holidays. Not far from that was a bathhouse, used for *shvitzing* and bathing, with a large mikvah.[29] A beautiful sukkah was appended to each of these houses. [. . .] In one corner [of the court] was a row of kitchens, [some] set apart for cooking meat dishes, and [others] for dairy meals, each appointed with all the appropriate utensils; to each was assigned its own staff—meat cooks and dairy cooks—who never switched over. In another corner, a row of houses for cleaning, [plus] stalls for the horses, wagons, and pens for the cows.

In short, the court in Tal'noe was like a small state within a big state, and from the salvific streams of this little state the larger state earned its sustenance, for the walls of the court were surrounded by inns, taverns, and all kinds of stores selling all kinds of merchandise; by tradesmen and coachmen; a large gang of the idle; collectors writing notes; temporary assistants to guests; emissaries collecting money for the maintenance of the court; and plain old ne'er-do-wells living out their days here while getting meals courtesy of the court. This entire large community—from the grandchildren and great-grandchildren and all the other VIPs who sit at the table of the rebbe, to the meat or dairy cook—all derive their livelihood from the network emanating from the court, that is, from the Hasidim of the *tsaddik*.

And who can count the Hasidim of the *tsaddik* of Tal'noe! Who can calculate their pride vis-à-vis all the other Hasidim descended from R. Motele Chernobyler! In those days the courts of the [other] Twerskys, descendants of the Maggid of Chernobyl, were almost barren in comparison to the court of the *tsaddik* of Tal'noe, who lead at such a high level. Many of his Hasidim were among the wealthy in the communities of Israel, and they gave with wide-open hands [to support] him, his children, all that were connected to him. They gave him the silver chair with the gold inscription "David, king of Israel, alive and well" (on which they spent tens of thousands of silver rubles),[30] and this seat of glory attracted the eye of the government to the point where the *tsaddik* was turned over to the secret police and imprisoned in Kiev on a charge of sedition. It took great effort to get him released. [...]

Only an expert in the goings-on of the *tsaddikim* and their courts can truly appreciate the extent to which the *tsaddik* of Tal'noe exercised influence far greater than his peers. R. Dovid'l was one of a kind, filled with the spirit of life, distant from all the waywardness and lazy idleness that prevailed then in all the courts of the *tsaddikim*. He could immediately understand the soul of his Hasidim, such that he could distinguish between the honest Hasidim, who believed in his power and *tsidkus*,[31] and the Hasidim who merely flattered him and admired him for their own benefit.

R. Dovid'l was the greatest optimist among the descendants of R. Motele, and this spirit emanated to his Hasidim as well. He despised weeping and sadness; among the spiritually ill who came to him for healing he chose to display his influence on those who were manic, but despaired of helping those who were depressed.

I remember when we sang before the *tsaddik* for the first time, with Nisi, the "u-nesaneh tokef" together with the "ki ke-shimkha" [...] prayers that are well known throughout Israel — in the key of F minor and rich with primal and Eastern animation, and especially when we reached the part "man comes from dust and to dust he shall return" that moves up a fifth to C minor like this:

and there was not a dry eye in the house. Suddenly the *tsaddik* opened his eyes and got Nisi to stop by telling him, "Nisi, you want to make me cry? Enough!" He did not allow him to finish and began engaging in jocular conversation. [...]

R. Dovid'l would spice his conversations with sharp riddles, and enjoyed jokes; jocularity was so precious to him that he retained the jokester Leibele-Michaels in the role of "court jester"; his role was to visit [R. Dovid'l] every day at the hour set aside for his mundane chatter — when he would lie down on his bed in his green silk *kapote* with his broad, white collar opened a bit to his breast, with important guests around him who would update him about the news in the town and the state. The "jester" would offer some joke, and the *tsaddik* would laugh with his mouth wide open. [...]

He loved music and song with all his soul. He spent lavishly to bring Hirshele Tulczyner — an excellent *ba'al tefillah* with a beautiful voice — to lead the services for the High Holidays. He also retained a permanent *hazzan*, Yosele des Rebbes, to attend to the "need of the tables," who was tasked with composing for each and every Sabbath a new melody for one of the poems of the [standard] Sabbath *zemiros*.[32] This melody (*nigun*) was then accepted and spread as a kind of holy tradition among Tal'noe Hasidim wherever they were, as this Yosele was, in the eyes of the Hasidim, a kind of *golem* of the *tsaddik*, through whom this melody emerged from the "overflow" of the *tsaddik*,[33] the master of the treasuries of the temple of song. The proof [that Yosele was merely the *golem* of the *tsaddik*]: after the death of R. Dovid'l, when Yosele moved on to the Rachmastrivka court of the *tsaddik* R. Yohentsi,[34] the divine presence left him and the melodies he produced were defective and tasteless to the point that he became a laughingstock and ultimately shut up.

Beyond these two *hazzanim* he had a coterie of *hazzanim* who sang in all the [surrounding] *shtetlakh*, who had the merit to provide the *tsaddik* with new musical nourishment practically every Sabbath and holiday. His Hasidim would always try to entice *hazzanim* from other hasidic courts to come and visit Tal'noe, if not as an actual "member" then at least as an occasional guest who comes to honor and sing for the rebbe. Even Nisi Belzer, although he was a Habad Hasid with the *Tanya*[35] always on his table, was, nevertheless, one of the pillars of song in the Tal'noe court, and paid his regular tribute to the rebbe by visiting once a year. Even the best instrumental musicians [. . .] honored the *tsaddik* with their fiddles. Thus, the court was always filled with life and vibrancy, and boredom did not dare approach the threshold of the court. [. . .]

The matter of pilgrimages to the *tsaddikim* rest on three pillars: prayer, redemptions, and "tables." The prayer of the *tsaddik* was, of course, his power and strength. Indeed, the world of Beshtian Hasidism was based on the belief that the *tsaddik* in prayer rises into the heaven and repairs worlds, and reaches such a level that God decrees, and the *tsaddik* annuls [the decree]. But when he prays he stands alone in his private room throughout the year, except on specific occasions when he comes out among his followers, for example, to call out the sounds of the shofar, or encircle the pulpit before Kol Nidre calling out *or zarua la-tsaddik*, or during *hoshanes* and *hakafes*, among others.[36]

The redemptions are a simple matter: a Jew acquires the blessing of the *tsaddik* by paying the price of the redemption, and, of course, each type of blessing had its price. But all this was a private matter, as each Hasid had his own distinct needs and wants, and it was these that led him to submit a "note" [request] to the *tsaddik*.

But the great hour of unity of the *tsaddik* and his Hasidim — the critical point in the descent of the divine presence to the *tsaddik* before his Hasidim — was always the public "tables" on Sabbaths and festivals. This was the sacred thread that brought near the hearts of

thousands of Hasidim and wove them together into a single cord. Each of the three Sabbath meals in Tal'noe had its own distinct splendor.

Already on Friday afternoon the everyday and tumultuous life in the court came to a stop, and in its place people began to taste a new life, the preparations for the Sabbath. On this day no one was permitted to come in to receive greetings and blessing from the *tsaddik*, and redemptions were not received either, except when there was danger to life or a difficult labor, and the like. In the winter, at 3:00 in the afternoon before sunset, the *tsaddik* "received the Sabbath"[37] in his room in his home with some important minyanim[38] and honored guests, who prayed in the other room. After prayers, he went off by himself to an inner room, and remained there in total solitude for a number of hours, and the others also went off to the guesthouses, the homes of their hosts, or to the inns in which they were lodging to relax until the time of the "table" (or *tish*).

The candelabra were burning bright in the large dining hall, and to their light the staff was setting the tables. Slowly, slowly, groups of Hasidim from all classes entered and sat on the long benches surrounding the tables. Only a row of seats was left open at the head of the table for the *tsaddik* and his family, with some other places behind them left for the guests and community leaders. All were waiting for the desired time, when they would hear the herald call out that the rebbe had opened the door to his room and was preparing for the *tish*. The guests and the leaders who were each at their place of lodging, upon hearing that the rebbe was heading to the dining hall, got up, dressed, girded themselves, washed their hands, and had a piece of bread after reciting the blessing. They rushed to precede the rebbe, receive greetings, and enjoy the splendor of the divine presence [that was felt] at the meal of the *tsaddik*.

How splendid was R. Dovid'l as he appeared accompanied by his family and entourage, so beautifully dressed! [. . .] He walked slowly, with purpose, on the path covered with boards that they built for him; as he was tall, and walked alone on the short elevated bridge between two camps of escorts who adorned him on each side, he seemed head and shoulders above everyone else. As he neared the dining hall, and the call went out, "the rebbe is coming," hundreds of hands belonging to the guests who had not yet received greetings from the rebbe were extended to him, and he responded with charm and grace, with the eyes of one deep in thought, "Aleichem shalom." On the path to the hall the whole community stood, each person in his place, and cleared a path for his Holiness and his family.

The *tsaddik* sat in his place and closed his eyes in concentration. He extended his right hand and beckoned, and his only son, R. Motele, beckoned and offered the wine goblet to the *tsaddik*, who recited *kiddush* with reverence. [. . .] After sipping the wine, the leftover wine was distributed, drop by drop, to hundreds of cups in the hands of the Hasidim. He then washed his hands with the cup that was brought to him by the server, [. . .] broke off a piece of bread, and offered the blessing, "ha-motzi." Immediately the *hallah* was cut into slices, pieces, and crumbs — all according to the luck of the recipient.

The *tsaddik* opened his mouth and softly sang "Askinu sa'adusa,"[39] closing his eyes, supporting his head with his right hand, in the softest of voices chirped each stanza in the melody of *devekut*;[40] for the most part the words collapsed in his teeth, but the assembly followed after him, reciting the verse loudly. After eating the fish and sauce, and "grabbing the leftovers," the *zemiros* began. [. . .] After the *zemiros* Yosele des Rebbes sang the new tune that he composed, generally [built on] two or three themes that repeated every week.

Then the *tsaddik* began to teach Torah, at first in a very soft voice, so that those sitting at a distance could not hear anything, but then we would repeat each clause several times, with his voice rising a half tone each

time. [. . .] With each elevation the dynamic strength and fieriness of his words increased, so that by the end his delicate voice filled the entire expanse of the hall, with each word burning like fire, amazing the audience. The content of the "Torah" was beside the point; the main thing was who was speaking and how he spoke. Much of his Torah was published in books, but with these things the effect is only on those who hear it directly from the speaker, and they are of almost no value when they are soulless words on a page before a reader. In general, R. Dovid'l's Torah aroused an unusual excitement among his admirers, for no one ever saw him with a book in his hands, and yet, in his discourses, he cited rabbinic and kabbalistic sources.

If the first two Sabbath meals held such excitement for his admirers, the third meal exceeded them in holiness and Torah. Amid the dimness of the twilight, the hall filled on all sides, with people standing and others sitting on the floor, benches, and windowsills, the *tsaddik*'s face glistening as the light of the moon. [. . .] The deathly silence of the congregation was broken by sweet, soft, deep, ebullient [. . .] sounds, piercing and penetrating the hearts, and stirring the minds to supreme enthusiasm and the "negation of the existing" of all worldly trifles. All this through the spiritual sounds that came forth from his holy mouth, that emphasized every syllable, not according to the phony grammatical rules the *maskilim* and *apikorsim* invented, but rather according to the rules of the heart that burns and bursts over the exile of Israel, the exile of the *shekhinah*, and the many kinds of exile of the soul; [sounds that burst out in song] arousing an earthly awakening, like this:

In short, the third meal was the crown of the Sabbath meals; here were expressed emotions and yearning for the presence of the "extra soul," as well as the soul's pain at the [impending] separation from the Sabbath. [...]

After the meal, different groups left for their homes or place of lodging, or to the *kloyz* [for prayer], or they stayed for the evening prayer in the hall, after the *tsaddik* was led to his home. At all of the houses of the *tsaddik*'s family they began serving hot drinks, singing *zemiras ha-mavdil*,[41] engaging in friendly conversation, and telling wonder stories about the *tsaddikim*, especially the Besht.

The *tsaddik* prayed the evening service and made *havdalah* in his home, and at a late hour [...] VIPs and honored guests gathered around him for mundane chatter, just as on weekdays. They found him with an entirely new countenance, the face of a sage more than that of a *tsaddik*, the signs of seriousness having departed from him [...] it seemed his heart was ready to hear some news, or a joke from the court jester.

One Saturday night, the *tsaddik* was lying on his bed [...] and in the room many visitors were around him, including five prominent rabbis. Suddenly, the door opened and [the jester] Leibele-Michaels entered, uttering the [standard Saturday evening] blessing, "good week." A kind of smile began to emerge in the Rebbe's eye.

"Rebbe," he said, "I have found a very serious question in the "Kaddish de-rabbanan."[42] Why does it say, 'for Israel, and for the rabbis'? No matter which way you look at it there is a problem. If the rabbis are Jews, the prayer should only say 'for Israel' and this would include the rabbis. And if the rabbis (he said pointing to the assembled rabbis) are *goyim*, it should say 'for Israel and for the *goyim*' and everyone would understand that 'Israel' refers to the Jews, and '*goyim*' refers to the rabbis?"

The rebbe smiled, and one of the assembled rabbis turned to Leibele-Michaels and asked,

"So, what's the answer?" But Leibele had already turned around and disappeared the way he entered. All that was heard was a muttered, "Teyku!"[43]

NOTES

1. ["Shatz" is an acronym for *shaliah tsibbur*, the traditional name for a prayer leader or cantor.]

2. [Pini is short for Pinhas; Motel Gadis refers to the writer's father, Motel (short for Mordechai), son of Gadi.]

3. [The traditional name of Yom Tov Lipmann Heller (1578–1654), best known for his commentary on the Mishnah, called *Tosafot Yom Tov*.]

4. [SHu"B (pl. SHuBim) is an acronym for *shohet u-vodek*, (kosher) slaughterer and inspector.]

5. [That is, reading musical notation.]

6. [All leading *hazzanim* of the second half of the nineteenth century.]

7. [This is apparently an adoption of a Hebrew word meaning "you shall dwell," to denote the Latin *descant* or *discantus*, which sounds similar.]

8. [The name of a hymn that is sung to introduce the Musaf service on the Festivals of Passover, Shavuot, and Sukkot.]

9. Nisan Blumental (1805–1902) became the head cantor in the Brody synagogue in Odessa in 1841 and remained in his post for fifty-five years.

10. [A charity named for the Mishnaic rabbi, Meir, known as a miracle worker. The collection boxes were to benefit the Jews of Palestine. They were named for this sage because, according to tradition, before he died he proclaimed that he would intercede in heaven for those who give charity in his name to benefit the poor of the land of Israel.]

11. [Mordechai Twersky (1770–1837), the Maggid (preacher) of Chernobyl, succeeded his father, Menahem Nahum, as the leader of the hasidic dynasty of Chernobyl. Each of his eight sons became a hasidic rebbe in Ukraine. One of the eight sons was David, or R. Dovid'l, of Tal'noe, who was the topic of secret government discussions in document 2.]

12. [Literally, "at the table," meaning the shared meal of the Hasidim. For more, see below.]

13. [*Ha-melits* was the first Hebrew newspaper in Russia, beginning publication in 1860. It was an

important vehicle for the dissemination of Haskalah ideas.]

14. [Salomon Sulzer (1804–90) was a cantor and composer in Vienna. His two-volume work, *Songs of Zion* (Shir Zion), contained music for Sabbaths and festivals, as well as various rites of passage. His melodies spread throughout the Jewish world, East and West].

15. [A call to prayer that initiates the morning and evening services, and the congregational response.]

16. [A *meshorer* (pl. *meshorerim*) served as a prompter and accompanist for the *hazzan*. Generally, they were a pair: a boy soprano and a bass. See Wendy Heller, "Cantors," in *The YIVO Encyclopedia of Jews in Eastern Europe* (http://www .yivoencyclopedia.org/article.aspx/Cantors). Other information relevant to this memoir may be found there as well.]

17. [Yeruham Blindman (1798–1891), better known as Yeruham ha-Katan, was a cantor and composer. Genrikh Sliozberg describes his splendid tenor voice in document 7.]

18. [It is not clear precisely what Minkovsky has in mind here. He is presumably referring to the period after 1881, but this is uncertain.]

19. [Alexander Zederbaum once criticized the choral synagogue (built in the 1830s) during his visit to Berdichev. According to Mikhail Krutikov, he found the architecture, zodiacal signs on the walls, and pictures of klezmer instruments on the western wall jarring to his religious sensibilities. Zederbaum remarked: "It is a shame and disgrace to see in the synagogue pictures of a violin, a string bass, a clarinet, a flute, a drum, with little *marshalik*'s drumsticks for beating the rhythm during the procession from the wedding canopy, as if they were a sign over a house of a klezmer or a manufacturer of musical instruments." He also expressed surprise at the Torah reading, which was divided into thirty rather than seven *aliyot* to garner more contributions. See: Mikhail Krutikov, "Berdichev in Russian Jewish Literary Imagination: From Israel Aksenfeld to Friedrich Gorenstein," in *The Shtetl: Image and Reality* (Oxford: Legenda, 2000), 101.]

20. [An old Jewish saying. For this and other aspects of the claim about Odessa offered here,

see Steve Zipperstein, "Odessa," in *The YIVO Encyclopedia of Jews in Eastern Europe* (http://www .yivoencyclopedia.org/article.aspx/Odessa); Jarrod Tanny, *City of Rogues and Schnorrers: Russia's Jews and the Myth of Old Odessa* (Bloomington: Indiana University Press, 2011).]

21. ["The Friedmans" refers to the hasidic dynasty that originated in the Ukrainian town of Ruzhin and then moved to Sadigura (Sadhora in Ukrainian).]

22. [Levi Yitzhak of Berdichev (1740–1809) was one of the students of the Maggid of Mezritch, who established the first hasidic courts throughout Eastern Europe.]

23. [Psalms 146:4.]

24. [Literally, text or version, but here used to denote mastery of the liturgical traditions of the service.]

25. [From the Russian state rabbi (*kazennyi ravvin*). See Azriel Shochat, *Mosad 'ha-rabanut mitaam' be-rusyah* (Haifa: University of Haifa Press, 1976); ChaeRan Y. Freeze, *Jewish Marriage and Divorce in Imperial Russia* (Hanover, NH: University Press of New England for Brandeis University Press, 2002), 95–128.]

26. [That is, they would argue that he had violated some minor point of law or custom.]

27. [A play on the traditional law code called the *Shulhan Arukh*, meaning set table. The pun means that the choral cantor was not held to the standards of this code.]

28. [That is, the community would fill the *kloyz*, while the rebbe would pray in a private space, able to hear the prayers of the community and its prayer leader.]

29. [A Jewish woman is required to immerse herself in a mikvah (ritual bath) after her menstruation to purify herself before she has sexual relations with her husband.]

30. [The silver ruble was the legal monetary unit in nineteenth-century Russia. The paper ruble, which also circulated, was valued at approximately 1.60 to the silver ruble in 1890.]

31. [An abstract noun from the same root as *tsaddik*, meaning his *tsaddik*-like qualities.]

32. [*Zemirot* refers to poems and prayers sung at

each of the three Sabbath meals. Then, as now, they circulated in prayer books, and also in stand-alone booklets.]

33. [That is, Yosele, the golem, was the conduit through which the effluence of the *tsaddik* passed.]

34. [Yohanan Twersky (1816–95), youngest son of R. Motele.]

35. [The Tanya or *Likute amarim* (Compilation of Teachings, 1797) was the main work of R. Shneur Zalman of Liady, the founder of Habad Hasidism. It was notable for its distinction between the *tsaddik*, who has a completely pure and divine soul, and the *benoni* (average person), who struggles to keep the commandments.]

36. [When the shofar (ram's horn) is blown on the New Year, it is customary to have someone well-versed in the rules call out each sound before the shofar blower blows the sound; on the evening of Yom Kippur, it is customary to initiate the service by reciting the verse above from Psalm 97:11; on the Sukkot holiday it is customary to encircle the pulpit reciting prayers for salvation, which begin with the Hebrew phrase *Hosha na* (please save), leading to naming the ritual *hoshanes*; on Simhat Torah it is customary to encircle the pulpit (*hakafes*) holding Torah scrolls (accompanied by much dancing). On all these occasions the *tsaddik* would appear in public and lead or participate with his followers.]

37. [That is, recited the Sabbath prayers; this service has come to be known as "receiving the Sabbath."]

38. [A minyan is a group of at least ten men, required for a prayer quorum.]

39. ["I have prepared the meal," the opening words of an Aramaic formula that introduces the Sabbath *zemirot*.]

40. [*Devekut* (literally, cleaving or attaching) refers to the state of communion with God that stands as the goal of much of hasidic life.]

41. [A traditional song noting the movement from the holy to the profane.]

42. [This refers to a version of the kaddish prayer recited publicly after the study or recitation of a rabbinic text.]

43. [A Talmudic term, meaning the question stands unanswered. Humor was an often-accepted way of poking fun at rabbis and rabbinic discourse.]

---

[2]

Secret State Reports on the Twersky *Tsaddikim* in Kiev and Volhynia Provinces (1861–68)

"Secret Memorandum of the Governor of Kiev, Lt.-Gen. Ress, to the Military General of Podolia and Volhynia (21 June 1861)."

TsDIAK-Ukraïny, f. 1423, op. 1, d. 6, ll. 49–51.

From the information sent to me by the heads of the district and county police about the existence of a secret sect of *tsaddikim* among the Jews, the main leaders of this sect appear to be members of the revered Twersky family, who reside in the towns of Chernobyl, Korostyshev (Radomysl' district), Cherkassy and Rotmistrovka (Cherkassy district), Tal'noe (Uman district), Makarov, and Skvir (Kiev province).[1] The merchant Ios' Mandel', who lives in the town of Rzhishchev, is considered to be one of these leaders. These individuals, who are called *maggidim* [. . .], are distinguished by their particularly fanatical convictions and wield considerable influence over all the Jews (except for the few who have received a [secular] education). The followers and worshippers comprise the sect of the *tsaddikim*, who have a baneful influence on the civil and moral development of Jewish society. The *tsaddikim* mainly pay attention to the education of males, giving them an exclusively religious upbringing and making them into complete fanatics; the latter in turn entice others [to join the sect]. They ignore the education of women, [who] engage in housework and sometimes commercial activities while their husbands—the Hasidim—only indulge in reading spiritual books.

Jews from neighboring towns travel to the Twerskys and spend a few days in prayers. They consult them about various commercial matters and consider the latter's decisions as law; they request their prayers in the case of childless marriages, illness, and other circumstances. They give money to the *tsaddikim*, and disburse part of it to the poor for the greater success of their prayers. If the Twerskys travel to a Jewish settlement, [the residents] organize a reception and show special hospitality; in general, the Jews consider their visits to be important for their holidays. The Twerskys are [registered] as merchants but [in fact] do not conduct any commerce. These people are so steeped in fanaticism that they speak only Yiddish and, if need be, use translators. In general, the *maggidim* bequeath their title and thereby perpetuate fanaticism from one generation to the next. The *maggidim*'s power and influence on the Jewish population is so great that the majority of Jews, predominantly the illiterate, believe that they are speaking with God and that their prayers—for those suffering, for the childless, the persecuted, and those in other straits—will have a salutary effect. The *maggid*'s verdict is almost always fulfilled; even Christians who lack evidence turn to the *maggid* with complaints against Jews and receive satisfaction. The *maggidim* look after the poor, giving them part of the offerings, [while] they

themselves gain in stature. That the office is beneficial is apparent in the [case of] the Gornostaipol' Maggid, one of the Twersky brothers who moved from Radomysl' district to Cherkassy at the invitation of the local Jews, who gave him every advantage and comfort, even making him stay in a rather expensive house in Gornostaipol'.

In Lipovets district, Jews among the *tsaddik*'s followers exhibit special fanaticism: Gdal' Reznik, Ovsheii Reminnik, Shulim Shakhna Shekter, Itsko Borshchagovskii, Arii Tul'chinskii, Berko Vaznekskii, Levii Rabinovich, the son of Iankel Rozenfel'd, and Mendel Reznik. These people secretly collect monetary donations. Gdal' Reznik sends the monetary assessments to Avrum Iankel [Avraham Yaakov], son of the former rabbi of Ruzhin, Fri[ed]man in Austria, in the town of Sadagura. For this reason . . . last May, upon receiving a passport from the Tarashcha town council in the name of Gdalia Zhenskii, Reznik left through the Gusiatinsk customhouse in the town of Sadagura. Allegedly, Levii Reminnik and Mendel Reznik delivered the money to Mendel Reznik at Khodorov's office in Berdichev; from there they sent the remittance to Sadagura to Iankel Friedman, and the latter transmitted it to Jerusalem for the restoration of the temple for the Messiah and also for distribution to poor Jews.

"Governor's Report (on Behalf of the General Governor) about the Tsaddikim in Volhynia (31 October 1861)."
TsDIAK-Ukraïny, f. 1423, op. 1, d. 6, ll. 53–55.

1. Avrum Twersky of Turiysk [Trisk, in Yiddish], the Turiyskii Maggid (preacher), fifty-one years old, enjoys great influence in Volhynia and Kiev provinces and in the Kingdom of Poland. All his sermons are directed against the state Jewish schools and the entire class of educated Jews. Despite his own wealth, he demands money from those who seek advice and also enjoys other material benefits. Among his numerous sons, the most

notable is Nukhim, who is considered the father's heir. . . . He already has many followers.

2. Itsko Shapiro of Nesukhotzhakh [Nesukhoyezhe], Kovel district, is seventy years old, the nephew of the Twerskys, one of the *tsaddikim* of Kiev province, and a miracle worker renowned for curing all infertile women. Intelligent, distinguished for his knowledge of the Talmud. He is embroiled in a territorial dispute with the *tsaddikim* of Turiysk. He has 100,000 silver rubles in capital. People also come to him to resolve matters of religious uncertainty, commercial matters, and childlessness.

3. Itskhok Mikhal'novich Berezna, Rovno district, is a decrepit old man, honest, constantly engaged in the study of Talmud; he does not pose as a miracle worker; he has hardly any followers. He is impoverished. His son Iosif, who lives with him, has begun to attract [attention] because of his debauched life and the charlatan ways of many Hasidim.

4. Lev Itskhok Katsenelenboym of Stepan, Rovno district, lives in luxury, carries on a debauched life, and has many followers.

5–6. Avrum and Itsel', brothers from Ostrog. Both are ignoramuses but have many followers. The first engages in reading spiritual books; the second, "being wealthy," leads a profligate life.

7. Gersh Leib Olyka, Dubno district, a miracle worker and ignoramus, has few followers.

8. Ios' Mendelevich Shtarson of Orshansa, second-guild merchant, son-in-law of the Cherkassy Tsaddik Twersky. He has lived in Ostrog since 1860. Not having much capital, he engages in lending money on interest; he does not have influence on his coreligionists. . . .[2]

"Denunciation from 'Jewish Progressives' to the General Governor of Kiev, Podolia, and Volhynia (1864)."

TsDIAK-Ukraïny, f. 1423, op. 1, d. 6, ll. 62–64.

1. The desperate and audacious swindler, one of the Twersky brothers, Tsaddik Duvid Twersky from Tal'noe (Uman district) spent ten days with the Jews in Vasil'kov, fleecing the Jewish fanatics there. He passed through Belaia Tserkov' on 7 August in order to influence the fanatical Jewish masses, most of whom are capitalists.

2. This remarkable Tsaddik Duvid Twersky has already been arrested in Vinnitsa. At the request of Your Excellency, he was sent to Kiev to provide a deposition. However, thanks to the patronage of the one who serves Your Excellency's person and enjoys the special trust of Your Excellency (who goes by the name of Fedorov), Tsaddik Duvid was released and even given a passport to travel with those chosen by him to disseminate pernicious homilies.

3. Special attention should be accorded to these *tsaddikim* as weapons of Russia's current political foes. Together with Polish landowners, they strive to prevent Russians from acquiring estates in local districts.[3]

4. They travel around the district with books to collect money, on the pretext that it is for poor Jews (who will not receive a single kopeck), and everywhere they preach about the promised fatherland in Canaan and abjure loyalty to Russia as a temporary [residence], citing the energetic activities of Poles as a model for the restoration of their own country.

5. The Polish insurrectionists and *tsaddikim* feel mutual sympathy for one another. Insurrectionists leaving for the forest run to the charlatan *tsaddikim* for their blessing. When locusts appeared in Vasil'kov district, the local governor of the town, the Pole Z . . . , implored the *tsaddik* to destroy the locusts. One constable in Kiev province, G . . . , invited the *tsaddik* to his house, honored him like a holy personage, gave him fifteen rubles, and implored him to bless the fields and crops.[4]

6. In general, the *tsaddikim*, wielding control over much capital and the minds of fanatical Jewish capitalists, have official agents in St. Petersburg and followers who serve in the higher courts. To achieve their ends, they

submitted the contents of a letter (in Yiddish) from someone, a trusted individual, serving under the auspices of Your Excellency. The letter pertains to Tsaddik Twersky of Makarov. Here is a translation:

DEAR BLESSED, PIOUS RABBI,
IAKOV ITSKHOK TWERSKY,

I received your letter [and] reply in a few words. You may travel throughout Kiev province without concern. I am your defender and protector. I am your right hand so that no calamity will befall you.

Signed: N. signifying the beginning of his name and surname; in his former Jewish status, he was Girsh Grinshtein.[5]

7. The well-known *tsaddik* from the Twersky family, Nukhim, arrived on Saturday in T[arashcha], Kiev province. He stopped at the final post chaise station Trotskii where a mob of fanatics met him; from here the *tsaddik* began to negotiate (through his envoys) with the authorities of T[arashcha] for permission to enter the town. The authorities agreed upon condition of payment from the fanatical Hasidim. However, when the latter did not keep their promise, the ingenious police superintendent of T[arashcha] placed four policemen in full uniform at the *tsaddik*'s apartment upon his arrival — as though to protect him from the grievances of the Jews. Meanwhile, the constables were ordered not to admit anyone to the *tsaddik* or to let him leave to see anyone. In this way the police superintendent did not free [the *tsaddik*] until the Jews made full payment to a salaried worker at T[arashcha] Square. Moreover, the town's court counselor received a whole *pud* [16.38 kilograms] of sugar and five rubles. The [authorities] then released the *tsaddik* and allowed all to enter.

8. On 7 August, Tsaddik Duvid Twersky's guide from Vasil'kov to Belaia Tserkov' was the district solicitor Sulevskii.[6] As is clear from his treatment of the *tsaddik*, he is a resolute and desperate Pole, who came to Belaia

Tserkov' to protect the *tsaddik*; he and a constable received a decent payment for this.

9. Duvid Twersky remained in Belaia Tserkov' on Skvir Street in the home of his follower Srul'-Shulim Kharash. On 8 August, there will be a ceremonial service with an enormous assembly of fanatical Jews; a booth was set up for that purpose. In [F]astov, the *tsaddik* with his sect will recite blessings in the name of the protector and patron of all *tsaddikim* in general but Duvid in particular.

In conclusion, the Jewish progressives earnestly request Your Imperial Excellency's order to banish the nine [*sic*][7] Twersky brothers — the *tsaddikim* — from the local region as the most harmful for all Jews living here and even for the region itself. Relocate them in distant provinces in Russia where Jews are forbidden to settle.

To convince you of the need to banish the *tsaddikim*, we request that you immediately appoint an honest and unbiased official of Russian descent to go to Belaia Tserkov' upon receipt of this petition so that he may apprehend the Tsaddik Duvid [while he is] still here. But it should be done without informing the solicitor Sulevskii and local constables.

"Secret Report Number 5261 to the Military General of Kiev Province (20 August 1864)."
TsDIAK-Ukraïny, f. 1423, op. 1, d. 6, ll. 64–65.

I received a denunciation from Belaia Tserkov' in a special report signed by "Jewish progressives" about the unlawful activities of the Jewish *tsaddikim*, in particular about the Jew, the Tsaddik Nukhim Twersky, with information about their dealings with the Polish patriots. [There was also information] about the reprehensible actions of the official O. Federov under my auspices,[8] the district police superintendent of Tarashcha, the district solicitor Sulevskii, and other people aiding Twersky and the fanatical Jews.[9] They are identified in the denunciation either by the first letter of their surnames or by the position they hold.

As I forward a copy of the above denunciation to Your Excellency, I ask you to note the facts in the report, find a trustworthy individual to verify the above, and to report the results of the inquiry and conclusions to me.

"Secret Report [of the Military General] to the General Governor of Kiev, Podolia, and Volhynia (20 August 1864)."

TsDIAK-Ukraïny, f. 1423, op. 1, d. 6, ll. 65–66.

A sect of *tsaddikim* exists among the Jews in the local region, as is evident from the cases before my administration; this has long been well known to provincial authorities. Its main leaders are members of the Twersky family, who are revered by the Jews living in various places of Kiev province.[10]

To be sure, what the denunciation of Jewish "progressives" says about the significance and pernicious influence of the *tsaddikim* on the Jewish population does not contain anything new—that is, we already have this information in our administration. On that basis, the late Prince Vasil'chikov, as well as Your Excellency, ordered surveillance over the *tsaddikim*, especially Duvid Twersky (about whom you had offered comments on 28 January 1863 and 29 March 1864 in nos. 160 and 2154). However, one should note a few items in this denunciation that provide evidence not only of the *tsaddikim*'s continued unlawful conduct and the reprehensible assistance offered to them by a few officials. Some places in the denunciation accuse the *tsaddikim* of ties to the Polish patriots. I recognized the need for a thorough verification by an expert criminal investigator (to be presented in an extract by the commanding official).

Independently, aware that the unrestricted travels of (Duvid) Twersky—which is absolutely harmful—can no longer be tolerated, I deem it necessary to terminate such wrongs immediately: to confiscate the official [letter] from the Society for the Assistance of the Poor (established by His Imperial Majesty in Kiev) for Twersky to collect money for the Jewish hospital, to forbid him to leave Tal'noe (with a sworn statement), and to intensify the police surveillance over his activities and relations.

"Report of the Lieutenant Colonel Palitsyn to the Governor of Kiev (30 September 1864)."

TsDIAK-Ukraïny, f. 1423, op. 1, d. 6, ll. 68–71.

It is reported that Duvid Twersky traveled to Boguslav, where he was received; his agents (who are listed) were constantly with him. Many followers, in large numbers, came from Rzhishchev, Belaia Tserkov', Kagarlyk, Tal'noe and other places. Having collected up to two thousand rubles here, Twersky—accompanied with great honor by a crowd of followers (among whom were the poor, whom his agents gave money for the trip)—departed for Kagarlyk; there additional admirers arrived from Tarashcha, Rakitna, Belaia Tserkov', Obukov, Vasil'kov, Germanovka, and other places. Twersky arrived here with the goal of "taking the *shtetl* into his possession," [but] a clash between his supporters and opponents erupted over his election to be one of the local *maggidim*. Moreover, at night a mob of Twersky's followers attacked their [opponents'] homes, smashed windows, and beat the homeowners themselves. The main instigators of the fights (Arii Dovgolevskii, Iankel Uritskii, and others), having hired a military band, went around the houses with joyful shouts: "Duvid, *melekh yisroel* [King of Israel] lives forever. . . ." Dovgolevskii rode on horseback ahead of the wild mob shouting "Our Kagarlyk!" Then they drove the local rabbi Iankel out of town because he would not agree to sign [a statement] in favor of Twersky. Twersky himself ordered the community not to pay Iankel a salary and to prohibit him from leading prayers in the prayer house. After such a rampage, on Monday Duvid Twersky (accompanied by a crowd) consecrated the place designated for a cemetery, where they brought out vodka and shouts resounded again: "Kagarlyk for us and Duvid—the Jewish tsar!"

Twersky left from here for Rzhishchev, with the whole crowd and his agents, . . . the goal being to "take possession of the *shtetl*." Along the way, in the village of Rossov, a quarrel broke out between Twersky's supporters and Jews who did not agree with him; the result was that the *tsaddik*'s followers violently beat up their opponents. Twersky rewarded the instigators of this assault. One received the post of assistant rabbi in Rossov; the second became the head of the local prayer house. In Rzhishchev they repeated the same story. . . . When Twersky proposed to the local Jews that they banish the local rabbi Mindel' and certify Twersky's election as the *maggid*, . . . a ferocious brawl lasted through the night (during which they bound up and beat one of the Jews).

Upon Twersky's arrival, the local constable left on a horse; his assistant also left on the day of the fights and disorder, leaving orders to "the rural policeman, the Jew Leib, and ten peasants . . . to remain . . . with Twersky for his protection." Twersky's influence over the local police is evident from the following examples: the Jew Tevel, who had not agreed to sign the decision in Twersky's favor, was compelled to ask for his forgiveness (on pain of having his shop closed)—and the police knew full well about this. He thus was forced to pay two hundred silver rubles in front of the entire town and authorities. They left some honey at the door of another Jew Kiianich and declared that it was stolen—all because Kiianich's wife spoke disapprovingly of Twersky's activities.

On Saturday, Twersky's agents (surnames to be included)[11] burst into the prayer house during services, demanding that they sign an agreement in Twersky's favor. In the face of stubborn resistance, they smashed all the windows in the prayer house and Rabbi Moshko's apartment.

Twersky spent eight days here (in Rzhishchev) and collected more than 1,400 rubles; from here he left for the village of Rossov, escorted with great fanfare by a whole crowd (led by three men on horseback). Here the mob also created great tumult; it attacked the house of Rabbi Vaskov (who refused to certify [Twersky's election]), smashed its windows, demolished the stove, and destroyed the rabbi's candle factory (where they released a dog, which devoured all the tallow; they took the wax for themselves). Rabbi Vaskov managed to flee, but his wife and children hid in a ditch. The mob also broke the windows in Tsak's house and took 123 rubles. The victims reported all this to the judicial investigator. Here is the police report: in accordance with the requests of Twersky's agents, the assistant police officer Babintskii arrested the victims and their relations and departed for the police station in Boguslav. He locked up the prayer house (as not legally registered) but subsequently allowed it to reopen. [Rabbi] Vaskov was held under arrest for two weeks and remains under police surveillance. As punishment, Twersky deprived Vaskov of his rabbinical post; one of his followers, Galperin (although illiterate [in Russian]) was elected [the new rabbi].

"Secret Report of the Kiev Governor (No Addressee, 12 November 1865)."

TsDIAK-Ukraïny, f. 1423, op. 1, d. 6, ll. 76–77.

Having received permission for a temporary absence [from his hometown of Tal'noe], Twersky did not comply with the conditions placed on him "not to ride to other places, to make trips with unauthorized people and crowds, and to disturb the peace. . . ."

To illustrate the violation of his travel conditions, the governor of Kiev gives this description of the reception for the Skvir *tsaddik*, Itsko Twersky, and the Chernobyl *tsaddik*, Aron Twersky, who had arrived in Makarov for the wedding of his grandson Borukh Meier. The crowd met them, some on foot, others in carriages and [on] horseback, while the mounted Jews surrounded his carriage as bodyguards. After prolonged salutations, the offering of hands with blown kisses, the entire . . . crowd together with the *tsaddik*'s entourage . . . made for Makarov with shouts, noise, and a great tumult, while the *tsaddik*'s carriage was accompanied by an orchestra of Jewish musicians. . . . The wedding feast lasted for four days, attended by local inhabitants and out-of-town [guests]—more than a thousand Jews. Counting those from out of town [who came only to offer their] congratulations and donations, the total was probably more than three thousand people. For food . . . [they had] thirty pud (49.14 kilograms) of fish, three times that amount in beef, and they set down alcoholic beverages in the courtyard and other places for all the residents, regardless of belief and religious confession. Moreover, the peasants and Jews got completely drunk together. . . . The peasants, despite the prohibition placed on them by the local authority, furtively presented the bride and groom with bread and salt,[12] explaining that "the rabbi is our benefactor; he helps us [when we are] in need of money and so forth. . . ." The wedding cost up to three thousand rubles, furnished of course by the donations of the followers. Everything went off with great pomp and circumstance. The celebration was adorned by the presence of Prince Romual'd Gedroiuts, the landowner . . . from the town of Stavishch. Acrobats and masked Jews entertained the guests. Because Aron and Itsko Twersky violated their sworn agreement, the governor intends to prohibit them to leave from their places of permanent residence "absolutely and forever."

"Report of the General Governor of Kiev, Podolia, and Volhynia to the Governor of Kiev (15 November 1865)."

TsDIAK-Ukraïny, f. 1423, op. 1, d. 6, l. 77.

The general governor finds it impossible to declare to the Twerskys that they are forbidden absolutely and forever to be absent from their place of residence; he asks the governor to refuse henceforth their requests for permission to leave their places of residence.

"Secret Report of the General Governor of Kiev, Podolia, and Volhynia to the Governor of Kiev (30 July 1866)."

TsDIAK-Ukraïny, f. 1423, op. 1, d. 6, ll. 79–80.

After examining Your Excellency's memorandum of 12 July (number 7069), I find that the investigation conducted by the special commission (which you authorized) does not present [sufficient] facts to indict Tsaddik Duvid Twersky for illegal activities as prescribed in article 1204. . . . [The report] only provides a general understanding of the pernicious influence of both Duvid Twersky and other *tsaddikim* on the Jewish population and the harmful education of Jews—which was already well known before the beginning of this case.

Given the state of affairs, I do not find sufficient grounds to remove Duvid Twersky from the district as you have proposed, all the more so as this measure would hardly eliminate the belief of the Jewish masses in the holiness of the *tsaddikim* in general. If one does not succeed in the latter, all repressive measures would of course have scant effect. The example of the former Tsaddik of Ruzhin [Israel] Friedman serves as proof: he has been abroad since 1841 but has not lost his influence on the local Jewish community.[13] On the contrary, he recently brought two new localities, especially the towns of Kamenets and Mogilev-Podolsk, under his influence.

Hence I propose to limit the measure to what has already been adopted in respect to all *tsaddikim* (per the proposal of 24 June 1865, number 3171): namely, to prohibit their travel without special permission. Given the prospects of possible resistance [and] harmful activities on the part of the most influential of the local *tsaddikim*, Duvid Twersky, I humbly ask Your Excellency to give him a forewarning. He must not instill the idea of his own elevated calling among the Jews and not dissuade them from educating their children in state educational institutions, otherwise he will be sent to one of the most remote provinces at the first indication of such conduct on his part.

"Report to the Ministry of Internal Affairs (22 August 1868)."

TsDIAK-Ukraïny, f. 1423, op. 1, d. 6, l. 80.

In a report of 24 July (number 1477), V. P. reports that the Jew Duvid Twersky, owing to [his] extremely harmful influence on the Jewish population, had been designated for exile from the region. He has been left alone, only because of a personal petition on his behalf by Count Suvalov, proprietor of the aforementioned town [Tal'noe]. On his guarantee, Twersky will henceforth conduct himself prudently. Neither Duvid Twersky nor his brothers are under house arrest. They have only been forbidden to leave their places of permanent residence without special permission in each case from provincial authorities. This measure was adopted with respect to all the *tsaddikim* of the southwestern region.

"Report of Major Count Kleimkhel' to the General Governor of Kiev, Podolia, and Volhynia (5 October 1869)."

TsDIAK-Ukraïny, f. 1423, op. 1, d. 6, l. 81.

In accordance with Your Excellency's order, I have conducted an investigation because a rumor has been circulating among the Jews of the southwestern region that the new general governor of Kiev, Podolia, and Volhynia wants to deport all the *tsaddikim* from the region. The rumors arose for the following reasons:

(1) The former general governor, General-Adjutant Bezak's directive, which exiled *tsaddik* Rabinovich[14] from the Lipitsk region, was implemented.

(2) Remarks by General Governor Katakaz to the *tsaddik* Rabinovich's wife, who had come to petition on behalf of her husband: "Your brothers allow themselves too much liberty; now he [her husband] has fallen but another will fall next — it will be the same for him."

(3) Comments by Lieutenant Colonel Demidov to Nemirovskii: "The case of the rabbis is in a bad way. General Governor Prince Alexander Mikhailovich will be angry."

The statements by Governor Katakaz and Lieutenant Colonel Demidov were communicated to the Tsaddik of Tal'noe, Duvid Twersky. Seeing that they had already exiled one of the *tsaddikim* (because of the order by the former general governor, General-Adjutant Bezak), and that they had made him swear not to leave [his home town without permission], Twersky sent Nemirovskii to St. Petersburg with a recommendation letter from Count Shuvalov to the minister of internal affairs. It contained a petition for him and the *tsaddikim* in general. The alarming rumors among Jews that their *tsaddikim* would be expelled from the region have gradually abated.

NOTES

1. [The Jewish Historical-Archeographical Society transcribed and typed these handwritten documents in the 1920s. Although the transcriptions included many ellipses (ellipses in the transcriptions are not in brackets), the sentences were complete without the missing phrases or words. In most cases, the ellipses represent editorial decisions (for example, to omit repetitious words and phrases). Orthography was also inconsistent; the name "David" and "Duvid" appeared interchangeably (the translation here will use just one version for clarity and consistency). Although the correct Russian transliteration for the surname is Tverskii, the more familiar spelling Twersky will be used here. ChaeRan Freeze thanks Jan Surer for obtaining these files for her in Kiev. See also Viktoriia Khiterer, *Dokumenty sobrannye evreisoi istoriko-arkheograficheskoi Komissiei* (Kiev: Institute Iudaika, 1999).]

2. [The document continues to list people who are not recognized as *tsaddikim* but who enjoy great influence and respect among the communities of Volhynia province.]

3. [The two authors of this letter were Vol'f Komrad and Vul'f Bugii, teachers at a state Jewish school.

Their arguments about the *tsaddikim*'s connection to the Polish nobility and disloyalty to the Russian state refer to the Polish Uprising of 1863. See the introduction and documents 162–164]

4. [The writers were clearly reluctant to include the full names of the people they were describing.]

5. [This suggests that Grinshtein converted and now served the general governor of Kiev.]

6. [The district solicitor (*uezdnyi striapchii*) represented the government's financial and legal interests at the local level. The judicial reform of 1 November 1864 abolished this office.]

7. [R. Mordechai Twersky (1770–1837), the son of Menahem Nahum of Chernobyl (1730–97) who founded the dynasty, was the first to adopt the Twersky surname. He had eight sons, who established courts throughout Kiev province: Aharon of Chernobyl (1787–1871); Mosheh of Korostyshev (1789–1866), Ya'akov Yisrael of Cherkassy (1794–1876); Nahum of Makarov (1804–51); Yohanan of Rotmistrovka (1816–95); Avraham of Turiysk (1806–89); Duvid of Tal'noe (1808–82); and Yitshak of Skvira (1812–85).]

8. [In a later report, Lieutenant Colonel Palitsyn reported that "it is only known that he [Federov] merits great trust among the Jews, and they turn to him in many instances as their mediator before the authorities" (TsDIAK-Ukraïny, f. 1423, op. 1, d. 6, ll. 66–68).]

9. [None of these individuals was found guilty (ibid.).]

10. [The report lists several *tsaddikim* and refers to the report dated 21 June 1861 above.]

11. [These names do not appear in any subsequent report.]

12. [Presenting the bride and groom with bread and salt was a Russian custom.]

13. [Israel of Ruzhin fled the Pale of Settlement in 1842, moving to Austrian Bukovina, a relatively short distance away. He did indeed continue to exercise influence on the Russian side of the border.]

14. [This is a reference to the exile of Itsko Rabinovich. He and his father (Gdal-Aron Rabinovich) are described in the documents as "minor *tsaddikim*." The latter succeeded in fleeing to Galicia, allegedly to the Sandagura court.]

[3]

The Vurke Hasidic Court in Otwock: The Memoirs of Ita Kalish

Ita Kalish, *A rebishe heym in amolikn Poyln* (Tel Aviv: I. L. Peretz, 1966).

Chapter One: My Mother and Her Family

I recall my mother mostly as a sick, weak woman, lying for hours on the couch in our long, dark dining room — and in later years — in the long hammock at the villa of my grandfather, Rabbi Simhah Bunem of Vurke [Warka, in Polish] in Otwock, of blessed memory.[1] She was sick for many years; she always had a special nurse and frequently traveled to spas abroad. She was often sarcastic and critical of people, ready with a caustic phrase for anyone whom she did not like, but redeemed by a genuine sense of humor and innate wit. She was especially disparaging in her accounts of Galician Jews, whom she encountered at Austrian spas. "The Jews over there," she would say, "consider themselves to be real 'Austrians'; they speak '*datsch*,'[2] their men shorten their coats, and their women wear wigs instead of traditional Jewish bonnets." My mother's nurse Freydl, who happened to come from Galicia, once created a major stir in our house. This happened on Yom Kippur eve, right after "Kol nidrei," when my father, together with his eldest son, brothers, relatives, disciples, and old Vurke Hasidim—all wrapped in their *tallis* adorned with silver crowns—returned home from the great synagogue. They came to rest after Kol Nidrei and to prepare for the long Yom Kippur night and discovered Freydl washing herself with soap in the kitchen.[3] I remember my mother's scathing remark at this desecration of the holiday: "What do you expect from a *Galitsianer*?" The day after Yom Kippur, Freydl packed up her belongings and left our house.

The one who remained to take care of my mother was her older and beloved sister, "Feygele the Pious" as she was known in her hometown of Kozienice. Every year Aunt Feygele used to fill the cellar of our house with bottles of raspberry juice for the sick and poor people. Raspberry juice was considered a sure way to induce sweating, which was thought to be an effective remedy against all kinds of colds. In the wintertime, any poor resident of Kozienice could receive a bottle of raspberry juice from Feygele. Aunt Feygele was very modest and humble. With a gentle smile on her pale lips, she was always ready to forgive the world any wrongdoings, even those committed against her own person. For thirty years—ever since the day of her wedding—Aunt Feygele lived together with her husband's parents, and her old mother-in-law, not Feygele herself, was in charge of the house. Yet during all those years, no one heard the two women raise their voices at each other. Aunt Feygele would often leave her husband and children in Kozienice and spend weeks sitting at the bedside of my sick mother, smiling good-naturedly and telling her all kinds of stories.

The town of Maciejowice, where we lived for a few years, consisted of a circular market-

place, a few narrow streets, and a big road leading to the surrounding gentile villages. It had a synagogue, a mikvah, two trustees, a Jewish mailman, a Jewish population with enough men for a few minyanim, and a river, the Dzika. The town's women told each other with fear that the Dzika demanded an annual sacrifice; each year someone would drown there. My mother, a daughter of a wealthy family from a big city, always felt antipathy toward the *shtetl*, which only increased after her own daughter nearly became another victim of the Dzika. This happened on a hot summer evening, when my mother took me along to the river. Children of every age were having a wonderful time, bathing and splashing in the water. Every moment, my mother would remind me that I should hold on to her. I have no idea what happened later: all I remember is opening my eyes and finding myself lying on the grassy riverbank surrounded by all the women and children of the *shtetl*, with my terrified mother and a Polish doctor next to me. We never went swimming in the Dzika again.

Mother came from a wealthy hasidic family in the Polish-German border town of Będzin [Bendin, in Yiddish]—the "Bendiner Orbachs," as one used to call the family in that border region. I first saw my grandparents from Będzin when they were already elderly and nothing remained of their former wealth. Grandmother's pride and sagacious silence, and Grandfather's humor and wit—his grandchildren enjoyed immensely. I remember him once on a summer Sabbath morning, strolling around the yard in front of our great synagogue during the intermission between the Shacharis and Mussaf prayers. He beckoned to me and, smiling broadly behind his large gold-rimmed spectacles, reached into the pocket of his long coat. "So what would you like?" he asked me innocently. "Ten *grozsy* or a *złoty*?" I remained standing, frightened and cried out: "But it's *Shabbes*!" I immediately realized that Grandfather was only joking and both of us, the eighty-year-old man and his little granddaughter, burst out laughing, pleased with each other's great sense of humor.

My aged, medium-built, and corpulent grandfather, Pinkas Orbach, white as a dove — a whiteness accentuated by his satin caftan and large black velvet hat — was grateful to God all his life for the great privilege of marrying off his daughter to a member of the celebrated Vurke court. He was proud of his youngest daughter, my mother Beylele, the oldest daughter-in-law at the Vurke court, and even more proud of his Vurke grandchildren, as children in our family are called to this day. In addition to Grandfather Pinkhes and Aunt Feygele, another member of my mother's large family, her only brother, known as Bunem Sosnovtser, would often come to visit us, staying for weeks at a time. Uncle Bunem's big black eyes were always smiling, sometimes sarcastically and sometimes humorously. He was very handsome: tall and slender, distinguished by his elastic, almost dance-like walk. As the only son in a household with six daughters, he was very spoiled from his earliest childhood, and his whole life; even after he had several children of his own, he paid little attention to the mundane necessities of life. He spent most of his time in various hasidic practices at the house of his brother-in-law, the rebbe, and had the reputation of a genteel young man — very popular and beloved among the Hasidim.

The chief breadwinner in Uncle Bunem's family was his wife, Miriam. Aunt Miriam required neither a bank nor bank clerks to conduct complex commercial and financial transactions. Her hometown of Sosnowiec had a large number of thriving money exchange offices, and she was able to make the most difficult and confusing exchange calculations in her head, without pen and paper. She was very clever, energetic, and renowned as a *laytishe yidene* [a resourceful Jewish woman]. Once, at my father's request, Aunt Miriam went with my youngest sister, who

was then suffering from a childhood disease, to a professor in Berlin. When they returned, the entire family surrounded Aunt Miriam, waiting impatiently to hear what the professor had said. Aunt Miriam stood in the middle of the room, smiling playfully, and said, "The professor, you say? He said it's nothing. It's something for a rebbe to deal with."

In later years, when my father was already the rebbe, Uncle Bunem performed various important duties at our court, including the "investigation" of the marital matches offered to my father for his younger daughters. My father was very proud of his children, and in response to offers of matches with Poland's great hasidic courts or business magnates, once remarked: "Whatever match I pick for my daughter, I will always lose." Uncle Bunem, his devoted "secret messenger," would bring a lot of news about the candidate to become the rebbe's son-in-law. Once it actually happened that Uncle Bunem failed miserably in his task. Here is how it happened. An almost certain candidate to become the son-in-law at the Otwock court, a young man of about sixteen to seventeen years of age and closely related to a famous rebbe in Poland, came to recuperate at one of the large, expensive *pensions* in Otwock following a severe cold. My father, always concerned about the health of his children, immediately ordered Uncle Bunem to go to that *pension* as a "visitor" in order to find out directly whether the potential groom's stay there was indeed for nothing more than ordinary recuperation after an ordinary cold. With great effort and with the help of various stratagems, my Uncle Bunem succeeded in moving next door to the young man. After several days of enjoying the great culinary art of the famous *pension* of that time, he discovered several little bottles of medicine prescribed by a great Warsaw doctor on the potential groom's night table. Before my father had enough time to make up his mind concerning this serious matter, the boy's father became aware of the whole "espionage racket" and, feeling terribly insulted, refused to discuss further the match with the "Vurke granddaughter."

Chapter Two: The Vurke Dynasty

The "Vurke grandchildren" traced their *yikhus* [lineage] to Rabbi Yitskhok of Vurke, "the Swarthy Yitskhok" as he was called in the hasidic court of Rabbi Bunem of Pshiskhe [Przysucha, in Polish].[4] Why was Rabbi Yitskhok swarthy? Thereby hangs a tale that my father's mother, Grandmother Goldele, explained in the following way: An ancestor of Rabbi Yitskhok of Vurke, the author of the *Levushim*,[5] was an exceptionally attractive man. Once, a young gentile woman—a noblewoman—saw him while walking on the street and followed him until he ran inside a house, climbed on top of the roof, and came out through the chimney covered in soot from head to toe. Upon his arrival home, he washed himself of the soot and exclaimed: "Master of the Universe, I beg you that all my descendants should be dark!" And therefore—grandmother concluded—everyone in our family was a brunette.

My grandfathers' great-grandfather, Rabbi Yitskhok of Vurke,[6] was renowned for his humility and good nature. Love for the Jewish people remained the dictum of the Vurke court in all subsequent generations. The Hasidim used to relate numerous oddities in connection to Rabbi Yitskhok's piety and modesty. All his life he traveled throughout the Polish cities and towns to intervene on behalf of Jews in distress: to government authorities in order to free a Jew from prison, to Jewish communities to save a Jew from a slanderous accusation, to help an *agunah* locate her husband,[7] or in general to help a Jew in times of difficulty. His piety and humility even influenced the notorious zealot and avowed *misnagid*, Azriel-Meir Grodshteyn of Lublin. R. Azriel-Meir was a great scholar and God-fearing person, but extremely irascible and dreadfully pedantic. A look from him made his family tremble with awe. One morning, an extraordinary thing occurred in his household: his son-in-law, Leybele Eyger of blessed memory, became a Hasid and stealthily left to visit the Kotsker rebbe. All hell broke loose in Azriel-Meir's house, for the man was beside himself. Neither his family's pleas nor his daughter's bitter tears helped. He prohibited his son-in-law—"the sectarian," as the *misnagdim* called the Hasidim in those days—from entering his house and commanded that he immediately divorce his wife.

Young Leybele Eyger remained in Kotsk for a while. Anxious and penniless, he decided—no matter what happened—to return to Lublin. He came into his father-in-law's house quietly, trying to stay unnoticed, and went to his room. Suddenly Azriel-Meir saw him and, approaching him quickly, grabbed him and wanted to toss him out the second-story window. After Leybele's wife and mother-in-law began screaming for help, several people ran in and led Leybele out of the house. When this terrible incident became known to Rabbi Yitskhok of Vurke, he immediately traveled to Lublin and spent long weeks without leaving Azriel-Meir's house until he persuaded this fanatic *misnagid* to annul the decree of divorce for his daughter.

The Hasidim used to tell a story characteristic of Rabbi Yitskhok of Vurke. Once, on a frosty winter night, he arrived in the Polish capital of Warsaw on some business regarding a Jewish matter. Lying in bed at an inn, he had a sudden desire for a pinch of snuff. The room was bitter cold, and he was shivering. As he lay in bed, Rabbi Yitskhok argued with himself: "The desire for a pinch of snuff is very strong. To rise now and take the snuff would be to yield to desire. But not to get up would be sloth." And so he decided: "I will come to the table, but will not take a pinch of tobacco." And so it was: he got up in the bitter cold, approached the table, but did not take a pinch.

In contrast to Rabbi Yitskhok, his wife, grandmother Rokhl, was a strict, taciturn woman, who frequently reprimanded her husband for his infinite kindness and readiness for sacrifice. She was particularly critical of his indulgence toward their two sons: Mendele (later the "Middle Vurker") and Dovidl (the rabbi of Amishinov [Mszczonów, in Polish])—both of whom at the time were still young, boisterous boys, who frequently exasperated her with their mad pranks, particularly the first-born Mendele.[8] "Your Mendele is impossible," she once told her husband angrily. Rabbi Yitskhok stopped in the middle of the room, smiled good-naturedly, and calmly replied: "Very well, then, let us divide. In the world to come, I shall have Mendele and you—Dovidl. Agreed?" Grandmother Rokhel left her husband's room satisfied with this promise of the world to come. The Hasidim would say that Rabbi Yitskhok's kindness was hereditary. His father, an ordinary pious Jew, was known as Shimen the Merciful.

My great-grandfather Rabbi Mendel Vurker, the "Middle Vurker" as he was called in the hasidic world, was attractive—the tallest and most graceful figure among his tens of thousands of followers. On cold winter nights, my father used to stand for hours in front of the steaming tile stove in our dining room, listening to the various stories that his mother, my grandmother Goldele—sitting in her large, soft armchair—would tell about the Middle Vurker. In particular, my grandmother would relate stories about the rabbi's extraordinary neatness, which bordered on true elegance. Every Friday afternoon he would go for a ride in a carriage with two pairs of horses harnessed in tandem. His white socks were smeared with tallow candles to achieve the proper shine. His entire appearance and behavior were those of a great aristocratic personality. With special reverence, Grandmother Goldele would tell of the great friendship between the old Gerer rebbe (the author of *Hidushe ha-Rim*)[9] and the Middle Vurker. The Gerer rebbe passed away in the winter. In the Vurke court, they waited the entire Sabbath for news, anticipating the appearance of the first three stars so that they could send a messenger to Ger to find out the latest developments. Gloom enveloped the Vurke [household]. On that Sabbath afternoon, Rabbi Mendel locked himself in his room, admitting no one. The Hasidim were walking around the large court, saddened and orphaned. At twilight, suddenly the door opened; the Middle Vurker came out of the room and walked over to the window of the long room, stopped with his back to the people, and exclaimed: "Oh what a pity! And I thought that the two of us would bring the Messiah! It certainly would have been right: he the older rebbe, and I the younger." Mendel Vurke died at the age of forty-nine. The Hasidim recounted that he died of a superhuman longing for an unattainable goal—the coming of the Redeemer. According to Grandmother Goldele's pious description, her father-in-law was the embodiment of human perfection.

My grandfather, Simhah Bunem, the successor of the Middle Vurker, was not seen by his grandchildren until the day of his departure for Eretz Israel.[10] Based on everything I had heard at home, in my childish fantasy, I imagined a kind of mythological figure, dwelling in a tall tower in the middle of an ice palace, from which emissaries came out occasionally with various orders for his wife and children, all of his family, and the entire world. For years, my grandfather was separated from his wife and children. He had left the old Vurke court and moved to his villa, located in the middle of the thick Otwock woods extending for miles all the way to the Polish capital. He stayed there alone with his *shamosim*, intimates, and other Hasidim, until his departure. No "stranger," not even his wife and children, was allowed to cross the threshold of grandfather's villa without his special permission. When his disciples challenged him on this point asking, "What will the world say?" R. Simhah Bunem of Vurke exclaimed: "The world? Who is the world? *I* am the world!"

During World War I, when Polish Jews were standing in a queue to receive provisions, the old Vurke Hasidim in our house used to quip: "There is nothing new under the sun. [R. Simhah Bunem] of blessed memory had introduced the custom of waiting in line long before them." They would tell of hundreds of Hasidim who would come to grandfather's villa from all over Poland and on *yontef* evening after the services would stand in line for hours to greet the rebbe. The line extended through the long *shammes* room, through the large *beit midrash*, and far out across the yard outside. His youngest son, Dovidl, a lean, consumptive young man who was on *kest* at his in-laws, once came for *yontef*; immediately after *Maariv*, he went to greet his father. My grandfather, who had not seen his weak son for weeks, raised his long eyebrows to look at him, and exclaimed sternly: "There are Jews who are standing in line ahead of you." The weak Dovidl went back to wait for hours in the line to greet his father.

The two-story house in Grandfather's villa [compound] was subdivided into dairy and meat rooms, and Passover and *hametz* rooms. The *caftan* for meat meals was not worn for dairy meals. The "Gerer pranksters," as we used to call the Gerer Hasidim, would make fun of the fact that the rabbi of Vurke would wait six hours between studying the laws of eating meat and laws of dairy.[11] From the large, solitary villa, Grandfather would send couriers to his wife and children, who remained in the old court in Vurke. The couriers brought garments for the women, along with strict orders, which referred mainly to the women's clothing. A special tailor, who worked under grandfather's supervision, sewed them at the villa. These feminine garments consisted of black and red satin or silk coats: the black ones for adults, the red ones for children. No less grotesque was the headgear for the women, a kind of veil with gold and silver threads and finishing in a large brim, studded with precious stones and pearls. Such a veil

was valued at several hundred rubles. Grandfather would send the allowance for his wife and children through a special envoy, a close Hasid. Once he noticed that the latter put the money in his pocket without first counting it beforehand. He called him back immediately, took the money, and told him: "He who takes money without counting it is not a trustworthy messenger." He never again sent money to Vurke through this Hasid.

My grandfather's outlook and lifestyle undoubtedly had a lot to do with his constant physical suffering. He was born with a blemish: he had a clubfoot and later had to sit in a specially constructed chair, with his foot tightly clamped in braces that were supposed to straighten his crooked bones. The famous Polish-Jewish sculptor [Henryk] Kuna, a former devout Vurke Hasid, told a friend Moyshe Mandel from Lodz many years later that when he created his famous ascetic figure, it was the image of my grandfather that served as his model.

Chapter Three: Grandmother Goldele and Her Family

My grandmother Goldele, Rabbi Simhah Bunem's wife, was the antithesis of her husband. A fashion maven, she had a predilection for elegance and an innate sense of beauty. In her later years, when she was running our Otwock household, she would order her hats from a special milliner in Warsaw, in precise accordance with her own models. It often happened that the hats would be sent back and forth (from Warsaw to Otwock, from Otwock to Warsaw) if ribbons, pins, or brims were not exactly as she desired. She was, however, by nature spontaneous and extremely sensitive; she regarded everything that did not completely accord with her wishes and tastes as an insult to her honor. Whether her anger was justified or not, my father would always try to appease her. Grandmother was particularly restless and worried during the Days of Awe. She was preoccupied with begging God for a good year for her children, grandchildren, and the whole family, and she was also anxious about the High Holiday prayers. Grandmother was afraid lest, God forbid, she should fail to articulate the words of the prayer correctly; thus, every Sabbath and *yontef*, particularly on Rosh Hashanah and Yom Kippur, she would have a grandson stand next to her for hours in the *shammes* room, which served as the women's synagogue, and he would help her with the pronunciation. It often happened that she repeated her prayer "On Account of Our Sins" or "Let Us Relate the Power" until she felt that she had succeeded.

My grandmother Goldele was the daughter of a well-known Warsaw magnate, Elihu Hertz, a distinguished Vurke Hasid, a scholar who was completely divorced from worldly affairs. His extensive business, which was mismanaged by his administrators, left him bankrupt. Thereafter my great-grandfather devoted all his time to study, taking great delight in his endless peace in God's world. My [great]-grandmother Sorele, the wife of Elihu Hertz, was a small, plump woman who wore a tall hat [*kapki*, in Yiddish] and always sat quietly, neat and tidy, wrapped in a long, black shawl. She had a reputation of being very wise. She would often tell me, with much humor, that when her mother-in-law came to "view" her as a prospective bride for her son, she brought along a large, tangled ball of wool, asked her to untangle it, saying, "My child, you should know that one needs a lot of patience with a man, a lot of patience." Untangling the ball of wool was sort of an examination of the twelve-year-old bride's patience.

Prior to his gruesome bankruptcy, Reb Elihu Hertz still succeeded in making good matches for his daughters. The best was considered that of my grandmother Goldele, although it did not turn out well. My grandmother used to tell how one of grandfather's closest Hasidim once had the nerve to ask why he never divorced his wife — to which he responded calmly and pensively: "I would have

done it if I knew who would be the brother of my Mendele."

From childhood, my father Mendele was not only his firstborn, but his chosen son — a compensation for unfulfilled hopes and shattered dreams. However, because of my grandfather's merciless consistency, the relationship to his son, the quintessence of R. Bunem's emotional life, assumed strange forms and led to major strife in the family. When his son Mendele turned one, my grandfather sternly and categorically demanded that grandmother immediately wean the child from the wet nurse. His firstborn would not nurse more than absolutely necessary — namely, a year. In those days, when children would not be weaned until the age of two and older, my grandfather's order seemed like stubborn tyranny to his wife (a trembling Jewish mother who had waited for her firstborn for quite a while) along with those around her. My grandmother was frightened that the early weaning would harm the infant. She categorically refused to obey her husband's demand: "Under no circumstance could I reconcile myself to the child's early weaning," my grandmother used to say in a quivering voice about that strange incident. "On an early frosty morning, I woke up startled from my sleep. Near my bed stood the wet nurse who whispered amid sobs: "Rebbetzin, rebbetzin — the child, the child . . ." I leaped off of my bed and went to his room. "He, of blessed memory," my grandmother would continue, but with a mild smile to describe that moment, "sat at the table smoking his long-stemmed pipe and just said: 'I have sent away Mendele to be weaned.'"

My grandfather strictly forbade all members of the household to tell my grandmother the whereabouts of the child. She suspected an innkeeper in an adjacent village, an intimate of my grandfather, and immediately ran to that village in a housecoat and slippers. Upon arriving there, she found the door locked and the shutters down. She knocked violently on the door. The innkeeper appeared at the door, confused and frightened, and began to calm her: "Rebbetzin, be calm. The child is all right." But my grandmother would not budge from the door. Moved to pity, the innkeeper's wife opened a small porthole and held up an infant saying: "Here Rebbetzin, see the child is all right." My grandmother ended the extraordinary story sadly: "The child that she showed me through the window was not mine." And she whispered almost inaudibly, as if to herself, "That child, the child she showed me, did not survive the year."

In her latter years, grandmother apparently seeking to understand the discord between her and her husband, the renowned Vurker rebbe, would also talk of better times in her family life. A radical change in the relations between her and grandfather came later, after the death of their oldest daughter, Rokhele. "After Rokhele's death," my grandmother would say with sorrow, "he, of blessed memory, became an altogether different person." My grandfather loved Rokhele, his first and oldest daughter, exceptionally. Even when she was still an infant, she had to be present at his meals, which he usually had once a day, often late at night. According to my grandmother, Rokhele was the embodiment of everything perfect in the world. Through Rokhele, he forgot his physical suffering and his bitter disillusionment. Rokhele died when she was sixteen.

Despite the rift in my grandparents' family life, relations between their respective families always remained most cordial. Reb Elihu Hertz, the father-in-law, used to come for all the holidays to his son-in-law, the rebbe. He would sit at his table, had a separate room in the villa, and his own *shammes*, a *beit midrash* youth. My grandmother's older sister, Aunt Eydele, was sometimes even the mediator to resolve differences of opinion between her brother-in-law, the Vurker rebbe, and his wife. Aunt Eydele was the opposite of my grandmother: calm, relaxed, self-confident,

always with a smile on her lips. She was the brain of her house on Freta Street in Warsaw and raised her children with dignity, made decent matches for them, and had the respect of all. Her husband Reb Borekh Klepfish, a close relative of the famous Rabbi Klepfish, was a noble-minded and learned man, but was a stickler and flighty—as we used to describe him in my family. He was always rushing: he spoke rapidly, walked fast, and became angry quickly. When Aunt Eydele would tell him of a match for their grown-up daughters, proposing that he go and meet the future in-laws, Uncle Borekh would "nod" his long yellowish beard and mutter, "Nu, nu, enough Eydl. Leave me alone." After a while he would ask her: "So Eydl, where do you want me to go to meet the in-laws?" Aunt Eydele would smile and give him the address along with his holiday caftan.

Relations between grandfather's family and my grandmother were likewise good. My grandmother was especially cordial and loving to grandfather's sister Itele. She would often say that Itele was to her like her "real sister." Aunt Itele the Tsadekes [pious] as she was called in our family, was the opposite of her brother: humble, good-natured, and lovably helpless—with respect both to the outside world and to the incessant bickering between her strict and pedantic brother, the rebbe, and her proud and obstinate husband, Nekhamye of Vurke, as he was called in court. Reb Nekhamye of Vurke was cheerful, with a zest for life, but a great egoist; he was inordinately proud of himself and contemptuous of others. He had a great gift for music and would travel to Italy and visit La Scala [the opera house] in Milan. Upon returning [to Poland], he sang tunes from Italian operas at the Vurke rebbe's table. He regarded the Vurke court with a great deal of irony and mockery, and his attitude toward his brother-in-law, the young rebbe, was one of open scorn and contempt. He believed that only his "profane lineage"—not having descended from rebbes — prevented him from succeeding his father-in-law, the Middle Vurker. Nekhamye actually presided over his own hasidic *tish*; he had his own followers, whom he would regale with good, old wine from his own cellar. Nothing ever bridged the abyss between the contradictory natures of the two brothers-in-law, and for many years they remained angry with each other. Only shortly before his death, did Nekhamye agree to allow his brother-in-law, the rebbe, to pay him a visit in fulfillment of the commandment of visiting the sick. Reb Nekhamye's lifelong ambition was never realized: he did not bequeath to his generation his own hasidic dynasty.

Chapter Four: Rabbi Simhah Bunem of Vurke Departs for the Holy Land

News of my grandfather's extraordinary plan to leave everything and everyone in his large rebbe's court to go to Eretz Israel reached his wife and children shortly after the Russian Revolution of 1905 — on the day when my father's life was actually hanging by a thread. "It was a cold and snowy morning," my grandmother would begin describing that day in a trembling voice. Suddenly, we heard rifle shots and heart-rending screams. Everyone was running toward the shul, while Cossacks on high horses with whips in their hands were galloping through the town shouting wildly — the pounding of the horseshoes getting mixed with the wild shouts of the Cossacks. Some entered our house, ran up to my father, and yelled: "Where are the strikers?" Without waiting for an answer, the Cossaks went on to search the house. Precisely at that moment, Tsivye our cook, a tall, skinny, and constantly worried woman, whose husband was serving in the military while she served the rebbetzin in town, went down into the cellar — [whose entrance was] located right in the middle of the dining-room floor — to get a cord of firewood. Suddenly there was a big bang from a heavy object falling down, accompanied by a horrific cry: a young Cossack was lying in the

cellar. He had fallen right on Tsivye the cook. He grabbed her and dragged her out as if she were a herring. A terrified Tsivye was screaming: "Gevalt, save me! A Cossack!" Grandmother Goldele concluded her story: the Cossack spat three times and uttered a vulgar curse in his native Russian. The Cossacks took my father away to a small church, where the arrested priest of the town was already sitting.

Shocked by her husband's radical decision to depart for distant lands, this time my grandmother resolved to ignore his strict prohibition on entering his residence and traveled to Otwock. Grandfather's villa was always guarded by a Jewish watchman, who — following the rebbe's orders — refused to admit her. After pacing in front of the metal gate for several days, it was only by an extraordinary incident that she sneaked into the court. The watchman's daughter, a young girl about eighteen years old, had left her parents' house angrily and had not returned home in weeks. On the very day that the girl suddenly arrived in a droshky, the watchman, in his happy confusion, failed to notice my grandmother sneak in while he was opening the heavy, iron gate for his daughter. Realizing his mistake, however, he ran to block her way, grabbing her by the sleeve, and categorically ordered her to leave the premises immediately. Furious and insulted, my grandmother stood in the middle of the large court, looked sternly at the watchman, and with a loud voice cried: "Show respect, I am the rebbetzin!"

A short time after my grandmother's visit to the villa, an order arrived from my grandfather to come and take leave of him before he departed for Eretz Israel. For the first and last time his grandchildren saw their grandfather R. Simhah Bunem of Vurke. In the enormous, large hall with a ceiling of white beams and bare, whitewashed walls, surrounded by six high windows through which tall, snow-clad pines were visible, my grandfather sat in a colorful, red silk armchair: a tall lean figure with a high forehead, a black velvet skullcap on his head, a long graying beard, two large melancholy eyes, and a deathly pale complexion. Near him was a long light wooden table and two long benches, and around the bare walls — endless doors reaching to the ceiling and leading into the other rooms of the house. The only things that interrupted the extraordinary space were the huge copper chandeliers with eight branches hanging from the middle of the ceiling.

For quite a while, my mother and her two tiny daughters stood mute in my grandfather's hall, waiting to say farewell forever. Suddenly, the silence was broken by a subdued weeping. My mother pleaded plaintively to her father-in-law, the rebbe, that she be healed in order to raise her small children. Grandfather was silent for a long compassionate time. During the last farewell, he gave his grandchildren beige leather chamois purses with a ten-kopeck coin in each. One grandchild quickly stepped forward and reached out for the purse. But grandfather slowly moved back in his armchair, shook his head, and said: "Show respect, the older one comes first." Seeing that "the older one" was shyly standing to the side and with downcast eyes, he smiled, moved the skullcap on his head, and said quietly, as if to himself: "Oh, she is modest." The Vurke Hasidim would for years repeat what their rebbe had said of his grandchild.

On the day of his departure, the villa was surrounded by tens of thousands of his own and other Hasidim, and other Jews who had come from all over Poland to bid farewell to the Vurke rebbe. Suddenly thousands of voices shouted: "Be well, rebbe!" The mass of people who came to see him off surged forward, unhitched the horses, lifted the coach on their shoulders, and carried it all the way to the train station. The last whistle of the locomotive pierced the air and drowned out the desperate sobbing of an orphaned community of Jews.

R. Simhah Bunem began his journey to Palestine nineteen years earlier when he was still young and had small children. He then packed a crate of books, a little sack of money, and some household goods, and departed with his wife and children, leaving his oldest sixteen-year-old married son, my father, in his place. Grandfather and his family journeyed for weeks — by rail, ship, camel, and donkey until they finally arrived in Safed. At that time, the law of the Turkish government permitted a foreigner to stay in the Holy Land for no longer than three months, and grandfather was not allowed to remain. To avoid capture, he traveled through mountains, villages, and towns throughout Eretz Israel, bribed Turkish gendarmes, and expected friends to intervene on his behalf with Turkish authorities. Finally, he was arrested and incarcerated at the Acre prison. After several weeks of imprisonment, my grandfather and his family were deported back to Poland.

The reason for his first departure from his home, court, and Hasidim to Eretz Israel, according to my grandmother's narrative, is as follows: the Middle Vurker had died after nineteen years of being the rebbe; my grandfather viewed it as an insult to his father to "lead" for longer than he, and he left in order to create an interruption. The second, final journey to Eretz Israel after another nineteen years he made alone, disillusioned, solitary, a stranger to the world and kin. On the Sabbath before his departure, he proclaimed in the *beit midrash* before his group of Hasidim: "Jews, a fire is raging and no one sees it!"

Chapter Five: My Father
the Rebbe of Otwock

My father, the successor of Reb Simhah Bumen, bore the image of his grandfather, Reb Mendel Vurker, and was also named after him. He was one of the handsomest men that I have ever seen. Even in later years, when walking the streets, surrounded as usual by Hasidim and followers, Jewish and non-Jewish passers-by would admire him. He had a sense of beauty and delighted in beautiful things. The caftans that he wore at home, made mainly of green moiré silk, were always gleaming. Green was indeed his favorite color. When, following her engagement, his daughter embroidered a *tefillin* bag — a gift for her future husband — my father told her to use green velvet. "Green is a color that affords pleasure," he told her.

He was very cordial, radiating a personal charm, adored by both Hasidim and those who were not Hasidim. He was not just the rebbe and the leader, but also a devoted friend. I remember him once approaching the sink to wash his hands when a Hasid ran ahead of him to empty the bowl, which was already full of water. My father took him by the hand and asked him in an earnest tone: "Why you? Why not me?"

He ate his breakfast very late, quite often already in the evening; after the *shiur* [discourse] and many hours of prayer, he would immediately receive the people who used to come to him to seek advice, to request a favor or just to bring oneself to the rebbe's attention [*mazkir zayn*, in Yiddish],[12] and only then would he eat. In the difficult days of World War I, after we were already living in Warsaw, when everybody was suffering from hunger daily, my father would send half of his meals, which he only ate twice a day, to a poor Jew who stood at the gate of the house and made a "living" by selling matches.

In his early years, when he was still young, my father was the rabbi of the town of Maciejowice.[13] My father's tender spirit was greatly oppressed by the little town with its petty concerns and his large family with its concomitant worries. But he was most heavily weighed down by the tyranny and fanaticism of his father, my grandfather R. Simhah Bunem of Vurke. My father's dream from youth was independence — from the small town with its communal officers and from his strict father. He decided to learn Russian and to take the exam to become a state rabbi[14] in one of the district towns of Poland, with greater possi-

bilities for independence. This daring plan was kept in utmost secrecy, lest God forbid, grandfather Simhah Bunem should discover it. Late at night, my father would lock himself in the innermost rooms with Mordkhe the Teacher to study the rules of Russian grammar, and pacing with heavy steps around the long room, he would repeat every night the declensions of the noun *stol* [table]: *stol, stola, stolu*. Mordkhe the Teacher was a learned man, dressed in merchant garb, and with a trim beard; he subscribed to the Yiddish daily *Fraynd* and tutored boys and girls in prayers and writing.

It did not take long before grandfather learned that his firstborn, the rabbi of Maciejowice, was studying a gentile language, and preparing to become a state rabbi. One chilly morning, two emissaries appeared in our house with an order for my father to come at once to grandfather. I am not privy to the particular content of that conversation between father and son, but for a long time, they heard grandfather's harsh screams: "So you too disobey me. You too are siding with your mother!" The Russian grammar by Nemtsevich disappeared from our house, and with it my father's youthful dream of learning Russian and becoming a rabbi in a district town. After a while, father left Maciejowice and — with the consent and help of grandfather — became rabbi of Sobienie Jeziory [Sobin], a *shtetl* with more favorable financial prospects, that is, until these disappeared because of an incident that was partially characteristic of my father's nature. On a certain evening, a *din toyreh* took place in our house between two litigants from the town. Both sides were shouting, creating a racket, and insulting each other. Suddenly, one of them turned to my father and said: "Rabbi, he was boasting before the neighbors that my youngest daughter resembles him!" Trembling, my father was shocked; he strode with great intensity to the other litigant and cried: "Adulterer!" A frightening silence fell upon the courtroom chamber, pierced by the bitter wailing of the offended litigant standing in the corner. Pale as a sheet, father quickly turned around, looked about as if in search of help, and hastily left the room. It was already late at night that my father was still standing before that litigant, begging him for forgiveness. From then on, he resolved never to adjudicate cases alone; at his own expense, he hired a *moreh hora'ah* [judge] out of his meager income as the rabbi of Sobin.

Several days after grandfather's second and final departure for Eretz Israel, Hasidim entered our house, drank ninety-proof alcohol [*spirt*, in Russian], danced in a ring, and cheerfully toasted father: "*L'chaim*, Rebbe!" With singing and dancing, the town of Sobin (where my father had been rabbi for a brief period) saw our two carts off—one carrying men, the other women—to our new house in grandfather's villa [compound] in Otwock. Several Hasidim, close disciples, and *tishzitsers*, who all these years sided more with grandmother than grandfather, went to father's bedroom with a saw, and while toasting, cut off the four high poles of my father's canopy bed. This symbolized the first departure from the view and way of life of my grandfather, the "Rebbe of Eretz Israel" as he was subsequently called. Keeping the canopy bed was one of my grandfather's strictest orders to his children.

In the many chambers of grandfather's villa in the large Otwock woods, they began to hammer, saw, plane, polish, expand, renovate, redesign, and build in various fixtures in every room. Throughout the subsequent years, all sorts of craftsmen would come and go, creating the cleverest changes to the design and structure of grandfather's two-story building with all of its annexes. Everything was done in accordance with father's plans and intentions. The painters and masons worked especially long and diligently on rebuilding and decorating our villa's great *beit midrash* with all kinds of artwork—for instance, a big *shi-visi* plaque on the eastern wall with two large lions that almost looked alive, gazing in all directions. At the time, it was rare for a hasidic rebbe's *beit midrash* in Poland to have such artistic decorations. Many of the older Hasidim began grumbling at the young rebbe's sharp break with the ascetic ways of his father. Heading this opposition was my oldest brother Yitskhok, whose "different [disposition]" from his father in his youth took pronounced forms, especially with regard to matters of the court lifestyle.

My brother considered the court a bastion of tradition, which one must strengthen and protect. During the engagement of his eldest sister to a member of another prominent rebbe's family from Poland, he demanded of the groom's wealthy father that, after the wedding, the young man stop visiting the "other" rebbe—a stipulation that almost ruined the match between the Otwock hasidic court and the aristocratic follower of a different rebbe. The groom's father, who was a wise, learned, and sensitive person, refused to accept the idea that his son, the "prodigy," would not be sitting as usual on Saturdays and *yontef* at the *tish* of his rebbe, a close relative. However, since the match with the Otwock court and mainly the bride greatly appealed to the mother-in-law, the two sides reached a compromise on the young man's future participation in the hasidic ceremonial gathering [*praven*, in Yiddish]: he would go to his own rebbe on the Sabbath, but remain at his father-in-law's Otwock [court] for the holidays.

The mother-in-law, herself from a prominent lineage that included Yoynesn Eybeshitz,[15] was a beautiful and elegant woman, known for her erudition. In her youth she had read works by Goethe and Schiller, and was very tasteful, but also somewhat conceited about herself, her beautiful family, and her big hasidic house on a wealthy estate, and especially her fair daughters and scholarly sons. For the "viewing of the bride" [*kalleh zeyekhts*, in Yiddish], she brought along special mavens, her recently married daughter and a young daughter-in-law—an elegant, cheerful, and wealthy young hasidic wife from Warsaw. The young daughter-in-law immediately tried to strike up a conversation with the fifteen-year-old rabbinic bride about the works of Gabriella Zapolska, the famous Polish author of spicy romances.

After the wedding, the young son-in-law, despite the agreement, packed up his *kapote* and *shtremil* and went to spend the holidays with *his* rebbe; when my brother learned of this, he opened the door of his sister's room, and standing on the threshold, shouted with great conviction: "Divorce him, divorce him immediately!" My father, seeking to end this unpleasant incident at his court, smiled good-naturedly, and said, addressing himself to Moyshl the Shammes, "Nu, nu, Moyshe. It is better to have a Hasid of a different rebbe than no Hasid at all."

Of the three *shamosim* at our court, Moyshl was the most efficient and my father's right-hand man. He was a learned man and in his youth had the reputation of a "prodigy." He already served as a *shammes* of my grandfather Simhah Bunem and later remained with my father. At our court, Moyshl was the "educated one": he wrote addresses in Polish and read telegrams sent by Hasidim in times of trouble or joy, as for example: "In need of mercy," "Pray for a complete recovery," or "She gave birth to a son." He was a very dear person, always smiling and often joking a lot, and remained forever young. Moyshl the Shammes was the first to present his rebbe's daughter with a book: the Bible with [Moses] Mendelssohn's commentary.[16] Even though Moyshl was persuaded that Mendelssohn had been a heretic [*apikores*, in Yiddish], he forgave the latter's heresy on account of his keen mind.

Our second *shammes*, Moyshe Tuvye Kalushiner, was the opposite of Moyshl—gloomy and reticent. As we used to say, when he did speak, he was terse, stern, and to the point.

He was a clever person with a pair of piercing gray eyes that saw and understood much and were seldom forgiving. He was the only person at our house who supported the Russians against the Germans in World War I, arguing that the Germans were Amalek, and if Amalek were to rise, Israel would fall. The womenfolk in our house did not particularly care for Moyshe-Tuvye, but his wife Khaye-Sore, "the Modest" as she was called in Otwock, worshipped him. Her mission in life consisted of two tasks: ensuring her husband's perfection and fulfillment of her rebbe's promise that she would be "helped" [by divine intervention]. Although she remained childless, to the very end she never ceased to believe in the rebbe's promise.

The third *shammes* at our court was Mendel Lodzher, a man of a totally different cut. He was the warm, down-to-earth type, and a great schmoozer, with a hidden sadness in his eyes. He was a man with many worries, a lot of children, and a great zest for life—the very opposite of his "ephemeral" wife, Khane. Khane was a quiet, refined, and weak woman who ate little, groaned a lot, and worried constantly. She was very afraid of thunder, but accepted it with love since she heard someone say that during thunder cucumbers would fall from the sky. Mendel the *shammes*, who was a stranger to his own family, used to spend most of his time at the house of his rebbe, telling all sorts of interesting stories and occasionally singing in his beautiful baritone. His talents were later inherited by his two sons, Zishe and Pinkhes Katz. One became a talented actor on the Yiddish stage, and the other a well-known journalist, a contributor to Yiddish humor magazines in Warsaw. Both were tragically murdered in Hitler's Holocaust.

Our *shamosim* were mainly engaged in matters related to the functioning of the court—my father's rabbinic and personal tasks. Matters pertaining to the family and the household were managed by two loyal family friends: Khaim Moyshe, the *melamed*, and Berish Kohen. Khaim Moyshe was a *besmedresh-zitser*—always studying in the synagogue with the *bokherim*. He was an austere and serious man whose refined, pale face rarely showed a smile, and he kept to himself. Quietly, so no one would notice, he watched my father's every step and paid attention to his every word, writing down every word of "Torah" that my father delivered to his Hasidim at the rebbe's *tish* on Sabbaths and holidays. Berish Kohen was an entirely different kind of man. His fresh ruddy face was always lit up with a good-natured smile. He let his wife worry about making a living, while he himself would sit in our house, often in the "women's section," engaged in friendly chats with members of his rebbe's family. He would also accompany us on our various shopping trips to the capital. He was privy to all the domestic matters and was always prepared to take the trouble for the sake of his rebbe or rebbe's children.

In the midst of this hubbub in the new rebbe's court life (the *beit midrash*, Hasidim, intimates, family), my father, the new rebbe, suddenly spun a new dream—a dream of peace and harmony, to establish a small farm, his own field with vegetables. He was especially concerned with the good health of his tenderly protected children: he wanted them to drink fresh milk, straight from the cow, and to eat the freshest eggs. Soon afterward, a barn was built, then a chicken coop; soon a large fat cow, a white goat, and a large number of fowl began promenading around the rebbe's courtyard; it was the beginning of the farm of peace and tranquility. At the head of this farm, father appointed one of the younger members of our synagogue, Reb Alter's Pinkhesl—a young, slight, snub-nosed fellow with round shoulders but with a cheerful smile ever on his face. Pinkhesl spent his entire youth at our court, together with his aging father, Alter, one of the first Vurke Hasidim. After his wife's death, Alter packed his *tallis* and *tefillin*, took his only son by the hand,

and went to his rebbe in Otwock, where he remained in an attic room of our villa to the end of his days. Pinkhesl was a joyful person; he had a fear of God and loved his rebbe, his rebbe's children, and all the living creatures in God's world. Our court was Pinkhasl's world, our house his home. On the day of the rebbe's daughter's wedding, he came running out of breath, and gave the bride a *kvitel*, requesting her blessing.[17]

But less than a year after our arrival at grandfather's villa, on a rainy autumn day, 12 Heshvan 5667 [1907], my mother died at the age of thirty-two, leaving five young children. In those preceding heavy and sad days, when my mother would lie quietly and pensively in the hammock in the dense pine forest at the villa, my father would often be standing next to her, arguing that "a mortal danger takes precedence on the Sabbath." Only then did she agree to taste some of the special meat cutlets that doctors had prescribed her as a remedy against her grave illness. My mother was my father's second wife. His first wife was the daughter of the rabbi of Radomsk (the author of *Hesed le-Avraham*), who died in childbirth with her firstborn child, shortly after grandfather's journey to Eretz Yisrael. Many years later, when father already had married children, I heard him say to an intimate of his: "Radomsk? That was the only happy year in my life."

As opposed to the ascetic life in the Vurke court, life in Radomsk was under the "female domination" of the rebbetzin. In contrast to my grandfather's austerity and despotism, my father encountered the joy of life and practical wisdom at Radomsk. My grandfather's orders of how to structure his eldest son's daily existence while he was supported by *kest* at his father-in-law's court—impinged on the son's self-assurance and independence of the Radomsk rebbetzin. At the time of my father's engagement, my grandfather stipulated that after the wedding the young couple must accompany him on a trip to Eretz Israel. But when his daughter-in-law's mother categorically refused to let her pregnant daughter undertake the long journey, my grandfather pointed to the palm of his hand and exclaimed: "Sooner will hair grow here than she will remain my daughter-in-law." The young daughter-in-law died in childbirth a year after her wedding. My father, not fully seventeen, lapsed into a deep depression. His father-in-law, the Hesed le-Avraham mourning over his oldest daughter, exclaimed: "Losing this son-in-law is just like losing my daughter." My grandfather declared that he would no longer marry his children into rabbinic courts, but only to the daughters of his own Hasidim, who would undoubtedly obey him in everything.

Chapter Six: After Grandfather's Death

Several months after mother's death came the news of my grandfather's death in Tiberias. He had lived in Palestine for only one year in simplicity and isolation, and no longer allowed others to address him as "rebbe." His only companions were a few old Hasidim, including an elderly man from Vurke, who had traveled with him and remained near him until his last minute. On the second of Shevat 5667 [17 January 1907], he breathed his last at the age of fifty-seven, seated in his chair, and wrapped in his *tallis* and *tefillin*. During his first visit he had selected his grave—in Tiberias, next to Rabbi Menachem Mendel of Vitebsk.[18] The sudden death of Grandfather brought a radical change in my father's mood. He mourned his father's death deeply and was filled with sorrow. Deep in his heart, his earlier opposition to his father's worldview started to mellow, and a new plan began to form in his mind: travel to the Land of Israel in order to visit his father's grave.

My father's third wife hailed from the small Polish town of Przedborz. She came from a family of modest means but distinguished lineage, which included members of the Raspsher, Kuzmer, and Medzhbizher families, whose *yikhus* extended all the way to the Yid ha-kodesh.[19] When I first saw my stepmother, who at the time was nineteen or twenty years old, I was frightened by her long and thin figure, and felt like telling her to be careful to avoid breaking apart. She was probably frightened as well—frightened of the big court, the small stepchildren, the numerous children, the many rooms—and she suddenly burst out in a loud laugh. In our house, no one laughed loudly like that. My stepmother brought into our house her old widowed mother, a thin, small, quick woman with a "man's head," as the Raspsher hasidim used to say about her. She hoped that all her ambitions that had failed and dreams that had vanished would now be realized in her youngest daughter, Yokhevedl, who had married into the famous Vurke court. Later on, I would frequently find my young stepmother sitting on the sofa and weeping—probably over the loneliness in her own house, burdened with a mother-in-law, stepchildren, relatives, Hasidim, and a cumbersome retinue, and over the abyss between her and her husband with his complex personality. She had undoubtedly envisioned things differently.

My father's dream of peace and contentment soon proved illusory. Discord arose between my stepmother and her mother-in-law, my grandmother Goldele, and wrangling over the estate erupted among my father and his three younger brothers. My father always found himself helpless against the conflicts raging between his beloved mother and his young wife. My grandmother, or chief housekeeper ever since my mother had died, managed our household on a grand scale. The villa became home to the entire extended family, from both my father and mother's sides. The house was always teeming with relatives—close and distant—especially in the summer months, when they would come to "our dacha."[20]

All of our "dacha guests" observed their specific diets, according to the recommendations of their particular physicians. One aunt from my grandmother's side was especially strict about her "egg diet": twice a day she ate two soft-boiled eggs, and, at every meal, in the interval between eating the first and the second egg, she would murmur to herself quietly: "Hmmm, two eggs? The doctor told me that two eggs equal half a pound of meat." And with a little silver spoon, she would zestfully scoop out the soft yoke from the eggshell. Our court was also full of younger "dacha guests." Most of them were young marriageable girls, suspected of deviating in some way from the traditional path of their parents. The parents would often send their daughters to our villa for the winter months as well, hoping that the court's holy atmosphere would have a favorable influence on their children.

We once almost had a serious family conflict over Ester Hertz, the daughter of my grandmother's brother, a smart and energetic girl. Ester had finished a Froebelian school [*fribel shul*], was well read in Yiddish literature and acquainted with Jewish artists, and had always aspired to enter the big world. Yet her extraordinary and limitless love for her frail, intelligent, and noble mother destroyed all of Ester's youthful dreams. Her every plan of leaving home was ruined by her constant worry: "And what will become of my mother?" In the wake of the October Revolution, Ester left for Russia without so much as a goodbye and worked there as a teacher, hoping until her last day for a chance to see her mother again.

Ester Hertz was the first to bring Yiddish newspapers and books secretly into our house. She told us about the Yiddish theater, about the concerts of Shneur's chorus at Hazamir in Warsaw, and about Poalei Zion on Karmelicka Street. My father quickly found out about it, became gravely concerned about the influence Ester might have on his children, and in the strictest terms ordered us not to spend any more time with her. Instead, he bought us editions of the *Chimushim* [Pentateuch]

with a Yiddish translation—the ones published by "Beys Yehuda." Every Friday night he would examine his little daughter on that week's Torah portion and would be proud of her "smart little head," as he would put it. He also allowed his youngest and most beloved son to study the *Tanya*.[21] Father hoped that the Yiddish version of the Bible along with the religious philosophy of Habad would serve in his house as a bulwark against the new tides of the outside world.

In this comfortable atmosphere at the court, my grandmother Goldele felt at home for the first time in her life. Yet after my stepmother's arrival, she sensed that the house was slipping out of her control and coming under the authority of her young daughter-in-law. Both of them—my grandmother in her long-held bitterness and my stepmother in her unrestrained [manner] and inexperience—made life bitter in our house.

In his inheritance battle with his brothers, my father was uncompromising and stood his ground firmly, demanding that my uncles recognize his right to a double portion of the inheritance as the firstborn son as well as their sister's right to a part of the estate. My father fully supported my aunt Tsivyele, asking for an equal portion for her, and finally demanded a *beit din* to resolve the matter. From her earliest years, my aunt Tsivyele found in her oldest brother a loyal protector. She hardly knew her father. Her childhood years were hard and joyless. Nothing was permitted in her father's house—playing with other children, romping in the woods, climbing the tall fence that surrounded and isolated the estate from the world. Once panic ensued in my grandfather's court from a prank played by Tsivyele. Disregarding her father's strong injunction, she climbed over the fence. When she was brought back, R. Simhah Bunem of Vurke exclaimed: "Praised be the Lord for giving me only one daughter."

Tsivyele was tall and slender, and had large black eyes, whose sadness would not depart even amid the heartiest laughter. And my aunt Tsivyele laughed very frequently, quietly, and heartily. R. Simhah Bunem married off his only daughter at the age of fifteen. Her husband, two years her junior, Isheyele the Prodigy, the son of the rabbi of Solec, was puny and looked like a child of eight. Under the canopy, he reached up to the bride's waist. [. . .] Hasidim from all over Poland came to the wedding of the only daughter in the Vurke court. The guests had to be attired according to grandfather's instructions: women in coifs, not wigs; the men in soft, unstarched shirts, large velvet skullcaps, with black silk sashes around their waists. The dining tables were set outdoors, in the middle of the wood. The bridegroom was led to the wedding canopy over the set tables, for fear of being crushed by the huge mass of people.

Tsivyele did not experience happiness in her family life. Her first two children were born prematurely and died. Shortly afterward she left her fifteen-year-old husband and returned to her mother in Vurke. My grandmother Goldele never liked her only son-in-law; rarely did she ever speak a word to him. She blamed him for all the tragedies that befell her daughter's life. Tsivyele later returned to her husband and became a God-fearing mother of several, healthy, good-looking children, frequently praying to the Master of the Universe that she should deserve to have "a household full of children" and a bag full of money for them. Ishayele the Prodigy, who later became a prominent rabbi in the town of Bialy Brzeg, was knowledgeable both in Jewish and in worldly matters and had the following psychological quirk: he never looked anyone straight in the eye. While talking to someone, male or female, my uncle's eyes were always turned down and half-closed. In his later years — probably as a way to flee from himself — he became an Uman Hasid, a follower of the "dead rebbe" Rabbi Nahman of Bratslav, at whose grave Hasidim would gather and study all day, dance all night, and drink brandy. My Uncle Ishayele, his wife, and their three beautiful children perished in one day at the hands of Nazi murderers.

Chapter Seven: From Otwock to Wyszków and Back

Awaiting the decision in his inheritance case, my father and his family left the villa for Wyszków. This was one of the more progressive towns in Poland at the time: it had schools, cinemas, dancing halls, and even a few assimilationists. The Wyszków Hasidim received my father with great honor, proud of having the privilege of entertaining a rebbe in their town for the first time. It was in Wyszków that the strange incident of an open desecration of the Sabbath occurred in our house. According to the old Vurke tradition, Sabbath and holiday meals would begin very late in our family. All the people in the house, and especially our cooks, would retire to their rooms immediately after lighting the candles and take rest after the hard work of preparing for the Sabbath, which would begin as early as Thursday night with the baking of hallahs and cakes, koshering poultry, cooking fish, preparing the cholent, filling the Sabbath teakettle, and various other preparations for the meal for the entire family and the large number of Hasidim, who would come to visit their rebbe.

It often happened that my uncle would be standing with a glass of wine in his hand, surrounded by a large group of men, waiting until the very last woman, following her Sabbath eve nap, would join the rest behind the door of the big *shammes* room to hear the *kiddush*. On one such Friday night an odd thing happened. One chief cook — a big, healthy, plump woman — suddenly fainted, and was lying with unmoving eyes, groaning heavily. The entire household, along with the neighbors, came running to her, trying to resuscitate her by yelling, calling, and pouring ice-cold water on her, but none of these or any other method had the slightest effect. She lay unconscious and motionless. Someone ran to call a doctor.

When the town doctor, an elegant young man with golden spectacles on his nose and glossy black hair parted in a straight line, entered our house on Friday night right before *kiddush*, our hasidic boys and young men gathered in a corner and began to whisper. The doctor looked around, ordered the windows to be opened, and demanded that a special medicine be delivered immediately. The Hasidim were in shock, looking helplessly at one another, as if petrified. My father, however, quickly went to the money cabinet and told me in a serious and confident tone: "Remember, a mortal danger supersedes the Sabbath." He ordered that the medicine be immediately delivered from the gentile pharmacy.

Our servants were essentially an integral part of our hasidic court, and they always maintained good relations with the children. We would share with them our childish "issues" and worries, and they with us their own problems and concerns. Especially faithful and devoted to the children was our cook, Zisl Przytyker, "the Half-Deserted Wife" [*Di halbe aguneh*, in Yiddish], as she used to be called. Soon after her wedding, Zisl separated from her husband and stayed with us for many years. Her responsibility was to take care of the children's eating. Zisl would stand behind the door of the *shammes* room and lament loudly for my father to hear that "the children don't eat." Her loyalty often resulted in comical situations. Once on a wintry Thursday night, when our cooks and various helpers had already completed all the Sabbath eve preparations, and the clock had struck two, I awoke and saw Zisl sitting next to me with a big, hot meat patty on a plate. "Take it, eat something," she pleaded with me, "you haven't eaten anything today." When, the following day, others tried to make fun of her, Zisl looked at them with a virtuous expression in her eyes and exclaimed: "You people

laugh! But do you know how many heavens the rebbe searched through till he found *this* girl's soul?!"

After the *beit din* confirmed my father's special inheritance rights as the firstborn son, he immediately gave them up, but on condition that Aunt Tsivyele's right to inherit part of the estate be recognized. After that we left Wyszków and returned to grandfather's villa in Otwock.

In addition to the two-story building in the middle of the woods in which we lived, grandfather's villa [compound] included several other smaller houses. Father immediately designated one house for his youngest brother, the sickly Dovidl. Uncle Dovidl's illness had threatened his life for a long time and weighed down the spirits of the entire family. Grandmother hoped that the galipot of the Otwock pine trees would heal the cavern in her youngest son's lung. But shortly after moving to our villa, Uncle Dovidl died at the age of twenty-nine, survived by a young widow and four orphans. Shortly before he gave up his spirit, he called my father and told him: "If God grants me to live, I promise that from now on, I will eat early and pray early." Uncle Dovidl used to sit wrapped in his *tallis* and *tefillin* and pray until late afternoon, sometimes until evening, despite the complaints of his dear wife, and in spite of the official permission from his brother, the rebbe, "to taste something" before praying. His final words were indeed, "to pray early and to eat early."

Uncle Dovidl's wife, Aunt Gele, was the daughter of Moyshe Tevye of Stanislow—not a particularly learned man, but a great benefactor, and one of the most devoted Vurke Hasidim. Moyshe Tevye was a huge man—tall and wide, with a disheveled yellowish beard, and a black velvet skullcap on top of a giant head—and he always commanded fear and respect. When he appeared on the streets of Stanislow[22] Jews and non-Jews alike would remain standing in awe, while one of his intimates ran in front, waving his hands and shouting: "Women, Moyshe Tevye is coming!" This was a warning to all women to step aside and make room. Aunt Gele would recount various funny incidents involving her father with great wit. Every Friday after lighting the candles, when everything in the house was prepared for the arrival of the "Sabbath Queen" (swept, clean, with the silver candlesticks standing atop the white tablecloth), Moyshe Tevye would enter the kitchen with a loud "*Gut shabbes*!" splash a bottle of scented water onto the floor and exclaim: "What a pleasure! The smell of *shabbes*!"

My grandfather Simhah Bunem of Vurke arranged for his two youngest sons, Uncle Moyshele and Uncle Dovidl, to be engaged to Moyshe Tevye's two beautiful and cheerful daughters, Royze and Gele. He was certain that the two girls, who were neither daughters of a "different" rebbe, nor of a wealthy man, but from the family of one of his own faithful Hasidim would always obey him in everything. After Uncle Dovidl's death, my aunt Gele suppressed her widow's sorrow deep in her heart and began building her life anew; she opened a dry-goods store in downtown Otwock,[23] raised her children in the tradition of a rebbe's family, and was very prominent and respected in town. Merchants considered it both a duty and a pleasure to do business with "Rebbetzin Gelele," as she as called—who was capable of resolving the most difficult business problems with a clever word and sweet laughter. Her youthful dream of becoming a true rebbetzin was realized only many years later, after she had married off her children but was still relatively young. She married the Kromolow rebbe, Nosn-Nokhem Rabinovitch from the town of Zawiercie, and became the mistress of a big, beautiful house, where she was beloved both by her stepchildren and the Hasidim— until they were all murdered by the Nazis.

My father's second brother, my oldest uncle Yisroel-Yitshkok, went to Vurke in order to prepare to revitalize the old, neglected Vurke court and to become the rebbe. However, one year later he died in the town of Piaseczna, leaving a young widow and three children by his first wife, Rivele, who had died young. This first wife was the beautiful daughter of a Lodz magnate, a woman of good taste and keen sense of humor, which frequently helped her dodge the severe injunctions of her father-in-law. They were mainly concerned with her manner of dress. The garments she received from the Vurke court she wore only in the circle of her husband's family and Hasidim. In her father's house in Lodz, she would exchange the veil for a modern bonnet and the housecoat for a beautiful, modern dress. Soon R. Simhah Bunem learned of the strategies of his daughter-in-law, and placed her under the supervision of his intimate, Leybush Turker, the precentor in the Vurke court on the High Holidays. He was a clever and jovial man, who often indulged in ridiculing the hasidic courts, including his own. He would notify my aunt of his official visit to Lodz. She took the hint, and upon his arrival, would be dressed in accordance with her father's-in-law instructions. A favorable report would then reach the Vurke court.

After the early death of my aunt Rivele, my uncle wanted to marry her younger sister Tsivye. He had loved his first wife dearly and wished to maintain a connection to her family. Besides, he hoped that his sister-in-law would make a good stepmother to her sister's children. My grandfather opposed the match, arguing that the second wife would also disobey him. My grandmother Goldele sided with her son. To all the pleas of the Hasidim and intimates, my grandfather would turn a deaf ear, adding: "I am, praised be the Lord, obstinate." After the death of my grandfather, my uncle married his sister-in-law, Tsivye. Their happiness was short-lived. Two years later, my uncle (in his early thirties at the time) died. The young widow went back to her father's house in Lodz, and the three orphans came to live with us. My father's first order was that under no circumstance was there to be any difference between his own and his deceased brother's children. Above all, he assigned close surveillance over the attitude of my oldest brother, Yitskhok, to his oldest cousin Mendele. The contrast between the two cousins was enormous: Mendele was a sickly boy, kind, humble, and full of pity for the whole world. My brother Yitskhok was egotistical, primitive, smug, and secure.

After the engagement of my brother Yitskhok to a girl of a hasidic court in Aleksander, my father sent a special emissary to the same court to arrange a match for his nephew. Great care was taken to see that no distinction be made in the preparations for the weddings of the two grooms, or in their bridal gifts.

Chapter Eight: The Wedding in the Aleksander Court

My brother's wedding was Father's first joyous moment since those long past but never forgotten days of his youth in Radomsk. It was a wedding on a grand scale and in splendid form, in stark contrast to the ascetic tradition of the Vurke court. For weeks, the house was teeming with people: caterers, cooks, bakers, waiters, neighbors, and ordinary women making preparations for the first great festivity in the Vurke court. The pantries, balconies, and anterooms were jammed with sacks of flour, cartons of sugar, baskets of eggs, tubs of butter, bags of almonds and raisins, and various assortments of fruit to be taken for the wedding in Aleksander, and for the following Seven Days of Festivity.

Especially festive and substantial was the "meal of the poor" [*orem moltsayt*, in Yiddish] for all the destitute in and around the town. Father personally took part in the two preparations for this feast and made sure that the big, long tables, arranged so as to form the Hebrew word *chai* [life] were placed in two separate rooms (one for men, one for women); they were covered with new white tablecloths, and had burning candles in silver candlesticks

and chandeliers, as well as large amounts of wine. "It should not be just for show," he kept reminding us and ordered us to put on our festive attire and join the poor women at the tables. He sat at the head of the table together with the groom, surrounded by the poor, and led the feast for hours, with the best food and drink. After the meal, the groom distributed money to the poor and joined them in a hasidic dance.

Excitement ran high especially among the women in the family on each day of the celebration: they were caught up in a maelstrom of seamstresses, milliners, and hosiers. The passion for clothing and the desire of ostentation broke through in full force as a reaction to the austerity of R. Simhah Bunem's court. For months, female processions wended their way from the rebbe's court to the most exclusive tailoring salons in Warsaw for wedding apparel, travel apparel, morning-after apparel, dresses for the Seven Days of Festivity, and ordinary dresses for aunts, cousins, marriageable girls, and small fry. These garments, of the finest silk, velvet, wool, and tulle, were made under the direction of my grandmother Goldele, one of the greatest mavens in matters of female fashion.

This female activity resulted in many curiosities. Our chief tailor, Madame Keller from Twarda Street, was notorious for always being tardy — a trait that caused many inconveniences to her customers. Throughout many years of tailoring, she was never able to finish a dress by the deadline, and her store often became the site of rows and altercations. Young brides would get cramps, future mothers-in-law would faint and cry, and all would be waiting forever for the dresses they had ordered. Madame Keller, more of an artist than a tailor, remained fully composed, as if she had nothing to do with it, and would remark serenely: "It's not ready yet," causing her customers to sink deeper into despair.

With the time of my brother's wedding approaching and not a single dress ready, my grandmother grew alarmed. After long consultations, we all decided to go to Warsaw and not leave Madame Keller's store until our dresses were finished. And we did precisely that: grandmother, Aunt Tsivyele, my cousins, the brides, and the younger children all went to Madame Keller's and stayed there all night, measuring, trying on, and measuring again the endless dresses. Before the last locomotive whistle of the chartered train, a panting Madame Keller arrived at the station in a cab laden with valises, boxes, trunks, and bags—the wedding garments for the family. There also came Hasidim, intimates, and wellwishers with bottles of brandy. They drank to the health of the bride and groom and began a hasidic dance at the Vienna Station in Warsaw.

When my tall, brunette, and stately Aunt Tsiyvele entered the wedding hall of the Aleksander court in her lemon-yellow satin dress, embroidered with blue velvet flowers, with a long train, a hush fell over the hundreds of women. But soon a malicious murmur arose: such a dress was better suited for an actress than a Vurke rebbe's daughter, and only such a short time after his departure. Under hasidic pressures and possibly even frightened by the drastic change in court, the next morning my father pleaded with his sister to put aside the "actress" dress, and out of great love and devotion to her brother my aunt yielded. For years that dress was hanging in my aunt's closet, sewn up in a white sheet. Years later, when the incident with the "actress dress" had been completely forgotten, my aunt was invited to a procession of leading the bride—the daughter of Rabbi Zilbershteyn of Vurke—to the synagogue. She went over to the closet to put on that dress and stopped perplexed. The dress was sewn up in the sheet—and it was the Sabbath. Never again did my aunt wear that dress.

Aunt Tsivyele was an excellent housekeeper [*goldene baleboste*, in Yiddish]: her clothes were always meticulous and her wardrobe was like an exhibit. After every washing, she would carefully inspect each article of clothing to make sure that not a single spot remained, and if she found even the slightest imperfection, she would tell grandmother in an angry tone: "If I only knew Polish." This meant that had she only known Polish, she would have had it out with the laundress. The laundress, an old gentile woman employed at grandmother's house, would understand what Aunt Tsivyele meant and would quickly leave the room, giggling.

My brother's wife, Malkele, was an extremely attractive woman: medium height, slender, two large sky-blue eyes on an alabaster white face, with a head of golden blond locks. She was the most accomplished woman in the Aleksander court and inordinately proud of the fact that her husband was considered by the Hasidim to be the image of R. Simhah Bunem in character and appearance. Her mother, the oldest sister of the Aleksander rabbi (author of *Yismah Yisrael*) and called Shevele Cossack by the Hasidim, was the administrator of the entire court, the advisor of her brother, and the manager of her large hosiery mill. She was a prominent woman in the hasidic world of the time. With motherly pride and courtly self-assurance, she would frequently describe how the wealthy merchants of Russia used to plead with her for the hand of Malkele, offering their large fortunes. My brother and his bride saw each other for the first time under the wedding canopy. They remained the happiest couple, in love to their last day.

Chapter Nine: In the Days of World War I
That Friday afternoon, the first day of World War I, our house was filled with people: old mothers, young women, and frightened little children were packed at the door to my father's room, crying bitterly and begging the rebbe to promise that their sons, husbands, and fathers would safely return from the war. Father stood by the window, looked at the

thick woods, and silently wiped tears with his big handkerchief.

The war lasted longer than had been anticipated. The Jews gradually began to leave their well-established homes and flock to Warsaw in the hope of finding greater security and protection, both from the general threat of hunger and from the specific threats affecting the Jews — pogroms and persecution.

My father fought stubbornly the idea of leaving grandfather's villa, the home of generations with the large stacks of holy books accumulated over many decades. He grew more serious, pensive, and melancholy. The waves of pogroms, the slaughter of entire Jewish communities in Russia and Poland, the streams of refugees driven out of cities and towns, and lastly, the news of the horrible death of Fayvele, the oldest son of R. Shmuel Hersh of Aleksander (hanged by tsarist soldiers in Radomsk) broke my father's resistance. The last straw came when Cossacks entered our synagogue, searched for arms in the Holy Ark, and confidently declared that, "the rabbi is a German spy." The following day, the doors and windows of our large house in Otwock were boarded up, the large silver utensils were buried in the woods, and the entire family left for Warsaw. My father was destined never to come back.

One of my father's faithful Hasidim, Yosl Rozenblat, let us use his six-room apartment on Grzibow Street, where we stayed for a long time until we had a suitable apartment of our own. After the war, when Yosl Rozenblat returned from the Soviet Russia, whither he had fled, and went to see his rebbe's children, he exclaimed: "I am coming back from Russia, but the true world revolution is right here!"

The complicated character of my father and even more complicated conditions of life deepened the split in his personality — in contrast to the steely intransigence and consistency of his father. When new winds began to blow in the Jewish Pale [of Settlement] in the years just before World War I and penetrated our court (the citadel of hasidic piety), and when the inescapable conflict between generations began to cast its shadow over his children, my father became terribly frightened. He would often recall my grandfather's words before he journeyed to Eretz Israel: "A fire is raging and no one is aware of it." He reproached himself for failing to grasp the import of these words, and late at night could be heard pacing the floor and repeating to himself: "Father, you were right." He stood trembling on the threshold of the next generation's new and alien world, while his world was collapsing. Once after the High Holidays, he said to me: "On Yom Kippur, I prayed that if my children, God forbid, no longer be good Jews, then let them remain childless. May the family come to an end."

My father fell gravely ill. The first to learn the diagnosis of his fatal disease was Moyshe Leyzer Khosid — my father's former rabbinical assistant and close friend. Moyshe Leyzer Khosid, as the Vurke Hasidim called him, had been a regular at the court since the days of my grandfather, R. Simhah Bunem. He was learned, often served as an arbitrator among Jews in Warsaw, and was well read in Jewish and non-Jewish philosophical literature. At his narrow desk in his dark room on Ogrodowa Street, Moyshe Leyzer searched for the meaning of life, trying to arrive at the secret of creation, and in the end forgot about his own physical existence. But above all he was devoted to his only son Mikhl, a smart and gifted boy. Young Mikhl was the essence and the greatest dream of his father's life. When Mikhl became a communist, in the years when being a communist in Poland was extremely dangerous, Moyshe Leyzer helped him pack a few necessities and smuggled him across the German border, realizing that never again would he see his only son.

During his frequent and long conversations with Moyshe Leyzer, my father often revealed his deep anxiety about the future of Judaism in Poland. "*Yiddishkeit* is going under,"

Father would say sorrowfully and wipe away his tears. All the consultations with the great doctors in Warsaw and professors in Berlin, where they brought my father in the last days of the war, were of no avail. The fatal diagnosis was unanimous. Silence and gloom descended on our lively home. My grandmother became bowed down and shriveled. Every time she approached her darling son's sickbed, he would make a desperate effort to change his agonized expression into a wan smile and say: "*Mame*, today I am much better, thank God."

For the first and last time, I brought a flower into my father's room: a big and fragrant purple-red azalea. On Lag Ba-Omer 5670 (1910), my father passed away at 14 Dzielna Street in Warsaw at the age of forty-nine, the same age at which his grandfather, the Middle Vurker, had passed away. His term as the rebbe was slightly shorter than his grandfather's — less than nineteen years. At the funeral procession through the Jewish streets of Warsaw, in which thousands participated, all the way to the Gensa Cemetery, my grandmother kept on saying quietly: "It will not be long now and I shall see you again." And she sobbed bitterly. A day after the Seven Days of Mourning, Hasidim came to our house, drank brandy, and toasted my oldest brother Yitskhok. "*L'chaim!*" "Long life, rebbe!" My brother and his family now occupied the villa in Otwock. There also resided our young stepmother with her five small children. We, the older children, left home for faraway places by entirely new paths, never to return.

After my father's passing, his only surviving brother Moyshele from the town of Palenica near Warsaw became the rebbe. Uncle Moyshele was a good-natured, warm, and quiet person. Following the untimely death of his beloved wife Royze, he remained alone with his young children and never remarried. When I was leaving home for the last time and came to say goodbye to my uncle, he said to me with a sad smile: "You see, now everything is different. Why did you need to be first?" To which I replied that the advantage of being first is having the opportunity to smooth the way for others who come after you. My kind uncle liked my response very much and took leave of me very heartily.[24]

NOTES

1. [Ita Kalish (1903–94) was the daughter of R. Mendel of the Vurke Hasidim, who succeeded his father Simkha Bunem as the rabbi of Otwock. Her memoir describes everyday life in the Vurke court, with special attention to the lives of women prior to World War I. Following the death of her father, she left her husband and child (whom she kidnapped later) to live with her sisters in Warsaw. She moved to Berlin and then to Palestine in 1933. Most of the selections here are reprinted, with editorial revisions, from Ita Kalish, "Life in a Hassidic Court in Russian Poland toward the End of the 19th and Early 20th Centuries," *YIVO Annual of Jewish Social Science* 13 (1965): 265–78. Some additional sections were translated by Yuri Vedyapan for this volume. The final text was revised with the assistance of Rabbi Ben Zion Gold, who meticulously went over most of it.]

2. [A sly allusion to the fact that these "German" Austrians speak not *Deutsch* (German) but "datsch" (Yiddish-German).]

3. [Washing is forbidden on Yom Kippur.]

4. [He was a companion of Rabbi Mendel, the founder of the Kotsk dynasty.]

5. [Mordekhai ben Avraham Yafeh (1525 or 1530–1612) was also known as the Ba'al Levush for his halakhic writings, collectively called *Levush malkhut* (Royal attire).]

6. [Yitshak (or Yitskhok) Kalish (1779–1848) established the Vurke dynasty and became one of the most important intercessors for the Jewish community. He successfully persuaded authorities to reverse a ban on *eruvim* in 1835, requested leniency for Jewish conscripts (so that they not be compelled to violate Jewish law), and so forth. See Marcin Woziński, "Hasidism, *Shtadlanut*, and Jewish Politics in Nineteenth-Century Poland: The Case of Isaac of Warka," *Jewish Quarterly Review* 95, no. 2 (2005): 290–320.]

7. [As explained in the introduction to part 2, an *agunah* is a woman who is unable to get a legal divorce.]

8. [Ya'akov David (1814–78) of Mszczonów, who was actually the oldest, established the Amshinov dynasty. The younger brother Menahem Mendel (1819–68), also known as the "Silent Tsaddik" became the rebbe of Vurke.]

9. [Yitshak Meier Rothenberg (1799–1866), known by his multivolume text, *Hidushe ha-Rim*, founded the Ger hasidic dynasty, which had one of the largest following in Central Poland, especially in the Warsaw area.]

10. [Simhah Bunem of Otwock (1851–1907), the successor of Menahem Mendel, left for Eretz Israel in 1905 over the strong objections of his family, especially his wife and children.]

11. [According to Jewish law, one must wait six hours between the consumption of meat and of milk.]

12. [This process entailed approaching the rebbe with a petition to gain his attention.]

13. [The translation in the *YIVO Annual of Jewish Social Science* notes that this town "consisted of a market place, a ritual bathhouse, two synagogue wardens, a Jewish postman, and several score Jews."]

14. [A state rabbi, who had knowledge of the Russian language, was elected by the community to serve a three-year term and perform a host of religious, administrative, and police duties. His duties of principal interest to the state pertained to record keeping and performing marriages, divorces, circumcisions, and burials. In 1853 the state decreed that all "marriages and divorces not performed by the state rabbi and his assistant will be considered illegal." In general, Jews viewed state rabbis as government servitors rather than spiritual authorities. In contrast, the Jewish community recognized "spiritual rabbis" as the real religious authorities. See Freeze, *Jewish Marriage and Divorce in Imperial Russia*, 95–124.]

15. [Jonathan Eybeshutz (Kraków 1690–Altona 1764), Talmudist, kabbalist, and rabbi of Altona, was accused—especially by Rabbi Jacob Emden—of being a secret follower of the false messiah Shabbatai Tzvi. Eybeshutz published his *Luhot edut* (1755),

which denounced the slanderers and justified his innocence. He was recognized as the chief rabbi of the congregations of Hamburg-Altona-Wandsbec in 1756 by the king of Denmark and the Senate of Hamburg.]

16. [Moses Mendelssohn's *Biur* (*Sefer netivot ha-shalom*, in Hebrew; Book of paths to peace) was his German translation of the Bible in Hebrew characters with accompanying Hebrew commentary. Both remained faithful to tradition, drawing on the exegetical methods of Sephardic rabbis. He intended the work to serve as a way to expose traditional Jews to modern culture.]

17. [On her wedding day, a bride was considered to be special and could provide blessings.]

18. [Menahem Mendel of Vitebsk (1730–88) was the prominent disciple of Dov Ber, the Maggid of Mezeritsh, and was the founder of the hasidic community in Safed and Tiberias.]

19. [Rabbi Ya'akov Yitshak Rabinowitz, or "the Holy Jew" (1766–1813), founded the Pshiskhe dynasty, which focused on Talmudic study. He declared that the task of being a "good Jew" was more challenging than miracle making and introduced a rigorous course of Talmudic study and self-scrutiny among his disciples.]

20. [In other words, the relatives treated the family's villa like a summer vacation house.]

21. [See document 1, note 30.]

22. Stanislow-Mazowiecki [this note is by Ita Kalish].

23. Otwock was divided into two sections: on one side of the train station was the downtown area, with the stores, synagogue, ritual bath, etc.; on the other side were the famous spas, with lavish villas and expensive *pensions* [this note is by Ita Kalish].

24. [The memoir ends with Kalish's last visit to her home in Otwock before World War II. She describes her brother's dream to make a pilgrimage to Eretz Israel, but his cabled appeal for a visa came too late. His entire family died violently at the hands of the Nazis. The last line reads: "The site of grandfather's villa and its large synagogue, which stood for nearly ninety years on Berek Joselewicz Street in Otwock, is now a grassy field cultivated by a Polish peasant. O Earth cover not thou their blood!"]

Yehoshua Heschel Levine's *The Ascents of Eliyahu* (Gaon of Vil'na)

Yehoshua Heschel Levine, *Sefer aliyot Eliyahu: toldot ha-adam ha-gadol ba-anakim . . . Gaon mi-Vil'na* (Vil'na: Yehuda Lev ben Elie'zer Lipman, 1875. Originally published in 1856.)

The Story of His Life and Activity

As the sun rises in the morning, so did an eternal
  light rise
And the earth shone from the glory of the great
holy one in Israel

On Tuesday, the first day of Passover, 5,480 years after the creation of the world [1720], a child was born, a son was given to the great rabbi, the saintly Reb Shlomo Zalman of Vil'na, born to him by the saintly woman Mrs. Trayna from the city of Seltz near the Holy Community of Brisk-of-Lithuania, and they named him Eliyahu. A shoot came out of the stock of the *gaon*,[1] our teacher Reb Moshe Rivkes of Vil'na, the author of the *Be'er ha-golah*,[2] and a limb from the root of the exalted *gaon*, the light of Israel and its holiness, our teacher Reb Moshe Kramer, "father" of the court and head of the yeshiva in the Holy Community of Vil'na. He was his father's first-born, and superior to all the *geonim* of the generation. His four brothers, whose names were known throughout the world for their splendor, eminent rabbis and *geonim*, made him their champion.

From the day of his birth he gave signs that he would be an eternal light, the joy of each generation. The glow of his face was like an angel of God, entirely beautiful and handsome. From his youth all who saw him were pleased by him, for a man's wisdom will brighten his face. His deeds also showed that he would raise the yoke of Torah, reveal deep things, and satisfy craving souls. Even in dis-

tant lands, the reputation of his holiness and restraint increased daily.

He studied with a teacher only until he was six years old, and from then on the voice of God called in the ears of the greatest scholars, "Keep an eye on this lad, a source of illumination, from whose mouth pearls of wisdom shall emerge, whose lips are lilies in the company of sages." At the age of six and a half he lectured in the synagogue on a portion that his father taught him. At the third Sabbath meal his father brought him before the *gaon* Reb Heschel, head of the court of the Holy Community of Vil'na, who tested his ability to say such things on his own and to generate his own novel interpretations. He gave him an hour to think. After this, young Eliyahu demonstrated wonders, raising more questions — which he would ask and then answer himself — all in a singular manner. The great scholars who were sitting before him saw and were dumbfounded; they wanted to hug and kiss him. After hearing all this they proclaimed that there was no one as intelligent or as wise as he.

At the age of eight he began to delve into esoteric matters to understand the words of the *aggadot* of our Sages, which are in the form of parables. The principles of true knowledge lit his path, and all his ways were peaceful without strain or difficulty.

By the age of nine he was fluent in Scripture, Mishnah, and Gemara. He satiated himself with their reasoning and with the aggadic midrashim that sprout from it. His intelligence served him in difficult matters [to be found in]: Talmud and legal literature, the responsa, the commentaries of the early and late authorities.[3] Who knew the secrets hidden from all in the book *Ets Hayyim*?[4] If they were sealed from the eyes of all living things, God would show them to him. He succeeded in studying books of the revealed and the hidden,[5] and he studied all the writings of the *Ets Hayyim* in half a year; he was assisted by God.

At the age of ten he had a permanent companion, closer than a brother, his neighbor, the famous rabbi and *gaon*, our teacher Reb Aryeh Leb of blessed memory, head of the court of Tsekhanovets [Ciechanowiec in Polish] who was his partner in the study of *gefet*.[6] They set up appointed times for study. He set aside only a few hours a day, to study faithfully that which flows from the wellsprings of knowledge, all the sections of the *Zohar* and *Pardes*[7] and the writings of the Ari of blessed memory. He stretched out his hand and encountered it by himself, without a companion. In six months he went from chapter to chapter, covering all of the *Zohar*'s teachings, and the light of his mind spread over it, arriving at the first principle, knowledge of God.

By the age of eleven, any praise would be damningly faint. None of the men of wisdom and knowledge could clearly comprehend the spirit of his mind, which flowed like a spring. On the day of his rejoicing, which was the night of Simhat Torah,[8] he remembered that some time ago he had pledged to study the tractates *Zevahim* and *Menahot*,[9] and to complete them by Simhat Torah. But he had not yet begun his work, for during the entire year his mind was occupied with *gefet*, the first four orders of the Mishnah,[10] and with the legal writings of the early and later authorities. At that moment he was driven by intense love for God, and his eyes remained open that entire night. A good and noble person slept there, the pride of the generation, wise and erudite, knowledgeable in secrets, our late teacher Mikhel of blessed memory of Datnów

[Dotnovo in Russian]. He awoke in the middle of the night and wondered where the boy had gone. He entered the room, which was nothing less than the house of God, wherein he found him preoccupied with the study of Torah, in its glory and splendor, on page fifty of tractate *Zevahim* [which is less than halfway through the tractate]. Upon seeing all this before him, Reb Mikhel raised his voice: "In only two hours you studied fifty pages of difficult matters?" [. . .] He began testing him with questions on the complex passages in the *gefet* of those fifty pages. On each of those complex passages he gave satisfactory answers and multiple possibilities. After testing him thus ten times over, Reb Mikhel said to himself, "I am now certain that his light will shine on all those who dwell on earth, for even in his youth his brilliance confounds the moon and shames the sun."

He returned before dawn and found that he had begun tractate *Menahot* and that he had studied more than half of it. He said to himself, "Who could match your ambitions?" and said to himself as before, "Who could believe the quickness of his learning?" He began testing him again on the complex passages in the half that he had studied that night and found him more than proficient, indeed, extraordinarily keen. He concluded that he was nothing less than an angel, for he could resolve any Talmudic query. He blessed him and said, "Your name shall be blessed in the community of the upright." He was not still until he fulfilled his pledge; he completed the tractates *Zevahim* and *Menahot* before the morning prayers and prayed with the congregation with great joy and gladness in his soul, rejoicing on Simhat Torah.

At the age of twelve it was not known that he had internalized all the seven sciences with ultimate precision and accuracy. The elders of that generation, all pious performers of God's will and giants of Torah, decided in their old age to study Maimonides's "Laws of the Sanctification of the Month"[11] with its commentaries, for they knew how useful this study would be for many issues. They were occupied with this for half a year, when they decided to see the ways of God. They instructed that [model] spheres be constructed for them in order to understand the movement of the planets: their conjunctions and oppositions, their moons and the length of their periods, their positions in each of the constellations, and the times they set and rise. The month arrived when they convened, each with his sphere in hand, and they attempted to analyze the subject. But they failed and could not determine the paths of the planets, for the craftsmen, who were foiled in their construction of spheres, due to their lack of comprehension, did not anticipate the errors that would arise at the end, and in this difficult work he did not adjust the axes and the horizons, without which there can be no correct wisdom.

A few days before they convened—he was about eight—[. . .] the power of his superior and boundless wisdom led him to think that he could construct a heavenly sphere by his own intelligence and by his own good and correct thinking. He had dabbled in astronomical works for a few days, about half an hour daily. In these hours he would examine the book *Tekhunat ha-shamayim*[12] and he became aware of the problems, the simple as well as the complex; he found that in this science a few words signify much. Because he was astute he waited for the day of their convention and kept the matter to himself while the great scholars of the generation were preoccupied for many hours with numerous problems concerning the project. When they had nowhere to turn he entered the worthy council. He made a request, saying, "May I say something? Not to increase my honor or to detract, God forbid, from the honor of the gentlemen, [. . .] I merely seek a technique of making a heavenly sphere from wooden hoops using a proper method, in order to grasp this wisdom perfectly. [. . .]" He pointed to a particular branch [of the model that presumably was

not placed correctly], and the craftsmen, who erred in their construction of the spheres, saw the resolution of their perplexity and attended to their work with a great diligence, as befit their intellectual level, finding that his words were completely accurate. Seeing that he was on target, they all agreed that he was exceedingly brilliant in *gefet* and that he was facile in all the exalted sciences. [. . .]

At the age of thirteen and a day he took upon himself great piety and restraint. Who was his equal in offering novel interpretations in *halakhah* and *aggadah*? [. . .] He advanced frontiers of Torah by training numerous and honored students who delved into the complexities of the *halakhah*, but none of them even reached [the height of] his ankle. [. . .] All his days and moments were spent studying God's Torah, and his soul cleaved to it. He listened to its true language and resided in its depths.

For six years he researched and carefully examined the Babylonian and Jerusalem Talmuds, the *Tosefta*,[13] *Mekhilta*, *Sifra*, and *Sifre*.[14] He illuminated the obscurities of the variant texts and had no equal in Talmudic analysis. He opened it wide, and all said, "Happy is the people who have one such as he." [. . .]

For another six years he occupied himself with the words of the early and late legal authorities. [. . .] In attempting to account for the difficulties in their works, he did not defer to their greatness, wisdom, or holiness. Rather, he strove with all his might to understand the holy words of the Talmudic sages whose words are all crackling embers of fire. With one letter of the sages he pushed aside many words of the later authors. [. . .]

He was exceedingly learned in grammar: verbs, pointing, cantillation marks, and the cantillation of Job, Proverbs, and Psalms.[15] [. . .] He first mastered arithmetic and triangles,[16] algebra and geometry, and subsequently music, as our teacher, may he rest in Eden, mentions in his commentary on the

Tikkunim.[17] He stated that the cantillation of the Torah, the songs of the Levites, and the secrets of the *Tikkune ha-zohar* cannot be known without it. In medicine, he knew anatomy and its related subjects. But as regards practical pharmaceutics, he wanted to learn it from the contemporary physicians, but his father decreed that he should not study it in order not to squander time from his Torah study—for after mastering it he would have to go out and save lives.

Above all he knew astronomy, turning to it in his youth, telling it, "You are my servant." For the early prophets prophesied, "Lift up your eyes on high and see: who has created these? He who brings out their host by number, etc."[18] [. . .] and this knowledge also complements the statements of the sages regarding the sanctification of the month[19] [. . .] and is necessary for understanding the secret of intercalation[20] in complex passages of the tractates *Rosh hashana* and *Eruvin*. [. . .]

He knew philosophy completely. He once said that he derived two things from it: the seventy forces within man and one other thing. There was no science too advanced for him in either natural philosophy or mathematics, for his strong hand ruled over them all. Even witchcraft, which the Sanhedrin[21] and the *tannaim*[22] knew in their day [. . .] he knew and investigated; he was only missing the knowledge of the composition of grasses and their final construction.

Now that we have described a small part of his vast knowledge and intelligence, let us return to his numerous deeds, which are more important than his wisdom. Just as his spiritual powers were boundless, surpassing the human limit, so did he restrain his physical desires, saying, "Come no further!" His beholders were amazed at his endurance and at how one so weary from a day full of Torah and devotion was able to take on such an unbearable burden. Yet his face was not depressed and the brightness of his appearance cast a light about him. [. . .]

From the age of thirteen and a day until the day of his death, he did not look further than his four cubits.[23] If we carefully consider all the actions that he performed throughout his life, from beginning to end, we would see that they were all done with ultimate diligence and perfection. This pertains to the personal peril he took on in his war with the physical desires, as well as the difficulty of the commitment he took upon himself throughout his life, not to sleep more than two hours per day. He never slept more than a half-hour at a time, and during that half-hour his lips would whisper *halakhot* and *aggadot*. When the half-hour was over he would gather strength like a lion, wash his hands,[24] and begin studying aloud; then he would sleep for another half-hour. This was the quantity of his sleep: three half-hours during the night and one during the day. He employed strategies against his desires, commanding them at will, so that he distanced himself from what was not truly good. He tolerated the pain of hunger, desiring not to enjoy this world. In his youth he would eat a thin piece of bread soaked in water, the size of two olives, eating this in the morning and at night. He did not taste it, but would swallow it whole.

His manners were like those of the early authorities, may they rest in Eden. He never walked four cubits without Torah or *tefillin*, and never spoke idly. Even when he sat in the company of learned men, he would listen only to true Torah. From youth, he would study for long periods in the forests, in a desolate house, secluding himself in a place unknown to others. God chose for him a wife, the pious Mrs. Hanna, the daughter of the wealthy Rabbi Judah of blessed memory of Kaidan; his helpmeet in holiness was pure. Only she would occasionally visit his secret place, staying there to keep her eye on him and sustain him.

When he was still young, he took upon himself to go into exile, to be a wanderer. For many years he roamed in exile, in holiness and purity, cloaked in a *tallit* and crowned with *tefillin*. He even passed through Berlin and Lissa [Leszno in Polish]. Wherever he passed, great things were told of him.

On his return from exile he hired, due to his weariness, a carriage for traveling day and night. He paid the driver a fee for the time that he waited while he said the *amidah* prayer.[25] Once, when the Gaon was standing and reciting the prayer, the carriage driver rode off with the horses and with all of his possessions, leaving him empty-handed. When he returned home he studied Torah in great poverty. During the day he would close his shutters while studying and study by candlelight in order that no one disturb him. This was his way in his youth, studying Torah for its own sake. He would review the entire Babylonian Talmud each month.

There occurred the following incident: In his large populated city, the Holy Community decided to give him a weekly stipend for the sustenance of his family. A certain communal officer, whom the Holy Community would send to deliver the stipend, kept the money for himself and did not deliver it. This went on for some years, but the Gaon told no one. He suffered such poverty that his pious wife and his small children had nothing with which to keep themselves alive. She came to him, and he instructed her to go with her small children to his neighbors during mealtime; as it is the manner of children to ask for food when seeing others eating, they will be given food. He did not wish to reveal the matter of his stipend being cut off, due to his great faith, and so that no one would be humiliated on his account. Finally, when that officer became ill and was close to death he confessed before all that for a number of years he did not give the Gaon the stipend that was sent with him. The officer then died. [. . .]

His great intelligence and exertion in the service of God allowed him to resist any adversary and removed from his heart all worry and sadness; he served God with joy and gladness of heart all his days. [. . .]

How committed was he to distancing himself from the company of his family, his sons and daughters! He sought the pure fear of God as his neighbor. [This reached] the point that he never inquired of his sons and daughters as to their livelihood and their condition. If one of his sons ever came to town, although he would rejoice greatly, not having seen him for a year or two, he would not ask him about the state of his livelihood. [. . .] His son, the great rabbi, a man of Torah and *yirah*, our late teacher Shlomo Zalman of blessed memory, when about five or six, was gentle and his father's favorite; he was loved by his father and was his joy all the time, for he recognized his goodness and saintliness. Once the boy became ill, and before he regained his strength the Gaon decided to travel to his place of seclusion. [. . .] There the wellsprings of nature were shut up, to the point that he forgot his family for days. One day he went to the bathhouse—where, as is well known, one is forbidden to contemplate Torah matters—and he began to consider his affairs. He remembered that he had left his home for more than a month and his precious son was left lying on a sickbed. Overwhelmed with compassion, he directed that his carriage be prepared to return to his home in order to inquire about his son.

Because of such things it is fitting to call our teacher a Hasid and Kadosh.[26] It is impossible to describe his exertion in Torah study; he reviewed what he learned hundreds and thousands of times, each chapter and each tractate. Out of love for the Holy Torah he once, during a long night in Tevet,[27] reviewed one Mishnah in the tractate *Taharot*[28] all night long. In his youth—during the winter when the cold was fierce—he would study in a room where no furnace was burning in order to prevent sleep. Who could relate his saintliness and piety—that he not once engaged in idle talk, and never took on the yoke of the community or the rabbinate, or any burden. He was a hater of ill-gotten gain.

Even greater than his enormous learning, relative to the great scholars, was his sense that he was inferior to any man on the face of the earth. One can discern his great humility in the fact that he almost never cited any scholar with whom he disagreed; rather, he simply discussed the matter according to his usual method, as if he were discussing the word of God, in order not to be glorified by the shame of the criticized scholar or author. He studied the holy words of the sages with the flame of the love of God and the fear of His majesty, in holiness and purity and inestimably wondrous *devekut*. While studying Torah and serving God he was enraptured and overtaken by love for it, to the point that his soul nearly left his body. [. . .]

His major disciples, from the day they entered his study house, tried to shorten the distance between themselves and the source of their life. They were not idle in their course and were not wearied by their pursuit, for they sensed their immense distance from him, and they knew that they had a long way to reach their destination.

The premier student was the *gaon*, the saintly light of the exile, our teacher Rabbi Hayyim of blessed memory, "father" of the court and head of the yeshiva of the Holy Community of Volozhin. He gazed upon the beautiful splendor of his Torah with a discerning eye. Though he was very powerful — for he slept in the valley of *halakhah* from youth — and skilled in the analysis of Torah and basked in its shade, he was unwaveringly humble and reverent toward God. When he came to stand before the Gaon to hear from his mouth words of the living God, the Gaon's lucidity and sharpness passed over his face and purified it, shattering its pride. Since he first perceived the awesomeness of the Gaon's mind, how great were his deeds! How deep were his thoughts in the revealed and in the hidden! He desired to dwell in the shade of his tent. [. . .][29]

Our teacher, a holy and ascetic man, [. . .]

encouraged his disciples to study in a proper sequence, so that their legs would not falter.

First, he directed a student to serve God, to be fluent in the twenty-four holy books[30] with the pointing and cantillation marks carefully noted, and he tested him on all these. The science of grammar was a priority. Many intelligent and worthy individuals realized that when they discussed the science of grammar with him they could not hold their own. [. . .]

Then he instructed that the six sections of the Mishnah be fluent in his mouth, with the prominent commentaries; the correct version of the text was of foremost importance. His major disciples saw that the knowledge of God was within him [. . .] that he expounded new interpretations that our fathers the early commentators never imagined. [. . .]

After this he directed him to study the methods of analysis in the sea of Talmud; to examine closely Rashi's commentary, for it is very precise to those who understand; to study the comments of the Tosafists of blessed memory, on condition that it be done honestly. He detested the excessive asking of questions.[31] He required him to acknowledge what was true, even that which came from schoolchildren; indeed, he should never insist on his own theory in the face of the truth. [If he followed this advice] he would succeed and be enlightened in his studies. [. . .]

At the age of forty he acquired an additional measure of understanding, becoming like a flowing spring; time does not permit the writing of all that was revealed to him. From then on he neither wrote nor composed, except by means of his disciples. All the compositions that he himself wrote were written before he reached the age of forty. [. . .]

Our holy teacher was like one of the early authorities.[32] Since the period of the Saboraim[33] and Geonim[34] no one had arisen like him in terms of his Torah and his prolific compositions on both the written and oral laws. He composed more than seventy volumes on esoteric matters. All his words were clear and concise, like the stars in the heavens; the entire world lay beneath him.

He opened the doors of the house of God with his complete commentary on the Bible; he provided a wonderful aid with his commentary on the entire Mishnah, using a method unimagined by our fathers. He removed the obscurities impeding a clear understanding of the Babylonian and Jerusalem Talmuds, the *Sifra*, *Sifre*, *Tosefta*, and *Mekhilta*; in vain did the earlier builders exert themselves to resolve the difficulties, ultimately producing forced interpretations. [. . .] His commentaries on *gefet* dripped sweetness [. . .] and he wrote great commentaries on many passages of the *Zohar* [. . .] on the *Shulhan Arukh*[35] [. . .] and on the *aggadot* of the Talmud. [. . .] He wrote a long composition on astronomy [. . .] explaining the constellations, [. . .] and wrote 303 new principles in algebra, never before seen in the Land of Judah. [. . .]

A lover of mitzvot such as he is never satiated [with] mitzvot: he decided to travel to the Holy Land and set out by way of Prussia and Hungary. When he arrived at Koenigsburg he sent a letter to his family, full of ethical teaching, *yirah*, and proper guidance in the fear of God. [. . .] In his old age they asked him many times why he did not go to the Holy Land, but he did not answer. Once, after much entreaty, he answered: "I do not have permission from above." [. . .] When he set out for the Holy Land, many wealthy individuals provided [money to cover] his expenses, and when he returned he reimbursed each one. [. . .]

The greatest of all his awesome deeds is that he did not gratify himself with anything but his own labor in wisdom, knowledge, and skill. When, after his great toil, the Heavens pitied him and the wellsprings of knowledge were revealed to him, he considered this a gift from God. Without his own exertion he eschewed such heavenly communications, even though the Heavens wished to confer them on him without labor or exertion, by means

of revelations. But he did not pay attention to this; it was near him, yet he distanced himself from it. His disciple—the *gaon* and saintly man, our teacher Rabbi Hayyim of Volozhin, may he rest in Eden—testified that he heard him say many times, "I do not wish to comprehend Torah through the agency of any intermediary at all. Rather, my eyes are raised to Him, may His name be blessed, awaiting whatever He wants to reveal to me [as a reward] for all that I have striven [to do] with all my might. [. . .] I want nothing save that which is in His mouth." [. . .]

Moreover, our teacher used to say that even that which the soul perceives during sleep [. . .] by means of an ascent of the soul [. . .] was not very significant in his opinion. What is most important is what one apprehends in this world, by means of exertion [. . .] but that which the soul perceives during sleep, without exertion or free will, is but a reward in which God gives us a taste of the world to come in this world. [. . .]

In order to perfect his generation he established a house full of Torah, that men should at all times be posted at their watch [. . .] studying Scripture, Mishnah, Gemara. He would sit at their head at scheduled times and set out before them [. . .] a program of how to be fluent in the entire Talmud within a few years, and to know the sources of the laws perfectly. He cautioned them against engaging in too much *pilpul*, saying that occasionally it is used for provocation, God forbid; that it is very destructive to the will of God, for by its practice iniquity multiplies and sin increases, and pleasant fellowship is ruined, and truth is driven out of God's community, when its purpose should only be to arrive at the *halakhah*. They accepted this upon themselves and studied for eighteen years during his lifetime. He was pleased that his good will was followed and they, by gazing day and night at the light of his Torah, merited the wondrous pleasure and light that is indescribable.

When he reached the age of seventy-one—

this was in the year 5551 [1791]—the weakness of old age weighed heavily upon him; his strength was increasingly deteriorating. His bodily powers weakened, and he became ill. Our teacher did not then seek out doctors nor did he turn his attention to worldly delights to amuse himself, to distract his thoughts from his sickness, for the powers of his soul were not dissipated. They strove to be delighted only by the love of God and his Torah, which was planted in his heart since his youth. He sought the company of the rabbi, the holy Maggid[36] of Dubno, sending him a letter in his own hand, requesting that he come to him to calm his soul with his pleasant parables that delight both God and men. [. . .]

In the year 5558 [1797] on the eve of Yom Kippur, he called to his children and said, "Gather near me and I will bless you." All his sons, daughters, and grandchildren gathered near him, and he placed his hand on the head of his oldest son, the great, learned rabbi, Reb Avraham. He blessed him and began to cry. All those in attendance were amazed; they were gripped by fear. "It is incredible," they said, "he has never acted this way." But they did not dare to ask him. On the day following Yom Kippur he was seriously ill; each day he became more ill. Even the Sukkot[37] holiday was made sorrowful and all happiness was darkened. On Monday, the third day of the intermediate days of Sukkot, he was exceedingly weak. But our teacher, despite his physical frailty, was invigorated by love, and he gathered strength in order to fulfill the mitzvah of *lulav* and *etrog*[38] in its proper time, with immense joy of the spirit, as he always did. While these were still in his hands, he straightened his legs and passed away. He died at a ripe old age, at the age of seventy-eight. All those in attendance, seeing that the angel of death had prevailed, that their crown had fallen, broke out crying. The joy of the holiday turned to mourning, and through all the streets of Vil'na one could hear only wailing. All those in the city, from young to old,

came out to accompany him to his final resting place. Wherever the bad news reached that the eternal light had been extinguished, there was great mourning and lamentation for the Jews. The great *geonim* in each and every city arose to eulogize him and tell of his glory. They called for crying, lamentation, and intense mourning. [. . .]

After the sun set, his disciples spread forth from their shepherd. They made their champion the *gaon*, light of the exile, the pious and erudite man, our teacher Rabbi Hayyim of Volozhin, may he rest in Eden, disciple of the Gaon. He began to disseminate his Torah. [. . .] A number of the Gaon's disciples went to the Holy Land and set up their study house there in order to illuminate the Eastern lands with the eternal light, the Torah of their teacher the Gaon, the Hasid, may he rest in Eden. There they increased and were successful, and cast a new light on Zion and Jerusalem.

His sons, the great rabbis, his son-in-law the great rabbi Reb Moshe of Pinsk, and his major disciples labored together to disseminate his Torah through his numerous compositions, publishing many of them. But many more books remain in manuscript. [. . .] The wealthy and generous men here in Vil'na also labored to realize his idea and establish his large study house; they expanded its structure and its floors, making it a great sight. They also collected a large library there. To this day, great Torah scholars and men of *yirah*, who day and night are never silent in their Torah study, are cloistered there. [. . .] The leaders of Vil'na stream to the holy study house and have set up groups: some study Alfasi;[39] some study Talmud; and some Mishnah, Scripture, or midrash. They have also set up nighttime watches. They are not silent for even one second [. . .] so that the study of the Holy Torah may not cease for even one second in the study house of the great Gaon. [. . .]

Happy are you, exalted city of Vil'na! Everyone, from the old to the young, received some spiritual benefit: each according to his capacity. All their efforts in Torah study and charity were inspired by him — by the power of his piety and the standard he set. [. . .] Through his guidance and stern example they became a large community of Torah disseminators, of people who are painstaking in mitzvot, who detest mastery over others, and give honor to God. Their wealth did not make them arrogant, they pleased all those who seek God, they made their Torah primary and their professions secondary; Torah and the worship of God were their only occupation. Then nearly all his fellow residents decided to tell the outlying people — for his teaching was primarily to those nearby — that they should not squander their time; that every man should keep an eye on his schedule, judging the seconds, and that their time should be used only for the most precious things, which are Torah study and the worship of God; to be zealous and very diligent. For all effort and skill besides this will not benefit at all; nothing but Torah and the worship of God, which restrain the machinations of one's desire and its schemes. [. . .] We must give thanks to God who sent before us a pillar of fire to illuminate our dark times [. . .] with true Torah and pure reverence of God, without whom who knows what would be our present lot. [. . .] May the good God bestow goodness, may what He planted bear fruit for us and for our children forever, to grasp the tree of life of Torah and *yirah* of God, to walk on the true path that He has shown us, for our good always.

NOTES

1. [*Gaon* (pl. *geonim*) literally means "eminence " but it was used in this period as an appellation for a particularly learned scholar. Because of his extraordinary erudition, Eliyahu of Vil'na is referred too simply as "the Gaon" or "the G"RA" (acronym for Gaon Rabbi Eliyahu).]

2. [A gloss on Joseph Karo's code of Jewish law, the *Shulhan Arukh*.]

3. ["Early" authorities are rabbis from before c. 1600, before the publication of the *Shulhan Arukh*.]

4. [*Tree of Life*, by Hayyim Vital, a sixteenth-century kabbalist of Safed, containing the teachings of his teacher Isaac Luria (known as "Ari," an acronym for Ashkenazi Rabbi Yitshak).]

5. ["Revealed" Torah includes Talmud and *halakhah*; the "hidden" wisdom is kabbalah.]

6. [An acronym for Gemara, Perush ("the commentary"— that is, the commentary of Rashi [d. 1105] and Tosafot [12th–13th century French]). A page of Talmud is composed primarily of these three texts.]

7. [The *Pardes Rimonim* (Pomegranate orchard) of Moses Cordovero, a sixteenth-century Safed kabbalist.]

8. [Rejoicing of the Torah, the holiday in which the yearly cycle of the Torah reading is completed and begun anew.]

9. ["Animal Sacrifices" and "Meal Offerings," respectively, two difficult tractates of the Talmud.]

10. [The Mishna is divided into six sections: seeds, festivals, women, torts, holy offerings, and purity. The last two sections were not commonly studied, as they pertain mainly to the Temple service. *Zevahim* and *Menahot* are in the fifth section.]

11. [A selection of the *Mishneh Torah*, the Code of Maimonides, which contains astronomical calculations.]

12. [*The Construction of the Heavens*, by Raphael Halevi of Hanover. This book was first published in 1756, when the Gaon was thirty-six, making the details of this story impossible.]

13. [A legal text contemporary with the Mishnah.]

14. [Halakhic midrashim on Exodus, Leviticus, and Numbers/Deuteronomy, respectively.]

15. [The entire Hebrew Bible is noted with cantillation marks that punctuate each verse and also serve as musical notation for public reading. Job, Proverbs, and Psalms have their own, more complex cantillation system.]

16. [Presumably elementary geometry as opposed to the more advanced geometry mentioned immediately below.]

17. [*Tikkune ha-zohar*, a part of the *Zohar* that

is structured as commentary on the first portion of Genesis.]

18. [Isaiah 40:26.]

19. [The Jewish calendar is based largely on the phases of the moon. In the rabbinic period, a new lunar month was "sanctified" after witnesses testified that they had seen the new moon.]

20. [The lunar year lags behind the solar year by about eleven days, but the lunar-based holidays must fall in their solar-based seasons. In order to correct this discrepancy, an extra month was inserted or "intercalated" in the lunar year at certain intervals. The knowledge of this procedure was considered difficult to master.]

21. [The highest court in the Jewish commonwealth of the rabbinic period, composed of seventy-one elders.]

22. [The sages of the Mishnah.]

23. [In rabbinic literature, an individual's space is four cubits (about six feet). Within this space one was constrained by the demands of the *halakhah*, giving rise to the expression, "the four cubits of *halakhah*." The point here is that the Gaon did not aspire to anything beyond his own space, in which he was thoroughly immersed in the halakha.]

24. [This refers to the ritual hand washing required after sleeping.]

25. [Literally, "standing." This prayer, also called the Eighteen Blessings, is the central prayer of all three daily services and is said standing.]

26. [A pious and holy man.]

27. [A winter month in the Jewish calendar.]

28. [A difficult tractate in the mishnaic section on purity.]

29. [A discussion of other students of the Gaon follows.]

30. [The books of the Hebrew Bible.]

31. [A reference to the classic *pilpul* method of study, in which theoretical questions were raised for the sake of demonstrating one's intellectual prowess and erudition.]

32. [Talmudic authorities from circa 1000 to 1600 CE. The opinions of these rabbis carried great legal weight.]

33. [Babylonian rabbis following the compilation of the Talmud (c. 500–700 CE).]

34. [Rabbinic leaders of Babylonian Jewry between circa 700 and 1038 CE.]

35. [By Joseph Karo [1488–1575], the *Shulhan Arukh* is the most commonly used code of Jewish law.]

36. [An itinerant preacher; the Maggid of Dubno was known for his use of everyday parables to illustrate the meaning of a biblical passage.]

37. [The seven-day Festival of Booths, commemorating the erection of booths by the Israelites during the exodus and celebrating the fall harvest. It is an especially joyous holiday.]

38. [Palm branch and citron, two of the four species that are taken in hand during prayers on Sukkot.]

39. [The Talmudic code of the North African halakhist, Isaac Alfasi (d. 1103).]

[5]

Memoirs of R. Elijah ben Benjamin Rabinowitz-Teomim, the Aderet (1845–1905)

Elijah David ben Benjamin Rabinowitz-Teomim, *Seder Eliyahu: Korot hayyav ve-hanhagotav shel ha-Aderet* (Jerusalem: Mosad ha-Rav Kuk, 1983).[1]

5628 [1867–68]

When we met I had a quarrel with Rabbi R. Shalom.[2] I held a grudge in my heart against him and broke off relations with him, each of us having bad feelings toward the other. It reached the point where I went to pray in the study hall rather than in the synagogue together with him as we had done up till then. However, on Yom Kippur Eve I very much regretted this. I overcame my will, battled my instinct, and went from the study hall to the synagogue where I prayed to reconcile with him, as the Torah commands. It was hard for me to overcome my will in this act and publicly make that move. But my love for him was never the same as it had been before.

When he saw that the place was too small for the two of us, he left the town of Lipnishki [Lipnishok in Yiddish] after the Sukkot holiday, and went on his way. We then were joined by our brother-in-law, the erudite scholar Mordechai Zvi Hirsch Pagirsky (may his candle shine), husband of my sister Esther Leah (may she live a good long life). The three of us [me, my brother, and my brother-in-law] studied very closely together. I made great progress in my studies once I came there, discovering new Torah insights every day and recording them in my notebook, until my scribbles did not suffice for keeping track of all that was occurring to me.

In that period my every thought and attention was focused on the Torah. I had almost no distraction from my studies, and when speaking to someone would still be thinking about some piece of Torah scholarship. I told myself: maybe that is what the Scripture means when it says, "And you should think of them day and night": that thought and mind shall be only on Torah matters—which is close to the statement of the Vil'na Gaon (may he rest in peace) on *Orah Hayim*, chapter 47.[3] So we studied the order of *Kodashim* together[4]—I (may God single me out for a long and good life) and my late brother—from the time of evening prayers till 1:00 or 2:00 in the morning without interruption; then we ate dinner and slept till morning and after morning prayers studied till noon when we ate lunch, then napped for a half-hour and studied till afternoon prayers. Our souls knew no end of joy at that time, from our friendship and our studies. I can almost say that in my whole life I never had days as good as those.

At the time I wrote *novellae* on the tractates *Zevahim* and *Menahot*,[5] which we studied together, and after the period of my residence in Lipnishki I wrote *novellae* on *Ketubot*, *Nedarim*, *Rosh hashanah*, *Yoma*, and *Sukkah*, and the rest of the tractates in the Order of *Kodashim*, which I studied myself, until the arrival of my brother the rabbi (of blessed memory): together we studied *Zevahim*, *Menahot*, and the rest of the tractates; we went over each tractate four times. I entitled the manuscript I composed *Kodshei David*.

During 1865–66 and 1866–67, I wrote *novellae* on the *Mechilta*[6] and the books of Numbers and Deuteronomy, and while I was in

Dinaburg in the summer of 1865 I purchased the *Sefer hasidim*[7] printed in Lvov in large folios; I studied it twice and wrote a proper commentary on it and an index, until it became a perfect work that the wise examined and praised. I called it *Mishnat hasidim*; I then wrote *novellae* on the book of *Yereim*[8] and gave it the title *Sod yereim*.

The winter of 1867 was very fierce. Once, while pacing up and down in my room, it suddenly became very bright while the moon and the stars were out shining in the sky; I was greatly frightened. Two stars had collided, and it was reported that somewhere stones had fallen from the skies—this was printed in the newspapers at the time. The following day, the Holy Sabbath of *Shemot*, the daughter of the innkeeper, the late M. Shaul Shtaler, came to my room and asked fearfully about a dream she had dreamed before daylight, in which a tooth had been extracted from her cheek causing her great pain (may it not befall us). As we had heard several times from our father and master of blessed memory that such things happen for the best, we told her as much, and to pay no attention to it. But during the week, her only daughter, who was seven years old, fell ill with the disease of diphtheria (may the Merciful protect us) and then passed away. We were indescribably anguished by this, for we had not been firm and did not oblige her to fast as the *Shulhan Arukh* writes. Ever since, I am careful never to make light of a dream like this; may the Lord protect us from all evil and show us His beneficence and salvation forever.

Many are the thoughts in the heart of man, towers I built myself, etc.; while seated in the earth's glory and the fullness of tranquility we studied together without interruption. I came to think that none was my like, as I had been privileged to study thus for several years, and would soon acquire perfection of soul; but such was not the decision of the Blessed Lord, for by my sins my eye trouble returned and kept me from my studies. And as we studied by the light of a bright candle, using the new Vil'na editions of the Talmud, which had very white pages, and as I was not warned to take a break from time to time, I consequently was obliged early in the month of Shevat[9] to take a holiday from my studies. My brother (rest in peace) studied within while I listened to him from without.

Once, in one of our conversations while we were dining, my brother-in-law R. Tzvi (may his candle shine), told me that he had heard and seen one of the most celebrated doctors in Vil'komir drink large quantities of cold water even in mid-meal, saying that this greatly improves human health. I then began to do the same and frequently drank cold water from the barrel that stood in the hallway, which sometimes even had ice in it. I drank during meals, before going to sleep, and in the morning too when I awoke. Soon I saw how healthy I was; although I did not yet know what foods to abstain from, all was good and fine, nothing was lacking from me in health (thank God).

On the day of the Fast of Esther[10] as I awoke in the morning, there was suddenly something new that thank God I had never experienced before. I coughed up bits of dried blood (may it not befall us), blood like in the liver. I immediately went to the doctor, the most honest among men, the God-fearing M. Kalman, who is fondly remembered. That gentleman prescribed me a spoonful of medicine to drink every two hours, as well as almond milk, and thank the Lord, by His glorious mercy, I recovered my health.

The day after Purim, one day after I had observed the commandment of getting drunk in its literal sense (God be blessed), I noticed that my eyes had not returned to their former healthy condition. I got ready to go back home. I left my brother (of blessed memory) in Lipnishki and set off home, accompanied by my brother-in-law.

After Passover I sought help for my eye trouble from an old and expert Polish doctor in the town of Ponevezh. This did me much good (thank God). He gave me specific instructions to bathe in the river as often as I could.

On the 15th of Av [some four months later], while bathing in the river, it happened to me again (may it not befall us): an expectoration of blood. I hurried to leave, and the next morning I asked the doctor, who said it was nothing. But for two days it did not cease and after beseeching him to give me a prescription and thus put an end to this coughing of blood (may the merciful protect us), he instructed me to take as much as a handful of *brost* tea (called a *speces*), to pour hot water on it from a boiling teapot, and to cover it well until it was cooked like tea; then to place in it a spoonful of pure *shalayic geist*, until it dissolves, and to drink a tablespoon of this potion every two hours.[11] This helped me (thank God), and I then noticed that this was the same prescription given to me by the doctor R. Kalman. This medicine is tried and true, I have already told it to several people who suffered from the same problem (may it not befall us), and it has helped them all. It is a mitzvah to make this information public on the principle that "thou shalt love thy neighbor as thyself."

Thus passed the days of summer unfruitfully. In correspondence with my brother the rabbi (of blessed memory) we resolved that the next year, 5629 [1868–69], we would sit in the house of our father and master (of blessed memory) to study together. We would fulfill the injunction to glorify ourselves through Torah study, perfect ourselves in the Law, and earn our keep.

In the year 1868, a great famine struck several districts of the country, especially Kovno district and the [rest of] the land of Lithuania. There was as yet no railroad here, and many died just from hunger (may it not befall us). Loaves of straw bread were sold in the main streets, and grist was imported from the southern lands and sold to the poor. The famine lasted two years, one after the other; in 1867 the rains had been plentiful but stopped completely in 1868. With-

out the aid of our brothers in Germany, who showered tens of thousands of coins on their brothers in Zamot[12] and Lithuania and the border regions, who knows what would have happened? Each and every week hundreds of silver rubles would arrive in every town to rescue the poor and the indigent. Who is like your people Israel?

At the time many rabbis permitted the poor to eat *kitniyot* on Passover,[13] and the rabbi and *gaon* R. Shimon Traub[14] of Koidanovo [Kaiden in Yiddish] (of blessed memory) opposed this, and demonstrated to his community that this was unnecessary as wheat flour [for matzos] could be obtained at cost without the need to release from prohibition something that had been banned since the time of our ancestors. My father the *gaon* was likewise uncomfortable about permitting this, although he did not object to the practice in other people.

5629 [1868–69]

The financial condition of my father-in-law (may his candle shine) deteriorated greatly during the Polish rebellion and the famine years, and through a loan scheme, he lost my property too that he had taken from me. My wife (may she live) was the manager of all his commercial business, and I became financially liable for it. My father-in-law had to wander away from his house to earn a living. He left for Warsaw and (thank God) succeeded at his business, and his condition improved.

During the winter months we lived together in the home of our father and master (of blessed memory). But even then I had difficult dealings with the stepmother, and could not bear to see how my father suffered from her and from the youth who had become related to him by marriage in the summer of 1867. In midwinter, I therefore left the home of my father and master (of blessed memory) in distress.

In the summer of 1869 I was forced once again to seek medical attention and was advised to go to Warsaw. I visited the *gaon* R. Dov Ber Meisels[15] but discussed no Torah scholarship with him; I found him (may it not befall us) mourning the death of his daughter (may she rest in peace); but I spoke with the *gaon* R. Y. E. Gezundheit (of blessed memory),[16] author of *Tiferet Yaakov* on Torah scholarship for two hours — and likewise met with other dignitaries of Warsaw, including the grandson of the *Hemdat Shlomo*;[17] Rabbi Zeev, author of *Trumat zahav*; and Rabbi Yosef, son of the *gaon* R. Hayim Davidson.

On my journey home during the Repentance Period [September], I took a detour from Zizeva[18] to Lomzha to see my brother-in-law and my sister (rest in peace). It was there that I first met the *gaon* R. Eliahu Hayim Meizel (may his candle shine),[19] who was then the head of the court of Lomzha, and his in-law R. Gabriel Levine, who was a rabbi in Sniadovo [Śniadowo in Polish] (both are now in Lodz), as well as R. Noah Yitzhak Dushkin (may his candle shine). From there I traveled to Kovno, planning to go from there to Vil'komir, and then home.

In Kovno, I again visited the *gaon* R. Israel Lipkin of blessed and righteous memory (he is the *gaon* R. Israel Salanter), and found him studying the tractate *Rosh hashanah*. [. . .] From there, I continued on to Vil'komir. I lingered there until the eve of the day before Yom Kippur, and as a carriage chanced my way I was obliged to travel lest I spoil the joy of the Sukkot holiday,[20] for carriages are not easily obtained. While there, I marveled at the concentration of my father and master the *gaon* of blessed memory, although this was not news to me. From the [forty days from the] beginning of the month of Elul until after Yom Kippur he would speak of no unholy matters; still the level of concentration I saw in him now was unlike anything I had ever seen in all my days. Indeed his sacred hand did not move nor did his mouth cease from engrossment in his studies; his Talmud continuously was in his hand; he was always glad to talk Torah

scholarship with us, although even then he was not really paying attention, so that he was not distracted from his studies and did not lift his eyes from the small Talmud that he held in his sacred hand. Apparently realizing that he was not long for this vain world, he forced himself to labor mightily to complete all the six orders of Mishnah by Simhat Torah, as was his habit every year.

5630 [1869–70]

When I left him on Yom Kippur Eve, he accompanied me down [to] the bottom of the steps to the yard and blessed me. I set off and immediately my heart struck me, why did I not say to him, "May it be that we shall be privileged to meet again"? Not for nothing did my heart register this pain, for on Thursday the 16th of Marheshvan the celestial lights dimmed, and on the morn of this bitter and urgent day I was summoned by telegraph to Vil'komir as the crown had been removed, and the glory of Israel and his holiness was lifted: my father, my master, had been called to the heavenly yeshiva.[21]

The members of my household did not reveal to me that the holy tabernacle had gone, and I hurried to hire a post chaise to arrive for afternoon prayers. I found them already occupied with cleansing his sacred body. Then the entire community went to the great synagogue for the eulogy, and the old preacher the *gaon* R. Yitzhak Aharon, may his candle shine (now residing in the ancient holy city of Jerusalem), delivered the funeral oration there. Among the large, tightly packed crowd, I too was asked to say some words, but was unable to say anything, save for a little idea that occurred to me about the phrase "Father lives" [*Pesachim* 3b] and a few other comments on other phrases, which I no longer recall. [. . .]

The funeral was held at night after evening prayers, and as I walked I discussed with the aforementioned preacher rabbi whether to go or to heed the opinion of the kabbalists, who are strictly against [contact with the dead, which defiles]. We concluded that it was a positive commandment for an Israelite [not a Cohen or Levi] to defile himself for a father; and as there was a possibility here of a positive commandment I went, for there was no opportunity to seek counsel about this.

To this day I am chagrined at having done so, and may heaven forgive me, for I meant to do right by heaven. At the time all or most of the community of Vil'komir were my followers, and so they asked me to speak on the occasion of the completion of the order of *Nezikin* in the Talmud society in the *kloyz* there, for they had completed the tractate of *Makot*. I gave a splendid sermon, [and] all the town's scholars were bowled over and stunned by it as they had not expected this—including the gifted young Mr. Zvi Hirsch Volk Hacohen (may his candle shine), who was there (he is now my dear friend the *gaon* head of the court of Pinsk). They immediately began to talk about appointing me as their rabbi and [to ask] why are we hesitating. I easily could have settled this to my advantage.

Yet in my heart, under no circumstances did I want to be anywhere near the stepmother and her daughter, all the more because of the groom destined for her daughter, who was already the bane of my father (rest in peace), and who had already been kicked out of his home. Only because he was the fiancé of the daughter of that woman was he sent for and brought back again; afterward, however, a fight broke out between her and the young man. Especially after the passing of my late father, to my distress, quarrels and hostility erupted between both of them over the fiancé. I saw that no good would come if I were to reside there and especially if I were to accept the rabbinical offer. Hence, I left the town of Vil'komir, to my heartfelt joy, after nine weeks, and returned home, thank God.

An inherited rabbinate is not a good thing at all. The Lord has fulfilled in me, by the grace of my fathers, the saying: "You shall be called by your own name and settled in your own place." [. . .]

When I returned home, I began to give Talmudic lectures at the *kloyz* in Ponevezh. I reviewed the commentators and especially the Jerusalem Talmud on each chapter daily and at the time discovered many novel interpretations (thank God) and wrote them in my notebook and also lectured in honor of my father (of blessed memory) using his *novellae*. I then wrote my great composition *Seder Mishnah* based on the large accumulation of quality Torah sermons (thank God), and hastily wrote it up in the year 1870 and the first half of 1871.

[. . .] And last but not least—this year I was blessed with a male child, whom I named after my father. I fulfilled the commandment of circumcision as required, and it was most pleasant and enjoyable.

In the middle of this year I was summoned to Vil'komir on a matter involving my younger sister (may she live) whose engagement had been broken off. I had much unhappiness from this, and my studies suffered as a result.

5631 [1870–71]

In the winter of 1870–71 I took yet another trip to Vil'komir, and from there went to the home of my brother-in-law R. Zvi (may his candle shine). [. . .] I lingered for several weeks with them; from there I went to Utsiany [Utena in Yiddish] to the house of the rabbi so well spoken of, the son of the *gaon* P. T. (of blessed memory). There I met the son Rabbi Binyamin (may he live a good long life) who occupied his father's seat, filling his position with honor. He told me about a difficulty that his father (of blessed memory) had told him in my name having to do with ritual immersion.

In the summer of 1871 I journeyed once more to Warsaw for the treatment of my eye ailment (may it not befall us); there I met a notable by the name of R. Zelkind, famous among the Lithuanians: a wise and smart person who does much to strengthen the bonds with our Lithuanian brethren living in Warsaw, who at the time were still few in number. I heard from him once that he had had the book *Pirhon* by R. S. Pirhon, with [handwritten] commentary and references by the *gaon* R. David Luria, (of blessed memory), but that while in his possession it got burnt, which he much regretted on account of the notes that were penned in it. I told him to give me [another] copy of this *Pirhon* and that (by God's aid) I would try to annotate it to the extent of my meager ability. He lent me the book, and I sat in the house of my father-in-law for one of the days in the month of Tammuz and went through the whole thing writing in the margins all of the references, omitting only a few items for which I was then unable to identify the source. It pains me greatly that I do not know what became of that book *Pirhon* with those marginal notes of mine; may the Lord restore me my loss.

After staying there several weeks, I saw no sign of improvement from my treatment by the Warsaw doctors, and I was advised to go to Vienna, capital of Austria. After a proper breakfast I drank coffee and beer; I did all I needed to prepare myself for a slow and long journey but did not think to take measures against stomach weakness along the way. At the time, there were still no restrooms in the railroad cars and, as a result, I nearly missed the train at the Chernovitz Station where I had to get off to relieve myself. In my haste I approached the cars after the third bell and clung to the doorway: one of the policemen came to shove me back down to the platform, but a soldier who was traveling with me signaled to the policemen, who eased off of me. He then realized he had confused me with someone else and grew very angry with me: I had quarreled with him earlier, in the section of the trip between Warsaw and there.

I then observed one of our brethren of the new generation riding with me; he had seen the very long braids of my *tsitsit*, which, thank God, I was not ashamed to wear despite the ridicule of some people; he was dressed in his manner with his *tsitsit* hidden under his outer garments, as is the fashion. I challenged him: why is he ashamed of a divine commandment, bless His name? But he pointed out that he was wary of the travelers who are not of the faith, and it was not, heaven forbid, that he be contemptuous of a commandment. And he showed me his little boy, four years old, who was dressed like a non-Jew: he lifted his clothes and underneath them was a fine and ornamented garment with *tsitsit*, which pleased me. But I did not change my behavior, although the soldier kept his eye on me. I have written this story so that we may learn not to regard anyone with suspicion, even those of the new generation.

As I knew no one in the city of Vienna, I had brought with me several messages to help speed my meeting people in a foreign land: from the *gaon* R. Zevil Klepfish (may his candle shine), a rabbi of Warsaw, to R. Shimon Sofer (of blessed memory) the head of the court of Krakow; also, from the venerable R. Yehoshua Levine of Warsaw (father of the rabbi, R. Yudel, may his candle shine, who is now an authority in Warsaw), and his brother R. Gavriel (may his candle shine) in Lodz, to the Krakow *gaon* [the aforementioned Sofer], requesting him to write to his brother-in-law the rabbi R. S. Z. Spitzer, who was a rabbi in Vienna.

From the *gaon* R. Eliahu Hayim Meisel (may his candle shine) who was then head of the court of Lomzha, I had a letter to the *gaon* R. Spitzer himself; to deliver that, I made a detour to Krakow to give the letters to the *gaon* R. Sofer, and to ask him for a letter to his brother-in-law. When I arrived at his [Sofer's] place I found that he had gone for an evening stroll in the fields; [after] relaying my wishes I was told to come back the following morning, but the next day I did not find him and was told by members of his house that he had been obliged to go off to Padgorza [Podgórze in Polish] to see his daughter. Yet the members of the household promised he would meet me in Vienna.

When I went to see him one other time I found him eating lunch and waited till he had finished his meal, speaking meanwhile with [the members of] his righteous court, one of whom was the *gaon* R. Hayim Natan Dembitzer (of blessed memory).[22] I told him the purpose of my visit and who I was, and he related to me that he had already heard of this from his father and master (of blessed memory), which seemed to me a remarkable thing.

When I arrived early Friday morning at the great city of Vienna, I was as empty as a riverbed in the desert; I went off to one of the inns, at a place called Saltz-Gris. I had no acquaintances there and was secretly glad of that but sad that I had no wine over which to make the Sabbath blessings.

I did not find the *gaon* R. Spitzer at home because he was in the baths near Vienna. So I was alone with no one whom I knew, and none who knew me. I myself prepared all that I needed: I bought raisins to make a wine for the Sabbath blessings as the Law requires. Little by little I adjusted to a town that was alien to me and was glad of my fate, for I remained anonymous. Every day I went to the eye doctor, famed throughout Europe, known by the name of Arald. I paid him five *gulden* a week.

I prayed every day in the study hall of the Talmud Torah in central Vienna. Soon I met the venerable rabbi R. Shlomo Neter, a bookseller and (I believe) a native of Yagustav, who in earlier times, as a boy, had left Russia to avoid military conscription and had wandered to Hungary where he studied for two years in the yeshiva of the Hatam Sofer (of blessed memory). With him I had the pleasure of bantering and conversing on Torah scholarship, sitting always in his shop where I saw many books from abroad that I had not known even by name. He showed me one small, fine book, the *Toledot ha-Rambam* (of blessed memory) (I believe),[23] and I wrote many comments in

it; as I did with *Zera Yitzhak* on the Mishnah;[24] in its margins I wrote many comments, thank God. [. . .]

After residing there for several weeks, I learned of the study hall in Ships' Lane (called the Schiff [ship] Shul) and went there every day to perform afternoon and evening prayers; even in midday I went to look at the many books they had there.

And then, one day while walking there I met on the bridge the *gaon* R. Shimon Sofer (of blessed memory), the head of the court of Krakow. He immediately made my acquaintance and apologized for not keeping his promise to me at the time, for he had been obliged to travel from his house—and his promise would be fulfilled now as he would introduce me to his brother-in-law R. Spitzer in person; I mentioned this to R. Shlomo Neter, and he was quite amazed by this—the latter told me that the two of them had been as friendly as brothers and that when he had studied with the Hatam Sofer, Shimon was a little boy, whom he used to beat and lash with whips sometimes on the orders of his father (of blessed memory).

[. . .] A fine youth from the Pressburg yeshiva came to the same inn. He had studied at Pressburg for several years and had real talents, among them, the ability to give a commentary on every passage of Scripture presented to him on the spot without looking anything up, as I was able to observe in person several times. I heard him praise that yeshiva so often that a fierce desire arose in me to travel to see it.

When I told this to my friend Rabbi Neter (of blessed memory), he gave me a letter of introduction to the *gaon* R. Avraham Rosenbaum (of blessed memory), one of the greatest and wealthiest men in Pressburg. In it he praised me for he had seen my prowess in Torah. [. . .] I traveled by ship on the eve of the Sabbath, and as soon as it began to move I recited the travelers' prayer. A distinguished God-fearing gentleman there with me pointed out that the ship had not yet left town and that the prayer ought not to be recited until it had done so. I replied that the requirement for waiting until leaving the city center applies only to land-based departures, lest the speaker return home and hence cause the blessing to go to waste. But in a ship or steam train where there is no possibility of return one should pray immediately, as was my case here.

When I arrived at Pressburg, I did not know where to turn as I knew no one and no one knew me. I followed a person who had accompanied me and whom I had seen on the way perusing a book of Eighteen Benedictions in abbreviated form (this was not yet published in Russia); with his consent I went to his home.

And at once all the chambers of my heart filled with light and gladness, for I found in his house darling youths dressed in might and glory: delighting in the Torah, working on the novel interpretations of the yeshiva head and leader of the court, and being preoccupied only with the Lord's Torah. I began to talk with them about Torah scholarship.

[. . .] I was sleeping in the house of a poor person near the Street of the Jews, not far from the synagogue. I ate only lunch (at the home of R. Rosenbaum, of blessed memory), as was my custom, to avoid having more comforts than other people. When it came to be known indirectly that I was living a poor and difficult life on a meager budget, and that I had not come there to collect funds, nor to travel further to Hungary, they made efforts to grant me as much as twenty-four rubles out of their kindness, which was twenty-six gold pieces in Austrian money. [. . .] They did me a great honor as they saw me off back to Vienna, for I do not crave money.

[. . .]

Before I set off for home via Warsaw, the drafting of terms was concluded for the engagement of my younger sister, Sarah Hanah (may she live), to Mr. Reuven Zilber (may his candle shine), for the sake of which I had trav-

eled to Vil'komir. The terms were written in the courtyard where the father-in-law lived, and his brother-in-law happened by: Rabbi Mendel Levine (may his candle shine), who is now the head of the court of Shiravent. For almost two days no sleep came to my eyes, literally two days when all the guests spoke to me one after the other on Torah scholarship and were greatly impressed by my talents, thank God.

The marriage date was set for the first of Elul. At the time I was in Vienna, and fearing they might postpone the marriage date, I hastened to return home. From Warsaw I sent a telegram to Vil'komir that I wished to come home but, if not for the marriage, would linger in Austria. I had a mind to detour to L'vov to meet the *gaon* R. Yosef Shaul Natanson, of blessed memory, or to Sanz to visit the *gaon* R. Hayim Sanzer, of blessed memory[25] (and some in Vienna wanted to cover my expenses), but I feared that the marriage would not take place and would be postponed until my arrival. God forbid that the orphan girl should suffer on my account, and the fiancé was, alas, like the sons of the [biblical character] Eli.[26] So I hurried like the eagle and made great haste to return home. Yet my haste was in vain. They did not reply to my telegram, and when I suddenly came to the house of the father-in-law on the eve of Sabbath, I did not find anyone of in-laws and relatives who had come—they had gone home. If I had known this on the way, I would have gone off to Ponevezh directly from Warsaw; unaware of this, with a heavy heart, I spent that Sabbath in the house of the father-in-law. From there I set off to Chesarka to my sister Esther Leah, may she live, until after the annual memorial for my righteous mother (of blessed memory) which is on the fourteenth of Elul; and from there I went home by a different route, not via Vil'komir so as not to meet up with the stepmother. I had told her that I had much bitterness in my heart about their failure to announce my return. I suffered many trials and tribulations and long travels because of her, and this was the reward for my endless years of toil. Therefore she would never see my face again. I felt great regret in my heart for having acted honorably and, as a result, had not been graced to meet the abovementioned mighty Torah *geonim*. And all my life I shall not be able to forget or forgive her for this.

5632 [1871–72]

At the time of my return to Russia, a cholera epidemic (may the Merciful protect us) was raging there. So in my passage from Warsaw homeward I took a detour via Lomzha to visit my brother-in-law and righteous sister in the town of Piatnitsa; there too the cholera (may it not befall us) was widespread. I took along their son Moshe Michal (may his candle shine) to stay in my town and study outside my home. When I came to my town I found traces of the disease there as well, and on the night of Yom Kippur I too suffered from it, heaven help us. I had to take medication yet continued to sleep on the floor in the *kloyz* as has been my practice long since. By day too I took only drops of the medicine in cups of water, and thank goodness recovered.

Toward daybreak on the night after Yom Kippur, my daughter, the five-year-old child Elta, fell ill with all the signs of the disease. I hurried to the medical council building and brought back medicines, but by evening her pulse had already stopped (may it not befall us). The doctors gave up on her, but the sole and trustworthy Doctor watched over her and sent His aid from the skies as a true miracle. Everyone said they had witnessed a resurrection.

On the second day of Sukkot, the bookcase tipped over and was about to fall on my son Binyamin, but the Lord saved him from this. But he too fell ill with a disease similar to cholera, may it not befall us, and by the fault of the medical people who took a long time to come, he was severely afflicted by the disease (may it not befall us) until he passed away and

was lost to us and to all of Israel on the night of the fifteenth of [the late fall or early winter month of] Kislev, to our endless sorrow. He was already a darling child who went with me to the *kloyz* and knew all the blessings and answered amen properly to any blessing he heard, and was handsome and good-looking and pleasant and was thought well-mannered by all who knew him. Given his talents, he would have been great in Torah and worship had I been privileged to raise him. The Lord took him, blessed be His Name. The Lord gave us another son, born around the chapter of *Mishpatim* [in the dead of winter]. A male child was born to us: I named him Azriel after my father-in-law, the righteous rabbi Azriel Ziv (of blessed memory), who was the prayer leader in Grodno and whose name is such that all those named after him grow to old age. I gave the boy the further name of Binyamin, after my late father and master. [. . .] Everyone called him simply Azriel.

This boy greatly surpassed the first one in his talents, was quite good-looking and sharp and quick in all his manners and actions, and would specially watch my every step to see how I acted, and would always ask about everything and why I did it that way. By the spring of his boyhood he was thoroughly conversant with all of the blessings and quick to carry out the commandments to the extent of his ability. When he would come back from his lessons—which we both greatly enjoyed, for I had the privilege of seeing my son going to a Talmud Torah—we would walk toward him and say, "here comes Azriel" (as I used to say affectionately). He would get angry at this, and several times reprimanded me: who was he that I should come for him? He was of a naturally modest frame of mind.

My tranquility and joy from him did not last, owing to an ailment that befell him and suddenly affected his legs. He would cry out in the middle of his sleep in a bitter voice, when I did not know what was happening to him; nor did he know about it afterward. Several times while shouting he would open his eyes and look about and did not know about this afterward; by day he would complain of a slight pain in his right knee.

In the summer of 1873, I was honored by the holy community of my hometown of Pikelin [Pikeliai, in Lithuanian], which sent me the offer of a rabbinical appointment via the dignitaries R. Zvi Hirsch, H. D. Ben Zion, and his brother-in-law R. Kadesh. For their rabbi, R. Avraham of Kraz (of blessed memory) had been bedridden (may it not befall us) for many years with the disease of paralysis (may it not befall us), and they were compelled to find another rabbi, for whom they could not pay more than five silver rubles a week plus expenses. Although I desired to fill the place of my late great father and master (of blessed memory), I replied that I could not accept their offer until I had made a thorough investigation to see if this was acceptable to the rabbi R. Avraham; in no way (heaven forbid) would I act against his will even if the world should end. So I set the date of my final response until after the Sabbath of Nahamu. It turned out that this was not in accord with the will of the preacher R. Avraham (of blessed memory). As someone informed [me] a year and a half later, he had written to his dear friend the *gaon* R. Y. M. of Ragli (may he live a good long life) that as the latter and I were close friends I would surely heed his words. Therefore he (the *gaon* R. Y. M.) should write to tell me that I should not go to Pikelin as he did not wish it and that his adversaries there wanted to make him angry about this. But the *gaon* R. Y. M. did not write to me at all and told me nothing about it, as he was certain that I would by no means do this.

Before they had received an answer from me, some other rabbi of great scholarly repute, who was a skilled preacher, was hired by them, although he was not at all to the liking of the rabbi R. Avraham (of blessed memory), who greatly regretted that I myself had not agreed to accept the rabbinical appointment. For then he would have been much better off. [. . .]

5634 [1873–74]

Before the Purim holiday of 1874, the town of Felkrai[27] was left without of a rabbi, and my brother the rabbi (of blessed memory) asked me to go there with him as it was just some six leagues from Ponevezh. But before I was able to leave, another rabbi had already taken the job, and I wrote my brother that I would not go there alone without him. Later on, accordingly, when the community of the town of Ligumy [Ligumai in Yiddish] in the same vicinity needed a rabbi, he again wrote to me to take a trip there; I replied, I would not go by myself and if you yourself did not come with me, neither I nor you would get anything.

But I went anyway, accompanied by a preacher as a middleman, and arrived one morning after prayers, passing through the town of Radzivilishki [in Kovno province]. The innkeeper told me that a scholar who resembled me had already come into town and had already said prayers in the study hall. I went there and it was — his honor, my brother. We lodged together in the home of the wealthy R. Zvi Yannover — and again things turned out differently than we had discussed. It was concluded that he would loan the townsfolk four hundred silver rubles, which they would repay him along with his salary over two years.

We left there with the letter of rabbinical appointment he had been given. He had to go to his town of Telz [Tel'she] and I to Ponevezh. We were late in getting under way and arrived at Shavli at three in the afternoon. In our haste he continued to Korshany [Kurshan in Yiddish] but did not manage to take along his things so that they were left on the platform. I was told of this by another coachman and went to the stationmaster to ask for the belongings back, but he did not oblige me even though I told him all of the contents. So, the next morning when the steam engine again returned to Shavli and had to stop there, the saying of the rabbis of yore was fulfilled: "Good thing for me my cow broke its leg."[28] For while he was at the home of his friend, the *gaon* [Yosef Zekharyah Stern] the author of *Zekher Yehosef* (may his candle shine), the latter informed him that there was a rule to be found in the laws of "Transfer of Fines and Confiscated Property," which prohibits the giving of funds in any manner for the sake of obtaining a rabbinical appointment. Accordingly, he withdrew the acceptance, saying, "Whatever happens to me, God forbid that I should transgress against an edict of our *gaon* rabbis of blessed memory." And thus, through the mediation of our friend the *gaon* Zekher Yehosef (may his candle shine), the townspeople agreed to appoint him without any loan whatsoever.

Toward the end of the summer of 1874 I traveled there to visit him and to pay him respects before the elders of his town. I took along my daughter Elte Bat Sheva and lingered there for some weeks.

In the month of Marheshvan [some two to three months later], 5635, I went there on the occasion of the circumcision of his son Binyamin Eliezer (may his candle shine) and then too lingered a month. We took great pleasure from each other's company.

On the eighth of Shevat [about one month later] my spouse (may she live) gave birth to a girl whom I named Esther Friedl. Following the Passover holiday of 1875, Rabbi Hillel Milekowsky departed from Ponevezh, having served as the rabbi there since the Shavuot holiday of 1869. The word going round was that I was the only candidate they would take to replace him, but even so they asked my advice about every rabbi who had been proposed to them, and I gave them my opinion, for I no longer dreamed of the rabbinical business. Especially in so great a town as Ponevezh, the burdens of a rabbi are onerous, and my income sufficed for me to live respectably through the shop that my wife (may she live) managed.

But the voice of the masses is like the voice [of the Almighty], and all said as one: is this not David who leads out and brings in,[29] etc., and already they began to beat on my door to trouble me with the cares of the rabbinate.

I did not speak with a soul or did not discuss this with anyone—until a time came when the community's dignitaries scheduled a special assembly to confer about the appointment of a cantor. One person there held a grudge against me, and upon hearing that I was the subject of much conversation in town, secretly had great fears that I might be appointed as the rabbi. So he too came to the meeting and berated them: why are you talking about a cantor when what you need is a rabbi?

The honorable town elder R. Shmuel Kisek, and then the wealthy Hayim Broda replied that there was no need at all to discuss a rabbi as we already had in our town someone suited to the crown of the rabbinate. The words had scarcely left his mouth when everyone followed suit and began to sign the rabbinical appointment. The signature papers went around to hundreds, all that was missing was to transmit this to me. It was agreed to delay this till the return of R. Hayim Broda from the wedding of his son, born in late age, for which he had gone to Petrikov for two weeks—so as to give him the honor of delivering the document to me in person. Meanwhile the document took up a full folio sheet covered with signatures on all four of its sides.

On Friday, the eve of the Holy Sabbath, the twenty-third of the month of the sign of Gemini, my birth month, all the town dignitaries assembled at the community hall dressed in their Sabbath and holiday finery, and the paper was transmitted to me in grandeur and glory, with great love and incredible overflowing affection—the merits of my fathers redounded to my benefit. I gave an elaborate sermon on a text of the *Sifre* to Deuteronomy. [. . .] They all cheered.

There were some who wanted to have me brought in high style under a regal canopy with a musical accompaniment to the study hall, to be seated on the throne of the rabbinate. But under no circumstance did I agree to such an honor.

The following day, in the Great Study Hall, I gave an elaborate sermon for two hours about the phrase by R. Elazar ben Azariah "behold I am some seventy years of age," part of which I drew from my writings from the end of reading *Beshalah* of 1869 by the grace of God. From then on I prayed in the Great Study Hall, in the seat of the leader of the court; I left the *kloyz* I had been praying in since my marriage.

At the end of the summer I took a trip to Vil'na, seeking medical treatment for my eyes, and lodged in a household in Bubezisak, twelve *versts* [12.84 kilometers] from Vil'na, at the home of my brother-in-law R. Zvi, may he live. We went to Vil'na for two days where I had the pleasure of meeting the R. Bezalel Hacohen, the foremost authority on all things in Vil'na. He urged me to join him in permitting the *etrogim* of Corfu.[30] I replied that since I was one of the junior rabbis it would be inappropriate for me to stick my head in among the mountains, all the more as I am fond of *etrogim* from the Land of Israel. I have the habit of saying, that even if an *etrog* is finest of the fine in appearance, what matters is the spiritual "fineness" I possess when I say the *hallel* and *etrog* blessings, holding an *etrog* from the Land of Israel in my hand and the memory of Zion in my heart — no glorification is greater than this. [. . .]

5637 [1876–77]

On Thursday the twenty-fifth of Shevat my son Mordechai Yonah was born to me; I named him thus after our family patriarch Rabbi Mordechai Yaffe, of blessed and righteous memory, author of the *Levushim*. I added the name Yonah after my late and righteous mother, but everybody just called him Mordechai. I then held a large circumcision party and gave a Torah sermon (thank God). [. . .]

5638 [1877–78]

In the summer of 1878 I went to Riga for treatment of my eye ailment and also because I began to suffer from pains in my throat (may it not befall us). I took along the child Azriel Binyamin, who had aches in his right knee, and we were accompanied there by my brother, the rabbi (of blessed memory), who was seeking doctors for his own ailments. I lodged at the family of my uncle, the dear and generous Mr. Pinhas Cantor (may his candle shine). My brother lodged with the children of Toiba Natanson, who lived together in the same house. We lingered there for a month or six weeks. At the time, the *gaon* R. Levi Shapiro (of blessed memory), who was head of the court of Novo-Aleksandrovsk, was away in Dublen [Dubeln in Yiddish] to bathe in the sea, and we took a trip to visit him and meet with him. As we had been friends some long years before, we stayed with him for a day before returning to Riga.

5639 [1878–79]

My son Avraham Moshe Levitt (may he live) was born [on the Sabbath when the portion of the Torah] Vayehi was read [in the early winter]. I named him after my ancestor, the author of the *Levushim* (of blessed memory), and after the *gaon*, author of the *Pnei Moshe* commentary on the *Yerushalmi*,[31] who is associated with the family of my father-in-law (may he live).

Before he was born I had resolved to perform his circumcision myself, but afterward this plan was called into doubt as he was born on the Sabbath: there is a ruling that one does not perform one's first circumcision on the Sabbath. Yet I considered this to apply only to one who is not specially obliged to carry out this commandment [such as a mohel], whereas the father of a son does have such a special obligation, so perhaps the first time is permissible. I found support for this idea in the work of the *gaon* R. Jacob Emden (of blessed memory). [...] But I feared to take responsibility for this on my own and consulted my dear friend the *gaon* of Shavli (the aforementioned Yosef Stern, may he live a good long life), who nearly prevented me from doing this, and I concurred that it would be improper to issue a ruling on a matter that would perplex the public as it runs contrary to the *Shulhan Arukh*.

In the summer of 1879 my son Azriel Benyamin suffered great pains in his leg, so we decided to take him to Warsaw. I went with him in the [summer] month of Tammuz, and the doctors decided to put his foot in a cast (as is usually done for treating a dislocated bone).

Words cannot describe the pain and suffering of this pleasant, tender child, who pleased everyone who saw him with his fine speech and looks. His handsomeness and the charm cast by his face and his movements captured the hearts of all who saw him, since he spoke only in a Torah-related and God-fearing manner. When we traveled from the station in Warsaw to the home of my father-in-law (may his candle shine) I told him: look at all the wonderful and attractive houses and towers. He was not at all amazed for nothing caught his attention; but as soon as we came to the house at the fifth hour of the morning, he took the Bible and studied the Book of Joshua in it—just as at home, where he would concentrate and try to study as much as he could. By my sins he was not able to study the Torah with Rashi's commentary beyond the reading of *Beshalah* [in the middle of the book of Exodus]—but he knew many of the books in Yiddish.

Before we went to Warsaw he had great pains in his leg (may it not befall us) and had to stay in bed (may the merciful protect us) in great distress. Nevertheless, the small books written in Yiddish did not move from his hands. [...] I and my spouse (may she live) watched over him in shifts every night. One time he recalled something from the Rashi commentary in the chapter on *Vayera*, that

the Holy One, blessed be He, listens more closely to the prayers of the sick. He accordingly asked me to show him where in the Eighteen Benedictions one prays for the sick; I showed him that it was in the blessing "Heal us," and told him it was enough to pray this in Yiddish as it is still a prayer in any language. He prayed thus; countless were the many tears from my eyes. And afterward he said that it was true, he had relief from his pain by means of his prayer. He believed with a whole heart that the Holy One, blessed be He, had heard his prayer, and chastised me: why had I not told him of this before, for then he would have been healthy and whole?

In Warsaw he did not want to eat before he had prayed and said that when you eat or drink before praying the prayer is invalid — only if I told him it was permitted would he eat. [...]

I left my son Azriel Binyamin in the care of my father-in-law (may his candle shine), as they were planning to travel in the month of Elul for the wedding of his daughter, my sister-in-law (may she live) in Shavli, and would take him along; so I returned home. On the first of Elul, the wedding was held in Shavli, and there too they were amazed by how careful the boy was with his eating. He would not eat any of the summer's fruit before it was checked for worms [which are not kosher], and took no one's word for it, but said if my father eats it then he will eat too; nor would he drink milk that had been milked on the Sabbath, and so on and so forth: he amazed his hearers and seers by such things.

5640 [1879–80]

On the first night of the Sukkot holiday of 1879 I took him with me to the sukkah that was in the yard, far outside my house, carrying him in my arms. And from my great joy that he too was sitting with us in the sukkah I forgot about the blessing "to sit in the sukkah," and instead said the blessing "that he has kept us alive . . ." before "to sit in the sukkah. . . . ." The next day on the second night I said the blessing "to sit in the sukkah" first, as our rabbi the Vil'na Gaon (of blessed memory) instructs and as has long been my own practice — and then I was asked by this bright boy, why did I do the opposite of what the *Hayei Adam* says (he knew no other book): on the first night you are supposed to say the sukkah blessing first and later "Time" [kept us alive] and on the second night "Time" and later "Sukkah" — whereas I had said these blessings in the reverse order. Tears streamed from my eyes at his talents.

Yet as the holiday ended my joy ceased. This darling boy fell ill on Simhat Torah, more ill than before, began to vomit when eating, and we did not know that he had been stricken with meningitis, may the Merciful protect us. The next morning he lost the ability to speak, and showed by his fingers in the prayer book that he should be given water so that he might ritually wash and pray, and silently recited all the morning blessings, tasting nothing and taking no medications whatsoever, as is the manner of this awful illness, may it not befall us. And afterward he had a seizure [convulsion], may the Merciful protect us.

He had a seizure and began to speak, but was no longer of sound mind; it seems the illness had jumped from his foot to his brain and triggered the infection there, causing the vomiting and the seizure (may it not befall us). His eyes were open; he looked around but saw nothing. He did not cease to speak for several days, but without reason or order. Only infrequently would he respond to what he was asked — he spoke always in the Torah-study and God-fearing manner of his studies and prayers, and it was wonderful to hear him speak as he said nothing during all those days except biblical verses and the speech of the God-fearing. He recited hymn verses, the "Shema" prayer, the Eighteen Benedictions, [. . .] and all that he had read in the Yiddish books. And from this, everyone who heard him could see that he had no thoughts apart from the Lord's Torah and His commandments — one time he "accepted the Kingdom of Heaven" by saying the "Shema" with such love and awe that those who heard it feared to listen and their hearts melted. Another time he asked in a loud and joyful voice, "My father, when will the Messiah come," and his thoughts and speech were all likewise. I did not refrain from praying and giving alms, I prayed prostrate on the ground, maybe God would answer me and take pity on me, but God did not hear my prayer, He hid in a cloud beyond my hopes, and on Thursday the sixth of Marheshvan of the year of bitterness 5640[32] his soul departed in purity to the anguish of everyone who knew him and was familiar with him, who shared in my grief. My heart overflows with sorrow. For on the first day of the *slihot* prayers [recited before Rosh Hashanah, some six weeks earlier] it seemed to me in my dream that my daughter Esther Friedl and my son Azriel Binyamin were being carried off to be buried, and I began that very day to fast the Dream Fast (may it not befall us), but I could not complete it because of the weakness of my heart, and fasted only till noon, and maybe the verdict would have been torn up if I had been able to.

In my judgment, I had sinned greatly with the commandment "honor thy father," and possibly had not acted as I should have during his funeral [see above]. I therefore was not privileged to raise my son who was named after so righteous a figure as my great father of blessed memory, may the Lord forgive me, and guide me with Thy salvation to raise my remaining sons to the Torah and the *huppah* and to good deeds.

NOTES

1. [Elijah David Rabinowitz-Teomim was a major rabbinic figure in Lithuania, serving the Jewish community of Ponevezh as its rabbi starting in 1875. Beginning in 1893, he was also *rosh yeshiva* in Mir. He is perhaps best remembered today as the father-in-law of Abraham Isaac Kook. He left the Russian

Empire in 1901 to serve with R. Shmuel Salant in Jerusalem. This memoir (unusual for a member of the rabbinic class) begins with his time in Lipnishki, before he assumed his post in Ponevezh. As the "Teomim" in his name indicates, he was a twin; his brother Tsvi Yehudah (also a rabbi) and he were very close.]

2. [R. Shalom (no family name recorded) was a rabbi in the town of Lipnishki.]

3. [This is an abbreviated reference to the commentary on the *Shulhan Arukh* of the Gaon of Vil'na, chapter 47, paragraph 4.]

4. [*Kodashim* refers to the order of the Talmud that deals (mostly) with matters of sacrifice and Temple procedures. Although rarely studied in European yeshivot, it became a favorite of Lithuanian Talmud scholars (as it demonstrated that the Talmud was to be studied for its own sake and not for the sake of practical legal matters, since sacrifice was not practiced by Jews after the first century CE) and was part of the curriculum in Volozhin and other *misnagdic* yeshivot.]

5. [Two Talmudic tractates that are part of the order of *Kodashim*. The list of tractates that follows come from the more conventional part of the rabbinic curriculum.]

6. [An early rabbinic commentary on the book of Exodus. It is another of those texts rarely studied in yeshivot that was to become part of the Lithuanian elites' regimen.]

7. [A classic work of Jewish mystical and ethical reflection, most of which was written by Judah he-Hasid of Germany (1140–1217).]

8. [A twelfth-century commentary on the commandments by Eliezer of Metz, one of the Tosafists.]

9. [A month in the Jewish calendar that generally overlaps with January and February in the Julian and Gregorian calendars.]

10. [A fast day that occurs the day before the Purim holiday.]

11. [Despite our best efforts, we are unable to determine precisely what is being described here, and we include it in the hope that someone can identify it.]

12. [Żmudż in Polish and Samogitia in Lithuanian. This was northwestern Lithuania, known in Old Russian as the *zamot'skaia zemlia*.]

13. [Ashkenazi Jews have, for centuries, extended the prohibitions on Passover, so that not only leavened forms of grain are prohibited, but also legumes and other grain-like foods (*kitniyot*). Thus, Ashkenazic Jews do not eat rice, corn, lentils, and beans on Passover, although Sephardic Jews do. These foods were not actually prohibited but were forbidden by custom. Some rabbis felt that in a year of famine it would be acceptable to relax these customary restrictions, while others disagreed. The latter were often the recipients of scorn at the hands of the *maskilim*.]

14. [Shimon Traub (d. 1876) was the author of a commentary on the halakhic classic, *Halakhot gedolot*.]

15. [R. Dov Ber Meisels (1798–1870) became a rabbi in Krakow in 1832 and then served in Warsaw, beginning in 1854. He ran afoul of the Russian government for his support of Polish independence, and he spent the last years of his life under strict government supervision.]

16. [Y. E. Gezundheit (1816–78), chief rabbi of Warsaw.]

17. [*Hemdat Shelomo* refers to the author of the book by that name, R. Shelomo Zalman Lipshitz (1765–1839) of Warsaw.]

18. [This town may be Cyców or Czchów in Polish.]

19. [R. Eliahu Hayim Meizel (1821–1912) became the rabbi of Lodz in 1873.]

20. [The Sukkot holiday begins just four days after Yom Kippur; if he had not traveled in this carriage, he might not have made it home for the holiday.]

21. [Rhetorical flourishes such as these are common ways of describing the deaths of the pious.]

22. [R. Hayim Natan Dembitzer (1820–92) was a rabbi and judge in Krakow.]

23. [Aderet was wise to add, "I believe" as he seems to have confused this event with some other. There were two works with the title *Toledot ha-Rambam* published in the nineteenth century — both in Vienna, but both a decade or more after 1871. Isaac Hirsh Weiss's (1815–1905) work appeared in 1881, David Holub's (1818–90) in 1884.]

24. [The work of Isaac Hayyut (Chajes; c. 1660–

1726), published in Frankfurt-an-der-Oder, 1731–32.]

25. [Natanson (1808–75) was the rabbi of L'vov (Lemberg) and author of the responsa collection *Sho'el u-meshiv*; Hayim Sanzer, or Halberstam (c. 1797–1876), was the founder of the hasidic dynasty of Sanz (Nowy Sącz in Polish) in Galicia. Although tensions between Hasidim and *misnagdim* (like Aderet) remained, the Sanzer rebbe was widely respected in *misnagdic* circles.]

26. [See Samuel I, chapter 2, and BT *Shabbat* 55b and 56a.]

27. [This town could not be identified.]

28. [Talmud Yerushalmi, Horayot 3:4.]

29. [See II Samuel 5:2, referring to the biblical King David.]

30. [See the Hebrew article by Yosef Salmon, "Pulmus etroge corfu ve-rik'o ha-histori," *AJS Review*, 25, no. 1, (2000–2001): 1–24.]

31. [Moshe Margolies (c. 1710–80), originally of Lithuania, authored the commentaries *Pnei Moshe* and *Mar'eh penim* on the Talmud Yerushalmi.]

32. [This year is generally written in Hebrew with the letters TR"M in that order; Aderet rearranges the letters, MR"T to spell out the Hebrew word for bitterness.]

[6]

Tkhines [Supplicatory Prayers] for Women

Tkhine *for a Woman Who Collects* Tsedoke *[Charity]*[1]

Reprinted from Tracy Guren Klirs, *The Merits of Our Mothers: A Bilingual Anthology of Jewish Women's Prayers* (Cincinnati: Hebrew Union College Press, 1992), 100–103.

Riboyne shel oylem [Master of the Universe], You have commanded and directed us in Your Holy *Toyre*: "You shall open," and "You shall give."[2] This means we should open our hands and give the poor man what he lacks. Giving *tsedoke* — having mercy on poor unfortunates — is one of Your holy attributes, for You are compassionate and gracious and You have mercy on all of Your creatures. When You inflict poverty on someone, You do not do it — *khas ve-sholem* — with bad intent or out of cruelty, but out of love. As it is written: "Those whom He loves, God reproves."[3] Therefore, since You love the poor man, we must love him too, and we must help him and support him with all our means.

Tsedoke is one of the three *mitsves*, which remove the evil decree.[4] If something bad is — *khas ve-kholile* — decreed against a person, he can redeem himself by giving *tsedoke*. Perhaps that is why there are always poor people, as it is written: "For the poor will not cease from the land"[5] so that others may have the merit of giving *tsedoke*.

Since not everyone is able to give *tsedoke*, collecting funds and encouraging other people to give is as meritorious as giving *tsedoke* yourself, if not even more. As the holy *gemore* states: "Someone who initiates is greater than the doer":[6] he who encourages someone to perform a *mitsve* is greater than he who does the *mitsve* himself.

I, Your maidservant, who now stands before You, have taken upon myself, as a vow, to collect funds for *tsedoke* and to help the poor and needy. As God is my witness, I do this with all my heart for the sake of the *mitsve* itself and not — *khas ve-sholem* — for honor and recognition. I beseech You, God, who is good and does good, to deal with me graciously and to strengthen my heart, that I may be like You, always good and ready to do good to others. Strengthen me and encourage me, make me strong and brave, so that I may be able to devote myself to this *mitsve* as long as I live. I now submit my supplication before You. I place my request before You, kindhearted Father in heaven, that one of Your good angels may accompany me when I go about collecting for *tsedoke*; may I not approach those people who have nothing to give; may they not feel ashamed before me. I beseech You, *riboyne shel oylem*, may no suspicion fall upon me that I am dishonest in my holy mission. May I be received politely wherever I go, with no suspicion or doubt, for I do my work in good faith. Guard and help me, watch over me, and protect me that I may not — *khas ve-kholile* — misuse *tsedoke* funds in error. Help me so that those who receive *tsedoke* will not be shamed because of me. Good God, may that which is written come to pass for me: "And the act of *tsedoke*[7] shall be peace." May all that I do for the sake of *tsedoke* be done with a full heart and a clear conscience. Praised be You who love *tsedoke* and justice.

"Musar *for Women," in* Eine shas tkhines *(1900)*

Eine shas tkhines (Vil'na: [s.n.] 1900).

I, a woman named Sarah, beseech young women not to talk in our beloved synagogue, for it is a great sin to talk about anything in the synagogue from the moment of *Borekh she-omer* [Baruch she-amar, or Blessed-be-He-who-said] until the end of the *Shimenesre* [Shmone esre, or Eighteen Benedictions]. I therefore warn you, lest you be punished, God forbid, the way that I have been punished, a homeless wanderer. Thus, consider my example and confess your sins to God. I likewise beseech you to have compassion on widows, orphans, captives, the old, and the sick. When you are fasting and your heart is pained and embittered, think of the poor man

who suffers, lacking enough food to give his wife and children. I therefore implore you to pray to God, to set your hearts straight so that you may fulfill with great care the commandments of giving alms to the poor. God, blessed be He, will then also provide for you. I pray to God to provide for me in my old years and days. May my sins be forgiven, just as I have composed this *tkhine* for you. May God grant us life when we remember our sins.

I remember all the instances when I came to the synagogue adorned with precious stones and did nothing but mock and laugh. Today, I remember that God, blessed be He, is just. For it says, "Haktsar bezaam umaarikh af," which means "He waits long and repays quickly." Today, I am homeless and my heart roars within me, for I remember that God grants to everyone that which is just. I therefore implore you to heed my words and take into your hearts that when you come to the beloved synagogue, you should feel great fear, and you should know before whom you have come, to whom you pray, and who will answer you regarding your lives. [. . .] Therefore, I, Sarah, implore you to do this for the sake of dear God, blessed be He, so that He may provide for you generously. For I, along with all the poor, trust in God's promise and pray to dear God to provide for me in my old age, lest our children be driven away from us.

I have composed still another beautiful new *tkhine* that we may be delivered this year from our sins and from the Angel of Death and that God grant us life.

NOTES

1. [Worship of God through gendered modes of prayer took place in the home and public institutions such as the prayer houses and synagogues. Women usually recited *tkhines* in Yiddish, the vernacular of Eastern European Jewry. In contrast to the obligatory Hebrew liturgy that men recited at set times in a public congregation, the *tkhines* for women were voluntary, personal, and generally recited at home. Moreover, the prayers addressed issues of specific

concern to women (such as pregnancy, childbirth, child rearing, visiting the cemetery or mikvah, petitioning the dead, baking bread, and other domestic rituals), and invoked the biblical matriarchs as models of piety and advocates in times of trouble (see Chava Weissler, *Voices of the Matriarchs: Listening to the Prayers of Early Modern Jewish Women* [Boston: Beacon, 1998]).]

2. See Deuteronomy 15: 7–11. [This and subsequent notes for this document are by Klirs.]

3. Proverbs 3:12.

4. Repentance, prayer, and charity; see Midrash, Genesis Rabbah 44: 14 and High Holy Day liturgy.

5. Deuteronomy 15: 11.

6. Babylonian Talmud, *Baba Batra* 9a.

7. Isaiah 32:17.

[7]

The Cantor of Poltava Choral Synagogue: The Memoirs of Genrikh Sliozberg

Genrikh B. Sliozberg, *Dela minuvshikh dnei: zapiski russkogo evreia*. Vol. 1 (Paris, Izd. Komiteta po chestvovaniiu 70-ti letniago iubileia G. B. Sliozberg, 1933), 23–24.

[. . .] Because of the fairs in Poltava, renowned cantors arrived to perform prayers in the synagogue.[1] One of them, who had come to the fair with his choir, remained as the permanent cantor in the large synagogue. This was the celebrated cantor of Berdichev, Yeruham—who was called ha-Katan [The Small] due to his unusually short stature; I do not recall his surname.[2]

Poltava possessed a monumental choral synagogue.[3] It was a very large building in three colors with a high dome. One male section accommodated more than a thousand people. Inside, the walls, ceiling, and dome were covered with paintings of sacred emblems and inscriptions; a grand chandelier lit up this spacious room. Especially luxurious was the decorated holy ark [*aron ha-kodesh*, in Hebrew], which occupied a large space on the eastern wall [*mizrah*, in Hebrew]. Broad gilded stairs with carved handrails led to the platform in front of the ark. The curtain of the ark shone gold and silver; on the inside lay numerous scrolls with rich silver adornments.

Each time the ark was opened with the corresponding prayers, my imagination was kindled, and it seemed like invisible light clouds of divine blessing flowed by on the thousands of bowed heads.

The small and poor population of Poltava could not have built such a wealthy synagogue without the I'linskaia fair. The cantor Reb Yeruham ha-Katan sang in this synagogue, surely pouring out his soul before God. He had a large choir. It is difficult to convey the beauty of Yeruham's tenor voice when he chanted the prayers without the choir. The prayer before Musaf Yom Kippur, "Hineni he-ani memaas" [I am the man of little merit]—its contents always struck a chord and touched my soul, but from Yeruham's lips, they produced a deep impression. I melted into emotional tears, reaching the highest level of ecstasy that an eight-year-old boy was capable of. But such dread enveloped me when Yeruham conveyed the grandeur of the days Rosh Hashanah and Yom Kippur in a haunting voice with the words of the prayer

"Unetaneh tokef"[4]—how the Everlasting in the highest place, with the sounds of the great shofar, sits to judge the world and all living things in it to determine the fate of each person in the coming year: who will live; who will die at his predestined time, who by beast, who by famine, who by sword; who will be enriched, who will be impoverished; who will be exalted, who will be degraded. But hope arose when all the people gathered and exclaimed, "Repentance, prayer, and charity remove the evil decree. [. . .]"

The lot of a *zinger* [chorister] was enviable. It seemed to me that there could be no higher honor than to be a *zinger* for Yeruham, and in my childish vanity, I earnestly tried to make strangers think that I was one of these fortunate ones. To do this, I would sing the opening of the prayers in my thin, childish voice, standing at the door of our house.

NOTES

1. [Genrikh B. Sliozberg, born in 1863 in the town of Mir (in Minsk province), graduated from the law school at St. Petersburg University. As a lawyer, he was very active in Jewish social and political affairs. The first chapter of his memoirs describes his family, which came from the town of Naliboki (in Oshmianskii district, Vil'na Province), the fairs in Poltava, the relationship between Jews and the surrounding population, Jewish life in "Little Russia" (Ukraine), Jewish education, and his childhood in Poltava. This selection is from chapter 1.]

2. [Presumably this is Yeruham ha-Katan, mentioned by Pinhas Minkovsky (document 1). His actual name was Yeruham Blindman (1798–1891).]

3. [Choral synagogues were elaborate buildings with the bimah and ark as the focal point by the eastern wall. They were especially known for the male chorus that replaced individual chanting during prayers.]

4. ["Let us recount the power of the holiness of this day."]

[8]

The Cantor of Vil'na and Cantorial Competitions: The Memoirs of Avraam Uri Kovner

Avraam Uri Kovner, "Iz zapisok evreia," *Istoricheskii vestnik*, 91: 3–4 (1903): 1002–1004.

Having returned to Vil'na [from Stolbtsy, in Minsk district], I lived at my parents' home for two years, amid a large family that steadily increased. Mother gave birth exactly every two years, and the children were all healthy: they lived and grew. However, the material position of my parents not only failed to improve, but deteriorated. Poor father just wasted away, and mother, burdened with the cares of the brood of children, grew nastier and nastier.

[. . .] My sole diversion was visits on the Sabbath and holidays—though not always—to the main Vil'na synagogue, where the cantor performed the prayers with a choir of choristers, especially when the main Vil'na cantor happened to be the cantor from Lomzha, who possessed a marvelous tenor voice and knew how to read music. I considered his singing and compositions to be of the acme of perfection.

This very cantor of Lomzha, by the way, happened to be the subject of a deep and stormy dispute between the Jewish parties in Vil'na. The Orthodox—and they were the vast majority—were satisfied with the old cantor, who with his tremulous voice and dissonant singing aroused irrepressible laughter among the worshipers; but they did not want any innovation. The progressive party, however, which had gained strength after the Crimean War [1853–56] stood solidly behind the cantor who had arrived from Lomzha, charming his listeners with an extraordinary voice and operatic melodies.

One must say that they often leased out the synagogue for cantorial competitions. If a vacancy opened up for a cantor in a large Jewish town, then the aspirants with their choristers set out to make a debut at such-and-such a synagogue, on such-and-such a holiday or Sabbath. A crowd of a thousand showed up at these free concerts so that there was not enough room, and depending on the merits of the debutant, the audience expressed its approval or disapproval, but not with applause or booing, rather with quiet expressions of satisfaction and rapture, or with clucking and laughter.

And at these [competitions] there were not only the debuts and sample of voices! Some debutant cantors struck the audience with thunderous basses, others with thin trebles, still others with unusual trills, some with a resemblance to a flute, and so forth. From some, the songs came out quite harmoniously, while others emitted such mournful sounds from their throats that one wanted to flee the synagogue. The homespun melodies and tunes of the composers did not always fit the text of the prayers: either they sang a dance tune when the words of the prayer expressed reverence to God, or they struck up doleful sounds when the prayer expressed the joy of the soul. If you add the fact that both the cantor and the choir were singing with their cheeks propped up with their hands and a fat finger resting on the windpipe, then you get a picture of the solemn service in a prereform synagogue. However, I return to the new Vil'na cantor.

To [my] surprise, the young Jewish party in Vil'na gained the upper hand. They accepted the cantor of Lomzha into the Vil'na synagogue and set a decent salary for him. He went about performing his duties. At first, after the terrible dispute, lovers of good singing were not admitted into the main synagogue, which was always jampacked at the time when the new cantor was performing the service. The Jewish community even took into its head to exploit this passion of its members and organized paid tickets for entrance into the prayer house, which was not very expensive, however (from ten to twenty kopecks a ticket). Subsequently, however, they canceled the ticket [system]; it was only kept for the semiholiday of Hanukkah [Festival of lights], when they organized a formal vocal and instrumental concert about which it is worth saying a few words.

Hanukkah is celebrated by the Jews to commemorate the victory that the Maccabee brothers won over the terrible yoke of Antiochus and the restoration of services in the Second Temple. Legend has it that when the High Priest was to light the holy fire before the altar of the temple, there was no holy oil anywhere so a miracle took place: the seven-branched lamp suddenly were filled with oil on their own accord and the High Priest was able to perform the rite.

So here, in commemoration of this victory and miracle that took place two thousand years ago, the Jews honor the holiday of Hanukkah, which continues for eight days. However, not having a religious basis in the Pentateuch, Hanukkah is not considered a "holy holiday," but is celebrated with general prayers and with the following kind of ritual. On the eve of Hanukkah, every Jew is obliged to light one branch of the menorah adapted for this purpose or one wax candle, on the second day two lights, on the third three—and so on until the eighth. These branches or candles must burn no less than half an hour; the public lighting of the lamps in the synagogue and prayer houses is carried out solemnly with singing and music. This is the only instance when musical instruments are permitted within the synagogue walls.

In this way, every town, depending on the musical abilities of its cantor, organized annual vocal and instrumental concerts. These were renowned in Vil'na, especially during the tenure of the cantor of Lomzhin; everyone in town gathered at his concert. In the main synagogue, where they admitted those without a ticket, such a stampede occurred that many suffocated and fainted; the unconscious had to be brought out from the synagogue, passed from one person to another over their heads.

The cantor himself, his small choir, and a few violinists, two to three flutists, and two to three double basses participated in the concert. In the majority of cases, the cantor sang concerts of his own compositions, though one often came across the melodies of Meerber and Ha-Levi. However, still more than the choir or the ensemble [of musicians], the cantor distinguished himself in the highest degree with his original recitatives and enchanted audiences. They performed the same concert on the day of Hanukkah in various prayer houses, when the public was admitted only by tickets, which sold like hot cakes. These concerts, as I have said, afforded me the greatest pleasure. Never having a lump sum of 10–15 kopecks at my disposal, I saved up this amount during the course of a month from pocket money that my father gave to me, to the tune of one *grosz* a day.

Religious Dilemmas and Jewish Law

[9]

Yehudah Leib Gordon, "The Mouth That Forbade Was the Mouth That Allowed"

Yehuda Leib Gordon, "Ha-peh sheasar hu ha-peh shehitir," *Kol shire Yehudah Leib Gordon* (St. Petersburg: Be-defus G. F. Pines, 1884) 2: 160–62.

The Rabbi's cow — allowed
(people say)[1]

"It's a scandal, Rabbi, among Jews, that took
   place
An imp of a youth broke the Sabbath,
   bare-faced."
— What'd he do, pray tell, what has
   gone on? —
"The woman standing, just over yon
Saw him while out, while walking apace
Carrying a time-keep in a public space."
— A time-keep's an implement, hence its
   transport [we say]
Is strictly forbidden
(Ruled the rabbi — law-keep, a.k.a.)
Its carrier sternly must be punishment given
To serve for the youth of the times as
   example
Lest they on the words of the Wise do
   trample.
Hurry, you beadles, go find him,
Go catch him,
To me you must bring him.
And the beadles hurried and ran and
   spread out
And one *melamed*[2] caught him and brought

Him back to the rabbi who looked — to
   discover
The criminal here was his son, and no other.
His heart turned about and his fury passed
   soon,
He smoothed down his beard, and shifted
   his tune:
"Contrariwise, nay? A time-keep [no doubt]
Is an ornament, which one's allowed to
   take out.
And no spaces are 'public' in the present age,
   why
All are twixt-and-tween, having few
   passers-by."[3]
And the rabbi's son thus came away clean
By having a father so sharp and so keen
Who could twist around words of the
   living God
As a man twists a shoe to his foot, to be shod.
If the beadle who found him hadn't been a
   melamed
He'd never at all to his dad have been trotted!
Haven't they guessed how with rabbis it is?
The Torah interpreted has many faces.
The beam that's poking in our eyes
To them is a pick, that their teeth divides;
What for us and our sons is clearly forbidden

Is quite allowed to them and their children.
The *gaon* rabbi of Havila (holy town)
By our great sins, prayer turns down.
What do folk say? "That's his might!
He won't pray, when in his brain there's a
sprite."
In Susa-court, forbade Rabbi Ishmael
Etrogim that come from the Land of Israel.
And why's that? — well, his uncle and
dear kin
Has his *etrogim* from Corfu to trade in.
The son-in-law of Rav Pesach the luminary
Takes from the indigent 50 percent usury.
In Gamla-town there's a ban on all Passover
wine:
The rabbi's daughter trades in the
raisin-juice line.

NOTES

1. [The point here is to suggest that the rabbi's
cow will always be considered kosher, although
people may be quite strict in ruling on the status of
the cows of others. It is impossible to say how widespread this allegedly popular saying was.]

2. [A *melamed* is a schoolteacher. Melamdim (pl.)
were frequently the target of Jewish enlightenment
writers; they were reviled for their lack of pedagogical sophistication, wisdom, cleanliness, and just
about all other virtues.]

3. [In Talmudic law a true public domain, in
which carrying objects is biblically prohibited, is
extremely rare, as it requires that the domain be a
contiguous space in which 600,000 people pass by
every day (this is the definition according to the medieval sage Rashi [1040–1105], which was widely if
not unanimously accepted). Spaces treated as public
spaces for the purpose of the Sabbath laws are thus
only rabbinically prohibited, and one may therefore
be more lenient concerning what may considered a
vessel versus an ornament.]

[10]

Responsum of R. Naftali Zvi Yehudah Berlin of Volozhin: Oaths

Naftali Zvi Yehudah Berlin, *Meshiv davar*, 2: 45 (Warsaw: [s.n.] 1894).

Q. On the question that was brought to me: A
son was born to a man, and he took an oath to
set aside a set amount each week for eighteen
years; once the entire sum was saved he would
use the sum to purchase a Torah scroll. But
when two and a half years had passed, and he
had amassed seventeen rubles, the child died.
The question is whether he is still bound to
his oath, and whether he is permitted instead
to spend this money for the purchase of other
books. May God enlighten my eyes.

A. [. . .] As to whether he is allowed to buy
other books with these coins, that is easy: if
this man has not yet fulfilled his commandment to write [purchase] a Torah scroll he
certainly may not exchange this for anything.
In the opinion of most adjudicators the commandment to write a Torah scroll has not
ceased to apply to this day. Even though according to the Rosh[1] it is a greater mitzvah
to purchase other Talmudic works, that is explained by the *Turei zahav*[2] and the Vil'na
Gaon in *Yoreh Deah* as applying only with regard to donating a Torah scroll to the syna-

gogue, not writing one for himself; however, if he already owns a Torah scroll, then surely it is a greater mitzvah to benefit others by means of books of the Talmud and the later commentators. In any event, that whole discussion is relevant only to the case where he is asking us what sort of mitzvah he can fulfill with his money. But if he has already taken an oath to purchase a fine Torah scroll, certainly one may not deviate from what has issued from his mouth: know that a person who takes an oath to bring a sacrifice of *shelamim* and instead brings a sacrifice of *olah* has not delivered himself of his oath, even though *olah* has greater sanctity than the *shelamim*. In any event he must fulfill his oath. Moreover, [given the language of his vow] even in the category of Torah scrolls, he must buy only

a single one with this sum, a fine expensive one, and not buy two Torah scrolls and give them to needy synagogues, which would otherwise be the right thing to do. If he vowed to buy a single Torah scroll he has no right to deviate from this. So he must purchase a Torah scroll with this sum, and do that which has issued from his mouth. I am the overworked:[3] Naftali Zvi Yehuda Berlin.

NOTES

1. [The acronym for Rabbenu Asher, or Asher ben Yehiel (c. 1250–1327), one of the leading halakhic authorities of the Middle Ages.]

2. [The name of a commentary on the *Shulhan Arukh*, produced by David ha-Levi Segal (c. 1586–1667).]

3. [A common closing line from Berlin.]

[11]

Responsum of R. Yitzhak Elhanan Spektor[1]:
Etrogim

Yitzhak Elhanan Spektor, *Ein Yitzhak*, Orah Hayim 1: 24 (Vil'na: [s.n.], 1888).

I was asked by several rabbis about *etrogim* stored under the bed. Tractate *Pesachim* explains (112b) that foodstuffs and liquids stored under a bed have an evil spirit hovering over them. Hence the *etrog* under the bed, which is not serviceable for consumption owing to the evil spirit in it, would not be eligible for fulfilling the ritual obligations of *etrog* use; and as tractate *Sukkah* (35a) explains, an *etrog* that cannot be eaten cannot be used for ritual pur-

poses; likewise *Orah Hayim* chapter 749 section 5 says if eating it is forbidden, it does not qualify. Hence the same should apply when consumption is prohibited because of an evil spirit.

NOTE

1. [Rabbi Yitzhak Elhanan Spektor (1817–96) of Kovno was one of the leading rabbinic figures in the Russian Empire and Eastern Europe generally.]

[12]

Responsum of R. Yitzhak Elhanan Spektor:
Hametz

Yitzhak Elhanan Spektor, *Be'er Yitzhak*, Orah Hayim 1: 1 (Koenigsberg:
Ba-defus he-hadash shel Gruber et Longriyen, 1858).

Q. Someone was not at his home on the eve of Passover, and was in a location from which he was unable to sell his *hametz*;[1] and he believed he would be able to get back home in time to sell the *hametz* but was late and arrived only after the time *hametz* had become prohibited. The court in charge of the business of selling *hametz* made efforts on his behalf and sold all his *hametz* following the policy that a person may be granted a benefit without his being present. I was asked whether the sale is valid.[2]

A. The response, by the aid of God. We find in tractate *Pesachim* 13a that *hametz* that has been placed in the charge of a trustee is, at the fifth hour, to be sold; and as is explained in the *Orah Hayim* chapter 443 and the *Hoshen Mishpat* chapter 292 section 17, even if [the trustee] is not liable for damages, he should sell it; and even if there is a great quantity of *hametz* that is not about to be used up prior to the time of prohibition, the sale of the trustee is nevertheless valid as is explained there. This seems problematic: Who gave the trustee permission to sell? For one may not sell what is not one's own; [. . .] thus, who gave him permission to sell? And do we not expect at least an indication from the owners granting a right to sell [rather than choosing] to be in transgression of "Thou shall not have [*hametz*] in sight [on Passover] . . ."—All of this necessarily proves that the principle of "a person may be granted a benefit without his being present"[3] is in force here, and we accept the opinion of the trustee that this person would certainly be pleased with the sale so as

not to lose his property, and that this is a valid sale, and "Thou shall not have in sight . . ." has not been transgressed upon.

NOTES

1. [It is forbidden to have *hametz* (products containing leavened grain) in one's house during Passover. As financial and practical considerations made it difficult, if not impossible, for most people to comply with this ban, the custom developed of selling the *hametz* in one's possession, putting it out of sight, and then buying it back after the holiday; thus, during the holiday, the householder did not own it, and therefore did not transgress the prohibition. In this case, a traveler was delayed and could not get back before the deadline to sell his *hametz*.]

2. [The question revolves around the Talmudic principle that one may act as another's agent, even without being asked to do so, to provide a clear benefit for that person. That is, if one is certain that another person would want this beneficial thing done for him or her, one may do it without a formal request or appointment. Given the difficulties in communication, this kind of *post factum* question—we did XYZ, was this right or valid?—was quite common. Local rabbis could not contact the primary deciders in a timely way to ask the question before deciding.]

3. [This is a principle in Jewish law that states that one may serve as an agent for another—even if unappointed—in order to procure what is unequivocally a benefit for that person. Not losing the value of the *hametz* is clearly a benefit for the person who was away and could not get him in time.]

[13]

Responsum of R. Yitzhak Elhanan Spektor: Share of Books in the Study Hall

Yitzhak Elhanan Spektor, *Be'er Yitzhak*, Orah Hayim 1: 24 (Koenigsberg: Ba-defus he-hadash shel Gruber et Longriyen, 1858).

Whether individuals praying separately can demand their share of the books in the study hall. [Here is] what I answered another rabbi.

[In this] case, there is a town that has long had a synagogue, and recently several people left this synagogue to pray by themselves. They are now demanding their share of the income from the old synagogue and also demanding their share of the books and the sacramental utensils of the old synagogue. Your honor ruled that they may not at all sue and diminish the rights of the old synagogue and expounded on this with sound arguments; and I concur, for it is clear they cannot transgress a boundary[1] set down by predecessors. For even *ab initio* if a minority of people wish to build themselves a new synagogue in a location where there is an old synagogue large enough to hold everyone, the majority can prevent the minority from being able to separate off and build another synagogue [. . .], and I have found the like in *Pahad Yitzhak*,[2] citing several authors who wrote at length that if the new synagogue would cause damage to the old, they may be restrained from building it on the grounds of threatening its ability to sustain itself. Accordingly if some congregation splits in two over differences of opinion all the sacred objects are to be given to the larger party, and even those held by the smaller one may be removed from them and handed over to the majority. But if they split because the space is not large enough to hold them all, it would be proper to divide [income and property] according to the number of males. For as your honor wrote explicitly [. . .] if there was a good reason for splitting in two, the rule is that all the sacred objects are to be divided up, etc. For it is different if the split was for a real reason such as the space is not big enough and so forth; but if they split only because of differences of opinion, they do not have the right to demand their share. And in any case there is a principle that the townspeople can impose their will on any faction, and the majority may compel the minority; and although there is an opinion [. . .] to the effect that a town's selectmen may not introduce legislation that causes profits to this one and losses to that one, it is nevertheless accepted that the majority may compel the minority. Clearly, therefore, the minority may not diminish the rights of a majority, rights it has long since held.

NOTES

1. [In rabbinic tradition, the biblical prohibition on transgressing a neighbor's boundary (Deut. 19:14, 27:17) also limits competing with one's neighbor economically. For example, the Talmud notes (*Baba Batra* 21b) that one may not set up a fishing net too close to another person's net. Spektor is applying the principle to opening up a competing synagogue or prayer house.]

2. [A Talmudic encyclopedia written by Yitzchak Lampronti (1679–1756) of Ferrara, Italy.]

[14]

Responsum of R. Naftali Zvi Yehudah Berlin of Volozhin: Counting a Minor in a Minyan

Naftali Zvi Yehudah Berlin, *Meshiv davar*, 1: 9 (Warsaw: [s.n.], 1894).

FOR THE LOVERS OF OUR TORAH AND THE CHAMPIONS OF THE WORD OF GOD, FOREMOST OF WHICH IS THE DEAR RABBI ETC. IN THE TOWN OF TSARVISTAN.

I was asked to venture a decision about whether a minor can be counted for ritual matters requiring a quorum.[1] I was surprised: how can a decision be set down on a matter over which both the early and late rabbinical authorities of blessed memory were divided? Anyone acting one way may not be faulted, nor may anyone acting the other way. Yet it is probably best if a minor is not counted. For if one rules thus permissively in times of duress [when the community is too small to have a quorum] one might assume this is acceptable practice even after the urgency has passed, such as when the minor achieves majority [when it would be wrong to count a minor because a quorum is possible]. Your honor should not be upset by the inability to recite the sacred passages requiring a quorum; for just as one is rewarded for doing what is required when it is possible, one is rewarded for refraining when it is impossible. [. . .]

But as to whether you can include the BILU [antireligious Zionists][2] who desecrate the Sabbath in public, and have them join you, heaven forbid, in anything that involves religious worship: even though it is explained in the *Shulhan Arukh* (chapter 55, section 11) that a transgressor or one who has sinned may be counted for a quorum of ten—that applies only to someone whose apostasy is confined to one single issue. For while "the sacrifice of the evil is repugnant" we nevertheless accept sacrifices brought by the sinners of Israel, as is said in tractate *Hullin* (5a), so that they might repent. And [if that applies for sacrifices] all the more so does it in the case of prayers, which are of lesser significance. But someone who believes in idols[3] and publicly violates the Sabbath, someone from whom a sacrifice would not be accepted since it is taken for granted he shall never repent—the prayer of such [a person] accordingly is repugnant. How then can we join with him [in prayer]? For in a place where his prayer is repugnant, the obligation for prayer has not been satisfied even after the fact; see *Brachot* (22a).

NOTES

1. [In traditional Jewish law a quorum of ten adult males is required for several matters, especially for the recitation of certain prayers. There are those who would support counting a minor (under thirteen years of age) when ten adult males are not to be found (here described as "times of duress").]

2. [A student group who were members of Hibbat Tsiyyon; their name was taken from the Hebrew letters of the verse: "House of Jacob, let us go up."]

3. [This phrase is not to be understood literally; rather, it is a term used to designate an apostate. Here the term does not require the embrace of another religion, but simply a rejection of the Jewish tradition.]

[15]

Responsum of R. Naftali Zvi Yehudah Berlin of Volozhin: A Separate Study Hall and Synagogue

Naftali Zvi Yehudah Berlin, *Meshiv davar*, 1: 11. 1 (Warsaw: [s.n.], 1894).

GOD BE BLESSED THE 8TH OF TEVET 5643 [1882], VOLOZHIN.

TO THE RABBI ETC. AND HEAD OF THE COURT OF THE HOLY COMMUNITY OF LAHOYSK [LOGOYSK].

I received your letter with the accompanying documentation yesterday, in which the complaint came to me about the small town of Gayna [Heyna in Yiddish], which is a suburb of and adjacent to your community; they heretofore accepted and contributed toward the salary of your rabbi. But they have grown and now have a community of ten [men] and more; they built themselves a separate study hall, and recruited a young man—a preacher and teacher—and appointed him rabbi. This has caused a loss of income to the rabbi, the chief of the court [of your town], may his candle shine; and your honor and those with him have appealed to me for justice to your honors.

Before answering, I must clarify the matter of whether they did a good thing in building a separate study hall and synagogue. For even in a single town, if it was necessary to form a new synagogue, the *Magen Avraham* in chapter 154 writes (citing the Ribash)[1] that one is prohibited from blocking another, and he who prevents or delays construction is classed as one who prevents the masses from fulfilling a mitzvah. All the more so in a case of people living ten versts [10.7 kilometers] from town: surely it is a great mitzvah to establish among them a special place for prayer. And the fact that they hired themselves a preacher to give sermons and homilies each and every Sabbath is right and fine on their part: after all

what shall the faithful masses do on holy days if not go to the study hall to hear the word of the Lord? In the Jerusalem Talmud tractate *Eruvin* (5:1), R. Hia cites R. Shimon asking, how is it that people traveled to the study hall of Moses—for Moses was near the Holy Tabernacle, and the Jewish public were as far away as one *mil* [0.9 km]. They explain, that Moses built them three huts and way stations. Here, too, given the great urgency, they are required to [take measures to ensure that there is] "a teacher of righteousness" [rabbinic leader] in their midst; although it would have been best if they had sought permission from the honorable Head of the Court (may his candle shine) who could have seen to it that the person is fit to be a teacher and is God-fearing. Likewise, the heads of the community should have looked to the needs of the satellite community, and seen how they could have brought a source of income and a little aid from the coffers of the larger community, for instance by sharing proceeds of the [kosher] meat tax [*korobochnyi sbor*] to which they contribute. Then the honor of the community and concern for the rabbi and his income would have also been part of their obligation. But if your honor did not attend to them, then surely they had to transfer their obligations to the local rabbi, to the teacher who would carry on his holy labors for them. And even though it is not clear whether they had the right to withdraw their obligations to the rabbi of the big city, we can do nothing about it now, and they will not listen to us—indeed they are not bound to listen to us. Why then should I flatter myself falsely that they will be satisfied with what I say and will not check to see if I am right? Accordingly, [rather than to issue a contested ruling, I find that] there is no recourse except to take the case to the large court nearest to your community, and follow whatever verdict they issue. But it would be better to collect opinions from everyone and to appeal to a great sage who is wise and knowledgeable in worldly matters such as these and to reconcile the adjacent community to the leaders of the larger one. He will determine in a proper manner what issues may be decided by the local rabbi without requesting permission from your honor in the big city, and what issues he needs to ask of [you, the rabbi of the larger community who is] someone greater than he and the author-ity of the region. Such a great sage would also be able to mediate the issue regarding what is to be paid to the "teacher of righteousness." And your honor should set his heart on maintaining tranquility in the community and surrounding areas and must not let matters go until there is a wide rupture, God forbid. He who restores peace to Israel shall bring peace to their residence and into their midst—and my heart too shall rejoice.

NOTE

1. [*Magen Avraham* is the name of a commentary on the *Shulhan Arukh* produced by Avraham Gumbiner (c. 1635–82) of Poland. Ribash is the acronym for Isaac ben Sheshet (1326–1408), a Spanish authority.]

Conversion to Christianity

[16]

Petitions for Conversion

"Petition of Vil'na Townsman, Vulf"
Iankeliovich Portukh to Aleksandr
Bogdanovich Efrey (Head of the
Preobrazhenskii Guards Regiment),
5 August 1863"
LVIA, f. 378, d. 314, ll. 1–4.

My underage son, Iankel, prompted by childish stupidity, caused sundry mischief and went into hiding. [. . .] Based on the search that I conducted, I learned that he was in hiding at the barracks of Your Excellency's section of the Preobrazhenskii Guards Regiment, which evidently intends to exploit his minority, to violate the freedom of conscience, and to tear asunder by force the natural ties between my son and his unfortunate parents.

In the name of the magnanimous Sovereign, our great Alexander II, who has most graciously granted complete freedom of conscience to all loyal subjects, I dare to pray with bitter tears that Your Excellency will make an order [. . .] that my son, who has been kidnapped, will be immediately returned to me.

"Statement of Iankel Vul'fovich Portukh"
[n. d.]

I, Iankel Vul'fovich (the son of a Vil'na townsman), swear and attest that I have not been taken by force and will convert to Russian Orthodoxy. This was [always] my desire; only before, there was no such opportunity to realize [this desire]. Now, however, with

an opportunity before me, I entered the 5th company of the Preobrazhenskii Guards Regiment. No one is forcing me to embrace Russian Orthodoxy; I myself am of sound mind and wish to embrace the Russian Orthodox faith. My father, Vul'f Iankeliovich, declares in his petition that I have been taken by force. This is not right. I told my father, in the presence of the commander (Col. Gel'freikh) that I want to convert to Orthodoxy [voluntarily], not by force. I have my own understanding of my wishes and ask the authorities to bring this to fruition.[1]

"Petition of the Merchant's Wife Freida
Srolovaia Poliakova to the Bishop of
Kovno for Baptism (29 July 1866)"
LVIA, f. 605, op. 4, d. 485, l. 1.

For a long time, I have nourished a desire to embrace Christianity. I fully understand that the promised Messiah in the Old Testament—Jesus Christ—has already come and is revered among Christians. I believe in him with all my heart and soul and can no longer remain in Judaism, although [baptism] brings a loss of external privileges. But I hope that the Lord God will not leave me without His Holy Providence and, since it remains impossible at present, that He will give my children a Christian direction in the future.

With these feelings and the recognition of the above-stated truths, I left my husband in Minsk and arrived here [in Kovno] in order to realize my wish, at least without any impediments. I see that the Lord God has already helped me in this charitable place — through the kind people at the St. Mary's Convent [in Kovno]. [. . .] My daughter Mariia (known as Merka in Judaism), who is seven years old, is with me. My daughter and I are already preparing to receive the saving baptism of the Russian Orthodox faith because we have studied all the principles of the Christian faith, life, and prayers for a long time by ourselves.

I humbly beseech Your Reverend Grace to give orders about instructing me and my daughter for Christian holy baptism at the place where we receive charitable care [the convent].[2]

"Memorandum from the Dean of Novoaleksandrovsk, Priest Afanasii Kovalevskii, to Bishop Aleksandr of Kovno (12 April 1866)"

LVIA, f. 605, op. 4, d. 123, ll. 1–17.

In his report on 10 April of this year, the priest of the St. Il'insk Church submitted the correspondence with the staff of the 3rd Infantry Battalion of the Vladimir Regiment about a Jewish girl, Khaia Essimovna, from the Dolginov community (Vil'na District) and a deposition that the priest took from her. He reported that this Jewish girl has sufficiently studied the principal truths of the Orthodox faith, and he asks for official permission to give instructions on the holy baptism of this Jewish girl: "[. . .] I have the honor to ask Your Grace to give an order [. . .] about this Jewish girl, who is now in the town of Vidza, and who endures many troubles from [the Jews] because of her intention to embrace Christianity.

"Statement of Khaika [Khaia] Essimovna (6 August 1866)"

My name is Khaika [Khaia]. My father was called Essim but I do not remember his surname. By religious confession, I am Jewish, but once the desire to embrace Christian-

ity awoke in me, I no longer followed [the rites of Judaism]. I am eighteen years old. By birth and place of residence, I consider myself a resident of the village Dolginov [Vil'na district] where I should be registered in the census because my father lived in Dolginov permanently as far as I know. I do not have any [document] that refers to me and have never had one. There is no way that I can obtain it from the Dolginov Jewish community. I do not have parents; I lost them when I was still very young. I was brought up by relatives. [. . .] When I had grown up a little, they placed me in service [as a domestic servant] in Dolginov, and I was there all the time until the fall of this past year. But from the fall until my arrival in Vidza, I was sent to the Jews in Vilensk, where I feared the persecution of the local Jews because of [my desire] to embrace the Christian faith. I ran away and arrived [here] without even my passport — for the sole purpose of being instructed in holy baptism. I seek holy baptism not for some kind of temporary passport but for the sake of salvation for my soul. I believe that God's promised Messiah has already come long ago — Jesus Christ, the true God incarnate from the Holy Virgin Mary, who is worthy of a place in the Holy Orthodox Church.[3]

NOTES

1. [The father sent another petition to the general governor of Vil'na, but there was no resolution in the file. In all likelihood, it was rejected as the son signed a statement in Russian (written in his own hand) declaring his desire to convert.]

2. [Poliakova's passport showed that she was thirty-two years old, of medium height, with dark hair and eyebrows and brown eyes. The mother and daughter were baptized on 5 September 1866. The former signed a declaration that she would always remain a Christian and promised to raise her daughter in the Orthodox faith. On 28 March 1867, the Lithuanian Spiritual Consistory wrote to the city police of Minsk to confirm the news that the husband of the new convert Poliakova had remarried.

It asked for details about the new wife and date of marriage. The city police of Minsk replied that Srol' Poliakov had indeed been remarried in March 1867—to Khana, the daughter of a merchant's son, Aron Liubarto.]

3. [The Dean of Novoaleksandrovsk reported on 20 August 1866 that Khaika [Khaia] was baptized and renamed Elena. On that very day, the bugler from the 3rd Battalion of the 61th Infantry of the Vladimir Regiment of Prince Gorchakov "proposed to her and she accepted immediately." However, since the battalion was moving from Vidza, she followed him to the village of Karslav (Vitebsk province) where he would be stationed for summer work. The dean had not received any news about whether they had celebrated their wedding yet.]

[17]

Missionary Activities to Convert Jews in Lokhvits (1903)

"Report of the Head of the Department of Police (25 July 1903)"

GARF, f. 102, 3 d-vo, d. 1307, ll. 1–7 ob.

On 13 July of this year [1903], His Imperial Majesty received a telegram in Peterhof from Lokhvits addressed to "Your Loyal Imperial Majesty," from a member of the Russian Orthodox Missionary Society, Court Councilor[1] Fedor Shishkov. The telegram read: "Tsar of Russian Orthodoxy, appointed by God! Please order a strict inquiry into the actions of the Jewish population in the town of Lokhvits and the Jewish rabbis, toward whom certain agents of the local police are overindulgent, to prevent a disturbance by the population."

His Majesty had sent this telegram to Your Excellency; at your command, the governor of Poltava was to provide information about both the substance of this telegram and the person of its petitioner, Shishov.

In a memorandum of 11 July of this year, the governor of Poltava reported that a retired Court Councilor, Fedor Nikitin Shishkov, settled in the town of Lokhvits (Poltava province) in 1899, having served as the government rail-road controller in the city of Ashkhabad. He lives on a pension from the State Treasury in the amount of fifty-nine rubles plus interest, together with a small amount of capital in his possession. He is a moral person and extremely religious. Having settled in Lokhvits, Shishkov began to help Jews who desired to convert to Russian Orthodoxy, instructing them in the dogmas of the Orthodox faith and giving them shelter in his own home. During his four years in Lokhvits, through his mediation ten Jews (six girls and four men) converted to Russian Orthodoxy; he adopted two of these through legal procedures. The majority of new converts live at Shishkov's, treating him as their own father, and are completely under his moral influence. The Jews of Lokhvits have been extremely upset by such activities and have repeatedly complained to provincial authorities that Shishkov has allegedly converted their children by force. However, the local assistant to the district chief of police did not corroborate the Jews' claims; and those who converted to Russian Orthodoxy attested that they did so out of conviction.

Among the Jews of Lokhvits, all this generated hatred toward Shishkov—which they expressed by repeatedly hurling insults at him and those who converted to Christianity. For example, on 2 November last year, after the Jew Khazanov converted to Russian Orthodoxy, two of his brothers assaulted Shishkov on the street. On 13 May of this year, as Shishkov made his way to the priest Gladkom with the Jew Khaimovich, who subsequently converted to Russian Orthodoxy, the latter's relatives hurled insults at Shishkov and Khaimovich. [. . .] When two converts to Russian Orthodoxy, Khaimovich and Aronov, were walking down the street, Iankel and Mordukh Livshits began to fling mud at them.

From the cases presented here about Shishkov's conflicts with the Jews, the first in particular merits attention: when Khazanov's brothers dealt blows to Shishkov, the Christians who saw this, indignant at the action of the Jews, rushed home to carry out reprisals, and only the timely appearance of the police prevented a possible disorder.

All these incidents, as well as the fact that the local clergy of late do not regard Shishkov as someone normal in terms of religious sanity and refuse to perform [the rite of] holy baptism on the Jews whom he brings [to them]—all this gave grounds for Shishkov to send the telegram addressed to His Majesty.

In addition, the governor of Poltava added that the local district chief of police has taken necessary measures to prevent any kind of conflicts between the Christian and Jewish populations in a timely manner.

NOTE

1. [Court Councilor was an upper-middle title in the pyramidic Table of Ranks—hierarchical positions introduced in 1722 by Peter the Great to determine status through military, civil and court service.]

[18]

Jewish-Peasant Conflicts in Stepashek Following the Conversion of Anastasiia Lerman (Shimanskaia) and Her Marriage to a Peasant (1901)

"Report of the Governor of Podolia to the General Governor of Kiev, Podolia, and Volhynia (24 August 1901)"

GARF, f. 102, 3 d-vo, g.1050, ll. 7–9.

In a telegram of 3 August 1901, the chief of police in Gaino district reported to me that on 30 July the peasants from the village of Stepashek (Kuniansk township [*volost*]), a mob of about two hundred people put the belongings of eight Jewish families residing in the village onto carts, headed for the Bug River, and dumped them on the shore. The reason was that the daughter of one of the Jews, Lerman, having converted to Russian Orthodoxy in January and married a local peasant, Shimanskii, disappeared this past July. The peasants are convinced that she abandoned her [Christian] faith and that the Jews persuaded her to do this and assisted in hiding her. Despite all the persuasion of the local chief of police about resettling the Jews [in the village], the peasants do not agree to this.

As a result, I was dispatched to [Stepashek] where the incident took place, to calm the peasants and establish order. A member of the Provincial Agency for Peasant Affairs, State Councilor Chervinskii, who set off for the village of Stepashek with the district chief of police and deputy Justice of the Peace candidate, Tsukkerman, found the following [facts] at a full peasant assembly. Eight Jewish families, numbering around fifty people, live in the village of Stepashek. Five families live in peasant houses and three in the manor house; they are engaged in the mill arenda [leaseholding] of the owner Elovitskii, small trade, the purchase of products from the peasants, and brokerage [*faktorstvo*, in Yiddish]. The peasants explained that, in addition, [the Jews] engage in different types of theft by using the peasants' children (tempting them with candies and toys).

The daughter of one Jew, Lerman, converted to Russian Orthodoxy, [was renamed] Anastasiia, and married the local peasant Shimanskii, a teacher at the parish church school in the village of Guz'kin in the same district. At the time of a visit to the home of Shimanskii's father-in-law [that is, her own father] during the summer holidays, Anastasiia suddenly vanished to some unknown place. The peasants presume that the Jews kidnapped her at the instigation of her father, the Jew Lerman, and acted upon her according to their own Talmudic law—that is, if she renounces Russian Orthodoxy and returns to Judaism, they carry her off somewhere far away and give her in marriage to a Jew there; however, if she remains a faithful Christian, then they kill her. This incident strongly aroused the indignation of the peasants, especially peasant women, who—without the participation of the men—took all the Jews with all their belongings to the edge of the village,

on the other side of the Bug River, left them there, and forbade them to return to the village. What is more, they touched neither the property nor the persons of the Jews. As a result, a few of the Jews resettled in the nearby town of Ladyzhin, but others have remained camped on the banks of the Bug River.

After the peasants' explanation of the facts, State Councilor Chervinskii ordered that the Jews who remained on the riverbank be resettled with their belongings in their former places [of residence] and that it be carried out by members of the local police in his presence, without any resistance on the part of the peasants. He ordered an announcement to those who had relocated to the nearby town of Ladyzhin that, if they desired, they could return to the village.

The matter of peasants who had taken the law into their own hands was transferred by the district chief of police to the court investigator for further instruction. State Councilor Chervinskii, however, proposes that such a resolution will not reconcile the peasants, whose agitation arose on religious grounds. The legal decision, no matter how wise and just it may be, will neither calm the indignant conscience of the peasants nor shed light on the truth of the entire case, thanks to the thousand-year experience of Jews and their communal solidarity. With complete confidence in the peasants' explanation, he concluded that the only correct and expedient solution to this case would be an administrative removal from villages and settlements in the Pale of Settlement—if not all Jews, then certainly this Jewish family Lerman, from which the missing Anastasia Shimanskaia had come.[1]

NOTE

1. [The minister of internal affairs marked up another copy of the same report (31 August 1901) and put a large question mark in the margin next to the proposal to remove villages and settlements from the Pale of Settlement. In a letter addressed to Mikhail Ivanovich Dragomirov (the general gov-

ernor of Kiev, Podolia, and Volhynia), the minister stated that although he would have been prepared to remove the village of Stepashev from the Pale of Settlement, he could not do so based on "one available rumor about the kidnapping and concealment of Shimanskaia." He feared that such measures would "present difficulties and perhaps bring about disorders" (DAKO, f. 1, op. 1, d. 258, l. 9–9 ob.).]

[19]

Disorders Following the Secret Conversion of Gitlia Korn in Lublin (1904)

"Report of the Governor of Sedletsk Province to the Ministry of the Interior (22 July 1904)"

GARF, f. 102, 3 d-vo, d. 1, ch. 18, 1.B, ll. 18–28 ob.

On 10 July [1904], the Jews engaged in disorders in the town of Parchev [Parczew] (Vlodavsk [Włodowa] district), in the province entrusted to me. These disorders were due to the arrival of the converted Jewish woman Antonina Korn, who was summoned by the Justice of the Peace Court for a trial on alleged theft.

The inquiry into these disorders is being conducted by the court investigator of the Sedletsk [Siedlce] District Court for major offenses (under the direct supervision of the procurator of the Sedletsk District Court). Based on the information collected by judicial and administrative authorities, the incident—which arose exclusively on religious grounds—occurred in the following way: the eighteen-year-old Jewish girl Gitlia Korn from the village of Sestrozhov (Iashchev community, Lublin district) by birth, intending to convert to the Christian faith, left her parents and took up residence in a workhouse [*dom trudoliubiia*] in the city of Lublin.[1] During the course of seven weeks, she prepared for her conversion to the Roman Catholic faith

with the priest Klopotovskii. During Gitlia's stay at the workhouse, her parents attempted to seize her, and for this purpose they filed denunciations with the Lublin authorities. As these denunciations lacked any grounds, the authorities took no action. Then the Jew Shiia Pankevich, a permanent resident of Parchev married to the cousin of Gitlia (now Antonina Korn), charged her with stealing ninety rubles. In the words of the plaintiff, this theft was committed in the town of Parchev, and that is why the case must be heard in that town, but, as it turned out, she had never been to Parchev in her life.

The Justice of the Peace for Vlodav and Parchev, Makarenko, set the hearing for this case on July 19 and summoned the accused to court. The head of the Lublin city police, Captain Merling, sent her on July 7 from Lublin to Parchev under the supervision of a constable. Father Klopotovskii, fearing violence on the part of the Jews, sent the organist of the Dominican Cathedral with them, providing the accused with the metrical registration of baptism, which was performed that very day, namely on the morning of July 7. These people arrived at 12:00 p.m. at the Parchev station, invited another railroad gendarme [to join them], and then set off for the city to the mayor. The latter, fearing that the Jews would set fire to or demolish the detention cell, found it safer to place Korn in a local tea shop. To conceal Korn's whereabouts, they brought her to the mayor around 3:00 a.m. from the tea shop to the constable Karpov's apartment at the other end of the city.

The following day, the staff captain Protopopov, chief of the rural police, arrived in Parchev by chance on another matter. When he received a report about events there, he shared the mayor's fear that the Jews would discover where Antonina Korn was staying. Approving the proposal to send Korn to the Milianovskaia Hospital (as did the mayor and prior of the Catholic parish, Father Verzheiskii), Protopopov left Parchev. On the night of 8–9 July, Korn was moved without a guard to the Milianovskaia Hospital, four versts [4.28 kilometers] from Perchev. There someone told Korn that she would depart for Lublin on 9 July at 5:00 p.m.

Upon arriving in Lublin at 9:00 p.m., Korn stopped at the workhouse. Father Klopotovskii, learning about her return, immediately reported this himself to the assistant lawyer Zdzennitskii, who was to leave for Parchev to defend Korn. Mr. Zdzennitskii, not knowing the reasons for Korn's release from arrest (which she could not explain), went to the procurator of the Lublin district court for advice. The latter counseled him to return with the accused to Parchev. The defender Zdzennitskii, Antonina Korn, and the servant Martin Damil set out from Lublin to Parchev with the coachman Iosif Goral'skii at 11:00 p.m. the same day, 9 July. They stopped at the home of the Catholic parish prior, Father Verzheiskii, where Mayor Tokarskii, the senior constable, and the gendarme had also come. Korn's relatives showed up here and tried to persuade her to remain Jewish, but she categorically refused.

Before the defender Zdzennitskii and Antonina Korn arrived in Parchev, Mayor Tokarskii personally asked the Justice of the Peace to postpone Korn's trial because of the agitation among the Jewish population, but (according to Mayor Tokarskii) the Justice of the Peace rejected his petition. Hence the moment that the defender Zdzennitskii and Korn arrived in Parchev, Mr. Tokarskii personally dispatched a cart to the rail station [at] Milianov, completely confident that Korn was there and not in Lublin.

With the time set for the hearing approaching (that is, around 10 a.m.), Antonina Korn left for the Justice of the Peace Court, accompanied by Mayor Tokarskii, the defender Zdzennitskii, the servant Damil, the constable, gendarme, and coachman Goral'skii. Soon two local priests arrived there. According to the testimony of various people, approximately 200 to 300 Jews were at the court building. At the conclusion of the case, which the Justice of the Peace examined during the arrival of these people, the matter was decided and she was vindicated. At this time, a crowd of Jews (approximately 700 to 1,000 people) gathered on the street and around the courthouse, with the number growing by the minute. Christians (some 30 to 50 people) summoned to the trial were near the court.

With the announcement of the verdict, Zdzennitskii sent his servant Damil for the coachman. When the latter arrived, the Jews offered him fifteen rubles if only he would leave; when he refused, they tried to overturn the carriage. After that, the coachman drove off. When Zdzennitskii demanded a second time that the coachman come, the latter (who had been persuaded by the servant) made for the courthouse again, but could not reach it since the Jews came up to him; one of them, threatening and pointing to the courthouse, said that those who are there will be killed and if "you drive up, then they will kill you." In view of this, the coachman Goral'skii went back to the priest's courtyard, but the servant went to Zdzennitskii and said that there was no help available.

In the interim, between 11:00 a.m. and

2:00 p.m., the mob of Jews had increased to 2,500 people. No measures were taken by the Justice of the Peace and mayor to block the influx of Jews from the town to the courthouse. The mayor's actions to this point were limited to sending telegrams to the chief of the district about the gathering of Jews. The measures taken by the police were the same — viz., a polite request by the constables to disperse. Not only did the Jews disobey this request but, on the contrary, cries from the mob of "Stand [your ground]!" could be heard in Yiddish. So many Jews pushed their way into the chamber [of the court] that it was impossible to pass.

With such a concentration of Jews, they succeeded in seizing Antonina Korn twice in spite of the fact that she stood in the corner behind the judge's chair and was guarded by the constable and Zdzennitskii with a revolver in his hand. Mayor Tokarskii and Zdzennitskii barely succeeded in tearing the victim away from the hands of the Jews and placing her back in the corner. Then, a resident of Parchev, Mendel El'baum, threatened the mayor with a knife; the latter evaded the attack, shielding himself with a chair. All this took place in the provincial court at the time of another trial at the Justice of the Peace Court. They did not honor Zdzennitskii's request to compile a report about the disturbance, despite the fact that the crowd's behavior on the street, in the courtyard, at all the windows, and even in the chamber of the court was provocative in the highest degree. According to Antonina Korn, a Jew (a paramedic) pricked her in the side with some sharp instrument during the trial; however, upon her examination in Lublin, no mark or wound was found. Apparently, the local private lawyer, the Jew Adler, restrained the infuriated mob until the justice left the court.

At 2:00 the justice announced a break and said that he was leaving for lunch. Zdzennitskii requested that he stay and dine in the court in view of the fact that his presence was a guarantee against violence by the infuriated mob of Jews. The justice replied that guarding them was not his business and left. As soon as he exited the chamber, the Jew Adler, opening the window, yelled: "The justice is no longer here. Now it is possible." Then the mob, which had only been restrained by the presence of the justice, immediately broke the door hinges, smashed the windows, and shattered and overturned the railings in the courtroom. Such a mass of people filled the consultative meeting hall, through the doors and windows, that releasing Antonina was out of the question. No one was even able to observe how they pulled her out of the court. Those who had been in the chamber — the mayor, Zdzennitskii, and others — are convinced that they pulled her out through the window, while Korn herself says that they carried her through the door.

Having seized the victim, the whole mob, surrounding her in an impenetrable circle, began to run to town. Then the mayor called the Christians to save the Christian girl and, pressed by the mob, stumbled over a Jewish boy and fell. The Christians in court, armed with pistols, broke the lattice surrounding the front garden at the courthouse, rushed toward the Jews, and dealt blows to whomever fell in their hands. At this point, the city treasurer Omul'skii — in his own words — fired four shots from a revolver into the air. His example was followed by the young constable Kharkevich, who also fired one shot, but the senior divisional inspector of the police, Skakun, ordered him to conceal the revolver. Omul'skii and Kharkevich's statements about firing into the air are confirmed because the medical examination of the injured did not find a single bullet wound.

Two hundred and twenty steps from the courthouse is Moshka Faigenbaum's brewery, with basements and underground passages. Running past this factory, the Jews with Korn separated from the mob and went to Faigenbaum's house; but the mass of Jews headed for the town. The Christians did not notice this maneuver and pursued the Jews, inflicting blows on them. Only one townsperson of Parchev, Ivan Tyshkovich, apparently aware of the entrance to the factory, began to suspect that the Jews had hidden Antonina Korn in the factory. His suspicions were justified because after a few minutes Antonina appeared at the window, which was located in the courtyard of the stone factory building. The Jews, in their haste, did not realize that the window of this building was visible from the street. At Antonina's cry, "Christians, save me," a few people rushed to the gate next to Faigenbaum's house, tore off the gate, and approached the window of the building. The constable Ordynets helped Antonina down from the window. Exploiting the fact that the entire Jewish mob being chased by Christians had run into town, constable Ordynets along with the Christians who rescued Antonina set out for the priest's apartment, where the coachman was standing. Not tarrying a moment, all those who had traveled to Lublin [. . .] (in the company of two townspeople) set out for the railway juncture Milianov and departed on a train to Lublin.

According to Antonina Korn, when she was taken from the court chamber to the factory, she asked them not to torture her but kill her right away. To this they replied: "That's impossible. We first need to consider how to do it." In Faigenbaum's apartment, Antonina saw a few old Jews dressed in rabbinical clothes in a dark room (with closed shutters), presumably preparing to judge her.

As a result, twenty-nine Jews were injured from beatings, but the local doctor Krzhimovskii judged the beatings to be superficial and not life threatening.[2] It was rumored that some Christians also received blows, but not a single person reported it — most probably for fear that they would be held responsible for participating in the disorder.

According to the report of the district court procurator about the disorder in Parchev, [. . .] ten residents were accused of criminal offenses: Mendel' El'baum, Moshko Liberman, B'iumen Vil'boim, Iankel Faigenbaum, Motel' Faigenbaum, Gdal' Tenenbaum, Abram Rapoport, Khemia Rozenfel'd, Shiia Pankevich, and Shlema Vainberg. Of these, prior to interrogation by the court investigator, Moshko Liberman had hid until being taken into custody by the investigator, and Mendel' El'baum, having been arrested, escaped from the rural constable Karpov who was guarding him; six people were questioned, placed under unconditional arrest, and sent under strict guard to the prison in Sedletsk. To search for the fugitives El'baum and Liberman, the police undertook the most energetic measures. An inquiry about El'baum's flight was carried out where the incident took place by the head of the rural police, Staff Captain Protopopov.

On 17 July, I personally traveled to Parchev to familiarize myself with the mood of the Christian and Jewish populations and to calm their minds. I made the strictest reprimand to the state and spiritual rabbis, and members of the "God patrol" [chelami boznichnago dozora, in Russian] for allowing the disorder; I also asked the local prior of the Catholic parish, Father Verzheiskii, to use his spiritual authority to promote a quiet, peaceful mood among the Christians. I told the leaders of the Christian population — the lavnik[3] and city mayor — that the sad incident of 10 July should be forgotten and that amicable relations between Christians and Jews (for which they had always been distinguished) be restored.

Taking into consideration that the disorder in Parchev began on 7 July but that I received a report about this only on 19 July (and not from the responsible individuals but from the assistant lawyer Zdzennitskii), upon an examination of the case, I made the strongest reprimand to the district head for his nonfeasance in this matter. The head of the rural police was placed under arrest for five days for failing to take measures to prevent the disorder and for not reporting it to me in a telegram on 8 July. I reprimanded the mayor of Parchev for failing to inform me and the district head about the agitation of the Jews immediately upon the arrival of Antonina Korn (that is, 7 July).

At present, the town of Parchev is completely peaceful, and I can affirm that order will not be breached again. I have presented similar information about this case to the General Governor of Warsaw.

NOTES

1. [The *dom trudoliubiia* (industrial home) was a refuge for the unemployed, which provided work and housing for the poor who could not find employment (Adele Lindenmeyer, "Charity and the Problems of Unemployment: Industrial Homes in Late Imperial Russia," *Russian Review* 45 [1986]: 1–22).]

2. [In contrast, in another report, the head of the local police reported greater numbers of injured Jews, some of whom were seriously injured: "At the time of the conflict, there were some forty Jews who were injured and hurt. Three victims suffered seriously: one elderly sixty-year-old Jewish woman whose lips were badly cut and head punctured; one Jew with a broken arm; and another Jew with a punctured head. The doctor concluded that the Jewish woman and Jew [with the punctured head] might die. They caused no Jewish [property] losses with the exception of five houses whose windows were smashed" (DAKO, f. 1, op. 1, d. 258, l. 20).]

3. [A *lavnik* was an elected peasant judge who was in charge of the *gminnye sudy* (*gmina* [municipality] courts) in the Polish provinces.]

[20]

Apostasy: Reconversion from Christianity to Judaism

"Report of the Volhynia Consistory about the Retired Soldier Sergei Ivanov Kotliar to the Procurator of the Zhitomir District Court (27 January 1884)"

DAZhO, f. 24, op. 13, d. 380, g. 1884, ll. 1–30.

The Volhynia [Orthodox] Consistory received a petition on 16 February 1883 from the retired soldier Sergei Kotliar about converting from Russian Orthodoxy to Judaism. Kotliar reported that he was taken as a cantonist to serve in the army. In Kiev in 1854, by order of the authorities, he was baptized against his will. Kotliar explained that although he was registered as a Christian, he did not understand anything about the religion and emphasized that he was baptized by force. He asked for permission to convert back to Judaism and to marry according to the Jewish rite. The petition was rejected based on the 1876 statutes. [. . .][1] According to point 40 of that statute, as an apostate from Russian Orthodoxy, he is required to meet with a priest, who would strengthen and reconfirm his faith. [. . .] As the [local] priest reported, Kotliar declared that he adhered, adheres, and will adhere to the faith of his birth, no matter what kinds of reprimands, treatment, or punishment he would receive from the commanding officer.[2]

Interrogation and Verdict:

Question: Is Sergei Ivanov Kotliar guilty? He converted in 1854 as a cantonist and returned to Judaism in 1883.

Answer: No, not guilty. [...] The procurator does not find him guilty based on the following: (1) the law of 4 December 1862 prohibits the baptism of children younger than fourteen years old;[3] moreover, it demands that they be conscious of the act and not be forcibly baptized; (2) the young must be educated about baptism before the act; (3) Kotliar was baptized thirty-nine years ago, when he was eleven or twelve years old and against his will. He is not guilty.

"Petition of Anatolii Kolodnii to the Volhynia Consistory (27 July 1907)"

DAZhO, f. 1 op. 35, d. 1786, l. 1.

In April 1893, I converted from Judaism to Russian Orthodoxy in the town of Rol through holy baptism. However, I was practically unable to relate to Russian Orthodoxy due to the manner of thought and childhood education that I received. I remained a Jew all this time in spirit. In view of this and guided by the Decree of 17 April 1905 on the Freedom of Conscience,[4] I am taking the liberty to request that you exclude me from the Russian Orthodox [community].[5]

NOTES

1. [The document was torn here, so the statute number was impossible to read.]

2. [Sergei Ivanov Kotliar (formely Leizer Khaimov Kniaiev) stated that "in the first year that I entered military service as a cantonist in 1854, I was introduced to an older man for instruction, and he began to pressure me to adopt the Christian faith. Thinking that this was necessary for service, I agreed to convert to the Christian faith. I was baptized in Kiev but do not remember in which church. I served in the military for eighteen years [during which time] I did not take part in any Christian rites." He explained that the Jewish community did not want to take him back as he was, and he was not registered to any Jewish community; as a result he wanted to return officially to Judaism.]

3. [On 4 December 1862, the state ruled that "Jews who are fourteen years old may convert to the Christian faith without permission from their parents or guardians" (see *Sbornik uzakonenii kasaiushchikhsia evreev* [St. Petersburg: Tip. Ministerstva vnutrennikh del, 1872]).]

4. [Until the Law of Religious Toleration (17 April 1905), it was illegal for converts to return to their original faith (*any* faith, not just Judaism). The new law enabled Jews and adherents of other confessions to renounce Orthodoxy and convert to other faiths (see Eugene Avrutin, "Returning to Judaism after the 1905 Law on Religious Freedom in Tsarist Russia," *Slavic Review* 65, no. 1 [2006]: 90–110).]

5. [This part of the document was defective, making the statute number impossible to read.]

[21]

Responsum of Hayim Ozer
Grodzinski: On Converts in America[1]

Hayim Ozer Grodzinski, *Responsa Ahiezer*, 3: 28 (Jerusalem: [s.n.], 1959).

On the issue of conversion: it has been a general practice to convert to Judaism the non-Jewish women who have married a Jewish man in a civil ceremony, even though strictly by law they ought not to be converted as their aim is cohabitation [rather than living a traditional Jewish life] and she [the wife] should be prohibited to him [the husband] even after the marriage, as is explained in the responsum of the Rashba, chapter 1205.[2] Elsewhere I have been inclined toward leniency and have found a basis for this in a responsum of Maimonides in *Pe'er ha-dor* number 132; R. Shlomo Kluger has come to similar conclusions in practice in *Tuv taam va-daat*.[3] But here is the problem. There is no presumption that she will accept the burden of mitzvot, as it is clear that they have no such intention and that they will violate the laws of Shabbat, *niddah*, and prohibited foods, as I wrote in my previous letter. The *gaon*, our teacher, R. Yitzhak Shmelkes,[4] has already drawn attention to this, and the ruling he issued was that a proper religious court should not get involved in such [a conversion].

But regarding the gist of what your honor wrote, that small children may be converted, for once they reach majority, legally they will be in a position to protest formally to [their conversion], and breaking the Sabbath counts as objection, [some other authorities take a different position]: [. . .] in truth, the Hatam Sofer[5] indicates in a responsum, *Yoreh Deah* chapter 253, that if the father and mother or just one of them brings the children to be converted, they cannot protest this when they

reach their majority; and he draws support for this finding from [various major rabbinic figures]. In any case, it might be argued that this applies only if [the converted child] behaves as a Jew, so that conversion was an absolute benefit for him, in such a case he has no right of protest; but if he violates religious law even though [the conversion is still] a benefit, it may not be an absolute benefit, in which case he has the right to protest on reaching his majority. In fact, however, someone who breaks the Sabbath and commits other sins is not to be considered as protesting his conversion but violating the law as a Jewish sinner, and certainly his status [remains that of] a convert. Yet your honor is quite right that a proper court should not become involved in conversion cases like these, although I do not find it proper for the rabbis of the age to clamor about this and openly challenge such conversions, for the common folk will regard it as a desecration of God's name that the rabbis are not letting women be converted, or the children in particular, who can in truth be converted by law.

NOTES

1. [Hayim Ozer Grodzinski (1863–1940), the rabbi of Vil'na, was the preeminent halakhic authority of the early twentieth century in Russia.]

2. [In the absence of civil marriage in Russia, intermarriage without the Jewish partner's conversion to Christianity was not permitted; non-Jews were not allowed to convert to the Jewish faith, so it was always the Jewish partner who had to convert. The situation was different in America. There,

as in the rest of Europe, Jews and Christians could intermarry civilly. There are numerous cases in the literature in which the non-Jewish spouse wishes to convert to Judaism, often after the birth of children. Although generally conversion to Judaism for the sake of marriage — where there were no grounds to presume that the convert would observe Jewish law — was forbidden, in cases where a civil marriage has already taken place, rabbis were often lenient in the matter. Although not a practical concern in the Russian lands, the fact that questions of this kind came to the rabbi of Vil'na is of interest, as are his reflections on the nature of the identity of a converted child.]

3. [R. Shlomo Kluger (1783–1869) was rabbi of Brody.]

4. [Yitzchak Yehudah Shmelkes (1828–1905) was rabbi of Przemyś.]

5. [Moses Sofer (1762–1839) was rabbi of Pressburg (Bratislava).]

Jews and the State on Religious Matters

[22]

State Rabbis

"Petition of the Jews of Buki to the Governor of Kiev (5 February 1896)"
DAKO, f. 1, op. 136, d. 258, l. 4.

Given the consistent prohibitions on private [spiritual] rabbis, *mohelim*, and [other functionaries] to perform the Jewish religious rituals of circumcision, burial, marriage, birth, and divorce for our community, it is extremely difficult to turn to the state rabbi for each of these instances because he resides with other public [officials] in the town of Tal'noe, some 33 versts [35.31 kilometers] from our town. To send for him, one has to rent a horse-drawn cart for such a trip to and fro.[1]

Meanwhile, based on the number of residents in our town, it would be possible to have a local state rabbi—whose lack has been extremely onerous for the residents in our town. This is especially true since we have two capable individuals for the office: the local pharmacist and doctor. As a result, we have the honor to ask Your Excellency for permission to elect a state rabbi for our town of Buki.[2]

"Petition of the Residents of Korsun, Kaney District, to the Governor of Kiev (1899)"
DAKO, f. 1, op. 138, d. 501, ll. 19–29 ob., 23–24.

Until 1898, the town of Korsun belonged to the rabbinical district of the town of Boguslav. However, given the large number of people in the town,[3] and the great distance (thirty versts [32.1 kilometers]) from Boguslav, we requested the separation of Korsun from the Boguslav rabbinical district and the establishment of an independent rabbinical district. We made our request, first and foremost, because of this circumstance: our town is in acute need of a doctor. The large population in our town has only one doctor (who serves on the estate of Prince Lopukhin Demidov) who cannot satisfy the great need for medical assistance, especially in times of epidemics. But we do not have special resources to maintain a doctor. Therefore we resolved to elect a privately practicing doctor to the recent opening of the office, who would combine both the duties of doctor and rabbi in his own person. With this aim, we invited the privately practicing Dr. [Arkadii] Vinnitskii from Kiev, who expressed a desire to be elected for the office of state rabbi. On 29 September 1899, the election by representatives took place in the prayer houses in the presence of the assistant police superintendent of Kanev and a local police officer. It was our fervent desire to have as our rabbi Dr. Vinnitskii, an individual with higher education in general and a special knowledge of the Hebrew language and the laws of the faith, who would have brought unquestionable benefit to our population. However, our representatives (for personal reasons and contrary to the wishes and will of our population) put Dr. Vinnitskii on the ballot but elected some unknown [Moshko] Ziskind from the town of Tarashcha, who appeared an hour before the election.

Under the law (point 3, article 1325, volume 9, part two on the Spiritual Affairs of Foreign Faiths), a state rabbi is obliged to perform all the rituals of the Jewish faith personally, including the ritual of circumcision.[4] This ritual, owing to its substance, must be performed exclusively by a special doctor, not some private individual, because in the majority of cases when a private individual performs the above-mentioned ritual, our children suffer and very often even fatalities occur. Although the law does not explicitly require that state rabbis know Hebrew and the laws of the Jewish faith, it goes without saying that the law intended people with knowledge of this language and law because all this enters into the direct sphere of the state rabbi's activities—for example, the translation of Hebrew into Russian and also the performance of well-known rituals. For rabbis who do not know Hebrew, translations are done by others. Although the translations are approved by the rabbi, the translations—made by people who are not under oath—lose any kind of moral significance. [One must also take] into consideration that:

(a) Dr. Vinnitskii is a person with higher university education;

(b) he has a solid knowledge of the Hebrew language and all the laws of the Jewish faith better than a spiritual rabbi;

(c) Dr. Vinnitskii is a good doctor, and in the course of the eighteen months that he has been in Korsun, he has brought much benefit in this regard;

(d) our representatives obviously ignored our wishes and all the above considerations and, on the contrary, elected a person whom none of us knows and who pales in comparison to Dr. Vinnitskii in terms of his educational and moral value.

Given the foregoing, we declare the following: Ziskind, who has been elected to the office of state rabbi and who does not know a word of Hebrew (not to mention his scant education),[5] is incapable of performing the necessary rituals, especially that of circumcision (on which the lives of many hundreds of children depend). Given all this, we have the honor to ask Your Excellency humbly not to confirm the election for state rabbi, which was held this past 29 September in Korsun and in which Dr. Vinnitskii was a candidate. This is because our population, as stated, is in great need of a doctor and does not have the means to provide a separate salary for a doctor. [Signed by forty residents].[6]

NOTES

1. [A decree of 1826 made state rabbis, who were elected by their communities, responsible for maintaining registers of births, deaths, marriages, and divorces; therefore, candidates had to demonstrate their knowledge of Russian to occupy this post. Starting in 1853, only the state rabbi or his assistant had the right to perform marriages, divorces, circumcisions, and burials. A ritual performed by anyone else was considered void and had no legal validity (see Freeze, *Jewish Marriage and Divorce in Imperial Russia*, 95–128).]

2. [The governor of Kiev allowed the Jews to elect an assistant state rabbi on the grounds that there were 4,237 Jewish residents in Buki at this time. Tal'noe, the closest town with a state rabbi, had 5,294 Jewish residents. The community was responsible for the assistant state rabbi's salary, which came out of the kosher meat tax.]

3. [According to the 1897 census, there were 8,262 residents, of whom 3,799 were Jews ("Korsun," in *Evreiskaia entsiklopediia*, reprint [St. Petersburg, 1991], 9: 773–74).]

4. [In a special circular, the Kiev governor stated that state rabbis could designate a special person for this task. See GAKO, f. 1, op. 129, d. 537, ll. 1–11.]

5. [Moshko Ziskind, a resident of Tarashcha (originally from Belaia Tserkov'), submitted his educational certificates, which showed that he had

completed seven years of school at a Belaia Tserkov' school. He was twenty years old at the time of the election.]

6. [The petition was denied because the representatives had elected Moshko Ziskind. There were fourteen votes in favor of Moshko Ziskind and four votes against him; there were five votes in favor of Arkadii Vinnitskii and thirteen votes against him.]

[23]

Synagogues and Cemeteries

"General Governor Vladimir Dolgorukov of Moscow on the Petition of Rabbi Zelik Minor and the Board of the Moscow Jewish Prayer House (31 February 1879)"

RGIA, f. 821, op. 8, d. 69, l. 31–32 ob.

TO THE HEAD OF THE MINISTRY OF INTERNAL AFFAIRS:[1]

The Moscow state rabbi and board members of the Moscow Jewish prayer house submitted a petition for permission to construct a synagogue for the religious community in Moscow on the model of St. Petersburg and to acquire a building in the name of the community, which would house a synagogue and school on its premises. This is all to commemorate the twenty-fifth year of the successful reign of the august monarch, which will happen in 1880. They have presented the findings of the Moscow Jewish community on this subject made on 14 January.

Regarding the above request of Rabbi Minor[2] and the board members of the Moscow Jewish prayer house, I have the honor to report this for the consideration of Your Excellency and am forwarding the petition and the attached finding [of the Jewish community], asking that you honor me with a notification [of the action taken].

"Notice of the Chief Secretary, L. S. Makov, to Prince Vladimir Dolgorukov about the Rejection of the Petition of the Representatives of the Moscow Jewish Community (10 April 1879)"

RGIA, f. 821, op. 8, d. 69, l. 39–39 ob.

TO THE GENERAL GOVERNOR OF MOSCOW,

I am pleased to report to Your Excellency regarding the memorandum of 3 February 1879 (number 695) about the petition of the rabbi and members of the Moscow Jewish community for permission for them to acquire a building in the name of their religious community to house a synagogue and a school to commemorate the twenty-five-year reign of the sovereign emperor. I have the honor of informing you that at the present time in Moscow there are discussions about forming an organization of Jewish religious communities outside the Pale of Settlement. Therefore the satisfaction of the above request from representatives of the Jewish community in Moscow would require a decision beforehand on one of the essential questions in this case — viz., granting the Jewish religious community outside the Pale of Settlement the right of a legal entity [corporation], that is, the right to acquire property in its own name and the corresponding right to appear in a court of law as plaintiff and defendant.

Given this [ongoing] discussion, which is of general legal significance, and recognizing that the juxtaposition of the upcoming joyous event for Russia next year [the commemoration of the emperor's rule] with questions about purchasing land and houses under [the auspices] of the synagogue is completely untimely. [. . .] I would propose to reject the present request of the representatives of the Jewish religious community.

"Second Petition of Rabbi Minor and Board Members of the Moscow Jewish Religious Community to Prince Vladimir Dolgorukov (22 March 1880)"

RGIA, f. 821, op. 8, d. 69, ll. 43–44 ob.

TO THE GENERAL GOVERNOR OF MOSCOW,

In February 1879 we presented Your Excellency with the finding of our religious community about the urgent need for us to have our own building to house a synagogue and to establish (with the state's permission) an orphanage and school. We humbly asked Your Excellency to obtain permission for us to construct a synagogue and to purchase a building in which to house a synagogue and school on its premises. However, to our great regret, such permission has thus far still not ensued — on the alleged grounds that no relevant law recognizes the right of Jews living in Moscow to appear (if the circumstances warrant) as plaintiffs and defendants.

Such a rejection has greatly dismayed us: on the one hand, the prayer house seems more crowded every year, while on the other the rent rises on both the premises of the prayer house and the school with each contract renewal so that it is extremely onerous for our community. Given the lack of our own building with the requisite hygienic and educational conditions, the school has already moved three times to new places. The prayer house — because of the difficulty of moving its pieces [for example, the bimah and seats] — is causing greater and greater expenses for us.

As Your Excellency knows, the arrangement of our prayer house differs from other prayer houses in having its own choral service and Russian sermon; in the orphanage and school, abandoned orphans and children of poor parents are educated in the Russian spirit. These two institutions were and are the most productive means for the regeneration of our community. The Russian school and reformed house of worship, in the opinion of even our enemies, are the most fruitful levers to merge the Jews with the dominant people; our humane government always favors the development and well-being of such charitable institutions among the Jews. The house of God, in particular, can develop and support religious sensibilities in our young generation, which is necessary to protect them from the pernicious influence of the latest false social teachings.

The circumstance — that there is as yet no general law recognizing the right of Jews living in Moscow to appear as a juridical entity — does not serve as a serious obstacle to our acquisition of a building and to construction of a synagogue for the following reasons:

1. On the basis of the existing laws on the Pale of Settlement, Jews are able to build synagogues, prayer houses, and so forth and to acquire real estate as a religious community. For merchants of the first guild, for those who have completed courses at an institution of higher education, and for retired Jewish soldiers, the interior provinces (not excluding the capitals) are considered a place of permanent residence. People of all the foregoing categories may acquire real estate like the rest of the citizenry. If each of these said persons is permitted to acquire immovable property individually, then why should a religious community, consisting of these individuals, not have the same right to acquire a house as a charitable institution?

2. The St. Petersburg Jewish community was permitted to acquire real estate in the

name of the community and to construct a synagogue. Why then are we not permitted on the same grounds whereby the St. Petersburg Jews were given permission?

Your Excellency! Under the protection of our humane government and under the auspices of the religious tolerance of the Russian people, every confession has its own corner here in Moscow: the Lutherans, the Reformed, Catholics, Muslims—they all have their own place of worship and their own philanthropic institutions.

Given the foregoing, we humbly venture to ask Your Excellency to obtain permission from whomever necessary to construct a synagogue and to purchase a building for a synagogue and orphanage and school, as was permitted for the St. Petersburg Jewish community.[3]

"Petition of the Jewish Residents of Gorodets to the Minister of Internal Affairs to Expand the Jewish Cemetery in Gorodets (Mogilev Province), 1903."
GARF, f. 1286, op. 46, d. 896, ll. 50–50 ob.

The town of Gorodets (Rogachev district, Mogilev province) has a Jewish cemetery, which, periodically, has an excess of corpses, and it is absolutely impossible to bury the deceased. We therefore feel the extreme and urgent need to have a new place allocated for a Jewish cemetery; otherwise the poor Jews of Gorodets in particular will cast out the deceased to the mercy of fate or simply on the street. This would have a harmful impact on the moral condition and health of all the residents in general in Gorodets. Consequently, three years ago we already submitted a petition to the appropriate authorities to allocate land from the place assigned to us (as there is absolutely nothing else) for the expansion of the Jewish cemetery. Finally, we were informed that the head of Mogilev province filed a statement to Your Excellency on 17 November 1899 (number 8879).

We therefore take the liberty to appeal to the person of Your Excellency and humbly to ask that you graciously issue, as soon as possible, an order to satisfy our request regarding the allotment of the requested land from the indicated place in order to expand the Jewish cemetery. This is urgently necessary with respect to the religious and primarily sanitary health of the people.

"Department of Medicine (MVD) to the Department of Police (13 September 1903)"
The memorandum of the Department of Police of 29 May 1903 (number 1329) on the question of expanding the Jewish cemetery in Gorodets (Rogachev district) was sent to the Medical Council for resolution. Upon examining the case, and taking into consideration the suitability [of the cemetery] in sanitary terms as certified by the local medical department, the Council sees no obstacles to expanding the aforementioned cemetery. [. . .]

NOTES

1. [The author of this memorandum, Prince Vladimir Andreevich Dolgorukov, was the general governor of Moscow from 1865 to 1891. He had close ties to the Poliakov family; according to Aleksandr Poliakov, Zinaida's mother once opened the winter ball with Dolgorukov—a sign of appreciation that her husband had paid off the debts of Dolgorukov's adjutant. He was replaced in 1891 by Alexander III's conservative brother, Grand Duke Sergei Aleksandrovich, who initiated a mass expulsion of the Jews from Moscow.]

2. [Zelik Minor (1826–1900), who served as the state rabbi of Minsk, attended the state rabbinical school in Vil'na and became the state rabbi of Moscow in 1869. He was among the first rabbis to deliver his sermons in Russian (see Efim Naumovich Ulitskii, *Istoriia Moskovskoi evreiskoi obshchiny* (Moscow: KRPA: OLIMP, 2006) 37–40).]

3. [Prince Vladimir Dolgorukov sent another memorandum to his superiors, who again rejected the petition.]

[24]

Petitions to the Governor of Kiev Province about High Holiday Services (1907–13)

"Petition of the Residents of Budaevka to the Governor of Kiev Province (23 July 1907)"

DAKO, f. 1, op. 141,d. 740, l. 10–10 ob.

With the permission of the chief [the governor of Kiev], there is a prayer house in the village of Budaevka, Glevakhsk townships, Kiev district. During the regular time of year, according to its capacity, it is so crowded that there is really no access to it for the throngs of worshipers due to the lack of space and air. It has affected us in the most intolerable way, for we are not all completely healthy people and are not able to endure it. This is all the more so during holidays such as the New Year [Rosh Hashanah] and the Day of Atonement [Yom Kippur], and the holiday of Sukkot [*kushchei*, in Russian] — days when [even] a Jew who has not visited the prayer house all year comes to pray. That is why we have the honor to request Your Excellency to permit us to assemble for prayer in the house of Mr. Nikolaev, in the apartment of the townsperson Usher Meerovich Kanevskii [. . .] in a separate [space] from the prayer house, which is not accessible. We ask you to inform us [about your decision] on this.[1]

"Petition of the Jewish Residents of Kiev to the Governor of Kiev Province (26 August 1913)"

DAKO, f. 1, op. 147, d. 686, g. 1913, l. 11.

According to Jewish law, every Jew must pray to God in the upcoming holidays of Rosh Hashanah, which will be on 19–20 September, and Yom Kippur, which will be on 28 Sep-

tember this year. The existing meetinghouse on Lybedskii [Street], which is in a distant district, is not an obstacle for all worshipers. However, children are absolutely deprived of the possibility of entering a prayer house. Hence we humbly ask Your Excellency to allow us and our families and relatives to pray in a rented accommodation for this purpose on Malaia Vasil'kovskaia Street in house number 7.

"Petition of the Jewish Residents of the Village of Glebovka to the Governor of Kiev Province (25 September 1913)"

DAKO, f. 1, op. 147, d. 686, l. 36.

In the upcoming Jewish holidays: 19–20 September (Rosh Hashanah), 27–28 (the eve and day of Yom Kippur), 3–4 and 9–11 October (the first and last days of Sukkot), it is obligatory for Jews to be at the prayer house. We do not have such [a prayer house] in the village, and we travel every year with our families to the small town of Dymer if we do not have permission for a prayer assembly. In the meantime, there is an epidemic of dysentery and scarlet fever in this small town [Dymer], and it is dangerous to travel with the children for fear of infecting them and returning with the danger of spreading the epidemic.

In view of this, we are forced to turn with this most humble petition to the mercy of Your Excellency, humbly requesting to allow an assembly for prayer on the aforesaid days in the apartment of Iosif Pilevskii in the village of Glebovka, Dymer township, Kiev district.[2]

DAKO, f. 1, op. 147, d. 686, l. 45.

I am submitting the attached certificate from the doctor and humbly request Your Excellency to permit me to establish an assembly for prayer in my apartment on Pushkin Street, number 12, on 19, 20, and also 28 September of this year, in view of the fact that it is impossible for me to leave my home. I have the honor to add that only my relatives will be present at the assembly for prayer.[3]

NOTES

1. [The decision was not included in the file; however, most requests for permission to gather outside the established prayer house were denied. The state cited a law, statute 206 of the General Establishments of the Province, in this case and other instances to justify the rejection.]

2. [An official added a note on the left side of the document that the medical department confirmed cases of dysentery in Dymer on 22–23 August 1913; he added that there were lingering cases on 22 and 23 August.]

3. [This petition was rejected.]

---

[25]

Trial of Girsh Sagalevich for Insulting the Russian Orthodox Faith in Vil'na (1869)

LVIA, f. 447, op. 1, d. 4092, ll. 1–14.

On 5 March [1870], by the Order of His Imperial Majesty, the Vil'na Chamber of the Criminal and Civil Court heard the criminal case of the Jew Girsh Sagalevich convicted of denigrating the Russian Orthodox faith. It was reported publicly. Signed: Assistant Deputy A. I. Oznabishin.

Circumstances of the Case

On 24 February 1869 the *feldsher* [paramedic] Shevel Shinder lodged a denunciation with the priest Flerov that, during an argument with the Jew Girsh Sagalevich, the latter said that the Russian Orthodox faith was dog shit [*govno sabach'e* in Russian]. Iurkevich, Rybinskii, and Ivanitskii were witnesses.

The Jew Sagalevich testified that in February 1869, the *feldsher* Shinder came to him at the tavern to argue with his mother and himself about money, and in connection [with

this] Shinder said to him that his uncle [Sagalevich's] had converted to Russian Orthodoxy, but this was said in the form of a reproach. To this, Sagalevich replied that his uncle had indeed embraced the Orthodox faith and observes it strictly, whereas he, Shinder, does not profess any kind of faith and is just like as a dog. These words were about Shinder, not the Russian Orthodox faith.

Of the witnesses interrogated under oath, the [following] testified: (1) Rybinskii: that when Sagalevich argued with Shinder, the former said that Orthodoxy was like a dog's faith. For what purpose he uttered this offensive comparison, he does not know; (2) Iurkevich: that Shinder had an argument with the tavern keeper Sagalevich. When the former said to Sagalevich in the form of a reproach that his uncle had converted to Russian Orthodoxy, the latter replied to this that his uncle had indeed embraced Orthodox faith and adheres strictly to it, and that he, Shinder, does not adhere to any faith, and his faith is dog shit. Hence, this foul language related strictly to Shinder's person, not to the Russian Orthodox faith; (3) Ivanitskii: that he was not present at the beginning of the argument, although he heard Sagalevich tell Shinder that his faith was dog shit but did not make out to whom these words were strictly directed and cannot say definitively. During a comprehensive search, [people] approved of his behavior and also testified that they never noticed a lack of respect toward the Russian Orthodox faith.

Having examined the circumstances of the case, the chamber finds that the accusation against the Jew Sagalevich for denigrating the Russian Orthodox faith was refuted by two sworn witnesses. Thus, the court decrees to free from prosecution the Jew Girsh Sagalevich, who has been accused of denigrating the Russian Orthodox religion. This decision will be explained to him, and he has the right to appeal through the Vil'na District court.

[II]
Family Life

The Jewish family differed from its Russian Orthodox counterpart not only in customs and patterns but also in legal status. In the absence of civil marriage in Russia, Jewish marriage and divorce was regulated by Jewish law (*halakhah*) and the rabbinical authorities. In spite of its patriarchal character, the Jewish family was the site of competing interests and negotiations over rights and responsibilities between parents and children, and between husbands and wives — as the following documents illustrate. Indeed, the family served as a testing ground for the reinforcement or rejection of social and gender hierarchies in Jewish society. Although the traditional family resisted the challenges of modernity, it could not stem the tide of new ideologies and values that derived from secular education, cultural change (such as a new secular print culture), industrialization, urbanization, and migration — powerful forces that were reshaping tsarist society, including Jews.

This part offers documents to illuminate the daily challenges of childhood, parenting, marriage, and divorce; marital questions, such as the crisis of the *agunah*;[1] conversion and the family; and the impact of death on spouses and orphans.

NOTE

1. [*Agunah* is a Hebrew term that denotes a woman "anchored" to her husband because she is unable to get a legal divorce — which requires the husband to give her a *get*, or bill of divorce. In the absence of a *get* given by the husband (or his agent) to the wife (or her agent), there is no mechanism for freeing the woman from her marital status. And without a legal divorce, she can never remarry. The status of *agunah* applies to a woman whose husband refuses to give her a *get* and to a woman whose husband has disappeared (presumed dead or otherwise; there is no legally valid presumption of death in Jewish law).]

Parents and Children

[26]

Kvitlakh¹ Addressed to an Unknown Rabbi in Vil'na (1839)²

LVIA, f. 1250, op. 1, d. 36, ll. 1–3.

"Petition of Yekhile son of Zara and Zlata to an Unnamed Rabbi (1839)"

From the depths of my heart, I submit this petition to our rabbi (long may he live!) so that he pray to God that He renew our bodies, souls, and lives with well-being, children, and abundant sustenance, that I be favored with a son in old age. For is anything impossible for God? May the patron of parents bring good for our nurturance in the coming year. You have shown me a genuine love in life and [. . .]³ [even] now are not distant from us. [I ask] that you pray to the Almighty for our well-being, that my heart will be inspired by the love of God. May my prayer be true and sincere. [. . .] As a priest intercedes in prayer, so may you turn your face on us with your pure heart. Knowing your concern for us and the entire Jewish people, I draw to a close.

"Petition of Nokhim Son of Feiga and Sara Daughter of Reizele to an Unnamed Rabbi (n.d.)"

DEAR RABBI,

I ask you on Yom Kippur to pray to God that He send down a living, healthy infant to me through my wife this coming year. Long have I lamented this but could find no help. So now, at this time of goodwill, I ask you to secure God's love for me, so that I may be counted among the people of Israel and given a living baby. May He send down blessings on my work and affairs, on both my body and soul. May He preserve me from malevolence at the time of prayer, and may He destine me for a happy and full life.

NOTES

1. [*Kvitlakh* are short notes requesting advice, blessings, or cures.]

2. [The file included sixteen letters confiscated by the censor; the governor of Vil'na, believing them to contain harmful material, sent them to the Jewish assistant of the Belorussian educational district chief for translation into Russian.]

3. [This line in the microfilm copy was blurred; the Lithuanian State Archive no longer has the original.]

[27]

Metrical Book Registration of Births by the State Rabbi (1906)

GASO, f. 11, op. 4, d. 1593, l. 1.[1]

"Petition of Townspeople Sherko and Mera Zysman to the Ekaterinburg District Court"

Our son was born 17 May 1894 in the Nizhnii Tagil factory [settlement] from our legal marriage (in 1876). According to the precepts of our religion, the ritual of circumcision was performed; however, this boy was not registered in the metrical books—partly because of our distraction, but mainly because the rabbi's residence (to which one must travel to register a baby) is located at a great distance from Tagil (in the city of Perm). Encumbered by a large family, we were in no position to travel and hence were deprived of the possibility of observing all the formalities required by the law. We were limited to entering him only in the family register [*posemeinyi spisok*, in Russian], from which he would then be registered in our passport.

Now, when the time has come to educate the boy, when he has displayed an aptitude for primary education at the public school and is yearning for the city school, the question about the future fate of this boy naturally arises for us parents. We would like to provide an education for him, but for this it is necessary to have either a metrical registration of birth or some substitute document.

In light of this and the additional attachment, we humbly ask the District Court to recognize Pinkhus as our legitimate son, who was born on 17 May 1894: (1) a copy of the family register of 20 November 1906, from which it is clearly evident that we the undersigned are a legal couple [and] that we really have a son Pinkhus, born in 1894; (2) a notarized copy of the passport, issued to us by the elder of the Dubrovensk townspeople on 18 November of this year, in which Pinkhus is also listed in the record; and (3) the certificate of the Gorets rabbi of 9 November 1906, number 176, which shows that the metrical books in the town of Gorky, in which our marriage was recorded, were destroyed in a fire on 12 May 1891.

To confirm that this infant was born to us, we ask that you question the Jewish witnesses Iuda Evseev Zil'berg and Solomon Samsonov Bliutshtein, who live in the first section of the Nizhnii Tagil factory settlement; among other things they participated in the Pinkhus's circumcision ritual. In addition, we are attaching a copy of the present petition and supplements to it.[2]

NOTES

1. [This is published in Irina Antropova, *Sbornik dokumentov po istorii evreev Urala iz fondov uchrezhdenii dosovetskogo perioda Gosudarstvennogo arkhiva Sverdlovskoj oblasti* (Moscow: Drevlekhranilishche, 2004), 300–301).]

2. [The Ekaterinburg District Court approved the petition to recognize Pinkhus Zysman (Zislin) as the legitimate son of Shmerko and Mera Zysman (Zislin) after questioning the witnesses and examining the supporting documents (GASO, f. 11, op. 4, d. 1593, ll. 27–28). For similar cases, see GAZhO, f. 24, op. 11, dd. 20, 26, 39, 596.]

[28]

A Jewish Boyhood in Odessa: Memoirs of Lazar B. Gol'denberg (b. circa 1845)

Lazar B. Gol'denberg, "Vospominaniia L. B. Gol'denberg," in *Katorga i ssylka. Istoriko-revoliutsionnyi vestnik*, ed. Vladimir Vilenskii, reprint (Moscow, 1971), 10: 89–98.

I was born in the village of Poplavok, Kherson province.[1] I do not know the exact date of this event but heard that it transpired during the time of Hanukkah. Apparently then, it was in December. It is more difficult to determine the year of my birth: some say that I was born in 1844, others in 1845, and still others in 1846. In the long run, what difference does it make — whether a person was born in December or some other month, a year sooner or later?

My ancestors did not belong to the aristocracy; they would not even be considered among the ranks of respectable Jewry. Both grandfathers hailed from simple folk. Grandfather on my mother's side arrived in Odessa, from God knows where, and earned a living as a water carrier. Grandfather on my father's side rented a parcel of land in Anan'evsk district. It is possible that at the time of my parents' wedding, my grandfathers enjoyed some prosperity because, as I heard afterward, my mother received a dowry of three hundred rubles in cash and a down-filled featherbed. I do not remember my father at all but heard that he was a learned man, who passed all his free time studying the Talmud. On the day of the wedding, my mother was thirteen years old and my father fourteen. Imagine how great was their worldly life and experience! Besides, they did not need to be in love or to decide the question about the date of the wedding or how to settle their own destiny; their parents decided all these questions for them. The young couple met for the first time on their wedding day.

My paternal grandfather took my mother into his home and supported the young couple for a period of three to four years.[2] Father continued to study, but they opened a small store for my mother in their home so that she could learn life's lessons and be somewhat prepared for the time when the cares of earning an independent living would fall on her after father's death. Mother told me that father knew the Talmud well. He died of cholera in 1848. My mother remained a widow with two small children — my older brother and myself.

I still remember the small store, especially the apples sold there, together with honey, multicolored kerchiefs, ribbons, and dried fish. The apples were etched into my memory because I became adept at stealing them (for which I once received a severe thrashing). I also recollect the kitchen behind the store where they baked bread in a large brick oven. According to the Jewish custom, they baked white loaves of different shapes and varieties for the Sabbath. When the bread came out of the oven, it was set out to cool on tablecloths spread out on the floor. Once I entered the kitchen and, struck by the magnificent sight of this peculiar flooring, I began to jump on it. The cook, who glanced back at me, was horrified; she struck me with such force that I fell onto the opening of the oven full of hot coals. I was in no condition to leave; they carried me to another room where I lay in bed on my stomach for several weeks until the burn on my back had healed.

I do not know how long my mother remained a widow. I only remember how my mother, brother, and I once arrived in Odessa and settled in a house with a small fragile boy and a deformed man (who was no spring chicken) with a flattened nose and a great, black beard. I was told that the delicate boy was to be my brother and the man my father. I was very strong and robust, plump and ruddy, whereas my new brother was sickly and weak. Naturally, after the first acquaintance, I often beat him. Once I obviously overdid it for he bawled and complained to Father, who gave me a good and proper thrashing, which he repeated so often that I gradually began to lose my well-fed appearance.

The story of my stepfather was as follows: he fled from Iampol to evade military service and arrived in Odessa without a penny to his name. As he was used to hard physical labor, he became a stonemason. I do not know how long he worked in this craft; however, by the time he married my mother, he was already a money changer. He usually sat on Evreiskaia Street [Jewish Street] behind a small, green table, and the Jews called him "Itsko the money changer." As far as I remember, on the street corners in the Jewish quarter there were a few such green tables with a wooden box in the middle. Through the netting, one could see the copper and silver coins and also the one-ruble notes, three-ruble notes, and other notes. Evreiskaia Street was the lively center of small trade, conducted predominantly by Jews. Kalachnyi was the center for Jewish migrants from Poland and Lithuania. Here, the Jewish poor huddled together in terribly cramped and filthy quarters. The streets were full of beggars and cripples. They did the dirtiest work and always lived half-starved. The orthodox institutions were located here as well: the *beit midrash* [house of study], every kind of synagogue, the slaughterhouse, the Jewish market, and schools. Consequently, the rabbis, cantors, and so forth also lived here.

I do not recall how old I was when I was first sent to the *heder* — that is, the Jewish primary school of instruction. I only remember that it was not far from our house. It was located on Ekaterininskaia Street in a large three-story corner house with a courtyard, which went out on to Evreiskaia Street on one side. Every kind of Jewish store was housed on the basement floor. The pavement was covered with the rags of old-clothes dealers and stands in which they sold pickles, halva and other sweets, rolls, fruit, vegetables, old dresses, and multicolored kerchiefs. Here too were the money-changers with their green tables. The draymen stood on the corner. On market day there were wagons and carts from Moldova with covered tops, loaded with charcoal. German colonists in their two-wheeled carts and all sorts of other people arrived. The street was overflowing with sailors, buyers, middlemen, pickpockets, beggars, and people who were unloading the contents of two-wheeled carts onto wagons. Often one could see well-dressed Jews in long *kapotes* with great beards and curly *peyes*, who collected money in a multicolored handkerchief for some poor family, for the residents of Palestine, for some new synagogue, or for some other Jewish social cause — for example, for a bribe to a police superintendent or officer in order to rescue passportless Jews from expulsion or other ordeals. Here too one could see matchmakers, boasting extravagantly about the beauty of the brides for whom they sought partners, their *yikhus* [lineage], the size of their dowry. [. . .] Another type of Jew — sick, bent down, pale — appeared on Fridays. There was also the *melamed*, who would collect his weekly fees — in money or kind — from the parents of his pupils. He also received payment from the relatives of the deceased for whom he said a prayer for the dead. The policeman also came to collect the weekly bribe for fulfilling his duties of surveillance as did other police officials, who strictly followed them to ensure that their source of income did not dry up.

The internal courtyard of this house consisted of a separate, peculiar world. Here lived every kind of artisan—all impoverished, often without any livelihood; however, they were distinguished for their remarkable ability to adapt to circumstances. Because the courtyard was large, it had exits to both streets [Ekaterininskaia and Evreiskaia]. In addition to this, the house of Ianopulo with its proximity to the commercial quarter was extremely convenient for small traders and artisans to sell their wares. Jewelers, watchmakers, cobblers, bakers, old-clothes dealers, and a store for Jewish prayer accessories all took refuge here. It also housed religious teachers [scribes], who copied the Torah on parchment for synagogues and manufactured the small boxes (*tefillin*, or phylacteries) that Jews fasten to their forehead at the time of prayer to protect against the devil.[3] At the end of courtyard was even a place for the *shochet*, where he slaughtered chickens according to Jewish rituals, just as there was a place for leaders of the burial society, who organized funerals, meals of consolation, and so forth. There were also hired mourners [*klogmuters*, in Yiddish], coffin makers, and the collector of alms for the poor during a procession. Here too lived a midwife, a middleman for hiring servants, a person who read prayers in the synagogue on major holidays, a *mohel*, a female matchmaker, and a woman who measured the graves in the cemetery and prepared special wax candles from the thread with which she measured the graves. These served as a talisman against the angel of death among pious Jews. These female measurers accompanied funeral processions to the cemetery and recounted afterward what miracles and visions had appeared before them. Sometimes, they even returned with complaints entrusted to them by the deceased if the children did not pray for them according to the established ritual and so forth.

I remember one such measurer of graves: a small, thin, old woman who once brought a waxed thread to sell to mother. She immediately began to tell a story about a dog who howled for three days in their neighborhood, and then Moishe Balshem died on the third day. Everyone wailed at the top of their lungs for the loss of such a learned and holy man. When the pious Jews gathered at the cemetery, it suddenly began to grow dark—exactly an Egyptian darkness descended on the earth, and everything became desolate. But from time to time something quietly moved in the sky. When everyone looked closely, they saw the dark cloak of the angel of death, which covered the sun. In the darkness the people barely managed to get to the grave. As soon as the body was lowered into the grave and the rabbi began to recite the prayer, a red disk of sun suddenly revealed itself and the entire sky appeared to be flooded with red light. It was obvious that, just like the prophet Elijah, he had gone up in a magnificent chariot of fire in a din of thunder and lightning; suddenly the bright-eyed angels flew with flaming wings and joyful smiles. Now the entire people understood clearly that God loves devout Jews, and each felt sure that the deceased had ascended straight to heaven. Those who had gathered then composed a prayer to God for the soul of the deceased. The storyteller did not forget her affairs and began to measure the grave by the time of the prayer.

My school was located in this courtyard: it consisted of a large entrance, two inhabited rooms, and a kitchen. The first class was in the entrance, which exited into the courtyard. This is where the assistant *melamed* taught us the art of differentiating the right hand from the left and instructed us to offer the right hand for a handshake. In addition, he taught us the Jewish alphabet and reading by syllables. The unique feature of this pedagogy was that he taught the boys to yell out in different ways the letters of the alphabet: *alef*, *beis*, and so forth. The children repeated the letters in a singsong voice countless times. The *melamed* sang: "Tell me, my children, tell me, which one is *alef*?" and the boys sang after him. Sometimes he tried to enliven us with a joke like, "Who wants a bride with four legs?"

At the end of the "syllables," we moved to the second room, to the same *melamed* who instructed us to read the prayers; we repeated after him the morning and evening prayers. He also taught us which prayers to read before eating fruit or a plant growing in the ground such as a pumpkin, watermelon, and so forth. He taught us about washing our hands before eating, what to say during this prayer, and what prayers [to recite] after eating. We learned to sing a prayer that they recite on Friday evening over a glass of wine before the first Sabbath meal. The *melamed* instructed us that upon meeting a stranger, we should offer him our right hand, and say "Sholem aleichem" [peace be unto you]. All the prayers were in Hebrew and we repeated them after the *melamed*, without understanding the meaning of the words. That is how we passed into the second class in knowledge and learning.

The assistant *melamed* and the *melamed* himself were very amiable people and conscientiously fulfilled their obligations. Sometimes we received a box on the ears or a blow on the head with rebbe Shulim's pipe for inattention; however, I must admit that this happened infrequently and that it was not especially painful. This was not a system [of punishment] but random incidents. I do not remember how many hours we spent at school but I recall that the assistant *melamed* came for me and the other children around 8:00 in the morning. At this time, one could often see the assistant *melamed* in the rain with a throng of children, whom he led by the hand through the streets because he was fearful of letting go of a little one through the impassable puddles. I think that I was at this school for two years, where I learned to read the prayers in Hebrew; with this, my initial education came to an end.

The second *heder*, where we went through the Torah and translated it into Yiddish, was starkly different from rebbe Shulim's *heder*—both in terms of the conditions and manner of teaching as well as the attributes of the rebbe, Srul Volochiskii. First, rebbe Shulim taught 200 boys and carried out the instruction according to a well-known routine. He comported himself with distinction, conscious of his own dignity. This second *heder* was located in one of the filthiest parts of the city—in Kalachnyi, a fetid, rear courtyard surrounded by boardinghouses and meat stores. The building reminded me of some kind of two-story barn, which had been thrown together. The first floor consisted of a spacious barn with a large oven for baking matzo for Passover. We had to clamber up a ladder to get to the second floor, which consisted of two rooms and a kitchen. In the first room stood a big, white table and two benches; this was our *heder*. The kitchen was half the size of our room; it contained a bed, a small table, two chairs, and an arm chair. This room served as kitchen, dining room, and bedroom for my new *melamed*, Srul Volochiskii, and his wife, a sick hunchback woman. She not only carried out her household chores in this room and prepared food in it, but she also set up her business here. She sold down feathers from dead birds (it was not known where she obtained them). Here too she plucked the feathers. This occupation of the rebbe's wife may have appeared innocent at first glance, but it played a major role in the course of our education. I shall return to this subject.

Rebbe Srul Volochiskii was a genuine representative of the breed of *melamdim*—that is, after his failures in all other spheres of activities, he turned to theology, the instruction of children in the *Tanach*, and the reading of prayers in the synagogue for the dead. Sometimes, he even tried to treat fevers with the help of round rye rolls on which he drew the shield of King David in black ink. On the first, he made three marks, on the second, five and so forth, adding two marks on each new roll, and only on the last roll did he draw a complete shield. Drawing these lines, he muttered some kind of secret words. The patient ate the roll with the three marks first, then the one with the five, and so forth. When he got down to the last roll with the entire shield of David, the accursed illness abated and he recovered. This was natural, as the Jewish proverb goes: "Purim is not a holiday and a fever is not an illness." I should note that rebbe Srul was not a charlatan; he piously believed in the curative properties of his medicine.

He was fifty years old, quite stout, with a broad, thick graying beard with long *peyes*, a narrow face, and vacuous lifeless eyes. It was as though it were engraved on his forehead: "There is nothing on earth that is worth worrying about: that which God entered in his book of fate will take place; I will attempt to hold out on this anthill until it pleases God to call me away." Despite the various occupations of rebbe Srul and his wife, they were terribly poor. His clothes consisted of a long, black *kapote*, which was faded and worn, but even on cloudy days, it had a glow. He wore a yarmulke on his head and a fur hat on top of it. Under the outer *kapote*, he wore a night-shirt, always stretched too tight across the chest; over it lay the ritual attire, the *arba kanfot*—a four-cornered garment with an aperture in the middle for the head, with four corners to which the fringes are attached. In place of pants, he wore voluminous drawers, which were tucked into long, white stockings, invariably with holes in the heels, gaping open with every step in his night slippers. As you see, rebbe Srul's wardrobe was not particularly grand and allowed for ventilation. His clothes got soaked through and through in the rain, and he would turn everything upside down in search of anything dry in the house. He was good-natured and treated the children well. Sometimes when he was upset about something, he blew his nose in the hallway and wiped his nose with his hands on his shirt. When he slipped quietly into the room,

he struck the students' backs with the mouth-piece of his long pipe. They never protested but applied themselves even more diligently to learn Torah by rote.

Friday was a day of joy for the boys. In the morning, rebbe Srul made rounds to his pupils' parents in order to collect the weekly payment and to pick up the children for school. On the road, he bought loaves and so forth for the Sabbath, gave them to a pupil, and sent him home with instructions to give the change to his wife. In such a manner, every five to ten minutes, one student after another was sent to school carrying fish, fire-wood, a chicken, a piece of meat, and other things, supposedly for the Sabbath. An hour and a half passed before all the pupils were gathered at school. If rebbe Srul were lucky enough to receive an order to read memorial prayers for some deceased Jew, he set off to do this in the synagogue and came back to school two hours later. The boys were very happy in the *heder*: they played, argued, and even had a fight. However, to calm them down, the rebbe's wife organized a reading. She called the children to her "classroom"—that is, the kitchen, where she sat on a box of lemons and plucked feathers. The boys seated themselves around her and she pulled out a Yiddish book, *Bove korolevich.*[4] One boy read aloud and the others helped her pluck feathers. I was considered a good reader. We discussed the miraculous adventures of Bove the prince, and everyone had a say about what he would do in Bove's place. The readings and conversations kindled our imagination: we built castles in the air and were very happy. The entire situation seemed extraordinary. The more rapturous the other places in the books, the more rapidly the children's fingers worked, picking up the cloud of *pukh* [fluff] in the kitchen until after an hour or an hour and a half of work, the rebbe's wife and all the children were absolutely covered with feathers and we resembled a hen with chicks.

I remember being in this school for a year

or a year and a half. Once the rebbe brought a pot with hot coals from the bakery, which was located under us, and placed it in the iron stove that stood in the room. As a result, all the children were nearly asphyxiated [from the charcoal fumes]. After this, I was removed from this school. Apparently my stepfather's business flourished at this time. He left the money-changing business and rented a large house with a courtyard and began to trade in lumber, stone, and other building materials.[5]

NOTES

1. [Lazar Borisovich Gol'denberg was an early Jewish revolutionary who worked with Aron Liberman on the populist journal *Vpered!* The two also created the Hebrew Socialist Union in London in 1876. In this selection from his memoir, Gol'denberg describes his childhood in Odessa. In contrast to most *maskilic* narratives of the *heder*, which criticized it as a site of abuse and violence, Gold'enberg remembered his *melamdim* with some fondness, even mild amusement. His life story also suggests that children were vulnerable to being orphaned or semi-orphaned because of the low life expectancy in the child-bearing adult population and the high mortality rate from disease and childbirth. It was not uncommon for children, during their early years, to become "blended" into another family with a stepparent and stepsiblings because of death or divorce—new family arrangements that led to the kind of conflicts that Gold'enberg describes.]

2. [This period was known as *kest*—the obligation of the bride's or groom's parents to provide room and board for the new couple for a specified period. *Kest* enabled couples to accumulate the means to establish an independent household or to allow the husband to immerse himself in traditional Torah studies.]

3. [*Tefillin* are leather-boxes that contain a parchment inscribed with verses from the Torah; they are worn on the forehead during prayer to make the worshipper cognizant of God. To protect against the devil, as Gol'denberg states here, was not the primary purpose, but this belief was evidently widespread among the population.]

4. [*Maaseh Bove* or *Bove korolevich* (Bove the prince) was a popular, romantic Yiddish story that adorned many a family's bookshelf. According to Buki ben Yagli (Judah Loeb Kazenelson), books like *Maaseh Bove* and *Centura Ventura* whetted his appetite (his "evil inclination") for fairy tales: "The subject of the *Maaseh Bove* tale surely is known to all, and if they do not know it, then they have not missed a thing. For surely it is a goyish legend. What is told therein are tales of wars and bloodshed, and these matters are in any case not an issue for Jews" (quoted in Iris Parush, *Reading Jewish Women: Marginality and Modernization in Nineteenth-Century East European Jewish Society* [Waltham, MA: Brandeis University Press, 2004], 139).]

5. [There is a gap in the narrative between his education in the *heder* (presented here) and the one-paragraph description of his gymnasium years. He notes that when he was thirteen years old, he was in the second year of gymnasium. In 1863, influenced by the Polish Uprising, he began to read social and political literature—including Nikolai Chernyshevskii's novel *What Is to be Done*—that led him to the revolutionary path.]

[29]

A Jewish Girlhood in Moscow in the 1870s and 1880s: The Memoirs of Roza Vinaver

Roza Georgievna Vinaver, "Vospominaniia Rozy Georgievna Vinaver, zheny chlena 1-oi gosudarstvennoi dumi Maksima Moiseevicha Vinavera," Hoover Institute Archives, Stanford, California. Collection V. Maklakov, box 15, folder 3 (January 1944).

I was born in Moscow in 1872.[1] My father, Gendel' Simkhovich Khishin, was one of the first migrants from Lithuania, one of the first Jews who dared to travel to the capital of Moscow in the beginning of the 1860s. Father told us that at the time Jews were allowed to move freely in the city only during the day; at night they were locked up in one house — the so-called Moscow compound (*podvor'e*) of the Glebov monastery, located near the Moscow River. Initially father arrived in Moscow alone and only after a few years moved his family with him; at that time, I can remember that we already lived freely in an apartment. Jews, for the most part, lived in a special quarter, the so-called Zariad'e. The more affluent lived in Kitaigorod, the commercial section of Moscow adjacent to the Kremlin. At the end of the 1890s, this entire section was demolished and turned into high-class businesses.

I came into the world after my parents had buried two of their sons (who had died from diphtheria, all in the course of one week). They transferred all their love to me and spoiled me to no end. This indulgence produced its own fruit because of my lively temperament and wild imagination. I made life impossible for everybody at home, turning everything upside down. Not one chair was left standing in its place: I overturned them, building trains and towers. Even living creatures got it from me. Once, some poor relative with a long beard somehow came by our house. It immediately came to my mind that it would not be a bad idea to put a braid in his long beard. Without giving it much thought, I climbed onto the knees of this poor man and made the braid, but he was afraid to protest — he saw that no one was going to stop me. When the braid was ready, it sent me into raptures. The old man was afraid to unbraid it and walked around with it, but no one punished me; they were only astonished at my ingenuity. There was a still worse [incident]. I caused a lot of trouble for my elderly grandmother. We lived in a summer house in Petrovskii Park on the second floor. Mother went to town, leaving me with grandmother. Suddenly it occurred to me that it would not be a bad idea to get dressed in my new muslin dress; but mother had locked it in a trunk, taking the key with her, and grandmother was not able to get it for me. Again, without giving it much thought, I climbed up to the roof through the window and yelled at poor grandmother that if they did not give me the muslin dress immediately, I would jump off the roof. Grandmother was distressed; what was she to do? She ran to the policeman, and through various tricks he managed to entice me back and to remove me from the roof. I remember that at this time some guests arrived, a woman with a girl, but they quickly left. It was apparent that the woman did not want her daughter playing with such a spoiled girl.

Because I was unmanageable, the domestic servants persuaded my mother to send me — an absolutely young [girl] — to school. The schoolmistress was called Agrafena Davydovna. She was angry, angry — and I was terribly afraid of her. The children stayed there until 3 p.m.; at 12:00 was lunch, which one brought [from home]. Until lunch there was reading; after lunch came penmanship and crafts. I especially loathed penmanship and crafts: penmanship was full of blots, and crafts was so dirty (as though you were holding a chimney sweep in your hand). Then I thought up the next stratagem — I told our servant Tat'iana to come to the school after 12:00 and say: "The guests have arrived, and they request that the girl come home." She did so, and I returned home after lunch happy with my prank. The following day, encouraged by my scheme, I asked Tati'ana to repeat it. Again I was happy to be freed from penmanship and crafts. And on the third day I risked repeating this prank. I arrived home, but Agrafena Davydovna had followed me home to my mother, and she asked her why she took her daughter home for a third day after lunch. And here, my pranks were revealed. They punished me severely: at the entrance to the school where everyone entered, they placed me for an hour in the corner on my knees — it hurt me, and it was shameful, shameful.

All the same, I did not turn over a new leaf. Next they sent me very early to the German gymnasium, renowned for its strictness, together with my cousin who was four years older than me but not taller. She was in the first class while I was in the preparatory class. When they brought these two girls with the same surnames, they [the staff] did not know whom to place in which class. My cousin was a timid girl whereas I was bold, so I said: "Place her in the preparatory class and me in the first class." They did so [. . .] and told me to write down my surname. I knew how to write but only in print [not cursive] — so I printed my surname on the board with a flourish. Everyone laughed, and they sent me back to the preparatory class while they settled Sonia in the first class.

But I was sly: at school I behaved in an exemplary fashion, but at home I was forever naughty. They would go to complain to the director Frau Kerber, but she replied that at school I behaved well and that she could do nothing to help at home. My pranks were countless. At that time my parents were in no position to hire a governess for me and my younger sister, and we were happily left to ourselves. In our free time we played in the courtyard and on the street; how blissfully we spent this time! How many resources did this courtyard provide, such as the haberdashery store. Every day they swept [into the courtyard] the litter from the store, which was full of treasures. We found lovely beads, turquoise and red buttons. And games? The unfortunate children who grew up under the supervision of any governess never played such delightful games: for the courtyard gave us countless corners in which to hide, [and to play games of] I spy with my little eye [*palochka ruchalochka*], golden gates [*zolotnyia vorota*], and games of catch [*gorelki*]. All of this so enchanted us that they could barely lure us to come home in the evening.

With such gaiety, learning did not enter my mind, and until the third grade I was a poor student at the German gymnasium, always the last student. But in the third grade an incident abruptly changed my behavior: I was forced to repeat it. At that time this was a major disgrace. In the gymnasium everyone teased me for being a failed student. I understood then that the time had come to abandon my pranks and come to my senses. Farewell to my collection of beads and feathers! I needed to bear down and read books. And wonder of wonders: a book did not seem that boring to me. I immediately began to study well and improved with every year until I was no longer in rank of the elementary pupils. However, the disgrace of having to repeat a class did not leave me for many years; I hid it from my husband, and I still experience [the shame] as though it were today — when I am already a great-grandmother.

Jews lived freely in Moscow in the era of the 1870s and 1880s. In the Jewish quarter, it was impossible to imagine that you were living in the heart of Great Russia. Jews gained the right to live in Moscow in different ways: registration in the merchant or artisan guilds, or simply through a private deal with the police. My father soon occupied a very honorable place among the Moscow merchants. He had a reputation for honesty, and the Moscow banks entrusted him to verify the signatures of Jews whom the banks did not trust because they had come from the Pale of Settlement but were unknown to the police. I remember that Father had a money box in which each placed ten kopecks for every such "visa" [verification] and he collected a lot of money for the poor in this way.

Although my father came from a fairly democratic [modest] family—his parents had something akin to a hotel in Novogrudok (which was located in a building called "the Palace" in my grandmother's words)—my mother came from an aristocratic family. She treated the Moscow Jews with a little suspicion; as for their "diversity" [in social origins], she always added that her relatives ate off golden plates. Indeed, she received a broader education: she knew German and loved to recite Schiller. She was embarrassed to admit that her teacher was [Iakov] Brafman,[2] notorious after he was baptized and, like a true renegade, provided false information to Russian antisemites. Our mother was very reserved because of her aristocratism. She only considered a few worthy enough to approach us, and I remember scenes when the young people surrounding me were expected to withdraw quickly when she appeared. When we went to the ball, we had to promise that we would dance only with those whom she had pointed out to us. Of course, we did not keep the promises and thoroughly enjoyed ourselves with our "democratic" acquaintances.

My mother was extremely religious, perhaps more religious than my father. The house was kept in a strict religious spirit. Preparations for Passover took place in such a feverish atmosphere that even smallest oversight would seemingly lead to ruin. I remember one such tragicomic incident. In those days Moscow did not have running water; instead water porters delivered the water and poured it into a barrel. On Passover all the holiday dishes along with the Passover barrel for water replaced the everyday dishes and barrel. Once, when the Passover barrel was full of water that had already been used to prepare the Passover dishes, they discovered that this barrel, which had been brought from the basement, was not for Passover but for sauerkraut. Everyone was in shock: life in the house came to a stop. No one was able to put anything in his or her mouth. They immediately sent for the rabbi so that he could decide this difficult question. The rabbi apparently was an intelligent person and decided that the barrel was allowed to remain [kosher for] Passover and nothing—neither the dishes nor the food—had to be discarded. I do not know whether he took the sin on his own soul or he actually decided according to the law. However, everyone in the house was joyous and began to celebrate Passover.

Thus I grew up in a very Orthodox environment. All religious rituals were strictly observed, and we children knew them very well. We were very fearful of the Jewish God and knew perfectly what kind of punishment awaited us for each kind of sin. I dare say that if you eat a piece of bread [during Passover], God will punish this sin by reducing the days of your close relatives. God forbid that you should drop the Bible; when you pick it up, you need to kiss it. We observed all the fasts very strictly. From the age of five, I studied Hebrew, and until the age of sixteen or seventeen, I punctiliously observed all the religious rituals. Even [though I was] sent to the gymnasium, I was deeply imbued with Jewish culture. When I was older, I grew very fond of the Hebrew language and Jewish history;

I became a strong Jewish nationalist. At that time there was no such thing as Zionism, only Palestinophilism, and I dreamed of traveling to Palestine to devote my life to the benefit of the Jews.

There was still another side of our education, which had an influence on my entire life. My father was one of those people who suffered over social inequality, and that is why he arranged our lives in an extremely austere manner. He sent part of his earnings to his family in the town of Novogrudok, where he established a hospital and interest-free loan office. Two times a year, on the holidays of Passover and Sukkot, he sent money to an entire group of people and so forth. He always instilled in us children never to allow any luxury and to use only what is necessary. Sweets were an indulgence [allowed] only on Saturday. Our linens were made from the same thick material that was sent to the hospital in Novogrudok. What was instilled [in me by my father] has remained with me all my life, although I was never able to accept the social theories [of the day]. At this time, the Jewish youth in Moscow were inclined to be extremely idealistic—just like the Russian Orthodox youth. It was thought disgraceful to pay attention to the external conditions of life and instead one focused on two mottos: spiritual improvement and preparation for future service.

Simultaneous with the influence of this Jewish atmosphere in the family that surrounded me was life outside the family. School with its pupils and friends as well as Moscow itself with its people, theaters, and gatherings—all this was Russian, purely Russian. Our language was purely Russian, and even in the family this Russian culture deeply pervaded our soul beginning from the earliest age. We did not know the Jewish people, just individual Jewish families. But the people around us were Russian. We did not experience any antisemitism whatsoever. We lived a common life with our Russian Orthodox friends, with our [Russian] nannies who took us to church, and with our teachers; we were imbued with Russian interests, literature, and history. As I grew older, I strayed from Jewish national interests. Already in childhood, our Russian reader *Our Word* with its "God's Bird Does not Know"[3] spoke to our childish imaginations much more than the Bible, which I had to read in Hebrew. I remember how my old rebbe suffered when he came for a lesson, and I hid from him under the bed. Hence the conditions of education tended to create people with a Russian-Jewish soul; such a synthesis of two cultures existed only in Russia. In some periods one of these sides dominated. During the dark days of the pogroms, I felt all the bitter resentment of the Jewish national self-consciousness. But this resentment did not cry for vengeance: on whom would we avenge ourselves? We knew that the government organized the pogroms, and that our Russian friends were ashamed and grieved with us. [. . .][4]

NOTES

1. [Rosa Vinaver was the wife of Maksim Vinaver, a lawyer and member of the First Duma. In contrast to Gol'denberg's narrative, Vinaver's memoirs portray her childhood in a more privileged family in Moscow, which included her education in a secular gymnasium. She describes the strict observance of Judaism in the family despite their use of Russian at home and interactions with Russian society.]

2. [Iakov Brafman (1825–79) was a convert from Judaism; he was best known for his notorious *Book of Kahal*, which described Jewish exploitation of Russians and a diabolical scheme to take over Russia.]

3. ["Ptichka bozh'ia ne znaet ni zaboty ni truda" (God's bird knows neither labor nor worries) first appeared in Pushkin's poem "Gypsies" and later in Lermentov's "Demon Song."]

4. [Vinaver echoes the sentiment of historians such as Simon Dubnow who blamed the government for organizing the pogroms. In her memoir, she continues to describe the major changes for the

Jews under the liberal general governor of Moscow, Prince Vladimir Andreevich Dolgorukov (who served in that post from 1865 to 1891, until he was replaced by the archconservative Grand Duke Sergei Aleksandrovich, the brother of Alexander III).]

[30]

Petition of Khaia Saetovaia for Material Support from Children (1846)

LVIA, f. 456, op. 2, d. 382, ll. 37–38 ob.

"Petition of Khaia Saetovaia to Emperor Nicholas I (15 March 1846)"

ALL BLESSED SIRE, THE GREAT
SOVEREIGN NIKOLAI PAVLOVICH,
AUTOCRAT OF ALL RUSSIANS,
MOST GRACIOUS SOVEREIGN!

In this petition, the Vil'na resident, the widow Khaia Aronovna Saetovaia, requests the following:[1]

1. I lived in marital union for fifty consecutive years with my now-deceased husband, Aron Saet, a resident of Vil'na. For fifteen years, we belonged to the merchant class, and by our mutual labor we acquired capital of no small significance, which consisted of cash, silver plates and dishes, valuables, and substantial personal property—with a total value of approximately 4,000 rubles. We also owned the following real estate: in the first quarter of the city (house number 236), in the second quarter (part of Ekzdevizorskii's house number 237 on Iatkovaia St. and number 380 on Nemetskaia St.), and in the fourth quarter (a stone one-story house, number 1253 by the Konn Market, purchased with the income from an inheritance and with an annual yield of approximately 800 silver rubles). In addition to loans to different people, all this amounted to a significant sum of money. Moreover, ten years ago my husband died suddenly, having failed to deal with the acquired property in a proper will, leaving me with our two sons: Iudel Aronovich Saet-Pokasevskii (who lives in the Kingdom of Poland in the town of Kalvárii) and Gabriel Saet (who lives in here in Vil'na). They took possession of all the hereditary property. In particular, the oldest son Pokasevskii takes the income from the real estate during each visit to Vil'na. Apart from this, as I was recently informed, Pokasevskii received a sum of 700 silver rubles in Warsaw from a Vil'na resident, Ilia Dovidovich Kenigsberg, on a loan owed to me and my deceased husband from the local "Mass" Jewish printing house. This money was part of the property I acquired together with my husband. I am also dissatisfied with the court decision regarding the Jew Mordukh Eremiashevich Maizel, [whose case] was put together in the name of Iudel, my oldest son. [Iudel] also received the same [repayment on loan] from the Jew Shimsel Moze, about 2,000 silver rubles and so forth. He seized directly debts owed to the deceased, a cash sum of approximately 7,000 rubles.

2. In spite of everything, however, the fact is that by the power of the law [. . .][2] one-quarter of the hereditary personal property and one-seventh of the real estate were apportioned to

me, and I have repeatedly sought [to receive] this allotment. However, my oldest son Pokasevskii often deceived me with firm promises; meanwhile, however, he has moved his residency to Poland, where he has been amusing himself for a year or two. But he collected all the money here [in Vil'na], failing to provide his aged and decrepit mother with the means for daily sustenance, other than the apartment in which I have continuously lived with my husband for fifty years.

These circumstances forced me to file a complaint with the Vil'na city police in humble petitions of 1 June, 11 June, and 18 June 1845, which led to a decision of 24 September of this year (number 22,842). The police ordered the first Ostrobramska police office to have my sons Iudel and Gabriel Saet swear that I would not suffer from want, and that they would properly provide for me as a mother, in accordance with the property bequeathed by the deceased. To fulfill this order, the supervisor Semkovskii required that several lodgers [residing] in the inherited rooms sign a statement that they will bring me the rent — twenty silver rubles a month for my support. However, my oldest son Pokasevskii, who became more aggressive in constraining me, took the liberty of filing a complaint against me with the city police: the twenty rubles a month for my maintenance, which consists of 5 percent a month, would be excessive for me. He neglected to say that from this money I must pay the apartment dues and city taxes, as well as the repair of the lodgings. After the deduction of these expenses, the net sum of money that remains for me is hardly about three rubles a week — at a time when, having reached the age of seventy-five, I have already been deprived of a healthy body. I hope for the very best benefits (with servants and other vigilant care) to pass the rest of my days. I hope for all this from my sons.

In addition, the city police should have been more concerned about my welfare. As a defenseless widow, I yielded to the petition of my son Pokasevskii. According to [the police chief's] new resolution, the decision of the supervisor, who obliged the lodgers to bring me twenty silver rubles, was groundless. Incidentally, he ordered that no action be taken and that my petition be assigned for investigation by the Conscience Court.

Given these circumstances and seeking the protection of justice, I humbly ask you [. . .] to order the seizure of the rent money from all the indivisible property of my son Iudel Pokasavskii.

The Vil'na townsman Girsh Aronovich Kachergiskii wrote this petition [on my behalf] since movement is very difficult for me because of my decrepitude and old age.

"Resolution of the Conscience Court (23 July 1847)"

[. . .] On the basis of the *Svod zakonov Rossiskoi imperii* [. . .],[3] the Conscience Court concluded that children are obliged to provide sustenance and support for their parents. In the petition to the city police, Iudel consented to give his mother the apartment (in the house jointly owned with his brother Gabriel) and with the latter to provide her support. To monitor the fulfillment of these conditions (order number 109, dated 20 March 1846), the police proposed that both Iudel and his brother Gabriel Saet provide their mother with the specified maintenance (four silver rubles a month each).[4] He will announce this to all three persons [and obtain their] signatures.

[The court] ordered the Vil'na city police to confirm the time that they will implement the court's proposal for the demanded signatures, without further confirmations.

NOTES

1. [Parental authority and filial subordination were not only Jewish patriarchal values but were also embedded in Russian state law. As the next two cases in this and the next reveal, the courts upheld a parent's right to respect and support regardless of

the child's age. This case came before the Conscience Court (*sovestnyi sud*) that Catherine the Great established to consider such issues as family strife and sexual misconduct. Apart from sensational matters like infanticide, the court was busy mediating family conflicts over finances and personal honor. For a similar case, see the 1851 suit brought by the widow Tsivia Ioseleva Rozensonova against her son for support (LVIA, f. 456, op. 2, d. 1130).]

2. [*Svod zakonov Rossiskoi imperii* (Digest of the laws of the Russian Empire), 9: 967 (1842 edition).]

3. [Ibid., 10: 188.]

4. [In short, the court gave the mother the apartment in which she resided but reduced the monthly allowance from her sons from twenty to eight rubles a month.]

[31]

Trial of Mordukh Eliashberg of Vil'na for Rebellion against Parental Authority (1859)

LVIA, f. 447, op. 19, d. 8558, ll. 1–6 ob.

"Petition of Iosel Eliash Vul'fovich Eliashberg and His Wife Iodes Eliashova Eliashberg of Vil'na to Tsar Alexander II (28 January 1859)"

BLESSED SIRE, GREAT SOVEREIGN ALEXANDER NIKOLAEVICH, AUTOCRAT OF ALL RUSSIANS, MOST GRACIOUS SOVEREIGN!

The third-guild merchant and resident of Vil'na, the Jew Iosel Eliash Vul'fovich, and his wife Iodes Iosel-Eliashova Eliashbergova present their petition on the following points:

1. Our son Mordukh Eliashberg, twenty-six years old and having reached his majority, began to abandon himself to drunkenness, perpetual disobedience toward parental authority, a dissolute and profligate life, and overt vice — despite being supported by us and our benevolent concern to ensure that he lead an honorable life. Simultaneously, he repeatedly allowed himself to offend us personally with curses and to insult us at our table, cruelly and even violently. His absent-mindedness, combined with his indecent involvements, give the appearance that he desires to abuse us elderly people.

2. Such treatment of us elderly parents by our son Mordukh is extremely offensive. Although we lost patience over time and in bitterness intended to hand him over to the law, in the meantime we took various admonitory measures to improve his behavior. For a long time we could not overcome our parental feelings and decide to have him prosecuted. Placing our hope in the excellent, honest upbringing that we gave him (and having provided for all his needs), we expected him to improve his behavior and return to a decent way of life. Sometimes, even among people of depraved morals, [decency] is restored; in some cases they come to their senses and abandon vice. But our son does everything in defiance and, to his public disgrace, sinks further into all kinds of explicit vice, which deprives him of feelings of humanity. His

unbridled passions have increased the danger to us parents, subjecting us to harsh insults and battery. Had he not been arrested, we would have been exposed to such dangers when he was in a state of agitation. To forestall such consequences and in compliance with the [law],[1] we turned first to the city police of Vil'na to arrest our aforementioned son, whom they have taken away.

3. Overcome with grief and dread, and being in no condition to endure the insults from Mordukh's cruel and extremely obstinate treatment, we humbly request that you order that the actions of our son Mordukh Eliashberg, who has been detained by the police for the crimes against us, be held accountable.[2] In addition, in hopes that he return to a moral life, allow us to reduce the personal penalty, based on our parental feelings and [the law].[3] In the same way, regarding the decision [. . .] on his fate, in the event that he repents and reforms his behavior, do not deprive us parents of our natural concern for him and permit us to prevent his association with the pernicious people in Vil'na with whom he has become acquainted. Allow us to settle him in a sparsely populated [place], at our discretion, where he will be under proper supervision until we are persuaded of a real reform in his behavior. In the meantime, direct the city police not to release our son from arrest until our petition has been examined, and not to allow him to have contact with other imprisoned criminals (who may have an influence on his further obstinacy against parental authority). Keep him separate from the others under arrest, and in particular, restrain him from his insulting actions against us.

"Ovsei Fridberg and His Daughter Basia Eliashberg to Tsar Alexander II (4 February 1859)"

BLESSED SIRE AND GREAT SOVEREIGN, ALEXANDER NIKOLAEVICH, AUTOCRAT OF ALL RUSSIANS, MOST GRACIOUS SOVEREIGN!

The townsman of the Vil'na Jewish community, the Jew Ovsei Fridberg, together with his daughter Basia (married surname: Eliashbergova)[4] request the following:

1. The Vil'na resident and third guild merchant Iosel Eliash Vul'fovich Eliashberg and his wife Iodes Eliashbergova, who are immensely wealthy and obviously resentful, are prosecuting their son Markus [Mordukh] Eliashberg (the first petitioner is the father-in-law and the second his wife Basia Ovsegovna Fridberga). The [couple] married against their [Markus's parents] wishes this past January 19. Being malevolent toward their son Markus and us, whom they have unjustly slandered even though they have been innocent since the day of the wedding, [the Eliashbergs] had him arrested in the 3rd Zarechnoi section through the agent Movshe [. . .] although he has committed no crime. Either tomorrow or the 20th, mercilessly and with no substantial facts, only the bald assertion and unsubstantiated complaint of the parents (who incidentally are merchants), their only son will be subjected to a frightening and unjust doom. He is incarcerated with various criminals; until now he has become emaciated without grounds for [allegedly] resisting the order of his parents. The matter is now before the Criminal Court. [. . .]

2. The merchants Eliashbergs, Markus's parents, have acquired property through commerce. Notwithstanding the fact that their son has already been married twice (divorced from the first and widowed by the second wife, with whom he had two children — nine and three years of age), and is in his majority — all this was quite enough for us, knowing his good

side and [understanding] that the immature behavior stemmed from alienation throughout the years. Before their marriage, Basia loaned him 200 silver rubles in cash at his request, supported him in almost everything when he was ruined, and incurred considerable expenses without committing any sins [sexual relations] with him. Even Markus's own parents are capable of knowing enough about this and did not contradict it. Based on real mutual love, the marriage was conducted with its own ritual on 19 January of this year. This is the only reason the Eliashbergs became malevolent toward their son, led him to a [marital] separation, and indeed desired to end the marriage. . . . They have defended the rank of the merchant estate such that they use their wealth to inflict slanderous persecution of the innocent and subject him to imprisonment, knowing that they would frighten him [with the threat] of being drafted as a soldier or being sent to a prison cell in Siberia.

3. The merchant's son Markus Eliashberg married his present wife, Basia Fridberg, who was single. She is also the daughter of a former merchant, but who no longer has that status due to God's will. Her position is modest but was achieved through honest conduct; poverty is the status of such a person. To a merchant with wealth, the marriage of my daughter to a merchant's son cannot be considered a vice; [the marriage took place] after thoughtful reflection based on common, benevolent sense, albeit without the consent of the parents. It is no offense, yet a hatred has been aroused only in the Eliashbergs toward us. They have unjustly discredited their son, who has been enervated by the arrest; they have groundlessly caused legal expenditures and have been a burden to authorities. Given all these circumstances, persecution by the Eliashbergs has brought insults and ruin to their son by depriving him of the right to belong to the family and denying [him] his inheritance — because of his marriage to Basia, the daughter of the plaintiff and the peti-

tioner. As for the detention of the innocent, the slander and injury asserted in the merchant Eliashbergs' petition derive from pure malice and are improbable in and of themselves. At the same time, we consider them severe and extremely offensive, all the more so since their son Markus is a part of the family. Moreover, at present the state census places him in the rank of the merchant class and as someone who has no vices. Had that [not] been the case, neither I, Ovsei Fridberg, nor my daughter Basia would have decided to enter into such a marriage. Of course, the wedding of Markus Eliashberg and Basia Fridberga was absolutely based on Jewish rituals, good-natured agreement, and even love; it is also a matter that lies within the purview of a rabbi. [. . .][5] The innocent do not deserve this treatment, all the more so since the marriage — even without parental approval — cannot be considered a crime. [. . .]

We humbly ask that it be ordered: the Criminal Court, having heard our petition, issue a legal directive so that the petition of the merchants Iosel and his wife Iodes Eliashberg regarding their son (who is guilty of nothing), which is full of the most false and unjust [accusations], be disregarded [. . .] and remain without validity. Free Markus Eliashberg, the son-in-law of the petitioner and the husband of my daughter Basia, even if it be on bail. In accordance with the established ancient law of Jewish ritual, allow our rabbi to resolve the Eliashberg suit and to administer an oath that they filed the complaint against their son solely because the marriage to his present wife was against their will. Subject the guilty to legal responsibility and punishment. [. . .] We ask for a gracious resolution.[6]

NOTES

1. [*Ulozhenie o nakazaniiakh* (Code of Punishments), (St. Petersburg: n.d.). vol. 10, statute 16; vol. 15, statute 2165 (1857 edition).]

2. [Ibid., vol. 15, statute 2164.]

3. [Ibid.]

4. [The document spells the name Eliasberg instead of Eliashberg, but the latter will be used for consistency here. This document was written in convoluted Russian, with numerous spelling errors, strange words that do not exist in standard Russian (such as *venchatel'stvo* for wedding), and repetitive sentences.]

5. [Here the document has several repetitive sentences that reiterate the injustice of the complaint against Markus.]

6. [In the last document in the records about the case, the son—who was still in prison—was even contemplating conversion to gain his release.]

Marriage and Divorce

[32]

Tenaim (Engagement Contract of Esther Machlevich and Aharon Rozenshtein)

"Handwritten Tenaim *(Engagement Contract) of Esther Machlevich and Aharon [Aron] Rozenshtein*"

Private Collection of Carolyn Rosenstein.[1]

With *mazel tov*. We will rejoice like a watered garden: you have found a wife, you have found goodness with God's will and blessings. He who led the Jews from slavery to freedom will give you a good name and the contract with the words of the *tenaim* and marital union, the terms of which have been agreed upon by the two parties.

Therefore one party is the honorable and learned rabbi, R. Zev (son of the late R. Yitskhak) on behalf of the bridegroom Aharon [Aron], and the second party is the honorable, wealthy, and learned R. Yechiel (son of the late R. Shraga) on behalf of his daughter, the laudable virgin Esther (may she live).

The honorable, learned student Aharon will marry the laudable virgin Esther (may she live) with *huppah* and *kiddush* according to the laws of Moses and Israel. May they be honest with each other, live in love and friendship, and manage their assets wisely.

R. Zev, son of the late R. Yitskhak, agrees to provide his son, the bridegroom, with Sabbath and holiday clothes, and in addition to the necessary clothes to make gifts to the bride as is the custom.

The honorable R. Yechiel, son of the late R. Shraga, father of the bride, obliges himself to contribute a dowry of 400 rubles cash immediately after the *tenaim* is signed. That sum will be tripled in treasury bonds by the time of the wedding. He is also to provide his daughter with Sabbath and holiday clothes and, in addition, the important necessity of jewelry as is customary for wealthy people.

The wedding will be at a happy and fortuitous hour, if it pleases God, fifteen days in the month of Tevet of this year. Expenses for the wedding will be fully paid by the bride's father.

Half of the [400-ruble] sum will be a fine [paid] to the injured party if one party defaults. The bridegroom's side will not be responsible for half of the dowry and the fine. [The responsible party will be] R. Yisrael [Machlevich], son of the late Shraga Faivish, may the memory of the saint be remembered. And from the bride's side, [the responsible party will be] Rabbi Menahem Mendel [Bakrinsky], son of Rabbi Yona Meir. And the sides are obligated to compensate the sum so that they should not sustain any loss in the world.

Everything in this contract is legal and
binding.
Tuesday, 14 Marheshvan 1900
The Sides:
Witness: Signed by Yisrael Machlevich
Witness: Signed by Mendel Bakrinsky

NOTE

1. [Another translation of this document can be found in *Secrets, Sorrows, and Survivors: Aron Rosenstein's Russian Letters for His Son, 1889–1923* (Baltimore: Gateway Press, 1997), 49–50. Note that Aron Rozenshtein is the formal spelling of the name in Russian documents and letters. Hebrew documents use his Hebrew name Aharon. Aharon Rozenshtein will be used throughout the book for consistency.]

[33]

Responsum of R. Naftali Zvi Yehudah Berlin of Volozhin: An Ambiguous Betrothal

R. Naftali Zvi Yehudah Berlin, *Meshiv davar*, 4: 30 (Warsaw: [s.n.] 1894).

BY THE AID OF THE BLESSED LORD
TO THE RABBI,
MONDAY 2 SIVAN 5644 [1884]
TO THE HONORABLE RABBI ETC.,
CHIEF JUSTICE OF THE COMMUNITY
OF MOLODETCHNO.

I have seen a letter of your eminence (may your candle shine) and have answered your letter on the bad business written therein, whereby one witness testified that the man told the maiden Esther (daughter of R. M.) at first that "I would like to take you as my wife," and afterward asked her whether she wanted to take him as her husband, to which she replied that "I don't want to take an old man as a husband." He then told her: "I am giving you twenty-five rubles," and she said, "give them." He gave them, and she accepted them without saying anything. And the witness is not sure whether he explicitly said, "If I give you twenty-five rubles, will you marry me?" Or whether he just said "I'll give you twenty-five rubles."

The second witness testified that he posed it to her as a question: "Do you want to take me as a husband?" And she replied, "I don't want you." After that he told her that "I am giving you twenty-five rubles," to which she

replied "good," or more precisely "recht" [all right]. He gave her the money, which she accepted in silence.[1]

Where your honor writes that use of the language, "do you wish to take me as a husband" is invalid for purposes of marriage, it is written (Deut. 24:1), "When a man takes a woman" (not when a woman takes a man). What you say is right and clear. But there may still be an issue of "speaking of the business of marriage" where he began to say, "I wish to take you for my wife" [which might have validity].

It is indeed true that the *Rosh* [R. Asher ben Jehiel] and the *Shulhan Arukh* have written (Siman 27 section 6) that "I hereby am your husband" is worse than other bad formulas and is invalid even if uttered while discussing the matter of marriage. However, has not the *Beit Shmuel*[2] cited the opinion of R. Hananel that there are reasons to worry about the formula "I hereby am your husband" when the two have been discussing the same matter [of marriage]? Nonetheless, in Siman 136 section 102, the *Beit Shmuel* ruled that the principle accords with the *Shulhan Arukh* . . .

Furthermore, it seems that even according to R. Yeruham, who holds that this bad formula (like other bad formulas, where "dealing in the same matter" confers some arguable validity) nevertheless does not count as "speaking with her about matters of marriage" unless the two are already in agreement. That is not true of the present case, in which she had already replied: "I do not want to take you for a husband since you are older than me," along with his bad formulation "Do you want to take me as a husband?" Hence there is absolutely no reason to fear that this is a valid marriage.

Moreover it should be known that the entire concern here pertains only to the testimony of the first witness, who said he was unsure whether the man said "If I give you twenty-five rubles will you take me as a husband?"; hence when she said "Fine," the marriage is suspect in terms of the Ran and the Rema's commentary (29:10). But the second witness did not remember hearing when the money was given: "If I give it to you, will you take me as a husband?" when the money was given. So, obviously, there is no concern [that she accepted the money as a token of betrothal], since she had explicitly said that she does not want him for a husband. Her later statement "recht," as all agree, is not valid for marriage. So at most this would be a suspect marriage attested to by only one witness; hence there is no reason at all to be stringent about this.

I therefore concur with the ruling of your eminence (may your candle shine) that there is no cause to fear that this was a marriage; this maiden is free to engage herself to any man who comes forward. May the Lord protect us from errors of judgment (heaven forbid) and set us upon the beam of truth.

NOTES

1. The issue here is whether her acceptance of the money was tantamount to accepting his offer of marriage. To understand this, it is probably best to think of this as if she had accepted something of value, such as a ring. There are different legal issues at play here, but the primary one is whether his formulation, "do you want to take me as a husband," has validity, since, if the answer to that is no, none of the other issues will matter.

2. A commentary on the third part of the *Shulhan Arukh*, written by Samuel ben Uri Shraga Phoebus (second half of the seventeenth century) of Poland.

[34]

Responsum of R. Naftali Zvi Yehudah Berlin of Volozhin: A Betrothal in Jest

R. Naftali Zvi Yehudah Berlin, *Meshiv davar*, 4: 31 (Warsaw: [s.n.], 1894).

The case concerns a Jewish soldier: he saw a maiden selling pastries, played a prank on her, and bought some pastries from her for a few pennies. When she came to collect the money, he took out a silver coin, held her hand and said [the marital formula]: "You are now consecrated to me . . ." giving her the coin. She laughed and went off with the coin. But when the matter became known, her father and mother — and she too — raised an outcry, declaring that she had not understood at all what he had said.

Marriage witnesses were as follows: first, the scoundrel in question saw two people walking along [. . .] and invited them to be marriage witnesses. They were two brothers, the younger a boy of about fourteen. The older one said: "Look, we are brothers, so you will have to find yourself another witness."[1] So he attempted to find a second Jew in the area while he engaged in mischief. And now the man refuses to give a divorce, and this is clearly an urgent matter that involves *igun*; the day will come when he will have to leave, and who knows where our respected government will be inclined to send him.

It seems that there are no grounds to fear that a marriage took place, either because of the witnesses or because of the content of the marital ceremony. May the Lord in his mercy show me the way of truth.

First, even if she had understood that he was marrying her, she could have replied, "Yes I took [payment], but I took what was mine"—that is, she took the price of the pastry, played a game with him, and left. Although under the circumstances the coin was worth more than the pastry, why should *she* worry about that? He presumably would come after her for the change, or she would get change and give it to him.[2] We do not need for him to have said, while giving the coin, "come take it for the pastry." Obviously, so long as there was no engagement and she was joking, there is no cause for concern, as explained in . . . [the *Shulhan Arukh* 28:3]; even if he says

"take this coin and you are sanctified [betrothed] to me with it," [it is not a marriage]. And the Rema's commentary explains that, although in a situation where the man owes the woman money and he pays her [while uttering the correct wedding formula], she cannot later say I took it as payment of the debt. However, this apparently obtains only when the debt was long-standing and had come due. But where there is no proper loan and he has incurred his obligation during that very same transaction, even when he does not explicitly say "take what I owe you" [and thereby makes clear that he means a commercial, not a marital, transaction], this will not work [as a wedding formula]. He needs either to have had an engagement with her or to obtain her consent.

Thus, it seems to me in my humble opinon. When to my opinion are added the verdicts of two other rabbinic decisors, this maiden will have the status of a marriageable woman who is freely available to any Jewish man without any reservations.

NOTES

1. Two immediate relatives may not serve as witnesses to the same matter.

2. The issue here is that, although the money that covered the price of the pastry was already hers (and so she received nothing of value, and thus could not be married through that exchange), the extra money might be considered as a marriage token.

[35]

Responsum of R. Yitzhak Elhanan Spektor: Breaking Off an Engagement

R. Yitzhak Elhanan Spektor, *Ein Yitzhak*, 1: 37 (Vil'na: [s.n.], 1888).

A great rabbi asked my opinion on the case of a person who gave his daughter in marriage to a certain man from an important family and spared no expenses in showering him with a large dowry. But now, after his fortunes fell, he engaged his younger virgin daughter to someone else. Then the married daughter died, leaving two young girls — one a mute twelve-year-old and the other a five-year-old. The widower would like to marry the second daughter, who was already engaged. Your honor has been asked whether the father can terminate the engagement and conditions without the groom's consent. For the father weeps at his misfortune that his offspring and grandchildren will be subject to an outsider [if his former son-in-law marries outside the family], and especially since one of the girls is mute. The orphans also cry bitterly over how it would be living under a stepmother. All this and more cause depression and a waning life for the old man and the souls of the poor orphans. Your honor's opinion is that the engagement can be broken without penalty and without worrying about the general ban against breaking engagements (as is explained in the *Noda bi-Yehudah* [. . .]), for that is only a generalized, not specific, ban. Here is a summary of my response.

A. The law applying to cases of *force majeure* befalling the father of the betrothed (per *Even ha-Ezer* 50:6) is that he is free of penalty. Its source is *Yoreh Deah* 232:12, which explains that if a son falls ill, this also counts as a *force majeure* that releases one from an oath (see tractate *Nedarim*, 27). Likewise

the Rashba's responsum attributed to Nachmanides, question 273, holds: the illness of a brother or sister also counts as *force majeure*. [. . .]

B. In this case, if the illness of a brother or sister is considered to be analogous to the illness of a son (as Nachmanides wrote), such is all the more the case when the issue is his grandchildren. As the *Midrash Raba* explains, our mercies extend thus far and so forth. Now the rabbis in tractate *Brachot* (56) hold that the curse in Deuteronomy ("Your sons and daughters shall be given over to a stranger") refers to stepmothers. We also find in *Yoreh Deah* (392:3) that if [a widower] has small children and his late wife's sister is willing to marry him, they can marry immediately, even within the seven days of mourning. That is because the aunt is mercifully inclined toward her nieces and nephews more than any stranger is. [. . .] Given that this reasoning (being more merciful toward her sister's offspring than an outsider) allows for an exception to the Laws of Mourning, for it is deemed to save the orphans from a cursed existence, in the present case as well, it falls under the principle of an oath that can be broken on account of *force majeure*. For the father would not knowingly accept the ban [on breaking engagements] when the saving of his daughter's daughters was at stake. It is like the case of the brother or sister falling ill. [. . .]

C. Your honor wrote nicely that we collect a penalty for breaking off engagements because of the shame suffered by the injured party (as explained in *Even ha-Ezer*, chapter 50 section 6 and in *Hoshen Mishpat* chapter 207 section

16). But in this case there is no shame: everyone knows that the father had no choice but to cancel the engagement to save the orphans from a cursed existence. As to the ban, your honor wrote this was only a generalized ban (as is explained in the *Noda bi-Yehudah* on the *Yoreh Deah* chapter 148), and surely does not apply in a case such as ours. We have found (in *Bechorot*, 31) that when it is necessary to aid orphans, we revert to Biblical law [devoid of rabbinic restrictions, as the ban on breaking engagements]; as the responsum of the Hemdat Shlomo wrote (Part *Even ha-Ezer* Chapter 7) . . . on behalf of orphans [guardians] may [collect the forms of] interest that are prohibited by rabbinical law. Moreover, we have seen that, for the sake of orphans (because a sister takes pity on her nieces and nephews more than another), an exception is made to the rabbinical laws of mourning, for it is important to save the orphans. Therefore,

as the sages never intended that their enactments would cause harm to orphans . . . surely they did not insititute the ban for a case such as this. And since the father of the betrothed is released from any obligations to the potential groom, by extension she is too for obvious reasons. [. . .] One must also take into account that these matters affect the very life of the old, depressed father.

Thus, if all this is taken together, one may break the bonds of engagement and let her marry the husband of her deceased sister. [. . .] It would be still better if your honor were to involve himself to ensure that the [rejected prospective] groom reconciles himself to this without any financial compensation. It would be proper that the [prospective] groom not harden his heart against agreeing to this. And the Lord shall surely draw to him a fine spouse as his heart desires.

[36]

Loss of Residence Rights: Marriage to a Jew without the Right to Live outside the Pale of Settlement (1909)

RGIA, f. 1412, op. 213, d. 1, ll. 1–11.

"Petition of Anna Mikhlina Babaeva by Her Husband to Tsar Nicholas II, Submitted to His Imperial Majesty's Chancellery for the Receipt of Petitions (25 August 1909)"

TO HIS IMPERIAL MAJESTY,
THE SOVEREIGN EMPEROR,
NICHOLAS ALEKSANDROVICH,
A HUMBLE PETITION

Being of the Jewish confession and having an ardent desire to convert to Russian Ortho-

doxy, I attempted to fulfill this dream, but my mother—upon learning of this and wishing to prevent the conversion by every means, at first began to admonish me. Then, seeing that the admonition was not helping, she took up the idea of marrying me off to a Jew. For this purpose (and together with my relatives), she found a groom—a townsman from the town of Temir Khan Shura [in Dagestan district], a certain Izgiia Il'iago Ogly Babaev.

Taking advantage of my inexperience (I am just sixteen years old),[1] through exhortations and various threats, but mainly through [arguments] about the personal benefits (since I am a poor woman), they were hoping for support from Babaev, who presented himself as a merchant—that is, the owner of a store and workshop. I acquiesced to the coercion; the wedding took place on 17 July 1909. Although yielding to my mother's nagging, I categorically told her that I would not live with my husband because I do not love him, and cannot possibly love him, after our three-day acquaintance, and that she makes my life unhappy. But my mother was not moved by these entreaties, answering with the well-known but bitter proverb: "Get used to it, you'll come to love him."

Given that I did not want to live with my husband after the wedding, he reported it to the police, who then arrested him, explaining that my husband was living "secretly" because he did not have the right to reside in the town of Rostov-na-Donu.[2] I was arrested with him on the basis of the law that a Jewish woman who has the right to reside in certain places [outside the Pale of Settlement] loses this right following a marriage to a Jew [who lacks this privilege]. Thanks to the attention of the local administration, I was released from arrest and began to ask my husband to give me a divorce. At first he agreed, but then categorically refused because of slander by some of his acquaintances at the rabbi's.

I thus found myself in a terrible position: first, I lost the right of residency in the town of Rostov-na-Donu, and if I do not leave voluntarily, I will be deported; second, I cannot receive a separate passport without the agreement of my husband. On the grounds of the above, I fall to the feet of Your Imperial Majesty and take the liberty to request humbly that you order [the following]:

(1) conduct a detailed inquiry into this case, with the purpose of securing my divorce;

(2) grant me the right to reside in the town of Rostov-na-Donu until the end of the divorce case;

(3) issue me a passport (separate from my husband) for the town of Rostov-na-Donu.

THE LOYAL SLAVE OF
YOUR IMPERIAL MAJESTY,
ANNA IOSIFOVNA BABAEVA
[SIGNED IN HER OWN HAND]

"Protocols Recorded by Assistant Police Officer Naumov of Rostov-na-Donu (25 August 1909)"

By order of the city administration of 24 August (number 12278) (pursuant to the resolution of His Excellency, the city governor [*gradonachal'nik*]), the assistant police officer of the third section of Rostov-na-Donu, Naumov conducted an inquiry based on the petition of the wife of the villager from Temir Khan Shura—Anna Iosifovna Babaeva, born the daughter of the engineer Mikhlin. I questioned Babaeva, who explained that she is fifteen years old, of the Jewish confession, literate, and has lived in the town of Rostov-na-Donu since the day of her birth (with her mother, the widow of the mining engineer, Liubov' Isaakovna Mikhlina). On the question about her reason for entering into the first legal marriage with the villager from Temir Khan Shura (Dagestan district), Izgiia Il'iagu Ogly Babaev, she explained the following: "On 13 July of this year, I set out to the home of my distant relative, Genia Lazaerva Laivint, who lives in house number 126 on Nikol'skaia Street, who introduced me to Babaev and proposed that I marry him. However, I categorically declared that I would not marry him. Nonetheless, Laivint began to influence my mother, no matter what, to give me in marriage to Babaev; my mother, in turn, began to insist on my marriage to Babaev. As a result, I had daily fights with my mother, and it reached the point where she hit me. In light of my mother's insistent wish and various threats, I decided—against my will—to marry Izgiia Babaev, whom I do not love or know."

The deposed witness, Dmitrii Matveevich Mishchenko (a provincial secretary living on Sennaia Street number 200 in Mikhlina's apartment), explained the reason for Anna Mikhlina's marriage. She married Babaev because of the unrelenting demand of her mother Liubov' Isaakovna Mikhlina, who insistently demanded every day that her daughter marry Babaev; moreover, every day they quarreled, which sometimes led to fights. He added that Mikhlina once declared to her daughter that, if she did not marry Zabaev, she would be poisoned.

The widow of the mining engineer, Liubov' Isaakovna Mikhlina, living at 200 Sennaia Street, explained that around 10 July of this year her cousin Genia Lazarevna Laivint (who lives at 126 Nikol'skaia Street) called on her and proposed a groom for her daughter Anna. She explained that the groom was a good person with means. Moreover, she began to persuade her that it was better to give the daughter in marriage than to live in poverty. At first she turned down this proposal but, under pressure from Krichevskaia and others, she subsequently agreed to marry her daughter to Babaev, which took place on 17 July of this year.

The townswoman from Kremenchug, Rokhel Itskovna Krichevskaia, living at 30 Bagatianskii Lane, explained that her niece Anna Iosifovna married on July 17 of this year under the following circumstances. On 12 July her niece came to her apartment, accompanied by an unknown young man, who subsequently turned out to be Babaev, whom she presented as the groom. In the following words she begged her: "Aunt, get me away from this den. I am sick of living like a tramp." Moreover, she added that "this young man is my future husband"; however, in order to marry, she needed material support. Krichevskaia agreed to this, but under the absolute condition that after the marriage

she must leave with her husband to his native Temir Khan Shura. This was because she had learned from different conversations with the groom that he was a newcomer and staying temporarily at the home of her niece's mother Liubov' Isaakova at 200 Sennaia Street. After her niece's first visit they began to call on her daily before the wedding, which took place on July 17. After the wedding, her niece not only refused to depart with her husband to his native town but even hid from him for two nights. To the above account, Krichevskaia added that no one forced Mikhlina in a deceptive way to marry Babaev, except her mother, because her niece had carried on a dissolute life since she was thirteen years old. Even she had once seen her with a drunken appearance; moreover, the entire Mikhlin family is well known to her [for their] wanton behavior.

The townswoman from Brainsk (Minsk province), Rozaliia Solomonovna Glukhovskaia, who resides at 45 Bagatianskii Lane, explained that Anna Babaev's mother — Liubov' Isaakovna Mikhlina — appeared at her apartment on 11 or 12 July of this year and declared that her daughter Anna was going to marry and began asking her to persuade Krichevskaia to help her financially because the bride had positively nothing in the way of undergarments, shoes, and also dresses. In response to her question to whom she was giving her daughter, Mikhlina replied that she knew the groom well as a good person, that she was glad to give her daughter in marriage, and that after the wedding the newlyweds must leave for Temir Khan Shura, so that she thereby would be rid of one daughter. She did not know where Mikhlina became acquainted with Babaev but does not suspect that Anna Mikhlina was given in marriage in a duplicitous manner by her acquaintances, with the exception of the mother.

A Vil'na townswoman, Genia Lazarevna Laivint (who resides at 126 Nikol'skaia Street), became acquainted with Babaev on Nikol'-

skaia Street and invited him to the home of her mother, who engages in trade at a kiosk on the corner of Sadovaia Street and Tkachevskii Lane. She presented Babaev to her as a future husband; upon Anna Mikhlina's meeting with Babaev, she (Laivint) also presented Babaev to her as her future husband.

Izgiia Il'iagu Ogly Babaev refuses to give any testimony except [to confirm] information that [the wedding] took place in July on the grounds that his marriage with Mikhlina led to troubles and the destruction of his health.

"Report of City Governor of Rostov-na-Donu to the His Imperial Chancellery for the Receipt of Petitions (4 November 1909)"

In addition to the legal statements of the police inquiry, produced as a result of the townswoman Anna Babaeva's petition for the right to live separately from her husband, I report to the Chancellery that the petitioner is sixteen years old and does not have a definite occupation. She entered into marriage on 17 July 1909, and the conjugal life with her husband lasted only three days. The marriage ended because of Babaeva's desire not to depart with her husband to his hometown and, most important, because her entry into marriage was coerced. At present Babaev lives in the town of Mariupol but his wife lives in Rostov-na-Donu with her mother. Although the legal statement contains an indication of Babaeva's immoral way of life, I am inclined to think otherwise — given the contradictory testimonies of the witnesses on the one hand, and the testimony of the petitioner (who lives with her mother) on the other.[3]

NOTES

1. Babaeva claimed that she was sixteen in this petition but stated that she was fifteen years old in the interview recorded in the protocols (see document 37). The police confirmed that she was indeed sixteen years old.

2. [Since 1888, Rostov-na-Donu was excluded from the Pale of Settlement; however, residents who were already living there before 19 May 1887 were allowed to remain.]

3. [The governor of Ekaterinoslav reported to the Imperial Chancellery that they were unable to locate the husband Babaev in Mariupol despite a thorough search (20 February 1910). In the final resolution, the Imperial Chancellery rejected Anna Babaeva's petition for a separate passport but gave no explanation. The file does not indicate whether the authorities located her husband or if Babaeva was deported from Rostov-na-Donu, where she no longer enjoyed the right of residency. In the end, she lost her residency rights in Rostov-na-Donu and became an *agunah*, chained to her husband without a proper divorce and unable to remarry until she received a *get*.]

[37]

A Rebellious Wife? (1904)

RGIA, f. 821, op. 9, ll. 41–60 ob.

"The Decision of One Hundred Rabbis on Permitting David Khaim Geller to Enter a New Marriage [Although Not Divorced] from His Present Wife: Translated by A. S. Tsunzer, the Learned Jew for the Governor General of Vil'na, Kovno, and Grodno" [undated]¹

With God's help! It has already been more than a year that the tormented David Khaim Geller, the son of Isaiah, cried out before us in the affliction of his soul as a result of the suffering caused by his wife, Khaia Iudis Geller, with whom he has not known peace for a period of five years now. They live separately: he resides here in Warsaw where he earns a living, while she lives in the town of Koidanovo [Minsk province]² and does not wish to live with him. We wrote repeatedly that she should come here to live with her husband, as is generally accepted. At first she replied through the local rabbi that she does not want to go to her husband and demands that he come to Koidanovo to live. Afterward we wrote that he could not live with her in Koidanovo in any way because he earns his living here, and that he could not possibly have any occupation there. Then the local rabbi announced to her that she was obliged to go to her husband in Warsaw because she did not have any grounds to think that it was better for her to live in Koidanovo than in Warsaw. After that we wrote again that she was obligated to come here, either to live together with her husband (as is generally accepted), or to receive a divorce after settling the question of how much money he should give her, with a warning that if she does not arrive within a certain time,

then we would deem her to be a "rebellious" [wife].³

1. and 2. Her husband's representative appeared together with her before the rabbinical court in Minsk, and this court ruled that she was obliged to arrive in Warsaw or obtain a divorce from him. Indeed, she came here and lived with her husband for a few weeks. Suddenly, in the absence of her husband, she collected all her clothing and ran away to the home of her parents, who live here. Then she came to us and declared that under no circumstances would she henceforth live with her husband. When asked why, she replied that her husband wanted to slash her to death at night but that she did not let him kill her. Because she fears that he will do something similar while she is sleeping, she will never return to him. When we proposed that she invite her husband and personally press her claims, she replied that she absolutely does not wish to see him and will take her complaint against him to the procurator. She then left. We informed her that she did not have the right to leave before the rabbinical court heard their case. We warned her, through two messengers, not to leave before the hearing, and if she left, we would deem her to be a rebellious wife and permit her husband to remarry, notwithstanding the absence of the wife [in court].⁴

3. We sent for her mother and announced to her that she must tell her daughter that if she left earlier rather than personally bring all the claims against her husband, then she would be deemed "rebellious" and lose her right to the *ketubah* and dowry;⁵ we would permit him to enter into a new marriage. But

none of this helped, and she left. We also did the following: we sent for the neighbors who lived with [the couple; that is, near them], who testified that they did not hear any fights between them during the whole time. On the contrary, she insulted him in the presence of the neighbors before their eyes. When we charged her with this, she replied that she could not tolerate him and that he forced her to live with him against her will. She does not desire a divorce from him but wishes and constantly prays to become a widow.

4. We once again wrote to the rabbi of Koidanovo to warn her that she is obligated to come here to explain the reason for her departure or to be done with her husband through a divorce. If she fails to come here in the course of two weeks, we will allow her husband to marry another woman. However, she ignored this and for several months has failed to come. Moreover, the rabbi of Koidanovo wrote to us that she will not be coming here.

The law treats this case as follows: Khaia Iudis ran away from her husband and does not wish to live with him. To receive a divorce, Khaia herself told us that she demands 5,000 rubles. Under the law, she is deemed a rebellious [wife] if she does not have an aversion toward her husband but wishes only to vex him (as stated in Ramo [Rema] 77: 2).[6] She thereby forfeits her right to the *ketubah* according to general opinion (also according to Ran; see also Beit Shmuel, 8).[7] If, as in the present case, the wife also declares that her husband is repulsive to her, then according to the religious authorities (Rambam, Rif, and Joseph Karo)[8] there is no need to wait. This is all the more true in this instance, where the case is indisputable because the fixed twelve-month period has long passed from the time we announced her warnings. The return to her husband and desire to live with him were not out of sincere repentance but prompted by her desire to make claims and various accusations against him. This is demonstrated

by the following circumstances: she did not take all her dresses and things with her [from Kaidanov], as the rabbis of Minsk have established. She took only the most necessary clothing, as she herself admitted. After all this she abandoned her husband for no apparent reason. However, as will be explained below, we do not have any need for such considerations and believe we had the right to free the husband David Khaim from the ban on polygamy (established by Rabbi Gershom[9]) for all Jews and from the obligation to deliver the bill of divorcement [*get*] through a third party.

In the work of the illustrious [R. David] of Novogrudok, *Galya mesekhet* [1844], I also found an analogous case: the rabbi (in section 16, page 70) writes about a woman who decided to run from her husband's home to that of her mother in a different region; her intent was to condemn her husband to eternal celibacy [to leave him as an *agun*] or to receive a large sum of money from him. In addition, it was extremely difficult for her husband to relocate to the place where she lived. The Novogrudok rabbi writes in his "decision" that the woman's manner of acting is even more reprehensible than the behavior of a rebellious wife: the ordinary rebellious wife does not have an aversion toward the husband but only wants to vex him. However, here the woman does not want to live with her husband, and her intention is to condemn him to celibacy; she is motivated by the desire to coerce him into giving her a large sum of money. Thus, Rabbi Gershom's ban on polygamy does not apply to this case. There is an absolute opportunity to permit the husband to do one of two [things]: deliver the bill of divorcement to the wife without her consent or to enter into a new marriage [without giving the first wife a *get*].

Although the author of the work *Galya mesekhet* does not indicate the sources upon which he based his opinion, that judgment obviously employed the words of Ramo (1: 10): if a wife should be divorced from her husband according to the law, but does not want to accept the divorce, is it possible to permit the husband to enter into a new marriage? In the author's opinion, *Galya mesekhet* makes it preferable to permit a forced divorce than to free [a husband] from the ban on bigamy. Confirmation for this is found in the commentaries of *Helkat mechokek* [by R. Moshe Lima of Brest] and *Beit Shmuel* 77: 19. It is absolutely clear that this specific meaning is established by the Maharam Padua[10] (whose words are cited in Ramo, 119: 6 and also in the commentaries of Baer Hetev).[11] However, this opinion appears strange to me. Why impose a service on her against her will at a time when we have another way out; there is no need to run after her and in haste to risk concluding the divorce improperly. Such accuracy always depends on observing numerous stipulations: in the event that an error is made, her remarriage would be deemed illegal. But such a situation cannot obtain if the husband is permitted to enter into a new marriage, as this always rests with the discretion of a rabbinical court. The correctness of our opinion appears even more apparent from the text of the *takkanah* by the Maharam Mintz (number 102)[12] that the prohibition against giving a wife a coerced divorce should be punctiliously observed, and if one performs such a divorce, it will be deemed null and void.

The author of *Noda bi-Yehudah*[13] (second edition, number 129) dwells on this ban in detail and develops two positions: (1) a coerced divorce does not free the husband from his obligations to his wife; (2) if the scribe of the *get* and the witnesses know that such [a divorce] was carried out against the wife's will, the divorce is considered null and void because the ban on executing a forced divorce is applicable both to the husband and other individuals who participate in it. The witnesses who violate the ban are considered invalid, and a divorce without witnesses is considered invalid (as can be adduced from the text on the ban in Maharam Mintz's responsum, number 102).

The first position of the author of *Noda bi-*

Yehudah—that a coerced divorce does not free the husband from his obligation to his wife—seems strange. After a wife and husband receive the right to remarry whomever they please, after any ties between the couple are completely sundered; can he have any obligation toward her, and what do they have in common? In the opinion of the Rif, Rambam, and the majority of other religious authorities, a husband is free from any obligation toward the wife, even if he has not yet paid the *ketubah* because she, the wife, is torn asunder from him. It is difficult to think that the author of the above position is guided by the principle, "let not the sinner profit from his new position" ([. . .] שלא והוא חוטא נשכר). Because of the authority accorded by Jewish law to the rabbinical court, it is not possible to release the man from his responsibilities to his wife since the man, in any case, obtains the advantage after the divorce has been recognized (in the sense that the connections between him and his wife are terminated). He acquires the possibility of remarriage whereas, until this tie has been eliminated, it is impossible for him to remarry (as stated in [the Talmud] *Ketubot* 64, 1). If one adheres to the above principle, one can realize it through another means — viz., by regarding the coercive divorce invalid because the rabbinical court, given its authority, can declare all of the chancellery supplies (paper, ink) used to compile the *get* constitute the wife's, not the husband's, property; in that case, the validity of the divorce is *ipso facto* nullified because, according to the law, the *get* must be composed with the husband's own means (as explained in Maharam Mintz, number 120).

A more likely opinion is that the forced divorce is considered invalid both for the above reason and for a case where the scribe who draws up the *get* and witnesses who participate in it know that the divorce is coercive. The opinion cited above follows from the text of the *takkanah* in which the invalidity of the forced divorce is unconditional.

All the above statements apply when a husband violated the established ban and gave the wife a divorce against her will. If the dispensation of one hundred rabbis permits the husband to carry out a forced divorce, this should be considered correct. However, one should pay attention to the following circumstance: the text of the *takkanah* regarding the forced divorce is presented so that this ban also applies to the witnesses and to the scribe of the *get*, whereas the *ban on bigamy* does not apply to the witnesses, the person officiating at the wedding, or even the wife.[14] In such a case, why should we rabbis lift the ban [of a forced divorce] from the husband, which encompasses a greater number of persons and is more stringent, when we have the possibility to free the husband from a less stringent ban [the ban on bigamy] in a similar way indicated in the Talmud (tractate *Yoma* 83, on the question of forbidden foods)? And indeed I found in the first edition of the work *Noda bi-Yehudah* (*Even ha-Ezer*, chapter 1), the same opinion that the ban on a forced divorce is more serious than the ban on bigamy.[15]

Regarding the opinion of Maharam Padua, whom I cited above, the author of *Noda bi-Yehudah* refers to this opinion in the case when a forced divorce is desirable according to the law—for example, when the wife is a convert [to another religion]. In such a case, the ban of Rabbi Gershom absolutely does not apply; hence there is no need for one hundred rabbis to permit a forced divorce. However, the permission of one hundred rabbis is certainly required to enter into a new marriage because it is possible that the first wife will turn to the right path. Then the husband would have two legal wives and thus be subject to the ban of Rabbi Gershom. Based on the cited words of the author of *Noda bi-Yehudah*, that seems true; in my humble opinion (forgive me, great scholar), however, a small correction is required here. His words indicate that, even in the opinion of those who think a divorce desirable from the perspective of Jewish law, the ban of Rabbi Gershom on bigamy is not binding. If someone under these circumstances entered into a new marriage and the first wife returned to the right path, the husband is then subject to the force of Rabbi Gershom's ban. If these words were not written by the holy hand of our luminary author of *Noda bi-Yehudah*, I would have said that such a claim could not be possible. If at the point when a husband enters a marriage it is absolutely legal, then how can the ban be reinstated? After all, it is said about the Torah: "Her ways are the ways of pleasantness."

As for the question of the obligation of the mandatory oath, it was written long ago by Ramo [Rema] in *Yoreh Deah* (*Shulhan Arukh* 228: 42) that in the case of releasing someone from the oath, this release remains in force forever. One vowed to give his daughter to another person [in marriage]. After that person became morally corrupt, the father turned to the rabbinical court with a request to release him from his vows. If even the morally corrupt man reforms himself, the father's release from the oath remains in effect. [This is] all the more so, as the question that interests us derives from common sense—that the force of the ban is obligatory at the moment of entering a marriage. If at this moment, a husband enters [a marriage] illegally, then he is subject to the force of the ban henceforth. The other position is this: if the husband acts absolutely legally at the time of the marriage, then his first wife's turn to the path of truth cannot have any meaning because she can receive a divorce from her husband. Why should he be afraid of the possibility of a reform on his wife's part when he has the legitimate means to divorce her? However, if she does not wish to receive a divorce, then there is nothing left for him to do. He cannot possibly divorce his new wife whom he only recently married. Thus it is possible to state positively that if the ban of Rabbi Gershom did not exist at the moment of entering a marriage, then the husband is not subsequently subject to its force.

However, one side of this question bears a very great significance: there is a danger that the wife will display a moral improvement in the intervening period between the betrothal or engagement and the wedding with the second wife. Then the husband will be deprived of the right to marry the latter. If, however, the husband enters into a new marriage with the permission of one hundred rabbis, then — even if the first wife improved [morally] after this, the husband will not be [under] Gershom's ban. This conclusion follows from the words of Ramo [Rema] and *Noda bi-Yehudah*. There is another possible challenge of this kind: if the first wife takes the path of truth, then the husband may relinquish his second wife and resume life with the first. But to allow such a position is impossible because no one would agree to be betrothed to him, not wishing to subject oneself to the risk as is stated in the Talmud tractate *Kiddushim* 64. It therefore follows that the one hundred rabbis remove the ban from the husband. This is possible based on the words of the Marmap [Maharam Padua]. Finally, the Maharam Padua may have agreed that it is better to remove the ban of bigamy than to give a forced divorce.

I also found in *Noda bi-Yehudah* (section 77, *Even ha-Ezer* 100?)[16] that the ban on the forced divorce is by far stronger and that its force is *applicable to all of Israel*. And so he wrote again in his second edition (number 102). See the analogous case, which states with absolute clarity: if a wife does not wish to accept the divorce and *ketubah* or if she agrees to receive the divorce on condition that the husband give her a monetary sum higher than [that stipulated] in the *ketubah*, such behavior on the wife's part is regarded as a general reluctance to accept the divorce. Although this case seems quite clear, I cited this opinion for a better understanding of the cases that interest us. I also found the following words in the work of the Hatam Sofer[17] (part 2, *Even ha-Ezer* 167): Because, for dif-ferent motives, it is far better to remove the ban of Rabbi Gershom regarding bigamy by the force of the *heter me'ah rabbanim* than to give a coerced divorce, and because the ban on the coerced divorce is considerably stronger and the range of its effects much wider, I absolutely cannot yield in favor of permitting a coerced divorce. However, it seems absolutely clear to me that it is possible to permit the entry into a new marriage. In this sense, there are instructions in Hatam Sofer (part 6, section 70 — at the end). Similarly, in the words of the text of Ramo ([Rema], 1: 10), in all cases where one is supposed to grant a divorce according to the law, but the wife does not desire to receive it, one should permit the husband to enter into a new marriage (per the clarification of Rashba).[18] However, this does not mean that the husband is permitted to transmit the *get* to his wife by force. However, according to the Rambam (as he is understood in *Noda bi-Yehudah*), it ought to read: "if the wife does not wish to receive the divorce, there is no way to impose this divorce on her by force." But that does not follow from the plain meaning of the statement. Surprisingly, however, the later religious authorities[19] fail to mention that the opinions of Ramo [R. Moses Isserles] (77), the author of *Helkat mechokek*, and the author of the commentary *Beit Shmuel* 18, do not correspond to their opinions: if a husband gives a wife a *ketubah*, then they permit him to give her a forced divorce, *without waiting for the expiration of the twelve months*,[20] but they do not permit him to remarry. The same idea is stated in the commentary of *Beit Shmuel* (117: 22). It is surprising that the author of *Noda bi-Yehudah* and the Hatam Sofer are silent about the fact that their opinions differ from those of other scholars. However, the explanation of the Rosh[21] (cited in *Even ha-Ezer*, part 1, 117: 11) contains the following: "If a man learns that his wife suffers from epilepsy, and he wishes to be divorced from her for this reason, but he is unable to pay her *ketubah*, then they compel the wife to accept the divorce and the husband must pay the amount he is able to in his condition and the balance when his means allow. If, however, she refuses to accept the *get*, then the husband may withhold her maintenance, clothing and conjugal rights." It turns out that the compulsion lies in withholding her maintenance, clothing, and conjugal rights, but not in giving her a *get* against her will. The author of *Helkat mechokek* (20) explains: "The Rosh did not decide to state that the husband can give his wife a forced divorce and that the wife, thanks to this divorce, is made free and receives the possibility to remarry."[22]

Ramo (77) indicates the explanation of Rashbo (860), and this is borrowed from the explanation of Meir of Rothenburg.[23] I looked there and found that toward the end he wrote in the name of Raban, and that he allowed a husband to marry another woman and doomed the first wife to eternal celibacy. Herewith he notes that this opinion was very well founded. In that case, his opinion corresponds completely to what I wrote: [permission for the husband to remarry] is far better than a forced divorce. Even according to opponents, which he cites from the explanations of the *geonim*, the wife—even in our time—has the right, before the expiration of twelve months, to receive the property that she gave to her husband for safekeeping when they married if she declares that her husband is repulsive to her. However, this opinion contains no hint that it is better to give a forced divorce than to allow remarriage. Thus I am extremely surprised that the authors of the commentary of *Helkat mechokek* and *Beit Shmuel* perceived in their opponents' opinion a ban on remarriage and permission to allow a forced divorce, whereby the *ketubah* is issued to the wife *before* the expiration of twelve months and without the giving the [*ketubah*] *at* the expiration of the twelve months.

Common to the questions is this: what outcome is more acceptable—a forced divorce or remarriage [without a divorce of the first wife]? And should the *ketubah* be issued or not? Obviously, the difference between that and the other opinion concerns only the question [of] whether it follows in our times, in the complete absence of bigamy among the Jews, to wait twelve months. According to some, there is no need to wait, and even if he does not give her the *ketubah*, he is permitted to remarry before the twelve months. According to others, in our time, a husband cannot be permitted to remarry before the expiration of the twelve months if he does not give the *ketubah*; if, however, he gives the *ketubah*, then he is undoubtedly permitted to remarry immediately, after the announcements of the warnings to the wife prescribed by law. Thus, according to the first opinion set out by Ramo [Rema], it is more desirable to permit [the husband] to remarry for it is written: "If the wife does not wish to receive the divorce, then they permit the husband to enter into another marriage." But it is not written that they cast the *get* on her [by force]. And according to the second opinion, there is a recommended twelve-month waiting period, in light of the inducements of the husband to give his wife the *ketubah*; if the husband gives [the *ketubah*] before the twelve months or is freed from giving the *ketubah* at the expiration of the twelve months, one ought to free the husband from the ban of bigamy without hesitation but not from the ban of a forced divorce. [. . .][24]

The final conclusion from our discussion of this question is that we must permit the husband to remarry another [woman] about which the author of *Hatam Sofer* 167 wrote. As for the wife's *ketubah* and dowry, long ago we explained that according to the law a rebellious wife does not have the right to the *ketubah* and what she has brought to her husband, and therefore there is no need to wait twelve months (?).[25] In addition, as written above, the twelve-month period has already long passed [in Khaia Geller's case], and it has been even longer since the announcement of the first warning to her (?).[26] According to the law, one is not supposed to wait more than twelve months, as written in *Hatam Sofer*. Even if we recognized that the wife's return to the husband in Warsaw was from her sincere desire to begin a conjugal life with her husband, and if we were to ignore her true intentions (as revealed in her actions and speech), even then we would not force the husband to wait for twelve months at the present time (?).[27] I have already explained that the purpose of the prescribed twelve-month waiting period is to encourage the husband to pay the wife's *ketubah*. However, the waiting period may have a role in the event that a wife declares that the husband is repulsive to her. By virtue of this declaration, she loses her *ketubah* and dowry only after the expiration of the twelve months. If, however, the wife declares that she does not feel aversion toward her husband but wishes to cause him pain, and still more, if she demands more money to receive the divorce, this deprives her of the right to her *ketubah* and dowry for such a declaration and demand. Hence we should not force him to wait and condemn him to celibacy, if only temporary.

However, we are not engaged in resolving the conflict between the couple regarding her *ketubah* and dowry at the present time — that is, does she have such rights? We are now examining the question as to whether he can marry another wife, notwithstanding the present wife. Therefore we now free him from the ban of bigamy in agreement with the rulings of our ancient religious authorities. We leave the question of her *ketubah* for another rabbinical court, which will arbitrate this case between the couple. We therefore take from the husband the sum of her dowry in agreement with the decision of the rabbinical court in Minsk. We accepted the said amount under the following conditions: after the signing of the present permission by the first rabbinical court, we will notify the wife through the rabbi

in Koidanovo or Minsk that we have freed her husband from the ban of bigamy and received the *ketubah* for her. This *ketubah* will stay with us until her hearing on the present case during the twelve-month [period] from the day of the signing [of this decision]. If their case is examined during the course of this established time, and if she receives her divorce from him, then we will act in accordance with the instruction of the rabbinical court that considered their case. If, however, a rabbinical court does not examine their case by the termination of the twelve-month period because of her (not her husband), then we will return the received sum to the husband, and she may not present any claims to us.

Once we have explained our case, we believe that others will join in our decision to free David Khaim from the onus of celibacy in order not to hurt or offend him without cause and to spare him the loneliness that he does not deserve. We hereby permit him, notwithstanding his present wife, to marry another [woman] under the following conditions: (1) if he finds more rabbis — one hundred individuals from three different regions, in conformity with our ancient religious authorities; these rabbis must join themselves in this decision; (2) if he finds a person who will prepare a translation of the present decision in compliance with the law of the government and state; (3) if the rabbis who join this decision are certified in the rabbinical ranks as great scholars [that is, those with *smicha* or rabbinical ordination], not those who are counted among the common Talmudists without a rabbinical rank. As it says in the books of *Noda bi-Yehudah* section 3 and *Hatam Sofer* section 4, those who join themselves to the rabbinical decision must be among the group of the learned, worthy of the rabbinical rank. The head of the rabbinical court in each town should take care to join the [signatures] of the worthy and verify the signatures with his stamp — about which my great teacher from Stavisk [Rabbi Hayim Aryeh Loeb] wrote in his book, *Pnei ha-aryeh ha-chai*, section 26, published by the author of this document. After there are a sufficient number of signatures, this document of permission should be returned to us and we will approve it in the proper manner.

> Monday night, 29 Elul, on the eve of the new year 5665, Warsaw.
> We the signatories in fulfilling the will of Rabbi Gershom, free from the ban [David Khaim Geller], subject to compliance with all the conditions of government and state laws.
> Rabbi of Warsaw, Ieguda Galevi [Yehudah Halevi] Segal
> Rabbi of Warsaw, Solomon David Kagan
> Rabbi of Warsaw, Isaac Rozmarin
> Rabbi of Warsaw, Ieguda Leib Gutner

> I join with the above-signed rabbis and permit Khaim David [David Khaim] to remarry under all the conditions prescribed by them with the permission of the state authorities.
> On the eve of Sabbath, Bereshit, 5664.
> Rabbi of Warsaw, Khaim Iegoshua [Yehoshua] Gutshekhter [. . .][28]

"Journal of the Rabbinic Commission" [1910]

Account of the Case: On 11 August 1904, the General Governor of Vil'na, Kovno, and Grodno forwarded the complaint of Khaia Iudes Geller[29] (number 5676, submitted to the procurator of Vil'na on 7 July 1894 with addenda) to the Ministry of Internal Affairs for review by the Rabbinic Commission.[30] [Appealing] the improper dissolution of her marriage by the rabbi of Lida, she declared that she had lived with her husband David Khaim Ishaev Geller in the town of Koidanovo (Minsk province) for more than ten years and had five children with him (of whom two sons remained living in 1904). In 1904 her husband moved to Warsaw where he began to earn more money, but she remained with the children in Koidanovo; initially her husband sent her the necessary means for living but then began to send less and less. Finally, he became completely cool toward her and her family and decided to marry another [woman], offering to part from her peaceably (whereby she would receive 2,000 rubles for the divorce). However, she rejected the deal, [and] he decided to divorce her against her will. From the supplementary attestation in the case of the Warsaw notary Bushinskii on 16 April 1904, it is clear that the latter declared to David Khaim Geller, under the authority of the wife, that she unexpectedly learned at the Koidanovo townspeople [meshchanstvo] administration (to which she had applied for a passport) that her husband had submitted a certificate of divorce from the metrical book, issued by the [state] rabbi of Lida, R. A. Kraminka, with the request to exclude Khaia Iudes from his family registry.

She submitted all this in writing to the procurator of Vil'na on 7 July 1904. Moreover, she added that, under Jewish law, a divorce is not possible without the agreement of both spouses, that the scribe writes the *get* only at the request of both spouses, and that the witnesses sign [the *get*] only at the request of the spouses. She, Khaia Iudes, was never in Lida, does not know the state rabbi of Lida (R. Kraminka), and did not apply to him to perform the rite of divorce, and therefore the rabbi had no legal grounds to grant the divorce solely at her husband's demand and to record the divorce in the metrical book. She considers Rabbi Kraminka's explanation (last in a letter to her brother Iakov Kliorin on 4 July 1904) that the divorce was carried out on the grounds of a certificate presented to him about the five-year absence of the spouse and the permission of one hundred rabbis to be groundless and illegal. [She rejects the explanation]: on the one hand, these rabbis are imposters to whom she did not turn; on the other hand, the spiritual rabbis of Minsk, who heard her divorce case, decided that her husband must continue to cohabit with her as before. In addition, she indicates in a supplemental petition of 2 August 1904 to the General Governor of Vil'na that her husband lives in Warsaw and she in the town of Koidanovo; [Rabbi Kaminka] had no grounds to divorce her in absentia without her consent.

On the basis of this, Khaia Geller seeks an investigation of this case, the annulment of the registration of her divorce from her husband David, and the legal prosecution of the guilty. Moreover, she asks to be summoned to a meeting of the Rabbinic Commission to provide her explanation when it considers her divorce case. [. . .]³¹

Conclusion: Based on the above consideration, the Rabbinic Commission proposes the following:

1. An investigation of the actions of Rabbi Kraminka is not included in this present case because of his death [on 7 November 1906].
2. The decision of the Jewish rabbis of Warsaw in the divorce case of David Khaim and Khaia Iudes Geller is considered correct and subject to execution. The complaint of the petitioner Khaia Iudes Geller does not merit respect and no action will be taken. Above all, the Rabbinic Commission considers it a duty to express its wish that the rabbi take the responsibility when registering this kind of act [*heter me'ah rabbanim*] in the metrical book, to note that the wife is not considered divorced, and does not have the right to remarry before the actual receipt of the *get*.³²

NOTES

1. [The file does not contain the original Hebrew text.]

2. [The Russian name for this town is Koidanovo, but the archival documents also use the name Kaidanov in the text.]

3. "Rebellious" [*moredet*] is a juridical term that designates such behavior on the part of a wife for which she should be divorced with limitations on the conditions for her. [The previous sentence and other

material not in brackets in the notes for this item are Tsunzer's footnotes. The language of the original Jewish law is ambiguous and vague: "If a wife rebels against her husband, the [lump sum] alimony provided in her marriage contract is to be reduced seven *dinarim* a week" (Mishnah Ketubot, 1:2). The critical issue was the meaning of the word "rebel." Some rabbinical authorities interpreted the term to include the wife's refusal to perform "the seven types of household duties" specified in Jewish law. Another interpretation in the *Shulhan Arukh* by Joseph Karo [1488–1575], the most commonly used codex of law in Jewish society, stated that "a woman who denies her husband sexual relations is the one who is called rebellious" (*Shulhan Arukh, Even ha-Ezer*, 77: 2).]

4. [The husband could remarry with the permission of one hundred rabbis, called the *heter me'ah rabbanim*. After the husband received this *heter*, he had to deposit the bill of divorcement (*get*) with the rabbinical court for delivery to his first wife, who could accept this divorce if she desired to remarry.]

5. The marriage contract is called [the *ketubah*], which is to support the wife in the event of her husband's death or divorce; a significant sum [for which he is liable] on his part but also the very capital that is guaranteed for the wife in this document. [According to the Jewish marital contract, the husband was potentially liable for three types of payments in the event of a divorce: (1) restitution of the entire value of his wife's dowry (*nedunyah*); (2) the *ketubah* payment, usually a lump sum as a one-time divorce settlement; and (3) the *tosefet ketubah*, any additional monies on which the two parties had agreed. The minimum *ketubah* settlement for the northwestern provinces of Russia was seventy-six silver rubles for virgins and thirty-eight rubles for previously married women; to deter rash divorces, wealthier families stipulated significantly higher sums in the marital contract. The *ketubah* could be reduced in the case of the *moredet* who rebelled against her husband. See below for the amount in this case.]

6. Ramo [the Polish R. Moses Isserles, known as the Rema (1520–72)]—(lived in the 16th century): included the significant glosses to the religious code [of law], the *Shulhan Arukh*.

7. Ran [R. Nissim ben Reuven of Gerona (1320–1376)] (lived in the 14th century): his explanations on religious questions was used with great authority; Beit Samuel [R. Samuel ben Uri of Furth]—commentary on the religious [codex], the *Shulhan Arukh* [by Joseph Karo].

8. Rambam [R. Moses] Maimonides (lived in the 12th century [d. 1204]), a great religious authority; Rif [R. Isaac Alfasi (1013–1103)] (lived in the 11th century), author who produced a digest of Jewish law; and Joseph Karo [1488–1575] the author of the codex, the *Shulhan Arukh*. [According to Maimonides, "If she says, 'I have come to loathe him, and I cannot submit willingly to his intercourse,' [the husband] must be compelled to divorce her immediately for she is not like a captive who must submit to a man that is so hateful to her. She must, however, leave with forfeiture of all of her *ketubah*" (quoted in Michael Berger, "Maimonides on Sex and Marriage," in *Marriage, Sex, and Family in Judaism*, ed. Michael J. Broyde and Michael Ausubel [Lanham, MD: Rowman and Littlefield, 2005], 158).]

9. Rabbi Gershom of Mayence (who lived in the second quarter of the eleventh century) issued a ban on polygamy and dispatching a *get* to a wife without her consent.

10. Maharam Padua [R. Meir ben Isaac Katzenellenbogen (1482–1565), an Italian halakhist originally from Germany] composed a collection of responsa on questions in the sphere of religious law.

11. [R. Moshe Mat (1551–1606).]

12. Maharam Mintz [R. Moses Halevi Mintz (1415–80)], (lived in the 15th [century] and composed a collection of responsa on questions in the sphere of religious law.

13. [Ezekiel ben Yehudah Landau (1713–93) was a Polish-born rabbi best known for his collection of responsa, *Noda bi-Yehudah* (Laszczow: Bi-defus Yitshak Rubin Shtain, 1818).]

14. [The distinction here is between the ban on forced divorces and the ban on bigamy.]

15. [This is in contrast to the opinions of Maharam Padua and R. David of Novogrudok in *Galya mesekhet* that "it is preferable to permit a forced divorce than to free [a husband] from the ban on bigamy."]

16. [Tsunzer placed a question mark next to this reference because he could not find it.]

17. [Moses Sofer (1762–1839)] see Hatam Sofer, *Even ha-Ezer* 1: 3. Where this question is decided in this sense, under no circumstances is it permissible to allow a forced divorce. It is explained by the fact that the author was unfamiliar with the text of the regulations printed in the book by Maharam Mintz, where it is said that with the agreement [of rabbis of] three communities, it is possible for such a permission to be granted.

18. Rashba [R. Shlomo ben Aderest (1235–1310) of Barcelona] lived in the 13th century.

19. Beginning in the 16th century, religious authorities are called the [*aharonim*] or later authorities in contrast to the early authorities [*rishonim*].

20. [According to BT *Ketubot* 63b, "we also make her"—the rebellious wife, or *moredet*—"wait twelve months for her divorce and during those twelve months, she receives no maintenance from her husband."]

21. [R. Asher ben Yehiel, born in Germany 1250 or 1259–1322] lived in the second half of the 13th c. and beginning of the 14th c., authoritative expert of Jewish law.

22. [This was the translation provided in the Russian.]

23. Lived in the thirteenth century [1215–93], the greatest legal mind of his time.

24. [The text includes more examples from other rabbinic authorities such as Josef Karo to reiterate the point that a husband can be freed from the ban of bigamy but not from the ban of a forced divorce.]

25. [Question mark in the margin of the archival document.]

26. [Question mark in the margin of the archival document.]

27. [Question mark in the margins of the archival document.]

28. [The rabbis used this formulation to add their name to the document. They were from numerous towns and cities, including Warsaw, Belostok, Sokolov, Grodno, Shavli, Aleksot, Slonim, Pumpian, Eishishok, Kamenets-Litovsk, Sokol, Kharkov, Kovno, Selib, and Vasilishek. Some rabbis (especially Rabbi Nison Iablonskii of Eishishok) insisted that the

husband wait for the complete twelve months before he remarried. Rabbi Sabbatai Sheftel of Aleksot also noted that "it is necessary to deliver the *get* to the rabbinical court for the first wife" so that she would not be left an *agunah*.]

29. [The report spells the name Giller rather than Geller as in the rabbinical decision above, but the latter will be used for consistency here.]

30. [The Rabbinic Commission was a consultative body established in 1848 under the supervision of the Ministry of the Internal Affairs to resolve matters such as divorce laws, schools, the synagogue, and the status of the rabbinate. It evolved into a kind of supreme appeals court to review rabbinic decisions—above all, in cases involving divorce.]

31. [The text next summarizes the decision of the Warsaw rabbis with a summary by the learned Jew Moisei Kreps, which confirmed the decision as correct. The text also notes that according to state law (*Svod zakonov Rossiskoi imperii*, vol. 11, part 1, statute 1324, 1896 edition), "the duty of the rabbi [. . .] is to carry out exclusively all rituals under his jurisdiction [. . . including] the dissolution of marriages." In other words, the state recognizes that this case belongs to the legal jurisdiction of the rabbis.]

32. [The state rabbi Kraminka did not have the right to register the divorce of the couple since the wife did not accept her *get*, a point that the Rabbinic Commission made in their conclusion. The husband may have asked for a legal certificate of divorce for several reasons. First, he needed the certificate to recreate his family register and exclude his first wife from it. Second, despite the rabbinical permission to remarry, he may have requested an official metrical registration of divorce for fear of prosecution in state courts for bigamy. Hardly unique to Jews in the Russian Empire, the issue of bigamy became a matter of increasing concern and figured prominently in government reports and in the Russian-Jewish press. According to Russian law, bigamy was a criminal offense only if the perpetrator's own faith condemned it or if the victimized spouse belonged to such a faith. If both spouses belonged to a confession that tolerated bigamy, and if its rules for making and dissolving the marital union posed no problem, Russian law did not prescribe any secular punishment. In this case, the rabbis clearly supported Geller's right to remarry without divorcing his first wife. But many cases are more ambiguous. See ChaeRan Y. Freeze, *Jewish Marriage and Divorce in Imperial Russia* (Hanover, NH: University Press of New England for Brandeis University Press, 2002), 226–30.]

[38]

Petition for a Separate Passport on Grounds of Spousal Abuse (1900)

RGIA, f. 1412, op. 213, d. 101, ll. 1–5 ob., 30–39 ob., 55–55 ob., 57–60.

"Petition of Shura Broun, Resident of Shuia [Vladimir Province] to Tsar Nicholas II, Submitted to His Imperial Majesty's Chancellery for the Receipt of Petitions[1] (27 November 1900)"

Four years ago, my husband—Iosif Moiseevich Broun, a former veterinarian of the Shuia *zemstvo* [an agency of local self-government]—suffered a stroke that paralyzed his left hand and leg and most severely affected his character. As a result, my husband began to behave in an intolerable manner: acting capriciously, cursing indecently, displaying a strong hatred toward me in every possible way, and creating scandalous scenes that made it impossible to live with him, all the more so since his outbursts have intensified. At present, my husband has rented a separate apartment from me in the Litvinov Hotel in Shuia, but he still shows up every day and makes scenes that have a harmful influence on my weak health (I have developed heart disease). Above all, my husband's behavior may have a negative impact on the upbringing of our nine-year-old son, Viktor, who is in the first year of the Shuia gymnasium: he is often an involuntary witness to these terrible scenes created by my husband. Then he has to hear his father's expressions and words, which are not suitable for children. Finally, my husband sent him an awful letter, which I fear could influence the child in the most corrupting way and beget a loathing in his soul toward me, his own mother. The director of the Shuia gymnasium, Mr. Sitarskii, will attest to this latter circumstance.

At present, I live together with my children (son Viktor and daughter Mariia) at the expense of my relatives and on my wages from needlework. My husband receives a pension of three hundred rubles from the *zemstvo* [rural self-government] of Vladimir province and lives on that. He does not contribute to the expenses for the upbringing of the children.

My husband's behavior is well known to everyone in the town of Shuia, including the following people: (1) Raisa Davidovna Damskaia, a woman's doctor; (2) her sister Bella Davidovna Mizebreit; (3) the constable of Shuia, Mr. Bulai; and (4) Mariia Antonovna Il'icheva, a peasant woman who lives with me as the nanny.

Given the above, I fall at the holy feet of Your Imperial Majesty and take the liberty to present this most humble petition with hope in Your boundless mercy and beg You, by Your gracious order, to grant me and my children a separate passport from my husband.

This petition is in the words of Shura Leia Broun, written by the townsman of Shuia,

Sergei Kuz'min Petrov [signed in her own hand].

"Petition of Iosif (Osip) Moiseevich Broun to the His Imperial Majesty's Chancellery for the Receipt of Petitions (30 December 1900)"

HIS EXCELLENCY!

My wife, Shura Leia Moiseevna, in her petition to His Imperial Majesty for a separate passport, reports that I rented a separate apartment for myself, that I do not provide money to support the family and a passport for residency, which implies that I abandoned the family without any means to live and without a passport. But this is an absolute lie. The following [actually] took place:

When my wife was convinced that my illness (paralysis on the left side) was not healing and when I lost my position and retired with a pension from the *zemstvo*, she began to cohabit with the doctor, Dmitrii Sergeevich Malyshev. She received a notarized power of attorney from me in a deceptive way and forced me to visit her relatives in Kherson province, where they attempted to secure a divorce for my wife — to which I did not agree. However, when I returned to Shuia, in order to sell the belongings and take the family back home, my wife informed the police that I had gone mad and called one of her friends, who beat me mercilessly and took my wife and oldest child from the house before my very eyes. After this, the district and city doctors examined me illegally and deemed me insane. The police therefore arrested me on the street and took me to the county hospital; from there they intended to send me to the insane asylum. However, my wife — fearful of the consequences — bailed me out on condition that I not sleep at home and that I leave Shuia within twenty-four hours without her, the children, and the belongings. She promised to sell the belongings after the completion of my son's examinations and to come with the children to live with me in my hometown. Fearful of such violence and illegal commitment to an insane asylum, I agreed to her conditions and left for my hometown. She sold off the belongings, received my money by proxy, and arrived at her relatives' home. However, at the end of the vacation, she returned with the children to Shuia and demanded a separate passport from me, again threatening to place me in an insane asylum. I sent her a passport for three months after I myself returned to Shuia, but she did not let me in the apartment; hence I was forced to stay in the hotel where I presently reside. She receives Malyshev daily at night and lives beyond her means.

On the basis of her petition, by the order of the governor of Vladimir, the assistant constable of Shuia conducted an investigation. On the questions he put to me, which I answered, I did not reveal the true state of the case, so her false denunciation that I abandoned the family without support and passport remains in force. I wanted to append to my testimony a general memo with documents for a complete and detailed elucidation of the case, but he refused to accept them — under the pretext that they would get lost. Having made a postscript to my testimony that "I wish to append a memo with the documents," I have the honor to ask Your Excellency to permit me to submit the memo and documents, entrusting them to Your Excellency's Chancellery in the event that the police do not take them. [I would like to do this] without the knowledge of the police, all the more so since the Shuia police forcibly separated me from my children at my wife's request on 17 December and permitted her to live in Shuia without a passport and residency rights. [The police] have demonstrated partiality in this case to the benefit of my wife, who robbed me, took possession of the children, abandoned me sick and helpless on the street, and is now attempting to obtain a separate passport — all for her unhampered illegal cohabitation. Thus, given the bias of the police in my wife's favor, I humbly ask Your Excellency to order an examination of the investigation and actions of the police in this case by a separate body of gendarmes, which merits greater trust than the police.

"Iosif Broun: Memo with Supporting Materials"

1. [. . .][2] I am forced to report that among us Jews, for whom divorce is possible by mutual agreement of the couple (according to religious law), there is no need [. . .] to issue a separate passport to the wife to the detriment of the civil legal rights of the husband. But only my wife needs this, wishing to separate from a sick husband in order to enter into a new marriage or to carry on her illicit cohabitation because of her constant pursuit of a luxurious and disgraceful life (for example, riding around on trotters [horses trained for harness racing]). If she consents to the proposed conditions for a divorce, she would receive a divorce and be free. However, as is evident from the enclosed letter, her relatives wanted a forcible divorce or separation that they could not obtain through their prolonged application from the rabbi of Elisavetgrad. They also wanted to alienate my son from me through the separate passport.

2. I will describe everything that took place during our marriage and served as the reason for our separation and the people who were responsible. I was married on 31 October 1887 at a time when I was in service with the local *zemstvo* in Chernigov province. Although I heard information and rumors about the suspicious behavior of the girl whom I had chosen as my bride, I did not attach any significance to them. If the rumors were true, I hoped to reform her through a quiet family life and by introducing her to the society of intelligent and educated people. Regarding her family, I did not have any information about them except that her older sister, for whose children my wife served as the governess for several years, often participated in philanthropic institutions.

And indeed, many literally envied our marital happiness. Even family tragedies such as the death of three children that followed the birth of our firstborn—whose deaths must partly be blamed on their mother's lack of desire to breast-feed them and her abnormal way of life with endless card games—did not destroy our family happiness. All the residents of Shuia, who have known us from the first day of our arrival in town, can confirm this, among whom I will point out in particular Vera Nikolaevna (the wife of the *zemstvo* board chairman, Mr. Balmont) and Nadezhda Filaretovna (the wife of the secretary of the board), because these two women were often at our house and we at theirs.

Thus continued our conjugal bliss until 21 February 1897, when I suffered a stroke that left me paralyzed on the left side. The circumstances at the moment of the stroke served to make me an incurable cripple. As a doctor I never had confidence in the treatment of R[aisa] D[avidovna] Damskaia, a woman's doctor, who had prescribed poisonous dosages of medicine for my children. As a result, I asked my wife never to invite Damskaia to our house again as a doctor. When I collapsed from the stroke, Damskaia showed up first—at my wife's invitation. She placed a hot rather than a cold compress on my head, and she personally held it on my head together with my wife. Fully cognizant of the harmfulness of the hot compress but having lost the ability to speak, I tore at the compress on my head and, in annoyance, tore out my hair. So they held the compress for three hours until Dr. Zvezdin arrived, who changed the hot for a cold compress. However, such a prolonged application of the hot compress had already succeeded in having a harmful influence. It increased the rush of blood to the broken vessels, which hemorrhaged copiously, followed by the complete destruction of the brain tissues in the right hemisphere of the brain (the movement and sensation center for the left part of the body). That left me an incurable cripple. Thus, the primary perpetrators of my paralysis are my wife and her friend Dr. R. D. Damskaia.

I deem it my moral duty to give my wife her fair due: in the first year after my illness, my wife made every effort to cure me, but all attempts were in vain because medicine is powerless to restore destroyed brain tissues. After four months of bed rest, I went to work again as the county veterinarian of Shuia despite being crippled. Our lives assumed their previous appearance, the only difference being that I participated less in the carousing and card games. However, I did not meddle in my wife's arrangement of soirées and receptions for card games, or being wherever she wanted so that my illness did not interfere with the continuation of our previous happy life. No matter how difficult, I continued my previous work, despite the introduction of the law of 28 April 1897 on provincial veterinarians and subordination of the *zemstvo* veterinarians to the provincial administration.[3] The work increased significantly, and the relationship between the [provincial] administration and *zemstvo* became strained as a result. We *zemstvo* veterinarians found ourselves caught between the devil and the deep blue sea: on the one hand, the [provincial] administration demanded the complete, legal subordination of *zemstvo* veterinarians; on the other hand, local activists demanded that we not interfere in routine abuses and in veterinarian and sanitary affairs. This resulted in conflicts between *zemstvo* veterinarians and local activists in almost all the districts of Vladimir province, and led to the dismissal of more than half of the *zemstvo* veterinarians. I had such conflicts with the marshal of the nobility,[4] Mr. N. A. Poroshin, and the city doctor, A. K. Zvezdin. As a result, the governor of Vladimir (through the provincial veterinarian and *zemstvo* veterinarian) proposed that I submit my resignation. Acquiescing to these demands, I resigned on 16 September 1899 and turned in my files on 18 October. In lieu of my previous salary (114 rubles a month), I began to receive a pension of 24 rubles a month, effective 1 October.

During 1899 the doctor Dmitrii Sergeevich Malyshev wormed his way into my home, first under the pretext of microscope work (as I have the county microscope) and later in the capacity of a doctor: our ailing son had been treated by Dr. Zvezdin. However, when I left the district one day, my wife again invited Malyshev, who remained as the overseer [of my son's care] at the insistence of my wife. The illness was a partial inflammation of the lungs, which had passed but which Malyshev alleged (for more than a half year) was a residual dry bronchitis. I was not able, with all my effort, to verify the sound. Malyshev's fabricated bronchitis thus gave him the opportunity to visit our house three times a day at the insistent demand of my wife. Moreover, during the evening visits, he led my wife away until 3:00 or 5:00 in the morning. As a result of these visits, he even left his work at the factory in the village of Kolobovo, where he traveled earlier on certain days. And then, at the demand of the factory owner, he was to move to Kolobovo, which did not correspond to his interest in visiting my wife. He did not live long at the factory but left his job and returned to Shuia.

My son, thanks to Malyshev's false diagnosis, missed 260 lessons in the gymnasium — that is, more than 100 days in nine months. Only thanks to his exceptional abilities did he advance to the next grade in the gymnasium.

I regarded Malyshev's visits to my house as suspicious. My wife, instead of reducing expenses because of my resignation, increased them (in the first two months after my resignation, October and November, she organized endless soirées and did not end her card games). Hence I began to demand that my wife end her disgraceful life and reconsider her relationship to Malyshev. I was personally convinced of her cohabitation with him, which gave cause for a major argument. Meanwhile, she wrote to her relatives in the south to summon me.

Upon receiving the letter from my wife's mother with an invitation to join them, I put

my affairs into order until the spring. I did not suspect any malicious intent. On 4 December I gave my wife a notarized proxy to dispose of the belongings and receive my money. I left on that very day for Bobrinets (Kherson province), where my wife's family was then living and went then to their estate in Gertopanov (Ketrosanov township, Elisavetgrad district).

I spent until 28 March at her relatives' home, and for these four months I could not make sense of the situation. Every day they pestered me with demands to give my wife a divorce, which I refused under the conditions they proposed or rather without any conditions. Because of this they caused me great distress. Once, after such troubles, I went into the servants' kitchen where I cried bitterly, and one of the former farm laborers, whose name and surname I do not know, turned to me with the following words: "I see, sir, that you are a good person, and I pity you. Therefore I advise you to leave for the good of your health." With such pity did their cook, the noblewoman Aniusha,[5] treat me, with words that made me surmise that they [the wife's relatives] were plotting against me.

At this time I received a letter from my brother in Elisavetgrad with information that my wife's relatives were making strenuous efforts at the rabbi's for a forced divorce. From my wife's letter [which I also received] I sensed a total disregard for my interests and a hostile relationship toward me. All this was why I decided to return to Shuia and to bring my family back to my hometown. I left Gertopanov on a cart that I rented from a peasant on 28 March. A courier on horseback with letters, sent from the estate to Bobrinets, overtook me on the road. As it later turned out, these two letters were sent to Shuia: one was from my wife's brother David Morgunovskii to her. Also enclosed in this letter was a most important document. The other letter was sent by my wife's mother to Dr. Zvezdin, as my wife told me herself, informing her that I was going to kill her.

I arrived in Shuia on 1 April in the morning. The first thing that struck me was that the apartment was excessively filled with smoke (my wife does not smoke) and cigarette butts were all over the place—of these, one brand was very prevalent. Picking up these cigarette butts, I compared them to the cigarettes that I took from Dr. Malyshev, who appeared immediately; I was convinced that among my wife's guests from the previous night, Malyshev had stayed the longest. And from the servants I learned that Malyshev had taken my wife out every day during my absence until 5:00 a.m., which led me to the conclusion that he had finally possessed her and replaced me.

Convinced of this, I asked Malyshev to visit my apartment less frequently. On 3 April Dr. Damskaia and Malyshev came to my apartment, insulted me, called me insane, and threatened to place me in an asylum. Moreover, Malyshev took great liberties and acted as though he were at home in my apartment—namely, he ordered the cook Maria to move my wife's bed to a special room (separate from mine) and to secure this room from both sides with locks. I threw him and Damskaia out for doing all this. After this, my wife very often left to go somewhere and was at Poroshin's. However, in the evening she sent for the assistant forest warden of Shuia, Nikolai Vasil'evich Romonovskii, who came to start a quarrel with me. He beat me, threw me to the ground, and before my eyes took my wife and oldest child, a student at the Shuia gymnasium. Knowing that my wife earlier had prepared my son's vacation from the gymnasium and afraid that they had taken him somewhere during the night, I could not sleep all night. I went to Damskaia's apartment, where all the doors were locked and the bell was broken, and demanded that they give up my son; not receiving any answer, I knocked on the window. Only toward morning did my wife appear with Damskaia at the window, and the latter told me that she and Malyshev had decided that I was insane, that I would not hasten to the asylum but that they would send me [there] in evening all the same. And my wife declared that she was no longer my wife, that she would take the sin upon herself if only to obtain her divorce, and that I would no longer see my son. [. . .][6]

Having fully described my wife's actions, I deem it necessary to add some information about her family, for the question comes down to this: having [custody] of the son, she would live separately from me. Her whole family, as I learned after the wedding, shows all the signs of mental degeneration with a proclivity toward immorality and crime. Of her four brothers, only one completed his education as a doctor, although all were sent to educational institutions. The rest were expelled from school for academic failure and bad behavior. What is more, even the physician, her brother Ruvin Morgunovskii, who was a military doctor in the Caucasus, killed an officer and was tried by court-martial. Her other brother, David Morgunovskii, the author of the letter attached here, has been the main instigator in our family conflicts. When he served as a soldier in the town of Nikolaev, he committed an offense while in military formation against his head officer (it appears that he tore off his epaulettes). To avoid a court-martial, he shot himself while in military formation, wounding the right half of his face, a scar that he still carries (in the form of a defect in his jawbone). Moreover, several times he intended to shoot his own father, who once filed a complaint with the procurator of Elisavetgrad but, at the instance of the family, withdrew it. Afterward this same David Morgunovskii often served time in prison in Elisavetgrad district as punishment for assaulting various people.

My wife herself, when she was a governess for her sister in Elisavetgrad, brought up three young children (Fedia, Lela, and Misha), who were often dismissed from school despite the intense care and enormous amounts of money that their father, Boris Slobodskii, wasted on them. None of them finished secondary school.

All this information about the upbringing of the children in my wife's family and about the criminal activities of her family members leaves me trembling for [my son's] fate and his future if he remains with his mother without me. What will become of my only son if my wife is given a separate passport? The fact is that even now my wife already teaches the child, under various false pretenses, to neglect his lessons in gymnasium. During one year without me, the pernicious influence of his mother (and, during holidays, of her criminal brothers) already revealed itself on 23 November of this year, when my son struck Katia Abramova, a girl who was serving him. When the girl complained to his mother, the latter hit the girl and dragged her by the braids through three rooms instead of instilling in my son the necessary respect for other people. When the girl's mother arrived on 24 November with a complaint, my wife ended up beating her too. I interpret this fact as the beginning of the moral destruction of my son under the influence of his mother's upbringing and her criminal brothers. My wife has always been accustomed to beating the servants, and many of our former cooks can attest to this.

As I do not have a formal list of my thirteen-year service in three provinces, I enclose eight documents that characterize my work from the time that I graduated from an institution of higher education until my illness, as well as the day of my retirement. For the sake of my honest and true service to the Tsar and fatherland, although [my work] was not in state service, as an incurable cripple I now take the liberty to *beg you most humbly, Tsar, to show sympathy, mercy, and charity toward me, so that I do not lose my family* at a time when I — having given my younger years, health, and strength for the sake of work and benefit of the family — am a sick person who is unable to work in my former position. In

particular, do not allow my only son, who is now the sole purpose of my life, to be subjected to the influence of my wife's criminal family, the Morgunovskiis. He would soon embark on a criminal path because already, under the upbringing of his mother, at the age of ten he does not have any understanding of moral principles and religion. He does not know a single prayer because his mother herself spurns all — moral and state — law. I thus beg you not to alienate me from my family, for this would be akin to a death sentence for me. [. . .][7]

True, I am sick and such a nervous illness requires, in everyone's opinion, an absolutely peaceful and quiet family life. However, I constantly worry, and it is the limit that they want to take the children away from me. Again, I beg for sympathy, mercy, and charity toward me, a sick person. In my illness, I am innocent. I am an involuntary slave of the disease.

Composed and written personally,

Signed Iosif Broun.

"Testimony of Shura Leia (Sonia) Broun (24 April 1901)"

My name is Shura Leia Broun. I am thirty-one years old, of the Jewish confession, resident of Shuia. Here are my responses to the questions: I married Iosif Moiseevich Broun on 31 October 1889 on my parents' personal estate in the town of Gertopanov. Apart from a complete wardrobe, I brought a dowry of 200 rubles, which was deposited in the Treasury of Shuia in my own and my husband's names. I had five children, of whom two are alive: a ten-year-old boy, Viktor, and a two-year-old girl, Mariia.[8] I moved with my husband to Shuia on 20 August 1890. We had a small circle of acquaintances — E. S. Liktorskaia, the Iushovs, and Damskaia. I met Dr. Malyshev at the Iushkovs' house; he was at our home both as a guest and as a doctor. He treated my son for a long time, earlier together with Dr. Zvezdin (when my son's life was in danger) and then alone. My husband was discharged from work in 1899; the main reason for his dismissal was a denunciation against the marshal of the nobility, Mr. Poroshin. Damskaia read the document [the denunciation] and attempted to persuade my husband not to send it, but he did not listen and sent it all the same. For the letter, he was immediately dismissed from service by the governor.

Earlier my husband was not sick with any serious illness. Perhaps he was ill before the wedding, but it was unknown to me. But after my husband became ill, I took him to a doctor, who said that the illness was due to syphilis, and he prescribed a mercury treatment that my husband did not want to undergo. I believe that Dr. Zvezdin knows about this.

Living with my husband, I never enjoyed any freedom of action; even the smallest manifestation of will led to scenes and abusive language. I ran the household, but my husband controlled everything—so, although he gave his salary to me, I could not buy anything. A few times, exasperated by the constant control, I refused to do the housework and returned the money to my husband. We were not short on grievances in life, but there were emergency expenses; for example, my husband traveled to bury his mother in his hometown, bought her a tombstone, and then traveled to Moscow for a vaccination against rabies (he had cut his finger during a postmortem examination of a dog). He gave his brother 200 rubles from my money. All these expenses were taken from my dowry; that is, they took my money from the treasury. While I lived with my husband, I never traveled to visit my family by myself because my husband always said that a decent woman does not travel alone to her family, but [. . .] with her husband. In ten years, I was at my parents' one time with my husband and son. To all my requests to let me go to my family, my husband always answered the one and the same [thing]: a decent woman does not travel without her husband when he is working and cannot travel to visit the family. My husband

really could not go in the winter, and it was impossible to go then with the little ones. Of course, I would not have agreed to leave my son.

My husband was short-tempered from the day of our wedding. Only now and then was he not irritable when everyone carried out his demands. The smallest failure to meet his demands led to a scene. After one and a half years with my husband, thanks to the constant troubles, I fell ill. My throat started to bleed. Prof. Povlinov treated me. Because of my illness, my husband sent for my sister, who sensed that my family life was not good. For some reason, however, I felt it necessary to conceal my husband's relationship to me from her and all those around me. To all her questions, I gave evasive answers.

After this illness, his short temper became unbearable. Not only did his jealousy provoke abuse but, for example, my husband demanded that I accompany him to the train station for his weekly trip to work in the city of Ivanovo. I complied, of course. However, having awakened at 5:00 a.m. for this, having come to the station, and being unhealthy, I left to go to the dressing room to lie down until [the train] arrived. He was irritated and cursed me right there at the station: why did I not sit with him? In general, my husband insisted that I never be absent from him.

I persuaded my husband to visit my relatives' estate because life with him became intolerable, and I simply wished to take a break "morally"—for I had begun to entertain thoughts of suicide. My husband became suspicious when I fell ill before his departure and asked the doctor: "Has she not been poisoned?" Only pity for my son, who is very attached to me, stopped me from taking this step. Up to this point, my life was unbearable. When my husband left for the family estate, he was not seriously ill but in his present condition. I received letters from my husband from the estate but, because these letters could harm him, he forcibly took them from me when he arrived in Shuia and burned them. A few of the last letters have been preserved, and I am enclosing them.[9] Until the time of his disgraceful behavior, I did not think about a separate life. Perhaps one can conclude that, as he left me a full power of attorney certified by a notary when he was leaving, I would receive a passport from him, but I did not.

When my husband arrived back from his estate, I was standing at the door of the gymnasium where I took my son, something that I do every day. Although my husband knew that I always take my son to the gymnasium myself and saw me leaving, he nonetheless met me with curses and asked where I was wandering about so early in the morning. This was his constant refrain wherever I went. After his arrival, my husband began to hurl anything that came to hand at me and to yell that I had been baptized and wanted to baptize the children but that he would kill me: as long as he was alive, he would not allow them to be baptized. Out of fear for my son's life, I summoned Mr. Romonovskii, and in his presence my husband yelled: "I will kill you, whelp." Earlier he threw books at him and whatever came to hand. At my son's request, "Papa, let me sleep," (it was already 11:00 in the evening and the boy is always asleep by 9:00), he replied: if a father so desires, his son should not go to sleep. I asked Mr. Romonovskii, with whom my husband has enjoyed the best relationship until now, to persuade my husband to release me and my son to Damskaia until he had calmed down. But my husband replied to him with curses. Romonovskii only stood at the door until my son and I left for Damskaia's. [. . .] But my husband called him a scoundrel.

I did not manage to put my son to sleep after arriving at Damskaia's because my husband showed up and, with the most vulgar curses, began to bang on the window of Damskaia's apartment. At the apartment he smashed my wardrobe, began throwing dresses into the

trash bin, and of course damaged everything. I reported my husband's violent conduct to the police personally, but not in writing. I did not receive my husband's examination from the doctor. My husband asked me by telephone to bail him out, which I did.

[The following] can confirm my husband's rough treatment of me: Damskaia, her sister, Mr. Bulai, the policeman (whose surname I do not remember because I was so upset that I forget it), and the nanny who serves me. I live at my parents' expense and receive as much as I need to live with two children. Sometimes I receive money in the guise of a present from my sisters and brothers, who are all wealthy. Documents about the amount of money that has been sent to me have been preserved; however, as they are not complete (because my husband destroyed the rest), you can inquire about it at the postal administration of Shuia and also at Tiubrinets where I receive my money. I received 565 rubles, which my relatives sent to the Shuia post office, but only 140 rubles here. As I conclude my testimony, I should add that I have long [desired] to convert to Russian Orthodoxy. I was imprudent enough to say this in the presence of my husband, and now he threatens to get even with me. If my petition is not fulfilled, then I will be forced to live with him.

"Report of the Head of the Vladimir Gendarmes to the Chancellery (17 June 1901)"

Submitting herewith additional [information] produced by an investigation of family discord case of the Broun couple, I have the honor to report to the Chancellery of His Imperial Majesty that a thorough secret surveillance found that Mrs. Broun maintains a close relationship to Dr. Dmitrii Malyshev at the present time. In town it is openly said that she has a [sexual] relationship with him and plans to embrace Russian Orthodoxy to marry him; however, it is practically impossible to confirm these relations.

Iosif Broun is absolutely healthy psychologically, but physically he is a completely sick person: he can hardly walk. He is extremely irritable and short-tempered about his wife's relationship with Dmitrii Malyshev (as Captain Vinogradov explained). He cries all the time and curses her vulgarly. Captain Vinogradov, who carried out the investigation, suggests that with such an illness and short temper, it is hardly possible for the son to remain with Iosif Broun, and that his means are extremely limited (even for his own sustenance). It is impossible to explain the true reasons for the conflict that arose between the Broun couple; however, based on public opinion, it follows that the conflict arose for the following reasons: (1) Iosif Broun is insanely jealous; (2) Iosif Broun is slovenly and, at any rate, gives an impression of being an uncultured Jew; and (3) Iosif Broun is a member of the Jewish religion. It appears that these reasons served as the source of family conflict, all the more so since Mrs. Broun is the complete antithesis of her husband. She became acquainted with a few cultured families in Shuia and previously felt hatred toward her dirty and coarse husband, and now toward a half-alive husband. One can judge as much by her character. To seize her son or to force her to live together with her husband may lead to suicide.[10]

"Report of His Imperial Majesty's Chancellery for the Receipt of Petitions (24 January 1908)"

Your Imperial Excellency, based on my humble report of 24 February 1905 [an account of an investigation of family strife], it pleased Your Excellency to approve, *inter alia*, my proposal to grant Shura Leia Broun (the wife of the veterinarian doctor, Iosif Broun) the right to separate residence from her husband for four years, leaving the minor children Vidgor [Viktor] and Mariia under her guardianship.

The conditions of the Broun couple's family life as the subject of investigation by His Imperial Majesty's Chancellery go as far back as 1902, when an inquiry established that their life together was impossible. Suffering from a nervous disorder and suspecting his wife of violating her marital fidelity, Iosif Broun felt malice toward her and, in fits of rage, began resorting to violent actions against her. As a result, as a temporary measure, Shura Leia Broun was permitted to live with her children separately from her husband for a period of a year. As I informed Your Imperial Majesty, Iosif Broun's treatment of his wife had not lost its hostility after the specified period; returning her to her husband might have led to extremely severe consequences, as was explained. So the first term of living under a separate passport was extended for four years (per article 12 of the secret instructions sent to me on handling cases of family discord).

Iosif Broun has now appealed to Your Imperial Majesty with a humble petition about the restoration of his family rights, about the transfer of guardianship over his son Vigdor, age seventeen, and about determining an educational institution for both the latter and his daughter Mariia, age nine. He cites his wife's participation in the revolutionary movement, thus influencing the children in a corrupt manner, to justify his petition.

From the collected information, it has been established that Shura Leia Broun (age thirty-seven), who lives with her children, has been in illegal cohabitation with an individual who participated in revolutionary propaganda and who is now the subject of criminal proceedings.[11] Herself sympathetic to revolutionary aims, she has allowed her son Vigdor to be carried away on the path of criminal deception; as a result, he has been expelled from the student body at the Shuia classical gymnasium and placed under investigation for belonging to the Shuia group of Socialist Revolutionaries.

Given that Shura Leia Broun maliciously abused the favor granted to her, her guardianship over her son Vidgor and daughter Mariia can no longer be tolerated. As the petitioner has been restricted in his own family rights and deprived of the possibility to change the conditions of his children's upbringing, I consider it just to satisfy Iosif Broun's petition and to change the 1905 decision that permitted Shura Leia Broun to live for four years separately from her husband and to have custody of her children. It will be explained to the petitioner that on the question of transferring his son Vigdor under his guardianship and placing his son and also his daughter Mariia in an educational institution, he is required to be guided by the existing legal order.

To implement my proposal I must ask for Your Imperial Majesty's consent.[12]

NOTES

1. [The chancellery, established in 1884, issued separate passports to women in exceptional instances of abuse and neglect thereby circumventing state laws that denied wives the right to reside apart from their husband or gain employment without their permission. In the late nineteenth century, the number of petitions seeking legal separation rose dramatically, more than doubling between 1881 and 1896 (from approximately 1,500 to 3,469 per year). The majority of requests (80 percent) originated from the wives of peasants and men in the lower urban estates; petitions from privileged groups constituted the rest. The motives of Jewish women seeking legal separation varied: some could not obtain a formal divorce; others wanted to retain their social, residential, and legal rights (based on the husband's status) but be free from reciprocal conjugal obligations. This particular separation file is 812 pages long.]

2. [Broun repeats the points made in his first petition, reiterating that the accusations of his wife — that he deserted the family without any means or passport — are fallacious.]

3. [The *zemstvo* counter-reform of 1890 encroached on the rights of local government because the provincial government gained greater control over *zemstvo* decisions. See Terrence Emmons and Wayne Vucinich, *The Zemstvo in Russia: An Experiment in Local Self-Government* (Cambridge: Cambridge University Press, 1982).]

4. [In the Charter of the Nobility (21 April 1785), the nobles obtained the right to elect a marshal of the nobility to represent their interests in local government.]

5. [Some impoverished noblewomen were reduced to working as cooks even as they retained their hereditary noble status.]

6. [Broun repeats the events that led to his arrest and illegal examination by the state doctors who diagnosed him as insane.]

7. [Broun repeats the description of his illness and his wife's "immoral behavior" for three pages.]

8. [In a later petition, in passing the husband mentioned a daughter Ida, who died on 18 June 1895.]

9. [There were several letters in the file, all similar to this undated note: "Sonia! After all your crimes against me, your telegram was rather cheeky. I just told you that I will not give you a separate passport, and I demand that you live together with me and the children — not only because I can demand it based on statute 103, part 1, volume 10 [of *Svod zakonov Rossiskoi imperii*]. I demand that you come to my place of permanent residence not because you prevented the transfer of Vitia [Viktor] and he needs to study in gymnasium. I agree to come to Shuia but only if you give a certified commitment to the police that you will not run away from me and not take the children away, and that we will conduct a normal way of life. Otherwise, I won't come. But if I come, at the very first violation [. . .] I will leave."]

10. [The wife received a separate passport for one year, during which time the couple were to resolve their differences either through reconciliation or divorce. In March 1903 Iosif Broun brought his wife and Malyshev to court on charges of adultery, but because all the witnesses rejected the accusation, Shura Broun and Dmitrii Malyshev were acquitted (RGIA, f. 1412, op. 213, d. 101, ll. 137–138).]

11. [A gendarme report from Vladimir province stated that "Sonia [Shura] Broun" was living "in illegal cohabitation" with a pharmacist's assistant, Vladimir Afroimov Drobinskii (ibid., l. 197).]

12. [Despite the wife's counterpetition to protest the accusation of her involvement in the revolutionary movement, the Imperial Chancellery upheld its ruling about the transfer of guardianship over the son to the father and the father's right to assign the daughter to an educational institution of his choice.]

[39]

Questions to R. Yitzhak Elhanan Spektor on Marriage and Divorce

Yitzhak Elhanan Spektor, *Ein Yitzhak*, *Even ha-Ezer* 1: 3 (Vil'na [s.n.] 1888).

I was asked about someone who, immediately after the wedding, set off for her brother's in a distant land; it has been over a year now and she has not returned to her husband. Her husband went after her to the same location, but she has not responded. According to the testimony of a single witness, she is violating the laws of Moses, has embarked on an evil path, and is rebelling against her husband. Her husband claims to be certain that she is adulterous, but he has no clear evidence — only endless rumors that she is on an evil path. I am asked whether he is permitted to remarry.[1]

Divorce of a Childless Wife

Yitzhak Elhanan Spektor, *Ein Yitzhak*, *Even ha-Ezer* 1: 4 (Vil'na: [s.n.], 1888).

I was asked about someone who lived with his wife for over ten years, without her ever having given birth: should he be allowed to marry another? The husband also says that he knows for certain that the wife is an *aylonit* [lacks a female sexual feature], as listed in tractate *Yevamot* (80). The husband has a reputation of being honest and God-fearing. I was also shown a writ from the local community court, whereby the said woman agrees that if she lives two more years with her husband and does not give birth, she agrees to accept a bill of divorce from her husband and to allow him to marry another, without any protest on her part. And now that the two years are up she has retracted all this. I was asked whether to permit him to marry another by law on the basis of one hundred rabbis.[2]

Divorce of an Insane Wife

Yitzhak Elhanan Spektor, *Ein Yitzhak*, *Even ha-Ezer* 1: 5 (Vil'na [s.n.] 1888)

I was asked about someone who married a woman, and immediately after the wedding it was apparent that this woman had gone insane, quite visibly so to all those at the wedding. During the actual ceremonies the groom did not discern this at all. But during the *yichud* [time in private for consummation] the groom said that he had no intercourse with her, and that she sometimes replied to him sensibly but other times spoke insanely. The day after the wedding and *yichud* they each went to their respective homes and separated from each other. It became clear from further testimony that before the wedding she had had episodes of melancholia; at times she was well but at times insane. However, the husband and his relatives were unaware of this because the bride's family and parents concealed this fact. There is also testimony that during the wedding the woman was seen to have the upper sign [breasts, indicating maturity], as listed in tractate *Niddah* (48) in the Mishnah ("Upper indications . . . ," etc.). I am asked whether the husband is permitted to marry another woman even without the hundred rabbis. Your honor proposes a lenient solution on the grounds that there is a double doubt: it is possible that during the ceremony she was insane, and if so the wedding is entirely invalid. Alternatively, during the wedding she was sane, but possibly had a defective condition that people are normally wary of [raising issues of fraud]; in a case of marriage and discovery of serious defects, she is not considered married but only by reason of doubt, as explained in tractate *Ketubot* (73b) and in *Even ha-Ezer* 39: 5. Accordingly, here is a double doubt, which is grounds to permit marriage to another woman. This is the essence of your honor's arguments.[3]

On the Divorce of a Convert

Yitzhak Elhanan Spektor, *Ein Yitzhak*, *Even ha-Ezer* 1: 1 (Vil'na: [s.n.], 1888).

TO THE RABBI AND *GAON*, ETC.

I received your letter about a woman who has a husband and who has abandoned the faith, etc. The husband has been trying to divorce her legally through a bill of divorce, but she refuses to accept this divorce by any means and shouts that she has no desire to gain the benefit of a divorce from a Jewish court. R. Meir Isserles in *Yoreh Deah* 1: 10 explains that when a woman has left the faith, the court appoints a beneficiary who accepts the divorce on her behalf and [the husband] can remarry, etc. In this case, however, she is explicitly shout-

ing that she does not wish the benefit of this divorce, and she cannot be granted the right against her will. As the *Shevut Yaakov* wrote (1: 120),[4] in such a case the husband does not have the recourse of granting her a divorce by benefit. But obtaining a special permission from a hundred rabbis is not possible in their region [given the dearth of rabbis there], so your honor has asked me to render my opinion on this.[5]

NOTES

1. [Spektor permitted him to remarry, but, since there was only one witness to her infidelity, he required the approval of 100 rabbis; he also insisted that he set aside all that he might owe her in a divorce settlement, and that the rabbi overseeing the matter ensure that all was done according to the laws of the state.]

2. [Spektor permitted this, provided that the government agreed. See document 37 for another case that involved the permission of one hundred rabbis to remarry.]

3. [Spektor agreed with this argument, accepting that he may marry another without the permision of the one hundred rabbis, with the proviso that he set aside all that he might owe her as a divorce settlement, and that all is done to comply with the laws of the state.]

4. [The work of Yaakov Reischer (1661–1733), rabbi of a number of European cities and towns, among them Worms and Metz.]

5. [Spektor permits him to marry another, arguing that the *herem* of Rabbenu Gershom forbidding bigamy does not apply in a case such as this. Hence he may marry without the approval of the one hundred rabbis.]

[40]

Divorce by Mutual Agreement, Child Custody, and Support

"Petition of Mosei Isaakovich Azer'er (Dentist) and Zlata (Zinaida) Izrailevna to the State Rabbi of Moscow, Iakov Maze (7 September 1904)"

TsIAM, 1467, op. 1, d. 16, ll. 34–34 ob.

We wish by mutual agreement to dissolve our marriage, which was concluded on 23 May 1900 by the rabbi of Vil'na. We have the honor to ask you to order the drafting of the *get* and its delivery according to Jewish law.

In addition, we declare by mutual agreement that our daughter Natalia, born on 7 March 1901, will always remain in the care of her mother. As for the dowry in the sum of 10,000 rubles that I, Mosei Azer'er, received, I am obliged to deposit it in the State Bank in the name of our daughter at the first opportunity, or to return this sum to my divorced wife in agreement with her request in the form that she wishes. Similarly, if my material circumstances allow, I am obliged to contribute to the expenses of the support and upbringing of my daughter.

Moreover, we present the following documents: a marriage certificate from 23 May 1900, [and] a certificate from Khar'kov University from 9 July 1903.

"Petition of Engineer-Technologist Grigorii Samuilovich Grodskii and his wife Sofiia (Sara) Shulimovna, born Rakhmilovich, to the State Rabbi of Moscow, Iakov Maze (28 June 1915)"

TsIAM, f. 1457, op. 1, d. 50, ll. 24–25 ob.

We wish by mutual agreement to dissolve our marriage, which was concluded in the town of Piatigorsk on 11 August 1906. We humbly ask you, Gracious Sir, to order the dissolution of our marriage. By mutual agreement, the son born to this marriage, seven-year-old Evgenii, will be given to his mother Sofiia (Sara) until he is eighteen years old [with the support of] 50 rubles a month and a separate payment for our son's studies of no more than 120 rubles a year. Moreover, we have no other claims toward one another.

[41]

Prison Divorces

"Petition of Abram I. Shapsovich Shtromberg, Held at the Moscow Central Peresylnskaia Prison, to the State Rabbi of Moscow, Iakov Maze (4 February 1909)"

TsIAM, f. 1458, op. 1, d. 16, ll. 2–3.

My wife, Beila Shtromberg, who lives in the town of Dubno (Volhynia province), wishes to request Your Honor for a divorce from me in view of the fact that I am in no condition to take her to Siberia with me or to give her and the baby any kind of assistance. Beila wishes to submit to Your Honor the documents regarding the divorce but does not have your address and asks you to inform her about it. In light of the above, I have the honor to request humbly that Your Honor inform my wife about your address [. . .] and to make your decision on the divorce, adding that you will not meet any obstacles on my part. [. . .]

"Letter of the Petrograd Provincial Prison Inspector to the Petrograd State Rabbi, Moisei Grigor'evich Aizenshtadt (25 August 1915)"

TsIAM, f. 1457, op. 1, d. 50, ll. 32–33 ob.

The provincial prison inspector informs you that your assistant, a scribe, and two witnesses will be permitted to visit the Bureau of the Petrograd House of Pre-Trial Detention to conclude the divorce between Lev Gershon Mikhailov Khinchuk, who is being held in this prison, and his wife Roza Verkova Khinchuk.

---

[42]

Responsum of R. Yitzhak Elhanan Spektor:[1]
An *Agunah* Whose Husband Has Been Exiled

Yitzhak Elhanan Spektor, *Ein Yitzhak, Even ha-Ezer* 2: 6 (Vil'na: [s.n.], 1888).

WITH THE GRACE OF GOD. WEDNESDAY THE 10TH OF AV 5728 [1868] TO YOUR HONOR THE RAV AND *GAON*, ETC.

A. After extending my best wishes to you, I received your letter, in which you sought my opinion on the matter of the *agunah* in your area, where the woman's husband several years earlier was sent for his crime to a land of punitive exile, to a place where no [Jewish] court existed to arrange a divorce. Nor could the woman travel there because of the great distance. So the only means you have to obtain a *get* granting her release is by means of handwritten instructions from her husband to the scribe and witnesses in your area instructing them to write and sign and deliver the divorce to his wife. Your Torah Eminence went to great lengths to permit this rather than create an *igun*,[2] as is explained in the responsum of the Maharam of Padua, of blessed memory. Actually, I do not have this responsum of his available to me. I myself, owing to the gravity of the situation,[3] did not wish to insert myself and issue a ruling on this point of law. But now that your eminence writes me that without my opinion he will not involve himself [and rule on the matter], and it would be a great *igun*, I must therefore briefly respond to you on the main issue — whether it is valid to have a bill of divorce prepared at the written request of the husband. [On this matter] the *get pashut*[4] in section 120 urges a lenient stance where *igun* is concerned and the *Knesset ha-gedolah*[5] on the *Even ha-Ezer* writes likewise.[6] In truth, it might seem that the opponents are correct [. . .] for even the *Tosefta*[7] explains that a husband's handwritten instruction is not valid. Even though one might claim that the *Tosefta* is corrupt, this is countered by the *Pri Hadash*,[8] which notes that the *Tosefta* in question is cited in the *Yerushalmi*,[9] *Gittin* 7:1, and *Terumot* 1:1. Indeed, this is a significant argument against those who would be lenient in cases of [relying on the] handwritten [instructions] of a competent writer. Moreover, the *Yerushalmi* there uses the [stronger] language "is not a divorce" rather than the *Tosefta*'s language ("is invalid"), suggesting that the invalidation is a matter of biblical law.[10] Hence I did not wish to insert myself into this issue. [. . .]

B. [. . .][11]

C. Therefore in the matter at hand, one should be lenient in a case of great *igun*. [The husband] must explicitly write that he is not writing this out as a mere draft[12] but rather writing it in full seriousness; also, at the end of his letter, he must write that all this was verbally stated by him explicitly [it is not clear to whom it must be stated]. He must write that he takes it upon himself by an eternal oath never to recant any of this, and that he takes it upon himself by a strict oath that everything here was said in full seriousness. [. . .][13]Accordingly, where an oath has been taken, we may say that the stringency of the

Yerushalmi is entirely irrelevant, and all the more so when [the husband] is writing from a location other than that of the scribe and witnesses [and has no other recourse], as in the case at hand. [. . .] And so I agree to your statements on this.

D. Nevertheless, there is cause for concern in the case at hand because in [the husband's] town there was only one witness, not two, to certify the husband's signature [as required by Jewish law]. With regard to what Your Honor wrote [one may be lenient with regard to non-Jewish courts that validate the husband's signature]: in fact I have affirmed this in my book *Be'er Yitzhak*, part *Even ha-Ezer* section 5, regarding the testimony in non-Jewish courts about the death of a husband. However, one must distinguish between the case of a witness to a death, where [in Jewish law] a single witness is trusted, and a relative or a wife [or any other woman] are likewise trusted; this suggests that a more lenient stance is to be taken about [death certifications by] non-Jewish courts. This is not the case in a divorce, where the requirement [in all cases] is for two valid witnesses who are not relatives; this indicates greater stringency regarding the suitability of non-Jewish courts. In my book (section 6) I cite the Maharik[14] as saying that non-Jewish courts are not acceptable for bills of divorce only because they are not subject to the Jewish laws of divorce,[15] not because they lack trustworthiness, etc. [. . .] This is in line with the [Babylonian] Talmud in *Gittin* (10b): "Yet they are not subject to the Jewish laws of divorce." [. . .][16]

E. Nevertheless, there is still room for discussion, as we find that the ancient sages, of blessed memory, have taken a lenient stance on the validation of a *get*, for the messenger alone is trusted to declare "it was written before me." As is explained in the beginning of *Gittin*, to avoid *igun* the rabbis were lenient. This [is so in matters of divorce] even though with commercial contracts the sages did not bestow similar trust on the messenger. Hence, the sages were more lenient about validation of a *get* than the validation of promissory notes or deeds of sale. Thus we may also conclude that the same applies to non-Jewish courts: just as they are to be trusted for the validation of contracts [in general], they are, a fortiori, to be trusted for the validation of a *get*. [. . .][17] In truth, the validation of a divorce by non-Jewish courts is to be trusted, since validation is only [required by] rabbinic law, although this proof is indeed superfluous since it follows logically, as I have written, from the fact that a messenger is trusted for divorces and not trusted for contracts (see above).[18] Therefore one must be lenient in the case at hand about the validation by non-Jewish courts of the husband's handwritten instructions. [. . .]

H. Regarding what Your Honor wrote about the textual formula for all this: for lack of time, I have not looked into the matter at all. Accordingly, my opinion is that your honor should form a court of three important rabbis from this region to determine how to behave in all this in every particular. So far as I am concerned, what I have written should generally suffice. And it would be better still if the [rabbinical] court of three would request that the non-Jewish court of their region write to the non-Jewish court in the husband's region. For there are grounds to worry that the husband has decided to divorce her only for fear of the authorities there. [. . .][19]

YOUR FRIEND, YITZHAK ELHANAN,
RESIDING IN KOVNO.

NOTES

1. [Spektor handled questions of all kinds, but we are especially interested here in the many questions directed to him, and his many responsa, on matters of marriage and divorce. This responsum is an important document in that it illuminates many aspects of Jewish life in Imperial Russia. A Jewish prisoner, presumably in Siberia, wishes to divorce his wife, who is a great distance away, presumably in one of the western provinces. This makes it impossible for the husband and wife, not to mention

the necessary rabbinic authorities, to be in the same place at the same time. This presents all kinds of legal challenges, described and resolved below. Along the way, we get a sense, albeit limited, of the intersection of Jewish legal and personal matters with the authority structures of the Russian state, at least as imagined by a prominent rabbi. We have removed the most technical legal material, while attempting to give the reader the flavor of Spektor's legal discourse. The recipient of this letter is unknown; the contents allow us to assume a town or village rabbi of limited authority, one who is unwilling to make such a momentous decision as sanctioning a divorce that is anomalous without the support of Spektor, one of the leading rabbinic authorities of the day.]

2. [*Igun* (related to the more familiar word, *agunah*, which shares the same root) refers to anchoring the woman to her marriage, as there is no way to dissolve the marriage without a *get* delivered by the husband.]

3. [Throughout the generations, the rabbis have generally tried very hard to avoid creating the status of an *igun* and this responsum is another example of this effort.]

4. [A work by Moses ben Solomon ibn Habib (ca. 1654–96) on the rules of preparing *gittin* (plural of *get*).]

5. [An encyclopedic work by Hayyim b. Yisrael Benveniste (1603–73), chief rabbi of Smyrna. The section on *Even ha-Ezer* was published posthumously in Smyrna in 1731.]

6. [Spektor cites other authorities who disagree.]

7. [An ancient work, probably from the third century, which contains many traditions of the *tannaim*.]

8. [A work by Hezekiah de Silva (1659–1695), rabbi of Jerusalem.]

9. [The so-called Jerusalem Talmud; *Gittin* and *Terumot* are the names of two tractates within this Talmud.]

10. [The language "is invalid" could be interpreted as suggesting that the *get* is invalid because of some technical problem, and thus runs afoul of rabbinic, rather than biblical law. The urgency of avoiding *igun* might override such technical concerns. The language "is not a divorce (*'eino get*)" suggests that the *get* is invalid on its face, in turn implying

that its disqualification adheres to the demands of biblical law.]

11. [In this paragraph Spektor explains that he looked into the *Yerushalmi* passage in greater depth and realized that, according to one opinion (that of R. Avdimi), the *Tosefta* passage applied only to a deaf mute. Even according to the opinion of R. Yossi b. R. Bun this is not so: the *Tosefta* applies only when the writer could have spoken to the scribe and the witnesses. In that case it may well be that he was only writing a draft. But our case would be different, as the husband cannot speak to the scribe, but can only instruct him in writing. It therefore seems unlikely that he was merely writing his instructions as a draft rather than as a full expression of his wishes.]

12. [Literally, as a way of "passing the time."]

13. [Spektor goes on to consider at some length objections to this ruling, and parries them to his satisfaction. He then concludes this section.]

14. [Joseph ben Solomon Colon (c. 1420–80), an Italian halakhist.]

15. [Since there is nothing comparable in non-Jewish jurisprudence to a *get*, the authenticating mechanisms of gentile courts are not valid, unlike with other contracts. This is a formalistic requirement that is difficult to get around.]

16. [After some complex legal argument, Spektor concludes that it seems unlikely that one can rely on gentile courts for the validation of the signature; thus the problem is unresolved.]

17. [Spektor presents further arguments on the question of validation and whether it is required by biblical or rabbinic law, leading to the following conclusion.]

18. [Were validation biblically required, either the opposite relationship would prevail, or messengers would not be trusted with any contract.]

19. [Spektor explains that, although there is sometimes room for coercion by a Jewish court in matters of divorce, coercion by gentile authorities renders a divorce void under Jewish law. If, however, the gentile authorities acted at the behest of a Jewish court, even if only in the most formal sense, their coercion would formally be that of the Jewish court and hence would not render the divorce invalid.]

[43]

Responsum of R. Yitzhak Elhanan Spektor on the Disappearance of a Husband

Yitzhak Elhanan Spektor, *Ein Yitzhak*, *Even ha-Ezer* 1: 20 (Vil'na: [s.n., 1888])

I was asked about a certain *agunah*: her husband, R. Shmuel the son of R. Moshe Epstein, disappeared last Marheshvan[1] from where he was being treated for illness, as he was subject to insanity (heaven forfend). He had been staying for some time at the Tatar's hotel called Tatar's Sarik and then disappeared; he has still not been found (after searches in the adjacent Bialeh River). Just before the last Shavuot holiday, word spread in the Vil'na community that [the body of] the man in question had just been found, in the said river near the said hotel, and near the path where he had been seen wandering about. He was immediately examined and seen to be dressed in all his clothes, with the four-fringed garment underneath; a folder was also found with many letters inside. Also found on his person was a small key to his safe with a small metal ring that held this key. There were also many letters written to him by acquaintances and relatives addressed to this person, Shmuel Epstein. There was also a letter from his wife in her own handwriting and a letter from his brother-in-law and his visiting card with his name in German letters. His notebook contained some accounts in his very hand that he had in his house (along with Arabic numerals that he had written out by hand). But no identifying signs could be found on his body as his entire face had decomposed. An acquaintance of his said that by his height and frame he had no doubt that it looked like the disappeared R. Shmuel. Also when he was buried they found on his undergarments and pants his monogram Shmuel Epstein. The hairs on his head were black; there was also much hair around his navel (just like the disappeared person). Around his neck was found the amulet that the Tatar had given him to heal his ailments and on the amulet was inscribed his name and that of his mother—Shmuel son of Haya Shena. I was asked whether to release her from the chains of *igun*.[2]

NOTES

1. Marheshvan is the eighth month of the Jewish year, and corresponds to October-November.

2. Spektor released the woman from the "chains of *igun*" despite the absence of definitive identification, and thus direct proof that her husband was dead.

[44]

Responsum of R. Naftali Zvi Yehudah Berlin of Volozhin: A Male *Agun*?

Naftali Zvi Yehudah Berlin, *Meshiv davar*, 4: 5 (Warsaw: [n.s.] 1894).

BY THE GRACE OF GOD AND FOR THE HONOR OF HIS BLESSED NAME
3 KISLEV 5723 [1862].

A man married a wife and before long, as it turned out, she took a position as a domestic servant in the home of a wealthy man in Vil'na. When her masters sent her to get change for a 200-ruble bill, she absconded with [the money]; her location has not been ascertained for over a year. She has been searched for extensively in Vilna, but without success. And her husband is bereft and grieving that the joy of offspring is denied to him. He seeks to marry another wife and to build himself a home.

In his commentary to the *Even ha-Ezer* (siman 1), the Rema [R. Moshe Isserles] writes as follows: in a case where a first wife is undivorceable (for example, she has gone insane; or if he is obligated to divorce her but she refuses to accept the divorce from him), one may be lenient and permit [the husband] another wife. Our Rabbi [the Rema] is describing two modes. In the first, he has no means of divorcing her and no remedy. In the second—the case where she is unwilling—in principle it is possible to persuade her with a pile of money (as prescribed by the Talmud in *Gittin* (30); that case discusses a situation where the money might lead her to reconcile with him; a fortiori the same applies to persuading her to accept a divorce. [Thus, we might conclude that in a case such as ours, we cannot permit him to marry another, as a proper divorce remains possible. But] as the Rosh writes (in *Yevamot*, Ch. *Ha-isha raba*, Ch. 4), great is the hatred of the women who hate and the love of those who love. From this [we infer] that our master does not require him [to attempt to find her and persuade her to accept a divorce].

In the second mode, I might say that since she is a sinner who refuses to follow the law — which differs from the case where she had suddenly gone insane [which is beyond anyone's control] — there are grounds to be lenient. [It would be different] if she were not a sinner and some sort of resolution — however unlikely — seemed possible; he would be obligated to take all possible measures and would not be readily permitted to marry another. [Such a case might be if] the woman had gone missing, and might have been willing to accept a divorce were it not for the great mountain separating the two. Hence if he is willing to expend a great sum to search for her and to inquire about her in distant markets, he might be able to find her. This appears to be the reasoning of the *gaon* the *Hatam Sofer*, *Even ha-Ezer* (volume 1), who wrote that when a woman has gone missing, a single witness to her death suffices to permit remarriage, to avoid his *igun*,[1] which is not the case if she has become insane and there is one witness to her death; in that case he already has a recourse available [because he would be permitted to divorce her; hence there is no *igun* to avoid]. But in my humble opinion a woman gone missing is no worse than one who went insane, for in the latter case too she might recover sanity [and reject the divorce,

just as a missing woman, once found might do]; hence the two cases are not so different. . . . But in our case one can say that even the *gaon* R. Moshe Sofer (of blessed memory) would admit [that leniency is appropriate] as she is deliberately hiding herself out of fear. It also seems certain that when she hears he is searching for her wherever he has received word about her, she will just run off farther.

Moreover, there are grounds for likening the case at hand to the case of a woman who has become an apostate. There the Rema similarly wrote that the husband is permitted to remarry without divorcing the first wife, except that in Austria the practice is to grant her a divorce by receivership, [the Rema] reasoning simply that this would be of benefit to her. So it is a relatively easy matter to offer a remedy that will not result in bigamy on his part. Thus everyone agrees that if he has no possibility of divorcing [the converted wife], he should be permitted to remarry; they do not oblige people to try and talk her into accepting a divorce from him [and by analogy we need not force the husband in our case to search high and low for his wife]. . . . In this case, where she has betrayed him and taken herself far from him to the point where he cannot divorce her, he is not obliged to go out and shout at the hills and the like. Rather one may be lenient, and allow him another wife.

NOTE

1. The implication is that without the witness he would have no recourse, meaning that we would not permit him to marry without a divorce.

[45]

Question to R. Yitzhak Elhanan Spektor about a Husband Killed in War

Yitzhak Elhanan Spektor, *Ein Yitzhak*, *Even Ha-Ezer* 1: 19 (Vil'na: [s.n.], 1888).

I was asked by a certain scholar about an *agunah*: a single witness testified that a Jewish soldier told him that [the husband] had been killed in battle; the soldier was his friend and standing beside him during combat. Information from military officers also report that her husband was killed in battle. Your honor considered this matter in depth and concluded

that she is permitted to remarry; you have asked me to render my opinion on this.[1]

NOTE

1. Spektor agreed that the woman may remarry, specifically noting that the military's notification has strong probative value.

[46]

The Unwilling *Levir* and *Halitsah* (1893)

RGIA, f. 821, op. 9, d. 35, ll. 4–4 ob., 9–10 ob., 21–23.

"Petition of Itsko Moiseev Pergamenshchik, of Nezhin (Chernigov province) to the Governor of Poltava (15 October 1893)"

TO HIS EXCELLENCY, THE GOVERNOR OF POLTAVA

My daughter Roza, after a year of marriage to the townsman Elia Sholem Leibovich Varshavskii, suffered the misfortune of being widowed in the twenty-first year of her life, with the onerous religious obligation of receiving a [levirate] divorce through the ritual of *halitsah*[1] from her brother-in-law Aron Dovid Leibovich Varshavskii, as a result of her childlessness. Until she receives this [levirate] divorce, she is doomed to remain un-

married. However, this Varshavskii demands 500 rubles from me, an impoverished family man, for performing *halitsah* for my daughter, without which he obstinately refuses to grant [my daughter] her personal freedom, despite the fact that he is obliged according to the demands of the Jewish religion and general human morality.

Appealing to the protection of Your Excellency, I beg you to save my daughter from eternal solitude with all of its terrible consequences and humbly ask you to instruct the rabbi of Gadiach to perform the ritual of *halitsah* for my daughter, without which her young life is in peril of moral fall [because she cannot marry].[2]

"Petition of Roza Itskov[na] Varshavskaia (née Pergamenshchik) of Nezhin, to the Governor of Poltava (27 July 1893)"

1. On 24 February 1892, I was married to the townsman from Gadiach, Elia Sheelia (Saul) Leibov[ich] Varshavskii, then being twenty years old. After the wedding, I moved with my husband to the town of Gadiach where my husband lived with his oldest brother, the townsman Aron Dovid Leibov[ich] Varshavskii. On 4 March 1892 he concluded a written agreement in which they proposed to open a soap factory (as a partnership) in the town of Gadiach. For this purpose my husband invested 500 rubles in capital—the dowry that he had received from me—which was managed by his brother.

At the end of February 1893, my husband suddenly became seriously ill. According to our [Jewish] law and custom (and what I learned), my father sent for the spiritual rabbi of Borzny, who after his arrival invited the state rabbi of Gadaich to obtain a divorce. Together, they proposed that my husband grant me a divorce.[3] My husband's brother, Aron Dovid, intervened in this [matter], demanding 300 rubles from my father for this divorce. My father received a telegram about this from Rabbi Khaitin. However, it was already too late to conclude this matter: my husband died on 17 April. As a result, I remained a widow who was not divorced—that is, a *halutsah*.[4]

According to our Jewish law, as Your Excellency can verify from the issued statement of the state rabbi of Nezhin (number 114) if you please, it says [the following]. The fifth book of Moses [Deuteronomy 25: 5–10] states: if a man dies without leaving children, if he has one or more living brothers, then one of them is obliged to marry the wife of the deceased brother. If, however, he does not wish to marry her, then he should give her a divorce through the ritual of *halitsah*. Until this ritual has been performed, the wife of the deceased

has no right to marry anyone.[5] Therefore one of the brothers of the deceased husband must free the widow through the ritual of *halitsah* so that she can enter into a second, legal marriage.

2. Meanwhile, despite the fact that the brother of my deceased husband Aron Dovid Varshavskii has used his capital of 500 rubles (the dowry that my husband received from me and invested in the soap factory), he does not wish to permit me to remarry under various pretexts and therefore, in his opinion, I must forever remain a widow despite my young age.

As proof of the above, I refer to the contract cited above, an anonymous letter, [and] two telegrams from the two rabbis.[6] Given the foregoing, I humbly beg Your Excellency to order whomever is responsible to insist that my *levir*, Aron Dovid Varshavskii, be compelled to give me permission—that is, a divorce through the ritual of *halitsah* and to grant me the possibility or remarrying.

"Journal of the Rabbinic Commission" [17 January 1894]

The townsman from the town of Nezhin, Itsko Pergamenshchik, and his daughter Roza, the widow of the townsman Elia Leibov Varshavskii of Gadiach (who died childless on 17 April 1893) interceded to compel his older brother, Aron David [Dovid] Varshavskii, to perform the Jewish religious levirate divorce for his sister-in-law. According to the petitioner, he has refused, demanding 500 rubles for the performance of this ritual.

This circumstance has been confirmed, and the witnesses' testimonies are in the file. Moreover, the assistant [state] rabbi of Gadiach, Madievskii, explained that he—recognizing that Aron Varshavskii is obliged to free his sister-in-law through *halitsah* according to the laws of the faith—exhorted and admonished him to comply. However, he did not succeed because of some financial dispute between Varshavskii and the father of his sister-in-law; in his own statements he does not consider himself responsible to perform this divorce.

Regarding the reason for the refusal, in the protocol of inquiry on 19 November 1893 he testified that, although Jewish law imposes [the responsibility] on the brother of a childless couple to take the widow as his wife, as there are three brothers in his family (of whom he and the next brother are married while the third is single), he does not consider himself obliged to marry the widow of his brother or consequently to give her a divorce.

Upon examination of the case, the Rabbinic Commission adopted the following considerations: according to Jewish law, a woman who has been left a childless widow does not have the right to remarry until one of her brothers-in-law frees her from this marital [bond] through *halitsah*. In addition, the following order is observed in obtaining this divorce: if the position of the brothers-in-law is such that they are all married or all single, the request for *halitsah* is presented by the widow to the oldest among them. If this *levir* cannot fulfill the ritual with the sister-in-law because he is married to her sister or absent, then the request for *halitsah* is presented to the next brother, in the order of seniority, until one of them gives her a divorce. However, when there is even one unmarried brother among them, then the request for *halitsah* must be presented only to him, even if he is the youngest, only if he is of age and legal capacity to grant this divorce and is not absent.[7]

Conclusion: Applying the stated principles to the case under examination of the widow Roza Varshavskaia, the Rabbinic Commission finds that the brother-in-law of the petitioner, Aron Varshavskii, has grounds to avoid performing the ritual of *halitsah* for her according to Jewish law, and the request should be made not to him but to his youngest, unmarried brother, if he is in his majority. If, however, this *levir*—out of some financial calculation—does not wish to give his sister-in-law Roza Varshavskaia a levirate divorce (which would be contrary to moral and religious laws), then she should turn to the rabbi in the hometown of the brother-in-law with a petition for an amicable settlement of their mutual claims and an inducement for the *levir* to fulfill the divorce. However, if the brother-in-law does not then carry out his religious obligation, they may apply measures of compulsion based on Jewish religious law, as the Rabbinic Commission laid out in the journal in the case of Gitla [Gitlia] Mogilevskaia, namely:[8]

(1) a prohibition on the obstinate brother-in-law to marry until he has freed his sister-in-law;

(2) forfeiture of his right to claim the deceased brother's inheritance;

(3) an obligation to provide the widow Roza Varshavskaia with a decent level of material support from his own means.

NOTES

1. [A Jewish woman whose husband died before they had children (called a *yevamah*) was chained to the husband's brother, who was referred to as a *levir*; that is, she was not permitted to marry anyone else until her husband's brother released her from her obligation to marry him. According to ancient Israelite custom, the brother-in-law was obliged to marry the childless widow of his brother and name their firstborn child after the deceased "so that his name is not obliterated from Israel" (Deuteronomy 25: 5), or to release the widow through a ceremony of *halitsah*, or levirate divorce. In Russia, the option of marriage (*yibum*) was not available to an already married *levir* due to restrictions on polygamy, and in contemporary Jewish practice, as well, levirate divorce was the much-preferred option; hence the levirate divorce was the only alternative. The ceremony of *halitsah* required the widow to remove a shoe from her *levir*, spit on the ground, and declare: "Thus shall be done to the man who will not build up his brother's house!" (Deuteronomy 25:9) If a surviving *levir* refused to perform this ritual, as in

this case, the widow became an *agunah*, unable to remarry for the rest of her life.]

2. [The following three pages of the petition contain various supporting documents from the state rabbi: wedding and death certificates and other information about the identities of the petitioner, the daughter, and her brother-in-law, as well as a letter confirming that Roza Varshavskaia requires the ritual of *halitsah* in order to remarry.]

3. [The state official reading this file penned marginal question marks next to this statement. The reason the father summoned the spiritual and state rabbis was so that the husband could grant a conditional divorce (*get al-tenai*) in case of death so his wife would not require a levirate divorce from her brother-in-law. As the metrical books of Khar'kov show, some husbands gave their wives conditional divorces before they embarked on a long journey or entered the military, so that the wife would not become *agunah* in the event of the husband's unconfirmed death. Some ailing husbands (as in this case) who were childless also granted their wives a conditional divorce to save them from the complications of a levirate divorce. See DaKhO, f. 958, op. 1, g. 1872, ll. 6 ob.–7; op. 1, d. 1871, d. 10, ll. 30b–4, and many more.]

4. [She misuses the word *halutsah* here. A *halutsah* is a woman whose brother-in-law refuses his levirate duty to marry her (*yibum*) but rather performs *halitsah* (levirate divorce) instead. The point is that one cannot be a *halutsah* unless one has undergone *halitsah*. The importance of the status is that a *halutsah* cannot marry a kohen.]

5. [Deuteronomy 25: 5–10 reads: "When brothers dwell together and one of them dies and leaves no son, the wife of the deceased shall not be married to a stranger, outside the family. Her husband's brother shall unite with her: he shall take her as his wife and perform the levir's duty. The first son that she bears shall be accounted to the dead brother that his name may not be blotted out in Israel. But if a man does not want to marry his brother's widow, his brother's widow shall appear before elders at the gate and declare, 'My husband's brother refuses to establish a name in Israel for his brother; he will not perform the duty of a levir'. [. . .]" If he insists that he will not marry the widow, "his brother's wife shall go up to him in the presence of the elder, pull the sandal off his foot, spit in his face, and make this declaration, 'Thus shall be done to the man who will not build up his brother's house!'" (Jewish Publication Society translation).]

6. [The anonymous letters and telegrams are not included in the file. Rabbi Iosif Magievskii of Gadiach stated that the telegrams (sent during the husband's lifetime) dealt with the conditions of the divorce, especially the matter of the 300 rubles and the husband's belongings. However, the contract of the two brothers about the soap factory is included, as well as the undated letter from the state rabbi of Nezhin, which was translated from Hebrew. It informs Roza Pergamenshchik that her husband died on Saturday and will be buried on Saturday. She must observe the seven-day mourning period (*shiva*). He also warns her that since it was too late to obtain a divorce from her husband, "you may remain with your father for a long time"—a reference to the problem of securing a levirate divorce from her brother-in-law.]

7. [If the *levir* were a minor, the *yevamah* had to wait until he came of age to perform the ritual of *halitsah*.]

8. [This was a similar case in which the brother-in-law demanded a large sum of money to perform the ritual of *halitsah*. As the Rabbinic Commission informed the Ministry of the Interior: "This symbolic rite often plays into the hands of unscrupulous people as an instrument of extortion from widows, dooming them to live in celibacy" (See RGIA, f. 821, op. 9, d. 21, ll. 6–36 ob).]

[47]

Emigration to America and Desertion of a Pregnant Wife

RGIA, f. 821, op. 9, d. 581, l. 2; f. 821, op. 8, d. 296, ll. 64–65.

"Petition of Tema Iankelevna Mezhibovskaia to the Kiev Provincial Board (18 October 1905)"

My husband, the townsman Khaim Aronov[ich] Mezhibovskii of Fastov, left for America about five years ago, leaving me pregnant and with two children in Russia. Approximately three years ago, my husband sent a *get* in accordance with Jewish law, addressed to one of the spiritual rabbis of Fastov. I was to receive this document through Tevel Iankel Kobal'chuk. In the presence of the latter and other individuals, two spiritual rabbis of Fastov carried out the ritual of divorce. Considering myself divorced, I live by my own labor and raise my two children.[1] However, this is already the third year that I have not succeeded in obtaining a certificate of divorce. The spiritual rabbi will not give me a [*get*] *petur*[*in*][2] — that is, a certificate in Hebrew about my freedom [to remarry]. Nor will the state rabbi give me a metrical certificate of divorce because [he does not] consider me to be divorced. Thus it turns out that I am neither divorced nor married. According to the teachings of the Jewish religion, [my] divorce is considered legal and authentic; therefore it should be recorded in the metrical books of divorce. However, I do not know why the document of my divorce has not been registered and who is the cause of this. Meanwhile, I am deprived of the possibility to marry, and I live under onus of being an illegally divorced woman. [. . .][3]

"Journal of the Rabbinic Commission" [1910]

We heard [. . .] the complaint of [Tema] Mezhibovskaia against [state] rabbi Kligman for his denial of the dissolution of her marriage with Khaim Mezhibovskii.

Account of the Case: [. . .] Rabbi Kligman explained that a rabbi is permitted by law to carry out a divorce upon the presentation of a written statement by the divorcing parties, not otherwise. Thus he, as the rabbi, specifically demanded on this occasion her husband's statement and evidence of his signature on the bill of divorcement sent from America. Mezhibovskaia refused to fulfill these demands. Hence the rabbi, finding this divorce to be illegal — which was performed without his knowledge — did not consider himself authorized to register this in the metrical book.

Deliberation: Based on a thorough examination of the circumstances of this present case, the Rabbinic Commission dwelt on the following considerations. Neither civil law nor the regulations of Jewish dogma require a written statement from the husband to dissolve his marriage. Although [state] law[4] demands a decision by the [state] rabbi or his assistant to dissolve a marriage, in fact this kind of case is resolved by experts on Jewish law on marriage and divorce or by spiritual rabbis (according to the special regulations of Jewish legal proceedings).

Moving then to a discussion of the actions by the Fastov rabbi Kligman [. . .] it is necessary to recognize the rite of dissolving a marriage through the delivery of the divorce document to the wife by a messenger in the presence of witnesses and two spiritual rabbis, performed with the observance of all established religious regulations. It would be proper to suggest that Rabbi Kligman himself does not question this; he explains his refusal to register the divorce of the Mezhibovskii couple in the metrical book on the basis of his demand that she submit an official, certified, written application of the husband, which [condition] Tema Mezhibovskaia did not fulfill. Notwithstanding the circumstances, Rabbi Kligman, from the point of view of Jewish law, had no grounds to refuse Tema Mezhibovskaia's request. If he has doubts about the proper delivery of the divorce document to Tema Mezhibovskaia, then in any case he would have been obliged to examine the present case and for this purpose find out by asking the messenger (in the presence of witnesses and rabbis). If the divorce document is considered legal, it should be recorded in the metrical book.

Conclusion: Upon thorough deliberation, the Rabbinic Commission comes to the conclusion that the actions of the Rabbi Kligman of Fastov should be recognized as incorrect and that the rabbi should reexamine Mezhibovskaia's request.

NOTES

1. [It is not clear what happened to the child with whom she was pregnant when her husband left. She only mentions two children here.]

2. [A *get peturin* (document of conclusion) or *get* for short is a bill of divorcement.]

3. [She goes on to request a certificate of divorce.]

4. [The document made reference to the *Svod zakonov Rossiskoi imperii*, vol. 9, part 1, article 1328.]

Family Life after Conversion to Christianity

[48]

Divorce of Jewish Spouses

"Petition of the New Convert, Nadezhda Nikolaevna Maksimova, to the Archpriest of Nikolaevskii Cathedral in Vil'na (4 July 1844)"

LVIA, f. 605, op. 2, d. 456, ll. 10–11 ob.

The Most Reverend Bishop of Kovno [. . .] announced to me on 30 June of this year the claims lodged by the husband of my former faith, Judaism — Meer Shein, a Jew and townsman of Volpo [Grodno province]. I have the honor of replying that I have become a faithful sheep in His flock in the Russian Orthodox Church by the mercy of the all gracious Lord God and salvation of our Jewish Christ and have received the sacrament of the body and blood of Christ. I do not wish to continue my marital life with my former husband, the Jew Shein. Moreover, I consider myself absolutely free from everything in Jewish law and the rituals of the [marital] obligation in question. I also flatter myself with the hope that the authorities — civil and, in any event, spiritual — will recognize me in accordance with the reasons given below:

(1) The age difference between Meer Shein and myself is enormous. He is more than sixty years old, which he himself admitted before Your Excellency. This is clear from the fact that he is completely gray in appearance. I ap-

pear no older than thirty to all who know me, even though the Grodno district police registered me as thirty-three years old for some reason unbeknown to me. If not based on law but on experience, I make so bold as to explain that many people in such marriages are celibate, which I would wish to be from my soul, but I would not dare vouch that I am. If the government would be content to force me to remain married to this old man, I fear that this coercion will abet the possible violation of my sexual probity.

(2) The sacrament of marriage demands from people who are married: (a) harmony; and (b) mutual conjugal relations except in the case of unequal ages; without this, a marriage cannot be considered solid.

(3) Can I have love for this Jew Shein, despite the teachings of Jesus Christ to love your enemies? When he learned that I intended to be baptized, he cast the most extreme aspersions on me, which were not only linked to him but to all Jews in this case — that allegedly I had taken 600 silver rubles during our previous Jewish marriage. But he could not have given that to me because he had nothing to give. Can I live with him in love and harmony when he thanks God daily in his morning prayers, according to the Jewish customs, and will most certainly always thank God

daily that He did not make him a Christian or a heathen (which is all the same to them), but a Jew?[1] Can it be pleasant for me to hear such disparagement [and] scorn every day toward those people who have faith in the son of God and to whom I now belong, redeemed by His priceless blood? What spouse does not fall ill at heart, knowing that her husband despises not only her fellow Christians but her too? He considers all who do not follow the teachings of the Talmud to be eternally lost, and that is why he is unafraid to threaten not only the property but the lives of all Christians, as those who do not observe the instructions of the Talmud. This is because he does not answer before God, but even expects to receive an eternal reward for this.

Can he be my husband when on the holiday of Passover, according to Jewish ritual, I as the wife should pour and pass a glass to my husband. But as a Jew he should not drink from, let alone take in his hand, a vessel touched by a Christian if he does not want to violate the laws of his faith. Indeed, he only became my husband to deprive me of life more quickly, for the Talmud allows the slaying of any Jew who has embraced Christianity.

There was no sanctity in my conjugal relations with the Jew Shein because I did not succeed in preparing myself for such relations through the ritual of immersion [in the mikvah], which is required by Jewish law. This was well known in the synagogue. But now insofar as I no longer am a Jewish but a Christian woman, there can never be such conjugal relations: as a Christian woman, I can never fulfill the ritual of immersion. That is because I scornfully renounced all the teachings, rituals, immersions, and even conversations, eat-

ing, and drinking with Jews, according to the Church rules in the first and second banns.

(4) Here are the reasons why it is impossible to fulfill the indicated [demands] in the Jew Shein's petition (*Svod zakonov Rossiskoi imperii*, volume 10, article 39). Because I am wed to Christ and have given my oath to the universal Church of Christ, I cannot and do not want (and indeed no one can force me) to violate it, either by word or deed. So I subject myself to accountability before the Church according to its regulations and [if I abjure my oath] will be condemned to eternal death with the devil and all the Jews who repudiate Christ, the Son of God.

Presenting all this to Your Grace, I have the honor to ask that my petition be presented to the Most Eminent Platon, Bishop of Kovno and Kavaler, so that Your Grace will defend me from all of the Jew Meer Shein's claims and encroachments. Reject his petition and permit me to enter freely into a legal marriage with a person of the Christian confession, if that comes to pass.[2]

NOTES

1. [She is referring to daily benedictions in which traditional Jewish men bless God for not making them non-Jews, slaves, or women.]

2. [In his petition to the Bishop of Kovno (30 June 1844), the husband, Meer Izraelevich Shein, demanded the return of his wife who had converted in accordance with civil law: "It is forbidden to enter into another marriage when the first legal marriage exists and has not been dissolved." He made reference to the *Svod zakonov Rossiskoi imperii*, vol. 10, statute 15). There was no final resolution to this case, although the bishop scribbled in the margins to investigate it.]

[49]

Petition of Roza Vil'ken of St. Petersburg for a Separate Passport from Her Lutheran Husband (1887)

RGIA, f. 1412, op. 214, d. 57, ll. 1–4; 60–64; 152–57 ob.; 170–78 ob.

"Petition of Roza Vil'ken (née Nakhmanova), Resident of St. Petersburg, to Emperor Alexander III (received 11 November 1887)"

ALL GRACIOUS MONARCH!

My extremely desperate position and fear for my life and health force me to resort to Your Emperor's mercy. Having married the collegiate registrar, Emil Gustavovich Vil'ken in 1879, a short time after the wedding I already became convinced that I had cast my fate with a person of an extremely egotistical and unrestrained disposition, who looks upon his wife as a house servant whom he can treat like a slave who has no rights.[1] To characterize the irrational despotism of my husband, I cite only a few examples. When our first baby was born in 1893, my husband meddled in the pettiest detail from the very moment of her birth. Caring for the baby in the most offensive manner with curses and threats, he demanded that I blindly submit to his will in every respect, as though there was nothing unreasonable about his demands. He forced me to breast-feed the baby when I suffered mastitis — in spite of the fact that the baby was satiated and there was no need to nurse her at all. As a result, I experienced terrible pain. Also, until the birth of this first baby, I had a few miscarriages solely because of his senseless demands to travel with him by coach and, despite the doctor's admonition, to make a journey that was too long and wearisome for me during pregnancy. When I felt extremely tired and sick, he did not allow me to consult a doctor or midwife, considering that to be a completely superfluous waste of money. During my pregnancy last year, he forced me to take cold summer baths although I begged him not to insist on this: I suffered from leg cramps and knew that the baths would be harmful to me. Whenever he is dissatisfied with me about something, he prohibits me from seeing my closest family members. So this past winter he forbade me to correspond with my own sisters who were abroad, and now he does not permit them to visit me or (for that matter) me to call on them.

Having been educated at the Riga City Institute for Girls and then having completed a program at the St. Petersburg Conservatory, I feel the need to occupy myself with reading. But he deprives me of this pleasure and absolutely forbids any reading, even journals to which he himself has subscribed. Reading, in his opinion, is only a frivolous waste of time, which I should devote exclusively to housework, and [I] should spend the whole day in the kitchen. In addition, I should sew the dresses and undergarments for both our children; he even refuses me the modest request to bring a seamstress, even for one week, to help me.

Last year, our oldest three-year-old daughter began to cough at night. My husband woke me up and told me that the child was sick with croup. Without saying a word, I got up from bed and went to the child. Convinced that her temperature was completely normal, I returned to the bedroom and told my husband that she had a slight cold but not croup.

My simple observation infuriated my husband in a terrible manner; despite that it was nighttime, he began to shout frightfully and curse. He would have certainly hit me if my sisters, who were visiting us then, had not run into the bedroom, where they saw my husband preparing to fling himself on me with his fists, screaming furiously: "If you dare contradict me again, I will surely kill you." The next morning, in the presence of my sisters, he repeated coldbloodedly: "I repeat to you again, with your sisters as witnesses, that if you dare to contradict me, some day I will kill you."

During my last pregnancy, he did not allow me to lie down to rest during the day and at night awakened me in the crudest manner if I moaned in my sleep, yelling at me that I did not let him sleep. My husband's despotism reached a point where I did not dare to express my opinions on any household affairs. If I say one word to justify myself, attempting to explain the correctness of an action that my husband does not approve of, he views this as recalcitrance; his terrible rage is the inevitable consequence of any innocent word that I express. It is enough for someone to break a dish to provoke his rage. He hurls the crudest curses at me, swearing at me with vulgar words, raising his fists and threatening "to smash my head." And indeed his threats turn into acts. He repeatedly hit me, without any cause on my part, when we went visiting; he was angry that I had not locked the door. He himself was holding the key in his hand before we left.

Another time when I was pregnant, as I sat on the floor in front of the dresser sorting undergarments, he pushed me so hard that I fell on the floor. Similar incidents recurred often; his premeditation is evident from the fact that he sends away the household or waits for an opportunity—when I am alone with him—before subjecting me to physical and moral torment. Also, not long ago, as in October of this year, he threw a solid chair at me with such force that one of the legs broke off. Fortunately, it did not fall on me; otherwise it would certainly have maimed me. At that time I was still completely weak and had not recovered from giving birth. My husband not only failed to show the slightest remorse for his behavior but began to demand that I ask him for forgiveness. After he insulted me deeply, he forced me to ask his forgiveness on my knees. It is impossible to recount all the humiliation and insults that I endured during the eight-year period of conjugal life. I never complained to anyone; nor did I allow myself to think of separation from my husband because of the children (so as not to deprive them of their family hearth). But now I am losing strength and see no end to my suffering. The thought that the children, who are growing up, will witness their father's barbaric treatment of their mother inspires in me a determination to end the conjugal life, which promises nothing but grief and unhappiness.

Although not all the circumstances set forth here can be proven, some may be supported by the testimony of witnesses. I am sending these testimonies: my brother Maksimilion Iulianovich Nakhman, my sisters Mariia and Fanni Nakhman, Edla Lendevist, Friderika Kekolainen, and the peasant woman Varvara Fedorovaia. Although the latter already served as our nanny for two years and should know about the facts set forth here, for many reasons I allow for the possibility that she may decline to give testimony altogether or may not tell the truth.[2]

On the basis of the above, I humbly ask that you give me and my minor daughters (Valeriia, age four, and my still unbaptized six-week girl) a separate passport from my husband. Summon my husband to the Chancellery to hear his testimony but not before my preliminary interrogation because I am living in his apartment on the corner of Sapernyi Lane and Znamenskaia Street (the Liteini section, 3rd district, house number 13); once he learns about the contents of my present petition, my life will obviously be in danger. I humbly ask that you send the notice not to my husband's apartment but to the apartment of my brother, the candidate of law, Maksimilion Nakhman, Bol'shaia Morskaia Street, house number 39, apartment 21.

This petition is in the words of Roza Iulianovna Vil'ken, as transcribed by her sister Mariia Nakhman.

"Emil Vil'ken's Petition to His Imperial Majesty's Chancellery for the Receipt of Petitions (24 January 1888)"

Not having received the summons to the Commission [Chancellery] for Petitions in the Sovereign's name for an explanation, I submitted my petition on 14 December 1877.[3] Separated from my children (whom I have not seen for more than two months), in this petition I take the liberty to explain the circumstances of the case.

I married a Jewish woman, who was baptized at the time of her marriage to me. Before the wedding, there were disagreements and misunderstandings about the dowry, in which my in-laws showed me such a bad side that I did not want to become related to them. At that time, my wife completely shared my opinion on this matter. However, after a time her relatives managed to gain my forgiveness and began to visit us almost every day. I forgot all about the past and treated my wife's two unmarried sisters like my very own sisters. I loaned them money upon their arrival [in St. Petersburg] and helped them to arrange an apartment, hung pictures, and so forth — in a word, I was like a loving brother to them, at times proving more of a brother than their own brother.

In 1886 one of the sisters became dangerously ill, and on the doctor's advice, she had to be sent abroad quickly. Her brother, a lawyer, could not help them obtain the necessary money at this time. So again I loaned them 200 rubles (which I borrowed); although I was repaid, nonetheless I did them a great

service, again demonstrating my great devotion to them.

Having been abroad for a year to convalesce from the illness, they began preparing to return to St. Petersburg. During the time of separation, my wife greatly longed for her sisters and began to carry on an intense correspondence with them. It was as though she were writing to a lover, not her sisters; at times that aroused a jealousy in me, for this kind of love for a sister seemed excessive and somehow affected me. During that year, my wife and I had misunderstandings, as is common with all married couples, so that once I even asked her brother to speak with her and bring her to her senses. We worked out everything and began to live together, amiably and amicably. In February my wife became pregnant and, being predisposed to miscarriages, lay in bed for two and half months out of precaution (three and a half months for the first child). Happily thinking that God would give us a second baby, I attended to my wife with complete attention and love. I brought her various delicacies, put her to bed myself (and we have two servants), fluffing up her pillows and providing books for reading. Sitting on her chair next to her bed, I had dinner, drank my coffee and tea, and spent all my free time away from work near her. She repeatedly asked me to go to the theater but I refused — so as not to leave her alone.

If one takes into account that I performed my spousal responsibilities, was always close to my wife, and was full of tenderness (when I found reciprocity), it is clear that our relationship was the very best and serves to refute my wife's testimony that "the disagreement between us allegedly began four and a half years ago." The conception and birth of our second daughter on 14 September serve as proof [that] we lived in complete harmony until her sisters returned from abroad!!

The month of May came and the arrival of the sisters approached. To make my wife happy, I suggested that she invite them to stay with us at the summer cottage in Terijoki [Finland], which the sisters immediately accepted. Having received a leave [from work] and knowing that my wife was in the company of her sisters, I often traveled to St. Petersburg to rent an apartment while visiting my parents, where I spent a week or a week and a half. My wife spent entire days with her sisters and in their conversations probably told them about the disagreements between us the previous year [1886], which she had provoked. Under their influence, my wife made up her mind to write a letter with the most outrageous contents to her brother abroad. Thus was a ruinous step created for me (I only learned about this now and have witnesses). Not knowing anything about the conspiracy against me, I continued to be courteous and kind—I bustled about and brought meat, vegetables, delicacies, and other things from town.

As Jews, my wife's sisters will be converting to Russian Orthodoxy this 19 January in order to obtain the right to live in St. Petersburg. They intend to open a shop for children's attire. My wife became enthusiastic about this idea and began to sew clothes, hats for dolls, and things that would be profitable to sell at once. I am certain that they had a definite plan. My wife had decided to leave me, gain [custody of] the children, and no longer be parted from her sisters who always lived at her expense.

I myself was pushed away from my wife because the sisters and midwife slept with her. They always left the bedroom *after* I left for work. I was deprived of seeing my wife as I would have liked—in a word, disorder and anarchy were introduced into my house, and I began to wish strongly that the sisters would leave us, all the more so since my wife had fully recovered from giving birth. They paid no attention to my request that the sisters move to their own apartment in view of [our apartment's] crowdedness. My wife was becoming indifferent, ungracious, and querulous, and finally I am convinced that the reason for

this was the sisters. To put an end to this, I forcefully asked them to leave and not to visit us until harmony had been restored between me and my wife. Nevertheless, they began to come—against my wishes—after I left for work. Learning about this, I was forced to ask them in writing not to visit my house any longer in view of the agitation against me. Further, when I reproached my wife that she and her sisters had turned against me, that her sisters divided us to destroy our family happiness, and asked that she give up her sisters, she showered me with the most unfair accusations. She declared that, "she does not love me and would sooner be parted from me than from her sisters!" I then realized how wrong it was to take the sisters into the house. All my efforts to calm my wife, all the arguments, the persuasion—all were in vain.

My wife's sisters secretly prepared a shelter for my wife and children in revenge against me; they invited their brother, the lawyer Nakhman, the lawyer Liven, and another person with whom I am completely unfamiliar, and these people kidnapped the children, who are the most precious to me. The barbarians destroyed my homestead, dragging along a sack crammed with property that they had stolen with their own hands.

My wife acquiesced to her sisters: lacking her own character and losing willpower, she followed the plan drawn up in advance. Someone else's family expected her at a designated time. The brother, who occupies a social position, took on the case, and his friend (the lawyer Liven) were invited to wage a terrible, unequal battle with an abandoned and grief-stricken husband. After the kidnapping of the children, Mr. Liven came to Boike (my place of work). Handing me the key from my writing table, he declared to me that I would find in it all the keys to the house (in fact all the keys were locked in the table). However, they had completely emptied all the cupboards and chest of drawers. Then he declared (18 November) that a petition was to be filed about me in His Majesty's name [. . .]; in fact, it had already been filed on 11 November.

I [then] persuaded and consoled my wife by saying that I could forgive her sisters. But she replied: "It is too late now (recalling the filed petition) to run away, not from the cruelty of a husband but from his embrace!"

The case against me was managed by the laywers Nakhman and Liven.

My wife disappeared to some unknown whereabouts. As a result of the petition to the city governor (*gradonachal'nik*), the police detective informed me where my wife and children were, and it turned out that they were at a family friend of my wife's sister (whose doorkeeper of this house had been bribed [not to say my wife and children were there]). Having lived there for more than a month, my wife disappeared again, giving a false [forwarding] address. Only through a police detective did I learn that she had settled at 41 Mukhovaia Street, in a furnished room, and had been inscribed in the house register, together with her sisters, as a Jew (although she is of the Lutheran faith).

They spoiled my wife as the youngest in the family and did not accustom her to anything—neither housework, nor saving, nor neatness—and all these shortcomings in her upbringing have been bitterly repulsive [to me] during my whole life. Having a headstrong and persistent character, she constantly provoked arguments and always kept the last word for herself.

The neglect of housework was the motive and reason for our disagreements. How many times did I ask her to consider my needs, to feed me properly—the worker [that is, breadwinner] of the house—for my strength, at least for my good? How many times did I remind her about her slovenliness, carelessness, and forgetfulness? I asked her to try as she promised, if not to make me happy then for all of my care, labors, and worries for her good, if only not to give me a reason to consider myself deceived and unhappy in everything.

Abandoning her home, housework, responsibilities, and her own husband, violating the oath that she gave in her relationship to him, before God and his sanctuary, my wife still shows cruelty and evil to her husband, even resorting to lies! Standing with me on this ground, she now sees in me only the strength—if only to find legal support in my rights—that can compel her to return the kidnapped children. To prevent this, I am sure that she would not find it reprehensible to portray me as a criminal. It has been two months since I have seen my adorable children. The youngest daughter is now five months old, [and] I cannot baptize her. I cannot note her as my own legally born [girl] in my documents. The most convincing request to see them was heartlessly rejected (I attach an original copy of the letter and response to it).[4]

My poor children are in a furnished room, but deprived of everything good and vigilant care. They are deprived of their beds, indispensable things for small children, and bath. They feed the oldest daughter, a four-and-a-half-years little one, food from a cafeteria. My wife has no means, not only for the children but for herself, and has agreed to live on someone else's bread and depends on the charity of her brother. I earn more than 3,000 rubles a year, having a complete household and every comfort. I do not want my children to be destitute; as their legal father, I demand them back from my wife.

Given the above and in defense of my rights, I have the honor to report that: (1) for the sake of the children whom I love more than my life, I am prepared to forgive my wife for all the offenses that she has afflicted on me and am prepared to accept her in my house, which she left against my will; (2) I do not consent to give my wife a separate passport for residency; and, (3) I humbly ask the Commission [Chancellery] to become irate at my enormous grief and to order the quick return of my oldest daughter Valeriia, leaving the youngest with the mother while she is breast-feeding.

I am certain that the question of our marriage depends on the decision regarding this question [of the children]. In that case, my wife would abandon all unnatural bonds and willingly follow the child to me at home. I will be redeemed from the terrible grief.

"Emil Vil'ken's Petition to His Imperial Majesty's Chancellery for the Receipt of Petitions (18 July 1888)"

In the addendum to my petition of 24 January of this year and in light of the intention of the Chancellery to reconcile me and my wife, I take the liberty to report that I do not want to reconcile with her at all and that all my attempts on this subject have been in vain. Neither the most convincing requests nor the poor condition of my health, nothing — nothing moves my wife. After our discord, her sisters even broke their own promise to their dying mother that they would not convert to the Christian faith and embraced Russian Orthodoxy in order to paralyze my anticipated protests that my children were in Jewish hands, and in order to carry out their plan for great success.

After an agonizing terrible five months, my wife decided to allow me to come to the children but only with this purpose — with the strict demand that I report about this every time and do not come without her permission.[5] I have the honor to include my wife's written reply to my request. Thus only in April did I begin to see my children again. My wife was untouched by tears over my broken life, my grievous position, or the staggering scene of my visits with the children.

My wife declared to Pastor Findeizen, whom I had asked to reason with my wife and to reconcile us, that in light of her sisters' conversion to Russian Orthodoxy, she would not return to me under any condition. What kind of indissoluble tie should exist between our lives and the lives of her sisters? The pastor did not act on my request. The pastor, who had advised me at first not to reconcile with such a wife but

to get divorced, did nothing about my request because he had gone over to her side. Not long ago, I was at a loss regarding a strange occurrence — because it turned out that one of Mrs. Nakhman's (the wife of the lawyer) friends, a Mrs. Russova, had a close, friendly relations with the Findeizen household.

The sisters, wanting to occupy a fashionable house, deferred their intention until this fall, merging their fate with that of my wife. Receiving sufficient support from their brother, they know neither need nor deprivation. They rented a summer cottage in Lesnoe and took their furniture out of storage. They have two servants and live in contentment. They have one interest, one fear, one plan, one means — one undivided life.

However, I must endure a small portion of happiness, with the highly arrogant need to ask permission to be a guest in the house, to visit my legal children. It was such a bitter and difficult visit! When I brought some kind of children's toy, my wife commented that she did not want this. Another time, when I gave my daughter candy, my wife commented that she forbids this and at my question: "Do I really need to ask your permission about this?" she replied, "Yes! And if you will not do this, then you may not come at all. Do not forget that you are in my house and with my permission!" I cannot even caress my child in the presence of my wife, who comments that the child is no longer so young that she needs to be kissed so much.

When I want to leave, my daughter clings to me and does not let go. "Papa! Is it not true that you are having dinner with us? Well then, do me a favor: have dinner with us. I will give you my candy! Do not leave yet! Darling papa, you are my dear! Well then, live with us!" There you have it: the words of my unhappy child, who is not guilty of anything, tear at my whole soul! This has no effect on my wife. She stands there, listens to this, sees the tears welling up in me, and can stand like a statue — cold, unwavering.

In my opinion, it is in my wife's interest to show that we had constant disputes, that I was allegedly "eternally" grumpy and angry. This is a lie and not the truth! On the contrary, we lived peacefully and amicably, and if there were disagreements, then it was when she argued in the wrong. Not only at present do I testify to this but already in my petition of 24 January of this year, I said that there were misunderstandings and fights between us — purely of a household nature — that could cause such great unhappiness for me.

We are all sinners! And if there is a couple anywhere, where does this [kind of discord] not happen? I repeat that I got along well with my wife, that I loved my wife more than anything until the last moment; I placed her above all else. If you were to find out anywhere we lived, if you were to call to account the people who served us, then this question would be cleared up completely and everything about her untruthful testimony would be revealed!

During all this time, my wife's relationship to me was haughty, crude, and even impertinent. She always said to me that she would obtain a separate passport from the Chancellery for the Receipt of Petitions, that she would receive a judgment on the children and then she would not let me see them. Well, think then! I said to my wife: "It is not like I am married to three [women]. I am married, but to one!" My wife said to me: "For the loss of all three!" This response explains everything!

It boggles the mind how the representatives of the defenders of "truth and law" — such as the lawyers Nakhman and Liven — violate the law [. . .][6] and, after outrageously fabricating the case, decided to petition in His Majesty's name — to the All Gracious Protector of the law.

As for the accusation about the chair, I long considered reporting that when I pushed back hard on the chair, one of the legs broke off, that I was completely alone in the room when this happened, and that subsequently, when I

went to work, only then did I hide it behind the door. My wife and her sisters, the three of them, laughed loudly, clapped their hands, and exclaimed, "Thank God! Thank God!" in the kitchen — in the presence of the cook and nanny. In addition, Fanni Nakhman importunately and at length persuaded the nanny Varvara Fedorova to testify that I allegedly threw the chair at my wife. "Well, nanny, let's go to our brother's to testify against the master. You are not afraid. Our brother is clever! He will not leave you for the entire century for this." If I really lived so dishonorably with my wife, is there any reason to think that, of my own volition, I would have taken into my home my wife's sisters, who would have been the most dangerous witnesses?

Regarding the witness Nikolai [Maksimilion] Nakhman, I listed him not as a witness for my side but as a witness against me: it is natural for a brother to support his sister's side. I would add that Nikolai Nakhman, having heard this from me, concluded the case; he immediately ended the correspondence with me. Incidentally, he said that he saw and felt how I was an obliging husband and father, and no one would know better than he to witness this, for he constantly came to our house.

Given the merciful and gracious words of His Excellency Davydov, who deigned to say to me: "You should not be arguing! You have a hot-tempered character, but of course your wife has no right to run away!" and equally His Excellency's hint "that I should wait while the baby is still breast-feeding," I place all my hope that my family will soon return.

They have affected my strength and health, which, according to the opinion of the doctor treating me, poses a great danger. Hence I have decided to ask the Chancellery for the Receipt of Petitions in the Sovereign's Name respectfully: have mercy on me and my grievous position and return at least my [older] daughter to my home — that is, if my wife herself does not wish to return, adding that as soon as [my daughter] is with me, I will positively agree to everything that only a wife can demand of her husband: (1) I will forget and forgive her from my soul if she would only want to return to my house, and will continue to treat her with the same respect with which I treated her earlier; (2) I would agree, if my daughter were with me and if my wife were to demand it, even to divorce on the grounds of her action. I will agree to all this! Only I cannot live without my children, even if only one! I cannot destroy my heart and love for the children!

I beg the Chancellery for the Receipt of Petitions submitted in the Sovereign's Name to recognize my right—the right of fatherhood—and not to take away the purpose of my life. Do not deprive me of my children. *This would be like my death sentence!* Have mercy, Your Imperial Majesty, All Gracious and Great Sovereign, and heed the weak voice of an innocent child who calls to her father: "Dear Papa, you are my dear! Live with us!"

"Report of the 'Family Office' of His Imperial Majesty's Chancellery for the Receipt of Petitions (29 July 1888)"

In my opinion, multiple interviews with the Vil'ken couple have established that the most salient deficiencies of the husband consist of his egoism, stubbornness, and stupidity. He does not even understand that his wife may have a certain sphere of activities upon which he has no right to intrude. He constantly interferes in all household questions. Vil'ken does not allow contradiction because he considers himself clever in everything—more than his wife. He is convinced that only his orders are appropriate. He does not understand that his wife had grounds to be offended when he allowed himself to yell and to create scenes over every trifle because the egoism in him has developed so much that he considers it his *right* to do everything that *pleases* himself. The awareness that his wife is dependent on his arbitrariness and meekly submits to all his demands gives him a certain plea-

sure. Being despotic at home, he can easily seem like a kind and gentle person to other people. Sometimes he really gave presents to his wife and was kind toward her, but he only tried [. . .] to show that he was a exemplary husband and that, as such, he had the right to demand complete submission from his wife to his caprice. However, there is no doubt that he himself is convinced of his sincere love for his wife, but his egoism and limited mind imagines that he must direct all her activities and thoughts. It is mainly in this aspiration that he turned her into a dehumanized object, a slave.

Mrs. Vil'ken creates the impression of being an oppressed woman with difficult family circumstances. She has a kind character; she is smarter than her husband, but she does not have enough energy to fight his despotism successfully. Based on her modest character, she undoubtedly did not show her husband all the resentment provoked by his tyranny and the danger brought out by his new crude antics; she does not even dare to speak openly about her opinions. The moral torment that she daily endured finally drove her to protest openly against her husband's treatment, shown by leaving his home together with her children.

Conclusion: Taking into consideration Vil'ken's abnormal view of his marital rights and responsibilities, it would be unjust to force the petitioner [Roza Vil'ken] to continue her life with him, and Mrs. Vil'ken is better suited to direct the proper upbringing of her children than her husband. His separation from the family for a certain time may have a beneficial influence on his character and make this dissolute man listen to reason. I propose that the humble petition of Emil Vil'ken for the return of his daughter Valeriia be rejected; that Roza Vil'ken be granted the right, without the consent of her husband, to live together with her children anywhere in the empire on a separate passport from her husband for a term of one year. The passport will be renewed if the husband does not reform and during the designated time is not persuaded of the extreme anomaly of his relationship to his wife. This order will be explained to the Vil'ken couple through the St. Petersburg city governor; I have also asked him to issue an order to provide Roza Vil'ken and her daughters Valeriia and Regina with a separate passport from her husband for a term of one year. The case will thereupon be considered closed for further execution.

NOTES

1. [Roza Vil'ken converted to Lutheranism, whereas her sisters converted to Russian Orthodoxy. His Imperial Majesty's Chancellery for the Receipt of Petitions, which investigated this case, noted that there was a ten-year age difference between the couple. According to a report of His Imperial Majesty's Chancellery for the Receipt of Petitions on 29 July 1888 (that is, a year after her Roza's first petition), the wife was thirty-three and her husband was forty-four; their daughters were Valeriia (five years old) and Regina (ten months old). RGIA, f. 1412, op. 214, d. 57, l. 170.]

2. [At the summons to the His Imperial Majesty's Chancellery for the Receipt of Petitions, the wife explained that the husband had destroyed their "marital trust" because he had a closer relationship to the nanny than with herself (RGIA, f. 1412, op. 214, d. 57, l. 170 ob).]

3. [In his first petition, the husband explained that he had learned just a week before that his wife had submitted a petition to the Chancellery. He complained that his wife and her relatives had taken everything from his apartment (except for the furniture) and had taken his children into hiding. He asked for the return of his children, at least of his oldest daughter, "so that I am not deprived of a purpose of life and brought to despair" (ibid., ll. 22–23).]

4. [The letters were written in German.]

5. [The note in German from his wife read: "Since you want to see the children, I have nothing against it. Come on Tuesday at 3:00 p.m. to my place. Roza Vil'ken."]

6. [The document cited *Svod zakonov Rossiskoi imperii*, vol. 11, part 1, 251 and 256, point 3.]

[50]

Petition of Sofiia Zil'berman of Dvinsk to Change Jewish Surnames of Converted Children

RGIA, f. 1412, op. 8, d. 345, ll. 1–10b, 2–20b.

"Petition of Sofiia Zil'berman of Dvinsk (Vitebsk Province) to Emperor Nicholas II (1896)"

Many years ago, I had a sexual relationship with the now deceased collegiate secretary Petr Nikolaevich Petrov, with whom I had two children. Because my deceased lover thought about consecrating our union in marriage (and repeatedly said this to his acquaintances and even his spiritual father), I — someone who then professed the Jewish faith — received holy baptism according to the rites of the Russian Orthodox Church and also baptized my children. However, as he was constantly sick and had a very weak will, Petrov postponed his intentions from day to day until he died in March 1889. So in the end he did not marry me.

Meanwhile, our children have already grown up: Vladimir is studying in the third year of secondary school, and my daughter Liubov will complete her studies in the gymnasium this year. The poor things suffer from ridicule and questions from their peers for carrying a Jewish surname, "Zil'berman." They will have to endure this even further when it comes to earning a living. So my daughter, upon completing her studies in the gymnasium, will have to find a position if only to earn a living. What if my dove should want to obtain a position as a teacher's assistant or governess? Even now she encounters [questions]: is she not Jewish? what was her father? and the like. And bitterness toward her mother and father has crept into her soul. Why did they not give her [his name]? Why should she suffer for sins she did not commit and constantly feel the backhanded glances of those around her?

Great Sovereign! A poor, exhausted woman dares to fall at the foot of the throne and prays for a gift of mercy. Let it be ordered that my children Liubov and Vladimir Zil'berman adopt some Russian name—Petrov or Serebriakov (a translation of the surname Zil'berman), if only as some protection from their illegitimate origins of which my poor children are completely innocent.[1]

"Record of the Chief Assistant of the Gendarme Administration in Dvinsk (1896)

29 March 1896, the town of Dvinsk. I, Lieutenant Colonel Priklonskoi (the assistant head of the gendarme administration of Vitebsk province for Dvinsk, Drissa and Lepil'sk districts) on the matter of the petition of Sofiia Zil'berman, a townswoman of Dvinsk, to change her surname submit this report (based on a strict, secret investigation):

In 1874 Sorka Bentsionova (a townswoman from the town of Iakobshtadt, Kurland province; a Jewish woman) married Elia Abrumov Zil'berman (a townsman from Dvinsk; a Jew). After living with her for two and a half years, [the husband] died, leaving a daughter Dveira with Sorka. After his death, Sorka began to lead a dissolute life and, among other things, cohabited illegally for eleven or twelve years with the retired official Petr Nikolaevich Petrov and allegedly had another son and daughter of the Jewish confession with him. Before Petrov's death on 1 April 1889, Sorka was baptized on 4 September 1888 for protection from the authorities and for possible assistance. Receiving the name Sofiia with the name Petrova after her godfather, she also baptized her children. At present, her twenty-three-year-old daughter Vera Aleksandrova (a village teacher by status), sixteen-year-old daughter Liubov (who is completing her studies at the Dvinsk Gymnasium for Girls), and fourteen-year-old son Vladimir (a student at the Dvinsk secondary school) live with her. All her children have been educated by charitable gifts.

The townswoman Sofiia Petrova Zil'berman petitioned the Vitebsk Financial Chamber about registering with her children in the Dvinsk Townspeople Society and about changing the surname. It is said that she was denied the latter, although that is not evident from the decree of the Vitebsk Financial Chamber (number 11783, 11 May 1893). The lawyer Srol' Iakobson wrote a petition in the Sovereign's name for her. Although the townswoman Sofiia Petrovna Zil'berman was baptized with her three children, until now they have been moving around in the Jewish community.

NOTE

1. [The petitioner offers as one option to keep the Yiddish root word for "silver" and replace it with the Russian equivalent, *serebro*.]

Death : Orphanhood, Guardianship, and Property

[51]

Family Letters of the Rozenshteins and Machlevichs (Kiev Province, 1890s)

Private document of Carolyn Rosenstein[1]

Yechiel Faivishevich Machlevich
to His Son-in-Law Aharon Vulfovich
Rozenshtein (11 February 1902)

OL'SHANKA [OL'SHANA, KIEV PROVINCE]
SHALOM!

I cannot describe our sorrow and sadness when we learned from your postcard that you have not received our letter. Since the day our mother [Esther] died,[2] we have sent you three letters and were impatiently waiting for your answer. Clearly, the postman deliberately did not give you the letter.

My poor son! Hadassah [Esther] has died and left us to suffer, and how can I console you, when I myself have not received enough condolences. Your grief is my grief. Your pain is my pain, As the Sages said: "A sigh breaks half the body of a person,[3] and we are forced by our Holy Torah to guard our souls." We cannot recover our loss because it can never return. Because of that, we have to exert ourselves to make our grief easier for us, and only her memory will be saved for us in all the days to come.

According to our faith, she is better off than we because she is free from an ugly and troublesome world and has gone to the world of truth, and her soul is still in the prime of life with all the holy souls of Paradise. Certainly, her soul was not touched by sins and crimes because she was only one year old.[4]

Her soul will pray for [her] son, whom we shall raise according to our faith and shall call him in her name, and we shall be blessed by light in our life.

From your father who is writing with tears in his eyes and sorrow in his heart.

[Postscript from Chana Machlevich,
Aharon's mother-in-law]

Best greetings to my son Aharon Rozenshtein from your mother, Chana Machlevich. Your old father and Yaakov send their greetings.

[Postscript from Uncle Israel Bakrinskii
and his family]

My greetings to my brother-in-law Aharon. Your Uncle Israel, his wife, and their daughter, Rachel.

[Postscript Yechiel Machlevich to A[ha]ron
Rozenshtein]:

When we came home, people at home began to complain about why we did not bring you with us, and if they could have seen you, it would make their plight easier. I excused myself before them and told them that it is impossible for you to leave all your business. Then they were reconciled [to the fact].

Because of that, my dear, do not think that with the death of my daughter our bond fell apart and that we (God forbid) stopped loving you. We love you now as we loved you in the past and in spite of the distance between us. Our correspondence will keep us in touch because this is our consolation, and we will not stop writing to you.

Letter of Shayndel Machlevich [Sister-in-Law] to Aharon Rozenshtein (12 February 1902)

DEARLY BELOVED BROTHER-IN-LAW
AHARON ROZENSHTEIN,

With trembling hands, I take my pen in hand in order to write to you a letter, dear brother-in-law. From the time mother returned from you, we have already written you two letters, but have not received any reply. I broke into tears for my broken heart that in such a short time, you have forgotten us. My pen informs you that on the 11th of this month, mother and I visited your son and our child Moishele. Thank God, he is healthy. He has begun to put on weight and sleeps in a very clean place. We go to see the child every week.

Dear brother-in-law, I am asking you to write letters to us more often than you have written. You will console us with your dear letters. You should write a separate letter for me [and send it] to Kiev because I will come there on the 12th of this month.

I would have written more but the tears are choking my heart. Stay well.

[Postscript from Rachel Machlevich]:

I greet you, dear brother-in-law. From me, Rachel Machlevich.

Postcard from [Chaim Zvi][5] to Aharon Rosenshtein (13 March 1902)

TO KIEV, ZHITNOI MARKET,
TO THE STALL OF MR. ISTOMIN
FOR MR. GLUVSHTEIN FOR
AHARON ROZENSHTEIN

VASIL'KOV [KIEV PROVINCE]

TO MY LEARNED AND INTELLIGENT
AHARON ROZENSHTEIN AND FAMILY!

I have received your letter. I am surprised that you write that you have not received any letters from me. I am writing to the same address that you have given me, but when I received your other postcard, I understood that you did not go to Kiev.

Today I want to inform you that your son Moishele, thank God, is healthy and putting on a little weight. The money is being spent for sugar, dried bread, potato flour, and soap. The wet nurse is asking for money. She needs it by Passover. Please try to send it to my address because she asks me every day if I have mailed a letter to you already. I do not have any more news. My daughter Tzirel went to the wet nurse to look at your son Moishele.

My wife Feigi, daughter Tzirel, and I wish you all the best.

Postcard from [Chaim Zvi] to Aharon Rozenshtein (19 March 1902)

VASIL'KOV [KIEV PROVINCE]
TO MY LEARNED AHARON!

We received your postcard and want to inform you that we are looking for another wet nurse because this one absolutely cannot nurse. Nor do we like her [lack of] cleanliness. When you come, you will decide what is best for yourself. In the meantime, Moshe is well and healthy, but he is not putting on enough weight. My daughter Tzirel goes to [see him] every day and so does your mother-in-law. Chana was at the house in Vasil'kov and Shaynder [also] visited him. They went three times a day. Moshe sends you his best greetings, Feigi also.

Best greetings to all the members of your household.

Postcard from Yechiel Machlevich to Aharon Rozenshtein (9 April 1902)

TO MY DEAR AHARON ROZENSHTEIN,

I want to inform you that we are all well. Your mother-in-law returned home. Her foot is almost healed, and we hope that she will be completely well very soon. Concerning the child, I want to inform you that the doctor said that there is no danger, and it is only necessary to give him breast milk in a bottle. And the hundred-ruble [note] — I lent to a trustworthy person for 1.25 percent interest a year. When I am in Kiev, I will give the promissory note to your brother Israel Dov. How is my friend Israel Dov now?

FROM ME, YOUR FATHER-IN-LAW
YECHIEL MACHLEVICH

Postcard of Chaim Zvi to Aharon Rozenshtein (11 April 1902)

HIGHLY RESPECTED AND LEARNED
MR. AHARON ROZENSHTEIN,

I have received your postcard. I have never yet received such a letter. I want to tell you that Mrs. Feigi was at the doctor's with Moishele. He examined him well and said that, God forbid, he does not have a bad disease, but he ordered us to feed him every two hours with a rubber nipple, to keep him clean, and the child, thank God, is fine. The wet nurse came to my home during the holiday, and I saw to it myself. There is no other news.

YOUR CHAIM ZVI

Postcard from Chaim Zvi to Aharon Rozenshtein (23 April 1902)

TO THE RESPECTED AND LEARNED
MR. AHARON ROZENSHTEIN,

I received your letter today and want to inform you that the wet nurse almost cast your son Moishele into my house. She said that she cannot feed him. I found out that the neigh-

bor's firstborn had died on the eighth day. I sent my wife Feigi and they have already agreed on 75 rubles a year; she is happy that God sent us such a nursemaid. Moishele simply came back to life. His face is completely different. She is childless and very clean! The baby is bathed every second day in a big [tub]. The other wet nurse was a big murderess. The most important thing we want to find out is how you will be sending money. What if she demands money, where will we get it? You do not have to look for another wet nurse because Moishele is already used to her and her milk.

Stay well.

My wife Feigi and Tzirel and all the others send their greetings.

NOTES

1. Another translation and additional documents can be found in Carolyn Rosenstein, *Secrets, Sorrows, and Survivors: Aron Rosenstein's Letters for His Son, 1889–1923*, 199–218.

2. [Esther Machlevich was married to Aron (Aharon) Rozenshtein on 25 January 1901, as shown in the wedding invitations and metrical registration by the state rabbi of Vasil'kov. Correspondence about their family business can be found in document 128. (Rosenstein, *Secrets, Sorrows, and Survivors*, 95–107). Esther's father refers to her as "our mother" because she died shortly after giving birth to her son, Moshe. Carolyn Rosenstein observes, the congratulatory letters "express concern about her postpartum illness," 199.]

3. [*Ketubot* 62a.]

4. [Rosenstein suggests several possibilities for this statement that Esther was "only a year old": perhaps it refers to the duration of her marriage (one year), her pregnancy, or length of time since Aron had asked Esther to marry him (*Secrets, Sorrows, and Survivors*, 200).]

5. [According to Rosenstein, Chaim Zvi [surname unknown] may have been Esther's uncle because her aunt's name was Feigi; Esther stayed with an Aunt Feigi during a trip to Vasil'kov to meet Aharon at the state rabbi's office on 25 January 1901 (*Secrets, Sorrows, and Survivors*, 207).]

[52]

Legalizing a "Homemade" Last Will and Testament

LVIA, f. 447, op. 27, d. 235, ll. 1–3.

"Petition of Etka Leibovna (Movshova Rafal'sonova by Marriage) to Emperor Nicholas I (7 April 1842)"

Your Most Exalted Highness and Majesty, Great Sovereign Emperor Nikolai Pavlovich, Autocrat of All the Russias, Gracious Sovereign! The Vil'na townswoman, Etka Leibovna, Movshova Rafal'sonova by marriage, submits a petition about the following:

My deceased mother, the townswoman of Vil'na, Basia Eliashevich Leibovaia Kovnorova, in agreement with her husband and my father, the Jew Leib Iudelevich Kovner, signed her will on 8 December 1841 in the presence of witnesses (Vil'na residents): nobleman Iuri Pepkovich, Iu. Kotorek, and the Jews Izrael Girsh Movshovich Aizenshtadt and Osher Berkovich Gordon. She bequeathed to me, the petitioner, in perpetuity, one room and also a small part of the courtyard in a one-story stone patrimonial house. She bought them with her husband (my father) in the city of Vil'na on the street leading from Zashkovaia Street to Zelenyi Bridge, number 797, at a value of 200 rubles. As my mother Basia Kovnerova has already died, I enclose (in addition to my mother's aforementioned will) my mother's death certificate issued by the state rabbi of Vil'na (3 April [1842], number 24) to strengthen my legal position to gain possession of the room and section of the courtyard. I humbly ask that you order my petition to be accepted in the chamber of the civil court in Vil'na, having completed the legal procedure in the matters of this chamber, and to return it to me with the proper certificate.[1]

NOTE

1. [The state declared that it could not recognize a homemade will because it had not been signed by the deceased and had only been signed in Polish (by two witnesses) and Yiddish (by the other two witnesses), without any Russian words in the document.]

[53]

Guardianship of a Grandchild in the Kiev Orphans' Court

DAmK, f. 164, op. 1, d. 1197, ll. 1–4, 7–7 ob., 14–16.

"Petition of Khaia Berkova Burshtein, Resident of Kiev, Kuznechnaia Street, to the Kiev Orphans' Court (received 7 May 1899)"

On 2 May 1899, my daughter Dvoira (that is, Debora), who was formerly married to the civil engineer Samuil L'vovich Betgilel died in Kiev. She left behind her young daughter, my granddaughter by the name of "Liubov'" (Liuba), who was born on 20 September 1888. As I report this, I have the honor to request humbly that the Orphans' Court pay favorable attention to the following circumstances.

(1) My deceased daughter, who was in no condition to tolerate the indescribable troubles to which she was subjected by her husband, was forced to live separately from him; she lived with her only daughter in Kiev with my family. For her part, she announced her demand for a formal divorce from her husband.

(2) My former son-in-law Betgilel, not having a permanent residence, constantly travels from one city to another, often going away on business to the remotest parts of Russia.

(3) During the whole time that he was married to my daughter, my former son-in-law never sent support for her and the baby. In 1897, my deceased daughter had to submit to her husband's demand that she leave her daughter with him in order to obtain a passport, which was necessary for a trip to some health spa for treatment. Instead of taking care of the child himself, he sent her to his sister who lives in Saratov, where they treated my granddaughter with such indifference that to this day she cannot recall the period that she spent with her father and his sister without shuddering, and begs me not to send her to them any more.

(4) The property left by my deceased daughter consists of money and items that she received exclusively from me and her deceased father; she did not acquire anything from her husband.

(5) My former son-in-law, in all likelihood, will remarry and then my granddaughter's position in his home will be even more difficult than [it was at] the time she was with his sister's family.

Given these circumstances, I have the honor to request humbly that the Orphans' Court appoint me as the exclusive guardian over the property and the person of my minor granddaughter Liubov' (Liuba) Betgilel. In addition, I enclose: (1) a metrical certificate of my daughter Debora's death;[1] (2) a certificate of Liubov's birth.

"Report of Khaia Burshtein to the Kiev Orphans' Court (19 May 1899)"

In compliance with the decree of the Orphans' Court (12 May 1899, number 1387), I have the honor to report that the property left after the death of my daughter Dvoira (Debora) Betgilel consists of following: (1) a piano; (2) six oilcloth-covered chairs; (3) a cabinet with glass [doors] for books; (4) a small collection of various books; (5) various diamond objects (earrings, ring, diamond brooch with a little chain, a gold brooch with diamonds), a gold watch with a chain, acquired by her long ago, and also a pair of diamond earrings that she acquired in April 1899; and (6) cash in the sum of 28,708.98 rubles.

In conformity with the attached copy of the arbitration court's decision, it is clear that her share [of the inheritance from her father Iosef Burshtein] amounts to 35,000 rubles, but in agreement with my own account [. . .] taken from the formal book of the heirs of Mr. [Iosif] M[oshkovich] Burshtein, my deceased daughter spent a sum of 11,017 before her death. In agreement with the decision of the arbitration court (6 November 1898), my deceased daughter expressed her wish that the money remain with the heirs, who agreed to manage Burshtein's case. They will disburse [the money] for the minor Liuba Betgilel's use — all the capital at 7 percent per annum — so that I can raise her respectably, and during this time her capital will increase. Until her illness, my deceased daughter in private conversations told me that she has still some other financial documents and that she would receive them from Yalta, where she spent all winter; upon receiving them, I shall present them to the Orphans' Court. I entrust my son Tobian Burshtein to file this report.

"Protocols of the Suit against Debora Betgilel for Violation of the Passport Laws (Kiev District Court, 1892)" [Earlier Case]

Deposition of Samuil Betgilel (19 March 1892): My name is Samuil L'vovich Betgilel. Rank: civil engineer of transportation. Forty years old. Confession: Jewish. Place of residence: temporarily at the Hotel Angliia in Kiev, but in a few days I am traveling to Vil'na to search for a position. Literate. Never prosecuted. Debora Betgilel is my wife. I wish to give my testimony.

I have already lived with my wife for five years. For more than a year we have not lived with each other in harmony. Since November 1889, I have been working with building contractors and travel often on business. On

22 or 23 December of last year [1891], I left for Odessa and Tiraspol' and traveled to some other cities. I returned to Kiev on 9 March 1892. During this time I wrote my wife two letters. When I returned, not knowing where she was, I filed a statement with the police; it turned out that she was living in Bershtein's apartment number 19 on Zhandarmskaia Street, which she had rented. It also turned out that the baby and nanny lived with her. I do not know whether my wife lived under the name Burshtein, but she is the daughter of the merchant Iosif Burshtein. When I left, I did not give her any passport, and because the term for the apartment on Sofievskaia Street expired on 20 January, my wife probably moved to a different apartment. Before my departure from Kiev, my wife and I did not talk about a divorce; we only decided to separate temporarily until I found a job. If my wife lived on a document under the name of Burshtein (that is, her maiden name), she was forced to do so because she did not have any document [bearing her married name]. The term on the apartment had expired, I was not in Kiev, and her position was hopeless. If so, she lived as the daughter of the merchant Iosif Burshtein — that is, [the name on] the passport she would have received if we had formally divorced. I do not wish to subject my wife to trial for this case and would ask that the process be terminated. I have nothing more to add.

Deposition of Iosif Moshkovich Burshtein (no date): Fifty-six years old, Jewish confession, first-guild merchant of Kiev. I live permanently in the town of Dubno (Volhynia province) and temporarily in Kiev at 9 Alekseevskaia Street. Literate. I have never been prosecuted.

Deberta Betgilel is my daughter. I wish to testify in this case. My daughter Deberta has been married to Samuil Betgilel for four years. She did not live in harmony with her husband, and her husband offended her very much. In December last year, her husband abandoned her and went somewhere. I was not in Kiev at the time; I arrived here only when I learned about the hopeless position of my daughter and the fact that she was living on a document that my brother Iudko [Iudel] Burshtein obtained for her from the Kiev Municipal Office. I have nothing more to add.

Following my signature, I add that my daughter's name is Deberta, not Debora. She called herself Debora because this is how her husband called her. Her real name, I repeat, is Deberta, as it is listed in my family register.

Deposition of Iudel Moshkov Burshtein (no date): Fifty years old. Jewish confession. Second-guild merchant of Brest. I live at 9 Alekseevskaia Street. Literate. I have never been prosecuted.

Deberta Betgilel is my niece. Deberta had a very stormy relationship with her husband. Her husband constantly insulted her. In December last year Samuil Betgilel left Kiev, deserting his wife and without leaving her a residency passport. After her husband left, Deberta came by, told me about her position, and I stopped by the Kiev Municipal Office with her and requested them to issue her a document as the daughter of Iosif Burshtein, a first-guild merchant. They issued her a document at the municipal office, and she resided on this document after her husband's departure. Samuil Betgilel said that he would give his wife a divorce. After the divorce she would have lived on the document of her father and under the family Burshtein. I have nothing more to add.

Deposition of Deberta [Debora] Betgilel (19 March 1892): My name is Deberta (and not Debora) Iosifovna Betgilel, the wife of an engineer. I am twenty-two years old. Jewish confession. My place of residence in Kiev is 19 Zhandarmskaia Street, but in a few days I will be moving to Dubno to live with my father. Literate. I have never been prosecuted.

I have been married for five years to the engineer Samuil L'vovich Betgilel. My husband and I had a stormy relationship, and he offended me very much, for no reason being jealous constantly of my attachment to others. More than once I asked him for a divorce, but for a long time he did not agree. In December of last year, he agreed to a divorce, but after a time he retracted his word. He left, after collecting all his belongings and selling the rest. He did not give me a passport, thus leaving me in a hopeless position. I went to my uncle Iudel, and we decided to obtain a residency document as "Deberta Burshtein" at the Kiev Municipal Office because my father is a first-guild merchant of Kiev. I have lived on this document for three months. When my husband was leaving, he told me not to go by his surname. I did not know that I was not permitted to live on a document based on my father's family register. If I had procured a divorce, then I would have adopted my maiden surname. I have nothing more to add.

After my signature, I add that my name is Deberta, and I have always been called that but my husband called me Debora.

"Petition of Samuel L'vovich Betgilel (Railway Track Engineer, Permanent Resident of St. Petersburg) to the Kiev Orphans' Court (2 July 1899)"

On 2 May 1899 my wife Debora (Dvoira) Iosifovna (also Ios-Gershova) Betgilel (born Burshtein) died in Kiev. My wife's brother [. . .] Tobian informed me of my wife's death in a letter dated only on 5 May 1899 and sent from Kiev on 8 May 1899, as is evident from the postmark of the Kiev Post Office. Upon receiving this letter in St. Petersburg on 10 May 1899, I quickly left for Kiev, where I arrived at 11:00 a.m. on 12 May, and only on 19 May did I petition the Kiev Orphans' Court to appoint me, on the basis of the law, as the guardian of the *property* of my minor daughter Liubov', who was born to my legal marriage with my deceased wife Debora on 25 September 1888.

I did not ask to be named guardian over the *person* of my minor daughter Liubov': they explained to me that the custody of my daughter belonged to me as a father, by virtue of the laws of guardianship established in family procedures and does not demand a special appointment by the Orphans' Court.

As I reviewed the case, I discovered that my petition of 19 May 1899 had still not been granted, and that on 7 May 1899 the mother of my deceased wife, my dear mother-in-law Khaia Burshtein, had already petitioned the Kiev Orphans' Court (in her capacity as my daughter Liuba's grandmother) that she be appointed as the sole guardian over the person and property of my minor daughter (and her granddaughter) Liubov'. The Orphans' Court upheld Khaia Burshtein's request, according to a decision made on 12 May 1899, and sent her a decree (number 1387) appointing her as the guardian over the person and property of the minor Liubov' Samuilovna Betgilel.

Such feverish activity of Khaia Burshtein, who counted on obtaining a guardianship edict in time, serves as the most eloquent explanation for the following: (1) why Khaia Burshtein was not good enough to inform me by telegram about the death of my wife Debora; (2) why her oldest son [. . .] Tobian, on her instruction, informed me about my wife's death in a letter, which was sent from Kiev to St. Petersburg with such calculation that between the time the letter reached St. Petersburg and my arrival in Kiev all the procedures in the Kiev Orphans' Court to appoint Khaia Burshtein as guardian over the person and property of my daughter would have been concluded, and she would have the decree of guardianship; (3) why, during my stay in Kiev, the existence of the decree of guardianship of 7 May 1899, which was in Khaia Burshtein's hands, was concealed from me; (4) why I turned to the Orphans' Court with the above-mentioned petition, knowing nothing about what had transpired and waited

for over a month for notification from the court.

A priori, [this look at] Khaia Burshtein's nature and purpose of action serves as clear proof of how much the contents of her petition correspond to reality and the truth. I would be in the right to limit my remarks and indications to the extreme speciousness of each of the five points in Khaia Burshtein's petition of 7 May 1899, which she submitted with the sole purpose of smearing my moral character before the Orphans' Court and obtaining a decree appointing her as the *sole* guardian of the person and property of my minor daughter Liubov' in a completely unseemly manner.

However, I do not wish to make use of this right, so formal in character, and have the honor to explain the following: my marriage to Debora, née Burshtein, took place on 26 May 1887. From the day of our wedding until the beginning of 1892, we lived together first at the Mozheika Station on the Libavo-Romenskoi Railway (where I served in the post of the division chief of railway repairs) and then in Kiev (where I was employed in construction work). From 1892, for lack of work in and around Kiev, I was forced to go to the Saratov steppes for the construction of the Tambov-Lamyshinsk line, where I worked again as the chief of the railway division. As is well known, this entailed constant traveling, moving around, and a life fully devoid of the most basic necessities. That is why one with the slightest love and respect for his family does not demand that the family necessarily live in the place where the husband resides; that would entail a sacrifice in general, especially for a sick wife suffering from severe ailments, tuberculosis of the lungs, female diseases, and other illnesses. Since then, our family life developed in this manner: owing to my professional specialty and the types of positions that I held, I had to be on the road constantly for long periods of time, while my wife had to live here [in Kiev] for the treatment of her physical ailments, where it was possible to have serious and reliable assistance at any time, and at the first possibility to travel to some health spa abroad or in Russia.

For a complete description of my wife's illness, I can and must cite this sorrowful page: soon after the wedding, for lack of good medical care at the Mozheika station, she lived for over two years in Kiev where she received treatment. Despite the fact that the Mozheika station is considered a country holiday location, I was forced to send my wife to Libava in 1888 and 1889 for the spa baths on the advice of the doctor, to Franzensbad [Františkovy Lázně] and Bad-Feslau in 1890, to the Andreevskii estuary in 1891, to the springs in Odessa and the estuary in Shabo [Ukraine] for a vineyard treatment in 1892, 1893, and 1894, to Franzensbad and Shandau [on the River Elbe] in 1897, to Bad Reichenhal and Interlaken in 1896, to the Caucasus and Crimea in 1897, and finally in 1898 to Franzensbad, Baden, Bad Ischl, and the Crimea, where she remained almost until her death. My deceased wife obviously spent a large part of the year and our marriage, voluntarily or not, separated from me so that our actual life together was strained of its own accord. Moreover, because of a serious illness like tuberculosis of the lungs, she was strictly forbidden to have a true married life [sexual relations] to avoid having consumptive offspring; I was to stay away from her. In general, though our ties were not sundered (even at the beginning of 1892, when I left for work in the Saratov steppes as indicated above) while my wife and daughter went to her parents in Dubno, I sent money by post as much as possible as evident from the list that I preserved, which I enclose. Often, at the smallest possibility, I took leaves [from work] and traveled to see my wife and personally to provide her with money and a temporary passport for trips abroad. In the summer of 1896, I stayed with my family in Interlaken [Switzerland], and in 1897 my daughter was with me in Saratov for almost a year while my wife was in the Caucasus and Crimea for more convenient treatment (without the distraction and worry about our daughter). In May 1898 my wife stayed for two weeks with me in Moscow where I was on a business trip, and I spent the Christmas holidays with my family in Yalta.

I always expressed sympathy and compassion toward my wife in everything and sacrificed myself a lot for the true good of my family. Not only did I not receive a "demand for a formal divorce" (which my wife allegedly told to someone, somewhere, sometime), but I did not even receive a request to give my wife a separate passport for residency. Hence our marital state was legal and continuous. It cannot, and should not, be considered torn asunder in light of some unproven attempt to obtain a divorce, especially when according to [the law][2] a marriage can only be formally dissolved by a spiritual court [the *beit din*]. [. . .]

That I lived with my wife at Mozheika Station can be certified by the former arbitrator of the Justice of the Peace Court in Shavli district at the time, Mr. Seleznev, who resides in Kiev and serves as manager at the Kiev Region of Transportation. He knew me even before my marriage to Debora Burshtein because I was one of the founders of the school at the Mozheika Station. A list that I have preserved (with various sums of money that I sent from my place of work for the years 1893–96) attest to my concern for my wife; incidentally, I sent 220 rubles in the name of Iakov Kagan, whom my wife's sister married, as is evident from the decision of the arbitration court on 12 May 1898.

The wife of the doctor for the Bobruisk Reserve Battalion, court councilor Dr. Grigorii Iakovlevich Abramivich, can testify about how they cared for my daughter in Saratov from August 1897 to 25 May 1898 at the home of my sister's family, and also about the intellectual and respectable upbringing of their own children. Of the latter the son is already a doctor; the oldest daughter completed her studies at the gymnasium and is now continuing her musical education at the Saratov Music School, while the youngest graduated from the gymnasium this year. Similarly, the fact that my daughter Liubov' took her exams in May 1898 at the Mariinskaia gymnasium in Saratov and entered into the first year [of school] can be attested by: all the members of the Major General Shreitffel'd and Deibner families, the brigade doctor (state councilor Shreder), and family members of the honorary citizen Iosif Alekseevich Perl'man, and doctors Kaplan and Shulman (the latter is the state rabbi of Saratov) with their own private practices. Compared to this, it is impossible not to notice that Khaia Burshtein *herself* and all the members of her family have not received any education, and only her youngest son studies at the gymnasium.

I myself was educated at a secondary school, completed the course of study at the Institute of Engineers of Transportation, and am now an employee of the Ministry of Transportation in the Department of the Railroad, with a salary of 5,400 rubles a year (see the list of ranks in the official publication of the Ministry of Transportation for 1898). I serve on the Saratov Board of Guardians for children's shelters under the patronage of Empress Mariia, thus bearing concern for other people's orphans. I therefore possess all the qualities to have custody over the person and property of my own daughter, who is left without a mother.

At my insistence, the arbitration court resolved on 13 May 1898 that, of the inherited property of my wife's deceased father Ios-Gersh (also known as Iosif) Moshko-Vol'fovich (also known as Moiseevich) Burshtein, my wife Debora (Dvoira) was allotted 35,000 rubles and an additional 3,000 rubles of the deceased Burshtein's real estate, [which she would receive] upon the death of the living owner Khaia Burshtein. For this reason, the widow Khaia Burshtein and other members of her family nurtured and still display manifest animosity toward me. They cannot abide the thought that our young daughter Liubov' will obtain such a significant sum of money after the death of Debora Burshtein. To reduce the [inheritance] to the minimum somehow, a plan was devised to name Khaia Burshtein the guardian over the person and property of Liubov'. This goal has already been achieved, as revealed in the account that Khaia Burshtein presented with a debit of 11,019 rubles. Such a debit provoked bewilderment on the part of the Orphans' Court, which demanded supporting documents from the guardian Khaia Burshtein. Significantly, this happened *at the first opportunity* and the question inevitably arises: how the guardian will act in the future; it is especially important in light of [the law],[3] which requires that "guardianship in all its parts is arranged so that it is for the true benefit, not for the ruin and destruction, of the person and estate of the minor."

Khaia Burshtein clearly belongs to the category of people who do not give hope [that she will provide] care [for] my daughter's health, moral upbringing, and sufficient maintenance appropriate for her status. It is impossible to expect from her parental care of the minor. This is all the more true since Khaia Burshtein has not been shy about putting words in my daughter's mouth that are beyond her comprehension and diverge from the truth, and she slanders not only me but my relatives. She [Khaia] is guilty of nothing less than nurturing malice in the soul and thoughts of my daughter toward her own father and his completely cultivated and morally trustworthy relatives. Such an environment is inconceivable for a child. It goes without saying that it is harmful for her and may corrupt her morally.

According to . . . [the law],[4] the parents of minors—before other individuals—are primarily responsible for performing guardianship obligations for their own minor children. The parents are individuals whose concern about the person and property interests of minors is most appropriate because of their natural parental feeling, relationship, and attribute of parental obligations toward their children in general. That is why guardianship over the person and property of my minor daughter belongs to me, as the father, based on the regulations of the affirmative law and natural feelings, regardless of whether I remain a widower or remarry. One or the other position cannot and should not weaken my natural parental feeling in relation to my own child, my daughter Liubov', and the possibility of my remarriage cannot be considered legal grounds to deprive me of the right of guardianship over my daughter according to the law. It is impossible not to add: what guarantee can Khaia Burshtein give that she, as a widow, will not remarry? What then will be my daughter's position and her care in this new family?

The care of my daughter will be conducted according to the rules provided in [the law],[5] avoiding superfluous and luxurious whims, and the management of her property will employ the specified rules.[6] As for turning her capital into state interest-bearing securities at 7 percent per annum (with its risks, if you please), as proposed in her petition, I will not be tempted to lose this capital.

The care of the person of my minor daughter urgently calls for placing her in one of the institutes or gymnasiums in St. Petersburg for the coming school year. That is why my daughter should be taken away from Khaia Burshtein no later than 1 August 1899 from Kiev, where I will go specifically to take my daughter to St. Petersburg, where I have permanent residency at the place of my employment.

On the basis of what has been presented, I have the honor to ask the Kiev Orphans' Court: (1) to change the decision of 12 May 1899, discharge Khaia Burshtein from the responsibility of guardianship over the person and property of my minor daughter Liubov', and appoint me as the *sole* guardian of my daughter. Give us a decree about this with an explanation addressed to Khaia Burshtein

that she is obliged to bring my daughter to Kiev no later than 1 August 1899 (according to the old style calendar) and to hand her over to me; (2) if my appointment as the sole guardian to the property of my daughter demands, regardless of the completely unsubstantiated petition of Khaia Burshtein, then investigate the circumstances that I have set forth. But, in any case, appoint me immediately as the sole guardian to the person of my minor daughter Liubov'.

"Decision of the Kiev Orphans' Court Sent to Khaia Burshtein (11 October 1899)"

On 10 August 1899, the Orphans' Court changed its decision of 12 May 1899 about appointing you with complete guardianship over Liubov', the daughter of Betgilel, in view of the fact that in agreement with the precise instructions of the law, Liubov' Betgilel's father is alive, which changes the guardianship over his minor children. Thus your role as the guardian of the minor Liubov' Betgilel must be considered terminated. You were informed about the decision of the Orphans' Court of 10 August 1899 in a decree of 11 August 1899.

Independent of this, the Orphans' Court asks you to appear in its presence to answer various questions about the guardianship over the property of the minor.

"Samuil Betgilel to the Kiev Orphans' Court (Received 20 October 1904)"

On 3 October 1904, Khaia Berkovna Burshtein (of the first-guild merchant estate) died in Kiev. She is grandmother of the minor [Liubov'], who is her heir by right of being the representative of her deceased mother Debora Iosifovna Betgilel, née Burshtein, daughter of the deceased.

The property bequeathed by Khaia Burshtein consists of: her share of the businesses and timber operations of the company "The Heirs of I[osef] Burshtein"; 24 percent of the general returns on all the businesses in accordance with point b of the arbitration court record, drawn up between the heirs of I[osif] Burshtein on 12 May 1898 and confirmed by the Kiev District Court on 6 November 1898; the furniture, silver, gold, diamond jewelry, and other objects of the deceased's toilette.

From the attached copy of the balance of Khaia Burshtein's accounting book on 1 January 1904, it is apparent that: (a) the deceased's share in the businesses of the company amounted to 59,327.37 rubles; (b) from the period 1 January to the deceased's burial on 6 October, her personal debit taken on credit at various times was 3,543.33 rubles, and the expenses for the burial and attendant ritual necessities totaled 1,980.74 rubles. A total of 5,524.07 rubles will be deducted from the balance of the deceased; (c) in addition, [the following] will be deducted from the balance of the losses of the company: the differences in foreign exchanges in interest-bearing securities and the timber fusion materials at a sum of 2,500 rubles, and two personal promissory notes in the amount of 2,500 rubles — for a total of 5,000 rubles; (d) with the general agreement of all the heirs, in fulfillment of the repeated wish of the deceased, a significant share of income is to be left to her relatives of modest means, and also spent on the erection of a monument—a provision that deducts 4,803.30 rubles from the inheritance.

Thus the value of the deceased's property based on her participation in the business of the company [. . .] after the deduction of the indicated expenses comes to 44,000 rubles (59,327.37 rubles minus 15,327.37 rubles). Her property of furniture, silver, gold, diamond items, and other objects of the deceased's toilette is assessed at 4,000 rubles by agreement of all the heirs.

The total value of all the decedent's property is 48,000 rubles (44,000 rubles + 4,000 rubles).

Because the deceased Khaia Bushtein did not leave a will, by law the inheritance must go to my minor daughter, who is in my custody, as the legal granddaughter by the maternal line of the deceased, and thus her legal heir. In addition in agreement with point a of the arbitration court record (a notarized copy of which is preserved in the file of the arbitration court), the estate property at 21 Kuznetskaia Street that remained after the death of I[osef] Burshtein was obliged to pay each of the daughters 3,000 rubles; consequently, my daughter in my custody, as the representative of her deceased mother, the daughter of Khaia Burshtein, also has [the right] to receive 3,000 rubles.

Altogether, 9,000 rubles should go to my minor daughter, Liubov' Betgilel, in trusteeship.[7]

NOTES

1. [The death certificate used the daughter's acculturated "Dora" instead of Debora or Dvoira (as her mother called her). "The wife of the civil engineer of transport, Dora Iosifovna Betgilel, died in the city of Kiev on 2 May at the age of thirty-three from tuberculosis of the lungs." DAmK, f. 164, op. 1, d. 1197, l. 3.]

2. [The document referred to the *Svod zakonov Rossiskoi imperii*, vol. 10, part 1, statutes 45 and 46.]

3. [The document referred to the *Svod zakonov Rossiskoi imperii*, statute 287.]

4. [Ibid., statutes 180, 226, 229, and 230.]

5. [Ibid., statutes 263 and 273.]

6. [Ibid., statute 268.]

7. [The file includes a power of attorney whereby Liubov' Betgilel gives her father the right to act on her behalf in all financial matters.]

[54]

Petition of Dveira Zelikman of St. Petersburg to Adopt an Orphaned Grandson (1912)

RGIA, f. 1412, op. 8, d. 299, ll. 1–2, 5–5 ob.

"Petition of the Townswoman Dveira Meerovna Zelikman, Residing on Voznesenskii Avenue, to Emperor Nicholas II (Received 31 January 1912)"

On 31 October 1910, my son Meer Zelikman (twenty-two years old), my daughter Mina Lebenshtein, and her husband Izrail Lebenshtein—who was in the third company of the Izmailov Regiment—were killed in St. Petersburg. After the murder of my sole breadwinner, my son, I remained without a livelihood, along with the son of my murdered daughter and my minor grandson, Solomon Lebenshtein (born in March 1904), my responsibility. With the death of the boy's parents, I was the sole remaining relative of this unfortunate orphan, and the St. Petersburg Orphans' Court appointed me as his guardian. I can only fulfill the responsibility to maintain and raise this complete orphan as his grandmother and sole appointed guardian by having him in my home. In view of Your Imperial Majesty's sincere concern and lofty attention to the unfortunate, innocent victim of a villainous murder, I humbly beg Your Imperial Majesty for your merciful and thorough attention to [my petition] to adopt my grandson Solomon Lebenshtein in the place of my murdered son because in my approaching old age, my breadwinner should be my grandson after the death of my son. Appended are the decree of guardianship, two certificates about the death of the father and mother of the minor, a birth certificate of my grandson, and the marriage certificate of my daughter.

"Ministry of Internal Affairs to His Imperial Majesty's Chancellery for the Receipt of Petitions (25 June 1912)"

In a communication of 29 February 1912, we asked Your Excellency for a decision on the humble petition of the townswoman of Vladimir, Dveira Zelikman, about the adoption of her grandson, the minor Jewish orphan, Solomon Lebenshtein.

Based on the law,[1] Jews living outside the Pale of Settlement may adopt only those among their coreligionists who themselves have the right to live anywhere in the empire on the basis of the general laws of the empire. The Jew, Solomon Lebenshtein, whose parents were registered to the Vitebsk townspeople community, does not have the independent right to live outside the Pale of Settlement. Thus, seeing no particular or exceptional circumstance in this present case to satisfy Zelikman's petition for an exception to the law, I propose to deny [her request]. At the same time, I see no obstacle to allowing Solomon Lebenshtein to live with his guardian, his grandmother Zelikman, until he comes of age per article 263 of the Civil Law (Senate resolution of 15 March 1905, number 2606, in the case of Levintan).

NOTE

1. [The document cited Aleksandr L'vovich, *Zakony grazhanskie* [Civil Laws] (St. Petersburg, 1886).] (1900), vol. 19, part 1, article 145.]

[55]

Petition of Izrail' Nemen of Kiev for the Appointment of a Guardian (1900)

GAK, f. 164, op. 1, d. 1309, ll. 1a–6.

"Petition of Izrail' David Moshko Itskovich Nemento the Kiev Orphans' Court (November 1900)"

After divorcing her husband (my father, Moshko Itsko Nemen), my mother continued to reside in Kiev and engage in handicrafts, having received a legal certificate from the Artisan Board. I lived with my mother because the location of my father was unknown, and it is now rumored that he has died.[1] In December 1899 my mother died in Kiev, and at present I remain without any guardianship; no one worries about my fate or arranges some kind of trade for me.[2]

Thus, having reached the age of fourteen, I have the honor to ask the Orphans' Court to appoint the private lawyer Melekh Govshievich (Mikhail Evseevich) Kailisman, who lives in Kiev at 11 Alekseevskaia Street, as my guardian. I also attach a copy of my birth certificate, and I ask that you return it through Mr. Kailisman.[3]

NOTES

1. [In a copy of his birth certificate, the state rabbi recorded the father's occupation as soldier transferred to the reserves after serving in the 45th Infantry Battalion.]

2. [The passport book showed that Izrail' Nemen's mother was Khana Rokhel Viner. She came from a farmer's family in the Jewish colony of Vil'sk (Volhynia province). In 1897 she had several children: Mania (seventeen), Doma (fifteen), Brendlia (fourteen), and Izrail' (eleven). The rabbi added a note that she died in the Jewish hospital in Kiev in 1899. Izrail' does not mention any of his older siblings as potential guardians in his petition.]

3. [Although the petition was granted, the lawyer noted that the petitioner's name had been misspelled and requested a new guardianship document from the court.]

[56]

Suit of Tauba Aizenshtadt of Kiev against a Spendthrift Son (January 1910)

GAK, f. 164, op. 1, d. 2096, ll. 6–9.

"Journal of the Kiev Provincial Administration (22 January 1910)"

The widow of a pharmacist, Tauba Aizikovna Aizenshtadt, submitted a petition to the general governor on 7 September 1910, with the following content: "My husband, Il'ia Vul'fovich Aizenshtadt, died on 19 January 1907 in the city of Kiev, bequeathing his property to me, my son Vladimir, and my minor daughters Dora and Sofiia (each with an equal share). My son's share, based on the present condition of our inherited property, may be determined at approximately 25,000 to 30,000 rubles. My son Vladimir (about twenty-one years old), who completed the Kiev Business School and is now a student at the Kiev Commercial Institute, recently began to live a most dissipated life. He signed promissory notes without any need (because he receives 150 rubles a month for his personal expenses and lives at home, with full room and board) to various shady characters and signed them under immensely difficult and ruinous conditions. Squandering his property at the instigation of people who took an interest in him (which cannot last long, obviously), my son dooms himself in the very near future to inescapable indigence because of his extreme frivolity and weak character. Independent of this, such a dissipated way of life threatens me and my young daughters with complete ruin. The promissory notes, which my son is signing and has thoughtlessly signed with such ease, will not come to an end in the near future. He receives pitiful pennies for every ruble of debt, and in the end [the promissory notes] will be presented for collection. To sat-

isfy the numerous claims on my son's debts to various rapacious sharks, our mutual inherited house will be sold at public auction. Then enters an unfamiliar and most likely a very nasty person as co-proprietor of this indivisible property, who could easily ruin me and my minor children.

Given what has been presented, I have the honor to request Your Excellency humbly to conduct a proper investigation and to transfer the present case to the Provincial Administration, the goal being to establish a trusteeship over the property and to prevent my son's further squandering [it], which entails the ruin of the entire family. If necessary, I can name witnesses to confirm the justice of my statement. In addition, I attach a notarized copy of the decision of the Kiev District Court about the execution of my husband's last will and testament."

From the attachment to Tauba Aizenshtadt's document, it is clear that the pharmacist Il'ia Vul'fovich (Vladimir) Aizenshtadt bequeathed his property—moveable and immovable—to Tauba Aizenshtadt, his son Vladimir, and his daughters Dora and Sofiia in equal portions. At the investigation, carried out by the constable of the Bul'varnyi police district in Kiev (at the order of the Provincial Administration [. . .] and upon Tauba Aizenshtadt's request), the following people were interviewed, and they testified [as follows]:

The petitioner Aizenshtadt, confirming her request in the name of the general governor, added that after his death, her husband Il'ia Aizenshtadt left immovable property consisting of an estate with a house in Kiev at

8 Kreshchatik Square, worth about 120,000 rubles. This property, according to the approved will and testament, belongs to her, her son Vladimir, and her daughters, Dora (seventeen) and Sofiia (eleven), in equal portions. The portion of the son (who will be twenty-one years old on 8 February 1911 and reach his majority), comes to approximately 30,000 rubles. Until May 1910 her son received 50 rubles each month for minor expenses with complete material support and lived a normal manner of life. Since May, falling under the influence of suspicious company who lead a fast life, he began to carouse, returning home in the morning [rather than at night]. Her admonitions as a mother and guardian had no effect. Through her acquaintances, she learned that he spent the entire night in *cafés chantants* with singers and squandered money. Since May he began to demand money from his mother, who was forced to give him 150 rubles a month for expenses. However, it turned out that this money was not enough for him, and he began to incur debts, signing promissory notes with various people. Moreover, he received paltry sums from his creditors but signed promissory notes for very significant amounts. Moneylenders, who supplied him with money, intend to present the promissory notes by bringing claims against him when he reaches his majority in February 1911, making claim to the immovable property that belongs to him. To whom specifically he has given promissory notes and for what sum, she still does not know. It is rumored that he signed promissory notes for a sum exceeding 10,000 rubles. The loans were made with the assistance of a well-known stockbroker in Kiev, the Jew Mark Il'ich Mazor, who lives at 31 Mariinsko-Blagoveshchenskaia Street and allegedly received a promissory note for 9,000 rubles on a 2,000-ruble loan. In addition, the following hold promissory notes in significant sums: the Jew Kopel Moiseevich Borochin, who lives in Odessa, and the singer Charskaia, who is departing for the town of Rostov-na-

Donu. The Jew Semen Breitbard contributed to the prodigality of her son and squandered money with him. They squandered borrowed money at *cafés chantants* and other such establishments. The son left bills at the *cafés chantants*; they brought the bills from Olympa and [the city garden] "Chateau," but [the mother] refused to pay them. She asks to establish a trusteeship over her son.

To support her testimony, Tauba Aizenshtadt presented to the constable two bills from the city garden "Chateau" bearing the signature of V. I. Aizenshtadt—one from 7 October 1919 for 90.20 rubles and another from 2 October for 115.80 rubles. She declared that these bills were presented to her for payment. With the consent of the owner of the bill, she paid 44 rubles for them. Moreover, Aizenshtadt presented a note on a scrap of paper from a certain Fishbein, inviting her son to his place for some important business, and she asked me to investigate the relationship between these people and her son. She is certain that, apart from the monetary [tie], there can be no other relationship. Her son is a student at the Kiev Commercial Institute, but does not attend lectures and continues to lead a dissolute life, disappearing for the entire night and returning home at dawn.

The singer, Ekaterina Mikhailovna Kislovskaia (Charskaia is her stage name), [testified] that she became acquainted with Vladimir Aizenshtadt in August 1910 in the city garden "Chateau," where she worked on stage. She spent time with him almost daily at that garden, and they often had dinner together. The Jews Semen Breitbard and Mark Il'ich Mazor participated in these dinners. Aizenshtadt always paid the bill. To all appearances, there was a close relationship between Aizenshtadt, Breitbard, and Mazor. She did not receive any presents or money from Aizenshtadt. In September she asked Aizenshtadt to change her earrings for more expensive diamond ones, but he said that he did not have the money and proposed to give her six of his promissory notes for 500 rubles each — for a total of 3,000 rubles. Consequently, she learned that it was impossible to receive the money in its entirety for these promissory notes, and she sold them for 1,200 rubles to her acquaintance, the assistant barrister Iosif Sergeevich Chertov, who lives permanently in Khar'kov at 8 Petrovskii Square. Aizenshtadt always passed himself off as a rich person and said that in January 1911 he would receive a substantial sum of money.

Srul' Liebovich Avrikh [testified] that he has known Vladimir Aizenshtadt for approximately five years, when he was still a student at the Business School. He met with him in different places, and they established a good relationship. In July 1910 Aizenshtadt, learning that he (the witness) had earned 1,800 rubles on the sale of a house, asked to borrow 500 rubles for a period ending on 20 January 1911, when he was to receive money [on his inheritance]. On 20 July the witness loaned him 500 rubles, receiving promissory notes with Aizenshtadt's signatures as a security for the loan (one for 500 rubles, another for 150 rubles). Within two weeks Aizenshtadt asked to borrow 100 more rubles. The witness, not having his own money, borrowed this sum and gave it to Aizenshtadt, receiving a promissory note for 300 rubles as security. Just as the witness did not know that Aizenshtadt was a minor, he did not know for what necessity he borrowed the money.

The dentist Moisei Fishbein [testified] that in the summer of 1910 his acquaintance Semen Moiseevich Breitbard asked to borrow 25 rubles for his landlord Aizenshtadt; he loaned Breitbard this sum on his word of honor. The witness was not acquainted with Aizenshtadt and had not even seen him. In a note he invited him to his place, wishing to receive back the loan, but Aizenshtadt did not appear. He knows nothing about Aizenshtadt's prodigality.

Itsko Surlev Sklovskii [testified] that he has known Aizenshtad for three years. In the summer of 1910, Aizenshtadt asked to bor-

row money; the witness loaned him 100 rubles one time and 175 rubles another time, for which he received two promissory notes (for 150 and 175 rubles) for security. He did not know that Aizenshtadt was a minor or for what purpose he borrowed the money.

Mordko Gerts Eleevich Mazor [testified] that he met Aizenshtadt through Semen Breitbard in the summer of 1910 in the restaurant "Semaden." Moreover, Aizenshtadt had been recommended as a landlord. Breitbard asked the witness to help Aizenshtadt borrow money from someone. In August the witness introduced Aizenshtadt to Kopel Vorochin, who loaned Aizenshtadt 1,500 rubles in cash (for a term ending in January or February 1911). As security for the loan, Aizenshtadt gave Vorochin six promissory notes for 500 rubles each (for a total of 3,000 rubles). He does not know on what conditions and for what need he borrowed the money; he also does not know that Aizenshtadt is a minor. The final sum of money received from Vorochin immediately turned up at Breitbard's. Apparently, Breitbard had a great influence on Aizenshtadt. For helping to borrow money, the witness did not receive anything from Aizenshtadt, but he received about 30 rubles from Breitbard. He never had dinner in the company of Aizenshtadt, Breitbard, and the singer Charskaia. He did not know anything about Aizenshtadt's prodigality.

Usher-Moshko Iosevich Shmorgun [testified] that he has known Aizenshtadt since childhood. In the summer of 1910 he asked to borrow 100 rubles, but the witness did not loan him money or accept promissory notes from him.

Vladimir Il'ich Aizenshtadt, who is accused of prodigality, testified that he lives with his mother. Until May 1910 he received 50 rubles a month from his mother for his personal expenses, but since then he has been receiving 150 rubles. This increase was made so that he would not incur debt. In the summer the witness often attended balls and was fond of playing billiards, winning a sufficiently substantial sum of money. In addition, he visit the city garden "Chateau," where he spent a lot of money on food and other things in the company of friends and female acquaintances, including the singer Charskaia. When he had no money, on the advice of his friend, he began to incur debts with the assistance of stockbrokers. Thus, he borrowed: 200 rubles from Itsko Srulev Sklovskii (giving him two promissory notes for 175 and 150 rubles), 550 rubles from Srul' Leibovich Avrikh (for three promissory notes of 500, 300, and 140 rubles), 1,500 rubles from Kopel' Vorochin (for six promissory notes, worth 500 rubles each, for a total of 3,000 rubles), and 200 rubles from the Jew Shmorgun (for promissory notes of 300 rubles). From the money borrowed from Vorochin, Mazor received 300 rubles as a brokerage fee. In addition, he gave the singer Ekaterina Mikhailovna Kislovskaia (Charskaia on stage) as a present six promissory notes for 500 rubles each (for a total of 3,000 rubles). People who loaned him money knew that he was a minor and gave him the money for a term that ended in February 1911, when he would turn twenty-one years old, and counted on recovering the money from his share of the inheritance. The Jews Breitbard and Mazor often spent time with him and at his expense. He now recognizes his mistake and does not issue any more promissory notes. He had a close relationship with the singer Charskaia, and under the influence of this relationship, he gave her the promissory notes as gifts. Apart from the obligation of the promissory notes, he also has some minor debts in a small sum. In contrast to his mother's testimony, he can only object that he did not issue promissory notes to Mazor. [. . .]

The Court has decided to establish a trusteeship over the property of the student Vladimir Il'ich Aizenshtadt. For the appropriate instruction, inform the Orphans' Court about this, requiring that it impose an interdiction on the real estate of Aizenshtadt in the established order, and announce [this decision] to Tauba and Vladimir Aizenshtadt through the Kiev police chief.

[III]

Health and Sexuality

Starting in the eighteenth century, Jewish health and sexuality attracted intense interest as European states sought to construct and control a new social order. From the time of the Enlightenment, a host of observers—doctors, state officials, and members of the educated public—criticized the physical condition of the Jews and their low level of productivity. They agreed that the so-called degenerate state of the Jews—evident from their poor biological development (low birth weight, infection, and weakness)—was partly due to the tradition of early marriage.[1] Proposals to abolish early marriage occupied a central place in the Haskalah vision of a modern bourgeois family—exemplified in Mordechai Aaron Guenzburg's memoir about the failure of his wedding night (document 78). Critics blamed the unproductive nature of Jews on their poor hygiene and health practices, especially in their homes and schools. As a result, prescriptive literature—advice books, manuals, and pamphlets—began to proliferate in the nineteenth century. They provided medical guidance on a host of issues: how to plan a nutritious diet, how to maintain a clean and tidy apartment with good ventilation to prevent disease, and so forth. These manuals also sought to provide a scientific guide for young women as they passed through pregnancy, childbirth, breast-feeding, and child care.

The intrusion of modern science into everyday life practices encountered considerable resistance among Jews, who had a rich tra-

dition of folk medicine and magic. As early as the mid-eighteenth century, Jewish physicians like Dr. Moses Marcuse (educated at the University of Koenigsburg) complained about people's reliance on folk healers: "I have already warned you in my book against ignorant *baalei shem*, Tatars, wax-pourers, exorcisers of the evil eye, fortune-tellers, and worthless little doctors [. . .] I also warned you about the old midwives."[2]

Israel Kasovich described his wife's skeptical response to his purchase in 1880 of such a manual after the birth of their first child:

> For my wife I ordered a Russian book entitled, *What Every Young Mother Ought to Know*. She did not want to follow altogether the suggestions contained in the book. This may have been due to the difficulty of carrying into practice the instructions given in the book, and it may also have been due to the fact that raising children in accordance with rules laid down in a book was then still unknown in those parts [Poltava, Ukraine]. Be that as it may, I had to use a great deal of persuasion before she yielded.[3]

Indeed, even when Jews were exposed to new medical information, they still tended to rely on folk remedies and advice.[4] In response, Jewish physicians and psychologists made selective use of Western medical discourse, often in combination with traditional views. Thus, Moshe Shtudentski of Warsaw defined masturbation both as a "sin" that derived from an evil impulse as well as a pathological disease that caused excessive weakness, paleness, and memory loss (document 59).

But traditional views of health and sexuality faced growing challenges, not only from the medicalization of health and sexuality but also from broader socioeconomic and cultural changes. One major sphere of change was the treatment of mental health. According to the All-Russian Census of 1897, Jews reported a slightly higher rate of mental illness (0.098 percent) than the general population (0.094 percent). The care of the mentally ill fell mainly on the shoulders of the family or sometimes the communal *hekdesh* (which often served the dual role of poorhouse and hospital). In Vil'na province, families sent their mentally ill relatives to Tatars for healing (with charms, herbs, and incantations) or to the Jewish agricultural colonies (where the healthy air was supposed to have a "salutary effect" on the nerves), or paid poor families to take care of them.[5] Many mentally ill people simply wandered the streets. By the late nineteenth century, however, more families were turning to the Jewish hospitals in large cities, such as Vil'na, Kiev, and Warsaw for care for their mentally ill relatives. To be sure, contemporary observers noted that most respectable Jews shunned hospitals, which tended to attract only "the most destitute, those engaged in heavy physical labor, and those without their own kin."[6] However, as the documents here show, families could expect a medical diagnosis and hospitalization of family members if space permitted. Reflecting the preoccupation of specialists with mental health and sexuality, psychiatric reports at the Jewish hospital in Vil'na routinely included a woman's reproductive history (dates and experiences of menstruation, birth, and sex) alongside questions about her religious and family life.

Another change pertained to Jewish sexual mores and practices because of the rise in the age at first marriage, urbanization (which led to more young women leaving home for domestic service and factory work), education, military service, and revolutionary activism. The Jewish population boasted one of the lowest rates of illegitimate births in 1897 (0.3 percent, compared with the national rate of 2.4 percent). However, premarital sex, especially with the promise of marriage, was becoming more common—or so, at least, was the perception. There was even one rabbinical responsum by Rabbi Zekharyah Stern (document 83), expressing explicit disapproval of another rabbi's request to allow a young man to have a concubine; the responsum reminded the rabbi of the difficulty of supporting more than one wife. Couples who had children out of wedlock had no possibility of adopting their own children—even after they married—without the extraordinary intervention of the emperor, something that occurred but rarely.[7]

As in most societies, women bore the brunt of social stigma for premarital pregnancies and found little sympathy in official circles or the Jewish community. In fact, state courts relied on the collaboration of medical experts to expose women who had violated the norms of sexual propriety. An especially intrusive mechanism of control was the modern gynecological examination that a suspect (or rape victim) was forced to undergo to determine her guilt or innocence. Registered prostitutes, who held what was called the "yellow ticket," were also forced to submit to regular medical inspections in an effort to contain the spread of venereal diseases.

This part of the book explores these issues. The first three sections deal with health, addressing traditional healing and folk medicines; diet, hygiene, and exercise, including modern advice manuals; and mental illness. The following four sections focus on sexuality, with materials on modesty, marital sex, extramarital sex (both premarital sex and adultery), and sexual crimes such as rape and prostitution.

NOTES

1. Jacob Goldberg, "Jewish Marriage in Eighteenth-Century Poland," *Polin* 10 (1997): 14. Angst about early marriage was hardly confined to Jews but was a general concern, as the Russian state sought to ensure that its subjects would multiply. Hence in 1774 and again in 1830, the state raised the minimum marital age for female and male Orthodox Christians (first to fifteen and seventeen, respectively, and then to sixteen and eighteen). See Gregory Lee Freeze, "Bringing Order to the Russian Family: Marriage and Divorce in Imperial Russia, 1760–1860," *Journal of Modern History* 62, no. 1 (1990): 714–15.

2. Quoted in Israel Zinberg, *A History of Jewish Literature* (Cleveland: Press of Case Western University, 1972–78), 3:158.

3. Israel Kasovich, *Days of Our Years, Personal and General Reminiscences, 1859–1929* (New York: Jordan Pub. Co., 1929), 150.

4. Lisa Rae Epstein, "Caring for the Soul's House: The Jews of Russia and Health Care, 1860–1914," PhD diss., Yale University, 1995, 99–106.

5. Dina Abramowicz, *Profiles of a Lost World: Memoirs of East European Jewish Life Before WWII* (New York: YIVO Institute for Jewish Research, 1999), 110.

6. V. S. Perlis, *Meditsinskii otchet po rodil'nomu otdeleniu pri Kievskoi evreiskoi bol'nitse za 1891, 1892, 1893 god* (Kiev: Tip. N. Piliushchenko, 1895), 4. On women giving to illegitimate infants at the Jewish hospital in Vil'na, see ChaeRan Y. Freeze, "Lilith's Midwives: Jewish Newborn Child Murder in Nineteenth-Century Vil'na," *Jewish Social Studies* 16, no. 2 (2010): 1–27.

7. The problem of illegitimate children applied to subjects of all confessions and was attracting the growing attention of reformers by the early twentieth century. See William Wagner, *Marriage, Property, and Law in Late Imperial Russia* (New York: Oxford University Press, 1994), 72–73.

Traditional Healing
and Folk Medicines

[57]

R. Pinchas Katzenelbogen: Remedy
for a Fever in *Sefer Yesh Manhilin*

Rabbi Pinchas Katzenelbogen, *Sefer yesh manhilin*, ed. Yitzhak Dov ben
Ephraim Fischel Feld (Jerusalem: Mekhon Hatam Sofer, 1986), 101–2.[1]

For one sick with a fever, heaven forbid, purchase a pot with a lid for whatever price the seller demands, and pour seventy-seven grains of legumes into the pot, and you shall recite "nit einz, nit zwei" [not once, not twice] etc. until you reach seventy-seven. After that, the owner of the pot should urinate into the pot on the legumes, then put soft mud around the lid of the pot so that lid adheres to the pot. Next they will bury the pot and the cover with all that is in it deep in the earth where no one shall pass over it (for instance, close to a wall), and this is tried and tested with the help of God.

NOTE

1. [R. Pinchas Katzenelbogen (b. 1691 in Dubnov) composed *Sefer yesh manhilin* between 1758 and 1764. While this publication was published before the tsarist period, its remedies were similar to popular folk remedies promoted by traditional Jewish healers in the nineteenth century. See Lisa Epstein, "Caring for the Soul's House: The Jews of Russia and Health Care, 1860–1914" (Ph.D. dissertation, Yale University, 1995), 99–132.]

[58]

Moshe Shtudentski: A Pediatrician on Puberty in Adolescent Girls (1847)

Moshe Shtudentski, *Rofe hayeladim: kolel 'etsot tovot ve-ne'emot li-shemor beriut ha-yeladim* (Warsaw: Gedruckt bei H. N. Schriefigtesser, 1847), 264.

The training of girls during these years is a matter of guiding them in manners of morals and modesty. The most essential is this: pay close attention and keep a most watchful eye on them. And here is the helpmate of men, and the success of human history, the parent and giver of life in the womb. One must doubly supervise and watch over their ways during these years of their life for their benefit and for that of their children after them. For when they corrupt their ways, not only do they corrupt their own souls, but the offspring of their wombs too shall be heavily tainted by the effects of their sin.

At that stage of childhood, a force of intense development awakens in the girls along with the enlargement of the body: the breasts enlarge and assume their natural shape. It is therefore necessary to keep an eye on the girls, and to remove all types of blockages from that growth lest the youthful breasts be squeezed by tight clothing that is confining and uncomfortable to the body or by things that obstruct them.

When the girls reach the time of their first menarche, a profound change takes place in their bodies. Therefore it is necessary to watch them and avoid anything that can cause a constriction of the uterus and a change in its structure. An incorrect timing of menstruation is most damaging to a girl's health, so parents are advised to avoid feeding their daughters all manners of food and drink which heat up the body, as well as [using] excessively warm clothing, especially for the lower part of the body as that will prevent

them from arriving at [this stage of] their adolescence. May they know no evil and let affliction not approach their tents.

And here I shall write about one further disease that may strike girls during these years of their lives. It is a fairly common illness, and fathers will do well to keep an eye on them to keep them from all evil—the illness of paleness. This term is used to describe a kind of illness that affects girls between the ages of fifteen and eighteen years. It may be recognized by the following symptoms: a pale and silvery facial appearance, pale lips, a swollen body, pain in the loins, tremors of the limbs, loss of appetite, depressed spirits, desire for excessive sleep, and weakness throughout the body. Besides all these, menstruation will be irregular—that is, either it will not occur at all or it will be diminished and light in appearance. The causes of this illness are [the following]: eating the kinds of food that weaken [the body]; insufficient physical exercise in the open air; and sitting to excess in a small unkempt room. Excessive sleep [. . .] can cause fever, colds, anger, anxiety, and depression.

If this illness has not already turned into a more serious one, it is easy to treat by means of home medications, but if it has already revealed itself in its strength, or if it has turned into *zviah memit* [possibly jaundice], then one must consult a trained physician.

No illness benefits so much as this from a proper diet; thus, the parents of such girls should pay particular attention to this matter as they may sometimes succeed in eliminating this ailment without any other treatment or medicine. They should instruct the sick girl to get out from time to time into open air, and should feed her with nourishing foods, especially meat and eggs. However, cabbage, jelly, salads, fruit, and the like are damaging for this ailment. Strengthening types of drinks such as beer, wine, and alcohol are most beneficial to her. Apart from a correct diet and a proper organization based on natural manners, the most beneficial cure for this disease is training in morals and modesty. The parents of such an ailing girl should make ef-forts to create for her conditions of happiness and merriment and keep her away from negative associations; her clothes should keep her from catching cold but not be overly warm. If she has constipation, it is best to clear this up with medications. [. . .] If the weakness greatly intensifies, a trained physician should be consulted; if one cannot be obtained, long-duration *calamus* baths should be employed. For internal medication, she should be given water in which *kina* [an herb] was boiled, and she should drink watered-down wine.

[59]

Moshe Shtudentski: A Pediatrician on Masturbation (1847)

Moshe Shtudentski, *Rofe hayeladim: kolel 'etsot tovot ve-ne'emot li-shemor beriut ha-yeladim* (Warsaw: Gedruckt bei H. N. Schriefigtesser, 1847), 264.

Of the things that have a special ability to corrupt health and damage all spiritual strength, first and foremost is the evil of deliberate ejaculation (the sin of masturbation). This evil instinct will, by its wrath, lay waste to all of the best forces of the youth's body, destroying his spiritual strength as well and ruin the power of all parts of the body by arresting and interfering with their function and growth.

Happy is the youth who knows not of this sin! And woe to the boys who corrupt their ways and sin often with this evil; theirs shall be an eternal punishment. Therefore, fathers, watch your sons with a careful eye over all the youth's manners lest he fail and fall into evil, for if the body already reveals visible signs indicating that he has already failed [. . .] redemption will be far and his posterity will not flourish speedily.

The signs by which we may recognize those who give in to this sin are [the following]: a pale and silvery facial appearance like the face of an ill person; a blueness around the eyes, pale lips, weakness of strength even if he has an appetite, feeble hands, a shaking of the limbs, especially the hands when he tries to grasp something; a fatigue that seizes him after any minor chores; and greatly diminished mnemonic powers.

The illnesses that result from this sin are [the following]: a particular form of physical emaciation called spinal emaciation, dullness of thought, confusion, depression that leads this unfortunate individual to despair of his life and commit suicide. There is, however, hope for a cure if he repents of his sin early and never returns to its folly, which was the cause of all his illness and suffering.

The training and appropriate medicine for warding off this bitter and evil sin and uprooting it from the youth's ingrained instinct is to train him in the manner that the Creator has implanted in man's nature, and to guide him in the ways of morals, propriety, and modest manners. When efforts are made to apply this medicine—why then the vast corruption that draws so many of our youth to itself shall depart speedily. And fathers should look after the welfare of their sons so that they will flower like a rose, well fed and alert; their offspring shall go forth and flourish like their parent's planted olive.

[60]

Birth Control Advertisement (1908)

Dr. Lesser, *Vos darf men thon um oystsumayden shvangershaft* (Warsaw, 1908), back cover.

Important for men and women: he who wants to protect his wife from pregnancy should always use only authentic American condoms made out of the strongest silk rubber, 15 kopecks a piece. Another good protection against pregnancy are Dr. Schweitzer's chemical pessaries—1.20 rubles a dozen. For women, menstrual pads (for use during menstruation) with soft filling, 1.25 rubles a dozen.

[61]

Dr. Nisse's Medical Advice about Birth Control (1908)

Dr. R. G. Nisse, *Gegen shvangershaft: meditsinishe eytses und mitlen vi tsuferhiten fun shvanger veren un kinder hobe* (Warsaw: Ha-tzefirah, 1908), 17–31.

Chapter IV

Simple domestic means: avoidance of sexual activity and the impractical nature of this method.—"Quick surprise."—*Coitus interruptus* and the terrible results thereof.—Various diseases caused by artificial infertility.—The ejection of the semen through movements of the body.—Sexual intercourse in a sideways position.—Keeping relations close to menstruation as a measure against conceiving; practical evidence that this is ineffective.

All methods of contraception can generally be divided into two main categories: *passive*, or simple, in which no external medical instruments or measures are employed; and *active*, exercised through various medical and chemical means. We shall begin by analyzing the first category—the passive methods.

(1) The simplest method from this category is separation: the couple, fearing pregnancy and childbirth, completely abstain from any sexual relations and live like strangers. This method is obviously the most natural, the safest, and also less harmful than all other methods used for this purpose. Yet it cannot be recommended for the broad masses simply because it can be practiced only by people who possess a very cold temperament and remain completely apart from the pleasures of this world: only such individuals can accustom themselves easily to the lonely and ascetic lifestyle. For an ordinary human being, this method cannot be any good. The sex organs, like all the other human organs, demand to be used in accordance with their nature. If left unsatisfied, they often look for alternative, unnatural, routes such as masturbation (onanism), which leads to quite terrible results, as we shall later describe in detail. In the best case, such separated life leads to a lack of harmony in the family: the husband and wife become increasingly estranged from one other and constantly feel offended and unsatisfied, nervous and moody. Voluntarily robbed of its greatest pleasure, life loses all its charm and becomes a burden, until in the end the person falls into incurable melancholia or hysteria, etc.

(2) In the higher aristocratic circles the following method, known as the "quick surprise," is often employed: unexpectedly and without any preparation the husband embraces his wife, before she is even ready for anything, and does his business. In many cases such unexpected sexual intercourse leads to the desired goal of avoiding pregnancy, since practice shows that the more aroused a woman is through various kinds of loving kisses and caresses, the more easily she becomes pregnant. This method does not completely go along with the conditions of family life and is a great offense to the woman's gentlest feelings and self-respect, and it is for this very reason that this method has never gained popularity among the wider population.

(3) Interrupted intercourse (*coitus interruptus*), when the penis is withdrawn before the final and most important moment of the sexual act—the ejaculation of the semen—can be regarded as the most harmful of all contraceptive methods. This method is very common and is especially fashionable in France and in the Siebengebirge region in Germany. Its effect is equally harmful for the man and the woman. The former is forced to make an effort in his mind, especially in the final moment preceding the ejaculation of the semen, and this in itself has a negative effect on the main organs of his nervous system— the brain and the spinal marrow, which have to apply their strength in two directions and as a result naturally become weakened. This method is especially harmful for nervous individuals, in whom it often leads to hypochondria and severe marrow diseases. The most frequent result of this method, however, is a disease called sexual neurasthenia. One begins experiencing general weakness and melancholia, the ends of one's limbs turn numb and cold and then hot again; one shakes while walking and tires easily. At a later stage the functioning of one's inner organs becomes weakened, with the appearance of irregularities in digestion, including constipation and hemorrhoids.

The woman, too, becomes weak and sickly because of the method's ill effect on the spinal marrow, and her sex organs cease functioning properly. Her period lengthens, continuing for six, eight, or even ten days; the bleeding increases and the blood becomes paler or darker. Other symptoms include white discharge, pain in the lower part of the stomach, and deformation of the uterus. Doctor Valento of Laibach observed in such women a whole number of nervous disorders with signs of hysteria, accompanied by a gross deformation of an enlarged uterus.

This method of artificial infertility has the worst effect on the middle and lower parts of the spinal marrow, upon which sexual activity, digestion, and blood production are dependent. Irregularities occur in all three of these functions, as the power of the nerves begins to deteriorate. Sexual passion is reduced first, and after a few years the male begins to suffer from impotence. Along with the impotence come indigestion, hemorrhoidal bleeding, and a disturbance in blood production. The stomach and the spleen no longer function properly and affect the properties of the blood. The patients' faces start looking pale and their skin — as if worn out. They become liable to catch a cold at the slightest opportunity; any physical activity makes them sweaty and tired. Furthermore, they develop various nervous diseases such as headaches and migraines — especially individuals from the wealthiest classes. Many women complain of migraines one or two days after intercourse, and it does not even occur to them that this was caused by an abnormal or incomplete sexual act.

A trembling in the face, the hands, the shoulders, and elsewhere, is another neurological symptom of a deteriorating spinal marrow. From the middle and lower parts of the marrow, the inflammation spreads either up to the neck and the brain, or down to the lowest part of the marrow. Eventually, the person loses sleep, and even if he does sometimes manage to fall asleep — after numerous efforts and using various sleep inducers — his sleep is light, superficial, filled with dreams, and brings ennui and weakness instead of refreshment and strength. The brain is thus also affected, which results in dizziness, headaches, and heaviness in the head; the eyesight deteriorates; the person is often attacked by unconscious fear, etc. In addition to all this one must also consider various phenomena related to the heart, the stomach, the intestines, the bladder, etc.

(4) No less harmful than the method just mentioned is a custom common in some regions of France: at the very moment ejaculation begins, the woman forcefully squeezes the urethra of the male sex organ with her finger, as a result of which the semen, instead of being ejected from the penis, flows back into the urethra, from where it flows into the bladder and later comes out along with urine. From a moral standpoint, one need not even comment regarding the harmfulness of this method. People who allow themselves to satisfy their animalistic urges in such a coarse and lowly fashion increasingly bring destruction to their nervous systems. This brutal method weakens and quickly exhausts the strength of the erection, the spiritual powers, and the memory, and leads to a general deterioration of the entire body.

(5) Some women try to avoid pregnancy in the following fashion: shortly after intercourse they sit up straight in bed, cough intensely, and, tightly pressing the stomach, attempt to expel the semen. This measure is widely used among the aborigines of northern Australia, who in this manner try to prevent the consequences of their sexual relations with white Europeans. To achieve this goal the woman gets up immediately following intercourse, spreads her legs widely, and using an energetic winding movement expels a thick white mass, which is in fact a mixture of the male semen and the sticky fluid from her own sex organs. This method is not particularly harmful, and yet it is little known or used, and this is because of its total dependence on the woman, who in this case has to strain her mind at the very moment of her delight and forgetfulness, when her pleasure reaches the highest point, intoxicating her and making her unable to think of anything else.

(6) Finally, one must also mention a method recommended by Dr. Damm, which he calls *cohabitation lateralis*, that is, intercourse in a sideways position. To execute this method, the man lies on his right side and the

woman on her left, and lying thus they engage in the sexual act completely naturally, without using any additional methods of contraception. Since this position prevents the male organ from entering deeply into the female sex organ and reaching the cervix, the semen does not come into the uterus and therefore no pregnancy occurs. Yet this method, as Dr. Damm himself acknowledges, is not completely reliable in preventing pregnancy, and also has certain negative consequences. Because of the extreme strain placed on the spine and the spinal marrow, excessively frequent relations of this sort lead to dull shoulder pain that continues to increase. To avoid this, one must become accustomed to the following conditions, as recommended by Dr. Damm: (1) do not use any alcoholic beverages before coitus; (2) never protract intercourse; and (3) do not engage in it too often. By following these safety precautions one can be certain that sideways intercourse will not bring any more harmful results than a slight tiredness of the spine. We will conclude by quoting Dr. Damm himself: "We cannot reject sideways intercourse, although from a moral perspective it is not completely right to recommend this method since it is not completely harmless. One should not, however, forget even for a moment that this method cannot fully substitute for natural sexual intercourse. This method has the only advantage of being, out of all the substitute methods, most similar to the act prescribed by nature, and it is therefore less harmful than all the other methods."

Before concluding this chapter, we shall cite one more method that has long been considered an almost unfailing protection. It still has many adherents, even among members of the educated class, who proceed on the assumption that the woman conceives most easily when she has sexual relations soon after the end of her period, and with each day the possibility of her getting pregnant decreases until a few days prior to her next period, when the chances of pregnancy once again increase.

Thus, according to the calculations of the physiologist Raciborsky,[1] of a hundred women who have relations precisely during the middle days between the end of one period and the beginning of the next, no more than six to seven become pregnant. Therefore, to avoid unwanted pregnancies, one need only systematize the sexual relations and accustom oneself to a certain amount of restraint. Thus, teach such physiologists, one should avoid sexual relations for two whole weeks after the period and three to four days before the next period.

There generally is nothing to be held against this method from any perspective, whether moral, physical, or hygienic. The only drawback is that it is no method of protection at all, and the best evidence is supplied by our own people. We Jews have always done it this way, as commanded by our Torah, and yet our fertility is at least as good as among the other nations.

Chapter V

Mechanical and chemical methods: Dr. Hasse's "*pessarium*" and the caution to be exercised when using it. —"Condoms" and their influence.—The insertion of a mushroom to absorb semen.—The need to keep the sex organs clean.

Much less harmful from the perspective of hygiene are the methods of the second, active category, that is, those exercised with the help of various mechanical and chemical measures; they are also to some extent more effective and safer than the passive methods discussed in chapter 4. First, we will consider the method of Dr. [Carl] Hasse[2] of Flensburg, who devoted much effort to the issue of artificial infertility and invented the following:

(1) *Pessarium occlusivum* is a round rubber dome, in the shape of a little cap, with a steel spring. One first smears it with lather from high-quality soap, and the outer sex organs of the woman are also smeared in the same way. It is best to use Askanas's Health Soap, which

is remarkable for its antiseptic properties and ought to be recommended generally for washing the face and the hands—especially for skin that is tender and sensitive, as for instance that of newborn babies and the like; for that purpose the Health Soap has practically no equal. After this, the sides of the dome are squeezed and it is inserted very carefully into the widely opened hollow of the sex organ so that it covers the cervix and prevents the seminal fluid from entering it. When choosing the "pessary" one should make certain it is of the proper size. It should not be too big, so that it does not cause pressure and pain in the sex organ; nor should it be too small, since it can be easily displaced from its correct position and thus fail to serve its purpose. The pessary should be removed twice a week for cleaning; this can be performed by the woman herself, while sitting between two chairs or on the edge of one chair. Smearing her finger with oil or soap, she carefully inserts it into the opening of her sex organ and, grabbing the edge of the pessary with her finger, she pulls it out. With some practice this becomes quite easy. However, when the woman is inexperienced and clumsy, it can also be dangerous. It can easily happen that when the device is inserted into the vagina, a part of the uterus can get caught between the dome and the cecum. Hasse himself acknowledges that the doctor who recommends this method to a woman should draw her attention to a number of precautions, explain them well, and maintain further supervision.

Although this method is not fully satisfactory (morally or aesthetically), it is nevertheless much more useful and practical than many others.

(2) Far more disgusting and harmful, both aesthetically and hygienically, are the condoms (so called after their inventor, a certain English doctor).[3] These are very thin little sacks, made of rubber or air bladder, which firmly cover the male organ, unto which they are pulled in the final moment before sexual intercourse. The purpose of the condom is twofold: first, it serves as protection against infection from suspicious relations, and second, it prevents the male semen from entering the sex organ of the woman and in this fashion protects her from pregnancy. There are also shorter condoms, which only cover the glans penis and remain securely in place thanks to the thick rubber rim on their bottom end. The semen is ejected inside the little sack and following intercourse it is discarded. When buying condoms, one should make sure they are of the best and strongest quality, for there are also fake ones made of material that is too weak and can easily break, thus rendering the whole effort futile. One should not pull a condom on tightly to the very end but should instead leave some room for the semen to be freely collected in it, otherwise it can be quite harmful to one's health.

Without lingering on this utterly disgusting method, we will note only that just as with the previous method (the pessary), it is the female who suffers the most. And this is only natural: the woman is thereby deprived of the ultimate moment of the sex act, namely the ejaculation of the semen into her organ, which gives her pleasure of the highest degree. An alien entity intrudes between the male and female reproductive organs, blocking and interfering with their natural functions. Besides, this method results in a prolonged physiological arousal of the nervous system, which has a very bad effect on a person's organism.

(3) Equally unaesthetic is the following method, employed by many women to prevent the entry of semen into the uterus: one takes a soft, round mushroom, well cleaned so that it contains no sand, and measuring from three to seven centimeters across, depending on the breadth of the sex organ's opening. One then dips it in water into which some vinegar has earlier been added, and before intercourse one inserts it into the opening of the sex organ as deeply as possible; right after intercourse the mushroom is pulled out by

means of a long silk thread tied to it. Although this method often protects against pregnancy, it cannot be considered entirely safe.

(4) Apart from the mechanical methods, various chemical acids are also employed, such as carbolic acid, sulfuric acid, and the like, a certain proportion of which is dissolved in water and, soon after intercourse, injected into the woman's sex organ through a syringe or irrigator. The purpose of these methods is to destroy the sperm (the life power of the tiny particles of the semen) quickly before they are able to join with the eggs of the woman and create an embryo. Practice has indeed demonstrated that these methods can completely block the movement of the sperm; one forgets, however, about a very important factor—namely, in healthy women, as the scientist [Samuel] Kristeller[4] has demonstrated, a flow of thick fluid is discharged from the uterus in the direction of the sex organ and joins immediately with the viable semen during intercourse. It is therefore quite doubtful whether the mechanical and chemical effects of the aforementioned methods are capable of counteracting these fluids, and since this question has not yet been resolved, it is not possible to give the final verdict on the usefulness of these methods. Besides, one must consider a factor that we have already cited in the previous chapters: because of the woman's excited and absent-minded psychological state at this moment during sexual intercourse, she is incapable of attending to anything.

Overall, douches are very effective from the perspective of hygiene, for there is no organ that becomes so filthy and dirty as the uterus, and every woman who neglects the cleansing of her sex organs is later punished by various diseases and weakening discharges. It is therefore imperative to rinse with cold water after intercourse, even though this procedure, especially in the winter, is quite unpleasant. It is also beneficial to add a chemical substance to the water, as for example alum or *cuprum sulfuricum* dissolved in 10 percent water.

For the same purpose, it is also advisable to wipe the sex organs thoroughly with a finger wrapped in thin linen, or with a piece of absorbent cotton.

(5) To block the movement of the sperm at the entrance to the woman's sex organ, one can also employ small blocks or caps made of easily dissolvable substances such as gelatin, cacao powder, and the like. These are first steeped in strong chemicals, such as quinine or alum, which have the capacity to destroy the life power of the sperm. About ten minutes before intercourse, a block is inserted into the sex organ of the woman, where it very quickly dissolves and fills the entire bottom part of the organ. Under the influence of the chemicals, the semen soon loses its life power and the movement of the tiny sperm stops.

(6) For the same purpose organ blowers have recently come into use to blow various powdery chemical substances into the woman's sex organ and to disable the semen. Of all such various devices, Dr. Justus's apparatus, known as "Atakos," deserves mention. It is a kind of rubber balloon with a long curved tube containing a reservoir into which the powder is poured, at the top of which are many tiny holes. The tube is inserted quite deep into the organ about ten minutes before intercourse. Then the balloon is squeezed, blowing the powder inside and filling the cervix and all parts of the organ so that the semen encounters the powder everywhere and thus loses its vital power.

(7) As a "home method" for women who are truly burdened by a large number of children or who must not give birth because of disease, Dr. Schroeder recommends tampons made of absorbent cotton with salicin, which are sprinkled with three to five drops of wine vinegar and inserted deep into the organ (up to the cervix). After intercourse the tampon is removed and the organ is rinsed with an irrigator.

As can be seen from the Talmud, this method was known even in those times and was widely used among the people. The Talmud mentions it quite often under the name of "תשמיש במוך" (intercourse through cotton), as something commonly known.

There are also various other contraceptive methods—one can say that hardly a week passes without a newly invented method being publicized. To enumerate all of them is practically impossible; we have included only those methods that are most used. Anyone interested can obtain details on all the other methods in the major stores that sell these devices.

In such cases it is generally beneficial to consult the owners of such stores: they are well informed about these matters through their constant customers and know which methods are more effective and practical.

NOTES

1. [Adam Raciborsky, *Traité de la menstruation: ses rapports avec l'ovulation la fecundation, l'hygiene de la pubertè* (Paris: Baillère, 1868).]

2. [Carl Hasse, *Über facultative sterilität beleuchtet vom prophylactischen und hygieinischen Standpunkte. Für practische Aerzte und Geburtshelfer* (Neuwied u. Leipzig: Heuser, 1883).]

3. [Recent scholarship has debunked the story of a seventeenth-century "Dr. Condom." See Aine Collier, *The Humble Little Condom: A History* (Amherst, NY: Prometheus, 2007).]

4. *Berliner klinische Wochenschrift*, 1871, No. 27. [Kristeller also published *Belegstellen zu den Grundsatzen der judischen Sittenlehre* (Berlin, 1882).]

[62]

Report of an Illegal Abortion in Vil'na: Trial of Feiga Noskin (1886)

LVIA, f. 448, op. 1, d. 5228, ll. 45–46.

Basia Lindenblit [the illegal midwife] asked [Mikhlia Girsheva] Baryshnikova in great detail when the rape [by her employer] had occurred and how long [after it] she ceased to have her menstruation.[1] She [Lindenblit] remarked that [Baryshnikova's condition] was not serious and that it was not too late to help her. Because Baryshnikova was poor, she [Lindenblit] only took five rubles [for the procedure]. During the course of eight or ten days, Baryshnikova visited Lindenblit for a few hours as the latter "dug" into Baryshnikova's sexual organs, first with a white, bent metal rod (the thickness of a pencil), and then with a white bone rod, which was slightly curved with holes at the tip. This "digging" took place every day, first with the bone, and then the metal rod. It was painful, but not very much, and there was some blood. Although Mikhlia Baryshnikova continued to work as before, she changed as a result of this treatment; her mother, not knowing anything, was quite surprised. Then Baryshnikova confessed everything.

NOTE

1. [The trial indicted a group of Jewish women for running a lucrative baby-farming business in which they hired out wet nurses and extorted their salaries in exchange for the care of their illegitimate off-

spring—most of whom died from neglect and abuse. The court interviewed Mikhlia Baryshnikova in relation to the case. Anecdotal references in trials suggest that illegal abortions were one method of getting rid of an unwanted pregnancy. For more on this trial and abortions, see Freeze, "Lilith's Midwives."]

[63]

Moshe Shtudentski: A Pediatrician on Breast-Feeding (1847)

Moshe Shtudentski, *Rofe hayeladim: kolel 'etsot tovot ve-ne'emot li-shemor beriut ha-yeladim*), (Warsaw: Gedruckt bei H. N. Schriefigtesser, 1847).

In the first days after childbirth, the breast milk is as thin as water: it is like colostrum (*servodka*). There is also little of it, and it is very good for the newborn as he is spitting and defecating the liquid tar-like stool [meconium] that follows birth, and it also prepares him for subsequent digestion when the milk thickens. [. . .]

Problems with lactation. Helpful treatments for this condition include: try to have nursing women rest and maintain their tranquility, proper living arrangements, and avoidance of rich foods and drinks (which do not promote lactation). Also, a light preparation of strong salts (English salts) may be made for her, and she should support and bind the breasts upward so that they do not hang down. If milk remains in the breasts after nursing, it must be emptied—viz., by feeding another infant, or by the assistance of another woman, or by a puppy that has not yet grown teeth. If these three are unavailable, then the milk may be emptied by a glass vial, called a milk pump.

If the breasts lack sufficient milk, the cause is the mother's nature, frailty, or the great loss of blood during delivery, or it may be that the breasts are constricted. If there is little milk in the breasts, it is neither necessary nor helpful to use medication except when the milk suddenly decreases or the mother has a fever. Then the concern may be about a transfer of milk to the internal regions of the body (such as the lining of the brain); in such cases it is therefore necessary to consult an educated doctor. But if the breast milk is not sufficient to quiet the infant from the first days of nursing, an attempt to increase the quantity of her milk will be to no avail. In that case it is better to hire a healthy wet nurse with ample milk or to accustom the infant to liquid food.

The quantity of milk may change for the following reasons: extreme anger, contracting a cold or drinking strong spirits like wine or liquor, which all cause much hardship for the nursing body and give the infant stomach aches, diarrhea, palpitations, and contractions of the organs (cramps). Women who tend to be short-tempered or like to take a glass should not breast-feed their children because of the bitter venom they are giving them in place of nourishment. Accordingly, the nursing mother should control her temper and not get angry. If she should have a bout of rage or take sudden fright, then she must not nurse. She simply should first empty out the milk in her breasts and only later nurse her child.

[64]

Circumcision of a Sixteen-Year-Old Jewish Boy with Hemophilia (1894–1908)

RGIA, f. 821, op. 9, d. 39, ll. 1–11 ob.

"Report of the Governor of Podolia to the Ministry of Internal Affairs (31 March 1894)"

The state rabbi of Bogopol'sk (Balta district) informed the Provincial Board subordinate to me in a report of 21 July 1894 (number 290) that the Jew Mordko Savranskii, a resident of the town of Golovanevska, submitted a petition to perform the ritual of circumcision on his son Avraam, who was born in the town sixteen years ago.

The information collected by the rabbi on this case revealed that the ritual of circumcision had not been performed on the boy because two of his older brothers died as a result of the circumcision (from hemophilia). Consequently, according to Talmudic law, he was not allowed to perform the ritual on the latter at an early age. Because [state] law does not provide exact instructions on this matter, the rabbi asked the Provincial Board to explain how to proceed.

The question raised by the state rabbi of Bogopol'sk concerning the regulations and rituals of the Jewish faith may be resolved only by the special Rabbinic Commission, which is attached to the Ministry of Internal Affairs (in conformity with the Statutes of the Spiritual Affairs of Foreign Faiths). [...] I therefore present the stated circumstances for Your Excellency's consideration and have the honor to ask humbly to be informed about the subsequent [decision].

"Report of the Learned Jew, M. Kreps, to the Department of Spiritual Affairs of Foreign Faiths (19 March 1908)"

Given the attachments sent by the governor of Podolia (31 March 1894, number 821), it is evident that [state] rabbi of Bogopol'sk — for want of exact legal instructions on whether to perform the ritual of circumcision on the sixteen-year-old Avraam Mordko Savranskii (resident of the town of Golovanevska) appealed to the provincial board of Podolia on 21 July (!)[1] to inquire about this case. The rabbi also indicates that the ritual of circumcision was not performed on time because Avraam's two older brothers had died from the circumcision (because of hemophilia).

For my part, with respect to this matter I should note that Jewish law (*Shulhan Arukh, Yoreh Deah*, chapter 252) establishes a specific date — that is, the eighth day after birth — when the ritual of circumcision should be performed. However, if it is not performed on time (because of illness or other special reasons), then there is no fixed age for performing this ritual. Furthermore, according to [state law],[2] it is evident that after the ritual has been performed it is to be recorded in the metrical books; the preface to article 913 provides that under special circumstances birth and circumcision can be registered separately. Since the circumcision may be performed at any age under Jewish law, in my opinion the rabbi may do this if he were to perform the circumcision on the sixteen-year-old Savranskii.

Regarding the possibility of performing circumcision on a hemophiliac, under Jewish law they absolutely do not perform circumcision on the third son if the parents' two sons died earlier from this operation. According to the *Shulhan Arukh, Yoreh Deah* (chapter 253), it may be possible to perform the ritual on the third son with hemophilia when he grows up and becomes stronger. However, the Talmud (*Tosefta Hullin* 4, 2) does not permit circumcision even at an older age if it has been established that the first two sons died from the circumcision (regardless if they were completely healthy). Meanwhile, in [this] case there is no information about whether Avraam's brothers, who died after the operation, were healthy at the time of the circumcision. Thus the Rabbinic Commission can hardly come to a definitive conclusion regarding this case.[3] At the same time, given that fourteen years have passed since the governor of Podolia submitted the question about transferring this case to the purview of the Rabbinic Commission in the Ministry of Internal Affairs, it is now inopportune to attend to this personal matter, but it is a matter of fundamental importance. Therefore I propose that the Rabbinic Commission proceed to discuss the following questions:

1. At which age is it possible to perform the rite of circumcision according to Jewish law?

2. Is it possible to register the ritual of circumcision when it has not been performed?

3. Can a rabbi be allowed to perform the ritual of circumcision in the case of hemophilia and, if so, until what age and under what conditions (for example, in the presence of a doctor)?

"Draft of the Rabbinic Commission's Deliberation" (undated)[4]

If two sons of the parents die from the circumcision due to hemophilia from hemorrhaging (although the latter were not from same father and mother), or even if both sons of the mother's sister died, or all the more so if one son of each of her sisters died, then usually the ritual is not performed on the third son in the prescribed manner and time (see *Yevamot* 64b, *Shulhan Arukh, Yoreh Deah* 263, 2, 3).

There are three opinions about whether and when to perform this ritual (in effect, when the infant grows up and gets stronger), namely: (a) in general, one is effectively not permitted to perform the ritual of circumcision on the third son (see *Tosefot*, tractate *Gittin* 20b, *Zevahim* 75a, *Minachot* 62b, and *Berachot* 61a); (b) if the aforementioned infants died after circumcision, having been healthy, then it is not appropriate to perform this ritual on the third son (see *Tosefot*, tractate *Hullin* 4b); (c) in all cases it is proper to perform this ritual on the third son around the age of three (see Maimonides, *Hilchot milah* 1, 18 and *Shulhan Arukh, Yoreh Deah* 263, 2; Responsa *Noda bi-Yehuda*, vol. 2, *Yoreh Deah* 165).

Under these considerations, the learned Jew [Kreps] proposes that in this case, when the rabbi, parents, or the very individual who faces circumcision insists on the necessity of performing circumcision, then this ritual might be permitted, but only at the age established by a medical institution and in the presence of a medical specialist, especially since that would not contradict the demands of Jewish law.

"Certificate" [n.d.]

Explanation of the Cassation Department in the State (26 March 1902): the circumcision may be performed by a surgeon.

"Governor's Report to the Department of Spiritual Affairs of Foreign Faiths (24 June 1908)"

According to the assembled information, the ritual of circumcision was apparently performed on the Jew Avraam Savranskii (the son of Mordko Savranskii, resident of the town of Golovanevska) ten days ago at the city hospital in the city of Odessa. At present, Avraam Savranskii, who is married and has children, has already been working as a carpenter for two years.

NOTES

1. [Here M. Kreps notes an obvious mistake in the dates: the rabbi allegedly sent his petition on 21 July 1894, and the governor issued his papers on 21 March 1894.]

2. [The document cited *Svod zakonov grazhdanskikh* vol. 9, statute 914, published in 1899.]

3. See *Tosafot, Gittin* 20b, *Zevachim* 5a, *Minachot* 62b, and *Berachot* 61a; see also *Yevamot* 64b, *Shulhan Arukh, Yoreh Deah* 263: 2–3; Maimonides, *Hilchot Milah* 1: 18; Responsa *Noda bi-Yehuda*, vol. 2, chapter 6, which is cited in *Piske teshuvah* to part 2, chapter 263, *Yoreh Deah, Shulhan Arukh.*

4. [After summarizing Kreps's report, the Commission upholds his opinion that circumcision should be performed eight days after birth but, in the case of illness or another important reason, can be deferred until it becomes possible. It authorized the registration of circumcision at a later point only if the state rabbi had previously recorded the birth.]

Diet, Hygiene, and Exercise

[65]

Dr. Gottlieb's Advice for Good Health (1911)

Dr. Meir Gottlieb, *Zeit gezunt* (Warsaw: A. Gitlin, 1911), chapter 3.

How does one protect oneself from consumption?— Cleanliness of the air and apartments.—Our orthodoxy and the houses of study.—Summer colonies for Jewish children and farms.—Our private schools.

It is much easier to protect oneself from consumption than to treat the disease after it has already developed. I hereby suggest principles to preserve one's well-being—rules for protecting one's health, which are very important for parents who want to raise healthy children.

In our time people believe less in pharmaceutical means and attach much greater importance to hygienic measures, which can protect us from many diseases and give our organism the strength to battle diseases that have already developed.

Apartments. Our apartments must be clean, well lit, and dry.

Air. The air that we breathe must be clean.

Nourishment. Our nourishment (food) must be varied (different every day), fresh, and sufficient for nourishing our organism.

As the reader is well aware, poor people have difficulty obtaining apartments, nourishment, and clean air adequate to promote good health, but in this regard I have no advice as a physician. Only the improvement of our economic situation can help in this re-spect. But a certain part of our middle class also lives in dirty, damp apartments, breathes and allows their children to inhale stuffy air and so forth, because they do not know how harmful it is for their health.

Our apartments must be clean. Why is dirt in apartments harmful? I do not speak in an aesthetic sense—the frequent lack of beauty among our masses. But dirt brings all kinds of infection.

I have already demonstrated above that consumption is a contagious disease: we become infected through the stuffy unclean air, unclean food, dirty handkerchiefs, clothes and underwear, unclean glasses, plates, towels, and so forth. All this creates conditions for becoming infected not only with tuberculosis (consumption), but also with typhus, smallpox, diphtheria, various skin and venereal diseases, etc.

Our teacher Moses placed great emphasis on purity: whenever he gave admonitions about purity, he always said, "for thou art a holy people." Unfortunately, we are now no longer holy and clean. The sages of the Talmud placed even greater emphasis on purity: [1]"תלמיד חכם שנמצא רבב על בגדו חייב מיתה": "a scholar (who should be a model for the entire nation) who has a spot on his garments deserves to be killed." This is hyperbole, but one can see from it how much cleanliness mattered to them, whereas now everything among us has changed. Let us consider ritual hand washing as an example. The sages of the Talmud, for the sake of cleanliness, greatly stressed hand washing and made it obligatory immediately upon awakening as well as before eating ("the first waters" and "the last waters"). Here they concur with modern scientists, who say: "The amount of water and the weight of the soap used by every nation shows to what degree it is civilized (developed, rational). Many a contagious disease, including cholera, typhus, consumption, etc., is caused by bringing dirty hands to our mouths, for masses of harmless and harmful bacteria (fungi) remain on the hands, especially when earlier we held dirty objects. But we must conclude that ritual hand washing is simply a matter of form: one pours water on the hands, but whether the hands become clean does not concern us. How often do we witness our common tradesmen switching from work to eating with dirty hands, without even the ritual hand washing. Without soap, the hands cannot be clean after work; along with the food, we are liable to bring infection into our mouths. This behavior stems from our lack of rationality and thoughtfulness. We do not think, but do it as "a commandment of men taught by rote"—that is, without thinking, merely from habit.[2]

Dirt has become second nature to our masses. For what can compete with the Jewish neighborhood and dwelling when it comes to filth? He who hath not seen Warsaw's Franciszkanska and Krochmalna Streets or Jewish and Yatkever [Butcher Shop] Streets in Vil'na, and other such, he hath seen no garbage from since he came into the world!

Praised be God for giving us Passover. If not for Passover, who knows how Jewish dwellings would look! But this is also the reason why we keep the dirt under the beds, in the corners, under chairs, as if we were afraid that on Passover Eve we would have nothing to

use in the ritual of burning leaven. In so many Jewish dwellings, especially in the provinces, the floor is washed only once a year (on Passover Eve). In our houses of study we are followed by the same dirt: one only sweeps once a week on Sabbath eve, and since there are no spittoons everybody spits wherever he pleases. This is the state inside the house of study, but outside it is even worse. Every nation reveres its places of prayer, but among our people in the provinces and even in big cities, heaps of garbage pile up next to synagogues, so that the words of the prophet are fulfilled: "And, lo, they put the branch to their nose" (Ezekiel 8:17). Often there is an inscription on the synagogue wall: "No urinating on the wall," but from this our average Jew finds out where he should urinate, forgetting what the prophet says about those "urinating on the wall." These things must be remedied! What can you expect from people who lack sufficient understanding to respect the house of God?

Our dwellings must be clean! But this is only half of what is needed, for the same applies to our clothes and undergarments. One often sees wealthy Jewish women dressed in velvet and silk, but wearing dirty underwear. Every doctor (semite or antisemite) who examines Jewish patients knows this.

Compare two poor sick maids who come to a hospital for advice. Without even seeing the face or hearing the "voice of Jacob," we can determine who is the grandchild of Jacob and who is that of Esau—based only on their clothes. Jacob's hands, which are none too clean, are also different from the hands of Esau.

Just look at how a Jew binds his wounds! A wound should be kept clean, otherwise it can lead to erysipelas (St. Anthony's fire), gangrene, and the like. Yet our fellow Jews use a dirty handkerchief or dirty old rags, smearing the wound with bull's gall and soiling it with old wives' remedies. The poor people! They do not know "כי בנפשם הוא," that is, this is a mortal danger. If they do not infect the wound, it is only because "שומר פתאים ד'" (that is, God takes care of all fools), yet miracles do not happen every day. As the rabbis of the Talmud say: "It is not every day that a miracle comes to pass." How unclean is our environment and how little does it bother us! Years ago, as a student, I served on a sanitary commission (which occupies itself with health issues); it visited, examined, and described (for statistical purposes) every apartment in Warsaw. I worked on a Jewish street (Mila St.), where the majority (95 percent) of residents were Jews. Once I was in a one-room Jewish apartment that housed an entire family; as usual, it was very dirty: the floor was wet; there was enough garbage in the corners that it could be shoveled; cockroaches and other small creatures were crawling on the walls; dirty linens covered the beds. On one wall hung the portrait of a rabbi, but this could be ascertained only from the inscription under the portrait, for the rabbi was smeared from top to bottom by flies. On the opposite wall hung a *mizrah*.[3] In its earlier days it must have been a very beautiful work of art, but now it was a true "memory of destruction," utterly destroyed by age, dust, and cobwebs.

"Why have you so neglected your household?" I asked the mistress. "May you be well," says the lady, who was wearing a wig with feathers. "It is after all a month before Passover. Come to us on Passover and you will see how clean and fine our home really is."

On the same corridor I went to see another apartment, also consisting of a single room and housing an entire family, and imagine my surprise at my finding quite the opposite of the first apartment. The floor was washed clean; a pure, white cloth covered the table. There were white linens on the bed, holy pictures in clean glass frames on the walls; everything was in its place and everything sparkling; the mistress was dressed poorly, but tastefully and cleanly. The difference from the first apartment was like day and night. I was naive enough to ask the Jewish lady, who also came into her neighbor's room: "What is the reason for this? Why is your place so dirty while it is so clean here?" I did not receive an answer from her, for she felt ashamed, but the other woman looked carefully at my nose and having certainly noticed that it was "of long dimensions" and hooked (woe to us!) said, with great haughtiness, as though she were Countess Potocka: "I am a Christian, and she a Jewess!" This explained everything I had seen; there were no more questions; everything was accounted for. But how much shame for us!

Here I want to mention a beautiful custom. I do not know whether it is different in big cities; I have observed it many times in the provinces. You come to a sick person who has been in bed for several weeks; he lies dressed in a shirt that he has been wearing for two to three weeks. Under a microscope (a type of magnifying glass), one can detect on him exquisite articles from a zoological museum, small and large (one can find them by Rabbi Judah's signs).

"Why don't you put on a fresh shirt?"

"What do you mean? People say it is dangerous to change the shirt on a sick person," says a female relative who has come to visit the sick man.

Let us return to our initial point: whether consumption has already developed or whether we aim to protect ourselves from the disease, it is very important that our apartments, furniture, clothes, and underwear be clean.

Air purity. Clean, fresh air is a necessity for our bodies, just as bread and meat are.

A person cannot remain healthy in stuffy air, just as he cannot remain healthy if he always eats spoiled or non-nutritious foods. The stuffier the air, the less the room is ventilated (aired), the more the carbonic acid [carbon dioxide] collects and the more harmful it is for the organism. Air consists of various gases, of which the most beneficial for us is oxygen and the most harmful carbonic acid. What is clean air, and how important is it for the organism? Of this our common people do not have any notion. Our masses understand that a sick person should have good refreshment, wine, but they fail to grasp that the healthy and especially the sick should breathe clean air. The worst rooms are usually designated as bedrooms, which often have no windows or ventilation. We forget that we spend one-third of our lives in the bedroom; moreover, our breathing is weaker when we sleep! Our usual methods of ventilation — opening a window, stoking up a fireplace — at night are complicated for several reasons. We therefore should designate our best rooms as the bedrooms. The recent trend among our middle classes, to place the beds in the living room, is very good; it is better to sleep in a large room than to open such a room for guests once a week or even once a month. Our common folk cling to the misconception that one may not open a window when there is a sick person in the house, especially one suffering from a lung disease, for the person can catch a cold. In summer, spring, and autumn, when the weather is mild, the sick person will not catch a cold; in winter, spring, or fall when it rains, snows, or is windy, one can open a small window panel (or the whole window when it is not cold) for fifteen to sixty minutes, having moved the sick person during this time to another room. If there is only one room, one can cover the sick person's head with a bedspread and open the window.

For ventilation it is good to stoke the fireplace daily, so that fresh air enters the room. When there is artificial ventilation, one should use it; it is not for decoration, but for freshening the air, especially in buildings for schools, *hadarim*, yeshivot, factories, and elsewhere. One should be especially concerned about good fresh air in places where large numbers of people gather. In schools, *hadarim*, and yeshivot, windows or small window panels should be opened every day; in summer they should be kept open all day and in other seasons from one-half to two hours (depending on the weather) before the congregation gathers for prayer, or before the children come together for classes and for the same duration after they leave. One should also sweep the floor (before opening the windows) and wipe the floor and furniture with a damp cloth both before and after.

As early as fifty years ago the best people of our nation observed that our *heder* with its steamy air, its dirt, the rebbetzin's hens, roosters, and geese (which always leave traces of their presence on the table, tablecloth, floor, etc.) — is killing our children and often leaves them scrofulous, consumptive, and hunchbacked (many Jewish writers have long been complaining about this). How can children be healthy, how can they not be narrow-chested, if they have to sit all day under the teacher's supervision as if chained to the table, and in winter several hours at night as well? How can children have broad chests if they do not move for hours on end? How can their spinal columns be straight if the children sit for hours hunched over; how can they have healthy lungs if twenty to thirty children study in a room that would scarcely allow fifteen to breathe freely? In the provinces in winter and often in summer no windows are opened in the *hadarim*, and the reason is quite simple: the houses are built and the windows are made without any regard for the health of the residents. If one did not know who lived in these houses, one would think that these were cattle barns.

When the room is swept, the dust gets into the children's throats. To run around and climb, to get into mischief, to play and have fun — these are all sins, for which only a whipping with a belt can compensate. Poor Jewish children! When will you also breathe clean air? When will someone see to it that you develop physically (in your bodies) like others?

In winter one studies at night by a tallow candle; how can the children not become nearsighted when they have to stare for hours with a lowered head (the blood rushing into their heads) at Rashi's letters? The last words of the famous German poet Goethe before his death were: "More light! More light!" We too must demand: "More light and clean air!" For ourselves and for our *heder* children.

Our apartments should have enough light! The sunlight destroys the bacteria that cause consumption and other contagious diseases. In dark rooms, in contrast (as our bedrooms often are), harmful bacteria thrive best. Recent scientific experiments demonstrated the great importance of sunlight for organic life, for animals and plants. Accordingly we find that many plants grow only in sunlight and wither in darkness. Other plants grow straight in sunlight and crooked in darkness. We encounter the same among people: dark dwellings produce deformed children with humps, crooked legs—that is, children suffer from the English disease (rickets) or consumption of the spinal column. As an Italian adage goes: "If a dwelling has light, the doctor does not come there!"

Our apartments should be dry! Dampness in a room often causes rheumatism, the English disease, and scrofula. One should not live in a house that has only recently been built. One should wait for a year or two (until the walls have completely dried). One should not build houses in a damp or low place; it is best to build a house on sandy soil or in a hilly location. When an apartment is damp, but not equally in all rooms, one should sleep in the drier room. When all the rooms are damp or if the apartment consists of a single room and this room is damp, one should move the beds away from the wall and cover the wall with a carpet or boards; one should also keep the windows open all day in summer and in other seasons for one to three hours daily (depending on the weather) and stoke the ovens once or twice a day—good ventilation is the best measure against dampness.

Consumption, as statistics show, is much more common in big cities than in small towns or villages, and much more widespread in industrial districts than in agricultural ones. Thus statistics show that in industrial cities in Switzerland three out of a thousand people die yearly, whereas in villages it is only one out of a thousand. These numbers show that patients with consumption are found three times less often in villages than in industrial cities. From this we can see the importance of clean air for people's health. It is therefore very good to send the children away to the country in summer. Indeed, that is a necessity for scrofulous children (that is, for those who have swollen lymph glands on the neck and are disposed to diseases that come from colds, for those with a cough, etc.).

Rich people can easily follow my recommendation, but the poor find it very difficult. However, the latter can send their children for daily walks in city parks or in the woods outside the city. Recently, societies have been founded in all big cities to fund sending poor children to the country for six to eight weeks in the summer. Such a society has existed in Warsaw for eight years and in Lodz for six years. Each year the Warsaw society sends up to 3,000 children, both Jewish and Christian. Last year it was 2,500, and this year it will be even more. The children usually gain from eight to fourteen pounds; they become more cheerful and lively; their cheeks gain color; their muscles gain strength; and their character improves—usually such children have no supervision at home. The parents toil and sweat all day long and often at night as well (as in the case of tradesmen) to support the family and have no time to instruct their children. I am surprised that in Vil'na, Minsk, and the like, where our fellow Jews are stuck in narrow and filthy streets, and where there are many great Jewish almsgivers (as is fitting for "the merciful sons of the merciful") and Jewish societies are formed every day, there is still no society to care for poor children and send them to dachas in the country in summer. We hope that with time such societies will be founded in Lithuania and will save hundreds of children from consumption.

Here I want to point out a recent novelty in Jewish upbringing. Six years ago a farm was founded in Odessa to teach Jewish children gardening. The farm is outside of town, has several *desiatina*⁴ of land, and works the land using its own resources (that is, the students work it under the supervision of their teacher, who is an agronomist—a specialist in agriculture). The students plant trees and various annual plants. The farm has two goals: one is to accustom city children to gardening and to train them as good agriculturalists, and the second is to give poor children the chance to breathe fresh air for a year or two and to develop muscles and broad chests. Everyone understands how good it is for a child's organism, and everyone sympathetic to this cause can feel happy that such farms have already been established in other cities (including, as far as I recall, Kherson, Akkerman, Bender, and Mogilev). We learn from Jewish newspapers that other Jewish communities also intend to open such farms this year.

One should strengthen children while they are still little by letting them outside in any weather. Why does a village peasant let his children walk barefoot in the severest cold? Why do our children catch a cold from the slightest rain or wind, even though they are wrapped in kerchiefs, shawls, and furs? The tender mother thinks she does a favor to her children by always keeping them inside, unless they are dressed, or rather overdressed, in all kinds of warm kerchiefs. She is greatly mistaken and does her children a disservice, for the children become accustomed to it; if such a child later catches a cold after forgetting to put a shawl on the neck, the responsibility rests with the loving but ignorant mother.

What of our private schools, the craftwork of our girls? How healthful is it to sit all day in the same spot and embroider Saul with Jonathan or Haman with Mordecai? I talked

earlier about *hadarim*, but the other private schools that most of our children attend leave much to be done with respect to health. Children spend six to seven hours sitting in class, and many get headaches from the stuffy air. Only at noon during the long recess do children go into the yard to breathe fresh air (although the yard is often small and dirty). After these six to seven hours, when the student comes home, often with a headache, he or she has another hour before dinner. After dinner they have to prepare lessons for the next day's classes, or to take additional private lessons in other languages, Hebrew, and music. Thus the day passes until 11 to 12 at night, when the child goes to bed and will spend the next day in the same manner. How can one develop physically while living like this? How can one have a broad chest? How can one acquire muscle strength? What we just described is in fact a relatively tranquil period; during the examination period, female students often sit up all night and study world history, geography, etc., and some stay up until 3:00 a.m. We know that sitting quietly in closed rooms and getting too little sleep at night are the best agents of consumption.

If you want to know how good movement, fresh air, and gymnastics affect the state of a child's health, compare our *heder* children or even the students of our private schools with English students. The latter are strong, cheerfully dexterous; color plays on their cheeks; for them life is movement. Playing ball, riding boats, riding horses, jumping, running, doing gymnastics—these are for them as important as science. And not only school pupils but also university students play ball. Breathing fresh air for three to four hours, and simultaneously doing gymnastics or climbing, running, and the like—that is needed by all *heder* boys and all students of private schools; it vitally necessary for children who come from consumptive families, who have swollen lymph glands, and who have scrofulous rashes or nose and eye catarrh. For the latter it is not enough to take a walk; the boy or the girl must engage in thorough gymnastics and, if possible, rowing — not only during vacation but also during the school year. It is better for the boy to skip a few pages of the Talmud or a few poems than compromise his physical development. How much health he will gain by it!

Poor people! When you are ill, you seek help from professors and ask them to give you a prescription to remedy an illness. But the pharmacy has no cure for consumption or other such infectious diseases, whereas nature provides many ways to stay healthy. We consider these natural means worthless (because they are free); our people respect only what is expensive. The doctor is judged by the cost of his horses and carriage and the prescription by its price; fresh air and exercise cost nothing and for this very reason are considered worthless.

Dear reader! Do you have brothers or sisters who suffer from (or have died from) consumption? Perhaps your brothers and sisters are healthy, but your wife is consumptive or has a sick brother? Or has your father or grandfather suffered from consumption? Are you yourself healthy? But has the disease, leaving the consumptive person's son in peace, reappeared in his grandson, as in the case I described in the chapter on heredity? Or is there no heredity of consumption in your family, but your children are scrofulous or suffer a consumptive ailment in their joints (the joints are swollen, hurt, and the illness lasts a long time and can, God forbid, require the amputation of an arm or a leg, or is one leg shorter upon recovery)? So, when the time comes for your children to pick occupations and decide which of their talents they will use to make a living, it is not enough to consult with your wife or even your other relatives — one should first of all listen to one's family doctor or any doctor. The choice of profession often makes a difference for a healthy person, all the more so for a son who, through heredity or scrofula, already bears the seed of the

terrible disease, consumption. If the soil is fertile and rain falls at the right time, the seed will sprout and bloom, but it will die if the soil is full of sand and rocks or if no rain falls. Your son, if possible, should choose an occupation that will always allow him to enjoy fresh air, to live in the village, and to exercise — whether he be a farmer, a gardener, an agrarian, a forester, estate manager, or the like (which is possible in Poland, since Jews there may live in villages).

Your daughters should take a daily stroll, engage in gymnastics if possible, and avoid sitting constantly inside making handicrafts, embroidering some trifle that will do nobody any good. Embroidering yet another Saul with Jonathan on canvas (which her mother-in-law will perhaps look at once) or some little dog or cat takes hours of hard work. Embroidery is regarded a life necessity without which no young girl can attain perfection; yet she deserves little praise for being some kind of artist. A clever young lady would rather spend her time jumping, dancing, and doing gymnastics. She will not be as romantically pale, but will put on color to be a healthy young lady — which is beautiful, for healthy is beautiful. The handicrafts, without which a woman cannot attain perfection, have now become very common, even among the upper classes. Every young lady from a wealthy family has to spend all day chained to the piano, even if she has no ear or ability for music; she must paint on paper or on porcelain even if she has no talent. (I am not speaking of craftswomen such as hat decorators or necktie makers who make a living from it.) But because of these pursuits, she can be presented as the perfect bride. "It's no laughing matter," says her mother, "she plays like Meyerbeer and paints like Rubens." "She is pale," you say, "and anemic." "Do you want my daughter to be fat and red, like a peasant?"

Dancing, as a form of gymnastics, can be allowed and even recommended, but only under the following rules: (1) one should only dance for a one-half to one hour, but no more than two hours with breaks and never all night long to the point of experiencing shortness of breath and a pounding heart; (2) one should dance in the open air or in a big hall, where no more than five to ten couples are dancing; when twenty-five to one hundred couples dance in the Warsaw halls, the air becomes increasingly worse because of the carbonic acid from breathing, the lighting, and the dust, so that by 3 or 4 a.m. the air is quite stifling. The dust collects in the throat, lungs, and nose. Then it often becomes difficult to utter a single word because the nose has been filled with soot like a chimney.

The ball is over (the party at the Warsaw Muscat Hall in Swiss Valley[5] has concluded), and one goes home (thank God), perspiring, soaked, exhausted, and barely alive. People have a heavy heart and the next day are often prostrate in bed. At this point pneumonia, bronchitis, and coughing up blood are liable to commence in those who were completely healthy before and in those who are predisposed to consumption. I am not against dancing; to some degree, dancing can even substitute for the gymnastics that most people practice so little. However, dancing all night—while squeezed into corsets and later walking home perspiring and dressed in ballroom dresses and a thin mantelet (and doing this every month or even every week) is certainly not a healthful activity for our ladies.

When I say that one should consult a doctor about the choice of profession for young people from ailing families, the reader should not conclude that these are mere words and that the occupation really has no effect (as something invented by doctors sitting in their offices). Do you want to hear facts? Then consider the following story about a consumptive family, which the famous German physician practicing in London, Hermann Weber,[6] describes in his lectures. Dr. Weber treated a teacher and his wife, who both came from consumptive families and who died one after the other from consumption. They were survived by six children (one other child had died of consumption while the parents were still alive). The six orphans, aged one through twelve, were healthy; they had eleven cousins, nine of whom died from consumption, and none of whom lived beyond the age of twenty-eight. A more awful heredity is indeed difficult to find; everyone can imagine what a terrible fate awaited the unhappy orphans. The children were raised by their relatives in Silesia (in Prussia), in a mountainous area. The doctor explained to the guardians how the children should be raised, and everything was done according to his recommendations: they remained in the country, enjoyed fresh air and movement, engaged in gymnastics, and so on. We can now see the effects of their upbringing:

1. The oldest son was healthy as long as he remained in the country. This was until he turned twenty-three and began his studies. He would study inside the house day and night and stopped taking healthful walks and engaging in gymnastics. They even brought food to his room. A few months later this young man fell ill with a galloping consumption and died one year later.

2. The second son remained an agriculturist until the age of twenty-nine and was as healthy as a fish. However, he was dissatisfied because he earned little from farming and joined a firm in a big city and started to work in an office, spending all day in a stuffy room. He began to cough and would often spit blood; he died two years later.

3. The third child went to serve in the army, became a cavalryman, and is healthy to this day.

4. The fourth, a girl, married a shepherd in a village; she is in entirely good health.

5. The youngest son is a farmer in Canada ([North] America); he is a fine, healthy young man.

6. The youngest sister, who lives with her brother in Canada, is healthy and strong.

The story of this family, observed by Dr. Weber for over thirty years, shows how important it is for children in consumptive families to be raised not according to their own or their parents' wishes, but according to a doctor's recommendation.

Professor [Vilém D.] Lambl, a learned physician who died in Warsaw in 1895, told his students: "It is not true that consumption is incurable." As the professor said, "I knew students and scientists who had been ill with consumption in their youth, but who later left their jobs in the big city, went to the village, became landowners, and engaged in agriculture. A few years later I encountered them; they were healthy, strong, and content with their fate."

I myself know a Polish woman who comes from a sickly family and who was consumptive in her youth (she constantly coughed and often spit blood). She then married and settled in a village. She is now wealthy and has enough time for walks and sleep; she drank a lot of milk (three to four quarts a day) and soon recovered. She gave birth ten times; she is now sixty years old and in good health.

So far the discussion has focused on the general principles of protecting children from consumption. It should be added that milk from cows that suffer from pearly tumor (especially those with sores on their udders) is contagious, and it often infects adults and children with consumption. Hence milk should be boiled for five minutes, thereby destroying the fungi and bacilli so that they can do no more harm. Every mother, when giving her child cow's milk, should stand by the fire herself and allow the milk to boil for five minutes. She should not rely on her cook, who often just warms the milk up but says it has already boiled.

NOTES

1. [*Shabbat* 114a.]

2. [Isaiah 29:13.]

3. [A picture with a scene from the Land of Israel designating the wall facing the direction of Jerusalem.]

4. [A *desiatin* is equivalent to 1.07 hectares.]

5. [*Dolina Szwajcarska*, a park in Warsaw that offered a variety of musical entertainment.]

6. [Sir Hermann Weber (1823–1918), a British physician born at Holzkirchen, Germany, made a career in England, where he became famous for his open-air treatment of tuberculosis.]

[66]

Dr. Gottlieb's Advice for a Healthy Diet

Dr. Meir Gottlieb, *Populere algemeyne higyene* (Warsaw: Ha-or, 1908), chapter 4.

From time to time, man must assuage his hunger and thirst through eating and drinking. However, there are many kinds of food, and they affect a person's health in different ways. Some foods are more nutritious and strengthening than others. The more nutritious the food, the faster it makes one satiated and the easier it is to digest. The contrary is also true: the less nutritious a food, the more one must consume to feel satiated and hence the harder it is to digest. Moreover, some foods taste better than others. Yet one cannot always make judgments based on taste, since the pleasant and tasty are not always healthful.

Under normal circumstances, one-fifth of a person's nourishment should consist of solids, such as bread, meat, cheese, butter, eggs, potatoes, and fruit; and four-fifths of liquids, such as water, milk, soup, tea, coffee, etc. One should ingest primarily plant foods, adding eggs, butter, cheese, meat, and the like. All food should be salted, for this makes it more agreeable and easier to digest. Plant products should be combined with animal products: for instance, bread with butter and eggs, bread with cheese, etc. Bread should be a person's main food; it is easily digestible and very nutritious. The crust is digested in the stomach more quickly than the crumbs, especially when one eats in haste. It is therefore preferable to bake bread in loaves that are as small and as elongated as possible (and thereby minimize the amount of crumbs).

Bread also facilitates the digestion of other foods. It is thus very important that meat and other foods, especially those rich in fat, be eaten with bread. Bread that is too sour from sitting uncooked for too long and has undergone excessive fermentation is unhealthy, as is bread containing too much bran or too much water (more than 35–40 percent): moist bread spoils quickly because harmful microbes develop in it. Bread containing potato flour or legumes is also unhealthy, for it is very difficult to digest.

The healthiest meat is beef, best eaten when roasted. Boiled meat loses all its nutritional power to the broth during cooking. One must be very careful, however, to avoid spoiled meat and sausage. Spoiled sausage can be recognized by the following signs: it has a somewhat sweet or sour taste; dark spots appear in places; the fat is tinged with green, red, blue, or dark yellow.

A good supplement to meat is vegetables cooked in fat and bread, for both facilitate digestion. It is better to eat first the cooked vegetables and then the meat, because liquid food more quickly stimulates the stomach juice[s] (highly necessary for digesting the more solid foods). For dessert it is always healthy to eat fruit, best of all cooked as a compote.

It is absolutely necessary to designate specific times for meals. One should be aware of the general principle that it is good to eat every four hours. If one takes breakfast at eight, one should eat lunch at noon, have a snack at four, and supper at eight. This is the best daily regimen. One should eat breakfast no later than a half hour after rising.

One should eat in moderation and never overeat: overfilling the pot makes cooking difficult. *It is better not to eat one's fill than to eat too much.* Overeating causes various stomach illnesses. One should always eat slowly, without haste, and chew well, because only this ensures that the food is sufficiently soft and soaked in saliva, which is absolutely necessary for digestion. *Well chewed is half digested.*

It is harmful to eat while standing or sitting hunched over. When one is standing, the stomach muscles are too stretched; when one is sitting hunched over, the stomach is pressed too much together. In both cases the stomach cannot do its work properly. It is also harmful to eat where the room is dusty or the air is stale. Many people like to read while eating, but this is a very bad habit: that forces the stomach and the brain to work simultaneously. Even an angel, let alone an ordinary human being, cannot accomplish two tasks simultaneously.

To aid digestion, it is very helpful to rest for an hour after each meal and especially after lunch rather than immediately start to work. However, to sleep immediately after eating is not good either. Since not everyone can afford to rest after eating, one should remember to eat somewhat less and not to stuff one's stomach excessively if one has to work immediately afterward.

In addition to bread and meat, the most nutritious foods include the following. Cheese is very nutritious, but one should not eat a lot of it since it causes severe constipation. Cheese that is moldy or has yellow, green, or blue spots should be avoided. It is also inadvisable to drink hot tea right after consuming cheese. Butter is also quite nutritious and healthful, but must be very fresh. Sugar is very healthful for adults and even more so for children: it warms the body; however, one should not consume too much of it. Eggs can serve as a substitute for meat. The white is more nutritious than the yolk. It is better to use eggs that are raw or slightly cooked: hard-boiled eggs are difficult to digest and require extensive chewing; one should not eat hard-boiled eggs at night, or even in the evening, because it takes a long time to digest them.

Peas, beans, and lentils are the most nutritious of all plants. It is advisable to cook these legumes in fat and consume them with bread. Potatoes and other foods containing a large amount of starch should be consumed sparingly.

As for liquids, beverages are necessary for a human being, and the most important one is water. Just as air is necessary for our body, so too is water. The largest part of every liquid consists of water, and water also accounts for three-quarters of our bodily weight. Without water there would be no life in the world. It is very healthy to drink a glass of pure water every morning after rising and every night before going to bed, as well as after every meal. This regulates the functioning of the stomach and the intestines. The water must, however, be clean and fresh and come from a flowing water source. Water from a nonflowing source, such as a lake or a ditch, as well as running water that flows through muddy, slimy, or peaty soil, or that contains factory waste is very harmful: it is filled with microbes that can cause various diseases. Bad water disrupts digestion, harms the blood, and makes the face pale. Good water has no color or smell; nor does it leave any sediment on the bottom of the container. If there is a yellow, gray, or brown sediment on the bottom of the vessel, it is not clean and as such [is] dangerous, especially if it is not boiled. It is highly advisable always to boil water before use.

Milk is the most nutritious of all drinks. It contains all the substances beneficial for the body—viz., nitrogen, fat, and sugar. Hence it is the best nutrition for children and for the weak and sick in general. It is better to use boiled milk.

Black coffee refreshes the nerves and gives energy. It is therefore very healthful to have a glass of black coffee once a day, especially in the winter, for it warms the stomach and facilitates its functioning. Cocoa contains a copious amount of fat [. . .] and is therefore a very nutritious beverage. All drinks and foods when ingested should not be too hot or too cold. Foods that are too hot or too cold cause stomach catarrh and ulcers.

As for strong drinks (such as wine, vodka, cognac, and all liqueurs), it is better not to consume them at all, with the exception of every Simchas Torah and Purim, when a Jew is obliged to have a little drink. These beverages deprive a person of his strength, weakening the marrow, the nerves, and the entire body. Uncertain movements, confused thoughts, and stomach catarrhs are the sad consequences of consuming liquor. During or right after a meal one may, however, permit oneself to have a glass of good beer.

[67]

Responsum of R. Naftali Zvi Yehudah Berlin of Volozhin: Polluted Water and Wells (1880)

Naftali Zvi Yehudah Berlin, *Meshiv davar* 2: 27–28 (Warsaw: [s.n.], 1893).

GOD BE BLESSED, THE THIRD DAY OF
THE INTERMEDIATE DAYS OF PASSOVER,
5640 [1880], ZVINIKRADKE

TO THE HONORED RABBI,
THE TRULY GREAT GENIUS. [. . .]

Question: I recently became rabbi and righteous decisor of this community, and I found that the members of the community do not avail themselves of the water from the river that runs through the town, because they said that years ago swarming creatures were discovered in the water, smaller than sesame seeds, such that they could not be seen by the eye except that when one shakes the jug, they are seen to be moving up and down through the water. In a glass jar one will see only one or two, perhaps three, of [these creatures]; yet, this clearly shows empirically that the creatures can pass through a filter. Thus until now people have declared the water [from this river] unfit [for consumption].[1]

People of the town are thirsty for water, as there are only two good wells outside the town, and these belong to one man, who will provide water only for as high a price as he can get. The cry of the destitute is great, for they cannot afford the water; they are forced to drink the water of broken and turbid wells.[2]

Hence they have asked me to review this urgent matter, and to ask the giants of the generation if perhaps their wisdom will be sufficiently great as to permit [consumption of] water from the river. Based on what I heard, I realized that the water had not been tested for a long time, so I went many times to check this water — thoroughly and with discerning eyes — and I found it clean and pure, with no creatures in it. I therefore permitted them to consume the water, but only through the Passover holiday, after which I will recheck the water, as I am concerned that as a result of melting snow or the summer heat, the creatures may reappear. This matter begins with the insignificant, such as I, and will be concluded by giants like him.[3]

Response: Regarding the matter of the river, once the water has been carefully checked it may be used. [. . .] But the water must be examined periodically, during both winter and summer, for it is possible that the air [weather] is the cause. It is also necessary to examine the water as the river leaves the town: if one checks it as it enters the town, we would have to worry that air pollutants in the middle of the town or at its outskirts cause the swarm. But if one checks the river as it flows out of town, there is no cause for concern: if the swarm emerged at the entrance of the town, it would still be discernible at the exit.

NOTES

1. [The halakhic issues are complex here. The critical point is that although, in general, a tiny amount of forbidden food is nullified by a permitted amount that is sixty times greater and that in general one must consume an olive-size measure of forbidden food to violate the law, these rules do not apply when the forbidden food consumed is a complete creature, such as an ant. In that case, the smallest amount is forbidden. Thus, these nearly microscopic swarming creatures would mean a ban on the consumption of this water.]

2. [The meaning here is that the plaster of the wells had breaks in it, and mud (and perhaps plaster chips) were to be found in the water.]

3. [Referring to Berlin; it was customary to address rabbis of high reputation in the third person. Evidently to indicate the urgency of the matter, the rabbi adds that even if the creatures were found again in the water, on various legal grounds it would still be possible to permit consumption of the water.]

Mental Illness

[68]

Moshe Shtudentski: A Pediatrician on Nervous Illnesses (1847)

Moshe Shtudentski, *Rofe hayeladim: kolel 'etsot tovot ve-ne'emot li-shemor beriut ha-yeladim*), (Warsaw: Gedruckt bei H. N. Schriefigtesser, 1847).

The nerves are the name for the tiny threads that originate in the brain and spinal cord, whence they spread and branch out to the entire body until they reach the epidermis (their outer extremity). Thus the brain and spine are the source and origin of the nerves, and the skin their outer limits. The nerves are the most precious of all human body parts, and their servants act mightily on their behalf, for it is by means of the nerves that we feel both suffering and pain. [. . .]

Convulsions of laughter may suddenly strike children. The child's face will contract, his cheeks will be sucked inward, and he will make laughing motions with his mouth; a mother might think that a child is laughing in his sleep if she is not aware of this illness of convulsions. A sealing of the mouth is one type of convulsion, wherein the lower palate is sucked toward the upper one quite tightly, and the child ceases to breast-feed; the lips take on a bluish hue. He foams at the mouth, and he moves but is unable to shout or cry. Stiffening of the body is when the entire body becomes rigid as a result of convulsions.

Convulsions occur when there are palpitations in the muscles of the face, the hands, or the feet. The child does not feel any attendant pain and retains consciousness and reason during the entire duration of the episode.

Internal cramps have a different manifestation, for they occur when the entire nervous system has been overcome by the disease. Superficially, this has the appearance of strange contractions and movements — especially when the eyes roll about in their sockets or remain utterly motionless. Convulsions and palpitations suddenly wrack the entire body; the head nods this way and that; the teeth grind; the breathing becomes heavy; foam comes from the mouth; consciousness and reason are lost for the duration of the illness.

Above we have already explained why children are susceptible to convulsive disorders, which involve excessive excitation and stimulation of the nerves. Indeed, the factors that turn the illness from potential to actual are the following: bad food, an increase or decrease in bowel movements beyond what is proper, colds, improper dress, and hyperactivity or excessive emotions (for example, anger, fear, fright, and even sudden joy) on the part of the mother or nurse. All these affect the child, and if the mother expresses any of these emotions, and nurses right afterward, the child will be seized with intense tremors or palpitations (cramps) for an hour. Hence it is necessary to warn the mother or wet nurse who experiences any of the above and is in a state of great excitement lest she extend a breast to nurse the child. Instead, she must empty the milk in her breast, wait until her emotions are calm, and only then approach to breast-feed the child. Likewise, any illness such as fever, flu, and skin ailments can cause the potential cramp to be realized. We have already seen that this disease happens in eight days after the implantation of the *fakei hagana* (*shutz fakkeh*).[1] In the second phases of childhood, it is intestinal worms that cause this ailment.

Making a prognosis of this illness in children is difficult and dubious. We have seen children [who are] attacked by this illness week after week for a whole year eventually become healthy, but children who contract this disease frequently die (statistically, one in six). We can make a prognosis for the disease based on the duration of the illness once it appears and on the frequency of its symptoms (whether they appear at short or long intervals). Children who have the disease of convulsions when suffering from cranial meningitis, or who have their eyes open while suffering an episode, are in an extremely dangerous state.

NOTE
1. These terms are unclear.

[69]

Petition to Hospitalize Dvoira Zlotoiabko for Mental Illness (1895)

LVIA, f. 383, op. 5, d. 451, ll. 2–9 ob.

"Petition of Enta Pushner of Vil'na (Illiterate) to the Governor of Vil'na (5 April 1895)"

My mother, Dvoira Zlotoiabko, who lives with me, has gone mad. She breaks everything, hits, causes arguments, so that it is impossible to keep her in the apartment where I have my own small children who are scared to death. I keep my mother in a cold storeroom in my house where she could catch some other dangerous disease. She will not accept my request to place her in the section [of a hospital] for the mentally ill.

That is why I have the honor of humbly asking Your Excellency to sympathize with my unfortunate position and order the acceptance of my mother in a place for the mentally ill in Vil'na.

"Preliminary Information about the Suspicion of Mental Illness (16 April 1895)"

TOPICS AND QUESTIONS
THAT REQUIRE DATA

Responses Containing Data
1. Age according to physical appearance, testimony of relatives, or documents[?]
   Approximately sixty years old according to external appearance.
2. Religious confession?
   Jewish.
3. Single, married, family. Does [the patient] own real estate or property—

personal or common? Family relationships?
Married. Three married daughters. Husband is destitute. Relationship [with family] is good.

4. What province, city, district, township, or village [is the patient from originally]?
Oshmiany [Vil'na province].

5. When and who reported doubts about the healthy mental capacities [of the patient [and for what reason]? Was [this] psychiatric disorder observed earlier and how did it manifest itself?
The daughter of the patient, Enta Pushner, submitted a petition to the governor of the province on 5 April 1895 on account of the [. . .] patient, who complains that street urchins throw rocks at her.

6. If [the mental disorder] was observed for a prolonged period, why was it not reported until the present time?
She has allegedly been sick for around twenty years, and during this time she was treated for mental illness four times at the Vil'na Jewish Hospital in the section for mental illness.

7. When, where, and who conducted the preliminary examination?
Unknown.

8. What has the health of the patient been until the present time?
According to the daughter's statement, she has been sick for about twenty years.

9. Education?
Illiterate.

10. Did the patient have any special pursuits [hobbies]?
Unknown.

11. [Is the patient engaged] in work-related, social, or domestic activities?
Unskilled labor.

12. At the present examination, does the patient display any signs of psychiatric disorder and namely what [symptoms]?

The patient conducts herself in a submissive manner. She replies incoherently to questions. She talks a lot about herself, but it is impossible to understand what she is saying.

13. Should she be placed in the hospital for treatment or could she be left at home?
In light of the absence of a shelter and appropriate domestic care, the patient should stay in the hospital for treatment.

14. Is there any information on the subject that is not included in the questionnaire?
The patient was found locked up in a shed; she herself complained about this. Her daughter explained that it was necessary to keep her mother locked up because her apartment is small and does not have the appropriate conditions. Her mother wanders about town and conducts herself indecently, provoking street urchins to throw rocks at her.

"Petition of Enta Pushner to the Governor of Vil'na (21 April 1895)"

I submitted a petition to Your Excellency requesting [you] to place my mother, Dvoira Zolotoiabko, in one of the Vil'na hospitals for the mentally ill. Apparently, the commissioned doctor and assistant police officer of the fourth district station, who were persuaded of her insanity, recognized her as mentally ill. But for some reason she was not accepted at this time at the hospital, despite the fact that she is now worse and severely beat up two [people]. It is difficult for me to watch over her, especially since she grabs a knife in her hand with the intention of stabbing everyone.

This compels me to turn to Your Excellency again with a petition to order that my mother Dvoira Zlotoiabko be assigned to a hospital section for the mentally ill.

"Report of the Vil'na Jewish Hospital to the Medical Department of the Vil'na Provincial Administration (23 July 1895)"

The Office of the Jewish Hospital has the honor to report to the Medical Department

[...] that the patient Dveira [Dvoira] Zlotoiabko died on 29 May 1895 from pneumonia. She suffered periodically from mania.

---

[70]

Petition to Hospitalize Rivka Khaimovna Arliuk of Oshmiany for Mental Illness (1902)

LVIA, f. 383, op. 3, d. 268, ll. 5–10.

"Statement from the Residents of Oshmiany to the District Police (11 September 1902)"

The townswoman Rivka Khaimovna Arliuk, who lives in the town of Oshmiany near the Borirskii bridge in the house of Leib Arliuk, is afflicted with utter madness and as a result exhibits unimaginable disorderly conduct: [she] beats passers-by and neighbors, throws stones at people, and tries to set fire to the house where she lives. She has bitten several people. In a word, she is a threat to public safety.

To prevent a possible misfortune that might occur (for example, a fire) and to protect the residents of Oshmiany from further violence (which will inevitably lead to an entire series of misfortunes), we have the honor of humbly asking the police administration to order that the violent and insane Rikva Arliuk be sent to the Vil'na Jewish Hospital for treatment.

NISEL MOVSHOVICH BOGCHZ (MERCHANT), ARON ABELOVICH, IVAN SOSLIDEV, KONSTANTIN PREVEDKOV, KHAIM KAUFMAN (MERCHANT), MORDUKH ZELMANOVICH BUPIMOVICH, ABRAM STRUZHAN (MERCHANT'S SON), NOTEL FAIVUSHEVICH ARON, VUL'F REZNIKOVICH (TOWNSMAN), I. B. STRAZDIM (PEASANT), AND OTHERS.

"Examination of the Patient Suspected of Mental Illness: Townswoman Rivka Khaimovna Arliuk (15 September 1902)"[1]

TOPICS AND QUESTIONS THAT REQUIRE DATA

Responses Containing Data

1. Who, when, for what reason, and for what purpose was the mental illness reported?
The residents of the town of Oshmiany submitted a statement about the disorderly conduct of Rivka Arliuk on the grounds that she throws stones at people, bites them, etc., with the purpose of placing her in the Jewish hospital.

2. Age?
30 years old

3. Religious confession?
Jewish

4. Place of birth, place of residence, background, rank, and occupation?
She was born in the village of Zhukh (Vil'na district) and lives in the town of Oshmiany. Status: townsperson (by her parents) and townsperson (by her husband). Occupation: engages in housework.

5. Education?
[Educated at] home

6. Family status (single, married, children and relatives, widow) and relationship with relatives?
She has been married for eight years and has three children. She has a bad relationship with her husband but gets along well with her in-laws and her own parents.

7. Material position:
Her husband has a wooden house with a dirt floor in generally poor condition.

8. Has [the patient] ever been prosecuted for any crime?
No

9. When did illness begin and how did the illness manifest itself (behavior, conversations, change of character, and so forth)? Did it have a continuous or periodic character?
The illness began six weeks ago: [the patient] began to run around on the streets, grab and curse passers-by; ripped apart a pillow and scattered the feathers. Sometimes she calms down but then is despondent, according to those around her.

10. Did [the patient] suffer earlier from diseases of the nerves prior to this (headaches, dizziness, deafness, loss of speech, paralysis, convulsions, loss of consciousness, epilepsy, spiral dancing, hysteria, sleep walking)?
She had headaches and generally suffered from irritability.

11. What kind of physical illnesses did [the patient] suffer (including syphilis)?
Unknown

12. [Has the patient] been subject to physical violence (contusions, wounds, shaking) or mental abuse (fright, grievances, insults, unhappiness, and so forth)?
According to family members, she was afraid of her own mentally ill brother and was sick herself.

13. Did [the patient] abuse hard liquor, smoke, [or engage in] sexual excess or masturbation?
No

14. Have any relatives ever had a mental illness [or been involved] in a crime or other circumstances that would legally influence the resulting diagnosis of psychiatric degeneration?
A mentally ill brother

15. In what year did [the patient's] first menstruation appear and were there any abnormalities? How many pregnancies and births have there been and what were their durations? Did one observe a disorder in the [patient's] mental capabilities at this time?
She has given birth four times; no disorder in her mental capabilities was observed at the time.

16. Have any symptoms of illness been discovered during the present examination?
The [patient] breathes heavily, screams, beats [her] fists on the table, curses, and fights. She says that she feels bad [while] everyone is well. In general, she complains about her own fate. She declares that God is one, and the second [important thing] are the commandments.

Conclusion: The examined patient is afflicted with mental illness and thus has a disorderly character. The sick individual should be placed in a hospital.

[SIGNED:] THE CITY DOCTOR
S. GEL'VEROV

"Report of the Vil'na Jewish Hospital to the Provincial Medical Department (8 October 1902)"[2]

The Office of the Jewish Hospital reports to the Medical Department of the Provincial Board that Rivka Arliuk exhibits an excited mental state. Her smiles, jokes, grimaces — all indicate a very cheerful mood. The patient chats a lot, especially if they [the medical staff] engage her in conversation, but this talk is not logical speech. She is very lively: she runs around the ward, touches the patients and servants, sometimes even fights with them so that it is necessary to isolate her temporarily. The patient is tidy and eats well. On the basis of what has been stated, she has been diagnosed with mania.

NOTES

1. [This was the new standard questionnaire included in all the files (used at least since 1902), which was different from the old one used in the previous document. The examination of the patient was conducted by Vil'na city doctor and used by the Medical Department of the Provincial Administration to determine whether hospitalization was necessary.]

2. [The Vil'na Jewish Hospital reported on 26 September 1902 that Rivka Arliuk had been admitted to the hospital two days earlier.]

[71]

Petition to Hospitalize Meer Mendelev Ginzburg of Bobruisk for Mental Illness (1902)

LVIA, f. 383, op. 3, d. 224, ll. 2–20b, 11–11 ob.

"Petition of Mordukh Baskin of Vil'na to the Governor of Vil'na (Received 5 August 1902)"

From among the victims who lost their property in a fire in Bobruisk, my relative—twenty-year-old [sic] Meer Mendelev Ginzburg—came to me and is psychologically disturbed. I arranged for him to reside in a furnished room on Kiev Street, [...] near the train station. I wish to have him admitted to the section for the mentally ill at the Vil'na Jewish Hospital. For his treatment, I am obliged to pay according to the determination of the hospital [because] the senior doctor at this hospital examined the patient for admission without Your Excellency's permission. That is why I have the honor to ask Your Excellency to order, as soon as possible, that my relative be admitted for treatment in the section for the mentally ill at the Jewish Hospital. [...]

"Report of the Vil'na Jewish Hospital to the Provincial Medical Department (24 September 1902)"

The Office of the Jewish Hospital reports to the Medical Department of the Vil'na Provincial Administration that Meer Mendelev Ginzburg, age twenty, comes from a healthy family. This is the fourth month that he has been ill. The illness evidently began in a rather acute form. The patient has an average build and diet; the skin is scratched in places. In physical terms, he appears to have no abnormalities. During his first visit to the hospital, the patient tore his clothing, fought with patients, and became agitated. Recently, he has become much calmer. He answers questions. He recounted that he had studied massage in Riga and completed six years of the gymnasium. He studied on his own, meaning that he prepared for the examination to receive a certificate of graduation.[1]

His mental capacities are diminished. The patient speaks in an incoherent manner and smiles. He has a defiant expression on his face. His memory has not been impaired. Apparently he does not have hallucinations. In addition, the patient is sensitive; he often cries, especially when talking about the disagreement with his father. He has not sufficiently adapted [to being hospitalized]. He evaluates his sick neighbors thus: at one time he considers them to be healthy people and devious pretenders; at another time he considers them to be as neurotic as himself. The character of psychiatric suffering in the patient has not yet become definitively clear. One may suggest that we have a case of treatable neurasthenic psychosis, which arose on account of mental fatigue, material want, and moral shock (the quarrel with his father, a postman in Bobruisk).

NOTE

1. [In the questionnaire, he replied that he had a home education and had "gone up to six years in gymnasium."]

[72]

Petition to Hospitalize Sholom Peisakhovich Shmuskovich of Vil'na for Mental Illness (1902)

LVIA, f. 383, op. 3, d. 217, ll. 1–4.

"Petition of Rivka Shmuskovich to the Governor of Vil'na (30 September 1902)"

My son, Sholom Shakhno Peisakhovich Shmuskovich, who is *mentally ill*, recently began to display *signs of madness* of the most severe character: (1) he often disappears from the apartment, hiding in the concealed remote corners of Vil'na; (2) he frequently flings himself on people; and (3) he has different domestic weapons in his apartment. He is absolutely dangerous.

The Assessor's Office in Iakobshtadt (Kurliand province) has agreed to pay for my son's treatment. Given that my son is in the town of Vil'na, I have the honor to beg Your Excellency graciously to order his examination and admission for treatment at the local Jewish hospital.

Signed by A. Sharin for Rivka Shmuskovich, who is illiterate

"Report of the Vil'na Jewish Hospital to the Provincial Medical Department (24 December 1902)"

The Office of the [Jewish] Hospital informs the Medical Department of the Provincial Board that Sholom Shakhno Shmuskovich is of medium build and [suffers from] malnutrition.[1] No symptoms of degeneration have been observed. The reaction of the pupils and the reflexes of the tendons are normal. According to his family, he was extremely ill two and half years ago. The family is from Kurliand [province]; the patient studied there and received his master's degree, then he traveled to London, attended the law faculty at the university in Berlin, and returned home two years age before the illness. He spent time at a hospital in Mitav for half a year, where the illness worsened.

The patient conducts himself properly, answers questions, and allows himself to be examined. He speaks excellent German; reluctantly speaks Russian despite an adequate command of the language. He calls himself by a different name and surname (Fridrikh Rozental') because, in his opinion, each person has the right to choose any name he pleases. He also gave his mother a different name and surname (in German). He considers himself to be German and responsible for the dissemination of the German language and culture. He calls Vil'na Riga because [in his mind] both cities have already been united. The patient considers himself a "volunteer"[2] and hopes to rise to the rank of officer, grand duke, or honorary citizen of foreign cities such as Vienna and others.

He describes how he allegedly studied in Bonn, where he usually taught children of high-ranking individuals ("It is a matter of career"). Continuing the conversation, one can get the patient to recognize that he is in the hospital because of illness. He complains that all of his "I's" have been destroyed, that everything has been shattered.

The patient has been very calm and decent; he rarely converses with anyone on his own initiative. He has little appetite and lies in bed all day. He neither reads nor writes nor expresses his wishes. His mental capacities are slightly diminished but he accurately calculated $8 + 7 \times 19$. The patient apparently suffers from hallucinations but does not say what they are.

On the basis of the observation of the patient, it is possible to conclude that he suffers from *vesania melancholia* (melancholy insanity).

NOTES

1. [The preliminary examination by the city doctor found that the patient, who was born in the town of Iakobshtadt, was twenty-nine years old. He was single and had four brothers.]

2. [A volunteer, not a conscript, in the army.]

[73]

Petition to Hospitalize Rivka Gefter of Vil'na for Mental Illness (1902)

"Preliminary Information about a Patient Suspected of Mental Illness: Rivka Aizikovna Gefter (10 June 1902)"
LVIA, f. 383, op. 3, d. 188, ll. 1–6.

TOPICS AND QUESTIONS
THAT REQUIRE DATA

Responses Containing Data

1. Who, when, for what reason, and for what objective was the mental illness reported?
   Her mother Feiga Gefter seeks to place her mentally ill daughter in a hospital for treatment.

2. Age?
   19 years old

3. Religious confession?
   Jewish

4. Place of birth, place of residence, background, rank, and occupation?
   She is a townswoman of Vil'na. She was born and lives in Vil'na with her parents. She was a seamstress.

5. Education?
Literate

6. Family status (single, married, children and relatives, widow) and relationship with relatives?
Single. She has parents and a brother.

7. Material position:
Impoverished; her father is in the hospital and her mother is a petty trader.

8. Has [the patient] ever been prosecuted for any crime?
Allegedly no

9. When did illness begin and how did the illness manifest itself (behavior, conversations, change of character, and so forth)? [Was it] chronic or episodic?
The illness began one year ago; she stopped working, ran away from home, and occasionally created disorders.

10. Did [the patient] suffer earlier from nervous ailments (headaches, dizziness, deafness, loss of speech, paralysis, convulsions, loss of consciousness, epilepsy, spiral dancing, hysteria, sleep walking)?
Allegedly no

11. What kind of physical illnesses did [the patient] suffer (including syphilis)?
No indication of syphilis

12. [Has the patient] been subjected to physical violence (contusions, wounds, shaking) or mental abuse (fright, grievances, insults, unhappiness, and so forth)?
She allegedly became ill out of fear of dogs.[1]

13. Did [the patient] abuse hard liquor, smoke, [or engage in] sexual excess or masturbation?
Allegedly no

14. Have any relatives ever had a mental illness [or been involved] in a crime or some other circumstance that would legally influence the resulting diagnosis of psychiatric degeneration?
Allegedly no[2]

15. In what year did [the patient's] first menstruation appear and were there any abnormalities? How many pregnancies and births have there been and what were their durations? Did one observe a disorder in the [patient's] mental capabilities at this time?
Her menstruation appeared when she was sixteen years old and was always normal; only a year ago, after the stress [of being afraid of dogs] was her period delayed. Now it is regular again. She has not given birth.

16. Have any symptoms of illness been discovered during the present examination?
The patient undergoing examination stands on her feet. During the conversation, she behaves submissively, smiles at questions, and answers them sensibly, but then begins to talk gibberish. Seeing the portrait of the tsar, she says: "Why is he sitting and not going to America?" She keeps repeating: "I want to go to America." Over time she becomes agitated and wants to assault people around her.

Conclusion: The examination of Rivka Gefter [shows that] she evidently suffers from a disorder of her mental capacities. For lack of supervision over her, it is necessary to place her in the section for the mentally ill.

NOTES

1. [The archive has a later, separate file on Enta Rivka Aizikovich Gefter (LVIA, f. 383, op. 4, d. 90). This file (from 1904) includes the same name for the mother (Feiga Mirle Gefter) and other information; the only discrepancy is in the patient's age (which appears as twenty-four, not twenty-one because she was older). This file also states that the illness began after she was bitten by a dog and became extremely frightened; ever since then she had suffered from "fits of madness."]

2. [In contrast, the 1904 report states that her father was "feebleminded but there are no other mentally ill members of her family."]

[74]

Petition to Hospitalize Leib Girshev Ioffe of Vil'na for Mental Illness (1902)

"Report of the Vil'na Jewish Hospital to the Provincial Medical Department (20 August 1902)"
LVIA, f. 383, op. 3, d. 300, l. 8–8 ob.

The Office of [the Jewish] Hospital informs the Medical Department of the Provincial Administration that Leib Girshev Ioffe displayed absolutely no abnormalities in psychiatric terms during his entire stay in the hospital.[1] He prays and fulfills all the Jewish rituals like a completely healthy person. He mastered the Jewish book that he was given to read and conducted a discussion that was sufficiently sensible. He wrote a letter to his family that was also sufficiently sensible. The only thing that came to my attention during the conversation with him was some awkwardness and slowness in speech, but that corresponds well with his intended career—as a candidate at a Jewish seminary.

Based on what has been stated, the conclusion follows that Leib Girshev Ioffe does not present anything abnormal in psychiatric terms and does not currently require treatment at a hospital.

NOTE

1. [The preliminary examination showed that Ioffe was born in Dvinsk and had lived in Vil'na for two years. He was twenty years old, unmarried, and a student at an unnamed Jewish school, where he was studying to be a rabbi. He had good relations with his parents, who were still alive, but had no siblings. His mental illness had allegedly begun two years before, in 1900, when he was hospitalized five months for mental illness. He claimed that none of his family members or relatives suffered from mental illness.]

Modesty

[75]

Petition of a Rabbi and Merchants of Zhitomir to Count Kiselev [Chairman of the Committee for the Organization of Jewish Life], against the Zhitomir Police (1853)

"Materialy i soobshcheniia. Goneniia na zhenskie golovye ubory, (1853)"
Evreiskaia starina 8 (1915): 400–401.

The Zhitomir city police, without announcing the state order that is the basis for their actions, demand that Jewish women appear in public with uncovered heads, and they accompany this requirement with every kind of coercion and unprecedented violence. Thus the district supervisor and policemen tear off the wigs, bonnets, and other headdresses of Jewish women; they drag them by the hair to the police station or guardhouse, pour several buckets full of cold water over their heads, keep them under arrest for several days, and finally force them to sweep the streets. They drove the merchants' wives from the theater with humiliating mockery and personal insults for appearing in wigs rather than in their own uncovered hair. These public insults and torture of the weaker sex — women — without distinction, without the smallest respect for age and status, have had very harsh consequences: some have fallen gravely ill from shame and fear, and they have also paid with their health and perhaps their lives to observe their [religious] law, without committing any civil crime.

Jewish law absolutely forbids women to dis-

play their hair, and we see the manifest mercy of our Sovereign Emperor, the All Gracious Monarch, in his imperial law of 12 April 1851: he only prohibited Jewish women from *shaving* their heads, but without ordering that they appear in public with uncovered heads. In other words, His Majesty does not want us to violate our law. We piously obey His Majesty's will: all of our women wear their hair; they do not have it shaved and cut.[1] However, they do cover their hair with wigs or other headdresses when appearing in public and do not differ from local Christian women of various ranks.

However, to evaluate the unfairness of the Zhitomir police, one should note another imperial directive from 19 August 1852, which ordered that Jewish women who shave their heads despite the prohibition be fined five silver rubles. Hence, for violating the sovereign's will, His Imperial Majesty established only a monetary fine. But the Zhitomir city police, for ignoring its whim, subject them [women] to public insult and torture without a trial (to which no criminal is subject and for which there is not even a designation in the Code of

Punishment) and compels our women to violate their own [religious] law. What is more, by insulting women publicly, the police themselves are committing a criminal act for what is not even a mere misdemeanor in any law or decree.

Our extremely difficult position gives us no choice but to seek the protection and patronage of Your Excellency, as the chairman of the Committee for the Organization of Jewish Life. We humbly ask you to issue the appropriate order to end the capricious demand of the Zhitomir city police (which has no basis in the exact meaning of the Imperial injunction promulgated by a decree from the State Senate on 12 April 1851) and to protect us from the violent coercion and torture to which our women are subjected for observing their law.

NOTE

1. [The editor of *Evreiskaia starina* notes that this statement was only partially true: it was mainly the elderly who continued to observe this ritual of shaving their hair; the cutting of the hair occurred when a woman was getting married, at which time they cut off their maidenly braids. In later times, observance of this custom declined.]

[76]

On Crinoline: The Memoirs of Avraham Paperna

Avraham Paperna, "Iz Nikolaevskoi epokhi," *Perezhitoe* 3 (1911), chapter 17.

Under the threat of a *herem* [excommunication], the hasidic rabbi of Bobruisk, R. Gilel [Hillel], issued an edict forbidding local Jewish women to wear crinoline.[1] Perhaps not all contemporary male and female readers know the meaning of the word "crinoline," but in the late 1850s and early 1860s it was on everyone's lips. These were women's skirts with a ravishing form: very narrow at the waist, they widened steadily and the bottom was spread out by a fish bone or steel hoop, several *arshins*[2] in circumference, thereby creating a kind of pyramid with a narrow peak. The upper part of the body (from the waist to the shoulders) also became wider (naturally or artificially), thereby representing an inverted pyramid. In a word, this fashion was fantastic and luxurious. Ever since the time of the prophet Isaiah, the daughters of Israel have been zealous admirers of fashion; no sooner had this fashion made its long passage from Paris to the Pale of Settlement than they seized upon it with all their might. As usual, they took the dimensions and exaggerated them, bringing the width of the hoop to an extreme size. However, nothing is perfect in this world. This marvelous fashion had its own small inconvenience: when sitting and especially in a lying position, the lady's hoop together with the skirt rose upward. Here is why our rabbi, indignant at the temptation caused by the crinoline, issued his strict edict. It is difficult to describe the misery that overtook the representatives of the fairer sex of the hasidic sect with the announcement of this prohibition. The misery intensified still more with envy toward the neighbors and friends of the *misnagdic* sect for whom the order was not binding and who continued to strut around in their crinolines. Induced to feel sympathy for the sufferings of the fair sex and indignant at the interference of the religious authorities in the alien sphere of a woman's toilette, I described this chaos in a humorous-malicious tone in a letter to the editor of [the newspaper] *Ha-melits*, Alexander Tsederbaum. He immediately published it, together with a long, sarcastic commentary on his part. This letter, as one might expect, provoked a storm of indignation among the Hasidim of Bobruisk. Fortunately, I was [...] careful [about signing my name]; forgoing an author's fame, I signed this letter with a pseudonym. However, everyone pointed their fingers at me as the author of this impertinent article; only the absence of explicit evidence saved me from the *herem*. My friends — secret freethinkers among the Hasidim — warned me not to go out on the streets alone at night.

NOTES

1. [Avraham Paperna (1840–1919), a Hebrew poet and literary critic, was drawn to the Haskalah movement and became one of its important supporters. His memoir describes the Nikolaevan period from the perspective of a *maskil*.]

2. [An *arshin* is equivalent to seventy-one centimeters.]

[77]

Secret State Report on Tsaddik Twersky's Disciples and Crinoline (1863)

"Report of Court Counselor Vladimir Fedorov to the General Governor (13 September 1862)"

TsDIAK-Ukraïny, f. 1423, op. 1, d. 6, ll. 56–58.

The Tsaddik Twersky lives in the town of Tal'noe, not far from Uman. His influence on the Jews is so strong that when the Jew Lifshits recently set fire to his own house in Uman (out of greed because of the high value of the insurance) and embittered all the Jews (who were ready to denounce him to the authorities), the Tsaddik Twersky gave an order not to give evidence against Lifshitz. [The latter] had already succeeded, by various means, in extricating himself from the hands of justice.

Encountering no obstacles to their activities, the *tsaddikim* have become demanding and unbridled from day to day. This is corraborated in the following incident. A few weeks ago in Berdichev, the *tsaddik* arrived from Rotmistrovka to collect the customary tribute (it is said that he took up to 5,000 silver rubles). His followers, overjoyed to have the *tsaddik* among them and in all likelihood with his permission, attacked women who were wearing crinolines on the street, inflicting insults and blows. One girl barely escaped with her life from the fury of the mob. She managed with difficulty to get home under the escort of the police attendants and a soldier.

Marital Sex

[78]

Early Marriage and Sexuality:
The Memoirs of Mordechai Aaron Guenzburg

Mordechai Aaron Guenzburg, *Aviezer* (Tel Aviv: Universitat Tel Aviv, 1966), pp. 74–107 with omissions.

Chapter 25

Friday, the fifth of the month of Adar came — and with it the end of my world![1] Yet my time was not the time of lovers; my labor was that of a man but my power only that of a boy — Fathers, oh my Fathers! What were you thinking when you wronged the boy to put a man's burden on his shoulders! I was fourteen years old and never had my heart been tempted to gaze at a maiden. I knew not of the vast change to be made by adding [the letters] F-E to the letters M-A-L-E beyond what the Talmud taught me. My heart had none of the desire that nature had forged in the hearts of men to uncover that which is concealed among daughters of their species. Indeed, kissing a pretty girl would have had no more effect on me than the pleasure of kissing a handsome boy, and for what foolish purpose does one force nature to open her flower before its time? You destroy the fruit prematurely when you squeeze out an unripe seed that will not germinate and may yield no fruit; leave nature alone and arouse not love until its time comes.[2] Let nature take its course slowly; do not force the boy to walk in the footsteps of a man.

Who is wise enough to know the happy median between the road of the House of Israel and the road of non-Jews in this great matter? For as our brothers, the inhabitants of Poland, have tilted the scales very far from the median to one extreme,[3] so our brothers the sons of Ashkenaz [Germany], who follow in the non-Jews' footsteps like a farm animal in a valley, have tilted the scales in the other direction and will not marry wives until they are on the verge of being elderly — after they have exhausted the force of their youth among harlots and prostitutes and have expended their might upon adulteresses. They waste their youthful strength and grow used to their corrupt ways until their might is dry as a potsherd and their sins afflict their very bones — only then do they dare approach the high fortress of maidenly beauty, divinely secured. He decides to set up a household but lacks the strength; he is flaccid and impotent. They are like a youth who opens a bottle of wine and happily gives the first clear glass to a filthy whore while setting aside the goblet and the residue for the wife of his bosom. Has so great a crime ever been heard of? And who would cast blame on this poor deceived woman — should her passions be aroused — were she to go off and seek to slake her soul's thirst with a different cup?

Moreover, those people who kept themselves in youth from the sin of drowning in the seed of their loins, marriage is not about to chase after them once their youth has passed: it is clear as the sun in the sky that just as two people do not have equal features in their faces, so are they not equal in their minds. Only in youth is one's nature still soft and pliant as a reed, so it is easy to accommodate the qualities of another. Yet that is not the case in later age, once a person's nature has become set in its ways and is no longer sufficiently flexible to adapt to its partner's will.

Marriages made in youth will in most cases thrive and succeed even if the minds of the couple differ, for the man will incline his spirit slightly toward the mind of his bosom bride, and the wife too shall control her spirit to bend it to the will of her husband. Each sacrifices just a little of their will for the other's will and, when the minds overlap for some time and the two have lost some of their individual sensibilities, a new nature shall have been born in which the two minds are fused.

Not so are marriages made in advanced age: then minds are set on the path to which they were destined and will not budge. Neither will yield before anything: he goes his way and she hers. They pull against each other like a bull and a donkey; they come apart rather than fuse, and all their days are filled with opposition and struggle.

The median between these two paths, and the time most favorable to those innocent travelers who have not tasted the bread of discord, is the age of twenty for young men and the age of fifteen for young women. In these years the body has reached the full measure of its growth and nature has refined extra quantities of fuel for the sparks of love: that is, the time to enjoy the pleasure of the fierceness of first love, and oh how good and how fine it is! Nor need they worry that the blaze of love shall diminish in the smoke of marriage, for the fire will burn steadily in their hearts like a flame without bellows. It is only the excess fire that dies down and fades; the flame itself burns on forever.

This day too has fled and passed me by like all the others, with full festivities for the guests but scant comfort for me. The musicians came and hurt my ears with their music, and the poet my heart with his nonsense rhymes; the townsmen came with their scroll and imposed on me duties—I did not know the meaning and nature of these, but assented contractually to all that was said in the scroll without knowing what was written. I was led with the noise of the celebrants under the *huppah* of honor arranged for me in the town street, where the text of marriage arrangements was read out in front of the community. I placed a gold ring on the finger of the bride (ah, and a steel cable of many strands round my neck); I returned home fainting in her arms—and became a man. In all this I did not know how I had turned instantly from a boy into a man, like a peasant who is drafted into military pursuits: the moment he puts on the uniform, he is instantaneously transformed from a field hand into a heroic warrior.

On the Sabbath of the sixth of Adar I gave the sermon in public and read from the Holy Torah, now being called "our teacher and rabbi" [as married men generally were] by the boy rabbi who then sat on the rabbinical seat there. Afterward, I went, along with the beadle, to greet each of the townsmen in his home, as was then the practice. [. . .]

Having told you from the outset that at the time my nature had not yet awoken to a craving for women, there is no need to draw back for you the curtain on my bridal chamber and show you that I went up Sunday night, seventh of Adar, to my wife's bed for the nuptial eve in the very same state as I descended from it on eighth of Adar in the morning. Nor on the second night was I able to gather my strength to become a man; although I had seen the castle so accessible that I almost could have called to it and it would have opened its gates, and the military maneuvers I knew properly (as set forth in the Talmud), I nevertheless did not gather the forces in my soul to rise to the castle and bring down its inner sanctum — for great is the distance between knowledge and ability.

Chapter 26

Tuesday, the ninth of Adar, I awoke in my wife's arms and my spirit shook, for my heart feared the things my wife had whispered guilelessly in my ears regarding the order in her father's household, which was as distant from that of my own father's as is heaven from earth.[4] I arose and with sullen face earnestly poured forth my prayer to God, and drank the morning drink blended with tears. O Lord! My father's servants are loading up the carts to return home; my heart melted within me and my eyes became two fountains; I bitterly wept seventy-seven times as much as I had cried upon leaving my native town. My mother approached to console me, and while consolation was on her lips and water in her eyes, much did she secretly lament over her prized possession that she had placed in the hands of strangers. As for the information that I had casually elicited from my wife regarding her father's household, my mother had been explicitly told by others. She voices consolation one minute and offers advice the next: it does a man good to carry something of a burden in his youth; and it prepares him for later life if he should submit to the spirit of others and not become dry and rigid. These words would have been meaningless to me had I not related them to the words of my wife, which I remembered as condiments that added a taste of bitterness; thus were the words of consolation flowing from her mouth transformed into a kind of melancholy.

While we were sitting in the party hall and eating the bread of melancholy,[5] the *badhan* [comedian][6] and his musical entourage heroically attempted to stir up a festive spirit in us, but this time the musicians' talents fell flat and the *badhan*'s rank cleverness failed to elicit laughter from the party: the groom sat as someone grieving over the loss of his mother, his mother, in turn, was as in mourning for an only child,[7] and his sisters' tears were streaming down their faces, so how, where was cheer to be found? The guests tried to lift the spirits of the downcast with wine; they drank, celebrated, and moseyed about, but all this was like the mascara that a prostitute applies to pretty herself up after the natural rouge of her cheeks has passed and that one recognizes at a glance for the contrivance it is, as meant to conceal nature's deficiency.

Two hours later, with eyes wide open and tears streaming from them, we accompanied my parental entourage in carts and carriages until we reached the inn where the townsfolk had received us upon our arrival. I took leave of them and watched their departure for as long as I could see them; then I returned to town, accompanied by my father, who was staying behind in my in-laws' house until a carriage would chance to carry him to Vil'na. I wiped a tear from my face and resolved to forget my parental home and to take the wife of my bosom for my pleasure; this concludes the tale of my wedding.

For two or three weeks the wedding mood stayed with me, and I did nothing but eat delicacies and drink sweets on scarlet cushions to embrace my spouse's home with love. Winning the affection of my father-in-law was my entire hope and desire; the sole objective I aimed at and devoted my heart to in these days of rest was to learn the rules of my father-in-law and mother-in-law, so that I might direct my behavior in a manner that most pleased them.

My father-in-law was a man from the poor masses, with a keen mind in worldly affairs born of the experience of ignorance and boorishness. And once he acquired wealth, he devoted himself diligently to the world of books, taxing his limited skills so as to join in his hands both the virtue of wealth and the honor of study.

By nature he was passionate and could not force himself to obey the Torah's discipline as his books directed. In order to quiet his conscience (which sometimes pricked him for having done something contrary to the Law), he also took to his bosom the foreign lady of philosophy and dipped the *maror* [bitter herb] of Torah in the *haroset* [condiment] of sweet philosophy to dilute its bitter taste somewhat. He became a quasi-philosopher of a new creed: whereas the teaching of the ancient philosophers was to bend the heart to obey the head, and to subordinate passion to the regime of the mind, the members of this creed invert that method and force the head to follow the heart's desire, thus enslaving the brain to passion and making philosophy the maidservant betrothed to her mistress's appetite. No sooner does the heart pursue an evil passion than the head is used to justify its action. And if I did not fear to befoul my mouth I would say that a philosophy of this species comes not from the head but from the pe[. . .].[8]

It became a depressing sport for me to see how this hybrid bounces back and forth, like a frog that hops from shore to sea out of fear of the predatory bird, and from sea back to shore out of fear of the ravenous fish. Where faith posed troubles for his passions he took refuge in the stronghold of philosophy, and where philosophy caused him difficulties faith returned to give him sanctuary. [. . .]

Chapter 31

One day I came back from my synagogue and sat down in my room to take breakfast — a bowl of milk and some bread, instead of the compote juice and butter cake that had been my customary breakfast since the first days of my existence. And here comes my mother-in-law and shuts the door behind her, as if she has some secret to tell me. But I, who had begun to scorn her in the recesses of my heart, did not rise from my seat and ignored her until she took the lead and said: "Tell me, what is your interest in money?"

"And who has asked you for money?!" I proudly parried her question.

"If only you had asked," she replied angrily, "for it is better to ask than to st . . . st . . . steal, to steal."

The word had left her mouth, and streams of blood broke forth like a flash-flood to deluge my heart. An unnatural passion raised me forcefully from my seat and to my feet, and placed the following words in my mouth: "Is it a *theft* that you are asking me about?" I grabbed the bowl and poured the milk to the ground before her eyes, and who knows where my youthful fury would have led me had my mother-in-law not rushed out of my sight, and let me take out my wrath on the wood- and stone-work of the house. In short order I left in fury from the house and went to the house of R. Simhah, my teacher, to complain about my troubles. They kept silent and did not offer consolation, for they saw that my misery was too great for me to be consoled. I was still pouring forth my anguish to them when one member of my in-laws' household who liked me came and whispered in my ear that they had found the stolen object that I had been suspected of taking (based on my wife's slander). A stream of tears then gave relief to my distressed heart and calmed me a little.

The master of the house, R. Simhah, then gave vent to his wrath: through that servant he sent my mother-in-law angry words (of which the messenger kept nine measures to himself while transmitting only a tenth to her). Driven by his love of tranquility, my teacher expended much effort until he persuaded me to return to my in-laws' house and have lunch there. [. . .]

But the façade cast by my wife had also fallen from my mother-in-law's eyes. Her eyes no longer prejudiced by love of her daughter, she now saw and realized that her daughter had attempted to slander me and worried about the damage to her reputation should word get out in town about the plot against a son dear to his parents. She especially feared her husband, for she knew that he truly loved me. Her heart turned against her daughter, whom she punished with words and fierce blows. When I returned home at noon bitterly scowling, I found my mother-in-law greeting me with a smiling face and kind words. From that day onward I recovered my proper status and earlier semblance of dignity.

The anger on my face did not pass, and I did not inquire about my wife, whom I had not seen that entire day. She had secluded herself in her grandfather's house to ponder the shame that her mother had heaped on her. When I [later] went angrily and scowling to my bedroom, she slithered in, fell to my feet, and, with cheeks red from weeping and shame, took me by the hand and asked me if my anger over the insult had abated (for which her mother, with the fist, had taken her to account). If my desire for revenge was not sated, she added words that were a mixture of joking and desolation: she was now ready to suffer a second time at my hand, but I must not bring my case to her father in writing. Her words overcame my rage to the point where I promised to forget all her transgressions against me.

My mother-in-law repented with all her heart the ill she had done me, and resolved to behave really well toward me in order to atone for her previous maltreatment. She saw that so long as my bed was not complete, her daughter would not direct her love toward me. She had the idea of using medical means to arouse male potency in me. However, typical of her simple ways, she consulted not doctors but rather wise women, who cleverly discovered that the root of my halting powers was in some bewitched potion that an enemy of my in-laws had made me drink on my wedding day, and that I would never be able to have a proper erection until I had removed that spell.

This message from my mother-in-law was conveyed to me by one of the brothers of my father-in-law whom she knew had the power to bend me to his will. This man implored me to remove the charm within me by a vomit-inducing herb that one wise woman had prepared.

These words have a great impact on me. I told myself that, since a verbal spell was cast upon me by the casual utterance of a witch, a whisper from the lips of a holy magician (*baal shem*) would remove it. I therefore gave my nose to his incense and my ears to his vain whisperings, and now a *physical* magic lingers like a stone in my intestines — which I must eject by the force of violent and frequent vomiting. All this quite serious medicine was for an illness that I did not feel!

The marvelous result that the potion was to have [as the woman had promised] is effective only to the mind of someone who believes anything. She ordered that all the vomit that spewed from my throat was to be collected in a vessel, that it be poured onto a bonfire stoked for that purpose. And when the bewitched substance comes in contact with the fire, the heart of the sorcerer will burn; it was only extinguishable by waters drawn from the home of the victim of the witchcraft — an idea that the wise men of Egypt and the doctors of Gilead had never heard of![9] Although there is no counting and no cataloging the vast acts of madness that men commit for love of women (love has neither vision nor understanding), a man like myself not yet inflamed by the spirit of lust would be completely insane to wander after such inanities as these (all just to discover a lust unbeknownst to him!). All right-minded people, beware of such idiocy!

Nevertheless, my powers of resistance faded before the entreaties of my wife, who brought this love potion to me in my room, her cheeks scarlet from embarrassment, and forced me to take the potion if there was a single shred of love left in my heart for her. I reflected on my ways and found that I ought to do as she wished, if only out of decency. I shut my eyes tight, opened my mouth, and swallowed the entire contents of the cup.

Chapter 32

Running for its life, the terrified hare is chased by a ferocious dog that catches it and bites it once or twice vigorously and fiercely until it collapses unconscious. Then the dog loses its ferocity and hovers over its prey, calmly licking the blood running from its flesh. Oh leave me alone and do not kiss me, cries the hare, for your kisses hurt more than your bites.

I apply this fable impartially to my wife: her new love was worse than the hatred she had hitherto shown. The full effect of her animosity extended only to my exterior and clothing, but her cup of love penetrated to my very soul. When the contents of the mother-in-law's potion reached my innards, all my insides disintegrated, spilling out as water from this side and that; my heart raced and shook from its place; fountains of phlegm opened and spewed unceasingly — until my soul grew weak from the ailment.

The members of the household, rejoicing over the wonderful news that was soon to come, busied themselves with their labors of love for me: one built the fire, another got a vessel ready, and several stood armed with clubs and sticks waiting for the witch to arrive to extinguish the flames of his burning heart with waters from the house.

I imagine that if, at the moment they cast the vomit onto the fire, a neighbor had come by to ask for some water to quench his thirst, he would have received furious blows at their hands. However, the eye of fortune shone on them and did not penalize them for our idiocy; I alone — my teeth bent by the unripe fruit that I ate — was punished.

Into the afternoon the herb did its work deep in my innards. Afterward, it emerged from the holes in which it was hiding and acted brazenly, in full view: all my insides had turned into fountains of water and my throat into a fountain of vomit that flooded and filled all the vessels that the members of the household had sacrificed (until I had practically vomited up my mother's milk). Even when my mother-in-law relented and tried to stop the retching by a citron-fruit concoction, she only managed to shift its path from the upper exit holes to the lower ones — the intense medicine did not free me from its grasp until late at night. After that I slept a deep sleep — but not one of rest — until morning.

At dawn I suddenly awoke and tried to move my hands and feet, but my powers failed. I tried to regain my strength with the appetizing foods that my mother-in-law set forth copiously before me. But my lust for food failed to stimulate the lust for sex that they meant to enhance. I turned my head to the wall and lay down until noon. As the sun rose higher, my strength slowly returned. I rose from my bed to walk around the house a bit in fits and starts. I even tried to eat a light snack, but as soon as the food entered my throat, it was engulfed by the pain of swallowing; any pleasure from eating was outweighed by the pain of swallowing. Although to comply with the wishes of my mother-in-law (who verbally pressured me to eat to the full) I stuffed my mouth with food and forced myself to swallow some, the rest I turned around and covertly spit out, until I had emptied more than half my plate — not to restore myself but to calm the heart of my mother-in-law. Then I went back to bed and stayed there.

I slept badly that night, for I was beset by violent and frequent chills that wracked all my organs. I drew no heat from the multitude of blankets and pillows that the members of the household had showered on me. Nor could I see the light of the stove that they moved close to my bed. I rejected the hot drink they brought up to my mouth, concerned that it would further hurt my throat. In vain I carved out a "grave" in the depths of the pillows and blankets to protect me from the cold outside air, but the stormy chills coming from my insides could not be stopped.

Around midnight the grip of the chills had weakened, and an unnatural heat took me forcefully in its grasp and squeezed my marrow, like rivers of burning pitch twisting in my veins. A raging fire came out from my deepest innards to boil my blood; soon I shook off my blankets and clothes and rolled about naked in my bed as on burning coals. As all the members of the household were dozing, there was nothing to stop me from grabbing a pitcher of cold water and drinking it to the very last. Although my throat hurt from each mouthful of water, the pain burning in my belly was still worse than that in my throat. But just as before my clothes had lost their power to block out the cold, so now did the water lose its power to quench my blazing fire. Hence cold and heat kept changing their guard over my depleted body, until early morning, when a troubled sleep descended on me, I slept the sleep of the wicked in hell.

With daylight I awoke tired and oppressed: the fever had left me, but a dry and wracking cough exhausted me and the swelling kept growing in my throat. I looked in the mirror on the wall and beheld the illness had brought forth a white flag on my face to mark its territory. Through all this my mother-in-law did not deign to seek a doctor, but only the old ladies whose coals had already singed me were present. I fought with her as hard as I could and resisted taking medicines from them. My teacher took my side to keep me from being handed over to these ladies on matters of internal medications; only one external treatment, the washing of feet, was I persuaded to receive from their hands.

Chapter 33

But Oh! Even these waters of salvation drawn for me at the counsel of the women became waters of affliction: the first waters into which I put my feet were not hot enough for curative purposes. As they rushed to pour in the additional water that was beyond boiling, I did not manage to withdraw my feet quickly enough before some boiling water fell on my right foot and instantly scalded it. Soon I was ailing in all my organs inside as well as out, from my neck to the sole of my foot. Such is my reward for heeding my mother's-in-law follies!

Either this external pain or the fright it caused evidently hindered the illness from its intended course, so that that day the fever was late in coming; I even allowed myself to imagine that it would never return. Similarly, the household experts congratulated themselves that this external pain had rescued my soul from its inner torments; so they did not worry about me until the following night and kept firmly to their beds in a deep sleep. I alone could not find sleep in my eyes, I rolled about hurting from the bandaged foot and every few minutes alternately tied and untied my leggings to change the bandages they had placed on it, in order to dispel the heat. In the middle of the night the fever returned and burned my bones with greater fire and greater might— both the pain in my throat and the burns on my leg were forgotten in the distress of my soul. I melted in the fire of the fever; I tried to awaken the sleeping with calls and found that the throat roared but no one woke up. I thought of extinguishing the fire with cold water, but the experience of the previous night showed me water could not extinguish such a fire. And my damaged foot would not let me budge from my place; I lurched and moaned, I opened my mouth and inhaled a dragon's breath until I despaired of salvation. I uncovered my arms and legs and wrapped my head in my blanket and lay down as if comatose.

Oh, how I suffered that night and how exhausted I was from thirst! To this day I imagine that if I had then seen my brother (my mother's son) bleeding to death, I would have fallen upon him to quench my thirst with his blood. With the last shred of strength I managed to throw the blankets to the ground and fell crawling on hands and knees to beg for water. But my strength failed and I collapsed, my dry tongue sticking out of my mouth.

At the sound of my fall, my mother-in-law woke up and aroused the remaining household members who hastened to lift me up and put me back in bed. But I shouted in their ears: "Carry me and throw me into the water." But, following medical rules unbeknownst to me, they refrained from reviving me by filling my mouth with cold water! I begged them, wept bitterly, fought with them, cursed and screamed until despite themselves they relented and gave me some lukewarm water. To compensate, they forced me to drink large quantities of hot water to banish the internal heat with the external. A curse on you witchdoctors!

Before morning nature won out against all its foes internal and external, and cast me into a deep sleep. As the fever had left me before dawn, my sleep was uninterrupted until noon, when I woke up, rubbed my eyes, looked around at all my surroundings, and behold: my father-in-law too was standing above me, having returned from his travels in the morning! Then all the stones [that were sealing] my heart rolled away; I held his hand and kissed him; tears of joy dripped from my eyes. Not in vain did my heart swell, for his first words were: do not play around any more with home remedies. He sent for a doctor, who would address the matter of my illness with the diagnoses of medical science.

With all that, my cure was late in coming, and my soul found only a feeble voice, for the doctor took his time in relieving the power of the fever by his medications. In the goodness of his heart my father-in-law did not spare any expense. The eyes of the entire household were on me, their hands ready always to serve me all day. At night too they hourly changed guards in maintaining a vigil over me; only my wife, who had caused this tempest, did not share my troubles, despite the eyes of her mother; [instead] she turned her attention to her enjoyments and youthful games in her grandfather's house. Indeed, I was secretly grateful to her for this: just then she was a thorn in my side.

I had a few more sleepless nights, and several hours of fever that sent hot steam to my brain to the point where, at times, I became incoherent and spoke nonsense before nature gathered its powers to combat the illness and pushed it out through the pores of the skin by means of heavy sweat. The afflicting fever then passed.

Chapter 34

The impairments of this disorder linger in my memory. Here is one of the mysteries that I offer to scientists who study psychology to determine its solution. The mystery is as follows.

While the hand of the illness ruled over me, my soul detested all desirable foods, some seemed bitter and others acidic to me. Nothing tasted good except apple juice mixed with water and honey. In my youthful mind's eye I could only imagine the reason for this to be the spoilage of the food; but then a malicious spirit overtook me and made me conclude perversely that my wife in her hatred and evil heart was spoiling all the foodstuffs being prepared for me (rather like the suspicion that the common masses felt toward elites in the cholera days). As I was harboring this suspicion in my heart, my mind — burning with the flames of the fever — generated groundless ideas like this, to the point that the idea became anchored in my heart like a well-placed spike.

It was night, and the servant was preparing a pot of chicken soup in front of me. My wife came and tasted the concoction. At that moment the power of imagination took control of my eyes, and the force of illusion passed before me, and I saw my wife pouring vinegar into the pot! With my own eyes, not a stranger's, I saw this. My heart had not yet seduced me to judge based on what I saw; I waited for my palate to render the true verdict. But once I tasted it and my palate sensed something like vinegar, my thinking no longer equivocated since I possessed certification from two authorities — my eyes and my palate. In vain did all those then at home (including my faithful teacher) taste the pot of soup and swear that nothing was wrong with it: what were their beliefs worth compared to the direct evidence of my senses?

Will I ever again be surprised by the wondrous apparitions seen by the feeble-minded — terrifying pictures visible to those who believe in them? Let me never suspect that those who profess such visions are inventing them! Not so! They truly see ghouls and the spirits of the dead that they talk about. [. . .]

I had just begun to breathe the air of health when my father-in-law slipped away once more to his place of business. Just as I had wept tears of joy when he arrived, so I wept tears of sadness when he left. My heart feared that my wheel of fortune — turned toward the good by his hand — might be turned backward once his controlling hand was removed. [I worried that] my tears were offensive to my mother-in-law, who might consider them a silent rebuke, but on this occasion I was proven wrong: my mother's-in-law love truly returned to me, and she showed me pity after my days of illness as a woman pities the fruit of her own womb. She did not withhold from me any nourishment that the doctor had prescribed to help me, and in the course of six weeks the bloom of health again began to surface on my cheeks as of yore.

This [episode] was the first thorn that time had cast on my boyhood days; as it was a true not imaginary affliction, and my heart was soft and prone to unrestrained excitement, it impressed itself very deeply on the furrows of my heart, such that it would take a long time before I could efface it. I had the memory of those awful days, and the cause of them, before me always. Nor was I wrong to surmise that double trouble would yet arise: for what good was it that I loved my mother-in-law or father-in-law, if my wife's heart was not mine? So long as I do not win her affections I shall be considered a foreigner in this house, and how shall I be attractive to her and draw her to me with bonds of love? As my soul lacks the allur-

ing gemstone that draws the hearts of maidens toward young men, such ideas pressed like stones upon my heart and did not permit a joyous spirit to return to me for many days after I had regained my strength.

Throughout all this it never occurred to me to call my parents to rescue me, as I knew they had enough troubles on their own. I took my private courage as my strength and relied on my patience; I said that either I shall save myself or I shall suffer what I cannot prevent. Therefore my letters to them contained nothing more than a brief "Hello" and "All is well." But one of father's faithful friends, who was living in my in-laws' town and who knew what I was enduring, did not act in this way: when he happened to go to my father's town, he told him in full that I was not lying in a bed of roses and revealed to him the illness that I had suffered. My parents heard this and took fright; my father soon resolved to come and meet me.

So one day, I was sitting on my seat lost in thought, my head in my hands, wondering what the Lord had in store for me, when a man dressed in traveler's garb came to the house. I lifted my eyes to the arriving visitor, and good Lord! "Father!" I called, and he answered, "Son!" and instantly we were wrapped in each other's arms. I stood astounded and stunned and could not bring a thing out of my poor lips, but my father kept greeting me. All my excitement, all my strength, my feelings, and my revived spirit came together at their proper destination — my heart, leaving almost no other trace of life in all my other limbs. This was the moment of ecstasy that forcefully overcomes years of pain and anguish!

Chapter 35

It took two or three days with my father before I opened my heart to him; I kept quiet — he began to open the mouth of the mute and to arouse me to unload my sufferings on his breast; and I was as one who had not in his heart any complaint nor rebuke to express, for my mother-in-law's efforts to cultivate my affections had worked upon me, had made me forget all that she had done to wrong me, therefore I spoke naught but good things of her, and likewise when my father disclosed the secrets of his heart to me, and revealed to my ears that he had not traveled in vain to visit me, but to rescue me from affliction; then too I took refuge in lies and denied that any distress had befallen me; and even those matters which I was unable to deny, I deflected with apologetics: I said of my mother-in-law that it was an accident and the same problem would not occur again, and even she, the evil one who sleeps by my side, I defended saying that her complaint was not false, since through the weakness of my potency I was keeping from her what was justly hers, namely the very essence of marriage, therefore it was my duty to bear her grievance until time shall bless my loins with manly might, at last! I stood to the right[10] of my in-laws' household like a defense attorney and did not allow my father to condemn them, and even when my father wished to reprove them directly with choice words, I kissed his hands and asked him to resist tarnishing the sanctity of his visit here with words of rebuke, for these are good days for me, not days of judgment; eventually, my father relented on the matter though he did not wish to leave me to be tortured at the hands of my wife till fortune smiled — he went back home upset and angry at the weak-heartedness of his son who embraced his wife as his master; for he had wished to untie the knot with which he had unwittingly bound me.

This was the consequence of the child marriages that were customary in Polish backwaters, leading to the manifold writs of divorce in this land that came to be piled high, despite the tears falling from the altar's eyes upon them, and despite the priests tending the altar who did not like to see so many women rendered unfit for the priesthood.[11] There is no counting the divorcées in this land. If you see two young women sitting in their father's house, you need not inquire if each of them sleeps in her first husband's bosom — for one of them doubtless has had two men. You can tell this from the way they mark time, for if you ask one of the old people about some case (asking "when did such-and-such happen?"), he will reply innocently that it occurred before my daughter's *first* marriage.

My mother-in-law did not forget the harsh words R. Simhah had sent to her via her servant. She resolved to keep me away from his home, and as she knew she could not prevail over me in this by force, she made cunning her fortress, and induced those who did her bidding to foul the scent of his home in my eyes. These slanderers were quick in their labors: *here* I was told that the members of that household had laughed over the feebleness of my manly powers; *there* it was hinted to me that they did not approve too of my Torah knowledge. I was told that my righteous teacher had offended my father-in-law over the matter of his inclinations to philosophy — similar slanderous words, till in the course of time I came to hate this virtuous teacher, who was full of love for me. By my own choice, without waiting for my father-in-law, I switched to another instructor — so far had my foolishness led me to sin against my instructor, with whom I had been comfortable and who had repaid me only with kindness in every way that he could. May my right hand that is writing these words fall off in testament to this wrong if ever in all my days I forget this sin of mine! And if ever I fail in the recesses of my heart when I remember him to say that I sinned against my teacher, and the righteous [whom] I have maligned! Nor did the cup of recompense delay in coming to avenge itself on my teacher's behalf: for no sooner did the shadow of my teacher depart and the light of his brother's home was lost to me than I returned to the dark, oppressive rule of this woman who governed me to the point that I hope that I have already drawn double the punishment due me [as opposed to the next world, where more punishment can be expected.]

My father returned to his home and took his seat in the family council, to discuss what was to be done with me. Yet they were of divided opinions, some took a harsher and some a more lenient stance. My mother consulted the book inscribed on the table of her heart, and found there written explicitly in the Book of Maternal Mercies that her duty was to remove me from my house of torture. My grandfather, who studies *halakhot* every day and found an explicit ruling that it is prohibited to divorce the first wife if nothing adulterous has been found in her,[12] rendered the verdict that I was to be left to be tortured by my wife's hands until things got better: for she would never abuse me, and she needed to fear the words of the Torah which say "and he [the husband] shall govern you." And my father who examines every issue with straightforward good sense, did not rely on religious law this time, for he considered my masculinity, and concluded that I would never conquer my wife through the laws of marriage, and in vain do builders build a house if one part does not fit the other — therefore he made the decision to act as my mother had said, but not for her reasons. And as the dignity of others was dear to him he kept his plans to himself, and waited till the days of Passover neared, and on Tuesday the 8th of Nissan 5571 suddenly a fine carriage arrived with a letter to my father-in-law, stating that my mother misses me very much, having heard of the illness that befell me, and in order to please her he has sent the carriage to carry me and my wife to joyously join them for the coming holiday. My father-in-law heard his words and believed them, as he knew he had not sinned against the child whom my father had deposited with him, and in all his actions he had been good to me; my mother-in-law too trusted in the goodness she had shown me in latter days and had no fear I might remind her of the sins of the former ones. Yet the rest of the members of the household glanced at each other, and whispered that I was going and would not come back; and so did my teacher and his brother's house as well as the rest of the townspeople who knew that my wife's heart was not in accord with mine: they predicted that my wife would return from my father's home alone. Yet my wife herself in her foolishness did not understand what awaited her, and welcomed the trip: she knew that while many were her crimes and vast the sins she had committed against me, nevertheless she thought that in the house of my father they were preparing for her days of love and honor; she could not see the sun due to the power of its light.

And I, anxious and glad, did not look forward to my trip with any comfort, for I loved my father's home and I loved my father-in-law, and knew perfectly well that I could not oblige them both: if I did as my father saw fit I would cause pain to my father-in-law, and my teacher too tried to keep me from leaving, and urged me in his wise counsel to inform my father-in-law of all that my wife was doing to me, for if the cure was to be found near at hand why must I trouble to get it from a distant land? But who shall take such advice, who shall listen to him on such a matter? The horses are fed, the carriage awaits, my parents are whistling for me, the friends of my boyhood have marked my arrival date: am I to be cooped up to attend the whistling of a shrew?[13]

NOTES

1. [Mordechai Aaron Guenzburg (1795–1846) was one of the leading *maskilim* in Russia. The author of works on history and geography, Guenzburg is best remembered today for his autobiography, *Aviezer*, a portion of which is reproduced here. It was written in the 1820s but published posthumously in 1863. Covering just the first sixteen years of his life in short chapters, it is a remarkable reflection on many aspects of Jewish life in Eastern Europe. The portion here discusses his marriage at the age of fourteen, which was not unusual for his class, to an older woman, which was unusual, and his ef-

forts to adjust to her family's home in Shavli (now Šiauliai, in Lithuania).]

2. [This is a phrase found in the Song of Songs (2:7, 3:5, 8:4), a biblical book widely quoted or paraphrased in the Hebrew of the Haskalah.]

3. [That is, they marry too early.]

4. [It was customary for learned young grooms to live with their in-laws, as in this case.]

5. [A traditional term for matzo, but intended here to convey his own private affliction.]

6. [Comedians or jesters were a common feature of Jewish weddings.]

7. [Although Guenzburg was not an only child, he here uses the phrase *evel yahid*, meaning the unique pain one suffers upon losing an only child.]

8. [He writes the Hebrew letters zayin-yod with ellipsis dots — most probably referring to *zayin*, the slang for penis.]

9. [Gilead, a place in contemporary Jordan, is associated with healing in the Bible; see Jeremiah 8:22.]

10. [To "stand to the right" is to stand in support of someone.]

11. [In Jewish law, a divorcée is not permitted to marry a *kohen*, a man of priestly descent. Thus each time a woman was divorced, she was rendered unfit to marry a priest.]

12. [This is one of the three classical opinions on the question of legitimate grounds for divorce, and the most limiting. It is not the accepted opinion, and it is interesting that Guenzburg's grandfather would invoke it.]

13. [In fact, Guenzburg went on live a total of 6 years in his in-laws' home.]

[79]

Petition to Divorce an Impotent Husband (1910)

TsIAM, f. 1457, op. 1, d. 29, l. 2–2 ob.

"Petition of Rozalii Savel'evna to the State Rabbi of Moscow, Iakov Maze (20 April 1910)"

I married a student [of the Imperial Moscow Technical University], Abraam Slepian, on 19 March 1909 in [Nizhnii] Novgorod and am not able to continue a conjugal life with him given that my husband suffers from impotence. I have the honor to ask you humbly, Gracious Sir, to send for my husband and declare to him my decisive and irrevocable demand for a *get* according to the rites of the Jewish religion. For my part, I am prepared to appear for the performance of the Jewish ritual.

"Response [of] Abraam Slepian to Rabbi Yakov Maze (12 April 1910)"

I hereby declare that the accusation of impotence by my wife Rozalii Savel'evna Slepian is a lie and that she has only raised this as grounds for a divorce. For my part, I declare that I do not desire to grant a divorce on those grounds, for I took a vow in synagogue obliging me to live together [with her] until the end of our lives. I cannot insist at the present that she is obliged to live with me in one apartment.[1]

NOTE

1. [In the final document in the file, the rabbi states that the case has not yet been heard but that he had taken it under consideration and would render a decision.]

[80]

Responsum of R. Yitzhak Elhanan Spektor: A Mikvah near a Turpentine Factory

Yitzhak Elhanan Spektor *Ein Yitzhak, Yoreh Deah*, 1: 19 (Vil'na [s.n.] 1888).

Your letter reached me regarding your question about a mikvah in a certain village that is several *parsa'ot* [10–12 kilometers][1] from town, so that it is hard for the inhabitants to come to town each time [to use the town's mikvah]. There is a turpentine factory and nearby a large natural spring and a pool with forty *se'ah* [293 liters][2] of water even in the dry season. But when they wish to warm up this cavity, they pour the warm turpentine from the outlet pipe of the factory, which warms up the water and flows into the cavity. As a result, the water in this cavity always has a smell of turpentine and a somewhat revolting appearance. Your honor has asked me to venture my opinion about this.

Here is my reply: as explained in *Yoreh Deah*, chapter 201, section 25, if you wash some utensils and the color of the water changes, that does not render the mikvah unfit; only if the actual object falls into the mikvah and changes the appearance [of the water] is the mikvah to be disqualified. And it is stated in the Mishnah, tractate *Mikvaot* 7:3: if baskets of olives or grapes were washed in the mikvah discoloring it, it is [nevertheless] kosher. And this position is affirmed by Maimonides in the *Laws of Mikvaot*, 7:5. . . . The BaH[3] notes that, even if utensils washed in the mikvah contained some liquid causing discoloration it still does not invalidate the mikvah, the implication being that this is the case even if some residue from the liquid adhered to the utensils. As the *Shach* has written in *Yoreh Deah* (chapter 95, subsection 1), utensils being washed are presumed not to have been scrubbed. As this plain language implies, it makes no difference whether the liquid adhered to the insides of the vessel. In any case, they have said that washing the utensils in it does not render the mikvah unfit. Only if some of the actual turpentine remained there should one be strict and consider it equivalent to a case of the actual object falling into the mikvah and changing its appearance. Unless this is the case, one ought not to be stringent, for the mikvah is one of flowing waters. As explained in *Yoreh Deah* (chapter 201, section 28): a spring does not become unfit by a change in appearance. [. . .] Hence, if it is known that the turpentine has been entirely vacated from the outlet, even if there is some turpentine residue in the outlet pipe, that is no cause for concern in my opinion. Certainly, the odor does not pose a problem as explained in Maimonides (*Laws of Mikvaot*, 7:1).

NOTES

1. [A *parasa* (pl. *parsa'ot*) is equivalent to 3.84–4.608 kilometers.]

2. [A *se'ah* is equivalent to 7.33 liters.]

3. Yoel Sirkes (1561–1640), rabbi of Krakow, among other places.

[81]

Responsum of R. Hayim Ozer Grodzinski: Manicures and the Mikvah

Chaim Ozer Grodzinskii, *Responsa Ahiezer*, 3: 33 (Jerusalem: [s.n.], 1959).

On your question about women who have the practice of growing their nails (manicure). You were asked by two women who wish to uphold the laws of purity and immersion properly [to permit them to do so] without trimming their fingernails. As it is explained in the Rema *Yoreh Deah* (198:20): where there has been a long practice of trimming the nails (either out of concern that some dirt may be stuck under the nail; or as the Siftei Cohen wrote, citing statements by the Raavad, on the grounds that a growth that is destined to be trimmed later counts now as an obstruction), even if a single long fingernail is left on her hand and she immerses herself, another immersion is necessary.

My friend, your honor really has raised a difficult question, and the right thing to do is to try and persuade them not to change the custom of those women who trim their nails prior to immersion. But if that is impossible, and if there is a chance that they may fall into error and avoid immersion on this account, then it would be acceptable if these women thoroughly clean their nails and are quite careful even without trimming them. It is only where the majority of people are scrupulous that we follow the majority (as was written in the top of chapter 198 and in the *Turei zahav* chapter 102). Indeed, most people are not careful to trim their nails and even the women are not, except for the time of immersion, [but even then] only because of the desire to follow the law punctiliously. . . . [A case in which] we are strict about this even after the fact in a case where she herself is normally careful about this but [in this hypothet-

ical case] has simply forgotten. In the case where she is careful (even when most people are not), [the extended nail] counts as an obstruction. (And this is the position of Maimonides, the Tur, and the Mordechai cited in the *Siftei Cohen* Chapter 102.) This is not the case where she is not at all careful [about observing this rule] and here, on the contrary, especially desires not to trim the fingernails and to immerse in that state; if most people do not take care to trim their nails even if most of those who immerse do, that [the latter condition] does not constitute a majority. Since she is not careful, it is not an obstruction. To this we may add the principle that her state of mind is to be considered. . . .

Regarding the proper practice of the law, the statements of the author [of the *Shulhan Arukh*] suggest that a fingernail does not count as an obstruction, even in cases where women have the practice of trimming them. As stated in the *Beit Yosef* and in the *Shulhan Arukh* (ibid.), there is no clear way of determining what counts as pressed against the flesh and what is not pressed against the flesh. Women developed the habit of trimming nails at the time of immersion: it seems that even where this custom is followed, it does not become an issue if the nail is clean (as written in sec. 20: the fingernail itself is not an obstruction; see the *Shaarei dura*). Only the Rama took a strict position when the practice was to remove nails out of concern for a little dirt; it came to seem a binding rule to be sure to trim the fingernails. And it appears that this is the reason the *Turei zahav* (chapter 121) is lenient if the woman had to immerse herself on Shabbat, a holiday, and *hol hamoed,* and has made a thorough cleaning [as nails cannot be trimmed then]. . . . For the same reason we can be lenient if she is not careful about trimming nails: people with manicures especially want to retain their nails.

Thus, we need not concern ourselves with the stringent approach of the Raavad (cited in the *Siftei Cohen* ibid.) that the fingernail counts as an obstruction because it is about to be trimmed, as in this case it is not about to be trimmed.

[82]

Responsum of R. Yitzhak Elhanan Spektor: Marriage of a Man without A Right Testicle

Yitzhak Elhanan Spektor, *Ein Yitzhak, Even ha-Ezer* 1: 9 (Vil'na: [s.n.], 1888).

BLESS GOD, MONTH OF ADAR 1861 BY OUR CALENDAR.

The question is about a man who had a diseased right testicle and took medical treatments. He traveled to the imperial city of Vienna, and there the doctors saw that his illness was beyond remedy, as the testicle had became rotten and soft. They amputated the right testicle, and he was healed. I have been asked whether he is permitted to marry a woman.[1]

NOTE

1. [After lengthy discussion of the issues, Spektor permits the man to marry.]

[83]

Responsum of R. Yosef Zekharyah Stern: Paternity Determination for the Child of a Raped Wife

Yosef Zakharyah Stern, *Zekher Yehosef, Even ha-Ezer* 20 (Vil'na: [s.m. 1898–1901).

TO THE RABBI OF TOKMAK, R. ELIMELEKH

At issue is your question from a woman who had been ill, who, after nearly eight years of marriage, had yet to give birth, and who went to a doctor specializing in women's matters, who laid her down on an apparatus built for this, and who used some instrument (the length of the male organ) to examine her illness; he ordered her to lie face down and pushed this instrument into her. She felt that he had inserted some mechanical object into her; it was very warm; she was lying face down, and did not know all that he was doing to her. When she returned to the inn, she told the innkeeper's wife about these things and also showed her smock (which was sullied with semen). The [latter] replied that it did not appear that any vile matter had been done; the dirty stain on the smock might be from the kinds of ointment that the doctor rubbed on the tool. Later, when she again came to the doctor and he ordered her to lie on the bed like she had done a few days before, she managed to see that he was standing before her with his member exposed, wanting to do the act, and she rose from the bed and knocked him down with her hand and began to scream. The doctor took fright and let her out of his room; she then went to the inn and realized that a few days earlier she must have had intercourse with the doctor. She came to [the rabbi] asking if she needed to do penance; he ruled that she was permitted to her husband and that she has the legal status of someone raped (per *Even ha-Ezer* section 178c), she had not lost her presumption of property by having secluded herself with him for there were no witnesses to that seclusion and "the mouth that forbids is the mouth that permits."[1] A still more severe case appears in the responsum of R. Haim Cohen (*Even ha-Ezer* chapter 10), who permitted her to [have sexual relations with] her husband: there is no need even to do penance. [Thus far the position of R. Elimelekh.]

[Stern responds:] On the issue of seclusion, one ought not at all to be stringent. See the *Shev Yaakov* part *Even ha-Ezer* chapter 19 on the issue of road travel on a non-Jewish coach when two upstanding Jewish men are present etc., notwithstanding that some authorities demand that in the field three upstanding men are needed [to avoid seclusion], etc. Shall we really disqualify a woman who travels with a lone trustworthy male guardian? In such a case of "seclusion" we do not prohibit her to her husband; otherwise, there would be no daughters of Abraham left, as I have stated at length elsewhere.

But your eminence is sensitive to what is written in *Even ha-Ezer* section 13 subsec. 6, where the Rema, in his comments on rape, states that if she had not had prior intercourse with her husband, she must wait [before having relations with him] for the sake of a [paternity] determination. The later authorities point out that the legal principle of "majority" [as in the majority of instances of intercourse with a virgin do not result in pregnancy] are not applicable here, since a test is needed to settle matters conclusively. A suggestion to this effect is in the *Yeshuot Yaakov*, Chapter. 13. But in this case, seeing as she had cohabited with her husband before going to see the doctor, no test [of waiting to resume relations with her husband] is needed as its outcome would necessarily be inconclusive.

NOTE

1. An adulteress is forbidden to her husband (and her lover), but a married rape victim is not considered an adulteress. In this case, because she willingly secluded herself with her rapist, one might have thought that that would undermine her claim of rape; but the ruling of R. Elimelekh of Tokmak is that she is believed when she claims she was raped, and permitted to her husband.

[84]

Responsum of R. Yosef Zekharyah Stern: On the Issue of Intercourse That Endangers the Wife's Life

Yosef Zekharyah Stern, *Zekher Yehosef, Even ha-Ezer* 37 (Vil'na: [s.n. 1898–1901).

IN RESPONSE TO A QUESTION TO ME BY ONE OF THE GREAT SCHOLARS.

FRIDAY EVE OF THE HOLY SHABBAT, 5746 [1886]

On a ruling in the case of a woman who became seriously ill from pregnancy and delivery. The couple was still young and not interested in divorce; [the wife] had already given birth to five boys and a girl, and the doctors declared that she would be in grave danger should she become pregnant again. [The rabbi who wrote me] told them that it was completely forbidden to follow the doctor's counsel of external ejaculation; drinking sterility potions in the manner of R. Hia's wife [*Yevamot* 65b] was also precluded by the doctor, who said this too would pose a danger for her. This left no other recourse but to use an absorbent [for contraception] as in the "three [types of] women ruling" [*Yevamot* 12b][1] over which Rashi and Tosafot disagree, and your honor does not know which opinion is decisive.

The *Shulhan Arukh* [*Yoreh Deah* chapter 196, section 13] states that it is permissible [for a woman] to bathe to extract [sperm]. Accordingly, in the case at hand, she may turn herself over (as per the *Rambam*) [to keep the sperm from advancing], rinse in hot water, and wipe with a fine cloth, or to walk around after [intercourse]. But to insert an absorbent into "that place"[2] before [intercourse] — that is prohibited. (See the responsum of the Hatam Sofer, *Yoreh Deah* Chapter 172 regarding post-coital usage of an absorbent, etc.).

R. Akiva Eger wrote in his responsum (at the end of chapter 72) "one may permit the insertion of an absorbent after intercourse in the manner of a menstrual examination only as far as the penis penetrates, since the Rashba and the Rosh permit a removal of semen to allow the count of the menstrual days to begin [to assure that it is menstrual fluid, not semen, that is being discharged], and the *Shulhan Arukh* chapter 196 section 3 sealed that into law. Although there is no benefit to this [as a contraceptive method], since whatever can be extracted from the vaginal canal would not have impregnated her in any case, the rest cannot be extracted in this way; and frequent examinations using an absorbent is truly prohibited." Apparently his permission was limited to the specific case he was addressing, in which the question was raised regarding a difficult or disturbed woman for whom each labor was harsh and involved great suffering and who was constantly in danger. He allowed her to use an absorbent in that place after intercourse etc., as that case fell into the category of [alleviating] labor pains as she always gave birth with great difficulty. This state of affairs is similar to that of the wife of R. Hia.

However, in the responsum of the *Hemdat Moshe* part *Even ha-Ezer* chapter 46, [the author] is similarly asked about a woman of whom it was determined (in the doctors' unanimous opinion) that becoming pregnant would place her at great risk: pregnancy would place her in mortal jeopardy. That woman was permitted to insert an absorbent before coitus: in a situation deemed by the doctors to be one of great risk, we do not have the right to issue a prohibition. There is no need [for the husband] to divorce her on this account: even though the medical requirement is to insert the absorbent long before intercourse, the ejaculation of semen is not considered "destruction of seed" as there is no alternative to this mode of intercourse because of the health hazard. [. . .]

Hence, where it is known that there is a mortal danger, and known that there are dangers to the unborn child as well . . . it is not to be considered "destruction of seed." The rabbis [who prohibit the absorbent in the case of the three women] in Yevamot 12b clearly did not have in mind cases of severe endangerment—otherwise how could they have relied on a miracle [rather than an absorbent to save a life]? But where, according to the doctors, there is the indubitable danger of her becoming pregnant, we have no reason to suppose that the rabbis dispute the position of R. Meir, who permits the use of an absorbent even before intercourse. In any event, in a case that generates such great duress, [R. Meir] is to be relied on. See the responsum of the *Meshiv davar*, chapter 88. If it had been possible (with the doctors') consent to use a sterility potion without fear [of side effects], this would have been better; even with an absorbent great care is needed [to avoid pregnancy].

Regarding such a potion, the *Shulhan Arukh* (*Even ha-Ezer* 5:12) gives a ruling that a sterility potion is permitted to prevent pregnancy . . . But allowing such a potion is disturbing: I have heard that it entails serious hazards, whereas I have allowed the use of an absorbent after intercourse with the permission of the husband. . . .

The *Birkei Yosef* allows himself to consider the possibility that, where there is a great need, the *husband* is allowed to drink a sterility potion. However, this is completely rejected and inconceivable; [male sterilization is] certainly not permitted because of "And in the evening relax not your hand," which con-

tinues to apply even once the commandment "Be fruitful and multiply" has been met. [. . .][3] See the *Turei even* on *Hagiga*, which says that although he is not obligated to divorce his wife [if she wants no more children], in any case he is never permitted to sterilize himself. That is not the case for a woman, as is affirmed by the *Tosefta* in *Yevamot* chapter 4 and the *Rambam* chapter 21 paragraph "Laws of Prohibited Sexual Relations," which even permits a woman to marry a eunuch. [. . .]

I was subsequently asked about all this by the rabbi of Shomrik, his honor Alexander Yonah b. R. Shalom Yudkowsky: A woman who suffered [probably from uterine cancer] underwent three operations at a clinic in Khar'kov over three months. She recovered, but would be endangered were she to become pregnant; so the doctors advised her to use an absorbent prior to intercourse. I replied in brief that in the event of a hazard the *Hemdat Shlomo* is to be relied on. I have also been asked several times by various petitioners about this; since the question had not been directed to me by the [local] rabbi, I did not wish to reply to individuals who do not have the right to adjudicate—especially in cases like these, which cannot be ruled on except by exercising judgment as to the gravity of the danger. It also seemed to me that the question had come from the husband himself, and that quite possibly he had already been given an answer by his rabbi. I therefore declined to enter discussions with these people by letter in response to their question.

NOTES

1. [In the passage R. Bebai stated before R. Nahman, "three [types of] women may use an absorbent while having intercourse: a minor, a pregnant woman, and a nursing woman." A *mokh* or absorbent is inserted into the vagina to absorb the semen and prevent fertilization.]

2. [The standard rabbinic euphemism for a vagina.]

3. [That is, even after the biblical commandment

has been met (there are differing opinions on how many children this requires), one may not "relax one's hand" meaning one must continue to reproduce as nature allows. This obligation falls on the man alone; while women, of course, are needed for reproduction the *obligation* to reproduce falls on the man. Hence, he may take no action to curtail his ability to reproduce, even as his wife may.]

[85]

A Husband with Syphilis (1872)

GAZhO, f. 19, op. 8, d. 11, l. 1–2.

"Complaint of Mendel Treibich against His Wife Dvoira to the Justice of the Peace Court (1872)"

In 1865, I married a single townswoman from the town of Kozen, Dvoira Zdenbaum. Having lived for three years in the town of Radzivilov, I took a lease on a tavern located in the village of Boratim, where I lived with my wife in love and harmony. Meanwhile, this past August 1871, one of our children was ill and needed to go to Radzivilov, [as we did not] have the means to treat him in the tavern. Before my departure, wishing to take some money with me, which was located in a chest, I unlocked it and saw that there was no money or documents about the maintenance of the tavern. When I asked my wife where the money and documents had gone, she replied, "You need to go, but when you return, you will find everything." Not having the necessity for this money and being certain that both the money and documents were with her, I left. Having lived for a few weeks with the sick child in Radzivilov, I suddenly learned that the tavern had burned down, and when I arrived at the place where the tavern used to be, my wife was not there. I learned from a neighbor that she had taken all the belongings and left for her parents in the town of Kozen.

Knowing that I had always lived in love and harmony with my wife and attributing the fire to an unfortunate event, I set out for Kozen to fetch my wife and belongings to live in Radzivilov. In the meantime, she decided everything, not wishing to live with me as the circumstances of the case revealed. She has made me so indigent that now I do not even have my daily livelihood. Despite my bitter situation and repeated trips to the town of Kozen to make peace with her, she [refuses to do so] every time.

"Verdict of the Court (31 October 1873)"

The decision regarding termination of the investigation into the complaint lodged by the merchant's son Mendel Treibich of Radzivilov against his wife Dvoira for her refusal to cohabit [is as follow]: Mendel Treibich filed a complaint in the Justice of the Peace Court of Kremenchug District against his wife for refusing to cohabit and for leaving him. At the proceedings of the Justice of the Peace Court, the Jewish woman Dvoira Treibich testified that she was forced to live separately from her husband because he is infected with syphilis to the degree that his nose has undergone disintegration and his appearance aroused an aversion in her and made her lose her appetite. For his part, Mendel Treibich declared that he has been infected with syphilis for five years but does not know from whom he got it; he suggested that it was from his wife. [. . .] Concurring with the opinion of the investigator, I propose to terminate this case with no further examination.

Extramarital Sex

[86]

Responsum of R. Yosef Zekharyah Stern:
On Concubines

R. Yosef Zakharyah Stern, *Zekher Yehosef, Even ha-Ezer* 38
(Vil'na: [s.m. 1898–1901).

12 ADAR 5755 [1895]

On the matter of your question that reached me earlier.[1] Although I am greatly concerned to ease this man's plight, I have nevertheless firmly decided not to respond at all, for the entire basis of your argument relies on the responsum of Yaakov Emden Ben Zvi, part B chapter 15. The latter intervened in a dispute of the medieval authorities after they had already decided clearly in favor of the Rambam's position (vigorously rejecting the positions of the Ribash and the Radbaz on the issue of concubinage).[2] [R. Emden] has already been shouted down by the entire scholarly community . . . the honorable thing to do here is to keep quiet. Likewise your eminence ought to resist offering remedies to single individuals; you do not pay attention to how far things reach and how many disasters can get into circulation by doing such things. As I did not know your name until now (owing to the remoteness of the place where this matter first arose), it was hard for me to imagine that any rabbi would inject himself into this issue and allow it. Also it once happened to me that someone included in his letter a *convert* [envelope], with the inscription that the sender was the town rabbi; I later discovered that he had deceived me, although my responsum reached him (based on the name and honorific written on the envelope). Now, once more your letter openly comes to me [stating that] you are perplexed by my lack of response and that it strikes you as all the more amazing since, as you write, all the great rabbis have always had the pleasure of engaging you in halakhic discussions. Hence you presumably must have written similar letters to others, and Israel is not bereft of *geonim* [great rabbis] closer to your place. You ought to have shown a copy of some letter of the great ones of our day who have exchanged words with you on this matter if such had reached you. By rights you have no ground for complaint against me for having withheld a response from you on this matter, since I do not know of you other than from your opinion on this issue.

[Many authorities][3] have gone to great lengths to prove that concubines are not permitted for commoners, [even] by Torah law . . . It would be superfluous to pile on argumentation on these matters as if a halakhic decision was to be required. This is all the more so because of your further argument that a concubine is not included in the ban against taking a second wife. That is nonsense! The whole point of the ban was that a man cannot provide for [more than one wife] and disputes [among wives] will multiply; as the later authorities wrote, on this matter the rabbis have the authority to demand inaction[4] as a protective measure and to meet the needs of the times. So this enactment is not considered to supplant biblical law. The responsum of the Maharam Padua (chapter 14) states that the rabbis took care to aid the daughters of Israel during our exile: if [a man] has many wives and many children, he will not be able to provide for them. Even according to Rava in *Yevamot* 65a, whose position is adopted into law, a man can take more than one wife only if he can provide for them all. That is precisely what worried our predecessors while we are in exile. Everything balances [precariously] on the antlers of the deer. . . . And why should there be a requirement to gather permissions from a hundred rabbis from three different countries, each of whom sees a clear reason to allow it (see the responsum of the *Beit Yosef, Laws of Ketubot* number 14), if we had decided there is no restriction whatsoever against having a concubine? R. Yaakov Emden Ben Zvi casts doubt on the basis for the ban on polygamy, writing that it only arose out of the threat of non-Jews, who fear that we will multiply and spread among them. Hence [he argues] that the ban should be rescinded; he also disagrees with the majority and accepted position that in a case when an Ashkenazi Jew travels to a community where this ban is not practiced [that is, a Sephardic community], since the surrounding nations there do not uphold the ban, there is surely no reason to add strictures to what is made law by the Torah. But who will listen to him about this? He has gone his own way, arguing that the ban was introduced only to prevent trouble in places where the non-Jewish authorities would in any event not allow a man to marry two wives, and not as a measure for societal improvement, as the medieval authorities have written. . . .

NOTES

1. [No recipient is identified in this responsum. It appears that a married man wanted to take a concubine, as a way around the prohibition on having two wives. Stern rejects this forcefully, and notes that the whole procedure of requiring one hundred rabbis to allow a second wife would be rendered pointless. The responsum contains insight into the nature of Jewish law and its intersection with the conditions under which Jews live in the diaspora.]

2. [That is, this is a clearly settled matter of law, and there is no basis for reconsidering it.]

3. [Stern cites several sources such as *Yeshuot Yaakov, Birkei Yosef, Atzei Arazim*, and others to support his case.]

4. [That is, contemporary rabbis have their authority to demand that one "sit and do nothing" — a lower level of authority than demanding that one "get up and do something." That is to say, the authority of the rabbis to ban a polygyny, including concubinage, is airtight.]

[87]

Questions to R. Yitzhak Elhanan Spektor about Adultery and Rape

"The Offspring of an Adulterous Marriage and Halitsah"

Yitzhak Elhanan Spektor *Ein Yitzhak, Even ha-Ezer* 1: 6 (Vil'na: [s.n.], 1888).

I received your letter with the question about a woman who had lived with husband ten years without giving birth and who was later rumored to be in love with some laborer. Witnesses reported about flirtations with her, and one witness testifies that the laborer was seen entering a secluded space with this woman. She subsequently gave birth to a child. The husband says she admitted the offspring was not his; they have since divorced. Later the husband married another woman and then died without issue. I was asked whether *halitsah*[1] is needed, as maybe the offspring was not his but the laborer's [in which case the second wife would need *halitsah*] or perhaps we say that the child is from the first wife's husband [i.e., the now dead man, in which case], the second wife does not require *halitsah*. Your honor wrote that we should be strict in this matter [i.e., require *halitsah*, which would also render the first wife's child a *mamzer*, as we would be saying that the husband was not the father] . . .[2]

"The Identity of the Child of an Adulterous Affair with a Non-Jew"

Yitzhak Elhanan Spektor, *Ein Yitzhak, Even ha-Ezer* 1: 7 (Vil'na: [s.n.], 1888).

The question concerns a couple who quarreled and fought for many years and then separated. The woman lived alone for many years, and the husband resided far away in a distant land. After some time, the wife traveled to where the husband lived and a year later gave birth to a son. The wife claims the child is that of the husband, who allegedly had been in her house several times. The husband claims the child is not his, but another's. He says that he surmises the child's father not to be of Jewish seed. I was asked to render my opinion as to whether the child is eligible "to join the congregation" [i.e., whether the child is a *mamzer*].[3]

"The Illegitimate Child of a Mute Woman"

Yitzhak Elhanan Spektor, *Ein Yitzhak, Even ha-Ezer* 1: 8 (Vil'na: [s.n.], 1888).

I was asked about a woman who had been divorced for some years and who became pregnant extramaritally and gave birth. The woman is mute; she hears but cannot speak, so we do not know who made her pregnant. In her town there are no *mamzerim*, but many close relatives. Do we have grounds to worry whether this child is fit to be a member of this congregation or not?[4]

"The Rape of a Betrothed Virgin by a Non-Jew"

Yitzhak Elhanan Spektor, *Ein Yitzhak, Even ha-Ezer* 1: 15.

TO THE HONORABLE RABBI AND *GAON*:

Your letter reached me about this bad business that (because of our sins) occurred in your community: some non-Jew raped a betrothed virgin and made her pregnant (still her present condition). The fiancé wishes to marry her, but on condition that he not have to wait twenty-four months from the date of the birth; if he must wait the twenty-four months, he will not marry her and the engagement will (God forbid) be canceled. This (heaven help us) presents a grave threat to the girl and shame to her venerable family. I was asked by your honor to attend to this question.[5]

NOTES

1. [*Halitsah*, or levirate divorce, is the ceremony whereby the living brother of a dead man releases that man's childless widow from having to marry the brother. See document 46, note 2.]

2. [In this case, Spektor averted the tragic consequences suggested by the unnamed questioner, deciding that the second wife does not need *halitsah* and that the child from the first wife is not a *mamzer*.]

3. [Again here, Spektor permits the child to "enter the congregation," finding that he is not a *mamzer*.]

4. [The question is whether a child is a *mamzer*. A person can become a *mamzer* by being the child of a *mamzer*—which does not obtain here, since there are no *mamzerim* in the town—or by being the product of an adulterous or incestuous marriage. Adultery does not obtain here, as she is not married, so the question is whether there are grounds to worry that the child is the product of incest. Spektor, predictably, decides that there are no grounds for worrying about that.]

5. [The issue here is that Talmudic law prohibits marrying a woman who is pregnant with or nursing the child of another man. A woman is expected to nurse for twenty-four months. Hence the concern that he would have to wait twenty-four months. Spektor permits him to marry her after she gives birth—that is, he must wait until then—and further says that she may not nurse the child but must hire a wet-nurse, who in turn must swear to fulfill her twenty-four-month contract.]

[88]

Trial of Sosha Lubshitz of Trokai Accused of Suffocating an Infant Conceived before Marriage (1879)

LVIA, f. 447, op. 1, d. 28157, ll. 3–4.

"Indictment of the Procurator of the Vil'na Criminal Court (31 May 1879)"

In May 1878 the police and head of the gendarme administration of Trokai district were informed that on 7 May the body of an infant, who had been strangled on 6 May in the tavern at Movshishko, was buried in the Trokai Jewish cemetery. The baby's mother, who was pregnant at the time of marriage, delivered a child five months after she married (the purpose [of the marriage] being to free herself from disgrace). The baby was strangled with the full knowledge of her husband and family. Ekaterina Lipnitskaia, who lives in Movshishko, served as the midwife for the sick woman [Dvera].

In the wake of the above notification, an investigation revealed [the following]: in 1877 the daughter of the tavern keeper Mones Lubshitz of Movshishko, Dvera, married the townsman of Sventsian, Shliomo Shapiro, who lived at the Lubshitzes' tavern for a few weeks prior to marrying Dvera. On 6 May 1878, a Saturday, they summoned Ekaterina Lipnitskaia and Petrunelia Gruzhevskaia to the tavern to Dvera Shapiro. Upon arriving at the tavern on Saturday evening, they found Dvera Shapiro sick and in bed. Around 12:00 Gruzhevskaia left to go home while Lipnitskaia remained with the sick woman. On the morning of Sunday, 7 May, Dvera delivered a child—an infant of the female sex. Having bathed and wrapped the baby in swaddling clothes, Lipnitskaia placed the newborn in the birth mother's room on the pillows of another bed. She herself left, leaving the baby with the birth mother Dvera Shapiro and her mother Sosha Lubshitz. That same day at 6:00 in the evening, Lipnitskaia lifted the baby from the pillows, but the newborn already appeared to be dead. On the morning of 8 May (Monday), Dvera's father, Mones Lubshitz, took the baby's body to Trokai, where it was buried in the Jewish cemetery by the local prayer house that very day (8 May).

The examination and autopsy of the baby born to Dvera Shapiro (conducted on 12 May by the court doctor) revealed the following. [The doctor] found a bluish mark the size of the soft part of the finger on the right side of the baby's neck, a finger width beneath the lower jaw. After an incision was made, this mark proved to be a superficial bruise. The cerebral sinus membrane was filled with blood. The brain exhibited many red dots. Upon the extraction of the brain, the blood poured into the cranial cavity in a rather abundant quantity. The trachea contained fine vesicular foam. The mucous membrane of the larnyx was reddish. The vessels of the neck were intensely overfilled and the thyroid gland contained a lot of blood. One observed pinpoints of bleeding on the membrane under the ribs, on the sternocostal surface of the heart. Upon incision, the lungs made a crackling sound and emitted a bloody foam; placed into water, the lungs floated.

According to the doctor's conclusion, which was confirmed by the Medical Department of the Vil'na Provincial Administration, the infant was not completely carried to term and was born in the ninth month of uterine life,

alive and capable of living. The death of this infant occurred from the flow of blood to the brain and lungs (to judge from the signs found in the internal organs); the blue mark on the right side of the neck was the result of suffocation. The defendants on trial for taking the life of a newborn infant—Dvera Monesov[n]a Shapira (seventeen years old) and her mother, Sosha Iankelov[n]a Lubshitz (forty years old)—plead innocent to suffocating the baby; they say that they do not know the cause of the baby's death. Moreover, at the first deposition the former [Dvera] responded with ignorance and lack of comprehension about all the circumstances, related or unrelated to her indictment.

The townsman of the Davgov community, Mones Girshovich Lubshits (fifty years old), who is on trial (being charged with burying the baby born to Shapiro at the end of three days, without an examination of the court doctor), pleads innocent and testifies that he took the baby to Trokai on the second day, but that burial was on the third day after the death.

The elder of the Jewish cemetery of Trokai, Leizer Oremovich Breinaliad (forty years old), questioned under oath in the capacity of a witness and then put on trial by the court investigator as a defendant (for burying the body of the infant born to Shapiro), also pleaded innocent for the premeditated burial of the body brought to him by Mones Lubshits, without the examination of the court doctor. He testified that he did not know that one ought not to bury a fetus without the permission of the police.

The husband of the accused Dvera, Shlioma Shapiro (Sapiro), testified that the baby had cried at the time of birth. His wife was pregnant with the baby two months before the marriage. Dvera acknowledged this latter circumstance at her reinterrogation at the investigation. When the baby died, Shlioma Shapiro was not at home. He had gone to Trokai at that time.

The witness Petrunelia Gruzhevskaia testified under oath that on Sunday, 7 May (around 7:00 a.m.), when she went by Lubshitz's tavern, she found the mother lying in the common room. Dvera was ill, but fully conscious and alert. Gruzhevskaia remained in the Lubshitz tavern for half an hour; all this time, the newborn slept peacefully. During her second visit to see Dvera that very day at sunset, in her presence Lipnitskaia took the baby from the bed, wishing to swaddle her again, but the baby appeared to be dead.

Ekaterina Lipnitskaia also testified under oath that after the baby was born in the morning on Sunday, 7 May, she swaddled her and placed her on a pillow on the bed, and the baby was alive. Visiting the sick Dvera that very day around noon, the witness also saw that the baby was sleeping. That same day Lipnitskaia came by to see Dvera at sunset. When she took the baby to swaddle her again, she saw that the baby was not alive. At that time, apart from the mother Dvera, her mother Sosha, and father, there were no other people in the house.

On the basis of the statements by the townswomen of Sventsian, Dvera Monesev[n]a Shapiro and Sosha Lubshitz are charged with the crime of suffocating the newborn baby. [. . .] Mones Lubshitz [. . .] is charged with burying the baby at the end of three days, without an examination by the court doctor. [. . .] It is proposed, given insufficient evidence, to terminate prosecution of Leizer Oreliovich Breinsliad for the premeditated burial of the baby.[1]

NOTE

1. [The procurator found that the evidence suggested that the baby was born alive (albeit a little early) and had the capacity to live. The death was caused by a rush of blood to the brain and lungs as a result of suffocation. He argued that the Dvera Shapiro and her mother should be arrested immediately and detained until the end of the investigation and trial.]

[89]

Trial of Rivka Khaet for Infanticide in Vil'na (1897)

LVIA, f. 448, op. 1, 3, d. 12707, ll. 2–5.

20 MARCH 1897, BY THE ORDER OF HIS IMPERIAL MAJESTY, THE VIL'NA PROVINCIAL COURT, CRIMINAL SECTION IS IN SESSION:

Senior Chairman: K. I. Karnovich
Members of the Court: Ia. Ia. Propopovich
                          and V. V. Lupolov
Procurator of the Court: P. P. Dobrinin
Assistant Secretary: B. M. Akhmatovich

[The Court] heard the case of the townswoman Rivka Khaimov[n]a Khaet, charged with the crime anticipated in the Penal Code Part 1, article 1460 [infanticide], and acted on the proposal from the procurator of the Court Chamber (number 1930, dated 14–15 March 1897).

On 2 February 1897, in the town of Vil'na the yardman of Kobchevskii's house on Rudominskaia Street, Ivan Solov'ev, and his wife,

Agaf'ia, found the body of a newborn baby in the outhouse on top of the frozen sewage. In the courtyard not far from the outhouse they noticed drops of blood in the snow. In addition, Agaf'ia Solov'evskaia also observed part of a placenta in the same place so she had no doubt that someone had delivered a baby and then cast the child into the outhouse, where there were no traces of blood (with the exception of a few drops). A few days before this Rivka Khaimov[n]a Khaet—a townswoman from Ol'kenik (Trokai district), who was pregnant—had come to work as a servant at the home of the Jews Elia and Khaia Bakshtanskii. After this event [the discovery of the dead infant] she had disappeared somewhere. That gave rise to the conjecture that the baby found in the outhouse was hers.

Rivka Khaet was found in the Jewish hospital in a postpartum condition. Upon an inquiry by the assistant policeman Gorlov, she acknowledged giving birth to the baby but declared that the birth had happened unexpectedly, while she was defecating. The postmortem on the baby's body showed that he was born at full term, alive, capable of life, and his death was a result of being left without assistance in low temperatures. An examination of Rivka Khaet found her to be in a postpartum stage. Dr. Ianovskii, who conducted the examination, also determined that she had given birth many times.

Interrogated in the capacity of a defendant, Rivka Khaet, who did not plead guilty, testified that she does not remember where she gave birth to the baby, in the courtyard or outhouse, and does not know how he fell into the privy. She became pregnant with this baby by her own legal husband, who is now deceased. She also had a son with him, but does not know whether he is alive or dead. Also, she does not know her husband's patronymic or where he was registered; his name was Israil and his surname Pil'nik. She had not seen her husband before the birth for about a year. He died in Russia but she does not know specifically where. She does not know why her passport indicates that she is not married.

The accused Khaet acknowledges that the above-stated evidence is quite incriminating. She explained that on 2 February 1897 she gave birth to an illegitimate child in the courtyard of the Kobchevskiis' house. Under the influence of shame and fear, she left him without help in the outhouse where he died. [. . .] The Court rules that: (1) the townswoman of Ol'kenik, Rivka Khaimov[n]a Khaet, twenty-eight years old, be handed over to the Vil'na Civil Court for a jury trial of a crime foreseen in the Penal Code (Part 1, article 1460); (2) the court investigator [is to] summon [the following] witnesses to testify about the accused Rivka Khaet: Agaf'ia Antonovna Solov'evskaia, Ivan Andreev[ich] Solov'ev, Khaia Antselevna Bakshtanskaia, Elia Mendelevich Bakshtanskii, the assistant policeman Grigorii Grigor'evich Gorlov, and as experts the city doctors N. Grinevich and Ianovskii; and (3) a copy of this decision along with this case be handed over to the procurator of the Provincial Court.

[90]

A Russian Orthodox Couple's Aid Request for an Illegitimate Baptized Jewish Child to the Russian Orthodox Church (1903)

GAZhO, f. 1, op. 31, d. 251, ll. 1–1 ob.

A Jewish woman living in the town of Ostrog became pregnant and gave birth to a male infant out of wedlock. Being extremely poor and without any relatives, she did not have a shelter where she could place the child or the means to support or feed the child, and so she gave the infant to us. [. . .] She found employment at another home[1] and paid [us] the agreed-upon sum to feed her infant for a period of one year. She then left Ostrog, concealed her whereabouts, and thereby stopped paying us for the maintenance and feeding of the baby. We appealed to the local civilian authorities for advice and, at the suggestion of the chief official in Ostrog, we turned to the local church authorities. Last year we converted the baby to the Russian Orthodox faith; he was baptized in the Bogoiavlenskii Cathedral in Ostrog and named Viktor. Because of our extremely destitute condition, we lack the means to maintain and raise this boy, who is already four years old. Thus we appeal to you with our humble petition [. . .] and request that you provide us some means to support this child from charity for three years and designate the payment for us in the near future.[2]

NOTES

1. [The most common employment for single Jewish mothers who gave up their illegitimate children was wet nursing (see Freeze, "Lilith's Midwives").]

2. [The response read that the petitioners "have not been denied [in their petition] to shelter and bring up the baptized Jewish boy, but only in their request for a stipend for his maintenance." Due to a fire the previous year, the church did not have the resources to provide the funds that the couple had requested. The Volhynia Ecclesiastical Consistory suggested that the child be turned over to the Zhitomir orphanage. The couple rejected that offer and asked to adopt him without paying any adoption fees.]

[91]

Petition of Rafail Veisman about His Illegitimate Russian Orthodox Children (1902)

RGIA, f. 1412, op. 3, d. 326, ll. 1–1 ob., 5.

"Petition from Rafail L'vovich Veisman to Emperor Nicholas II (2 September 1902)"

I am of the Jewish faith and for six years have had an extramarital relationship with the doctor's widow, Elizaveta Iakovlevnaia Mal'shevskaia of the Russian Orthodox faith. From our relationship, we have had two sons: Evgenii (born 4 February 1901) and Iurii ([born] 31 March 1902). Without the legal right to adopt my illegitimate children, I grieve deeply because my children will carry the stigma of being outcasts as illegitimate. That is why I, falling at the feet of Your Imperial Majesty, beg you to allow my children to adopt my patronymic and surname. Their mother will raise my children in the spirit of Russian Orthodoxy. Placing all my hopes upon the mercy of Your Imperial Majesty, I fall at Your feet.

"Letter of Elizaveta Iakovlevnaia Mal'shevskaia to Emperor Nicholas II (28 August 1904)"

Oh, Great Sovereign! Laying my loyal feelings at the feet of Your Imperial Majesty, in joy on the birthday of an heir—the tsarevich—I ask you [to hear] the supplication of a mother about the adoption of my firstborn son from an illegal marriage (*nezakonnyi brak*) with the lawyer Rafail' L'vovich Veisman.

The father of my son is a Jew. But I, Elizaveta Mal'shevskaia, am Russian Orthodox, the widow of a doctor. Two years ago, my son's father appealed to the mercy of the monarch, but his petition was rejected. I beg you, Sovereign, for the happiness of my son [. . .] to allow him to assume his father's name [patronymic] and to bear his surname. My son, Evgenii, born on 4 February [1901] in the town of Tomsk, was baptized at the cathedral by the priest Sidonskii. I will raise my son as a sincerely believing Christian in the spirit of the Russian Orthodox Church.[1]

NOTE
1. [There was no final resolution in the file, but it is likely that the state rejected the petition, especially since the petitioner was asking for her Christian son to adopt a Jewish surname; moreover, Jews were not permitted to adopt Christian children.]

[92]

Petition To Legitimize a Child Born Out of Wedlock (1916)

RGIA, f. 1412, op. 3, d. 325, ll. 1–7.

"Petition of Mordukh Davydov Gofman and His Wife Mar'em Gofman to Emperor Nicholas II (Received 23 April 1916)"

On 28 January 1907, Mar'em Peisakhovich, now Gofman, gave birth to a baby by the name of David in the city of Berlin. As our offspring, he has lived with us as our son from the day of his birth, with equal rights as a member of our family. We were united in a legal marriage on 13 April 1914 and bear one surname, but our son David, born before our marriage, has his mother's former surname. Our very one and only son, blood of our blood, flesh of our flesh, only now, with the beginning of a conscious life, experiences feelings of estrangement, induced by the difference between the surname of the parents and the child. With age, this feeling cannot but become stronger and embitter a young heart.

The only solution is to legitimize our child. Thinking of ourselves as Russians, as children of one great common motherland, we intended to legitimize our child through the means indicated in the law, which is common to all citizens of the Russian tsar. However, as a result of the shortcomings of the law, and the absence of specific instructions that would allow the non-Christian population to enjoy the same rights established for the Christian population of the empire regarding the legitimation of their illegitimate children, the court, which we petitioned about legitimizing our son David refused. [. . .] The child about whom we petition to legitimize is born from us, his natural parents, and should be called by their name and by their documents.

Great Sovereign, Tsar, *Batiushka* [Little Father], father of your loyal citizens, allow us to be called the parents of our only child. May the Tsar's grace not abandon us and order that we [may] legitimize our only son David, born on 29 [*sic*] January 1907. With great faith in the ineffable grace of the Russian Tsar, we beg our Sovereign, the original source of truth and law, whose holy will creates the norms of society, to order that the stigma of descent from an unknown father be removed from our innocent child and grant us the great happiness of seeing our child as a member of our family. In addition we attach notarized copies of the following: a metrical certificate of birth of our son David; a metrical certificate of our marriage; and our signatures about our son David as our offspring.[1]

NOTE

1. [The archival file breaks off inconclusively.]

[93]

Alleged Rape of the Domestic Servant Rakhil Krupen by Her Employer in Moscow (1885)

RGIAgM, f. 142, op. 17, d. 388, ll. 6–13.

"Petition of Rakhil Krupen to the Procurator of the Moscow Court" [n.d.]

I, [Rakhil] Krupen, have lived for about two years as a cook at the home of Girsh Kolodnyi, who lives in the house of Kuznetov (11th Piatnitskii district, on the Naberezhnyi). During my entire time at Girsh Kolodnyi's, I carried out my duties with all diligence, and they observed no reprehensible behavior. Recently, my master, Girsh Kolodnyi, began to display a special predisposition toward me and began to [try to] talk me into an adulterous relationship with him, I refused (despite his repeated pursuit of me). However, despite all this and despite my refusals, Girsh Kolodnyi burst into the room that I occupy at night and raped me. Despite all my efforts and resistance, I was not able to stand up [to him] and had to submit to his will. He took advantage of my weakness and violently deprived me of my virginity and honor. After some time, Girsh Kolodnyi, observing the signs of pregnancy in me and wishing to hide his vile behavior, dismissed me from the house. At present I find myself in the most impoverished position and do not even have a shelter.

Owing to all of the above, I humbly ask Your Excellency to make your authoritative order to the proper channels to investigate my case and to bring Girsh Kolodnyi to trial for his action. Due to the illiteracy of the petitioner, her petition is signed by the military clerk Viktor Petro.

"Police Report to the Procurator of the Moscow District Court (24 August 1885)"

In fulfilling the order of the procurator of the Moscow District Court (14 August, number 14279), regarding the petition of the Jewish woman, Rakhil Krupen, about her rape by Girsh Kolodnyi, I the policeman (with my signature below) of the first district carried out this inquiry, which showed:

The townsman of Pinsk, Girsh Movshovich Kolodnyi (forty-four years old), explained when asked that he has lived for one year in the Novo-Moskovskii inn, where he did indeed employ the Jewish woman Krupen as a cook. As a family man, he has children from ages one to nineteen years old and a wife Golda, twenty-nine years old. He has never dreamed of a special predisposition toward the cook Krupen, and the accusation that she has ascribed to him is a lie and a slander. She often disappeared from the courtyard; strangers saw her with some young people, even with servants at the above-named inn, with whom she carried on freely. However, he did not know what kind of relations she had with them. Recently, with their move to the house of Kutsnetsova in the same district, he dismissed her on the order of the police because he did not have the right to keep Krupen (for lack of permission from the general governor of Moscow to keep a servant from among his coreligionists).

Kolodnyi's wife, Gilda Moiseeva, during her interrogation explained that of late she had begun to notice that Krupen often spent time with the servants, and some young people came to her. Not wishing to have such a servant with her children, she rejected her, all the more so as [the police] informed them that they did not have the right to keep a servant from among their coreligionists without special permission from the general governor. As for Krupen's complaint, she is sure that one of her acquaintances instructed her to make this slander.

The peasant woman Praskovia Ivanovna Kondakova (twenty-four years old), from the town of Gorodishche (Spassky township), who lives at the Kolodnyis' as a wet nurse, explained that Rakhil Krupen lived with her at the Kolodnyis' for about four months. All this time she behaved like a streetwalker; [Kondakova] often saw how [Krupen] carried on with the servants and yard men; a few times she herself reprimanded Krupen that this was indecent. Sometimes Krupen went out for water and wasted an hour or two, and the mistress sent [Kondakova] to find her. She always found her in the courtyard, where she carried on with yard men and other men who were unknown to her. During the four months, she let Krupen out into the courtyard at night after the mistress had gone to bed. [Krupen] said that she was visiting an uncle during these absences. She returned at 4:00 or 5:00 in the morning, and [Kondakova] let her in the door. The mistress did not know anything about these absences. She never observed the master having a special predisposition toward Krupen; on the contrary, he did not like her because she went out with strangers, sometimes half dressed. Through her, the wet nurse, he ordered [Krupen] to get dressed and not go out with a disgraceful appearance.

Itsko Berkov Galperin (nineteen years old), a townsman from Minsk, lives at the Kolodnyis' apartment and explained that he once saw how Krupen complained about some servant Iliusha. He did not know who this servant was or where he lived. She [Krupen] sometimes came to him [to open the door so that she could] go out at night to relieve herself. The door appeared opened, but the cook Krupen was not in the kitchen. At his call, she appeared from the corridor. He did not know where she had been during this time. He also thinks that her accusation against Kolodnyi is slanderous because her behavior was not at all modest.

Gesel Borukhovich Itskovich (twenty-two years old), a townsman from Turetsk (Novogrudok district, Minsk province), explained that he knew Rakhil Krupen for a year and a half when she lived at [the] Kolodnyis' in the house of Shakhovskii. She is absolutely an immodest girl who became involved with various people. He sometimes remained to spend the night at the Kolodnyis' and had sexual relations with Krupen, who herself persuaded him [to do so]. He had nothing good to say about her. Her slander against Kolodnyi was raised on instructions from people who are ill-disposed toward the Kolodnyis.[1]

NOTE

1. [The file ends with a short note that Rakhil Krupen's whereabouts were unknown.]

Prostitution

[94]

Inspection Report of Sixteen Brothels in Vil'na (1871)

LVIA, f. 383, op. 1, d. 20, ll. 53–57.

"Report of the Vil'na Provincial Administration to the Vil'na Medical Department (20 November 1871)"

Pursuant to the general governor's proposal of 17 February 1871 (number 1488), a Commission under the chairmanship of Colonel Izmailov (and created by order of His Excellency) was established in Vil'na to inspect craft shops, artisan shops, taverns, and brothels. He presented a report [. . .] to the chief of the province about his inspection of distilleries, breweries, tannery factories, fish and meat markets, taverns, and brothels.

The inspection of brothels in Vil'na revealed that there are sixteen of them in Vil'na, in which seventy-seven prostitutes (including forty Jews and thirty-seven Christians), between the ages of nineteen and thirty-nine, reside. All these establishments were located either on the outskirts of the city or on out-of-the-way streets. Half of the establishments are kept by Christian women, the other half by Jewish women. The condition of all these establishments, with respect to their buildings, were found to be extremely unsatisfactory upon inspection; their maintenance was far from corresponding to the published regulations on this matter. The inspection of all these establishments showed that:

(1) The majority of the houses in which they [the women] live are in a dilapidated condition and thus, in the winter, must be extremely cold. The entrances to them are vestibules; the staircases, with few exceptions, are not neatly maintained.

(2) The internal rooms of these houses for the most part are not tidy; dirty, damp, and cramped, they are far from corresponding to the number of prostitutes who live in them.

(3) At the inspection one of the madams did not produce the permit for the right to maintain her establishment. The permits [for the other brothels] were examined subsequently; they proved to have been issued and signed by the district doctor appointed to examine these establishments and by the district constable. According to the regulations, however, the permits should have been issued by the police (who are well aware of these women's reliability). [. . .] The doctor's role should rest in responsibility for examining the facilities and the arrangements of these establishments with respect to hygiene and sanitation (in conformity with the existing regulations).

(4) The bedrooms in most establishments are dark and crowded; rarely are they occupied by a single person, but generally have

two and even three beds, [with] no partitions between them.

(5) In a large number of the establishments, the bed linens were in an abominable condition: filthy or badly laundered, covered with stains. The mattress covers were torn, badly washed (if at all), and also covered with stains. The underclothing on many of the women was slovenly in appearance.

(6) At the inspection, it turned out that three Jewish prostitutes live in the brothel of the Christian madam Sof'ia Tukernes (in Karlesa's building on Mostovaia Street). There was one Christian prostitute for every [Jewish] prostitute at the brothel of the Jewish madams, Genna Grinberg (on Raiskii Lane in the building of Rubazhevich) and Golda Makhlotskaia (on Nikodimovskii Lane in the building of Kovalskii).

(7) The madams do not have lists of prostitutes; that is why the verification of their numbers should be made on only one medical card.

(8) Rarely do the buildings have *fortochki* [hinged panes in windows for ventilation]; as a result, the air in these establishments proved to be extremely heavy and putrid.

(9) In one of the establishments of madam Sof'ia Tukernes (in the house of Parnes, located on Mostovaia Street), we found that her husband was living with her and residing in a common room designed for the women. At the time we therefore requested the local constable to have him immediately removed.

(10) In one of the establishments of madam Natalia Krasnitskaia, it turned out that because of her enmity toward the retired soldier Dmitrii Voronov (who was living with her in the house), [Krasnitskaia] neglected her establishment and settled in another place. The Commission reported this to the Vil'na police for the appropriate order to close this establishment.

(11) At the inspection of the brothels located on the following streets [on Novaia Sveta Street in the house of Gilels; on Tatar-skaia Street in the houses of Shul'man and Fliaks; on Kozhevskaia Street in the houses of Bass and Afronovich; on Mostovaia Street in the house of Parnes; and on Sofiannaia Street in the houses of Gurliand and Sokher], we found that taverns are open in the same courtyards; there is direct access through the courtyards to the brothels.

(12) In all the brothels, the women take half of their revenues—that is, one half remains with them and the other half is given to the madam. In return, the latter is obliged to give her tenants beds and bed linens. They may supply their own board or pay the mistress individually for this (up to twenty kopecks a day).

(13) Out of seventy-seven prostitutes in sixteen brothels, verified medical certificates showed that at the time of the inspection, only four prostitutes were in the hospital for venereal diseases. Those admitted to the hospital are obliged to pay for their own maintenance and treatment (about 6.60 rubles a month). As far as is known, hospitals in the capitals do not take any payment for the treatment of prostitutes.

(14) The medical inspection of the brothels, as is evident from the signatures on the medical card, is conducted at least twice a week. The best brothel (with respect to cleanliness, tidiness, and order in upkeep) appears to be the establishment located on Raiskii Lane in the house of Rubakhsevich, which is operated by the townswoman Genna Grinberg. However, there is one difficulty: it is situated in two different buildings, which prevents proper surveillance of the establishment.

Apart from the prostitutes who reside in the brothels, other women in the city live separately (individually or in pairs). They are settled more on the main street or nearby in private houses or inns under the guise of being ordinary women. Incidentally, some entire houses are rented and occupied almost solely by single prostitutes. All these houses are usually leased by Jews, who rent them out to such women (one or two rooms), furnished and with bedding that is extremely filthy. Of the private homes rented for such premises, the best known are the houses of Broit, Ialovtsev, and Nishkovskii on Pokrovskaia Street. These houses, which are inhabited mainly by single prostitutes, have the general character of a brothel in which the owner (a Jewish man, not the madam) shows up and [exploits] the unfortunate victims and other residents [by demanding an] excessive price for these premises. For a room in such houses, prostitutes pay between twenty and thirty rubles a month, with payment [required] a week in advance. However, inspection of several of these accommodations revealed that the prostitutes who live there enjoy greater comforts than those confined in the brothels: the bedding and bedclothes were found to be sufficiently clean enough, although the mattresses in their apartments were extremely filthy.

The medical examination of prostitutes who live separately is usually performed in their living quarters, which constitutes one of the most important difficulties. It is hardly possible for a doctor to conduct [the exam] with complete accuracy in the designated time, with the unrestricted absences of prostitutes from their apartments at any time, day or night. It seems that it would be useful and more appropriate to conduct such examinations at the same time, at designated hours, two or three times a week in a specified location prescribed for this, even the city hospital. Although the women who live separately (only 120 in the city, according to the list of the doctor who supervises the prostitutes) are rarely admitted to the hospital with a venereal disease, it is impossible not to think that many are exposed to infection. As the medical cards and supervision of madams show, those living in a brothel—who are tested by more accurate examinations—have an annual turnover of this disease; their admission to the hospital, as the doctors have indicated, is 150 per-

cent.[1] One must assume that the women living separately resort to private advice when they are ill. Based on the state's overall view of this immoral but necessary business, one can conclude that the supervision of prostitution in Vil'na appears to be clearly irregular and unsystematic. This business is certainly not subject to close [surveillance] in any respect—sanitation or (if this can be said) in moral terms. [...] Perhaps there are some factors that prevent this. However, the measures to establish regular maintenance of the brothels and regular supervision of prostitutes who live separately clearly demand better requirements given the ease with which [people] develop depravity and given the advantages of the present conditions in these shelters.

The establishment of a special committee, which would acclimate itself to local conditions and adapt the statutes that exist in the capitals and cities of Warsaw, Odessa, and Riga concerning supervision of this business, would [help to] prepare permanent statutes. [...] For Vil'na, that would represent one of the beneficial administrative measures that local authorities actively seek to establish better order (to the maximum possible extent), thereby promoting the maintenance of the city's welfare with respect to the people's health. Immediate measures should be adopted, for the sake of sanitation and removal of vice:

(1) The madams of brothels, according to the local premises of their establishments, should limit the prostitutes kept there to a smaller number or should find more spacious lodgings.

(2) They [the measures] should place both the madams and those who rent out furnished apartments that are usually inhabited by prostitutes under a strict obligation to put the mattresses into the proper order.

(3) Pay strict attention to greater cleanliness in the maintenance of undergarments and bed linens.

(4) The brothels that share a courtyard

with a tavern should relocate to another place or the tavern should be banned.

(5) Prostitutes residing in the inns should move to private accommodations.

(6) For prostitutes who live separately, establish a fixed location for medical examinations at set times and twice a week.

(7) If possible, hospitals should admit gratis prostitutes infected with venereal diseases.

(8) Require madams of the brothels, without fail, to keep a list of prostitutes living with them (noting as well their religious confession).

(9) In addition to the basic responsibilities of police constables, they should supply the medical department with a list (as detailed as possible) of all the prostitutes living in the district and maintain strict supervision

so that the latter are furnished with medical cards without delay.

Colonel Izmailov presented the above to the general governor [. . .] and asked that the latter inform him about his instructions on this matter. He also proposed that: (a) the medical examination of women living separately from the brothels should take place on a day determined for them, not in their homes but at the Hospital Savich; (b) the police confirm that they will not be lax in enforcing the law with precise execution.

NOTE

1. [Presumably this means that among the seventy-seven prostitutes in brothels, there are 116 annual hospital admissions for veneral disease (150 percent of 77 is 115.5).]

[95]

Petition by Homeowners to Close the Jewish Madam Mil'shteinova's Brothel in Kiev (1871)

DAmK, f. 802, op. 7, d. 89, ll. 2–4.

"Homeowners' Petition to the Kiev Administration (5 April 1871)"

On Kozinaia Bolotnaia Street, four houses from the crowded Kreshchatik market square, the townswoman Mil'shteinova maintains her own house as an open establishment of depravity—a house of prostitution. It is across from the windows of state councilor Kelenovskii, the merchants Stepan and Vasilii Mzchenkov and Shulgin, collegiate secretary Zhitnitskii, and in close proximity to other houses (including ours, the petitioners). This establishment subjects us, our families, and other families who lodge in our houses

to a grievous moral offense, and we [blame] this situation for the material decrease in the value of our homes. That is why we humbly ask the city council to close down the prostitution in Mil'shteinova's house, to protect us and our families from disgrace and offense, and to give us the possibility to enjoy peace—which is violated day and night by the outrage of this depraved establishment.

"Report from Kiev Senior Constable to the Kiev Municipal Board (14 April 1871)"

With respect to the [report] of 8 April 1871 (number 3460), I have the honor to inform the municipal administration (and I am simultaneously writing to the police officer of the Old Kiev district), that the madam of the brothel on Kozinaia Bolotnaia Street, the townswoman Natalia Mil'shteinova, has been ordered to move to another distant and remote place in the course of twelve days; if Mil'shteinova does not comply, her establishment will be closed.

[96]

Khanne Gershator's Application for a Prostitute's "Yellow Ticket" (20 December 1877)

RGIA, f. 594, op. 1, d. 213, l. 5.

I, the undersigned soldier's wife Khanna Gershator, state in the presence of the medical and police committee that I wish to be placed under medical and police surveillance.[1] I will take up residency in the Shchekin brothel, house number 18, Narvskii District. I have a passport from the Vil'na City Duma. Until this time, I was under medical and police surveillance and resided on Voznesenskaia Street 4, apartment 30.

NOTE

1. [When a woman registered with the police and medical authorities as a prostitute, she received a "yellow ticket" (*zheltyi bilet*) and was subject to physical examinations twice a week for venereal diseases.]

[97]

Residents' Denunciation of Guta Mekler for Prostitution in Vil'na (1882)

LVIA, f. 383, op. 1, d. 65, l. 9.

"Petition of Residents of Vil'na to the Vil'na Provincial Administration (5 February 1882)"

We consider ourselves obliged to inform the Municipal Board that on Vil'komirskaia Street, in part of Ilia Vul'f[ovna] Ol'kin's house belonging to Iosel Leizerovich Katz (number 1015), a woman — Guta Feige Mekler — is acting as a prostitute. We therefore ask whether it would not be desirable for the board to take measures to remove from our street this woman — who does not undergo medical inspections and who does not have a [yellow] ticket for such an occupation. She corrupts young people and soldiers whose barracks are located nearby; in this manner, she may have a harmful influence on her frequent visitors.[1]

NOTE

1. [A note in the margin orders that the denunciation be sent to the city police for further investigation by the Medical Department.]

[98]

Prostitutes in Antokol' Accused of Infecting Soldiers with Syphilis (1882)

LVIA, f. 383, op. 1, d. 65, ll. 28–39.

"Report of the Vil'na Police Chief to the Medical Department of the Vil'na Provincial Administration (15 August 1882)"

Pursuant to the report of 12 August (number 5570), I have the honor to inform you that in view of the private report of the senior doctor of the regiment (which took up its position in the camp by Vil'na) about the infection of low-ranking soldiers at Rivka Lobanovskaia's brothel in the suburb of Antokol', I have instructed the local police to keep strict surveillance over the named brothel and to follow the low-ranking soldiers [to learn] where they predominantly go and where they may have become infected.

In a report of 27 July (number 2484), the police of the seventh district informed me that in the suburb of Antokol' there is only one brothel, maintained by Lobanovskaia. In this brothel there are four prostitutes on [yellow] tickets, who have notes written in the hand of the city doctor about their examination twice a week (on Wednesdays and Saturdays). From the doctor's notes, the prostitutes of Lobanovskaia's establishments are found to be healthy. From the surveillance over the lower-ranking soldiers, it turned out that they frequent a tavern kept by the Jew Aizik Levin; it is possible that they were infected there. The tavern, which is at a distance of 500 meters from the gates of the suburb of Antokol', is in the house of the owner Liepliav, almost across from the same [military] camp.

Music is always playing in the tavern kept by Levin, and as a result many different people always gather, including young girls who have sexual relations with the lower-ranking soldiers, none of whom are examined [medically]. On 25 July at 12:00 p.m., the gendarme Grechin, a noncommissioned officer, escorted two women to the seventh district police. They were arrested for prostitution at Levin's tavern. For the convenience of communication between the camp and Levin's tavern, there are constantly a few boats [available], including one that belongs to the Jew Levin.

On the basis of information of the seventh district police, I made a report to the Vil'na district police because Levin's tavern is located outside the city.[1]

"Report of the Assistant Provincial Medical Inspector to the Vil'na Medical Department (8 October 1882)"

Pursuant to the order of His Excellency, the Head of the Medical Inspectors, I set out at 11:00 on 2 October to be present for the medical examination of prostitutes by the second city doctor, which was being conducted in the Dominikomskii building of the police prison. I found these premises extremely inconvenient. They consist of two small, bright but dirty rooms: in one there is no floor, while the second houses some kind of archive of old papers with a large quantity of dust. Moreover, the staircase leading from the corridor to these rooms is steep and completely dilapidated. The second room has a tall chair made of ash wood (with steps in the front), on which the

examination would take place. It was inconvenient: it had a vertical back so that the witness could not lean back (which would have been convenient for looking at the sexual organs). There was no equipment for the examination: no speculum, no basin, no washstand, no uterine douche, and no towels. Without this equipment, it was easily possible to transfer the infection from the exterior labia of an infected prostitute to a healthy one through the hands of the doctor or *feldsher* [paramedic]. The examination was conducted by the second city doctor with the help of a *feldsher* in the presence of a policeman and sometimes the constable (who was not present on 2 October). The doctor conducted the exam as diligently as possible, but without the necessary equipment it was a superficial examination, which did not include the vagina and cervix. Moreover, both rooms were full of the prostitutes who had assembled, forming a busy flea market, and that made it possible for them to deceive the constable, who was recording the results of the doctor's examination. I also observed that many of the prostitutes did not show up at all for the examination (approximately a quarter of them); among those who appeared I did not notice the more prosperous prostitutes.[2]

NOTES

1. [There is a note at the bottom of the document that the Medical Department immediately dispatched a doctor to the tavern to carry out a rigorous examination. He found infected prostitutes whom he sent to the hospital for treatment.]

2. [The file ends with an order (dated 1 November 1882) for all military doctors to report every case of syphilis among the lower-ranking soldiers immediately, to prevent the spread of the disease. The lower-ranking solders were to be subjected to a monthly examination by the medical officers to ensure that they had not contracted a venereal disease (LVIA, f. 383, op. 1, d. 65, ll. 55–58; 62–63).]

[99]

Report of the Vil'na City Doctor on Two Prostitutes (1893)

LVIA, f. 383, op. 1, d. 205, ll. 203–4 ob.

TO THE DOCTOR OF THE FIRST MEDICAL SECTION OF THE POLESSKI RAILROAD,

Dr. Ianovskii, the primary city doctor of Vil'na, informed the Medical Department in a report (12 August, number 272) that:

(1) in Natina's brothel on Poplovskaia Street there is a prostitute, Brokha Kagan (Jewish; brunette), who goes by the name Roza in the establishment. From the day that she joined the establishment (18 February of last year [1892]), she has never been ill, has never had any symptoms of syphilis, and was not considered syphilitic on the list. She appeared punctually for the examination twice a week. Apart from her, no one in the above-named brothel fits the details of your memorandum. Based on Dr. Ianovskii's account, it is not possible for a healthy prostitute to infect her guests with syphilis. Perhaps with some stretch of the imagination one could propose that following sexual relations with a syphilitic [client], she had sexual relations with another man, and that afterward he became infected, but she remained healthy. Natina's establishment at present has only one prostitute who has been infected with syphilis (Palinskaia, a blonde). However, she has not had a visible recurrence of syphilis for three years.

(2) The independent prostitute, the "Hungarian Melania" (her real identity is Apoloniia Gigl) mentioned in your other memorandum, has resided in Vil'na since 18 February of this year as a legal independent prostitute and has never been ill. In the beginning, she showed up precisely on time for the examination, twice a week, but only once a week in June and July. The last notation about her health in the book was made, in the absence of Dr. Ianovskii, by the second city doctor Ogievich on 31 July. After that time, she did not appear until 11 August of this year; at the examination, she proved to be healthy. It is possible to assume that during this period she may have caught a mild chancre [and] infected the guests with it, while she herself recovered. Because she missed two examinations, Dr. Ianovskii reported [her] to the manager of the prostitutes, instituting legal proceedings against her. The Medical Department of the Provincial Administration has been notified about this.

[100]

Denunciation of Sheina Zlata Accused of Infecting Men with a Veneral Disease (1894)

LVIA, f. 383, op. 1, d. 211, ll. 93–93 ob.

"Denunciation by A. Polevich to the Inspector of the Medical Administration of Vil'na (19 March 1894)"

TO HIS EXCELLENCY, HONORABLE INSPECTOR OF THE MEDICAL ADMINISTRATION OF VIL'NA:

I have the honor to inform Your Excellency that in our neighborhood in the town of Voronov (Lida district), there is a young woman, twenty-four years old, by the name of Sheina Zlata, the daughter of Shimelia Leib Gol'danskii. She was married in February 1893, but because she was accustomed to a dissolute life, she abandoned her husband five weeks after the wedding. She leads the most dissolute life in Voronov, where she now lives, and she has infected many people who suffer terribly from an infectious disease because of her. The more this disease is spread, the more people will have the disease. I myself know this from experience; therefore I have decided to inform Your Excellency about this and to ask for your order to summon her to the hospital immediately to have the disease treated. Otherwise, still more innocent men will suffer from this disease because of her.[1]

NOTE

1. [The Vil'na Medical Department informed the police of Lida about the denunciation. There was no follow-up document about whether the state subjected the young woman to a medical examination.]

[101]

Physical Examination of Jewish Prostitutes

*"Weekly Register: Examination of Women Who Are Employed
in Prostitution in the Town of Lida (15 January 1889)"*

LVIA, f. 383, op. 1, d. 614, l. 7

Name and Surname	Examination of 10 January	Examination of 14 January
1. Teofiliia Balshevich	Healthy	Healthy
2. Tofiliia Puidakova	Healthy	Healthy
3. Mera Klet	Healthy	Healthy
4. Reiza Kliatskaia	Healthy	Healthy
5. Adelia Grinevetskaia	Healthy	Healthy
6. Rivka Pukhoril'skaia	Healthy	Healthy
7. Sora Vainshtein	Healthy	Healthy
8. Ekaterina Gernetskaia	Healthy	Healthy
9. Mikhalina Shul'ts	Healthy	Healthy
10. Viktoriia Baron	Menstruating	Healthy
11. Mariia Balevich	Healthy	Healthy
12. Aleksandra Vrublevskaia	Healthy	Healthy
13. Viktoriia Nosovich	Healthy	Healthy
14. Khana Fein	Healthy	Healthy
15. Mariia Zhukovskaia	Healthy	Healthy

*"Weekly Register: Examination of Women Who Are Employed
in Prostitution in the Town of Disna (31 May and 3 June 1889)"*

LVIA, f. 383, op. 1, d. 614, l. 107.

Name and Surname	Examination of 31 May
1. Sonia Katz	Healthy
2. Mariia Kovalevskaia	Healthy
3. Feodora Martsinkevich	Healthy
4. Feodora Zhuravskaia	Healthy
5. Shul'ka Rokhman	Healthy

Name and Surname	Examination of 3 June
1. Sonia Katz	Healthy
2. Mariia Kovalevskaia	Healthy
3. Feodora Martsinskaia	Healthy
4. Feodora Zhuravskaia	Healthy
5. Shul'ka Rokhman	Healthy
6. Gesia Smushko	Infected with syphilis, in the city hospital for treatment

[102]

Denunciation of Jewish "Prostitutes" in Stoklishki (1899)

LVIA, f. 383, op. 1, d. 342, l. 97–97 ob.

"Denunciation of 'Prostitute' by an Anonymous Resident of Stoklishki, Trokai District, Vil'na Province to Vil'na Medical Administration (1899)"

TO HIS HONOR, THE INSPECTOR OF THE VIL'NA MEDICAL ADMINISTRATION,

I have the honor to report to Your Excellency that [two] unmarried girls—Tsivka Berel-Iankelevna Kats and Shtirka Tsertselevna Maliarskaia, who live in the town of Stoklishki (Trokai district, Vil'na province)—lead a depraved life [but] do not go for inspection, since the town of Stoklishki has no sanitary surveillance. Because these girls are frequented by many residents of Stoklishki, they will eventually be able to infect the entire village. Apart from the residents of Stoklishki, quite a few travelers also visit them because both girls live in a wayside inn, where many travelers are constantly infected with various infectious diseases. I humbly ask Your Excellency to take notice and to issue an order about the girls Tsivka Kats and Shtirka Maliarskaia. Summon them for a medical examination because they have enticed many innocent girls into a shameful business.[1]

NOTE

1. [There was no final resolution to this file.]

[103]

The Russian Society for the Protection of Women: The Jewish Section (1900–1901)

"Report on the Creation of a Jewish Section in the Russian Society for the Protection of Women (1900–1901)"

RGIA, f. 1335, op. 1, d. 2, l. 37.

At the beginning of 1901, the question arose before the Committee of the Russian Society for the Protection of Women about the desirability of organizing a special section for the care of Jewish girls in St. Petersburg under the auspices of the Society.[1] As the idea of forming such a trusteeship met with great sympathy, in a meeting of 12 February 1901, the Committee examined and approved a proposal for instructions, which were confirmed by the august chairperson of the Society [Princess Elena Georgievna of Saxony-Oldenburg].[2]

1. Under the auspices of the Russian Society for the Protection of Women, a section for the care of Jewish girls in the city of St. Petersburg has been confirmed; its purpose is to protect girls from activities harmful to the moral condition of life and contribute to their moral development.

2. Accordingly, the [Jewish] section may provide assistance: (a) by taking legal measures to protect girls from ill treatment, oppression, and insult; (b) by constructing premises where the girls may spend their free time, as well as a dormitory, inexpensive lodgings, rooms, parts of a room, kitchens, and summer colonies; (c) by organizing for them, with the appropriate permission, recreation and educational courses; (d) by rendering support to girls seeking a position or occupation and by establishing for them artisan collectives (*arteli*) in various trades. The section will not provide monetary assistance. [. . .]³

"Questionnaire of the Russian Society for the Protection of Women for Participating Applicants" [n.d.]

RGIA, f. 1335, op. 1, d. 28, l. 1–1 ob.

1. Number:
2. Year, Month, and Date:
3. Surname, Name, Patronymic, Status, Religious Confession:
4. Year, Month, and Date of Birth:
5. Age:
6. Address:
7. Biography: [a large space was provided for information here]
8. Response to the proposal of assistance by the Russian Society for the Protection of Women:
9. Were any ties or relations with relatives made and were other measures taken?
10. [When was she] placed under [police and medical] surveillance for the first time? Sanitary ticket number:
11. Why was she placed under surveillance?
12. Under what circumstances did she spend her childhood?
  a. Favorable, satisfactory, difficult, very difficult [in these and other questions below, one option was to be selected].
  b. [Does she] come from a family that is well-to-do, middling, needy, very needy, impoverished; does not remember family?
  c. Might she have inherited or obtained a propensity toward an immoral life from her surrounding circumstances in childhood or acquired a moral dissoluteness from her father, mother, both parents, or other people?
13. Education: received a middle-school education; matriculated in a middle-school institution but did not complete the courses; completed elementary school; literate, semi-literate, illiterate.
14. Professional occupation:
15. The loss of virginity was [. . . :]
  a. at an age younger than 10, 10, 11, 12, 13, 14, 15, 16, 17, 18, 20, 21–25, 26–30, older than 30.
  b. with an individual who was younger than 20 years old, 20–30, 30–40. 40–50, older than 50.
  c. with an individual of a higher social position, equal social position, lower social position.
  d. with an individual with whom she was well acquainted earlier, little acquainted earlier, completely unfamiliar.
  e. with an individual who was a husband, groom, father, brother, stepfather, uncle, relative, guardian, caretaker, household head, foreman, member of the master's family, an individual who had power [over her] for other reasons, an individual without power.
  f. with an individual who was an army officer, official, student, educator at a

middle-school institution, landowner, merchant, doctor, lawyer, pedagogue, engineer, journalist, actor, owner of a theater, choir, or entertainment establishment, servant in [one of] them, intelligent individual of a different profession, intelligent individual without a definitive profession, individual living on revenues from capital or immovable property, office clerk, trader, cart driver, soldier, police servant, lackey, cook, coachman, yard man, porter, watchman, factory foreman, factory worker, artisan, urban unskilled laborer, village unskilled laborer, an idle poor person living with parents or relatives on the formers' means.

g. with an individual who lived in one room with her, in one apartment, in one house, in different houses;

h. in the apartment where she lived, a different apartment, a hotel, a compartment of a train, a steamer boat, garden, woods, [on the] floor, in the courtyard or on the stairs of an urban house, on the street, boulevard, in a city park, in a den of iniquity [illegal brothel].

i. in St. Petersburg, in a provincial town, in a district town, in the village.

16. At the moment of the loss of virginity [. . . :]

a. she lived with her parents and had both parents, lived with one father, mother, father and stepmother, mother and stepfather, one stepfather, one stepmother; she did not live with her parents but with close relatives, with distant relatives, with friends; with someone else's family for a position [that is, as a servant], for an apprenticeship; she was a homeless orphan; lived independently.

b. she did not experience material hardship, experienced hardship but was not in desperate need, was in desperate need, was extremely destitute.

17. What prompted her to give up her vir-

ginity the first time? She gave up her virginity to her husband; in hopes of getting married; in hopes of continuing relations; being strongly enticed by money; being caught off guard; owing to a threat or coercion; she was taken by force.

18. Did someone participate in the capacity of a middleman in the loss of her virginity? Her parents, close relatives, distant relatives, acquaintances, friend, professional procuress [madam] participated; no one participated.

19. With the person to whom she lost her virginity: she got married; was in extramarital relationship for more than a year, more than three months, more than a month, less than a month, no longer had sexual relations.

20. After the loss of virginity, she began to engage in prostitution: in the next few days, after a month, after half a year, after a year or more.

21. The beginning of engagement in prostitution was in direct connection to the loss of virginity, in remote connection, in no connection.

22. Until the engagement in prostitution, (a) she had one lover, two, three, four, five or more; (b) was married, was on financial support, was not on financial support; (c) had children, was pregnant, was not pregnant.

23. Profession until engagement in prostitution: she lived on the means of her parents, husband, lover; she was a domestic servant; worked in the village, factory, mill, in an artisan workshop; handicrafts at home; actress; member of a choir; singer; served as a vendor at a clerical office, bureau.

24. Taking up prostitution [. . . :]

a. she continued working at her previous profession, stopped working at the former work.

b. [was a result] of extreme material need, loss of work, not having work, difficult conditions of labor, difficult conditions with the parents, husband, roommate [or lover], relatives; innate sloth (natural repugnance toward labor); being spoiled in life; a desire for a merrier life; aspiration for luxury and apparel; envy; owing to moral dissoluteness; heightened sensuality; being compromised; infected with syphilis; deserted by a lover but not pregnant, pregnant, with a child; being deserted by a husband; for feeding the children, husband, lover, parents, close relatives; under the influence of the evil influence of her mother, sisters, friends.

c. [was the result] of her own conviction; persuasion to engage in the profession of a procuress [madam] by parents, husband, lover, relatives, acquaintances, friends; persuasion of prostitute friends, landlady of the apartment in which the prostitutes live, professional procuresses, owners of brothels, dens of iniquity [illegal brothels], agents and servants of dens of iniquity, owners of choruses, entertainment establishments, hotels; under the influence of coercion on the part of a husband, lover, parents, and owners of brothels and dens of iniquity.

25. Until being subjected to [police and medical] surveillance, she engaged in prostitution for less than a month, 1–3 months, 3–6 months, up to a year, more than a year, more than two years, more than three years.

26. [She] was infected with syphilis prior to becoming engaged in prostitution, in the first half year, in the first year, during the course of one year, two, three; does not have syphilis.

27. Recruits clients: in the theater, entertainment establishments and gardens, visits to dens of iniquity [illegal brothels], on the street; guests visiting the apartment in which she lives.

28. Does she have general rules in the sexual relations with her clients: in her own room, in the hotels, in the baths, in the dens of iniquity [illegal brothels], in different places.

29. Has she appeared before the medical and police committee for submission to surveillance: owing to the demand of the committee, landlady of the apartment in which she lives, the owner of a den of iniquity [illegal brothel]; being brought to court for illegal depravity; for greater ease in streetwalking.

NOTES

1. [The goal of the Russian Society for the Protection of Women, which was created following an international conference in London on white slave trafficking, was to prevent girls in St. Petersburg and other large cities from falling into prostitution. The Jewish section was led by Baron Goratsii Osipovich Gintsburg and Baroness Roza Sigizmundova Gintsburg.]

2. [Princess Elena Georgievna (1857–1936), wife of the prince of Saxony-Oldenburg, resided in the capital.]

3. [The remaining points deal with issues of finances, trustees, and relationship to the larger Society.]

[IV]
Education and Culture

Beginning in the late 1820s, under Emperor Nicholas I, the Russian state intervened to support the Haskalah's program of Jewish educational reform that would profoundly challenge traditional learning and culture, then already in flux but afterward much more so. From the late eighteenth century on, distinct pedagogical ideologies divided rabbinic scholars in the north from the Hasidim in the south. As Michael Stanislawski points out, the Lithuanian scholarly elites envisioned reforms that the Haskalah movement would later advocate: "a stricter emphasis on the study of Hebrew grammar and the Bible, in addition to the Talmud; a moderation in the use of hermeneutical technique of *pilpul*; the admission, on some level, of the study of secular subjects and languages."[1] These changes help to explain the greater ease that intellectuals educated in this milieu would later have in accepting Russian education. The *maskilim* indeed portrayed the Hasidim as the most serious obstacles to secular education and enlightenment—as was demonstrated when "Jewish progressives" denounced the Twersky *tsaddikim* (document 2).

Despite their initial reservations and fears about conversion, many Jews gradually came to view secular education as the path to greater opportunities, especially during the era of the Great Reforms, when university students obtained permission to leave the Pale of Settlement. Jewish women, in particular, flocked to university courses open to female auditors[2] and sought new intellectual horizons and autonomy from their constricted lives in the Pale. As the documents in this part show, Jewish success in secondary and higher institutions of learning elicited sharp criticism from Russian authorities (especially in the Pale), who feared that educational opportunities would lead to Jewish domination of the economy and other spheres of society. Russian officials also emphasized the role of Jewish students in the revolutionary movements, an argument that resonated strongly in St. Petersburg. In response to such reports and the violent pogroms of 1881, the state imposed quotas on Jewish students and resisted calls to abolish or reduce them. It even maintained them during World War I, when gymnasiums had an abundance of vacancies. Nevertheless, the Ministry of Education did make some exceptions. For example, it allowed Jewish students who had studied in foreign universities to take final examinations in medicine and technology.

This part examines the diverse paths that Jews traveled in their quest for knowledge and learning. It includes the intellectual journey of *maskilim* like Moshe Leib Lilienblum, who shifted from the study of religious texts to the critical exploration of philosophy and literature (document 104); the yeshiva experience of Ben Zion Dinur (document 109); the traditional *melamdim* who taught under stricter state regulations, the rise of private Jewish schools and state rabbinical schools, the increasing matriculation of Jews in Russian gymnasiums and universities, and the impact of the *numerus clausus* regulations that limited Jewish access to education and upward social mobility.

NOTES

1. Michael Stanislawski, *Tsar Nicholas I and the Jews, 1825–55* (Philadelphia: Jewish Publication Society of America, 1983), 51.

2. Although Russian universities did not admit women as regular students, beginning in the early 1860s they were allowed to attend as noncredit auditors.

Institutions of Jewish Learning

[104]

Moshe Leib Lilienblum, *The Sins of My Youth* (1873)

Moshe Leib Lilienblum, *Hatot neurim*, in *Kol kitve Moshe Leib Lilienblum*, vol. 2 (Krakow: Joseph Fisher, 1912; originally published 1873), pp. 206–243 (excerpted), 251–256 (excerpted), 323–408 (excerpted).[1]

Days of Chaos[2]

After my father divorced his first wife, without providing the settlement that was usually required[3] (because she had stayed in the house of a gentile without a chaperon), he married a second woman. After five years, their one and only son was born, the author of this work, on the 29th of [the Hebrew month of] Tishre 5604, or the 10th of October [Julian calendar]; (the 22nd according to the foreign [Gregorian] calculation) 1843. [. . .]

My father's mother always said that she was the granddaughter of two great and wealthy rabbis (even *geonim*). [. . .] My mother's father was a *kohen*,[4] distinguished in Torah learning and in fear of sin; he never uttered a falsehood in his life. [. . .] My father, even though he was great in poverty, was not great in Torah; he was a laborer, who lived by the work of his hands, who enjoyed his studies; he was quite proficient in Mishnah and *aggadah*;[5] he would attract his friends of various occupations to Torah study, and he had quite a good reputation in his native city. [. . .] It is superfluous to say that my father tried with all his might to raise me, his first and last son, to be a great Torah scholar and fearer of sin. [. . .]

In 5611 [1850–51] my mother's father began to teach me Talmud, and I lorded it over my friends who had not yet merited beginning Talmud study. In 5613 my mother died in a cholera epidemic, even though she carried an amulet, on which was inscribed letter pairs, that were coupled from the letters of verse 30 of Psalm 106,[6] and from the letters of the four-letter name of God; folded within the parchment was some grass, which was cut with a golden key. This catastrophe did not make such an impression on me, since my father and my mother's father did not wish to be estranged, and my mother's sister, a virgin of sixteen, did not want her dead sister's only son to be raised by a stepmother. Therefore, my father, who was then forty-seven, married my mother's sister, the virgin previously mentioned. This foolish woman wasted her life because of me, never attending to the fact that in another twenty years my father would be old and weak, and she would be a subject to a miserable fate in the prime of her life.

There was nothing unusual about my education. [. . .] I learned Talmud, and its commentaries. In 5613 [that is, before he was ten] I began to prepare a page of Talmud by myself, before the lesson with the teacher, and in 5614, I could decipher by myself a certain Maharsha.[7] [. . .] My parents saw this and were elated, and those in the town who knew me predicted that I would be a great scholar in Israel.

It is superfluous to add that beside Talmud I learned nothing, except some [Hebrew] grammatical rules that my grandfather taught me; he was an expert in grammar. [. . .] My place of birth, even though it was not a city or a town, still had a gymnasium, in which some Jewish boys studied, and nobody thought to challenge them. But my father thought it would be crazy to take his only son, who would grow up to be a great Torah scholar in Israel, to a gymnasium in order to learn things that a Torah scholar could learn in the bathroom without even trying. For my part, I would not have been happy in a gymnasium in which children were routinely and cruelly flogged, as I heard from my friends (who undoubtedly heard it from their parents and teachers, who fabricated the lie to scare them); not only that, but those who were hit were not permitted to cry. Similarly, my friends claimed that when a student was flogged, the teachers at the gymnasium closed a drawer on his head so he would not flinch; who could hear of such cruelty and want to be a gymnasium student?

My father the expert in *aggadah*, would give a lesson in it, gratis, to the other laborers every Sabbath and holiday. Therefore, we had [the basic library in this area]. [. . .]

Through the kindness of my father and grandfather, I also acquired some worldly wisdom, beyond Talmud. My father taught me the means to calculate the seasons, and the influence of the seven planets on cold and warmth, the weather conditions of each month, together with some geographical rules pertaining to the river Sambation and the ten lost tribes of Israel. I was exposed to stories such as the tailor who broke away from these lost tribes and killed a wicked man by invoking the divine name, or of the son of a Shimon the son of Yitzhak, the liturgical poet, who was captured by gentiles, and went on to become a pope. My grandfather told how he saved a man from demons, to whom he had sold his soul for a large sum. [. . .]

This was how they educated me in the early years, due to the terrible and benighted stupidity that surrounded the people of my village, including my ancestors. When I was four years and three months old, before my tender powers had developed, I was already burdened with the study of Torah learning and with teachers, and from that day forward I was imprisoned in my study room. They did not permit me to enjoy my childhood; they did not reinforce my abilities with some liberty, and children's play; they deprived me of the pleasures of word games that I innocently desired; they deprived me of all knowledge and interest that was not related to Talmud study. Instead they filled my mind with all kinds of nonsense, and filled me with a damaging poison, to the point that when I was twelve, I was already heartbroken regarding the travails of the *shekhinah* cut off from the light,[8] as if such nonsense is relevant to a child, as if they need to sadden his heart. My father's innards were elated by his only child, who was destined to be a great Torah scholar in Israel. They did not even teach me the letters of the European alphabets; on my own I learned the Russian and Polish letters, since I found out incidentally that the name of every [Hebrew] book is printed also in Russian letters or Polish letters (in the Warsaw district). [. . .]

On Sunday, 17 Elul 5617 [in the summer of 1857], I awoke, but with the laziness of an only child I rested on my bed, until my father said to me, "Get up, groom! Why rest? Go say your prayers; your future mother-in-law is coming." I did not understand him at all, and I did not try to, for I thought he was joking. I got up, dressed, washed my face, took my prayer book and *tefillin* and went to the synagogue. With a calm heart I said my prayers, and together with a group of children my age, I climbed up to one of the beams in the synagogue, to see the insignificant goings-on that children delight in seeing. I climbed down, returned to my home, and my father's mother told me a new story that I could never have imagined even in a dream. She told me that a rich woman from city X had come, together with her daughter, a virgin of eleven, and she wanted to take me as a groom for this daughter. I asked my father about this, and he told me with great joy and happiness that it was so. I did not agree with my father's plan and pleaded heartily that he not make me a groom, even though I had no idea why I did not wish to be a groom, just as my father had no idea why he wanted to enter into a marriage agreement for me. It could be that I simply did not wish to change my situation, as is my nature, and maybe my reluctance was due to something else. Be that as it may, I simply did not wish to enter into a husband-wife connection. After breakfast, I went, as was my custom, to the yeshiva where I learned. I spent that day as I spent every other day. In the evening, I went to the synagogue, where I studied the talmudic tractate of *Rosh Ha-shanah* [the Jewish new year, which was two weeks away from the date on which these events occurred] by myself, for this was the way of all those boys who were destined to become great Torah scholars in Israel—they learn the tractate of the New Year before the New Year, and the tractate dealing with the reading of the Book of Esther before Purim [the holiday on which this biblical book is read]. During my studies, someone came from my father's house and called me home. I went home, and my father changed my clothes and took me with him. I asked, "Where are we going?" "To write the 'conditions' [of the marital agreement]," he answered with satisfaction. My heart pounded within me, and after a few minutes we came to the house of a relative of my future mother-in-law, which was the designated place for writing the conditions. I sat

on a bench, and from a distance I could see a little girl, who seemed to me to be three years old; I understood that she was the bride. The conditions were written, and the person who read them announced to all that the woman [that is, the future mother-in-law] representing the bride was obligated to provide me with 300 silver rubles as a dowry, and to provide them before the actual wedding ceremony, [as well as] two years of support before the ceremony, and six years of [support] after. The ceremony would take place, with good luck, three years from the date noted below, and all is valid and proper. [. . .]

The women hurried to break a plate, and, like thunder, their mouths called out *"mazel tov."* [. . .]

Congratulations to you, dear reader; the boy destined to be a great Torah scholar in Israel had become a groom. [. . .]

For Sukkot I went to my fiancée's town. Her father was furious with his wife for her schemes. "My daughter is but a child of eleven, and I am a poor money-lender; why place my neck in a yoke and pay up front? [. . .] But his wife kept on babbling and drew him to her point of view. So, her father also agreed to the match, but he changed the conditions. Instead of six years of support after the wedding and a payment of three-hundred silver rubles, payable before the wedding, he agreed to five years of support, and two-hundred silver rubles, to be paid during the period of support. My father was not with me because of a headache, so my maternal grandfather, a simple *melamed*, represented me, and his way was to nod his head at whatever was said to him; thus, he nodded his head [in agreement] to what my fiancée's father said. [. . .] The mother slipped me a one-hundred silver ruble bill—without her husband's knowledge—to fulfill her commitment of three-hundred rubles. When, after the holiday, I returned to my father's house, he let my grandfather have it for selling me without any money [up front]. [. . .] Samuel David Luzzatto[9] once wrote that biography is superior to fiction. A novel is the product of the writer's imagination, whereas biography describes events that actually happened. Though I do not completely agree with Luzzatto, having read many biographies—including his—and gained nothing from them, while I learned much from the many novels I read, Luzzatto is right on the whole. A biography recording a person's actions and behavior, his opinions and mode of thinking, his sufferings, and an analysis of his experiences and their effect can be more enlightening than the best novel.

There are two sorts of biography: the biography a famous person writes for his admirers, because the public likes to know everything about celebrities, and [the] autobiography, usually written because the events are worth recording for themselves, not because of the person to whom they have happened.

Of biographies of famous people written in Hebrew we have many, but I know of only two autobiographies—Luzzatto's and Mordechai Aaron Guenzburg's *Aviezer* [see document 78]. Luzzatto's autobiography is as hollow as the parched ears of corn in Pharaoh's dream, whereas *Aviezer* was written to tell about events—the system of Jewish education in our country. But *Aviezer* is limited to the author's childhood and boyhood, and tells nothing of his later life, which might have been instructive for the young people of my native land. This defect I wish to repair: I want here to set down events in my life, from my childhood until I became a mature man.

I am an ordinary man. Hebrew is the only language [in which] I have written—some articles in periodicals and a few books. I have no particular distinction, yet my experiences can be instructive, even though they are not spiced with tall tales and extraordinary accomplishments. My life is a sort of Jewish drama. I came on stage and played it for my readers. They ridiculed me, shook their heads in disapproval, and held me up as a horrible example. [. . .]

My troubles did not arise from passion or evil, as in a French drama, but out of foolishness, for that is the basis of Jewish drama. A *maskil* once wrote, "The life of the Jew begins in triviality and foolishness and ends in sorrow and woe; the beginning a comedy and the end a tragedy." My life was a tapestry woven of small and large errors my parents made and I myself made, of idle dreams that I dreamed about myself and that others dreamed about me. The threads became warped and tangled round my neck, sapping my strength.

Now I am twenty-nine, and old age has already overtaken me. I have given up the idea of living a vital life. My eyes have become heavy with weeping, and the source of my tears has dried. But my self-esteem does not let me rest. Perhaps my tears and despair can serve as a lesson to others. That is why I am writing the story of my life.

Who am I? What is my name?

A living person am I, not a nonexistent Job, nor Ezekiel's dry bones. I belonged to that dead talmudic world that brought Hebrew literature back to life. Yet it was a dead literature, whose life juices were too weak to restore life, sufficient only to keep it hovering between life and death. I am a Talmudist who sinned and went into seclusion, a believer who repudiated the lovely visions and joyful hopes handed down by my ancestors. I am a failure and an unfortunate man who has abandoned hope of anything good. And my name? I have said before that in autobiography not the name but the events are the point.

I passed through four periods: the days of chaos in my native town when I was still unformed clay waiting to be shaped; the days of darkness and the beginning of the transition, when I lived in Miroslav with my in-laws.[10] There I stuffed my head with harmful nonsense. The world became dark, and its monstrous darkness began to oppress me. Then came the time of disbelief, when I thought I had discovered the truth and fought for it, as Don Quixote fought the windmills. I was satisfied with myself, though I had nothing with which to be satisfied. Finally came the time of crisis and despair, when I traveled and discovered a new world that I had never known in dream or reality.

Days of Darkness and the Beginning of the Transition

I have already said that in my first period I was matter, ready to take on form. Even though I had already learned much Torah for my age, I knew nothing of anything else. [. . .] Even so, a good teacher could have made of me a good merchant, or a secular scholar, or an artisan who knows his craft. I am not a light-hearted person. [. . .] On the contrary, I am very serious. [. . .] Even so, had I been accustomed to interacting with different types of people, I would have been more gregarious than I am now; I would have been able to engage in small talk, rather than the way I am now, devoid of anything to say when I come into contact with people who are not my peers. In other words, if indeed I was talented enough to be a great Torah scholar in Israel, a good educator could have made of me a person useful to society and to himself, so that I would have been happy all my life. In truth I myself was certain that I was already fully committed to the lifestyle they inculcated within me. When my future mother-in-law asked my father, "We see most of the brilliant youngsters are being led astray by their sharp minds that mislead them, and they become heretics. What guarantees do I have that my son-in-law will not be transformed, God forbid, into a heretic?" I answered innocently, this terrible thing could not happen to me, for I am certain that the path on which I walk is true. The Berliners [*maskilim*] have bequeathed falsehood to us, the Hasidim [have bequeathed] nonsense; the way of the *misnagdim* is correct, and how is it possible that I would depart from the path that I am certain is superior to all others? What I believed then is no longer sufficient, for I now see the fruit of my certainty in my way of life. [. . .] In my second period, any educational system could impress me, and it is self-evident that "poverty chases the impoverished," and after confusion came darkness.

I spent the winter of 5618 (1857–58) studying the tractate *Baba Kama* with all the commentaries, and writing letters filled with riddles, rhymes, and anagrams to my father-in-law-to-be. Then my mother-in-law [to-be] asked that I come before Passover to settle in her city, without returning to my father's home. My father honored her request, and I was sent there to settle. [. . .]

In the city of Miroslav, my in-laws' home, and now mine as well, lived an uncle of mine, a great Torah scholar and fearer of sin, who was also a total fool—one would have to search with a bright light to find such a fool. He was much loved by the local preacher, and this preacher handed him all kinds of nonsense and frightening stories, which he received from the luminaries of Lithuania, and my uncle believed them all. Obviously, my uncle became my guardian and educator. From him I heard all kinds of terrible and frightening stories, which he received from the preacher, and I wholeheartedly accepted them as truth. From him I came to recognize Samael, and Lilith and all her demonic virgins, who come to men when they are sleeping and bring them to sin. [. . .] He told me all about the *Gaon* of Vil'na, and the great battle between Rabbis Jacob Emden and Jonathan Eybeshchutz, and thousands of wondrous stories about all the luminaries and rabbis. I was very excited by these stories, and I pressured my mother-in-law to buy me the *Ascents of Eliyahu* [see document 4], and after she did so I could not take my eyes from it, and the matter that was ready to accept any form began to take on a defined form, which created its days of darkness. [. . .]

I spent most of my time learning Talmud and arguing with my uncle about vitally important matters. He claimed that all the interpretations of scripture that we find in rabbinic literature are genuinely grounded in scripture. [. . .] I, who had some training in grammar, said that most of the interpretations were contrary to the rules of grammar, and cannot possibly be true. We engaged in this dispute and many like it just about every week, and to this day we have not resolved it.

[. . .] You are laughing at me, discerning reader, and indeed you have reason to laugh; but am I at fault? What could I do if fate put me in the hands of foolish educators, and I was but fifteen years old? Now I know that while I was depleting my strength and wasting my time with nonsense, other boys my age were involved with matters that were truly important: they learned in the [government-sponsored] rabbinical seminaries, in [the] gymnasium, in trade and vocational schools; I also know that such boys grew into happy men; they see goodness and they see life. As for me, I shall not succeed as a man and will remain miserable. Could I know then what I know now? [. . .] Around springtime my mother-in-law heard rumors that my father wanted to abrogate the contract, and so she devised a plan to expedite the wedding, that according to the "conditions" was not to be held until the end of 5620, and to hold it at the end of 5619. I did not oppose this, although I did not assent to it until something altogether unusual happened to me. Listen, and laugh!

Once at night after I recited the great confession in the proper manner, together with the first four parts of the book of Psalms, sleep overcame me, and then I woke with a start—and my heart died within me! I realized that I had suffered a nocturnal incident! This was like an arrow in my heart, for I already knew from my uncle that Lilith and her cohorts travel around every night and tempt the children of Abraham, Isaac, and Jacob. And I knew that this sin caused many souls to go around naked, and wander through the world until they fall prey to the external hands [that is, demons], God protect us; and

that this sin is beyond repentance. My heart melted within me, and my innards throbbed, for the demonic lasses had found me and because of me the souls of many pure and righteous people were imperiled by demons, God protect us! I cried terribly, and fasted that entire day; perhaps God would see my suffering, and forgive my sin. As an added precaution, I changed the location of my bed; perhaps the demonic lass would not find me in my place and would leave me alone forever.

But the Good who brings good [that is, God], who desires the repentance of the wicked, did not attend to me or my fasting, did not accept my blood and fat that were diminished that day, and in the course of the next couple of weeks, the same accursed incident recurred. I fasted once again, and once I realized that my fasting was in vain—I too agreed with the plans of my mother-in-law to move up the date of the wedding, in order not to aid Lilith and her cohorts.

[. . .][11] After much fighting and bickering, my father returned to his home, and I obviously remained in the home of my in-laws. Were I not the type who valued my liberty, I would not have felt any difference in my life. But I valued my freedom very much, and about two weeks before the wedding I began counting the days in which I could feel free, and I would count each day: "For X many days I will be free!" Thus, immediately after the wedding I felt that I was no longer free, and that a burden was placed upon me, which I could not characterize. Not a few weeks passed and I began to drink of the poisoned cup that came from my mother-in-law's hand, and from which I drank for nine consecutive years.

No doubt, the reader has already noted that my mother-in-law was the active force and my father-in-law the peripheral one. Indeed, this is so: my father-in-law did not "wear the pants" in his house, but was subordinate to his wife. My mother-in-law was a person of inferior character and spirit. All the defects that we find in Sarah the wife of Ephraim[12] are found in my mother-in-law. [. . .] She wasted my father-in-law's money in a manner you would not believe. For many years she requested of doctors, *baalei shem*, magicians, and anyone who was an "expert" that they try to help her have a son. Frequently, she spent seven silver rubles for "medications" that were in fact nothing but dust and water, and often she paid for medicines that she never took because someone would tell her that the medicine was a deadly potion. [. . .]

It should not surprise [anyone] that this accursed woman extended her dominion to a fifteen-year-old boy, such as I was at the time, and she made my life bitter with her curses, her fiery tongue, her contentious screaming at my wife, me, and my father-in-law. No doubt this contributed to the emotional weakness that still plagues me.

That summer I reviewed Maimonides's introduction to his Mishnah commentary. I read it and reviewed it, and enjoyed it greatly. [. . .] This led me to desire deeply to know the investigations of the earlier scholars, but there was little available to quench my thirst. The book *Duties of the Heart* did not grab me because a dark spirit hovered over it, and Maimonides's *Guide of the Perplexed* I did not dare touch lest I become a heretic. [. . .]

That winter [5620, or 1859–60] I purchased *Tsemach David* [a historical chronicle], and also *Melekhet mahshevet* of R. Moses Chafetz. The first book contained nothing new for me. [. . .] But the second book gave me great pleasure, for it contained many investigations that pleased me greatly. I realized that many good Jews deny the existence of demons and magic, even when these explanations conflict with the Talmud, and yet they are not considered heretics — this was wondrous to me, and I guarded it in my heart.

In the winter of 5621 I learned in a study hall and there made the acquaintance of a rich boy, who loved to buy books. Once he asked me whether I had any books. I listed all the books I had, including the *Melekhet mahshevet*, which I praised greatly. "Does it contain Haskalah?" he asked me. "What is Haskalah?" I answered innocently. "There is philosophy and independent investigation, but Haskalah, I don't know what it is!" The boy answered me that the meaning of Haskalah was Haskalah, and that he had books of Haskalah. I asked him to lend me one of these books, and he lent me the periodical *Ha-maggid* from the first three years of its run, bound together, although missing many issues. I read about some matters and some news, but the rest of the stuff I did not fully understand, and what I did understand did not grab me, and I returned the Haskalah book to him. [. . .]

Once, in the summer of 1861, a friend and I happened to talk about the disagreement between Rashi and Rabbenu Tam about the order in which to insert into the phylacteries the parchment slips with the biblical inscriptions. There was a legend that Moses came down from heaven and sided with Rashi in this dispute. I had read this story long ago, but only now did I disbelieve it. I said to my friend, "the Tannaim in the Talmud disagreed about many things. Because of a dissent he, Tanna Eliezer the Great, was excommunicated by the Sanhedrin, yet Moses was never brought down to give his opinion. The Talmud itself says: 'the Torah is not in heaven.'" We talked a lot more until I said the whole story was a lie and even convinced my friend of that. For a whole day I rejoiced that I had the high privilege of finding the truth, not as it is in books or accepted by the common people. Eight years later, when I rejected Maimonides's articles of faith, I did not rejoice.

[. . .] In those days I bought the responsa of the Rashba. I read it a lot, and much in it was new to me, some even beneficial. With curiosity I read the bans directed at the scholars of Provence due to their study of philosophy, things about which I knew in general from rumor and from [stray reference in] books.

But Bedersi's defense I read many times, and with great joy.[13] Anyone who has read Bedersi's defense can understand the impression that it made on an unsophisticated seeker of truth such as I was. I ceased to believe in strange *aggadot*, and, moreover, I made no attempt to provide any explanation for these *aggadot*; it was clear to me that these stories had some meaning that conflicted with the literal one, a meaning that I had no responsibility to discover. If the appropriate explanation was X or Y, whether I knew it or not, made no difference to me, as long as I knew that the literal explanation was to be rejected.

Obviously, I did not reject all the strange *aggadot*. Bedersi himself acknowledges that he accepts all stories that describe miracles that occurred to the Talmudic sages; I never suspected him of saying that merely to appease his enemy, and I was scared to continue alone on this path, which was illuminated by the earlier authorities.

My belief in the efficacy of amulets and other prophylactic measures was gradually dissipating; [. . .] but I continued to believe in metempsychosis even though Bedersi explicitly rejects this. My reason was that belief in metempsychosis was a fundamental aspect of kabbalah, and if I rejected it, I would be rejecting the kabbalah and the Zohar! And if Bedersi did not believe in metempsychosis, he did not know kabbalah, and if the Zohar had been known in his day, he too would have believed in it.

In general, I did not understand enough to be able to blaze my own trail in the manner of the books of the sages of Israel that were so important to me. In no way did I wish to be a heretic, and when I came to doubt something that was mentioned in the Talmud, I sought an authority from among the great teachers of Israel on whom I could rely. When I could not find such an authority, I forced my mind to believe. Of course you cannot really force a mind to believe, but that is only true of a fully developed mind, which was not the case with

my mind, which was a treasury of nonsense and of vain philosophical investigations, together with a cowardly submission to the luster of the Talmud and the great sages of Israel. My mind at that time was like a publishing house, in which many independent ideas are developed in response to many questions, and before they are published, they come before the judgment of the censor who affirms them or negates them, based on the laws of so-and-so. I already possessed an inchoate idea of what was possible and what was not, but I did not know the boundary that divided between these extremes.

I must say that the personal revolution regarding *aggadot* and the [superstitious] prophylactic measures, etc., did not take place quickly, but over some years. I am by nature rather conservative, and I decide things only after lengthy consideration. Studies in Maimonides and Bedersi [and others] ignited an internal battle between everything I read and heard, and the determinations of my own beclouded mind that was gradually clearing. The latter prevailed only over time, yet my heart was calm only for a short while, for as soon as I solved one problem another emerged. The battle started all over again. Thus did I live for nine years. Throughout this period I lived with anger, inner pain, boiling blood. At the end, from the time I became a heretic, [I lived] with a cold and calm spirit.

[. . .] On Rosh Hashanah in 5622 [1862], I was filled with religious ecstasy. Wherever I was, wherever I went, I concentrated on the Tetragrammaton. The two days of Rosh Hashanah and the Sabbath of Return I was in this frenzy. On the fourth day, a frightening idea suddenly floated into my consciousness: "Who can prove there is a God?" Had this thought arisen out of rational doubts, my question might have been put this way: "We assume nothing happens without cause and all causes derive from the laws of nature. What, then, do we gain from the belief in Providence? We assume that nature has always gone on its accustomed way, and we know neither its beginning nor its end. From what ground, then, do we deduce a Creator and a Maker? It is hard to understand how nature first originated, but the question can be put about the Creator Himself. It is easy to say God created nature and His Word created the heavens, but it is hard to comprehend how the Creator created something from nothing with a word. Left without a reasonable answer, we ask who can prove there is a God?" Had I found rational answers to rational questions, I might have eliminated the doubt in my heart. But my doubts had their source in my total concentration on the Tetragrammaton. This cruel thought "who can prove there is a God?" must have come to me only because I concentrated on God's existence. My heart was tormented by this inner voice: "Who can say there is a God?" I tried to still this cry by immersing myself in religious books, but everyone knows that no matter how hard one tries to banish a hateful idea, it keeps returning. Then came the Day of Atonement.

After the Kol Nidre service, I recited the Great Confession and the first four Psalms, as was my custom to prevent nocturnal emission, and I went to bed. In the middle of the night I awoke suddenly and my heart died within me at what I saw. I would be in anguish for a whole year.

That Day of Atonement I was as if struck by thunder. Obviously God had punished me for my evil thoughts, for doubting His existence. Yet that thought persisted, and my heart quivered at that remorseless voice: "Who can say there is a God?" The cantor chanted the prayer [that opens the Musaf service], "Here I am, poor in good deeds." The congregation trembled at his voice. I saw everyone lifting hands and heart to God, while I — where was my God? I covered my face with the prayer shawl and dissolved in tears. The day after, I began to recite certain Yom Kippur liturgical poems that were supposed to be a sure remedy for someone who had had an emission.

These prayers were to be repeated for thirty consecutive days. I vowed that if that cruel doubt would return to plague me, I would reject it and immerse myself in the Talmud.

[. . .] In the summer [of 1863] the Polish rebellion broke out. My friend who lent me the Haskalah books [. . .] and some of his friends decided to publish a Hebrew weekly devoted to the news, in particular the foolhardiness and defeat of the Poles. [. . .] I was asked to participate in this venture, to write poems, for no Hebrew periodical could be devoid of poems, and they already knew that sometimes I wrote poetry. I nodded my head, and at the head of the first issue of the weekly called "Timely Matters" there appeared a poem that I wrote in praise of the Hebrew language, in which I exhorted the Jews to come to the aid of our holy tongue. Obviously, the poem showed no taste or poetic talent; it was just a group of phrases, although I am sure that it was not any worse than many poems that are published in [other periodicals]. Since poems of this type could not appear in every issue, they asked me to write a [different kind of] poem for each issue that pertained to the weekly Torah reading. [. . .] I, who had nothing better to do, agreed, and each week submitted a moralistic poem. My first poem was for the week of Be-ha'alotekha [Numbers 8–12]. There I preached about the evils of slander, and the punishment of Miriam the prophetess, who slandered her brother Moses. I went on preaching in this manner until we reached the week of Devarim [six to eight weeks later], at which point the periodical became known to the Talmud learners, for whom we the writers, and the editors even more so, were the subject of taunts and gibes. Our periodical died before I finished my poem for the week.

[. . .] On Yom Kippur 5625 [1864] the remembrance candle that my mother-in-law lit went out. At night I came home to revive after the fast, and after my mother-in-law spread the fragrance of honey to all the corners of the house as a sign of a good and sweet year, as she always did, she despondently reported the catastrophe that befell us, that the remembrance candle went out! I answered her smugly, "We should never know a worse catastrophe than the extinguishing of the Yom Kippur candle." My mother-in-law heard and said nothing. The next evening, as I was sitting over a book, I heard my mother-in-law's voice, in the plaintive tone reserved for the special supplications, saying "every Jew prays on Yom Kippur for the well-being of his wife and children, but this lout stands and requests that the Yom Kippur candle shall go out — it should only be that no harm comes to his wife and child, but to him alone!" I heard this and mimicked her. [. . .] Obviously, my mother-in-law did not allow me the last word; she poured out all kinds of curses on me, and I was not slothful in responding, not with boorish curses, but with humor and sarcasm that angered her even more. This business went on for about a month, every night, and then new matters would arise to fight over. [. . .]

In addition to my fighting with my mother-in-law, I was also engaged in the [modern] study of Judaism. I asked my friend once again for the first three years of *Ha-maggid*, and I read then carefully, and was filled with much joy and pain. I was particularly irked by an article [. . .] in which [the author] poured out scorn on R. Shlomo Kluger because he forbade the use of machine-made matzos on Passover. I particularly enjoyed an article by Eliezer Zweifel, the title of which I do not remember, [. . .] which served as a kind of confessional of one of the *maskilim*, as he recalled the joys of his earlier life, when he was close to God and his religion, while now his heart was like ice. This article was like honey in my mouth, I read it many times, and copied it so that it would be with me at all times. I was happy with my lot, that God had not departed from my heart; I blessed his great name, for having separated me from those in error, and I did not realize that in another six years God

would depart from me as well, and my heart too, would be as ice! [. . .]

In those days I bought some books, among them a Russian-Hebrew dictionary by [Leon] Mandelstamm. I tried to read Russian books with the help of this dictionary but was not successful, for I knew nothing of the grammar or structure of this language, and without this knowledge it was difficult even to find words in the dictionary, for you had to be able to isolate the root. When I came upon a noun or verb [in an inflected or conjugated form], I was like a wanderer in the desert. I abandoned this endeavor, and said to myself if I ever succeed in becoming a great Torah scholar in Israel, then I will study external subjects, in order to increase the honor of Torah and to understand it even better. But if I remain a simple teacher or shopkeeper — I will have no need for languages and secular knowledge, for what interest has a shopkeeper or teacher with such things? On the basis of this healthy logic, I made no effort to master any new areas of inquiry, and I continued to spend my time writing poems and *pilpulistic* investigations.

[. . .][14] During this time I came into contact with a number of books I had never seen before, among them *Behinat ha-dat* of Elijah Delmedigo [1460–97; the book is an attempt to reconcile faith and reason], together with the commentary Isaac S. Reggio [1784–1855; an important Italian *maskil*], as well as *Ari nohem* [see below]; and *Shorshe ha-levanon* [by Isaac Baer Levinsohn; the book contains discussions of linguistic matters, as well as Jewish and human affairs]. I had already read *Ari nohem* before, and it had made no impression on me; indeed, I considered its author [Yehudah Aryeh de Modena, 1571–1648] as an unworthy person. Now, however, my mind was more developed, and since I read those three books in a few days, and they are all unanimous in proving the fraudulent nature of the kabbalah, and that together with these three books I read the *More nevukhe ha-zeman* of [the Galician *maskil*] Nachman

Krochmal [. . .] which I considered very important because Rabbi Zvi Hirsh Chajes mentioned it with approbation in his book, [. . .] I ceased to believe in the kabbalah. [. . .] I accepted Krochmal's proofs that the kabbalah had originated among Jews who converted to Christianity. These four books succeeded in overwhelming my firm faith in the kabbalah. The darkness, which blanketed the Torah and the Talmud because of my belief in all kinds of occult and esoteric matters, was diminished. I began to see some light. I now saw the Torah simply, the Talmud, also simply, and the Zohar I considered fraudulent darkness. There were no secrets and hidden doctrines beyond what is accessible to human cognition, beyond what a human can affirm as true; as for the rest, were it a genuine tradition [the actual meaning of kabbalah is "tradition"] from the prophets and the sages, we would accept it, and if not, it is nothing but falsehood! These investigations caused me much pain, although in actuality, I remained the same captive of the study hall that I had always been; when I, that winter, first came into possession of the book *Ahavat Zion* [the first Hebrew novel, by Abraham Mapu], and I had the opportunity to read it on Sabbath eve, but first searched in the *Shulhan Arukh* for permission to read such books on the Sabbath, and after searching I relied on the opinion of [a particular authority] who permitted reading such books on the Sabbath if they facilitated learning the language. [. . .]

I was weary and exhausted from studying the Talmud, its disputations and various absurdities. When I heard of something new that was rational, I was drawn to it, just like an escaped prisoner coming upon a field of flowers. Every Haskalah book I came upon, I devoured like the fruits of summer. It was not that I loved the Haskalah, for at that time I did not rightly know what it was, but so weary was I of the casuistic books and their sophistries that I looked for spiritual sustenance in other sorts of books.

I had no teacher or guide in studying the literature of the Haskalah.

In my town, I was the first to show public interest in the Haskalah, and I did not care what the fanatics said. There was no one to advise me wisely, "Stop sleepwalking and chasing shadows. Live, for you are a living person." Undiscriminating, I read everything that came into my hands, oblivious of how the days were slipping away.

Days of My Disbelief

Here is a letter, with all its foolishness and high-flown rhetoric, which, in my naiveté, I wrote to a friend, and which shows what I was going through that summer [of 1869]:[15]

"I want to tell you what I believe, and I want you to uphold me or condemn me as you see fit. I am not the hypocrite the rabbi accuses me of being.

"I believe in the Holy Torah that was given by Moses, that he wrote down from God's words, and in the songs that he sang with His Holy Spirit, like the Song of the Sea, Hazinu, and his blessings before his death, for in all these the Spirit of God spoke.

"I believe in the words of the prophets in whom God's spirit spoke. I am loyal to the tradition and disapprove of the reformers. I do not believe in the new critics who say that the words of comfort in Isaiah are not his, that chapter 40 and after were added later.

"I believe that God will shed His spirit upon a man of the House of David who will rule over us in our land. But I do not believe in the messianic legends of our Talmudic sages, nor do I believe in the other Talmudic legends.

"I believe that our dead will be resurrected, that the good and the pious among the gentiles will partake of the world to come.

"I hold sacred all the laws based on the Talmud. But I have no regard for customs not based on the Talmud.

"I have told you, dear brother, everything I believe. Hide this letter; do not show it to anyone. There are enough fanatics in your town to say even you have been snared by the words of the impious."

The whole town was in an uproar over me. It hurt me to see my wife's suffering because of my conduct, and I was very worried about my little boy's health. But neither the uproar of my townspeople, nor my wife's weeping, not even the pleadings of my Torah-true friends who tried to convince me to yield to the rabbi, swayed me one bit. They decided, once and for all, that I was an unbeliever and they kept clear of me. I was satisfied that an iron wall had arisen between me and my Torah-true friends. I ceased to be under their watchful eye and became free, free to write whatever I wanted. In clear Hebrew, I began to describe the barbarities of my townsmen and their foolish deeds. To all these articles I signed my name. The townspeople made even more of an uproar [and] threatened me, but I ignored them.

[. . .] Then my heart was seized with a new sorrow, for Judaism was dying, and with it the Jewish people would perish. One must seek a cure for this curse. I concluded that the only remedy was to make it easier to observe Judaism, so Jews could always fulfill the commandments as written in the Torah — not as interpreted in the Talmud. Though some fences around the Torah were needed, the encumbrances and customs that make Judaism difficult to practice and unattractive to people who cannot tolerate absurdity ought to be removed.

If I regarded each nation not as a world in itself, but as a part of humankind that people, rather than nature, separated into groups, I would make peace with the idea that the end of the Jews would be like the end of all other peoples, that eventually all groups would revert to a common substance. They would cease being peoples and become just people. If I did not love Judaism in which I believed with my whole heart, I would not care if it disappeared. But now, wanting to preserve forever the Jewish people and Judaism, I was

convinced the cure for the disease was lifting some of the Talmudic restraints and fences. I had a tested cure for the mortal illness, but there was no one to administer it to the patient. [. . .].

Since my eyes were opened and I perceived the darkness, I have been persecuted. The foolish rabbi of Miroslav aroused the whole town against me because I had secular books in my possession. They regarded me as a Berlinchik. In one moment I, the head of a yeshiva, was turned into an unbeliever. The desire for revenge, a natural and human thing, made me expose them in the newspapers. At this, too, my townsmen were enraged. Yet I always observed the commandments and never intentionally violated the slightest prohibition of the later Talmudists. Even now, I never eat cheese less than six hours after eating meat. [. . .] I imbued the young people of my town, over whom I have had influence, with love for the Jewish people, respect for Judaism, and aversion toward evil. Yet I was considered the town heretic and endured affliction and sorrow, poverty and hunger. When I wrote about reforming Judaism, bringing the practice of religion closer to reality, my mind was full of ideas but my stomach was empty. My reward for this article was disgrace and dishonor, shame and sorrow. The town elders tried, on false charges, to have me banished to Siberia. The kinder ones were ready to contribute fifty rubles for my children's welfare if I would disappear. [. . .] They incited street urchins against me; wherever I went, young rascals trailed me, shouting "freethinker, unbeliever." Scurrilities about me were scribbled on the walls of the prayer houses, the kiosks, the outhouses. Every Saturday, preachers agitated the people against me. Some people informed government officials against me. Some said I issued false receipts, while others said I was teaching deceit to the young. Some Hasidim even tried to poison me. They called my children offspring of unclean parents, and the other children bullied them. Everyone fled from me, and even my friends were afraid to speak with me on the street. [. . .] That was how I passed that summer, until I could no longer earn enough for bread. Then the [maskilic] community of Odessa invited me to come there. [. . .]

All my life I was never beholden to anyone nor had I taken gifts, until last summer, when the committee helped me settle in Odessa.[16] Nor did they instruct me to write in one way or another. They saw the troubles I suffered at the hands of the fanatics, and they found a place of refuge for me, where the reach of the fanatics would not extend. Had these not tried to drive me out of town because of my articles, the Odessa committee would never have heard of me. My only lament is that my upbringing had stunted my abilities and hung a millstone on my neck before I was sixteen. Now, with a wife and three children, I am a miserable creature unsuited to any kind of work.

[. . .] For many years I was tormented by an inner struggle that progressed step by step. After denying the power of amulets and charms, I then questioned the existence of other demons. Having finished off demons and magic, I turned to the Zohar. After Zohar and kabbalah, the existence of angels; then the *aggadot* in which I had believed. After that, the *midrashim* of the Talmud that relate to religious laws, and then, the traditional law. Then I had radical thoughts about Providence, about natural change, about reward and punishment, and about a man's soul. [. . .]

All my days passed in emptiness, without pleasure, for the rancid air and the polarizing spirit of the denizens of the *beit midrash* surrounded me always. I have scarcely any pleasant memories of my youth. Yet, except for the events of 1869 [when I was denounced and forced to leave my home], I found a deep satisfaction in prayer. I was raised as a *misnagid*, and our services were not marked by enthusiasm as those of the Hasidim were. Yet often ecstasy seized me, especially during the Rosh Hashanah and Yom Kippur services. When I recited [the section of] the [Musaf] prayer "U-ve-khen ten pahdekha," proclaiming man's recognition of God's sovereignty, the song of unity that most deeply touches the heart of everyone who loves God, I was immensely affected. I do not need to describe this rapture to those who are familiar with it. To those who do not know what this is like, I can tell them that it is like embracing one's beloved after crying one's eyes out pining for her; in great joy grabbing her and squeezing her to his heart in rapturous love. The heart of such a one will not race more than that of a true lover of God when he recites prayers such as these.

Now what am I? My heart is cold and dried like wood. It is all the same to me whether it is the Sabbath or Yom Kippur, Passover, the Fast of Esther, or a weekday. It is impossible for me to experience spiritual joy as I once did, just as it is impossible for me to once again be twenty years old, or to have three eyes; even poetry, too, has been torn out of my heart. [. . .] My heart is frozen with hoarfrost. How bitter for one who once was so passionate! If I had filled my head with pure science, or if I were rich and enjoyed worldly pleasures, perhaps I would not feel bereft with the loss of my illusory world, for then I would rejoice in the real world, which I understood. But I am only a poor ignoramus who denies all sense of the illusory and naive faith, and I cannot replace my deficiency with something else. [. . .] That was the result of the intoxication and of the illusions I had that stemmed from the chaotic Haskalah—to which I had been so susceptible only because of the bad education I had received. [. . .]

Once I lived with illusion instead of truth, but I did not know that it was illusion; I thought it was the truth. That is why I was happier then than now. [. . .]

I have written this book for myself and for others: for me—to lighten my heart's burden with this funeral oration on my wasted life; and to show others the mistakes and the sins of my youth that they should avoid. For others—to show the readers all the sins of my youth, so that they may avoid them based on the experiences they find in this book. Perhaps my desire to benefit my readers is only my residual intoxication, since, in truth, it is hard to accept the experiences of others as a guide; some things one needs to experience for oneself. Still, it is hard for me to believe that my book will make no impression on its readers. [. . .]

I hope that copies of my book will not be eaten by the moths in the bookstores but sold and read by parents and children. Some parents, I suppose, will draw an a fortiori conclusion: see what has become of this writer who had studied all of the Talmud by the age of eighteen, was steeped in the responsa literature at nineteen, and at twenty, subject to judgment of the Heavenly Court, he fasted and studied all day in prayer shawl and phylacteries so that he might enter the fifty gates of holiness. Though he lived among Talmudic sages and God-fearing men, where no one doubted God, yet even his Torah study and piety could not resist the Devil, and he became an unbeliever. How much easier, then— these parents will think—for their children to be corrupted?

If parents understand me, they will not prevent their children from becoming educated out of fear that they will be ruined, nor will they marry them off prematurely. If parents want to protect their children from heresy, they should keep them from speculative thought, bar them from studying even a page of Talmud, and teach them a trade instead. [. . .] Otherwise their children will come to the same end as I.

I would like to think that my book will influence the young people who have become absorbed in the futile chaos our writers call Haskalah. They must learn from my fate and turn to more practical things: learn living languages (I do not mean Hebrew—those reading this book know it already), mathematics,

penmanship, natural sciences, and a trade by which they can live. [. . .]

Boys ought to be prepared for the world while they are still young. Anything that cannot be understood as preparing them for life and does not provide them with real treasures—such as languages, the sciences, or vocational skills—should be strictly forbidden. [Now] those who flee from the Talmud run toward the chaos of the new literature. This flight has been going on for about a hundred years. [. . .] All the younger generation is fleeing, but they do not know to where. It is high time for us to stop a moment and ponder where we are running and why. Are we not fleeing into a bottomless pit? Have we no other way except flight? [. . .]

I am not the first victim of the Haskalah; many writers and *maskilim* secretly bewail the sins of their youth for it is too late to correct them. But they continue to lead new enthusiasts on the same futile path along which they went, calling on young people to build and repair the Hebrew language, raise the walls of Zion, serve in the temple of the Haskalah, and other such meaningless phrases. But I hide only my face, not my ruination, neither the sins of my youth nor the afflictions and sorrows that destroyed my life.

NOTES

1. [We wish to acknowledge benefiting from the edition of Shelomo Breiman, *Moshe Leib Lilienblum: Ketavim Otobiografiyim* (Jerusalem, 1970).]

2. [Moshe Leib Lilienblum (1843–1910) was born in Kaidan (Kedainiai), Lithuania, where he received a traditional education. He was married at the age of thirteen to an eleven-year-old girl; this early marriage was to be a source of complaint throughout his life, and was one of the "sins" imposed on him by his father (the other being an education limited to Talmud study). He moved into his in-laws home in Vil'komir. There he was drawn to the Haskalah (one of the "sins" he committed on his own), which led to his persecution and estrangement from family. Lilienblum became an advocate for reforming Jewish

law and education, but came to despair of achieving that. The memoir excerpted here was published when he was thirty years old, and was written to warn both fathers and sons to avoid the sins committed by his father and him.]

3. [In Jewish law, a woman may not be "secluded" with a male over the age of nine (as men are forbidden to be secluded with females). A woman who did seclude herself with a man would be suspected of adultery. This suspicion is enhanced if the man is a gentile. By staying at the house of a gentile without a chaperone (that is, by being secluded with him) Lilienblum's father's first wife forfeited her right to a proper marriage settlement.]

4. [A priest; a person who claimed descent from Aaron, Moses's brother, the founder of the priestly line.]

5. [Although certainly included in the Talmud, the Mishnah by itself and the *aggadah* were considered less challenging parts of it; a person proficient primarily in these areas could not claim to be a Talmud scholar.]

6. [The verse refers to the repulsion of a plague in the time of Moses.]

7. [The name of the author of a sixteenth-century commentary. Deciphering this commentary was obviously considered quite a feat for a young, budding Talmud scholar.]

8. [A kabbalistic doctrine.]

9. [Moshe Hayim Luzzatto, 1800–1865, was an Italian *maskil*, who wrote, among many other things, an autobiography.]

10. [Lilienblum's in-laws' home was actually in Vil'komir; however, in the text, he calls the town Miroslav.]

11. [Here Lilienblum briefly describes the preparations and the wedding.]

12. [A fictional character in *Fathers and Sons* by Sholem Y. Abramovich, better known as Mendele Moykher Seforim. Obviously, this woman was a detestable character to him.]

13. [Yedaiah Bedersi (c. 1270–c. 1340) was a philosopher and poet. In the wake of the ban that was issued in 1305 in Barcelona against the reading of philosophy, Bedersi wrote an apologia to the Rashba in which he strongly defended the study of philosophy and the pursuit of free inquiry.]

14. [Here Lilienblum describes how, in the winter of 5626 (1865–66), he taught different groups and individuals extensively, in order to make money beyond what his in-laws were providing to him.]

15. [By 1869 Lilienblum was widely identified as a heretic, and persecuted for it. For example, he describes how once he was the tenth man to enter the synagogue, meaning that a quorum had been reached, but the rabbi insisted on waiting for another man to arrive, as he would not count the heretic in the minyan.]

16. [This presumably refers to the Society for the Promotion of Culture among the Jews of Russia, which had an office in Odessa at this time.]

[105]

State Inspection of Private Jewish Schools in Vil'na (1870)

LVIA, f. 378, op. 1870, d. 882, ll. 10–21.

"Notes on Private Jewish Schools by Lieutenant General Prince Bagration (August 1870)"

Pursuant to the order of Your Excellency's former assistant (number 8440, dated 14 August 1870), which entrusted me with the hygienic inspection of private Jewish schools in the city of Vil'na, [. . .] I inspected all these institutions with the teacher of the [Vil'na State] Rabbinical School Uspenskii and the learned Jew Gershtein, who is attached to the administration of the general governor. I have the honor to report the following results of my examination:

Names and Number of Schools: The number of private Jewish schools in Vil'na under the jurisdiction of the school district include: (a) three boarding schools (*pansiony*) for girls; (b) two yeshivot (schools where Jewish youth are engaged exclusively in the study of the Talmud); (c) the philanthropic institution of the Talmud Torah; and (d) the Saturday school for artisans; [(e) *hadarim* and *melamdim*].

Girls' Boarding Schools: The female boarding schools are supported by the tuition paid by the students, with assistance from the candle tax. These establishments are sufficiently spacious and clean; they generally conform to hygienic conditions to an acceptable degree, with the exception of the two-room female boarding school on Rudnitskaia Street (in the house of Kozello and operated by Isaak German). The two small rooms are much too inadequate to accommodate seventy-six students; a crowded school cannot satisfy hygienic requirements.

Yeshivot: The two yeshivot represent a striking contrast. Both are situated in that part of town where the Jewish population is excessively congested and consists predominantly of the impoverished class. In the yeshiva maintained by Trotskii on Rudnitskaia Street, there are not even separate rooms for study and sleeping quarters for the students. Instead, everyone is together in the prayer house, where worshipers gather three times a day to conduct their prayers.

Although the other yeshiva, maintained by Peskin, has sleeping quarters with constructed bunks that are partitioned off from the study rooms, the quarters are nonetheless extremely crowded. It is apparent that these improvements were made recently, in all likeliness [in advance] of Prince Bagration's visit to this yeshiva. In general, judging by the numerous pupils studying at the yeshiva (who are predominantly from the lower class of Jews from other towns — that is, those without shelter find lodging for the night), one can conclude that contagious skin diseases, which are so prevalent among Jews, come from such crowded conditions, the filthy state of the establishment, and the stifling, stuffy air. In addition, it is not natural to grow up in such cramped conditions; Jewish youth are deprived of all necessary conditions to develop physical health, embark on life with broken health, and become incapable of hard labor.

The pitiful condition of the yeshivot is explained mainly by the lack of control over the resources used to maintain them. The source of a yeshiva's maintenance comes from voluntary donations of private individuals. These gifts are continuous or temporary; they are at the complete disposal of the yeshiva proprietors. It is a great pity that nowhere do they keep a credit and debit book of income and expenses, which could provide even a minimal understanding of the level of donations, the amount of student fees, and specifically if they might imagine that the revenues might provide sufficient resources to improve the maintenance of the yeshivot.[1]

The pupils receive sustenance from different pious Jews and, at the latter's homes, receive a meal for each day of the week (which the Jews call "eating days"). The pupils' breakfast consists of a piece of dry bread from the proprietor, the cost of which is covered by the donations mentioned above.

The studies of the yeshiva students (*yeshiva bachurim*) cannot but have a negative impact on the development of their intellectual and physical strength. They devote their youth exclusively to the study of the Talmud, engage in this mainly for the sake of studying, as something pleasing to God, and avoid all knowledge about the existence of other subjects (which would be more helpful in developing and acquiring intellectual capacities and adopting some kind of definite purpose for the future). Yeshiva students who complete their study of Talmud only become a burden to society as idle people lacking the capacity for productive activities.

Reflections on Improvement of the Yeshivot: Of course, the government cannot directly set about the destruction of these establishments, for the Jews would see such drastic measures as a violation of their religion. Nonetheless, one should not let rational measures disappear from view, for these could contribute to reducing the harmfulness of these establishments.

From the time of the establishment of [state] Jewish literacy schools in Vil'na and as a consequence of the order by the late Count Murav'ev (making study at such schools obligatory for all young Jews, including the ye-

shiva students), the latter have increasingly begun to devote several hours a day to the study of general subjects. This has led many of the yeshiva students themselves to abandon the yeshiva and to attend the [state] rabbinical schools or to be appointed as clerks in commercial enterprises. Such a phenomenon directly suggests that the most effective measure against the yeshivot would be to broaden the curriculum of the yeshivot by adding other general subjects to Talmudic study. Given these circumstances, it would be useful to adopt the following measures with respect to the yeshivot:

(1) Compel the owners of the yeshivot to keep a credit and debit book for recording incoming monetary donations and in general all allowances. These books should be kept in Russian.

(2) Induce the owners to build sleeping quarters separate from the study rooms for pupils who do not have another shelter and in general to keep the establishment as tidy as possible.

(3) As for expansion of the curriculum, first and foremost pay attention to Russian grammar and arithmetic.

However, implementation of these measures must be left to solely to the Jews—viz., those who by their own education have already acquired a progressive tendency and rationally take an interest in improving their coreligionists' way of life. One will not find a shortage of such people in Vil'na. Such Jews, conscious of the abnormal condition of the yeshivot, themselves are able to find practical means to improve them. For this purpose, it would be useful to establish a committee of Jews along with participation by officials from the government (including one from the department of the general governor and another from the school district).

Talmud-Torah: The school called the "Talmud Torah" leaves an absolutely different impression. It is in a special house belonging to the latter [the school]. The number of pupils who enroll from the childhood age amounts to 140 people, of whom 50 receive their entire upkeep from the institution. The rest receive only free instruction beginning with the Jewish faith, Russian grammar, and arithmetic. The 50 [stipendiary] pupils have special bedrooms with beds, a cafeteria, and kitchen, which are sufficiently spacious and relatively neat. Despite the fact that this institution is maintained through donations and is not subject to state control, it has nonetheless established a credit and debit book in Russian. I deem it my duty to present the following for Your Excellency's consideration at your discretion:

The Talmud Torah is supervised by a committee of trustees, which was established as far back as 1861 by former General Governor [Vladimir Ivanovich] Nazimov, who issued an order to the learned Jew Gershtein (attached to the office of the general governor) to oversee this institution in his capacity as a member of the secretariat. The committee envisioned many reforms in this institution (the goal being to raise it to the level of a comfortable children's shelter). Unfortunately, however, it had only initial and partial success. One cause was the inadequacy and instability in its support, which consisted of individual donations. Hence it is not surprising that the institution provides the most meager food, which is limited to bread and groats, and this in insufficient quantity. At the completion of their studies, Mr. Gershtein endeavors to see that these pupils enter training in various artisan trades; however, these people [artisans] —who are from the very impoverished class of Jews—often return their students earlier than the prearranged term, finding it unprofitable to support a weak boy, whose labor does not compensate for his upkeep. The children thus become homeless again.

Proposals to Improve the Talmud Torah: To avoid the foregoing, it is impossible not to approve the petition of Mr. Gershtein to allocate a certain sum from the kosher meat tax to build an artisan school at the Talmud Torah.[2] This institution would correspond fully to serving as a well-equipped children's shelter and ensure the future of its poor pupils.

Saturday School: The Saturday School for Artisans consists of one small room where artisans of every age gather for instruction in their faith. Although the gathering reaches up to 150 pupils, the space cannot accommodate so many people. However, since the assembly meets once a week, this does not pose a danger in terms of hygiene.

Hadarim and Melamdim: With respect to the private Jewish schools [*hadarim*], which are led by *melamdim*, I was guided by the list furnished by the chancellery of the Vil'na School District for the first half of 1870. According to the list, every *melamed* is registered at an address where he maintains a *heder*; however, it was difficult to find the addresses as one should: in the second half of the year, the majority of the *melamdim* had moved the premises of their *hadarim*, and very few remained in the place indicated on the list.

The *hadarim* under review, where Jewish youth receive their primary education, represent a sad picture. With the exception of thirty *hadarim* located on orderly streets in the suburbs, the rest—up to 200—were on the filthiest narrow streets and in crowded, dark, and musty rooms that simultaneously serve as classroom and lodgings for the numerous members of the *melamed*'s family and residents of the apartment. They do not pay the slightest attention to the hygienic conditions of the *hadarim*. The *melamdim* clearly do not even know how to bring about such [hygienic] conditions. The filth is staggering. Obviously, such an environment can only have a negative impact on the health of the boys being educated there. Indeed, the faces of most boys are pale, emaciated, and frightened; their hands are covered with scabs from scabies. The *melamdim* apparently regard all this with complete indifference, as if it [hygiene] were something ordinary and simply unnecessary [to maintain]. The savagery of the *melamdim* toward their pupils reached the point where in one, when I entered, the boys hastened to hide themselves under the desks; only after some time did they begin to crawl out, one by one, and follow me out of a dim curiosity laced with fear. The Russian language is so alien to the *heder* that I could hardly understand not only the boys but also the *melamdim*. As an exception I can point to the *hadarim* maintained by the *melamdim* Tiktin and Dronzik, which are in relatively better order and much cleaner. These exceptions can be explained by the fact that Titkin and Dronzik are not deprived of some education, and by the fact that the boys who study at their premises belong to the more prosperous class of Jews—which gives the material resources to keep these *hadarim* at a more decent level. The other *hadarim*, run by individuals who are absolutely ignorant and who have no understanding of order, cleanliness, and other conditions of educational institutions, create an extremely painful impression on visitors. In such institutions a large mass of Jewish youth are obviously perishing, physically and morally.

Proposal for the Reform of the Hadarim: Given the extremely poor conditions of the Vil'na *hadarim* in hygienic and pedagogical terms (both the complete ignorance of the majority of *melamdim* and the equally limited material means of the latter), one must conclude as follows. To reduce the harm described here, it would be advisable to merge several *hadarim* into one big *heder* and [it woud] thereby resemble more the organization of public schools. Appoint head teachers from the *melamdim* who are more appropriate for the rank of public [school] teachers, with assistant *melamdim* under them, who because of the proposed mergers would be deprived of running independent *hadarim*. The mergers would increase the resources of the reformed *hadarim*. The owners will have more resources to ensure the proper environment. In hygienic terms, at least, the head of the school will [be able to] ensure strict observance of order and proper methods of organizing the educational institutions. One may assume that this measure will not meet any obstacles from Jews in particular after it is discussed with their very help (that is, in the commission mentioned above).

NOTES

1. [For a comparative perspective on the funding of the Volozhin yeshiva, see Shaul Stampfer, *Lithuanian Yeshivas of the Nineteenth Century*, trans. Lindsey Taylor-Guthartz (Oxford: The Littman Library of Jewish Civilization, 2012), 31–36. See also document 109.]

2. The report contains the following note: Mr. Gershtein's proposal is at the Chancellery of the General Governor.

Certification of *Melamdim* (1869)

RGIA, f. 733, op. 189. d 321, ll. 1–15.

"Memorandum from the Ministry of Education to the Second Section of His Imperial Majesty's Chancellery (23 April 1869)"

In the course of 1863 the *Svod zakonov [Rossiiskoi imperii]* [Digest of the laws of the Russian Empire] (volume 11 on Laws on the [Social] Estates, footnote to article 1410, published in 1857) states that "in this foresaid footnote, a certificate will be issued to a *melamed* (a home schoolteacher) on the basis of a special procedure established by the Ministry of Education. However at the expiration of ten years (calculating from 4 May 1859), the issue of certificates must be limited only to former *melamdim*; as for those entering [the profession], it will be given only to those who have been educated in the [state] rabbinical schools or general higher or secondary educational institutions. From 1875 *melamdim* may only be Jews who have been educated in the said educational institutions." In the supplement [to the law] of 1864, this footnote was still in force, but [it] was not included in the supplement [to the law] of 1868.

Bearing in mind that this May is set as the time to restrict the issue of certificates to previous *melamdim* on existing grounds (as shown above), I deem it my duty humbly to ask Your Excellency to inform me whether the Ministry of Education is guided at present by the footnote to article 1410, according to the supplement of 186[4], or should consider the resolution changed and, if it is the latter case, by virtue of what arrangement.[1]

"Petition (Translated from the Hebrew) of Iakov Iakovlevich Gotlib of Videopol to Minister of Education Dmitrii Andreevich Tolstoi (4 July 1874)"

To Dmitrii Andreevich, Herr [*sic*] Tolstoi (who, to the honor of the great Sovereign, is respected, elevated, universally known for his loving mercy and truth, whose intellect is erecting an edifice of enlightenment and to whose wisdom people cling, whose lips disseminate knowledge and augment learning, whose honest sobriquet is the Minister of Education):[2]

To the dust of thy feet, Great Sir, do I reach out with outstretched arms and legs to ask your forgiveness for taking the liberty to approach your honorable Sir with the present letter. As the heavens are my witness, and God knows, I do not even have a kopeck to my name to pay a clerk to write this petition in the Russian language for me. This is all the more so because the town in which I live has very few residents, and we do not have someone who would properly know a little about a Russian letter and the Russian language. Although I myself know a little Russian, I am in no position to draft my petition because it is being submitted to such a lofty gentleman as yourself. For a proper letter, I would have had to spend about two rubles to travel to Akkerman or Odessa, which I absolutely cannot do at the present time when I am short of a morsel of bread. That is why, Sir, I decided to submit my present letter to you in Hebrew. I depend upon the mercy of His Excellency, that he would forgive me for this, for a suffering person should not be punished.[3] I suffer ever so much. May God take pity on me first and then on you, Your Excellency.

I am Iakov Iakovlev[ich], son of Gotlib [*sic*] from the town of Pinsk (Minsk province). It has already been twenty-five years that I have worked as a *melamed*—that is, I teach Jewish boys the Hebrew language with grammatical pronunciation of words according to the vowels [*nekudot*]. I also teach a little biblical grammar as well as all the conjugated verbs with their aspects and pronominal suffixes (using the simplest method, namely the system of the teacher Mapu).[4] In the same manner I also teach the Russian and German languages as much as this is requested for five- and six-year-old boys. During the entire course of my work, I had permission, a *Schein* (the German term for certificate). Only recently, when I was a teacher in a village near Khotin, a big fire burned all my possessions, including the trunk where I kept my passport and certificates. If I were to undertake to obtain a new certificate, I could easily do so. However, it would be necessary to spend money for a trip to Akkerman (where I obtained my first certificate), but I am not in a financial position to do. Meanwhile, a year and half have passed and my petition for a new certificate that I sent to the inspector in Akkerman has been rejected on the grounds that the time limit has expired. I also applied for a new certificate to replace my old one in Kamenets-Podol'sk, where I was last year, but they too denied my petition, saying that they do not have the right to issue a new certificate because a long time has passed since I lost my old one in the fire.

I now prostrate myself before Your Excellency, with this petition: Oh Sir, save me for the waters have risen up to my neck,[5] for I am unfit for any other work and am in no condition to assume any kind of burden. Teaching is my only hope. I now live in the town of Videopol [Ovidiopol] Kherson province, with my wife and children, who are starving to death as they have no means to buy bread, and who remain as barefoot as the time of their birth by their mother. So what am I to do now? If I had the certificate, I would be able to gather here five or six boys, who are wasting their time without a teacher and who do not even know how to speak properly; then I could earn three rubles a week to feed my family. My only hope now is Your Excellency. Thus I fall before You and beg You to take pity on me, to help me in my unfortunate time and to order the authorities to issue me a *melamed*'s certificate at least until the next year (1875) according to your great mercy. Then all that will happen to the remaining *melamdim* [without secular education] will also happen to me.[6] Only for the said six months, I beg you Sir for the *melamed* certificate in order to support myself and my family. This will be the salvation of eight souls who would [otherwise] perish from poverty and anguish.

May Your Excellency be rewarded by God (may You be blessed)! May Your good fortune rise higher and higher; may God extend a tent of peace over You in this world and the world to come. May His sun shine eternally from age to age according to the wish of Your Excellency and according to the wish of Your servant, who is prostrate before Your great honor from afar.

NOTES

1. [The next document in the archival file states that the instructions in the supplement to statute 1410 in 1868 were a mistake.]

2. [The translator attached this note to the Minister of Education: "In accordance with the request of the department, I have the honor to submit together with the original petition in Hebrew, a Russian translation of the aforementioned letter. Due to the metaphoric, hyperbolic style, and numerous platitudes, it is difficult, if at all possible in general, to convey the literal meaning in many places. I have attempted as far as possible to maintain the special style of this present letter; however, a few expressions cannot be conveyed at all in Russian."]

3. [The translator noted that this was a Talmudic

saying. A more literal translation of the original Hebrew letter would be: "He who is extremely distressed, God has mercy on him."]

4. He was a teacher from Kovno who died a few years ago. [The reference is probably to Avraham Mapu (1808–67), one of the most important figures of the Haskalah movement. Gotlib may be referring to Mapu's children's textbook, *Hinukh la-no'ar* (1859), which was used for teaching Hebrew.]

5. Psalms 69, 1.

6. [The reference here is to the law stipulating that, from 1875, only *melamdim* who graduated from the state rabbinical school or other similar institution would qualify to receive the certificate.]

[107]

Trial of Girsh Korobochko for Teaching without a *Melamed*'s Certificate (1888–89)

LVIA, f. 445, op. 1, d. 729, ll. 9–11.

"Sentence of the Criminal Section of the Vil'na Provincial Court (12 December 1888)"

[The court] heard the case of Girsh Korobochko, accused of [teaching children without a *melamed*'s certificate] in accordance with an appellate review.

On 13 May 1887, the constable of the fourth police station of Mozyr District—owing to a letter from the Mozyr state rabbi about requiring *melamed* Girsh Korobochko to provide information about his occupation of teaching Jewish children how to read—was in the town of Lenin. He demanded that Korobochko present the legal certificate required of *melamdim*. Korobochko, who did not deny teaching Jewish children how to read, declared that he did not have the certificate. The village constables questioned as witnesses during the preliminary investigation (Ivan Migai and Liokim Slutskii) confirmed that Korobochko's occupation was teaching Jewish children to read. Subject to investigation as the defendant, Girsh Korobochko did not admit his guilt. On the basis of the testi-

mony, Girsh Leibov Korobochko, a townsman from Gorodok, Pinsk district, came to trial on 5 September 1888 in the Minsk District Court, without the participation of a jury, on the charge that he engaged in teaching Jewish children to read and [recite] prayers in the town of Lenin without a certificate for the office of *melamed* as mandated by a decree by the imperially established committee of the Ministry of Education (9 March 1879). Under oath, the witnesses testified as follows:

> Constable Ivan Migai: Although Korobochko was illiterate [in the Russian language], he nonetheless engaged in teaching Jewish prayers to children and for his work he received compensation in the form of produce.

> Constable [Liokim] Slutskii: Korobochko does not know how to read everything and does not engage in teaching children everything: he only takes on the task of teaching children [to recite] prayers at school.

The district court has examined the present case and taken into consideration the law (which prosecutes individuals who engage in any teaching of children without permission from authorities, whether it be teaching Jewish children how to read or [recite] prayers). The court found that the testimonies of the witnesses Migai and Slutskii were completely verified. [. . .] Given the circumstances of the case, the court deemed it warranted to assess a monetary fine of twenty-five rubles on Korobochko. In the event that Korobochko was too poor to pay this fine, then he was to be subjected to detention by the police for two weeks in conformity with [the law]. Because of a revised decision of the district court, the townsman Girsh Leibovich Korobochko is [now] subject to a monetary fine of twenty-five rubles for the benefit of charity for individuals who have acquired the right to teach the youth in private homes. If he is too poor to pay the fine, then he is to be subject to arrest for two weeks. [. . .] If he is too poor to pay the expenses for the court, the Treasury will pay it for him.

Korobochko brought the decision of the district court for appellate review to the provincial court, on the grounds that the decision [of the district court] was erroneous: he taught Jewish children [to recite] prayers orally in town of Lenin for free. He was not able to know that this was a crime [under the law], which was made known to him on the day he received the indictment. If a certificate is required for the right to open a *heder*, then it does not follow from this that he should be liable to punishment for [his] decision to teach a few children of poor parents based on religious inclination. Keeping in mind that teaching the children [to recite] their prayers orally was without [monetary] compensation, [. . .] Korobochko requests the provincial court to acquit him [of the charges] or at least decrease his punishment, which would be ruinous for him to fulfill.[1]

NOTE
1. [His request was rejected, and the court upheld the ruling of the district court.]

[108]

Apprenticeship of Buki ben Yagli to a Scribe in Slonim

Yehudah Leib Katzenelson, *Mah she-rau 'einai ve-sham'u 'ozenai*, (Jerusalem: Mosad Bialik, 1947), 37–46.

One day, during the festival of Sukkot, all my many aunts and a few of my uncles gathered in the Korhin house to oversee my plans and decide "what to do with the orphan boy."[1] I recall that when one of the assembled suggested that I be apprenticed to a craftsman, all the women raised their voices in a cry and called out in horror: a *craftsman*—who ever heard of such a thing? Praise be to God, so far we have not had a craftsman in our family, and now we are going to turn Miriam's son into a craftsman? Just because he is an orphan do we have to cloak him and all our family in eternal shame? What possessed you to say such a thing? In vain did the man try to justify himself, declaring that he was not suggesting, heaven forbid, to turn me into a tailor or a shoemaker, but to have me learn a clean and easy craft like watch repair or gold-smithing. The women did not want to hear his words and would have torn the hair from his beard had he not made a hasty exit from the house. Korhin then rose from his seat, bade the women to be quiet, and spoke:

Indeed it would pain me greatly to turn the boy into a craftsman, but not because craft work is shameful to those who engage in it: God forbid—the greatest of the Tan-naim were shoemakers and metalworkers and thought it no shame. But this boy has a brain in his skull; he was created to be a son of Torah. It pains me greatly that we are unable to guide him in the path that he was destined to take from birth. There are no good instructors in Chernigov, and even if there were, we do not have the money to pay tuition for him. His inheritance money is tied up in the state orphan's court and will not be available to him until he is eigh-teen years old. And who is to feed him now, who is to clothe him and put shoes on him? For lack of choice, the boy himself must find his food and satisfy all his needs. We just have to find him a trade that will not carry him far from the Torah and the fear of God. There is such a trade, in which flour and Torah are mixed together: that is the holy work of the STaM scribe,[2] and the boy al-most knows it now and will be able to earn a living from it right away. A few months ago the scribe from Slonim suggested that I send the boy to apprentice with him. He had seen his Assyrian handwriting[3] on the margins of the pictures he draws, and he thinks that if the boy learns this craft with him, after a long while he could become one of the great scribes in the land. I have not been able to send him until now, as the boy had not reached thirteen years of age, and by religious law may not engage in this sacred work. In another month the boy will have his bar mitzvah and then may proceed to this sacred labor.

I doubt whether the women agreed in their hearts with Korhin's advice, but the man was greatly respected by all those around him, and none dared oppose him. Thus did I become a scribe.

The scribe from Slonim (thus was he called by all: his actual name escapes my memory) was sharp at his job, sharp with his tongue, and sharp in his scheming. He was then a man of about forty, sturdy as an oak, with a red face, yellow hair, and eyes full of cunning and energy. His broad beard and his thick paunch all commanded respect. He knew how to win my heart with his smooth flattery, turn me into his indentured servant, and im-pose harsh labor on me, by the sweat of my brow [he turned] his profit. For two months I trained my hand to imitate his handwriting (which really was strikingly beautiful) until even a sharp expert eye could not distinguish between our handwriting. He was then writ-ing a Torah scroll for a certain wealthy man. This job took several months. Thus he could turn to his daily pursuits and have me write the Torah scroll without anyone knowing.

So he says to me: Binyamin, how many *me-zuzot* can you write in a single day? Ten, I an-swer. Ten? No, that is beyond your ability. To show him that my pen is that of a rapid scribe, I rise early the next morning and all through the hot and dry day sit hunched over a table, from 5:00 a.m. to 9:00 p.m., when I give him thirteen *mezuzot*. From that point on, the daily quota of *mezuzot* is thirteen, and if I fall short of this number, the scribe from Slonim shows me a furious face that I cannot bear.

In truth, I did not make my master wealthy by the sweat of my brow. There is a Talmudic saying that a curse of God lingers over STaM scribes and the teachers of babes: they shall never grow wealthy in order that they never leave their posts. The scribe from Slonim for all his talents and cunning lived in impecu-nious circumstances. I do not know the price of sacramental objects nowadays, but then, fifty-five years ago, the scribe from Slonim would sell a bookseller a hundred *mezuzot* for five silver rubles and a *mezuzah* for five kopecks. Raw materials for a single *mezuzah* then cost two and a half kopecks. Shall a man grow wealthy, shall his house gain in stature from such a business? Yet in time I learned that even the business of sacramental artifacts could sometimes be done fraudulently, and this knowledge allowed me to free myself from bondage to the scribe from Slonim—even as he did not get rich from such fraud.

Nevertheless, during the first year that I was an apprentice to the scribe from Slonim, something happened whose consequences for me would not be apparent until long after. As the reader may recall, at the time there was a privatized system of liquor taxation in our country. The tax collection office in Chernigov was then headed by someone called Yitzhak Blumberg, apparently one of the first crop of Vil'na *maskilim*. For his birthday the clerks of the collection agency (all of whom were Lithuanians, who themselves had whiffed the scent of the Haskalah) sent him a thank-you note in rhymes, written on parchment in Assyrian characters by the hand of the scribe from Slonim. At the suggestion of its composer, a friend of Yitzhak Blumberg, I personally drew an ornamental frame around the rhymes in various colorful forms. My drawing pleased the recipient, and he desired to see me.

Why did you choose to be a scribe, he asked when I came to him, instead of trying to be a painter? Has no one told you that you have a painter's skill?

I did not know that there was such an occupation in the world. Every Jew needs phylacteries and *mezuzot*, but who would want a painting? Moreover, it was not I who chose the trade of a scribe; my relatives chose this trade for me. I did not want to be a scribe. [...]

And what did you want to be?

I wanted to be a Talmudic prodigy, I answered in all innocence.

A prodigy, said the man without managing to suppress his laughter. You wanted to be a prodigy? But is there such an occupation in the world?

Prodigies do not need to make a living, I answered in a voice of someone who knows the matter thoroughly. A wealthy man takes the prodigy as a husband for his daughter and provides for all his needs, and when he grows up, he becomes a rabbi or a judge, and then too he does not need to make a living. The community provides for all his needs.

Have you studied Talmud?

I have studied a little.

A little? Why have you not studied a lot? A prodigy needs to study a lot of Talmud.

But in our town there are no good teachers who could turn me into a prodigy. There was this Rabbi Gershon, who liked me, and I also liked him a lot. But illness got the better of him; he stopped being a teacher and went off to be a merchant in another town. I was left without a rabbi.

But why did they not send you to one of the yeshivot in Lithuania?

What is a yeshiva? I have not heard that term before today.

Blumberg described the business of a yeshiva as if it were a factory that turns out prodigies, and from that day on the yeshiva became the focus of my imagination and the object of all my aspirations when I awoke and went to bed, when I sat and when I walked. [...]

Is there a yeshiva in Bobruisk too? I asked.

Not one yeshiva, but three. I lived a long time in Bobruisk. But why do you ask me about Bobruisk? There are yeshivot in other towns that are better than the ones in Bobruisk.

My father was a native of Bobruisk and I have many relatives in that town.

Who was your father?

I told him his name.

Ah. I knew him; he was a great scholar and a *maskil*. I also know his close friend, Yaakov Katzenelson ("Kuli," as everyone calls him). If you go to Bobruisk, I will give you a letter of recommendation to him, but he is your own flesh and blood and even without my letter would receive you warmly. He too is a very honorable man as well as a *maskil*.

Maskil—what is a *maskil*? This was the first time I had heard the term. But I did not dare ask Blumberg to explain what it meant. In my youthful innocence I assumed that it was simply a special kind of trade. In Chernigov I would often hear that people differed from one another only on the basis of their employment and trade: shopkeeper, instructor, cantor, or peddler, so maybe a *maskil* was like one of those. I did know that in Lithuania there were some very bad people, called *misnagdim*, who do not believe in great hasidic rabbis and who recite the prayer "blessed is He who said . . ." before the prayer "be thankful. . . ."[4] But I had yet to hear anything about the cult of the *maskilim*. With respect to the conversation with Blumberg, I cannot refrain from relating an amusing story I heard from him that day, although it does not bear on my memoirs. One of the office's clerks did something improper that had aroused Blumberg's ire, and in his fury he wanted to fire him. The man was burdened with many children, and the expectation was that he and his family would have to endure shameful starvation. The accountant intervened and sought to mollify Blumberg, asking him to forgive the man's transgression and leave him at his post. Blumberg apparently was easy to mollify, summoned the guilty clerk, and in front of everyone told him: you are keeping your job, but please remember that it is not I who is doing you this kindness, but he, the accountant. Please remember and do not forget it. And when it occurs to you to repay kindness with malice, pay it to him, the accountant, and not to me. I have done you no favor.

A few days later I accidentally found in the drawer of one desk a packet of letters from my father to my uncle Korhin, of whom I have already spoken. The letters took my heart with their easy and attractive style, and the riddle

of the *maskilim* was almost completely resolved for me. A *maskil* and a prodigy seemed to me synonymous: a *maskil* is a prodigy who knows how to write lucidly and finely in the Holy Tongue. Chance soon lent support to my conjecture. My appetite for acquiring small books had not dulled, and one of the itinerant merchants found for me the book *La-yesharim tehilah* [Glory to the righteous] by R. M[oshe] H[ayim] Luzzatto. I knew Luzzatto from his book *Mesilat yesharim* [Path of the righteous] to be a holy and God-fearing man, and if such a man had spent his time writing poems, especially fine and noble poems, then without doubt clear writing in the Holy Tongue was one of the commandments that God favored most. [. . .] Would that I might write poems such as these, or write in the manner that my father of blessed memory wrote!

And as I sat bent over the desk and for the thousandth time wrote out the script of the *mezuzah* or the verses for the *tefillin* (mechanically and without religious intention), my thoughts drifted on the wings of the imagination further and further from the parchment in front of me, and I dreamed pleasant dreams about the invisible yeshiva, which in my thoughts I conjured as an Eden, a garden of God where youths sit, every one of them loved and chosen, sitting and enjoying the radiance of the Torah that shines upon them from the head of the yeshiva, who looks like the Angel of the Lord of Hosts. It was neither from love of possessions nor love of honor that my soul yearned for the Talmud and the Holy Table. I was then a youth full of faith; strange ideas, like becoming a bridegroom in the household of a wealthy man, were already remote from me; the numerous homiletic texts that I found in the library of the scribe from Slonim had turned me into a devout believer. The sole object of my soul was to become one of the Thirty-Six secret righteous people of the world who study Torah for its own sake without any alien incentives.

I revealed my dreams to no one, not even my relative Shimon Moshe, whom I loved as a brother. I feared that I would become a laughingstock if I revealed my soul's aspiration. For in the end I was only a simple craftsman. My trade might be clean, but it was not easy; it enslaved my body and soul from morning to night. So when was I to work to advance myself, when and who was going teach me the Talmud and the Bible? How was I to guide my empty soul to become both a prodigy and a *maskil*?

Thus did I walk about, oppressed by the burden of my schemes. But I never ceased to dream and hope. The tale *La-yesharim tehilah* I knew almost by heart. This noble poem gave wings to my imagination and lifted me above the life in which I was mired. Indeed, if in the end "glory" came to "the righteous," despite all the obstacles in one's path, why should I not likewise have hope? [. . .] Suddenly some words came from the mouth of my uncle Korhin, and I fell from heaven to earth.

The booksellers had slowly begun to bring Haskalah books in their bundles (perhaps there was a certain demand for them from the liquor tax officials). The first such book to come into my hands was *Harisot beitar* [The ruins of Betar][5] by Kalman Shulman.[6] On the basis of the Talmud and the midrash, which the author cites in the introduction to the book, I could not for a moment doubt the truth of the tale just as I could not for a single moment think that the stories in the Book of Samuel and Kings were all invented. That was particularly so after I saw the characters in the book: Rabbi Akiva, Rabbi Eliezer of Modai, and Bar Kochba. For I had known all of them since long ago. The book came into my possession on the morning of Hoshanah Rabbah. The book's contents stole my heart: it was the first such story I had ever read, and also the language was precisely that of the Sabbath scripture readings. It enthralled me: "a cloud pregnant with thunderbolts nestles o'er the castle of Beitar." Would that I could someday link together words like these! With great effort I pulled back my hand from the object of my desire so as to pray with the community. For is not Hoshanah Rabbah one of the Days of Awe, according to hasidic teaching? On that day the souls of humans receive the slips with the verdicts written on Rosh Hashanah and sealed on Yom Kippur. I could barely wait until the end of the prayer to run home to read *Harisot beitar*. On Shabbat and holidays I would always take meals at the table of my uncle Korhin. During the afternoon meal in the sukkah I could not turn my eyes away from the book for a minute.

"You bring the nonsense of Kalman Shulman into the holy sukkah," my Uncle raised his voice at me, "or do you seek to uplift the sparks of the meal by his nonsense?"[7]

Had a jug of cold water been poured on my head I would not have been as startled as I was by my uncle's short words. A great tempest shook within me. "The nonsense of Kalman Shulman?" Can a book based on sayings from the Talmud and the midrash be all nonsense? Can a book written in the Holy Tongue, in the language of the Torah and the Prophets, not be sacred but rather secular? Is the book *La-yesharim tehilah* similarly secular rather than sacred, although it was written by a holy man? What is the bedrock standard that distinguishes between one book and another, between sacred and secular?

All day long I went about oppressed by the contradictions that had been aroused in my heart. At night in the study hall I asked one of the junior hasidim, who was said to have some knowledge of the kabbalah, what did he think of R. Moshe Hayim Luzzatto? And what did he think of Kalman Shulman?

"I have heard nothing about R. Kalman Shulman, but R. M[oshe] H[ayim] Luzzatto was undoubtedly a holy and pure man, who also wrote the kabbalist text called *138 Doors of Wisdom*. But the members of our close group, the Habad Hasidim, do not subscribe to his kabbalist teachings."

Why not? Because once my father (of blessed memory) was visiting the Lubavitcher Rebbe, and saw the *138 Doors of Wisdom* on his table. The Rebbe was drinking tea and placed a piece of sugar on the book. If his kabbalist teachings were true, the Rebbe would not have treated it so disdainfully as to put something on it.

This response did not calm my soul. Not long afterward one of the booksellers delivered to me the books of Mordechai Aaron Guenzburg: the *Kiryat Sefer* [1835] and the *Devir* [1844], as well as a certain small book called *Methods of Arithmetic*. I read these books in my free time with intense interest and great concentration. The Guenzburg books lit up my eyes, and the science of arithmetic became a joy and an entertainment for me. I then came to realize that there are sacred books and secular books, and that reading sacred books was obligatory while reading secular books was voluntary. But no one in Chernigov told me, nor did anyone there know that the secular books were written by *maskilim*, and that the *maskilim* were all unbelievers, and that reading them was considered a sin. I learned all that only when I came to Bobruisk.

The difficult and tedious scribe work did not leave me time to study Talmud, even on Shabbat and holidays. On my rest days I could only read *Ein Yaakov* or peruse the homiletic texts [that were not considered demanding or part of an elite education]. I had already forgotten the little Talmud that I had learned three or four years earlier. I had already despaired of becoming a prodigy (prodigies are generally little boys, whereas I was already fourteen), but continued to dream about going to a yeshiva. Blumberg's words had struck deep roots in my heart. I could not explain to myself what was pulling me with such force to the yeshiva, which I had never yet seen. I knew only one thing: staying much longer with the scribe from Slonim was something I could not do, even if I had to face

starvation. I had formerly loved and also respected that man for his fine speech and his God-fearing qualities. Then something happened that exposed his religiosity as a mere mask: when no one was looking, he saw fit to sell his soul to Satan for the price of a few copper coins. A man had ordered from him a set of phylacteries that were to be written specifically by his hand. He did not know that I was at home, and I saw him take scribe texts out of the rejects basket and insert them into the chamber of the phylacteries. At first I thought I was not seeing things properly, but I soon found that he did this routinely and was causing the public to sin by wearing nonkosher phylacteries. From that day on I could not look him straight in the face, as if I myself had done something wicked.

NOTES

1. [Yehudah Leib Benyamin Katzenelson (1846–1912), also known by his pseudonym Buki ben Yagli, was born in Chernigov. Despite early difficulties after the loss of his father, he went on to study at the yeshiva in Bobruisk, the state rabbinical school in Zhitomir, and medical school in St. Petersburg. He wrote regularly for the Jewish press and was a leader in the Society for the Promotion of Enlightenment among the Jews (Hevrat Mefitse Haskalah).]

2. [STaM: Sfarim — books of the Torah; Tefillin — phylacteries; and Mezuzot.]

3. [This is the Talmudic name for the form of Hebrew orthography found in Torah scrolls.]

4. [In other words, the *misnagdim* followed the traditional Ashkenazic liturgy, while the Hasidim followed the liturgy of the Lurianic kabbalists.]

5. [This was an adapted translation of a book by Rabbi Samuel Meir of Achingen.]

6. [Kalman Shulman (1819–1899) was a Hebrew writer and *maskil*.]

7. [The kabbalists say that the material world is a sort of shining *kelipah* (or shell), that is, a mixture of good and evil. The whole existence of the material world depends on the sparks of light that broke from the Infinite Luminescence and fell into the Other Side. Whenever a Jew gets pleasure from

the material world while being at the same time engaged in the performance of some commandment (for instance, while making a blessing over enjoyments or eating in the *sukkah* or the like), he uplifts the sparks of light that had fallen into uncleanliness and returns them to their source, and thereby builds the courage of the Heavenly Entourage.]

[109]

Ben Zion Dinur's Yeshiva Memoirs[1]

Ben Zion Dinur, *Be-'olam she-shaka: zikhronot u-reshumot mi-derekh hayyim 5644–5673* (Jerusalem: Mosad Bialik, 1958), 62–76

Two Years in the Telz Yeshiva

When I returned home I found a minyan [ten male Jews] in our house, and Father sitting *shiva* [for the seven days of mourning]: grandmother Hanna, his mother, had passed away a day before I arrived. She died suddenly in the town of Gadiach [Poltava district]. That was also the town where my father's brother lived, Leib Dinaburg, who had been exiled from Moscow, along with my uncle R. Yosef-Hayim Madievsky, the town's state rabbi. I told my father about the idea of the trip to Telz [Tel'shi in Russian; in Kovno Province] after the mourning period. He agreed to the idea. Although Mother expressed reservations about a trip "beyond the mountains of darkness," ultimately she also agreed.[2] As was customary, the matter was brought to the "family," especially the "uncles," for deliberation. My uncle the rabbi not only agreed, but decided that along with me and my brother, his son Leib (who was older than I by three years) would also go with us to the Telz yeshiva. It was decided that we three would set forth immediately after the Sukkot holiday. After Yom Kippur my father went to Gadiach to take care of my grandmother's estate. Father took me along. We lodged with Uncle Leib, and they examined me once again [along the lines described earlier in the memoir]: Uncle R. Elia Zephrin, a learned layman . . . , the town rabbi, R. Yosef (an utter fool), and R. Heshel (who aspired to the rabbinate and was a keen and sharp scholar). All the examiners had spread my name throughout town [by praising my Talmudic scholarship], and when I walked in the street, the boys would all run after me and shout: 'There he goes! There he goes!'"—which caused me discomfort as well as difficulties. Nor was my uncle at all pleased with these praises (the rabbi wrote of me that I was "one in a generation"); he was suspicious of the examiners, who were heaping praises on me in order to win the affections of my relatives, respected and influential people in town. At any rate, the recommendation letter from the rabbi seemed excessive to my uncle, and it was suggested that I travel to Romania and see R. Layzer Arlozorov, the rabbi of Romania, so that he could examine me and write me a recommendation for the Telz yeshiva. We had heard that without recommendations it was difficult to get into Telz. My brother had been given a recommendation by "the Great One," but because of my departure from Kherson I was prevented from receiving an "influential" recommendation. It was therefore decided that during the Sukkot holiday I would set out for Romania.

The son-in-law of my uncle Yossi (Madievsky), Misha Rotenberg . . . was a Romanian, who had completed a medical degree that year. He took me to Romania and treated me with great affection. That was on the second day of *hol ha-moed* Sukkot. He took me to Rabbi R. Layzer (my uncle Pinhas Ostrovsky seemed uncomfortable for some reason with the whole affair). The rabbi examined me for two hours in both Order *Moed* and tractate *Baba Kama*, as well as in the *Yoreh Deah*,[3] and gave me an enthusiastic letter of recommendation. Although he did not describe me as "one in a generation," in general his recommendation was not inferior to that of the Rabbi of Gadiach.

My uncle, R. Eliezer Moishe, was well acquainted with R. Eliezer Gordon, the head of the Telz yeshiva. He recounted that he came to know him in Warsaw, and that they had lodged together in the same hotel. Needless to say, he also gave a private letter to R. Eliezer Gordon recommending us and his son. Father's "inheritance" was the source of travel expenses for my brother and me, and on the 24th of Tishrei [right after the Sukkot holiday] we set out for Telz. Our uncle accompanied us to the train and took leave of us and his son with great warmth. The train goes straight from Khorol to Mozheika, the station from which one travels by coach to Telz. We passed the towns of Romny, Gomel, Bobruisk, Minsk, Smorgen, Vil'na — all towns that I had known of; I counted all the large and small stations and their number came to eighty-six. We left at 1:00 p.m. on Tuesday and arrived in the early morning on Thursday. The whole trip, with its transitions in landscape, climate, and even the look of the train stations and the passengers, made a deep impression on me.

And then we got off. Coachmen besieged us, offering to take us straight to Telz. If we agreed to wait for other passengers arriving in two hours on the next train from Libava,

the fare would be cheaper. My cousin did not want to wait. A coachman named Neta took us straightaway to his coach, and we set off. The hour was early, and the road went through forests; until then I had not had the chance to travel through forests. In Ukraine, my native region, there are not many forests. But here the entire road passes through forests; it is wide and pleasant (you would not find the like in our areas) and winds around — sometimes you see lakes alongside [the road]. This entire vista was new to me and made a great impression. The road goes from Mozheiki through the town of Siady (which the Jews call Shad) to Telz, and after I believe three hours, we already were in Telz. On the way Neta the coachman offered to take a detour to his house: he had a room for us and would gladly offer us lodging, and his young wife — whom he had recently married — would gladly cook for us. Negotiations with him were conducted by my cousin and my brother, and the affair ended favorably.

As soon as we arrived, we went to the yeshiva. We handed in our letters, but it turned out that the business of admission to a yeshiva is no easy matter. At the Telz yeshiva, the standard practice was for a student seeking admission to so inform the yeshiva administration in advance, to send the recommendations, and only upon receiving the acceptance letter to show up. Each student also had to guarantee a certain minimal income. The yeshiva students were not allowed "eating days" (or even "weeks") except on Sabbaths,[4] when a student could be the guest of a local inhabitant. The yeshiva administration was very strict regarding the terms of admission and never accepted students who had not applied in advance and who had not brought a letter of acceptance. Moreover, we were young, especially me; I would not celebrate my bar mitzvah until Hanukkah [some two months away], and boys of this age were not even in a yeshiva at that time. But because we had come from "a great distance" and had brought multiple recommendations, because Poltava district was a fair source of income to the yeshiva, and because we brought recommendations even from the "envoys" of the Telz yeshiva who in late summer had passed through our district towns, it was not easy for the yeshiva directors to deny us admission. Two hours later, after my cousin—the oldest among us who spoke for us all—handed over the recommendations and the letters, we were all led to the rabbi's house. The flat was extremely modest. First a small room (half of it a hallway and half a room), followed by a slightly larger room, with a small table, a window behind, and three chairs: R. Eliezer Gordon (I presume) sits in the middle, to his right R. Yosef-Leib Bloch, his brother-in-law, and to his left R. Shimon [Shkop].

We enter single file. My cousin stands before R. Eliezer, my brother is next, and I am last. They look at us, and laughter shows on all their faces.

"Why did not you apply in advance for admission and then come?"

"We did not know one had to."

"But notices were printed in *Ha-melits* and *Ha-tsefirah*."

"We do not read newspapers!"

"Your father does not read newspapers either?" R. Eliezer asks my cousin.

He remains silent. So I reply: "There were envoys from the yeshiva who visited us, they counseled and even encouraged us to go to Telz, and never told us we had to apply with a request in advance and wait for an answer!"

They all look at me, and R. Yosef Leib says: "We need to question them, one by one."

My brother and I were asked to leave the room. Ten minutes later my brother was called in, and ten minutes after that it was my turn—I had to report what I had learned. I listed the tractates: *Berachot*, the entire order of *Moed* (adding: I studied tractate *Eruvin* too, but I am weak in it; the rabbis laugh), *Ketubot*, *Baba Kama*, *Baba Metzia*, and *Hullin*. They tested me by asking me to explain the principle "a man may not transfer an object that has not come into existence": to explain the reasoning and definitions of the principle, as well as the statement "ownership of fruits is like ownership of the body."[5] I answered as best I could. I was satisfied, especially with my answer that if a man sells the fruits of a tree, even though they had not grown yet, this does not count as "something that has not come into existence," because the propensity of the tree to bear fruit preexists. But I did not know the answer to the [follow-up] question: "but he is not selling the propensity, only the fruits of one given year?" I likewise did not know how to respond [to the interjection] that my explanation would work only for "ownership of fruits is like ownership of the body," and not to the problem of "a man cannot transfer an object that has not come into existence," which stands [unresolved] . . . However, I noted precisely the location of the passages and issues I was asked about: by tractate, folio—recto and verso. In the end, I was asked by R. Eliezer: "Well, if we do admit you, to which *shiur*[6] would you like to be admitted?" "In Kherson I had studied in the third *shiur*, the highest." "So here at the fifth *shiur*?" They all broke out in laughter.

"Although," R. Eliezer concluded his exam, "you do know where the issues are stated and cited, you do not at all understand their content! The rabbis who wrote you recommendations are big ignoramuses; we would not admit them even to the first *shiur* but perhaps we will accept you to it!"

A few minutes later they informed us: my cousin and I were admitted to the first *shiur*, and my brother's admission would be postponed until after Pesach [almost six months away], since he had not applied in advance. [. . .] While we had not applied in advance either, my cousin and I did have the recommendations of the envoys, the yeshiva's representatives, and so they authorized our admission, but my brother did not have such a recommendation.

This decision caused us pain and anguish. It also stirred up emotions in town. The yeshiva was located in the great study hall [which was provided by the community] (the yeshiva's new building was then nearly completed). News about us spread and R. Ephrayim the blacksmith, a pleasant Jew, who taught a Talmud lesson to the local people every day, took a special interest in the fate of my brother, gave him a room in his home, and took it on himself to plead his case before R. Eliezer Gordon. I too went to R. Shimon and R. Yosef-Leib and complained about the unfair treatment of my brother, but to no avail. My brother was left outside the yeshiva till the end of the winter. From the yeshiva's funds I was given a monthly allotment of two rubles (that was a great sum!) and the students' aid association added another seventy kopecks a month; on Sabbaths I was a guest in the home R. Ephrayim the blacksmith, who along with his family members treated my brother and me most warmly. My visits with R. Shimon and R. Yosef Leib on the matter of my brother decided my attitude toward each of them, and apparently theirs toward me. R. Shimon greeted me warmly and told me he was glad of my visit, and even had asked the supervisor to send me to him. He wanted to tell me that my studies in the Talmud had thus far been superficial and that I had not delved into the issues as deeply as need be (which was certainly true), but that the method of study that gave me proficiency was not to be scoffed at. He sought to counsel me not to abandon my method of study entirely and to continue to learn more tractates on my own. I must make efforts to learn *Yevamot*—the tractate currently being studied in the yeshiva—as it is being taught here in Telz and to listen properly to the lectures. R. Shimon asked Nahum of Malaty [Molėtai] (Nahum, not his brother Shmuel), a student of the fourth level who was now moving to the fifth, to guide me in the study and investigation of texts (if I should need it) and to inform him from time to time

about my studies. If I wished, I could come to R. Shimon every Friday afternoon. At any rate, in a month's time I should come. He advised me to study by myself tractate *Gittin* ("Have you not learned *Ketubot*?") He very much values the virtue of love of Torah to which I am faithful and that I should preserve. It is a good and important quality. "And one of the ways to preserve it is the study you do on your own, which you need not be examined in and for which you do not have to give any account." I sensed that the friendship shown me by R. Shimon (he also asked the rebbetzin — Leah, I believe — to treat me to a cup of tea and blackberry jelly) aimed to encourage me after the [discouraging results of the] examinations and to soothe my mind over the attitude taken toward us—which, as we later learned from the students—was not to his liking and contrary to his opinion.

Only gradually did I absorb the method of study in Telz. First of all, the classes of R. Yosef-Leib and R. Shimon awakened in me an initial conception of Talmudic-juridical thinking. The influence of R. Shimon on me was especially great. His manner of lecturing, in which he would reveal, through each and every detail of the Talmudic passage, the fundamental conceptual issue: he would define it and ultimately determine a principle from it; and, in light of that principle, reconsider the details, examine in the light of these details the unfolding debates on the issue that were now to be seen in an entirely different light — one could see the remarkable artistry involved in this architecture. [. . .] In each lesson I had the experience of new doors opening before me. During the two years I studied [at Telz], I not only did not miss a single lesson by R. Shimon, but I had the privilege in my regular visits to his home to discuss his novel interpretations with him, to come to him with questions. To be sure, he would sometimes note if I did not properly grasp his reasoning or if I did not draw from his words the proper conclusion on the overall issue at hand. Yet, in general he would listen, smile, comment, and ask questions (not necessarily about what he covered in class). My happiest day in Telz was the day when Nahum of Malaty told me that R. Shimon had praised me, noting that he values the combination of excellent memory, quickness of comprehension, and delving spirit [that comes] from a desire to penetrate to the essence of others' thought (all powers with which I was blessed). That was a joyous day for me. Not only because I admired R. Shimon, but because essentially similar things had also been written about me by R. Eliezer of Romny (Arlozorov), things that, at the time, had aroused ridicule from the yeshiva heads (both R. Eliezer Gordon and R. Yosef-Leib Bloch).

The very study in the Telz yeshiva was a powerful experience: a large hall, broad and wide, row after row of benches in four columns along the hall and *shtenders* [lecterns] in front of each seat on the bench. Not a single place was vacant. Some three hundred and fifty young men were studying passionately, with the sounds of Torah filling the hall's expanse. [. . .] Narrow lanes ran through the whole hall between the columns of benches; the tall supervisor, R. Leib Hasman, whose head always tilted to one side, wanders among these aisles and casts an eye on this or that student; or one of the students stands up to look up another tractate. And so on, day after day, from dawn to late at night. I, the youngest of them all, my voice too is lifted in this mighty choir. [. . .]

It pained me that my brother was not admitted, and my heart was bitter toward the yeshiva administrators. "The rabbis respect only the wealthy." I felt that an injustice had been done to my brother. And my brother of course felt it all the more. He did not visit the lectures, and studied on his own in the *beit midrash* all winter long. It was my job to pass to him each and every lecture, with its novel interpretations and problems — in this way I introduced my brother to the "Telz way" even

before he entered the yeshiva. For the sake of that "way," we also studied *Kezot ha-hoshen*.[7] Actually my brother insisted on it. The book was expensive, and my brother borrowed an edition and decided to copy it out in his fine handwriting. Only after extended arguments with me did my brother agree that first we would study it and then, after each subject and issue, decide what was worthy of copying. We followed this practice for the whole two years that we were in Telz. Each and every day we delved into *Kezot ha-hoshen*, *Netivot ha-mishpat* (by R. Yaakov of Lissa),[8] the innovations of R. Akiva Eiger, and several other texts. In the course of our reading we determined what was worth copying, and my brother would copy it. We thus formed a sort of *shita mekubetzet* [anthology] of innovations in the "Telz manner," which acquired a reputation among our friends. . . .

My apartment mates were, as noted, the brothers Shmuel and Nahum from the town of Malaty near Vil'na. This Nahum, who then was already twenty-three years old and who had been released from the army two years earlier because of his short height, treated me with brotherly love. My budget was tight, as was his, and he would order lunch for the both of us; instead of meat the landlady would buy lungs, intestines, feet, and bones, all sorts of leftovers and make a soup out of them as well as a sort of meatloaf. At Nahum's instruction I would buy saccharine (very cheaply) instead of sugar, and with a few kopeks we would fill our needs for months. Very tactfully, he would also examine, week by week and sometimes more frequently, the extent of my progress in studies, both in tractate *Yevamot* and in tractate *Gittin*. He would also oversee my conduct: he would remark, as if in passing, on my attitude toward people, on my way of approaching people great and small; and he would also caution me about my "recklessness," my excessive haste in responding, and my sharp comments about friends, people, and opinions. . . .

Although I knew that he was genuinely interested in me, I also knew that the main thrust of his interest was on behalf of R. Shimon. This was the cause of satisfaction and happiness, but it also inhibited me: I felt that I was constantly under the eye of a supervisor, subject to the oversight "of one who sees and is not seen." I once hinted at this to Nahum. From experience I have learned the truth of the saying, "Let the fear of Heaven be upon you as the fear of flesh and blood":[9] it is not hard for us to imagine the fear of flesh and blood when one is constantly subject, night and day, to his supervision. Actually I meant my words to refer more to Shmuel, Nahum's elder brother, than to Nahum himself.

Shmuel was the complete opposite of his brother: his hair was yellow, his eyes blue — visible even through his glasses — and his face was tiny. He already had the certification to teach from the "elders" among the students and from the heads of the "moral masters" in the yeshiva. He was not at all pleased with me and did not share the special attitude toward me either on the part of his brother or R. Shimon. He would express this openly. "You," Shmuel once said seriously, "are too spoiled. You are used to being shown affection but are not an only child! A person cannot rely on anyone but himself. You always like to be with others and enjoy their company. You have too much fondness for fancy words and for joking. Life is serious, and a person should not enjoy laughter too much! This is the gateway to flippancy and even to frivolity! Do you think that someone who knows how to joke around, to be a smart aleck, is really smart? Sometimes he is a complete idiot!" He proposed that each day I study a chapter of *Mesilat yesharim*, and even gave me as a gift a copy of *Heshbon ha-nefesh* of Mendel Lefin, in the Vilna edition. [...] The hint about "the fear of flesh and blood" that I had made to Nahum marked the first step toward my departure from the apartment. The official reason was that with my brother's acceptance to

the yeshiva, I would be living with him in the same room.

My visits with R. Shimon did not cease afterward. I recall that during one visit R. Shimon noticed that a button from my coat was torn off and ripped out. He called to me and asked me to come closer to him. Looking at the coat, he said: "Did you get into a fight with your brother yesterday?" I blushed and confessed. "Did it actually come to blows? With hands?" I blushed even more. I confessed. R. Shimon grinned and said: "You see, the button is torn off with part of the cloth; it seems that force was used. [...]" "Leah," called R. Shimon to the rebbetzin, "could you please sew a button on for Ben Zion the Khorolian. I would not want him to walk about in the street in a coat without a button.... It is not fitting for a boy from the yeshiva of Telz!" I understood that "it is not fitting" referred not just to the button....

The years 1897–98 were years of upheaval in the Telz yeshiva: the yeshiva moved to its new building and began to teach *musar* studies, which fact aroused opposition among the students. There was a student "strike" and disturbances; students were expelled, and the Haskalah and Zionism spread among the students. The yeshiva heads fought against these trends....

The day that we entered the new building of the yeshiva was celebrated with special religious rites: the yeshiva heads and the students fasted, prayed, and recited special psalms; the Torah scrolls were moved festively to the new quarters. R. Eliezer Gordon delivered sermons twice that day, the evening prayers were recited in public, there were special study sessions and rotations, so that Torah study in the yeshiva would not cease even for an instant. As I regularly would wake up early, I had a noticeable place among the students of my study group and a role in arranging these rotations. The yeshiva administration made efforts to introduce the *musar* studies into the yeshiva, both on account of the importance of the subject in itself and as a barrier against the Haskalah and Zionism that had begun to spread among the students. A yeshiva supervisor, R. Leib Hasman of Chelm, one of the prominent *musar* men, [*musarniks*] was invited and students were made to study, each day between afternoon and evening prayers, a half hour, I believe, of *musar* texts: *Mesilat yesharim*, *Hovot ha-levavot*, the *Iggeret ha-musar* of R. Israel of Salant, *Heshbon ha-nefesh* of R. Mendel Lefin (which is actually a revised version of the [ethical program] in [the *Autobiography*] by Benjamin Franklin) and several other *musar* texts. This new arrangement aroused opposition among the students. One evening, while the students were studying, and the sound of Torah could be heard at great distances, a stone was thrown at one of the windows — the pane was smashed. This was a sign. A tumult ensued. All the older students said: Sh . . . sh . . . and studies ceased. Here and there lights went out, as if from the wind. The supervisors went about helpless, and ten minutes later R. Eliezer Gordon entered. In the storm and tempest he walked through the aisles. Who, who is it? Let the claimants, the agitators come out! Those responsible for the halt in the study of Torah! The boy from Kursk left. And a student from the third *shiur*. I did not hear what he said, although it happened close to me — all of a sudden I heard R. Eliezer's voice: Agent for evil!! And afterward: two ringing slaps in the face, the echoes of which filled the cavern of the yeshiva. [. . .]

The boy from Kursk and his friend, the boy from Krozhi , were expelled from the yeshiva. The yeshiva was closed, and students roamed about town. The townspeople said: the rabbis' "Cossacks" have appeared on the streets. Two or three days later studies resumed. The student leaders of the insurrection "graciously" accepted their traveling arrangements; *musar* study became voluntary, not obligatory. Things went back to normal. [. . .]

The first person who aroused in me a desire and eagerness to look for Haskalah books and even showed me a way I might find them was R. Eliezer Gordon, whose sermons would polemicize against the *maskilim*. The rabbi specifically referred to Graetz and Weiss; he often cited Wessely and praised his *Sefer ha-midot*. In his sermons he similarly liked to mention the names of other *maskilim*, the early ones.

I recollect how the rabbi burst into fury in one sermon at Graetz, who writes simply in his book *History of the Jews* about the Israelites' crossing of the Jordan River: "Joshua took the nation across via the Jordan on one dry day in spring." First, argued R. Eliezer, how does Graetz know that this was a "dry day"; might that day not have been overcast? What is not known he knows, but what is known he conceals: "took the people across via the Jordan," instead of "across the Jordan"! He conceals the miracle that is spoken of in detail in Joshua![10] We could perhaps accept, continued the rabbi, the fact that Graetz does not tell about the miracle of the parting of the Red Sea. That cannot be held against him: the parting of the Red Sea also involved the sheep and cattle that the Israelites took with them on leaving Egypt. Did the cattle and sheep behold the parting of the Red Sea? It is not enough to have lived at the time of a miracle; one must be at the level of fitness to behold the miracle.[11] [. . .] Another time the rabbi battled with [Isaak Hirsh] Weiss over the [rabbinic notion of] *halakhah le-Moshe mi-Sinai* [a law of Moses from Sinai, which Weiss understood in a non-traditional manner], and the oral law more generally, and also mentioned the book by Zechariah Frankel, *Darkei ha-mishnah*. From this I concluded that numerous Haskalah books could be found in the rabbi's home. I made friends with the rabbi's son Shmuel, who was a little younger than I, and he would regularly give me books to read. But he would lend me the books only for short periods — for one night, one Shabbat and no longer than that. That was inconvenient. I recall that Shmuel once informed me they had received an excellent book: *Uncle Tom's Cabin*, a tale about the liberation of the Negro slaves, translated by Avraham Zinger. He was prepared to lend me the book for one night only. I took the book and read it all night without stopping. In the morning I managed to get dressed and even before the yeshiva's beadle came to wake up the students; I was finished. My brother was not happy about the fact that I did not keep the book for one more day so that he could read it too. He was also concerned that I did not sleep the whole night. The beadle who "woke" the students went out of his way to praise me, that I was "properly diligent," and that I was ready before he came to wake me up. My brother teased: you are a classic example of "a sinner who benefits [from his sin]!"

Interest in the Haskalah also encouraged us to read newspapers, which were permitted. Fifteen students had a joint subscription. My brother and I, whose contribution was the smallest, were the fourteenth out of the fifteen [to read the paper], which reached us two weeks after its arrival—that is, almost eighteen days after it was printed. Still, we were informed about all that was happening in the contemporary world, especially all the details in the arguments about the Dreyfus case.

I received a very strong push toward the Haskalah during my visit to Romania for two weeks in the month of Elul, 5657 [1897; the month before the High Holidays]. I went home for the holidays; my brother stayed in Telz. On the road I was invited to be a guest in the home of Uncle Pinhas Ostrovsky. He had a pleasant residence; especially pleasant was his enclosed porch, three of whose walls were made of glass. Each wall was framed with multiple panes of glass. His library was especially well appointed and amazed me with its arrangement: each cabinet contained books of a different kind.

The first contained the Bible and commentators, along with language and grammar books; the Talmud and posekim, together with all sorts of midrash books (many of which I had never heard of); and a special container full of responsa.

The second cabinet, which was large and handsome, was full of Haskalah books (again, I had not heard of many of them). These included many new books that still emitted the smell of printer's ink.

The third cabinet of responsa texts was actually full of books that had belonged to my grandfather, with each and every book bearing the explicit inscription: "Zvi Yaakov Halevi Dinaburg, the Rabbi of the Holy Community of Khorol."

I was a guest in my uncle's home for ten days. I rose early, as was my habit. I would sit on the swing (which I saw for the first time in my life) and read. Over these ten days I read *Knesset Israel* by Shaul Pinchas Rabinowitz,[12] the volumes of *He-asif*, the *Pardes*, the *Luah Ahiasaf*, and historical works: Ben Avigdor's [Abraham Leib Shalkovich] *Lifne arba me'ot shanah*, *Emek ha-arazim*, *Rav le-hoshia*, and the *Zikhronot le-vet David*, booklets by [Avraham Shalom] Friedberg, and his *Korot ha-yehudim bi-Sefarad*.[12] My uncle's son-in-law was Yehudah Leib Gamzu—a poet who published poems and even two plays in Hebrew (*Abarbanel* and *Ezra o shivat Tsiyyon*, which were partly translated from Russian) and a regular contributor to *Ha-tsefirah*, under the pseudonym "the Lion in the Group," (he also wrote a few articles against Ahad Ha'am). He was held in high regard by my uncle. My uncle, Gamzu, and the whole household were at first entertained and amused at the sight of the hunger attack that made me devour these books, but after a while began to regard it negatively.

While I was sitting and reading early one morning, my aunt found me and began preaching morals at me. She told me that my grandfather, Zvi Yaakov, also used to rise early and that this had caused his illness and early death (he died at the age of twenty-eight). "If you behave as he does (heaven forbid), what happened to him will happen to you.[13] My father, Grandfather Abraham, was orderly: he ate on time, studied on time, and went to bed on time." She told of this at lunch, and my uncle said that he does not want my stay with him to last a full month as he had thought, especially because I am not engaged in Torah study (as he had expected) and I read Haskalah books — for this we already have many "little masters."

My brother was taken by the Haskalah even more than I was. He made friends with sons of several families of Telz's known *maskilim* . . . and they would often pursue him until matters came to the attention of R. Yosef-Leib. Once I even went to R. Yosef-Leib to put in a good word for him. The rabbi received me very nicely, reassured me that nothing bad would happen to me, and said that he did not accept malicious reports. "However, before you make guarantees on his behalf, please make sure that you will not be in need of a defender and guarantor yourself."

The Haskalah and "external books" also caused a rift between us and our cousin. The latter was quite alien to all that. He studied persistently and was distinguished by his fear of heaven; R. Leib Hasman drew satisfaction from him. Our cousin saw it as his duty to preach morals to us and to write about us to his rabbi father and say that "external books" were capturing our hearts. These two things caused us to separate completely and to break off relations.

My departure from the yeshiva was not like that of my brother. My brother got his bon voyage in "a clear and firm manner": you are to leave and never return. If you submit a request to return, we will inform you that you cannot return. As for myself, they repeatedly advised me not to leave. R. Yosef-Leib even called me specially and urgently advised me not to leave the yeshiva with my brother. Once I announced that I was leaving, they told me that if I should ever wish to return, I would of course have to apply and to wait for a re-sponse. But they hinted to me that I would be accepted because of my "love of Torah." My farewell from R. Shimon was most sad. He understood that I would not be returning and was sorry for it. He said to me that from the beginning, when I first came, he was convinced that I should be separated from my brother for the good of us both. He was sorry that I had left Nahum of Malaty. Maybe he was wrong for not intervening right away. He blessed me, saying that "the love of Torah" would never leave me, and would help me overcome obstacles, mainly internal "obstacles." He walked me to the door and shook my hand, and urged me to think well on the matter of my return, and that if I decided to come back to Telz and to apply in writing to the yeshiva, I needed to write him a private letter to tell him about this immediately and perhaps even sooner. From that I inferred that I had my own share of critics among the yeshiva administration. The image of R. Shimon has stayed with me all my life. When I reached fifty and they organized a party for me in Beit ha-Kerem [in Jerusalem], I mentioned his name in gratitude and was glad to receive congratulations from Grodno from R. Shimon himself, bearing his signature and saying that he has not forgotten his young student "Ben Zion the Khorolian."

NOTES

1. [Ben Zion Dinur (Dinaburg; 1884–1973) was born in Ukraine, and attended the Telz yeshiva for the two years described here. By his late teens he was involved with the Zionist movement, eventually achieving some prominence there. He left the Empire to study in Germany and Switzerland, returning to become a lecturer in Odessa in 1920. In 1921 he immigrated to Palestine, where he would come to serve in both academia (at the Hebrew University) and, later, the Israeli government, serving in the Knesset and as Minister of Education and Culture.]

2. [Dinur's family also lived in Poltava district in Ukraine.]

3. [One of the four parts of the *Shulhan Arukh*.]

4. ["Eating days" refers to the practice of having yeshiva students eat at a different house each day of the week. This was a way that the community could support yeshiva students. In general, the larger Lithuanian yeshivot eschewed the practice, preferring to keep the students within the ambit of the yeshiva as much as possible.]

5. [See BT, *Gittin* 47b. The issues here are very complex, and defy short explanation. "Fruits" here refers to the rights to the fruits a field produces without owning the field. The question is whether for the purpose of bringing the first fruits one recites the pilgrim's confessional (Deuteronomy 26). One opinion is that one does because "fruits" (i.e., rights to the fruits) is like ownership of the "body" (i.e., the field itself), while another opinion rejects this, and says that one does not recite the confessional as if one were the owner.]

6. [The word admits of more than one translation, but here "level" or "grade" seems what is intended. Telz was known for having multiple levels —up to five—and placing younger students, like Dinur, in the lower levels to start.]

7. [This is a commentary on the fourth part of the *Shulhan Arukh*, by Aryeh Leib Heller of Galicia (1745–1812).]

8. [This too is a commentary on the fourth part of the *Shulhan Arukh*, known, inter alia, for its sharp attacks on the *Ketzot*. Yaakov of Lissa lived from 1760–1832.]

9. [*Berakhot* 28b.]

10. [See Joshua 3–4.]

11. [The implication is that Graetz is no more discerning than the cattle and sheep present at the crossing of the sea.]

12. [1845–1910, Rabinowitz, best known today as the Hebrew translator of Graetz's History, was the editor of the annual, *Knesset Israel* from 1886–1888. *He-asif* (The Gatherer), edited by N. Sokolev, was published in Warsaw from 1884–1889 and 1893–94. *Pardes* was a literary Hebrew journal published in Odessa from 1892–1896, while the *Luah Ahi'asaf* was an almanac, published from 1893–1895 by Ben Avigdor, the author of historical tales entitled *Four Hundred Years Ago*. The other books on the shelves included translations of historical works into Hebrew by Avraham Shalom Friedberg including Grace Aguilar's *Vale of Cedars*; Ascher Sammter's *The Rabbi of Liegnitz*; and two compilations: *Memoirs of the House of David* and *The History of the Jews in Spain.*]

13. [It is worth noting that Dinur actually lived to 89.]

Jewish Private Schools

[110]

The Berman School for Jewish Children in St. Petersburg (1865–84)

RGIA, f. 733, op. 189, d. 170, ll. 2–3, 23–29, 65–66.

"Petition of Anna Berman to the Minister of Education, Dmitrii Andreevich Tolstoi (24 January 1867)"

With the permission of the all merciful Sovereign Emperor, the Ministry of Education provides an annual monetary allowance, levied from the candle tax, to the many male and female proprietors of Jewish boarding schools (*pansiony*) and schools to encourage my coreligionists to [receive] an education.

I have the good fortune of running an educational establishment in St. Petersburg for Jewish girls — the majority of whom are children of soldiers who are serving [in the army] or who have retired. In the short time of my institution's existence, it has received approval from educational authorities. However, due to the scarcity of resources (which consists of fees collected from the pupils, whose parents — as noted above — are poor), I am finding it extremely difficult not only to promote the school's further development but even to maintain its present condition.

Thus, on the basis of the imperial permission cited above, I take the liberty to appeal to the merciful consideration of Your Excellency and to ask humbly about the allocation of an annual allowance from the Jewish candle tax to maintain my educational establish-ment in St. Petersburg for Jewish girls [. . .] and to take into consideration that the cost of every educational institution in the capital exceeds that of those in the provinces.

"Memorandum of the Supervisor of the St. Petersburg School District to the Department of Education (25 July 1868)"

Owing to the letter from the Department of Education on 19 July (number 5896), regarding the allocation of an annual monetary subsidy from the Jewish candle tax to support Berman's Jewish school, I have the honor to inform the Department of the following:

(1) Mr. Berman opened the school for Jewish boys in 1865, and his wife has run the school for girls since 1866.

(2) The school for boys consists of three classes and a fourth preparatory class (for entry into the first class of school at this institution). Since 1865 it has had 195 students; of these, 22 and perhaps even more,[1] have enrolled in a private or general educational institution, including the gymnasium, even in the fourth class, to continue their education. Upon completing studies at this Jewish school, many enter a workshop. At present, the school has 71 students, of whom 51 attend gratis and 20 students pay a fee.

(3) The school for girls had 113 students, but at present has 49. The other students withdrew: 17 to enter into a general educational institution; 3 to learn the needle trade in a shop; and 44 to return to their parental homes. Of the 49, only 19 pay a fee.

(4) The school provides instruction in:
- Jewish subjects (with four teachers): Jewish law, the translation of prayers, rituals, biblical history, the Jewish language [Yiddish], and Jewish calligraphy;
- general subjects (with eight male and female teachers): Russian language, arithmetic, geography, history, natural history, German language, calligraphy, and needlework for girls. In addition, for those who desire to enter a gymnasium, lessons are given in French and Latin.

(5) For the maintenance of these pupils, annual expenditures include:
- salaries for teachers of Jewish subjects: 1,176 rubles
- salaries for teachers of general subjects: 1,112 rubles
  total: 2,288 rubles (14 rubles per class per year)
- rent for the apartments with courtyards: 1,200 rubles
- lighting: 72 rubles
- domestic servants: 288 rubles
- upkeep of class furniture and other housekeeping expenses: 250 rubles
  Total: 4,098 rubles

To meet these expenditures, the school receives: 1,560 rubles from Mr. Gintsburg's philanthropy, 1,740 rubles from the [St. Petersburg Jewish] community, and 1,000 rubles from instructional fees—for a total of 4,300 rubles. Consequently, the portion that remains for the directors of the school [Lazar and Anna Berman] for all their labor comes to only 200 rubles. However, these revenues cannot be considered reliable and are subject to change. Moreover, [the revenues] are paid in an extremely unreliable manner. For example, the community currently owes 700 rubles, but there is no one to whom one can appeal: the Jewish community of St. Petersburg does not have an organized structure and its members constantly change. In case of instructional fees, 200 rubles are overdue. Hence, instead of receiving something for their labors, the directors fall into debt as a result.

(6) During my personal inspection on 15 July, I found the school in the following condition:
- The third class had eight pupils. In the Russian class, the reading was sufficiently fluent and intelligible; for the most part, pronunciation was completely satisfactory. During the dictation of a letter with twelve lines, only one of the pupils made a mistake, which he himself corrected. In grammatical and logical analysis, the students' progress was satisfactory. They can make themselves understood in Russian without difficulty, although with mistakes. In arithmetic they have covered the rules of alligations [complex algebra]. The students' knowledge of the function of fractions was satisfactory, but they had not properly mastered the solution of math problems related to the rule of three [a method for solving proportions]. In my opinion, this is because the students are shown only the method of solving math problems by means of ratios. In geography the pupils' progress was not demonstrated as adequate because of the frequent turnover in teachers and the scarcity of school books.
- In the second class, the pupils read Russian and translated the Bible into Russian—in general, satisfactorily. The students' progress in calligraphy was satisfactory, but they are not yet trained to keep their notebooks neat.
- Students in the third class read Russian and recounted what they had read well. They experience a shortage of textbooks and teaching materials.

- The premises of the school for all classes — for both boys and girls — was satisfactory.

Based on all the above information, I find the school to be beneficial and therefore meriting support from the government. Since those educated there are the children of Jews from the western provinces, their parents pay part of the fixed candle tax. I therefore consider it my duty to request the allocation of an annual subsidy for the school, at least the same amount as that set to support state Jewish schools at the primary level. The money should be used predominantly for instruction in general subjects. I also deem it necessary to attach a list of male and female pupils with a report about the condition of the school.[2]

"Petition of Lazar and Anna Berman to the Minister of Education (28 July 1872)"

The number of poor Jewish children of both sexes studying at our two schools for boys and girls in St. Petersburg has increased each year. At present, they have reached 200 — three times more than before. This circumstance forced us to open a preparatory class in each school for incoming students who are not at all familiar with the Russian language, given that instruction in all classes is conducted in Russian.

In addition, we considered the need to introduce supplementary courses at our school beyond the obligatory subjects — such as *Latin* for boys (who are preparing to enter gymnasium), *French* for girls, and *Russian history* for children of both sexes. The constant increase in the number of students, the addition of preparatory classes, and the expansion of the curriculum entails an increase in expenditures to maintain our school. Rent for the premises with heating costs us more than 2,000 rubles a year. The salaries of the teachers (the majority of whom are university educated and individuals who have completed their studies at other institutions of higher

education), whose share amounts to a total of 175 lessons a week, in addition to covering other expenses to maintain both schools — amounts to approximately 5,000 rubles annually. The total comes to 7,000 rubles.

Our school's resources fall far short of the existing demands. Apart from the 3,600 rubles, which we receive as a voluntary gift from the St. Petersburg Jewish community for the education of its scholarship recipients, the school has no other reliable sources of income at its disposal. The dues collected from incoming students who pay an instructional fee are insignificant and one cannot count on this because of the proliferation of illegal *melamdim*, who lure away the resources of paying students to their *hadarim*. Under such unfavorable conditions, our work educating the Jewish youth in the capital not only goes unrewarded but will lead to the utter exhaustion of our personal resources (which, although extremely insignificant, were accumulated with difficulty during our twelve years of hard labor in educational activities in Mitav, Kurliand province). This constant shortage of resources undermines the stability of the school's existence.

Meanwhile, the benefit that the school brings in pedagogical terms is recognized by all people who are sincerely sympathetic to public education and will corroborate the following considerations: without these schools, the uneducated class of St. Petersburg Jews, because of their own prejudice, would decide not to send their children directly to a non-Jewish school, but would continue to entrust their education to an ignorant *melamed*. In our school, all the subjects of curricular courses, excluding Bible, are taught in Russian. Thus Jewish children at completely familiar with the Russian language at [our] schools; otherwise they would not be able to understand the Russian teachers at Russian educational institutions [in the future]. Finally, in favor of our schools is the fact that after completing their studies, the children demonstrate sufficient preparation to enter the third year of gymnasium or other secondary educational institution, or they apply the acquired knowledge to practical life. In this way our schools serve to bring Russian literacy to Jewish society in the capital—to serve both the future good of the students and the political demands of the country. Moreover, this serves as a transitional stage from the ossified condition of the Jews to a position that corresponds more to the present conditions of public life.

Apart from these considerations, one further circumstance compels our schools to seek complete success in the future: these schools are essentially the sole educational institutions in the capital open to children of poor Jewish parents,[3] who lack the means to give their children the best education and left them in deep ignorance before the founding of our school. Moreover, almost all the parents who resettle here are frequently from the western regions, where they appeal for monetary resources to educate Jewish youth (which they obtain from the candle tax). [...] Indeed, even the private Jewish schools in the provinces constantly receive a subsidy of more than 600 rubles per year from the government, while maintaining a similar school in the capital costs much more.

These considerations and the repeated, favorable assessment by the supervisor of the St. Petersburg School District about the benefit of our schools (which are recognized as worthy of encouragement and considerable support on the part of the government) give us the audacity to ask Your Excellency humbly to allocate us an annual subsidy of 800 rubles for each school—a total of 1,600 rubles a year—from Jewish capital [that is, the candle tax].

The sympathy and repeated visits by Your Excellency at our schools instill hope in us that Your gracious attention will not allow us to perish from insufficient funding and, in accordance with our petition, that you will provide for them in the near future for the benefit of future Jewish citizens of the Russian state.[4]

NOTES

1. [It is impossible to determine this number precisely at the present time due to the absence of information.]

2. [The Ministry allotted a one-time payment of 400 rubles each to Lazar and Anna Berman (800 rubles in total) for their respective schools.]

3. [The class registers show 159 males and 128 females for two years (1871 and 1872). Of the total of 287 pupils, only 10 (7 males and 3 females) came from the merchant or townspeople estates; 120 (46 males and 74 females) were from such categories as artisans, shop workers, and the like. The majority of students (157—106 males and 51 females) were from soldiers' families.]

4. [The state apparently granted the annual subsidy until 1884, when a letter from Lazar Berman to the Ministry of Education expresses dismay about the state's abrupt change in policy and refusal to renew support. The timing of this change coincides with the imposition of strict Jewish quotas in general Russian schools.]

[111]

Complaint of the Jews of Tel'she against Yehudah Leib Gordon's Treatment of Students (1867)

RGIA, f. 733, op. 189, d. 232, ll. 1–2.

"Superintendent of the Vil'na School District to the Department of Public Education (27 November 1867)"

Regarding the communication of the Department (31 October, number 8316), in the absence of the superintendent of [the educational] district, I have the honor to report that based on the order of the superintendent, the director of the Shavli schools [M. V. Fursov] conducted an inquiry in September regarding [. . .] a complaint by the Jews of Tel'she against the supervisor of the local state Jewish school of [Yehudah Leib] Gordon.[1] This inquiry seemed all the more necessary because, simultaneously with the complaint, the superintendent received a telegram, and then a petition from the Tel'she rabbi, merchants, and deputies of local community that declared: "Sympathizing with the success of the education of Jews and finding all the measures and actions of [Yehuda Leib] Gordon at managing both the state and also the private girls' schools to be prudent, successful, and fully in conformity with the goals of the state and their own wishes, they deem it their duty of honor and justice to protest against the so-called complaint of a handful of fanatics."

Upon arriving in the town of Tel'she, Fursov had the opportunity to be persuaded—by the testimony of all the Russian communities and the best representatives of the Jewish community—that Gordon's activities and his honest attitude toward his responsibilities were irreproachable. The director received a no less favorable testimony from the deputies of the Jewish community, excluding the merchant Khaim Raivid, the state rabbi, one of the *melamdim*, Lunts (who, as it turned out, is the sole *melamed* in Tel'she who knows Russian). Then the director summoned those who signed the telegram with the complaint against Gordon that had been addressed to the superintendent: the Jews Vul'f Press, Ion Kan, and Itsik Kopel. Instead of heeding the summons, they rudely replied that they did not want to speak with the director. At the second summons (transmitted through the police), they did not corroborate the denunciation that they had made. When the signatures of the petition to the superintendent were presented to the local rabbi and to deputies of the Jewish community for verification, the latter declared that those who [allegedly] signed—David Kagan, Itsik Kopel, Itsik Levin, Zal'man Sandler, and Kusil Litvin—do not know how to write. [. . .]

Among the eighteen people, the majority of those who signed the petition declared themselves to be deputies of the community. When Director Fursov declared that he had already seen the deputies of the Jewish community elected to this rank on a legal basis, the tax collector [Yankel] Gutman, in the name of all those at hand, declared that this is none of the Jewish deputies' business, and that they elected their own deputies to negotiate with the director. Without acknowledging their authority, Mr. Fursov nevertheless asked them, as private individuals, what business did they have with him? Khaim Raivid replied that if the director did not want to talk to them as deputies, then they declined to give any explanation. However, at the insistent declaration of the director that he would not permit insolent Jews to speak to him with impunity and demanded that they explain their claims, the Jews who had come proposed to talk in the name of the tax collector Gutman. Without permitting him to explain before his turn, the director asked each Jew individually what did he have against Gordon? It turned out that not one could express any claim against the supervisor. When it came to Gutman's turn, he—after many general phrases that did not prove anything—accused Gordon of allegedly saying that *it is possible to eat beef with milk*.[2] This conversation, according to Fursov, clarified for him sufficiently from whom the case originated and who had instigated the fanatics' complaint against Gordon. From the testimony of local Russian people and well-intentioned Jews, and from private information collected by the director, the instigators of the whole affair—which paralyzes the good measures taken by the government with respect to Jews—are Khaim Raivid and Gutman. These two individuals, having a fanatic crowd behind them, do whatever they want in Tel'she; this conclusion, as reported by the director, is confirmed incidentally by the military chief Fon Tsigler, the gendarme officer Martynov, the chairman of the verification commission (Voronov), the excise tax supervisor Golubev, Rabbi Khazanovich, the Jewish merchants Neftalin and Berman, and the deputies Bai, Gruslavskii, and Shul'man. The instigators Raivid and Gutman gather supporters not only from among Tel'she residents but also visitors; for example, those who signed the petition—Abram Shliom, Eliash Braude, and Vul'f Kliaf—are not Tel'she residents, and the latter does not even have a passport.

From the inquiry conducted in this manner, the director Fursov can discern no grounds for accusing the supervisor of the Tel'she state school, [Yehudah Leib] Gordon, of illegal wrongdoing. On the contrary, his accusers are exposed of violating his good name through libel and slander, for which the main instigators must be subjected to legal punishment.

Guided by this consideration (in the absence of the superintendent but based on his order), I am referring this case to the chief official of Kovno province, asking him to observe the instructions given to him and to put an end to the slanderous actions on the part of the named Jews and to press charges against them for the slanderous petition that they submitted. It is my duty to add that Gordon, who has been in service since 1863, has always—both by his manner of thinking and also his willingness to serve—been among the best Jewish teachers in the Vil'na School District.

NOTES

1. [The petition accused Yehuda Leib Gordon of such abuse as "the severe beating of one student, Nison Press, who was whipped so mercilessly by the supervisor Gordon that he lay in a sick bed for two weeks. Only he did not die from this one beating and feverish condition, which seized Press's entire body from extraordinary fright." They also accused Gordon of being a renegade from Judaism: "In the first place, he never attends synagogue, on the Sabbath he cooks his food, writes, and smokes cigarettes, which is patently forbidden in the law of Moses" (RGIA, f. 733, op. 189, d. 232, ll. 1–2).]

2. [In other words, he accused Gordon of saying that one could violate the laws of kashrut, which prohibit the consumption of milk and meat together.]

[112]

Petition of Eidlia Liubich of Grodno for Permission to Teach Hebrew Calligraphy to Jewish Girls in Grodno (1892)

RGIA, f. 733, op. 190, d. 449, l. 1.

"Report of the Superintendent of Vil'na School District to the Ministry of Education (31 July 1892)"

The townswoman Eidlia Liubich, a resident of Grodno, submitted to me a petition in which she explained that, after the law of 3 April 1892 on "secret teaching" went into effect, it became evident that the [Jews] in Grodno were striving to educate their children on a legal basis. She requests permission to teach Hebrew calligraphy to up to twenty Jewish girls in her apartment. She attached (among other documents) an attestation from the Grodno state rabbi that she is a pious woman and that she has good Hebrew calligraphic handwriting and the skills to teach the art of Hebrew calligraphy. In addition, she has free command of colloquial Russian.

According to the law, Jews may open their own private schools or societies to educate their youth in the sciences and arts and in the study of confessional principles. For my part, I have drawn up regulations, in agreement with the general governor of Vil'na, Kovno, and Grodno about the procedures for applying the law of 3 April 1892. It provides for various kinds of special schools that cannot teach general subjects without special permission under threat of legal accountability before the law. In general, the existing regulations do not prohibit opening a school of the kind that Liubich desires to establish. However, there are no exact instructions regarding this type of school.

In view of some preliminary instructions on Liubich's petitions, I have the honor to ask the Department of Education humbly to give orders on how to resolve this petition.[1]

NOTE

1. [The Ministry of Education noted that, "the art of Hebrew calligraphy is absent as a subject that is taught at the existing private Jewish educational institutions in Grodno. Various types of unknown people teach it without the knowledge and permission of the educational authorities." RGIA, f. 733, op. 190, d. 449, l. 3. Given her attempt to secure permission legally (in contrast to other teachers), Liubich received permission on 26 November 1892.]

[113]

A Private School for Jewish Boys in Siberia (1896)

RGIA, f. 733, op. 190, d. 589, ll. 1–2, 4–4 ob.

"Petition of the Teacher Naum (Nakhman) Dashevskii to the Minister of Education (19 January 1896)"

Upon arriving at Irkutsk in 1879 to enroll in a local cadet school, I satisfactorily passed the examination as a privately funded student[1] but was not accepted *because I am a Jew.*[2] Finding myself without any means in a strange town, I was directed by Providence to become a teacher in order to live: I began to teach Russian grammar to Jewish boys. God blessed my work. Given the shortage of elementary schools in Irkutsk, I was useful and lived comfortably. In 1887 the superintendent of the Western Siberian School District conferred on me the rank of private teacher, and I continued this work, which in my opinion is sacred. I taught the poor for free.

The long years of strenuous work ruined my health, and it became difficult for me to visit my students in their homes. I therefore appealed to the chief inspector of the Eastern Siberian Schools[3] with a petition for permission to open a private Jewish school for the study of Russian reading and writing. The chief inspector denied the petition; I attach the rejection. However, the general governor of Irkutsk granted me the right to petition Your Excellency. In view of the supplementary documents about my irreproachable behavior, I have the honor to ask Your Excellency humbly to permit me to open a private school to teach Russian reading and writing to Jewish boys in order to support myself and my family.

The new happy dynasty, the expansion of the tsar's family, the imminent holy coronation—these three happy events give me the audacity to hope that the Great All-Russian Sun among the enormous oak trees will look upon me as a withering cornflower and will illuminate me with his warmth through Your Excellency. Thus I humbly ask Your Excellency to place this enclosed petition at the feet of His Imperial Majesty.

"Memorandum of the General Governor of Irkutsk to the Minister of Education (12 February 1896)"

Pursuant to the note of 26 January 1896, I have the honor to inform Your Excellency (with the return of Dashevskii's petition and its attachments) that the reasons for rejecting this kind of petition, as the chief inspector of schools explained to Dashevskii on 14 January 1894, seem to be significant and well founded. Since the petitioner has not brought any new information to justify his petition, there are not sufficient grounds to permit the satisfaction of his request. That is all the more so since the opening of a special Jewish school in Irkutsk would be undesirable in the highest degree: it would intensify the deep isolation of the Jewish elements and might foster the development of Jewish fanaticism, which must be deemed absolutely intolerable.

Furthermore, it is my duty to inform Your Excellency that Dashevskii, as is apparent in the documents that he has submitted, is registered in the townspeople's community of Tomsk and does not even have the right to live in Irkutsk. Hence I have ordered an explanation regarding the grounds on which he is residing outside his place of registration. In view of what has been stated above, for my part I reject the petition from the teacher Dashevskii for permission to open a Jewish school in the town of Irkutsk.

NOTES

1. [As an independent, privately funded student he would not receive a state stipend.]

2. [This phrase was underlined in the original.]

3. [In the previous paragraph, he referred to the superintendent of the Western Siberian School District.]

[114]

Elite Home Education and Culture: The Diaries of Zinaida Poliakova

OR RGB, f. 743, k. 137, d. 27, ll. 7 ob., 14–16.

Moscow, 27 August 1875[1]

Yesterday, we had dance lessons; Varia also came. In the evening I read her my diary, which she liked so much that she even swore that today she would begin writing her own. She promised to write me a letter but did not keep her word; perhaps, however, I will receive it tomorrow. Today I had [lessons from] the teacher of calligraphy and French. Then I prepared tomorrow's homework for music and arithmetic.

The weather is quite good. I went on a half-hour walk with Mlle. Evgeniia (mother's chambermaid). But on the way to Uncle Lev, whom we intended to visit for a minute to tell him that Mother was not going to the concert today, we met Miss Cecilia. She had left the church and gone to the dentist.

Misha is taking his first lesson with the French teacher. Masha sulked the entire day (for reasons unknown). Lidushka [Lidiia Stepanovna][2] was not home. Today I managed to read *Grafinia Katia* [Countess Katia]. Variushka [Varia] brought me this book to read.

I gave her [. . .] a few books. Of late I have come to write my journal gladly, and yesterday I read it and liked it. I think it is better to write something than to sit on your hands or quarrel with your brothers and sisters. True, this is not practicing calligraphy because I am scribbling, but sometimes there is so much to write that my hand even gets tired. That is all.

Moscow, 20 September 1876

There was such a lengthy interruption of my diary—because of my prolonged illness, then a trip to the Crimea, and finally the stay at the dacha (I did not take along my diary). I do not know where to begin now: I have forgotten many things that I could have told my diary. First of all, I wrote "Crimean Impressions" in the Crimea, which I left at the dacha. I was sick for such a long time, and all this time I did not see my diary. Yesterday I was not at the duet. My head hurt so I missed the Russian language [lesson] and only took dictation because I do not like it when I have fragments in my notebook. Lidiia Stepanovna did not allow me to study today because my head hurt a little.

Today the weather appears good but we will not begin our strolls because it is terribly dirty [muddy].

Tomorrow I have a music lesson—a [piece] that I still do not know well. [. . .] Now I need to study Yiddish, but Mother will allow me to skip it because of my headache. However, it would be a pity for me to miss a lesson (I have only one a week).[3] The French teacher M. Bertrand assigned me a translation from the history of medieval feudalism.

Masha is in my room now, and I do not know what she is doing. She is probably embroidering a monograph on the pillowcase that Mother told her to embroider (she sulked about this many times). She will not thank me for that childish expression, but how else can it be expressed if it is true?

I have a lesson in arithmetic tomorrow instead of Monday.

In the Crimea we went to see Tatar inhabitants and were at the home of a wealthy Tatar named Mustafa.

But enough!

20 January 1877

Exactly on this day last year I fell sick at night. It is very pleasant now to remember my illness, and (thank God) I am healthy under mother's [care]. Mother promised to take us to the opera to the Lukks' benefit performance, but, to tell the truth, I do not believe it: "she promises a lot and does a little." Today at 3:45 I will have [lessons with] Klindvert. I think he will be very satisfied because I tried very hard to prepare his homework well; it would be a pity if he is not satisfied. I wrote Miss Cecilia a letter in English and do not think I made even two errors. We are all writing her that Mlle.

Evgeniia died because she knew her. Yesterday Anna was at Madame Novikova's[4]—who recently arrived from abroad.

The weather was poor today, so no one went for a walk. Bertrand brought books to show me—*Voyage autour du monde* [Jules Vernes's *Around the World in Eighty Days*] (which cost 150 rubles). But of course I would not buy them because they are too expensive for me.

Khaia is now writing her diary too. Lidiia Stepanovna is with Mother because she is not at all well and is lying down. Tomorrow is my first lecture in general history. I have not prepared my homework yet, so I must hurry. Mother is searching for a French chambermaid, but a Russian woman came today who knows French and German, asking if Mother needed a companion.

NOTES

1. [Zinaida Poliakova, daughter of the wealthy banker and railroad mogul Lazar Poliakov, kept a diary from the age of thirteen (eight volumes of which have survived). Her father attained the rank of hereditary noble (which was highly unusual for Jews), and the family hobnobbed with the Russian nobility and Jewish elites. Her diaries indicate that she was educated at home education by excellent tutors in English, French, Russian, German, and Yiddish. She also studied arithmetic, literature, handwriting, music, and piano.]

2. [Lidia Stepanovna was a paid companion.]

3. [Although Poliakova was extremely russified, she learned to read and write in Yiddish to correspond with her grandparents, who resided in Vitebsk.]

4. [Ol'ga Alekseevna Novikova. See Joseph Baylen, "Madame Olga Novikov: Propagandist," *American Slavic and East European Review* 10, no. 4 (1951): 255–71.]

Secondary School Education

[115]

A Girl's Gymnasium Education: The Memoirs of Mariia Rashkovich

Mariia Rashkovich, *Vospominaniia vrachei Iulii Al. Kviatkovskoi i Mariia Rashkovich* (Paris, [s.n.], 1938), 151–56.

My Family: Childhood Years

I was born in 1859 in Odessa.[1] My father was also born there. By the time of my birth he was managing a wholesale cloth warehouse. My mother's family hailed from Galicia; my mother came from there to [stay with] her orphan brother, shortly before her marriage. In our family of eight children, I was the seventh. Father died before I was even six years old. After father's death, our family found itself in the care of my older brothers. The oldest brother, Leonid, although lacking an education in law, worked for a long time in the office of an experienced and well-known lawyer in Odessa and devoted much time to self-education; they subsequently made an efficient and talented jurist out of him. The second brother, Ieronim, worked in the Odessa City Administration. Both of them fulfilled their duties to the family solicitously and conscientiously. Leonid was more interested in our material well-being while Ieronim was more concerned about our upbringing, although in reality no one raised us younger ones. Life itself educated us: work at the family warehouse, the model of Mother's endlessly kind and boundless devotion toward us children, the mutual loving relationships — beautiful and cordial — between the members of the family, and the deep respect and love of all toward Mother. Only the third brother Mikhail was sometimes a disappointment for our family, because he showed far greater interest in hunting and sports than in gymnasium studies.

We the youngest — my sister Susanna Pavlovna and I — were completely excluded from participating in our family housekeeping: the three older sisters were good helpers to Mother. As we were growing up and studying at school, they gave us special protection for fear of interfering with our studies. In the 1860s and 1870s the idea about the importance of children's participation in the practical life of housekeeping (and the significance of activity and manual labor) not only failed to penetrate into the family, but it was not discussed much in pedagogy. All my life, especially now in my advanced old age, I have regretted this deficiency in my upbringing and feel completely helpless in practical life. We, the youngest children, were also deprived of a religious education. Mother was very devout but could not counteract the influences of our surroundings. She did not adhere to enough outward rituals. She had grown up in a non-Orthodox family: her father, a pharmacist, gave his sons a commercial education;

his daughter (my mother) graduated from a Polish boarding school (*pansion*). From early childhood I have retained painful memories of cholera and the Jewish pogrom.[2]

Gymnasium Years

After completion of the primary school, I went to school at the Mariinskaia gymnasium. At the age of eleven I already felt independent. I found myself a female tutor, my sister's friend, who prepared us both for the second class. I recall the gymnasium with warm feelings; only in the final years did they take us in hand; at times the new headmistress—wanting to make us feel her power—poisoned our existence. The gymnasium curriculum was considerably less [rigorous] then it is now.[3] I succeeded in completing almost all the homework during the breaks between classes. In the fifth class, I began to give private lessons and gave the money that I earned to Mother to support the family. I devoted the free time from lessons to reading books, for early on I had become enamored with them.

We had a first-rate staff of teachers, including several senior lecturers from Novorossiisk University. The history teacher, B. A. Afanas'ev, a senior lecturer from Novorossiisk University, had the greatest influence on me. We began history lessons in the third class; the female students read a history book for the parallel course and asked [questions] about what they could not understand in the readings. In the sixth and seventh classes, the senior lecturer from Novorossiisk University did not give lessons but lectured on the history of the French Revolution and made us create summaries of the books on this. During the gymnasium years I managed to read the classical works on all aspects of history.

As for literature, things fared badly: our teacher was dry, uninterested, and limited to the contents of the textbook and its repetition. I became acquainted with Russian and foreign literature and the critics—Belinskii, Dobroliubov, Pisarev—independently, through a self-education circle that we formed in the fourth class. This circle for self-education was the brightest spot in my gymnasium life. It filled [my life] with exciting interests, gave it meaning and joy, and turned out to be fundamental in shaping my future life. Seven students participated in the circle; I was especially close to four of them. We met constantly, read together, and wrote reports; we did not have a leader. One of the students was Roza Iaron; we entered the gymnasium together and she eventually married my brother Mikhail. She was the head mistress of a well-established Jewish professional school in Odessa for many years.

The second and third members of the circle were the Belokopytov sisters, the twins Ol'ga and Ekaterina. I became close friends with them through curious circumstances. They came from a wealthy, landowning family, far from the new currents [of culture and politics], and the parents had intended to give the daughters a home education. However, under the influence of the governess, the daughters began to insist that they be allowed to enter gymnasium, and the parents eventually yielded. The girls entered in the third class; they arrived at the gymnasium, accompanied by a livery servant, and kept apart from everyone. This particularly upset one schoolmate, a member of our circle. Without saying anything to us, she waited for the right moment and struck one of the sisters. When we learned about this childish prank, we were full of indignation, and I was charged with providing an explanation to the sisters. This incident served as the reason for our friendship.

The fourth member of our circle was A. V. Baranovskaia, subsequently one of the best headmistresses of the Odessa city schools. Unfortunately, our school circle in its full composition lasted only until the middle of the sixth class, when the Belokopytov sisters left: Ol'ga Nikolaevna married Prof. I. I. Mechnikov, and her sister did not want to continue studying alone at the gymnasium. [...][4]

NOTES

1. [Mariia Rashkovich became a doctor after her medical studies in St. Petersburg.]

2. [The author did not elaborate on this final sentence, but perhaps she meant to comment on her "Jewish" memories, especially of the Odessa pogrom, despite her lack of a religious upbringing.]

3. [The author is referring here to the Soviet standard of secondary-school education under Stalin.]

4. [Here the author devoted two long paragraphs to "the great, erudite Russian, Ilia Il'ich Mechnikov" and his wife Ol'ga Nikolaevna, who married when she was sixteen years old. He was a widower; his first wife had died from tuberculosis in 1873.]

[116]

A Boy's Gymnasium Life: The Memoirs of Genrikh Sliozberg

Genrikh B. Sliozberg, *Dela minuvshikh dnei: zapiski russkogo evreia.*
Vol. 1 (Paris: Izd. Komiteta po chestvovaniiu 70-ti letniago iubileia
G. B. Sliozberg, 1933), 290–302.

Chapter Three

Father's *melamed* income was far from sufficient to support our large family, the struggle with Mother's illness, and the treatment of small, sickly children.[1] He needed a permanent income. Father was fortunate: the owner of the house where we lived was favorably disposed toward him and, as the former traveled from Poltava, he leased to [my father] the entire courtyard with all the buildings. Father sublet the apartments. From these operations he received a benefit in the form of a free apartment and 200 to 300 rubles a month.

One wing of the estate was occupied by old Slivitskii, a lawyer, very admirable person, and without a family. An elderly Polish woman lived with him as housekeeper along with a female relative and her daughter (a gymnasium student). These were the first Christians whom I ever met. The mother and daughter loved me and expressed their sympathies to me in every way possible. My father conversed with both the old lawyer and his female relatives for long periods of time. Appar-

ently, these conversations instilled the idea in my father and gave him the courage to commit a seemingly unthinkable transformation: he invited a student in the eighth class—then one of the few Jewish gymnasium students, named Ostrovskii[2]—to teach me all the rules of grammar and arithmetic. This was at the beginning of spring, after Passover. Soon Ostrovskii was replaced by another gymnasium student from the eighth class, Sheboldaev. The blond boy, extremely pleasant, inspired a great love in me for him; that circumstance, not his pedagogical talent, explains how, after four months, I appeared completely prepared in all subjects, including Latin, for the second class of gymnasium. I knew Russian grammar superbly; I wrote without mistakes in dictation; the course in arithmetic and the ability to calculate did not present any difficulties, of course, for a student of the Talmud. However, since I had not spoken Russian before, I did find it difficult to master Russian in a few months. I read fluently but did not know how to produce the proper accent. Studying with the chosen teachers, however, I did not cease my regular Talmudic studies and exhibited no change in my exterior way of life.

The intention of placing me in a gymnasium was my father's secret. And only for a short time before the entrance exams, which would take place in August, did father begin to occupy himself with obtaining a metrical certificate for me from the town of Mir [in Minsk province]. Because it did not exist, it was necessary to replace it with attestations from a few old residents of the town (which was usual at that time), who firmly remembered that "on 31 December 1863 (the fourth day of Shevat 5623), a son was born to Shai Borukh Sliozberg by his legal wife Esfir Nokhim Davidovna, née Oshmainskaia," and that they "were invited to the ritual of circumcision at which he was given the [Hebrew] name Genokh [Henokh]"[3] It is difficult to imagine receiving a discharge certificate from the Nalibok townspeople society (that is, a certificate whereby, per the decision of the community, I was released from the townspeople and would not encounter any obstacles to entering into an educational institution). This is how my father's scheme came to light.

A titanic struggle between my grandfather and other relatives against father commenced. Stormy explanations took place. They mourned my future apostasy, threatened God's retributions, appealed to father's conscience, and begged him not to destroy a Jewish soul, not to deprive Israel of a future light of the Torah. Of course they also pointed out the material ruin: it was impossible to imagine combining the title "father of a gymnasium student" with the title of "*melamed*." But nothing could affect my father's decision, despite his usual compliance to grandfather's influence. I remember that he cited the example of the late [Il'ia] G. Orshanskii, then in all his glory among the Jews; although born in Ekaterinoslav, he came from an old Poltava family, and of course that is the only reason why the Poltava Jews had any notion of him. With gratitude, they said that this renowned writer devoted his talent and learning to the Jews, defending his nation against oppression and lack of rights. Father gave a solemn promise that my matriculation in the gymnasium would not affect my piety. Thanks to an order published not long before this, Jewish gymnasium students (if they so wished) could be freed from written work on the Sabbath. My Talmud studies, although curtailed, would not altogether cease; not one Sabbath would pass when I did not go to the synagogue for the first order of prayers (which ended before the beginning of lessons at the gymnasium at 9 a.m.), so that I would not violate the Sabbath rest by carrying a book to gymnasium, etc. Father, confident that I would pass my examinations by the end of the Il'inskaia fair, spent a significant sum on blue cloth for my gymnasium uniform and gray cloth for the coat (purchased at the fair—at a loss, since manufactured goods were cheaper).

Finally, the day of 7 August arrived: the entrance examinations took place at the Poltava gymnasium. It was preceded by a sleepless night, passed in dreams about the new life in store. I remember the trembling that seized me when I appeared before the director of the gymnasium, [Nikolai Mikhailovich] Shul'zhenko, an elegant, relatively young man. They led me into an assembly hall. For the first time in my life I saw such a large building; the full-length portrait of the tsar, whom I had never seen before, created a huge impression on me. Pupils in uniform scurried about, stirring up fear. When I began to answer the examination questions, it seemed to me that the tsar himself was directing an inquisitive gaze at me. The presence of the German language teacher, L. K. Kan (who lived in the house leased by my father and hence was known to me) in the hall calmed me somewhat. Kan was a Jewish convert from Kurliand, a highly educated individual, an expert in German literature, and also a completely unsuitable teacher; he spoke Russian so poorly that his every utterance provoked laughter among the students.

I took all the exams, oral and written, with great success, and the Russian dictation did not contain a single mistake. The following day I had to take the Russian oral exam. They made me read a story from [K. D. Ushinskii's] *Rodnoe slovo* [Native word], retell it in my own words, and then make a grammatical analysis of several phrases. The latter was accomplished with such success that it astonished the examiners; however, my pronunciation at the reading and mangled speech at the retelling of what I had read cast the examiners into complete horror. I remember how they invited the director of the gynmasium to the examination table and reported to him in undertones about this phenomenal event: a boy displays an excellent knowledge of all the subjects, including Russian grammar, but his spoken Russian is incredibly poor. They decided that I had passed the examination for the third class, but would persuade my father to put me in the second class so that I could fill in the gaps and enable me to acquire fluency in the Russian language. Father had to agree. Thus did I—a trained Talmudist, having learned to master all the difficulties, even the commentary of Maharsha[4]—become a gymnasium student of the second class, having taken the stipulated number of classes and other such "pearls of wisdom."

At that time, the Poltava gymnasium had a certain reputation, having shown its darker side to the superior authorities. The very year that I entered gymnasium, the teacher of history, Chartoryiskii, was dismissed for political unreliability; I subsequently learned that he belonged to one of the circles (apparently, the circles of *Chaikovtsy* and *narodovol'tsy*).[5] He formed groups of the best students from the upper gymnasium classes; his influence on the young was irresistible. They loved him very much; his lessons sent his pupils into raptures. Thirty years after this, I happened to meet with him in St. Petersburg, where he was working at a small office. I learned that after the Poltava gymnasium, he led a life of

wandering: he was in exile in Siberia, served as a *zemstvo* statistician, and even landed in the Justice of the Peace courts in the Caucasus. From there he came to St. Petersburg, where he lived in extreme need.

Under the influence of this teacher, a circle of "progressive" young people formed that would have an impact on the entire gymnasium. The director of the gymnasium, Shul'zhenko, was a gentle and tolerant individual; he was universally loved. According to the authorities, he "let the gymnasium get out of hand." This was the epoch of the Minister [of Education] D. A. Tolstoi, who sponsored educational reforms that emphasized a classical education.[6] When I entered the gymnasium, I was in the last remaining classes, which did not yet [at that time] study the Greek language. The debate between the adherents of classicism and its opponents was still at its full height. As evident from the press and journals of this epoch (I entered the gymnasium in 1875), the publicists were still assiduously engaged in polemics over Count Tolstoi's reforms. The question of classicism determined the fate of many of us starting [gymnasium] in the 1870s until the end of the century. [...]

It is understandable that the controversy about classicism was an abstract debate, guided purely by principle, with no practical significance. The discussion of the principled side of the issue remained in the shadows of the practical questions about how to implement classicism in our school. Against the din of this debate, the implementation of the classical program was beneath criticism. Formal classicism had no spirit; in place of an actual classical education, the school taught grammatical rules, deadening the minds of the young people and resulting in the mindless memorization of texts by Latin and Greek writers and in absurd extemporaneous exercises of translating from Russian to Latin and Greek. These classical authors, excluding Homer, remained alien to the spirit of even the best pupils, who knew all the syntactical rules in detail. As a result, Russia remained with neither a modern nor a classical education.

In this respect, the Poltava gymnasium was no exception. With the departure of Chartoryiskii, there was not one notable figure on the teaching staff. The teaching of mathematics was more or less tolerable; only one teacher of Russian language and literature met modest pedagogical requirements. The relationship between teachers and pupils was limited to official class relations. None of the teachers could influence the youth and stimulate initiative and self-education.

Soon after I matriculated at the gymnasium, they dismissed the director Shul'zhenko and in his place appointed an old man, Sergei Nikolaevich Shafranov [1820–88]. Evidently, higher educational authorities hoped that he would take the gymnasium in hand—which, as I mentioned, had a reputation for having a dissolute, infectious free spirit. Until his appointment as the director of the Poltava gymnasium, Shafranov had been the director of the [secondary school] Galagan Collegium [Kollegii Galagana] in Kiev—that is, he served under the direct supervision of the superintendent of the Kiev [educational] district and was [considered] to be sufficiently informed of the government's views. He taught the sixth class when I studied Russian literature. Shafranov's personality, at any rate, was outstanding. Without any links to the students outside of school, it was difficult to appreciate the individuality of this interesting old man and to understand his *Weltanschauung*. He was not strict by nature, loved young people, even caressed the little ones, but we knew that he was very exacting in terms of the pedagogical staff. We maintained a great respect toward him with some measure of fear, which stemmed from incomprehension. As a teacher, he seemed like an eccentric to us. With him we did not learn literature according to the textbook; he did not set a fixed number of pages to be memorized from the ancient Church Slavonic manuscripts. However, in the course

of the entire year of teaching in the sixth class, he made us learn by heart the little-known *byliny* [traditional Russian heroic poems], fairy tales, and in particular hundreds of intricate proverbs, adages, and sayings. Woe unto the student who at the director's question, for example—which proverbs of the Russian people are devoted to the sea—did not know to answer with the corresponding series of proverbs, such as: "Whoever has never been to sea has not prayed to God." Shafranov apparently thought that the knowledge of *byliny*, fairy tales, and proverbs could satisfy all the developmental needs of young people and instill in them the proper literary tastes. The themes assigned for compositions did not go beyond that circle of popular epics and folk wisdom. We were astonished that the director himself did not adhere to an official course program, and we moved to the seventh class without knowledge of Russian literature. Director Shafranov, however, was undoubtedly a well-rounded, educated person. He had an excellent command of French and especially German ([he spoke with] no accent), and he was familiar with foreign literature. We did not know about the literary works by Shafranov himself.[7] As I later described Shafranov's personality, I realized that in him we had a representative of Slavophilism,[8] which had become stronger during my time at the gymnasium. He was one of those who believed in Russia's special path, who—beginning with [Ivan] Aksakov and then together with [Mikhail] Katkov (the journalist of *Tver Boulevard*, the editor of the *Moscow Gazette*)—gathered around the banner "Let's go backward and home," and who proclaimed a merciless war on Westernizers. [. . .][9]

After the announcement that I was admitted to the gymnasium, I immediately dressed in the requisite uniform—a short, single-breasted frock coat of heavy blue cloth with white metal buttons, with a stand-up collar and white lace, and a cap with the gymnasium coat-of-arms. Despite the distress that I must enter the second and not the third class, I considered myself the happiest person in the world. My appearance in the schoolboy uniform caused veritable grief for my family. Mother and grandmother burst into tears upon seeing me in such an apostate's attire.

The class lessons began. Practice makes perfect: I was dealt a severe blow. The geography teacher — one of the very worst pedagogues that I have ever met and, what is more, one who did not have a clear pronunciation — ordered me to point out the Bay of Bengal on the map with the pointer. Not understanding his question and not knowing what to do with the pointer, I did not satisfy the teacher. He gave me a grade of 2 [out of 5] — me, who had passed the third-class examination superbly and had dreamed that my triumphal march on a path strewn with "5s" would begin from the first day. My grief was infinite; I was prepared to consider myself lost. This event deeply distressed my father as well.

The most difficult matter, of course, was coping with Russian. To make things worse, the teacher of Russian language often forced me to read and narrate, apparently amused at my broken speech. However, I soon overcame all these difficulties and my gymnasium life flowed peacefully from class to class with awards, placement in the first tier for success, even in first place (for which I competed with other classmates, even Jews). In this way we reached the end of the gymnasium, taking turns holding this top position and not allowing anyone else to take it [from us].

The first year of the gymnasium and a considerable part of the second did not affect my religious conduct. In the beginning I even doubled my diligence in fulfilling religious obligations and rituals, in an attempt to show my aggrieved relatives that being at the gymnasium was compatible with the punctilious fulfillment of all that is prescribed for a pious Jew and to vindicate father's guarantee. Not only on Saturdays, but also on Mondays and Thursdays — days when the Torah is read after the prayers — I rose at 6:00 a.m.; at dawn I was already at the synagogue for prayers. After returning from class and before setting about my homework, for some time I continued the break by studying the Talmud. When the day of my bar mitzvah arrived (in the winter of 1876), in the presence of my relatives, acquaintances, and Talmudic authorities who gathered for the occasion, I delivered the usual *drasha* [speech], which was devoted to a complex interpretation of a few difficult passages of the Talmud from the tractate *Hullin*, and showed that a gymnasium education had not had a deleterious impact on my Talmudic knowledge.

On Saturdays, with the permission of the gymnasium director, I did not participate in written work. Our yard man — my great friend Matvei, a retired soldier in the service of Nicholas I — carried the books to and from class on Saturdays. For lack of another place, he slept in the same tiny room where my lessons took place (under the dull light of the tallow candles). This Matvei was a constant witness to my evening and early morning vigil over the Jewish books, over the memorization of Latin words, over something very difficult for me — learning poems by heart. I remember that *The Battle of Poltava* did not come easy for me; unable to do the accents properly, I could not master Pushkin's rhythm.

But then, as my Nalibok grandfather rightly predicted, my matriculation at the gymnasium immediately had an unfavorable effect on my father's material welfare as a *melamed*: the *melamed* career was closed to him, forcing him to find a different livelihood. That did not materialize, however, and poverty — acute poverty — began to knock at our family's door. In November, when the time came for the final term payment (approximately fifteen rubles) for the right to study at the gymnasium, father — despite the impending cold — had to pawn his fur coat to the wife of a rich Jew, the director of the Kremenchug branch of the commercial bank in Poltava (the bank subsequently went bankrupt) and to borrow fifteen rubles to deposit in the gymnasium cash office. The bank director's wife viewed herself as my benefactor, making the sacrifice only because her son studied in the same class as myself. True, they did not exact interest [on the loan].

Father's extreme poverty and the realization that I was the cause impelled me to search for an income. At the end of the school year, having been promoted to the third class, I began to give lessons, and my first [job] paid one ruble a month for daily lessons with two boys whom I taught to read and write Russian. After these lessons, others soon appeared; in the third class of gymnasium, I earned fifteen rubles a month, which proved a significant help to father. My reputation as a good teacher and tutor became firmly established, and in the fourth and fifth classes, my earnings already amounted to thirty to forty rubles a month, on which the entire family could subsist. Of course, this was from 3:00 p.m. — that is, directly after finishing school, I set out to give lessons and returned home no earlier than 9:00–10:00 p.m. At home [more tasks] awaited — working with my brother, whom I began to prepare for gymnasium and then "tutored." Only around 12:00 a.m. was I able to prepare my own lessons for the next day.

Gradually, study of the Talmud decreased and eventually, for lack of time, had to cease completely. I slowly turned into a freethinker, an atheist; from atheism I fell into mysticism — that is, I experienced the rupture that is ordinary for an intelligent boy of fifteen who was accustomed to meditating. It depressed me that I was not able to devote enough time to reading, being obliged to spend all my time running around to give lessons. With the greatest of effort and at the expense of sleep, I managed to read books. In the fifth class, I familiarized myself thoroughly with [Henry Thomas] Buckle's *History of Civilization in England* [1857–61]; this book gave me many

ideas and expanded my intellectual horizons. I managed to make up the reading only during vacations, but in the summer months I was intensely occupied with giving lessons and preparing students to enter gymnasium.

I want to mention one summer that I spent at the estate of that bank director, who for some time had held my father's fur coat as a security. I had been promoted to the fifth class of gymnasium and was invited to be the teacher for this banker's younger children. He had acquired the estate (located about twenty-seven kilometers from Poltava) from a ruined noble family, who had operated a large-scale enterprise on it. For the first time in my life, I came to spend a more or less prolonged period outside the city in the open air and, what is more, under exceptionally favorable conditions. The banker's family lived in the old country estate manor — a large, two-story stone house with spacious rooms, furnished with antique furniture. Behind the house was a vast park with a pond and immense fields covered with rolling waves of winter wheat. These beautiful things were new for me and left the most enchanting impression.

I spent all my free time away from lessons with the pupils (which took up five to six hours a day) lying in the grass in the solitude of a little corner of the park and did not tire of watching the birds flutter around, the movement of the leaves on the ancient oak and lime trees; in the evening I listened avidly to the song of the nightingale. I remember that in the fifth class, soon after vacation, the literature teacher assigned us an essay — describe a garden. I reproduced an impression from the garden in which I had spent so much time the previous summer. The teacher deemed this essay to be exemplary and assigned it a mark of 5 plus. My stay at this estate aroused in my soul a love for nature and country life for the rest of my life.

However, this summer was interesting for me in another respect: it was the first time that I came to live under circumstances of prosperity and well-being. I became more familiar with the life of well-to-do Jewish families and saw how wealthy people lived—those who did not have to worry about getting hold of a few rubles at the bazaar before the Sabbath. At the same time, there were no ideals, no past, no purpose for the future except the increase of capital. I saw how an environment in which profit serves as an idol corrupts. The wealthy man, in whose presence I lived, was a migrant from Kamenets-Podol'sk; he had nothing in common with Jewry and in general was a complete ignoramus. As a young man, he had worked as a vodka tax-farmer[10] and kept the largest storehouse of wholesale alcohol in Poltava. His wife knew how to speak French and considered herself an educated woman. She had a malicious character and treated the poor harshly. The governess, nursery governess, and music teacher lived in the house. Young people came to visit, and this entire company, together with the oldest son in the family (my classmate in gymnasium), was an example of unbridled dissoluteness. The marvelous nature that surrounded them did not inspire any feelings in particular. Incomparably superior to this ostentatious life in my eyes was the working life of a Jewish pauper who was materially starving but capable of uplifting the spirit to mental pleasures. Compared to such impoverished [people], my Amphitryon[11] was spiritually poor. And how many "poor rich" was I to meet afterward in life! They were only an excrescence on the Jewish national organism, the product of an abnormal Jewish life, the result of neglecting the true Jewish spirit. But, you know, the observation of this excrescence has, unfortunately, always fed antisemitic agitation.

The fifteenth year of my life was extremely painful for me in psychological terms. The difficult material circumstances and excessive labor for a boy damaged my health. Having been accustomed from an early age to introspection and self-criticism, I made up my mind (which was precocious for my age)

about a person's meaning and purpose; I began to reconsider and reassess all the former values taken from my hard-working and joyless childhood. My mother, whom I loved infinitely, was perpetually ailing, losing her strength all the more under the strain of poverty, hard work, and worry about her children. Shortly before, a five-year-old sister (to whom everyone in the family was attached) and then a three-year-old brother had died. My nervous condition began to assume a menacing character. I was afraid of the dark, but I was forced to give lessons in the dark evenings, returned home late, and even walked past a cemetery. I was ashamed to admit this illness—but I could not decline the lessons, which paid thirty rubles a month. I suffered unbearably. An elderly doctor provided me some relief; he was also a Jew who lived in such seclusion that his membership to the Jewish people only became known after his death, when he was buried in a Jewish cemetery. Due to his weak health, he did not practice medicine, and did not have any contacts with people. He lived in the corner of a garden of an estate, next door to my grandfather from Mir [Minsk province]. He loved to converse with grandfather, and this gave me the opportunity to make use of his medical advice. One of his main medical prescriptions was visiting a Russian bath as much as possible, which in his opinion had a salutary effect on strengthening the nerves. This doctor—who went by the surname Gerber—was an enigma to everyone. No one knew anything about his past. He lived in Poltava for many years, and the few who knew him considered him an outstanding doctor and learned person.

My mental condition had its effect: in reality I was completely alone. I was a good friend, and the friends treated me well; the good relationship with my classmates was based mainly on the fact that I did not refuse to help them with school work; I gladly let them copy my work and did not begrudge the work, arriving early to class, explaining to them the lesson that they did not manage or want to prepare, or translating the assigned places from Latin and Greek. My favors became so common that they gradually turned into an obligation: I "did not have the right" to arrive late because I needed to serve many friends before the lessons. However, I did not have the opportunity to meet with them outside of school. Neither was I at their homes nor they at mine, although among the friends, there were a few with whom I would have wanted to become close. Friendly relationships outside of school were not possible to create under the conditions in which I lived. I did not have time (even a little) for this at my disposal. Indeed, because of my development at the *heder* that I had attended and because of the serious, worldly school [of the gymnasium], I stood apart from my friends and was a stranger to them.

I gradually began to emerge from my difficult mental condition in my sixteenth year of life when, already a gymnasium student of the sixth class, I began to meet sometimes with pupils of the seventh and eighth classes, even with Jews, and became close to some of them. At this time there was a relatively large number of Jewish students at the Poltava gymnasium, especially in the older classes. The majority of them were from another town and transferred to us from other gymnasiums. Ours had the reputation of not being picayune and was free from displays of Judeophobia. The director of the gymnasium, Shafranov, as a Slavophile who believed in Russia's unique path, was of course an antisemite at heart, but he was so conscientious in the fulfillment of his responsibilities that I cannot remember one act on his part toward Jews that would have made his hostility clear to us. The influx of students from other towns in the older classes contributed to yet another very characteristic circumstance that I shall discuss later.

However, I was not able to spare much time now for intellectual relations with the new friends, among whom were very pleasant young people. A few of them were interested in political questions and apparently formed ties to the leaders of various circles, which had moved from the capitals to the centers of provincial universities and from there to the gymnasiums. The gendarme authorities in Poltava worked diligently. From time to time, rumors circulated about arrests that were taking place. I do not recollect such events among the gymnasium students. I myself did not participate in these circles and was not present at gatherings of young people. Only on holidays, free from studies, and during vacation time, was I able to unburden my heart in conversations with the new friends.

The gymnasium came to life and the pupils were enriched with the new impressions during the spring examination period because of the arrival of many externs — individuals who took the examinations to receive a diploma of certification from our gymnasium, but who did not matriculate as pupils. The majority of the externs were Jews. A few of them were in great poverty and turned to me for assistance, which I could provide thanks to my connections to the local Jews. These externs, in contrast to subsequent generations of externs, were people who had been expelled from different educational institutions or who had voluntarily left them in order to prepare at liberty — namely to pass the Poltava gymnasium examinations for the certificate. I did not encounter among them a self-taught person who had gone through Jewish school — the *heder* and yeshiv[a]. When I recall the numerous rows of these certificate seekers, I cannot think of one who was a more or less notable person.

NOTES

1. [Genrikh Borisovich Sliozberg (1863–1937), who describes his difficult beginnings in this section of his memoirs, later graduated with a gold medal in law from St. Petersburg University. He worked as the assistant in the Ministry of Internal Affairs and

attempted to defend Jewish rights within the legal system. See Benjamin Nathans, *Beyond the Pale: The Jewish Encounter with Late Imperial Russia* (Berkeley: University of California Press, 2002), 325–34.]

2. [Il'ia Davidovich Ostrovskii was later a famous doctor in Yalta.]

3. [See document 27 on how Jews obtained metrical certificates when the child's birth had not been registered with the state rabbi.]

4. [R. Shmuel Eliezer Edels (1555–1631), a Polish rabbi who wrote two important commentaries on the Talmud, including *Hiddushei halakhot* and *Hiddushei aggadot.*]

5. [The circles of Chaikovskii and the People's Will (Narodnaia Volia).]

6. [Dmitrii Andreevich Tolstoi, minister of education from 1866 to 1880, was charged with raising educational standards while containing the growing problem of student radicalism. As an antidote to the science and materialism that seemed to inspire the first generation of nihilist radicals in the 1860s, he laid particular emphasis on classical education. See Allen Sinel, *The Classroom and the Chancellery: State Educational Reform in Russia Under Count Dmitry Tolstoi* (Cambridge, MA: Harvard University Press, 1973).]

7. [Sergei Shafranov apparently published several books on Russian proverbs and education such as *O sklade narodno-russkoi pesennoi rechi, rassmotren-noi v sviazi s napevami* (St. Petersburg: [s.n.] 1879) and *Tri rechi o vospitanii v russkoi gimnazii* (Poltava, [s.n.] 1880). See Viktor Kelner, ed., *Evrei v Rossii XIX v.* (Moscow: Novoe literaturnoe obozrenie, 2000), 511.]

8. [Slavophilism was a diverse intellectual movement opposing the view that Russia must follow the Western model of development. Instead, Slavophiles argued that Russia must seek its own unique path, drawing on the strengths of its roots and history.]

9. [Here he breaks away from his narrative to provide a short account of Slavophiles and Westernizers during the Russo-Turkish War and the impact of Slavophilism as a "cultural-national" and "not a political" worldview.]

10. [The system of vodka tax-farming (*vinnyi otkup*) was a system for leasing to a tax-farmer (*otkupshchik*) the monopoly to distribute and sell vodka in a specific area. It was subject to periodic changes but survived until its abolition in 1861. See David Christian, *Living Water: Vodka and Russian Society on the Eve of Emancipation* (Oxford: Clarendon Press of Oxford University Press, 1990).]

11. [In Greek mythology, Amphitryon—son of Alcaeus, king of Tiryns—could not consummate his marriage to Alcmene until he fulfilled his duty to avenge her brothers. In the meantime, Alcmene was seduced by Zeus and gave birth to Heracles, whom Amphitryon could not claim as his own son.]

State Rabbinical Schools in Vil'na and Zhitomir

[117]

Avraam Uri Kovner: The Vil'na Rabbinical School

Avraam Uri Kovner, "Iz zapisok evreia," *Istoricheskii vestnik*, 91: 3–4 (1903): 987–90.

How and why our family came to be in Vil'na again, I do not remember[1]—I only know that Grandmother sold her "estate." However, nurturing a special passion for land, for "one's own" little corner, she bought some kind of shack in the forest (not far from Vil'na) and moved there. But it had no space for our family. Nor do I remember how I, a nine-year-old boy, suddenly turned out to be a student in the first class of the Vil'na Rabbinical School. Whether they required some kind of examination to enter this school and whether I took this examination are things of which I have no distinct recollection. I only know that one nasty day I found myself among little children, students of the first class in a large, bright room on the second bench.

However, a few words need to be said about this school. When it was established, it was meant to cultivate educated state rabbis and teachers for urban Jewish schools. The curriculum at the rabbinical school was eight years (like our gymnasiums), except for Latin (which apparently was not obligatory then—even at the gymnasiums under the Ministry of Education). However, German and Hebrew, study of the Bible, and some knowledge of the Talmud were obligatory, along with the fundamental principles of the Jewish faith according to *Hayei Adam* [The life of man] and the *Shulhan Arukh* [The prepared table],[2] which concisely and systematically laid out the foundations of the law of Moses.

The head of the school was the director, a Christian; the assistant inspector and all the teachers of general subjects were also Russian and enjoyed the rights of state service. Only the inspector and the teachers of Jewish subjects were Jewish; the inspector, moreover, was not invested with any power and [had been] appointed only for honorific reasons from [among] the prominent Vil'na Jews. Instruction, except for special Jewish subjects, was in Russian.

The school, which occupied a large stone building, had a dormitory that housed a certain number of the most gifted student at public (that is, Jewish) expense.[3] Among them was my older brother, subsequently well known in the medical world as the author of an extensive historical work.[4] How my brother ended up there, I do not know—all the more so since the rabbinical school was considered a hotbed of freethinking and atheism among Orthodox Jews (which my parents were), and none of them sent their children there. My parents' motive for sending their own first-born to this impious institution was undoubtedly the fact that rabbinical school students were exempted from military conscription (something that not only Jews deemed terrible—given the brutal conditions of the Nikolaevan era). Their sons, however, given that they knew neither the Russian language nor the Russian way of life, considered [attending] this school to be the greatest misfortune. A considerable incentive for my parents must have been the desire to be rid of an extra mouth to feed, all the more so since, as a special exception for the first class, my brother was admitted at public expense.

In terms of the Jewish subjects, I was better prepared than the others. But back then, Russian was completely alien to me, and hence I had absolutely no understanding of the lessons in general subjects. Soon, however, I began to make notable progress and would have fully mastered Russian had a severe illness not befallen me. I was a day student. Every day at 4:00 to 5:00 in the morning, I set out for school with my brother, who helped me prepare the homework; during these excursions in the winter, dressed extremely lightly, I caught a severe cold and came down with a fever. I stayed home in bed in dire circumstances for more than three months, all this time remaining nearly unconscious. When I finally recovered, thanks to a strong body, and showed up at school, the teachers did not recognize me and asked: who is this? After the illness, I did not remain for long at the school. My parents apparently took my illness as a punishment from above for attending the impious institution, so they withdrew me and planted me in front of the Talmud. "It is enough," said Father, "that one son of mine is an atheist; woe unto us if another (that is, I) becomes a goy ([which, according to him, meant] an apostate from the Jewish faith)."

The relationship of my parents to their oldest son was strange. Living in the dormitory at the rabbinical school, he rarely visited the parental home, and my parents never visited him at the rabbinical school. When my brother did appear at home for the big Jewish holidays, he felt like a stranger, remaining constantly reticent and sullen. My parents, considering him lost for the Jewish religion, were indeed ashamed of him. They tolerated him like an unavoidable evil: they never greeted him, caressed him, especially Mother, despite the fact that he was an extremely talented and hard-working student, quiet and modest, and most important—he did not cost them anything.

I will also recount an episode from my brother's life that characterized my parents' treatment of him at the time. Brother was in the sixth class when the school celebrated the first decade of its establishment [in 1847]. Apart from the educational authorities and the district superintendent, Adjutant General Nazimov (the former general governor of Vil'na) was present at the celebrations. Three of the best pupils of the school were to deliver a speech in Russian on this occasion. It fell to my brother's lot to deliver a speech in Russian. General Nazimov, having heard the speech, at first did not believe that a Jewish boy had spoken, but when the supervisor of the district confirmed this, the governor general beckoned for my brother to come to him, smothered him with kisses before the whole audience, hoped that he would perfect his learning, and wished him every success in life. News about this spread to all the Jews of Vil'na, and many came to congratulate our parents with an unprecedented celebration of their son. But as simple, religious Jews (who are not at all flattered by distinction), they naively declared that if their son had achieved such a triumph in the Talmud, they would have considered themselves far happier.

Having spent "a week short of a year" at the rabbinical school, I understandably did not come away with anything essential—neither an elementary concept of life and non-Jewish interests, nor even [the ability] to read Russian properly. The sole, powerful impression that I took away from the school during my short stay was the public birching of a third-class student, a lanky fellow of sixteen or seventeen years of age.

The matter came about in this way: the student, the most terrible scamp and idler, instigated caterwauling during the class of a Jewish teacher. No sooner had the lesson ended than the teacher went straight to the director to complain. The latter, who was not even convinced about the fairness of the complaint and refused to hear the student's excuses, ordered that he be flogged immediately in the courtyard and in the presence of all the students. The scamp became flustered, started to ask the teacher for forgiveness, and begged the assistant inspector to intercede on his behalf, but it goes without saying that nothing helped. Four guards appeared with an enormous bundle of birch [sticks] to carry out the corporal punishment. Pale as death, the culprit begged the director, who was right there, for forgiveness; in the end the student declared that he would leave the school entirely, but the director was unmoved. They stripped the culprit and laid him on the ground covered with snow; two guards held him by the head and arms while the other two inflicted the lashes. The unfortunate lad screamed with all his might, but the powerful lashes fell with a whistling sound on his bare body; he was flogged until he bled. Finally, the director yelled, "Enough!" and—indifferently and in recognition that he had carried his responsibilities—left. However, the punished student, who put on his clothes with shaking hands, ran out on the street, as though he were rabid, and never returned to the school.

Soon after leaving the school, I found myself in the small Jewish town of Mir (Minsk province), where the Jewish rabbinical seminaries [yeshivot], in which some two hundred Jewish boys studied, were flourishing.

NOTES

1. [Avraam Uri Kovner (1842–1909) was a literary critic who transferred to a Talmud Torah after a brief period at the Vil'na rabbinical school. He wrote extensively for the Jewish and later for the Russian press. He was also known for stealing money from his employer, the banker Avraam Zak of St. Petersburg. In prison, Kovner carried out a correspondence with Dostoevsky. See Harriet Murav, *Identity Theft: The Jew in Imperial Russia and the Case of Avraam Uri Kovner* (Stanford: Stanford University Press, 2003).]

2. [R. Avraham Danzig (1748–1820) of Gdansk wrote the *Hayei Adam*, an abridged summary of *Orah Hayim* in the *Shulhan Arukh*, to provide concise instructions on daily conduct, prayers, the Sabbath, and holidays. Joseph Karo's *Shulhan Arukh* was a codex of Jewish law, which Eastern European Jews studied with the glosses of Moses Isserles, reflecting the distinctions between Ashkenazi and Sephardic customs.]

3. [According to Shaul Stampfer, two of the first Jewish school dormitories in Eastern Europe were attached to the rabbinical seminaries of Vil'na and Zhitomir. Ya'akov Gurland found the dormitories at the Vil'na Rabbinical School to be impressive: "The residents of the dormitory reside in attractive spacious buildings. They are nice and clean and the floors are marble. Servants are at their disposal to do their bidding, their dress is attractive, their beds are comfortable, and their diet is healthy" (*Families, Rabbis, and Education: Traditional Jewish Society in Nineteenth-Century Eastern Europe* [Oxford: Littman Library of Jewish Civilization, 2010], 200).]

4. [His brother, Savelii Grigorievich Kovner (1838–96) wrote the three-volume *Istoriia drevnei meditsiny* (Kiev, [s.n.] 1878–88).]

The Curriculum of the State Rabbinical Schools in Zhitomir and Vil'na

"Memorandum of the Director of the Kiev School District to the District Superintendent (6 November 1848)"
DAZhO, f. 396, op. 1, d. 9, l. 1.

As is well known, a large part of the prejudices and superstitions of the Jewish people stem from false interpretations of the Bible, and hence the teaching of this subject is of particular importance, all the more so since the teachers usually add their own explanations during the reading of the Bible. I therefore proposed to standardize the lessons and ordered that the teacher of Hebrew, [Markus Moiseevich] Sukhostaver[1] teach Bible in all the classes. [. . .] Being experienced in matters of teaching, it seems that he would be beneficial for the students and capable of furthering the government's goal of extirpating the superstitions and prejudices of the Jews. [Rabbi] Segal, as the teacher of [Jewish] law, will remain for the teaching of prayers, Mishnah, short religious instructions, and Sabbath siddur.

"Journal of the Pedagogical Council of the Vil'na Rabbinical School (26 April 1862)"
DAZhO, f. 396, op. 1, d. 378, ll. 2–2 ob.

Having heard the director's proposal (accompanied by the special opinion of the senior teacher Sobchakov, which was submitted for consideration on 19 March 1862), and taking into consideration that the Talmudic subjects taught in the rabbinical classes are necessary only for rabbis, the pedagogical council of the Vil'na Rabbinical School proposes to introduce the [following] subjects: natural history, Latin, and French for everyone without exception, but especially for those who desire to matriculate in university after the completion of the seventh class. [The council] ordered:

(1) the addition of one class on Friday (from 12:00 to 1:00 p.m.) for all classes;

(2) the teaching of *Hayei Adam* as a subject in the preparatory classes and to discontinue the concise code of laws;

(3) the transfer of courses on Mishnah and the codes[2] from the rabbinical to the specialized classes, leaving the Jewish subjects—Bible, Hebrew, history of the Jewish people—in the [. . .] curriculum;

(4) the study of [Talmudic] tractates for rabbis is scheduled for three times a week (3:00–6:00 p.m.);

(5) for teaching the courses on natural history, Latin, and French, the annual salaries of the teachers will be set as follows: teachers of natural history: 650 rubles; Latin: 650 rubles; French: 550 rubles; total: 1,850 rubles;

(6) taking into consideration the fact that the preparatory classes at the rabbinical school correspond to the first three years of the gymnasium, those who receive state assistance in the preparatory classes [must study]: (a) Russian language; (b) mathematics and geography; (c) Bible and Hebrew; (d) Mishnah; and (e) the history of the Jewish people. [. . .][3]

NOTES

1. [Markus Moiseevich Sukhostaver was an Austrian subject hired to teach at the Zhitomir Rabbinical School on 2 December 1848. The Bible courses were supposed to be taught in German, but for practical reasons the director recommended using Yiddish instead.]

2. [The council may have been referring to the *Tur* and *Shulhan Arukh*, which were in the original program of study but not included here.]

3. [The rest of the report dealt with budgetary issues, such as decreasing the number of state-supported students and other cost-saving measures.]

[119]

Graduates of State Rabbinical Schools Who Had Received State Stipends

"Petition of Natan Gasman to the Minister of Education (2 June 1867)"

RGIA, f. 733, op. 1, d. 219, ll. 2–3

Having completed the course of study at the Vil'na Rabbinical School (with the rank of teacher of Jewish schools, tier two),[1] I petitioned the superintendent of the Vil'na School District for permission to continue my education in university, [. . .] which was approved by the Minister of Education. However, upon completion of my studies, I was to serve for a fixed number of years at the Vil'na Rabbinical School because as a student I had received a state stipend.[2] When I entered the law faculty at St. Petersburg University, I devoted all my time to the pursuit of jurisprudence and successfully completed the course of study. As I love to work in jurisprudence and being specially prepared for legal work, I would find it extremely difficult to serve in the field of Jewish education — customs, manners, and subjects that I have forgotten and views that I do not share. Thus, I have the honor to ask Your Excellency humbly to free me from the obligation to serve in the field of Jewish education, thereby granting me the opportunity to be useful to the fatherland and allowing me to earn my bread and butter through labor that would be all the more pleasant for me and for which I have trained — service in the juridical sphere.

"Petition of Oskar V. Gintsburg of Moscow to the Minister of Education (11 September 1867)"

RGIA, f. 733, op. 1, d. 219, ll. 14–15

My most extreme and desperate position compels me to trouble Your Excellency with my humble petition. On 5 June 1867, I had the honor of submitting a most humble petition to Your Excellency about freeing me from obligatory service. [. . .] Due to the procrastination in the examination of my case, I was forced to turn personally to Your Excellency during your time in Moscow with a request to accelerate my case; as a result, a second request was sent from the Ministry to the Vil'na District. However, because the proper order has still not followed, I have been prevented from starting work that corresponds to my rank and special education. So I am taking the liberty to ask humbly a third time for an urgent order from Your Excellency to free me as soon as possible from the obligatory service.

In addition, I take the liberty to base my humble petition on the following facts: (1) the previous precedents and customary law that have freed many of my other colleagues (such as the Gol'denveizer brothers, Gordon, Bomstein, and others) [from obligatory community service]; (2) the lack of a position in a Jewish school that would correspond to my rank; (3) the surfeit of people who complete their studies at the Vil'na Rabbinical School annually and who suffice to fill the teaching positions; (4) the general feeling of justice: if I were not released, it would be tantamount to the loss of my doctoral diploma and the rights that I acquired with my blood and hard life of suffering. I dare to hope that Your Excellency will sympathize with the position of a poor person who is without resources, documents, and work. Do not reject my *modest* request and be favorably disposed to issue an immediate order releasing me and to inform the administration of Moscow University about it.

"Superintendent of the Vil'na Educational District to the Ministry of Education (10 October 1867)"

RGIA, f. 733, op. 1, d. 219, l. 23.

The director of the Vil'na Rabbinical School informed me that there are very few vacancies for positions in the Jewish schools, and for each position there are several candidates. For their part, there are no obstacles to free former graduates of the rabbinical schools who were supported by the state from [obligatory] service: Natan Gasman, Girsh Verblovskii, and Oskar Gintsburg, who have completed their university studies. [. . .][3]

"Petition of Mark Lipman, City Doctor of Dubno, to the Minister of Education (28 November 1867)"

RGIA, f. 733, op. 1, d. 219, ll. 36–37

In accordance with the statement of the Superintendent of the Odessa School District, the former Minister of Education permitted me—a former student of the Second Odessa State Jewish School (first tier), who was educated at the Vil'na Rabbinical School on a state stipend—to enter one of the universities to audit medical courses at my expense. At the completion of the courses, I was to serve for the required number of years in the medical field for the education that I had received at the Vil'na Rabbinical School.

From the notification to the board of St.

Vladimir University [in Kiev] from the superintendent of the Odessa School District and the director of the former Ryshel' Lyceum [. . .] it is clear that I am obliged to serve in the medical field for seven years, five months, and twenty days.

After I completed my medical studies at St. Vladimir University with a doctor's diploma, I was assigned to the post of city doctor in the town of Dubno on 8 February 1867. However, due to various family circumstances—the harmful influence of the Dubno climate on my wife's health and the extremely deleterious impact of my wife's health because of the separation from her parents in Berdichev—I was forced to send my wife back to Berdichev and leave her close to her parents. Her separation from them could have subjected her to various fits of illness. Apart from the family circumstances that compel me to reside in Berdichev, my family matters may take an extremely harmful direction if I am required to live in another town.

However, because a fee-paying student in the eighth class of the Zhitomir Rabbinical School, Girsh Chernoburskii, has agreed to assume my obligation to serve as a teacher, I have the honor to ask Your Excellency humbly to feel my critical position [. . .] and to find it in your favor to order that my obligation to serve for my education at the Vil'na Rabbinical School [. . .] be entrusted to a student in the eighth class of pedagogy in the Zhitomir Rabbinical School—Girsh Chernoburskii.[4]

NOTES

1. ["Tier 2" (*razriad* 2) refers to the ranking of students into three groups—from the top (tier 1) to the bottom (tier 3)—each of which had corresponding rights and obligations. Tier 1 was the most privileged.]

2. [According to the regulations of 13 November 1844, students who received a full state stipend to study at one of the two state rabbinical schools were to serve as teachers in Jewish schools, or as doctors and so forth in the Pale of Settlement for ten years

after they graduated from the university. Those who received only half a stipend were to serve for six years. The state allowed exemptions based on illness and other extenuating circumstances; it also reduced the time for various reasons (see DAZhO, f. 386, op. 1, d. 1).]

3. [The decision was to free the three university graduates from obligatory service. Girsh Verblovskii had also studied law.]

4. [The general governor of Volhynia was not sympathetic to Lipman's petition, especially after a medical examination showed that his health was perfectly fine. In contrast to alumni who had chosen legal professions, doctors like Lipman found it more difficult to obtain an exemption from service obligations, perhaps because doctors were in greater demand than lawyers. The final order required Lipman to complete his medical service.]

University Life

[120]

On University Life: The Memoirs of Vladimir Osipovich Garkavy

Vladimir Osipovich Garkavy, "Otryvki vospominanii," *Perezhitoe* 4 (1913): 275–87.

At last, the question of my entering the university was settled.[1] My dream turned into a reality. Preparations for the trip commenced: Mother and my sisters prepared the linens with an air of concentration. Father looked on my future with pride and hope; it was as though the ideals of his youth, his striving for education and enlightenment, had converged in me. I was one of the first to depart for university from that milieu to which my father belonged — the intellectual and religious aristocracy.

Preparations for the trip and furnishing me with the necessary items took on a patriarchal character. They supplied me with a warm, heavy overcoat, warm boots, and even a sheepskin coat. Mother took leave of me with a quiet melancholy and reminded me of the promise that I had given — not to abandon Jewish learning or become carried away by nihilism, the denial of the past. My sisters, young men, and ladies my age looked on me as a future hero in a war without a sense of what constituted this heroism. For me, [the university] was a torch, a symbol of freedom for someone like me who wanted to escape from the ghetto, both geographically and mentally. Russia, which was unknown to us (in contrast to the Polish life of our environment), was radiant, comprised primarily of people imbued with the ideas of [Vissarion] Belinskii, the editor of *Otechestvennye zapiski* [Notes of the fatherland] and *Sovremennik* [The contemporary], [Ivan] Turgenev, and [Nikolai] Nekrasov and so forth.

It was decided that I should matriculate at St. Petersburg University. In St. Petersburg, I was initially to take up residence with one of our family's relatives. Before my departure for the university, my friends organized a party, which was a complete novelty for me. My friends were older than I; they had already experienced want, lived on their own modest incomes, and with some bitter cynicism, you can say, even scorned the religious beliefs of their parents and environment. For the party, they bought vodka, sausage, pork, and even invited some women. All this was disgusting to me. I refused to partake of the vodka [and the food], remembering my promise before entering the university that I would not violate Jewish laws and customs. The presence of women provoked disgust in me because I was completely innocent. Owing to this, a great conflict broke out between me and my friends. They called me an "aristocrat." However, my protest against "purchased love" gained the respect of a few people. This laid the foundation for my special friendship with Shlossberg and Doctors Kramnik and Gordon.

On the day of my departure, in the morning I set out to say farewell to my grandfather, [Samuel] Strashun. I went to him into the synagogue where, after the prayers, he read and commented on a section of the Talmud before a gathered audience. I remember this farewell and the situation vividly. The synagogue was located in Polavakh—a suburb of Vil'na. It was quiet on the street, without any movement. From grandfather's house, one heard only the splashing of the water from the mill and then babbling brook with crystal cold water; trees surrounded the old wooden synagogue. Grandfather sat, with a radiant, cordial, and affectionate face, in the place of honor near the ark, surrounded by an audience in prayer shawls. When I came up to him, he stroked my cheeks and said: "You know, we the elderly are afraid of the university; we are fearful that it will take you away from Jewry. However, new times and new paths have come, and we cannot oppose you. I respect science—especially medicine and astronomy. Farewell my child, but remember and do not forget that you are a Jew." The surrounding audience was very astonished. They had expected an irate reprimand, even curses. I sealed these words in my soul and in my heart, and tearfully bid farewell to Grandfather.

Father escorted me to the train, and there he introduced me to a Pole who was sending his son off to Moscow University. We traveled together. For the first time, I savored the feeling of equality: not a *zhid* traveling with a *pan* but two students. I became friends with this student, and we subsequently we ended up as colleagues on the juridical faculty in Moscow University. We conducted our conversation in Russian; he was offended that I did not know Polish.

It was the first time that I made this trip alone, and everything was new or alien to me: the passengers, the compartments, the stations, the buffet (which I entered with timidity and uncertainty). And then the faces of the passengers changed; the station, everything somehow moved sleepily, and I felt alone and abandoned. Despite the uplifting of my spirit, I looked at vast fields and peasant huts with sadness and even thought about whether to return home.

I arrived in St. Petersburg in the morning. The weather was rainy and damp. Of course, the city made a powerful impression on me. In the Petersburg hubbub, I felt even lonelier and alien. From the train station, I went to my relative P.'s house based on the address that I had. He received me very cordially. They occupied an apartment in a large St. Petersburg house, which seemed to me almost like the Tower of Babel because I had never seen such a big house before. Although the P.s were religious and observed Jewish customs, their atmosphere was already mixed: the porter, maid, and nanny were Russian; the family spoke Yiddish among themselves but Russian with the servants and children. The porter in his livery appeared to me like the type described in Nekrasov, and P. himself with his bureaucratic reception seemed to me the "uncle type" from Goncharov's *Obyknovennaia istoriia* [A common story; 1847].

Soon I moved to their dacha in Tsarskoe Selo. Here everything was novel for me and seemed somehow magical. The dachas were beautifully arranged: flower gardens, palaces, parks, stylish and plump coachmen, carriages, shiny droshkies—and no sign of poverty. I met there a few Jewish merchants who had their own small synagogue where they observed all the rituals, although somewhat stiffly and coldly. I spent the whole day in the park, where I prepared for the examination in Latin. My astonishment was indescribable when one morning I met the late sovereign Alexander II face to face. He was walking one of his dogs. He seemed so majestic, beautiful, almost divine. He answered my greeting with a smile. I was especially staggered by this when I compared it with the uproar and racket when General Governor M. N.

Murav'ev of Vil'na appeared on the streets — surrounded by Cossacks, with the contempt that the Vil'na authorities manifested toward local residents, especially Jews. After this I often met the Sovereign, who even began to salute me before I managed to bow.

One morning, a hasidic *melamed* in Jewish garb and boots with long *peyes* and, for some reason, a red knitted scarf around his neck, who was living at the home of wealthy Jewish contractors from Finland, was taking a walk at the same time as myself on the same road. He apparently caught the attention of the Sovereign, and within a short time after the meeting, some soldier came up to him and began to ask the *melamed* where he was from. After his humorous reply that he belonged to the Finnish family, the soldier proposed that he find a secluded street a little farther away for his walks. Then this solider came up to me, curious to see what kind of book I had; he returned my Latin grammar and wished me success in passing the examination.

One Sunday P. took me with him to Pavlovsk. There the orchestra played a Strauss piece — and Strauss was the conductor. This was something magical. Together with the crowd of many thousands, I reveled in the marvelous sounds to the point of intoxication, ecstasy. Pavlovsk at that time was an assembly point for all of St. Petersburg. The nobility, military, navy, dignitaries, and all of fashionable Petersburg with "the beggars and well dressed" of Nekrasov mingled together in one common crowd and went into raptures over Strauss. The ovation and summons were without end. I never again saw or experienced such ecstasy.

When the time approached for the examination in Latin, I moved to St. Petersburg and settled in a furnished student apartment. For me this was an abrupt transition. From the elegant and well organized dachas, I found myself in furnished rooms with a certain fetid smell, with a retired prostitute and carousing students as neighbors; still, for the first time I felt free from being under someone's wing and was infinitely happy because of the awareness that I was beginning to live by myself in this great city. At this time, my relative A. G., by then already a former student, took me to the *kukhmisterskii* [Russian eating house] where I tasted non-Jewish food for the first time. Although I did not acknowledge the Jewish laws of kashrut by conviction, I was nonetheless tormented by pangs of conscience for a long time.

I did not pass the examination in Latin. On the advice of my friends, I sent a petition to Moscow University and moved to Moscow. They accepted us [Jewish students] at Moscow University without [passing] the Latin examination owing to a letter from [General Governor] Murav'ev asking to exempt us from this examination (in the same way as seminarians) because of [our] excellent knowledge of the Russian language.

My move to Moscow on the Nikolaev railroad forms one of the most pleasant experiences. Here I immediately felt myself among the homogeneous purely Russian masses. The trip from St. Petersburg to Moscow lasted thirty-six hours. Sitting interspersed were peasants and nobles, women and children, on benches and on the floor. All the passengers had a lot of baggage, and in the coach they drank tea and sang songs. They nestled down for the night and with mutual agreement slept on the floor and under the benches with quaint sayings and jokes. I became acquainted with almost all the passengers with a naiveté that seems funny to me now. I read and explained Nekrasov and Nikitin to the peasants, who listened to me, sighing from time to time. I imagined that I had plunged into the heart of folk life. On the coach I made my first acquaintance with an intelligent Russian woman. She was returning from the countryside to Moscow with her child and nanny. We conversed about Russian literature — about Belinskii, Dobroliubov, Pisarev, Chernyshevsky, and about the female type in

Turgenev.[2] By my pronunciation and speech, she discerned that I was not a Russian, and when I told her that I was a Jew, she was astonished to no end. She could not understand how I had come to have such a love for Russian literature. She treated me with special attentiveness and invited me to visit her in Moscow. Her husband turned out to be a colonel, a teacher at the Aleksandrov School. I visited them on Sundays. They invited me to give lessons — an opportunity that I handed over to my friends because I was not in need of [giving] lessons and, moreover, did not feel that I was sufficiently prepared [to teach]. In their house I met many educated military people. [. . .]

When I arrived in Moscow, my friends from Vil'na met me: Shlossberg, Gordon, Kramnik, and Rogalin. I settled down with them in a student apartment on Ermolaia Street, in one small room with four beds and a couch; I paid seven rubles a month. I was the sole person who had brought money with him. My friends did not have any resources or things, but looked to their future with good spirits and assurance. We set off for the eatery where I paid 3.50 rubles a month in advance for meals — that is, for two courses and coffee. Of the four friends, I paid for two meals because every other day they had soup or stew. More than all, I became close friends with Shlossberg who was older than me and had already experienced plenty of need; by conviction, he was a materialist who recognized only natural science. Under the influence of Pisarev, materialists and realists thought that natural science would solve all the questions of life, philosophy, worldviews, and especially jurisprudence. I decided to enroll in the law faculty, which gave rise to disagreements between my friends and myself.

Two days after my arrival, I set out with Shlossberg for the university to take the "colloquium" examination in Russian language and mathematics. For the Russian language examination, I chose the theme of Peter the Great and wrote an enthusiastic and laudatory composition about him. Professor Leshkov,[3] a well-known Slavophile, examined my essay and told me that in terms of the form he approved my essay, but that in terms of content he hoped that I would study and change my opinion. There, for the first time, I learned about the different perspectives on Russian history, and the observation that the old professor with animated eyes made to me created a more enchanting impression: "Now, I thought, that is true of temple learning!"

Within a few days I was enrolled as a student and received a student card. When I exited the old university on Mokhavaia Street with Shlossberg, we crossed over to the opposite pavement, took off our caps, bowed before the temple that had accepted us, and exchanged kisses. We proudly went home and, to everyone we met, we were ready to yell, "Listen, we are students!" It was as though the feelings of alienation from the surrounding Christians immediately subsided. We felt included in a new corporation that had neither Jews nor Hellenes.

We decided to celebrate our admission to university and that evening set out for the Hotel Hermitage, which at the time was renowned. Stewards in white shirts, an organ, a wide staircase, luxurious lighting, and a wealthy public, sitting at various tables — we felt too shy to occupy a place and intended to leave. But just then some young man came up to us and said: "*Messieurs* students, please, sit down!" This moved us to indescribable feelings. We ordered tea with cookies for ourselves, and when we sat down, we heard the familiar sounds of home: a Jewish wedding dance. And such was our astonishment and joy when we saw a Jewish orchestra in the next room: the violin, *bandura*,[4] and drums. The familiar sounds from a remote home, from the far-away Pale [of Settlement], blended with our new impressions. We sat for a long time and talked about our past and future. [. . .][5]

Life in the university was not complicated. The relationship between students was simple, more like circles. Inspector Krasovskii was a dull-witted military man; his attitude toward students was outwardly formal but not disparaging. The assistant inspector very much reminded us of the supervisor of a gymnasium, and thus the students treated him rather condescendingly. In reality, for the most part, they were good people and always defended the students in conflicts over an inspection or with the police. The assistant inspector for law students was Barsov, who was very close friends with the Shchepkins[6] and Belinskii. He was well known as one of the best translators of historical works.

The first lecture that I attended was the "Encyclopedia of Law," taught by [Mikhail N.] Kapustin [1828–1908]. Subsequently, he also taught international law. He gave dry lectures but could excite curiosity in his own subject because he attempted to explain all his legal decisions by drawing examples from everyday life. He was a follower of German scholarship and recommended German books and philosophy above all. He received students once a week at certain hours and willingly furnished them with more instructions and books than they could use.

A completely different type were two other professors: [Ivan D.] Beliaev [1810–73] for the history of Russian law and [Vasilii I.] Leshkov [1810–81] for public (civil) law. Beliaev was small, very fat, pudgy, and resembled a priest's wife. His course was extremely extensive, and all the more so in terms of primary sources. Initially, he was incomprehensible to us, but after some time we became accustomed to his good-natured readings and gladly attended his lectures because they were rich in details about Russian life and the everyday. However, his lectures lacked broad horizons or illuminations. In his first lecture he led us into a scholarly dispute about communal and ancestral origins. Leshkov was by nature a greater fighter. A passionate opponent of the Petrine reforms, in the department he had furious disagreements with his literary opponents, the professors of Moscow University. A completely different spirit began to flow from the lectures of Professor [Stepan V.] Eshevskii [1829–65], who unfortunately soon passed away. Strict scholarship, lucidity of exposition, precision of definition — all that immediately attracted our attention, and right away we felt that before us was a true teacher, who was opening up horizons and worldviews that were previously unknown to us

Above all, the course by the professor of theology, [Archpriest Nikolai S.] Sergievskii [1827–92], which was obligatory for [Christian students in] all departments — drew in the students. Sergievskii won over the students with his handsome and elegant appearance, extremely pleasant voice, and especially his detailed exposition of the philosophy of Fichte, Hegel, Feuerbach,[7] and the latest materialists, who denied religion in general and Christianity in particular. Although his course was not obligatory for me, I attended it attentively. I was attracted to this public, open discussion of religious questions, and I must say that Sergievskii's lectures hardly tended to strengthen one's beliefs; rather, in their ambivalence, they strengthened doubts because his refutations and proofs bore more of a theological than academic character. Besides [the course by] Sergievskii, I attended lectures on physics taught by [Nikolai A.] Liubimov [1830–97]; this was a tribute on my part to the materialist mood of my friends. Liubimov held his audience with greater experience so that [the experience] was new for us.

Shlossberg, my other friends, and I continued to disagree about the superiority of natural science over the other fields. Every new article by Pisarev served as the cause of a new disagreement and an attack on me. However, I became attached to my subjects and began to study philosophy and history. Kapustin then gave a lecture to us on juridical entities.

This lecture made a powerful impression on me, for it brought out a whole series of new understandings and concepts. When I returned home I began to talk about this with passion. My medical friends disagreed with me and began to demonstrate how all this was sophism. When I began to demonstrate the necessity of such understanding, and pointed out the university as an example of a legal entity, Shlossberg asked me: "So is it possible to steal something from a university? If I were to take a small laboratory bottle for a chemistry experiment, then according to your opinion, I have committed a theft? From whom have I robbed it?" And when I began to maintain that in this case, he had robbed the university, as a legal entity, he was offended and we quarreled and even went our separate ways.

During the first year at the university, I began to become acquainted with a few students who belonged to various strata of society — from the seminarian to Count Komarovskii, from the subsequently famous Minister Bogolepov[8] to the current chairman of the State soviet Akimov.[9] Our acquaintance and merging was based primarily on grounds of religious questions and doubts. As it turned out, we were people of different circumstances, living in various conditions, experiencing the same torments of doubt. This was also a time of re-evaluating all of one's values, although this term was not well known. From conversations with friends and Sergievskii's lectures, I was convinced that the questions about separating secular from religious education and striving for freedom from the burden of a spiritual life and from the clerical worldview — all this was not the lot just of educated Jews. Rather, these questions also tormented and created suffering for thinking young Russians. In this respect, I met many seminarians in particular who had a lot in common with us. At the time social questions did not yet especially occupy us; they were still *im Werden* [coming into being], so to speak, and perceived only in some general, vague terms. The woman's

question moved forward very strongly; it was not understood in the sense of "equal rights" as it now is, but rather in the sense of the treatment of women as "human beings" rather than "females." In this respect, the great difference between me and my friends was probably caused by the differences in our family situations. I had not seen a drunken serf owner ridiculing his peasants; I had not seen drunken husbands and fathers losing all their fortune and abusing their wives. I was familiar neither with prostitution nor with kept women. I always witnessed the calm treatment of mothers and daughters, as well as employees. Only in one respect did men stand higher than women: the fulfillment of ritual obligations and religious ceremonies. A woman's life after death depended on the husband's virtue. Thus I had no doubts about the woman's question, and my friends observed a kind of special moral purity in my attitude toward women.

NOTES

1. [Vladimir Osipovich Garkavy was born in Novogrudok around 1846–47. He was the grandson of the famous Talmudic scholar Samuel Strashun (1794–1872). Garkavy attended Moscow University and was active in Jewish communal activities. He began his memoir in 1889 but, by the time he passed away on 6 September 1911, he had succeeded in writing only three segments ("Childhood," "Vil'na," and "My Entrance into the University"). This passage sheds light on the journey of a young Jewish man from the provinces to the capitals to pursue higher education.]

2. [These writers were members of the intelligentsia whose works had widespread appeal among the new generation: Vissarion Belinskii (1811–48) was a literary critic who idealized the notion of *narodnost'* (the "idea of the people"); Nikolai Dobroliubov (1836–61) was best known for his critique of the "superfluous man" in his essay "What Is Oblomovism" (inspired by Ivan Goncharov's novel *Oblomov*); Dmitrii Pisarev (1840–68) had a science degree from St. Petersburg University but became famous as a radical nihilist and journalist in the 1860s. He

served as a model for the nihilists, who embraced science, utilitarianism, and realism—ideals embodied in Turgenev's character Bazarov in *Fathers and Sons*. The radical youth were deeply influenced by Nikolai Chernyshevsky (1828–89); his novel *What Is to Be Done?* (1862) idealized the "new type" of men and women who embraced women's equality, socialism, and political activism.]

3. [Vasilii Nikolaevich Leshkov (1810–81) was a specialist in early Russian history and domestic jurisprudence.]

4. [A Ukrainian instrument similar to a lute.]

5. [Here the author describes how he fell in love with the city of Moscow, to which he devotes a few pages of vivid description. He observes that it was inexpensive to live there, especially as he received a state stipend of twenty-five rubles a month for his expenses.]

6. [The Shchepkin family included a mathematician and, more famously, a prominent journalist and publisher, Mitrofan P. Shchepkin (1832–1908).]

7. [Johann Gottleib Fichte (1762–1814) an eighteenth-century philosopher of transcendental idealism; Georg Wilhelm Hegel (1770–1831) also belongs to the period of German idealism; and Ludwig Feuerbach (1804–72) is best known for his critique of idealism and religion.]

8. [Nikolai P. Bogolepov (1846–1901), minister of education from 1898 to 1901, was assassinated by a terrorist while in office.]

9. [Mikhail G. Akimov (1847–1914) was chairman of the State Council from 1907 to 1914.]

[121]

The Impact of Women's Higher Education on Marriage

RGIA, f. 1412, op. 214, d. 104, ll. 1–2, 5–6.

"Petition of Chaim Davidovich Grinshtein (Son of an Odessa Merchant) to His Imperial Majesty's Chancellery for the Receipt of Petitions (Received on 1 December 1899)"

GREAT MONARCH!
MOST GRACIOUS SOVEREIGN!

I take the liberty to fall at Your Majesty's feet with this humble petition. I have been married to Revekka L'vovna Grinshtein for eleven years and have had two children with her—a daughter Raia (seven years old) and a boy Mikhail (three years old). Until the past year, our lives passed by happily and quietly, without storms and agitation; however, at the beginning of last year, my wife took it into her head, for no reason at all, to go off to a course in [dental] medicine and, in order to attain this, registered with the medical inspector, Dr. Korsh, in Odessa, who permitted her to practice with a dentist in the town of Korabel'nikov. All of my protests and appeals to Dr. Korsh not to permit my wife to practice without my consent were futile and had no effect. In the end, my wife left me and our minor children to the will of fate and devoted everything to the goal of studying dentistry. [This was] not due to necessity because I, thank God, am a man of means; I have provided and continue to provide for my family with abundance.

As a result of the illegal permission, my wife practices dentistry, and with each passing day

I am ruined, as my business fares badly; I have lost my head and the small children suffer worse than orphans, being left without the tenderness and care of their natural mother. The heart of any person with the slightest feeling would shudder involuntarily at the sight of my unfortunate position, living with my little orphans, who are susceptible every minute to dangers such as colds, illnesses, or injury without the care of their natural mother. The tears of the unhappy children calling in vain for their mother are endless; the sight of their tears and bitterness rends my heart. It is sad that in this case, as explained above, my wife's study of dentistry is not caused by any necessity and appears only to be the fruit of caprice.

Falling at your feet and appealing to the ineffable mercy of Your Imperial Majesty, I beg you, All Merciful Sovereign, to look mercifully on my unhappy children, who are perishing without [their] mother, and save them with your kind word: forbid my wife from engaging in the study of dentistry so that she returns to the bosom of the family, to the joy and happiness of our little children.[1]

"Petition of Revekka Grinshtein to His Imperial Majesty's Chancellery for the Receipt of Petitions (17 November 1901)"

Most Gracious Sovereign! Most August Monarch! Among the multitude of people who are shielded by the scepter of the Great Russian Monarch, seeking and appealing for salvation at the foot of the Throne, I turn my eyes to You, who serves as the source of good for all His loyal subjects.

In 1889, at the age of eighteen, I was married to the Odessa townsperson [Chaim] Nukhim Abramov Grinshtein with whom I soon had two children. After the passage of a few years, however, I had time to be convinced that my family life had turned out in the saddest way. Apart from the differences in personalities, I was especially oppressed by the disagreement in our moral worldviews, which became manifest with respect to the meaning of the family, the mother's role in it, and concern about the upbringing of the children. My striving for development and self-reliance met with desperate opposition from my husband, and I decided to study dentistry to satisfy my thirst for knowledge so far as possible and to support myself and the children with a source of livelihood, being compelled to separate from him. Now I have successfully completed my studies at the local dental school and must take the examination at one of the Russian universities. However, I have been deprived of the possibility of achieving this because my husband, who at first agreed to provide me with his written permission after long entreaties, now abruptly refuses to give me the requisite separate passport, which is necessary for this purpose. This refusal, which obstructs the path to the most cherished dream of my life and has already absorbed a lot of my labor, will leave me completely horrified.

But boundless despair inspires in me the audacity to entrust my fate to the powerful hands of the Father of the Russian lands. In addition, I am submitting four certified copies of certificates of marriage, [my] trustworthiness,[2] completion of dental school, and the agreement of my husband about the continuation of my education. I fall down at the feet of Your Imperial Highness with [this] supplication: make me happy by your gracious command to issue me a passport from the Odessa townspeople board. I am not attempting to dissolve our marriage but strive only for the possibility of living on my own labor and dedicating myself to the proper upbringing of our children.

This petition was written according to the petitioner's words by the townsman of Bender, Moishe Modko Surlev Finkel'feld.[3]

NOTES

1. [The Chancellery issued the follow decision (8 December 1899): "Inform the petitioner that his humble petition is denied." RGIA, f. 1412, op. 214,

d. 104, l. 3. When the husband received this very abrupt rejection, he refused to accept it and immediately resubmitted a petition to deny his wife the right to study dentistry. This prompted the wife to send a counterpetition to receive a separate passport, the next item.]

2. [The Chancellery of the Odessa City Governor submitted a certificate of good behavior on 24 September 19011. It attested to her moral quality and political reliability.]

3. [The couple signed an agreement that the husband would grant a separate passport with the understanding that his wife would return to Odessa after she received her dental certificate. The children would live with the wife's parents at their father's expense until their mother returned to Odessa. When the wife returned, the children were to move back to his home and the wife was granted the right of visitation and supervision over their upbringing. They left the decision about the future of their marriage for a later time: "Regarding our future way of life, this will depend on our future circumstances and mode of activities" (RGIA, f. 1412, op. 215, d. 104, ll. 14–15). A police report noted that the two were living separately at the time of the agreement: the wife resided in her parents' home, while the husband lived in his own house and managed a brick factory. It also mentioned that the Grinshteins had had an older child, Emilia, who was born in 1890 but who died five years later.]

[122]

Letters of a Female Medical Student in St. Petersburg to Her Admirer (1903)

TsGIA-St. Petersburg, f. 229, op. 3, d. 105, ll. 42–45 ob., 73–79 ob., 87–91 ob.

"Letter of Mania Lur'e to Isaak Lur'e (3 October 1903)"[1]

I am making an effort not to leave more than one promise unfulfilled, and thus I hasten to write you a letter in due course. I am much busier now than last year so it is easy to forget every promise. We now take twelve subjects, can you imagine? Namely: anatomy, physiology, physiological chemistry, organic chemistry, histology, physics, theory of motion, zoology, botany, mechanics, analytic geometry, and differential calculus. For each subject, I have a different professor; only [Professor] Lesgraft also teaches the theory of motion and [Professor] Dolbiia teaches analytic geometry and mechanics. In addition, there are still more labs for five of the subjects (I attend only three). Add to these, the three examinations that I should have taken last year but did not for lack of textbooks. That is why I will go by the library to get them for a limited time — so I need to hurry. There now, you have a clear picture of how much I must study. But do not be alarmed because, actually, apart from attending four hours of lectures [every day], I do not do anything else, the proof of which is that I have been here a month already and still have not prepared for the examinations, even in analytic geometry, which is quite an easy subject.

Moreover, the day goes by so quickly that you do not have time to notice the dawn before it is night again. Such a feverish lifestyle does a lot of good for me: there is no time to think and be depressed, no time to observe one's life, if one can put it like that. You spin around constantly like a squirrel on a wheel. I get along quite amicably with Imenitovaia, and things have worked out quite well. I feel closer to the female students this year; some are even nice to me, and I call on them with pleasure. But I do not have any personal relations with P. F. now, as though nothing ever happened, because his pedestal is beginning to totter slightly in my eyes and that does not attract me to him.

I have already managed to see the opera *Evgenii Onegin*[2] at the theater in which celebrities took part—Sobinov[3] played the role of [Vladimir] Lenskii. Sobinov sings marvelously. I have never heard anything like it, and so I took great pleasure in hearing him. It is a shame that you were not there; you will probably hear it but without such celebrities. I was also at the Malyi theater for "The Fallen" (Padshikh) and a literary evening. There (that is, at the latter), I had the pleasure to see and hear our contemporary authors, such as Chirikov,[4] I. N. Potapenko,[5] and so forth. Even Gorky[6] was there, but I did not have the good fortune of seeing him (I use the term "good fortune," ironically here of course).

Regarding Lev, I can write very little because, apart from a fleeting meeting by chance at the literary evening, I have not seen him; he came by at 3:00 in the afternoon, only I was not at home. I think he only dropped by because I had inquired at the Belinskiis' for his address, which your friend Khomskii had requested. Lev, probably thinking that I was intending to drop by and being embarrassed, hastened to forestall me; it is obvious that you cannot buy sympathy. However, I managed to learn from our common acquaintance that Lev already has one lesson and that they have offered him others, that he has a great circle of acquaintances, and that he has many "friends." Would to God that this were so! I would be glad from my soul. His cohabitation with Belinskaia also seems to be fine; however, in all likelihood she is completely under the influence of the Belinskiis (him

and her), people who are in some ways alien to me. But this is good because thanks to his "greenness" he absolutely needs to be under someone's influence—so indeed he is under theirs. This at least is well known. I ask you not to utter a word about me to Lev as though I never breathed a word about him to you. I hope that you will keep your word; otherwise, I will never write anything about Lev again. I have suddenly noticed that I have written two pages and have not asked anything about you. Please forgive me, and in spite of this, write to me about yourself in the same way that I write to you about my own person.

Well, stay well.

P.S. Please send me Kovner's address again. I lost it.

"Letter from Man'ia Lur'e to Isaac Lur'e (30 September 1904)"

I am surprised that you think that your message would seem strange to me. You know that I myself always take action and this time I was in a hurry, but in all probability I share the same views on this as you.[7]

Besides fasting, I still have not worked on Saturday and holidays up to now. All this (as it is not stupid, frankly speaking) constitutes my external bond with the Jews, my Jewish shell so to speak. You of course will say that it is not the external but internal bond that is necessary, and to be sure this is true. Such a bond does exist in me; otherwise my exterior would be false, and I have a feeling that I would have broken it because I am not capable of falseness. The question arises: why do I need my Jewish shell in this case, which makes me like the Pharisees? It is difficult to answer this question, and I cannot. It somehow makes me stand firmer on my own, forever reminding me that I am a Jewish woman. But because I am in constant need of strengthening, this indicates the weakness of my spiritual bond. However, I repeat, I cannot confess to this because Jews and Jewishness are infinitely close to me. My friends are surprised, of course, and say that I simply lack the strength to give up tradition. Is that really possible? It seems to me that if I jettison everything, I would somehow alienate myself from my people. I am probably wrong. Please write and tell me what you think about this.

I am further surprised that you should ask my forgiveness for taking the liberty to dwell on your spiritual world — strictly speaking, on one small corner of it. You know, I have asked you so many times to write to me about yourself or is your asking for forgiveness just an assumed trite form? After such a request, I will become ashamed that I constantly pour out my feelings to you.

Why do you always worry about my material situation? You know, I receive thirty-five rubles [a month]. Consequently, I can live like a bourgeois. Every day I have breakfast, lunch, and dinner, which are regular and sufficiently nutritious. I go to bed at 11:00 p.m. and wake up at 7:00 a.m., and in general I carry on a normal life, except that I do not take enough walks because I have no companions and it is boring to walk alone.

As for my studies, I attend four lectures, and for the rest of the time I am preparing for the examinations on last year's subjects. I also read and give lessons on therapeutic gymnastics to a boy who suffers from paralysis, because I want to be convinced about how much P.F.'s therapeutic method actually works. In addition, I prepare and study cadavers; I also study some German. I have practice with a German woman twice a week in all. Finally, I teach reading and writing to a female artisan at a seamstress shop where I eat lunch. And that is all. When you read this, it will seem to [you] like I am very busy, all the more so since I also spend an hour on physical exercise every day. But this only seems so, because there is much in quantity but not in quality, so to speak. On some days it seems that there is little in terms of quantity, so that there are hours when I do not know what to do with myself. So there you have it, all the details of my external life. I am writing almost nothing about my internal life.

The subjects of the courses are now interesting: they relate to the psychological life of a person, not only the physical, as it had been until now. I particularly like psychology, the history of pedagogy, and anatomy (since now P.F. speaks a lot about psychiatric functions). Embryology is also interesting. In this way, the courses this year do not cause me grief. But in lieu of that, my father causes difficult thoughts for me with his incessant and justified complaints that he does not have any more strength to work, and that it is time to place his yoke on someone else's shoulders. You, of course, understand what he wants to say by this.[8] Taking into consideration the inaptitude (to put it simply, the feeblemindedness) of our entire family, I am simply horror-stricken at the thought of what the future holds for us, because I know that father is far from being wealthy (as they think). Speaking like this, I have a premonition of my future guilt before all of my kin if I do not submit to father's plan, which undoubtedly is impossible. I have decided, in the worst case, to take a personally active role in the business, if only to assist in the face of a threatening future. Perhaps I am expressing the collapse of something grand now. I am just a shopkeeper — you know the saying: need springs up, need cries, need sings songs. True, this also means to sell yourself. However, this is the better of the evils that fate has presented me as a choice. Moreover, despite my apparent aversion to trade, there is a so-called merchant streak in me, so perhaps I will cope. I see, however, that I have entered a jungle and need to get out as soon as possible: the horizon is fully clear now, and it means there is no need to hide from the threat. On this basis, I ask you not to attach any significance to all that I have said because, to repeat, the storm is far off. For the time being, I live at my own pleasure. I see that there will be no end to my letter today if I continue in this spirit and so I will talk about something more objective.

It is terribly funny for you to write that I have an influence on Lev. You know Lev is already grown up and does not value me in the least. And how can I have an influence on him when I myself am still in need of a good guardian, for I have not stood on my own two feet until now. I am weak and do not have the ground under my feet; so how am I supposed to teach others? As for Rosa, I can make you glad: she is already almost healthy. But I cannot say anything about your grandmother because I did not see her before my departure. Now I think it is high time to end this letter, which answered all the points conscientiously.

NOTES

1. [This collection of letters was found in the files of Isaac Simkhovich Lur'e. In his handwritten autobiography, he states that he was born in Novgorod in 1875 and could not enroll in the gymnasium because of the strict quotas for Jews, but received a solid education at home. In 1902 he went to Paris to attend the university; it was during his time in Paris that he began to correspond with Mania Lur'e. After he returned to Russia, he served in the library of the Society for the Spread of Enlightenment among the Jews and later managed the archive of the Jewish Historical-Ethnographic Society. Mania was a medical university student from Vitebsk. Her letters indicate that Isaac knew her family well, and that they may have been relatives. She did not welcome his attraction to her and responded sharply to his declarations of love. There are over 100 pages of letters from 1903 to 1913 in the collection. The letters included here describe Mania's university life.]

2. [Tchaikovsky's opera (1879) based on Alexander Pushkin's novel.]

3. [Leonid V. Sobinov (1872–1934) was a famous tenor.]

4. [Evgenii N. Chirikov (1864–1932) was a prominent author, writing plays and short stories.]

5. [Ignatii N. Potapenko (1856–1929) was a playwright, novelist, and essayist.]

6. [Maxim Gorky (1856–1936) was among the most famous writers of the prerevolutionary era, with close ties to revolutionary Marxist circles.]

7. [The previous letter in the file does not indicate what her sentence here refers to.]

8. [She suggests later that her father wanted her to take up the family business in Vitebsk, meaning that she would have to abandon her studies in St. Petersburg.]

[123]

Complaints about Overrepresentation of Jews in Education

"Report of the Temporary General Governor of Odessa, Prince Aleksandr Dondukov-Korsakov, to Count Nikolai Pavlovich Ignat'ev (21 November 1881)"
RGIA, f. 821, op. 9. d. 149, ll. 3–4.

I cannot remain silent any longer but must draw special attention to the phenomenon of Jews who succeed in filling up the educational institutions, especially the secondary and higher educational institutions, thanks to their great material resources (in contrast to the Christian population). They are even supported by resources of the nobility and the *zemstvo*—to the detriment of spreading education among the Christian population. This fact carries the threat of Jewish intellectual predominance in the local districts in the near future, with which they undoubtedly will gain economic domination. Hence it merits the most serious consideration.

Acquiring, in addition to education, greater refined resources and instruments of exploitation in fields in which they hitherto had little access in Russia, this cosmopolitan people with their caste-like order and exclusive tribal interests pose a serious danger not only to the economic fate of the region but also to its civil and political development, even for the preservation of the moral condition of the government's [non-Jewish] tribes. This incentive generates the desire for a quick, definitive, and thorough solution to the Jewish Question, which is also a general Russian question, for it touches on the most vital, material, moral, and social interests of Russia in the present and future. The matter is urgent because any delay—if legal measures are not taken in proclaiming the state's guiding principles—can give rise to the belief that the authorities are indifferent to the fate of the masses of the population. The latter [the masses] would be quick to assert [its own] solution to the question, which is [the source of] its main anger, and open a vast field for instigators, who would pursue greater criminal goals.

I humbly ask Your Excellency to be assured of my true esteem and complete respect.

"Secret Memorandum of the Department of Police to the Third Section (27 January 1901)"

GARF, f. 102, 3 d-vo, d. 1035, ll. 1–1 ob., 6–6 ob.

In a communication of 14 July 1901, the chief of the Kiev Provincial Gendarme Administration stated the following: "The dental schools in Kiev are crammed full of female Jewish auditors, who obtain the right to reside in Kiev through the schools. They represent a den for those associated with political crimes, with Jewish circles, and with those who conduct criminal propaganda not only among the Jews but also among Russians. Above all, these female Jewish auditors at the dental schools in Kiev are the most impudent, audacious, and brazen participants in the street demonstrations, meetings, and assemblies. They conduct themselves provocatively at the investigations, with inexplicable impertinence toward the city police as well."

To confirm this, I relate a personal, verbal conversation that I had with the dentist Zandberg, whom I once asked why he so hastily resold the dental school that he had founded and organized in Kiev. He replied frankly that when he saw and experienced what his auditors—who began to organize assemblies for such purposes in the school—represented, he sold the school immediately, for fear of being held accountable for the consequences. This is because he recognized that the auditors were absolutely occupied with politics, not dental matters.

After that, the mayor of Kiev, Protsenko (one of the best doctors in Kiev, who had built up a large practice in Kiev until he assumed his duties as mayor), once posed the question, without any demand on my part: "For what purpose have we established dental schools that are comprised of Jewish women and led by Jewish doctors in Kiev? How is it that they have not been vacated and closed since the Jewish women positively study nothing but only obtain the right of residency through the school? Moreover, the Jewish doctors who direct the schools only make a profit for themselves, taking 200 rubles or more from the auditors."

In accordance with the above report [. . .], His Excellency has deigned to propose the following resolution: "On the schools, I request that the Third Section discuss [the report of] 18 July." Regarding what has been stated, I have the honor to report that implementation of the director's resolution rests with the Third Section of the police."

"Secret Memorandum of the Chief of the Kiev Province Gendarme Administration to the Director of the Department of Police (27 August 1901)"

The general governor of Kiev, reporting to me on 20 August 1901 about information sent to him by Your Excellency about the dental schools in Kiev, asked me to report to him with information that I had about the schools.

On 22 August 1901, I informed the general governor that the information conveyed to him by Your Excellency about the female Jewish auditors at the dental schools in Kiev has all been corroborated. [. . .] As an addendum to what I conveyed to Your Excellency on 14 July 1901, I have the honor to add the following about the named schools, which I obtained from completely reliable sources.

The city of Kiev has two dental schools that are filled with Jewish men and women: that of the Jew Dr. Blank, and that of the Jew Dr. Golovchiner. In the first Dr. Blank appears to be the head of the business; in the school of Dr. Golovchiner, it is run by a group of Jews who spend money on the school through its purchases. These consist of the Jews Dr. Golovchiner (a doctor), Golovchiner (a dentist), and Gol'denberg (also a dentist). The latter two, according to testimonies of those who ridicule them, are poor dentists.

The founders of both schools, in the nominal lists of people at their schools, never indicate all those who are Jews; there are by far more of the latter. It cannot be otherwise because based on the number of people indicated by name in the schools, it goes without saying that neither school could exist [without the Jews]. Not only among the male and female pupils of the schools are the Jews not indicated, but the list also includes many Jews who live in Kiev and have registered with the acquired rights of residency but are not at the dental school. Rather, they are [dealers] of bonds, clerks and saleswomen, workmen in shops, and so forth, so that in the school there is a riffraff of all possible personalities if only they pay money for the right to listen to the lectures by the founders, who cover up everything in order to take the money and make a profit. Substantial correspondence between the general governor and the Provincial Administration arose last year regarding the right of Jewish residence in Kiev.

In reality, there is absolutely no control over the dental schools in Kiev. It is how these schools form dens of Jewish men and women, where those without rights of residency assemble — people without passports who live in the city, across the Dnieper [River], and in the Nikolaev suburb. The female auditors of the dental schools even assume such a distinctive appearance that, when walking on Kreshchatik Street from school, it is impossible to mistake an auditor based on their singular appearance. They keep to the Jewish circles, workers, and student youth and undoubtedly have a destructive, pernicious influence, also strengthening the composition of the political committees, parties, and assemblies.

[124]

Numerus Clausus during World War I

GARF, f. 579, op. 1, d. 2010, ll. 1–2, 8–14, 15–16.

"Petition of the Jewish Students
David Beniamin-Ur'rev Meseli (Odessa)
and Froim Ber Sikhov Medvedovskii
(Kherson) to Duma Deputy Pavel
Miliukov (11 August 1915)"

Having completed secondary educational institutions in Russia, we were forced to leave to continue our education abroad because of the existing quotas on Jews in the universities. The outbreak of the war cut short our education abroad. Returning to the homeland at the beginning of the war, we submitted a petition to the Ministry of Education to grant us the opportunity to complete our education. This petition was approved only for groups of students who had taken at least *eight* semesters [of classes] in a medical department: they were allowed to take the state examination for the rank of doctor. The petition for the remaining mass of students was rejected.

For the past year of the war, many of these students were conscripted into the ranks of the army due to the loss of their deferment (since they had completed their education). Now there remain only people who were permanently exempted from military conscription or who enlisted in the irregular militias of the second rank but enjoy a temporary deferment.

Given that the school year is beginning, His Excellency, the Minister of Education, who was anxious about the question of increasing the number of doctors, issued a directive on 14 July 1915 about intensifying the work with students promoted to the fourth year at the medical departments in Russia so that they might take the government examinations in the spring of 1915 and replenish the ranks of doctors. This directive provides the opportunity for medical students who have taken *seven* semesters at a foreign university to be admitted to the indicated classes.

We students who have taken *six* semesters in a medical faculty abroad (and are working in the field hospitals in the city and *zemstvo* union or public hospitals) are eager to petition Your Excellency, Minister of Education, to accept us as nonmatriculated students [auditors] in the fourth year at the medical departments of the fatherland's universities.

Mobilization of all the national forces is now under way in the country to work for organizing victory. In this common cause, nothing must be left undone. Those of us who took six semesters in a medical faculty abroad now number about 150 people in Russia. Under conditions that would allow us to intensify our studies with the students at the university in the upcoming school year and then take the government examination, the country and the army have the opportunity after some time to gain 150 doctors — a large shortage of whom is now being experienced. The students who passed seven semesters and who are to be admitted are few in number. That can be explained by these circumstances: Russian young people who complete the gymnasium in May or June can go abroad only in the fall semester (beginning in September); [it is just that] a few tend to be compelled by one reason or another to postpone their trip until the next spring semester, which begins in April. The latter students, it turned out, had passed an odd number of semesters — that is, seven — at the beginning of the war.

The Ministry of Education indicated to us

that those who took six semesters abroad are less prepared than those who have taken the same number of semesters in Russian universities. Indeed, the structure of the curriculum in medical departments abroad does not all correspond to that in Russian medical faculties. For example, we students who have passed six semesters have not yet taken several theoretical subjects. [The foreign medical schools] do not lecture at all on the subjects of pharmacy and pharmacognosy abroad, but they do lecture on pharmacology and general pathology only in the seventh semester in many universities. However, we did receive substantial practical training. In German and Austrian universities, students in their sixth semester already work in a few clinics, and French universities even allow students to work in clinics in the third semester. Thus the vast majority of us have worked in hospitals and field hospitals during the course of the war, looking after not only the sick, but also ill or injured soldiers, and that has further augmented our practical training. We will be able to make up the few gaps in our theoretical knowledge in the course of the academic year.

The acceptance of those who attended one or two years abroad as students or auditors in the earlier courses can give them the opportunity to continue their education. [. . .][1] We take the liberty to hope that you will not reject us and will kindly support our petition.[2]

"Memorandum of Lev N. Azchenskii and Aleksander Davidovich to the State Duma" [1915]

Over 200 Jews who have completed [programs in] secondary educational institutions were allowed to take the competitive examination this year at the Khar'kov Technological Institute. Many of them had already been repeatedly examined. Others went to study at technical educational institutes abroad. Of this number, 163 individuals passed the examination with high marks, with scores no lower than 19 [out of 25].[3] Of these (given

the 10 percent quota), only 21 people were accepted; the remaining 142 people were denied admission. Khar'kov Technological Institute was the sole higher technical institution under the jurisdiction of the Ministry of Education that admitted Jews this year. Non-Jews who passed the examination with the minimal mark (15) were all admitted.

Due to the impossibility, under present conditions, of continuing our education abroad (where we studied by enrolling in foreign technical institutions), the remaining group of 142 individuals has been deprived of the opportunity of receiving a higher technical education.

As a result, this group—in our persons—has decided to submit a humble petition to Your Excellency to provide assistance to facilitate our acceptance in a technical educational institution. The present time, although it is hardly necessary to point this out to Your Excellency, appears to be exceptional. One can hardly fail to mention that our striving to receive a technical education, fulfilling the inclination in each of us, is valid from a general point of view, in light of the development of industry, which will occur as a result of the victorious war in which we Jews participate equally with others under the glorious Russian banner.

We are compelled to seek assistance from the head of the people's representatives [in the Duma] in the hope that the national conscience of the best representative in your person, Your Excellency, can scarcely be reconciled with the preservation of restrictions that place us Jews (who wish to devote ourselves to peaceful and useful labor for the homeland) in a difficult position. This at a time when the fatherland is put to the test, when the material position of a significant majority appears to be shaken, and when the struggle for existence is so exacerbated.

"Newspaper Clippings in 1915 about Jewish Gymnasium Applicants"[4]

Rech' (*8 August 1915*) Smolensk: On 8 August, Dr. Ratgauz turned to the Ministry of Education with the following telegraphed petition: "My son passed the examination for the first class of the Smolensk State Gymnasium, and my daughter passed the examination for the first class of the Mariinksaia Gymnasium. I participated in the Manchurian campaign and was awarded the Imperial Order of St. Stanislaw and Anna with the sword. I have worked for three years without pay as a doctor at the Number 3 Smolensk Upper School. Now I have been called up again to active duty. I request an order that my children be accepted above the quota and outside the lottery." Dr. Ratgauz received the following answer to the submitted petition: "Your petition about the acceptance [of your children] above the quota and outside the lottery was denied."

Rech' (*17 August 1915*) Ekaterinoslav: The Jew, Dr. Knirel, who was drafted in the war, petitioned that his son be accepted without the lottery, having received the highest marks on the examination at the nonclassical secondary school (*real'noe uchilishche*). Knirel's petition was denied.

Rech' (*1 November 1915*) Zhitomir: The Rovno City Duma submitted a petition to the head of the schools about the acceptance of twenty-six children of the Jewish confession above the quota at a male gymnasium. The petition was motivated by the war: many residents have left the town, and there are vacancies at the gymnasium.

Pravitel'stvennyi vestnik (*16 November 1915*): The Sovereign Emperor, according to the imperial report of the Ministry of Education, sanctioned awarding the name of Emperor Alexander I to the Odessa First Upper Elementary School, in memory of the Patriotic War of 1812, and halting the acceptance of Jews at this school. However, he granted the possibility of permitting Jews who had already been accepted at the school to complete their education.

Den (*15 November 1915*) Ekaterinoslav: The petition of the Mariupol' City Duma, with respect to Jews who had been drafted into the war, to accept their sons in the gymnasiums without quotas was denied [by the Ministry of Education].

"Newspaper clippings in 1915 about Jewish University Students and Graduates"[5]

Rech' (*3 September 1915*): The Ministry of Education denied the petition of the Council of Professors of the Higher Women's Courses to accept seventy-seven Jewish women, who do not have the possibility of receiving an education abroad owing to the war, above the quota.

Russkie vedomosti (*15 September 1915*) Petrograd: The following was published in the *Pravitel'stvennyi vestnik*: "In light of wartime circumstances, a large number of Russian citizens, who were receiving an education in technical and commercial schools abroad, have been forced to return to the homeland. The Ministry of Commerce and Industry recognizes the possibility of allowing those among them who have completed their courses to take the final examination as external students at a corresponding educational institution. Apart from them, however, there is a large number who have not completed their courses abroad and who have submitted a petition to the Ministry of Commerce and Industry about their acceptance at a corresponding educational institution. Moreover, a large group of these young people are of the Jewish confession. In light of overcrowding at educational institutions in general and the existing quotas, satisfying these petitions will be met with great difficulty."

Den (*4 October 1915*) Petrograd: This petition pertains mainly to Russian Jews who were studying in German universities and have now been forced to interrupt their studies. According to the survey conducted this past fall, in January and February of the current year there was a total of 3,364 Russians studying at German universities, including approximately 2,377 Jews. For the most part, the Russians studied at the University of Berlin (510 students, of whom 499 were Jewish). To go further by order: in Leipzig 408 students (of whom 350 are Jewish). They do not take one examination until the completion of the specialized higher educational institution. As is known, the educational committee petitioned to accept 103 students from the universities abroad without examinations and without the observation of quotas for Jews.

Rech' (*2 November 1915*) *Petrograd*: The Ministry of Education permitted 190 individuals of the Jewish confession, who have completed their studies in medical departments at foreign universities, predominantly in Berlin, Munich, Koenigsberg, L'vov, Breslav, and so forth, to take the examination for the rank of doctor under the state examination commission in different universities. All these individuals have been notified beforehand that the exemption from compulsory military service is granted to them for the conscription of 1915.

Den' (*16 November 1915*): On 15 November, the Council of Assemblies of the Representatives of Commerce and Industry presented the head of the Council of Ministers and the Minister of Commerce and Industry a second memorandum on account of students of higher technical educational institutions, who were studying abroad but did not succeed in completing their education [before the outbreak of war]. The Council of Assemblies requests to change the quotas for Jews — that is, for the former students of foreign educational institutions. In addition, the memorandum draws attention to the following.

A petition, submitted by young people who have not succeeded in completing their education abroad, was partly approved: those who were close to completing their course of study abroad received permission to take the final examinations at the Petrograd Technical Institute in the spring session on the same level

with individuals who have the right to take this examination as externs (nonmatriculated students). In agreement with the established regulations of such examinations, this would take place during the course of May and encompass all the subjects that they passed in the indicated educational institutions. One must take into consideration, however, that the position of young people who have been educated abroad will differ from that of those who, as a rule, take the final examinations as externs. They took some of the first subjects in the foreign universities that were more inclusive and passed the examinations in them. However, they did not take other courses at all or had less comprehensive courses. [Given all this], it is necessary to change a few requirements presented to the young people. This would namely necessitate [the following]: to establish a test for them in those subjects that they have successfully passed in the foreign universities, and at the same time, extend the period of the exam for those subjects which they must especially cover in order to pass the examination.

In view of the fact that only an insignificant part of the young people have been currently permitted to take the examination and all those in the lower and middle courses have not received permission (even in the capacity of auditors), it is necessary to permit foreign students of Russian citizenship who have taken the theoretical subjects and passed the midcourse exams abroad to take the exam with the permission in each individual case from the school authorities of the corresponding educational institution.

On these grounds, the Council of Assemblies [also] proposes that it would be just and expedient to facilitate acceptance in the technical educational institutions of young Russian citizens who have not studied abroad and who passed the fall entrance exams in special educational institutions but were not accepted because of the very high competition set specially for them.

Den (*28 November 1915*): Upon the advice of the institutions of higher education under its jurisdiction, the Ministry of Commerce and Industry circulated an order to permit former students at foreign higher specialized educational institutions to take the examinations as externs. The Ministry proposes that only those who have a certificate for the completion of Russian secondary educational institutions (received no earlier than 1911) be permitted to take the examinations. In addition, only students in the last semesters at foreign institutions [will receive permission]. The institutes may not issue residency passports to externs. Everyone, regardless of confession or nationality, will be permitted to take the examinations as externs. The time frame for completion of the examination will be no more than a half-year.

NOTES

1. [The students go on to reiterate the arguments made above.]

2. [There was no final resolution in the file, but the following newspaper clippings on the Jewish quotas were included in the file describe the decisions of the Ministry of Education on some of these issues.]

3. [The file included the list of the 121 Jewish students who received high marks (between 19 and 25). The highest scoring students included eight Jews who received a perfect score of 25 and forty-seven others who received scores of 24.0–24.75.]

4. [The clippings were collected and filed by the ministry itself, as it monitored public opinion on the issue.]

5. [The Ministry of Education collected these newspaper clippings.]

[V]
Work

Prior to the Polish partitions of 1772–95, the Jewish economy in Poland developed a particular character. Faced with bans on landowning and intense competition with Christian townspeople, but endowed with an ability to take risks and make investments, Jews concentrated in several main occupations in urban centers: commerce and moneylending (especially pawnbroking). So dominant were the Jews in trade that, according to one study, they occupied almost all the houses and stalls in the market squares of Polish towns. For instance, in Kopys, "seventy-five percent of the town's stalls in 1747 were owned by Jews."[1] Although the protective Christian guilds largely excluded Jews, the latter nonetheless carved out their own niche in the crafts such as the textile trades, leather tanning, butchery, bakery, and gold- and silversmithing. By the late seventeenth century, Jews began to move to the new noble estates and towns, where they negotiated lucrative positions in the rural economy as middlemen, tax farmers, and leaseholders, especially with a monopoly over the production and sale of alcohol as well as tavern keeping.[2]

Although the Jewish economy retained its general character after the partitions, it did exhibit some tendency to change. First, Jewish merchants sought to find new markets by expanding into the Russian interior — that is, outside the Pale. The documents reveal constant negotiations between individual merchants, local officials seeking to stimulate their local economies (for example, in Riga and Tomsk), and the central state. During the Great Reforms of the late 1850s and 1860s, Jewish first-guild merchants gained the right to reside anywhere in the Russian Empire and subsequently created a new class of Jewish entrepreneurs and bankers in the capitals. Second, with respect to the rural economy, Jews who engaged in traditional occupations encountered growing legal restrictions, especially in the liquor trade — which the Russian state viewed as the cause of peasant impoverishment and lack of productivity (even while it sought to appropriate this lucrative business for its own benefit).[3] Despite state decrees, court records reveal that illegal Jewish distillation and sales continued to flourish: as soon as inspectors uncovered one illegal brewery in someone's basement, another sprang up in someone else's kitchen, for every distiller sought to avoid the onerous excise duty. Third, Jews continued to run the majority of taverns.[4] As the documents in this part (and in part 4) show, taverns in the villages and remote areas represented a kind of "frontier space" permeated with wild entertainment, sexuality, and violence; it was a site where Jews and peasants mingled to drink and exchange news, to gossip, and sometimes to insult each other and get into brawls.

Other rural Jewish inhabitants resided in agricultural colonies, the vast majority created by the state after 1835 partly to "productivize" the Jews (that is, make them more productive subjects), and partly to colonize the newly Russian territories in the south. Exemptions from taxes and military service provided strong incentives for Jews to uproot their families and relocate to the sparsely populated regions of southern Ukraine and Bessarabia. The documents reveal that the Jewish colonists faced a life high in risk and low in reward. Some, frustrated by their inability to cultivate the land successfully, turned to trade and thereby lost their right to the plots. Those who continued working the land found that the combination of drought and infertile soil (at least on their allotments) made a bountiful harvest all but impossible. In the north (Lithuania and Belorussia), farmers such as the father of Mariia Shkol'nik were forced to send their children to toil in artisan shops and factories to augment the family's meager income (document 144). Still, more than 150,000 Jewish farmers (also known as *yeshuvniki*) had settled on the land by 1900.[5]

In urban centers, economic opportunities varied by skill and education: unskilled Jewish workers (like the girls at the Gal'pern factory in Pinsk; see document 149) worked longer for shrinking wages during the rapid industrialization of the late nineteenth century. The unfavorable terms of labor caused even the least politically conscious workers to strike (whether spontaneously, as the female workers insisted, or at the instigation of political radicals, as the factory owners claimed). Uncontrollable circumstances such as illness also threatened the existence of smaller artisan shops, especially in the capitals, where Jewish artisans had to demonstrate continual engagement in their trade or lose their residency rights. In large cities like Moscow, St. Petersburg, and Kiev, the number of Jewish white-collar professionals increased sharply,

especially in the fields of medicine, engineering, and law. The pressure to convert to Christianity, which would "open doors to state service," in Genrikh Sliozberg's words,[6] was particularly strong for educated elites seeking to make a career in the free professions.

This part focuses on the most important areas of Jewish economic life: commerce and trade, domestic service, farming and agriculture, factory and artisan trades, and the professions of medicine and law.

NOTES

1. Adam Teller, "The Shtetl as an Arena for Integration," *Polin* 17(2004): 35.

2. Gershon Hundert, "The Role of the Jews in Commerce in early Modern Poland-Lithuania," *Journal of European Economic History* 16, no. 2 (1987): 245–75; Moshe Rosman, *The Lords' Jews: Magnate-Jewish Relations in the Polish-Lithuanian Commonwealth during the Eighteenth Century* (Cambridge: Harvard University Press, 1990); Adam Teller, *Kesef, koah, ve-hashpa'ah: ha-Yehudim ba-ahuzot bet Radz'ivil be-Lita ba-me'ah ha-18* (Jerusalem: Zalman Shazar Center, 2006).

3. For instance, the Statute of 1804 sought to prohibit Jews from holding leases to sell alcohol and run taverns. A similar law enacted on 30 December 1812 extended this ban to the Grand Duchy of Warsaw.

4. See Magdalena Opalski, *The Jewish Tavern Keeper and His Tavern in Nineteenth-Century Polish Literature* (Jerusalem: Zalman Shazar Center, 1986); Glenn Dynner, "Legal Fictions: The Survival of Rural Tavern-Keeping in the Kingdom of Poland," *Jewish Social Studies* 16, no. 2 (2010): 28–66.

5. Jonathan Dekel-Chen, *Farming the Red Land: Jewish Agricultural Colonization and Local Soviet Power, 1924–1941* (New Haven: Yale University Press, 2005).

6. Sliozberg, *Dela minuvshikh dnei: zapiski russkogo evreia*. 1: 198.

Commerce and Trade

[125]

Jewish Commerce and Trade in Moscow (1790)

RGADA, f. 19. op. 1, d. 335, ll. 2–4 ob.

"Petition of the Moscow Mayor Mikhail Pavlovich Gubin and Chairman of the Moscow Merchant Society [on behalf of the Moscow merchants] to the Commander-in-Chief of Moscow, Petr Dmitrievich Eropkin (13 February 1790)"

TO HIS EXCELLENCY,
THE COMMANDER-IN-CHIEF OF
MOSCOW AND ALL THE PROVINCE
OF MOSCOW, GENERAL-IN-CHIEF,
SENATOR PETR DMITRIEVICH EROPKIN:

Your Excellency's patriotic efforts on behalf of the general welfare are quite well known to all. Your Excellency has denied none of our requests and has made evident Your paternal protection in all instances of public need. Feeling Your compassion toward us and knowing full well how You are burdened with state matters, we would not take the liberty to trouble Your Excellency. However, given the extreme danger now before our society, we are compelled to turn to You, gracious Sire, with our most humble petition.

According to the decree of April 1727, *zhidy* [Jews][1] may not enter Russia under any circumstances and are strictly admonished that this be observed everywhere. Moreover, a personal manifesto from Her Imperial Majesty, our most compassionate monarch, on 4 December 1762 permits foreigners of all different nations—except the *zhidy*—to settle in Russia. This imperial injunction was reiter-

ated in the imperial decrees of 23 May and 9 July 1763. Indeed, according to article 124 of the City Statute [of 1785],[2] the wisdom of the Russian sovereign, Her Imperial Majesty, established and confirmed the freedom of the non-Orthodox and foreigners to practice their faith. As a result of these decrees, on 21 May 1786 and 24 December 1789, the Governing Senate denied the petition of Belorussian *zhidy* to permit them to register in the tax rolls of a Riga suburb and in the Smolensk merchant estate.

Nevertheless, *zhidy* from abroad and from the Belorussian provinces have recently appeared here in the capital [Moscow] in considerable numbers. Living in inns that they have rented, they sell there (and distribute among private homes) various foreign wares that they import illegally from abroad that are cheaper than our own goods—in violation of the decrees of 30 October 1752, 29 April 1756, and 20 November 1760 that banned such retail trade. This has caused tangible harm and disruption to all of the local business. Their sale of cheap goods, in contrast to [the practice] of all Russian merchants, clearly demonstrates that they clandestinely smuggle [goods] across the border and do not pay custom duties. In addition, the whole world believes that any gold or silver coin, especially Dutch gold coins, that have passed through their hands, never remain intact and have always been reduced or debased. These very actions make [the Jews] absolutely intolerable in many well-organized societies. Herein lies the main danger—that the pernicious activities of the Jews will bring harm and the impermissible destruction of the government's gold and silver coins. They have long been known for this, as is evident from Her Majesty's personal decree of 26 April 1727 that expelled the Jews from the state and, at the border, specifically ordered a thorough inspection to ensure that they not take gold or silver abroad.

Above all, some of the newly arrived Jews — concealing their real origins from the state and identifying themselves only as new merchants arrived from Koenigsberg or Mogilev — secretly register in the Moscow merchant estate under the simple category of merchant. This false registration alone manifestly reveals their deceptive schemes and actions. Thereby many of those who do not rightfully belong to the local merchants not only engage in the wholesale and retail sale of foreign goods in various parts of the local city, but they also provide a convenient conduit for illegal retail trade by their coreligionists (as if they belonged to the local citizenry), whom they control and support.

We will refrain from giving Your Excellency a more detailed description of the Jewish trade in foreign goods that is harmful to the state and commerce. The Jews transport (by various subterfuges and deceptions) such imports through overland customs, which they use to satisfy their foreign creditors. Nor shall we delve into the circumstances favorable to their commerce; in this respect, one can believe public opinion. For now we only want to report that those coming from abroad, especially Polish and Belorussian Jews (who are generally characterized by the greatest poverty and moral depravity), conduct all their trade and business on the basis of lies, deception, and every kind of unacceptable means. They are capable of resorting to every kind of illegality, as can be seen in their secret reg-

istration in the local merchant estate. However, the real danger that they obviously pose already came to light earlier. That is because one of their society — a Belorussian *zhid* [Jew] named Not[a] Khaimov, better known informally as Notkin[3] — secured significant credit (through various subterfuges and forgeries) from the general public that he used to obtain goods worth 500,000 rubles from local merchants. He then sent the goods to a place known only to himself, secretly left Moscow, and fled abroad with everything (the significant capital) that he had manifestly stolen. He subjected many merchant households to pitiful ruination; some merchants died of grief, leaving behind poor wives and children without support. The rest lost all the property and credit they had accumulated over many years of hard work; bankrupted, they innocently lost their good name as citizens, while others remained with their families in extreme need and poverty.

Because of the manifestly perceptible danger posed to all of society by the pernicious Jews, who have illicitly entered the capital, but not because of any disgust or hatred of them that derives from their religion, the local merchant society seeks only to protect itself from an increase in their numbers over time and from their duplicitous activities, lies, and deception that are inherent to them and that are known to all. We cannot endure the overall damage and complete decline of local trade that they have caused. We find ourselves compelled to appeal to Your Excellency, as someone chosen by our Most Gracious Sovereign, to serve as the intercessor and protector of the decrees and public well being that She has promulgated. We humbly request, Gracious Sir, that you deign to order the appropriate authorities to find all the *zhidy* living here in Moscow and not only terminate the illegal retail trade but also legally prohibit them from residing here any longer; also exclude those who have registered illegally in the local merchant class and order an examination based on the imperial decrees published about this. Thereby, Your Excellency will save the entire community of local citizens from the [otherwise] inevitable calamity that threatens them. Sensing the patriotic favor of Your Excellency, we give you our eternal pledge to exalt You (as one worthy of praise for the concern about the common good and justice that are embodied in the person of Your Excellency) with our deep respect and devotion.

NOTES

1. [In the Polish-Lithuanian Commonwealth, *zhid* was the standard Polish word for Jew. In contrast, the Russian government chose to employ *evrei* (Hebrew) for standard legal usage, and *zhid* eventually gained a pejorative connotation in Russian, In this eighteenth-century document, the petitioners are not employing the term *zhid* in a pejorative sense. See: John D. Klier, "*Zhid*: The Biography of a Russian Epithet," *The Slavonic and East European Review* 60:1 (1982): 1–15.]

2. [A reference to the *Zhalovannaia gramota* (Charter to the cities) of 1785, which established a new system of urban self-government.]

3. [Nota Khaimovich Notkin (d. 1804) became one of the first influential Jewish figures to intervene on behalf of the Jews before the Russian state. In this document, the merchants of Moscow accuse him and other Jewish merchants of ruining their businesses and bringing harm to the capital city. Notkin moved to St. Petersburg in 1797 and served as a member of the State Committee for the Organization of Jewish Life under Alexander I. See David Fishman, *Russia's First Modern Jews: The Jews of Shklov* (New York: New York University Press, 1995), 52–56, 90–91.]

[126]

Jewish Contraband in Moscow

GARF, f. 109, op. 9, g. 1835, d. 53, ch. 1, ll. 1–2 ob, 24, 24 ob, 37–40 ob.

"Secret Report of Colonel Shubinskii of the Gendarme Corps, Moscow (26 February 1835)"

For some time we have seen an increase in the sale of forbidden goods in Moscow. An investigation revealed that Jews with contraband goods are staying at one of the inns beyond Dorogomilov on Mozhaisk Road. From there they allegedly bring the goods into Moscow and sell them in small quantities to avoid inspection. Although these circumstances have not yet been sufficiently verified, one agent determined that about thirteen kilometers from Moscow, on the Mozhaisk Road and behind the village of Setun'ia, near a tavern called Marfukh or Oborvikh, Petr Iorov and Ivan Sivertsov run two inns, where allegedly only Jews continually stay with [their carts full of] their products and goods.

According to the innkeeper Iorov's own words (in an indirect conversation), he intentionally has special horses and cart drivers for the Jews, similar to those of the Moscow stockbrokers—with whom the Jews purportedly leave the goods for delivery to Moscow in small quantities. They freely transport them through the military checkpoint and deliver various goods to the market and to the Glebov Monastery where the Jews stay. Above all, [people] say that the inns of Ivan Chushkin,

Abram Gushchin, Aleksei Kuznetsov, and Natalia Mostachikh were opened specifically for Jews in the same village of Setun'ia. Although it is impossible to confirm categorically the complete accuracy of these stories, one might find the means to uncover the contraband — a delivery is expected in two weeks. I considered it my duty to present this to the gracious consideration of Your Excellency and humbly request Your resolution on how to move forward in finding [the contraband] if the above stories are verified.

Moreover, I deem it my duty to add that a thorough reconnaissance leads one to conclude that if the *zemskii* [county] police and officials were to conduct the searches, one can certainly vouch that nothing will be found. Even in the event that they find something, they will use part of them in accordance with the law. Therefore I take the liberty of asking your permission to use gendarme officers for the search.

"Secret Memorandum of the Civil Governor of Lifland to the Moscow Chief of Police (3 November 1837)"

The chief of police, Colonel Reits, has informed me that Private Ivan Griaznov, a police officer from Riga who was passing through on furlough to St. Petersburg, reported [the following]: On 27 October he was passing through the town of Valka when he saw two *zhidy* [Jews] from Libava traveling in two carriages with forbidden foreign goods: raccoon fur coats in packages without customs stamps and other contraband goods in large suitcases, weighing over 200 pounds.[1] The coachman driving the carriage was Konstantin Goriachii from Moscow province (Klin district), and he was delivering the goods directly to Moscow. In one carriage with the Jews was a German woman; in the other carriage were two market gardeners from Iaroslavl province. Assured that his suspicions were correct, Private Ivan Griaznov stopped them with the word "contraband." But the Jews threw two

silver rubles at him, and at the coachman a silver fifty-kopeck piece; they lashed the horses and galloped off. According to an inquiry, the Jews were headed for Verro and Pskov.

Although the chief of police conveyed Private Griaznov's deposition to the Pskov police so that it could adopt measures, I, for my part, deem it necessary to inform Your Excellency of his statement and the measures undertaken by the Civil Governor of Pskov to seize the contraband and its transporters and to address the matter in compliance with the law. I humbly request, Gracious Sir, that You take the appropriate means in the capital (in the event that the Jews and coachman come to Moscow) to seize the transported contraband and enforce the law.[2]

NOTES

1. [The text gives a round figure of "six *pud*" (98.28 kilograms).]

2. [The file does not include a report about the arrest of the alleged Jewish smugglers of contraband. However, the case sparked further discussion about the rights of Jewish merchants temporarily residing outside the Pale of Settlement. As the Minister of the Interior noted in a letter to the civil governor of Moscow on 9 January 1838, the few heads of the provinces "were perplexed about how to proceed on Jewish petitions to travel temporarily outside the Pale of Settlement" following confirmation of the Statute of 13 April 1835. Such queries pertained primarily to third-guild merchants and to petty townspeople [meshchane]. The Ministry of the Interior responded by making several important clarifications. It noted that although third-guild merchants were forbidden to travel outside the Pale of Settlement, the military governor of Riga had made some proposals: "The military governor of Riga writes that the prohibition could prove harmful to the trade of local merchants, for example, in the city of Riga. Given that many Jewish families have lived there from time immemorial, and given the close proximity to Kurland province (where quite a few of them also permanently reside), [Riga] has a special relationship to other port cities. [. . .] I propose that

third-guild Jewish merchants and petty townspeople be allowed to travel to Riga and to sojourn there on the same basis as those that exist in the published Statutes of 1835." However, the Ministry of the Interior did not make the same concessions for the third-guild Jewish merchants of Zhizhmory and Mogilev who had requested permission to travel to Moscow (GARF, f. 109. op. 10, d. 53, ch. 1, ll. 58–59 ob.).]

[127]

Petition of a Jewish Merchant to Reside in Siberia (1855)

GARF, f. 1265, op. 4, d. 22, ll. 1–2, 3–4.

"Iosif Khaimovich of Tomsk to Emperor Nicholas I (7 December 1854)"

Before the promulgation of the Imperial regulation of 15 May 1837, confirmed by Your Imperial Majesty, which prohibited Jews from residing in the Siberian *krai* [territory], I voluntarily traveled to eastern Siberia, where I settled with my family and acquired real estate in the town of Tomsk. I have conducted considerable trade there for over two decades.

The general governor of eastern Siberia is personally satisfied with my commercial activities. I have earned the complete trust of all the Christian population, and all of our relations are in order and trustworthy. In November 1851 I petitioned the minister of finance to secure the most gracious order of Your Imperial Majesty to leave me and my family in the rank of merchant in the Siberian territory; however, Mr. Brok (who holds the rank of privy councilor) did not deign to make a satisfactory intercession on my behalf. My five sons, upon reaching the age of sixteen, are to return to the provinces open for permanent Jewish settlement [the Pale of Settlement]. So as not to remain without a rank and a settled way of life, I found myself forced to register as a first-guild merchant in Kishinev, and this registration obliges me—an extreme calamity—to conclude all my commercial affairs, to sell my own real estate, and to leave forever the territory with which I am so closely tied. With the move to Bessarabia (a land completely alien and new to me) and the Jewish people (with whom I have nothing in common except our religion), my entire business will suffer an inevitable decline, especially amid the present wartime conditions [of the Crimean War]. But [such is not the case] in Siberia. With tireless labor and strict integrity, I succeeded (thank God) in gaining the general favor and intercession of the local general governor, who finds me useful to his territory. Under these circumstances, I have decided to fall at the feet of Your Imperial Majesty and humbly request that the August Monarch graciously deign to permit me and my family to remain in eastern Siberia and enjoy the merchant regulations that were granted to all merchants (upon obtaining the information that has been presented) and to honor the request of the main head of eastern Siberia [the general governor] for my welfare.[1]

NOTE

1. [The governor general of Eastern Siberia had sent a petition requesting permission to allow Iosif Khaimovich to remain due to his usefulness to local trade; he pointed to the precedent of "the Jew Preisman" who was allowed to register as a merchant in Nizhneudinsk in Eastern Siberia on 1 August 1850. In 28 February 1850, Prince Golitsyn rejected his petition; however, on 25 April 1855, the "Siberian Committee" reexamined the case and arguments by the governor general and general of the infantry Gasford that "leaving Khaimovich in Siberia will be useful for the revival of trade in the region, where there is a shortage of capitalists and practically no competitors." This time the committee allowed Khaimovich and his family to remain in Siberia and to enjoy the rights of the merchant rank.] RGIA, f. 1265, op. 4, d. 22, l. 19–19 ob.

[128]

Aharon Rozenshtein's Correspondence on the Brick Business (1901)

Private collection of Carolyn Rosenstein.

Handwritten Letter to Aharon Vol'fovich Rozenshtein from M. M. Kalin (9 April 1901)

I humbly request that, upon receipt of our letter, you respond immediately about the price for selling bricks from Kiev and if you or your father will load them [for shipment] to Ekaterinoslav. I am now opening a warehouse with a partner. You should immediately answer me now. 100,000 bricks are needed.

Letter of Aharon Vol'fovich Rozenshtein from Kiev to M. M. Kalin (14 April 1901)

I have just received your letter of 9 April and hasten to reply: I intend to load the bricks [for shipment] to Cherkassy. If you agree to purchase 100,000 Mezhigorskii bricks from me for cash, then I can add this quantity to my barge. I can sell you this brick at 5.75 rubles per thousand at the Ekaterinoslav docks. I can also be your permanent supplier. If you wish to purchase [the bricks], send me a telegram. However, I forewarn you that [I will load the brick exclusively for you in Ekaterinoslav][1] I am sailing to Ekaterinoslav exclusively for you.

WITH GREAT RESPECT TO
SOKOLOVSKII AND DOBROLIUBOV.

Letter of Aharon Rozenshtein to his wife Esther Rozenshtein (8 June 1901)

VILLAGE OF KAMENSKOE,
FRIDAY, 9:15 A.M.

I am writing to you from [the village of] Kamenskoe and not from Ekaterinoslav as you of course expected. The reason is that the barge has not yet arrived in Ekaterinoslav. I overtook it on Wednesday at 8:00 p.m., 134 kilometers before Ekaterinoslav. [I am here also] because I learned from the captain of the barge that they did not unload the 10,000 bricks [out of the 100,000] in Burzhin, which I sold. I decided to visit a few places; perhaps I will manage to sell some bricks. I was in Verkhned[ne]provsk yesterday, spent the night in Pan'kovka, and did not sell anything there. Now I am here in Kamenskoe, and it seems that I will not sell anything here either, although I do not know for sure. I still have 90,000 unsold bricks. Eisenberg is ruining the price all over the place here.

First, I thought I would not write you until I had finished the business or at least until I arrived in Ekaterinoslav. However, knowing that you miss me and I miss you here too, I decided to have a chat with you on paper. I am sitting here in the café waiting for dinner and writing to you. I intend to tell you a bit about the places where I have been this week. But first of all, I want to let you know that I mailed the letter to your parents in Kiev, and that I purchased ninety pounds of sand in Kiev but did not manage to send it; I was forced to leave it in Kalin's small store on the riverbank. Srul'-Ber Liudmirskii promised to deliver it to you at home on Wednesday. The town of Verkhnedneprovsk bears the designation of a district town; in reality it is no bigger than a *shtetl*, but does have a pro-gymnasium (its lower forms) for girls. The residents are in the bakery business but, because of the bad harvest, these poor people are in extremely difficult straits. The environs are rather picturesque. Kamenskoe is precisely the opposite: it bears the designation of a village, but actually is an important town with a large foundry. Its condition, however, is bad: the dust is unbearable, stones are everywhere, and the heat from the foundry is terrible. The local dust is acrid because it is mixed with peat. The inhabitants here depend exclusively on the factory, which employs 14,000 workers.

Pan'kovka, where I spent last night, is a tiny village in a good forest, where the count (who owns Pan'kovka) has a large distillery and a large *dacha* [summer home]. Altogether three Jews live there: one, with whom I lodged, is a *feldsher* [paramedic]. His family was hospitable; I ate dinner there. They gave me a meal of black bread, genuine rye that I did not even touch, and fresh white bread, butter, sour cream, and milk. Of course, I was very

happy with such a dinner because I have not had anything like it for a long time.

Please write a letter to me in Ekaterinoslav: tell me how you are, how you spend your time, [and] whether you are bored. I saw Vol'ka Liudmirskii between Sekirna and Cherkassy. Please swim every day in the river. It is very healthy. I have not swum even once since I left. Greetings to Bentsion, Khava, the children, Zusia, Leib, Bliuma, Ravikovich, Rivka, and all the rest of ours [our relatives]. If you see my father, please send greetings from me. If I do not sell the bricks here, then I will leave today at 5:00 or 6:00 in the evening for Ekaterinoslav. I kiss your photograph and remain yours — Aharon

Letter from Aharon Rozenshtein to Esther Rozenshtein (10 June 1901)

KAMENSKOE

I wrote you a letter on Friday. Yesterday I sold 20,000 bricks for 6.24 rubles, and 5,000 bricks for 6.20 rubles, and 200 unloadings for 7.50 rubles per hundred [bricks]. Moreover, I sold 20,000 bricks for 6.00 rubles to a person from Ekaterinoslav. Altogether, I have only 45,000 unsold bricks left. According to what I have heard, I will be able to sell them for a good price in Ekaterinoslav. I will be earning 55 rubles more than I expected, if I am successful. The barge arrived here yesterday evening and is being unloaded today. I hope to be in Ekaterinoslav tomorrow.

I kiss you from afar and remain your loving Aharon.

Letter from Aharon Rozenshtein to Esther Rozenshtein (15 June 1901)

EKATERINOSLAV, THE OFFICE OF FRESHMAN, 1:30 P.M.

DEAR ESTHER,

I still do not know, even now, when I will come home. I am writing you only so that you should not worry about not receiving letters. I will tell you the details when I am home.

I visited Uncle Iosif twice and even promised to come once more. I think I will be there today. This week, a huge fire burned down two mills, six lumberyards, twelve lumber warehouses, a workshop on the railroad, two streets of houses, and still more. Today is the fourth day of the fires but even yesterday I saw flames. The ship docks and also our barge were taken away from the shore during the fire. Greetings to all of ours. Your A[ha]ron, who loves you.[2]

NOTES
1. [The phrase in brackets was crossed out.]
2. [See document 51 about the death of Esther and the hiring of a wet nurse for Aron's infant son.]

[129]

Theft and Violence at Jewish Stores in Warsaw Province (1883)

GARF, f. 102, 3 d-vo, g. 1883, d. 1014, ll. 7–14.

"Chief of Warsaw Province to the Minister of Internal Affairs (19 November 1883)"

This past 13 October, at the time of the fair, an unknown woman stole several meters of cloth from the store of the Jewish merchant Fromer. Having observed this, the store clerk drove the woman onto the street, took away the goods, and also began to beat her. Responding to the woman's cries, a crowd of 300 people who had gathered in the town square of Sokhachev shouted: "Have no mercy on the Jews" and attacked Fromer's store. However, they were stopped by the police constables who had arrived and managed to close the store's entrance in time. Nevertheless, some attacked and beat the Jews whom they encountered; the peasants threatened to resume the disorders at the next fair (3 November), but did not carry out the threat because of the [state] directive to intensify patrols during fairs.

On 1 November recruits from the communities of Kozlov-Biskup, Kliavinsk, and Ioroshin started an argument with the Jews. At noon, when the members of the district board for military conscription suspended their work, the recruits let themselves into the adjacent chamber and dealt several blows to the head of the Jew Leizer Efroimovich. Only the arrival of the mayor at that point saved Efroimovich, who was brought into the chamber hall.

On the same day, about ten people (recruits) came into Zil'berstein's leather store under the guise of purchasing leather and initiated an argument with the shopkeeper, followed by a brawl. The fight began because the recruit from the community of Mlodzheshin, Vikentii Gurestkii, stole a piece of leather without paying for it and intended to leave the store. The constables arrived at this point and restored order.

On that same date, a market day, Jews from Sokhachev (Aron Shoel, Iukel, and the Iablonskii brothers) bought straw from a Christian, Iakov Petrovskii (from the community of Khodakov). However, because the latter did not want to sell the straw at their proposed price, the Iablonskii bothers started a fight, and other Jews came running and took part. Christians passing by took Petrovskii's side. The police halted the fight.

On the following two days the public peace and quiet were violated only by recruits who directed vulgar curses at Jewish passers-by and by a fight at the small tobacco store of the Jew Gol'dberg. However, patrols put an end to the disorders.

Simultaneously, the police from the second precinct of Radimin followed ten intoxicated people from their village to the city. Along the way, the latter perpetrated disorders at taverns run by Jews, who did not want to open their establishments. In a few places, they broke glass and threw down a few small objects on the floor.

I have the honor to inform your Excellency about the above, with an addendum that the guilty have been indicted in court for perpetrating the above disorders.

"Governor of Vil'na to the Ministry of Internal Affairs (21 November 1883)"

The police superintendent of Vil'na district has informed me that on 9 November recruits called up for military service were summoned to the Maliaty *zemstvo* [county] administration to verify the conscription lists. Afterward, they set out for the small town of Maliaty, where they behaved violently in an inebriated condition. They also took off with baskets of apples and eggs worth three rubles and two rubles in cash from Khaia Vainer's [store]. At Gitlia Videtskaia's small store, they seized various goods worth eleven rubles and beat her. They also beat Shmuil Zhiv and stole goods worth five rubles. At Mortkhelia Gerberovich's or Segal's [store], they took three rubles in cash and locked [the latter] in the stall. Of the entire mob, the victims managed to identify only: the peasants Iurii Genis, Kazimir and Avgustin Slepikasov (from Maliaty, Kazimorov rural community). [...]

Your Excellency, I have the honor of adding that an inquiry will be conducted in the above case, and its conclusion will be conveyed to you through the proper channels. Taking into account that the village and county officials did not take appropriate measures to prevent the disorders, I have given an order to initiate proceedings against them according to [the law].

[130]

Anti-Jewish Disorder at a Jewish Store in Chenstokhov (1902)

GARF, f. 102, 3 d-vo, d. 1508, ll. 7, 11–24 ob.

"Secret Report of the Chief of the Gendarmes, Petrokov Province [Poland], (30 August 1902)"

As a supplement to my telegram, I have the honor to report that the street disorders in the town of Chenstokhov resulted when a Jewish trader swindled a Christian woman. The case was [as follows]: Yesterday, on 29 August, around 8:00 a.m., a peasant woman, Teofilia Kliuk[1] purchased a small barrel of fruit from a Jewish trader at the old bazaar. The bulk of it was spoiled; the only fresh fruit was placed on top. Kliuk returned to the trader and asked him to replace the rotten [pieces of] fruit with fresh ones. Although he agreed to satisfy the customer's request, another Jewish trader came up and convinced him not to comply with Kliuk's request. As a result, an argument broke out between the customer and her husband (Andrei Kliuk) on one side, and the Jewish traders on the other. The Jews who gathered there attacked the peasant woman, threw her down, and beat her. The police escorted the victim to the hospital.

The above circumstances gave rise to a false rumor that the Jews had killed a woman, who left behind five children. [. . .][2]

"Secret Report of the Governor of Petrokov Province to the General Governor of Warsaw (3 September 1902)"

On Thursday, 29 August, around 9:00 a.m.[3] the police officer Budogovskii of the factory district, while passing through the New Market, heard that the Jews had killed some woman at the Old Market. He rushed to the Old Market and from afar saw a crowd. When he approached, he found a woman lying on the ground in their midst, moaning violently, and three small children next to her. The husband of the woman (who turned out to be Teofilia Kliuk), Andrei Kliuk, and the city doctor Pisarzhevskii arrived almost simultaneously. The latter, having examined the victim thoroughly, found only minor injuries to the arms, inflicted by a stone or some other kind of blunt weapon. Seeing no need to send her to the hospital for treatment, the doctor expressed his opinion that she should be taken home. However, Andrei Kliuk did not wish to heed this advice and disappeared, leaving his wife and children. Then the policeman Budogovskii sent the local sentry to fetch a cart driver while he remained with the woman who was lying down, dispersing the crowd (primarily women) that had grown around her. The cart driver did not arrive for a long time, so the policeman walked toward the New Market in hopes of finding a free driver. At this point Andrei Kliuk reappeared at the Old Market and began to smash the small tables and barrels of fruit close to where his wife lay. Hearing the clamor and din at the site of the incident, the police officer hurried back, and once again Andrei Kliuk disappeared. Observing that the crowd had grown larger, the police officer called the rural police by telephone and ordered the police supervisor Goritskii to see to it that Teofilia was taken home, and proposed to maintain order in the place of the incident. After Teofilia was taken home, her husband expressed discontent that his wife had not been sent to the hospital. After an hour had passed, he hired a cart driver, seated his wife and three children in the droshky, and sent them to the hospital. Returning from [the hospital] around 12:00 p.m., he stopped at the Cathedral of St. Sigizmund as workers from a few factories were passing by; he showed them his small children, cried, and lamented loudly that his wife — the mother of these little ones — *had been killed* by the Jews.

As the initial investigation showed, the following circumstances had caused the conflict between Teofilia and the Jews. She had bought a barrel of plums from one of the Jewish fruit dealers to resell and paid him what they cost. Standing to the side, she began to examine the plums more closely and found that those in the lower part of the barrel were completely rotten. She hastened to return them to the seller and demanded that he either take back the entire barrel of plums and return the money that she had paid in full or give her part of the money for the rotten plums with which he cheated her. After much wrangling, the trader agreed to return part of the money for the [rotten] plums. At this time, the Jew Shternberg — an individual well known to the police for his brazen, contemptuous character — approached them as they argued. He began to hurl insults at his coreligionist, the trader, for yielding to the stupid demands of a *baba* [hag] and pushed her aside. When she attempted to protect herself, he beat her, together with other Jews, most likely by using stones.

The loud clamor and wailing of Andrei Kliuk and his children at the cathedral drew the attention and deep sympathy of the workers who were passing by the cathedral at this time, as stated above, as well as others. Soon a large crowd of people had gathered around them.

Hatred toward the Jews (nurtured in the hearts of simple folk who are often shamelessly exploited by the Jews) and fanaticism now poured out instantaneously. The crowd (among whom there was no one to reason with it) attacked Jewish homes and stores, giving no thought to the consequences of its brazen whim. They began to smash the buildings to smithereens, breaking the glass in the windows, brutally beating and trampling every Jewish man and women whom they met, not to mention the property that they stole or destroyed.

A few sentries who were nearby rushed to the clamor and din, and although the furious mob began to pelt them with stones, managed to disperse the crowd. However, the dispersed crowd began to form again as a mob on another neighboring street. It grew as the city rabble (mainly workers who had lost their jobs at the factory) joined and spread to the adjacent streets, curtailing production in the factories. There they began to cause bedlam.

The entire Chenstokhov city police that was available that day (thirty-seven people) were summoned to the sites of the disorders and responded very energetically; at first, it seemed as if they had managed to suppress the commotion. Then, the police officer Taboriskii, who had taken the place of local chief of police who was on vacation, sent me the following telegram, which I received at 4:05 p.m.: "A Christian woman was beaten by the Jews at the Old Market. In revenge, a large Christian mob conducted a riot in both markets; a

few people were injured. Measures are being taken."

I had returned from my holidays abroad the day before and was not in good health— indeed, to the point where I had asked the vice governor to take my place as governor for a few days. In addition, based on the tenor of the telegram, one might think that the disorders had already ended. I nevertheless considered it necessary to suggest to the vice governor, Count Liders-Veimarn, that he go immediately to Chenstokhov to clarify the situation and telegraph me a report. In the event that he found further disorders, he was to take decisive measures to suppress them. Simultaneously, I took into consideration the fact that the disorders might recur, the fact that the paltry forces of the local police were insufficient to suppress them in a town with more than 45,000 people (which is constantly crowded with pilgrims who flock there from all over the region), and the fact that the Chenstokhov garrison (two infantry regiments and one cavalry [unit]) is away conducting maneuvers and will not return earlier than 2 September. Given all this, I summoned a Cossack squadron, the 14th regiment from the town of Bendin, forty constables from Bendin district, and fifty policemen from the city of Lodz.

Upon receiving Count Lider-[Veimarn's] telegram at 8:40 p.m. reporting that the situation was serious and that the unruly conduct had escalated into open looting, I recognized my responsibility to go personally (despite my poor health) and take the first train to Chenstokhov.

When I arrived in Chenstokhov at night, I learned that the disorders had assumed a serious, acute character starting at 7:00 p.m., when the workers returned from the factories and mills. The rabble behaved desperately, and the pogrom steadily intensified. To help the police to quell the disorder, it was necessary for [Taboriskii], who was the acting police chief, to summon a small regiment stationed here in Chenstokhov. But rioters met it brazenly, [and] threw stones both at the soldiers and the police officers. According to Lieutenant Livotov, at two sites they even shot at the company with revolvers as they shouted: "Beat the *zhidy* [Yids] and the police!" Finally, they made a frenzied attack on the company under Lieutenant Livotov's command, with the aim of disarming it.

The company used only their gun butts initially, but when the rioters intensified the assault, Lieutenant Livotov repeatedly warned that he would have to resort to firearms. Loud laughter and shouts of "You would not dare!" resounded from the midst of the rioters, who showered the company with a hail of stones. By then Lieutenant Livotov realized that he had exhausted all means short of firearms in his attempt to subdue and pacify the mob. He therefore ordered a few riflemen to shoot at the crowd; two were killed and six others injured. After this, the crowd quickly dispersed. Further information about what took place in Chenstokhov after 7:00 p.m. has been included in the vice governor's report to me, a copy of which is attached.

It was quiet on 30 August. At 9:00 in the morning the 14th company of the Don Cossack regiment was dispatched by railroad from Bendin. At 10:00 a.m., together with Major General Baumgarten, who had assumed responsibility as the head of the garrison, I went around the towns and suburbs where there had also been attacks on Jews and, in particular, made a careful inspection of the Jewish quarter that had suffered from the pogrom.

The pogrom left major devastation in its wake: many Jews had been severely beaten, more or less by fists, stones, and various other weapons. According to the latest information, approximately one hundred Jews came to the local Jewish doctor for medical assistance; he found that eight people were in grave condition, with little hope of recovery. Not one home with windows in the Jewish quarter es-

caped damage: all the glass was shattered. In many Jewish stores and apartments, the mob had ripped the doors off their hinges, smashed everything, and looted the belongings. The Jewish community estimates the losses from the pogrom at approximately 150,000 rubles. The synagogue had had only its windowpanes broken and was full of stones that had been thrown at it. In the adjacent prayer house, all the books had been torn to shreds.

Here and there a crowd of Jews (especially Jewish women) surrounded me and showed me various bodily injuries (which were not, however, especially severe). With tears, everyone begged me to protect them from [further] destruction (which the Christians had vowed to perpetrate), and to order an inquiry about the looted property. According to them, the unruly Christians — as they beat and robbed them, as they destroyed their property — shouted that the state officials and Roman Catholic clergy had authorized the pogrom. They were plundered not only by the rabble, but also by the *zapasnye trubachi* [reserve trumpeters] of a dragoon regiment and the rank-and-file members of the voluntary fire society that had been summoned to extinguish two fires. General Baumgarten informed me about the trumpeters; he immediately ordered that the information be verified and that their lodgings be searched. However, the inquiry did not turn up the slightest confirmation of the report. As for the rank-and-file members of the voluntary fire society, the police indeed did arrest three of them on suspicion of robbery; thus far the preliminary investigation has sufficient evidence for a criminal indictment against one of them.

Upon receiving my reports, the Jewish community hopes that the full cost of their losses incurred during the riot will be recompensed through a compulsory assessment on the entire Christian community of Chenstokhov. It even proposes that the Imperial order on the compensation for losses, which the Khar'kov and Poltava landowners suffered during the recent looting of their property by peasants, be applied to this case.[4] The Jews did not present these proposals directly to me or to the public servants under my jurisdiction, so I was not able to dispel their unwarranted expectations.

A terribly frightened rabbi of Chenstokhov and members of the *chleny Bozhnichnogo dozora* [God patrol] appeared before me and tearfully asked that I defend all their coreligionists from further attacks by the Christians. As I calmed them down (averring that I would not tolerate a repetition of the disorders and violence), I could only declare that the Jews themselves are absolutely guilty, that the Christian population—especially the simple folk, who have been exploited at every step—has long nurtured a hatred toward them. The present events—which are sad for all—began when a Jewish scoundrel attacked a defenseless Christian woman. The Jewish population can thank him for the pogrom that has caused them such misery. In response the rabbi declared that Shternberg has long been well known in the community as someone who is brazen and contemptuous in the highest degree and who is prone to commit every kind of crime. Last year he raped a Jewish girl, which prompted a legal investigation; however, due to the lack of evidence required by law for a conviction, he avoided penal servitude. According to the rabbi, the entire Jewish community is convinced that this time he will not escape the most severe retribution under the law; it is fully content to get rid of him.

However, the assumptions of the Jewish community are hardly justified. In the procurator's opinion, proceedings against Shternberg (who has now gone into hiding) can be initiated in the Justice of the Peace Court either by a complaint from the victim who was beaten or by the police records showing a violation of public order. In either case (in the former, since the victim did not suffer mutilation or life-threatening injuries; in the latter,

even under the full extent of the law), Shternberg faces an extremely light punishment—a maximum three-month detention. For my part, however, I think that this scoundrel should not get off so easily, that he remains a danger to social order in the future: the peasantry will not soon forget that, first and foremost, he must be brought to court for many crimes and for shedding their brethren's blood. I therefore propose to request that he be permanently exiled from Chenstokhov as the punishment determined by the court.[5] [...]

During the inspection of the town, I visited the city hospital where Teofilia Kliuk and those suffering from bullet wounds (from the army's attack on the rioters) were undergoing treatment. Teofilia Kliuk's life is not in any danger; they found only marks and bloody bruises on her body, without any damage to the bones or internal organs. However, she is in a state of nervous agitation; that is the only reason they are keeping her in the hospital. [...][6]

By 31 August, those who had been detained (based the testimony of the police, officers from the military detachment, and the victims of the riot) numbered 137 (122 men and 15 women). That day the police released 16 people (14 men and 2 women) for lack of evidence in the crime. By the evening of 1 September, the court investigator found sufficient evidence to indict 60 of the detained for crimes.

In agreement with the procurator of the Court of Appeals, I ordered that all the detained be sent by rail to the Petrokov prison under a heavy police guard on 4 or 5 September. [...][7]

NOTES

1. [The documents spelled the surname in various ways (Kruk, Kriuk, Kluk and Kliuk). For the sake of consistency, the text here uses the spelling (Kliuk) used in the police reports.]

2. [The report goes on to provide a short descrip-

tion of the anti-Jewish violence that followed, which is reported in greater detail in the following item.]

3. [The earlier report had the time as 8:00 a.m.]

4. [The reference here is to the Poltava and Khar'kov disorders in the spring of 1902 — the first major wave of peasant rural disorders leading to the Revolution of 1905-7. To deter peasants in other provinces from emulating their peers in Poltava and Khar'kov, the regime engaged in demonstrative punishment, including steps to hold the rebellious peasants accountable.]

5. [Administrative exile indeed became a favorite extrajudicial device to quash disorders and to combat the revolutionary movement. See Jonathan Daly,

The Watchful State: Security Police and Opposition in Russia, 1906-1917 (DeKalb: Northern Illinois University Press, 2004).]

6. [The governor goes on to provide a list of seven men who were hospitalized for their injuries; two men were killed during the shooting.]

7. [The governor devotes the rest of the report to describing how to prevent further violence during the funeral of the two workers who were killed by the military. He warns that "the funeral can easily assume the character of a demonstration." He also describes signs of unrest among peasant workers in Chenstokohov and the neighboring towns of Lodz and Dombrov.]

[131]

Theft and Violence at a Jewish Store in Smela (1904)

GARF, f. 102, 3 d-vo, d. 1, ch. 16, l. B, ll. 38–40.

"Secret Report from the Governor of Kiev to the Department of Police (29 August 1904)"

As a supplement to the encoded telegram sent to the minister of internal affairs about the disorders in Smela [Kiev province], I report the following to the Department [of Police].

On Sunday, 22 August, peasants from neighboring villages as always came to the usual bazaar in Smela. However, the influx of arrivals was especially large this time because of the metropolitan's trip through Smela. On this occasion, townspeople and workers from Smela, predominantly young lads from the working class, held a celebration at the bazaar. The mood was peaceful; nothing indicated a threat to the Jewish population. Around 12 p.m., however, the peace was suddenly shattered by a dispute that took place in the small

store of the Jew Duvid Koval'skii at the center of the market. The owner of the store and his wife Feiga began an argument with a peasant woman from the village of Goloviatin, Feodora Trofimovna Pustovoitova (age twenty-six), who had stopped at the store and haggled over a few *arshins*[1] of cloth. According to the small storeowner Koval'skii, Pustovoitova took advantage of his distraction as he negotiated with other customers and managed to steal a kerchief and to hide it under her shirt (from which a small piece of the kerchief was visible). Feiga Koval'skaia pulled out the kerchief from under the shirt while Duvid Koval'skii threw Pustovoitova out of the store by her neck, as they themselves confirmed.

Pustovoitova says that she did not steal the kerchief, that the Jew Koval'skii unjustly accused her of theft, forced her out of the store, and slapped her twice on the face. Without leaving the shop, she began to scream and cry that the Jews had beaten her. At her cry, peasants and Jews gathered so that two crowds — Jewish and Christian — instantly formed. The crowd of peasants, aroused by Pustovoitova's tears and claims that the Jews had unfairly accused her of stealing a kerchief and that they had beaten her, began to threaten the Koval'skiis and to demand that they come out of the store and set things straight. At that very moment, however, the policeman Maksimenko and constable Fatenko managed to restrain the crowd and to protect the Koval'skiis. The crowd, which remained at Koval'skii's store, fell on the large storage bins that were nearby and that belong to the Jews. They overturned several bins and then began to destroy and loot Jewish shops among the trading stalls. As peasants and local workers arrived, the crowd of looters increased still further.

The disorders continued until 11:00 p.m.: the crowd looted and destroyed property in ten stores, smashed the windows, and in a few homes ripped off the window shutters. On Sunday the disorders subsided, but [they] resumed the next day (Monday, 23 August) with still greater force from 8:00 a.m. until 11:30 p.m., when a military detachment arrived. Approximately 2,000 people gathered to destroy and loot on 23 August. Several hundred people in the front split up into parties, went into town, looting and destroying goods in the small shops and the property in Jewish homes; they did not destroy the buildings but did smash windows and window frames, tore

off shutters, broke the doors, and destroyed the furniture and everything else in the homes and small shops. Over two days, 176 commercial establishments (including [shops selling] manufactured goods, grocery stores, secondhand stores, and storage bins), as well as 98 houses, were subjected to looting. The losses were considerable: the Jews estimate several hundred thousand rubles, although they exaggerate quite a bit. [...][2]

The local police, together with the police officers that I dispatched from Kiev, are conducting an investigation, searches, and proceedings against those accused of participating in the pogrom. By 27 August, twenty-six people have been implicated in the destruction, arrested, and indicted (by the order of the court investigator in accordance with the gravity of the offense). The arrest and interrogation of detained witnesses are continuing. Stolen goods have been found in the homes of seventy-seven people. People who did not participate in the looting report that many [stolen] goods have been thrown onto the streets and jettisoned. [...]

On 28 August, I traveled again to this site. In view of the menacing mood that persists among the local population and the danger that the disorders may break out in neighboring towns, I have left a full military detachment in Smela.

NOTES

1. [An *arshin* is equivalent to 71.12 centimeters.]

2. [Here the report devotes a few pages to the efforts of the police to quell popular unrest and the ongoing violence.]

[132]

Inaccurate Scales in a Small Jewish Shop (1909)

LVIA, f. 448, op. 1, d. 29314, l. 1.

"Indictment in Vil'na Criminal Court (1909)"

On 13 November 1908 the trade inspectors, policemen Frants Vasilevskii and Vikentii Voitkevich, conducted an examination of weights and measures in commercial establishments in the city of Vil'na. In a small store run by the townswoman Khasia Solomonovna Levin, located in house number 6 on Sirotskaia Street, they discovered a five-*funt*[1] cast-iron weight that was not the approved brand. Upon the examination, the weight proved to be inaccurate.

The preliminary expert examination, which measured Khasia Levin's five-*funt* weight with precise instruments, established that it was off by 105 *dolia*[2] and therefore exceeded the legally permissible margin of error, 10 *dolia* per pound. This scale is therefore false.

Indicted as a defendant for using a weight that is inaccurate and that is not the approved brand, Khasia Solomonovna Levin pleads guilty to the violation as due to an oversight and denies any intent to deceive [her customers]. She explained that she knew nothing about the inaccuracy of the five-*funt* weight in her small shop and that she was unaware that the weights needed to be a [particular] brand.[3]

NOTES

1. [A *funt* (an obsolete measurement) is equivalent to 409.5 grams.]

2. [A *dolia* is equivalent to 44 milligrams; there are 9,216 *dolia* to a *funt*. Levin's scale was off by roughly twice the permissible margin of error.]

3. [Khasia Levin, who was twenty-four years old, requested a court defender. The court could not prove that her motive was to deceive her customers with the inaccurate scales, but it found her guilty of violating the regulations of weights and measures in trade. She received a five-ruble fine; if she was unable to pay this fine, she was to be jailed for two days. The court ordered that her scales [including the weights] be destroyed. For a similar case, see LVIA, f. 448, op. 1, d. 29313a.]

[133]

Petition of Belorussian Jews about the Liquor Trade (1784)

M. F. Shugurov, "Istoriia evreev v Rossii," *Russkii arkhiv* 2 (1894): 157–58.
Reprinted from Gregory Freeze, *From Supplication to Revolution: A Documentary Social History of Imperial Russia* (New York: Oxford University Press, 1988), 96–97.

1. Some [Belorussian Jews] who live in towns engage in trade and especially in the distillation of spirits, beer, and mead, which they sell wholesale and retail. This privilege was also extended to them when Belorussia joined the Russian Empire [in the partitions of Poland]. Hence everyone active in this business used all their resources to construct buildings suitable for distillation and the pursuit of this trade in the cities. After the Russian Empire annexed the Belorussian region, the Jews in some towns constructed more of these in the same fashion and at great expense. The imperial monarchial decree [on Jews] emboldens them to request tearfully monarchial mercy.

2. According to an ancient custom, when the squires built a new village, they summoned the Jews to reside there and gave them certain privileges for several years and the permanent liberty to distill spirits, brew beer and mead, and sell these drinks. On this basis, the Jews built houses and distillery plants at considerable expense. The squires voluntarily farmed out the inns to Jews, with the freedom to distill and sell liquor. As a result, the head of the household and his family employed other poor people and paid their taxes. A new decree of Her Imperial Majesty on 3 May 1783 [and] a decree of the general governor of Belorussia have now forbidden the squires to farm out distillation in their villages to Jews, even if the squires wish to do so. As a result, the poor Jews who built houses in small villages and promoted both this trade and distillation have been deprived of these and left completely destitute. But until all the Jewish people are totally ruined, the Jewish merchants suffer equally with the poor rural Jews, since their law requires that they assist all who share their religious faith. They therefore request an imperial decree authorizing the squire, if he wishes, to farm out distillation to the Jews in rural areas.

3. Although, with Her Imperial Majesty's permission, Jews may be elected as officials, the imperial statute on provincial administration allots Jews fewer votes than other people, and hence no Jew can ever attain office. Consequently, Jews have no one to defend them in courts and find themselves in a desperate situation — given their fear and ignorance of Russian — in cases of misfortune, even if they are innocent. To consummate all the good already bestowed, Jews dare to petition that an equal number of electors be required from Jews as from others (or, at least, that in matters involving Jews and non-Jews, a representative from the Jewish community hold equal rights with non-Jews, be present to accompany Jews in court, and attend the interrogation of Jews). But cases involving exclusively Jews (except for promissory notes and debts) should be handled solely in Jewish courts, because Jews assume obligations among themselves, make agreements, and conclude all kinds of deals in the Jewish language, and in accordance with Jewish rites and laws (which are not known to others). Moreover, those who violate their laws and order should be judged in Jewish courts. Similarly, preserve intact all their customs and holidays in the spirit of their faith, as is mercifully assured in the imperial manifesto. [. . .]

[134]

A Violent Night in the Tavern (1878)

"Journal of the Court Investigator of the First Sub-district [Uchastok] of Vladimir-Volhynia District (12 December 1878)"

DAZhO, f. 19, op. 9, d. 84, l. 1.

The Court heard the report by a member of the provincial court, L. G. Zenetta, about the case of the peasant Feodor Stepanov Pilipchuk, forty-two years old, accused of delivering a severe blow to the [pregnant] Jewish woman Shnaidmel', which resulted in the premature birth and death of the baby.

The Court gave orders to examine the present case and found that on the evening of 23 March 1879 the peasant from the village of Zalis'ia, Feodor Pilipchuk, came by the tavern run by the Jewish woman Khaia Tovbe Shnaidmel' and demanded vodka. After he downed the vodka, being already quite drunk, he picked an argument with Shnaidmel's children, who were learning to read and write in the next room. Pilipchuk began to run around, having taken off his leather belt on which hung a knife. When Khaia Shnaidmel' sought to protect her children, Pilipchuk kicked her in the stomach so hard with his leg that she became ill. Three days later she gave birth to a baby, which lived for one hour and died. Witnesses Efim Prilep, Maria Prilep, Akim Morchuk, and Viktor Daniliuk confirmed that Pilipchuk had kicked Khaia Tovbe in the stomach. Moreover, they explained that her pregnancy was very evident and that Pilipchuk, although drunk, was not on the verge of losing consciousness. That Khaia Tovbe gave birth after she received the blow was confirmed by the witnesses Soldaiuk, Savchuk, Koltman, and Ivan Trachuk.

The peasant Fedor Pilipchuk, brought to trial for inflicting a blow on a Jewish woman and causing the premature birth and death of the baby, does not consider himself guilty. He explained that at the time he was so drunk that he has absolutely no memory of what happened at the tavern. He added that he had noted Shnaidmel's pregnancy. Concerning the day on which the crime took place, the accused Feodor Pilipchuk [claimed] that he was so thoroughly drunk that he did not remember anything, and said that he would refute the testimonies of the witnesses.

From the court's medical report on the newborn infant's body and also the mother, Khaia Shnaidmel' clearly gave birth to a baby girl at the end of the seventh or eighth month [of pregnancy]. The baby was born alive and breathed but soon died. The cause [of death] was a concussion to the fetus from a kick of the leg to the stomach.

On the basis of the above, the peasant Feodor Stepanov Pilipchuk is found guilty. [. . .] In addition, because there is no information to show malice aforethought in Pilipchuk's action and, on the contrary, given his agitated condition as a result of his alcohol consumption, the court finds that Pilipchuk did not act with premeditated intent.[1]

NOTE

1. [The court sentenced him to serve time in the workhouse, a subunit of the city prison, and then to be placed under the general surveillance of society. It gave Khaia Shnaidmel's husband permission to file a new suit for damages in civil court.]

[135]

A Secret Distillery in Briansk (1885)

"Sentence of the Vil'na Provincial Court of Appeals (5 September 1885)"

LVIA, f. 445, op. 1, d. 106, ll. 16–29.

On 22 August 1885, by His Imperial Majesty's Decree, the Criminal Department of the Vil'na Provincial Court heard in public session [. . .] the case of the townspeople Iosel Leibov and Geneida Liebovna Graf involving the construction of a secret distillery. The case has come before the [Vil'na] Provincial Court because of an appeal filed by [the defendants] regarding the verdict of the Grodno District Court of 8 March 1885.

According to the indictment statement, compiled by the procurator of the Grodno District Court (Serebraikov), the Grafs were tried in the Grodno District Court without a jury on the accusation of building a secret distillery in the village of Kersnov (Bel'sk district), which was discovered on 22 January 1885. During the course of three years, they clandestinely distilled alcohol without paying the excise duty. In the court sessions, Iosel Graf admitted building the secret distillery without paying the excise duty but [claimed] that he produced alcohol for only two months before they discovered his violation of the law. His wife Geneida Graf explained that she was away for three months, and her husband built the distillery in their house during her absence, without her participation or knowledge.

Among the sworn witnesses who testified, the peasant Kazimir Osipov Vonzhatel' said that before the distillery was discovered (some months ago—in any case more than half a year ago), his wife brought him a bottle of vodka from the Grafs. It was very strong and was probably *spirt*.[1] He and other residents of the village (Ivan, Aleksandr, and Pavel Kersnovskii) stated that Graf had constructed a tannery in his house a long time ago; recently, however, they had detected a heavy odor around the house as well as black smoke and steam coming out of the chimney and through other chinks in the windows and door of the house. However, they assumed that it came from the operation of the tannery. Vikentii Grinivitskii recalls that in his presence a year or less ago, Iosel Graf poured some kind of liquid from a bucket near his house; it produced the smell of vodka. According to the testimony of experts, based on an examination of all the equipment, [. . .] the distillery in this house had been operating for two to four years.

As to the question of the two defendants' guilt, the district court—on the basis of this information—found: (1) By virtue of his confession, which is completely in accordance with the information by the preliminary and court investigation, Iosel Graf personally built and secretly operated a full-scale commercial distillery in his house. According to the average assessment of experts, he distilled alcohol for three years; (2) On the basis [of this information], his wife Geneida, who lived with her husband in one house, collaborated not only in the production of alcohol but also in building the still; this is beyond doubt, especially since Geneida Graf is much more energetic and more intelligent than her husband. To determine the guilt of the defendants, it seemed necessary for the district court to determine the quality of the alcohol, its market value at the time, and the amount due in excise duties. Moreover, the law makes it necessary to determine the daily quantity of the distilled alcohol in order to determine the total quantity (provided that the still was in production every day for the entire period). It is also necessary to consider the possibility of a greater quantity from the daily distillation.

To decide these matters, [the district court] had to be guided by the inspection record, the measurement of the largest mash tub, the conclusions of the excise duty board responsible for Grodno province, and the regulations of the Ministry of Finance. The court concluded that: (1) with the capacity of a mash tub of 14 *vedro* [168 liters],[2] three *pud* [49.14 kilograms] of sugar beet residue can be squeezed out daily for a total of 3,285 *pud* [53,808.3 kilograms] over three years or 1,095 days; for fermentation and formation of the yeast for this volume, one needs 328.5 *pud* [5,380.83 kilograms] grain products on the basis of the proportional ratio. Given that one *pud* of sugar beet residue produces a 30 percent waterless spirit and that one *pud* of grain product yields 45 percent alcohol, one can conclude that if distillation continuously took place for 1,095 days, that would produce a 113.3325 percent grade alcohol [*sic*].[3] Supposing that the cost that is due for the graduated excise duty is 8 kopecks, but the market sale price for this grade of alcohol is 10 kopecks, one can deduce that the full excise duty due is 9,066.60 rubles and that the secretly distilled alcohol brought in 11,325.65 rubles.

As for determining the defendants' punishment, the [district] court observed that on the precise basis of [the law], the guilty are subject to: a penalty of twice the value of the excise duty; imprisonment from two to four months; confiscation and sale of everything that belongs to the secret distillery as well as the distilled alcohol (all for the benefit of the State Treasury). In the event that they have already sold their wares, there is not only a penalty for the value of the liquor but also compensation to the Treasury for the lost excise that would have been due on the secretly distilled alcohol. In addition, the de-

fendants are held mutually responsible for the penalties; in the event that neither are in the position to pay the monetary penalty (here twice the value of the normal excise duty of 9,066.60 rubles, or 18,133.20 rubles), then each must be sentenced to prison for a period concomitant to the sum in accordance with [the law] — in this case, two years in prison. However, irrespective of the definite and separate prison verdict that the court considers a just punishment for each of the accused, a middle measure would be three months in prison. On the monetary fines to compensate the Treasury for the losses incurred, accept the above-named excise duty and the cost of the vodka. The initial court costs will be exacted from the convicted in accordance [with the law].[4]

The Grodno District Court ruled that the townsman Iosel Leibov Graf, fifty years old, and Geneida, thirty-eight-years old, are each sentenced to three months in prison; moreover, they are to be penalized, bound by mutual obligation, for double the sum of the excise duty on the secretly distilled alcohol (18,133.20 rubles). If neither can pay, they are to be imprisoned for two years each, in addition to the confiscation and sale of the [wares] belonging to the secret distillery for the benefit of the Treasury (viz., the mash tub, three mead tubs, the boiler, rectificator, refrigeration plates, refrigerator, and distilled alcohol found at the secret distillery (552 liters) as well as their personal belongings. They are mutually responsible for the value of the excise duty for all the distilled alcohol during a three-year period (9,066.60 rubles). [. . .]

At the appeals review, Iosel and Geneida explained that:

(1) There was no precise evidence regarding the period during which they illegally distilled the alcohol. The conclusion of the experts that the distillation had taken place for two to four years on the basis of the [equipment] belonging to the distillery is of no merit: it is diffi-

cult, if not impossible, to determine this by examining the equipment. Rather, it is necessary to consider the conditions under which the equipment was used, but that could not be known to the experts. Thus the experts' conclusion cannot be accepted by the court to determine the level of punishment. Furthermore, even if one allowed that the experts were correct in their conclusions, that could not provide the basis for calculating proportionately the total excise duty for three years (the time that the experts determined that the equipment had been in use). The reason is that, at the opening of the distillery, they could have used secondhand equipment (as was done here). Consequently, in all cases, whether one attaches significance to the conclusions of the experts or not, the district court could not calculate the sum of the excise duty and determine the measure of punishment proportionate to this time.

(2) The District Court, which found them guilty for distilling alcohol secretly for three years, did not take into account the Sabbath and holidays on which, as is well known, Jews do not work. For these three years, that adds up to 213 days, which should be deducted from the number of working days by the court. Besides the Sabbath and holidays, it would be inconceivable to assume that the distillation proceeded without any breaks, especially in a secret distillery, where no one hesitates to take a break, not only in the course of three years, but even in the course of one month. The days off always exceed the working days. Thus, while the [district] court incorrectly calculated 1,095 days, it should have counted the Sabbath and holidays at the very least (213 days), not to mention the indubitable fact that the days off far exceed working days.

(3) The capacity of the mash tub set at fourteen *vedro* is exaggerated; that is three times more than its real capacity. Hence the court incorrectly calculated the sum of the excise duty and subjected them to such a severe punishment, which is in variance with the reality.

(4) Although, based on [the law], one should accept the largest possible quantity of daily distilled alcohol, the time required for distillation nevertheless raises significant doubts; according to the law, any doubt should be interpreted in favor of the defendant (per the footnote to article 671). In cases where it is impossible to determine even the time that it takes to produce alcohol, the fine is calculated according to the sum of the excise duty that a factory owner would owe for a designated period. The law allows taking into evidence [the time needed to produce] each kind of alcohol in a legally constructed factory that does pay the excise duty.

(5) In this case there was no dispository evidence of Geneida Graf's guilt in the illicit production of alcohol. The court found her guilty solely on the basis of its assumption that since she lives with her husband, this already proves her participation not only in the production of the alcohol but also in the construction of the factory. Such assumptions by the court should not and may not serve as evidence against Geneida Graf in the conviction, which involves such a severe punishment that it entails the loss of her parental care over her minor children and ability to earn a livelihood. The Grafs request a change the Grodno District Court's sentence on defendant Geneida Graf and exonerate her completely from responsibility for lack of evidence against her. With respect to the defendant Iosel Graf, they request that his punishment be changed and reduced.

Having heard the conclusion of the procurator of the chamber and the case of the lawyer on behalf of the defendants, [. . .] the Vil'na Provincial Court finds that:

(1) Neither the preliminary nor the court investigation uncovered any firm information that could provide grounds to persuade it of Geneida Graf's guilt in building a secret distillery with her husband Iosel. Regarding

the grounds that the [district] court cited for its verdict (that Geneida, as Iosel's wife, could not but participate in the criminal activities of her husband), that is inadequate, especially in light of the defendant's testimony. It is clear that she was away for three months when the apparatus of the distillery may have been built. Thus, on the basis of article 771 (Statutes of the Criminal Court), Geneida Graf must be considered innocent of the criminal activities of which she has been accused.

(2) The district court adopted an incorrect basis to calculate Iosef Gral's monetary penalty (namely, the conclusion of experts about the duration of the alcohol production) and hence its estimation is incorrect. Given that the district court [relied] only on an examination of the equipment as the basis [for its estimation], this Court holds that it cannot be sustained, [. . .] especially since the experts' opinion on this question (three years but perhaps one year more or less) is indefinite to the highest degree. Hence it is more appropriate to focus on the testimony of witnesses to determine how long the distillery operated. The confirmation by Vonzhatel' that the production of the alcohol proceeded for more than half a year must be [treated as] proof that the distillery operated for six months, to which, by law, fourteen days must be added, making a total of 194 days.

Taking 194 days as the basis [for calculating] the production of alcohol, the capacity of the mash tub of 14 *vedro*, the daily mash of sugar beet residue of three *pud* equals 582 *pud* for 194 days. Distillation and refinement of this quantity requires 58.2 *pud* of grain (taking into account that 30 percent waterless *spirt* is obtained by distillation per *pud* of residue); a *pud* of grain produces 45 percent alcohol. This leads to the conclusion that over 194 days a 200.79 percent alcohol was distilled [*sic*].[5] Assuming that the amount owed for the excise duty is 8 kopecks and the market price for the alcohol on sale is 2 kopecks

[*sic*], the excise duty for the entire duration of the illicit alcohol production amounts to 1,606.32 rubles.

As for the punishment set for the fifty-year-old defendant Iosel Graf, the Provincial Court finds that, on the basis of [the law], he is to be sentenced to prison; the duration of the imprisonment must be an average based on the circumstances of the case—that is, three months in prison and a monetary penalty of double the value of the excise duty for processed drinks: 3,212.64 rubles. In addition, to compensate the Treasury for its losses, the monetary fine is the value of the excise tax (1606.32 rubles) and the value of the alcohol produced at the distillery (401.68 rubles). Independent of this, the liquor, supplies, and materials in the distillery are to be confiscated. In the event that he cannot pay the monetary fine (3,212.64 rubles), Graf is to be imprisoned for one year in accordance with [the law]. Iosel Graf is liable for the court costs in this case; if he cannot pay, the Treasury will assume these expenses. The court pronounces thirty-eight-year-old Geneida Leibovna Graf, on the basis of the [law], innocent. The sentence of the Grodno District court in this case is changed.

NOTES
1. [*Spirt* is closer to pure alcohol than vodka.]
2. [One *vedro* (bucket) is approximately twelve liters.]
3. [They came up with this figure in the following way: 328.5 x 0.30 = 98.55; 10 percent of 328.5 = 32.85; 32.85 x 0.45 = 14.7825; 98.55 + 14.7825 = 113.3325 percent. It is unclear to what the percentage refers as alcohol cannot be over 100 percent.]
4. [The document lists numerous laws and statutes that the couple had violated and the corresponding laws on punishments.]
5. [The court came to this figure in the following way: 582 × 0.30 = 174.6; 58.2 × 0.45 = 25.19; 174.5 + 26.19 = 200.79. It is unclear what all these figures mean, as there cannot be alcohol that is 200.79 percent.]

[136]

Trial of the Nokhim and Khaia Gurvich of Vil'komir for the Illicit Production of Alcohol (1901)

LVIA, f. 445, op. 1, d. 2796, ll. 2–6 ob., 1–6, 113–17, 118 ob., 126–26 ob.

"Indictment (29 September 1901)"

On the night of 18 July 1901, police officer Indrik of Vil'komir discovered a secret distillery in Andrei Kozlovskii's apartment (located in Count Kossakovskii's brick factory near Vil'komir). As the inspector was approaching Kozlovskii's house, he observed the two small sons of the Vil'komir townsman, Nokhim Gurvich, in the courtyard. One of the children, the oldest, ran away at once. The inspector found Gurvich himself in Kozlovskii's apartment near the stove, where vodka was being distilled with the aid of the appropriate equipment. After completing a charge sheet on the basis of what was discovered and after dismantling the distillery, the inspector and policeman Romanovskii arrested Gurvich and Ekaterina Kevlich (who lives at the Kozlovskiis') and escorted them into town. At the inspector's order, two other policemen Valepko and Zemorzhitskii set out to investigate Andrei Kozlovskii.

They brought [Ekaterina] Kevlich, her two children, and Gurvich's young son on a small cart, onto which they piled all the distillation equipment that had been found. However, Gurvich, who was bound up so his hands remained free, walked. Around 3:00 a.m. they entered outskirts of the town of Pivonia and, at Gurvich's request, came up to his house to get his overcoat. The inspector stopped and sent Gurvich's son, who had traveled on the wagon with Kevlich, for the overcoat. Soon, Gurvich's wife Khaia Eta brought it out to her husband; he asked the inspector to free his arms so that he could put it on, but the latter refused. Gurvich then seized the left side of the inspector's beard while his wife Khaia Eta grabbed a tin canister of alcohol lying in the cart. Pulling with all his might toward the canisters, the inspector left half his beard in Gurvich's hands, and began to struggle with Khaia Eta, who grabbed the right side of his beard, ripped off his cap and glasses, and also scratched his nose. To free himself from her, the inspector bit her on the right arm above the elbow and then struck her on the face with handle of the revolver with a backhanded blow. Khaia Eta fell to the ground. Leaving her, the inspector rushed to help policeman Romanovskii, who was attempting to wrench his loaded revolver (which Gurvich had managed to seize from the holster) from his grasp. But Gurvich refused to let go of the revolver and began to take aim at the inspector; when the latter asked him to calm down or he would shoot, Gurvich replied that he would also shoot.

Then the inspector fired two shots in the air and a third arbitrarily at Gurvich, which struck him in the chest. Gurvich continued to resist, and another ten more minutes passed before Romanovskii knocked him to the ground. The inspector snatched Romanovskii's revolver out of Gurvich's hand. Taking advantage of the fact that the inspector and Romanovskii were engaged in a struggle with Gurvich, the latter's wife, Khaia, grabbed the boiler (which had been confiscated at Kozlovskii's apartment only that morning) and took it into the woods behind their house. The foregoing has been confirmed by the witness police officer Indrik at the preliminary investigation. The witness, police officer Romanovskii, confirmed the testimony of the inspector and also explained that when the inspector, who had torn [himself] away from Gurvich's hands, began to take away the canister from the wife from the side, Gurvich grabbed and choked him. Then he seized the loaded revolver from his [Romanovskii's] halter, intending to shoot the inspector; the witness, however, pulled his hand back and prevented him from shooting. During the struggle, Khaia threw stones, wood, and gravel at the inspector and witness, but Nokhim yelled at her in Yiddish: "Get the axe." The latter circumstance was described by the policeman Valepko, who came running to the site of the struggle after the shots had already been fired and the gun wrenched from Gurvich, and reported that Khaia Gurvich had dealt him a blow to his face.

The court medical examination on 20 July found a few scratches on the inspector's nose and wrist, and five small scratches on the right side of Romanovskii's neck and on the left side of his Adam's apple. A light wound was discovered on the left side of Nokhim Gurvich's chest (from the gunshot) and marks of light blows on different parts of the body. Similar marks of light beatings were found on different parts of Khaia's body; one bruise, the size of a palm, was on the lower side of her right upper shoulder.

Called to account as defendants, Nokhim and Khaia Eta Gurvich pled innocent: *Nokhim Gurvich* [testified that] on the night of 18 July, when inspector, Indrik, and three policemen came to the hut (which is located near Count Kossakovskii's brick factory), he and his sons were pasturing the horse. He was arrested by the inspector whom he had followed into this hut out of curiosity. After the secret distillery discovered in the hut had been disassembled, the inspector and policemen led him into town, with his hands bound behind

him.[1] When they stopped at the outskirts of town and his wife Khaia brought him his overcoat, the inspector for no reason hit in her face with the handle of his revolver and began to shoot; one of the shots wounded him in the chest. According to the defendant, the inspector fired at him and blamed him in order to create a case and thereby distinguish himself.

Khaia Eta Gurvich [testifed that] just when she approached her husband Nokhim with the overcoat in her hands, inspector Indrik began to beat her and threatened to shoot. She did not grab anything from the cart and did not commit violence against anyone.

Ekaterina Kevlich, who was questioned as a witness, testified that she had been arrested with Gurvich and was brought into town with him. When they stopped in the outskirts, she saw that Gurvich's wife Khaia did not scratch the inspector, grab his beard, or tear off his glasses and cap. She only took the inspector by the hand for some reason, but the latter struck her in the face and, to intimidate her, fired two shots from his revolver. She does not know what happened after this because she was preoccupied with her own children, who were frightened by the shots. She confirms that Nokhim Gurvich could not have held the revolver because his hands were tied behind him, and they did not free him. The witness did not see Khaia attempting to take something from the cart containing the equipment confiscated from Kozlovskii's apartment.

Iosel Epshtein, a witness for the defense, testified that at 3:00 a.m., as he sat with David Gutmakher on the front steps of his summer house on the outskirts of town, he saw how the inspector and policemen were leading Nokhim Gurvich, who walked behind a wagon on which a woman was sitting. They stopped in front of Gurvich's house. Gurvich stood near the inspector and did not commit any violence against him. A few minutes after they stopped, Gurvich began to cry "Gevalt!" and the inspector shot at him three times, and then Gurvich fell to the ground.

The witness [*David*] *Gutmakher* stated that he and Epshtein were on the front steps of Anolik's summer house but could not see the side of the road of Gurvich's house, which is about one hundred steps away. The inspector and the prisoners stopped when Gurvich began to yell and the inspector fired one shot; then the witnesses went into the street and saw the inspector shoot at Gurvich three times. He did not see whether Gurvich had a revolver in his hand but confirms that he did not point a revolver at the inspector.

The remaining witnesses—Khaia Levin, Al'fons Buchinskii, Gitlia and Israel Anolik, and Iankel Zimanskii—explained that they arrived on the scene after the shooting had already taken place, and the injured Gurvich lay on the ground. [. . .]

On the basis of the above, Nokhim and Khaia Eta Gurvich will be brought to trial at the Vil'na Provincial Court with the participation of representatives of the social estates.[2]

"The Verdict (27 February 1902)"

[. . .][3] Given the facts of the case, legal guidelines, and the particular harshness of the resistance (pulling out the beard, choking the neck, beatings to hide the signs of the crime), it appears just to set a higher level of punishment [. . .] in the third, fourth, or fifth degree.[4] The court designates a punishment for Nokhim Gurvich in the fifth degree according to article 31 of the Penal Code in the highest measure in view of his persistent denials. The townsman of Vil'komir, Nokhim Gurvich, is to be stripped of all his special rights and privileges and committed to the Corrective Department for Prisoners for 1.6 years. After he has served the term under the custody at the Corrective Department for Prisoners or in prison, Nokhim Gurvich is to be under the special police surveillance for four years with the corresponding restrictions. Gurvich was also sentenced by the Kovno District Court on 26 November 1901, which took legal effect: convicted for the illicit distillation of alcohol,

he was sentenced to two months in prison (in addition to the monetary fines). This latter punishment (that is, imprisonment for two months) [. . .] does not qualify him for a reduction in [the prison term].

The punishment set for Khaia Eta Gurvich corresponds to the second degree (in view of her extreme ignorance). [. . .] The townswoman of Vil'komir, Khaia Gurvich, is deprived of all her special rights and privileges and to be imprisoned for eight months. Upon serving her prison sentence, Khaia Gurvich is to be under the special police surveillance for two years. [. . .] Nokhim and Khaia Gurvich are mutually responsible for court costs. In the event that they both unable to pay, the Treasury will assume the court costs.

"Petition of Khaia Gurvich to the Procurator of the Kovno District Court (21 March 1902)"

On 27 February 1902, in the town of Shavli, the Vil'na Provincial Court of Criminal Affairs, with representatives of the social estates [. . .] sentenced me and my husband to the following punishment: me to prison for eight months, and my husband to a penal battalion for one year and six months. However, because we are burdened with six minor children, if we begin to serve our punishments simultaneously, there will be no one to look after the children and support their wretched existence and see that they do not starve to death.

Thus I have the honor of asking Your Excellency to pay heed to the situation of our minor children and to order that my husband and I not serve the court sentences simultaneously; so that my husband Nokhim Gurvich, presently in custody at the Shavli prison, will serve his term first; and then I shall serve my term. Moreover, I deem it necessary to state that at the beginning of this month [March], I gave birth; hence I am in poor health after the delivery and nursing the infant. I humbly request that you report the decision on my petition through the Vil'komir police.

"Decision of the Vil'na Provincial Court (24 March 1902)"

The petition of Khaia Eta Gurvich, on the basis of what has been stated in her petition, is approved.

NOTES

1. [In his petition to the court on 17 December 1901, Nokhim Gurvich argued that he could not have carried out the violence described by the inspector and policemen because his hands were tied behind his back, but the report claims that he was bound but his hands were free to move. He pointed out that Ekaterina Kevlich (in prison at the time) "was the sole witness" to the violence and testified that his hands were tied behind his back.] LVIA, f. 445, op. 1, d. 2796, l. 47.

2. [There was a trial of Nokhim Gurvich (forty years old), Andrei Kozlovskii (eighty-two years old), and Ekaterina Kevlich (forty years old) on 27 November 1901 in the Kovno District Court. Based on the testimonies and measurements of the equipment, the court determined the following sentences for the defendants: each was to pay a fine of 1,132.70 rubles for the excise duty they had failed to pay; if they were in no condition to pay the fine, they sentenced to two months each in prison (LVIA, f. 445, op. 1, d. 2796, ll. 30–48). The case of the alleged assault against the police was heard on 27 February 1902; both spouses were convicted as shown in the next item.]

3. [The document begins with a reiteration of the "facts" described in the indictment; the court clearly accepted the testimonies of the inspector and two policemen instead of the countertestimonies of the defendants and Kevlich.]

4. [Russian law designated categories of punishment depending on the seriousness of the crime. For a comparative case of sentencing in the case of arson and the degrees of punishment, see Cathy Frierson, *All Russia Is Burning: A Cultural History of Fire and Arson in Late Imperial Russia* (Seattle: University of Washington Press, 2002), 159–62.]

Domestic Service

[137]

Avraham Izrailevich Paperno's Nanny Roiza

Avraham Paperno, "Iz Nikolaevskoi epokhi," *Perezhitoe* 2 (1910).

Roiza, a middle-aged woman, an *agunah* whose husband's whereabouts were unknown, came to work for us as a *Mädchen für alles* [maid of all work]: she cooked, washed, baked bread, sewed, and because the mistress in the house was absent, [she] replaced her in everything.[1] In addition, the responsibility of taking care of me also fell to her. However, she regarded this obligation as the most gratifying duty: lonely and childless, she poured all her innate maternal love on me. She did not let me out of her sight lest something befall me, and in her free time pampered and carried me. The moment when I opened my eyes in the morning, I invariably saw her at my bedside. She instantly picked me up, washed me, and read prayers with me; with these prayers she put me to bed. In time I became her idol, her comfort, her entire life; and I reciprocated her love.

I especially loved her songs and stories: she was a walking repository of folk songs and tales, and dear God, how marvelous was she at singing and storytelling. I sensed that she had not only mastered these works of folk culture, but that they constituted the better part of her being. Through them, she expressed her own aspirations and wept copious tears over her own grief. Dusk (when the atmosphere that enveloped us was most harmonious with the substance of her songs) was usually the time that she chose to sing. Her mournful motifs and doleful tone corresponded to those prevalent in synagogue melodies in terms of substance. Songs of joy, happiness, and love were not in Roiza's repertoire; neither were heroic songs. The fundamental background of Jewish folk poetry in the diaspora is sorrow, misfortune, diminished hopes, eroded faith, and a feeling of national pride.

A melancholy tone also dominated the stories — for the most part about princes and princesses, rabbis and rebbetzins. The heroes and heroines, the perfection of beauty and kindness, nevertheless suffered and endured every injustice and persecution. In the end, however, they were rescued and rewarded a hundredfold for the insults that they had suffered. The virtuous were often subjected to onerous tests but, after bearing them with steadfastness and firmness, they prevailed over evil in the end for "there is no injustice with God."

Roiza knew how to tell countless stories about angels and demons, about the lives of *tsaddikim*, miracle workers, and holy martyrs who would gladly have been burned at the stake to sanctify God's name. She described heaven and hell and their inhabitants as graphically as if she had seen them with her very own eyes. She found a grateful listener in me. As I listened to her stories, I lived through all the grief and joys of her heroes, and under her influence the spirit of Jewishness—its aspirations, belief in God and His justice, and the absolute conviction that the people of Israel were the chosen people—percolated through me until I entered the *heder*. In short, I was already a complete Jew in miniature. But every cloud has a silver lining, and every silver lining has a cloud. The adverse side of Roiza's influence was that I became an incorrigible dreamer; fantasies often replaced reality; as I chased after cranes in the sky, I let go of the titmouse on the ground.[2]

NOTES

1. [During most of Paperno's childhood, his father was away from home and working for Isaak Zabludovskii, a wealthy lumber merchant in Belostok. His mother ran a textile store in Kopyl, where he grew up. Remarking on his father's absence, Paperno wrote: "As I indicated earlier, it was not unusual for wives to be left behind by their husbands; this was the order of things. Some left to complete their studies, others to search for work, so that ten months out of the year Kopyl appeared to be partly a town of *Amazonki* [Amazon women] or rather young female traders, waging a desperate struggle for existence without the help of the male sex." Avraham Paperno, "Iz Nikolaevskoi epokhi," in *Evrei v Rossii XIX vek*, 78–79.]

2. [This is a play on the Russian proverb "Luchshe sinitsa v rukakh, chem zhuravl' v nebe," or "a titmouse in the hand is better than a crane in the sky." Similarly another proverb goes: "Ne suli zhuravlia v nebe, a dai sinitsu v ruki," or "a bird in hand is worth two in the bush."]

[138]

A Russian Cook Accused of Observing Judaism in Moscow (1896)

RGIAgM, f. 203, op. 395, d. 12, ll. 1–5.

"Report of the Police Officer of the First Khamovnicheskii District (17 September 1896)"

I am honored to report to Your Excellency that the manager of Ganeshevin's buildings (numbers 18 and 20), the peasant Ivan Shiriaev, learned that the merchant Zak's cook, a peasant woman from the village of Kholmov, a certain Mikhailova who is Russian Orthodox, has begun to observe the Jewish religion.

I ordered the deputy policeman Felerov [...] to investigate the conversion of the peasant woman Mikhailova to Judaism.

The manager of the Ganeshevin buildings, the peasant Ivan Shiriaev (thirty-five years old), testified on 1 September 1896 that the Moscow Jewish merchant Shliomo Iudelevich Zak, his family, and servants moved from their summer place in Borogodskii to live [in Moscow]. When he took his passport to the housing office registry, he heard from a lackey who worked for the Zaks, Efim Mikhailov Bobylev, that the Zaks' cook Mariia Mikhailova Filipova, although listed as Russian Orthodox on her passport, partly observed the Jewish rituals. Not wanting to go into details about the case, Shiriaev reported it to the district police. He knows nothing more.

The lackey living in the home of the Jew Shliomo Zak, Efim Mikhailov Bobylev (twenty-eight years old), a peasant from Orlov province, under interrogation testified that he has worked for Shliomo Zak for eight months and that the cook Mariia Filipova has served at the Zaks for two months. When he once asked Mariia, "What is [your] faith?" she retorted: "That is none of your business; it is what it is and what it will be." Among other things, she once told Bobylev that she understands Yiddish, and he repeatedly saw her reading Jewish books and even reading them aloud. On Saturdays they lit the candles at Filipova's; after she lit the candles, she did not add firewood to the stove. [...] On one Jewish holiday this September, she was absent from the apartment and said that she had gone to the Jewish synagogue. [...]

Mariia Mikhailova Filopova (thirty-three years old) testified that she has worked for the Jew Shliomo Zak since 30 July 1896. Four years ago she moved from Moscow to the town of Libava (Kurland province), where she served an owner of a firewood [business] Brutskus; she does not remember his first name. His wife was called Anna Ivanovna Brutskus. She does not know his origins or religious confession.[1] Four years ago, this same Brutskus ran a leather factory near the Donskoi Monastery. She worked for Brutskus for two and a half or three years and returned to Moscow, where she settled in the house of Belova on Nizhnaia Street in the Lifortovo district. She lived there for two years, renting a two-room apartment, and engaged in the seamstress trade. [...][2]

She moved to the house of Veliankin, who lives on Kalanchavskaia Street and worked as a broker. Apart from her (Filipova), there were two other servants at the Veliankins': Evdokiia Danilovna and Fenia (whose surname and rank she does not remember). She worked at the Veliakins' for four months (from January to May 1896). On 26 May 1896, Veli-

ankin went abroad, and she continued to live with the other servants in the apartment. On 30 July she moved to a summer place in the village of Bogorodskoe to work for Shliomo Zak. She does not know how to speak Yiddish or read it; she did not speak to anyone or read in Yiddish; she did not tell anyone that she reads or speaks Yiddish. On Saturdays, she did not and does not celebrate the Jewish holiday of Shabbat. Although she lights the candles on Shabbat, she does so for the Jews, and after she lights them, she adds firewood to the stove.

According to Jewish law, it is forbidden to cook milk and meat products in the same pots, and Filipova observed this punctiliously with respect to herself, but this was because the masters of the house (that is, the Zaks) insisted on this.[3] She did not go to the synagogue this year but went once six years ago when the synagogue was located on Solianka [Street]; however [it was] out of curiosity, not religious duty. Filipova has not been to confession and communion for six years because she has not had time. The last time that she took communion was six years ago at the Grebenskii Mother of God Church on the corner of Lubianka Square. Presently, Filipova professes the religion in which she was baptized — viz., Russian Orthodoxy — and has never converted to the Jewish faith. [...][4]

The Moscow second-guild merchant, Nekhama Zak (twenty-nine years old), testified that she hired the peasant woman Mariia Filipova on 30 July 1896 when she lived in a summer place in the village of Bogorodskoe. When Filipova came to get the job, Nekhama Zak asked her where she had worked earlier; she replied that she had served in many places and named the heads of a few families with whom she was not familiar. Among these names, she hit upon the contractor Veliankin, whom she had heard was a good and wealthy individual, so she agreed to hire Filipova as a cook, provided that in her free time she sewed linens. Moreover, Nekhama Zak stipulated that all the pots used to prepare food not be mixed together—namely, the crockery designated for meat must not be used for milk products. During the time that Filipova worked for her (from 30 July 1896 until 19 September 1896), she did not notice the latter observing Jewish religious rituals and, in general, considered her to be Russian Orthodox, as appears on her passport. [. . .][5]

Evdokiia Danilovna Gorin (twenty-eight years old) testified that she works for the first-guild merchant Mikhail Morkova Veliankin as a chambermaid for his wife and children, and that she began this job on 13 November 1894. She testified that she knows Filipova, who worked for the Veliankins for four months at the beginning of 1896. During this period she never went to church and did not seem Russian Orthodox at all. Each Saturday she celebrated Shabbat and lit the candles; after lighting the candles, she did not add firewood to the stove because the Jewish religion forbids this. From Friday evening until the end of Shabbat (that is, Saturday evening) she not only failed to add firewood to the fire but did not perform any work. Because the Jewish religion forbids the mixing of meat and milk products, Mariia always became terribly indignant if someone mixed the pots and pans. She never used Russian meat but ate Jewish kosher meat (that is, butchered only by a Jewish slaughterer) and certainly never ate the anterior or rear parts as *tref* [nonkosher]. Did she know about the Veliankin family? No, but she only knew that Veliankin did not force Filipova to work on Saturday; every Saturday, she left the apartment. Veliankin and his family were at home, but Filipova did not work all the same. Did Filipova visit the synagogue and speak and read in Yiddish? She knows nothing about this and has neither heard nor witnessed it.[6]

NOTES

1. [Brutskus could have been a Jewish surname in Kurland: for example, Iulii Brutskus (1890–1951) was a political figure and historian from Kurland.]

2. [She then worked for three other people in Moscow and lists their addresses here.]

3. [Several Jewish memoirs attest to the strict observance of kashrut in the kitchen by Christian domestic servants. For instance, Genrikh Sliozberg recalled: "Those families [in Poltava] that could afford to have a servant relied on a Christian servant even in the kitchen: the cooks knew that one needed to salt the meat, not to mix milk and meat dishes, and attempted not to lead their employers into sin. Among those who did not have servants, a Christian would arrive on Friday evenings to extinguish the candles for a glass of vodka or a piece of a small loaf; in winter, they came to stoke the stove. Indeed, this was the relationship that they maintained with Jews not only in the towns of Ukraine but also in the villages" *Dela minuvshikh dnei: zapiski russkogo evreia*, 1: 26–27.

4. [Here another peasant, Iakov Vasil'ev Gorianchikov, testifies that Filipov appeared as Russian Orthodox on her passport, but she "prayed to God according to Jewish rituals."]

5. [Here Nekhama's husband Shlioma Iudelevich Zak (fifty years old) gives similar testimony.]

6. [The file ends with inquiries about Filiopova's parentage; her father's identity was unclear.]

[139]

Lawsuits in Zhitomir for Unpaid Labor

"Petition of Khaia Sura Shtatland against Borukh and Reiza Maizlish (1887)"

DAZhO, f. 169, op. 1, d, 53, l. 1.

Reiza Maizlish (a townswoman of Zhitomir) hired my thirteen-year-old daughter, who works to sew linen. Moreover, she agreed with me to [pay] 20 rubles per year. After she worked the entire winter (that is, half a year), [Maizlish] paid her 2.50 rubles but refused to pay the balance of 7.50 rubles. Taking into the consideration that I am now in extremely straitened circumstances, I petition [. . .] to have the couple Borukh and Reiza Maizlish pay the 7.50 rubles in my daughter's favor. I also have the honor of presenting the witnesses Berko Markus (who lives on Khlebnaia Street) and Baba Zidelshtein (Khlebnaia Street).[1]

"Petition of Brukha Gintsburg against Dveira Model of Zhitomir (21 July 1901)"

DAZhO, f. 170, op. 1, d. 338, l. 1.

I worked for nine months as a cook for Dveira Model according to an oral agreement for a salary of fifty rubles a year. On 6 June [1901], Dveira Model fired me, without paying me the salary for half a year (twenty-five rubles). Regarding this sum for which I am suing Dveira Model, I refer you to the testimony of witness Elia Nysa, who lives on Malaia Chudnovskaia Street in the house of Leizor Litvak. In addition, I am sending the court's fee and humbly request that Your Excellency summon the defendant Dveira Model to court.

"Response of Dveira Model to the Suit and Ruling (5 October 1901)"

Your Excellency's judgment in absentia in August 1901 ruled that I am to pay twenty-five rubles to Brukha Gintsburg for services and three rubles for administrative costs [court fees]. As for having the case reviewed, I have the honor to state that Gintsburg should have filed her suit against me in my local place of residence, which is on Chudnovskaia Street in the house of Gorits (that is, the Justice of the Peace Court for the fourth district of the Zhitomir region). In light of this, I humbly request a new trial, rejection of Gintsburg's suit, and an advisory that she file her suit in the Justice of the Peace Court in the fourth district of the Zhitomir region.[2]

NOTES

1. [The couple responded that the contract was for one year but the daughter did not work for the first part of the year, only the second. Moreover, the mother asked for 2.50 rubles to pay for some shoes—money that they had given her out of pity. The daughter did not return to work and owes them time for another half year. The archival file ends without a resolution.]

2. [The court apparently upheld its ruling in favor of Brukha Gintsburg because it terminated her employer's case and did not respond to her request for a new trial.]

[140]

"Fictitious" Jewish Servants outside the Pale of Settlement (1890–91)

"Report of P[etr Nikolaevich]
Durnovo[1] to the Governor of
St. Petersburg (7 February 1891)"
GARF, f. 1286, op. 46, d. 622, l. 98.

Gracious Sir! On the basis of Article 17 (in the Statute on Passports), Jewish first-guild merchants can bring their coreligionists from the Pale of Settlement to the internal provinces in fixed numbers as stewards and domestic servants. It is well known that these merchants enjoy the right, as stipulated in law, to conduct wholesale, retail, and petty trade. They leave their stewards to conduct various types of trade independently, and their service as a steward is only fictitious. This circumstance can be explained by an abnormal phenomenon: operating in the name of the Jewish first-guild merchants who deal in grain, they have stores and small shops with very diverse wares that have nothing in common to do with the occupation [of stewards].

Given the Jews' explanations about these activities, I have the honor of appealing to Your Excellency with a humble petition to inform me about the following: are there Jewish merchants in St. Petersburg, who, by the above evasion of the law, give their coreligionists the opportunity to conduct trade? If so, do not decline to apprise me about the number of such traders — namely, what trade they conduct, and also what trade do their fictitious masters conduct?

Respectfully yours, P. Durnovo[2]

NOTES

1. [Petr Nikolaevich Durnovo (1845–1915) was at this time director of the Department of Police (1891–93); he later served as deputy minister of internal affairs (1900–1905) and then as minister of internal affairs (1905–6).]

2. [For Jewish petitions for permission to bring Jewish servants to the Russian interior, see GARF, f. 102, op. 76a, d. 706.]

Jewish Agricultural Colonies and Farms

[141]

Exclusion of Jewish Colonists from Colonies in Kherson Province (1875)

"Report of the Ministry of State Domains (25 January 1875)"
RGIA, f. 381, op. 16, d. 21274, ll. 3–11.

The Committee of Trustees for Foreign Settlers in the Southern Territories of Russia reports that the Trustees of the Jewish settlements in Kherson province have presented the Committee with a confirmed list of fourteen families of the Jewish colonies who have neglected their agriculture.

According to this list, among those who do not engage in agriculture, the family or heads of families have abandoned their houses (many of which are completely destroyed or in a dilapidated condition). [These include] ten families in the colony Novo-Poltavka, one in Romanovka, one in Novo-Vitebsk, four in Gramokleia, three in Bol'shoi Nagartav, two in Malyi Nagartav, two in Efengar, one in Ingulets, three in Kamianka, one in Izluchistaia, two in Izrailevka, [and] four in Sagaidak. Altogether, thirty-four families in twelve colonies received a land allotment but are constantly absent and do not engage in agriculture. In addition, economic negligence also appears among outside ["registered"] families — that is, those who do not have a land allotment but who are registered with another colonist family (including twelve in L'vov, one

in Novokovno, thirteen in Novo-Poltavka, three in Romanovka, one in Novo-Vitebsk, one in Gromokleia, three in Bol'shoi Nagartav, one in Malyi Nagartav, three in Efengar, ten in Ingulets, four in Kamianka, one in Izluchistaia, and three in Israilevka — a total of fifty-six families out of a total of ninety families).

Given that these families do not live in the colonies and do not engage in agriculture, the Committee of Trustees attributes their negligence to personal blame and acknowledges that they are a burden to the community (as foreseen in [the law] of 1868).

On this basis, the Committee of Trustees proposes that thirty-four families in these fourteen colonies and fifty-six "registered" families (a total of ninety families) on the attached list [. . .] be excluded from status of farmers, even if they lived in the colony after being recorded on the list of *brodiazhstvuiushchikh* [vagrants]. It requests permission from the Ministry of State Domains to bring this about. [. . .]

The Law: Digest of Laws, vol. 9, article 1455 (laws of status): Every Jewish family that has settled on state lands by the order of the government, either at its own expense or at the expense of its coreligionists, is obliged to set up a kitchen garden as well as cultivate and sow a field of at least one *desiatin* [2.7 acres] one year after settlement; by the fourth year, each family is obliged to have a kitchen garden and a field of two *desiatin* [5.4 acres]; by the sixth year, to have a kitchen garden and a cultivated field of three *desiatin* [8.1 acres]. Moreover, they are to have agricultural equipment on the inventory, which is attached.

Article 1456: In general, Jews who settle on state lands are obliged to cultivate it themselves or may employ their coreligionists as workers; however, they are forbidden to hire Christian workers. Jews who are negligent in farming or who lack the corresponding plot size of [cultivated land] are to be placed under the supervision of the nearest rural authorities [in matters relating to their] economic livelihood, especially with respect to these instructions. Absence [from farms to work] in industry is forbidden as long as they do not reconstitute their agriculture and remain negligent; in this case, they are liable to the rural authorities for punishment, which will be determined by the rural court regulations for state peasants.

Article 1457 (per the 1867 supplement): If Jewish settlers do not have a complete economic livelihood in the course of six years, as prescribed in articles 1455–56 (that is, have not established their life accordingly and remain a burden on the community, which fulfills various monetary and natural obligations for them): based on the attestation by the Jewish administration of settlers (on pre-

cise legal grounds) that this negligence resulted from reasons that were not beyond the settlers' control, but solely because they personally neglected their farms or because they engaged in dissolute behavior, they are to be excluded from the rural status with the permission of the Ministry of State Domains. In such cases, Jewish settlers are to be handed over to the court and transferred to a corrective prisoner unit under civil jurisdiction.

Opinion: [. . .] With the permission of the Ministry of State Domains, the ninety Jewish families on the list of those who neglected their economies are to be excluded from the rural status. [The Ministry asks] that the Committee of Trustees report to the local State Treasury about the arrears owed by those have been excluded from the rural status. The land parcels that remain unencumbered after the departure of these families from the community to which they now belong are to be allocated at auction for quitrent; the income from these parcels will be held in a special account until a determination has been made about what should be done with the sums and lands (with responsibility for this given to the Committee of Trustees for the correct application according to permissible measures).[1]

NOTE

1. [The Ministry of State Domains upheld the request to exclude the ninety families from the rural status.]

[142]

State Loans to Jewish Farmers during a Drought in Ekaterinoslav Province (1885–86)

RGIA, f. 381, op. 22, d. 14507, ll. 4–5.

"Report of Mikhail Ostrovskii of the State Domains of Kherson and Bessarabia Provinces to the Department of General Affairs, Ministry of State Domains (16 November 1885)"

Due to the drought in southern Russia this past summer, the grain and grass on the land of nineteen Jewish agricultural colonies of Kherson district were so completely scorched that at present they [the colonists] lack supplies not only to sow the fields but also [to serve as] foodstuffs [for themselves] and fodder for the cattle until the next harvest. So impoverished were the Jewish farmers that the chief of state domains in Kherson and Bessarabia provinces was prompted to propose an interest-free loan of 30,816 rubles for these nineteen Jewish colonies for five years. This was to include mandatory terms of 15,508 rubles to assist 8,352 souls (male and female) and 15,308 rubles to purchase seeds to sow the fields and fodder to feed the cattle. In the chief's opinion, these 30,816 rubles may be transferred to the community treasury of the colony (26,416 rubles) and to community food-provisioning funds because of the lack of sources in some colonies (4,400 rubles).

Given the urgent need to assist the nineteen Jewish colonies of Kherson district that have suffered from the drought, the Ministry of State Domains (in agreement with the declaration by the head of state domains of Kherson and Bessarabia) accepts the duty to appeal to the gracious consideration of Your Imperial Majesty with this most devoted petition to issue these colonies an interest-free loan of 30,816 rubles against the capital in the community treasury and community food-provisioning capital (per the attached list).[1]

NOTE

1. [The Jewish colonies that would receive funds in their community treasuries were Bol'shoi Seidmenukha (536 people of both sexes), Bodrovyi Kut (468), Malyi Negartav (111), Efengar (1,039), Novo-Poltavka (816), Ingulets (754), Novo-Zhitomir (162), Komianka (351), Izluchistaia (361), Novo-Vitebsk (387), Novo-Kovno (207), Novo-Podolsk' (69), Izrailevka (799), Sagaidak (343), Gromokleia (93), and Dobraia (676). There was a total of 7,172 people in these colonies. The colonies that would receive funds for the communal food provisioning capital were Malaia Seideminukha (189), Bol'shoi Nagartav (485), and Romanovka (506), with a total of 1,180 people.]

[143]

Request for Land in a Jewish Colony in Kherson Province (1887–88)

RGIA, f. 381, op. 22, d. 15609, ll. 3–3 ob., 5–5 ob.

"Petition of Thirty-Five Jewish Residents of Novo-Ukrainka (Kherson Province) to Emperor Alexander III (16 July 1887)"

YOUR IMPERIAL MAJESTY,
ALL GRACIOUS SOVEREIGN!

Having received neither a rank nor commercial instruction from our parents, we have earned our livelihood until now as day agricultural laborers. Insofar as rural agriculture in southern Russia has suffered from a shortage of workers, we of Jewish descent did not encounter obstacles to finding work. However, the influx of fieldworkers from other provinces has devalued labor wages such that we and our families have been deprived of a livelihood.

Thrust into this critical position with unforeseen outcomes and yet capable of physical, agricultural labor, we thirty-five townsmen take the liberty of prostrating ourselves at the august feet of Your Imperial Majesty with our humble petition to apportion us state land in the Jewish colonies in Kherson Province, where we can settle, engage in cultivation, and prepare our children to do the same.[1]

"Report of Mikhail Ostrovskii of the State Domains of Kherson and Bessarabia Provinces to the Governor of Kherson Province (15 January 1888)"

The commander of the Imperial Headquarters has forwarded the humble petition submitted by thirty-five Jewish townsmen in Novo-Ukrainka (Elizavetgrad district, Kherson province) to the Ministry of State Domains through proper channels. They ask to allocate them state land so that they can settle in the colonies of Jewish farmers in Kherson province.

Taking into consideration that the opinion of the State Council (confirmed by His Imperial Majesty on 30 May 1866) has halted the further entry of Jews into the rank of farmers and finding that the free land in the Jewish colonies may be needed for Jewish farmers who are already settled there, the Ministry of State Domains proposes that the petition of the thirty-five Jews be rejected. [. . .]

NOTE

1. [Interestingly, all thirty-five of the male petitioners signed in both Russian and Yiddish. Although the signatures do not reveal their level of literacy, they suggest that all the petitioners could write in two languages.]

[144]

Life on a Jewish Farm in Borovoi-Mlyn: Memoir of Mariia Shkol'nik (1890s)

Mariia Markovna Shkol'nik, *Zhizn' byvshei terroristki* (Moscow: Izdatel'stvo vsesoiuznogo obshchestva politkatorzhan i ssy'lno-polselentsev, 1930), 11–21.

The small hamlet of Borovoi-Mlyn [Vil'na province] where I was born consisted of approximately thirty *khaty* (huts)—low, wooden structures with thatched roofs. Their walls— on the outside and inside—were plastered and whitewashed with lime. All the huts stood in one row and formed the only street in the village. The wide, dusty road passed through here, where the clucking, grunting, and snarling members of the commune gathered. Further on was a common meadow, a long, thin strip of land that followed the high banks of the small river Okena. Behind the huts were small kitchen gardens, surrounded by low wattle fencing, and immediately beyond that one could see the fields.

Our house stood on the very edge of this village. It was an old, dilapidated hut. Two small windows hung very low to the ground; in the winter, high snowdrifts lay against them, obscuring the faint light coming through the double window frames. For most of the year, a piece of cardboard replaced the broken glass to keep out the clouds of dust that rose up and penetrated the house every time a wagon went down the road. The straw roof was black and full of holes from age. When a strong wind blew, water seeped in and created a puddle on the dirt floor.

Like all peasant abodes, our hut was divided into two halves by a dark passage. One half was for lodging; the other served as a shed for horses, cows, farming tools, and provisions. The room for lodging was large and square. One corner was partitioned off with a long, red curtain. This was my parents' room, with two beds and a cradle.[1] The furnishings in the rest of the room consisted of a large table and a bench that stood against the wall. Another table had a copper samovar and a pair of candlesticks—the only objects of value in our house. An enormous brick stove occupied a considerable part of the room. Apart from its usual functions, this stove had another purpose: it served as a warm bed, and the children often fought over the privilege of sleeping on it. It was in this room that I saw the daybreak on a September day in 1885. I spent the first fourteen years of my life in this room.

Sixteen *desiatin* [17.44 hectares] of poor, largely clayey soil and a straw-thatched hut— such was the property that my grandfather bequeathed to his five sons and two daughters.[2] I do not know how the heirs divided up this "rich" inheritance among themselves; however, over time my father and one uncle remained the sole proprietors of the sixteen[3] *desiatin*. They were the oldest sons and were already married. With the partition of [the land], eight *desiatin* [8.72 hectares] and the house came into my father's possession.

Our belongings, apart from the land, consisted of two cows, one or two horses, and a dozen hens. When the harvest was good, eight *desiatin* produced enough grain and potatoes to last the entire year. However, because of my father's primitive methods of cultivation, insufficient manure, and drought (which was not rare in our parts), a good harvest was the exception rather than the rule. I remember a prayer taught to me when I was four years old: "God, send us rain for the sake of the little children."[4] Each morning, before our modest breakfast, we folded our hands and began to pray. However, God turned out to be cruel: the drought scorched our fields, [and] famine struck the entire region. Then Father drove our beloved cow to town and sold her there; our other cows subsequently met the same fate, and we were left without milk. The price for basic necessities was so high, however, that the money we made in this manner did not suffice. Then Father left to find work and was not at home the entire week. On Sabbath evening, the family waited impatiently for his return. The room assumed a festive appearance: the table was decorated with a white tablecloth; the candles were burning. In the corner stood the samovar, which had just been polished. However, when Father sat down without saying a word, without the usual affectionate smile on his face, we understood that he had earned nothing and was upset by this. We sat in silence around the table for dinner that Mother had prepared. This time, however, there was no meat for dinner as was usual on the Sabbath.

Indeed, it was an extremely necessary to earn at least some money to cover household expenses. A few *desiatin* of land that a peasant owned did not produce enough income to feed a large family and pay taxes. Our village was approximately two kilometers from the town of Smorgon, which had tanneries, tailor workshops, and other enterprises. In our world a child of eight was already considered able-bodied and sent off to the city, where he was apprenticed to a tailor or shoemaker or even went to work in a factory. A few had the opportunity to send their children to school. The parish school, which was supposed to educate [Russian Orthodox] residents, could boast of no more than a dozen students. The village priest, who knew little about education, was the teacher. But he was occupied with other, more "important" obligations and could not spare much time for teaching the youth. Hence students completing the fourth

year did not know how to read or write. However, this shortcoming was completely offset by the ability to sing the Psalms, which they knew by heart. Our boys started the Jewish school when they were six years old. My brother Vul'f "completed" his education when he was ten years old; girls did not study at all. I remained illiterate until I was thirteen years old; many remained illiterate longer.

Many peasants, our neighbors, lived in greater poverty than we did, and their grown sons and daughters did not go to the city but remained in the family. They did not send their children to the workshops. Their small land allotment, which was liable to high taxes, could not feed so many "souls." Nearby was the landowner's expansive estate, which covered several hundred *desiatin*, a large portion of which remained uncultivated. As a result, peasants were even deprived of the chance to earn a little money through day labor.

I remember a circumstance that perplexed me greatly, despite the fact that I was still very young. The meadow of our village was small, and the livestock often returned hungry. Next to ours was the enormous pasture of the priest, who had long left the church and did not even live on his own property. The pasture was guarded by a person who literally lived at our expense. He collected a ruble for every horse or cow that he found on his land. If [the owners] did not pay money, he locked up the livestock in his barn and held them without fodder. He starved one of our cows to death. When winter arrived, the wonderful grass in the priest's meadow was covered with snow, while our barns were empty.

Although a thick forest surrounded the village, we did not have enough firewood to heat our huts. The forest belonged to the state [and was therefore off limits]. The peasants were left to freeze to death or steal the firewood from the forest; as a result, the prison in the closest town was always full: some [people] remained there two years—just for attempting to steal logs to heat a cold hut.

When I was six years old, a great misfortune befell our family: my mother fell from the loft and fractured her head. She was sick for almost an entire year. For four months, she lay in a semi-comatose state: she did not recognize anyone and drove us away when we came to her bed. I do not know what would have happened to us if it were not for our sister Revekka. She took care of us like a mother and kept an eye on us to make sure that we were fed and dressed. She was eleven years old at the time. My mother's illness completely ruined us. She was the only person in our family who could run the household and, as they say, make ends meet. Father lacked this ability. Moreover, Mother's illness drastically increased our expenses. To pay for the doctors and medicines, we had to sell the cows and horses; we even mortgaged our land.

It was summer, and father worked in the field. Revekka and I stayed at home and took care of the year-old baby. We rose at the crack of dawn and worked constantly the entire day. Revekka milked the cows (they were later sold in the winter), and I drove them out to pasture. I remember how I responded to my friends when they called me to play with them with a serious expression: "I never play. My mother is ill."

One incident that occurred during my mother's illness made such an impression on me that I have remembered it to this day. It was haymaking time. Father was in field; mother lay in bed; Revekka and I sat on the threshold of our house, resting after a morning of hard work. Suddenly a wagon, harnessed to two horses, appeared on the road. We immediately recognized him [the driver] and understood that the tax collector had arrived. He had a wooden prosthesis and a long, black beard. The village children were terribly frightened of him. The periodic appearance of the tax collector, whom they called "the one-legged devil," was always the cause of many calamities. He stopped across from our house; we were terrified of him. On another occasion we would have fled and hidden somewhere in the barn; however, that happy phase of our lives had already passed. Feeling the great responsibility resting upon us, we remained and, standing up, valiantly met the uninvited guest. "No one is home," Revekka said as the tax collector approached us. But he paid us no heed and went straight into the house, producing an awful sound with his wooden leg. We went in after him. Examining the belongings in the room, he stopped in front of the table with the samovar and candlesticks. We held our breath and followed his movements. He knocked on the window with his fingers, and a young lad with a large sack entered the house, and before we could understand what was happening, our samovar, which decorated the house and constituted its pride, vanished into the dirty sack; next went the candlesticks. We were dumbfounded and stood gazing at the sack, speechless. Powerless to move from the spot, we saw him go to the door and leave. When we came to our senses, we could hear the clatter of the departing cart. Revekka sat down next to the barren table and wept; within a few minutes, I joined her. Without the samovar and candlesticks, the room looked more dismal than ever.

Mother's illness dragged on, and Father finally decided to call in a doctor from Vil'na. His visit cost us fifty rubles, but this doctor really helped Mother, who gradually began to recover. When she had recovered from her illness, Revekka was sent to town to work in a tailor's workshop, and I became Mother's primary helper at home. On long winter nights, I plucked feathers for pillows — some of which were to be part of Revekka's dowry. She left when she was thirteen years old.

Two years went by. During this time, our poverty was indescribable. All the earnings went to cover the debt and pay the interest. To earn some money, my mother decided to sell vegetables in the city. Every morning, she left for town and returned in the evening. The housework and care of my eleven-month-old brother were entrusted to me.

The death of my aunt, a young thirty-four-year-old married woman, forced me to start thinking about our general situation. It was harvest time, and my aunt went to the nearest village to hire day laborers. She departed before sunset; a few hours passed, night approached, and she still had not returned. Around midnight, the horse returned with an empty wagon. We raised the alarm and went to the village; however, the local peasants, who knew my aunt well, said that she had not been to the village that day. Finally, after an all-night search, they found her buried in a pit by the road, still alive. Her face was unrecognizable; her entire body had been beaten unmercifully and bore the signs of violence. The police arrived and began to investigate. Our courtyard was packed with peasants, young and old, from the neighboring village. Each of them was led to the bed on which my aunt lay with an indescribable expression on her face. She was unable to talk, but her eyes were full of suffering and silent reproach. Each time they led a peasant to her bed, she slowly shook her head. The investigation continued for a second day. My aunt tried to say something all the time, but our efforts to understand her were in vain. The police had already lost any hope of finding the perpetrator of the horrible crime. My aunt lost all her strength; the doctor could not give us any hope. Suddenly, she clearly articulated the word "Barchuk" and died. Barchuk! The word spread among the mob of peasants. They crossed themselves; now they knew who had committed the crime.

A short distance from the village to where my aunt was heading was a landowner's estate. The landowner had a son, who usually spent the summer in the village. He was the curse of the neighboring villages: when he appeared in the village, the peasants hid their daughters, but he found a way to insult them with impunity. My aunt had identified him as her murderer. He was arrested. All the peasants testified against him. Nevertheless, within three months he was freed: the landowner had bought off the investigators, and the case was closed.

As I have already said, they did not send me to school. When I turned eleven years old, my mother found a position for me at a small grocery store in town. The store was so tiny that when two customers dropped by, one had to wait her turn on the street where a large portion of the wares were laid out. I was responsible for carrying out many tasks: to take out and bring back the wares from the street, sweep the store, hand out purchases, and run errands. My wages were fifteen rubles for the winter. It was there that I first became acquainted with numbers and learned to add and subtract: my position as store assistant required some knowledge of arithmetic. At first the storeowner taught me; then my brother Vul'f guided my study of mathematics (in which he was especially strong). However, months went by, and I offered no hope that I could become a saleswoman in the grocery store. My mistress was very dissatisfied with me; she often reprimanded me for my inability to treat customers properly and called me a "boorish peasant." I did not understand what they wanted from me and was tormented because of this. However, I was very proud to be a store assistant and earn money. Every evening I went home. The town had a tavern where workers from our village gathered, usually around 8:00 p.m. There I found fellow travelers for the way back home.

Before Passover, the storeowner fired me; she had found another girl who knew how to treat the customers properly. This was a great misfortune for me, but mother tried to comfort me by saying: "Do not be distressed. I will place you at a tailor's workshop like Revekka. It is settled."

The summer passed. When the cold [weather] set in, mother took me to town, and I began my new career as an apprentice in a tailor's workshop. I was not used to the workshop, for I was accustomed to freedom, to the fresh air of the fields. The harshest, frigid weather and storms could not keep us children in the house. We never felt cold, although I was never dressed for the season. Here I had to sit all day under lock and key in a stuffy room. Sometimes my responsibilities kept me there until midnight. My boss did not think about teaching me to sew. Most of the time, I was occupied with the two children whom the mistress left in my care.

I was thus "apprenticed" for two years. They had agreed to let me go home in time for fieldwork. According to that agreement, in the first year I was to learn [the trade], without compensation; in the second year, I was to receive twenty rubles. However, fate played one of her pranks on me. At the end of the second year, when I began to think repeatedly about the money that I was supposed to receive shortly, something happened so that I never saw my hard-earned money.

In the spring of 1898, the workers of Vil'na began the struggle for a ten-hour workday. The Bund, a secret Jewish worker's organization that had been created shortly before this,[5] led a strike. It issued an illegal proclamation (titled "The Eight-Hour Work Day"), which it distributed to all the nearby towns, large and small. I found one of these proclamations on the street and [another] in our workshop. The workers in our tailor's workshop discussed it secretly. Workers from all the tailoring workshops met and decided to declare a strike before Passover and to demand a ten-hour workday. They did not admit me to these secret matters because I was too young or because they did not consider me a real worker (since I usually spent the summer in the village). But I managed to learn, without great difficulty, the secret that they concealed from me. I anticipated the strike with enormous impatience. Having returned home from work, I told my friends about the impor-

tant events and the preparations being made in town. The designated day finally arrived, and the workers of Smorgon went on strike. Much to the surprise of everyone in the shop, I also refused to work. The strike lasted only a few hours. The shop owners decided to concede because it was before Passover — the busiest season of the year. They agreed to all the demands of the workers. After Passover, however, they fired everyone and offered to let them work under the previous conditions. I was not taken back. This circumstance made a great impression on the workers, who saw me as a victim. When I think about this now, and what followed from this, I am deeply grateful to fate, but from that time I became a source of unhappiness and torment for our family.[6]

NOTES

1. [The presence of two beds suggests that the author's parents may have observed the laws of *niddah*, requiring the couple to sleep in separate beds during the wife's menstruation.]

2. My grandfather settled in Borovoi Mlyn, a village in Vil'na province. In 1851, the government granted the Jewish agricultural colonists a few privileges, including freedom from military conscription. At this time, the term of military conscription was twenty-five years, and the life of a soldier was terribly difficult. Not too many returned home. In order to save his sons from military service, my grandfather became a peasant.

3. [The text reads "fifteen," presumably a typographical error.]

4. [This prayer comes from the Talmud: "To Ḥanan, the grandson of Onias, the children came during a great drought, crying, 'Abba [Father], give us rain!' whereupon the saint prayed: 'O Ruler of the world, for the sake of these little ones who cannot discriminate between the Abba [the Father] who giveth rain and the Abba [the father] who can only pray for, but cannot give, rain, hear my prayer!' — and behold rain came" (*Ta'anit* 23b; from "Abba," *Jewish Encyclopedia* [1906]).]

5. [The General Union of Jewish Workers in Lithuania, Poland, and Russia, better known as the Bund was created on 7 October 1897.]

6. [Mariia Shkol'nik's narrative about how she joined the revolutionary movement, first the Social Democratic and then the Socialist Revolutionary movement, is continued in document 174.]

Artisans and Factory Work

[145]

Residence Rights of Children of Skilled Artisans

GARF, f. 102, op. 76a, d. 69, l. 262.

"Memorandum from the Minister of Internal Affairs to the Governor of Moscow (1889)"

Regarding the memorandum of 14 December 1889 (number 6563) on the question of whether Jewish children who reach their majority and who have no definite occupation can live in Moscow with their parents who are artisans, mechanics, and alcohol distillers, I have the honor to inform you of the following. In accordance with the law, children may not acquire from the parents the right to reside in the interior provinces. Thus, when Jewish children reach their majority, they must be returned to the Pale of Settlement if they do not engage in an independent handicraft or trade (in compliance with the regulations of the above law).

[146]

Expulsion of a Skilled Artisan from St. Petersburg (1890)

GARF, f.102, op. 76 a, d, 785, ll. 6–9 ob

"Memorandum of the Passport Department to the Ministry of Internal Affairs (16 April 1890)"

I am sending the attached petition of the Jewish townsman, Iosel' Abramov Azgud of Trokai, which was forwarded to me by the procurator of the St. Petersburg District Court on 6 April 1890 (number 8999). Azgud complains that he was improperly excluded from the St. Petersburg artisan guild and requests permission to reside in St. Petersburg. I have the honor to present this clarification about his complaint.

Azgud has lived in St. Petersburg since 1883 — first as a confectionery baker with the right to work as a sausage maker at the same time, then as someone who makes stuffed animals [taxidermist]. Based on information that Azgud did not practice this trade, the Artisan Board was directed to check on his occupation. Subsequently, the Artisan Board submitted a copy of its resolution (20 December 1888) to exclude Azgud from the guild because he had stopped working in his trade. Given that resolution and article 189 (the Statute of the Artisan Guild), the [Board] ordered that Azgud be expelled from St. Petersburg.

In April 1889, [the Passport Department] received a petition about Azgud's improper exclusion and forwarded it to the Artisan Board for an explanation. However, the latter reaffirmed its decision of 20 December 1888, adding that his workshop was fictitious, that Azgud did not work there, and that he does not engage in his trade. Rather, he used to leave daily for Tomar's butchery, where he worked as a salesman. Moreover, the medical certificate indicating that he was ill from 10 October to December does not appear to be accurate: on 20 November at 11:35 (the day that the report was compiled that he had abandoned his trade), Azgud was not at home; however, at 12:30 that day he left the butchery and went to a tavern.

In May 1889 Azgud submitted a complaint about his improper exclusion from the guild and expulsion from St. Petersburg to the State Senate. But his complaint was denied, and he was so informed by an order of the First Department on 4 October 1889 (number 12269). Recently, Azgud, who has no right to reside in St. Petersburg, arrived in the capital without permission. He was detained on 29 March and sent to the St. Petersburg District Administration for deportation (under police guard) to the place where he is registered to live.

"Petition of Iosel' Azgud to the Minister of Internal Affairs (3 March 1890)"

Having arrived in St. Petersburg in 1873, I opened a Jewish sausage shop and continued to work in this trade until 1884; at the same time, I stuffed birds (for which I had a license for 1889). During this entire time, I lived in the third precinct of the Spasskii police district. On 1 May 1899, I left with my family for a summer house in Shuvalovo. I returned to St. Petersburg in September and settled in a place in the fourth precinct of Spasskii district. Five days later, I fell ill with typhoid, an illness that persisted for approximately three months. During that time, I was treated by Dr. Spainerovskii from the Mariinskaia Hospital, who attended me for a month and a half; later, as I recovered from the illness, I began to visit a clinic for shop assistants on Gorkhovaia and Sadovaia Streets.

During the period of my illness, on the basis of a false denunciation, the police of the fourth precinct suspected that I was not engaging in my trade. On 29 November 1888, it compiled a report and forwarded it to the St. Petersburg Artisan Board, which appointed an expert (that is, one of its own members) to verify the report. That member, who came to my apartment, found me at my joiner's bench for dressing raw material. Nevertheless, they declared the arrangement to be fictitious, and also because I did not have apprentices.

I deem it necessary to explain the statement of the members of the St. Petersburg Artisan Board about the fictitious arrangement and the absence of apprentices. Before my illness, I always had apprentices (from one to seven people). However, because my illness entailed major expenses, I was forced to dismiss them. Indeed, the whole situation bore a different appearance. The police report, which asserts the following, was erroneous, and I can refute it completely: (1) "Iosel' Azgud leaves his apartment and works at Tomar's butchery where he engages in the sale of meat"—such is the explanation of the yard man in the house where I live. But I consider this testimony incorrect and unlawful since I was the owner of this shop until 1885 and, later, I was the owner of the workshop. Did I not have the right to go at any time to any place that I wanted? I do not deny that I visit Tomar's shop, but how could I not go there since he [Tomar] is my father-in-law and a person who extends monetary credit to me? That explains why I used to go to Tomar's shop. Because of my exclusion from the guild, I am deprived of my right to live in the capital.

The reasons for excluding me from the guild were as follows: (1) there were no apprentices [in my workshop]; (2) the police report; and (3) Berenshtein and Trok's desire to get money from me again for my admission to the St. Petersburg artisan guild.

I was ordered to leave St. Petersburg in three days but petitioned the governor with a request that he give me some time to explain the erroneous decision of the St. Petersburg Artisan Board. I received permission to live in the capital for three months (that is, until 14 May 1889). During that time I filed a number of petitions with the St. Petersburg Artisan Board. The first response was that everything depended on the governor. I sent him a petition and received a response that this was a board matter and that the police did not have any objections. Nevertheless, I was not admitted [to the guild] and all my petitions remained like a "voice crying in the wilderness."

I find it necessary to add that a certain Shvarts, a furrier by trade, was also excluded from the guild in the same manner; he was apprised of this on 25 December 1888 by the Kolomna Precinct (he lives at 49 Ekaterininskii Prospect). He was given two and half days to leave [St. Petersburg]. Here is what Shvarts did: he vacated his apartment, then with the help of bribes and a petition from the St. Petersburg artisans Trok and Berenshtein, he gained readmission to the guild, followed by an inspection of his shop. I must say that when the members of the guild (Osip Ivanov, secretary Gurov, and Trok) came through the back door, they found two apprentices and the senior yard man of the building where Shvartz lived. They issued a license for Shvartz but did not grant him residency; he received permission only on 8 February 1889.

After that, Trak explained to Movshe Ebich (who lives at 42 Bol'shaia Sadovaia Street) that if I gave him twenty-five rubles, I would be readmitted into the guild. After that I must say that Trako and Berenshtein slandered me before members of the St. Petersburg Artisan Board. The clerk of the tailor's guild, Vasilii Vasil'ev, can confirm this.

I therefore have the honor to submit this humble request to Your Excellency and to ask for your order that I be readmitted to the ranks of the St. Petersburg artisans' guild as someone who suffered for not working as an artisan but through no fault of his own. You will thereby give me the opportunity to live again with my family and young children, who pray to God for Your Excellency's health.[1]

NOTE

1. [There was no final resolution in this file. There are numerous cases like this one in GARF, f. 102, op. 76a, d, 69, gg. 1882–90.]

[147]

The Hemp Scutching Trade and Expulsion from Kursk Province (1890–91)

"Report of the Minister of Internal Affairs to the State Senate" (1890)
GARF, f. 108, op. 76a, d. 786, ll. 37–38.

The State Senate has sent me the complaint of the Jews Geiman and Gan regarding the decision of the Kursk Provincial Administration to expel them from the town of L'gov to be decided together with the Ministry of Finance.[1]

It is evident from the case that Gan and Geiman, townsmen from Tel'shi (Kovno province) settled in the town of L'gov (the former in 1874, the latter in 1878) [as] artisans engaged in hemp scutching and rope making. After receiving their certification and documents as second-guild [merchants] from the Kursk Artisan Board, they opened a hemp scutching and spinning business. However, the local provincial administration learned that these Jews must have certification as artisans from the place of their registration (that is, the Tel'shi Artisan Board) and that rope spinning and [hemp] scutching are not regarded to be handicrafts. It therefore declared identified Geiman and Gan to be illegal residents, subject to expulsion from L'gov to their place of registration.

The petitioners appealed this decision, with the explanation that: (1) having settled in L'gov until 1889 as artisans, they obtained the right to reside there on the basis of the circular of the Ministry of the Internal Affairs of 3 April 1880 (number 30), which directed police to suspend the resettlement of the Jews living in the interior provinces; (2) upon arriving in L'gov, they showed the police the requisite artisan certificates from the Tel'shi Artisan Board (of which the Kursk Artisan Board was then apprised) and began to collect certificates from the latter to engage in these trades; (3) the occupations of hemp scutching and rope making do not constitute manufacturing because, according to article 2 of the Statute of Manufacturing, production in a factory or mill differs from handicrafts because it entails a large plant and machinery—which artisans do not possess (apart from hand tools and instruments). The petitioners' businesses use only manual instruments.

The minister of finance (without discussing whether hemp scutching and rope making are handicraft occupations) concluded that the Jews Geiman and Gan cannot settle in the town of L'gov even as artisans if the legal regulations are strictly observed: Jews from artisan guilds seeking to work outside the Pale of Settlement may receive a passport to leave their permanent residence only on condition that they present a certificate of their rank as master artisan or foreman from a site in the Pale of Settlement. The petitioners' claim that they presented certificates from the Tel'shi Artisan Board to the Kursk Artisan Board appears to be unsubstantiated.

Given the foregoing, the Ministry of Finance deems the decision of the Kursk Provincial Administration to expel Geiman and Gan from L'gov to be correct, and the petitioners' complaint does not merit consideration.

I also have the honor to inform the Senate [. . .] that the petitioners' reference to the circular of 3 April 1880 (which, they claim, gives them the right to reside in Kursk) cannot apply in this case: that circular aimed only to suspend the mass resettlement of the Jews who had improperly settled in the interior provinces, and not to bestow the legal right for Jews of this category to settle permanently outside the Jewish Pale of Settlement.

NOTE

1. [This file included the cases of several Jewish expulsions from Kursk Province, including the expulsion of Sophia Ioffe, Gorelikov, Shapavalov, and Mil'ner from the town of Koroch. The first names of the latter three and Geiman and Gan were not provided in any of the documents. They were expelled because the police argued that their occupations involved petty trade (for example, in dairy products), rather than handicrafts.]

[148]

Prohibition on Jews in Mining Factories in Siberia

"Report of the Governor General of East Siberia to the Department of Police (3 September 1836)"
GARF, f. 109, 1 eksp. g. 1837, d. 103, l. 3–3 ob.

On 19 December 1835 an imperial decree took measures to exclude Jews from the state and private factories under the jurisdiction of the State Office of Mining.

On this basis, the former chief of the Nerchinsk mining factories (after receiving instructions about the imperial order) proposed to deport Jews whom the courts had sent there for various crimes. He dispatched all of them to the city of Nerchinsk and requested the head of Irkutsk province to send the Jews to remote places away from the factory boundaries and henceforth not to assign them to mining factories.

The civil governor of Irkutsk, for his part, found that this recommendation [. . .] has no basis in the imperial decree, which (in his view) pertains to free Jews, not to those whom the courts had sentenced to factory work for committing crimes. He sent a detailed statement to the former general governor of Eastern Siberia and per a decree of 25 April 1825[1] also addressed this question to the head of the Ministry of Internal Affairs. [. . .] Not having received any decision, I humbly ask Your Excellency for assistance in resolving this question. [. . .][2]

NOTES

1. [An earlier decree of 19 December 1824 prohibited Jews from working in private or public mining factories; it may have been repeated on 25 April 1825 (see Irina Antropova, *Sbornik dokumentov po istorii evreev Urala* (Moscow: Drevlekhranilishche, 2004), 155). This prohibition was repeated several times. In the 1870s only Jews who had the right to live outside the Pale of Settlement were allowed to be involved in gold mining (157–58).]

2. [The file ends without a final resolution.]

[149]

Female Workers' Strike at the Gal'pern Matchbox Factory in Pinsk (1901–2)

LVIA, f. 446, op. 3, d. 234, ll. 10–12 ob.; 85–87, 94–97, 125–28.

"Secret Report of the Assistant Chief of the Minsk Gendarme Administration (5 April 1901)"

On the night of 1–2 April 1901, a mimeographed appeal to cabinetmakers to join the struggle against the owners was disseminated in the town of Pinsk. It was signed by the Pinsk Social-Democratic Committee of the Jewish Workers' Union in Russia and Poland, and was dated April 1901. On the night of 3 April, the same Committee distributed appeals to workers of the plywood factory demanding an increase in wages and reduction in the workday. The appeal concluded: "Put an end to the domination of capital! Long live the workers' movement!"

On 2 April at the Gal'pern matchbox factory, before the start of the evening shift, the workers of the packing division informed the owner that they would not work and demanded an increase in pay given that the owner had reduced the thickness of the matches, making their work more difficult and slightly reducing their [piece-rate] wages. Four girls presented the demands to the owner: Ginda Vorona [Gleiberman],[1] Reizla Iuzik, Shosha Segalevich, and Sora Breitbord. When the owner proposed to deal summarily with the latter [that is, fire them], they declared that they would leave the factory—not alone, but with all the girls.

On 3 April, more than one hundred young women and adolescents in the packing department did not show up to work. Moreover, the owner was informed that the four girls named above (with the assistance of several youths) did not allow the girls into the

factory and threatened to beat them if they disobeyed.

After I and the chief of police arrived at the factory that day, the owner [Iosif] Gal'pern told me that he had known about the strike earlier: the previous day the girls had assembled in one of the courtyards, where they gave speeches and offered fifteen kopecks to anyone who wished to strike. In addition, in early March he received a mimeographed appeal (signed by the Pinsk Social-Democratic Committee) to the workers in his factory. He did not report this appeal to anyone but kept it to himself. Nevertheless, he was targeted by the workers: in January or February, a mimeographed newspaper of the same Committee, *The Pinsk Workers* (number 3) said that in view of the accumulated facts about the oppression of the workers in the plywood and matchbox factories, separate sheets would be released about the factories in the near future. The newspaper advised workers to unite and go to the owner. When I asked why Gal'pern kept this newspaper and appeal to himself and did not forward it to me or the chief of police, he replied that such are police and gendarme matters, but he is an absolutely a private person. When I demanded the newspaper, he replied that he had given it to his manager to read and would get it by evening. Further investigation showed that the strike did ensue and included the participation of the "Pinsk Committee," which distributed strike money on the first day of the strike.

On 4 April, at 11:00 a.m. almost all the girls came to work. With the assistance of the police, I took measures to discover the local meetings and chief activists of the "Pinsk Committee."

On the night of 5 April, they produced and distributed mimeographed appeals urging girls who had not yet come to the meetings not to accede to the owner, to continue the strike, and to give worker-informers the treatment they deserved.

Here is my assessment of the strike: (1) Gal'-pern himself is at fault because he changed the size of the matches in an untimely manner, even without the permission of the factory inspector; (2) his manager, Rom, who promised to increase the packers' piece-rate wages after the holidays [Passover], exploited this "Pinsk Committee" and the March appeal (which urged workers to demand a supplement for their piece wages from the owner Gal'pern once work resumed after the holidays and to strike if he refused). The appeal worked, and on the first workday after the Jewish holidays (2 April) they submitted the demand for a supplement; he refused, with the strike as a consequence.

Based on the circular of the Department of Police (2 August, number 7587), I initiated a formal inquiry [. . .]; I propose to combine it with my investigation of the "Pinsk Committee" (see my report of 18 December 1900, number 1028). To identify the other members of the Committee, I have taken the most energetic measures. I have placed the above-named girls under arrest until the facts of the case are clear.

"Deposition of Iosif Avraamov Gal'pern (4 April 1901)"

My name is Gal'pern, Iosif Abraamov. I am fifty-five years old, of the Jewish confession. My rank is first-guild merchant. I live in the town of Pinsk, district 2, in a private house.

Here is my response to the questions directed to me: On the occasion of the Jewish holiday of Passover, work ended on 20 March at my factory and resumed again on 1 April; however, as it was the first day after a break,

work proceeded at a slow pace. On 2 April work began properly, with the usual energy. A little later, the foreman of the packing division noticed that two girls, Gleiberman (that is, Vorona) and Segalevich, were somewhat excited and, fearing some kind of prank on their part, informed them that in fourteen days he would dismiss them and make the appropriate note in their labor books. That same day, around 2:00 p.m. (during the lunch break), twenty girls gathered in the corridor of the office. Hearing the ruckus, I opened the door; When I asked "What is going on?" the two girls, holding up their labor books, told me that their foreman had fired them because they had asked for a raise in wages. I told them that anyone who is dissatisfied with the factory could leave their jobs, and I would even free them from the fourteen-day [notice] period. In response the girl Leberkes, who was also standing there, asked me to note in her booklet that she was unwilling to continue working. Another girl, Breitbord, began to beckon to girls gathered in the courtyard. As I collected the labor books from these girls, I proposed that those wishing to work, return to the [packing] division and that those who did not, give me their books for notation. The four girls cited above began to demand that the other girls stop working, but except for these four, they all of course went back to work.

At my request, the police chief for the first district came to remove Gleiberman, Segalevich, Leberkes, and Breitbord, but when they declared that they wished to remain and resume work, he left them at the factory.

Seeing that the workers had calmed down, I went home. Within a half-hour of my departure, however, all the girls in the packing division suddenly stopped working and went into the factory courtyard. The factory administrator announced that she would make a list of all those who did not wish to work and advised them to go back into the [packing] division and get down to work. Eighty girls went in immediately, and the rest after a while. Work continued until the end of the evening.

On the evening of that same day, I was informed that the girls from my factory gathered at a meeting in the courtyard of some house on Goncharnaia Street. An unidentified speaker persuaded the girls not to work the next day. Some young people at the assembly promised to give them strike money. I did not manage to learn the details about the site of the assembly, which probably ended quickly because of a fire that broke out on the same street.

On 3 April work in all the sections of the factory proceeded as usual. However, only 25 girls showed up at the packing department (which always had up to 160 girls). I learned that many of the girls (including Segalevich, Gleiberman, Leberkes, and Breitbord) stood on the corner of the street to my factory and prevented others from coming to work by threatening to beat them. In the course of the day a few more girls appeared to work, but about 80 girls were absent. Some of those who were present at the factory office yesterday came with tears in their eyes, saying that the [strikers] had not allowed them into the factory under different pretexts, as you yourself have seen.

Moreover, I suggest that the cause of the strike was the mimeographed appeal that the Pinsk Committee disseminated in March about my factory workers. I see no other reason for the strike, because I did not offend the workers. I did reduce the size of the matchsticks, but the girls' wages did not decrease — because the size of the matchboxes was reduced proportionately. However, if it did seem that wages were reduced because of this, then of course I would have supplemented the wages.

On 4 April, before 11:00 a.m. up to one hundred girls gathered in the packing division and resumed the order of work. According to rumors, the agitators and members of the Pinsk Committee may consist of Ovsei Gurin and Borushok (the son of the barrister

for legal matters, Faivel Borushok). Not all the girls packed [the boxes] with the new matchsticks; only part of them did, because I introduced the new matchsticks only for a trial but did not establish them definitely.

"'The Pinsk Worker,' Number 3 (January 1901)"[2]

BROTHERS AND SISTERS!

The workers lead a sorry life! All our lives, we toil like animals: not a moment is free to think about ourselves; after our arduous labor they do not allow us to rest as they should. Each foreman, each scoundrel master robs us of the time to sleep and eat. We are forced to listen to their every curse and savage attacks on us. The factories and workshops are cramped and filthy; the ventilation is poor. During our difficult work, we must endure stale air. The cramped factories and onerous labor are the reasons for the terrible misfortunes that often befall us. The workers are tired. [. . .] The wages are so meager that they do not suffice for the most basic necessities. And we do not even receive them in full — they make penalty deductions for all kinds of nonsense. Our food is vile and gives us stomach illnesses. Our homes are cold, dirty, and squalid. The factories are like poison to us, but we do not have any pleasure at home either.

Our income does not make it possible to educate our children, whom we can send not to the *heder* but only to the factories, where they fall ill and die young. Hard labor dulls their young brains; the maltreatment of the foreman destroys their energy; for the rest of their lives they remain downtrodden, unhappy, and ignorant. In a word, we do not live, but suffer. Our lives consist of endless adversity and destitution. [. . .]

When the steam mill still existed, workers complained about a slimy glutton named Moisei Lur'ia, the manager of the mill who oppressed them. "Brothers," Moisei replied, "if it is bad for you, then it is good for me." For once in his life, Moisei Lur'ia told the truth.

He clearly stated that everything that is bad for us is good for our employers. All that is for our benefit is to the owner's detriment. We want to live like people, not like wild animals. We want to receive wages for our hard work so that we can eat until we are satisfied, buy shoes and dresses, and live where we are sheltered from cold and dampness. We do not want to labor all day like beasts; we want to have time for rest and education. [. . .]

Brothers and sisters! It depends on us to improve our position or to live in poverty as we have until now. To improve our position, we must unite; we must all come forward together against our employers and demand that they raise our wages, that they not penalize us for trivial things, that they shorten the working day, that they treat us with greater humanity. We must demand that they treat us like human beings. Then our employers and their foremen will not dare to deceive us as they have been doing until now. They will know that we will not allow the slightest [abuse] or tolerate a single injustice. Unity and consciousness—that is the strength of the workers. To the struggle![3]

"On Strikes"

Long have the factory owners oppressed the workers. They do not make them into people but into toiling beasts. Long have the workers borne the yoke of the factory owners—so long that the owners assume that it will always be this way. They think that the workers have already turned into workhorses and cannot protest against oppression and tyranny. But they are grievously wrong. For many long years the workers have nurtured a growing hatred toward their oppressors, and they have finally expressed this in amazing protests. The workers have shown their employers that they are not workhorses, but human beings with whom the owners must deal. Moreover, the workers have a firm grip on the employers, not vice versa. When workers do not hold a firm grip ([and are] each on

their own), the employer can do whatever he wants. He can deceive them, curse them, hold them like horses, and drive them to work with a whip. However, when the workers act together, when everyone stands up as one, that puts an end to the employer's domination and robbery. The workers understood this, began to unite, and organized as a close-knit group: "One for all and all for one," they said as they began to fight for their interests. Practice and time showed that the best way to improve their situation was to strike.

A strike is when workers stop work and stay away until their demands have been met. The workers do not lose anything because of the strike: all their capital, all their wealth, which is comprised of their ten fingers, remains with them (only if the employer's machine has not removed them). But the strike ruins the employer: he cannot deliver orders, machines are not maintained, the capital investment in the factory is idle and brings no profit, and the employer faces bankruptcy. Obviously, it is better for him to give in to the workers. [. . .] But one needs to know how organize the strike. English workers have already held numerous strikes and gained experience in this. All workers who strike are imitating our English brothers. Brothers and sisters! The workers in different cities and countries have already improved their position considerably through strikes. They are earning far more than the Pinsk worker; they labor less and are treated like human beings; no one dares to offend them. To improve our situation, we must embark on the path that our brothers and sisters in other cities and countries have taken.

First of all, we must unite, organize. We must create a *kassa* [treasury], which will provide money temporarily during strikes. The *kassa* is the best means to unite. Artisans whose masters keep an eye them may create a general fund for each trade; in factories where the foreman serves as a spy for the administration and follows every step of the workers, it is impossible to establish a big *kassa*. One should create a fund for five to seven people in the factories. Then, when there are already several *kassy* at the factory, they can unite them. Unite through the joint funds and prepare to strike. Show our cruel oppressors our strength!

The strike at the Gvirtsman Tobacco Plant: in the month of Av [July–August], the cigarette-rolling workers at the Gvirtsman Tobacco Plant organized a strike. Before the strike they received eighteen kopecks for every thousand rolled cigarettes, but five kopecks were deducted for the carton [in which they were packed]. The plant gave them poor material, removed two cigarettes from each hundred rolled cigarettes [for inferior quality], and at the end of the year deducted for the cartons. The owner's treatment of the workers was very bad. When a girl demanded that they give her good materials with which to work, Gvirtsman took offense that a worker had the temerity to demand something from him and replied: "Look, she is my girlfriend, but [she] began to raise objections to me—so I ordered the guard to throw her down the stairs." With that he went too far: all the girls stopped their work and announced their demands: (1) increase wages by two kopecks per thousand; (2) not deduct two cigarettes per hundred; (3) supply good materials; (4) make no deductions for the cartons. They announced that they would not return to work until their demands were met. The factory owner did not agree to this and ordered that none of the girls be admitted to the factory. "It is nothing," he thought, "they will yet ask for my forgiveness." But a few days passed, and no one came to work. The foreman began to run from one girl to another to persuade them to return to work. The girls firmly stood their ground. The owner threatened to hire other people and to install machinery. He told the girls: "Come to work; do not look at the older ones; they are rebels." When this had no effect, he began to dismiss the cigarette rollers from the factory. But the latter did not begin to work until the factory owner yielded.

They did not work for two weeks, and in the end he hired his own workers back. He added one kopeck to their wages, was to deduct only one cigarette per hundred, was no longer to charge for the cartons, and would supply good materials. Since then the treatment of the cigarette rollers by the factory owner and foremen has definitely changed. They cannot say a word to them; they remember well how they had to implore the workers [to return].

"Information Sheet and Statement of Ginda Itskova Gleiberman (11 April 1901)"

My name is Gleiberman, Ginda Itskovna.
Age: Seventeen years old
[Social] Origins: townswoman
Nationality and Citizenship: Jewish; Russian citizen
Time and Place of Birth: I was born in Pinsk
Rank: Townswoman of Pinsk
Place of Permanent Residence: Pinsk
Place of Registration: Pinsk [Townspeople] Society
Family Status (name, patronymic of wife or husband, names of children, their occupation, and place of residence): Single
Means of Livelihood: Personal earnings
Occupation: Packer at the Gal'pern Plant
Family Relations (name, patronymic, surname of parents, brothers, sisters, place of residence and occupations): Father Itsko Aron, manual laborer; mother Mera; brother—a minor [no name given]; sister Khaia Leia. They all live in Pinsk.[4]

Although my surname is Gleiberman, I worked at the factory under the name Vorona. The fact of the matter is that I entered the Gal'pern factory when I was not yet fourteen years old, hence [too young] for the factory administration to accept me legally to work. To circumvent the statutes of the law, I took the metrical record of a friend, Gnesha Vorona, who is older than I and used it to prove my identity; afterward I received a work booklet under the name of Vorona (the plant having no knowledge of my real surname). People usually resort to this method of evading the law with the knowledge of the factory, thereby enabling many minors work under an alien surname.

I will explain the essence of this case: I do not consider myself guilty of ties to the activities of the Pinsk Social-Democratic Committee, which initiated appeals to workers to struggle against the employers. On 2 April I wanted to organize a strike of female workers at the packing division of the factory; I therefore refused to work and encouraged other girls to follow suit and to demand higher wages from Gal'pern. Before the Jewish Passover, the manager Rom promised to increase our piece-rate wages when work resumed after the holidays (given the changes in the boxes and the reduction in the thickness of the matchwood). As a result, it became more difficult to work: we packed fewer boxes; but because the wages are based on piece-rate, these decreased. After Passover, because Rom did not uphold his promise, I turned to the foreman Levi to clarify matters. He sent me to the office, but [Gal'pern] refused me work. When I left to complain to the others in the packing division about the capriciousness of the owner Gal'perin, he declared that they would have me arrested. Afterward I did not go to work for several days, but then I went to the factory to settle accounts, and the police arrested me. I did not urge the other girls to stop working, but only made efforts on my behalf. I did not hear about the appeals to the workers and do not know who distributed them.

"Statement of Sora Vol'fovna Breitbord (11 April 1901)"

My name is Sora Vol'fovna Breitbord. [. . .][5] I do not consider myself guilty of having ties to the Pinsk-Social Democratic Committee.[6] [. . .] Before the Jewish Passover, the manager Rom promised everyone in the packing department an increase in their wages because the factory began to produce matches with thinner matchwood and had changed the size of the boxes. Those changes significantly reduced our wages. For example, before I received up to thirty-five kopecks, but now no more than twenty kopecks. After Passover Rom did not think to fulfill his promise: all the packers (including me) left for the office and demanded an increase in wages. In response, the owner Gal'perin fired me and declared that he would have me arrested.

I was afraid of this threat and for two days did not go to the factory. When I did go there to settle accounts, for some reason the police arrested me. I did not urge any of the other girls to stop working but only took the efforts for myself. I was not at the assembly and I did not hear about the appeals. I do not know who distributes them.

"Statement of Reizlia Abramova Iusik (1 December 1901)"

My name is Iuzik, Reizlia Abramovna, age 17, born in the town of Telekhany.[7] I do not consider myself guilty of having ties to the Pinsk Social-Democratic Committee. [. . .] Two weeks after Jewish Passover, I was dismissed from the Gal'pern factory — for what, I myself do not know: Rom, who handles the accounts, did not give me an explanation. On the first day after the end of Passover, my sister and I left Pinsk to live with our relatives (our father was in America, and our stepmother refused to support us any longer). Initially, in Telekhany we went to the tailor Iosel (whose surname I do not remember); he is now dead. After three days we moved to the estate "Somino" to our uncle. I do not remember his name and surname but I know that he runs a *pakht* (a milk business)[8] and leases land. After two weeks we moved to our relatives in Logishin, but [we] returned to Pinsk when our father returned from America and summoned us. I was not in Pinsk during the disorders at the Gal'perin plant and therefore could not have participated in them. No other people, apart from my relatives cited above, can confirm our stay in Telekhany and So-mino. I do not know Gurin and Borushok. If my sister said that we left for Telekhany be-fore Passover, she is mistaken; most probably, she simply misspoke because she absolutely does not have a good command of the Rus-sian language.[9]

NOTES

1. [The file records her name variously as Gneta and Ginda, but her legal name was Ginda Gleiber-man.]

2. [The police requested the state rabbi of Pinsk to translate the appeal and newspaper from Yid-dish to Russian. The police reported that they had not identified those who had distributed the ap-peals because the original activists, Gekel'man, Levin, Dezint, Sel'tser, and Gel'dzand were already in prison when the third issue appeared. The police also noted that the newspaper employed simple sen-tences, rudimentary vocabulary, and repetition in an attempt to reach the mass of workers.]

3. [The next article on the "long work day" warned the readers that "studies show that one should not work more than eight hours in a twenty-four-hour period," or one would risk permanently harming the body.]

4. [The second page of the information sheet in-cluded questions about education and travel abroad, which were not filled in because they did not apply

to her. The page also asked if she had ever been ar-rested or brought to trial, to which she replied no.]

5. [Breitbord filled out the same information sheet as Gleiberman: she was a permanent resident of Pinsk but registered in the Shereshevskii commu-nity. Her marital status was single. Her father Vol'f was a woodcutter at a woodworking shop. She had a mother, two brothers, and one sister. Her brother Leizer was married and lived separately.]

6. [The first part of her testimony is identical (almost word for word) to that of Ginda Gleiber-man (beginning at "I will explain the essence of this case") and other workers who were questioned.]

7. [The rest of the information sheet showed that Iuzik was registered in the town of Sviato-Vol'sk and lived in her father's house. Her father was Abram, a tailor. Her sister Khana was also questioned in this case.]

8. [*Pakht* is a Yiddish word meaning a lease on an estate; in this case, the uncle had a lease on a milk business.]

9. [The testimonies of Sosha Segalovich, Feiga Fuksna, and Sora Leberkes were identical to the bulk of Ginda Gleiberman's. The state dropped its investigation of the female workers, who thus were not punished for the strike. However, the state did arrest and imprison two political activitists, Ovsei Gurin and Iuda Borushok. Significantly, the police blamed the factory disorder on the owner's decision to change the terms of work and wages.]

Professionals

[150]

Permission to Open a Medical Clinic for Women in Vil'na (1907)

LVIA, f. 383, op. 2, d. 15, ll. 3–5, 17–17 ob.

"Petition of Midwives Ester (Esfir) Viktorovna Vysotskaia Gringauz and Pesia Abramovna Lipkovich to the Vil'na Medical Department (30 April 1901)"

Seeking to open a birthing clinic for women who are pregnant, in childbirth, and recently confined, we have the honor to request that the Medical Department grant us the proper permission.

[Handwritten note by Pesia Abramovna Lipkovich]

In view of the fact that I decline to participate in this, I ask that the present petition be denied.[1]

"Statement from Dr. G. Ratner to the Vil'na Medical Department (18 May 1901)"

I state that I agree to assume the responsibility to be in charge of the clinic for women who are pregnant, in childbirth, and recently confined, established by the midwife Vysotskaia Gringauz.

"Inspection of the Clinic (15 October 1908)"

We, the undersigned, after a visit and inspection of the private clinic for women who are pregnant, in childbirth, and recently confined, established in Vil'na by the midwife

E[ster] V[iktorovna] Gringauz, found the following violations of the articles of incorporation confirmed for this clinic on 2 June 1907: (1) The clinic Vysotskaia Gringauz has expanded without authorization: instead of two beds (article 3), we discovered five beds; (2) The clinic not only admitted women who were pregnant, in childbirth, and recently confined, but also women with gynecological illnesses; (3) The registration book is not properly maintained: it includes only the name and surname of the patients and no other notations; (4) Contrary to article 7, two midwives work in the clinic without the knowledge of the Medical Department: the founder Vysotskaia Gringauz and Feifits, a masseuse (an announcement about this has been posted); the following doctors were invited: Bomash, Shil'kret, Liapides, Tiger, Burak, Kon, Zal'kind, Vygodskii, Mil'kovskii, Gudinskii, to treat patients without the participation of Dr. Ratner, the head of the clinic; (5) Dr. Ratner, who assumed the responsibility for running the Gringauz clinic, to all intents and purposes appears only for consultations (on a level with the other doctors invited [to treat] patients); the midwife Vysotskaia Gringauz admits, treats, and discharges the patients and provides medical supervision of the clinic. The Medical Department has not received the information and registers required under article 12; (6) No trace was found of a register to record documents, money and items accepted from inpatients for the depository (article 15). According to the statement by the head, the patients did not leave anything in the depository. Not the [clinic] head but a midwife kept the list of [the patients'] afflictions, and it was absolutely incomplete.

In addition, it turned out that the clinic had no mortuary or sterilizers for dressings (which are carelessly stored in a cabinet); the medicines in the clinic pharmacy were of dubious quality and lacked stickers to show their origins. According to the head, the founder of the clinic personally obtained all the medicines (including the potent ones), without the required catalogs prescribed by the doctors and various pharmacies in Vil'na.

*"Statement of Dr. Vysotskaia
Gringauz to the Medical Department
(received 30 October 1908)"*

Because the inspection on 15 October 1908 of my clinic in Vil'na revealed several violations, which resulted because the individual points of the charter were not completely clear to me, I have the honor to request a one-month period to bring the clinic into complete compliance with the mandatory articles.[2]

NOTES

1. [Vysotskaia Gringauz wanted to establish her clinic with Pesia Lipkovich, who withdrew herself from the project. It is not clear why she requested that the petition should be denied.]

2. [The clinic underwent another inspection on 2 August 1912, when the inspector again found several violations, mainly with respect to record keeping and sterilization.]

[151]

Permission to Open a Dental Clinic in Kursk Province (1908–9)

RGIA, f. 1284, op. 224, d. 260, ll. 25–30.

*"Petition of Dentist Tauba Khaia
Korenblat, Former Wife of a Turkish
Citizen, to the Minister of Internal
Affairs (3 November 1908)"*

Since receiving my certificate (number 523) for the profession of dentist from the Council of Imperial Khar'kov University on 8 April 1883, I have opened dental offices in various towns of the Russian Empire, with greater accessibility for the poor class of people and for male and female students. I have always fulfilled my

responsibilities in dental treatment with precision. Apart from gratitude, I received nothing. I accepted the poor and provided assistance gratis. On 21 May 1907, I received from the Khar'kov Provincial Administration the most recent certificate (number 2599) for the right to open a dental office in the town of Chuguev, where I was until August of this year. On 12 August, I submitted a petition to the governor of Kursk for permission to open a dental office in the town of Koroch, in view of the fact that the town has 14,000 residents, two gymnasiums for males and females, but no dental office. Moreover, I presented my diploma and stamp for the reply. Then in hopes of receiving permission, I arrived in Koroch to find and rent an apartment for the dental office. As I did not receive any answer for a long time, I turned to the inspector of the Medical Department of the Kursk Provincial Administration to determine the status of my petition. The inspector replied to my telegram of 30 September with a telegram [saying] "An answer will be sent by mail," which I received on this date, concluding that my petition to the governor was denied, but did not explain the grounds and information [on which he based his decision]. Nor did they return my diploma.

Not encountering obstacles to opening an office during the twenty-five years of my practice, I cannot understand the impediment to my petition, all the more since I have never been observed doing anything illegal (as demonstrated by the fact that I have always been issued permissions to open dental offices without obstacles). No one has ever submitted a complaint about the treatments. I find the general governor's order forbidding me to open an office in Koroch to be oppressive (since I live only by my labor in dentistry and do not know another trade on which I could live). The prohibition to open a dental office is tantamount to depriving me of the right to practice dentistry, for which I expended my strength and health to receive the diploma.

Having explained and presented the [following] attachments (a copy of my diploma for the rank of dentist, number 523, and certificate from the Khar'kov Provincial Administration, number 2599), I humbly ask Your Excellency — given what has been stated about my circumstances and the hopeless position in which I presently find myself presently, to order that I be permitted to open a dental office in Koroch, and that I have not lost my right [to practice dentistry], which has not been revoked by a court or administration.

Regarding the order, I ask that you inform me through the Koroch district police administration (along with returning the attachments), and as soon as possible, especially in view of the fact that I am a woman without any means of support. I am living off my last possessions. I also seek to prove that, if deprived of my legal rights, I shall be forced to beg for a living, because — even though I have a diploma — I have not been allowed to earn a living through lawful labor.

"Telegram from [Tauba] Korenblat to the Ministry of Internal Affairs (28 November 1908)"

I humbly request that you inform the police not to obstruct my [dental] practice. The police are oppressing the dentist Korenblat.

"Report of the Governor of Kursk to the Ministry of the Interior (22 May 1909)"

In returning the telegram from the dentist Tauba Khaia Korenblat (in which she complains that the police persecute her [dental] practice in Koroch), I have the honor of informing the Department of Police that this dentist submitted a petition in August 1908, asking permission to open a dental office in Koroch. However, she was denied permission on the grounds that the population of Koroch, during the revolutionary movements [1905–7], demonstrated an especially intense revolutionary mood, reflected in the murder of the assistant constable on political grounds, the travel of *zemstvo* employees in the district to disseminate propaganda among the peasants, etc. In view of this, any newcomers to the town of Koroch, especially Jews, are extremely undesirable.

Thus, denied permission to open a dental office, Korenblat has no right to practice [dentistry], and her complaint against the police is groundless.[1]

NOTE

1. [In the document there was a marginal note scribbled by an official in the Ministry of the Interior: "Under the statutes pertaining to the practice of a specialty [that is, dentistry], she has the right

to live in Koroch and opened an office for that. [. . .] This order is incorrect." Although this official questioned the governor's decision, the file does not include an order countermanding his decision against Kornblat.]

[152]

The Law Profession in Russia: Memoirs of Genrikh Sliozberg

Genrikh B. Sliozberg, *Dela minuvshikh dnei: zapiski russkogo evreia.* Vol. 1 (Paris: Izd. Komiteta po chestvovaniiu 70-ti letniago iubileia G. B. Sliozberg, 1933), 190–204.

Chapter 10

[. . .] Once again I attempted to take several steps to enter state service, but did not succeed—and all for the same reason: the Jewish confession. Having decided to become an assistant to a barrister, I faced the question of choosing a patron. A beginning, young legal intern usually attempts to become the assistant to some famous barrister, not to acquire an abundance of practical experience and learn all the secrets of the profession from this barrister (with the hope of becoming famous oneself, presuming that one has grounds for this), but to acquire the appropriate formal affiliation. At that time, the probation entailed extremely abnormal conditions, and this has still not changed. The institution of barrister was created by the judicial statutes of 20 November 1864, which were based on the French model, albeit adapted to correspond to the political conditions of both countries. The imitation was totally inappropriate and, in my view, yielded unfavorable results. Far more practical and expedient is the situation in Germany, at least with respect to the length of the probationary period. According

to the law applicable in all German states, the probation is the same for barrister as it is for magistrates—that is, one must first qualify as *Referendar* and then *Asessor*.[1] Only after an aspiring candidate has held the rank of *Referendar* and has served in various judicial offices (even under a notary public) is it possible to become a barrister. There is no institution of patronage for these probationary lawyers. Nor is there such in France. In the latter case, the personal patronage is replaced by participation in so-called conferences—that is, assemblies of young lawyers convened under the guidance of people appointed by the *bâtonnier* (the head of the legal bar at a given appellate court). In Russia, upon graduation from the university, a young man—who has no practical preparation and who is armed with very weak theoretical baggage—must go for training to some barrister and serve as his assistant for a term of five years. The institution of assistant barrister appeared simultaneously with that of barristers: those seeking to be assistants announced their candidacy, but there were not enough barristers to take them. Absolutely nothing was specified with respect to the real conditions of the assistant (with few exceptions). Enlistment as an assistant to this or that barrister from the very beginning of the formation of our legal bar turned into a formality: there was never any relationship between the so-called patron and his assistant (the former never supervised, the latter never assisted). By the end of the 1880s St. Petersburg had virtually no barristers (with two or three exceptions) with whom young people could work as assistants and under their direct supervision. Therefore I did not make a special effort to be registered as an assistant to some "royal barrister." However, if I had had such a desire, it would hardly have been realizable for want of any recommendations or protection. The recommendations of professors, it seemed to me (and I was not wrong), did not carry much weight with practicing barristers; the protection of a rich client, in this respect, would have meant much more. I was listed as the assistant to the barrister A[leksandr] M[oiseevich] Brilliant; I knew the Brilliant family when I was still a student. The family consisted of a very elderly man, the head of the family, who spent almost his entire life in the service of Baron Gintsburg[2] and had already lived out his time when I came to know the family. Among his sons was one Aleksandr Moiseevich, a barrister, a man of high moral quality who enjoyed among his acquaintances a reputation as a lawyer punctilious in the highest degree and who had a small, but substantial practice in midlevel commercial circles. He was the legal consultant for one of the railroads. His distinctive quality as a person and as a lawyer was exceptional modesty and lack of pretentiousness.

Another member of the family, Semen Brilliant, was a young man who unfortunately lost his way and did not have any definite career. But he was of my age and ranked as a leading Petersburg connoisseur of belles-lettres. Endowed with exceptional gifts, he undoubtedly could have — with some self-discipline — occupied a prominent position in literature.

He was an extraordinarily kind person: he spent all his energy and time on performing endless tasks for others, seeking jobs for those in need, and giving protection to every kind of unsuccessful youth and aging talent. Constantly occupied with the interests of others, he did not look after his own fate and squandered his natural gifts by failing to concentrate on them.

In literary circles, S[emen] Moiseevich Brilliant was well known. He was constantly engaged in plans to address questions that evoked great interest. Unfortunately, however, he never realized these plans, for he was distracted by efforts to help various beginning talents. He compiled biographies of Krylov and Michelangelo for the Pavlenkov publishing house;[3] these were successful and showed the talents that could have been developed if the energy had in some measure corresponded to these capabilities. But it was precisely this energy that was lacking. He thus spent his life forever planning to realize plans but never managing to do so. Not long before the outbreak of war [World War I] he found himself in Switzerland — he was to study something, but once again failed to do so. He passed the entire period of the war under the horrendous conditions of an émigré. He did not engage in politics. At the end of the war, he had become a refugee. Upon his arrival in Paris, Brilliant devoted himself to propagandizing the ideas of the famous [Émile] Coué, who developed the theory of inspiration and autosuggestion. But this time there was no work to be done — he limited himself to conversations and gathering material. Of course, he had to live under difficult circumstances; however, he spent virtually his entire life in need. At the age of seventy-two he died — a crushed, sick old man; until the end he sought people who would support his ideas, did not find them, and died at the Rothschild hospital in 1930. Thus departed an endlessly good, talented person with a great education and incomparable moral qualities.

I valued him greatly. My contact with him led to closer ties to the Brilliant family and, in particular, to the barrister Aleksandr Moiseevich, who willingly agreed to list me as an assistant. This enlistment was of course a mere formality; I never received nor expected any guidance from him, and correspondingly, my patron did not expect any kind of help in conducting his affairs. However, I did not regard becoming a lawyer as something of any significance. I still calculated that, once I had passed the master's examination, I would succeed in embarking on an academic career in the faculty of criminal law.

The system of preparing young scholars for a professorship at the time was not different from what it is now—it is profoundly unsatisfactory. To hold a faculty position, it was above all necessary to pass the master's examination for a specialized scholarly field. The master's examination itself had no clear criteria; everything depended on the views of the professor or professors from the faculty of that specialization. One could not preclude the possibility that a well-prepared young scholar would fail the master's examination, while a candidate who was ill prepared but enjoyed the protection of a given professor would successfully pass the examination. The examination itself (in the presence of all the professors of the faculty) consisted in participating in a colloquium on a topic approved by the faculty. Some professors demanded full familiarity with all the literature (past, present, and, if possible, future) and of course exhaustive knowledge of works on this topic that the examiner himself had written his dissertation (master's or doctor's). Others compiled a special list of those compositions that the master's candidate should know in order to pass the test. Other faculties did neither of these: the examination had no set framework and reflected the personal discretion of the specialist professor. My master's examination occupied me from the fall of 1888 to the spring of 1889. The professors who con-

ducted the examination on criminal law were aware of my work abroad, placed no special demands on me, and were fully satisfied with the colloquium in which I participated (as an examinee in the faculty).

Simultaneously, I was searching for ways to earn a living. I cannot fail to mention one attempt, since it is characteristic and at the time had a depressing impression on me. Professor Foinitskii[4] was friends with the boss of the Tsarkoe Selo Railway, which was under Poliakov,[5] who had died shortly before my return to St. Petersburg. Fonitskii sent me (with the corresponding letter of recommendation) to one of Poliakov's heirs. I was received with minimal politeness and offered a position that was insulting (whatever my situation might have been): that of a ticket conductor on the passenger trains on the Tsarskoe Selo line. That was virtually an insult. Of course I rejected the offer. No doubt, given the laudatory testimonial of a prominent professor, if I were not a Jew (and if the person I approached were a more sensitive Jew), they would have found a position more appropriate for my educational level. Later, in my practice I encountered this heir of Poliakov (not his son) and became convinced that it would be difficult to expect any other attitude in such a situation.

In December my son was born in Poltava. In the interval between two examinations, I spent several months there. The birth of a son served as a new stimulus to determine more quickly my material situation. I arrived from Poltava with the determination that, no matter what, I would find some kind of job, even if [it was] that of a mere teacher. In the event I decided to take a position in a bank run by one of the Poliakovs—son of the brother of the "railway" Poliakov.[6] So, having dreamed that upon my arrival in St. Petersburg I would embark on a brilliant career as a scholar, I had to work in a bank writing form letters for routine banking correspondence. Having worked for two weeks I became convinced that, even if I am suitable to be a bank correspondent, the latter is not suitable for me. So I left the job at the bank.

I was registered to be an assistant to a barrister. To conduct business in the *okruzhnoi sud* [district court] it was necessary to have a certificate (that is, the court's permission); I obtained this certificate just before the government (based on an imperial memorandum from the former Minister of Justice Manasein[7] in 1889) prohibited the issue of certificates giving Jews the right to represent others in judicial institutions and to be admitted to the bar of barristers.

Manasein found that the legal profession was, [as it] continues to be, overpopulated by Jews, who drive out Russians and who (in his opinion) introduce into legal work methods that do not adequately guarantee the moral purity at the level that Manasein deemed necessary. To restore the estate of barristers to a healthy condition, he proposed to block future access for Jews to the legal profession. In order to avoid proposing this matter as a legal statute to the State Council, Manasein exploited the formula of "temporary measure," which was adopted "henceforth until the review of general laws on Jews." He proposed to make the acceptance of Jews as barristers and the issue of certificates for legal representation in the affairs of others dependent in each individual case on the permission of the minister of justice. Only later did the main detail of Manasein's note become known: the minister of justice will not use his right to permit the acceptance of Jews into the legal profession until a norm is established fixing the percentage of Jewish lawyers [in relation] to the total number in a given judicial circuit and until the proportion dropped to this norm. But the text gave hope that for individuals, against whom no moral objections might be raised, and especially in those places where Jewish lawyers are few in number (or entirely absent), access to the bar would be possible with the permission of the minister of justice. In reality, this hope proved to be illusory be-

cause of the supplementary statement (and, as it were, the obligation) of the minister not to exercise this right. This method of violating rights, contrary to the fundamental law about the order for publishing and applying new legal norms, became widely practiced with respect to Jews in other administrative branches as well. But this was especially so with respect to its application in this case by the minister of justice—the general procurator whose main function consisted precisely in ensuring the observance of laws in the empire.

The report of the Minister of War, Vannovskii,[8] requested an imperial directive to preclude the acceptance of Jews as military doctors. This was preceded by an order that Jews should not be made officers in military service.

Thus began a new era in the history of depriving the Jews of their rights in Russia. Previously, the government had taken measures to encourage Jews to obtain secondary and higher education; a series of legislative acts established that those who graduated from institutions of higher education would be exempted from restrictive laws with respect to residency, rights in trade and business, and even rights to enter state service. Henceforth the government openly adopted the reverse policy: it created obstacles not only with respect to entering institutions of higher education (by introducing percentage quotas in 1886) but even with respect to those who had previously received, or who in the future would receive, such an education despite the restrictions. The government now erected barriers for entering the free professions; it deprived these people of rights that, in formal terms, they continued to enjoy on the basis of laws that had not been abolished. But [the regime] simply ignored those laws through all kinds of imperial reports and through arbitrary directives.

It was perfectly clear that my dreams of an academic career were destroyed, that (regardless of any scientific accomplishments) a Jew will not be admitted to teach in the university and to hold an academic appointment. But in recent years I was so engaged in my scientific work that I had not noticed the spirit of antisemitism that had become so sharply expressed in official circles. I still nourished the hope (perhaps weak, but still dominant in me) that my scholarly preparation would nonetheless be used for the goals of science.

Chapter 11

Having passed the master's examination, I embarked on what was for me one of the most difficult periods of my life. My calculation that in the near future legal practice would give me sufficient income to support my family had proved unwarranted. I had no business connections, and my experience showed that professorial protection was of no great significance. Nevertheless, I had become so attached to the idea of scholarly work that I could not change course without a certain spiritual crisis. The professors, who valued the quality of my academic training and my abilities, began to insist and to give friendly advice on what they deemed a "formal" difficulty based on my Jewish origins: adopt (as some of them put it) "some kind" of Christian confession, which would open for me the doors both to state service and to a professorship, and ensure my career. Moreover, they referred to the fact that, by having made a career and gaining influence, I would be in a position to do much more good for my fellow Jews than would be the case if I were deprived of the possibility of making this career.

To be honest, I can say that I did not experience an internal struggle or, more exactly, temptation. The idea of converting to Christianity did not occur to me, but the very raising of this question and, above all, the idea that I must abandon my dream (because of my difficult material situation, after such a difficult youth) could not fail to have a depressing effect at the very point in life when internal energy demands a resolution.

Because of these circumstances, my life moved in different directions. [First], having become one of the assistant barristers and having become convinced that neither state service nor an academic career was available for me, I had to look on the legal profession as a source of income. [Second], it was impossible to abandon the scientific knowledge that I had acquired. I thought that my work in legal scholarship could prove useful for my legal work in general and for my material situation in particular. Third, the Jewish Question, which during my university years and time abroad had been only of tangential interest and had not engaged me, now proved so acute that it was impossible for me — someone raised in a Jewish spirit — not to take a deeper interest and to devote part of myself to this. And as often happens, oppression that is subjectively experienced, the impossibility of choosing a path in life according to one's own inclinations and capabilities solely because this is barred by restrictive laws about Jews, could only make this question personal and profoundly intimate. No sensitive person could ignore it; on the contrary, even if one has a certain sickly feeling, one wants immediately to expose all the pain caused by this injustice.

Before turning to recollections about my personal activity in these three areas, I will allow myself to characterize these three spheres in my era: the status of the legal profession in the capital, scholarly circles in the capital, and the circles that engaged the question of the Jews' lack of rights.

Above all, [some words about] the legal profession: The entire legal estate was divided into two categories, barristers and their assistants. The latter attained a certain autonomy and were governed by their own representative organ, the Commission of Assistant Barristers, which was the leading disciplinary authority over the young legal interns in the same way that the Council of Barristers, as representative of an estate, supervised the activity of its members (that is, barristers). General assemblies of assistant barristers adopted resolutions. These assemblies were of great interest to young lawyers; a large crowd gathered at these assemblies and, as was the custom, engaged in interminable conversations and adopted compromise resolutions. Moreover, one had to bear in mind that this or that resolution was subject to review by the Council of Barristers, who had to confirm certain resolutions. Membership in the ranks of assistant barristers depended, above all, on the consent of the Commission and, in turn, the Council, which adopted its own resolution. The members of the Commission consisted of the most popular representatives of the young lawyers. As I have already said, the assistant barristers were occupied with independent practice and rarely had the opportunity to be in contact with this or that prominent barrister who had a broad array of cases. In other words, personal patronage (the foundation of our institution of legal internship) proved utterly inadequate. The St. Petersburg Council of Barristers counteracted this lack of personal patronage by means of "estate patronage"—modeled after the Parisian *barreaux* (bars): young interns should gather at conferences under the leadership of senior barristers elected by the Council. Such conferences were conducted by groups. When I entered the estate [of assistant barristers], the conferences—despite their brief existence—proved a stillborn institution: very few attended them. The youth preferred to devote their free time to other activities and entertainment, which were plentiful in the capital. Nor was there much use from the Council's decree that only those who proved their readiness by personal participation in this or that group in the activities of the conference could join the rank of barrister. It all turned into pure fiction. The Council knew perfectly well that some assistants, in terms of preparation and abundance of cases, surpassed the practical knowledge of many, even senior, barristers. Of course, the

Council knew (and the entire legal profession knew) that activities in the conferences could not replace practical training, and, finally, everyone knew that these activities bore a completely formal character. It was necessary to present three *doklady* (papers), which were approved by the leaders of a given conference, and to prove attendance at a certain number of conferences. As for the latter, people who had been assistants for five years found it very easy to show the requisite number of attendances, all the more because this proof amounted to the registration that was recorded by the conference secretary—who, of course, could not determine if someone left right after signing in. As for the conference papers, the topics were usually abstract questions, which had nothing to do with legal practice; abstract questions were preferred because some kind of published sources were available. Unfortunately, there were cases when the assistants presented a report that copied pages or chapters of some little known (or even well-known) scholarly work, under the assumption that neither his colleagues nor the conference leaders (practicing lawyers, who did not keep up with scholarship) would review [the work] and notice the plagiarism. Finally, recognition of the conference paper as satisfactory was a formality: the leadership rarely declined to give out this confirmation, for it did not want to thwart a young lawyer—who had an established practice by the end of his internship—from becoming a barrister. Nor did visits to judicial offices prove to be of much value, although—if properly done—this could have been of real practical use to the assistant barristers. A lot of assistant barristers gathered in the court lobbies and, especially, in the room and buffet reserved for barristers and their assistants at the judicial institutions. (The latter were called "the Smirnov room," after the guard and buffet owner, Smirnov, a retired old man who had served the Petersburg lawyers to the point where it was impossible to conceive of the lawyers without Smirnov and vice versa.) To wander among the judicial corridors, however, was not tantamount to acquiring practical knowledge by being present at court proceedings and studying the activity of judicial organs and especially the work of lawyers in court. In most cases these were young people seeking cases (especially criminal cases), since only the latter were reported in the periodical press.

Incidentally, it should be noted that toward the end of the 1880s public interest in the work of the courts decreased significantly. This was no longer the time when the new courts had just begun to replace the previous parody of judicial institutions; all strata of society that encountered the judiciary, which they had not seen in the prereform era, followed the new reformed court with great interest. The courts were the liberal offspring of the first half of the reign of Alexander II. From the point of view of liberal ideas, the judicial statues of 1864 represented something fully complete, without any deviations, and gave every guarantee for the triumph of those principles that lay at the basis of the judicial system in the most liberal political regimes. Notwithstanding the fact that the entire judicial organization was of course borrowed and had almost no roots in the Russian past, it quickly became established and adapted life to itself (not itself to life). But soon, especially under the influence of political trials and their requirements, principles began to be applied to the organization of the judiciary that corresponded to the changed attitude in upper government circles. Already in the second half of the reign of Alexander II and especially from the beginning of the reign of Alexander III, the architecturally perfected system of judicial institutions was subverted by all kinds of add-ons, partial changes that contradicted its basic style. Politics, not more elevated considerations about providing justice, were injected into the judicial system. The composition of the magistrates, correspondingly, began to change for the worse; these were no longer select people, knights of Femida of the first category; entry into the judicial hierarchy became something routine for the usual service career. The rank of magistrate attracted, unfortunately, few who were called to this office and mostly those who were not.

During this period, however, the prestige of the court was high. The new judicial institutions, from the first moment of their activity, demonstrated by their very essence that they had absolutely no connection to the previous courts; no traditions (and there were no good traditions) carried over to the new courts; the judicial organs were completely free of suspicion of bribery and corruption. The intrusion of political attitudes into the sphere of the judiciary and its work resulted in the fact that, if the public preserved its interest in the courts, then that was precisely in the sphere in which "politics" could most glaringly be reflected — that is, in the sphere of criminal justice. Civil affairs, with few exceptions, were of no political interest. Therefore the press was more interested in the transformation of criminal affairs. It was rare to meet a newspaper reporter in the hall of the sessions of the civil department of the court; reports about criminal affairs were abundantly published, mainly in sensational trials and especially those with some kind of political character if they were conducted in open session and did not encounter any censorship obstacles. A young lawyer who sought to make a career for himself above all sought to be part of the defense in such cases, which would undoubtedly appear in the newspapers as a detailed report, with references to his name. At this time there had already developed an unpleasant method of self-advertising by young lawyers who had close ties to newspaper reporters and who engaged in an unseemly currying of favor. There were various ways to gain the opportunity of participating in such a sensational case: first, by constantly hanging around the chancellery corridors, one could obtain information about the review of an impending sensational trial;

second, by seeking ways so that the accused himself petitioned to have such-and-such a person on the defense [team]; third, if a famous lawyer had already been invited to be the defender, by finding a "back door" to this person and in one way or another be added to the case and have a role. In the hall of the sessions where criminal cases were handled, it was always possible to see many assistant barristers who were not participating in the cases; at the same time, it was almost impossible ever to find assistants who were following civil cases in the civil section. In the majority of cases, the pride of the young legal intern inclined toward the criminal case — which was easier, did not entail hard work, and did not require serious preparation.

NOTES

1. [In Germany, a *Referendar* was a candidate for higher civil service who had passed the first state examination; an *Asessor* was a civil servant who had served as a *Referendar* and passed the second state examination. The terms applied primarily to lawyers and teachers.]

2. [Goratsii Osipovich Gintsburg (1833–1909) amassed enormous wealth from financial and industrial undertakings.]

3. [Brilliant did publish these two biographies in the series called The Life of Remarkable People, published by Florentii Fedorovich Pavlenkov in St. Petersburg: *I. A. Krylov* (1891); *Mikel'andzhelo* (1891). He also published *Rafael'* (1891); *Fon-Vizin* (1892); and *G. R. Derzhavin* (1893).]

4. [Ivan Iakovlevich Foinitskii (1847–1913) was a specialist in criminology, professor at St. Petersburg University, and deputy chief procurator of the State Senate.]

5. [Samuil Solomonovich Poliakov (1837–88) was a prominent railway magnate, who first obtained railway concessions in the 1860s and then built an empire of several key railway lines.]

6. [The reference here is to Lazar' Solomonovich Poliakov (1842–1914), who was the head of various banks — the Moscow International Commerce Bank, the Moscow Land Bank, the Russian Commercial-Industrial Bank, and several others.]

7. [Nikolai Avksent'evich Manasein (1834–95) served as minister of justice from 1885 to 1894.]

8. [Petr Semenovich Vannovskii (1822–1904) served as minister of war in 1881–98 and was minister of education in 1901–2.]

[153]

Jewish Law Graduates from the Imperial University of St. Vladimir, Kiev (1912)

"Memorandum [of the State Duma] on the Question of Acceptance of Jewish Graduates of the Imperial University of St. Vladimir as Assistance Barristers" (undated printed document, 1912 or after)
GARF, f. 579, op. 1, d. 2101, l. 21–21 ob.

Until 1912, Jews who completed courses in the study of jurisprudence in the Russian imperial universities were accepted as assistant barristers without any restrictions, and Jewish students who entered a juridical faculty could be confident that they would be provided with the opportunity to apply their acquired knowledge in the field of juridical activities. However, in March 1912, the State Senate, on the order of the Ministry of Justice, explained that enrollment of Jews as assistant barristers cannot be carried out except with the consent of the Minister of Justice.

Since then, the Kiev District Court completely halted the acceptance of Jews as assistant barristers, and all the presentations by the Union of Barristers about the enrollment of Jews who have graduated from the Imperial University of St. Vladimir as assistant lawyers still have not received the approval of the minister of justice.

The definitive ruling of the Senate and the new state of affairs that has been created put the Kievan Jewish jurists, who graduated from the university in 1912 or earlier, in a more difficult position; until the very end of their course of study, they had no grounds to worry that they would not be allowed to engage in the work of law. The explanation of the Senate on 12 March 1912 was completely unexpected for them and sharply diverges from the order of things that existed for us in the last fifty years, from the time of the Great Reforms of Emperor Alexander II, when Jews were accepted as assistant barristers without any restrictions.

Whereas the present Jewish students of jurisprudence, knowing about the new state of affairs for them, still have the possibility to transfer to a different faculty, those who graduated from the university in 1912 or earlier, who were not forewarned about the restrictions that awaited them, having gained the knowledge and being prepared for those activities of a jurist, have the moral right to expect that their exclusive position will be taken into consideration and they will be given the opportunity to engage in those matters on which they have expended many years of their lives.

Being placed in a desperate position in the new order of things, a group of Kievan Jews turned to His Imperial Name at the beginning of February with a humble petition for an imperial order so that those Jewish jurists who graduated from a Kiev university in 1912 or earlier can be enrolled as assistant barristers in Kiev district.

[VI]

Jews, Neighbors, and the Russian State

In a petition to the Jewish Committee in 1856, Evzel Gintsburg and eighteen merchants argued that "useful Jews"—including graduates of Russian institutions of higher education, first- and second-guild merchants, skilled artisans, and retired soldiers—should be granted the freedom to reside anywhere in the empire. Appealing to the state's ambitions for "merging" (*sliianie*) Jews with the surrounding Christian population, the merchants stressed the impossibility of accomplishing this goal in Pale of Settlement: "The government wishes that the marked traits distinguishing Jews from native Russians be smoothed out, that in all matters the Jews adopt the way of thinking and acting of the latter. *But in the western territories, which alone are open to us, there is not the sort of group with which such a rapprochement of the Jews could occur.* We constitute there the entire middle group in the cities and hamlet. The Christians belong to the highest noble estate or to the group of rural dwellers [peasants]."[1]

Although these elites may not have imagined "merging" with the surrounding population, the archival records show that the life of Jews in the Pale of Settlement was intricately connected to that of their neighbors. Not only did Jews share the same physical space with Christians, but they also interacted with them daily, especially in the economic sphere.[2]

Coexistence (with occasional conflicts) was largely the norm until the late 1870s, but there were historical moments when Jews were caught between their long-time neighbors and the imperial state, whose aims clashed with local prerogatives, alliances, and customs. This was most evident during the Polish Uprising of 1863 when the former Polish lands—a hotbed of discontent and nationalism—erupted in rebellion against tsarist rule. As the documents below indicate, the Jews were inevitably drawn into the conflict and were later prosecuted by the state for giving the insurrectionists provisions (food and alcohol), money, shelter, and even travel directions, whether willingly or under duress.

Following the assassination of Alexander II, anti-Jewish pogroms, which were distinctly related to the state policies of the counter-reform period as described in the introduction, marked a shift in the way that neighbors expressed their growing hostility toward the Jews. Although in the 1880s pogroms primarily targeted Jewish property, they became increasingly violent—for example, during the Kishinev pogroms of 1903, the *pogromshchiki* murdered, mutilated, and raped Jews with unprecedented cruelty. The police reports below describe the day-to-day events that led up to Kishinev pogroms, revealing the human faces behind the ritual murder case in Dubossary that sparked the rumors leading to brutal violence. The reports also provide more nuanced details, such as the greater propensity of the Old Believers (more than Russian Orthodox Christians) in Bessarabia to commit violence against the Jews — a topic that requires further investigation. The documents also show that Jews did not respond passively (as traditional Zionist narratives would have it); rather, their mass purchase of revolvers, organization of self-defense groups, and the dispatching of hundreds of telegrams to local police alarmed government authorities, who requested advice from St. Petersburg about how to proceed.

Negotiating relations with the Christian population was indeed difficult, especially in the late imperial period; however, no less complex were the interactions within the Jewish community, which became increasingly fragmented in part due to state policies. In particular, this part examines the impact of the conscription law of 1827, which marked the state's first ambitious attempt at Jewish integration. State laws that made each community collectively responsible for delivering the quota of recruits eroded the Jewish trust not only in communal officials but also in neighbors and close family members. The Hebrew writer Yehuda Leib Katzenelson wrote about his grandmother's description of the *khappers* who snatched poor children off the streets to fulfill the recruitment quota:

> In ancient times, the gentiles who approached us, holding the cross in one hand and a sharp knife in the other, said: Cursed Jew, kiss the cross or be slaughtered. The Jews would stretch out their necks to be slaughtered for they refused to be converted. All this we can understand. [. . .] And now here come Jews, religious Jews with beards and sidelocks, who steal children and send them off to be converted; such a punishment is not even written in the list of the most terrible curses. Jews

spill the blood of their brothers, and the Almighty sits in the heavens and remains silent, and the rabbis [also] remain silent.[3]

Unable to negotiate with their communal leaders, impoverished parents and relatives flooded the provincial state offices with petitions about the illegal conscription of their children. To avoid military service, some Jews even resorted to self-mutilation, prompting one state official to propose that each family be held collectively responsible for the draft evader: when a recruit failed to show up, the official suggested that the family should offer another member in his place. Jews who committed desperate acts such as self-mutilation did so out of a real fear of coerced conversion to Christianity in the army. Despite the ability of some soldiers (especially men in the navy) to practice Judaism during military service, as one recent study has shown,[4] young cantonists were more likely to succumb the zealous pressures of their battalion officers. Rather than passively accepting the coerced baptisms of their sons, the documents reveal that parents tried to protect the right of their offspring to observe Judaism by appealing to the link "between filial and political allegiances which informed the effective exercise of social control in the empire."[5]

By the late nineteenth century, increasing disillusionment with state policies as well as sympathy for the plight of the working masses and peasants led a disproportionate number of Jews to join revolutionary movements in the Russian Empire. Featured below are police records and narratives of three female Jewish revolutionaries who sought to remake Russia according to their diverse political visions: Gesia Gel'fman of Narodnaia Volia, or the People's Will (document 171), Manya Vil'bushevich of the Bund and the notorious police unions of Sergei Zubatov (document 172), and Mariia Shkol'nik of the Socialist Revolutionaries (document 174). Although they adhered to different ideologies and strategies, all three had a deep hatred of the autocracy and believed in a new socialist order.

Unlike these women, who staked their future with Russia, some Jews opted to emigrate. As the documents show, leaving Russia was a complicated affair, especially when family members did not have the proper papers. A missing metrical birth certificate could prevent or at least delay the emigration of families who were unable to demonstrate that they were indeed related (especially in cases of parents and children). Would-be emigrants whose relatives had evaded military service and gone abroad discovered that the state held them personally responsible for the 300-ruble fine, which they had to pay to receive an exit visa. In cases of extreme poverty, the state annulled the fine for some women. Finally, emigration raised fears among the orthodox that Jews abroad would stray from religious observance, not only in America (document 182) but also in Palestine, the locus of Hibbat Tsiyyon's activities. As Rabbi Naftali Berlin wrote to Leon Pinsker, if Hibbat Tsiyyon desired unity, its members needed to insist that the colonist remain observant: "But we, the children of Lithuania and its environs — God's Torah is with us, and we know that we are obligated to force those whom we can compel to observe the Torah" (document 175).

To explore the nexus between the Jews, the state, and their neighbors, this part focuses on conscription, the Polish Uprising of 1863, pogroms (with special attention to Kishinev), political activities of the revolutionary movements of the late nineteenth and early twentieth centuries, and emigration.

NOTES

1. Quoted in Benjamin Nathans, *Beyond the Pale: The Jewish Encounter with Late Imperial Russia* (Berkeley: University of California Press, 2002), 52 (emphasis added).

2. See the documents in part 5 on conflicts in the marketplace. For more on neigbourly relations in the northwestern provinces, see Eugene Avrutin, "Neighbourly Relations and Imperial Russian Legal Culture," *Journal of Modern Jewish Studies* 9, no. 1 (2010): 1–16.

3. Yehuda Leib Katzenelson, *Mah she-ra'u 'einai ve-sham'u ozenai* (Jerusalem: Mosad Bialik, 1947), 14.

4. Yohanan Petrovsky-Shtern describes soldiers' prayer groups and synagogues, Jewish voluntary societies, and resistance to conversion (*Jews in the Russian Army 1827-1917: Drafted into Modernity* [Cambridge: Cambridge University Press, 2008], 61–128).

5. Olga Litvak, *Conscription and the Search for Modern Russian Jewry* (Bloomington: Indiana University Press, 2006), 20.

Conscription

[154]

Complaint about the Illegal Conscription of an Only Son (1836)

*"Petition of Beila Leibovna Faivilovich
to Prince Nikolai Andreevich Dolgorukov,
Military General Governor of Vil'na,
Minsk, Grodno, and Belostok
(13 January 1836)"*

LVIA, f. 378, op. 1, d. 45, l. 2–2 ob.

Last month, the elected officials of the Vil'na Jewish community for conscription seized my only son Sender, who gives me daily sustenance in my impoverished circumstances, and designated him as a recruit. Their illegal action[1] has now deprived me of my support and hope for daily sustenance. Your Excellency! Turn your merciful eyes upon a poor mother, who has been deprived of her only son, who sheds tears before the most precious feet of Your Excellency. According to the decree approved by your Excellency, the recruitment must commence with large families that have several sons; but these recruiters, without considering this, abducted my only son, my sole hope for my existence.

Therefore, in appealing to Your Excellency (as the protector, especially for the aggrieved) for protection and justice, I take the liberty to trouble the generous personage of Your Excellency to issue a decree regarding my only son:

take a recruit from a family that has several sons, and return my only son Sender (who is still here in the city). I await a gracious resolution.[2]

NOTES

1. [Under Russian law, an only son was exempt from conscription—a policy designed to mitigate the impact of military service and to avoid leaving families without any working-age sons to support them.]

2. [The governor conducted an inquiry and discovered that the two representatives of the Jewish community of Vil'na, Todris Rozenkrants and Mordukh Aizikovich, did indeed know that Sender Faivilovich was an only son and conscripted him all the same. Although there was no exemption for only sons who were the primary breadwinners until 1874, petitioners routinely resorted to the image of the childless parent without support to gain attention from the authorities. In this case, the state found that Sender was listed with another family as the "nephew," and that the representatives of the community had "oppressed" him and made "allowances for others." Rozenkrants and Aizikovich were to be prosecuted for their actions, but there was no mention of returning Sender home from the military (LVIA, f. 378, op. 1836, d. 45, ll. 8–9).]

[155]

Complaint about the Illegal Conscription of a Jewish Surgeon (1837)

LVIA, f. 378, op. 1837, d. 62, ll. 1–30b.

"Petition of the Midwife Khasia Iatskovaia to Prince Nikolai Andreevich Dolgorukov, the Military General Governor of Vil'na, Minsk, Grodno, and Belostok (18 March 1837)"

My nephew, Faivish Berkovich, who is registered in the Antokol' Jewish community as a barber, fulfilled all his responsibilities as a surgeon at the local military hospital and conducted himself honestly and decently, as the authorities of the Antokol' community have attested. Due to some outrage, the Jew Iudel Apatov, who does not even belong to the Antokol' community, came with the housing supervisor bearing an order and, for unknown reasons, forcibly took Berkovich off to prison; without the knowledge of the Antokol' community and without any directive based on the [recruitment] queue, they handed him over as a recruit. However, he suffers from an illness and is presently in the hospital. He has not yet been forced to take the oath because he was not drafted but was handed over because of Iudel Apatov's outrage. For that reason I bow to the feet of Your Excellency and with all earnestness request, if you please, that you issue an order to investigate this.

I affirm to Your Excellency that I submitted a petition on 3 March to you and respectfully have not yet received an order.

"Report of the Vil'na Chief of Police (7 April 1837)"

The Jew Faivish Berkovich was first in the queue to be handed over as a recruit in the previous recruitment from the Antokol' community. However, due to a petition from the Jew Apatov, he was freed from conscription by the *kahal*. When the civilian governor ordered that they prosecute him and hand him over as a recruit, Feivish disappeared every time there was a conscription. Finally, His Excellency Dmitrii Nikolaevich [the son of General Governor Nikolai Andreevich Dolgorukov] summoned Apatov and ordered him to find the Jew [Faivish] without fail. That is why Apatov took Faivish with the housing supervisor to His Excellency; on his orders, he was imprisoned and then sent to the conscription office. When doubts about his capacity for military service arose, he was sent to the hospital for an examination.

[156]

Observance of Judaism in the Russian Army (1843–44)

RGVIA, f. 405, op. 4, g. 1844, d. 8158, ll. 1, 3, 4–9, 10–11 ob.

"Memorandum of the Major General of Smolensk to the Department of Military Settlements (20 December 1843)"

I submit this report and have the honor to inform the Department of Military Settlements that I deem it necessary to instill the principles of Christian faith with measures of gentleness and suasion. [Jews] will be permitted to fulfill the rites of their faith in a special room at the rabbi's home in strict compliance with [the law].[1] With respect to their billeting, I confirmed the order to Major Titkov that he punctiliously fulfill point four of the order (number 111, issued in 1827) pertaining to the cantonist battalion.

"Report of the Commander of the Revel' [Tallin] Half Battalion of Cantonists, Major Titkov, to the Department of Military Settlements (Received 7 January 1844)"

[. . .] With respect to implementing the [orders][2] on the conversion of Jews to Christianity, the priest Ioann Golubov (who teaches religion in my half battalion) and I undertook measures of gentleness and suasion, but in vain (for now and forever more) because of the following reasons.

With the approach of the Jewish holidays, the commandant of Revel, Lieutenant General and *kavaler* [Cavalier Vladimir Grigor'evich] Patkul issued an order that, in accordance with decrees issued at different times by the military command and in compliance with [the law],[3] rank-and-file soldiers of [the Jewish] confession are to be released for prayer services in the *kahal* according to their laws.[4]

However, that directive was disregarded on the grounds that this decree does not mention cantonists, which the commander cited during his investigation of the ensuing complaint. The directive of 24 May 1844 (number 593) stipulated that Jewish cantonists be released immediately to fulfill the rites of their faith, and simultaneously that I report to Your Grace regarding the grounds on which I had acted contrary to the Code of Military Enactments and Your Grace's order (number 13). At the same time, I completed the report on the above and sent Jewish cantonists to that community. Their rabbi and [the] Jewish rank-and-file are recalcitrant toward Christianity because of their incorrigible habits. In all likelihood, they are being cajoled into observing their law. Above all, Jewish cantonists under my command live in defense barracks, which also house a considerable number of sailors from the naval crew who are also persuaded to remain faithful to their faith. As a result, I do not expect Jewish minors to be inclined to convert to the Orthodox faith. I have the honor to submit these circumstances to the most esteemed Department of Military Settlements for consideration.

MAJOR TITKOV

"Admiral Count L. P. Geiden to the Military Governor of Revel (31 March 1844)"

The commandant of Revel, Lieutenant General Patkul informed me verbally that the local commander of the half battalion of military cantonists, Major Titkov, prohibits Jews under his command to fulfill the rituals of their religion, especially during the days of Passover. I am responding to [his claim] that he has a secret directive from Your Excellency based on the belief that Major Titkov was unfair in his justifications, especially since the Imperial Sovereign strictly ordered that Jews in military service not be prevented from exercising the rituals of their faith by any means. I humbly request Your Excellency to inform me about this matter.

"Report of the Department of Military Settlements to [Admiral Count L. P. Geiden] (17 May 1844)"

[. . .] Information:

(1) Until 1 February 1844, the half-battalion in Revel had 147 cantonists of the Jewish faith. In February and March, 94 of them converted to Russian Orthodoxy; 54 [*sic*] individuals remained [in the Jewish faith].

(2) A comment about the calendar of the most important Jewish holiday dates:[5] "At all times when on leave from service, Jews in the military may fulfill any ritual permitted by state law. The superior will strictly observe that there are no impediments and reprimand [his subordinates for any infractions]."

(3) Along with the departmental directive (6 February 1843, number 8), a copy of an order of the former chief of staff of the military settlements (sent to the commander of the Smolensk battalion of military cantonists on 14 November 1827) regarding measures to spread the Christian faith among conscripted Jewish minors [. . .] was dispatched to the commander of the Second Training Brigade of military cantonists, for the knowledge and guidance of brigade units under his command. According to this order, His Majesty prohibits any coercion in the profession of faith. Nonetheless, bearing in mind that Jewish minors are not secure in their religion because of their young age and may desire to convert to Christianity upon finding themselves among Christians and seeing the superiority of the faith, His Majesty deigned to order [the following]. One should not hinder them in this; on the contrary, one should instill in them the principles of the Christian faith with prudent suggestions and didactic examples. Those who voluntarily express a desire to accept the Christian faith will be ushered into [the faith], according to the regulations of the Russian Orthodox Church.

(4) In 1843, His Imperial Majesty directed the Chief Procurator of the Holy Synod to issue the appropriate order to give special attention to the conversion of conscripted Jewish minors in the military cantonist battalions, but that one [should] act with all due caution and not engage in the slightest oppression. This has been made known to all the military cantonist establishments. Nevertheless, the attached order (number 17) was sent to all the commanders of these units.

Opinion: Taking into account the fact that Jewish military personnel are permitted by law to conduct prayer services according to their rituals and that His Majesty has graciously ordered the conversion of underaged Jewish cantonists to Christianity by gentle suasion, the division of military educational institutions proposes the following:

(a) Order that Major Titkov not prohibit Jewish subordinates to conduct the rituals of their religion, but that these rites be performed only by a rabbi in a special room for the half battalion; moreover, that Major Titkov has a responsibility to convert Jews to Russian Orthodoxy, to follow with precision the injunctions and regulations in the manual sent to the military cantonist units (per the order of 3 February 1844).

(b) Inform the military governor of Revel about the present order, with the stipulation that the conversion of Jews to Russian Orthodoxy requires greater attention to resistance and, whenever possible, to efface false understandings about the correctness of the Jewish faith so that these measures hopefully will make it possible to realize the emperor's will to bring Jews into the Russian Orthodox Church.

NOTES

1. [*Svod voennykh postanovlenii*, (St. Petersburg: Tipografii II-go otdeleniia sobstvennoi E.I.V. Kantseliarii, 1859), book 1, part 3, article 386.]

2. [The orders were dated 2 February, 29 April, and 31 May (numbers 18, 38, and 59, respectively) and explained the orders (numbers 291, 905, and 1067) from the commander of the second educational brigade of cantonists regarding the conversion of the Jews to Russian Orthodoxy.]

3. [*Svod voennykh postanovlenii*, book 1, part 3, article 392.]

4. [Ibid., supplement 3.]

5. [Ibid., book 1, part 3, supplement to article 392.]

[157]

Observance of Judaism in the Russian Army (1851)

RGVIA, f. 405, op. 4, d. 13028, ll. 1–2, 3, 4–6, 8–13, 14–15, 16, 18, 23, 24–27, 28–28 ob.

"Petition of Jewish Townspeople in Vitebsk and Nevel Districts to the Minister of War, Prince A. I. Chernyshev (8 September 1851)"

Absolutely confident in the boundlessness of Your Excellency's virtue and justice bestowed on those who report [to you] for protection, we surrender ourselves to the mercy of Almighty God. We make so bold with a dejected spirit and quivering heart to fall at the precious feet of Your Excellency as our father. We implore you to grant a few free moments to read our most humble petition, which consists of the following: Our children — juveniles from the ages of twelve and up — were handed over as cantonists to the Vitebsk Provincial Recruitment Office. Before the party of Jewish recruits (a half battalion of cantonists) left for Arkhangel'sk, each of the fathers furnished his son with everything required by Jewish law for prayer services. Giving them a blessing for a safe journey, we remained absolutely confident that our children in state service will be instilled with the parental injunction to practice the religion of their fathers[1] conscientiously and always remain useful soldiers because the loyalty of subjects [is] based on religion. We were horrified to learn about the strange fact that in Arkhangel'sk various pretexts have been raised to prevent Jewish prayer services, so that a half battalion of cantonists will not be treated as *Jewish* cantonists.[2] This concerns our children. Despite the Jewish faith and even prayer services, the erosion of religious feelings can cause them to convert to Christianity because of their minority and immaturity, without a proper understanding about the essence of faith.

Fully cognizant that infinite justice shines in our Russian fatherland and the Jewish faith has found protection and shelter from all impediments and diversions, we — as the parents of minor children — take pity on their fate. We dare to resort to the protection of the lofty person of Your Excellency. We implore you with bitter tears, if it pleases His Most Excellent Prince, to order the authorities in charge of the half battalion of military cantonists in Arkhangel'sk to permit the underaged Jewish cantonists to practice [their] religion freely and in accordance with Jewish law. By no means, under various pretexts, should he force them to renounce their traditional faith and convert to Christianity during the period of their minority and immaturity —not until they are eighteen years old, at which point they will be in the position as adults to think for themselves and to decide about the importance and preeminence of religion. Your Excellency, show us your infinite assistance by accepting this most humble petition, and we flatter ourselves with the hope of being favored with Your Excellency's gracious resolution.

IZRAIL LIBSON, IANKIL GOLDIN, IOSIL BLOKH, ZALMAN TSADKIN, SHEINA DUSINOVA, IZRAIL GINDIN, MOISHA ZABAROV, ZALMAN BUTMAN, SHLOMO FOMIN, MEER LEIBOV, ABRAM KACHTOV

"Memorandum of Lieutenant General Baron N. I. Korf (Department of Military Settlements) to the Commandant of Arkhangel'sk [Major General Baron Solov'ev] (7 November 1851)"

The Department of Military Settlements forwarded a petition of Jewish townspeople from Vitebsk and Nevel Districts (Libson, Blokh, Dusinova, and so forth), who complained that the chief of the Arkhangel'sk half battalion of military cantonists (under whom they [the sons] serve) was persecuting their sons for practicing their religion in accordance with Jewish law. The Department has the honor to ask Your Excellency to treat fairly what has been stated in the petition and to report the findings. I also am honored to return the forwarded petition.

"Military Governor of Arkhangel'sk to the Department of Military Settlements (7 November 1851)"

In response to the memorandum of the Department of Military Settlements, [. . .] the commandant of Arkhangel'sk, Major General Baron Solov'ev has submitted the explanation from the commander of the Arkhangel'sk half battalion (dated 6 November) and his conclusion regarding the complaint by the Jewish townspeople of Vitebsk and Nevel districts regarding the alleged coercion of their children, who are in the Arkhangel'sk half battalion, to convert to Christianity.

Having examined the assessment by the commandant of Arkhangel'sk of the complaint, I find it to be fair. Hence I am forwarding, as well, the original statement of Major General Baron Solov'ev along with the report of the commander of the half battalion. [. . .] I have the honor to inform the Department of Military Settlements that from among the petitioners' sons, seven have affirmed a desire to accept the Russian Orthodox faith. [. . .] When they appeared before me, they repeated this desire.

"Report of the Commandant of Arkhangel'sk, Major General Baron Solov'ev, to the Military Governor of Arkhangel'sk (6 November 1851)"

[. . .] From the time I joined the half-battalion establishment, I did not observe any obstacles to allowing Jewish cantonists to participate in prayer services according to their faith in this very institution. Here is evidence for the lack of such impediments: of the eight such cantonists, the son of one petitioner has retained his [Jewish] faith, without any constraints. This fact shows that Jewish cantonists who converted to Christianity did so voluntarily. Above all, this has confirmation from the priest and the cantonists' religious teacher. Moreover, as the commander of the half battalion reports, Your Excellency personally deigned to conclude that seven of the cantonists proved to be the sons of the Jewish petitioners.

I therefore see no grounds to conclude that the Jewish cantonists were ever hindered in [their] faith. However, the petitioners' complaints may have been incited by:

(1) false information about their children's situation that derived, on the one hand, from measures adopted by the machinations of the Jews in Arkhangel'sk who are secretly seeking to get in touch with Jewish cantonists (contrary to the rules regarding the surveillance of the latter on the part of their closest superiors); on the other hand, [measures seeking] to remove the influence of Jewish rabbis, *kahals*, and meetings on these cantonists. I had the unpleasant experience of receiving the report of the half battalion commander about the baseless complaints from someone serving as the rabbi of the first Arkhangel'sk garrison battalion.

(2) the characteristic Jewish determination to do anything for the benefit of their faith. This is demonstrated by their calculated demand that their children not be converted to Christianity before the age of eighteen. From that age, and sometimes even earlier, Jewish cantonists begin serving in the military; if they desire to convert to the Christian faith with all their heart, they encounter obstacles from their coreligionists — rabbis and parents who exert an influence. It is evident from the cases that: (a) those who expressed a desire to convert are rejected, and (b) by filing a complaint, they discourage and demean Jewish cantonists (who merit incentives) and the zeal of the immediate commander of Jewish cantonists seeking the means to convert them to the Christian faith. [. . .]

"Report from the Commander of the Arkhangel'sk Cantonist Half Battalion, Major D'iakonov II to Major General Baron Solov'ev (27 October 1851)"

[. . .] I have the honor to report to Your Excellency about my actions with respect to the Jewish cantonists.

1. Upon the very arrival of Jews in the half battalion, their personal money is immediately determined to prevent the loss of their property and to prevent unauthorized spending. My order is necessary and useful; however, their lack of understanding (because of their young age) causes them to feel from the outset that they are being persecuted. The Jews living in Arkhangel'sk, who have served a long time, encourage them to think this; in an effort to retain [the cantonists] in the Jewish faith, they resort to every measure and pursue secret dealings. They receive the money by post from parents to deliver personally [to the cantonists]; the Jews of the Land and Marine Departments have been repeatedly apprehended for doing this, especially during the current year.

2. When Jewish arrivals are assigned to a company, each time the general governor's order is repeated to the company commanders: they are to follow the fixed regulations in their actions with respect to the education [about] and conversion to Russian Orthodoxy.

3. Although prayer services are not prohibited in their own half battalions, the Jewish cantonists may not leave for the holidays to the *kahals* and Jewish assemblies. Nor are they permitted to go to the rabbi, who (out of ignorance of the fact that cantonists are bound by the same regulations as Jewish employees regarding freedom of assembly for public prayer) acts without authorization and contrary to the law. In this respect, Your Excellency is assured about the groundless complaint by the soldier Shlema Mamid, who serves in the post of rabbi for the first

Arkhangel'sk City Garrison Battalion. That is why they attempt in every way to incite their coreligionists to complain through letters.

4. The Jewish cantonists are not only allowed to have ties with their parents but are even given by the authorities the means to establish residency for their parents. [. . .] Above all, each general assembly reiterates the children's duties to their parents, in accordance with religion and civil law. The only restriction is that the letters be in Russian so that they can be examined by company commanders in memoranda (with my permission). They are to send [the letters] by mail; under no circumstances are they to permit mediation and delivery by private means through coreligionists. Such are my close ties and love toward the children, who are used to seeing a father [figure] in me. The authorities have aroused envy in the [Jews], which has prompted the complaint.

5. Given the significant number of Jewish conscripts in the half battalion, they cannot be released from singing prayers (according to the rites of the [Orthodox] Christian Church) in unison with other cantonists; this is an established cantonist custom. The rabbis deem this as an act of coercion.

6. Jewish cantonists who voice a desire to accept the Orthodox confession are first interviewed by the company commanders. On the basis of their report to me, the religious instructors are informed about this inquiry regarding their voluntary declaration to accept Orthodoxy; until then, they are not admitted to holy baptism. Once the religious teachers have been satisfied about the certainty of their intentions, instruction in the necessary prayers, and exhortation in the dogmas of the faith, the conversion to Russian Orthodoxy is to be performed (in every case with the permission of the diocesan head and in accordance with the law);[3] afterward the priest collects signatures, in accordance with the regulations of the Church about their absolute intention [to convert]. I have the honor to present a certified copy of the relevant correspondence (numbers 724, 795, and 1918).

7. The sons of the Jews named in the attached petition (herewith returned) lists thirteen individuals. They are in the present half battalion. One still adheres to the Jewish faith; he is among the eight who have yet to express a desire to convert to Orthodoxy. However, twelve have voluntarily accepted the Orthodox faith; of these, seven converted to Christianity before Your Excellency took command of the half battalion. In accordance with the order of the Military Governor Boil' of Arkhangel'sk, they were presented to His Excellency on 22 April of this year to confirm in person that they voluntarily desire to accept the Orthodox faith.

8. The demand of the Jewish petitioners to block the conversion of their children to Orthodoxy before the age of eighteen does not correspond to the directives on Jewish cantonists and contradicts the "Ustav blagochiniia" [Code of Good Order, 1782] (volume 14, article 97). Accordingly, those who express a desire to accept the Orthodox faith have the complete right to do so without any age restrictions. Parents do not have the power to prevent the conversion of the children, especially those in educational institutions.

Having detailed the reasons why the complaints are unfounded, I take the liberty to share my hope that Your Excellency, having most graciously investigated the recent status of the case and the existing statutes, will extend Your protection and defense from malicious denunciations, making it possible to convert the Jews successfully (as is required).

"Major D'iakonov II: List of Jewish Cantonists in the Arkhangel'sk Half Battalion Whose Parents Submitted an Unfounded Petition about Persecution (27 October 1851)"

Jewish Names and Surnames	Names and Surnames in Holy Baptism at the Time of Registration (6 April 1851):
1. Mordukh Libson	1. Mikhailo Burudukhin
2. Leib Goldin	2. Ivan Medvetskii
3. Abel' Blokh	3. Semen Aleksandrov
4. Abram Tsatkin	4. Ivan Iarygin
5. Iankel Dozhn	5. Konstantin Iakovlev
6. Movsha Gindin	6. Vladimir Shergol'd
7. Aron Slonimskii	7. Konstantin Golomberg
8. *Abram Zaborovskii*	8. *Remains in the Jewish faith*[4]
9. Iankel Butman	9. Aleksei Sokolov
10. Itsin Stromin	10. Aristarkh Bubnov
11. Davyd Magrachev	11. Nikolai Savliunov
12. Erukhin Leibov	12. Fedor Golyn
13. Movsha Khatstov	13. Luka Liubyshin

"Memorandum of Major D'iakonov to the Religious Teacher, Father Petr Kremlev (27 April 1851)"

On the basis of the reports from company commanders (nos. 37 and 41), I am forwarding a list of names of fifty-three Jewish cantonists who have voiced a desire to accept the Russian Orthodox faith. I ask Your Grace to examine these and to inform me whether they are all inclined, voluntarily and zealously, to accept the Christian faith. This is for the report to the [diocesan] consistory.

In addition, I ask Your Grace to schedule the times to teach them the prayers and to explain the dogmas of the Orthodox faith at your discretion, above and beyond the hours set for the [general] religious instruction.

"Memorandum of Father Petr Kremlev to Major D'iakonov II (7 May 1851)"

[. . .] I have the honor to report to you that the Jewish cantonists have expressed [a desire] to accept the Christian faith. I have examined the fifty-three individuals on the list of names; on the basis of this examination, they are inclined to accept the Christian faith and holy baptism voluntarily. They have studied the [Orthodox] creed and necessary prayers and may undergo holy baptism if the diocesan head [the bishop] grants permission.[5]

"Opinion of Prince Dolgorukov (22 December 1851)"

The Department of Military Settlements proposes that the petition of the thirteen Jewish townsmen from Vitebsk and Nevel districts about the alleged persecution of the Jewish cantonists by the chief of the Arkhangel'sk half battalion of cantonists in the fulfillment of the rites of their faith does not merit any action. It has been demonstrated to be groundless by a report of the Arkhangel'sk governor and commandant.

NOTES

1. [Although the term *prirodnaia religiia*, translated here as "religion of their fathers," literally means "natural religion," Olga Litvak translates it as "inherited religion" (*Conscription and the Search for Modern Russian Jewry*, 20).]

2. [Emphasis added.]

3. [*Svod voennykh postanovlenii*, book 1, part 3, article 311.]

4. [Emphasis added.]

5. [The diocesan consistory granted permission on 15 May 1851 (number 1918).]

[158]

Self-Mutilation to Evade Military Service

GARF, f. 109, op. 3, d. 2316, ll. 1–6.

"Secret Report of the Chief of the Gendarmes in Vil'na (10 November 1835)"

While residing permanently in the western provinces by virtue of my office (since 1831), I have attempted to focus on military conscription among the Jews. Hitherto, in general this class of people (as every Jew acknowledges) has been reluctant to fulfill its military duty. Until 1827, this duty had no precedents and was new and alien to them because of their religion and ignorance. However, in the interests of their social well-being and in fairness to others subject to the poll tax, the government found military service a necessity [for the Jews]. The Statute on Conscription (26 April 1827), for the implementation of conscription, prescribes limits to deal with abuses, draft evasion, or self-mutilation. [. . .]

If a self-mutilator is discovered in some Jewish family, and if that criminal is apprehended, he is to be punished: he is drafted *without an examination* and an additional recruit is to be taken from the same family. The community is responsible for paying an assessment *for both* for the state draft. Does the community willingly expose and prosecute self-mutilators and return those who evaded military conscription if there is neither a personal nor communal reward of some kind? It is self-evident that the Jewish community, *kahal*, and elders of the family make no effort to reveal

and prosecute these and others; they shield them in order not to be deprived of souls in vain or to pay unnecessarily for the conscription. In the latter case, they do not want to be held responsible for the arrears of the state dues. This is currently the general thinking of the Jews, which encourages many to evade the draft and to commit self-mutilation.

With respect to the present fulfillment of military duties, there appears to be an increase of abuses — such as hiding from their places of residence and, in particular, self-mutilation (a large part of the conscripts have several teeth removed — which the Jews easily perform). The latter abuse had spread to such an extent that when the Vil'na *kahal* compiled its eighth census last year, of the hundreds of young Jews, only a few appeared to be completely healthy and suitable for induction into military service. During the current military conscription, when the Jews of Vil'na owe up to eighty recruits, it is difficult to find suitable ones from the 1,800 individuals to fulfill this quota — because of self-mutilation and other physical shortcomings and illnesses (both premeditated and unintentional). Hence the Jewish community or *kahal* finds the administration of the conscription increasingly difficult. In particular, it has not found a means to avert the premeditated self-mutilations; if it were to prosecute each abuse on the basis of the law, such actions would yield no real benefit except for the loss of a few souls. The payment of the poll tax and accumulation of arrears would be irrelevant for them, whereas the others subjected to the poll tax [that is, ordinary Jews] would seek to expose every abuse. The [draft evaders] will not suffer: those who hide from the draft, if found, will replace the one who was conscripted even though the former is not next in line for recruitment, and the latter will be returned to the community. However, if the one who has evaded conscription is found and sent as a recruit to the troops, then his conscription counts toward the community's dues. When the self-mutilator is discovered, he will either be sent to military service or deported to Siberia (if incapable of military service), in either case counting toward the communal recruitment.

Taking into account all these circumstances under the existing law, I would deem it fair and even necessary to publicize [this law],[1] which was issued for the entire poll-tax-paying population, among the Jews. The community, *kahal*, and elders of the family, who accept this as a sign of the all-merciful care of the Sovereign Emperor, will probably attempt — with all the means at their disposal — to act against both those who hide from the draft and those who commit self-mutilation. The fate of both will inevitably be punishment for their crimes. The community that receives conscription certificates for this will receive a significant reward. Escape will be futile and the number of draft evaders will be reduced; the community will not be liable for unnecessary conscriptions and the accumulation of poll-tax arrears. Indeed every member of the [guilty] family who is not in the queue will become the next in line; those who deliberately hide from the draft or commit self-mutilation will not drag innocent people from other families into a premature conscription for military service.

NOTE

1. ["Ustav o sostoianiiakh," articles 336 (part 6), 337, and 468.]

[159]

Appeal against a Vil'na Court Decision on Draft Evasion (1893)

LVIA, f. 445, op. 1, d. 1705, ll. 1–4 ob.

"Appellate Decision of the Procurator of the Vil'na District Court (8 November 1893)"

In the case of townsman Khaim Berkov Shif and collegiate assessor Dr. Solomon Iakovlev Mandel (who were accused of violating articles 13,512, and 514 of the Criminal Code), on 27 October 1893 the Vil'na District Court found Mandel not guilty.

This part of the verdict appears to be erroneous, for Dr. Mandel was proven to have mutilated Khaim Shif's eyes: (1) medical experts testified that the blemish in Shif's eyes did not occur as a result of disease, but was produced artificially by an experienced hand; (2) Mandel knowingly gave Khaim Shif a false medical certificate that he had treated the latter for an eye disease (keratitis) in 1884,[1] and that the blemish in the eyes formed as a result of the disease. The verdict of the district court recognized the correctness of the first evidence. As for the second, the district court relied on the testimonies of witnesses: the feldsher Trestman, the shop assistant L'vovich, Shif's neighbor Levin, the home teacher Beilin (rope manufacturer and hairdresser), and Shif's boarder Shlezinger, who collectively testified that Dr. Mandel treated Shif for the eye disease in 1884.

Based on the finding of medical experts that the doctor was not an ophthalmologist and that he could have mistaken the artificial blemish in Shif's eyes as one caused by the disease, the district court concluded that Dr. Mandel treated Khaim Shif for an eye disease and that, because Dr. Mandel was not a specialist in eye diseases, he issued the above medical certificate. He made an [honest] mistake and accepted the artificial blemish in Shif's eyes as one caused by the disease for which he treated Shif.

However, the testimony of the witnesses does not merit trust because of their contradictions of Shif's own explanations at the preliminary hearing. In the first interrogation by the court investigator, Shif testified that he does not know whether someone treated his eyes. Then, the very same Shif, when confronted with the witness Trestman (the *feldsher*), declared that this person was absolutely unknown to him. The witness testified that Dr. Mandel's treatment of Shif's eyes took place in 1884, but the latter was then fourteen years old. This leads to the conclusion that he should remember this treatment; if not, then that proves no such treatment took place.

The second finding of the court that Dr. Mandel is not an ophthalmologist is entirely arbitrary. Although there is no evidence that Mandel was a well-known eye specialist, the witnesses (whom the district court believed) testified that Dr. Mandel had great experience and treated eye diseases, as indicated in the case of Khaim Shif. Moreover, as can be seen from Dr. Mandel's numerous written explanations in the case, he is so thoroughly familiar with eye diseases that he could challenge the findings of the best specialists of our region about the cause of the blemish in Shif's eyes. Subsequently, it became clear from the formal transcript of Dr. Mandel's service that he had served as a doctor at the Minsk Military hospital. In that capacity Dr. Mandel must have known what kind of mutilation would provide a reliable means to exempt Shif from compulsory military service.

These considerations lead to the conclusion that Dr. Mandel did not treat Khaim Shif for an eye disease, that he possessed enough information to produce Shif's artificial blemish, that he issued a false medical certificate about treating his eyes. [. . .] Under these circumstances, he is guilty of mutilating Shif's eyes. I therefore have the honor to ask the Vil'na Appeals Court to amend the verdict of the Vil'na District Court, to find that that Dr. Mandel is guilty, and to punish him for this crime.[2]

NOTES

1. [Keratitis is an inflammation of the cornea that can lead to scarring and the development of tiny blood vessels in the eye, loss of vision, and glaucoma.]

2. [The final conclusion was not available.]

[160]

Letter from Jewish Students to P[avel] N[ikolaevich] Miliukov [Kadet Leader in the State Duma] on Admitting Jews into the Officer Corps of the Russian Army (27 October 1916)

GARF, f. 579, op. 1, d. 2010, ll. 17–17 ob.

The [members of the] circle of Jewish Students at the Demidov Juridical Lyceum appeal to you as representative of the Russian people [. . .] on the troubling question of the status of Jewish students who have been called up for military service.

For more than half a year our fellow Jews who have been called up to fulfill their patriotic duty still languish in uncertainty about their fate. Having found ourselves alongside Christian comrades for several years, having shared the interests of academic and Russian public life during all this time, it turns out that now we are to be kept separate. At a time when our fellow Christians perform their great duty as army officers, all our fellow Jews still await a decision as to their fate.[1]

The newspapers report that the ruling circles have taken this question up for consideration, and we deem it our duty to tell you, highly esteemed Pavel Nikolaevich, as the representative of the Russian public conscience, our view on this question.

The circle of Jewish students considers it absolutely an unjust, bitter separation of fellow Jews and Christians with regard to the conscription for fulfilling the duty to the people of the fatherland and we appeal to you, highly esteemed Pavel Nikolaevich, with a request to exert your utmost influence to have this question resolved and solely in a just manner.

NOTE

1. [The Russian army did not allow Jews to become officers.]

[161]

Appeal by the Jewish Students of Petrograd University to Serve as Officers (c. 1916)

GARF, f. 579, op. 1, d. 2010, ll. 22.

Comrades, the Jewish people have been dealt another new and grave insult. The government, which enlists the services of the young students to serve as officers in the army, true to its age-old policy of national oppression, has decided not to call up Jewish students on the grounds that they do not have the right to serve as officers. This exception is the result of the general lack of Jewish rights; its meaning is perfectly obvious.

At the very outset of the war, the government placed Jews — a peaceful population — and soldiers in exceptionally difficult conditions. In order to justify and preserve for a later time its senseless, implacable policy of depriving an entire nation of its basic human rights, the government used all its power to belittle the meaning of the Jewish sacrifice of blood and dignity that the Jewish people have borne in this war. In order to blame someone for the military failures and disasters, it relied on irresponsible bureaucrats to disseminate fraudulent aspersions about "Jewish treachery." All Russia now knows the price of this accusation. It will not be long before all Russia knows how much desperate grief this false accusation has brought to the Jewish people.

One link in this heavy chain of anti-Jewish restrictions and repression is the new planned "exemption." Separating Jewish students in an insulting manner from fellow students, it attempts to create a poisonous national atmosphere of difference.

With all the energy at our disposal, we reject this blow to our national dignity. The Jewish people, who bear absolutely all the obligations, always demand equal civil, political, and national rights of every citizen in Russia. This demand for equal rights and equal responsibilities is now the sole answer that we must give to this new challenge. With the most profound indignation, we repudiate the offensive privilege [of the "exemption" from officer duty] that has been imposed upon us. Confident of the support of our Russian democratic students and all progressives in Russia, WE DEMAND THAT, IN THE EVENT STUDENTS ARE CALLED UP FOR MILITARY SERVICE, JEWISH STUDENTS BE ON AN EQUAL FOOTING WITH ALL OUR COMRADES.

The Polish Uprising of 1863

[162]

Tsirla Adelsonovaia's Petition on Behalf of Her Husband in the Trial of an Insurgent (1863–64)

LVIA, f. 438, op. 1, d. 247, ll. 8–9.

"Tsirla Adelsonovaia (Zhizhmor, Troki district): Petition to the Military General and General Governor of Minsk, Grodno, Kovno, Vitebsk, and Mogilev (25 June 1863)"

On 25 June 1863, I submitted a petition to Your Excellency and took the liberty to complain about the arrest of my husband, the Zhizhmor resident, Leib Adel'son, who is being held in the Vil'na citadel because of a false slander by the criminal insurrectionary, the nobleman Khristovskii.[1] The latter persecutes him and harbors unwarranted malice toward my husband for failing to pay him six rubles (which Khristovskii himself will admit), whereas my husband has never been found to do anything reprehensible. He is engaged in agriculture and the sale of various goods in a petty townsman's shop in order to support five orphans and myself (a petitioner who is ill). His behavior has been exemplary. I can offer assurances and guarantees about his reliability from the local Russian Orthodox residents and members of the Jewish community.

With respect to my petition, I did not have the pleasure of obtaining permission [to release him] and, in the interim, our entire household will come to ruin. The family will suffer destruction despite its innocence. Such is my pitiful position. I again take the liberty of making a request to the person of Your Excellency not to prevent the chief authorities from ordering my husband's release on bail, which I am obliged to submit.

"Testimony of Leib Adel'son (11 January 1864)"

The Jew Leib Adel'son, age forty-six, is under arrest by order of the military authority in Troki on the basis of an accusation by Khristovskii. At the inquest, Adel'son testified that Khristovskii nurtured malice toward him and had slandered him in accusations going back to 1861. He was summoned as a witness on several occasions. Hence, when they led Khristovskii under arrest through Zhizhmor, he spotted Adel'son and demanded the payment of money. However, because the latter owed him nothing, Adel'son did not give him any money. Khristovskii thereupon slandered him, alleging that Adel'son had provided information to the rebels so that they could attack the mounted patrol and seize its vodka. A colonel demanded that Khristovskii provide proof. He initially claimed to have slandered him out of malice but then claimed to have heard about this from some Jew. However, this testimony was not at all confirmed.[2]

NOTES

1. [This file concerns the investigation of the nobleman Mikhail Khristovskii, age twenty-six, was accused of being a member of the Visloukh insurrectionary band. He claimed that on the week before Pentecost he became drunk at a tarvern with some unknown men, who forced him to join the band in the forest; however, the other witnesses testified that he joined voluntarily. During the interrogation, Khristovskii accused Leib Adel'son of participating in the insurrection, an accusation that led to his arrest.]

2. [The file ended with the release of Abel'son along with a few other rebels: "Considering all of the above, the Vil'na Commission for Political Affairs proposes [. . .] that the Jew Leib Abel'son be freed on bail for lack of evidence." LVIA, f. 438, op. 1, d. 247, l. 4 ob.]

[163]

Investigation of Litka Abramovicheva for Supplying Gunpowder to Rebels (1864)

LVIA, f. 438, op. 1, d. 960, ll. 2–4 ob.[1]

"Memorandum Compiled by the Sventsian Commission for the Investigator for the Commission of Political Affairs [n.d.]"

By order of the military chief of Sventsian (15 January 1864), an investigation was conducted on the gunpowder found by the Jewish woman [Litka] Abramovicheva in a tavern in Milovka.

A noncommissioned officer in the Aleksapolskii-Egerskii regiment (now infantry), Mikhail Tomashev Aleshkevich (who was on leave at the time), gave this testimony: a Jewish woman, Litka Abramovicheva, whom he did not know, came to his tavern in Milovka on 11 January 1864. Upon entering the room where he lived with his family, she stood for a while, then went into the general room for travelers, and immediately went out into the courtyard. After a time, the witness went to the storehouse; hearing a knock at the gate, he unlocked it, let the same Jewish woman in again, and returned to the storehouse. However, he did not manage to return to the tavern because his wife came out. Handing him a sack of powder, she told him that the Jewish woman had given it to her, saying that she found it by the stove; the wife did not know what it was. The witness upon hearing this rushed into the tavern and found the Jewish woman. He asked her where she got this powder; she replied that she had stumbled upon the sack, which was lying on the ground; thinking that it was theirs, she gave it to his wife. Up to this point, he did not know what it was and to whom it belonged. The witness weighed the [sack of] powder, which turned out to be three-quarters of a *funt*.[2] He then [got the peasant on guard duty and they] arrested the Jewish woman and brought the sack of powder to the police station. The witness did not own any powder and other forbidden supplies; the police chief does not regard him as suspicious.

Aleshkevich's wife, Mar'ia Gradzko, testified that on 11 January she was in the small room with her family when a Jewish woman came in, stood for a short time, and then left. After her husband Aleshkevich left, the woman came to her a second time and handed her a sack saying, "Mistress, your sack," and the witness replied that it was not her sack and that she did not have one like it. When the witness asked the Jewish woman what it was, she responded that she did not know but that it must be filled with poppy seeds. Taking the sack, she untied it, but upon seeing the powder ran in fear to show it to her husband in the storehouse. The witness herself did not own the powder or forbidden things and has not had the occasion to observe anything or anyone suspicious for a long time (with the exception of the Jewish woman).

The peasant Petr Padumis' testified that he was the village guard at the tavern in Milovka on 11 January. When the Jewish woman Litka arrived at this tavern, he was in the small room of the tavern keeper and saw how the Jewish woman handed the sack to the mistress saying: "I found a sack of poppy seeds in your tavern by the stove on the floor." The tavern keeper's wife took the sack from the woman and brought it to her husband in the storehouse. The tavern keeper Aleshkevich then came back into the tavern and placed the sack on the table, which upon examination indeed turned out to be filled with powder. He began to question the Jewish woman about where she obtained it; she responded that she had found it on the floor by the stove. The witness himself does not know to whom it belongs. He did not observe anyone suspicious. [...][3]

Kazimir Adamov Noreiko, a peasant from the village of Lit'ian, testified that on 11 January a Jewish woman (a total stranger) approached him at the bazaar in Sventsian and asked if he would take her to the tavern in Buiki where she said her sister lives. She promised to pay him nineteen kopecks for this. Because the witness was heading to the tavern of Buiki, he agreed to this. En route, before reaching the estate of Strunoits where the

village guards have a post, the Jewish woman asked whether they conduct searches at the outpost. He replied that they always ask for a travel permit when they conduct a search. When they arrived at the tavern in Milovka, the Jewish woman went inside and then he also went in to eat. The Jewish woman was standing by the stove at this time. While he ate, he noticed that the Jewish women went into the courtyard twice and then resumed standing by the stove. He did not see anything else except that the tavern owner came in; he declared to everyone in the tavern that the Jewish woman had handed his wife a sack that she found by the stove, saying that it must contain poppy seeds. Upon examination, the sack proved to contain powder. The witness did not observe anything valuable about the Jewish woman; nor does he know to whom it [the sack] belonged.

Litka Abramovna Abramovicheva (age fifty), a Jewish woman from the Sventsian community, testified as follows: on 11 January 1864 she met a peasant at a bazaar in Sventsian. When she learned that he was traveling to the village of Buiki, she asked him to take her to the village and promised to give him fifteen silver kopecks for this.[4] The peasant agreed, and they set off for Buiki. They were ten *versts* [10.7 kilometers] from the village when they stopped at the tavern in Milovka, where they found six peasants warming themselves. The witness stood by the stove for a while warming up and then went into the courtyard to take care of her needs. When she returned, she noticed a small sack lying on the floor by the stove and felt it with her hands. Assuming that it was filled with buckwheat,[5] she gave it to the mistress of the tavern, explaining that she found it on the floor by the stove. The mistress examined it and went out to give it to her husband, who soon came into the room and asked her where she got the powder. The witness replied "on the floor" but [said] that she did not know if it was powder or something else. Then the soldier [Aleshkevich, the tavern keeper] summoned the peasant on guard duty, and they arrested her. She does not own any powder and does not know to whom it belonged. She did not ask the peasant with whom she had been traveling to the tavern whether the guards conduct searches of travelers. If someone testified that this was so, it was not true. She was going to her sister, who resides in the village of Buiki.

At the *ochnaia stavka* [a face-to-face confrontation of two witnesses] Nareiko bore evidence against Abramovicheva. On the way to the tavern in Buiki, they had not yet reached the estate of Strupoits where village guards are posted when she asked him if they conducted a search at the outpost. He replied that they always ask for a travel permit when they search. Litka Abramovicheva denied this evidence and reaffirmed her testimony.

At another face-to-face confrontation, Mikhail Aleshkevich gave evidence in the presence of Litka Abramovicheva that the [outside of] the sack handed to him was completely clean. At the time, the tavern was absolutely filthy. When he asked her where she obtained the [sack], she replied that she had stepped on it next to the stove. Similar evidence was brought against her by Petr Padumis, Iuzef Tseiko, and Ian Iunevich, who stated that they were together with the Jewish woman at the tavern. They did not see any sack on the floor. Abramovicheva responded to this evidence that she does not remember whether the sack was dirty or clean. She did not say that she stepped on the sack; this was not true.[6]

"Memorandum of the Military Chief of Sventsian to the Investigator for the Commission of Political Affairs in Vil'na (5 May 1864)"

I present the completed investigation by the Sventsian Investigatory Commission on the gunpowder found by the Jewish woman, Litka Abramovicheva, in the tavern at Milovka. I have the honor to add that Abramovicheva does not confess to the crime of which she is accused and that there is no clear evidence against her. However, due to the course of events, the court finds it necessary to conclude that she took the gunpowder for Kagot ("The Claw"), perhaps at his criminal demand. Thus I would propose to expel Litka Abramovicheva from the local region as politically unreliable.

NOTES

1. [The documents refer to the accused as both Litka and Letka; the former spelling—the most common form—is used here. For another case involving a Jewish woman (Sara Toruhini) accused of harboring the leaders of an insurrectionary group, see LVIA, f. 438, op. 1, g. 1864, d. 723.]

2. [A *funt* (an obsolete measurement) is equivalent to 409.5 grams.]

3. [Here, two other peasants confirm the testimony of the first peasant.]

4. [The peasant Noreiko testified that she had promised him nineteen kopecks.]

5. [The previous witness, Kazimir Adamov Noreiko, claimed that Abramovicheva handed him the sack, claiming it must have poppy seeds in it, not buckwheat as she claimed here.]

6. [A marginal note by an official reads: "It is difficult to imagine that a fifty-year-old Jewish woman, who has been engaged in transporting [goods] since birth, had three-quarters of pound of gunpowder for the insurrection. In all likelihood, this gunpowder belonged to some traveler who forgot or lost it at the tavern. No Jew, especially a woman, would knowingly take upon oneself the responsibility of distributing gunpowder."]

Investigation of Movshe Oreliovich Shur
for Supplying Provisions to Polish Rebels (1864)

"Report of the Vil'na Investigatory
Commission to the Military Governor of
Vil'na (30 May 1864)"
LVIA, f. 436, op. 1, d. 984, ll. 1–3.

The commander of the troops in Vil'komir and Ponevezh districts sent the Vil'komir Commission the case of the Jew, Movshe Oreliovich Shur, who is accused of supplying various provisions to a band [of rebels].

Examination of the case revealed the following: state peasants in the Ushpol'skii community, Iosif Varnas, Vikentii Sokolovskii, and Kazimir Vanichas, former rebels, testified that the Jew Movshe Oreliovich Shur supplied the Sava band three times with various provisions. For purposes of identification, Shur was placed [in a lineup of] five Jews who were shown to the accused [rebels]; all three identified him.

The Jew, Shur, forty-seven years old, did not confess to this accusation and called it false and attributed the accusation to their alleged hostility toward the Kamaisk community for not handing over the tax collector, whom they wanted to hang. This [claim] was supported by twenty-five Jews, above all by Shur's wife. In a humble petition to Major General Pokhomov, she explained that one of the rebels had slandered a certain Jew, Movsha Khaimovich, and that her husband Movsha Oreliovich had allegedly been arrested in his place and handed over [to the authorities] in the town of Ushpol. At the face-to-face confrontation, a certain leader of the rebels, who was at a different chancellery but not convicted, heard the name of her husband, who was convicted unjustly; he [admitted] that he himself supplied the band with provisions. In an opinion (number 1909), Major General Pokhomov explained that, as the information at his disposal makes clear, apart from the rebels above, Vitsentii Kakautskii (also from Sava's band) testified that Movsha Zel'man from Anikst and Movsha Khaim from Kama supplied the band with provisions. A face-to-face confrontation of Kakautskii and Shur did not occur because the former had already been expelled from Vil'komir.

Given these circumstances, Shur is strongly suspected of the [crimes] imputed to him, but legal evidence for a complete indictment is lacking. That is why the major general proposes to expel Shur from the district. The Vil'na Committee of Inquiry [...] reports that it concurs with the opinion of Major General Pokhomov to expel the Jew Shur from Vil'komir.[1]

NOTE

1. [Sarah Faige Foner (née Menkin) recalled similar events in her memoir: "One time, they [the Polish rebels] burst into a town not far from Kopishak where a Jewish family lived and cried to them, 'Give us food and if not, we will hang you from the tree that stands before your window.' [...] When the Jew returned with loaves of bread and handed them over, they said, 'If she [the wife] hadn't advised you to give us bread, you wouldn't have wanted to give it to us. Therefore you are loyal to the Russians.' They all united around the idea that they should hang him. [...] In the next moment, they hung him on the tree before his window. [...] The next day, the Russian army arrived with thunderous noise and they cried, 'Where is the traitorous

Jew who brought bread from the other towns to give the rebels, as we were informed by the shepherds?' So the unfortunate woman showed them the dead man, and they released her, but asked her to show them which way the rebels had gone, and she did so. [. . .] The Poles came and attacked her murderously, saying: 'You showed the Russians where our brothers were and they were killed, so have a dose of your own medicine,' and then they killed her." Foner says that she could relate "tens and hundreds of incidents like these which occurred at that time" (Morris Rosenthal, ed. and trans. *A Woman's Voice: Sarah Foner, Hebrew Author of the Haskalah* (Wilbraham, MA: Dailey International Publishers, 2001), 14–15).]

Antisemitism and Pogroms

[165]

Pogroms in Nezhin District, Chernigov Province (1881)

GARF, f. 192, 3 d-vo, g. 1881, d. 790, ll. 1–5.

"Telegram from Prince D[mitrii] I[vanovich] Sviatopolk-Mirskii in Kharkov[1] to Unidentified Addressee in Kostroma (2 July 1881)"

The Nezhin chief of police telegraphed today that disorders began yesterday evening in the town of Nezhin. In several taverns the windows were broken and property destroyed. In one extreme case, the troops opened fire, killing four people; toward 2:00 a.m. the disorders ceased. It appears necessary to send in the troops, mainly the cavalry, owing to the dispersedness of the town. Upon receiving this telegram, I immediately dispatched one battalion and two squadrons to Nezhin. Count Kutaiskov passed through today on his way to Pereiaslavl.

"Report of the Nezhin District Police [Chief] to the Governor of Chernigov (24 July 1881)"

23 July: Residents of the small villages of Naumov, Khimov, and Kalinov (located 12–15 versts [12.6–16.0 kilometers] from Nezhin) — viz., the peasants Ananiia Shatrovaia, Khodshton Zhezher, Roman Zheznebskii, Trofim Shugailo, Panteleimon Kemchenko, and Fedor Shevliugo — attacked the Jewish townswoman Koganovaia's tavern, which is adjacent to the village forest. Having destroyed Koganovaia's house and stolen her belongings, they set off for the village of Pashkovka, located 4 versts [4.3 kilometers] away. In Pashkovka they destroyed the tavern and plundered the property of the Jewish woman Khaninaia and her son-in-law Leizin (who suffered the loss of 1,600 rubles, according to their testimony). In Pashkovka, they were joined by local residents — the townsman Artel Savchenka, the Cossack Evsei Mishchenko, and the soldier Evstafii Sherbak. Armed with axes, they went together to the village of Kurilovka, 4 versts [4.3 kilometers] from Pashkovka, where they destroyed the tavern of the Jew Zil'berman and stole his belongings; Zil'berman claims that he suffered 800 rubles in damages. In addition to those named, the residents who participated in this robbery included: Vasilii and Ananiia Koty and Sergei Greben of Pashkovka; Moisei Ishchenko and Grigorii Levchenko of Kurilovka; [and] Kirillo Muz'chenko of the village of Doroginka. In the village of Kurilovka, measures taken by local residents to arrest the guilty proved ineffective because of resistance and threats, and the band of criminals dispersed.

Upon receiving a report about these events, Officer Gun'ko of the third police station immediately ordered an investigation of the accused. Seven of them were arrested in the village of Pashkovka, and the remaining eight who were working in the fields [were arrested there]. The investigation of those arrested was given to the court investigator on 24 July (number 1779). The general mood of the population is apparently peaceful, but to maintain the peace and prevent any [additional] disorders, I reported to the commander of the Kiev Hussars regiment, stationed in the city, about establishing mounted patrols.

"Secret Report of Chief of the Chernigov Gendarme Administration to the Department of the State Police (4 December 1881)"

I have the honor to report the following: On 23 December a county clerk from the village of Mrina, Konstantin Kononenko, reported to a noncommissioned officer from the supplementary staff in Nezhin district that several of his acquaintances were saying that there would be another Jewish pogrom in Nezhin on the upcoming Christian holiday. The investigation of this circumstance by the Nezhin police showed that these rumors were being spread by the Cossack Reshetsko who, however, denied the accusation against him. Reshetsko was arrested by the police and will be put on trial in a Justice of the Peace Court under article 37 of the Penal Code.

NOTE

1. [Prince Dmitrii Ivanovich Sviatopolk-Mirskii (1825–99) was a decorated Russian general who became a member of the State Council in 1880. In 1881–82 he was the military commander of the Khar'kov military district and the acting general governor of Khar'kov.]

[166]

Pogroms in Pereiaslavl, Poltava Province (1881)

GARF, f. 102, 3 d-vo, g. 1881, d. 742, ll. 1–18 ob.

"Report from the Chancellery of the Governor of Poltava to the Minister of the Interior (15 July 1881)"

At the outset of disorders in the town of Pereiaslavl, I foresaw that this disturbance might be reported in surrounding localities and provoke violence against the Jews there. I sent a telegram during my stay in Pereiaslavl, ordering all the police officers in the other districts of the province to intensify vigilant measures to prevent disorders from arising in the towns and districts; in addition, they are to recognize the need to deal with Jewish property that has been plundered and destroyed.

On 9 July, five homes in the villages of Semenovka and Lialiaka were smashed, with damages of 4,875 rubles. Finally, on 12 July, as I already reported to Your Excellency, disorders erupted in the highly populated town of Borispol, which is overcrowded with a Jewish population. It was necessary to use firearms, which had regrettable consequences: the death of four peasants and the injury of two others (of whom one has already died).

The former Kremenchug police officer in Borispol, a witness to the unruly behavior, submitted the following report about the course of the disorders. Until 12:00 p.m. on 12 July, all was well; he did not see any signs of possible disorders. Earlier that day, the township assembly began to disperse peacefully, and the police officer deemed it possible at 12 p.m. to leave Borispol for the village of Voron'kov (together with Lieutenant Plechko, the district police officer and aide-de-camp of the gendarme administration). However, en route he received news that disorders had broken out within an hour of his departure, and they immediately set off for Borispol, arriving there at 8:00 in the evening. There was a sense of general agitation: people were armed with axes, sickles, and clubs, and mobs were gathering in the streets. In a few places, fights broke out. In the market square, cellars were being smashed and cries could be heard: "That's it. We have come to cut up the *zhidy* [Yids] and *pani* [Polish landowners]." When the police officer and Lieutenant Plechko left under a Cossack escort to deal with the mob so that it would not attack them, someone from the crowd stabbed Lieutenant Plechko in the back and tore off his aiguillette. They also wanted to assault the police officer, but he managed to evade the blows. At this point Esaul Voitsekhovich and Lieutenant Kamenskii arrived, one of whom (the police officer did not notice which one) ordered the Cossacks to fire on the mob, and that resulted in four dead and two injured. The mob dispersed and at 8:30 p.m. order was restored.

According to information collected by the police officer of Kremenchug, the disorders began at 2:00 p.m. To ascertain what happened, eyewitnesses were summoned. These included the *zemstvo* doctor Goshkevich, the pupil Artem'ev from the Kiev Vladimir Military Gymnasium, and the assistant township clerk Onenko. Peasant boys playing at the square began to take down the tents that the Jews had put up (after a fire there the past July 9). This drew a crowd. Someone in the crowd threw a rock at the window of a Jewish house, as if it were a signal for disorder. The mob attacked the Jewish houses and began to demolish them, destroying everything (including the belongings inside). The thirty Cossacks posted there were in no position to restrain the unruly conduct of the mob and in turn were subjected to assaults and blows by the rioters. However, when the mob attacked the Borispol postal station to plunder it, the Cossacks did not allow them to go that far; it was only thanks to their efforts that the station was not plundered. Two priests attempting to exhort the mob were nearly assaulted themselves; thanks only to the use of arms was a general slaughter averted, so intense was the fury of the mobs. The wounded were given medical assistance; the bodies of those killed are at the [office of the] *zemstvo* board until special orders are given. The police officer of Kremenchug added that he had reported about the above the same day to the procurator of the Lubensk District Court (which is located in Pereiaslavl), the court investigator of the second administrative sector of Pereiaslavl district, and the Pereiaslavl police superintendent. He himself remained in the town of Borispol to maintain order.

Disorders simultaneously occurred in the village of Berezan (also in Pereiaslavl district); twenty Cossacks, along with the assistant police officer, went there.

In apprising Your Excellency of all this, I deem it my duty to report that the agitated condition of the peasants appears to be directed, so far as one can judge, personally against the Jews. In a telegram to the chief of the administration, Lieutenant Plechko (aide-de-camp of the gendarme administration) incidentally noted the damage to a landowner's estate in the town of Borispol. The significance of this report prompted me to send a telegram to confirm its accuracy and character. The police superintendent reported that, "according to Lieutenant Plechko, the estate in Borispol being leased by the Jews has been destroyed."

At present, there is a large gathering at the Il'inskaia fair in Poltava, which is in full swing.

Although there have been no threatening signs, individual incidents that erupt almost daily and that call for the requisite emergency measures did not allow us to regard the situation as peaceful. Therefore, not deeming it possible to leave Poltava, I authorized the vice governor, Zhukov (who holds the rank of active state councilor), to set out for Pereiaslavl district to adopt pacification measures appropriate for the local conditions and to suppress any disorders that might arise. Drastic, decisive measures will make it possible to prevent a further outbreak of rioting. In addition, I gave instructions to the vice governor to seek eyewitness accounts and make personal inquires to explain the real character of the Borispol disorders. Were they exclusively an anti-Jewish movement or suffused with other purposes and aspirations? Were there instigators and agitators? Was there a political undertone that led to dispatching of the troops and the use of firearms that resulted in the death of five peasants?

As for the other districts in the province, nowhere did the disorders erupt with the same mood and emulate Pereiaslavl district, but they still impelled me to take extreme measures beyond the framework of law in order to secure the peace:[1]

(1) On 2 July, the police officer of Priluk sent a telegram [reporting] that, beginning on 25 June, residents of Priluk, the townsman Lenskii and the peasant Trodoimenko, were inciting the town's population to engage in disorders and violence against the Jews. As a result, I sent a telegram to the police officer of Priluk to arrest Lenskii and Trodoimenko immediately. Upon receiving detailed information from the police officer (which absolutely demonstrated the guilt of these individuals in the agitation against the Jews), I sent the acting general governor of Khar'kov a statement about the need to punish these individuals.

(2) The police superintendent of Kobeliak district reported that a Minsk townsman,

Dreitser, had arrived again at the village of Kozelytsina. Despite all the attempts of the peasants to dissuade him and to insist otherwise, he opened his business[2] near the chapel that houses the icon of the Mother of God (which brought a miracle for the daughter of the local landowner Count Kapnist and for others). Thus the icon enjoys great respect by the Christians and every day attracts enormous crowds of pilgrims. The extreme outrage of local peasants and other pilgrims makes it impossible to leave the Jew Dreitser close to this image, if only because of the threat of disorders in the very near future. I shall thus order the police superintendent to remove Dreitser and implement this immediately.

"Petition from the Wife of P. M. Trodoimenko (a Cossack)[3] to the Minister of Internal Affairs (20 July 1881)"

Your Excellency, my poverty and that of my family and the harsh imprisonment of my innocent husband compels me to bow down before Your Excellency and report the following. Under orders from the governor of Poltava, the police officer of Priluk detained my husband Prokhor Mikhailovich Trodoimenko at the police station from 3 to 9 July. On 9 July at 9:00 p.m., he was imprisoned on the order of the police officer. His imprisonment was based on neither the decision of a court nor the person who ordered his arrest. This is demonstrated by my husband's request to know the crime with which he has been charged. He has personally asked the police officer to show him the court verdict. Our petition to have a copy of the resolution was denied. My husband was then summoned to the office of the procurator and there submitted the same request. However, the procurator, seeing that neither my husband nor I have legal counsel, did not give us a satisfactory answer. I filed a petition with the head of Poltava Province to transfer the matter for which my husband has been indicted for some unknown crime to the jurisdiction of the court and to prosecute those who unjustly ordered that he be deprived of his freedom.

In particular, I have heard that my husband is accused of allegedly inciting people against the Jews. He did not and does not acknowledge his guilt. During the police officer's inspection of our apartment, neither dubious papers nor anything compromising was found. On what this slander is based, I do not know; whatever led to the legal order of the governor general is buried in obscurity—whether the slander came from a private, unofficial source or was a denunciation based on the suspicions of the local police. About this and other matters, I can state positively and demonstrate to the court investigator that this probably emanated from the Jews with whom members of the police are extremely friendly. This is proven by the fact that they walk around the street arm in arm with rich Jews, are entertained at their Sabbath meals, pander to them in everything for their satisfaction, and circumvent the law at the expense of peaceful Christian citizens. These actions of the local administration unwittingly stir up religious people, who consider themselves the true patriots and the former indigenous residents, against the Jews. One cannot go one step without passing the disgusting [alcoholic] drinks of the Jews, not to mention [. . .] the Russians whom have been made drunk by the Jews, who file complaints with the local police about oppression. Take, for example, my innocent husband, who must languish in prison while my family and I [gave up] our rented apartment (which we could not afford) and go begging from door to door. Poverty is such grief. But wealth means something else before the law of the police: after my husband was arrested for inciting talk against the Jews, six merchants in the town of Priluk were arrested, but have since been released (so I have heard). Bringing forth the naked truth, I take the liberty [of attempting] to convince [you] of my truthfulness (and swear on the religious oath of a Christian woman). Falling at the feet of the person of Your Excellency, I have the honor to request humbly a legal order to free my innocent husband [from] illegal imprisonment in prison and to subject [. . .] this case to a legal investigation. I have the liberty to request on my knees and to beg Your Excellency to send your official to inquire into the truth of this case. Moreover, I make so bold as to beg to be informed of your order. Because of my poverty, I have sold my very last clothes. I submitted a petition to the head of the province and the general governor of Khar'kov but have received no reply, not even information about the crime of which my husband has been accused and why he has been deprived of his freedom and imprisoned.

NOTES

1. [As the next petition demonstrates, the measures "beyond the framework of the law" included the arrest and imprisonment of people suspected of being instigators of anti-Jewish violence without a legal indictment, which bypassed the normal court process. For more on extrajudicial measures used to quash disorders and combat the revolutionary movement, see Jonathan Daly, *The Watchful State: Security Police and Opposition in Russia, 1906–1917* (DeKalb: Northern Illinois University Press, 2004).]

2. [According to a similar report, he set up his small shop close to the chapel at a site rented from a nobleman Lipevik for three years at 1,500 rubles a year.]

3. [See the preceding item for the order to arrest him for instigating anti-Jewish violence. This petition from Trodoimenko's wife is replete with spelling and grammatical errors.]

[167]

Anti-Jewish Violence after Accusations of Ritual Murder in Dubossary, Kherson Province (1903)

GARF, f. 102, 3 d-vo, d. 731, g. 1903, ll. 8–8 ob., 16–19, 28–31, 48–50, 66–75.

"Telegram from Governor Lebashov to the Minister of the Interior (11 March 1903)"

Having arrived yesterday in Kherson, I received news that a ritual murder had been committed on a Christian boy in the town of Dubossary (Tiraspol' District) and that the population has been stirred up by rumors that the Jews had committed the murder for ritual purposes.[1] Today the inspector reports that on 5 March in the town of Pavlovka, which is 46 kilometers from Tiraspol, there were anti-Jewish disorders. Residents from neighboring towns arrived at the bazaar and became agitated by stories told by an unidentified person that the Jews had cut up a Christian boy in Dubossary to use his blood for Passover. People began to beat up the Jews and seize goods that they had delivered on carts. The village constable wanted to arrest the individual who spread the rumors, but the crowd snatched him away and hid him. Damages amounted to 3,000 rubles. There were no casualties among the population, however. The police restored order, arrested seven people, and seized some property. An investigation is under way. Proper measures have been adopted in Tiraspol' district, under the direction of a permanent member of the provincial office.

"Secret Memorandum of the Police Supervisor and Permanent Member of the Kherson Provincial Office to the Governor of Kherson (16 March 1903)"

Owing to the proposal of 10 March 1903 (number 1098) and the addendum to my telegrams of 11 and 13 March, I have the honor to report the following to Your Excellency. After arriving in Tiraspol on 11 March and receiving information from the district police administration that the mood of the population in Dubossary, Grigoriopol, and other population centers in Tiraspol' district was calm, I set out for the village of Pavlovka (Tumanovo) where the district police officer, the procurator of the Odessa District Court, and the court investigator of the fourth sub-district of Tiraspol' district were conducting a preliminary investigation of the anti-Jewish disorders that had occurred in this village of Pavlovka.

The police inquiry conducted by the chief of the first police station (Vorob'ev) and the preliminary court investigation showed that the disorder in Pavlovka took place in the following circumstances. On 5 March there was a bazaar in Pavlovka, and quite a few Jewish traders usually come here with temporary stands and cartloads of cheap manufactured items, haberdashery, and foodstuffs. Already in the morning (around 10 or 11 o'clock), rumors began to circulate in the market square that the peasants intended to attack the Jews because last February, the Jews [purportedly] murdered a Christian boy in Dubossary and used his blood for the coming Passover holidays. Soon a peasant from the village of Shibki, Mikhail Krugliak (who goes by his nickname Mishka), showed up at the square and began to tell the mob that the events in Dubossary—the murder of a boy by the Jewish population in order to extract his blood— actually occurred. The village constable tried to arrest Krugliak, but the mob did not allow him to do this; separate groups of peasant youths then began to deal blows to the Jews and to plunder their goods. Stealing only goods that were on display and in the carts, they left the Jewish houses and small stores in the town untouched. It was exclusively the village youth who joined in this disturbance of the peace, but partly also the women, who collected the goods scattered on the ground. Older peasants opposed all this; as soon as the noise and tumult erupted in the market square, they immediately rushed to their carts for fear of being blamed for the incident and quickly began leaving for home.

In general, the disorders were on a small scale; they consisted of scattered fighting and riots that the village lads initiated in different parts of the market square. This circumstance serves as proof: Jewish houses and stores in the village were untouched, as indicated above. The cheap goods laid out in open displays were subjected to plunder. As indicated in the telegram of the police superintendent, the damages amounted to 3,000 rubles (according to the statements of victims, which, however, were significantly exaggerated). In reality, the losses do not exceed 500 rubles. Nor were there injuries or casualties among the victims. The worst disorders continued only for a short time because of a rumor that the district police officer, the village elder, and police from the neighboring German colonies of Neidorf and Glikstal had been summoned. The disorders stopped long before the appearance of the police officer, who arrived in Pavlovka at 4:30 p.m. and immediately launched an inquiry into the plundered goods and arrested the guilty.

The preliminary investigation of the court is now being conducted; sixteen people face prosecution; of these, eleven have been taken into custody and five released under the surveillance of the police. Of those on trial, only one is head of a household; all the rest are village lads.

On the day of my visit to Pavlovka, the town had another bazaar, and the gathering was very important (for Jews as well): complete order reigned everywhere. The disorders that occurred a week earlier did not disturb the normal flow of local life in the least, thanks to the prompt and judicious measures taken by the police and court authorities. Thus the cause of the disorders—apart from a tribal animus of our peasant population [toward Jews]—was the rumor in the surrounding localities that the Jews had murdered a Christian boy in Dubossary for ritual purposes, an event that the peasant Mikhail Krugliak had repeated to people at the bazaar in Pavlovka.

Turning to the question of the police's activities in this case, I must report that in my opinion they fully merit approval. The village constable of the first police station, Alekseev, long before the outbreak of the violence, quickly sent a telegram summoning the district police officer to Pavlovka the moment the rumor spread. He ordered that Jewish homes, small shops, and the wine store be closed and wrote to the *zemskii nachal'nik* [land captain] about sending the village elders well as the *sotskii* and *desiatskii* [rural police] from the nearby German colonies. The district police officer, Vorob'ev, whose apartment is 25.7 kilometers from Pavlovka, appeared very quickly at the site of the incidents, immediately reported to his superiors, questioned the guilty, and conducted an investigation according to the advice of the court investigator and procurator. The same should be said about the work of the acting police officer, the assistant Tsybul'skii, who apart from the serious instance of nonfeasance noted by Your Excellency (his failure to send a report by telegraph), in all other respects acted entirely in a manner that deserves approval. Thus Tsybul'skii immediately sent a telegram to the police supervisor Evdokimov, who was on leave, and with the help of the police officer Seredinskii of the first police station, dispatched a [police] inspector from Tiraspol' to the site of the incident in Pavlovka.

One must also mention the absolutely ex-pedient preventive measure taken by the court investigator with respect to the eleven people under investigation in order to ensure investigation, trial, and incarceration. His actions made a very strong impression on the people, persuading them that those guilty of disorders will be held accountable in a township court.

Afterward the district police superintendent Evdokimov and I visited the towns of Dubossary, Grigoriopol,' and Tiraspol,' where we talked at length with representatives of the city administration and local Jewish population (per Your Excellency's orders). We impressed on the latter that, under the current situation (which, alarmingly, incites the Christian against the Jewish population), they must seize every opportunity to influence their coreligionists and explain to them about the need to avoid separate public clashes, which could give rise to general disorders against the Jewish population in these dreadful times.

In the specified towns, the mood of the population was absolutely peaceful and, according to the assurances of representatives of the city administration, there is no ground to fear disorders. In Tiraspol,' where the annual mid-Lent fair is now in progress, precautionary measures have nevertheless been taken: police surveillance has been intensified and Chief Garnizon has been warned, and the head of the town and members of the city board constantly visit the fair.

Regarding the incident in Dubossary in February—the murder of a fifteen-year-old boy (Mikhail Rybachenko) and outrage of the Christian population (thanks to the gossip and rumors about the ritual murder of the boy by the Jews)—the circumstances were as follows. An orphan, Mikhail Rybachenko (now deceased) lived in the home of his grandfather, Konon Rybachenko, a well-to-do local townsman, at the latter's expense. The other grandson (Mikhail's cousin, Timoshchuk, who is

nearly deaf) also lived there with his young wife (likewise at the grandfather's expense). Mikhail, who left with all his relatives for church on 9 February, disappeared without a trace; they discovered his body on 13 February in a garden not far from the Dniester River with signs of a violent death: he was found in a pool of dried blood, his clothing saturated with blood from two wounds in the back (1.5 centimeters long) in the vicinity of the liver, inflicted with a sharp weapon. On 14 February the Dubossary city doctor, Poliankovskii, conducted an autopsy of the corpse and concluded that the death of the boy occurred from the profuse hemorrhaging caused by the two indicated wounds. However, because Dr. Poliankovsii—a Jew—drew this conclusion, Konon Rybachenko continued to believe that his grandson had been killed by Jews for ritual purposes; he then submitted a whole series of petitions to the minister of justice.

Upon orders from the minister of justice, a second examination of the corpse was conducted. This second autopsy was conducted by the Tiraspol' city doctor, Man'kovskii, a man of the Christian faith, in a more rigorous setting and in the presence of a priest, police officer, procurator of the district court, the court investigator, and several witnesses. A second examination of the corpse confirmed the findings of the first autopsy; both doctors concurred that the boy died from profuse hemorrhaging caused by the two wounds in the vicinity of the liver. The only additional discovery was a minor bruise in the area of the brain, which occurred before death but did not disturb the integrity of the cranial bone and cover. This indicates that the deceased was stunned by a blunt, heavy weapon before the infliction of the lethal wounds. Therefore the conditions under which the corpse was discovered and the findings of the two forensic examinations of the corpse preclude any possibility of ritual murder.

The court investigator believes that the cousin Timoshchuk committed the murder out of material interests: he knew that their common grandfather had a special love and affection for Mikhail Rybachenko and that he intended to make him the sole heir (for that very purpose Konon Rybachenko had even adopted the deceased). For the time being, Timoshchuk obstinately denies this; in the investigator's opinion, however, [. . .] it will not be long before Timoshchuk comes to him and confesses. If this assumption is realized, that would undoubtedly be the best way to calm the entire local population. After the second examination of the corpse, many residents have now become convinced about the lack of grounds for suspicions of ritual murder in this case.

In accordance with these events, the district police superintendent Evdokimov went expeditiously to the site [of the disorders] and helped the police of Dubossary search for the perpetrators of the crime.

SIGNED BY THE POLICE SUPERVISOR OF GRIGORIOPOL AND THE PERMANENT MEMBER N. ANDREEVSKII

"Secret Memorandum from the Assistant to the Chief Gendarme of the Kherson Provincial Gendarme Administration (25 March 1903): On the Mood of the Population in Dubossary, Its Environs, and Bordering Region of Bessarabia"

To implement the verbal order issued by Your Excellency, on 19 March we conducted a secret investigation into the rumors that anti-Jewish disorders could soon break out both in Dubossary and in neighboring towns. The cause of the possible disorders is the mysterious murder of Mikhail Kopolov Rybachenko,[2] which was blamed on the Jews. On 21 March, I dispatched the noncommissioned officers Gorishchenko and Movchan, who are under my command, with the appropriate instructions. They returned to Tiraspol' on 24 March and then traveled to the villages of Tashlyk, Maloeshty, Pogreby, Doretskoe, Koshpitsa, Pererytoe, Magaly, Korzhevo, Rogi, Molovatoe,

Goiany, Doibany, [and] Lunga; then the villages of Rozovka and Il'ia; next the towns of Grigoripol' and Dubossary—in short, to all the localities that border on Bessarabia province. They reported the following to me about the source of the rumors. At the places listed above, except for Dubossary and the adjacent [village of] Lunga, everything was absolutely peaceful; the population was occupied with fieldwork and quite indifferent to the murder of Rybachenko. In Dubossary and the adjacent Lunga, however, the public mood was extremely agitated because of distrust toward the police and investigatory department; the population unanimously believed that Rybachenko's murder was ritual.

On 23 March, the victim's cousin, the deaf Ivan Timoshchuk, was incarcerated in the Tiraspol prison for the murder of Mikhail Rybachenko. This arrest was made by Galushchinskii, the investigator responsible for the most serious cases. But the Christian population cannot accept that Timoshchuk is the murderer and has become still more anxious. The latter view is fully shared by the grandfather and grandmother of the murdered child—Konon and Elisaveta Rybachenko. It is necessary to dispel the current homegrown views of the Christian population of Dubossary and Lunga that it was a ritual murder. That view was confirmed by stories by alleged witnesses to various aspects of the murder; these stories persuaded the population of the rightness of its views, namely:

(1) The townsman Grigori Kazimirov (cited in my report of 13 March) spread a rumor that the investigator proposed that he confess to the murder of Rybachenko and beat him. His father, Petr Kazimirov, confirmed this rumor and says that his son was so intimidated by the investigator that after the interrogation he lost his appetite and [ability to] sleep and would complain about the investigator's actions.

(2) Dar'ia Zakhar'evna Zhuchenko, a fifty-

three-year-old townswoman from Dubossary, vociferously declares that on 9 February of this year, on the day that Mikhail Rybachenko disappeared, she was at the bazaar near the grocery shop of Aizik Urman. She heard the Jew Meier Shender, who had come up to Urman, say to him in Yiddish: "We already have the one that we shall torment!" Urman hissed a reply: "*Sha* [be quiet]! [. . .] Some people understand Yiddish!" Zhuchenko is certain that "the one whom we shall torment" was Rybachenko. She also says that on 11 February, when Rybachenko's disappearance became the topic of general discussion, she went up to the fourteen-year-old daughter of the Jew Nukhim Khait (she does not know her given name but recognizes her as a resident of Dubossary). The latter allegedly told her: "Go quickly to the home of Ios'ka Filer. The boy is still alive but he will soon be murdered." To her question — "What boy?" — the girl explained: "The one for whom they search." Zhuchenko immediately reported this to Konon Rybachenko, who lives close by. The latter, as he himself states, went to Filer's home, situated in the garden near to the place where they discovered Rybachenko's corpse on 13 February. Finding a Christian man and woman in the house, they did not dare look into the cellar at this house. Konon set out to see the local police officer and request that the house be searched, but was rebuffed. Zhuchenko states that she reported all of the above to the investigator.

(3) Fedor Danilov Sevast'ianov (a twenty-seven-year-old townsman from Dubossory; an unskilled laborer who drinks but is not a drunkard) reported that in February (he could not remember the date but it was after the discovery of Rybachenko's corpse) some local Jews — Iankel Fishman, Tsalek Urman, Moshko Slavkis, and Mordko Nukhim Benderskii — invited him to Benderskii's home. They began to offer him drinks and a bite to eat; they proposed that he spread rumors that Rybachenko was murdered by his relative the deaf Ivan Timoshchuk not the Jew. To compensate him for doing this, they gave him 100 rubles and promised another 500 afterward. Sevast'ianov could not resist such a sum and agreed to the proposal. However, at this point someone's laughter rang out from behind a screen in the room where the transaction was taking place; Sevast'ianov, fearing a trap, threw down the 100 rubles and left — but with difficulty because the people named above restrained him. They calmed him down, and he agreed to the proposition. After a few days they began pestering him; however, he not only refused but gave an account to the investigator Galushchinskii. But the latter allegedly threatened to exile him to Sakhalin for spreading such rumors.

Given that Ivan Timoshchuk had been arrested by the most experienced investigator in the region, Timoshchuk was undoubtedly the murderer. Hence the unofficial clarification of details about this murder (which now appear not only superfluous but inconvenient) have been omitted.

In reporting to Your Excellency, I have the honor to add that I have presented a copy of this statement together with the preliminary reports (numbers 116 and 117) sent to the commander of the corps and the department of police. Given the obstinate conviction of the Christian population in Dubossary and village of Lunga regarding the ritual murder of Rybachenko (sustained by rumors and the sensational newspaper articles written by the secretary of the Dubossary city board, Krivenki-Ianovskii, a drunkard who incites the population in these places)[3] and taking into consideration the approaching holiday of Easter, it is difficult to say whether the holiday will proceed normally in terms of public peace.

"Chief of the St. Petersburg Criminal Investigation Department to Mr. Iazykov [Ministry of Justice] (13 May 1903)"

On 20 April [1903], in accordance with Your Excellency's personal orders, I sent two police officers (Nikolai Alekseev and Evgenii Afonas'ev) to Odessa on the basis of instructions from the Odessa Provincial Court. Upon arriving in Odessa on 22 April, they became familiar with the facts of the preliminary investigation in the murder case of the boy Mikhail Rybachenko in the town of Dubossary. The facts were as follows: On Sunday (9 February) the peasant boy from the town of Bolshoi Fontan, Mikhail Rybachenko, was at the cathedral in Dubossary with his grandmother Elizaveta Rybachenko, his cousin Ivan Timoshchuk, and the latter's wife Mariia. After matins, as always, Mikhail set out from there to the Dniester River to skate on the ice. That is where the boy Grigorii Stepanenko saw him; when the church bells rang for early Mass, he left Rybachenko, who was still skating. After that point (that is, 10–11 a.m.), he [Rybachenko] was never seen again. At first it was assumed that he had fallen through the ice and drowned; the river was searched, but with no success. On 13 February a resident of the village Usti'a (Bessarabia province), Serafim Kirillov, who was traveling down the Dniester on the side of Dubossary, stopped to attend to his natural needs in Zholubova's garden, which is enclosed by a fence. His attention was attracted to crows that were agitatedly circling around the old willow. Upon approaching this place, he discovered the body of Mikhail Rybachenko and reported it to the policeman Nikifor Osadchenko; the latter did not take steps to preserve the corpse but loaded it onto a wagon and transported it first to the hospital; when they did not accept it, he took it to the rural police headquarters. This tactless behavior fueled misconceptions that there was no blood on the body of the murdered boy.

An autopsy of the body revealed nineteen lacerations—nine on the right side of the head, the rest on the right side of the torso to the feet. There were also three additional wounds: in the liver, kidneys, and carotid artery, a cut that went all the way through and was absolutely lethal. All the clothes on the deceased were soaked in blood. The clothes were slashed precisely in the place of the wounds. The scarf was cut to shreds and drenched in blood. There were two pools of blood where the body was discovered. Nevertheless, the local Christian population, under the influence of repeated agitation, came to believe that Jews had murdered the boy and, having used the requisite blood, carried him into the garden and poured animal blood on him to cover up the murder.

This gave rise to anonymous denunciations of the investigation and inquiries, usually claiming that authorities were bribed, that the city doctor made an incorrect autopsy and drew false conclusions about the death, and so forth. All this led to the removal of the court investigator (Fediukin) from the investigation, the transfer of the rural police officer (Liaskovskii) to another district, and the appointment of the court investigator of the most important cases Golushchinskii. The second autopsy by another doctor yielded the very same result and clearly refuted the belief that the body had been moved from the place where it was discovered. According to the doctor's conclusions, the savage wounds were inflicted by someone who was not completely normal or who was under some extreme stress, and that gave reason to suspect and arrest the cousin of the deceased, the twenty-two-year-old Ivan Timoshchuk, who is deaf and stutters. He recently married and may have been jealous of his cousin Mikhail, whom his grandfather Konon Rybachenko adopted. It is rumored that the elderly Rybachenko planned to bequeath his entire fortune to Mikhail. Then Ivan, his father, and his five children from a second marriage would just [inherit] a small piece of land, which the old man had bequeathed to Ivan but that had remained under the guardianship of his father (Mikhail Timoshchuk) until he came of age. When he came of age, Ivan had initiated proceedings against his father to take the land, but the court ruled in favor of his father. The assumption that Ivan committed the murder is further collaborated by the fact that his father was at the local notary Rapoport's soon after Mikhail's disappearance; being extremely anxious, he inquired whether the elderly Rybachenko had drawn up a will in favor of Mikhail. Moreover, with respect to the site of the crime, one may surmise that Mikhail was summoned to the garden under some pretext by a person with whom he was acquainted — otherwise, he would not have stopped by the garden to attend to his natural needs. If he were in danger on the banks of the Dniester River, he would have had good reason to save himself by running toward the town, not the garden. The testimonies of witnesses are extremely contradictory; they merely report rumors. The investigation has had to resort to face-to-face confrontations, but so far these have not led to anything.

Upon obtaining the above facts, the police officer (in accordance with the supervising procurator), left for Dubossary (Tiraspol' district, Kherson province), but en route he learned about the arrival of some official from St. Petersburg. The population of Dubossary was already aware of this. This circumstance forced those who had been sent [to investigate] to carry out their assignment with the utmost caution. Moreover, the local population (comprised mainly of Jews, Moldavans, and Ukrainians) categorically refused to discuss Rybachenko's murder with outsiders. The two police officers, based on the information they nonetheless managed to collect from a few individuals, concluded that the murder was committed in order to gain possession of the inheritance and that there were no serious indications of ritual murder apart

from the vociferous accusations by the Christian population. In view of what has been stated, the procurator and investigatory authorities deemed a further stay of the police officers unnecessary. [. . .]

"Procurator of the Odessa District Court N[ikolai Mikhailovich] Levchenko to the Minister of Justice (1 July 1903)"

As an addendum to my communication of 30 June 1903 (number 5585), I want to inform Your Excellency that detective Matveev left for the town of Dubossary in May to investigate the murder of Mikhail Rybachenko. I acquainted him in detail with the circumstances of the case and, in accordance with Your Excellency's instructions, I recommended that he direct his inquiry along three lines: with respect to the mentally ill Bekker,[4] to boys of the same age as the murder victim, and especially to Ivan and Mikhail Timoshchuk, as the people most interested in the death of Mikhail Rybachenko. Even earlier Matveev speculated that the Timoshchuks were guilty; furthermore, his personal statements convinced me that his conjectures conveyed such certainty that I was worried about the one-sidedness of his investigation. Nonetheless, I supported his certainty all the more since the suspicions of the expert professor Sikorskii regarding Bekker had been completely dismissed. Moreover, it could not have been a ritual murder, and no information has been found with respect to the murdered boy's peers. Thus I advised Matveev to pay special attention to the Timoshchuks by establishing ties with all their relatives, especially the women in their family. Matveev carried this out brilliantly. Based almost exclusively on his personal impressions, not having any facts, Matveev repeatedly asked my permission to arrest Timoshchuk. However, I did not agree to this, for I feared damaging the case for which I had received Your Excellency's approval. I only gave my consent for the arrest on 25 June, as the term of Matveev's assignment was coming to an end. When I received a telegram from him on 27 June, reporting that Timoshchuk had been arrested and that in his house they had found a sheepskin coat with stains that looked like blood, I was skeptical of this news. I could not give serious weight to Matveev's telegram that I received on 29 June with the following contents: "Timoshchuk's accomplice confessed. I am conducting an inquiry." Concerned about Matveev's extreme enthusiasm, I did not allow myself to report this to Your Excellency in writing with a preliminary copy to the Ministry of Justice; instead, I limited myself to an oral report to you. In an urgent telegram I asked Matveev about the results of his inquiry. The same day I suggested that the court investigator and procurator leave for Dubossary; I ordered the latter to telegraph me immediately the actual, reliable facts established through the inquiry and investigation. In response to my inquiry, Matveev sent me the following telegraph: "The watchman Anton Tishchenko confessed that Mikhail Timoshchuk proposed that he participate in the murder. At Tishchenko's a rag with traces of blood was found. A detailed report [will be sent] by mail." The contents of the telegram and the rather evasive answer increased my doubts that the information uncovered by Matveev was substantive. The next Matveev sent me the following telegram: "The watchman Tischenko confessed a second time that Timoshchuk, with his help, committed the murder in the garden where the corpse was found; Timoshchuk threw the knife and cudgel in the Dniester River." The procurator later confirmed in a telegram that Timoshchuk and Tishchenko were arrested as suspects, that at the inquest Tischenko confessed to participating in the murder, that at the time of the murder he was on the lookout for anyone who might hinder [the criminals], and that Timoshchuk had not yet been interrogated. The same day that you deigned to report about this by telegram to the minister of justice, I sent Your Excellency a writ-

ten report with a copy to His Most Esteemed Excellency.

In conclusion, after observing the activities of the assistant chief of the Kherson detective division, Matveev, I can report that I believe he is not only the most diligent, experienced, and intelligent police officer but also that in this case he acted skillfully and with extreme zeal, energy, and devotion to the case. He has undoubtedly discovered the most valuable material for solving of this crime; if the information that he has gathered is confirmed, it contributes to determining the guilty party and [the credit for] this will belong to him. Thus I take the liberty of requesting that Your Excellency encourage Matveev with some kind of reward.

"Copy of the Testimony of Anton Tishchenko [to the Court Investigator of Odessa District] (29 June 1903)"

[Site:] Village of Lunga. The court investigator of Odessa District Court for the most important cases interrogated the defendant named below as the accused (in accordance with article 403 of the *Ustav ugolovnogo sudoproizvodstva* [Criminal Justice Code]. In response to questions, he explained:

I am Anton Nestorov Tishchenko, forty-three years old, and I was born in Poltava province in the village of Andreevka, Velikobuchovsk Township, Konstantinograd district. I am a soldier (private) in the reserve army. I live in Dubossary in Filer's garden where I am the watchman. I am legitimate, Russian, Orthodox, illiterate, and single. I do not have any real estate. I had cysts on my right hands, which were removed by an operation. I was on trial ten years ago for theft and sentenced by the Justice of the Peace Court in Dubossary to six months in prison. I served the punishment in the Tiraspol' prison. I do not consider myself guilty of the premeditated murder of Mikhail Rybachenko by prior arrangement with Mikhail Timoshchuk [Ivan's father] on 9 February of this year. However,

I consider myself guilty of standing guard in Zholubova's garden when Mikhail Timoshchuk killed Rybachenko with the task of warning him if some stranger approached.

It was like this: On the Saturday before the murder, I set out in the evening for the old bazaar to buy four *funt* (1.6 kg) of sunflower oil and one *funt* (0.4 kg) of buckwheat, because my wife[5] Evdokiia Liashenkova lay in bed sick after falling off a ledge. At the bazaar [. . .] I met Mikhail Timoshchuk, whom I did not know previously. He invited me to drop by the wine shop of the red-haired Jew Iankel "for a few words" and to drink an *oko* of wine.[6] In response I told Timoshchuk that, first, I did not have time and, second, I had all of twenty kopecks on me. The latter countered that he was not in need of any money, and that he would treat me at his expense. We dropped by Iankel's wine shop and requested an *oko* of wine. The shop consists of one small room; it has a table and two benches. No one else was in the shop. We drank the *oko* of wine; Timoshchuk ordered a second *oko* of wine, and then a third. We drank all this wine. A Russian woman, in whose name Iankel obtains the license, served the wine. She only served the wine and immediately left, so she did not hear our conversation. Indeed, there was no conversation as such yet. I attempted to leave but Timoshchuk detained me, saying that he had something to say to me. When we had emptied the third *oko* of wine, the woman demanded money and Timoshchuk paid her forty-eight kopecks (two fifteen-kopeck, one ten-kopeck, one five-kopeck, and one three-kopeck coins).

Timoshchuk ordered a fourth *oko* of wine, and after it was served, he asked whether I would agree to go to work with him as an assistant. Assuming that Timoshchuk had in mind the usual work of *papusha* [involving tobacco leaves, hay, herbs] or rocks, I replied that I would go if I were free. Timoshchuk then explained that it was "not work" but "hunting," and added that, "I have a grudge against the boy Mikhail Rybachenko.

I want to kill him and seek an assistant." I understood the word "grudge" to mean that Timoshchuk harbored hostility or malice toward the boy, but he did not exactly speak to me about this, and I did not ask him. I refused bluntly to help him in such a matter and said that I would not go. God preserve me. Hearing my refusal, Timoshchuk replied, "If you do not wish to, then I will manage by myself, but look here, don't say [anything] or else I'll kill you." Drinking another glass of wine, I bid farewell to Timoshchuk. Leaving him at the wine shop, I went to the market, bought the buckwheat and sunflower oil at the grocery shop, and went straight home. I was a little intoxicated. When my *baba*, who had been waiting for me, asked me where I had been, I replied that I had drunk an *oko* of wine with someone, but I did not say with whom, and I did not say a word about the conversation that I had had with Timoshchuk. By the time I returned home, it had already begun to get cold, but the fire had still not been kindled. After cooking lunch, I ate and gave my *baba* something to eat. I lay down to sleep on the stove.

The following day, Sunday, at 7:00 a.m., I left home for the market. Matins had still not begun at the cathedral. Buying two *funt* (0.8 kg) of sunflower seed oil and one *funt* of macaroni from the market and, without meeting any acquaintances, I returned home. As I walked home, the church bells for early morning services began to ring. At home I was busy preparing lunch; after the end of matins, people went by along the lane to the Dniester River to the ferry crossing. Having prepared and eaten lunch, I again set out for the Old Market without any specific business but only to walk and look. At this point they rang the bells for Mass. Having walked a little around the market, I returned home. My wife was groaning on the stove. I did not have any money, not a single kopeck. I lay down for a while on the bed and dozed off, then woke up and sat down by the window that faces the lane. The door to my hut was ajar and un-locked. Suddenly, someone knocked at the window where I was sitting. Looking out, I saw Mikhail Timoshchuk knocking. I went out to the courtyard to Timoshchuk, who appeared anxious and upset. He said: "Hurry up, the boy is already standing by the shore." A chill passed through my body. I began to waver: should I go or not? I was not fully awake when Timoshchuk called me. I decided that I would not strike the boy in any case and limit myself to being the lookout so that some stranger would not catch Timoshchuk red-handed. Timoshchuk urged me, saying, "Go, go, or else you're going to pay for it." We left through the gate in the lane to the ferry cross-ing. Liashenkova, who was lying on the stove, did not know where or with whom I left.

The boy Mikhail Rybachenko, whom I ab-solutely did not know until then, was in the lane nearby, climbing over the ditch to Zhol-ubova's garden. Apparently, he waited for Ti-moshchuk, but under what pretext the latter lured him there I do not know—he did not tell me anything. Saying to the boy, "Come," Timoshchuk climbed over the ditch to Zhol-ubova's garden. The boy followed him and I went behind the boy, who was thus between us. Mikhail Timoshchuk was holding a pitch-fork, 1.5 arshin [108.18 centimeters] in length with four tines. When they approached the stump of the old willow, Timoshchuk let the boy go ahead and then he raised his hand and struck the boy on the right side of his head. He "pounced on him" with such force that the boy fell unconscious to the ground, like a "chicken." He fell on his left side. Then Ti-moshchuk tore off the boy's overcoat, jacket, and waistcoat, next unfastened his shirt col-lar, pulled the shirt up to the head, dropped his trousers, took a knife from his pocket, and "scuppered"[7] both sides of the boy's neck and body. The knife was small, with a thin blade (about as long as a small finger) and a red wooden handle. One side of the knife was blunt, the other sharp and rigid. I did not hold it and cannot say whether it had a grooved blade; it seems to me that the blade was straight and even. This was not a shoe-maker's or kitchen knife; in general, it was not an "artisan's" but something of a "hunt-er's" knife. I stood five steps back as Timosh-chuk dealt the blows; I myself absolutely did not do anything. How many wounds and in which sequence Timoshchuk inflicted them I cannot say; however, it did not go on for long, three or four minutes. The boy showed no sign of life. After the boy had been "scup-pered," Timoshchuk unrolled the shirt, pulled up the pants, and dressed the boy as he had appeared earlier. I did not notice whether Ti-moshchuk slashed the overcoat and the boy's other clothes.

When I asked him why he undressed the boy and stabbed the naked body, Timosh-chuk replied: "It's just what the Jews would do. I am a Russian, they will not suspect me and will think it was the *zhidy* [Yids]." Hav-ing dressed the boy, he hauled him close to the wattled hedge near the old willow. He took some soil and leaves from under the willow and sprinkled large spots of blood on them near the path where we had walked. I think that altogether two cups of blood came from the boy. I saw only the one bloody spot that described earlier. I was afraid to leave because Timoshchuk said: "Stand here, don't leave." The blood did not splash on me, but there was blood on Timoshchuk's hands and cam-el's hair overcoat. I did not notice whether Timoshchuk was wearing a sheepskin coat beneath his overcoat.

Having finished with the boy, Mikhail Ti-moshchuk left Zholubova's garden by the path leading from the willow tree to the Dni-ester River. I followed him and stopped at the exit from the garden along the towpath, but Timoshchuk went up to the very edge of the precipice and, with great force, first threw the pitchfork and then the knife used to kill Mikhail Rybachenko into the Dniester River. Although the river was still frozen, there were already many ice-free "pools." Earlier the ice had moved but then stopped. The knife went to the bottom of the river. Although the pitchfork remained on top of the ice, no one could reach it: it was impossible to go on top of ice because of the "pools." Having thrown away the pitchfork and knife, Timoshchuk threatened me with his finger when we parted, saying: "Be quiet. Don't say a word to anyone; if you let the cat out of the bag, this will also happen to you." He did not go through Zholubova's garden this time but went along the banks below on the towpath and along the way passed Baptizmanskii's shop, climbed over the fence, and went somewhere through the garden, but I do not know where exactly he went—I did not see.

I myself returned home through Zholubova's garden by the same ditch that I had climbed over on the ferry lane and have already mentioned. I did not go past the murdered corpse but went around it.

I confirm that Timoshchuk did not return to Zholubova's garden, and I do not know how to explain the bloody handprints that cross over from Zholubova's garden to [that of] the neighbor on the right side. Perhaps Timoshchuk, who had already parted from me, made inquiries about the murdered boy and climbed over to the place; but I did not see this and I do not know. Exactly why did Timoshchuk murder Mikhail Rybachenko? He did not say. He only said that he held a "grudge" toward him. While striking the blows, Timoshchuk was very embittered and beat the boy "with the furious zeal" of a "wild animal." Until that Saturday I did not know Mikhail Timoshchuk. I was never at his house and he was never at my house. The first time that we became acquainted was on Saturday, 8 February. Evdokiia Liashenkova did not know anything about the murder of the boy; I did not tell her a word. The police seized Liashenkova's rag, remade from an old skirt, which covered a chest. This skirt had some old blood stains from her monthly menstruation. Liashenkova washed them out, but the old stains nonetheless remained. She was wearing this skirt at the beginning of the year when she was ill.

After the murder, I never went to see the corpse. Strangers do not go to Zholubova's garden in the winter, and that is why no one stumbled upon the corpse until Thursday. When Timoshchuk was with the boy, I entered Zholubova's garden from the lane and definitely did not see anyone. People and children on the banks of the Dniester were not visible at the moment when Timoshchuk threw away the knife and pitchfork in the river. As is already evident, it was God's will. When I returned to my hut after the murder, the church began to ring its bell—one peal for the [prayer], "*Dostoino* [*est'*]."[8] It meant that the liturgy was half over.

I did not speak about the murder of Mikhail Rybachenko, either to Liashenkova, to Konon Rybachenko (who came to me the next day), or to you during my interrogation as a witness because I was very afraid of Timoshchuk's threat that he would kill me if I shot off my mouth. I live alone on the banks of the river, in a garden. I do not have neighbors nearby. I do not have a dog. If Timoshchuk so wishes, he could easily carry out his threat. I firmly decided to keep silent until the authorities themselves got to the bottom of it. I suffered and endured what God gives. But now when they began to say that I killed the boy, I decided to tell the whole truth as before God and am prepared to confirm the truth under oath, even before the twelve Apostles. Regarding the other questions, I will say this. After the murder I never talked with Mikhail Timoshchuk. At a chance meeting, we made it appear that we absolutely did not know each other. I cannot say for certain why Timoshchuk turned to me for assistance when he absolutely did not know me, or why I listened to the request of someone who was a stranger, or why I stood guard while he killed the boy. Timoshchuk did not directly ask me to stand as lookout but only said, "come, come." However, I understood his invitation to mean that I was to warn Timoshchuk of any kind of danger. I do not know whether Mikhail was at church that Sunday, or in general how he spent his time before and after the murder. I do not know if Timoshchuk washed somewhere along the banks of the river and [if so], where. After the murder of Mikhail Rybachenko, I no longer saw the camel's hair coat on Timoshchuk. Mikhail Timoshchuk did not give or promise me money. I do not know if the death of Mikhail Rybachenko really saved Timoshchuk from giving [up] the hereditary farmstead to the stuttering son, and I cannot explain anything else.

"Report from the Procurator of the Odessa District Court to the Minister of Justice (24 July 1903)"

With respect to the murder of Mikhail Rybachenko, I report the following to Your Excellency. Though the indicted Anton Tishchenko confessed to the murder, his admission nevertheless did not inspire particular confidence because he immediately lapsed into several contradictions regarding the incontrovertible circumstances of the case. Soon after the first interrogation, he changed his first testimony and provided a new explanation, departing still more from the known facts of the case. He has persisted in repeating his latest explanation, which was manifestly absurd and utterly lacking in veracity. In view of this and his established penchant for drunkenness, and in accordance with Your Excellency's orders, we decided to conduct a psychological and psychiatric examination of Anton Tishchenko's intellectual and mental condition. For this purpose, first and foremost we invited Professor Lange from the Department of Psychology at Novorossiisk University to conduct an observation of Tishchenko in order to determine whether he somehow deviates from the norm. For this purpose, on 13 August the professor was given the appropriate documents from

the investigation, and after that the court investigator, in Lange's presence, ordered Tishchenko to recount exactly how the murder of Mikhail Rybachenko had been committed.

Tishchenko began his story very willingly, repeating his latest testimony about the murder of the boy in the cellar. However, when he was informed (as before) that his story was impossible (the cellar being pitch-black, too small, and too low to swing a pitchfork), Tishchenko abruptly broke off his story. He stated categorically that both this story and all previous testimonies were lies and fabrications, that he had not taken any part in the murder, that he knew nothing about the case, and that he did not know and had never seen the accused Mikhail Timoshchuk and the murdered boy. When asked why he had not only confessed but had earlier identified Mikhail Timoshchuk, he said that he himself does not understand how this happened and thinks that it was all due to the influence of detective Matveev, although the latter did not use force, threats, or deceitful tricks in his treatment. However, after his arrest, Matveev began to insist that it was precisely he and Timoshchuk who had killed the boy. Matveev so convincingly advised him to confess that, without thinking things through clearly, he began to say that indeed he and Timoshchuk killed the boy, conjuring up different stories about this murder as they popped into his head. He cannot explain why he constantly repeated his confession before the court investigator in the presence of the head of the Directorate of Public Prosecution and talked absolutely freely and voluntarily—even though no one forced him to say this. In fact, they explained both the gravity of the responsibility that he was taking upon himself as well as the incongruity of his stories. He has now reconsidered and cannot understand how all this could have happened. In view of this, Professor Lange considered it necessary to subject Tishchenko to a thorough observation with the participation of the prison doctor. I gave permission to the professor to have access to see Tishchenko in prison. I will report the results of Professor Lange's expert opinion.

Shortly, the court investigator and I will deliberate the question about the possibility of keeping both Tishchenko and Timoshchuk under arrest.[9]

NOTES

1. [For an account of the Dubossary ritual murder based primarily on newspaper accounts, see Edward Judge, *Easter in Kishinev: Anatomy of a Pogrom* (New York: New York University Press, 1992), 39–48. According to the 1897 census, Dubossary had 12,809 residents, of whom 5,220 (43 percent) were Jews; the rest were mostly Christian Moldavans and Ukrainians.]

2. [The memorandum used the name Rybal'-chenko instead of Rybachenko, as in the other documents. For consistency, Rybachenko will be used here.]

3. [The newspaper that circulated stories about the ritual murder was the daily *Bessarabets*, run by

Pavolachi Krushevan (see Judge, *Easter in Kishinev*, 30–33).]

4. [A mentally ill individual named Bekker was apparently considered to be a suspect.]

5. [He refers to her as his "lover" here and "wife" in other places in the document. "Wife" is used here for consistency.]

6. [An *oko* is equivalent to 0.77 liters.]

7. [The witness created a verb out of the word *shpenek* (scupper), a nautical term that refers to opening up the side of the ship to let the water run out. The court investigator added the word "stabbed" in parentheses to explain what the witness meant. He did this on many occasions when the terms used by the witness were not clear. The boy was clearly wearing special clothing for the church service (an overcoat, jacket, waistcoat, and collared shirt) as described by the police report about the murder of 13 May 1903 (above).]

8. [*Dostoino est'* (truly worthy) is the opening line of a prayer to the Virgin Mary.]

9. [There were no further documents in the file about the final resolution of this case.]

[168]

Eyewitness Accounts of the Kishinev Pogrom Recorded by Hayim Nahman Bialik (1903)

Hayim Nahman Bialik *Eduyot nifge'e Kishinov, 1903: ke-fi she-nigbu 'al-yede H. N. Bialik ve-chaverav*, ed. Ya'akov Goren, ed. (Tel Aviv: Ha-kibutz Ha-meuhad, 1991), 66–67, 165–66.

"The Testimony of Shlomo Zilberman, Who Lived Near the Chupili Field"

The disturbances began in our area on Sunday at 2:30 p.m. The thugs attacked a passing Jew, and a Christian saved him from their hands. The liquor shop of a young man, Yosef Kaushen, located on the corner of Gostinaia and Svechnaia Streets, was the first to be de-

stroyed. The *pogromshchiki* demanded wine; when he refused, they began to destroy [everything]. The violence then spread from there to the adjoining streets. [. . .] [The location of my home is such that] I shared a courtyard with the lieutenant commander of the Dugnov quarter, and I saw that this lieutenant had rounded up the crowd; in my heart I gave thanks, saying "this will save us." I gathered my wife and four children and brought them to his house to hide, but I immediately realized that he was unhappy with this. Meanwhile, his wife returned from the market dressed in her holiday clothes,[1] with a splendid bonnet on her head. As she stood there in all her glory she began to mock us and spoke in a haughty, scornful manner: "This is what you Jews deserve." Then the old nurse who lived with them said to us: "You Jews go too far; in vain do you seek refuge. They will drag you out from every hiding place and kill you — I heard that from the *pogromshchiki* themselves. First they will plunder your belongings, and then they will kill you." The lieutenant listened and was silent. My family and I sought refuge and salvation somewhere else.

"The Testimony of Berl Tsubis"

As we arrived for the *bris* of Israel Holman, we wanted to hasten back to our home because of rumors that we had heard, and a passing nobleman told us about what was happening in the city. I was the *sandek*, [one who holds the child on his lap during circumcision] and I rushed to finish. As we left the *bris*, we were attacked by two local *shkutzim* [pejorative for non-Jews] who were throwing stones. A Christian woman interceded on our behalf: "Why are they attacking people who are innocently walking by (we were wearing respectable clothing)?" Before this Christian spoke up, they threw me into a puddle with my coat on me. After Tsifris picked me up, I ran with him and his son toward my house. As we approached, we saw many Moldavans standing around. I left my *tallis* and *tefillin* in Leib Grinzberg's house. Afterward I found out that they dressed a dog in my *tallis* and *tefillin*, and marched him around the village. I saw a mob coming from the city, and I went with my wife and son to Kopel Krinsky's house. I said, "We'll assemble here and fight for our lives." Kopel said, "Jews, where will we go?" We were still debating the matter when two neatly dressed men came in, one wearing a fur hat, the other a woven cap, and requested an *oko* of wine. We answered, "There is no wine here." They went to the outskirts of [the city], to the first tavern, Hirshl's [. . .], and the man in the fur hat threw the first stone, and after that a whole group of Moldavans joined in. Where could we flee? We went to the courtyard of Dr. Stein. This doctor, and someone named Opitser, went out and looked on the disturbances from a distance. The doctor's assistant came out and said, "The doctor demands that all the Jews leave." And his wife said, "On your way! Out!" So we left and decided to go to the slaughterhouse of Shimon Vakhs; maybe he would give us a place to hide. He advised us to go to the inner slaughterhouse, but I thought that we needed to worry that [the *pogromshchiki*] would slaughter us with the butcher knives and hang us on the meat hooks. So I thought of sending all the women and children to the milking area, while Shimon Wachs and I would remain in the slaughterhouse. Shimon spoke on the telephone with the [police headquarters for the] fifth quarter, which responded: "We have no order with regard to this matter." Eight times we pleaded on the phone: "They are killing [people]." The response: *"Dezhurnyi ukhodil, zhdi"* [The supervisor left, wait]. So I also went to the milking area, and we closed the gates and the doors. By the fourth hour the pogrom in the town was over, and the mob headed toward us — led by Todor Pupinok, a guard at the slaughterhouse. They threw stones through the windows, pelting those hiding there. There was screaming and wailing! Pupinok called out "Open the door," and the mob broke through the door. I approached Todor, whom I knew, and said, "Todor Badi[2]" and he immediately broke my hand with a pipe, and yelled in Russian: *"Poshli von, zhidy"* [Get out of here Yids]. They drove us out into Kopel's courtyard, where they began to beat the Jews. Kostati Odriks smashed two iron hooks into my head (the kind used to draw up buckets from the wells). I forcefully pounded his hand and he dropped the hooks. Next to me stood Yakov Rosenberg, holding his two children. Another of them hit me once with a metal strip — my blood gushed out; Yakov Rosenberg also received this present. [. . .] I hid in a corner of the Kishchni courtyard and stayed there until the action was over. The Jews fled, and the gentiles pursued. Six *shkutzim* entered. They looked at me, and one of them said, "dead." A second said "no" and kicked me in the stomach. [. . .] They picked me up and wove braids from my beard, and cut it off. I wanted to kiss them — but they prevented it, lest I contaminate them with my flowing blood. A third came and said, "My Lord; the Savior has arisen!" With the brick in his hand he smacked me on my lower jaw near my right ear (as I, from fear, turned my head slightly), and another struck me with a metal strip on the shoulder, breaking my hand.[3]

NOTES

1. [This was Easter Sunday.]

2. [The name Badi (not Jagu as the note states in the Hebrew notes) was spelled out in Russian in the original. It may have been his nickname.]

3. [The testimony ends here. Obviously Berl Tsubis survived to tell the story.]

[169]

Violence in Bessarabia Province in the Aftermath of Kishinev (1903)

GARF, f. 102, 3 d-vo, g. 1903, d. 874, ll. 24–24 ob., 34–39, 40–41, 42–43, 45–45 ob.[1]

"Report of the Assistant Chief of the Bessarabian Provincial Gendarme Administration to the Chief of the Gendarme Administration (8 April 1903)"

This 8 April, around 10:00 p.m., several people — workers on the Kriuliansk Highway (which runs through the village of Gurshevo, Grotoposk township, Orgeev district) together with a few lads from his village — first attacked a house in which the Jew Moshka Grinshpun lives. Breaking the windows and doors, throwing rocks inside, they forced all the members of this Jew's family and a stranger there to flee. Then they set out for the house of another Jew, Iankel Grinshpun. After breaking the doors and windows, they burst into the residence with a grocery shop attached to it and completely destroyed all its contents — goods, furniture, dresses, dishes, and utensils. Having finished here, those who had committed excesses returned again to Moshka Grinshpun's and created such havoc that the kerosene from the broken lamp poured onto various objects and caught fire. However, the very same brawlers who started the fire quickly put it out.

During the devastation at the two houses, the attackers did not perpetrate violence on anyone. According to the victims, the [value of the] plundered [property] amounted to 2,260 rubles in cash and 840 rubles in gold objects and pearls. The local police are currently conducting an inquiry into the case and have arrested the main participants in the disorder, eight people.

"Report of the Assistant Chief of the Bessarabian Provincial Gendarme Administration to the Chief of the Gendarme Administration (17 April 1903)"

[. . .] Continuing with observations about the danger of anti-Jewish disorders in the districts entrusted to me, I have the honor to report to Your Excellency (in an addendum to the report of 15 April, number 401) that I received the following information by secret means:

(1) [REGARDING] IZMAILOV DISTRICT
On 12–13 April in Izmailov, four windows were broken at the house of the Jew Ioska Pul'ferman at night; that same night four windows were also smashed at the house of the Jew Shlezinger. But the guilty have not been caught, nor have any suspects been identified.

On 13 April swings were built in a town square in Izmailov. According to the custom from time immemorial, young people come together from the town and also the suburbs. Moreover, hostility between these parties [often] erupts because of a girl. That day youths from the suburb of Kopanaia Balka evidently decided to start a quarrel with the town lads; that is why even passers-by were apparently armed. But the police officials had forewarning and arrested several youths: Grigorii Chernyi (who turned out to have a loaded revolver), Evdokii Federov and Gavril Scherbin (who had large, new knives in their pockets), Lavrentii Sirot (who had a metal hammer in his pocket), and Dmitrii Iakovenko (who had a rock in his pocket). All of these people were immediately incarcerated in a guardhouse; an investigation will be undertaken with respect to them. These circumstances caused a panic among the Jews and rumors circulated around town that everyone

was preparing for a massacre of the latter; for the present, however, people think that these are rumors spread by idle people and old women gossipmongers.

At the same time, ten horse-drawn carts arrived in Izmailov (at night on 12–13 April from the town of Bolgrad) with Jews who were taking precautions to avoid being slaughtered (as they put it), for rumors had been circulating there among themselves. In general, the Jews and their families are highly anxious, but there have not been any special, well-founded intelligence and rumors about anti-Jewish disorders.

On 15 April, a delegation from the Jewish community came to me and, among other things, the merchant Lebedinskii gave me a quarter-sheet of paper that he had picked up near to his store, with the following written in ink:

Odessa Leaflet. 14 April 1903
I am informing you briefly that in an unknown town the Jews seized a Russian boy, sewed up his mouth, nose, and ears, inflicted eighteen stab wounds all over his body, and took blood from him for Passover. He had already lain in a closed box at their place, and on the third day they crucified him on a tree in his garden. That same night the dog howled, broke away from its chains, ran to the garden where [the boy] had been crucified, and would not let anyone near him. Informed of this, the governor arrived before permission had been given to bury the child; in Kishinev they have now beaten up around 500 Jews. Now the Jews are very frightened. They lay down to sleep at dawn (5:00 or 6:30 a.m.). One Jew, utterly exhausted, slept for fifteen hours. 14 April 1903.

On the night of 14–15 April, at 3:25 a.m., the Jewish merchant Kitsis, a permanent resident in the town of Kili but currently in Izmailov, appeared and asserted that he had just received a telegram that Kili is "restless."

I sent him to the police officer of Izmailov. At 4:30 a.m., the secretary of the Izmailov District Police, Mr. Varnitskii, came to me and showed me a telegram that the police station had received at 2:00 a.m. from the police officer in Kili: "The dead three-year-old child of the Old Believer[2] Bykov has now been found in a vacant house, a case that has aroused agitation. It is said that the child was strangled by the Jews. I am taking measures. I cannot answer for the consequences. [Signed]: Police Officer Vrzhezhevskii."

Upon [receiving] this telegram, the assistant police officer left Izmailov for Kili that same night in order to expose the crime as quickly as possible, and the commander of the Izmailov brigade sent a telegram to the commander of the division in Kili to assist in the event of disorders. A noncommissioned officer, Evmen Perets, who is my subordinate and serves as the elder in Kilii, reported to me that while there are presently no disorders, strong agitation is nonetheless apparent; it is also rumored that the Jews will be slaughtered. In Kili the mood of the Russian Orthodox population toward the latter has, in general, always been strained — as I reported to Your Excellency on 7 November 1902 (number 752) and 10 February (number 127) of this year. However, the noncommissioned officer also reported that on 14 April, between 8:00 and 9:00 p.m., the three- or four-year-old daughter of the Old Believer, Efrem Nikitich Bykov, a member of Kili City Board, was found dead in an empty house. That is why the Old Believers feel extreme outrage toward the Jews, believing that they strangled the girl. Effective 13 April, all taverns, wine cellars, and state liquor stores have been closed.

(2) REGARDING AKKERMAN DISTRICT

A noncommissioned officer, Daniil Strelets, who is under my jurisdiction and serves as elder at the unit in Akkerman, reports that the popular mood there has become agitated because of the disorders that occurred in Kishinev on 6–7 April. That is why many Jewish families temporarily left for Odessa, and many have armed themselves with revolvers and other weapons in the event that they need to defend themselves against an attack.

"Report of the Assistant Chief of the Bessarabian Provincial Gendarme Administration to the Chief of the Gendarme Administration (19 April 1903)"

To comment further on the danger of anti-Jewish disorders in the districts entrusted to me, I have the honor to report to Your Excellency (as an addendum to the report of 17 April, number 418) that I received the following information by secret means:

(1) REGARDING AKKERMAN DISTRICT

On 13 April, one company of the 37th Modlinskii infantry regiment, numbering 120 soldiers, arrived in Akkerman from Odessa. It is rumored that this company was sent to help the police, who believed that there would be anti-Jewish disorders on 13 and 14 April. However, for now, everything in Akkerman is fine.

(2) REGARDING IZMAILOV DISTRICT

Rumors have persistently circulated in the town of Kagul that there would be disorders on 13 April. Because the Old Believers in this town have always been extremely hostile to the Jews, the police officer of Izmailov went there. Low-ranking border guards rode around town on horseback; police officials allegedly warned the more suspicious personalities that they could be severely punished if there were disorders. For now, everything in Kagul has also been fine.

In the village of Leovo, where very many Jews reside, the mood of the latter has been extremely restless. That is why the police chief has reinforced the watch around town, calling in rural constables from the neighboring village of Primara, who were on duty on the streets day and night. All shops and taverns were shuttered on 13 and 14 April. The Jews even armed themselves with revolvers and all night roamed in throngs around their homes, stores, and shops. Because the Jews allegedly requested the governor of Bessarabia to send in troops, the vice governor arrived in the village of Leovo, [and] urged the Jews not to worry and to be calm because disorders had not broken out anywhere. He warned the Russian Orthodox to behave in an orderly manner. That same day he went back to Kishinev. So far, the situation in Leovo is good.

Rumors persist that the Jews in this town sent a flood of telegrams requesting protection (even to the minister [of justice]) and spent several hundred rubles on these telegrams.

A noncommissioned officer, Evmen Perets, who is my subordinate and serves in Kili, having made further observations about the reasons for the death of Bykov's daughter (age three-and-a half and named Stefanida), received information that continues to circulate in Kili. On 14 April, Stefanida left, apparently to take a walk at 4:00 or 5:00 p.m.; by late evening she still had not come home. That is why her parents began to search and to question neighbors. One Jew allegedly said: "Go look. Perhaps she fell asleep in that empty house." When they went there, they indeed found her dead. The dead body was still warm. Given this coincidence, the Old Believers raised an uproar, [saying] that the Jews — bitter toward Christians over the beatings in Kishinev — had strangled the girl. Police officials took measures to calm the Old Believers. On 15 April the local sanitary doctor Nemirovskii examined the girl's corpse. He allegedly declared that death resulted from a heart attack, but Bykov and the Old Believers do not agree with this medical opinion. They are still convinced that the girl died a violent death. Police officials are taking measures to maintain the peace, and mounted patrols of border guards ride around the town. How-

ever, the Jews remain very afraid; that is why many of them have armed themselves with revolvers. At night they do not sleep; several people gather near their homes, stores, and shops. Some are housing their families in Russian Orthodox homes as well as in the towboats and barges at the port. Moreover, a few families have temporarily left Kili; today, for instance, up to twenty people from prosperous Jewish families arrived in Izmail. Because the agitation had calmed somewhat, taverns and state liquor stores were opened on 15 April.

I can tell Your Excellency that the lower ranks subordinate to me are continuing to patrol their own area. Moreover, in all the other populated centers of the district with Jewish residents, it has been generally peaceful and fine for the time being, although the ferment and unrest persist.

The Jews in Vilkovo are still in an extremely anxious and agitated condition because this suburb is populated exclusively by Old Believers, who hold a permanent and even fanatical hostility toward the Jews on religious grounds. The greatest danger will be on 19 and 20 April (that is, Saturday and Sunday) when the local residents return from fishing and usually spend these days in debauchery and drunkenness.

In addition, I have the honor to inform Your Excellency that I am presenting a copy of this present report to the Commander of the Gendarme Corps and Department of Police.

"Report of the Governor of Podolia to the Minister of Internal Affairs (19 April 1903)"

On 13 April, after receiving information in Kaments-Podolsk about the anti-Jewish disorders in Kishinev during Easter, I dispatched a military detachment to Balta (two companies of the Kubanskii regiment) since there are no troops in the town. Meanwhile, anti-Jewish agitation has appeared there. The soil for anti-Jewish disorders appears to be the most fertile in Balta — both because a bitter plunder of Jewish property took place in 1881 (which all the local residents still recall) and because a significant number of Russian Old Believers live here and are far more inclined toward anti-Jewish disorders than are [Russian Orthodox] Ukrainians.

From the report of the Balta district police officer, which I received recently, it is evident that these military units arrived in Balta on the evening of 15 April. Their arrival immediately had a positive impact on the hostile agitation against the Jews. However, the ferment only abated; by no means did it end. In the town of Bogopol (Balta district) the odds of anti-Jewish disorders will soon increase because it is expecting the usual influx of migrant workers who come each year to this town. The hired workers from Bessarabia and Kherson provinces number up to 5,000 people. In the town of Rybnits (Balta district), which borders Bessarabia, there tends to be an influx of both migrant workers and also different unreliable elements of society during this season. That is why until the migrant workers settle down and go to work in these towns, one can always expect an outbreak of mass disorders that, for the most inconsequential reasons, could easily turn into an anti-Jewish movement.

I therefore asked the head of the 19th infantry division to leave two companies of Kuban regiments (which he had sent to Balta at my request) until the danger of anti-Jewish disorders subsides. Independently, [I requested] that he issue a corresponding order so that, if need be, at the demand of the Balta district police chief, the head of the military detachment would dispatch the required unit, at his discretion, to the towns of Bogopol' or Rybnits to prevent or suppress such disorders if they should arise.

I have the honor to inform Your Excellency about the above. It corresponds to article 24 on the call-up of military forces to assist civil authorities. Unfortunately, I received more trustworthy information about the disorders in Kishinev only on 15 April from private sources. An immediate notification from the administration of neighboring provinces (even by telegraph) about the outbreak of mass disorders would have been extremely desirable in order to take timely preventive measures in the most dangerous and densely popupulated centers in the province entrusted to me.

"Report of the Chief of the Provincial Gendarme Administration of Podolia to the Department of Police (21 April 1903)"

As an addendum to my report of 14 April (number 1273), I have the honor to report to the Department of Police that, owing to rumors about preparations for anti-Jewish disorders in Balta district, I personally traveled to the towns of Rybnits and Balta. Thanks to timely measures that were adopted, the day when the disorders were expected remained absolutely peaceful. Only on 18 April, in the Jewish colony (3.21 kilometers) from the village of Boronkovo in Balta district, ten peasant lads who were driving cattle began to assault Jews (but did not rob them) and said that "the Sovereign permits the beating of Jews." They were immediately arrested by the village authorities, who came quickly from the village of Boronkovo.

Nevertheless, the public mood remains extremely tense — the situation is further aggravated by the appearance of suspicious people who apparently fled from Kishinev after the disorders [there]. I have given instructions to arrest these people. However, the Jews are in a state of panicky terror: they greatly exaggerate the danger and attach significance to every trivial threat by the peasants and every foolish rumor.[3] Such was the case in the town of Okno, where the peasants did not manifest any hostility toward the local Jewish population. The anxiety of the Jews was absolutely groundless. The areas that do pose some danger of possible disorders are the towns of Balta (the site of an enormous fair on 25 May) and Bogopol (situated on the border of three provinces, it is the site where landowners and lessees hire migrant workers on 9 May). Up to ten thousand people will gather in Bogopol, and I have reported to the governor personally about this.

NOTES

1. [This file contains dozens of secret reports about pogroms all over the small villages and towns of Bessarabia in response to the pogrom epicenter in Kishinev (6–7 April 1903).]

2. [The text uses the term *lipovan*, used to describe the priestly (Filippovtsy) subgroup of Old Believers. The Old Believers (officially called *raskol'niki*, meaning schismatics and self-described as *staroobriadtsy*, meaning old ritualists) were religious dissenters who rejected the Orthodox Church reforms of the mid-seventeenth century. They subsequently divided into two groups, the "priestless"

(the more radical branch, which denied any hierarchy or sacraments and also tended to regard the tsar as the Antichrist) and the "priestly" (who first relied on renegade priests but later created their own hierarchy with regular clergy, recognized sacraments, and tended to be less politically radical). The *lipovan* belong to the priestly subgroup; they are now found today mostly in Moldava and other areas outside the former Soviet Union.]

3. [A police report from Kiev (28 April 1903) showed how Christians manipulated the rumors of ritual murder. One peasant girl, Mariia Kondratenkova, who served the Jewish family of Elia and Rivka Shtobskii, reported that she left her healthy six-month-old infant in the house only to find him dead when she returned. She accused the Jewish head of the household (the husband) of killing the infant and spread rumors about this among peasants in their town of Tsybulev (GARF, f. 102, 3 d-vo, g. 1903, d. 874, ll. 76–77).]

[170]

Reports of Armed Jewish Self-Defense Groups in Rostov-na-Donu (1903)

GARF, f. 102, 3 d-vo, g. 1903, d. 874, ll. 66–68.

"Secret Report of the Chief of the Gendarme Administration of the Don Region to the Department of Police (27 April 1903)"

I am sending a copy of a letter dated 13 April (enclosed herewith) that I received from Dr. Gintsburg (from Rostov-na-Donu), which he transmitted to the local police chief. I have the honor to inform the Department of Police that, according to reports, a considerable number of such letters have been sent from Kishinev to other Jews in the town of Rostov-na-Donu and that the Jewish population is extremely alarmed by rumors of possible anti-Jewish disorders. The local rabbi, for example, came to the police chief for advice: should not a Jewish delegation request the Cossack ataman of the Don troops to dispatch a company of Cossacks, serving near the Novo-Cherkasska Camp, to Rostov (at the Jews' expense). Masses of Jews are appealing to me with requests for permission to bear firearms. Rumor has it (and there is some basis for it) that the Jews are stocking up on weapons, and that they intend to form their own armed detachments for the sole purpose of defending themselves in the event of a pogrom.[1] The police are calming down the Jews as much as possible, explaining that they guarantee the public order through the adoption of measures and the presence of military units in Rostov.

"Copy of a Letter Appended to the Previous Document: 'Macedonians in Kishinev' (13 April 1903)"

We are all well and all our belongings are intact. The Jewish calamity in Kishinev defies description. The greatest misfortune has befallen us Jews—an unfortunate, solitary people.

The calamity took place as follows. At 12:00 p.m., an organized gang began to walk up and down through the entire Jewish quarter and the outskirts of the town, smashing the glass of the upper and lower floors with long sticks and rocks. They designated and marked only Jewish houses, which they destroyed in this way: they utterly demolished all the property—from the most important to trivial. The trees, such as the acacias, as well as the roads and roofs, were covered with down fluff [from destroyed down bedding]. All the streets were crammed with fragments of expensive furniture, piano keys, broken pieces of machines, metal cash boxes, pieces of silk, velvet, fur, curtains, hats, books, plates, and such utensils.

Almost all the stores in town were destroyed and their goods plundered, so that absolutely nothing valuable remained, not even the furniture. Not only did stores with metal bars and window-front shop shutters suffer; in many wine cellars, they poured [out] wine [worth] tens of thousands of rubles. The general loss reached tens of millions of rubles.

The leaders and organizers of these "Albanians" [Moldavans] were the local Russian intelligentsia, such as [Pavolachi] Krushevan and his colleagues: the notary Pisarevskii, Dr. Sinadino, the engineer-technologist Belinskii,

a few elected members of the *zemstvo*, and other privileged individuals. Moreover, students, pupils at the classical and nonclassical gymnasiums, and others also participated.

Regarding victims, to date approximately one hundred mutilated corpses have been found. It is beyond comprehension how such brutalities could have been perpetrated against people: some had their hands and feet severed, ears cut off, nails driven into the eyes, stakes plunged into the mouth. A girl's braids were torn off. A five-year-old girl had her legs ripped off, skull smashed, and tongue cut out. They split open the stomach of one person, yanked out the innards, and stuffed the corpse with feathers and the like. There were mass atrocities and more than 600 injured, of whom 200 were seriously wounded and were taken to the hospital to live out their final days and hours. The remainder had minor injuries.

No matter what street you walk on, you meet people with bandages on their arms, heads, and legs. Many women endured miscarriages and rape. Materially, they deprived many individuals of their cash by breaking into metal registers: from one they took 25,000 rubles and many valuables, from another 18,000 rubles, and from a third 2,050 rubles, and the rest amounted to smaller sums. The total adds up to an immense sum. The Feld'shteins suffered a loss of 15,000 rubles and barely escaped with their lives. Their entire store is full of glass and not a single whole bottle remains; afraid to go home, they are now living with the gendarme Colonel. Brk [*sic*] was left destitute. They cut down Dublinskii's garden and destroyed two buildings. Shvatsman, Perl'shuter, the Gal'perins, and a few wealthy people were left unharmed. They also stole 18,000 rubles from Shelzinger; his family has had no choice but to become vagrants.

Words cannot describe the tragedies that so suddenly befell our unfortunate people. On many streets they walk on down fluff as if it were snow. All the small wooden shops and stalls were overturned and looted. The shops left intact are closed and offer no goods [for sale]. Approximately 18,000 (of the victims) need food. The bakeries are still not working. The precious Torahs and holy books were torn to pieces. For the time being, only 150,000 rubles in donations have come to the Jewish Committee to help the Jewish victims.

The entire pogrom continued for a day and a half. Martial law was announced only on the second day at dawn; that was followed by an intensified guard in the entire town and outskirts. Until then, the police and military patrols looted along with the mob, and all this was encouraged by the antisemitic intelligentsia. The police asked the Jews not to denounce them to the chief procurator, who was responsible for the most important cases in the criminal section and who came from the Odessa Provincial Court. Next the director of the Department of Police arrived, who is conducting an energetic investigation. The police and patrols did not allow the Jews to defend themselves and if the latter had not meddled in this calamity, then it would not have reached such proportions.

The director [of the Department of Police] invited ten thieves from prison and asked them: Is it possible that they wanted to massacre all the Jews? They replied that the police ordered them to act in this way. One must suppose that they prepared for this pogrom for a few months because the entire town was drawn into the atrocities simultaneously with too much precision. The antisemites prepared the agenda.

All the Russian hotels are full of Jewish families in hiding and take sixty kopecks for a bottle of beer. Clearly, they are getting by on other vital supplies; [the hotels] charge two rubles a day for the most modest things.

The men and women in the mob who were not arrested dress up fashionably in the looted clothes and female adornments. One town policeman took a silver cigar case, silver watches, and bracelets. Such impertinence: "He did not take according to his rank." A few policemen were arrested for possessing [stolen] valuables. We were saved thanks to a priest who lives in the courtyard and is head of the house. For entire days we have been gone to look at the heartbreaking sights. For two days we did not sleep or eat but lived only amidst the din, the whistling of the mobs, the wails of victims—in other words, we were between a hammer and an anvil. Now, everything is calm.

NOTE

1. [On 3 May 1903 the head of the Poltava gendarme administration reported that the Jews in Pereiaslavl had organized armed self-defense groups against pogroms and "bought sixty-three revolvers at the stores of the merchants Kotelnikov and Marchenko" (GARF, f. 102, 3 d-vo, g. 1903, d. 874, l. 98).]

Jews in the Revolutionary Movement

[171]

Narodnaia Volia: Gesia Gel'fman's Trial in the Assassination of Alexander II (1881)

1 marta 1881 goda. Po neizdannym materialam (Petrograd: Izdatel'stvo "Byloe," 1918), 298–300.

*"First Testimony of Gesia Gel'fman
(3 March 1881)"*

My name is Gesia Mironova Gel'fman. I am twenty-six years old, of the Jewish confession. I am a townswoman from Mozyr, Minsk province, unmarried.

None of the questions pertain personally to me. I do not wish to answer questions about the person who shot himself tonight in the apartment where I was arrested and about the items found in this apartment. The photograph that you are showing me is really me.

*"Testimony of Gesia Gel'fman
(5 March 1881)"*

I do not know the individual whom you are showing me now (the townsman Nikolai Ivanovich Rysakov was shown to her). I acknowledge that I belong to the Russian Socialist Revolutionary Party, the program of the People's Will. I decline to provide any answers about my revolutionary activities and about my life and pursuits in St. Petersburg in general. I did not have and do not have any acquaintances — either in the apartments or in the different commercial establishments — on Malaia Sadovaia Street in St. Petersburg. I do not wish to answer the question of whether I knew about the existence of this plot.

*"Testimony of Gesia Gel'fman
(6 March 1881)"*

On 6 March 1881, the court investigator I. F. Knirim questioned the accused, named below, in an especially important case before the St. Petersburg District Court: My name is Gesia Mironovna Gel'fman, twenty-six years old, of the Jewish faith, a townswoman from Mozyr, single. I was educated in Kiev where I passed the midwifery course at St. Vladimir University. I was tried in a political case and sentenced in 1877 to a worker's home for two years by a resolution of the special office of the State Senate. I do not consider myself guilty of complicity in the explosion that took place on 1 March 1881 on the embankment of Ekaterininskii Canal, which resulted in the death and injury to the health of a few private individuals. I do not know Rysakov. They indeed found two jars of dynamite in my apartment, and I knew that this was dynamite. I decline to testify where these jars with dynamite came from. I decline to give any answers regarding the apartment and the person who shot himself there. Someone was seriously injured from the blast and died in the hospital. I do not know where he lived under the name El'nikov. "Special" should be crossed out. The amended "1877" is correct.

GESIA GELFMAN.

COURT INVESTIGATOR, KNIRIM.

"Reply of Gesia Gelf'man to the Testimony of the Yard Man (12 March 1881)"[1]

On 6 or 7 September 1880, I rented apartment number 25 in building number 27/1 on Troitskii Lane under the name of the Moscow townsman Andrei Ivanovich Nikolaev.[2] Previously, I lived for a few days in a furnished room (apartment 4 in building number 55/1 (I think) on the corner of Nevskii [Prospect] and Novaia Street. However, I decline to say where I lived in St. Petersburg previously. I was registered at the furnished rooms as Elizaveta Alekseevna Nikolaeva, as I am called by my husband, Andrei Ivanov, who lives with me in one room. When I rented the apartment at 27/1 Troitskii Lane, I gave my name as Nikolaeva and it was furnished. I do not know if it was old or new furniture because Nikolaev brought it. We did not have servants; I bought and prepared the food myself. I do not wish to name the person who lives with me under the name of my husband Andrei Ivanov Nikolaev. In the apartment with us were Zheliabov, Perovskaia, and someone else (the picture of the dead person is now being shown to me) whose surname I know but decline to say. [She was shown the picture of the corpse of the person who died from wounds on 1 March in the hospital]. I will say only that I knew this individual, also under the name Mikhail Ivanovich and under the nickname "Kotik." There were other people at our place but I decline to say who they were. My lover (or cohabitant), Nikolaev, left at the beginning of February from number 27/1 Troitskii Lane for a destination un-known to me. He "was summoned for some matter." I moved to apartment number 5, house number 5 on Telezhnaia Street, in the second half of February together with the person who also called himself my husband, Fesenko-Navrotskii. The man who calls himself Fesenko-Navrotskii is not the same person who calls himself Andrei Ivanovich Nikolaev. At the present time, I can say that Nikolai Alekseevich Sablin lived with me under the name Fesenko-Navrotskii. As is well known by now, I lived under the name of his wife Elena Grigor'evna Sablin. Nikolai Rysakov was never at my apartment at 27/1 Troitskii Lane. Nikolaev and I had a printing press for *Rabochaia gazeta* [The worker's newspaper] in this apartment. I decline to name the person in charge of the literary part of this newspaper or those who worked for this press. As for myself and Nikolaev, I can only say that, since I was familiar with typesetting, I was the typesetter and Nikolaev helped. Zheliabov, Perovskaia, and Kotik did not participate personally in printing the newspaper. I decline to say anything about their work in relation to the distribution of this newspaper except that as far as I know, Zheliabov was a contributor to the newspaper. Only the first issue of the newspaper and the *Program of the Worker's Party of Narodnaia Volia* were printed in my apartment, where the press was located. Two weeks before I left this apartment (shortly after the departure of Nikolaev), all the equipment belonging to the printing press that published the newspaper and program was removed from my apartment. After I moved from the apartment where we had printed the newspaper and program, I began to buy cardboard, which I used to make typographic boxes. As for my lover Nikolaev, I said that he served somewhere, but I do not remember where. I decline to add anything to this present testimony except that the apartment at 27/1 Troitskii Lane was clandestine.

"Testimony of Gesia Gel'fman (8 March 1881)"

I decline to answer the questions posed to me. As to the question whether I knew about the plot from the cheese store on Malaia Sadovaia Street in St. Petersburg, I declare that I did not participate in this plot. However, I decline to answer the question whether I knew about the existence of this plot.

"Statement of Gesia Gel'fman (after the Death Sentence on 30 March 1881)"

In view of the sentence that the Special Office of the Senate passed regarding me, I consider it a moral duty to announce that I am in my fourth month of pregnancy. I entrust this statement to the barrister Avgust Antonovich Gerke.[3]

NOTES

1. [Gesia Gel'fman was tried for the assassination of Tsar Alexander II on 1 March 1881. The yardman, Usman Gultov, testified that Gelf'man lived in the same house under the surname Nikolaeva with Makar Teterk (surname, Nikolaev).]

2. [Nikolaev was in fact another prominent populist revolutionary, Nikolai Sablin (1849–81), who shot himself just as the police were breaking into the apartment — presumably to avoid revealing information during interrogation.]

3. [Her death sentence was changed to hard labor for life on 2 July 1881; under the law of the time, capital punishment was prohibited for pregnant women because of the innocence of the fetus. Gel'fman gave birth in prison, but the infant was taken from her on 25 January 1882 and placed in an orphanage, where he died shortly afterward. Gel'fman, denied proper medical attention before and after the birth, died from an infection of the peritoneum on 1 February 1882.]

[172]

The Social Democratic Workers' Party (Bund): Police Files on Mariia (Manya) Vul'fovna Vil'bushevich

"Anonymous Denunciation[1] of Mariia (Manya) Vil'bushevich[2] [Postmark of 13 January 1898 on the Envelope]"

GARF, f. 102, Osobyi odel,

I have the honor of bringing to your attention the fact that a certain Mariia (Manya) Vil'bushevich is currently living in Minsk. She resides with her brother, the engineer Vil'bushevich on Zakhar'ev Street, in the building owned by Shapiro. She has close ties to foreign socialists. Recently, she took a whole suitcase of proclamations to Grodno, propagandizing [the idea of] assassinating

the Sovereign. She is always very circumspect and cunning; even her relatives are unaware of her activities. A search of her residence will not turn up a single paper. She wants to travel soon to Petersburg with extremely dangerous intentions. She gives the impression of being a naive girl, but this is simply an outward ruse to divert attention. My advice is that you arrest her as soon as possible, so that she does not slip away and the consequences are tragic.

As a friend of the fatherland and the Sovereign and as someone who hates socialists, I decided to bring all this to your notice so that [you can] destroy this evil at its roots once it is in your hands. I have fulfilled my duty.

RESPECTFULLY, "THE UNKNOWN"

"Second Anonymous Letter to the Minsk Gendarme Administration [Postmark of 18 January 1898 on the Envelope]"

GARF, f. 102, Osobyi otdel, g. 1898, d. 103, l. 6a–6a ob.

MOST HONORABLE COLONEL!

I have already had the honor of reporting to you about the presence here of Mariia (Manya) Vil'bushevich. I now wish to bring to your attention the fact that today she is supposed to receive from Zurich a program for action on how to attack the Sovereign. This program was prepared in Zurich by a large secret society. If her room is thoroughly searched tomorrow, it will be possible to catch her.

YOUR DEVOTED FRIEND,
"THE UNKNOWN"

"Secret Report of the Chief of the Minsk Gendarme Administration: Secret (22 January 1898)"

GARF, f. 102, Osobyi otdel, g. 1898, d. 103, l.5.

I have the honor to submit the many letters received today through the city post office pertaining to Manya Vil'bushevich and to add that today the Minsk Post Office received mail for the office of Zalkind and Vil'bushevich, two opened and one sealed letter from abroad. All the letters pertained to their business affairs.[3]

"Secret Supplemental Report of the Chief of the Minsk Gendarme Administration: (13 February 1898)"

GARF, f. 102, Osobyi otdel, g. 1898, d. 103, l. 4.

In the addendum to my reports of 18 January (number 134) and 22 January (number 159) about Mariia Vil'bushevich, I have the honor to report to the Department of Police that a careful surveillance revealed nothing objectionable about her. She works in her brother's office, sometimes goes strolling with someone, and in the evenings very often goes to the theater with the Zalkind family. The surveillance on her has been terminated.

"Appeal: The General Jewish Workers' Union in Russia and Poland"[4]

GARF, f. 102, Osobyi otdel, g. 1898, d. 5, ch. 16, l. 4.

We demand: equal rights for all nations in general and the abolition of the shameful exceptional laws for Jews in particular. We demand: freedom to strike, [freedom] of assembly, freedom of press and speech. We demand: a parliament, to which the people would send its representatives, elected on the basis of elections that are universal (equal for all), open, and secret.

"Secret Report[5] on Mariia Vil'bushevich from the St. Petersburg Gendarme Chief (9 October 1898)"

GARF, f. 102, OO, d. 103, g. 1898, ll. 10–11 ob.

Apropos of the letter from the Imperial Court Commandant of 10 June of this year [1898], number 303, to the Director of the Department of Police, I have the honor to report the following:

In January of this year, the head of the Minsk Gendarme Administration received a letter on Mariia Vil'bushevich's ties to socialists abroad and on the concealment of proclamations in her trunk propagandizing an assassination of the Emperor. The surveillance established over Mariia Vil'bushevich in Minsk revealed nothing objectionable. She worked in her brother's office and sometimes went out strolling with him, and in the evenings frequently went to the theater with the Zalkind family. An examination at the Minsk Post Office of correspondence addressed to Zalkind and Vil'bushevich's firm showed that all the letters pertained to business matters.

In the beginning of May, the chief city administrator of St. Petersburg received the same kind of letter and with the same kind of signature. Secret surveillance was established to determine Mariia Vil'bushevich's activities and relations in St. Petersburg; information was also obtained through police agents. All this revealed the following:

Vilbushevich, Mariia (Manya) Vul'fovna is the daughter of a Grodno townsman; nineteen years old. From the earliest years, she was sickly and had a hysterical temperament,[6] a circumstance that served to prevent her matriculation in a gymnasium. Two years ago she struck her head on the corner of a photographic display case, which intensified her illness, and later she began to be subjected to hysterical attacks. At the beginning of this year, while living with her brother, the engineer Vil'bushevich in Minsk, on two occasions she noticed a person on the street, similar to an insane man, who was following her with feverish attention. Her sister Anna Vul'fovna Tanenbaum, who lives with her husband (an engineer) in St. Petersburg at number 4 Kabinet Street, received word from her relatives about the deterioration in Maria Vil'bushevich's health and, loving the latter very much, decided to invite her to their home in St. Petersburg so that she could consult a local doctor of psychiatry, [I. P.] Merzheevskii.[7] As Mariia Vil'bushevich sat down in the train for Petersburg, she immediately noticed that same person who had followed [her] with feverish attention in Minsk was sitting in the same railway car. During the trip he tried to talk to her, but she responded unwillingly and feared him greatly, thinking that he was a plainclothes detective. Moreover, he told her that he could hypnotize her and learn her thoughts. This conversation upset Vil'bushevich deeply; by the time she arrived at her sister's, she was completely sick. The sister, Anna Tanenbaum, soon took her to the psychiatrist Merzheevskii, who began to treat her.

During Mariia Vil'bushevich's stay in Petersburg, Tanenbaum received a letter written (as it turned out) in the same hand as the letters to the head of the Minsk Gendarme Administration and the St. Petersburg chief city official. In this letter, the author proposed to Mariia Vil'bushevich that she immediately leave Petersburg, and also declared that she is being closely followed; the letter was signed "Your collocutor on the railway coach." This letter greatly upset Mariia Vil'bushevich; she then had a prolonged hysterical attack.

Her brother-in-law, Abram Tanenbaum, began to interrogate her and to implore her to confess whether she was acquainted with some suspect people in Minsk. But Mariia Vil'bushevich tearfully swore to him that there had never been anything of the sort. Both her sister and relatives know this girl to be completely open, incapable of hiding anything.

Tanenbaum immediately went to the office of the chief city official of Petersburg and requested permission for Mariia Vil'bushevich to remain in Petersburg until 15 June (on the basis of treatment by Dr. Merzheevskii). As for the letter, engineer Tanenbaum sent it to Mariia Vil'bushevich's parents, explaining to them its influence on Vil'bushevich.

Fearing new meetings between Mariia Vil'bushevich and the person mentioned above, Tanenbaum stopped letting her go out alone, but only in the company of her sister Anna or a relative, which included the students Lapin, Aleksandr Iakovlev (son of a Grodno merchant), and Burdo and Khaim Leibovich (also Grodno townsmen). The [police] have no files on these [individuals] and have detected nothing objectionable about them. On 11 June, Tanenbaun escorted Mariia Vil'bushevich (who had recovered significantly from treatments by the psychiatrist Merzheevskii) to her parents in Grodno, where she is at the present time.

A comparison of the handwriting of all the letters shows that they are written by the same person, and two of them (addressed to the emperor and the Petersburg chief city official) are signed with the surname "Trubovin," who in fact is not to be found in Petersburg.

On the basis of these facts, in all probability, one can presume that the person who wrote these letters is the same person who followed Mariia Vil'bushevich in the railway car and in Minsk, that he is mentally ill, and that for some reason he imagined Mariia Vil'bushevich to be a criminal and deemed it his duty to inform state authorities about this and continued to follow her himself.

"Two Surveillance Reports [of the Secret Police]: December 1899–February 1900"

GARF, f. 102, Osobyi otdel, g. 1898, d. 5, ch. 16, 1-B, ll. 33 ob, 37 ob.

At 8:30 in the evening, Shakhnovich left the workshop with Findyeler (who lives in house number 9), [went] along Zakhar'ev Street to the apartment of engineer mechanic Vil'bushevich, and the sister of the latter (daughter of a merchant in Grodno), Mariia Vladimirova Vil'bushevich ("Gray Collar"[8]). [. . .]

Mariia Vil'bushevich left at 7 p.m. from Petropavlovskaia Street with an unknown worker and eight female workshop employees. They went to number 20, Iur'ev Street, to the Passazh Hall where Dr. Gratsioanov delivered a lecture on coal.

"Telegram from the Chief of the Minsk Gendarme Administration (March 1900)"

GARF, f. 102, 7-oe deloproizvodstvo, g. 1900, d. 111, l. 52.

Searches were conducted at thirty [residences]; twenty people [were] arrested. A cursory examination at the residence of Girsh Shakhnovich and Borukh revealed illegal brochures (four copies) and compromising correspondence. Grodno has been telegraphed to arrest Mariia Vil'bushevich.

"Report of the Grodno Police to the Chief of the Grodno Gendarme Administration (7 March 1900)"

GARF, f. 102, 7-oe deloproizvodstvo, g. 1900, d. 111, l. 58.

I have the honor of informing the Department of Police that, as a consequence of the [the report of] the head of the Minsk Provincial Gendarme Administration (6 March), today [. . .], on the basis of the Statute of State Security, Mariia Vol'fovna Vil'bushevich was searched, arrested, and sent under the con-

voy of two junior officers to be placed under the control of the chief of the Minsk Provincial Gendarme Administration.

"Report of the Minsk Gendarme Chief (25 March 1900)"

GARF, f. 102, 7-oe deloproizvodstvo, g. 1900, d. 111, l. 75.

In her activity, Mariia Vil'bushevich is characterized by the fact that she engages in giving instruction to workers. Thus, having become acquainted with Izrail Geriu (an employee in the office of the aforementioned engineers), she urged him to study; in his opinion, this merits attention.

"Deposition of Berta Borisovna Bernshtein (12 December 1900)"

GARF, f. 102, Osobyi otdel, g. 1898, d. 5, ch. 16, 1-B, l. 71 ob.

I was at Girsh Shakhnovich's; Mariia Vil'bushevich came there and invited me to a meeting of propagandists, which was supposed to discuss the question of uniformity in propagandists' work with their groups. [. . .] This meeting decided to divide the workers into three categories. Category one was "instructional"—that is, one was to engage only in teaching literacy in Russian. Category two consists of workers with whom propagandists have already worked; this activity was first to focus on political economy but then involve reading illegal books such as Dickstein's *How Do Various People Support Themselves*. Category three are workers who should start by reading *The Erfurt Program* and then the *Manifesto of the Communist Party*. However, one cannot regard this question as conclusively settled because only eight, not all, propagandists came to the meeting.

NOTES

1. [The Gendarme Chief of Minsk forwarded this anonymous denunciation to the Department of Police in Moscow on 18 January 1898.]

2. [Mariia (Manya) Vil'bushevich (1879–1961) became an active member in the Jewish workers' movement, later participated in the "police unions"

of Sergei Zubatov, then lived in Italy for several years. She eventually moved to Palestine, where she became involved in the first militarized Jewish political movements. She died in Tel-Aviv in 1961.]

3. [An anonymous denunciation to the Department of Police reports that Vil'bushevich lives on Zakhar'evskaia Street together with Zalkind, who was already under police surveillance. At this address Vil'bushevich and Zalkind jointly opened an agency to establish mechanized factories.]

4. [This appeal was included next to a report from Minsk that "printed Jewish proclamations" had been disseminated around town, such as one titled "Appeal to the Male and Female Employees of Minsk."]

5. [The Imperial Court Commandant at Tsarskoe Selo transmitted a letter on 6 October 1898 from a certain Trobuvin to the emperor (not included in the archival file) that triggered this report on Mariia Vil'bushevich.]

6. [The medical establishment routinely diagnosed and treated "female hysteria" in nineteenth-century Russia and Europe more generally. See Mark S. Micale, *Approaching Hysteria: Disease and Its Interpretations* (Princeton: Princeton University Press, 1995).]

7. [Ivan Pavlovich Merzheevskii (1838–1908) was a prominent, internationally known psychiatrist in St. Petersburg at the time.]

8. [According to an secret police agent in Minsk, Mariia Vil'bushevich's underground code name was first "Zakhar'evskaia" but then changed to "Seryi Vorotnik" (Gray Collar). See GARF, f. 102, Osobyi otdel, g. 1898, d. 4, ch. 16, l. 129.]

[173]

The Jewish Independent Workers' Party and Police Unionism (1901–2)

"Report of Sergei Zubatov to the Deputy Minister of the Interior (23 June 1901)"
GARF, f. 102, Osobyi otdel, g. 1898, d. 5, ch. 16, 1-G, ll. 28–36.

At the end of last April, through the Moscow chief, I met with the Minsk gendarme chief, Nikita Vasil'evich Vasil'ev, who shares my views on the so-called workers' movement.[1] This agreement is especially good, because many of the people arrested last year are in Minsk, including Mariia Vil'bushevich, who in conversations with me agreed with my understanding of the contemporary state of the workers' movement and not only has remained faithful up to the present time, but has actively endeavored to realize it.

Colonel Vasil'ev distinguishes himself by his pure Russian initiative, intense energy, and full recognition of the seriousness of his own official position and the authority of his uniform. Since his arrival in Minsk, he has established excellent relations with the local governor, Prince [Nikolai Nikolaevich] Trubetskoi. The most recent situation has a special importance for him, for the revolutionary ferment has attracted artisans, whose relationships to their shop owners is regulated by the "Artisans' Statutes"; surveillance to ensure that the latter are observed is carried out not by the factory inspector, but by police officials, who are all under the jurisdiction of the governor. The political interests of the province demand from Colonel Vasil'ev special attention to the activities of the police in this sphere and his own direct involvement. With such an understanding of things, a metal craftsmen's strike took place this May and involved several hundred workers, who wished to limit the legal work period (in agreement with article 431 of the Artisan's Statutes) to twelve hours, in place of the current fourteen. Having learned about this [plan to strike for shorter working hours], Colonel Vasil'ev expressed his desire to meet with representatives of the metal craftsmen so that he could simultaneously invite their employers to come. A group of people who share my views (with Mariia Vil'bushevich at their head) conducted agitation for days on end until they were hoarse, and began to prove the whole usefulness of the intervention by Colonel Vasil'ev in the strike. At the same time, revolutionary agitators demonstrated such a clear grasp of their situation that their hair stood on end, and they attempted by every means possible to frighten the masses, fearing that the latter would respond to the summons by a colonel of the gendarmes (who, meanwhile, continued to send for the workers every day and invite them to appear). In the end, the workers held a meeting, elected deputies, and dispatched them for this purpose [to meet with Vasil'ev]. In the session for reconciliation in the Gendarme Administration, the entire incorrectness of the unauthorized work stoppage was explained to the workers; shop owners were informed that their demands were illegal. It was immediately proposed that the workers go back to work and that the owners introduce a legal workday. Both sides will be informed of all this by a special declaration of the governor of Minsk, Prince Trubetskoi; this declaration will be posted and in the morning work resume. As a result of such an expeditious and favorable outcome of the matter, the irreconcilable [radical] agitators tore out their hair, for they were in no condition to endure "a political slap in the face" (as they themselves put it). At the same time, the apartments of those representing peaceful tactics began to be inundated by workers, who came to talk things over and to learn about the new methods of action.

The incident described here showed how distant is the mood of the masses from being revolutionary. The workers understood that the workers' movement has nothing to do with the constitution, that they can follow their own path under any state system. There developed such a fondness for running to Colonel Vasil'ev ("for tips," in the phrase of one revolutionary) that it is almost necessary to use force to restrain them.

At the same time, after this incident the revolutionary faction of workers became contemptuous of strikes, saying: "We are not interested in the economic improvement of the masses; let the liberals be occupied with this. We need the political education of the people, and these so-called 'Vasil'ev' strikes will definitely kill the revolutionary spirit." As for revolutionary forces in Minsk, according to the information of my correspondent, at present there is absolutely no serious revolutionary leadership there, but they have a few agitators with the youth Solomon Chemerisskii at the head, who have tried in any event to exert influence on the working masses.

"Report of the Minsk Gendarme Administration (4 September 1901)"

GARF, f. 102, OO, g. 1898, d. 5, ch. 16, 1-G, l. 62–62 ob.

An underground circle has recently been formed in Minsk and identifies itself as the Jewish Independent Workers' Party. This organization has issued its own "Program" and "Letter" (in hectograph [that is, using a direct-process gelatin duplicator]); these publications are printed in parallel columns, in Russian and Yiddish. According to agents' reports, the circle is headed by a certain Mariia Vil'bushevich, who (about one year ago) was subjected to prosecution and after her release initially lived in Moscow. The main participants in the newly formed circle are local joiners and masons. This organization has purportedly even held a public meeting, under the guise of a "gathering" permitted by local authorities.

Among the revolutionary activities in Minsk, this Mariia Vil'bushevich is suspected as someone who agitates on behalf of a certain counter-revolutionary movement, which was recently evoked among the workers in accordance with the ideas of the head of the Moscow secret police [Zubatov].

"Program of the Jewish Independent Workers' Party"
GARF, f. 102, Osobyi otdel, g. 1898, d. 5, ch. 16, 1-G, ll. 63–64.

The Party Program
1. The Jewish Independent Workers' Party has the goal of raising the material and cultural level of the Jewish proletariat by means of cultural and economic organizations (both legal and illegal), to the degree this is possible. In practice, this goal amounts to the following: (a) development of broad economic organizations, treasuries, clubs, [and] associations; and (b) development of scientific and professional knowledge among the working class and rearing it for a collective life.

2. The party as a whole sets no political goals and raises political questions only to the degree that these concern the daily interests of the worker.

3. For economic and cultural work, the party unites workers of all political views as well as those without such.

4. The party's organization is democratic — that is, it is governed from below, not from above.

The Party's Views
1. No kind of theory is sufficiently powerful and incontrovertibly true that it gives its adherents the right to lead the unconscious masses to a goal that the latter do not understand.

2. At present, the Jewish working class demands bread and knowledge, and these demands should be satisfied.

3. It is criminal to sacrifice the material interests of the working class to the political objectives that, at the present time, are alien to it.

4. The worker, like every person, has the right to be the adherent of any political party he chooses, or to stand apart from every political party, and nevertheless has the right to defend his economic and cultural interests, to be an equal member of economic and cultural organizations.

5. The worker needs economic and cultural organizations as much as air and water. These should control his economic interests and provide him knowledge. They can only become such when they are a goal in themselves, and [do] not serve as the weapon of a political party, whatever it might be.

11[*sic*]. We find the contemporary situation abnormal, for economic organizations are under the control of the Bund, which is primarily political in its goals. For that reason, economic activity, so far as the Bund is concerned, is mainly a means to revolutionize the working masses. Hence, the Bund, in its economic activity, deliberately ignores many measures that are undoubtedly useful for the working masses.

When the Bund accepts a worker (who seeks only bread and knowledge) into what the worker sees as purely economic organizations, it imposes its own political views and aims on the worker — paying no heed to his psychology, preferences, and goals. The Bund does not admit into its economic organizations those workers who do not share its own views; rather, it frightens away the energetic, conservative part of the working masses because of its reputation as a political party. As a result, this practice of the Bund harms the organized masses and deals harshly with the remaining workers, who also seek union with their organized comrades.

The Bund is developing the workers in a one-sided fashion, shields them from non-

Bundist ideas, and thereby introduces a spirit of intellectual enslavement into the working masses. The Bund does not admit to the working masses intellectual forces that do not agree with its own political views. The Bund performed a great historical mission when it developed in the working masses a spirit of dissatisfaction with their economic condition. But when this was attained, and the entire working mass strove to organize, it became impossible to contain economic and cultural activity in the political vise of the Bund.

"Letter from Germany to Engineer M. Vil'bushevich 'For Sasha' (25 October 1901)"

GARF, f. 102, Osobyi otdel, g. 1898, d. 103, l. 22a–22a ob.

TO THE GENERAL [HEAD] OF THE JEWISH INDEPENDENT WORKERS' PARTY,

Your letter of 7 October was received. As for the transport of the printing press, you misunderstood me. I propose everything just as I advised you; I wanted only to have a metalworker, who could take the old cast iron from the train station (so that it would not attract attention). [A marginal note reads: "The printing press in Berlin is probably sold, but it will be possible to get another one."]

The fund of the Free Russian Press gave a negative reply, which I sent to you in a letter to B. I send the answers of the PPS [Polish Socialist Party] to the following questions:

1. Can one print and transport Yiddish brochures and proclamations, and on what topic? [The answer in the margin is: "Yes."]

2. Can one transport from various cities abroad into Russia literature, typefaces, and printing presses? [Answer: "Yes."]

3. Can one obtain a printing press 23 x 16, and at what price? [Answer: "Yes."]

4. If not, can you give the address of people engaged in contraband? [Answer: "No." Marginal note: "We are quarrelling with the Bund. The answer is satisfactory, as you see."]

"Memorandum of Sergei Zubatov to the Deputy Minister of Internal Affairs (18 October 1901)"

GARF, f. 102, Osobyi otdel, g. 1898, d. 5, ch. 16, 1-G, ll. 74–75.

I have received the following report from Minsk:[2] "Everything has worked out for us and has progressed so far that I am probably no longer even needed. The meetings of the joiners are going splendidly. [. . .] People are positive, interested, and have begun to work. Permission was given to all the artisans in Minsk to meet in private apartments (it only being necessary to report to the police precinct a few hours in advance that there will be a meeting in such a place). On Saturday, 20 October, a literary evening for workers is permitted in the auditorium Passazh, where 10,000 workers are expected. The program is interesting—with speeches and a workers' choir. In addition, a commission of workers has been given the duty of supervising the [implementation of] the twelve-hour workday and, in the event of infractions, of informing the police so that it can be officially registered. Colonel Vasil'ev surpasses even himself. I simply did not recognize him. He has, to an astonishing degree, grasped the spirit of the movement and is extremely consistent [in his actions]. In a word, a most essential and active person. The public has been so well prepared that it has abandoned all prejudices; in the gentlest possible way, it has come to terms with the authorities and has totally forgotten the antipathy it nourished toward the state not so long ago. The attitude toward our group has undergone a radical change. Shouts of "down with them" are no longer to be heard. The masons are almost entirely in our camp; the bookbinders too. The *slesari* [metal craftsmen] with their whole hearts, half the joiners and half the shop clerks, almost all the tinsmiths. We expected that the campaign would ferment, become excited, roar, turn around, and return entirely ours. And that is what happened.

Now people regard the Independent Jewish Workers' Party as a real force. All across the northwestern area the most amazing stories are making their rounds. Many come here to see if it is true; indeed, many come gnashing their teeth, some with an entire ocean of doubts. The Bund works very zealously. New forces came from somewhere and, instead of remaining silent, they are speaking up. The democratic intelligentsia is filled with malice, but this is almost harmless for our movement; we react quite calmly toward all this. Our sole strength is found in legalization and the press. I shall not conceal the fact that at one point we were in an onerous, painful condition; in our hearts we often cursed the cause we had begun. Both "ours" and "theirs" reached a stage of insane rage and got into street fights. Brother rose against brother; and with a blind rage poisoned each other's life. The Bund launched terrible espionage in order to determine what we are doing; it even reached the point of provocations. In a word, there was a filthy garbage pit instead of ideas, hatred instead of peace and love, confusion and mental chaos instead of lucid thinking; for many sensitive nerves that was terribly harmful. But now everything has calmed down. People have come to their senses, and the stormy sea became calm again."

"Memorandum of Sergei Zubatov, 'Report from Minsk,' to the Deputy Minister of Internal Affairs (24 October 1901)"

I received this report [from Minsk]:[3] "On Saturday, October 20, the workers' evening that I mentioned earlier took place—that is, a holiday of our independent party. There were about 1,600 workers, and the mass of democratic intelligentsia set many minds aflame. The Bundists found themselves in a terribly unpleasant situation. They conducted propaganda and agitation against this evening for a whole week preceeding this holiday. Some reached the point of fanaticism: they secretly gathered in apartments and ceremoniously burned tickets that they had bought for the evening; some bought up tickets and publicly tore them up at teashops. The [Bund] committee deliberately called for assemblies and meetings that evening in all their workshops. They disseminated rumors among the masses that the five-kopeck pieces from the sale of tickets were put at the disposal of Colonel Vasil'ev. Organized workers burned with a thirst for vengeance against these legalizers and destroyers. They also organized attacks on me—and not without effect. They wanted to give a thrashing to two girls, Bund members, who had participated in the [workers'] choir. In a word, they did everything possible and impossible to restrain the people. But nothing worked. There were horrendous scenes at the front door. The unfortunate policemen were exhausted from the pressure of the public, which wanted to enter, no matter what. A crowd of one thousand people stood around the doors in the hope that perhaps they could somehow get in. Those who attended the evening felt themselves free and acted free; despite this, no one exceeded the limits of the permissible. Excellent speeches were delivered; in the end, the result was a total triumph of legalization. Midway through the evening, Colonel Vasil'ev and the city's chief of police came, but they were sufficiently tactful so as not to enter the auditorium; they only spoke with me in a dressing room and requested that we behave properly, and ordered the police officers not to intrude. The holiday bore enormous significance for agitation that was difficult to expect. Next Saturday (27 October) meetings and talks are being organized for all artisans. Read the next issue of *Budushchnost'* [The future], the article about the joiners' club; it is very interesting. If only the government does not become frightened and take back what it has given, it will make the most enormous turning point for all Russia. In my opinion, what is now needed is a congress of gendarme officers, where they would receive the requisite instruction on how to conduct themselves with respect to the economic movement, especially during a strike."

"Proclamation of the Jewish Independent Workers' Party (4 June 1902)"

GARF, f. 102, OO, g. 1898, d. 5, ch. 16, 1-D, l. 74–74 ob.[4]

To all Jewish male and female shop clerks! The governor has rejected the request to close all shops at 9 p.m. In addition, police officers collected from many shop clerks a signed statement swearing that they agreed to sit in their shops until 11 p.m. [. . .] We must call a strike because we see clearly that no one wants to help us; therefore we must help ourselves — through force and unity, through our own struggle.[5]

NOTES

1. [The Independent Jewish Workers' Party (Evreiskaia Nezavisimaia Rabochaia Partiia) was created in the summer of 1901 in Minsk by former members of the Bund such as Mariia Vil'bushevich — who became the party's leader — at the initiative of Sergei Zubatov, who sought to create "police unions" as a way to channel the workers' movement in a monarchist direction (see Jeremiah Schneiderman, *Sergei Zubatov and Revolutionary Marxism: The Struggle for the Working Class in Tsarist Russia* (Ithaca, NY: 1976). For differences between the Bund and the Independent Jewish Worker's Party, see the latter's program below, which emphasized culture and education — in contrast to the Bund, which had shifted to political propaganda. Moreover, while the Bund

shunned Zionism, some members of the Independent Jewish Worker's Party, including Vil'bushevich, supported Zionist goals. Vil'bushevich even obtained legal permission to hold the Second All-Russian Conference of Zionists in Minsk in 1902 (see "Everiskaia nezavisimaia rabochaia partiia," in *Kratkaia evreiskaia entsiklopediia* ed. Itshak Oren, et. al. (Jerusalem: Keter, 1994), 2:414–16).]

2. [This report is obviously from someone in Vil'bushevich's circle and most probably from Vil'bushevich herself.]

3. [The report was most likely from Mariia Vil'bushevich.]

4. [The proclamation was translated from Yiddish into Russian for Sergei Zubatov.]

5. [Clearly, the enthusiasm about police unionism had given way to disillusionment. By 13 December 1902, the secret police reported growing activism of former police unionists and described the appearance of a proclamation "for the cessation of trade at 9 p.m., with an appeal to workers for a struggle against the government." The proclamation also instructed "workers who are planning to participate in the demonstrations to bring stones to throw at the police if they are detained or if the demonstrators meet with barriers on their way down Zakhar'ev and Governor Streets." The report stated that there was a demonstration planned for December 14: "The purpose of these disorders is to lift the spirit of illegal parties and a desire to claim for themselves success — which, in their opinion, the Party of Independents [the Jewish Independent Workers' Party] had attained" (GARF, f. 102, Osobyi otdel O, g. 1898, d. 5, ch. 16, 1-D, l. 133).]

A Female Socialist Revolutionary Terrorist:
The Memoirs of Mariia (Mania) Shkol'nik[1]

Mariia Markovna Shkol'nik, The Life
of a Former Female Terrorist

Mariia Markovna Shkol'nik, *Zhizn' byvshei terroristki*
(Moscow: Izdatel'stvo vsesoiuznogo obshchestva
politkatorzhan i ssy'lno-polselentsev, 1930), 31–88.

CHAPTER 2

[. . .] News that Mania, the daughter of Mor-dukh, was going to Odessa spread throughout the village like lightning. Our house was always filled with women. My mother showed them a long brown dress — my first long dress (sewn for this occasion) and three pillows. The three pillows and featherbed were essential components of the dowry for Jewish girls. "But she is still too young," my mother said to every visitor. "Who knows? Perhaps she may not want to return home soon; she will grow up and find her own happiness: the city is large."

The train left at 4:00 p.m. but I was ready by early morning. I wore my new brown dress and wove a red ribbon into my hair. The three pillows and a few coarse towels were the work of my mother; a piece of homespun linen was packed in a large suitcase, and my preparations were completed. With a heavy heart, I bid farewell to the fields and forest, to every corner, shrub, and path. "Will I see you see again?" I thought, walking in the green meadow. Everyone came to the station in Smorgon to bid me farewell: my parents, brothers, sisters, neighbors, even strangers. Hanna also came and brought me a letter addressed to one of her friends in Odessa. Bidding me farewell, father said to me: "I believe you will be happy, Manya." Mother cried and embraced me for a long time. My older brother Iokhim, who had come home on leave

(he was serving in the army) gave me his last fifty kopecks. At last the third bell sounded and the train started slowly, and soon everything disappeared in a cloud of smoke. Seeing only the strangers around me, I sat in the corner and began to bawl loudly.

On the third day, I arrived in Odessa. When I exited the station and saw the long line of coachmen with shiny peaks on their caps, my heart was full of joy: "How beautifully they are all dressed here," I thought. I went up to one of them and said: "Could you please take me to my uncle, Mr. Shkol'nik?" "Of course, young lady," he replied, casting a sidelong glance at me. "Give me his address." I was very surprised that he did not know where my uncle lived. I took a piece of paper out of my dress pocket and held it out to him. "Very well, young lady," and with a motion of the hand, invited me to sit in his carriage. When we began moving, he asked where I had come from. I told him why I had come to Odessa; sitting sideways, he listened to me and nodded his head approvingly.

After a long trip, we stopped in front of an old brick building. "Here is where your uncle lives," said the coachman. Disappointed, I looked at the dirty house, damaged by storms. As I learned later, my uncle lived in the poorest part of the city, called Moldavanka. I began to ascend the dirty staircase, accompanied by the coachman, who carried my suitcase for me. On one of the doors on the fourth floor, I saw a card with the inscription: "Samuil Shkol'nik. Teacher." I rang the bell. A thin man, a little taller than medium height, with a long beard and bright eyes, opened the door. For a moment, I thought it was my father standing before me, so great was the resemblance. It was my uncle. He greeted me very warmly; paying the coachman forty-five kopecks, he led me into the apartment. My aunt and cousins surrounded me and scrutinized me with inquisitive looks. Observing that I had arrived with an uncovered head, my aunt said: "You will need to buy a hat."

My uncle was a teacher of the Russian language at a Jewish school. He earned sixty rubles a month. Despite such a meager salary, he managed to provide the best education for all his children (six sons and one daughter). One of his sons was a civil engineer; the other studied in a gymnasium. Incidentally, his children themselves earned a living as tutors; otherwise, it would have been impossible. However, their earnings were irregular, and it often happened that the entire family lived on the sixty rubles earned by the father.

When I arrived in Odessa, revolutionary organizations had already established a solid position among the working population of the city. At their head were the Social Democrats. The work of secret organizations at the time consisted primarily of organizing educational circles among the workers and the publication and dissemination of forbidden literature — primarily proclamations. The latter were distributed through various means. Late at night when everyone was asleep, dozens of young men and women pasted them on lanterns and telegraph poles, on the walls of houses and fences; they scattered them on the streets along which the workers went to work and tossed them into the courtyards of the factories and mills. At the most interesting moment of action in the theaters, a cascade of leaflets suddenly rained down from several sides. This was the reign of paper terror, and the police were helpless to combat it. Before they could collect and destroy the proclamations, the audience greedily read these uncensored words against the orders of the governor, who had banned them on pain of six months' incarceration in prison. It is hardly necessary to say that the proclamations passionately assailed the tsarist regime, explaining to the workers that an improvement of their economic position was impossible under a political system that prohibited strikes and freedom of speech and assembly.

The letter that Hanna gave me at my departure was addressed to one of the leaders of the revolutionary organizations, a Social Democrat. When I went to him and declared that I wanted to study, he quickly gave me a few proclamations and promised to send someone who could teach me. Returning home, I gave a few proclamations to my uncle and male cousins to read. I was certain that both my uncle and his children shared the ideas set forth in them; how great was my astonishment when these people, whom I looked upon as highly educated, were horrified at my forbidden leaflets. "These things will lead you to Siberia," they cried out in unison. "This is not the countryside: do not seek truth here because it will take you to prison." I lost my head and did not know how to understand Uncle's words. "What do you want me to say?" I asked. "I left my father and mother, departed from my home village and turned up here in order to learn the truth; however, you forbid me in this. How can I agree to this?" His response: "You are still a child and understand little about these matters. I have grown sons, and you must not bring these things into my house. Besides, you came to me, and I am responsible for your well-being. There is no one else here who could take care of you. We all love you and wish you happiness. Despite the fact that I am a poor person, I want to help you; however, you must be very careful."

Two days after this conversation, a girl sent by comrade S. D. came to invite me to a secret meeting that was to take place at night. Saying nothing to Uncle, I left with her. The circle, which accepted me, consisted of nine workers and one intellectual, who lectured to the workers on political economy. I was happy and proud that they had accepted me.

This circle later played a significant role in the revolutionary movement in Odessa. It was already late when I returned home from the meeting. My uncle had not slept and apparently waited for me. "Where were you?" he asked, and I told him everything. "You must not have anything to do with these people," he said. "If you go out again, I will be forced to send you back home."

I found myself in a difficult position. I could not decline the books or people who taught me; at the same time, I did not wish to go home without having learned anything. I spent a few days in a quandary and did not know what to do. I finally found a way out of the position that had been created: I decided to leave Uncle's house. I revealed my intentions to one girl, a member of our circle, and she invited me to lodge with her, promising to find me a job in the factory where she herself worked. That very day, I brought a few things from Uncle's house and took up residence with this girl.

There was a section in the confectionery factory Krakhmal'nikov Brothers where my friend worked. Several hundred girls were wrapping candies in already-cut paper. The work was not very complicated, and within an hour, I already knew how to do it. At the end of the day, my fingertips had become so tender that contact with the rough paper caused me terrible pain. Drops of blood seeped out through the raw skin. I looked in despair at my hand, not knowing how to continue work. The girls tried to cheer me up: "Don't be afraid, this always happens in the first days. It will go away."

The workday at the factory lasted from 7:00 a.m. to 7:00 p.m. with a one-hour break for lunch. They paid the girls mere kopecks [for their work]. Girls who managed to wrap a whole pile of candies in the course of the day earned [just] thirty kopecks. This was considered a very big income; not many could work so fast and earn so much. Around 7:00 p.m., each brought her work to the top floor to be weighed. To my great astonishment, I had wrapped only a half a *pud* [8.2 kg]. When we left the factory, they searched us. This greatly embarrassed me. They conducted a search every evening: if they found candies on a girl, she was immediately fired. I worked for more than six months at this factory. My fingertips became as tough as parchment. The searches no longer bothered me. There were days when I earned up to thirty kopecks, to the great surprise of our circle.

We formed something like a commune out of the seven people: Zhenia, a twenty-two-year-old factory worker, who was a very ardent agitator and organizer of strikes; Sema, a factory worker; David [Roitershtern], a merchant's clerk; Aaron Shpaizman, a bookbinder who had already been in prison for distributing illegal literature; Nikolai, a painter who became a socialist and joined our circle after he was freed from prison after being incarcerated for teaching [Leo] Tolstoy's doctrines; Izrail, the sole intellectual in our circle; and me. It was a rare occurrence when we all had work. There were times when everyone in the circle lived off the earnings of one or two [of the] people. And there were times when none of us had work, and we all waited for Israel to come and place his final copper coin on the table. Then we sat down for *zavtrak* [breakfast].

However, such trifles did not trouble the members of our circle. They all took an active part in revolutionary work and were devoted to it. They established a secret printing press and then published and distributed proclamations by the thousands. They organized new agitation circles and conducted propaganda in workshops and factories. Of course, all were aware that prison, solitary confinement, and exile inevitably awaited them. Despite the fact that they expected to be arrested at any time of the day or night, they passed their free time happily, as if nothing special would happen to them. [. . .]² At that time, work in the Odessa Social Democratic organization did not correspond to my revolutionary mood. By then the Socialist Revolutionaries had become very active in Odessa, and under the influence of their literature, I crossed over to them. One of the urgent needs of our group was the establishment of a printing press. Literature from Kiev arrived irregularly and subjected one to great risk. It was impossible to set up a printing press in Odessa because the gendarmes were already following us. A few members of our group had already been detained; we therefore decided to set up the printing press in Kishinev, a few hours' travel from Odessa.

I arrived in Kishinev with a complete set of typefaces and various printing equipment. There I met a group of comrades, including Iasha Grinfel'd, Grisha Koff, and Aaron Shpaizman. With their help I settled in Brontman's apartment, which served as a refuge for the illegal items. My suitcase with the [set of] typefaces was hidden in Brontman's shed. Having settled and found work as a seamstress, I began to wait for the promised typesetter and materials. The revolutionary mood in Kishinev had already begun to emerge. Soon after my arrival, I managed to participate in a demonstration organized by workers and students in front of the governor's house to protest the exile of a student to Siberia.

Days and weeks passed, but the promised materials had still not appeared. I wrote letter after letter, but did not receive any answer. Finally, I decided to leave for Odessa myself on [a] reconnaissance [mission]. Unforeseen circumstances, however, prevented me from carrying out my intentions.

CHAPTER 3

At the beginning of February 1902, we were awakened at night by a deafening knock at the door. Before the elderly Brontman managed to lift the hook, a crack could be heard and the door flew open. Gendarmes and policemen filled the room. Without a word to us, they began to search the premises. The apartment consisted of two rooms and a kitchen. A long and thorough search commenced. Everything in the house was turned upside down. They slit open pillows and mattresses, ripped out the linings of old caps, and looked behind pictures on the walls. But they found nothing suspicious.

Disappointed, the gendarmes were preparing to leave when one of them picked up my dress lying on a chair. He fumbled in the pocket and pulled out a few letters of type. They were the type for capital letters that I had obtained from a typesetter acquaintance for the purpose of increasing my supplies. The faces of the gendarmes transformed instantaneously. Each of them carefully examined the ill-fated letters. They treated them with great care, as if they were not small metal letters but explosive bombs.

The gendarme officer sat down and began to write the charge sheet.

He only asked me: "Does this dress belong to you?"

"Yes."

"You are under arrest. Get dressed."

With these words he turned to comrade Shpaizman and the owner of the apartment. His wife and girl began to cry. With great emotion, I tried to explain to the officer that Brontman knew nothing about the letters that they had found in my pocket, but he brusquely interrupted: "You are not supposed to talk."

On the order of the officers, the gendarmes surrounded us and led us away. The mistress of the house sobbed. The girl, who threw herself at her father weeping, was cast roughly aside. The night was dark and cold. Surrounded on all sides by gendarmes, we walked in the middle of the road. We walked silently; for me, the silence was horrible. I could not figure out how I was guilty before comrade Brontman, but a sense of guilt grew in me. I completely forgot that I was going to prison. The sight of his gray head, bent before the gendarmes, pushed thoughts of my own position into the background.

At last we arrived, and the heavy gates of the prison slammed shut behind us. They took us to the office, where the chief of the prison registered our surnames and ordered one of the overseers to take us to the prison cells. The prison guard came to a halt in the half-lit corridor and opened one of the doors. I entered, and he quickly closed the door behind me and turned the key in the lock. I remained by the door, listening to the sound of his retreating footsteps. I stood in this half-dark cell with no desire to move from the spot. There was only one thought in my head: that the door was locked and I could not leave. [. . .]

A few days later, they called me for interrogation. The gendarme colonel met me very cordially. His broad face had a smile, and his small gray eyes looked insinuatingly [at me].

"Sit down." He indicated a chair standing by the table. "What is your given name? Your surname? How old are you?"

I told him.

"You are too young to sit in prison and it would be my pleasure to let you go, but everything depends on you."

"How?" I asked, surprised.

"You have only to tell who gave this to you, and I will set you free immediately." From a table drawer, he took out the letters of type that they had found in my pocket.

"I refuse to give testimony," I replied.

"It would be very imprudent on your part," the colonel said. "It will be bad for you, and you will regret this."

I was silent. The gendarme colonel pushed up a paper to me and said:

"Sign this paper."

"I refuse to give testimony," I repeated.

"Then it will be all the worse for you," he said, his tone changing immediately.

He stood, opened the door, and called the prison guard.

"The interrogation is ended. Take the prisoner to the cell."

I was filled with a pleasant sense that I had not fallen into the gendarme's snare. I began to walk around the cell, not knowing how to find an outlet for the feelings that filled me. It is possible that they will hold me here for a long time, I thought. I was not quite seventeen years old then. Life had only begun to unveil itself before me. Everything had seemed beautiful and attractive, and suddenly the stone walls of the prison had slid down and obscured the whole world. For a long time, I was unable to believe that I would have to stay here. From morning to evening, I dreamed about how my door would open and the prison guard would say, "You are free!" Three times a day, he came [and] brought me food, and every time I heard his steps near the door, my heart filled with hope that this time he would pronounce these magical words: "You are free." However, the days, weeks, and months passed, and the prison guard still brought me bread and kasha rather than freedom.

The gloom and dampness of the cell began to affect me. I started to suffer from insomnia. The twenty-minute walk in the prison courtyard was torture for me. The sun shone so brightly behind the walls of the prison, but I was deprived of light and freedom, without which I felt I could not live.

At first, I was alone in the women's section because all the other female political prisoners were in the men's block. Many comrades were already incarcerated there: [for example,] Leon Gol'dman, one of the active members of the Social Democratic Party. They found the secret printing press of [the newspaper] *Iskra* [The Spark][3] in his house. Together with him, they arrested his wife Mania Gold'man, Fenia Korsunskaia (who lived with them under the guise of a domestic servant), and Grisha El'kin. There was also Nina Globa, who was arrested as one of the organizers of the Kishinev demonstrations and also for her connections with the Kiev group Iskra.

I did not remain alone for long. Soon the arrests began, and they placed two more women in my cell: Zhenia Godlevskaia and Roza Rozenblium. Immediately after her arrest, the latter declared a hunger strike to demand freedom. Despite the fact that not everyone in the men's block was in agreement, we all united in a hunger strike, which lasted for a whole week. As a result of the hunger strike, Rozenblium was set free.

After the hunger strike, all the female political prisoners were transferred to our block. They placed Nina Globa, Fenia Korsunskaia, Mania Gol'dman with her young child, and a few others in our cell. I especially became friends with Nina Globa. She was a distinct type of revolutionary woman. She really burned with hatred for her jailers and did not lose a single opportunity to declare it openly. Despite her youth (she was eighteen years old then), she inspired respect from the authorities for her strong will. She often served as mediator between us and the prison authorities, and we were confident that she would protect our interests to the end, right up to isolation cells and hunger strikes. Thanks to her, we had constant ties with the outside. Her mother and sisters, who were sympathetic toward us, not only brought us letters and notes from comrades but also illegal literature.

In general, I remember my time in the Kishinev prison as a continuous struggle with the administration. They used harsh repression for the slightest offense, such as exchanging remarks with comrades from another block. Two comrades, Vasia Broska and Khaim Nakhmanberg, were once summoned to the office, severely beaten, and thrown into an isolation cell. When we learned about this, we stirred up a riot. The prison guards burst into our cells to drag us to the detention cell. When the prison guard wanted to take Mania Gold'man, she refused to go, saying that she could not leave the child. Then the chief ordered that she be taken by force. Accompanied by a few soldiers, he came into our cell. Gold'man held the child in her arms, clasping her to her bosom. "Soldiers," she turned to them, "Is it really possible that you have so

little heart as to take me away from my child?" The child, frightened by the sight of strange people, wailed with all her might; the soldiers retreated and did not dare move closer to her. Then the chief himself came, caught her by the arms, and gripped them above the elbows. After the struggle, which lasted several minutes, they tore the baby from the mother's arms.

"Take her," said the chief to the soldier, "and take her away from here."

Nina Globa and I grabbed the logs lying near the stove and began to hurl them at the chief, who jumped back. He ordered them to take both of us to the isolation cell. When they led us to the isolation cell the entire prison was in an uproar. The din of furniture being thrown, stamping, and screams was deafening. The criminals also joined in [the] protest with the political prisoners. Soon the procurator arrived. He made his rounds to the prison cells and assured everyone that Broska and Nakhmanberg would be released from the isolation cells. Indeed, after a few hours, they released all of us [from those cells]. All the political prisoners in the male block were taken to the isolation cell for two weeks.

Passover 1903 arrived—my second in prison. On the second day, unusual sounds reached our ears. Now at a crescendo, now at a lull, they seemed to penetrate into our cell on all sides. The prison guard began to run about more often past our doors. We were all anxious. What could this mean? We asked the prison guard. He looked at us for a few moments and then whispered: "Orders have been given to kill all the *zhidy* [Yids]—that's what it means." The blood flowed to my head at these words. I remained by the door, not having the strength to take a step. A strange spectacle greeted our eyes when they took us out for a walk. The whole prison courtyard was covered with feathers, which the wind had carried from town. These were the feathers from Jewish pillows and featherbeds, torn to shreds by the *pogromshchiki*. For two days and two nights, the slaughter of the Jews continued, and their desperate cries could be heard in our prison. Only on the third day did they [the authorities] begin to arrest the thugs.

After some time, they brought David Roitershtern to our prison. They had found my letters on him and arrested him somewhere in Poland, where he was performing military service. These letters served as the most serious evidence against me because [in them] I expressed my views on tsarism and discussed ways to struggle against it in the most definite terms. After a few days, they summoned me to an interrogation. The gendarme colonel met me with a solemn appearance. Pulling out a bundle of my letters to comrade Roitershtern, he asked: "Do you recognize these letters, which were found on Private Roitershtern and written in Yiddish by you?" I replied: "I refuse to give testimony." Then the colonel said: "The preliminary investigation into your case is concluded and, according to the order of His Excellency, the Minister of Internal Affairs, [Viacheslav Konstantinovich von] Plehve, you will be put on trial." The interrogation finished, they led me back to my cell. After the interrogation, it became clear to me that they would not be releasing me soon.

News that Gold'man, Korsunskaia, Grisha El'kin, Shpaizman, and I were to stand trial reached the comrades on the outside. This turn from the system of administrative exile, which had been practiced for a long time, aroused great interest among liberal circles in Russia. A few well-known lawyers — Maklakov, Kal'manovich, Ratner, and others — wrote to the procurator, proposing to serve as our defenders. Finally, they delivered a copy of the indictment to us. The articles on which we were indicted carried a punishment of hard labor for eight to twelve years. The trial was set for 6 October 1903. [. . .][4]

The judge entered, took his seat, and the trial commenced. The secretary read the indictment aloud. We were accused of establishing a secret printing press, of publishing [the newspaper] *Iskra*, and inciting a riot. When the chairman asked, "Do you admit your guilt?" we all answered, "No." Comrade Shpaizman and I declared that we did not have connections with the publication *Iskra*, which was the organ of the Socialist Democrats, and that we were members of Socialist Revolutionary party.

All the witnesses gave favorable testimony except the official translator of my Yiddish letters, the local rabbi. He confirmed that one of my [Yiddish] expressions said: "I will not rest until *I* spill the blood of the vampire," whereas one of the unofficial translators said that this expression meant, "I will not rest until the blood of the vampire *is spilled*." The rabbi reaffirmed that the disputed expression was written clearly and properly and that he had translated it accurately. [. . .]

My legal defender Ratner delivered this speech:

Private letters cannot serve as evidence for the court, in particular in cases when they express general ideals and convictions. Such letters have the imprint of individual moods and consequently cannot have the value of precise evidence. Can one really choose one statement arbitrarily and discard another, believe one and not the other? We must believe Shkol'nik when she declares that she is a Socialist Revolutionary; the secondary claim of the prosecutor that she is a Social Democrat is absolutely incomprehensible. There is a major difference between Socialist Revolutionaries and Social Democrats.

Under no circumstances could the workers' organ that she intended to publish (as stated in Shkol'nik's own letters) be *Iskra*. Everyone knows perfectly well that this organ is published abroad and began to appear much earlier than when Shkol'nik wrote her letters. Consequently, she could not have had *Iskra* in mind when she wrote about her intention and that of her friends to issue a newspaper.

As for [the use of] the word "vampire" (leaving aside the dubious scruples of the translation), it is juridically impossible to see it as an [act of] malice aforethought to carry out a terrorist deed. This is simply a poetic expression of the terrorist mood that has seized the young hearts in Russia at the present moment because of the circumstances. Whether she wrote "vampire" or "vampires" is of no significance to us because she expressed an abstract desire in the letter; no court has ever punished anyone for this desire [to spill the blood of a vampire]. The main idea of the indictment is that the accused had a definitive opinion, conviction, and general intention, and that this is clear if one looks attentively at her life. A worker from the age of fifteen, lively, and bold — she pondered the strange contrast between her position (and that of her fellow comrades) on the one hand, and the position of the customers on the other hand: she could not fail to see her personal intellectual superiority compared to these dressed-up ladies.

Thinking logically and without prejudice (which did not influence her), she came to some definite conclusions. Meeting with people who were more intellectually mature, under their influence she initially accepted Social Democratic doctrines. But her free, militant spirit could not settle on this; when she became acquainted with the views of the Socialist Revolutionaries, she joined them. In her place each of us would have undoubtedly craved liberation. One must note that, despite the specific oppressions to which she was subjected as a Jewish woman, the accused did not join a narrow nationalistic struggle. She had much broader views; the interests of all humanity were more precious to her. This is a talented nature, capable of everything good. [. . .] In some other country, she would have been happy but, alas, among us here, that is not possible. The court can, of course, convict her but this would hardly be a triumph of justice. This will be yet one more poor, contrived, unjust sentence about which history knows so much.

After two agonizing days of trial, a verdict was announced. We were sentenced "to the deprivation of all rights of status and exiled to settlement in Siberia."

CHAPTER 4

The thought that I would be sent to Siberia did not frighten me. The desire to leave these hateful walls was so great that I would have been happy to go not only into exile but even into hell itself. But day after day, month after month passed, and we all were still in the Odessa prison. [. . .] Contradictory rumors about the war with Japan began to reach our cells. [. . .]

In July 1904 [on the 14th] Plehve, the minister of internal affairs — the bastion of reaction who boasted that he "would free Russia from revolution" — was killed by a bomb thrown at his carriage by Egor Sozonov, a member of the Combat Organization of the Socialist Revolutionary Party. The prison administration itself brought us this joyous news. Not only the people but even his subordinates hated him. The appointment of [Petr Dmitrievich.] Sviatopolk-Mirskii as Minister of the Internal Affairs marked an end — albeit short-lived — to the repression of political [prisoners]. Soon after the assassination of Plehve, my comrades and I were unexpectedly appointed to a group to be sent to Eastern Siberia. [. . .]

The filthy prisoners' wagon was as overcrowded as could be. The prisoners settled down more comfortably and felt so free in this setting that it was obvious that it was not the first time that they had made this journey. The food given to prisoners consisted only of bread with herring. However, peasants —

mainly in Siberia—met the train and handed out charity to the prisoners, giving them bread, milk, pies, and so forth. [. . .]⁵

Winter had already begun when we set off on the road again. The prisoners' wagon was even filthier and more tightly packed than in European Russia. The harsh Siberian frost made our trip even harder. Here were the same, usual settings: one or two days in transit prisons, walking back and forth in half-torn boots on the road covered with ice and snow. It was here that we learned our destination. To my horror, I was destined for a hamlet in Aleksandrov district of Eniseisk province. I stood before the chief, listened to him, and could not believe that I was to be separated from my comrades and taken to a distant, deserted hamlet. [. . .]⁶

At last we arrived at a township in Aleksandrov district. The village constable and county clerk unfolded a piece of paper that the police officer brought in a stamped envelope.

"Here are the special instructions concerning you," the clerk told me.

"What sort of special instructions?" I asked.

"It says here that you must be placed under special surveillance," he replied.

I spent the night in the clerk's house, and the next day he took me to Aleksandrov, which was located 19.3 kilometers away. The village had approximately thirty huts and consisted largely of migrants from Russia. Peasant men and women had gathered at the house of the village elder where the clerk initially took me. They began to discuss the question about the arrangements for me. The women stood with their arms folded, and shook their heads sympathetically. A few of them offered to lodge me in their homes. One elderly peasant who stood pensively, pinching his long, gray beard from time to time, said: "I understand that she was sent to us for [her] entire life and we may do with her as we please. Did I understand correctly?" The clerk explained to the peasants how they were to treat me.

Finally, after lengthy disputes, it was de-cided that I would live in the home of the church watchman. The village constable ordered the rural police constable to show up every day to confirm that I was present. As he was leaving, he warned the peasants: "You understand that you are all responsible for her."

The peasants led me roughly to the house of the church watchman. For a long time, the women continued to express to me their feelings of empathy and sympathy saying: "Unfortunate orphan." Their fervent empathy could be explained by the fact that they themselves were from Russia and saw in me a fellow countrywoman, a fresh person from their native homes for which they pined very much. In the end, I remained alone. When they called me an "orphan," I actually felt very lonely, completely alone in the whole world. I sat down, looked around hopelessly, and a feeling of self-pity filled my soul. However, those around me did not allow this feeling to grow. I lived in a hut with the owners, and the peasants did not give me a moment of peace.

My landlord, a venerable man, gray as the moon, approached me and asked: "Do you know how to read?" Receiving an affirmative response, he took a letter out of a pocket. It was from his son, a soldier in the Manchurian army. News that I could read quickly spread around the village. The peasants collected every scrap of paper that had something written or printed on it and brought it to me so that I could read them. They surrounded me on all sides and listened with great attentiveness to each report about the war. They were deeply interested in these reports because almost every one of them had a son, husband, or brother on the battlefields, but they had not received word from them in months and were in despair.

Soon women began to come, bringing me pitchers of milk, earthen pots with butter, and other gifts. They asked me to write letters to their sons and husbands. As I listened to the sorrowful talk of these old mothers and young wives, who clutched desperately at any hope that their loved one had not been killed, but only injured and maimed for life, and gazed at the young orphans who already knew that they would never see their fathers, I forgot about myself and only thought about what I could do to lighten their painful grief. However, to my great distress, I could not conceive how I could be useful to them; all I was able to do was to write letters to people who might already be dead.

Some time after my arrival, the village priest came to see me. He was a robust man with a merry disposition, who must have been a great lover of drinking. He began to talk to me in a fatherly tone. "Just don't you despair. Nothing is forever in this world," he responded to my declaration that I had been sent here not just for a fixed period but for my entire life. "My daughter is about to get married," he continued, "and there is no one here who can sew her a dress. That is why it would be better for you if you moved to our home and helped her with the sewing." I agreed because I was glad to earn my own bread somehow.

I was no longer in prison and did not see prison walls, but I did not feel free. An aimless life in a remote Siberian village seemed even worse to me than prison. The peasants, together with the priest, usually drank heavily for two or three days a week. They spent all their money at the state liquor store and when they had no more cash, they pawned everything that fell in their hands at home. It seemed that only vodka allowed them to forget their poverty and pitiful existence. On these "drunken" days, I took refuge in a corner so that no one could see me, and I watched the snowdrifts that separated me from the rest of the world.

"I need to escape, I need to run away from here," the voice inside me resounded more and more urgently. The county clerk, village constable, and police constable were the only people who were responsible for guarding me. However, they apparently were quite negligent in their duties. As was clear, they thought that the enormous dense forest was the best watchman for me. "Run away, run away," I repeated to myself on long, sleepless nights, as I gazed into the dark, constructing one fantastic plan after another.

At this time news of Bloody Sunday [9 January 1905] reached our village. With trembling hands, I held the letter and read to the peasants about how the workers in Petersburg, led by [Father] Gapon, went to request their tsar to improve their living conditions, how they came with their wives and children, holding icons and portraits, and singing patriotic anthems, how all of a sudden, they came under fire without warning, how the Cossacks trampled them with their horses and beat them with sabers and whips, how the streets of Petersburg were transformed into a battlefield where hundreds of beaten and the dead lay about. Here the peasants stopped me.

"Is it possible," they said, "that the tsar could do this? Certainly, are his ministers not to blame?" As they thought about this, they asked me to read it all again from the beginning. On that day, their faith in the tsar was crushed, and they openly expressed their sympathy toward me, the direct victim of his despotic government. For me, the fact that the Petersburg workers went to request the tsar to improve their lives held a completely different meaning. I saw here an awakening of the laboring masses and looked upon this demonstration as the foreshadowing of the great revolution that would topple the tsarist throne. "It is not possible for the blood of children, flowing on the streets of Petersburg on 9 January, to remain unavenged," I thought. I saw that the Russian people could no longer endure the oppression of the tsarist yoke, that they were preparing for great changes in Russia, and I firmly resolved to run away and join with weapons in hand to struggle for the freedom of my oppressed country.

The township clerk was an intelligent, kind person and openly showed his sympathy toward me. The thought occurred to me to ask him to obtain permission for me to travel to Kansk with the constable. I hoped to find comrades there who could offer me help with money and a passport. "Yes," he said in response to my request, "I will obtain the permission for you. But if you run away, the responsibility will fall on me, for I am certain that the constable will try to prove in any event that I conspired with you. You know that I am a father of four children," he continued. "However, if you give me your honest word that you will return, I will try to persuade the constable to give you permission to travel to Kansk for a few days."

It was very difficult for me to accept his offer. If I gave him my word, I would have to return, but the sole purpose of my trip was to escape. For two days I tried to find a way out of this dilemma, but in the end I decided to agree to his conditions. It was absolutely essential to go to Kansk and obtain money and a passport, without which I had no way to consider escape. We went to the constable, and after a few questions he agreed to let me go to Kansk for a few days.

At the beginning of February 1905, I left the village on a wagon with peasants who were going to the town for their own affairs. I had no address whatsoever; I did not even know if there were any political exiles in Kansk. The peasants in Aleksandrov persuaded me that there were few "gentlemen" there. As I later learned, the politicals there were called "gentlemen."

We arrived in Kansk. For two kopecks, a boy whom I met took me to a blacksmith. The tall man in a blue shirt with hands and a face covered with soot received me with a friendly smile. I introduced myself to him, and he took me to his house. I explained to him the purpose of my visit. "Unfortunately," said the comrade, "It is unlikely that you will obtain anything in our town. There are only six political individuals here, and they are all starving. The only thing that we can do for you here is to give you a recommendation letter to com-

rades in Irkutsk. Many of them are there, and they will certainly help you." A few hours later, the entire colony of exiles in Kansk gathered at the house of this comrade. They began to discuss the matter and decided that I needed to travel directly to Irkutsk. They bought me a ticket there with their last money, and that very evening I was on a train with a recommendation letter in my pocket.

After a two-day journey, I arrived in Irkutsk. When the coachman stopped opposite a wealthy house on the main street, I momentarily hesitated. "What if they do not let me in?" I rang the bell. A pretty young woman opened the door and asked me to take a seat in the reception room. Soon a short, elderly man came out. He asked me who I was and what I needed. Persuaded that I was indeed who I claimed to be, he shook hands with me and proposed that I go to his wife and children.

This comrade K. was an old revolutionary who had been exiled to Irkutsk many years ago. Despite his past, he occupied a high post in Irkutsk at this time. On that very day, he handed me one hundred rubles and a passport that identified me as a "merchant's daughter." Such a passport was as good as a real one for Siberia since they did not subject documents to careful examination [there]. The wife of comrade K. helped me to change into her daughter's dress and gave me a watch as a present. In a word, I became unrecognizable.

I had to return to Aleksandrov. I knew that the clerk would be anxious because of my long absence. I did not want to think yet about how I would escape after my return. The challenge seemed insurmountable to me; however, I had given my honest word and had to return. With sorrow in my soul, I bid farewell to my dear comrades. One of K.'s sons went with me to Kansk for fear that they would arrest me en route. In the train compartment (we traveled second class) there were two army officers. They became friends with my traveling companion and entertained him with vodka and cigarettes. There was nothing in their behavior that would have aroused our suspicions. When night fell I lay down on my bench. The thought that I was going back to this desolate village gave me no peace. Suddenly, I felt someone pull at the small chain on which hung my watch. I opened my eyes and, to my great horror, saw the same officer who had been so courteous toward me a few hours ago. In one hand he had my bag, in which lay the hundred rubles and passport. I cried out loudly. The officer grabbed me by the neck and began to strangle me. I lost consciousness.

When I came to, my first thought was that the money and passport had vanished. I heard people talking next to me, but I did not want to look at them. "Why didn't they let me die," I thought. "What will I do without money and a passport?" I was not able to move my head even slightly; it felt like his fingers were still squeezing my neck. At the first station, they took us over to the gendarme department. The two officers were already there. It turned out that they were fugitive criminal convicts from Sakhalin disguised as officers.

"Why did you want to kill me?" I asked. "Didn't you see that I wasn't wealthy?"

"Then why did you scream" was the answer.

"I needed to save myself."

"In the end, I did not even strangle you to death."

They returned the bag with the money and passport to me. For my rescue, I was indebted to K.'s son, who first rushed to me when the vagrant began to strangle me. After a long absence, I returned to Aleksandrov. The county clerk and constable went into raptures at the sight of me. "But we already thought that you were not going to return," the constable said to me smiling.

The question about how I would run away did not leave me for one minute. The only people from whom I could hope to receive the necessary information were the Gol'dmans, who lived in the village of Rybinsk, and I decided to take off in this direction. I was afraid to ask the peasants for help despite their sympathy. Moreover, I knew that if the authorities learned that someone had taken me to Rybinsk, the poor peasants would have to answer for my escape. There was only one [option]: walk the distance of seventy-five kilometers that separated the two villages. I knew the road to Rybinsk quite well.

Some time after my return from Irkutsk, I set out on the road to Rybinsk at dusk, dressed as warmly as possible, with a few pieces of bread tied up in a kerchief. Everyone in the village was already asleep, but it seemed to me that the very huts were following me. Every sound made my heart beat faster, and I looked around in all directions expecting to see pursuers. Soon I reached the farthest end of the village. A smooth silvery road stretched before me. I drew myself up tall, inhaled a full breath of clean, frosty air, and quickened my pace. My terror vanished. I looked calmly at the snow-covered forest that stood on both sides of the road and I walked faster and faster, dreaming about freedom for me and for my homeland.

I do not know how long I walked. I only recall that a sharp sense of hunger interrupted my dreaming. I started to devour my bread, piece by piece without stopping. Suddenly, I heard the clatter of horse hooves behind me. Not stopping for a minute to think, I turned toward the forest, but the sleigh was already next to me before I managed to disappear into the forest. "Where are you going?" a voice asked me. I glanced back. It was a peasant from a nearby village. He knew me well. "I'm going to Rybinsk," I replied in an indifferent tone. "I didn't have money to hire a horse." "Have a seat," he said, "I'm also going there and can give you a ride."

Within a few hours, I was already at the Gol'dmans' house. A child's tiny hands embraced me. "I won't let you get away from us any more," he said, stroking my cheek.

When I told them that I had decided to escape they were glad for me. "And we ought to get out of here no matter what," said Gol'dman. He paced up and down the room, lacking the strength to control the agitation that enveloped him. "How can you run away with a child?" I said. "They would recognize you right away." Gol'dman replied, "Yes, that is the only thing that keeps us here."

I mentally regretted that such an active worker like Gol'dman should remain in an obscure little hamlet because of a child, and a happy thought suddenly dawned upon me.

"Listen," I turned to Gol'dman, "I will take your child with me and then you leave. The police will be searching for me *alone* and for you with a *child*, and this change of roles will save us all." Instantaneously, their doleful faces lit up with hope. "Boria," I said to the boy, "Do you want to go with me to grandmother?" He replied with a resolute look, "Yes, I do. I will go, and then mama and papa. I don't want to be here. It is cold here."

Within a few hours the matter was arranged. I was to escort the child to his grandmother in Vil'na. Upon receiving news from me that everything went well, the Gol'dmans were to escape. In the evening Gol'dman found a peasant who agreed to bring me to the nearest village. The following day, we made preparations for the trip. Just as soon as it grew dark, the coachman arrived for us. "Hurry, hurry," he urged us. Gol'dman took the child by the hand, kissed his crying wife, and we left. The night was still and cold. The snowdrifts blanketed the earth. We walked quickly, and the snow crunched under our feet. At the end of the village stood our sleigh. The horses pawed the snow impatiently.

The sleigh slid rapidly across the smooth road. The horses galloped, the coachman hummed a song. I clasped the child to my bosom, listening to his rhythmical breathing. Soon the coachman climbed out of the sleigh, and ran next to the horses, attempting to warm himself up. I resolved not to move, afraid of disturbing the child who quickly fell asleep. At 4 o'clock in the morning, we ar-

rived at a village and knocked at the door of the peasant hut. They let us in. To their questions—where was I from, where was I going—I replied in a plaintive voice that the child had been left as an orphan and that I was taking him to his grandparents in Russia.

Having stopped thus for the night at the peasant hut, we arrived finally safely at Ol'ginsk station, where I took a train. The long trip to Vil'na passed uneventfully. The child served as a splendid cover for me from the attentive eyes of the gendarmes. The spies who darted about at every large station ignored me; they obviously could not imagine the possibility of such a scheme. Only once, Boria almost gave me away. I didn't want to fulfill some kind of wish and he stated to me loudly: "If you do not do what I want, I will call you Mania Shkol'nik and not Sasha" (I was Sasha on the passport). After this, I yielded to his demands and did not let him get too far from me. When we arrived in Cheliabinsk and transferred to another train, our coach was suddenly locked; they began to take out the passengers one at a time and check passports. I held the child in my arms and the gendarmes let me go, without asking a single question.

At the beginning of March, I arrived in Vil'na; after I delivered the child to his grandparents, I sent a telegram to Gol'dman. Finding myself a short distance from my own home, I decided to see my family. I so wanted to see them that I threw caution and prudence to the wind. The same day I sent them a letter through a comrade, and in a few days they came to me. The joy of the reunion seemed to make us forget all the past sorrows.

"I won't ever give you back to them," my mother repeated, by now not even trying to hold back the tears that flowed like a stream down her face. Father pulled out fifty rubles and said to me: "I borrowed this money. Take it and go abroad. You'll be safe there." "Father, I cannot do this. What they did to me, and thousands of others, must not remain unpunished. I cannot leave it like this." Father took my face in his hands and looked me straight in the eyes. "My God, what have they done to you? You do not even cry, and there is so much hatred in your eyes that it does not disappear even in the presence of your old parents." I repeated, "I cannot, I cannot." My father's arms embraced me tighter and tighter to his breast. "Look here," he said with tears in his voice, "three years of your imprisonment turned me this gray. What will happen to us if you land in prison again?" The following day, father and mother left for home. I took a train for Minsk. From there, Jewish smugglers escorted me to the Austrian border. After sitting in a small frontier town for three days, I safely crossed the border into Brody.

CHAPTER 5

I decided to go abroad. I heard that the leaders of the Combat Organization[7] of our party were in Geneva at the time. I intended to join the Combat Organization and become a terrorist. My own life and the lives of my comrades led me to believe that peaceful methods of struggle against autocracy were no longer possible.

To be a member of a terrorist organization was a quite difficult matter. They only accepted people with an established revolutionary reputation. I arrived in Geneva with doubts in my heart. As luck would have it, I found comrade Shpaizman there, who had escaped from Siberia a few weeks earlier than I and who had already succeeded in getting in touch with people who had close ties with the Combat Organization. With his help, I obtained a meeting with [Boris] Savinkov and [Evno] Azef.[8]

Their mysteriousness and conspiratorial appearance made the most depressing impression on me. The lavish setting in which they lived shocked me; it did not correspond to my expectations of a revolutionary. Soon Savinkov set up a meeting for me with Azef. The latter came to see me in the apartment. I lived in a very tiny and impoverished room, so his massive figure was especially prominent. Corpulent, tall, with small darting eyes—the very sight of him almost inspired me with fear, and I experienced some feelings of revulsion toward him.[9] Mysteriously silent for a while, he turned to me and asked, "Why have you decided to join the Combat Organization?" Passionately, I began to try to prove the necessity of an active struggle against autocracy.

"You are a great agitator, and you could do more on this path." He questioned me about my personal life and family and then left, leaving me absolutely perplexed and uncertain about my acceptance into the Combat Organization. Within a few days, Savinkov sent me to Paris to see Azef. He lived on one of the best streets and occupied a luxurious apartment. His wife made a very pleasant impression on me. I spent a few days at their place, but then she placed me in a *pension*. I rarely saw Azef during these few days. He remained just as taciturn outside as he was inside the home. Finally, Savinkov arrived and informed me that Shpaizman and I had been accepted into the Combat Organization. We conducted all the preparatory work for our trip to Russia with him.

Shpaizman left for Russia first. He carried bombs and a revolver with him. He was detained at the border; they searched him and, despite the bombs and weapons that they found on him, let him go. After a few days, I left, also with bombs and a revolver on me, and safely crossed the border. In Vil'na I met comrade Shpaizman and he told me about this strange incident at the border. I took up residence in Druskeiniki, where I was to wait for Savinkov. When he arrived, I told him about the incident with Shpaizman at the border; Savinkov was suspicious of the latter. Soon, I received an invitation to appear in Nizhnii Novgorod for a meeting with Azef. Our meeting took place at the horse races. He immediately began to talk about the incident with Shpaizman, expressing his manifest suspicions about him. Despite my ardent assurances that Shpaizman was a devoted revolutionary, that I had known him now for several years, he repeated that Shpaizman needed to be removed because "the cause takes precedence over everything else." With difficulty, I managed to defend comrade Shpaizman. Only after the discovery of Azef's betrayal did we understand that the incident with Shpaizman was nothing more or less than Azef's cunning maneuvers, lest any suspicions fall on him. This was not the only case of this sort.

It was proposed that our first case be an attempt on the life of General [Feodor Feodorovich] Trepov, the general governor of St. Petersburg. The first and foremost condition of a terrorist's life was the strictest abstinence from relations with friends. A terrorist was not even supposed to correspond with anyone. The only reason for this precaution was the necessity of protecting the innocent from state persecution in the event that one of the organization's members was arrested. There were cases in which people were sent to Siberia or sentenced to long-term hard labor for just a single note that they had written to a terrorist or that they themselves had received from one.

This isolation and focus on a single idea affected me in a special way. The world did not exist for me. For me, the photograph of Trepov was a symbol of all of Russia's misfortunes, and his death was the only means against them. My brain could not imagine what inevitably awaited me. The very fact that I was sacrificing my own life had no meaning for me whatsoever. I did not even think about my own death. However, the thought of his [Trepov's] death — a person whom I considered the cause of thousands of deaths — never left me. Finally, after an entire month of agonizing suspense, a comrade brought me the unpleasant news that Trepov had somehow learned about the plans of the Combat Organization and had taken extreme precautions.

He did not receive anyone and almost never left his house. The executive committee decided to postpone the assassination until a more opportune moment presented itself.

It then ordered Shpaizman and me to organize the assassination of the general governor of Kiev, [Nikolai] Kleigels, who had brutally repressed every manifestation of discontent among peasants, workers, and students, who had organized Jewish pogroms, and who had become universally hated. It was decided that we would settle in Kiev—Shpaizman as a street hawker and I as a flower vendor. These jobs enabled us to be on the street at all times without rousing suspicions. From seven o'clock in the morning to eight o'clock at night I sat on the stones on the corner of Kreshchatik and Fundukleevskaia Streets, waiting for Kleigels. Shpaizman's place was on the opposite corner. A week passed, another, a third, but Kleigels had still not appeared. One day, two Cossacks on horseback flew past me; behind them followed a closed carriage, and behind them still two more Cossacks on horseback. The carriages stopped at the church; I hid behind the corner. Finally, Kleigels appeared, but his wife and son were with him. At this moment, my gaze fell on Shpaizman, who stood at the very entrance of the church. There was a look of despair on his face. Kleigels must have known that [Ivan] Kaliaev[10] risked his life but did not kill the Grand Duke Sergei because the princess was with him, and that he also used his family as a shield. For us this presented an insurmountable obstacle. Thus, our second attempt was doomed to failure.

At this time, the political agitation of the country reached unprecedented proportions. Frequent strikes on the railroads and other public and private enterprises merged into one great all-Russian strike. The entire mechanism of the great empire came to a halt. The authorities completely lost their heads, and within a short time the capital was run by a Soviet of Worker Deputies, elected by the workers of St. Petersburg. This open and general uprising [of 1905] forced the tsar to make concessions: on 17 October 1905 he issued the famous [October] manifesto, which granted Russia a constitution.

Suspecting nothing, I went out on the street with flowers as usual, intending to continue my surveillance of Kleigels when my ear was struck by the loud shouts of the newspaper boys, "The Tsarist Manifesto! Freedom!" Soon the street was flooded with a triumphant crowd. Throwing aside my small basket of flowers, I joined the crowd, walking with red flags. The following day, after the publication of the manifesto, the Black Hundreds, composed mainly of the dregs of society, with the cooperation of police agents disguised as gendarmes and spies, seized control of Kiev. They plundered and killed defenseless residents in front of the soldiers and police, who failed to intervene and help.[11]

To protect the population from these hooligans, the workers organized *druzhiny* [defense units]. I joined one of these defense units and, revolver in hand, dispersed the drunken crowd. After two days of this work, my position in the city became dangerous. They were already following me. Because the Combat Organization of the Socialist Revolutinary Party had lost its bearings after the manifesto and virtually ceased to function, I decided to go to Moscow. I did not remain there long. I saw Aleksandr Ivanovich Potapov and Abrasha [Avraham Rafailovich] Gots, who were then the heads of the Combat Organization, and they decided that I should travel to Chernigov to assassinate Governor [Aleksei Alekseevich] Khvostov, who was distinguished by the special ferocity of his suppression of peasant uprisings. I went with Nina Globa, who was sent by the Combat Organization; however, neither she nor I were informed about what the other had been sent to do in terms of the conspiracy.

Having arrived in Chernigov, we established ties with the local combat unit headed by Comrade Nikolaev, an old revolutionary associated with [Dmitrii] Karakozov.[12] The local committee decided that Nina Globa and comrade Shapiro, who was also sent from Moscow, would go to work in the countryside while I remained in town to carry out the assassination of the governor. When I proposed to recruit comrade Shpaizman; the comrades consented. After some time, I met with Nina Globa and comrade Shapiro, who told me about the terrible condition of the peasants after the suppression [of the uprisings]. [. . .][13]

Having received all the necessary information and money from comrade Nikolaev, I rented a house and settled down, not far from the governor—who lived at the edge of the city. His house stood on a knoll, surrounded by a garden.

My private residence was too large for me alone and, to avert suspicion, I told the homeowner that I was expecting the arrival of my mother and sister from Warsaw. I sent my passport as a Polish teacher to the police station for a residence permit, and it returned safely within a few days. Then I sent a telegram to comrade Shpaizman. He had been injured during the Jewish pogrom in Odessa after the publication of the manifesto and had only recently been released from the hospital. After a few days, Shpaizman arrived in Chernigov and settled across from the Noble Assembly. According to our information, the governor sometimes went there.

Sitting at my window, I studied the daily schedule of the governor's life. I knew when he would get up and when he lay down to sleep. I knew when and whom he received. I even knew the time when he had dinner. The governor did not leave his house for the entire week. He only came out for a walk in the garden. Alone with my thoughts, I walked back and forth around the empty house. I spent a lot of time compiling a list of the governor's victims. I collected like treasure the names of those whom he had killed or flogged to death.

I read and reread a thousand times the simple peasant stories about his horrific crimes.

Finally, we learned that the governor would leave for the Noble Assembly at 12:00, and we decided to kill him on the return journey. It was New Year's Eve. I sat at the window and looked at the street covered with snow. Only one thought was on my mind: he must die. All doubts disappeared. I knew and felt that this would come to pass. At midnight, I carefully pulled out the tube from the bomb,[14] dried out the powder, and loaded the bomb again. I placed the four-pound tin box in a good bag that had been brought specifically for this purpose, put everything in order, wrote a letter, and laid out money for the homeowner. Then I went to sleep. "I must sleep," I kept repeating to myself, and indeed I fell asleep.

A knock on the door woke me. I opened my eyes and the awareness that something must have happened filled my soul. I heard a second knock on the door. I got up and glanced at the window. A group of masqueraded children stood at my door. I realized that they probably had come to wish me a happy New Year and, as was the custom, to throw millet on the floor. They usually received a few kopecks for this. I received them and, in a frenzied haste, began to give away everything that fell into my hand. An irresistible desire to be in the company of these children even for a little while seized me, and I asked them to take off their masks and have tea with me. They hesitated, but when the oldest boy took off his mask, the others followed suit. I prepared tea and seated the children at the table. They became bolder and soon prattled without inhibition and scrutinized me and everything in the house with curiosity.

The samovar sounded off happily on the table, the children laughed noisily, the sun shone brightly in my window. At that moment, I forgot what was about to happen in a few hours. Suddenly, across the street, the Cossacks passed by quickly, [and] behind them, a carriage. I recognized it. The children continued to laugh but I no longer heard them.

"Go, go, children, time to go already," I exclaimed. "But first, let's say goodbye." They looked at me with surprise. Their sweet faces clouded with regret, their thin grubby hands stretched out to me. "Don't forget me, children," I said. They crossed themselves at the corner, wished me a happy New Year, and went home peacefully. I dressed hastily, took my bag, and went out onto the street.

The day was clear and cold; there was not a cloud in the sky. The street was almost empty, save for the appearance of occasional passers-by heading for church. Not far from my house was a bridge on which stood a policeman. Holding my bag in hand, I walked past him. Soon, however, I went back and began to walk back and forth not far from my house. A few minutes later, I saw Shpaizman from afar, walking in slow, measured steps toward me. He was carrying a box, tied up with a red ribbon: it was a bomb. He crossed the bridge and stopped seventy or eighty steps from me. I understood that he wanted to throw the bomb from the place where he had stopped. I continued to walk back and forth not far from the governor's house. Comrade Shpaizman caught up with me and whispered as he walked past me: "I see him. Remember, keep a little farther from me so that your bomb does not go off accidentally when mine explodes."

"Good," I whispered in reply.

"Farewell," he said and quickly went to his previous place.

I followed him with my eyes, turning slightly.

The street was empty as before. Suddenly Cossacks on horseback came into sight and between them was the carriage. Comrade Shpaizman quickly stepped off the pavement. At this moment, the carriage came up alongside him. He raised his hand and threw the bomb at the carriage. The bomb fell in the snow but did not explode. The police official, who went in front of the governor leaped at comrade Shpaizman and I heard the revolver discharge. The carriage stopped for a moment; however, evidently understanding the situation, the coachman began to whip the horses and let them gallop toward me. I stepped down the middle of the bridge and threw the bomb at the carriage window. A terrible blow stunned me. I felt like I was thrown in the air.

When I regained consciousness and opened my eyes, I was standing next to a coachman and some woman was supporting me. She said something to the coachman, but I was unable to catch what she said. She sat me down in the sleigh, and the coachman drove off. He went past my house, crossed the bridge where a policeman always stood — but at that moment he was not there. We went through all the streets and did not meet another living soul. "What does this mean? Where are all the people?" I thought. The coachman turned down some street and came to a stop before a house. The hospital sign momentarily brought me to complete consciousness. I realized that by some miracle, I had survived the blast and that they were taking me not to prison but to a hospital. I paid the coachman, waited until he disappeared around the corner, and walked farther. I walked for a long time, with absolutely no idea where I was or where I was going. I felt that my strength was draining away and that soon I would collapse in the middle of the street. By chance, I saw open gates. I went into the courtyard and sat down in the snow. I took no comfort in the thought that I had been saved. I knew that anyone who would want to hide me would perish together with me.

In order to stop the blood that was gushing from my head wound, I placed snow in a handkerchief and held it to [my] head. This revived me a little. Then I took off my fur coat and lay on it. I felt a strange weakness in my entire body and a heavy numbness envelope the limbs. I do not know if I had lain there for long when suddenly I felt someone tugging at my sleeves. With difficulty, I opened my eyes. Next to me stood a youth. He bent down to my ear and I clearly caught what he said:

"Was it you who killed the governor? You?"[15]

The youth got up, glanced at me again, and left, not saying a word. Five minutes had not passed when he returned together with a bent, old woman. They lifted me up and took me inside the house. The warm air and cold water, which she used to moisten my head, brought me completely to my senses. I took into consideration that these poor Jews were subjecting themselves to danger. "I must go from here," I said to the old woman, who persuaded me to lie down on their only bed. "But my son asked that we take care of you," she replied. The young lad (who was Iasha Leikin) and the old folks (his parents) returned from somewhere greatly agitated and said that the police were following me by my blood trail and no doubt would be here soon. "Oh, oh," moaned the old woman, and she began to run around the room in horror. I went up to the door with the intention of leaving but the old woman screamed, "What are you doing? The police will see you and we will all perish."

Suddenly, she opened a secret wardrobe, pushed me inside, and locked the door. Suffocating and growing weak, I leaned against the wardrobe door, unable to breathe. A distant noise reached me; it grew closer and closer. I heard the trampling of feet not far from where they had hidden me. My knees buckled and I lost consciousness. Late at night I found myself sitting at a table. One candle illuminated the room. The old woman whispered in my ear, "Thank God, I managed to show them out." I could not understand what she was talking about. I felt a sharp pain in the head; my whole body burned. I did not think about anything and only wanted peace.

Iasha Leikin came in, carrying a soldier's coat and hat in his hands. They dressed me and, supporting me with their arms, they led me to the courtyard. They seated me on a sleigh; Leikin sat next to me and we left. We traveled for a long time through town, passing patrols of soldiers and police here and there. Finally, we left the town safely and by morning arrived in Gorodnia. In this little town I boarded a train, which was stopped by a police official with soldiers. They took us to the police station and held us there until a Cossack detachment arrived. They placed me in a closed carriage and took me back to Chernigov. We arrived there in the evening. The prison cell at the police station where they first placed me was completely empty. I lay down on the floor. A gendarme with a drawn saber stood near me. As soon as I began to fall asleep, the gendarme awakened me and asked: "Who are your accomplices? What are their names?" Despite my weakness and absolute exhaustion, this question always brought me to my senses. I knew too well why the gendarme asked me this; I was silent. This kind of questioning did not last long. The gendarmes realized that their chicanery could not achieve their goals and they stopped waking me up.

During the interrogation by the procurator, I did not deny the attempt on [the governor's life] but refused to give my name and appeared in court as "the unknown." By concealing my name, I hoped to protect my parents from suffering for their daughter, who was to die at the gallows, and [my] comrades from arrest. I was soon transferred to a military prison. They informed me that I would be tried the following day. At 10 a.m. Shpaizman, Iasha Leikin, and I appeared before the military court. When they brought us into the courtroom, it was filled with gendarmes and police. In the corner stood the unfortunate old people — Leikin's parents. Apart from them, there was no audience.

The court ceremony did not last long. They offered us [the opportunity] to say "our final words." Comrade Shpaizman and I, confirming our membership in the Socialist Revolutionary Combat Organization unit and the attempt on Khvostov's life, categorically stated that Leikin had no part in the attempt and had no ties to the Combat Organization. Leikin pleaded not guilty. In his speech, the procurator called for the death sentence for all three of us. After this, the court recessed to deliberate the verdict; they took us away to the prison cells. Horror enveloped me at the thought that they could hang Leikin. For a few hours, I paced in my cell. The sun set. It had become dark, but the judges were still deliberating.

The clock struck midnight. Someone opened the door quietly. "Please come to the courtroom." The gendarme spoke in a whisper. The corridor was in semidarkness. One could hear the clinking of the spurs, the rattling of sabers, the noise of hasty footsteps. Gendarmes and police were everywhere. The courtroom was poorly lit; the faces of the judges looked weary and morose. At last, the chairman of the court, an old general, began to read the verdict: "The unknown male"[16] is sentenced to the death penalty by hanging. "The unknown female" is sentenced to the death penalty by hanging. Iakov Leikin is sentenced to ten years of hard labor.

We felt as though an enormous weight had fallen from our shoulders. We began to congratulate Leikin and say our farewells to him. "Ten years of hard labor!" I said loudly. "You will not have served a year before Russia is free." The judges looked with surprise at our animated faces and one gendarme whispered to another, "They obviously did not grasp their own sentences."

They took us back to our cells. "This is the death sentence?" I asked myself when I was left alone. "But why is my heart so light? Why do I not feel that which will take place in twenty-four hours?" I looked into the corners of my heart, I listened to its very secret movements and thoughts, but I did not find any signs of death there. Finally, I dozed off.

"Get dressed, get dressed!" This voice immediately brought me to my senses. "Surely, twenty-four hours have not passed already," I unwittingly asked the gendarme. "What time is it?" He replied, "Six o'clock in the morning."

I thought, "It makes no difference, does it, that they hang me a few hours earlier or later." The sun has not yet risen. But I so wanted to see the sun! "Where will this take place?" I asked the gendarme, but he looked at me in confusion and did not reply. Suddenly I remembered about the letter that I had prepared for my parents. They were my final words to them. I looked around. There was no one except for the gendarme. "Listen," I told him, "I cannot go peacefully to the gallows without sending this note to my parents. This is the final wish of a woman on her way to death and you cannot refuse her. No matter who you are, you have or had parents and you must understand their grief." I placed the letter in his hand. He concealed the letter and said, "Fine, I will send it. But now I will take you not to the place of the execution but to prison." I assured him, "They will hang me there." Later I learned that my family never received this letter. However, in any case, this gendarme was honorable, because the thought that my parents would receive my final words heartened me and I could die peacefully.

I was taken to the city prison in a closed carriage. "I must wait here the entire day," I thought. The day passed quickly and night fell. I lay on the bunk without getting undressed. Anxiously, I listened to the footsteps of the prison inspector in the corridor. The hours dragged by slowly. I heard footsteps all the time; often they grew close to my door but each time they passed by. At last I fell asleep. When I woke up the sun was high. The unrestrained joy of life enveloped me. I felt my arms and legs, and the happy awareness that I was alive was stronger than the death sentence that hung over me. Every sound that I was able to detect made me happy. A tiny piece of sky, which I saw through the bars, drew me to it. I passed through the cell, and my dreams carried me away far from the prison walls. A great feeling of love for life, love for every living thing, increasingly grew inside me and vanquished death.

"They will hang you this evening," I tried to persuade myself, but these words seemed meaningless to me. They were unable to vanquish in me the faith in life and in all that is living. My jailers no longer angered me; there was no more hatred in me for these deceitful people. I was in this state the entire day, but toward evening, I again began to prepare for death and to wait. In this manner, I passed six days in anticipation of death. On the seventh day, I heard a tap on the wall. My heart beat with joy; I had a neighbor.

"Who are you?" I tapped; and the answer followed clear and unmistakable.

"Shpaizman."

"Could it be?" I exclaimed. "He is here; they have not hanged him yet."

Soon we were already deeply immersed in conversation. He explained that he had spent all this time in a military prison and that they had only [just] transferred him here.

"This is the last day," he tapped.

"Yes, I am certain," I responded.

We hastened to share with one another all the thoughts and feelings—everything that we lived through during the years of our friendship, which neither prison nor exile had broken. "I do not want you to die," tapped Shpaizman, and the feelings deeply hidden in his soul until now were expressed freely in words at this moment of death. I could not stand at the wall any longer. Completely weakened, I threw myself on the bunk. Hour after hour passed. Night fell. An unusual sound could be heard in the corridor. I held my breath and clasped my hands to my heart. I heard as they opened the door of the neighboring cell. "They have come for Kolia." I thought. I listened. Someone was approaching my door. "Farewell my beloved. Farewell my dear!"

"Kolia! Kolia!" I shouted, but the thick walls drowned my weak voice. I pressed myself to the corner and listened. The sound of footsteps now became weaker and weaker and finally died away. I leaned against the wall through which I had conversed with Kolia. He was no longer there.

Someone carefully opened my door and entered the cell. "Finally," I thought, and leaping up I turned my face to my executioner. The dawn had broken, and the small lamp that illuminated my room barely flickered in the light of the newborn day. The chief of the prison came over and began to look me in the face, not saying a word. There was something evil in his gaze. I realized that he had come from the place of execution. He stood idle like that for five minutes and left.

I lay on the bed with eyes open. The prison clock rang ten o'clock. The door of my cell flung wide open and some kind of official entered. "I have brought you His Majesty's pardon. You have been given the gift of life," he said and left. The hours passed slowly. I lay motionless on the bunk, trying to grasp the enormous significance of this fact. However, a sudden emptiness arose in me. I did not feel anything [in] my soul. The threads of my internal life had broken, and I attempted in vain to collect the lost ends.[17]

"Report of Collegial Councilor of Special Commissions (Ministry of the Interior) to the Department of Police (30 January 1914)"

GARF, f. 400, op. 11, d. 270 t. 1, l. 77.

According to the information received from the secret service, a meeting in honor of the famous Socialist Revolutionary Mariia Shkol'nik will be organized at the initiative of a New York group with the assistance of the Socialist Revolutionary Party on 5 February in New York. The public speakers will be American, Russian, and Jewish socialists, but it is still not clear who they are.

"Report to the Department of Police (21 February 1914–6 March 1914)"

GARF, f. 400, op. 11, d. 270 t. 1.

According to the information received from the secret service, a meeting was held in honor

of Mariia Shkol'nik on 5 February in New York in the Cooper Union building (Third Avenue and Eighth Street [sic]). Approximately eight hundred people participated in the meeting.

Dr. [Pavel] Kaplan, a Socialist Revolutionary, was elected chairman and in his short inaugural speech declared that he, like all those displaced from their homeland, is proud of heroes like Mariia Shkol'nik.

"We must," he declared, "assist the Social-Democratic [sic] Party; we must send similar fighters and heroes again" (whistles and applause). He is certain that M. Shkol'nik will find herself in the first ranks of the revolution as soon as the movement begins anew in Russia.

Then the chairman gave the floor to V. Mikhailov, a Socialist Revolutionary who provided a description of Shkol'nik's activities.

"From the age of fifteen," Mikhailov began, "she was already working for the Bund organization and then, after her arrest and liberation from prison, [she] joined the Socialist Revolutionary Party [Combat Organization]. The party is proud of workers like Shkol'nik, but it is not enough to be proud of them; we need to bow down before them."

"They are heroes of the Combat Organization and only they have dealt the first serious blow to the Russian government. For us, Mariia Shkol'nik represents the swallow of a new spring, a new Russian revolution, and thus we can say, 'Long live Mariia Shkol'nik, long live the swallow of a new Russian revolution!'"

Then a certain Kenedi [Kennedy] and Vud [Wood], members of the Socialist Party of America, spoke in English. They concluded their speeches with compliments directed at Mariia Shkol'nik.

Mr. Gurevich, a former Social Democrat but now an independent socialist, spoke in Yiddish: "We should," he said, "learn from Mariia Shkol'nik how to fight our enemies. Here, in America too, not everything is good." He further appealed to workers to join workers' unions and to organize for the coming struggle against capital.

The final speaker was Shkol'nik herself. She declared that she was glad to come to America for here she could do so much for the relief of the fate of close comrades who were dying of hunger in convict prisons in Russia at the present time. Then Shkol'nik thanked everyone for the joyous reception and asked that we stand to honor the memories of [Grigorii] Gershuni[18] and Egor Sosonov; all those present did so. Then the chairman read the letter of apology from Messrs. Deich and Katz, who also should have appeared, and closed the meeting.

NOTES

1. [See document 144 for an earlier segment of this memoir. Shkol'nik joined a circle led by Hanna, the Smorgon rabbi's daughter and Bund activist. When her father discovered the clandestine books that she had been hiding for Hanna, Shkol'nik told him that she wanted an education, that she could not live in such poverty any longer: "I want to learn how we can improve our lives." However, she concealed her revolutionary activities from him. Her father suggested that she move to Odessa, where her uncle lived, to pursue her desires for an education and self-improvement.]

2. [Here Shkol'nik describes her activities in the circle as an agitator. Her small circle lost three of its members: Zhenia and Izrail were sentenced to prison and David was taken for military service.]

3. *Iskra* was the political newpaper of the Russian Socialist Democratic Labor Party (RSDLP), which Il'ia Lenin and other Marxist revolutionaries founded abroad in 1900 to unite their movement.

4. [Shkol'nik goes on to recount her meeting with her laywers Kal'manovich and Ratner, who are horrified to learn that she had written the letters when she was only sixteen years old. The police transported her from Kishinev to Odessa to stand trial. The trial took place at the beginning of November 1903. A few family members were present, as well as a few members of the general public were in the courtroom.]

5. [She goes on to describe the long journey with other prisoners — including thieves, murderers, and others who were ill with tuberculosis and other diseases — to Siberia (passing through Kiev, Kursk, Voronezh, the Urals, and Tiumen in Siberia). The extract here resumes after the convicts have begun to travel overland by cart.]

6. [Shkol'nik then traveled from Krasnoiarsk to Kansk and finally to a hamlet in central Siberia.]

7. [The *Boevaia organizatsiia* (Combat Organization) was the terrorist arm of the Socialist Revolutionary party founded by Gershuni; it was active in Russia starting in 1902.]

8. [Boris Savinkov (1879–1925) was head of the Combat Organization during the Revolution of 1905–7. His successor was Evno Azef (1869–1918), the notorious double agent who simultaneously planned terrorist attacks and collaborated with the secret police.]

9. [In Shkol'nik's interview with the *Forward* in 1914, she observed: "He was fat, ugly, with the appearance of some kind of repulsive bourgeois, which, however, I did not notice then. We so valued him, so respected him" (GARF f. 400, op. 1911, d. 270, t. 1, l. 193).]

10. [Ivan Kaliaev (1877–1905) participated in the attempted assassination of Plehve in 1904 and succeeded in assassinating Grand Duke Sergei Aleksandrevich in Moscow on 17 February 1905.]

11. [On pogroms in Kiev, see Natan Meir, "'The Sword Hanging over Their Heads': The Significance of Pogrom for Russian Jewish Everyday Life and Self-Understanding (The Case of Kiev)," in *Anti-Jewish Violence: Rethinking the Pogrom in East European History*, ed. Jonathan Dekel-Chen, David Gaunt, Natan M. Meir, and Israel Bartal (Bloomington: Indiana University Press, 2011), 111–28.]

12. [Dmitrii Karakozov (1840–66) carried out the first radical attempt to assassinate Alexander II in 1866; he was executed by hanging on 3 September 1866.]

13. [They related a story about how the peasants interpreted the October Manifesto as permission to take the extra grain from the landlords but were punished by an "important official" for rioting. The authorities flogged one peasant and shot eight

others dead. The peasants apparently knew Shapiro well and told him this story.]

14. This bomb was filled with some concoction supplied by Azef.

15. Khvostov was not killed by the explosion, but only injured. Apparently he lost his hearing and partial sight as a result of the Socialist Revolutionary attack. After serving in Chernigov since 1903, he was appointed a senator in 1906.]

16. Comrade Shpaizman was also tried as "Unknown."

17. [Shkol'nik's partner Aaron Shpaizman was hanged for his assassination attempt (despite the failure of his bomb to explode), but she received a reprieve from the death penalty because she was a woman. In the last two chapters of her memoirs, Shkol'nik describes how she was transferred to the Butryki Transit Prison in Moscow, where she was confined with other female prisoners, including five other Socialist Revolutionary (SR) female activists, who collectively became known as the *shesterka* (the "six"). These women, who had either attempted or succeeded in carrying out political assassinations, included Aleksandra Izamilovich, Lidiia Ezerskaia, Revekka Fialka, Anastasiia Bitsenko, and Mariia Spiridonova. Sentenced to exile in 1907, the *shesterka* traveled to the Nerchinsk penal complex in the Transbaikal by the trans-Siberian railroad until they reached their first prison in Akatui. Here they found other SR prisoners including the leader of the Combat Organization, Grigori Gershuni, and Yegor Sazonov, who assassinated Vlacheslav von Plehve. Shkol'nik includes a riveting description of Gershuni's escape from the prison in a barrel of pickled cabbage with only two rubber tubes for air. The women were later sent to the Mal'tsev women's prison, which was notorious for its harsh living con-

ditions and corrupt officials. When Skol'nik fell ill with appendicitis, the prison officials allowed her to be transferred first to the Zerenui prison and then to Irkutsk for surgery. Nine days after her surgery, she decided to escape rather than return to the horrific Mal'tsev prison. With the help of her SR connections, she fled the Irkutsk prison hospital to Manchuria in July 1911, traveled to Harbin and Dairen, and then escaped to Europe. See Sally A. Boniece, "Maria Spiridonova, 1884–1918: Feminine Martyrdom and Revolutionary Mythmaking" (Ph.d. Dissertaion, Indiana University, 1995), 80–191. Shkol'nik traveled to America in 1914 and gave an interview to the *Forward*. She was twenty-eight years old at the time. For the interview in Yiddish, see the January 1914 issue of the *Forward*. For a translation of it into Russian with comments from the translator (who referred to her as "the criminal"), see GARF, f. 400, op. 1911, d. 270, t. 1, ll. 185–202. Following the Russian Revolution of 1917, Shkol'nik joined the Left Socialist Revolutionaries who reconciled with the Bolsheviks, and she became a Communist Party member.]

18. [Grigorii Gershuni (1870–1908) was born in Kovno and studied to be a pharmacist at Kiev University. He was one of the founders of the Workers' Party for the Political Liberation of Russia. Later he helped to found the Socialist Revolutionary Party in 1901 and became the head of the Combat Organization in 1902. Betrayed by Azef, he was arrested in 1904 and sentenced to life in prison and hard labor, but escaped from Siberia to America in 1904. He died of tuberculosis in 1908 in Geneva. See Grigorii Gershuni, *Iz nedavnego proshlogo* (Paris: Tribune Russe, 1908); Anna Geifman, *Entangled in Terror: The Azef Affair and the Russian Revolution* (Wilmington, DE: Scholarly Resources, 2000).]

Zionism

[175]

Hibbat Tsiyyon: Letters between Leon Pinsker and Naftali Zvi Yehudah Berlin[1]

Naftali Berlin to Leon Pinsker

Alter Druyanov and Shulamit Laskov, eds., *Ketavim le-toledot hibbat tsiyyon ve-yishuv eretz yisrael* (Tel Aviv: Ha-kibbutz Ha-meuhad, 1988), 5: 431–33.

BLESS THE LORD.
1 KISLEV 5648 [NOVEMBER 17, 1887]

THE WISE AND HONORABLE, WHO SEEKS
THE BENEFIT OF THE HOLY LAND, WHO
DOES MUCH TO ESTABLISH ITS SOUL,
THE HONORABLE DR. PINSKER.

Last week I wrote his honor from Vil'na, and upon returning to my home [in Volozhin] I found his letter dated 19 Marheshvan [November 6].[2] I am compelled to repeat what I have said regarding the inhabitants of the colony of Gedera, for a letter has reached me from an important figure in Jerusalem, who is well known to our friend, Rabbi Pines, who is no fanatic, and speaks well of the settlements. All the same, he goes to great lengths to denigrate the inhabitants of Gedera, for one of them has the power to lead the many astray, who, were it not for him, would walk on the straight path. He also informed me that in [the settlement] of Rishon le-Zion, which is supported by the philanthropist (may he be granted length of days),[3] there were some inhabitants who were members of BILU [Beit Ya'akov Lekhu Ve-nelkha][4], and did evil and destructive things; the philanthropist opened his eyes and concluded that it would be bet-ter if they [the other inhabitants] were free of them, and if they were replaced by others. Thus, for whom do we toil, while they are destroying much good, for I know there are several holy communities that are sitting on a bundle of money, but refuse to send it until the Land is purified of its destroyers? [. . .][5] Thus, his honor will understand that all his suggestions regarding the [inhabitants of Gedera] are strange to us. Better to disperse a few thousand francs and allow them to settle in the diaspora, and to settle in Gedera worthy Jews from Jerusalem who wish to work the land faithfully; this will improve conditions for the inhabitants of Jerusalem as well, who are suffering from a lack of food there. We will be praised by the observant communities in these regions [in Russia], and the benefits will increase as it becomes known that we did this great thing regarding the service of the Lord in the Holy Land. [. . .]

As I wrote you in my previous letter, even though we do not agree about everything, we must strive to achieve equilibrium on that which brings us together [namely, Jewish settlement of the Holy Land]. We [the pious trustees] cannot concede anything with regard to our views, for the Torah is our guide, but his honor and those who share his views can concede on this matter. In this manner all the fruits of our efforts will call out to the

Lord, who watches over them from the beginning to the end of the year; we need the rains, and it is not like other countries in which drought is rare, and surely rain is not needed for drinking water in any event. In the Land of Israel, if, God forbid, there is no rain, there is no water to drink. [. . .]

In these matters, it is incumbent on his honor to come to a meeting of minds with me, for from that will flow consequences for the life of the [Jewish] community [in the Holy Land]. If things are not established as they should be, there is cause for concern that from one year to the next Hoveve Tsiyyon will be diminished in Lithuania and beyond, until, God forbid, it melts away entirely. Thus, we must gird ourselves and seal the breaches. God is with us and will not abandon us. [. . .] His honor will also be remembered well, for he has done much with strength and courage [. . .] his reward from heaven is reserved, for long life in this world, and eternal life in the next. [. . .]

Leon Pinsker to Naftali Berlin

Druyanov and Laskov, eds., *Ketavim le-toledot hibbat tsiyyon ve-yishuv eretz yisrael*, 5: 440–442.

ODESSA, 8 KISLEV, 5648
[NOVEMBER 24, 1887]

HIS HONOR THE GREAT RABBI AND *GAON*, LIGHT OF THE EXILE, ETC., OUR TEACHER AND RABBI, NAFTALI ZVI YEHUDAH BERLIN, MAY HIS LIGHT SHINE.

I received your letter. Regarding the words of the important figure of Jerusalem, who cast aspersions on the inhabitants of Gedera, I wish to convey to his honor the words of Rabbi Pines that I received today; seeing as there is no kosher slaughterer in Gedera, they refrain from eating meat from holiday to holiday, and thus he asked me to appoint a slaughterer and inspector so that they might enjoy meat from time to time. Of course I will honor this request and will employ a slaughterer, but how could one imagine that sinners and destroyers would refrain from eating meat from holiday

to holiday because they do not have a slaughterer who can provide them with kosher meat? I do not know if that important rabbi from Jerusalem relies on rumors—but I know, to my dismay, that many of our important rabbis rely on rumors that "bloom in the air" when it comes to desecration of the religion, without gathering evidence that is proper according to the laws of the Torah—or whether he is reporting as an eyewitness. [. . .] I am almost certain that now, under the supervision of Rabbi Pines, the people of Gedera will enjoy the approval of all the children of Israel.

In any event, God forbid I should insist on my position; I will present the honorable *gaon*'s proposal to replace inhabitants of Gedera with those of Jerusalem to the advisors and trustees.

Together with that, I must inform the honorable *gaon* that the tension in Rishon le-Zion, which led the philanthropist to bring in new settlers in place of veterans, had nothing to do with religious matters, but was caused by disagreements with the philanthropist's overseers [that led the settlers] to show disrespect to the philanthropist. [. . .]

The honorable *gaon* says that he and his colleagues cannot concede anything with regard to their views, for the Torah is their guide, thus it is incumbent on me and my colleagues to concede. Please know, honorable *gaon*, that were this between you and me, even given our differing views, we could arrive at a shared position. But we work with thousands of Jews from different parties, and what I would concede they never would. If there are many members of Hoveve Tsiyyon who tremble before the Lord, there are many, indeed thousands, of those who would not wish in any way to punish the colonists for disregarding the voice of the religious guardians as the honorable *gaon* suggested in his last letter; and were they to hear such a thing [that people were punished for religious transgressions] they would separate from us, and, in the end, Hoveve Tsiyyon would be diminished.

God forbid that I should suggest to the honorable and exalted *gaon* that he compromise on matters of Torah, but it is appropriate for the religious leaders of Israel not to overreach, to assert their views over the laws of the Torah, [to ignore the principle] that it is better to transgress unwittingly than wantonly, etc.[6] Why would the honorable *gaon* insist that the colonists give the tithe to the priest or Levite in perpetuity, when the Torah permits buying back the produce? Why will not the leading rabbis of Israel try to find a way to permit working the vineyards in the sabbatical year — not for consuming the grapes, but to preserve the vines when it is practically impossible to demand that the colonists refrain entirely from such work, for the vines would all be lost, and all the labor of past years would descend into oblivion — when undoubtedly the colonists will not listen to those who prohibit? I am not an expert in viticulture, and I do not know what labor is required to sustain them [the vines], but one can learn this from experts, and it is appropriate to find a leniency regarding those labors, for the existence of the vineyards depends on them. If the rabbinic scholars would do this, if they would strive to find a good and moderate path for the colonists to be reconciled with the pious, in such a way that the moderns would not consider it to be overreaching, all the parties would unite for the sake of the love of Zion, and, with the help of the God of Zion, we would accomplish great things.

Naftali Berlin to Leon Pinsker

Druyanov and Laskov, eds., *Ketavim le-toledot hibbat tsiyyon ve-yishuv eretz yisrael*, 5: 452–455.

Regarding my desire to be rid of [some of] the inhabitants of Gedera and to replace them with better people, this is only if they wish to leave, in which case we would pay a few thousand marks for their labor to this point. And this would be right, for while it may be so that the criticism is greater than is appropriate, all the same it would be worthwhile to be cleansed of the disgrace of our sinful brethren. [. . .] Therefore I suggested to his honor maybe there is room for this [banishing the sinful inhabitants of Gedera]. But clearly they cannot be forced to leave against their will.

Now may his honor please listen well. Our friend, Rabbi Pines, has asked for a slaughterer and inspector for Gedera, and his honor said he would fulfill this request. Now I would add that we should strive to find a slaughterer and inspector who is distinguished in his knowledge of Torah beyond [the rules of] slaughtering and inspecting, who knows and learns the practical laws that pertain to the sanctity of the Land, and what he cannot determine he would know to ask of the *geonim* of Jerusalem (may it be rebuilt speedily in our day). And this slaughterer and inspector should also be a prayer leader and Torah reader; of him it should be said in the words of Josiah the king in the book of II Chronicles, "serving God and his people Israel," meaning that he should be the intermediary between the residents and workers and their Father in heaven. And, [with all that] he will, of course, be able to expound words of *aggadah* and ethics to them on Sabbaths and holidays. [. . .]

If his honor were to ask my advice, I would recommend a man known to me, R. Yehiel David Asch, an expert slaughterer and inspector, who filled this role in Jerusalem (may it be rebuilt speedily in our day) when he lived there, and to this day he has a father and daughter there, although he left for the diaspora because he could not make a living and is now an emissary for the holy yeshiva [of Volozhin]. To be sure, it is contrary to the law to migrate from Jerusalem to the diaspora, and in my opinion he is capable of all the things I mentioned, and it be quite acceptable. May his honor please let me know his view on this, and I will suggest it to him [Asch] as well. [. . .][7]

Regarding the seventh [sabbatical] year, his honor knows that labor that is required to preserve the trees [. . .] is permitted in the seventh year, but one must know the details in this matter [. . .] and there is room to discuss. [. . .] His honor should not say that the rabbis are [unnecessarily] stringent and do not know of the travails of the settlers who want for a living. It is forbidden to say such a thing. When it is possible to rule leniently we do not refrain from saying so honestly, but when leniency is impossible his honor should not complain and belittle the honor of the Torah's sages, for they uphold the nation and Judaism, and were it not for the great Torah sages who strengthen every generation, the entire people would have become assimilated among the gentiles and the name of Israel would have been forgotten, God forbid. As long as the generation truly wishes to be assimilated, to become the same and imitate the ways of the nations of the world, the Holy One, blessed be He, instills a deep hatred in the hearts of the nations to alienate Israel from them, so that Israel will know who they are. [. . .][8] Given that we work as one in this exalted matter [settling the land], it is incumbent on us to converge as much as possible. [. . .]

I also mention today that it would be appropriate to try to settle in one of the colonies the people of Jerusalem (may it be rebuilt speedily in our day) who wish to work the land. This would be a great mitzvah, a life-saving act, that would bring gratification to the faithful Jews of Russia and Poland.

Leon Pinsker to Naftali Berlin

Druyanov and Laskov, eds., *Ketavim le-toledot hibbat tsiyyon ve-yishuv eretz yisrael*, 5: 479–481.

ODESSA, 4 TEVET, 5648
[DECEMBER 19, 1887]

THE HONORABLE RABBI, THE
GREAT GENIUS, THE LIGHT OF THE
EXILE, OUR TEACHER AND RABBI,
THE RABBI NAFTALI ZVI YEHUDAH
BERLIN, MAY HIS LIGHT SHINE.

I received the honorable *gaon*'s letter, dated 19 Kislev [December 5], and may the honorable *gaon* forgive me for being slow to reply, due to all my distractions.

The honorable *gaon* clarified his suggestion regarding the inhabitants of Gedera, that he meant only to suggest that they could leave only if they so desire. And now that we know the extent of the love of these inhabitants for the holy land — they have devoted their lives to it, and have cast off the pleasures of the world to endure want and famine in the land of Israel, and still today stand ready to endure all the travails under an open sky almost without any protection, and never leave the land that is the object of all their concern — the honorable *gaon* has withdrawn his suggestion, and, Lord willing, I will make this known in my next general update [to the advisors and treasurers of the movement].[9]

As for the Rabbi Yehiel David Asch, whom the honorable *gaon* wants to appoint as a slaughterer and inspector in Gedera, I have already written to Rabbi Pines about this [approvingly], and I requested that he let me know if this has not already been done. [. . .]

[In the December 5 letter] the honorable *gaon* said, "His honor should not say that the rabbis are [unnecessarily] stringent and do not know about the travails of the settlers who want for a living, and so on. When leniency is impossible his honor should not complain and belittle the honor of the Torah's sages." I do not know why the honorable and exalted *gaon* attributes such ideas to me. I do not harbor such negative thoughts regarding the rabbis, and all the more do I not belittle their honor, for what is it to me to interfere in matters of "prohibited and permitted" [that is, religious law]? If there is an area where I part company with the view of the [rabbinic] overseers, it is not in the area of "prohibited and permitted," but in the conduct of the interest of the Hoveve Tsiyyon. In my view, for example, we must take care to ensure that the colonists do not wantonly violate the laws of the Torah, and that in general they should be upright people. But we should not interfere too deeply in their affairs, to appoint for them a prayer leader, Torah reader, or preacher, or someone to watch over how they are fulfilling a particular commandment, as the honorable *gaon* suggests that we appoint a particular scholar from Tzefat to oversee the tithing in [the settlement of] Yesod ha-Maaleh. The colonists are not small children who need to be educated to watch their steps, and if we say that we should appoint an overseer for the tithes, or how they bake matzo, if their *tefillin* or *tzizit* are kosher, and the like, we do not have the means, and it is an embarrassment for them. The colonists are *kesherim* [worthy Jews] like all our brethren. No one from outside should interfere in their affairs. They should choose preachers; they should set aside time to study Torah; they should behave like pious and worthy individuals, but they should do that themselves. It is incumbent on Hoveve Tsiyyon to strive to provide those things that a Jewish community cannot do without. Thus, we have built a mikvah in Petach Tikvah, and we will do likewise, Lord willing, in Gedera. When there are enough husbands [and wives], and clear authorization to build houses and to dig wells, we will strive to build a mikvah, but we should not cast suspicion [on them] and to serve as guardians as if they were children. This view of mine, which is not mine alone, does not rest of the spirit of toleration of the new generation, nor on the large divide between rural and urban interests, but on the obligations that Hoveve Tsiyyon took upon itself. Some things are beneficial for any community, like preachers, schools, yeshivot, hospitals, artists, and so on, but none of these things are the responsibility of Hoveve Tsiyyon, whose goal is to support those who work the earth in the Holy Land. It is self-evident that those who are supported in the Holy Land by our brethren, the children of Israel [in the diaspora], must observe the commandments, and those who cast off their obligations are unworthy of support. But it is for the colonists themselves to ensure that they are worthy Jews, just as it

is done everywhere else; it is not for us to impose teachers, overseers, and guardians as we do with children, for Hoveve Tsiyyon was not created for that. "Grasp all, lose all."[10]

The honorable *gaon* can see that in this matter, generally, I am not relying just on personal opinion; I constantly confer with the other trustees of the movement, may their lights shine. And please believe me, honorable *gaon*, if the [religious] trustees would agree with me and my colleagues that it is not for us to be the kosher supervisors of the generation, just as we agree with them to separate from the [religiously] forbidden, all of Hoveve Tsiyyon would unite as one, and peace would reign over our righteous endeavor, and the settlement [of the land] would soar.

Naftali Berlin to Leon Pinsker

Yitzhak Rivkind, *Igrot Tsiyyon* (Jerusalem: [s.n.] 1923), 21–23.

BLESS THE LORD, 24 TEVET, 5648 [JANUARY 8, 1888], VOLOZHIN

THE FAMOUS, HONORABLE, AND WISE, WHO DELIGHTS TO DO KINDNESS ON BEHALF OF THE RESIDENTS OF OUR LAND [OF ISRAEL], DR. PINSKER, MAY HIS LIGHT SHINE.

Your honor's letter reached me on 7 Tevet [December 22, 1887], but I could not free up time from my many burdens until today. [...]

I see your honor, may his light shine, expressing views that for the most part are positive to us, however his remarks concluded thus: If the leaders [of Hibbat Tsiyyon] would agree with us on some matters, just as we agree with them on some matters — specifically, if they would agree that there is no need to appoint a guardian to oversee the [religious] behavior of the colonists [inhabiting the Zionist settlement of Gedera], just as we agree that these colonists need to be observant of the Torah — all of Hibbat Tsiyyon would unite with a full heart.

With all respect, these words are difficult to hear. Tell me, please, why are the colonists any more obligated to observe the Torah than any other Jews whose forefathers stood at Mount Sinai and the heard the words of the living God, "I am the Lord your God, etc.? Therefore [because I am your God] you must observe my commandments. We sealed a covenant on this at Sinai." [. . .] And what difference is there between those who live in the Land and those who live outside regarding the laws that do not depend on the Land? The prophet Malachi (3:12) says, "And all the nations shall call you blessed; for you shall be a land of delight, says the Lord of hosts." This means it is not our Land that makes us Jews, but we ourselves are a land of delight, and that is what makes us blessed in the eyes of the gentiles who reflect wisely on the matter. If we had separated ourselves as the Lord commands in Leviticus [. . .] we would not have come to all our troubles, and [experienced] the alienation they impose on us. They oppress us economically in all kinds of ways. All of this came upon us as a result of Divine Providence, to force us to separate from the gentiles, for the word of the Lord will stand. And if we do not embrace [that word] voluntarily it will come forcibly. [. . .]

That being the case, your honor and his colleagues have not conceded anything to us. And we cannot concede that there is no need for a guardian to ensure that they [the settlers] observe the Torah and its commandments. No, sir. If we could force our brethren outside the Land in this, we would be obligated to do so. But what can we do? It is beyond our reach. But surely those people whom we settle in the Land of Israel, whose lives and happiness depend on us, it is on the condition [that they observe] that we do this kindness for them.

Is it not clear to anyone with intelligence that we must force them to observe the Torah? Did not Nehemiah the governor do likewise when he set up guardians to ensure that they [the Jews of his day in the fourth century B.C.E.] did not violate the Sabbath? And when he forced them to separate from their foreign wives against their will?[11] And regard-

ing this new generation that we are raising, Dr. Erlanger (may his light shine) informed us that the Baron, the philanthropist, firmly warned them about observing the commandments. And when he heard that one of them was drinking TOTON on the Sabbath, he banished him from his land. And although I am not sure that he completely fulfilled his obligation in this matter, he is after all someone who grew up in Paris, who does not know how to impose his will fully on those who depend on him. But we, the children of Lithuania and its environs — God's Torah is with us, and we know that we are obligated to force those whom we can force to observe the Torah.

More astonishing is what his honor wrote, "We should not interfere too deeply in their affairs, to appoint for them a prayer leader, Torah reader, or preacher, and on on. The colonists are not small children who need to be educated to watch their steps, and so on. The colonists are *kesherim* like all our brethren. No one from outside should interfere in their affairs. They should choose preachers; they should set aside time to study Torah." To this I will reply by citing his honor's own words in his Hebrew letter that the colonists are poor who cannot afford to offer the tithe to the Levite as the Torah commands. Thus, how could they procure a preacher to sermonize to them, as the observant among them desire? Is it not incumbent on us — who tend to their worldly needs — to tend even more so to their eternal needs? To teach them the Torah and its commandments, which they would want to hear and do, if not for the fact that they do not know what is forbidden them? Behold, in every community in the diaspora we expend public or charitable funds to appoint qualified people to decide religious law, lead prayers, read the Torah, and more.

Those people who, while in Russia, embraced freedom from the commandments are like children who assimilated among the gentiles. We are obligated to educate them and help them understand their [religious] obligations in all things. It would be best if this could be done through preaching ethics and truth; but if they turn a cold shoulder to that, God forbid, we must separate from them and not tend to their needs. Attend to what I am saying, and do as we and all the contributors in these districts wish. If so, they will continue with their efforts on behalf of this mitzvah [building communities in the Land of Israel]. But if his honor and those close to him from this new generation, with their new ideas about Judaism, reject what we are saying, and a heavenly bird will spread the word that the colonists breach the fence of Torah and do as they please, there will be a sharp decrease in the Lovers of Zion in these regions. Of this I am certain.

NOTES

1. [The following letters are part of a series of letters between Pinsker and Berlin regarding the Eastern European Jewish settlers in the new Zionist community of Gedera, founded in 1884 by the Biluim. The land on which the settlement was founded had been purchased by Hibbat Tsiyyon, and the community relied on that movement for support. The correspondence, most of which may be found in Alter Druyanov and Shulamit Laskov, eds., *Ketavim le-toledot hibbat tsiyyon ve-yishuv eretz yisrael*, vol. 5 (Tel Aviv: Ha-kibbutz Ha-meuhad, 1988), provides insight into the interplay between elites and everyday life, both in Palestine and in the Russian Empire.]

2. [This letter was written by Pinsker to the six *yoatzim ve-gabbaim* [advisors and trustees] of the Hoveve Tsiyyon movement. In June 1887 the movement had been reorganized with Pinsker as leader and with six advisors, three of whom were important rabbinic figures: Naftali Berlin, Shmuel Mogilever, and Mordechai Eliasberg. Pinsker would send his

advisors updates on matters from time to time. It is important to recognize that Berlin is responding to Pinsker in his capacity as an advisor and trustee of the movement. The year 5648 (1887–88) was a crucial one for the movement, as debates surrounding religious observance dominated discussion — in part because this was an upcoming sabbatical year, one in which, according to Jewish law, the land is to lie fallow. The early Zionist settlers considered observing such law absurd on its face, especially so given the tenuous economic conditions of the early Zionist settlements.]

3. [The reference is to Edmond de Rothschild. In the literature of the time (and long after) he was referred to simply as *ha-nadiv* (the philanthropist).]

4. [Following the pogroms of 1881–82, a group of Jewish university students in Khar'kov decided to establish agricultural colonies in Palestine. The members of Bilu established two communities in Palestine.]

5. [In other words, Berlin is complaining that the non- and antireligious elements in the new settlements are leading traditional Jewish communities in Europe to withhold funds, undermining the work of Hoveve Tsiyyon.]

6. [This is a rabbinic principle that recognizes limits on rabbinic authority and suggests that there are times for rabbis to be silent, rather than press a position that the community cannot or will not bear.]

7. [In the end, the position went to someone else.]

8. [Berlin develops this theory of modern antisemitism in his *She'er Yisrael*, which he goes on to mention in this letter, offering Pinsker a copy of it.]

9. [He did so (see Druyanov and Laskov, eds., *Ketavim le-toledot hibbat tsiyyon ve-yishuv eretz yisrael*, document 1137).]

10. [This is a common rabbinic saying.]

11. [See Nehemiah, chapters 11 and 13].

[176]

Secret Police Reports on Zionist Activities in Synagogues

GARF, f. 102, Osobyi otdel, 1913 g, d. 44, ch. 19, ll. 13 ob.

"On the Jewish Question' Memorandum of the Secret Police, Number 32280 (30 October 1913)"

Glos Lubelski (Lublin, 1–11) reports the words of the Yiddish newspaper that in Belostok a splendid Jewish celebration has been organized for "the introduction of the people to the big synagogue." In the words of the Jewish press, all the houses were decorated with flags, illuminated in a manner supported by Jews with white and blue panels (national Zionist colors).

Up to 40,000 Jews with twelve baldachins [canopies] participated in the procession, accompanied by orchestral music and torch bearers. An enormous crowd of people in the synagogue were singing "Our hope is not yet lost."[1]

"Secret Memorandum to the Governor of Grodno Province (16 November 1913)"[2]

Regarding the letter of 31 October in the name of his Majesty, Major General [Vadim Nikolaevich] Shebeko, I have the honor to report to Your Excellency that the information presented in the correspondence of the newspaper *Glos Lubelski* was greatly exaggerated. The opening of the synagogue in Belostok took place with the permission of the former governor, Councillor of State, [Petr Mikhailovich] Boiarskii, under the follow-

ing circumstances. The celebration for the opening of the synagogue, with the local city head and chief of police present, began with the prayer "For the Tsar," after which a humble telegram was sent to His Imperial Majesty with expressions of [the] loyal feelings of the Jewish population of the city. A most gracious reply [from the tsar] by telegram was read in all synagogues and prayer houses in the city by order of the chief of police. The following day, after the opening of the new synagogue, the Holy Torah was transferred from the old prayer house. There were no illuminations and decorations on the houses along the path of the procession with the Holy Torah. They indeed carried the Torah scroll under canopies, accompanied by torch bearers. At the entrance of the synagogue, they were met by a few musicians. The songs were exclusively of a religious character. The celebration took place under the observance of a police detail headed by the chief of police, and the Jews did not have any kind of bands on their hands at the celebration.

NOTES

1. [The reference was to the Hatikvah; "our hope is not yet lost" (*od lo avdah tikavteinu*) comes from the refrain.]

2. [The signature on the memorandum is illegible, and the text does not indicate who sent it.]

Emigration

[177]

The Case of Mordukh Itskovich Berezovskii (1907)

RGIA, f. 1284, op. 224, d. 195, ll. 1–10.

*"Petition of Mordukh Itskovich
Berezovskii to the Minister of Internal
Affairs (12 February 1907)"*

In November 1905, a rumor arose in the town of Khorol, as it probably did in other towns, that the Jewish Colonization Society [*Evreiskoe Kolonizatsionnoe Obshchestvo*, or EKO], located at Zamiatin Lane 4 in St. Petersburg, would accept emigrants to Argentina[1] through its agents, with the permission of the government. One only needed to send fifty rubles for each emigrant to the EKO board or its agent. On 29 November 1905, I sent fifty rubles to the post office in Bozhedarovka (Ekaterinoslav province) addressed to agent Ofengendler of the EKO, as the enclosed receipt from the Khorol post office, number 611, shows. However, in response to this transfer of money, I received the attached letter from [Z. N.] Brunin of the EKO in Novo-Poltavka (dated 17 February 1906) that the board of directors would find it difficult to accept me as one of the emigrants. He did not mention a word about receiving my fifty rubles. After this, I turned to Z. N. Brunin and also to the committee in St. Petersburg branch about returning my fifty rubles if the society did want to accept me as an emigrant. To this, Brunin (the representative of the EKO) replied that he does not have means to intervene in the case. Despite my request to return my money (sent on 22 January 1907), the board of the EKO refuses to respond, although this society, its board of directors, or its representative Brunin in person earlier became involved in this case, informing me that it did not desire to accept me as an immigrant.

It is impossible to see the activities of the EKO and its agents (which operate with the permission of the government), as a simple violation of civil law, but rather [they] represent an abuse of power. This is because when I sent the money—fifty rubles to the agent of this Jewish organization who represents the society—he answered that the board of directors found it difficult to accept me among the emigrants. Ofengendler was therefore acting in the name of the society. I sent the money not to a private individual but to an agent sanctioned by the society, which is responsible for all the activities of its agents. From our district, many people (up to twenty) have sent a deposit of fifty rubles each and the money has vanished into thin air. I am a poor laborer, a tailor, an artisan who barely earns his daily bread to feed his large family with honest sweat and blood.

I am taking the liberty to submit this humble petition to Your Excellency so that you would sympathize with my position and order the EKO to return the fifty rubles that I sent to its agent in order that its agents not abuse the gracious trust of the Russian government in this society.

I hope that my modest request will not be neglected and that Your Excellency would order the EKO to return my hard-earned fifty rubles immediately so that I will not be ruined, because I do not have the means to recover it without the assistance of the state (which allows this society to function).

"Enclosed Document: Letter from
Z. N. Brunin, Representative of the EKO,
to Mordukh Itskovich Berezovskii
(17 February 1906)"

The board finds it difficult to accept you as one of the emigrants. It finds that your family does not have a sufficient number of workers and asks for additional information about the family's capacity for work.

I ask you to come to Novo-Poltavka to convey this information.

"Enclosed Document: Letter from Brunin
to Berezovskii (26 January 1907)"

Gracious Sir, as far as I know Mr. Ofengendler is not an agent of the EKO and I do not have any way to intervene in your business with him.

"Report of the EKO to the Department
of General Affairs (9 March 1907)"

Owing to the inquiry from Department of Special Affairs (23 February, number 4721) regarding the complaint of M[ordukh] Berezovskii about the actions of Mr. Ofengenden [*sic*], the Central Committee has the honor to report that Ofengendler has never been and is not a representative of the EKO. At the end of

1904, an independent group of Jewish settlers formed in the town of Bozhedarovka (Ekaterinoslav province). The group turned to the Central Committee with a request to give it plots of land in Argentina on favorable terms. The group elected as their leaders Aron Brodskii, Zelig Besedovskii, and Iosif Ofengenen [*sic*], who conducted negotiations with the Central Committee and are now in Argentina. The actions of the leaders, as a completely independent group that is not subject to the Central Committee, were not under the latter's control. They acted on their own. The obligations of the EKO to this group consisted of examining its staff's capacity for work and material welfare.

The name of the EKO is well known to the Ministry, and it periodically disseminates information about emigrants through publications in the Jewish press.

"Minister of Internal Affairs to the
Governor of Poltava (27 March 1907)"

The Department of Special Affairs requests that Your Excellency make an order to exact 1.50 rubles from the townsman Mordukh Istkovich Berezovskii of Khorol (Poltava province) for the stamp tax. Inform him that the Minister of Internal Affairs could not follow through with an order because Ofengenden [*sic*] is not and has never been a representative of this society. The damages incurred by the petitioner may be settled through a legal suit.

NOTE

1. [For applications to emigrate to Argentina through the auspices of the EKO, see RGIA, f. 1284, op. 224, d. 151.]

[178]

Problems with Exit Certificates and Foreign Passports

RGIA, f. 1284, op. 224, d. 195, ll. 26–26 ob.

"Ministry of Internal Affairs,
Department of General Affairs
to EKO (23 September 1908)"

The Central Committee of the EKO reported (number 489) about the difficulties experienced by Jewish emigrants in obtaining a police certificate about the absence of impediments to go abroad. In view of this, the Department of General Affairs asks you to indicate which kind of emigrants the Central Committee had in mind: Jews who leave Russia on the basis of point 16 of the Statutes for the Activities of the EKO in Russia [established on] 8 May 1892, or those who go abroad on a foreign passport[1] but intend to abandon the fatherland forever.

"EKO to the Department of General
Affairs (13 October 1908)"

In response to the memorandum from the ministry (dated 23 September, number 19962), the Central Committee of the EKO has the honor to report [...] that it had in mind emigrants who go abroad on an ordinary foreign passport. An individual who is provided an exit certificate on the basis of point 16 of the Statutes for the Activities of the EKO in Russia (established on 8 May 1892) does not need to receive a preliminary [police] certificate about the absence of impediments to go abroad. Nonetheless, they [such individuals] experience difficulty going abroad, primarily as a result of the ex-

treme slowness in obtaining the exit certificate, which usually takes several months. For example, the Central Committee submitted a petition on 3 June 1905 about issuing exit certificates for the families Aronov (from the town of Pochep, Chernigov province), Shevelevich (Belostok, Grodno province), and others. They received the exit certificates on 13 October. The petition submitted for the family of Kh. Shteinman (Chepovichi, Kiev province) was on 13 August 1906; they received the exit certificate only on 4 March 1907 (that is, after seven months). As a result of this delay, the majority of emigrants give up and leave on a foreign passport.

In view of the fact that the foreign passport is issued only upon submission of a police certificate about the absence of impediments to going abroad, the Central Committee requests assistance to deal with the difficulties associated with obtaining the certificate from the police.

NOTE

1. [Individuals who traveled on a foreign passport (*zagranichnyi pasport*) were Russian subjects visiting countries abroad but intending to return home. As shown in the document below, those who left on a foreign passport needed confirmation from the police that there were no impediments to going abroad (that is, no court cases pending, fines to be paid, financial obligations and debts, and the like).]

[179]

Tema Lysianskaia of Kiev and Her Children

RGIA, f. 1284, op. 224, d. 195, l. 45.

"Governor of Kiev to the Department of General Affairs (28 April 1909)"

I am informing the Department of General Affairs that I have rejected the petition to issue an exit certificate for the Jewish woman Tema Lysianskaia and her children, Meer Iankel and Zisel, because of the lack of a material birth certificate or other proof of a parental connection between Zisel and Tema Lysianskaia. I have reported this simultaneously to the Central Committee of the EKO.[1]

NOTE

1. [The mother and children received a certificate the following year, on 15 September 1910. This document shows the additional complication for families that did not register their children's births with the state rabbi.]

---

[180]

The Rights of Wives and Children Left Behind after the Secret Emigration of Husbands

RGIA, f. 1284, op. 224, d. 195, ll. 62–68, 90–93, 100–100 ob.

"Governor of Kiev to the Department of General Affairs (10 February 1909)"

I often receive petitions about issuing exit certificates to emigrants from Russia, based on the Statutes [for the Activities of the EKO in Russia] [established in] 8 May 1892, [. . .] from the wives and children of Jews who have surreptitiously emigrated or who left on a foreign passport for temporary travel, but who in fact remained there [abroad] permanently and now send for their families.

According to point 15 of the established statutes, entire Jewish families (that is, father, mother, and children) or individuals (that is, those with neither father nor mother) may emigrate. The [statutes] of 8 May 1892 did not foresee cases where a husband or father left Russia surreptitiously or on a foreign passport.

According to the laws on passports [. . .], a wife cannot use a foreign passport without presenting a certified statement from the husband granting his consent to her departure with the children abroad. The law did not foresee the emigration of wives and children alone beyond Russian borders on the basis of this document. I request the Department of General Affairs to report to me: (1) Can one issue an exit certificate to a wife and children in cases where their husbands have already left abroad for permanent residence? (2) Is it necessary to demand the presentation of a certified statement from the husband about his consent to the departure of the wife and children abroad? (3) Should the head of the family be considered to have abandoned the borders of Russia forever (irrespective of the reasons that may have impeded his legal departure abroad and that he evaded by emigrating secretly from the borders of Russia)?

"Ministry of Internal Affairs, Department of Police to the Department of General Affairs (3 May 1909)"

In cases where the head of a Jewish family emigrates from the empire and then sends for the remaining members of his family, in the Department's opinion this should be treated as the emigration of the entire family with all its members. Thus the questions submitted by the Governor of Kiev should be decided in the following manner: (1) an exit certificate may be issued to the family of a Jew who has gone abroad for permanent residency and then sends for the remaining members of his family; (2) a declaration from the head of the family giving his consent for the departure of the latter from Russia is necessary because, had he not emigrated earlier, then he himself would have requested an exit certificate for his wife or children; (3) in the event that the Jew sends this declaration, he should be deemed as one who has forever abandoned the borders of Russia.

"Petition of the EKO to the Minister of Internal Affairs (1 May 1909)"

In recent times, the emigration of Jews from Russia, which had abated somewhat because of the financial crisis in North America, has again increased. The heads of families who emigrated earlier to America have again begun to buy steamship tickets or provide the necessary means to send their families who remain here with invitations to go to America. At the same time, the EKO has once again become witness to the suffering that falls on those who wish to leave Russia if they observe all the requirements of the law. Thus, in a few provinces a woman who has a separate passport for residency (with the permission of her husband) must obtain her husband's special permission to go abroad when she applies for an exit certificate. The basis for such a demand could hardly be found in the law. If a wife has been issued a separate passport with the permission of her husband, then she has obviously been given complete freedom in her choice of a place to live.[1] In any case, this freedom cannot be limited when a woman sets off to join her husband, the provider of the family, which occurs with the emigration of the woman and her children.

The demand of local authorities for special permission from the husband to go abroad leaves the ignorant, unenlightened woman in a hopeless position. She must write to her husband in America and explain what kind of document is demanded from him. This paper may be certified by a local notary, but the signature of notary must be certified by the Russian consulate. In addition, one must take into consideration the fact that there is often no Russian consulate in the cities where the emigrants reside, and it is necessary to travel to another, sometimes extremely remote, city. The prospects of such red tape, which costs no small sum of money, frightens the poor woman in the majority of cases. She yields to the persuasion of a "benefactor" agent, who always pursues those who are preparing to go abroad with his own services. It is not difficult for the agent to persuade the inexperienced woman that it would be easier, quicker, and absolutely safe to travel with him — without a passport but with his assistance. So they win over the emigrant for secret passage across the borders. Thanks to this state of affairs, the treasury is deprived of the passport tax, which would be received if only it were possible to obtain a foreign passport more easily; the Russian steamship society (in Libava)[2] also loses passengers to the German and English lines.

The established order thus makes it difficult for a woman to receive a foreign passport. She not only travels to her husband illegally, but this contradicts the interests of the development of Russian maritime trade. To attract emigrants to Libava, it is necessary to facilitate the receipt of a foreign passport in every possible way and not to complicate it with excessive formalities.

In view of the foregoing, the Central Committee of EKO has the honor to request Your Excellency to explain to the heads of the provinces where the Pale of Settlement and tsarist Poland are located, that women who have a separate passport do not need to submit special permission from their husbands to go abroad when they request a foreign passport.

"Department of General Affairs: Information for the Report to the Minister [of Internal Affairs, September 1909]"

The Department of Police, in its own conclusion on this question, has opposed satisfying the request of EKO because the consent of the husband, regardless of whether he is Christian or Jewish, to issue a separate passport to his spouse within the boundaries of the empire does not predetermine his consent to the independent departure of his wife abroad.

In May 1909, as a result of the questions submitted by the Governor of Kiev, regarding emigration of Jewish families to America, where the head of the family was already in America, the Department received the following instructions: [. . .][3]

"Governor of Ekaterinoslav to the Department of Police (30 October 1909)"

The Department of Police informed me on 17 October 1909 (number 24248) that, to facilitate the emigration of Jewish families through the mediation of the EKO, the Ministry of Internal Affairs deems it possible to issue exit certificates to wives who wish to emigrate to their husbands in America, with the submission of only a written declaration that the head of the family wishes her to come, without [the signature of] a notary or a consulate certificate.

Both the Statutes on Passports and orders of the Ministry of Internal Affairs on this subject only provide for permits or free passports for residents of border regions and individuals of rural status, who set out abroad for agricultural work — categories to which Jewish wives residing in Ekaterinoslav province and whose husbands are in America, do not belong. Given this, I ask the Department of Police to inform me as to precisely what kind of documents are meant by "exit certificates," to whom should these certificates be issued, and what the fee should be.

NOTES

1. [A separate passport, which granted wives the right to reside separately from their husband, was equivalent to marital separation. Hence, the EKO argues here that this gave the wife the right to choose her place of residency.]

2. [Libava (now Liepja, in Latvia) is a port city on the Baltic Sea.]

3. [See the instructions of 3 May 1909 above.]

[181]

A Fine of Three Hundred Rubles for Emigrants Whose Relatives Evaded Military Service

RGIA, f. 1284, op. 224, d. 69, ll. 21–21 ob, 31–31 ob.

"Governor of Podolia to the Department of General Affairs (16 May 1913)"

Owing to the judgment of 18 January 1913 (number 1898), I informed the Department of General Affairs that [. . .] debtors who pay the 300-ruble fine [for a family member who evaded military service][1] nonetheless do not have the right to receive a foreign passport. In my opinion, however, the Jewish woman Khava Brukha Srilikhis cannot be denied a passport on the basis of regulations promulgated by the imperial orders of 8 May 1892 [. . .] for this reason: one obstacle to issuing certificates to Jews can be the presence of a settler's property on which there is a state lien. But in this case the emigrant has no property, as the investigation has shown.

Regarding the petition of the EKO to exempt Khava Brukha Srilikhis from the 300-ruble fine in the absence of any property, this cannot be satisfied in view of the explanation of the Department of General Affairs (17 September 1910, number 27612) based on the Decree of the State Senate (3 October 1891). Jews cannot be exempted from the 300-ruble fine based on their hopeless inability to pay because this was not foreseen in the law.[2]

"Governor of Minsk to the Department of General Affairs (30 January 1913)"

Khaia Sora Ioseleva Matusevich [of Smolevich] submitted a petition through the EKO for an exit certificate to emigrate to the United States of America with her seven-year-old son Srol'.

Meanwhile, according to assembled information, it turned out that the Matusevich family was assessed a fine of 300 rubles for the evasion of military service in the call-up of 1909 by the petitioner's brother-in-law, Leib Matusevich. Apart from the fine, I found no other property or capital belonging to the Matusevichs.

Deeming it impossible to issue Khaia Sora Matusevich the requested certificate under these conditions, [. . .] I have the honor to inform the Department of General Affairs that there are no other impediments to petitioner's emigration to America.

"Minister of Finance, Department of the State Treasury, to the Minister of Internal Affairs (11 March 1913)"

Owing to the memorandum (number 5170) on the question of annulling the 300-ruble fine of Khaia Sora Matusevich and her son Srol'. [. . .] I have the honor to inform Your Excellency that in view of her intention to emigrate to America with her son, with the assistance of the EKO, the Ministry of Finance for its part does not find any impediments to this exemption. [. . .][3]

"Governor of Minsk to the Department of General Affairs (27 April 1913)"

I inform the Department of General Affairs that I issued Khaia Sora Ioseleva Matusevich, a townswoman from Smolevich (Borisov district) an exit certificate on 27 April to emigrate from Russia.

As a supplement to the memorandum of 27
April 1913, I have the honor to inform the Department of General Affairs that Khaia Sora
Ioseleva Matusevich has declined to emigrate
from Russia to the United States of America.

NOTES

1. [In a later document, the Department of General Affairs explains that the woman in this case was
liable for the fine because one of her family members
had evaded military service. Jews were required to
pay 300 rubles as compensation to the state for their
family member's failure to serve when they sought to
obtain an exit certificate for emigration.]

2. [The Ministry of Finance allowed the exemption from the fine on 19 August 1913 because the
EKO had agreed to assist the woman in this case.
She refused to travel to America, according to the
governor of Podolia on 7 September 1913, but did
not specify why.]

3. [There were several cases in this file in which
the state waived the 300-ruble fine for evasion of
military service.]

[182]

R. Israel Meir Kagan,[1] *The Outcasts of Israel* (1893)

Israel Meir Kagan, *Nidhe Yisrael*, reprint (Bene Berak: Mishmor, 1986 or 1987).

It is written in Ezekiel: "O mortal, prophesy
against the shepherds of Israel. Prophesy and
say to them: [To the shepherds: Thus said the
Lord God: Ah the shepherds of Israel, who
have been tending yourselves! Is it not the
flock that the shepherd ought to tend?] You
partake of the fat [you clothe yourselves with
the wool, and you slaughter the fatlings; but
you do not tend the flock.] You have not sustained the weak, healed the sick, or bandaged
the injured; you have not brought back the
strayed, or looked for the lost . . . [For thus
said the Lord God . . .] I will take them from
the peoples and gather them from the countries . . . I will look for the lost, and I will bring
back the strayed; I will bandage the injured,
and I will sustain the weak."[2]

The scripture seems imprecise, as the order
[of God's actions] is different from the order
[of omissions] at the beginning. But when
we consider matters, we realize just how precise it is. For when we encounter a man who
is on his deathbed, we realize that the condition did not emerge in an instant, such that
he suddenly went from being a healthy person
to someone in grave condition. Rather, at first
his strength was sapped a bit, and then he became ill, and then the illness intensified such
that he became critical, and only then did he
become mortally ill. And when a skilled physician comes to him, his first job is to improve
his condition from grave to critical, and then
he can provide other therapies to improve his
condition to that of serious, and then on to
a cure.

To our point: This entire passage is an al-
legory of the community of Israel, and what
happens to them at the hands of improper
shepherds [that is, leaders] who do not tend
to the flock. First we will explain the alle-

gory, and the point will follow automatically. It is the way of a sheep in a weakened state, if nothing is done to strengthen her, in time, she becomes sick. If she goes untreated and walks with the other sheep she is likely to injure her legs, and if the injury goes unbandaged she will inevitably go astray, and if no one searches for her she will be entirely lost. When a reliable shepherd comes along to look after the sheep, he seeks the lost one to return her to the flock, and when he sees that her leg is injured he bandages it so that she does not remain damaged, and then he seeks to cure her of the underlying disease.

So too with people. There are people who are weak of soul, and if they are not strengthened their souls weaken further to the point that they are considered to have diseased souls; if they continue to go unobserved their souls will be damaged . . . and if they remain untreated further they will wander away from the community of Israel. That is, they will separate from the community, and will forge dangerous paths for themselves. Ultimately, they will be entirely lost, as they separate from God and his Torah, and assimilate among the gentiles. The main reason this came about is that the original weakness [of soul] went untreated. Thus, God, may He be blessed, says in His infinite kindness that He will awaken a pure spirit among His people; He will search for those who are lost, and will bring those who have gone astray back into the camp. Those whose hands or legs are injured will be bandaged, and their wounds cured, and even though they remain sick, God will strengthen them such that the disease will disappear entirely . . .

Even though the good Lord will have mercy on His people, and will [ultimately] bring back those who go astray, it is still to the great shame of the Jewish people that they are driven to the corners of the earth, places where there is no [commitment to the] Torah, where they remain damaged, denuded of Torah and *mitzvot*, and this is not to the greater glory of God. . . .

When we observe our current migrations to distant lands like America and Africa, and other such places throughout the world, we see the extent to which Ezekiel's vision was fulfilled. For when they first come there they are like weakened sheep, that is with weakened souls . . . and then they become wholly diseased of the soul, and in the course of time they abandon some of the *mitzvot*, and there is no one to bandage them, that is, to return them to strength. Naturally, in time, they go astray and separate from the ways of the community . . . such that eventually some are altogether lost. . . .

In our time we find a number of people wandering in distant lands who have faith in God and his Torah, but all the same have totally abandoned the Torah and its commandments. I am astonished by them, as their actions contradict their beliefs, and how is that they do not fear God who is the Lord of justice, and certainly watches over all things? Do they think that God is lost and not to be found in the [far off] corners of the world? [. . .] In truth, in the majority of cases it is because he [the immigrant] has come to a place that has no one who recognizes and redeems,[3] and he imagines that if he neglects a bit of the Torah and the commandments it will be easier for him to integrate among the inhabitants of the land and to achieve his goals. In the course of time he naturally gets used to this, such that he sees it as permitted to him to violate all the words of the Torah.

Thus, if one considers the matter carefully, one sees that this is the deception of the passions (*hata'at he-yetzer*). For could it enter the mind of anyone that the good Lord, who controls all, and without whom nothing on earth is done, would withhold good from those who walk with integrity? That He would not provide sustenance to those who walk in His ways and observe His commandments? To be sure, at this moment He has hidden his face from him, but in the end He will surely return and have mercy on him, providing him with what he needs in accordance with the laws (*be-hekhsher*). Even though those deceived by their passions will think that by refraining from fulfilling the Torah it will be easier to earn a living, when they consider the matter thoroughly they will ask if some transient pleasure is worth turning their backs on the teachings of the God of heaven and earth, who has created us and to whom we belong, to whom we shall return, to be eternally protected in the shadow of his wings.

In truth, those who revere the Lord will cry at the state of our holy religion today, which has declined astonishingly in these times, especially in the distant lands, where many have abandoned our holy faith entirely. To be sure in the past, when most Jews lived quietly and calmly in their places of domicile . . . we did not have to worry all that much about the few who were dispersed to the corners of the globe, most of whom, facing hardships, assimilated among the gentiles and adopted their ways, since most of the people remained at home [geographically and culturally]. For, thank God, in these lands all, from the youngest to the oldest, know the Lord, they all respect the Torah, submit to its commandments, and will still give their lives for it. But today, troubles increase from hour to hour, and, therefore, the flow of emigration to distant lands increases from day to day. Thousands, tens of thousands, of our brethren, are migrating to all parts of the earth, and their number gets larger every day. Thus, [unlike in the past] today we must take to heart the state of our people and worry what will be the fate of Israel there; will, God forbid, they all assimilate among the gentiles? Will all the pillars of our faith be destroyed? . . . What will be in the future, especially with the generation that was born there, that was raised and educated by parents who have contemptuously abandoned all the *mitzvot*, whose eyes have never seen the slightest sign of Jewish practice, in whom the holy religion of Israel has never taken root? Will they not assimilate entirely among the

gentiles there, and the name of Israel will no longer be remembered at all, God forbid?

What brought them to all this? Not the fury of the oppressor, for no tyrant has arisen to annul [forcibly] the laws of the Torah. Rather, it is of their own free will, as the desire for money, and other worldly pleasures, has overtaken them; they pursue them incessantly to the point that they forget the obligations of a Jew, who was born of the seed of Israel. How do they not cover their faces in shame when they remember the holiness of the Torah that was bequeathed to them, in blood, by their ancestors, who faced many oppressors and pillagers, who sought to cut them off from their Torah? They remained steadfast in support of its holiness, and submitted themselves to the sword and the flames; for every law the blood of tens of thousands was spilled. . . .

Now in this generation, when, through the grace of God, there are no oppressors or those who keep us from observing our religion, how can these people not be ashamed that for some insignificant and transient desire they scornfully reject the holiness of our Torah, the source of our spiritual lives for all eternity?

[. . .][4] My brethren, after all the words of this book that I put together to strengthen the hand of the migrants to distant lands so that they will not be careless in the observance of the commandments of the Torah, [I must] nevertheless [say] that the correct path for anyone who wishes to be truly worthy before the Holy One, blessed be He, is to have the fortitude not to settle in those lands. If he is driven there by economic desperation, when God helps him he should return home, and have faith that the God who provides for all flesh will provide for his household as well. He should pay no heed to his passions that are seducing him to stay there until he accumulates great wealth, for he is trading a permanent world for a transient one. For the entire time he remains there he is very likely to falter with some essential aspect of our religion, as do many others. . . .

In truth, any righteous man who migrates there will initially be in turmoil as he sees the breaches of the law that are common there; he will curse the day that brought him to see such outrages. His only hope will be that God will help him to flee from there. And God forbid that he should bring his children to assimilate among the gentiles, God forbid. But as time goes on, his thinking changes entirely. It is not enough that he does not leave, but he will bring his children over. And what causes this? Have the commandments of the Torah lost any of their value? No, they stand firm forever, with no change and no decrease in value, God forbid. It is the quality of the people that has diminished with the flow of time, for they have become habituated to the ways of their new country. . . .

But freedom of choice is given to all, and every man who fears God must find strength in God who will help him; he should return to his country and educate his children in Torah. He will thereby thrive in the world to come, as in this world, for God does not forsake his pious followers, the guardians of the covenant and its commandments!

NOTES

1. [Rabbi Israel Meir Kagan (1838–1933) published his work *Nidhe Yisrael* (The outcasts of Israel) in 1893, at the height of Jewish emigration from the Russian empire. Like many rabbinic figures, Kagan strongly opposed the migration. Recognizing he was powerless to stop it, he wrote a short halakhic work that lays out the basics of Jewish religious practice in the hope of strengthening observance among the emigrants. Here we reproduce excerpts from his introduction and afterword in which he inveighs against the choices the emigrants have made. It is an important, albeit tendentious, read on the motives of the migrants, and also provides a sense of the pressures some Jews faced as they considered the momentous decision to leave Russia.]

2. [Ezekiel, chapter 34:1–4, 13, 16.]

3. [The allusion is to the biblical character Boaz in the Book of Ruth; the idea is someone who takes responsibility and provides leadership. In medieval ethical literature, the phrase has been applied to God. Although that meaning is not impossible here, it seems more likely that Kagan is noting the absence of leadership, as he has already suggested that God is not absent from these distant lands.]

4. [Kagan proceeds to discuss other periods of Jewish history in which Jews sought to assimilate, especially Spanish Jewry, noting that they always end badly for the Jews. He then proceeds to explain that much of the abandonment of Jewish practice is the result of ignorance. This is his reason for writing this halakhic manual for those who emigrate. There follow many chapters dealing with the basics of different areas of Jewish law. We come then to the closing remarks of the work.]

Select Bibliography

General Studies

Avrutin, Eugene. *Jews and the Imperial State: Identification Politics in Tsarist Russia.* Ithaca: Cornell University Press, 2010.

Baron, Salo. *The Russian Jew under Tsars and Soviets.* New York: Macmillan, 1976.

Bartal, Israel. *The Jews of Eastern Europe, 1772–1881.* Translated by Chaya Naor. Philadelphia: University of Pennsylvania Press, 2005.

Dubnow, Simon. Translated by Israel Friedlaender, *History of the Jews in Russia and Poland from the Earliest Times until the Present Day.* 3 vols. Philadelphia: Jewish Publication Society of America, 1916.

Eisenbach, Artur. *The Emancipation of the Jews in Congress Poland, 1780–1879,* edited by Antony Polonsky. Translated by Janina Dorosz. Oxford: Blackwell, 1991.

Horowitz, Brian. *Empire Jews: Jewish Nationalism and Acculturation in 19th- and Early 20th-Century Russia.* Bloomington, IN: Slavica Publishers, 2009.

———. *Jewish Philanthropy and Enlightenment in Late Tsarist Russia.* Seattle: University of Washington Press, 2009.

Hundert, Gershon D. *The YIVO Encyclopedia of Jews in Eastern Europe.* 2 vols. New Haven: Yale University Press, 2008.

Klier, John. *Imperial Russia's Jewish Question, 1855–1881.* Cambridge: Cambridge University Press, 1995.

———. *Russia Gathers Her Jews: The Origins of the "Jewish Question" in Russia, 1772–1825.* DeKalb: Northern Illinois University Press, 1986.

Loeffler, James Benjamin. *The Most Musical Nation: Jews and Culture in the Late Russian Empire.* New Haven: Yale University Press, 2010.

Lohr, Eric. "The Russian Army and the Jews: Mass Deportations, Hostages, and Violence during World War I." *Russian Review* 60, no. 3 (July 2001): 404–19.

Löwe, Heinz-Dietrich. *The Tsars and the Jews: Reform, Reaction, and Anti-Semitism in Imperial Russia, 1772–1917.* Switzerland: Harwood Academic, 1993.

Meir, Natan. *Kiev, Jewish Metropolis: A History, 1819–1914.* Bloomington: Indiana University Press, 2010.

Nathans, Benjamin. *Beyond the Pale: The Jewish Encounter with Late Imperial Russia.* Berkeley: University of California Press, 2002.

Pipes, Richard. "Catherine II and the Jews." *Soviet Jewish Affairs* 5 (1975): 3–20.

Polonsky, Antony. *The Jews in Poland and Russia, 1350–1881.* Vol. 1. Oxford: Littman Library of Jewish Civilization, 2010.

———. *The Jews in Poland and Russia, 1881–1917.* Vol. 2. Oxford: Littman Library of Jewish Civilization, 2010.

Safran, Gabriella, and Steven J. Zipperstein, eds. *The Worlds of S. Ansky: A Russian-Jewish Intellectual at the Turn of the Century.* Stanford: Stanford University Press, 2006.

Veidlinger, Jeffrey. *Jewish Public Culture in the Late Russian Empire.* Bloomington: Indiana University Press, 2009.

I. Religious Life

Assaf, David. *The Regal Way: The Life and Times of Rabbi Israel of Ruzhin.* Stanford: Stanford University Press, 2002.

———. *Untold Tales of the Hasidim: Crisis and Discontent in the History of Hasidism.* Waltham, MA: Brandeis University Press, 2010.

Avrutin, Eugene. "Returning to Judaism after the 1905 Law on Religious Freedom in Tsarist Russia." *Slavic Review* 65, no. 1 (2006): 90–110.

Deutsch, Nathaniel. *The Maiden of Ludmir: A Jewish Holy Woman and Her World.* Berkeley: University of California Press, 2003.

Dynner, Glenn. *Men of Silk: The Hasidic Conquest of Polish Society.* Oxford: Oxford University Press, 2008.

Endelman, Todd. "Jewish Converts in Nineteenth-Century Warsaw: A Quantitative Analysis." *Jewish Social Studies* 4, no. 1 (1997): 28–59.

Immanuel Etkes, *The Gaon of Vilna: The Man and His Image*. Translated by Jeffrey M. Green. Berkeley: University of California Press, 2002.

———. *Lita bi-Yerushalayim: ha-'ilit ha-lamdanit be-Lita u-khehilat ha-perushim bi-Yerushalayim le-or igrot u-khetavim shel R. Shemu'el mi-Kelm*. Jerusalem: Yad Yitshak ben Tsevi, 1991.

———. *Rabbi Israel Salanter and the Mussar Movement: Seeking the Torah of Truth*. Translated by Jonathan Chipman. Philadelphia: Jewish Publication Society, 1993.

———. *Ba'al ha-Tanya: Rabi Shene'ur Zalman mi-Ladi ve-reshitah shel hasidut Habad*. Jerusalem: Zalman Shazar Center, 2011.

Fishman, David. "The Musar Movement in Interwar Poland." In *The Jews of Poland Between the Two World Wars*, edited by Yisrael Gutman, et al. Waltham, MA: Brandeis University Press, 1989.

Freeze, ChaeRan Y. "The Mariinsko Sergievskii Shelter for Converted Jewish Children in St. Petersburg." In *Jews in the East European Borderlands: Essays in Honor of John D. Klier*, edited by Eugene Avrutin and Harriet Murav, 27–49. Boston: Academic Studies, 2012.

———. "When Chava Left Home: Gender, Conversion, and the Jewish Family in Tsarist Russia," *Polin* 8 (2006): 153–88.

Green, Arthur. *Tormented Master: A Life of Rabbi Nahman of Bratslav*. Tuscaloosa: University of Alabama Press, 1978.

Katz, Dov. *Tenu'at ha-musar: toldoteha, isheha, ve-shitoteha*. 5 vols. Jerusalem: Feldhaim, 1996.

Klier, John. "State Policies and the Conversion of Jews in Imperial Russia." In *Of Religion and Empire: Missions, Conversion and Tolerance*, edited by Robert Geraci and Michael Khodarkovsky, 98–114. Ithaca: Cornell University Press, 2001.

Lure, Ilia. *Edah u-medinah: Hasidut habad ba-imperyah ha-rusit, 588–643*. Jerusalem: Hebrew University Magnes Press, 2006.

Mahler, Raphael. *Hasidism and the Jewish Enlightenment: Their Confrontation in Galicia and Poland in the First Half of the Nineteenth Century*. Philadelphia: Jewish Publication Society of America, 1985.

Nadler, Allan. *The Faith of the Mithnagdim: Rabbinic Responses to Hasidic Rupture*. Baltimore: John Hopkins University Press, 1997.

Rapoport-Albert, Ada. "On Women in Hasidism: S. A. Horodecky and the Maid of Ludomir Tradition." In *Jewish History: Essays in Honor of Chimen Abramsky*, edited by Ada Rapoport-Albert and Steven J. Zipperstein, 495–525. London: Halban, 1988.

Shapiro, Marc B. *Between the Yeshiva World and Modern Orthodoxy: The Life and Works of Rabbi Jehiel Jacob Weinberg, 1884–1966*. Oxford: Littman Library of Jewish Civilization, 1999.

Stanislawski, Michael. "Jewish Apostasy in Russia: A Tentative Typology." In *Jewish Apostasy in the Modern World*, edited by Todd Endelman, 189–205. New York: Holmes and Meier, 1987.

Wodzinski, Marcin. *Haskalah and Hasidism in the Kingdom of Poland: A History of Conflict*. Translated by Sarah Cozens and Agnieszka Mirowska. Oxford: Littman Library of Jewish Civilization, 2005.

Zipperstein, Steven J. "Heresy, Apostasy, and the Transformation of Joseph Rabinovich." In *Jewish Apostasy in the Modern World*, edited by Todd Endelman, 206–231. New York: Holmes and Meier, 1987.

II. Family Life

Biale, David. "Eros and Enlightenment: Love against Marriage in the East European Jewish Enlightenment." *Polin* 1 (1986): 49–67.

Deutsch, Nathaniel. *The Jewish Dark Continent: Life and Death in the Russian Pale of Settlement*. Cambridge: Harvard University Press, 2011.

Etkes, Immanuel. "Marriage and Torah Study Among the *Lomdim* in Lithuania in the Nineteenth Century." In *Jewish Family: Metaphor and Memory*, edited by David Kraemer, 153–78. New York: Oxford University Press, 1989.

Freeze, ChaeRan Y. *Jewish Marriage and Divorce in Imperial Russia*. Waltham, MA: Brandeis University Press, 2002.

———. "'She Done Him In': Marital Breakdown in a Jewish Family." In *The Human Tradition in Imperial Russia*, edited by Christine Worobec, 129–40. Lanham, MD: Rowman and Littlefield, 2009.

Hyman, Paula. *Gender and Assimilation in Modern Jewish History: The Roles and Representations of Women*. Seattle: University of Washington Press, 1995.

Stampfer, Shaul. "Ha-mashma'ut ha-hevratit shel nisuei boser be-mizrah Eropah." In *Studies on Polish Jewry: Paul Glikson Memorial Volume*, edited by Ezra Mendelsohn and Chone Shmeruk, 65–77. Jerusalem: Zalman Shazar Center, 1987.

III. Health and Sexuality

Bartal, Israel. "'Onut' ve 'ain-onut': Bein masoret le-haskalah." In *Eros, eisurin ve-irosim: miniut ve-mishpahah ba-historiyah*, edited by Israel Bartal and Isaiah Gafni, 225–33 Jerusalem: Zalman Shazar Center, 1998.

Biale, David. "The Lust for Asceticism in the Hasidic Movement." In *Jewish Explorations of Sexuality*, edited by Jonathan Magonet, 51–66. Oxford: Berghahn, 1995.

Epstein, Lisa. "Caring for the Soul's House: The Jews of Russia and Health Care, 1860–1914." PhD diss., Yale University, 1995.

Etkes, Immanuel. "Mekomam shelma giah u-va'ale ha-shem ba-hevrah ha-ashkenazit." *Tsiyon* 60, no. 1 (1995): 86–101.

Freeze, ChaeRan Y. "Lilith's Midwives: Jewish Newborn Child Murder in Nineteenth-Century Vil'na." *Jewish Social Studies* 16, no. 2 (2010): 1–27.

Mondry, Henrietta. *Exemplary Bodies: Constructing the Jew in Russian Culture since the 1880s*. Boston: Academic Studies, 2009.

IV. Education and Culture

EDUCATION

Adler, Eliyana. *In Her Hands: The Education of Jewish Girls in Tsarist Russia*. Detroit: Wayne State University Press, 2011.

Borzymińska, Zofia. *Szkolnictwo żydowskie w Warszawie 1831–1870*. Warsaw: Żydowski Instytut Historyczny, Instytut Naukowo-Badawczy, 1994.

Dohrn, Verena. *Jüdische Eliten im Russichen Reich*. Köln: Böhlau, 2008.

Dolbilov, Mikhail. "Russifying Bureaucracy and the Politics of Jewish Education in the Russian Empire's Northwest Region (1860–1870s)." *Acta Slavica Iaponica* 24 (2007): 112–43.

Goldstein, Yosef. "'Ha-heder ha-metukan' be-Rusyah ke-vasis le-ma'arekhet ha-hinukh ha-tsiyonit." *Iyunim be-hinukh* 45 (1986): 147–57.

Greenbaum, Avraham. "The Girls' Heder and the Girls in the Boys' Heder in Eastern Europe before World War I." *East/West Education* 18, no. 1 (1997): 55–62.

Ivanov, Anatolii Evgen'evich. *Evreiskoe studenchestvo v Rossiiskoi imperii nachala XX veka. Kakim ono bylo? Opyt sotsiokul'turnogo portreturivaniia*. Moscow: Novyi khronograf, 2007.

Kreis, Simeon. *Bate-sefer yehudiyim peratiyim: gorem rusifikatori o gorem yehudi meshamer? Hinukh ve-historyah: heksherim tarbutiyim u-politiyim*, edited by Rivka Feldhay and Immanuel Etkes, 285–96. Jerusalem: Zalman Shazar Center, 1999.

Levin, Sabina. *Perakim be-toldot ha-hinukh ha-yehudi be-Polin: ba-me'ah ha-tesha-'esre uve-reshit ha-meah ha'esrim*. Tel Aviv: Graphit, 1997.

Parush, Iris. *Reading Jewish Women: Marginality and Modernization in Nineteenth-Century East European Jewish Society*. Waltham, MA: Brandeis University Press, 2004.

Salmon, Yosef. "The Yeshiva of Lida: A Unique Institution of Higher Learning." *YIVO Annual* 16 (1974): 106–25.

Stampfer, Shaul. *Families, Rabbis, and Education: Traditional Jewish Society in Nineteenth-Century Eastern Europe*. Oxford: Littman Library of Jewish Civilization, 2010.

———. *Lithuanian Yeshivas of the Nineteenth Century: Creating a Tradition of Learning*. Oxford: Littman Library of Jewish Civilization, 2012.

Zalkin, Mordechai. *El hekhal ha-haskalah: tahalikhe modernizatsyah ba-hinukh ha-yehudi be-Mizrah Eropah ba-me'ah ha-tesha' esreh*. Tel Aviv: Ha-kibutz Ha-me'uhad, 2008.

Zipperstein, Steven J. "Transforming the Heder: Maskilic Politics in Imperial Russia." In *Jewish History: Essays in Honor of Chimen Abramsky*, edited by Ada Rapoport-Albert and Steven J. Zipperstein, 87–109. London: Halban, 1988.

CULTURE

Alter, Robert. *The Invention of Hebrew Prose: Modern Fiction and Language of Realism*. Seattle: University of Washington Press, 1988.

Balin, Carole. *To Reveal Our Hearts: Jewish Women Writers in Tsarist Russia*. Cincinnati, OH: Hebrew Union College Press, 2000.

Cohen, Tovah. *Ha'ahat ahuvah veha'ahat senu'ah: Bein metsi'ut le-vidyon be-te'urei ha'ishah be-sifrut ha-haskalah*. Jerusalem: Hebrew University Magnes Press, 2002.

Etkes, Immanuel, ed. *Ha-dat veha-hayim: tenu'at ha-haskalah ha-yehudit be-mizrah Eropah*. Jerusalem: Zalman Shazar Center, 1993.

Feiner, Shmuel. "Ha-'ishah ha-yehudit ha-modernit: Mikreh-mivhan be-yahasei ha-haskalah ve-ha-modernah." *Zion* 58 (1993): 453–99.

Fishman, David. *The Rise of Modern Yiddish Culture*. Pittsburgh: University of Pittsburgh Press, 2005.

———. *Russia's First Modern Jews: The Jews of Shklov*. New York: New York University Press, 1995.

Garrett, Leah V. *Journeys beyond the Pale: Yiddish Travel Writing in the Modern World*. Madison: University of Wisconsin Press, 2003.

Krutikov, Mikhail. *Yiddish Fiction and the Crisis of Modernity, 1905–1914*. Stanford: Stanford University Press, 2001.

Litvak, Olga. *Conscription and the Search for Modern Russian Jewry*. Bloomington: Indiana University Press, 2006.

———. "Khave and Her Sisters: Sholem-aleichem's Lost Girls of 1905." *Jewish Social Studies* 15, no. 3 (2009): 1–38.

———. *Haskalah: The Romantic Movement in Judaism*. New Brunswick: Rutgers University Press, 2012.

Miron, Dan. *A Traveler Disguised: The Rise of Modern Yiddish Literature in the Nineteenth Century*. New York: Schocken Books, 1996.

Moss, Kenneth. *Jewish Renaissance in the Russian Revolution*. Cambridge: Harvard University Press, 2009.

Murav, Harriet. *Identity Theft: The Jew in Imperial Russia and the Case of Avraam Uri Kovner*. Stanford: Stanford University Press, 2003.

Nathans, Benjamin, and Gabriella Safran, eds.

Culture Front: Representing Jews in Eastern Europe. Philadelphia: University of Pennsylvania Press, 2008.

Novershtern, Avraham. *Kesem ha-dimdumim: Apokalipsah u-meshihiyut be-sifrut yidish*. Jerusalem: Magnes Press, 2003.

Patterson, David. *The Hebrew Novel in Czarist Russia: A Portrait of Jewish Life in the Nineteenth Century*. Lanham, MD: Rowman and Littlefield, 1999.

Quint, Alyssa. "'Yiddish Literature for the Masses'? A Reconstruction of Who Read What in Jewish Eastern Europe." *AJS Review* 29, no. 1 (2005): 61–89.

Roskies, David. *A Bridge of Longing: The Lost Art of Yiddish Storytelling*. Cambridge: Harvard University Press, 1995.

Safran, Gabriella. *Rewriting the Jew: Assimilation Narratives in the Russian Empire*. Stanford: Stanford University Press, 2000.

———. *Wandering Soul: The Dybbuk's Creator, S. Ansky*. Cambridge: Harvard University Press, 2010.

Schachter, Allison. *Diasporic Modernisms: Hebrew and Yiddish Literature in the Twentieth Century*. Oxford: Oxford University Press, 2011.

Seidman, Naomi. *A Marriage Made in Heaven: The Sexual Politics of Hebrew and Yiddish*. Berkeley: University of California Press, 1997.

Shachar, Pinsker. *Literary Passports: The Making of Modernist Hebrew Fiction in Europe*. Stanford: Stanford University Press, 2011.

Sinkoff, Nancy. *Out of the Shtetl: Making Jews Modern in the Polish Borderlands*. Providence, RI: Brown Judaic Studies, 2004.

Stanislawski, Michael. *For Whom Do I Toil? Judah Leib Gordon and the Crisis of Russian Jewry*. Oxford: Oxford University Press, 1988.

Trachtenberg, Barry. *The Revolutionary Roots of Modern Yiddish, 1903–1917*. Syracuse, NY: Syracuse University Press, 2008.

Werses, Samuel. *"Ha-kitsah ami": sifrut ha-haskalah be-'idan ha-modernisatsyah*. Jerusalem: Hebrew University Magnes Press, 2001.

Wisse, Ruth. *I. L. Peretz and the Making of Modern Jewish Culture*. Seattle: University of Washington Press, 1991.

Zalkin, Mordechai. *Ba'alot ha-shahar: ha-haskalah ha-yehudit ba-Imperyah ha-Rusit ba-me'ah ha-tesha esreh*. Jerusalem: Hebrew University Magnes Press, 2000.

Zierler, Wendy. *And Rachel Stole the Idols: The Emergence of Modern Hebrew Women's Writing*. Detroit: Wayne State University Press, 2004.

Zipperstein, Steven J. *The Jews of Odessa: A Cultural History*. Stanford: Stanford University Press, 1986.

V. Work

Anan'ich, Boris V. *Bankirskie doma v Rossi, 1860–1914 gg*. Moscow: Nauka, 1991.

Avrutin, Eugene. "Jewish Neighbourly Relations and Imperial Russian Legal Culture." *Journal of Modern Jewish Studies* 9, no. 1 (2010): 1–16.

Bartal, Israel. "Le'an halakh tseror ha-kesef: ha-bikoret ha-maskilit 'al hebeteiha ha-kalkaliyim shel ha-hasidut." In *Dat ve-khalkalah, yahase gomlin: kovets ma'amarim*, edited by Menachem Ben Sasson, 375–85. Jerusalem: Zalman Shazar Center Press, 1995.

Kahan, Arcadius. *Essays in Jewish Social and Economic History* edited by Roger Weiss. Chicago: University of Chicago Press, 1986.

Lederhendler, Eli, "Classless: On the Social Status of Jews in Russia and Eastern Europe in the Late Nineteenth Century." *Comparative Studies in Society and History* 50, no. 2 (2008): 509–34.

VI. The Jews, the Russian State, and Neighbors

MILITARY CONSCRIPTION

Petrovsky-Shtern, Yohanan. *Jews in the Russian Army, 1827–1917: Drafted into Modernity*. Cambridge: Cambridge University Press, 2008.

Stanislawski, Michael. *Tsar Nicholas I and the Jews, 1825–55*. Philadelphia: Jewish Publication Society of America, 1983.

ANTISEMITISM

Aronson, Irwin Michael. *Troubled Waters: The Origins of the 1881 Anti-Jewish Pogroms in Russia*. Pittsburgh: University of Pittsburgh Press, 1990.

Avrutin, Eugene. "Racial Categories and Politics of (Jewish) Difference in Late Imperial Russia." *Kritika* 8, no. 1 (2007): 13–40.

Dekel-Chen, Jonathan, David Gaunt, Natan M.

Meir, and Israel Bartal, eds. *Anti-Jewish Violence: Rethinking the Pogrom in East European History*. Bloomington: Indiana University Press, 2011.

Goren, Yaakov, ed. *Eduyot nifge'e Kishinov 1903: ke-fi she-nigbe al'yede H.N. Bialik ve-haverav*. Tel Aviv: Ha-kibutz Ha-me'uhad, 1991.

Judge, Edward. *Easter in Kishinev: Anatomy of a Pogrom*. New York: New York University Press, 1992.

Klier, John. *Russians, Jews, and the Pogroms of 1881–1882*. Cambridge: Cambridge University Press, 2011.

—— and Shlomo Lambroza, eds. *Pogroms: Anti-Jewish Violence in Modern Russian History*. Cambridge: Cambridge University Press, 1992.

Rogger, Hans. *Jewish Politics and Right-Wing Politics in Imperial Russia*. Berkeley: University of California Press, 1986.

Weeks, Theodore. *From Assimilation to Antisemitism: The Jewish Question in Poland 1850–1914*. DeKalb: Northern Illinois University Press, 2006.

POLITICS

Almog, Shmuel, Jehuda Reinharz, and Anita Shapiro, eds. *Zionism and Religion*. Hanover, NH: University Press of New England, 1998.

Avineri, Shlomo. *The Making of Modern Zionism: The Intellectual Origins of the Jewish State*. New York: Basic, 1981.

Bartal, Israel. "Zikhron Ya'akov le-R. Ya'akov Lifshits: Historyografyah ortodoksit." *Milet* 2 (1984): 409–14.

Frankel, Jonathan. *Prophecy and Politics: Socialism, Nationalism, and the Russian Jews, 1862–1917*. Cambridge: Cambridge University Press, 1981.

Galai, Shmuel. "The Jewish Question as a Russian Problem: The Debates of the First Duma." *Revolutionary Russia* 17, no. 1 (2004): 31–68.

Gassenschmidt, Christoph. *Jewish Liberal Politics in Tsarist Russia, 1900–1914*. New York: New York University Press, 1995.

Goldshtain, Yosi. *Ben tsiyonut medinit le-tsiyonut ma'asit: Ha-tenu'ah ha-tsiyonit be-Rusyah be-reshitah*. Jerusalem: Hebrew University Magnes Press, 1991.

Haberer, Erich. "The Jewish People's Group and

Jewish Politics in Tsarist Russia, 1906–1914."
Modern Judaism 10 (February 1990): 1–15.
———. *Jews and Revolution in Nineteenth-Century
Russia*. Cambridge: Cambridge University Press,
1995.

Harriet, Davis-Kram, "The Story of the Sisters of
the Bund." *Contemporary Jewry* 5 (1980): 27–43.

Hertzberg, Arthur. *The Zionist Idea: A Historical
Analysis and Reader*. Philadelphia: Jewish
Publication Society, 1997.

Hoffman, Stefani, and Ezra Mendelsohn, eds. *The
Revolution of 1905 and Russia's Jews*. Philadelphia: University of Pennsylvania Press, 2008.

Lederhendler, Eli. *The Road to Modern Jewish Politics: Political Tradition and Political Reconstruction in the Jewish Community of Tsarist Russia*.
New York: Oxford University Press, 1989.

Levin, Vladimir. "Politics at the Crossroads: Jewish
Parties and the Second Duma Elections, 1907."
*Leipziger Beiträge zur jüdischen Geschichte und
Kulture* 2 (2004): 129–46.

Luz, Ehud. *Parallels Meet: Religion and National-
ism in Early Zionism*. Translated by Lenn J.
Schramm. Philadelphia: Jewish Publication
Society, 1988.

Mendelsohn, Ezra. *Class Struggle in the Pale: The
Formative Years of the Jewish Workers' Move-
ment in Tsarist Russia*. Cambridge: Cambridge
University Press, 1970.

Nathans, Benjamin. "The Other Modern Jewish
Politics: Integration and Modernity in Fin de
Siècle Russia." In *The Emergence of Jewish Poli-
tics*, edited by Zvi Gitelman, 20–34. Pittsburgh:
University of Pittsburgh Press, 2003.

Peled, Yoav. *Class and Ethnicity in the Pale: the Political Economy of Jewish Workers' Nationalism
in Late Imperial Russia*. New York: St. Martin's,
1989.

Pinson, Koppel, ed. *Nationalism and History:
Essays on Old and New Judaism*. Philadelphia:
The Jewish Publication Society, 1958.

Rabinovitch, Simon. "The Dawn of a New
Diaspora: Simon Dubnov's Autonomism from
St. Petersburg to Berlin." *Leo Baeck Institute
Yearbook* 50 (2005): 267–88.

———. "Russian Jewry Goes to the Polls: An Analysis of Jewish Voting in the All-Russian Constitu-
ent Assembly Elections of 1917." *East European
Jewish Affairs* 29, no. 2 (2009): 205–25.

Salmon, Yosef. *Religious Zionism: First Encounters*. Jerusalem: Hebrew University Magnes
Press, 2002.

Shapiro, Leonard. "The Role of the Jews in the
Russian Revolutionary Movement." *Slavonic and
Eastern European Review* 40 (1961): 148–67.

Stanislawski, Michael. *Zionism and the Fin de
Siècle: Cosmopolitanism and Nationalism from
Nordau to Jabotinsky*. Berkeley: University of
California, 2001.

Tobias, Henry J. *The Jewish Bund in Russia from
Its Origins to 1905*. Stanford: Stanford University Press, 1972.

Ury, Scott. *Barricades and Banners: The Revolution
of 1905 and the Transformation of Warsaw
Jewry*. Stanford: Stanford University Press,
2012.

Vital, David. *Zionism: The Formative Years*.
Oxford: Oxford University Press, 1989.

Weinberg, David. *Between Tradition and Moder-
nity: Haim Zhitlowsky, Simon Dubnow, and
Ahad Ha-Am, and the Shaping of Modern Jewish
Identity*. New York: Holmes and Meier, 1996.

Zimmerman, Joshua D. *Poles, Jews, and the Politics
of Nationality: The Bund and the Polish Socialist
Party in Late Tsarist Russia, 1892–1914*. Madison: University of Wisconsin Press, 2004.

Zipperstein, Steven. *Elusive Prophet: Ahad Ha'am
and the Origins of Zionism*. Berkeley: University
of California Press, 1993.

EMIGRATION

Alroey, Gur. "And I Remained Alone in a Vast Land:
Women in the Jewish Migration from Eastern
Europe." *Jewish Social Studies* 12, no. 3 (2006):
39–72.

———. *Bread to Eat and Clothes to Wear: Letters
from Jewish Migrants in the Early Twentieth
Century*. Detroit: Wayne State University Press,
2011.

———. "Journey to Early Twentieth-Century Palestine as a Jewish Immigrant Experience." *Jewish
Social Studies* 9, no. 2 (2003): 28–64.

Bartal, Yisrael. "Amerikah shel ma'alah: Artsot
ha-Berit ke-ide'al uke-mofet li-yehude Mizrah
Eropah ba-me'ah ha 19." In *Be-'ikvot Kolumbus:
Amerikah, 1492–1992*, edited by Miriam Eliav
Feldon, 511–22. Jerusalem: Zalman Shazar
Center, 1986.

Brinkman, Tobias. "Zivilgesellschaft transnational: Jüdische Hilfsorganisationen und jüdische Massenmigration aus Osteuropa in Deutschland 1868–1914." In *Religion, Wohlfahrt und Philanthropie in den europäischen Zivilgesellschaften, Entwicklungen im 19, und 20 Jahrhundert*, edited by Rainer Liedtke and Klaus Weber, 138–57. Paderborn: Schöningh, 2009.

Kobrin, Rebecca. *Jewish Bialystok and Its Diaspora*. Bloomington: Indiana University Press, 2010.

Kuznets, Simon. "Immigration of Russian Jews to the United States: Background and Structure." *Perspectives in American History* 9 (1975): 35–124.

Lederhendler, Eli. *Le'an?: zeramim hadashim be-kerev yehude Mizrah-Eropah*. Tel Aviv: The Open University, 2000.

Index

feeding the poor, 90; hasidic *pidyon* gifts disbursed to poor, 73; *hekdesh* as poorhouse and hospital, 262; "meal of the poor," 99; orphanage in Moscow, 159; raspberry juice for the poor, 81; R. Meir Baal ha-Ness collection boxes, 62, 70n1; Russian Society for the Protection of Jewish Women: Jewish Section, 347–50; Society for the Assistance of the Poor, 76; *tkhines* for a woman who collects charity, 129–30

Chenstokhov, 449–54

Cherkassy, 72–74

Chernigov, 5, 531–32

Chernobyl, 62, 70n11, 72

Chernov, Victor, 36

Chernyshevskii, Nikolai, 34, 421–22, 424–25n2

children: adolescent marriage, 19, 23, 261, 263n1, 305–16, 355–56; adoption, 254, 262, 334; bar mitzvah, 376, 382, 407; breastfeeding and weaning, 86, 207, 232, 236, 243–44, 261, 275; childhood games, 176; child illness, 208; child labor, 471, 479–81, 492; childlessness as grounds for divorce, 215; child mortality, 207, 244; children of divorced parents, 217; children of separated parents, 209–10; children of skilled artisans, 483; conscription of Jewish children (cantonists), 14–15, 508, 513–20; counting minors in a minyan, 140; guardianship over children, 98–99, 246–53, 255, 332; illegitimate children, 240, 241, 262, 327, 332–34; infanticide, 328–31; inheritance by sons, 256–59; metrical records of baptism, 148; metrical records of birth, 33, 168, 404; miscarriages, 232, 556; nannies, 467–68; narratives of boyhood, 169–74, 353–55, 375–76; narratives of girlhood, 80–103, 175–79; only-son exemption from conscription, 511; orphaned children, 174n1, 246, 254, 332, 375–76; paternity determination, 319–20, 327; pediatric nervous illnesses, 292–93; prayers for childbearing, 167; puberty in adolescent girls, 266–67; rebellion against parental authority, 181–82; support for elderly parents, 179–80; surnames of converted children, 241; wet nurses and, 243–44. *See also* circumcision; family

Chirikov, Evgenii N., 428, 430n4

Christianity. *See* Catholicism; conversion; Russian Orthodoxy

Chudnovskii, Solomon, 35

circumcision: accounts of, 118, 124, 125–26, 404; of boy with hemophilia, 276–78; under Jewish

legal jurisdiction, 59; mention during pogrom account, 549; metrical records of circumcision, 276; state rabbis and, 103n14, 156–57, 168

Cohen, Haim, 320

Colon, Joseph ben Solomon (Maharik), 219, 220n14

communal institutions. *See* charity and philanthropy; *kahal*; rabbinate; *and particular hasidic courts*

Constitutional Democrats (Kadets), 44

conversion (to Christianity): conversion to Catholicism, 148–49; conversion to Lutheranism, 240n1; conversion to Russian Orthodoxy, 16, 143, 146–47, 152–53, 212, 235, 237, 240n1, 333, 469, 514–15, 517–18; divorce and, 216, 230–31; forced conversion of Jewish soldiers, 15–16, 52n123, 152–53, 513–20; marital problems after, 232–40; missionary activity to convert Jews, 145–46; parental objections to conversion of children, 143, 190–93; reconversion to Judaism, 152–53, 154–55; residency rights and, 235; social tensions after, 146–52; surnames of converted children, 241

conversion (to Judaism): Jewish interfaith marriage in America and, 154–55, 154n2; Jewish observance by Russian servant, 468–70; reconversion to Judaism, 154–55

Coué, Émile, 499–500

crime: capital punishment, 560n3; criminal law sentencing categories, 446n4; criminal prosecution for pogroms, 453, 534–35, 535n1; inaccurate scales in shops, 452–53; infanticide, 328–31; murder of farm wife by peasant, 479–80; poverty as condition for, 47; prosecution for apostasy from Christianity, 152–53; prosecution for illegal alcohol production, 463–66; prosecution of illegal *melamdim*, 374–75; prosecution of political criminals, 525–30; rebellion against parental authority, 181–82; sale of contraband, 443–45; smuggling attributed to Jews, 5, 48–49n23, 442; theft from Jewish stores, 448–55; vagrancy, 11, 51n81. *See also* pogroms; violence

Crimean War, 25, 133, 445

Danzig, Avraham, 412, 414n2

Davis, Natalie Z., xviii

Dawidowicz, Lucy, xvii

death: cemeteries, 102, 131n1, 160, 171, 328–29, 409; estates and wills, 179–80, 245, 246–47,

military service and, 607–8; exit certificates and foreign passports, 603; Hibbat Tsiyyon settlements, 593–99; Jewish Colonization Society (Evreiskoe Kolonizatsionnoe Obshchestvo, EKO), 33, 601–7; metrical records required for, 509, 604; rejection of settlement applications, 601–2; separation of families by, 604–6.

DESTINATIONS: Argentina, 601–2; Great Britain, 42; United States, 56n242, 154n2, 228–29, 604–8. *See also* Palestine; Zionism

engineering profession, 247, 249–51

environment, 290–91, 3170

Eshevskii, Stepan V., 423

etrogim, 111, 125, 137

everyday life (*Alltagsleben*), xvii, xx–xxii, 7, 28, 31, 45–47

expulsion of Jews: from Kursk, 486, 487n1; from Moscow, 30, 160n1; from rural settlements, 5, 11; from St. Petersburg, 27, 483–85; during World War I, 45

extramarital sex: adultery, 212, 240; concubines, 262, 325–26; disputes over paternity, 327; as grounds for divorce, 215, 216n1, 315, 315n12; *halitsah* (levirate divorce) ritual and, 327, 328n1–2; illegitimate children and, 240–41, 262, 327; legal status of adultresses, 320n1; promiscuity of servants, 336; with Russian Orthodox partners, 212, 333; state court rulings on adultery, 214n10. *See also* prostitution; sexuality

Eybeshutz, Jonathan, 91, 103n15, 357

family: overview, 165; brothers, 16, 22, 39, 47, 52n123, 82, 86–87, 91–92–94–95, 97, 99–100, 102, 103n24, 104, 115, 116, 123, 125, 128n1, 169–70, 180, 189, 201, 208, 212, 215, 224, 225–26, 233, 235–38, 276–77, 285, 296, 311, 381–86, 388–89, 401, 408–9, 412–14, 478, 480, 560–62; Conscience Court for family issues, 180n1; disputes over inherited property, 179–80; father-in-law, 24, 27, 83–84, 87–88, 91, 93–94 116, 119, 121–22, 124–26, 147, 244, 307, 309, 312–15, 358–59, 485; marriage to brother-in-law after death of sister for orphans' sake, 98, 189–90, 353; mother-in-law, 86, 91, 94, 242–44, 249, 307–15, 354–59, 361–62; religious observance in families, 59; secret emigration of husbands, 604–6; selective integration and, xx, xxiv n22; sisters, 36, 82, 87, 91–92, 95, 100, 117–18, 121, 176, 206, 209, 211, 232, 233–38, 240, 307,

401–2, 409, 419, 493, 562–63; stepfather, 170, 174; stepmother, 94–95, 116, 121, 189, 353, 493; stepsiblings, 170; Vurke hasidic family life, 83–87; widowhood, 18, 97–98, 169, 179–80, 189, 224–27, 251–52, 256. *See also* *agun*; *agunah*; children; desertion; divorce; domestic servants; everyday life; *halitsah*; marriage

Feierberg, Mordekhai Ze'ev, 42

Feuerbach, Ludwig, 423, 425n7

Fichte, Johann Gottlieb, 423, 425n7

Fin (Feunn), Samuel Iosif, 22

Foinitskii, Ivan Iakovlevich, 500, 505n4

folk customs and superstitions: amulets and talismans, 6, 222, 353, 360, 365; demons, 6, 357; evil eye, 12, 171; evil spirits, 137; extinguishing of remembrance candles on Yom Kippur, 362; folklore and tales, 21, 173, 174n4, 357, 467–68; folk remedies, 172–73, 261, 265, 309–11, 359; government view of superstition, 357, 415; Haskalah view of superstition, 358

Foner, Sarah Menkin, 9, 529–30n1

food and dietary laws: advice manual on healthy diet, 287–89; breakfast, 308; designated rooms for maintenance of, 85; *etrogim*, 111, 125, 137; *hametz*, 85, 128n13, 138, 138n1; kashrut observance by Russian cooks, 468–70; kosher slaughter in Hovevei Tsiyyon settlements, 594–99; Passover dietary laws, 116, 128n13; Passover preparations, 177; polluted water and wells, 290–91; Russian eating house, 421; yeshiva student food budget, 385

Frank, Il'ia, 11

Franklin, Benjamin, 387

French language, 393, 399–400, 409

French Revolution, 5

Friedberg, Abraham Shalom, 388

Friedman, Israel, 78, 80n13

Galicia, 7, 80–81

Gamzu, Yehudah Leib, 388

Gaon of Vil'na (Eliyahu ben Shelomoh Zalman): birth and early life, 104–5; character, 107–10; commentary on *Shulhan Arukh*, 114; death and legacy of, 111–12; on hasidic prayer, 8–9; stories told about, 357; Torah study and, xxi, 104–7

Garkavy, Vladimir, 26–27, 419–25, 424n1

Gayna, 141

Gedera, 593–99

Gel'fman, Gesia, 35, 508, 558–60

gender: language acquisition and, 19–20; piety and, 129–30; reading practices, 19–21, 26, 28, 41, 44, 91, 95, 177, 402, 421–22, 424–25n2; system of traditional education, 19. *See also* women; masculinity

General Jewish Workers' Union, 561

geographic mobility: easing of restrictions during the Great Reform era, 25; modern transportation and, 3, 119, 249–51; patterns, 32; restrictions on, 30

Georgievna, Elena, 347, 350n2

Ger hasidic dynasty, 84, 85, 103n9

German language, 392, 404, 412, 423

Germany: famine of 1868 and aid from, 116; German higher education, 434–35; Jewish emancipation in, 44; Western musical influence from, 63

Gerondi, Nissim ben Reuven (Ran), 195, 203n7

Gershom of Mayence, 195, 203n9

Gershuni, Grigorii, 35, 591

Gintsburg, Goratsii Osipovich, 499, 505n2

Gol'denberg, Lazar B., 169–74

Goncharov, Ivan, 421–22, 424–25n2

Gordon, Eliezer, 386–87

Gordon, Yehudah Leib, 135–36, 395–96

Gorky, Maxim, 430n6

Gornostaipol, 73

Gorodets, 160

Gottlober, Avraham Ber, 19

Gozhanskii, Samuel, 37

Great Reforms: overview, 25; Jewish merchant restrictions, 439; Jewish policy of, 26; Jewish Question as consequence of, 1; judicial reform of 1864, 4; liberalization of censorship, 28; preparations in prereform era, 1, 6, 14; reformed courts, 25, 506; retreat from, 29, 207, 214n3

Grodno, 14, 397

Grodzinski, Chaim Ozer, 154, 154n1

Guenzburg, Mordechai Aaron, 19, 21, 23, 315n1, 380

Gurliand, Iakov, 22, 414n3

Habsburg empire, 12

halakhah (Jewish law): contracts, 220; converts to Judaism and, 154–55; dietary laws, 290; *heter me'ah rabbanim* (permission of one hundred rabbis), 194–204, 215–16; inheritance, 97, 245; jurisdiction over marriage and divorce, 165, 325; kohanim and, 118, 316n11; *mikvah* (pl. *mikvaot*),

46, 71n29, 81, 317–19, 597; *minyan*, 140, 140n1; non-Jewish courts in, 219–20; oaths, 136–37, 189; role of agents in, 138nn2–3; scribes, 171, 196–97, 201; seclusion, 320, 353, 367n3; witnesses, 186–88, 196–97, 218–19, 223n1, 224, 320, 327. See also *agun*; *agunah*; divorce; *halitsah*; marriage; rabbinate; sexuality; synagogues

halitsah (levirate divorce) ritual, 224–27, 327, 328n1–2

Hanukkah, 133–34

Hasidism: Aleksander hasidic dynasty, 99–100, 101; Amshinov hasidic dynasty, 103n8; Habad hasidic dynasty, 42, 62, 380; challenge to *kehalim*, 48n11; court life, 7–8, 62, 66–70, 84–85, 90–96; criticism by *misnagdim*, 8; defense of traditional dress, 24; doctrine of the *tsaddik*, 7, 62, 66–68; educational reform and, 351; founder of, 6; Ger hasidic dynasty, 84, 85, 103n9; Haskalah movement and, 19, 52n126; literature, 379–80; Moshe Lilienblum on, 357; music and, 61–72; mysticism and, 7, 8; pilgrimages, 8, 68; prayer, 8–9; Pshiskhe hasidic dynasty, 103n19; ritual slaughter in, 9; and the Russian state, 9, 72–79; Sabbath observance, 67–69; *tish*, 62, 68; Twersky hasidic dynasty, 7, 62, 70n11, 72–73, 72n36; Vurke hasidic dynasty, 83–85, 102n6; women's modesty and, 8, 81, 83, 302–4. *See also* Twersky hasidic dynasty

Haskalah movement: critique of early marriage, 19, 23, 261, 263n1, 305–16; critique of Hasidism, 19, 74–75; development in imperial Russia, 18–20; educational reform and, 21–22, 351; Hasidism and, 19, 52n126; Haskalah literature, 379–80, 387–89; Hebrew language renaissance and, 41–42; impact on liturgical music, 63; marriage reform proposals, 23, 261, 325n1; *maskilim*, 18, 377–78; Moshe Lilienblum on, 357, 359, 365–66; and the Russian state, 18; in Telz Yeshiva, 386–87

Hasman, Leib, 387, 389

Hayyim of Volozhin (Hayyim ben Yitzchok Ickovits), 9–10

health: advice manuals on good health, 287–89; breastfeeding, 207, 275; masturbation and, 267–68; personal hygiene, 279; physical exercise and, 284–85; polluted water and wells, 290–91; pregnancy and childbirth, 174n1, 232–33, 495–96, 560n3; puberty in adolescent girls, 266–67. *See also* illness and disease; medical profession; mental illness

Hebrew language: grammar, 18, 351; subject at state-sponsored schools and rabbinical schools, 22, 157, 412; as a vernacular language, 41. *See also* Jewish press

heder (pl. *hadarim*): harsh discipline in, 354; Haskalah reform program, 351; *heder* system, 19–20, 170–74, 282; hygienic conditions, 20, 282; Russian language in, 370–71; traditional Jewish lifestyle and, 19–20, 170–74, 282; views of *melamdim*, 136n2, 170–72, 370–71, 372–75, 404, 407

Hegel, Georg Wilhelm, 423, 425n7

Heshbon ha-nefesh (Lefin), 386

Hibbat Tsiyyon agricultural settlements, 40–42, 140, 140n2, 509, 593–99

higher education: complaints of overrepresentation of Jews in, 430–32; dental schools, 431–43; faculties of jurisprudence, 505–6; female auditors, 352, 427–30; student subculture of universities, 26–27; university life, 419–25; university quotas, 430n1, 432, 433–37; women's higher courses, 351–52

High Holidays: musical traditions for, 62, 67; permission for religious assembly for, 161–62; shofar, 68, 72n36; Vurke hasidic traditions, 85–86

Horowitz, Moshe Yitzhak, 63

Hovevei Tsiyyon (Lovers of Zion) societies, 40

Idel, Moshe, 7

illness and disease: bronchitis, 208; burns, 169; child illness and mortality, 206–7, 244; cholera, 122, 280, 312, 353, 402; clubfoot (congenital talipes equinovarus), 85; concussion recovery, 479; coughing up blood, 115–16; early marriage and, 19, 23, 261, 263n1, 305–16; eye ailments, 115, 118, 120, 125, 521–22; of Genrikh Sliozberg's mother, 403; head fracture, 479; hemophilia, 276–78; illnesses and cures, 115–17, 119, 125–27; impotence, 305–16; of Ita Kalish's mother, 80–81, 93; of Ita Kalish's uncle, 97; "paleness," 266–67; rickets, 283; seizures, 127; self-mutilation to avoid conscription, 15, 508, 520–21; sexually-transmitted diseases, 262, 323–24, 340n1, 342–46; stroke, 207; tuberculosis (consumption), 249, 250, 253n1, 279–286, 291n5; typhoid, 27. *See also* circumcision; death; folk customs and superstitions; health; medical profession; mental illness

Independent Jewish Worker's Party (ENRP), 38

industrialization: overview, 46–47; child labor in factories, 492; factory work, 33, 37–38, 400, 488–94, 572; female labor, 440, 488–94; impact on Jewish artisans, 32–33; industrial expansion of 1885–99, 29–30; pollution from a turpentine factory and, 317; strikes and, 33, 37–38, 488–94, 571, 572. *See also* artisans; economy; merchants

Irkutsk, 398, 487

Islam: under Catherine the Great, 2; Jewish policy and, 11; language laws and, 12; religious tolerance in Moscow and, 160

Israel Salanter (Israel ben Ze'ev Volf Lipkin), 10, 117, 387

Isserles, Moshe (*Rema*), 6, 195, 202n6, 222, 320

Jabotinsky, Vladimir, 46

Jewish Colonization Society (Evreiskoe Kolonizatsionnoe Obshchestvo, EKO), 33, 601–7

Jewish identity: confessional identity, 11, 47, 59; conversion to Christianity and, 15–16, 47, 143, 230–41; documentation and registration of, 12, 18, 168; military as vehicle to erase, 16; observance of Judaism in Russian capitals, 59–60n3, 177–78, 428–29; reconversion to Judaism, 152–53. *See also* acculturation; assimilation; names; registration

Jewish Independent Workers' Party, 565–68, 569n1

Jewish policies (Imperial Russia): Alexander I policies, 11; Catherine the Great integrationist policy, 4–5, 11–12; consistory-like administrative system, 17; Great Reform era policies, 26; Jewish Committee (Committee for the Organization of Jewish Life), 11, 14, 16, 17, 23, 25, 27, 302–3, 507; Nicholas I integrationist policy, 6, 14; Nicholas I utility and reclassification policies, 24–25; postreform era policy, 30; Rabbinic Commission, 17, 27, 201, 202, 204n30, 204n32, 225–29, 276, 277; religious tolerance and, 2, 12, 59; selective integration policy, xx, xxiv n22, 1, 12, 25–26, 30, 177, 507; social estates (*soslovie*) and, 4–5; Statute of 1804, 11–12; Statute on the Jews (1835), 16–17, 23, 52n126; taxation of Jews, 4, 5, 9; Temporary Regulations (May Laws), 30; terminology *evrei* versus *zhid*, 441, 443n1. *See also* dress and grooming; elementary (primary) education; higher education; Pale of Settlement; rabbinate; registration; secondary education; taxation

Lilienblum, Moshe Leib, 18, 23, 39, 40–41, 57n281, 351, 353–67

Lilienthal, Max, 21

Lipkin, Israel ben Ze'ev Volf (Israel Salanter), 10, 117–18, 387

Lipnishki, 114

literature: *byliny* (traditional Russian heroic poetry), 406; early modern Italian Jewish literature, 362; German romantic literature, 91, 177; Great Reform liberalization of censorship, 28; Haskalah literature, 361–63, 379–80, 387–89; Hebrew literature, 19, 28, 363; historical literature, 408; Jewish biography and autobiography, 356; kabbalistic literature, 379–80; *musar* literature, 387; Russian literature, 34, 44, 178, 399, 402, 421–22, 424–25n2, 428; subversive literature, 563; Yiddish literature, 19, 28, 95, 173, 174n4

Lithuania: Napoleonic wars and, 13; Polish Uprising of 1863 and, 28, 361; postreform anti-Jewish violence in, 31; reform of traditional Jewish education in, 351; stronghold of *misnagdism*, 351. *See also* yeshiva

Liubimov, Nikolai A., 423

Lodz, 32

Lokhvits, 145–46

Lomzha, 132–33

Lurianic Kabbalah, 6, 8, 49n36, 380n4

Luzzatto, Moshe Hayim (Samuel David Luzzatto), 355–56, 367n3, 378

Maimonides (Rambam), 154, 195, 203n8, 318, 359

Makarov, 72, 75, 77–78

Manasein, Nikolai Avksent'evich, 501, 505n7

Mapu, Abraham, 363, 374n4

marital separation, 204–15, 232–40

marriage: arranged marriage, 23, 98, 169, 190–93, 306–7, 355–56; betrothals in jest, 187–88; broken engagements, 189–90; courtship in hasidic families, 82–83, 87, 91–92; dowries, 169, 170, 185, 194–95, 199–200, 202n5, 210, 217; early marriage, 19, 23, 261, 263n1, 305–16, 355–56; genital imperfections as restriction to, 319; hasidic mercantile marriage alliances, 8; jurisdiction of state rabbi over, 17–18, 103n14, 156–58; *kest*, 85, 93, 169, 174n2, 355; *ketubah* (marriage contract), 194–202, 202n5, 355–56; metrical records of marriage, 18, 23; Pale of Settlement residency and, 190–93; parental

disapproval, 182–84; permission for remarriage without divorce from first spouse, 195–204, 203n9, 215–16, 216n1, 216n3, 216n5, 222–23; pregnancy by a man other than the husband, 327–28, 328n5; "rebellious wife" (*moredet*), 194–202, 202n3, 203n20, 215; spousal abuse, 204–15, 232–33; *tenaim* (engagement contract), 121, 185–86; tokens of betrothal, 186–87; women's higher education and, 425–27. *See also* *agun*; *agunah*; divorce; extramarital sex; family; halakhah; weddings

Marxism, 35–37, 39, 563, 591n3. *See also* socialism

masculinity, 42

maskilim. *See* Haskalah movement

medical profession: dentistry, 425–27, 431, 496–98; fear of domination by Jewish doctors in Bessarabia, 31; *feldshers*, 162, 343, 447, 522; folk remedies, 172–73, 261, 265, 309–11, 359; Jews as military physicians, 501; medical inspection of brothels, 338–40; medical training, 433–37; ophthalmology, 521–22; physicians, 46, 115–16, 119, 120, 126, 151, 205, 207–8, 211, 244, 250–52, 285, 319; physicians as state rabbis, 156–57; rape by a physician, 320; women's medical clinics, 495–96. *See also* health; illness and disease

Meir of Rothenburg, 199, 203n23

Meisels, Dov Ber, 128n15

Menachem Mendel of Vitebsk, 94, 103n18

Mendele Moykher-Seforim (Sholem Y. Abramovitsh), 41–42

Mendelssohn, Moses, 11, 19, 92, 103n16

Mendes-Flohr, Paul, xvii–xviii

Mensheviks, 36

mental illness: care of mentally ill, 262; demographic data on, 262; depression, 266–67; fears for public safety, 295, 298; as grounds for divorce, 205–6, 209, 215–16, 222; *meshugener* (insane person) figure, xx–xxi; pediatric nervous illnesses, 292–93; petitions to institutionalize for, xix, xxi, 293–301; phobia of darkness, 409–10; phobia of dogs, 300; treatment by Tatars, 221, 262. *See also* health; illness and disease

merchants: attraction to radical circles, 34; brick merchants, 446–48; competition with native Russians, 5, 441–43; contraband, 445; estate merchants, 4, 11, 27, 177, 183; fictitious servants of first-guild merchants, 272; first-guild, 23, 48n17, 52n126, 159, 177, 489; hasidic merchants,

Index [629]

Sabbath: hasidic observance of, 67–69, 81, 319; importance of music on, 62–63, 69; Sabbath meals, 67, 69–70, 71–72n32, 379

Sablin, Nikolai, 560n2

Sagalevich, Girsh, 162

Savinkov, Boris, 591n8

Scott, James, 11

secondary education: classical gymnasium reforms, 405–6; complaints of overrepresentation of Jews in, 414; corporal punishment in state rabbinical schools, 414; elite home education for girls, 399–400, 408; gymnasium for boys, 403–11; gymnasium for girls, 401–3; state rabbinical seminaries, 22–23, 374n6, 412–18, 414n3; state stipends for state rabbinical school students, 416–18. *See also* yeshiva

Sergievskii, Nikolai S., 423–24

sexuality: abortion, 274; abstinence due to illness, 321–23; *ailonit*, 215; birth control, 268–74; contraceptive methods, 321–23; early marriage and, 23, 263n1, 305–16; genital imperfections as marriage restriction, 319; illegitimate births, 240, 262, 263n4, 327, 330–31, 332–33, 334; intercourse that endangers life, 321–23; *keri* (nocturnal emissions), 358, 361; male impotence, 23, 309–11, 316; masturbation, 261–62, 267–68; menstruation, 71, 481n1; *moredet* (rebellious wife), 194–204; *niddah* (menstrual purity), 71n29, 317–19; obligation to reproduce, 322–23n3; pregnancy and, 320; puberty in adolescent girls, 266–67; questionnaire of women's sexuality, 347–50; rape, 32, 262, 319–20, 320n1, 327–28, 335; sexual freedom in radical literature, 34; sexual indifference/dysfunction in marriage, 23, 203n8, 230, 250; sexually transmitted diseases, 262, 323–24, 340n1, 342–46; sexual repulsion, 203n8, 230; sex with soldiers, 343; unequal ages in marriage and, 230. *See also* circumcision; extramarital sex; marriage; prostitution

Shafranov, Sergei, 406, 410, 411n7

Shalkovich, Abraham Leib (Ben Avigdor), 388

Shalom, Avraham, 388

Shaykevitch, Nokhem Meyer (Shomer), 21, 28

Shchepkin, Mitrofan P., 423, 425n6

Shereshevskii, Idel, 22

Shklov, 8

Shkol'nik, Mariia (Mania): account of farm upbringing, 477–82; arrest for illegal printing equipment, 573–77; as artisan worker, 440, 480–81; attempted assassination of Aleksei Alekseevich Khvostov, 585–90; Combat Organization activities, 36, 577, 583–85, 588, 590; confectionery factory work, 572; educational circle in Odessa, 570–72; exile to Siberia, 577–83; Kishinev pogroms and, 575–76; recognition as socialist luminary, 590–91, 592n17; Vil'na artisan strike, 481

Shlomo ben Aderet (Rashba), 154, 189, 198, 199, 203n18, 321, 359, 367n13

Shmelkes, Yitzchak Yehudah, 154, 155n4

Shneur Zalman of Liady, 9, 12

Shpaizman, Aaron, 36, 572–76, 583–89, 591n9

Shternberg, Lev Iakovlevich, 35

Shulhan Arukh, 40, 110, 112n2, 113n35, 115, 126, 128n3, 140, 142n1, 187n2, 188, 197, 276, 277, 292n3, 321, 322, 363, 412, 414n2

Shulman, Kalman, 379, 380n6

Siberia: Jewish commerce and settlement in, 445–46; mining in, 487; schools in, 398–99; as site of exile, 183, 218, 220n1, 405, 487, 577–81

Sirkis, Yoel, 317, 317n3

Skvir, 72

Slavophilism, 25, 30, 406, 410, 411n8–9, 422. *See also* Aksakov, Ivan

Sliozberg, Genrikh, 44, 132n1, 410n1, 440, 498–505

Slobodka, 10

Smela, 454–55

Smolensk, 1, 5, 435, 441, 513–14

Smolenskin, Peretz, 39

Smorgon, 478, 481

Sobinov, Leonid V., 428, 430n3

socialism, 174n1, 563. *See also* Bund; revolutionary movements; Socialist Revolutionaries

Socialist Revolutionaries (SRs), 35–36, 213, 558, 573, 576, 585, 588–92

Sofer, Moses (Hatam Sofer), 120, 154, 155n5, 198, 203n17, 223, 321

Sokolov, Mikhail ("the Bear"), 36

Sozonov, Egor, 577, 591

Spain, 611n4

Spektor, Yitzhak Elhanan, xix, 46, 137–39, 189–90, 215–16, 218–22, 224, 317, 319, 327, 328

Stanislawski, Michael, 351

Stepashek, 146–48

Stoklishki, 347

Stolypin, Petr Arkad'evich, 44–45

Acknowledgments, continued from page viii

Hundert, editor, *The YIVO Encyclopedia of Jews in Eastern Europe*, map on page 1312, "The Pale of Settlement, ca. 1855." Published by Yale University Press, 2008, and reprinted with permission.

Ita Kalish, "Life in a Hasidic Court in Russian Poland Toward the End of the 19th and Early 20th Centuries," *Yivo Annual of Jewish Social Science*, Vol XIII (1965), pages 264–278, reprinted with permission.

Rabbi Tracy Klirs, "Tkhine for a Woman Who Collects Tsedoke" in *The Merit of Our Mothers: A Bilingual Anthology of Jewish Women's Prayers*, translated by Ida Cohen Selavan and Gella Schweid Fishman, and reprinted with permission.

Ben Zion Dinur, "Be-olam she-shaka: zikhronot u-reshumot mi-derekh," The Bialik Institute, 1958, pages 62–76, translated and reprinted with permission.

Gregory Freeze, ed., *From Supplication to Revolution: A Documentary Social History of Imperial Russia*, pages 96–97. Published by Oxford University Press, and reprinted with permission.